THE CAMBRIDGE HISTORY OF IRISH LITERATURE

★

VOLUME 2
1890–2000

★

Edited by

MARGARET KELLEHER

and

PHILIP O'LEARY

CAMBRIDGE
UNIVERSITY PRESS

CAMBRIDGE UNIVERSITY PRESS
Cambridge, New York, Melbourne, Madrid, Cape Town, Singapore, São Paulo

Cambridge University Press
The Edinburgh Building, Cambridge CB2 8RU, UK

Published in the United States of America by Cambridge University Press, New York

www.cambridge.org
Information on this title: www.cambridge.org/9780521822244

First published 2006
Reprinted 2007

Printed in the United Kingdom at the University Press, Cambridge

A catalogue record for this publication is available from the British Library

Library of Congress Cataloguing in Publication data
The Cambridge history of Irish literature / edited by Margaret Kelleher and Philip O'Leary.
p. cm.
ISBN 0 521 82224 6 (2-vol. hardback set)
1. Irish literature – History and criticism. 2. English literature – Irish authors – History and criticism. 3. Northern Ireland – Intellectual life. 4. Northern Ireland – In literature. 5. Ireland – Intellectual life. 6. Ireland – In literature. I. Kelleher, Margaret, 1964–. II. O'Leary, Philip, 1948– III. Title.
PB1306.C36 2006
820.9′9417 – dc22 2005006448

Volume II ISBN-10 0-521-82223-7
Only available as a two-volume set

ISBN-13 978-0-521-82224-4

Contents

List of contributors *vii*
Acknowledgements *viii*
Chronology *x*

Introduction *1*
MARGARET KELLEHER AND PHILIP O'LEARY

1 · Literature and politics *9*
DECLAN KIBERD

2 · The Irish Renaissance, 1890–1940: poetry in English *50*
PATRICK CROTTY

3 · The Irish Renaissance, 1890–1940: prose in English *113*
JOHN WILSON FOSTER

4 · The Irish Renaissance, 1890–1940: drama in English *181*
ADRIAN FRAZIER

5 · The Irish Renaissance, 1890–1940: literature in Irish *226*
PHILIP O'LEARY

6 · Contemporary prose and drama in Irish: 1940–2000 *270*
MÁIRÍN NIC EOIN

7 · Contemporary poetry in Irish: 1940–2000 *317*
LOUIS DE PAOR

8 · Contemporary poetry in English: 1940–2000 357
DILLON JOHNSTON AND GUINN BATTEN

9 · Contemporary prose in English: 1940–2000 421
GEORGE O'BRIEN

10 · Contemporary drama in English: 1940–2000 478
ANTHONY ROCHE

11 · Cinema and Irish literature 531
KEVIN ROCKETT

12 · Literary historiography, 1890–2000 562
COLIN GRAHAM

Afterword: Irish-language literature in the new millennium 600
BRÍONA NIC DHIARMADA

Afterword: Irish literature in English in the new millennium 628
FINTAN O'TOOLE

Guide to major subject areas 643
Index 648

Contributors

Guinn Batten Washington University
Patrick Crotty University of Aberdeen
Louis de Paor National University of Ireland, Galway
John Wilson Foster University of British Columbia
Adrian Frazier National University of Ireland, Galway
Colin Graham National University of Ireland, Maynooth
Dillon Johnston Washington University
Margaret Kelleher National University of Ireland, Maynooth
Declan Kiberd University College Dublin
Bríona Nic Dhiarmada University of Limerick
Máirín Nic Eoin St Patrick's College, Drumcondra
George O'Brien Georgetown University
Philip O'Leary Boston College
Fintan O'Toole *Irish Times*
Anthony Roche University College Dublin
Kevin Rockett Trinity College, Dublin

Acknowledgements

Firstly, our thanks to all of our contributors: the excellence of their scholarship was the mainstay of our work throughout. We acknowledge with gratitude our editor Dr Ray Ryan, Cambridge University Press, who first conceived of this project and who encouraged us to the finish. Our thanks also to the anonymous readers of our initial prospectus who offered very useful suggestions, and to the Syndicate of Cambridge University Press for their support. We gratefully acknowledge the expert assistance of Alison Powell, Carol Fellingham Webb, David Watson and Maartje Scheltens of Cambridge University Press in the preparation of these volumes for publication.

To those who offered comments on specific chapters and assistance to individual contributors, sincere thanks; these include David Berman, Michael Clarke, Peter Denman, Aileen Douglas, Peter Garside, Raymond Gillespie, Nicholas Grene, the members of the Harvard Postgraduate Colloquium 2002–2003, Siobhán Kilfeather, Carla King, David Latané Jr, Joep Leerssen, Jane Moody, Jane Moore, James H. Murphy, Máirín Ní Dhonnchadha, Nollaig Ó Muraíle, Pádraig Ó Riain, Erich Poppe, Paige Reynolds, Maria Luisa Ross, John Valdimir Price, Diego Saglia and John Strachan. Our special thanks to Máire Ní Mhaonaigh, who offered wise counsel throughout. We acknowledge with gratitude the work of Matthew Stout, who provided the maps for this history. Amanda Bent, Denis Condon, Mike Cronin, Feargus Denman, Michael Kelleher, Niamh Lynch, Brian Ó Catháin and Andy Storey provided invaluable assistance in the production of these volumes. The views expressed, and any errors, are, of course, our responsibility.

We are very grateful for the support provided by our colleagues in the Irish Studies Program, Boston College, and the English Department, National University of Ireland, Maynooth. We gratefully acknowledge the assistance provided through the granting of the John J. Burns Visiting Chair in Irish Studies, Boston College to Margaret Kelleher in the academic year 2002–2003. Once again, we are indebted to the staff of the Burns Library and O'Neill

Library, Boston College; the staff of Maynooth University Library; and the staff of the National Library, Dublin. Financial assistance towards this volume was received from the Publications Fund of the National University of Ireland, and we gratefully acknowledge this assistance.

To Joyce Flynn, the Kelleher family (Mallow, Co. Cork) and the O'Leary family (Worcester, Mass.) we owe personal thanks. We acknowledge with gratitude the warm and longstanding hospitality provided by friends in Ireland and the US: Angela Bourke, Eleanor Byrne, Patrick Ford, Marie Kearney, Gemma Kelleher, Maeve Lewis, Tomás Mac Anna, Nollaig Mac Congáil, Deirdre McMahon, Mohsen Marefat, the Ní Mhaonaigh / Meissner family, Brian Ó Conchubhair, the O'Shea / Curtin family, the O'Sullivan / Fleming family, Kathleen Rush, Mary Ann and Bud Smith, Leslie Swanson, Alan Titley, Terri Trafas, Maura Twomey and Unn Villius. Our work on this project is dedicated to the memory of two distinguished friends and mentors, Professor Adele M. Dalsimer, Boston College, and Professor John V. Kelleher, Harvard University.

Ár mbeannachtaí leat, a scríbhinn . . .

Margaret Kelleher and Philip O'Leary
Dublin and South Yarmouth

Chronology

c. AD 130–80	Ptolemy's 'Geography' provides detailed map of Ireland
Fourth and fifth centuries	Irish raids on Roman Britain
431	Annals of Ulster (post-Patrician) begin
431	Pope Celestine sends Palladius as first bishop to Christian Irish
432	Traditional date given to beginning of St Patrick's mission
444	Traditional date given for foundation of Armagh
c. 500–900	Old Irish linguistic period (including Archaic Irish, Early Old Irish and Classical Old Irish)
546	Derry founded by St Colum Cille (Columba)
547/8	Clonmacnoise founded by St Ciarán
c. 550	Beginning of monastic Hiberno-Latin writing
563	Iona founded by St Colum Cille
Sixth and seventh centuries	Latin literature flourishes in Ireland
597	Death of St Colum Cille
615	Death of St Columbanus
697	*Cáin Adamnáin*, 'The Law of Adamnán' (of Iona), promulgated in Ireland
Seventh and eighth centuries	Writing of Early Irish law texts
795	First Viking raid on Ireland
806	Iona raided by Vikings; chief relics moved to Kells
837–76	Intense Viking activity in Ireland; semi-permanent bases established, including encampment in Dublin (*c.* 841)

900–1200	Middle Irish linguistic period
916–37	Renewed Viking activity in Ireland
1002–14	Reign of Brian Bóruma mac Cennétig
1014	Battle of Clontarf (Good Friday, 23 April)
c. 1100?	Compilation of *Lebor na hUidre* (The Book of the Dun Cow)
1101	Council of Cashel
1127–34	Building of Cormac's chapel at Cashel
c. 1130	Compilation of Leinster codex, Rawlinson B502
1142	First Irish Cistercian house founded at Mellifont
c. 1160–1200	Compilation of the Book of Leinster
August 1170	Richard de Clare (Strongbow) arrives in Ireland
c. May 1171	Death of Diarmait Mac Murchada; Strongbow (his son-in-law) succeeds as king of Leinster
November 1171	Henry II in Dublin; receives submission of kings of north Leinster, Bréifne, Airgialla and Ulster
February 1183	First visit to Ireland of Giraldus Cambrensis (Gerald of Wales)
c. 1200–*c.* 1650	Early Modern Irish linguistic period
November 1216	Magna Carta issued for Ireland
1224	First Irish Dominican foundations (at Dublin and Drogheda)
c. 1224–30	First Irish Franciscan foundations (at Cork and Youghal)
c. May 1316	Edward Bruce crowned king of Ireland (defeated and killed October 1318)
c. 1330	Compilation of British Library Manuscript Harley 913
February 1366	Statute of Kilkenny promulgated
1446	First known use of 'Pale' to denote area under Dublin control
1494	'Poyning's Law' enacted by parliament at Drogheda
1534–5	Silken Thomas's rebellion

February 1537	Silken Thomas executed in London
October–December 1537	Acts for the suppression of Irish monasteries
June 1541	Henry VIII declared 'king of Ireland' by statute of Irish parliament
June 1549	Order for use of English Book of Common Prayer in Ireland
1550–7	Plantations in Laois (Leix) and Offaly (established as Queen's County and King's County in 1556)
1555	Papal Bull of Pope Paul IV declares Ireland a kingdom
1561–7	Rebellion of Shane O'Neill; English campaigns led by Sussex and Sir Henry Sidney
1568–73	First Desmond rebellion
June 1571	First printing in the Irish language, in Dublin
1579–83	Second Desmond rebellion
December 1585	Scheme for plantation in Munster drawn up (amended scheme passed by Elizabeth I, June 1586)
September 1588	Ships of Spanish Armada wrecked off Irish coast
March 1592	Charter incorporates Trinity College, Dublin
1595–1603	Rebellion of Hugh O'Neill, earl of Tyrone
September 1601	Spanish army lands at Kinsale
December 1601	Tyrone and 'Red Hugh' O'Donnell defeated at Kinsale; O'Donnell leaves Ireland for Spain
March 1603	Surrender of Tyrone at Mellifont
September 1607	Flight of the Earls (including Tyrone and Tyrconnell) from Lough Swilly
1608–10	Preparations for plantations in Ulster counties
January 1621	Patents granted for plantations in Leitrim, King's County (Offaly), Queen's County (Laois) and Westmeath
August 1632	Compilation of the Annals of the Four Masters completed
October 1641	Outbreak of rebellion in Ulster

1642–9	'Confederation of Kilkenny': government of Catholic Confederates
August 1649	Oliver Cromwell arrives in Dublin as civil and military governor of Ireland
September 1649	Massacre at Drogheda
October 1649	Massacre at Wexford
November 1649	Death of Eoghan Ruadh Ó Néill (Owen Roe O'Neill)
May 1650	Cromwell returns to England
August 1652	Act for the settlement of Ireland
1652–3	Cromwellian land confiscations
1660–5	Restoration land settlement
July 1663	First of series of acts restricting Irish trade and exports
March 1689	James II arrives in Ireland
April 1689	Siege of Derry begins; ends in July
July 1690	Forces of James II defeated by those of William III at River Boyne
July 1691	Battle of Aughrim: Williamite victory
October 1691	Treaty of Limerick, allowing evacuation of Irish army to France and promising toleration to Irish Catholics
1691–1703	Williamite land confiscations
September 1695	Beginning of 'Penal Laws': Acts restricting rights of Catholics to education, to bear arms or to possess a horse worth more than five pounds.
March 1704	Further 'Penal Law' introduced, including 'tests' on Catholics and Protestant dissenters for holding of public office; amended and strengthened August 1708.
June–July 1718	Beginning of large-scale migration of Ulster Scots to American colonies
November 1719	Toleration Act for Protestant Dissenters
April 1720	Declaratory Act defines right of English parliament to legislate for Ireland
Winter 1740–spring 1741	'Bliadhain an Áir' ('The Year of the Slaughter'): large-scale famine, with

	mortality estimated at over 200,000, from a population of approximately two million
June 1758 – April 1759	Acts removing restrictions on some Irish exports
March 1760	Catholic Committee established in Dublin to advance Catholic interests
c. October 1761	Beginning of Whiteboy movement in Munster
March 1778	Beginning of Volunteer movement (local independent military forces); first company enrolled in Belfast
August 1778	Catholic Relief Act grants rights of leasing and inheritance
June and July 1782	Repeal of 1720 Declaratory Act and Poyning's Law amended
April 1783	British Renunciation Act acknowledges exclusive right of Irish parliament to legislate for Ireland (inaugurates 'Grattan's parliament', to 1800)
May 1785	First meeting of Irish Academy ('Royal Irish' after January 1786)
October 1791	Foundation of Society of United Irishmen in Belfast
April 1792 and April 1793	Catholic Relief Acts allow Catholics to practise law and give parliamentary franchise
June 1795	Act passed for establishment of Catholic seminary at Maynooth
September 1795	Foundation of Orange Order
December 1796	French fleet, with Wolfe Tone, at Bantry Bay
1798	United Irishmen rising: rebellion begins in Leinster (May); outbreaks in Ulster in June; French force lands in Killala (August); French force surrenders (September)
August 1800	Act of Union dissolves Irish parliament and declares legislative union
January 1801	Act of Union takes effect
July 1801	Copyright Act renders illegal the publication of pirate Irish editions of British publications

July 1803	Robert Emmet's rebellion in Dublin; Emmet executed in September
Autumn 1816	Failure of potato crop leads to first major famine since 1742; widespread typhus epidemic continues until late 1819
Autumn 1821	Failure of potato crop; fever follows in west of Ireland in summer 1822
May 1823	Foundation of Catholic Association by Daniel O'Connell
1825–41	Ordnance Survey of Ireland carried out
July 1828	Daniel O'Connell elected MP for Clare
April 1829	Catholic Emancipation Act enables Catholics to enter parliament and to hold civil and military offices
September 1831	State system of National Education introduced
June 1837	Accession of Victoria
July 1838	English system of Poor Law is extended to Ireland
April 1840	Repeal Association founded
June 1841	Census of Ireland: population of island 8,175,124
1844	Queen's University founded, with colleges in Belfast, Cork and Galway.
1845–51:	*An Gorta Mór* ('The Great Irish Famine'): mortality estimated at in excess of 1 million
September 1845	Arrival of potato blight in Ireland first noted
June 1846	Repeal of the Corn Laws
August 1846	Recurrence of potato blight, leading to large mortality in winter of 1846–7
May 1847	Death of O'Connell
July 1848	Abortive rising by William Smith O'Brien at Ballingarry, Co. Tipperary: beginning of short-lived Young Ireland rebellion
March 1851	Census of Ireland: population of island 6,552,385
March 1858	James Stephens founds Irish Republican Brotherhood (IRB) in Dublin
April 1859	Fenian Brotherhood established in USA

1867	Fenian rebellion: disturbances in England and Ireland in February; execution of Fenian 'Manchester Martyrs' in November
July 1869	Irish Church Act disestablishes Church of Ireland
May 1870	Isaac Butt founds Home Government Association: beginning of Home Rule movement
August 1870	Gladstone's first Land Act
1876	Society for the Preservation of the Irish Language founded
August 1877	Charles Stuart Parnell elected president of Home Rule Confederation of Great Britain
August 1879	Foundation of National Land League of Mayo by Michael Davitt
October 1879	Foundation of Irish National Land League by Davitt and Parnell
May 1880	Parnell elected chairman of Irish Parliamentary Party (IPP)
October 1880	Foundation of Ladies' Land League in New York
January 1881	Ladies' Land League established in Ireland
August 1881	Gladstone's second Land Act
May 1882	'Phoenix Park murders' of Lord Frederick Cavendish and Thomas Burke
November 1884	Foundation of Gaelic Athletic Association (GAA)
August 1885	Ashbourne Land Purchase Act
June 1886	Gladstone's Home Rule Bill defeated
October 1886	Announcement of 'Plan of Campaign' to withhold rents on certain estates
1877	National Library of Ireland established
1890	National Museum of Ireland opened
December 1890	Split in IPP, with majority opposing Parnell
October 1891	Death of Parnell
August 1892	National Literary Society established
July 1893	Foundation of Gaelic League (Conradh na Gaeilge)

September 1893	Second Home Rule Bill passed by House of Commons but defeated in House of Lords
August 1898	Irish Local Government Act
May 1899	First production by Irish Literary Theatre
September 1900	Foundation of Cumann na nGaedheal led by Arthur Griffith
March 1901	Census of Ireland: population 4,458,775
August 1903	Wyndham Land Act
December 1904	Opening of Abbey Theatre
April 1907	Cumann na nGaedheal and Dungannon clubs become Sinn Féin League
December 1908	Foundation of Irish Transport Workers' Union (later ITGWU)
April 1911	Census of Ireland: population 4,381,951
May 1908	Irish Women's Franchise League formed
April 1912	Third Home Rule Bill passed by House of Commons; twice defeated in House of Lords (January and July 1913)
September 1912	Solemn League and Covenant signed in Ulster
January 1913	Foundation of Ulster Volunteer Force
August 1913	Beginning of ITGWU strike in Dublin, becomes general lockout
November 1913	Formation of Irish Citizen Army and Irish Volunteers
March 1914	'Curragh Mutiny': resignation by sixty cavalry officers in the British army at Kildare
April 1914	Ulster Volunteer Force gunrunning
April 1914	Foundation of Cumann na mBan (women's auxiliary league)
May 1914	Home Rule Bill passes again in Commons
July 1914	Howth gunrunning by Irish Volunteers
August 1914	United Kingdom and Germany go to war
September 1914	Home Rule Bill suspended; John Redmond calls on Irish Volunteers to support British war; movement splits into National (pro-Redmond) and Irish (anti-Redmond) Volunteers
April 1916	Easter Uprising

May 1916	Execution of rebel leaders
December 1918	Sinn Féin victory in general election
January 1919	First meeting of Dáil Éireann at Mansion House, with Eamon De Valera elected president
1919	Irish Volunteer organisation increasingly known as Irish Republican Army (IRA)
1919–21	Irish War of Independence / Anglo-Irish War
January 1920	First recruits of British ex-soldiers and sailors ('Black and Tans') join Royal Irish Constabulary
December 1920	Government of Ireland Act provides for creation of separate parliaments in Dublin and Belfast
June 1921	George V opens Northern Irish Parliament
July 1921	Truce between IRA and British Army
December 1921	Anglo-Irish Treaty signed
January 1922	Treaty approved by Dáil Éireann (sixty-four to fifty-seven): establishment of Irish Free State
June 1922	Beginning of Irish Civil War between pro-Treaty (Free State) and anti-Treaty (Republican) forces
April 1923	Cumann na nGaedheal (political party) founded as first new post-independence party
April 1923	Suspension of Republican campaign
July 1923	Censorship of Films Act
September 1923	Irish Free State enters League of Nations
1923	W. B. Yeats is awarded the Nobel Prize for Literature
1925	George Bernard Shaw is awarded the Nobel Prize for Literature
November 1925	Findings of Boundary Commission leaked
April 1926	Census of Ireland: population of Irish Free State 2,971,992; population of Northern Ireland 1,256,561
May 1926	Foundation of Fianna Fáil
1928	Irish Manuscripts Commission founded
July 1929	Censorship of Publications Act

1930	Ireland elected to the Council of the League of Nations
February 1932	Fianna Fáil win general election
June 1932	Thirty-First International Eucharistic Congress held in Dublin
September 1933	Foundation of Fine Gael (replaces Cumann na nGaedheal)
June 1936	IRA declared illegal
June 1937	De Valera's new constitution (Bunreacht na hÉireann) approved; Éire declared official name of state
June 1938	Douglas Hyde becomes first president of Ireland
September 1939	Éire's policy of neutrality announced
1939–1945	'Emergency' years
April and May 1941	Air-raids on Belfast
February 1948	Fianna Fáil loses overall majority; replaced by Coalition government under John A. Costello
December 1948	Republic of Ireland Act under which Éire becomes Republic of Ireland and leaves Commonwealth
April 1951	Catholic hierarchy condemns 'Mother and Child' Scheme; resignation of Dr Noël Browne as Minister of Health
December 1955	Republic of Ireland joins United Nations
December 1956	IRA begins campaign on Northern border
1958	Programme for Economic Expansion introduced, encouraging exports along with private and foreign investment in manufacturing
June 1959	De Valera elected president
December 1961	RTÉ (Radio Telefís Éireann) begins television service
March 1963	Terence O'Neill becomes prime minister of Northern Ireland
1966	Ulster Volunteer Force (UVF), loyalist paramilitary group (taking its name from the 1913 movement), founded

January 1967	Foundation of Northern Ireland Civil Rights Association
August–October 1968	Civil rights marches in Northern Ireland; clashes between marchers and police in Derry mark beginning of 'the Troubles'
1969	Samuel Beckett is awarded the Nobel Prize for Literature
January 1970	IRA splits into Official IRA and Provisional IRA
August 1970	Foundation of Social Democratic Labour Party (SDLP) in Northern Ireland
August 1971	Internment introduced in Northern Ireland
October 1971	Ian Paisley founds Democratic Unionist Party (DUP)
March 1972	Stormont parliament in Belfast suspended; direct rule from London introduced
30 January 1972	'Bloody Sunday': fourteen civilians killed and twelve wounded in Derry by British army
21 July 1972	'Bloody Friday': twenty-two bombs set off in Belfast by IRA; nine people killed and some hundred and thirty wounded
January 1973	Republic of Ireland joins European Economic Community (EEC)
May 1974	Ulster Workers' Council declares general strike
December 1975	Suspension of internment without trial in Northern Ireland
29 September–1 October 1979	Pope John Paul II visits Ireland
October–December 1980	Hunger strikes in Maze and Armagh prisons
May–August 1981	Ten IRA and Irish National Liberation Army (INLA) hunger-strikers die, including Bobby Sands (elected MP, April 1981)
September 1983	Amendment to constitution passed by referendum, seeking to prevent any possible legalisation of abortion
May 1984	Report of the New Ireland Forum is published
November 1985	Anglo-Irish Agreement signed by Garret FitzGerald and Margaret Thatcher

June 1986	Referendum upholds constitutional ban on divorce
May 1987	Referendum approves Single European Act
November 1990	Mary Robinson elected president of Ireland
November 1992	Referendum held on three abortion-related issues: the right to travel and the right to information supported
December 1993	Downing Street Declaration signed by Albert Reynolds and John Major
August and October 1994	IRA and Loyalist paramilitaries declare ceasefires (later suspended and restored)
October 1995	Seamus Heaney is awarded the Nobel Prize for Literature
November 1995	Referendum allowing divorce is carried
October 1997	Mary McAleese elected president of Ireland
April 1998	Good Friday Agreement is negotiated and endorsed in referendums in Republic of Ireland and Northern Ireland (May)
December 1999	Northern Irish Assembly meets
2001	Census of population of Northern Ireland: 1,685,267
April 2002	Census of population of Republic of Ireland: 3,917,203

For a fuller chronology, to which this chronology is indebted, see T. W. Moody, F. X. Martin and F. J. Byrne, eds., *A New History of Ireland, Vol. VIII: A Chronology of Irish History to 1976* (Oxford University Press, 1992). For a detailed comparative chronology of Irish and international literary history, 1800–2000, see Joseph Cleary and Claire Connolly, eds. *The Cambridge Companion to Modern Irish Culture* (Cambridge University Press, 2005).

Introduction

MARGARET KELLEHER AND PHILIP O'LEARY

In 1875, one year short of the centennial of the American republic, the publisher George H. Putnam asked Moses Coit Tyler to produce a 'manual' of American literature. Tyler was to do much more than that. Convinced that it was now time to write an account of what he called 'the most confidential and explicit record' of the American mind, the record preserved in the nation's literature, he undertook a full-scale history of American literature from 1607 to 1765, a pioneering effort that was to mark the beginning of the serious study of that literature. Tyler himself was in 1881 to join the faculty of Cornell University as the holder of the first professorship in the United States devoted to American history.

We believe that now is the time for a similar pioneering effort to create a coherent and authoritative history of Irish literature in the two major languages of the island. The publication in 1991 of the three-volume *Field Day Anthology of Irish Writing*, the first attempt to formulate a standard if not definitive anthology of Irish literature, has in effect established a canon of Irish literature, a canon since expanded with the appearance in 2002 of the fourth and fifth volumes of the anthology, volumes dedicated to writing by and about women. The existence of such a canon, however contested, only makes more compelling – even urgent – the need for an accessible and reliable historical framework within which the newly canonical texts can be read, and marginalised texts, together with the reasons for their marginalisation, can be explored. Indeed the *Field Day Anthology* has created the anomalous situation in which Ireland now has a chronologically organised literary canon but no comprehensive literary history in light of which to think about it.

Of course that does not mean that there are not sound works of Irish literary history available. Unlike Tyler, we face a situation in which there is an almost baffling profusion of histories, biographies, critical monographs, and so on, dealing with various aspects of the literatures of Ireland. Yet for all this wealth of scholarly material, we have as yet no definitive literary history. To be sure, there are important and useful surveys like those by Jeffares and Deane for Irish writing in English, and for Irish writing in Irish by Hyde, de Blacam and J. E. Caerwyn Williams (the last translated into Irish and English from the original Welsh). In addition, there are, of course, histories of individual periods, movements, genres, themes, etc. But for the scholar or general reader trying to make sense of the bigger picture, looking for a reliable overview of the Irish literary tradition as it has developed in both Irish and English, there has been next to nothing.

Given the enormous scholarly and popular interest in Irish literature at present, now is the time to remedy this deficiency. Ireland's literary tradition spans more than fifteen hundred years. As we begin the new millennium, we have both a need and an opportunity to make sense of that long tradition by providing an authoritative chronological history that will enable readers to check facts on specific authors and literary works, to trace in meaningful detail stylistic and thematic developments and influences through time, or to explore the often neglected interrelationships between the two literary traditions that have shared the island over the past five hundred years. For as Homi Bhabha has pointed out in *The Location of Culture*, 'what is theoretically innovative, and politically crucial, is the need to think beyond narratives of originary and initial subjectivity and to focus on those moments or processes that are produced in the articulation of cultural differences'.[1]

At the moment, Irish culture is experiencing unprecedented visibility and acclaim on the world stage. Simultaneously, Irish Studies has developed as a respectable academic discipline in many universities, most notably in North America and Great Britain, but also in Australia, continental Europe and, curiously belatedly, in Ireland itself. Yet despite this visibility, not all those engaged with Irish culture share the confidence, even occasional complacency, that is the predictable by-product of such striking accomplishments. In fact, some have experienced a nagging ambivalence, a concern that superficial successes, however impressive, are actually obscuring rather than illuminating an authentic understanding of crucial questions called forth by those very successes. Are Irish writers in English the Anglophone flavour-of-the-moment for jaded cosmopolitan readers? Is translation a vital transfusion of cross-cultural energy that will make writing in Irish more visible and ultimately more viable, or is it a lethal injection leading to linguistic redundancy? Do the plays of Martin McDonagh give new voice to the ever-evolving vitality of Irish theatre, or do they cynically parasitise that tradition to propagate a (not all that) new species of stage Irishism? What does the controversy over the *Field Day Anthology* say about the possibility of thinking about Irish writing as a distinct and coherent literary entity?

It is, however, difficult, if not impossible, to think clearly and creatively, much less authoritatively, about these and other questions, large and small, without a specifically Irish context in which to read the literary works all too often seen as curious offshoots from a normative English tradition. At present, scholars and general readers alike lack such a context, with even those professionally involved in the study of Irish culture often experiencing an insecurity about finding a proper approach to thinking about Irish literature, about whether and how current developments relate to an ongoing tradition, and indeed about the existence and nature of that tradition itself. Given that those previous histories that do exist have concentrated exclusively on one or the other of Ireland's two major literary traditions, we see *The Cambridge History of Irish Literature* as a pioneering as well as a timely project. Far more than simply supplementing existing and forthcoming histories of English literature, it provides the first systematic and comprehensive overview of the Irish literary tradition as it has achieved expression over the centuries in both Irish and English.

The adherence to a chronological structure of organisation for the history means that the earlier chapters focus almost exclusively on Irish-language texts and writings in insular Latin and Norman French. Later chapters alternate between the Irish and English language traditions, with literature in English playing a considerably – and appropriately – more prominent, though never exclusive, role from the seventeenth century on. Our approach should, by its very novelty, generate new comparative insights, particularly in areas such as oral tradition, antiquarianism, translation or bilingualism, where the two languages have been, and still are, in direct and fruitful contact.

For general readers and even teachers and students, many of whom know only of an Irish literature in English, the relevant chapters provide a thorough and authoritative discussion of both familiar and less well-known texts along with an analysis of historical trends and current developments in the different periods. At the same time, readers of the *History* will also be introduced, many for the first time, to the diversity of the Irish-language tradition, a tradition many may have only encountered previously at second-hand through the uses and misuses to which it has been subjected by Irish writers of English. The older Irish-language material will thus not only be of interest to those with a special interest in the Gaelic past or to medievalists and scholars of comparative literature seeking access to seminal texts previously denied them. It should also enable those primarily interested in Irish literature in English to see how that literature has been influenced right up to the present by the older native tradition. We do not, then, see this as two discrete histories sharing the same covers, but rather as an integrated narrative addressing the needs of a wide readership from many different backgrounds. On the other hand, we have not tried to construct a unitary or teleological 'metanarrative' from the rich and often refractory reality of Irish literature. Rather, our intention is to offer a comprehensive and accessible survey of two thousand years of Irish literature in two principal and several incidental languages.

One controversy that the editors have had to face from the title page itself concerns the complex and often contested definitions of what an 'Irish' writer is. Our primary criterion for inclusion has been that authors were born on the island of Ireland or lived a significant and formative period of their lives there. Thus we include writings by Spenser, Moryson, Davies, Swift, Sterne, Goldsmith, Trollope and many others as important contributions to the history of Irish literature. In the case of representations of Ireland by English and other commentators (Carlyle, Engels, Gaskell, Asenath Nicholson, etc.), we are interested in the shaping role acquired by such representations, in particular their influence in Ireland and the response they generated from Irish authors. Obviously this definition by its very flexibility generates its own ambiguities. In cases of genuine uncertainty as to whether writers should be considered 'Irish' in any meaningful sense, we would prefer to err on the side of generous inclusion rather than to impose any kind of ethnic or ideological litmus test. Indeed, in some ways the very fact that an author's 'Irishness' is an issue worthy of debate is itself proof that he or she belongs in the *History*!

By defining Irishness on an inclusive island-wide basis, we are also asking our contributors to be sensitive to the existence of differing cultural, political and literary traditions on the island. By no means should this be seen as a genuflection to a transient political correctness. Given the rapid changes affecting Ireland today, in particular the still-embryonic growth of a newly multi-cultural society as a result of increasing immigration, this question of creating and living with a more fluid and embracing sense of Irish identity may well be *the* most important new theme in Irish literature confronting the editors of the successor to these volumes in the future. For now, however, we are attempting to subvert more familiar dichotomies. Thus, for example, we do not intend to marginalise writing from the unionist tradition in Northern Ireland by relegating it to a separate chapter as a regional or provincial offshoot of a putative dominant national tradition.

In keeping with the practice adopted in other *Cambridge History* volumes, we use the term 'literature' in an expansive sense, not limited to *belles lettres*, but also encompassing where appropriate a wide range of other forms of literary expression. We are not seeking to denigrate or subvert the term 'literature', finding it instead both a useful and a necessary term. The traditional genres of poetry, prose and drama are, as is proper, at the heart of this project. Yet by adopting a more comprehensive working definition of what constitutes literature, we make room for several forms of literary expression that have been more prominent in Irish literature than in that of other predominantly Anglophone countries. Could any comprehensive history of Irish literature fail to engage with autobiographical writings such as those by Wolfe Tone, Yeats, George Moore or Sean O'Casey in English, or the so-called 'Blasket autobiographies' in Irish, a genre memorably parodied by 'Myles na gCopaleen' in *An Béal Bocht* (The Poor Mouth)? In like manner, any discussion of Irish literature in either of the island's languages would be poorer for the absence of the many adaptations and reworkings of early Irish heroic tales by authors such as Standish James O'Grady, Lady Gregory, Thomas Kinsella and Seamus Heaney. And of course such adaptations provide a particularly rich illustration of an ongoing cross-fertilisation between the two traditions. Another example of an ongoing Irish cultivation of less traditional genres is the popularity of political writing from Swift and Burke, to the Young Ireland writers of *The Nation* newspaper in the mid-nineteenth century, to the contemporary social and cultural critics associated with Field Day and the Raven Arts Press.

We have asked contributors to address the question of generic ambiguity as a persistent and positive quality of Irish literature in both Irish and English. We hope to show that the Irish tendency to challenge, subvert, redefine and/or merge traditional genres is one of the major forces that gives Irish literature its distinctiveness and vitality, and by no means an indication that Irish writers have either failed to master the canonical genres or devoted an inordinate effort to the cultivation of miniaturist adaptations of major genres from the dominant English tradition. In fact, Irish experimentation with genre goes back to the very origins of Irish literature, to the often anti-climactic heroic tales that represent the oldest vernacular literature north of the Alps and that, despite the example of classical models of the epic, are almost entirely in prose. In this light, one could see Swift's satires, Wilde's subversions of the well-made play, Synge's violent comedies, Yeats's experiments with the *Noh* drama, O'Casey's blendings of high tragedy and farce, and the stylistic experiments of Joyce, Beckett and Flann O'Brien as only a few of the most conspicuous examples in a mainstream Irish tradition of revisioning and revising conventional genres.

The part played by literary works in the broader cultural sphere in Ireland, and their relation to the history and politics of their time, is of necessity an essential theme throughout. Chapter titles are used to help place the literary texts under discussion into a recognisable historical context. A fundamental theme of this *History* is the role of literature in the formation of Irish identities. (And again it should be noted here that we are not positing any unitary or essentialist definition of what it means to be Irish.) Of particular interest throughout the *History* is how literature has been shaped by and in turn has helped shape the political and social developments of its time. Literature in Ireland has often provided a forum in which issues suppressed or neglected in the political arena can continue to circulate. On the other hand, literature has also been the subject of state control and censorship under both colonial and native governments. One of the more fruitful contributions of the *History* is its exploration of these themes through history, showing, for example, how intricately contemporary political issues were woven through the early literature in Irish, how the works of writers as diverse as Swift, Goldsmith, Wilde and Shaw take on different resonances when read in a specifically Irish context, and how Free State censorship blended moral and political objections to suppress dissident voices in the first decades of native rule in the South. By no means do we read the interplay between literature and politics as straightforward and unambiguous. Rather, we hope to explore how this interplay has generated its own traditions in Irish writing – past and present, in Irish and in English, North and South – traditions shaped by diverse, complex and shifting impulses which somehow manage to co-exist, however uneasily and at times all but invisibly.

The contents of this history span work from the sixth century to the year 2000, interweaving literature in Irish and English. Using this scheme readers should be empowered, in a way that was never possible while the two linguistic traditions were treated in isolation, to note and trace the existence of parallel or contradictory trends in the literary development of two languages sharing a single small landmass. Needless to say, the complexities and discontinuities of Irish life as expressed in two very different languages under the stress of a colonial hegemony seen very differently by different segments of the population often render any simplistic linear narrative inadequate, if not downright misleading. But these gaps and disjunctions are at the very heart of the Irish experience, and can therefore be far more interesting, challenging and suggestive, not only for specialists in Irish literary studies, but also for an international audience. Among the practical consequences of the acknowledgement of such gaps is that chapters do not always flow together seamlessly, a development we see as inevitable and beneficial.

The break between volumes occurs just before the commencement of the Literary Revival (*c.*1890). Volume I ends with a transitional chapter on the reciprocal relationships between oral and literary traditions in Irish and

English. This chapter looks back to the nineteenth century (and earlier) and forward to the twentieth century from this dual-language perspective. The opening chapter in volume II is also organised around a crucial theme, in this case the interplay between literature and politics in Ireland. In like manner, the final two chapters of the entire *History* are intended to continue this thematic focus and indeed extend it into the future. These chapters, one dealing with literature in Irish, the other with literature in English, provide an assessment of the current state of Irish writing as well as a projection of possible future trends, all in light of current critical and theoretical methodologies that have radically changed the way we think about Irish literature at the turn of the new millennium.

The allocation of an entire volume to the period 1890–2000 obviously represents a bias. We are aware of this bias, and see it as almost inescapable. Many readers will doubtless consult the *History* for an understanding of the place and significance of modern and contemporary authors in an evolving tradition. Deprived of the luxury of a critical consensus formed over time, we may well have attributed an importance to writers of the recent past and the present that future historians will find inappropriate. But thus has it always been. We believe our decision to devote so much space to twentieth-century literature is justified both by the extent and quality of that literature and by what we believe will be significant reader interest in it. Moreover, readers drawn to the *History* primarily by an interest in the recent past may find especially illuminating and empowering the opportunity to explore the traditions and circumstances that shaped twentieth-century Irish literature in both languages.

One of the potentially more enlightening and provocative aspects of the *History* is its commitment to acknowledging the centrality of canonical figures, while also noting and discussing the contributions of less well-known writers, including those in the process of being retrieved from what now seems inexplicable obscurity and those previously marginalised for reasons having nothing to do with literary merit, but instead based on religion, gender or sexual preference. Indeed a recuperative impulse has been a fundamental motive throughout these two volumes.

Moses Coit Tyler's 1875 history was a pioneering effort, although one whose path can no longer be blindly followed, in large part because he was so sure of where that path would lead – to an ever-clearer, uncontested definition of what it meant to be American. The American tradition in literature will be more accurately explored in the pluralist and multivalent *New Cambridge History of American Literature* (edited by Sacvan Bercovitch) than it ever could be, even in its own time, by the monochromatic and teleologic approach of Tyler. Of course an emphasis on living tradition always looks to the future as well as the past, though the parameters of that future can only be suggested, never defined, much less guaranteed. Nevertheless, as Linda Hutcheon points out in her essay 'Rethinking the National Model', the traditional national model of literary history, one that lays down 'a familiar bedrock of development' and 'historically guarantees a sense of cultural legitimacy', may have to be created 'before competing, correcting, or even counterdiscursive narratives can be articulated'.[2] In this *History* we have tried both to lay down that 'familiar bedrock' and to suggest where 'competing, correcting, or even counterdiscursive narratives' might begin to reshape our understanding of the past. A future *Cambridge History of Irish Literature* will look very different from this one. We hope, however, that its editors will not find their intellectual forebears an embarrassment.

Notes

1. Homi Bhabha, *The Location of Culture* (New York: Routledge, 1994), p. 1.
2. Linda Hutcheon, 'Rethinking the National Model', in Linda Hutcheon and Mario J. Valdés, *Rethinking Literary History* (Oxford and New York: Oxford University Press, 2002), p. 13.

I

Literature and politics

DECLAN KIBERD

The artist and the social world

When Seamus Heaney was awarded the Nobel Prize for Literature in 1995, that story received front-page treatment in the Irish broadsheet press and on news programmes of the electronic media. This was but one indication that creative writers are central to the self-image of Ireland. Another might have been found on the national banknotes still circulating in that year. These featured such figures as W. B. Yeats, James Joyce, Douglas Hyde and Jonathan Swift, as well as the nineteenth-century political leaders Daniel O'Connell and Charles Stewart Parnell. The number of artists far exceeded the number of political figures, such as were to be found on the currencies of most other European countries. In the modern Republic of Ireland, culture is often seen as healing, whereas history is viewed as divisive. If the last national currency before the arrival of the Euro in 2002 projected writers as part of the self-description of a people, the design of the very first set of coins for the Free State back in the 1920s had been entrusted to a committee chaired by W. B. Yeats. That same author was, even then, putting the final touches to *A Vision*, his attempt to write a personal imaginative system which might also function as a Celtic constitution for the emerging nation. Nor was there anything immodest about the ease with which Yeats identified his intellectual project with that of the nation. After all, by then James Joyce had presented his first collection of stories, *Dubliners*, as 'a chapter of the moral history of my country' and had ended *A Portrait of the Artist as a Young Man* with the protagonist's promise to forge in the smithy of his soul 'the uncreated conscience of my race'.[1] Against that backdrop, it may not have been surprising that the question most often put to Seamus Heaney in interviews during the quarter-century leading up to his Nobel Prize was this: what was his solution to the 'troubles' of Northern Ireland? A poet was expected to propound an answer to a problem which had defeated the best intelligence of political science for generations. As far back as 1972 Richard

Rose had called Northern Ireland 'a problem without a solution'.[2] In Ireland, however, artists are expected to see things other mortals don't see and the social powers accorded to the artist are of ancient lineage.

Catastrophism and art: the sense of an ending

The *filí* or poets stood second only to the chieftain in the power-structure of Gaelic Ireland, carrying rods as symbols of their vatic powers. They composed while lying on pallets in darkened huts and their job was to praise a good prince, rebuke his enemies and memorialise dead heroes in immortal lines. After the collapse of the old order in 1600 and the Flight of the Earls in 1607, all that changed: and so the *filí* became the first 'dandies' of Europe, which is to say courtiers dispossessed of a court. Deprived of their aristocratic audiences, the *filí* had no choice but to aim a reconfigured lyric at the wider public and to submit to the conditions of the marketplace. In other parts of Europe, the tradition of literary patronage would last for many more decades – in Germany for two whole centuries – but in Ireland it was now destroyed. Much of the writing of the Irish Renaissance between 1890 and 1925 is an attempt to reverse this reel and to restore elements of the old Gaelic order. The use of actors by Yeats, Synge and Augusta Gregory at the Abbey Theatre recalls the employment of the *reacaire* as a formal reciter of lines by the *filí*, with the audience replicating the old convivial gatherings in the prince's hall.[3] Even a figure as unlikely as James Joyce seems to have been caught up in this project: his Stephen is described in *Ulysses* as a 'youthful bard' complete with vatic cane, just as Joyce himself wished to re-enter what he called 'the fair courts of life' (pressing gullible but monied bluestockings into service as replicants of the old princely patrons).[4]

All of this revivalism was of course wish-fulfillment. After 1607 it was clear to those who had eyes to see that the old days could never return. The serfs had been freed in 1605 and from that moment on could save money, press cases in court or even buy land. They were no longer obliged to provide free field labour to princes but must now be recompensed for all work done. With pastorage giving way to tillage, there was good money to be made and life became easier for many. Soon the former serfs were outbidding fallen noblemen for tracts of land. A centralised administration was being established in Dublin. As primogeniture took the place of custom, the old rule of poets as interpreters of rightful sovereignty was lost. Under the new laws, there was no place for them. Small wonder that these ruined aristocrats floated their poems on the market in a heavily ironical search for a buyer. Over two centuries before Charles

Baudelaire lamented a similar loss of aura among French poets, now turning tricks like harlots desperate to please a passing customer, Mathghamhain Ó hIfearnáin asks:

Ceist! cia do cheinneochaidh dán?
  a chiall is ceirteolas suadh:
an ngeabhadh, nó an áil le haon,
  dán saor do-bhéaradh go buan?[5]

A question! who will buy a poem
  whose content is the fit learning of scholars?
Will anyone accept or does anyone even want
  a fine poem that will last forever?

The *filí* had been futurologists, as that last line wryly implies. As part of their prophetic function, they proclaimed the honour of their chief for the coming generations. It was through the poet's vibrant lines that a ruler or warrior left 'names upon the harp'.[6] Now there was a sense that that future was annulled: the ruined *filí* were among the first poets of the world to abandon the comforts of tradition and to seek an originality that was market-oriented.

Much of the art produced by the *filí* between 1600 and 1660 anticipates those elements of Modernism rehearsed in 1840s Paris. The broken dandies tried to appear unperturbed amidst the collapse of old securities but were now lamenting the death of an entire civilisation, while desperately seeking any new patrons who might suddenly emerge from the chaos. Instead of the old duty of keening this or that personage, they were now lamenting the end of culture itself. Yet their dirges were somewhat paradoxical. The need to address a wider audience had a tonic effect upon their art, infusing it with a new vitality of diction and urgency of rhythm.[7] These desperadoes took pleasure in stating the worst but with such eloquence as to throw the diagnosis into question. For many, death was just another career move. The old mortuary traditions were thus given a new set of inflections, becoming in effect one of the most potent of all rhetorical devices in the cultural politics of the next 400 years. That rhetoric would inspire the Fenians of the 1860s, who found Ireland like a corpse on the dissecting table and kissed it back to life. It would explain Patrick Pearse's use of the grave of O'Donovan Rossa to indicate that the patriot dead would ensure that an unfree land could never be at peace. It would stoke the phoenix-fires of more recent republicans and hunger-strikers in Northern Ireland who said 'Éireoidh muid arís' (We shall rise again). If the search for the means to put an end to things, as Samuel Beckett wittily observed, is what enables discourse to continue, then the Irish have known that better than most. For centuries their culture has been surviving near-death experiences in a state of augmented vitality. The ruined bards made their verses grow fat on negation. Perhaps it was in their poetic achievement that the notion of 'the triumph of failure', which would animate not just the Easter Rising but the aesthetic of Beckett, was so strangely born.

The nomad as sign of the modern

One of the central figures in the texts of Irish Modernism, the tramp or nomad, also has roots in the fall of the bardic order. Both Yeats and Synge saw in the tramp a version of the decline of the Anglo-Irish gentry: and that equation was all the more telling if the tramp were taken as a version of the ruined bard/turned *spailpín* poet, travelling from place to place with song and story. The tramps of Beckett are men who sound as educated as any bard, and as *déclassé*, rather in the manner of people whose self-image is exalted even as their fate is humble. 'You should have been a poet,' says a sardonic Didi to Gogo in *Waiting for Godot,* only to evoke the reply, as his partner gestures at his rags: 'I was. . . . Isn't that obvious?'[8]

Synge, in particular, saw in these learned nomads early types of the artistic sons of mercantile families and took to signing his own love letters: 'your old tramp'.[9] The degree of identification by twentieth-century authors with the toppled bards of the early seventeenth is remarkable: in both cases the collapse of an order signalled a major revival in literature, which sought to come to terms with all the turbulence. The narrators of Beckett's texts ('A voice comes to one in the dark. Imagine')[10] often evoke the compositional practices of the *filí* on their pallets, even as the wanderers of Yeats's poetry lament the philistinism of middle-class arrivistes in 'The Curse of Cromwell'. The lesson of the *filí* wasn't lost on these authors: by over-identifying with a single political regime, they ran the risk of falling with it. The more intrepid Irish Modernists could see a further analogy: between the ruined bardic poets and the cakes-and-ale aristocrats of Shakespeare. Both groups were displaced in due course by Malvolio-style puritans, seeking revenge on the whole cavalier pack.

Meltdown: literary form and social change

Whenever one order falls and another eventually takes its place, there is in art a period of 'latency' when forms go into meltdown and all kinds of innovation are attempted. In most parts of Europe, the transition from aristocracy to bourgeoisie happened with relative speed, so that the new forms of literature thrown up by the changes (notably the form of the novel) soon stabilised into formula. In Ireland, however, conditions were somewhat different. The native aristocracy was toppled after 1600, two or more centuries before equivalent events elsewhere in Europe, but a truly comprehensive native middle class didn't emerge until well into the twentieth century. Between these dates, the key works of Irish prose were collections of micro-narratives cast in the appearance of a novel but without its sense of a completely connected plotline. Swift's *Gulliver's Travels* is really four short *contes* and *Castle Rackrent* describes many generations in sixty pages. Works as varied as *Siabhra Mhic na Míochomhairle*, *Ulysses*, *At Swim-Two-Birds* or *Cré na Cille* are structured around episodes and anecdotes which never quite shape themselves into a novel. If epic is the genre of warrior aristocrats and the novel that of the bourgeoisie, then it is in the troubled transition period between these orders that a radical innovation of forms becomes possible. In most lands that transition was managed smoothly, but in Ireland it took more than three centuries.

The radical innovations in Irish begin with the writings of Seathrún Céitinn and Eochaidh Ó hEodhasa. Two centuries before Wordsworth's 'Preface' to the second edition of *The Lyrical Ballads*, they were compelled to address their lines to the masses rather than the classes. They were able to think like wise men, yet express themselves like the common people. Some (such as Céitinn) who might have been bards now became priests, adding a millennial element to their narratives. Proclaiming themselves at the end of a whole era, they brought a modern sense of crisis to Irish writing. In their eyes (as in the view of the English planter-poet Edmund Spenser), Ireland was a site of apocalypse. If Spenser saw 'mutabilitie' as the mark of all created things, and the deaths of rebels as a version of the Last Judgement, so did a priest like Céitinn. Both men, after all, were courtiers without a court.

For the next three centuries, writers would know only dire stress, forever proclaiming themselves at the end of an era. Yet the promised apocalypse never came on cue. Instead, its terrors were absorbed back into art-works, by intellectuals who would learn how to make destitution sumptuous. The less of Ireland there was to write about, the more copious and gorgeous was the documentation about it.

Virtual worlds

With the Gaelic lords either fled or on the run, the *filí* were reduced through the seventeenth and eighteenth centuries to the condition of journeymen or day-labourers. Yet in another sense they were more important than ever, for now they maintained the consciousness of a proud underground people. Their lyrics were promissory notes or blueprints for a restored Gaelic Ireland which might re-emerge at some future time – and thus the prophetic element of the tradition was maintained. The virtual world of the fairies, who were believed to exist beyond the 'rational' social order (perhaps even underground in the 'unconscious' of the people) became itself a practical zone of alterity, in which it was possible to 'think otherwise'. If the colonisers had a secret police who spied on rebels and insurgents, as Angela Bourke has shown, the natives had access to fairies who might spy back on the enemy, being (like the police) everywhere and nowhere at once.[11]

It would be hard to overestimate the social power of the virtual worlds often created by writers within the colonial scheme. For instance, the courts of poetry set up in Munster in the eighteenth century were not only serious attempts to reconnect with bardic tradition but also subversive parodies of the despised English law. In these courts a self-appointed sheriff often signed a pompous 'warrant', in a mocking throwback to the ancient days when *file* and *breitheamh* were one. In similar style, the court presided over by fairy-women in Brian Merriman's poem seems another parody of the hated parliamentary processes which had brought such misery to Ireland. The poem was also, however, a return to the old sovereignty myths, as well as a radical prophecy of a future when women might be fully empowered.

Texts like these had a palpable influence on the insurgent leaders of Ireland in the nineteenth and twentieth centuries. The setting-up of a revolutionary Dáil in 1919, with its own republican courts within the overall British structure, may have been suggested by readings of Merriman's poem, or of texts like it. Nor did that tradition die away with the attainment of independence in 1922. The novelist John McGahern has suggested that within the censorious land of the 1940s many young people created their own pockets of freedom and experiment. McGahern contended that in the summer months after local dances 'there wasn't a hay-rick safe for miles around, but the whole place filled with couples going off like alarm-clocks'.[12]

It was inevitable that there would be two versions of everything in a colony – official and unofficial – but once again what often seemed like contrary realities turned out upon inspection to be alternative versions of the same thing. Opposites had a habit of turning into doubles. For example, the tradition of the 'wake' might have seemed to rationalists a deeply superstitious exercise and an excuse for drunkenness. However, it also functioned as a sort of unofficial autopsy, as Maria Edgeworth noted in *Castle Rackrent*, giving people time to ensure that the person mourned really was dead.[13] Likewise, Edgeworth remarked on how fairy raths in which valuables were stored by local people were trusted more than banks, whose role they mimicked. What seemed like foolish superstition to the sceptical outsider often had a perfectly rational explanation. If fireside tales were told of a hand reaching out of rough sea to pull unsuspecting oarsmen to their deaths, this was really a practical warning to sailors about a particularly treacherous tract of seawater along the coast.

Underground codes: the Gaelic samizdat

Words were among the most potent weapons of a disarmed people, who resorted to modes of irony, deceit and wordplay as methods of self-protection. Sir John Davies was perhaps the first to notice that coercion made the Irish grow crafty, for, he said, 'such as are oppressed are ever put to their shifts'.[14] In a contested land, poets said one thing while actually meaning another. They praised the beauty of Síle Ní Ghadhra or Cáit Ní Dhuibhir or Caitlín Ní Uallacháin, while secretly celebrating the island imagined as a woman. This was a throw-back to a bardic conceit, according to which the chieftain was married to the land, which was itself female, and so (as we have seen) beautiful or barren depending on the quality of his rule. And that concept was in turn intimately connected with the old sovereignty myths, according to which an ugly crone might meet a young man and offer him the lordship of all Ireland, if only he would sleep with her and thus make her young and beautiful again. A strong echo of that tradition was to be found in the *aisling* poems of Gaelic Ireland in the eighteenth century, which depicted a passive, wan *spéirbhean* (skywoman), whose weakness would only be brought to an end when her true prince emerged from across the sea to save her. The *aisling* became increasingly formulaic through the period, being often parodied by poets who recognised that there was little or no chance of a foreign deliverer: but the underlying images remained astonishingly vibrant. They were to be reworked by W. B. Yeats and Augusta Gregory in the play *Cathleen ni Houlihan* (1902), in which an old woman will once again walk like a ravishing young queen if only the young men are willing to die for her. To Constance Markievicz, the socialist leader of 1916, this play was 'a kind of gospel', to the young republican P. S. O'Hegarty 'a sort of sacrament', but the constitutional nationalist MP Stephen Gwynn was less enamoured. Though conceding that Maud Gonne's impersonation of the old woman was deeply moving, he was troubled by the long-term implications. Such plays should not be staged, he averred, unless people were willing to go out of the theatre to shoot and be shot at.[15]

There were many who believed that there was a definite link between the play and the Rebellion of 1916. Even in old age, Yeats fretted about this:

Did that play of mine send out
Certain men the English shot?[16]

One nationalist who did his best to break that link was the Celtic scholar and leader of the Irish Volunteers, Eoin Mac Néill. Just some weeks before the Easter Rising, he told the men under his command during manoeuvres at Rathfarnham that there really was no such person as Cathleen Ní Houlihan or a poor old woman. There was merely the physical reality of a land that they might all one day fight for.[17] That he should have felt such a deep need to counter the poetic tradition suggests just how tenacious a hold it had on the popular imagination of nationalist males. Perhaps the conceit fed the cult of machismo among young men who might otherwise have felt themselves emasculated by the long pre-1914 peace and by the daily humiliations of life in a down-at-heel colonial backwater.

There were other, even deeper codes at work in the Gaelic songs and poems of the seventeenth and eighteenth centuries, but they all had one common element: they showed how public events were swamping private lives, to such an extent that the personal and political meanings of a text were often wholly intertwined. This would become a feature of much poetry in twentieth-century Europe, but it had many precedents in Irish. Poets like Stephen Spender who praised Yeats's 'Easter 1916' as a text which was at once love lyric and political statement thought that this was a new combination in English-language poetry – what Spender called the raising of an 'occasional' poem to the status of a political lyric.[18] Perhaps it was a new moment in English, but such a combination was of ancient lineage in Irish.

As far back as the seventeenth century, the Tipperary rebel and Gaelic aristocrat Éamonn Ó Riain was beseeching his lover to shelter him from the storm, a storm which turned out on inspection to be the superior fire-power of English guns:

'Cé hé sin amuigh
A bhfuil faobhar ar a ghuth
  Ag réabadh mo dhorais dúnta?'
'Mise Éamonn an chnoic
Atá báite fuar fliuch
  Ó shíor-shiúl sléibhte is gleannta.'
'A laogh ghil 's a chuid

Cad a dhéanfainnse duit
  Muna gcuirfinn ort beinn dem ghúna?
Mar tá púdar go tiubh
Dá shíor-shéideadh riot,
  's go mbeimis araon múchta.'[19]

'Who's out there in the night.
His voice sharp with fright,
  Beating on my locked door?'
'I'm Ned of the Hill,
Half drowned and chill
  With walking the mountain and moor.'
'My love and delight
How can I ease your plight
  Only shelter you under my gown?
For powder and shot
Are forever your lot
  And together we may both go down.'

In the figure of this toppled aristocrat may be found yet another precursor of the *déclassé* wanderers of a later age:

'Is fada mise amuigh
Fé shneachta 's fé shioc
  'S gan dánacht agam ar éinne;
Mo sheisreach gan scur
Mo bhranar gan chur
  Is gan iad agam ar aon chor.
Níl caraid agam
Is danaid liom san
  Do ghlacfadh mé moch ná déanach;
Is go gcaithfidh mé dul
Thar farraige anonn
  Ós ann nach bhfuil mo ghaolta.'

'It's long I am lost
In the snow and the frost
  And none who will give me a hand;
My plough-team is gone,
And my sowing's not done,
  And I've small claim enough to the land.
It's a sorrowful end
Without even a friend
  Who will shelter me late or soon;

And so I must flee
To the east over sea,
 Where none of my kindred is gone.'

These evicted Gaelic leaders often lamented the felling of the woods by the new English overlords and middlemen:

Anois tá an choill dá ghearradh
Triallfaimid thar chaladh
'sa Sheáin Uí Dhuibhir an Ghleanna,
 Tá tú gan géim.

But now the woods are falling;
We must go over the water,
And John O'Dwyer of the Valley,
 You have no game.

The code is never difficult to crack, for the planters were often puritans and killjoys, seen to be at war with the world of nature itself. If for Edmund Burke, as later for W. B. Yeats, a tree with its branches symbolised the slow, patient evolution of a complex society and its institutions, then those who cut down trees and sold them off at sixpence a time were persons with no understanding of tradition or order. The woods as a whole had both a literal and metaphorical meaning. At a practical level, they were places in which rebels on the run from the crown forces might hide away; but in a more symbolic guise they also represented the unconscious, that place of secrecy where instincts were liberated. Anyone who sought to clear them was simply attempting to roll back and control the instinctual, to make way for the daylight world of reason and commerce. No wonder that the lament for the deforestation of Ireland (famously recycled in the Cyclops episode of Joyce's *Ulysses*) was linked with so many other losses, as in the song 'Cill Cais':

Cad a dhéanfaimid feasta gan adhmad?
 Tá deire na gcoillte ar lár;
Níl trácht ar Chill Cais ná a teaghlach
 Is ní chluinfear a cling go bráth.
An áit úd ina gcónaíodh an deigh-bhean
 Fuair gradam is meidhir thar mná,
Bhíodh iarlaí ag tarraingt thar toinn ann
 Is an tAifreann doimhin dá rá.[20]

What shall we do without timber?
 The last of the woods is down;
Kilcash and the house of its glory

And the bell of the house are gone.
The spot where that lady waited
Who shamed all women for grace,
Had earls come sailing to meet her
And Mass was said in the place.

These lines – and others from the Gaelic poet Aogán Ó Rathaille – lie behind Yeats's reworking of the theme in 'The Curse of Cromwell'. There the poet makes a telling comparison between boorish bailiffs who dogged the Gaelic writer in the eighteenth century and the philistine councillors who curbed the artist in the Free State of the 1930s:

The lovers and the dancers are all beaten into the clay
And the tall men and the swordsmen and the horsemen, where are they?
And there's an old beggar, wandering in his pride,
His fathers served their fathers before Christ was crucified.[21]

Overground codes: Anglo-Irish anxieties

On the planter's side, too, there was much scope for metaphor and innuendo. In a land where there were two contested versions of reality, neither side enjoyed complete dominance. The English planters had control by virtue of military power, but they were nervously aware that the native Irish constituted a four-fifths majority of the population. The external confidence proclaimed in the architecture of the big houses erected by planters could not completely conceal an inner anxiety as to just how long their power might go unchallenged – the Anglo-Irish may indeed have been the first 'provisionals'. Many of the planters assumed over time the airs of an aristocracy but Gaelic poets were quick to point out that most of them were irretrievably middle-class and no true replacement for the toppled Gaelic princes. This ambiguity about their true social identity added to their inner uncertainty – and thus to their exterior swagger. One consequence was that what sometimes looked like a clash between official and unofficial Ireland was often more accurately a contest for hegemony between 'unofficial' and 'unofficialer'.

This anxiety can be deduced in the rhetoric of the Penal Laws enacted against Catholics after 1690. The ferocity of the measures and extremism of their language may have been attempts to compensate for their inoperability in those areas which lacked a secure prison or a working police force. For instance, one enactment compelled Catholics to work on church holidays, but any officer who refused to implement this law could be thrown in jail. 'The law acknowledges that it is simply one way of looking at life,' writes Andrew Carpenter, 'and seems to accept that the other perspective is de facto to remain in existence.'[22] Maidens who married Catholics were to be considered dead (as in effect were all Catholics themselves) – though the great majority clearly continued to breathe after the experience.

If these measures were to some degree rhetorical, it may not be surprising that such exercises in radical irony were also performed by creative writers. The most famous case is probably *A Modest Proposal* by Jonathan Swift, in which the author suggested that all children under the age of six be provided as roasting-meat from Ireland for English tables. With tongue in cheek, Swift insisted that he could not be accused of having a vested interest in the scheme, since he had no children of eligible age and his wife was now past the age of childbearing. However, *Gulliver's Travels* is the paradigmatic text with its tale of a rather unimaginative Englishman caught among tiny Lilliputians and gigantic Brobdingnagians. One source was a folk anecdote heard in the townland of Quilca, County Cavan (and one which has persisted down to our own time in Irish), but Swift gave the narrative a truly Anglo-Irish inflection by foregrounding in it the question of perception. Making great play with Gulliver's pair of spectacles, he showed how readers identify with the big people in each phase of the story but forced them also to consider what the world must be like for those who feel themselves tiny in the face of overweening power. The ever-shifting perspectives allowed by the story might be applied also to Anglo-Irish relations, with Swift seen as offering an early instance of imperial feedback to the metropolitan centre of London (where the book was first published). A similar obsession with ways of seeing is to be found in the philosophical writings of George Berkeley, the Anglican bishop of Cloyne. His mantra – 'Esse est percipi, To be is to be perceived' – is but another way of saying that the forms of perception determine the nature of the thing seen and that such forms are fluid, subjective, ever-changing. Being a spiritually hyphenated people, the Anglo-Irish were doomed to seem forever English in Ireland and Irish in England. That outsider status led to a certain coldness and to a sense of aesthetic distance of authors from subjects, as if they were taking an anthropological view rather than a merely cultural one. Again and again from Swift to Beckett, writers ask exactly what kind of a creature man really is. Such coolness of approach was also conducive to laughter, for, as Horace Walpole said, the world is a comedy to the man who thinks and a tragedy to the man who feels.[23] The Anglo-Irish were sharp, edgy thinkers, whose art turned often to mockery, satire and the comedy of manners.

To live in a state of hyphenation was to experience perpetual insecurity, but that was a state propitious for the production of a rich literature. Because London was the despatch-point for most publications, the books and texts so issued were almost invariably read as comments on British society. So *Gulliver's Travels* was taken as a mordant commentary on high politics in the time of Queen Anne and after, or Goldsmith's 'The Deserted Village' was interpreted as a protest against the changes in small-town England. These analyses unnecessarily limited the possible range of interpretations of major works. It is only in recent decades, with the emergence of a cadre of Irish-based scholars, that analysts have rediscovered Irish bearings in the writing of someone like Richard Brinsley Sheridan, a republican sympathiser with the 1798 rebellion as well as a friend of the English royal family.

The tradition of Anglo-Irish comedy, in particular, ran from William Congreve, through George Farquhar, down to Oscar Wilde and Bernard Shaw. Because these artists existed at an angle to English society, their accounts of it had for many the interest of familiar but objective commentators. They were like but not too like their English subjects. So Goldsmith, as a Longford man in London, was in a position to imagine how that city might appear to a Chinese visitor in *The Citizen of the World*. If the criticisms voiced by the Anglo-Irish authors seemed fair, the writers could be accepted as valid and thoughtful commentators: but if they went too close to the bone for comfort, they could be instantly disregarded, on the grounds that the Irish were merely being whimsical and feckless once again. Much of the tradition of British comedy across the centuries has been an experimental laboratory in which the Anglo-Irish tested certain lines of argument, just as back in Ireland the colonial administrators from the same class tried out new policies on their underlings, which might in due course be introduced in Britain too.

Some write to the future

One effect of all of these manoeuvres was to make literature even more socially significant than ever, among the Anglo-Irish as well as the Gaels. A novel by Jane Austen was read by young people in the nineteenth century not only for its vivid plot and sparkling dialogue, but also as a sort of etiquette manual. Close study of it might teach an ambitious young man how to speak to a lady of title or how to walk across a crowded ballroom. Literature, in such applications, was believed to carry the blueprint for a civil society which might be made over in its image.

Such a utopian element was, if anything, even more present in writing in the Irish language. The *aisling* was but one form among the 'poems of the dispossessed' which kept the hope of a recovered and vibrant Gaelic system alive. An oppressed people could not identify themselves with most of the great state formations, whether law, army or police: but literature was one social institution through which they might project past values and future aspirations. The act of writing or reading or reciting a Gaelic work meant that, for the duration of its enunciation at least, the artist or receiver was in a world elsewhere, a virtual space, in which all injustices might yet be set to rights. The *filí*, despite their identification with a toppled aristocracy, became for many persons of humbler origin through the seventeenth and eighteenth centuries the figures who maintained an underground consciousness. For these people, also, literature was supremely important because it offered a utopian vision based on a visionary understanding of tradition.

The pressures of expectation placed in consequence upon all forms of writing in Ireland help to explain their extraordinary involutions of form and style. They may also account for that strange blend of the conservative and the radical which would lead Terry Eagleton to dub Irish Modernism a case of the 'archaic avant-garde'.[24] That blending, however, had occurred well before the twentieth century, for the colonial conditions saw to that. Whether they wished it or not, the Gaelic poets who yearned for a return of the old leaders were by that very volition seen as subversive of the new regime. Hence that strange mixture of nostalgia and radical protest which may be found in texts like *Cúirt an Mheán Oíche* or *Caoineadh Airt Uí Laoghaire*, a conjunction also apparent in 'The Deserted Village' by Goldsmith. The upholders of ancient Gaelic value often felt obliged to find new forms – such as 'Trí Rainn agus Amhrán'(Three Stanzas and a Song) – in which to address the Irish-speaking masses, so that their old ideas would have the protection of up-to-date metres. This tradition of securing a hearing for aristocratic ideology under the protective cover of a radical form would also link a writer like Swift to a much later example such as W. B. Yeats. But there was a fairly predictable corollary: republicans like Richard Brinsley Sheridan or socialists such as Sean O'Casey would find it equally opportune to use tried dramatic formulae to promote their left-wing social philosophy. In this context, there were some amazing texts in Irish which seemed to have things every way. Merriman's *Cúirt*, as we have seen, rigged itself out in an ancient sovereignty myth, but only to promote libertarian modern ideas about the need to fulfil all bodily instincts. What emerged in the end from all these manoeuvres was a sense of the writer, whether in Irish or in English, as a masked rebel, playing off form against content for some ulterior purpose, a Tory Radical or a Radical Tory. In this, as in so much else, the two language traditions, in superficial ways so opposed, were often in the deeper structures of thought and feeling much closer than their practitioners seemed to realise.[25]

Which is to say that the Irish evolved some techniques of literary Modernism decades before its appearance in other parts of the world – and some decades at least before the process of social modernisation began in the 1830s. That decade saw not only the mapping of the countryside by the Ordnance Survey but also the launch of a statewide system of primary schooling (both subjects to be treated with great understanding by Brian Friel in his play *Translations*). In the 1840s a state postal service was instituted and, like the school system, it was a pilot scheme, well ahead of similar measures in England. Local Anglo-Irish landlords had proven in many cases delinquent, unlike their counterparts in England, and so the move to centralise power in the state was made sooner in Ireland, leading to a whole set of 'national' narratives, often from women writers like Maria Edgeworth or Lady Morgan (Sydney Owenson). Because Ireland was a laboratory, many modern experiments were tried there first – some bad (coercion, cat-and-mouse acts) but others good (some so good that they have yet to be fully implemented in Britain, such as the disestablishment of the Anglican Church as state religion in 1869 or the widespread expropriation of the landlords in the 1880s and after).

Yet, for all these innovations, Ireland remained in the nineteenth century, as in the age of Swift, overtaxed and under-capitalised. Here was another case, now in the socio-economic realm, of cultural modernisation existing side by side with material backwardness. It was out of such discrepancies that the art of Irish Modernism at the end of the nineteenth century would emerge. A youth like James Joyce was at once the beneficiary of an impressive system of education and the victim of an economy which had little use for graduates such as he. If you educate a populace to high levels but leave them with few outlets for their talents and qualifications, you are creating the conditions for three things – endemic emigration, cultural efflorescence (as the powerless seize control of discourse, as only the unarmed can) and, eventually, rebellion.

Writing as exile: exile as writing

Joyce once had Stephen Dedalus say that the shortest way to Tara, epicentre of Gaelic Ireland, was through Holyhead,[26] port of disembarkation for Irish emigrants to Britain. More than a predictable witticism about the difficulty of reviving cultural traditions, this was also a recognition that Irish people discover themselves as such only in some foreign country. Given that no people can ever fully define itself from within, exile has indeed been the cradle of nationality. This has interesting implications. Irishness is like Jewishness – whatever people say it is. To be Irish in such a context is simply to be called Irish; and to know what that means, you generally have to ask the English or, failing them, the Americans. Though berated sometimes for their simple-mindedness, emigrants in the nineteenth century, such as Oscar Wilde, were aware of the hybrid sources of nationalism: only through contact with the art of another country or countries, said Wilde, could a modern Irish literature be shaped.

Some writers went overseas to achieve that distance which allowed them to recast earlier experiences with the same sort of detachment achieved by the Anglo-Irish on the island. Whether the culprit was British rule, censorship by clergy, or the common middle-class distrust of art, they felt (in the words of Frank O'Connor) that 'an Irish person's private life begins in Holyhead'.[27] Bohemia, a place filled by definition with exiles, rather than Ireland was these artists' native country. It was the 'note of banishment'[28] which Joyce detected in Shakespeare, whose whole canon he read as a narrative of exile and loss. This was Joyce's way of converting Shakespeare and his own self into versions of Colmcille: for the story of the saint's exile and eventual surreptitious return became a paradigm of Irish culture, to be repeated in every generation. Thus the *Jail Journal*, written by the patriot John Mitchel during his transportation to Tasmania in the 1850s, would become a defining document of modern Irish nationhood.

Those who stayed at home were, nonetheless, transformed by this migrant experience too – and for a simple enough reason. Those who left solved two problems. By moving on, they often secured greater comfort for themselves but also made life better for those who stayed, since if they had remained, many would have been a drain on finite resources. If the one in two who left since 1841 had stayed, Ireland would today look more like an underdeveloped country and the United States or Australia seem a lot less prosperous. Wherever emigrants went they took with them something which the stay-at-homes seldom bothered to shoulder: *an idea of Ireland*. Yet the usual paradox of the exile's life was to be noted: in England, Australia or North America, those who had emigrated because of a refusal or inability to conform to norms of Irishness at home were, nevertheless, expected to represent precisely that type they had not managed to be. Further simplifications occurred. Aware of the image of the stage Paddy, migrants in England played up to the role, in order to know themselves, assuming an identity in order to prove it on their pulses.

As early as 1818, the poet John Keats observed that 'the Irish are sensible of the character they hold in England and act accordingly to Englishmen'.[29] They worked the stereotype, if only because it made an initial relationship possible. Modifications and subtleties could come later. Many found it easier to don the mask of a Paddy than to reshape a complex urban identity of their own. For them once again, Wilde spoke when he quipped: 'Mask and it shall be given to you'.[30]

Bringing it all back home

In such a fashion was a modern culture reshaped out of the hybrid experience of the Irish among nationalities in England, Australia or North America, the double-exposure working, in the words of Benedict Anderson 'like a white-on-black photographic negative'.[31] The longing for a sod of Sligo earth felt in a London street by the young W. B. Yeats was one manifestation of the phenomenon: and Australian ballads about Ned Kelly were another. All fed the forces of an emergent modern nationalism. By the close of the nineteenth century, a group of activists decided to return and print a photograph of the negative exposure 'in the dark-room of political struggle'. The centre of gravity in Irish culture was to be shifted from London and New York back to Dublin, as writers would look henceforth for publication in their own land first of all. In the words of Yeats:

> All day I'd looked in the face
> What I had hoped 'twould be
> To write for my own race . . .[32]

He believed that the creation of a national literature necessitated the gathering of a national audience. That audience didn't always welcome the art so offered. When Synge's *The Playboy of the Western World* was rejected in 1907, Yeats bleakly observed that whenever a country produces a man of genius, he is never like the country's idea of itself. He began to suspect that the artist is often an internal exile.

For many artists, the act of writing was not only a measure of their estrangement from official versions of Ireland, but also of the removal of that Ireland from its own past. Unlike other emigrants from Europe, the Irish chose to learn English and abandon their native language *in their own land*. The result was that kind of compulsory Bohemia described in a letter from Friedrich Engels to Karl Marx: 'the fellows begin to feel like strangers in their own country'.[33] Learning English was a desperate bargain made with modernity: it prepared children for emigration, commercial life or higher education. The famines of the 1840s hit Irish-speaking areas very hard, destroying many Victorian ideas of history as a straight line based on progress and reintroducing the notion of history as an ever-retraced circle – a model which would have huge influence on Yeats in *A Vision* and on Joyce in *Finnegans Wake*.

By a brutal paradox, English became the language in which the nationalist case was put. If Benedict Anderson is right in saying that print-language creates a nationalism, and not a particular language of itself,[34] then English was the ideal medium through which the abstract bonding of people into a unified movement could be achieved. Through newspapers, ballad-sheets, handbills and pamphlets, the very technology which underpinned nationalism was available in the English rather than the Irish language. For a rebel who wished to write a threatening letter to a landlord or defend himself in court, a knowledge of English was essential. Even a fluent Irish speaker such as Daniel O'Connell used English in addressing large crowds for much the same reasons that Arab protestors hold up placards to CNN cameras in English, in the hope that their sentiments would prick the conscience of hesitant liberal well-wishers in the imperial centre.

Yet acceptance of English as the major medium of Irish nationalism seemed to undermine the very basis of the separatist claim, leaving the Irish Question to be treated as more economic than political in nature. In part to combat such simplified interpretations, Douglas Hyde and others founded the Gaelic League in 1893.

A masked modernity?

It was as if the people had moved too far too fast in cultural terms. To give up a language and learn another would perforce become one of the defining features of modern life for many peoples in the twentieth century, but for hundreds of thousands of Irish this happened in the nineteenth century. To have begun life in a windswept village on the western seaboard and to have ended it in Hammersmith or Hell's Kitchen was to have experienced the deracination that would be for many millions the central 'progress' of the twentieth century. Not necessarily sympathetic to the modern by temperament, the Irish were among the first to be caught in a modern predicament. If at times they evinced a nostalgia for a 'lost' Gaelic past, they did so as the natural human response to being hurtled into the future at break-neck speed. Those who suffer from motion-sickness may take some comfort in the rear-view mirror.

For such a people modernisation has been not so much an option as a *donné*. The sense of being asked to improvise a set of values in a terrifyingly decontextualised space is the subtext of John Montague's lines about the loss of Irish in his native Tyrone of the nineteenth century:

> All around us shards of a lost tradition,
> The whole countryside a manuscript
> We had lost the skill to read,
> A part of our past disinherited
> But fumbled like a blind man
> Along the fingertips of instinct.[35]

A similar crisis underlies the plight of Beckett's tramps, who must invent on an open stage a set of instant traditions: 'Yesterday. . . . In my opinion. . . . I was here. . . . yesterday'.[36] These tramps also have to imagine the missing details of a landscape, details filled with hints as to how they might behave, when what actually confronts them is a blasted, near-empty setting. Their condition is rather like that of the *filí* after 1600.

This culture is never more modernising in practical purpose than when it appears most nostalgic in its official self-description. The Easter Rebellion of 1916 is the central example, now lamented by fashionable historians as a foolish military misadventure, conducted as an attempt by sentimentalists in open revolt against the modern world to return to a Gaelic order. Nothing could have been more romantic than the symbolic choice of Easter and springtime for a resurrected and revivified land, yet the date also made pragmatic sense too, since Easter Monday was a public holiday, leaving the authorities vulnerable, as police and soldiery spent the day at the horse-races. A similar mingling of the idealistic and the practical may be found in the Proclamation of the Irish Republic by the rebels. It began 'Irishmen and Irishwomen', including women in the body politic at a time when they still hadn't the vote but when suffragism was at its height. Over fifty women fought as volunteer soldiers in the Rising. Another woman, Hanna Sheehy Skeffington, was appointed to the inner cabinet of five ministers, should the provisional government come into administrative being. She would in fact have been the first female government minister anywhere in the world (a full year before Alexandra Kollontai in the Soviet Union). Yet the opening sentence of the Proclamation, in which Ireland was imagined as a woman summoning her children to her flag, was as old as the Gaelic poetic tradition. So the ambivalences persisted. The Rising was home-grown but unthinkable without the help of 'gallant allies overseas', not to mention the example of other republics such as France and the United

States, nor indeed the 'dulce et decorum' rhetoric of World War I. Like much else in the country, it too was an effect of the emigrant experience.

The rebel leader Patrick Pearse might summon the Celtic hero Cuchulain to his side, but only to validate his idea of a social-democratic state which would 'cherish all the children of the nation equally'.[37] That vision had as much in common with Rosa Luxemburg as with Cathleen Ní Houlihan, and the Irish Modernist who shaped it was yet another who knew how to have things both ways. He was after all a man who had studied child-centred methods of liberal education in Belgium, before importing them into his own college of St Enda's, with the blithe assurance that they amounted to nothing more than a return to the sort of fosterage systems practiced in ancient Ireland. Pearse realised that if he had something radically new to offer, it was wise to present it as a reassuring restoration. History would in this way take on the contours of science fiction and the past become the future, as for the *aisling* poets.

In those very years, James Joyce was learning how to gift-wrap *Ulysses*, arguably the most subversive narrative of the age, in the structure of one of Europe's oldest tales, *The Odyssey* of Homer. Although the actions and texts of the national renaissance often seemed both modern and counter-modern in the same gesture, it was the underlying modernity which ultimately set the agenda. Far from being fixated on the past, people like Pearse and Joyce relished their power over it, their capacity to make it answer current and future needs. In effect they chose to see past and future as complementary rather than opposed, much like the Gaelic poets who knew how to remember a future. This both/and philosophy was really a form of translation, of a culture being 'carried over' from one code to another, while refusing to surrender what was good in either, however discrepant their elements might seem to the analytic mind.

Here lies yet another explanation of the awesome complexity of many texts of the Irish Renaissance. Artists were willing to take extreme liberties with the forms inherited from English literature, to improvise without undue deference to that tradition. Jorge Luis Borges likened the freedom taken by Latin Americans with Spanish literature to the Irish handling of English forms. The same freedom accounted for Joyce's unprecedented blend of magical and realist narrative modes in *Ulysses*, with the consequence that his art anticipated Rushdie and Márquez as much as Mann or Eliot. He employed myth to expose the limits of European realism, and he used realism to expose the limits of ancient myth-making. His steady conviction was that more might be gained than lost in the act of translating Homer into the realities of everyday life in the twentieth century.

A central tenet of postcolonial writing – that the more translated a text may be, the richer it becomes – is implicit in many cultural projects of the risorgimento. The new species of man dreamed of by Yeats was intent on a perpetual becoming, his art a process rather than a product, his identity less a stable entity than a way of moving through the world. The image of the migrant, tramp or traveller is taken up from Gaelic tradition not just because displacement is a condition of the modern intellectual but more especially because such a figure is adaptive. Of such characters one might say what Salman Rushdie observes of postcolonial exiles in *Imaginary Homelands*: 'they are people who root themselves in ideas rather than in places, in memories as much as in material things; people who have been obliged to define themselves because they are so defined by others – by their otherness; people in whose deepest selves strange fusions occur, unprecedented unions between what they are and where they find themselves'.[38] The migrant is not simply transformed into a hybrid by travels; she or he creates a wholly new art by virtue of multiple locations.

The politics of dialect

One example of the 'added value' made possible by translation is to be found in the uses of Hiberno-English by the revival generation. The Irish taught one another English, mainly out of books, and since English orthography is a poor guide, often with major mispronunciations. Hence the notorious 'brogue' – since there is no 'th' sound in Irish, 'this and that' became 'dis and dat'. To allay possible feelings of inferiority, the hedge schoolmasters had often resorted to 'jawbreakers', multisyllabic words which would advertise their learning in the absence of paper diplomas. And not just hedge schoolteachers. Goldsmith's village schoolmaster was a further example of the type:

> While words of learned length and thunderous sound
> Amazed the gazing rustics ranged around;
> And still they gazed and still their wonder grew,
> That one small head could carry all he knew.[39]

The characters of Synge's plays show a marked liking for such jawbreakers: 'potentate', 'bedizened', 'stratagems'.[40] The change-over from one language to another happened so fast in many areas during the nineteenth century that people continued to think in Irish while using English words. One consequence was a radical restructuring of English grammar and syntax along Gaelic lines. In standard English, emphasis is achieved by vocally underlining a key word in a sentence: 'Are you going to town tomorrow?' but in Irish the word-order is shifted and the crucial term brought forward: 'Is it to town that you are going tomorrow?' These effects seemed poetic to an ear trained on standard English locutions. George Moore even went so far as to claim that if you translated Irish word-for-word into English, the results were always poetry.

There was undoubtedly an element of psychological compensation in all this. The reputation for eloquence given to Irish users of English stilled some guilt-pangs among English liberals about the effects of their country's policy in Ireland. Even more poignantly, the praise for Irish mastery of English helped to still the sense of shame among those Irish who had quite deliberately decided to abandon their native language. Writing in English, the majority could now hope to win a sympathetic hearing in Britain as well: ever since Swift, writing by Irish persons was designed to be heard in Ireland but also overheard in England.[41]

Having a double audience presented some dangers, especially when the number of potential readers in Britain was often far higher than in Ireland. The fear was that an author might defer excessively to Anglo-stereotypes of Ireland, thereby exploiting rather than expressing the national personality. For centuries the British had evolved a theory of antithesis between all things English and Irish, using the attributes of the latter as a foil to set off their own virtues. If England was rational, modern, analytical, it followed that Ireland was irrational, backward, superstitious. These binaries were wittily dismantled by the two great geniuses of late-Victorian theatre, Oscar Wilde and George Bernard Shaw. Wilde mocked them by turning himself into a very Irish kind of Englishman and by writing plays whose males were womanly and whose women were manly. In an age when the Irish were deemed a feminine race (and therefore incapable of self-government at a time when women had no vote), the political implications of his plays were not very hidden. Shaw made such an analysis even more obvious in *John Bull's Other Island*, where the Irishman Larry Doyle is a sardonic rationalist and the English Tom Broadbent a hopeless heedless romantic. Doubtless, the internationalist perspective of those two socialists helped to account for their mocking inversion of national categories, since they made the English seem more Irish and the Irish more English.

W. B. Yeats, as leader of the home-based Irish Renaissance, was less likely to abandon notions of a national personality. He accepted the ancient antithesis, on condition that he might be allowed to reinterpret it along lines more flattering to his people. So, instead of seeing the Irish as irrational, he described them as healthily instinctual; rather than backward they were intelligently traditional; and far from being superstitious they were simply religious and mystical. This was a subtle enough tactic, which took much of the sting out of a racist typology. As a manoeuvre it would be repeated by the black-is-beautiful movements in the United States through the 1960s and by Seamus Heaney in his positive reinterpretation of the 'bogman' symbol in his poetry of the 1970s. Perhaps the ultimate way of disposing of the Anglo-Irish antithesis was that favoured by Joyce. He simply ignored it, joking in *Finnegans Wake* that he was a 'farsoonerite' who would 'far sooner muddle through a hash of lentils in Europe than meddle with Irrland's split little pea'.[42]

Irish Modernism

The national Renaissance has often been called a 'Revival', but in many ways this is a misnomer, based on a false view of the Irish as a people fixated on the past. While it's true that Cuchulain and other heroes walked again not only on the boards of the Abbey Theatre but also in the General Post Office at 1916, the underlying urge was to unleash the still-unused energies from past images into the present. The socialist leader of the Easter rising, James Connolly, warned against the worship of a past which was no more than a ruse to escape the mediocrity of the present. He counselled against a fetishising of Celtic Studies, which might be 'glorious and heroic indeed, but still *only* a tradition'.[43] He argued that socialism would be itself a revival of the old Gaelic system, whereby the chieftain held land in the name of all the people, except that henceforth it would be the state and not the prince holding the land in this way. Like Pearse and Joyce, Connolly was an Irish Modernist who remembered (in the sense of piecing-together) his own desired future. Connolly saw the invocation of the Gaelic past not simply as an urge to repeat but as a compulsion to form constellations between past moments and present ones, thus opening up a revolutionary future. His notion of the past was rather like that of an old Connemara woman who said that people get wrinkles not as a punishment for the nights of debauchery in youth but for all those wasted moments in the past when the passions knocked and there was nobody in to answer them.

If anything, the deeper underlying thrust of Irish Modernism was against the overweening power of the past. Joyce's treatment of Homer is, for all his love of *The Odyssey*, highly aggressive – he wishes to convert Homer into a ur-version of himself, much as Stephen Dedalus claims that his father Simon has 'my eyes' (and not the other way around).[44] The rather harsh handling given to fathers and father-figures in the writings of Wilde, Shaw, Yeats and Joyce suggests a generation devoted to self-invention rather than ancient lineage, as suggested when Stephen Dedalus opts to become 'himself his own father'. This Oedipal theme was strong right across Modernist literature around the year 1900, and given added depth by the emerging notion of a 'generation', each possessed of its own identity and charged with its own life-task. However, there were particular conditions in Ireland which gave the father / son conflict an added poignancy. In a more autonomous society, the revolt of the young against the old can be translated into social progress, because both groups have hands on the levers of power, but in an oppressed community such a rebellion is strictly meaningless, since it can produce no significant change. Instead, it merely lapses back into the squabbles of family life, which are accordingly magnified, as in the battle between Christy Mahon and his 'da' in Synge's masterpiece. It is, as Deleuze and Guattari might say, less a case of Oedipus producing neurosis than of neurosis producing Oedipus.[45]

The usual method of international critics of Joyce or Yeats was to elide this major difference and to treat them as part of a great Euromodernist generation which included Mann, Lawrence and Kafka. Richard Ellmann, in particular, identified the crucial importance of the father / son conflict in his studies of Yeats and Joyce, but he used it to suggest analogies with Dostoevsky, Samuel Butler and the Euromodernists. More than that, there is a paradigm in each of his great biographies which suggests that Yeats, Joyce and Wilde became modern (i.e. European) to the extent that they ceased to be knowingly Irish. It isn't difficult to see *why* Ellmann might have adopted that view. An American humanist of Jewish background, he was a member of the US forces which liberated Europe and uncovered the Nazi death-camps. He was attracted by the idea of a European high art as a student in the 1930s, and then appalled in equal measure in the 1940s to learn just how many of its exponents had been complicit with barbarism. His whole career was a sort of rescue-operation on behalf of Euromodernism, leading him to introduce new Irish recruits (first Yeats, then Joyce, later Wilde and then Beckett) to the empty spaces in the pantheon. His project was to protect the humanist content of Euromodernism in the decades after the Holocaust and to assist in the building up of the new Europe. No wonder that each of his biographies sold copiously at Dublin Airport bookshop, where civil servants and administrators intent on linking Ireland ever closer to 'Europe' in the last three decades of the twentieth century could purchase witty, charming volumes which seemed to exhale the very spirit of *their* project too.

So literary history was slowly rewritten and the Ireland of the renaissance was gradually portrayed (by F. S. L. Lyons, R. F. Foster and others) as an intolerant, narrow, backward place which drove free spirits like Joyce into permanent exile. Yet the facts suggest something very different. Joyce left because he could find no post commensurate with his qualifications. In later years, from Paris he looked back longingly on the Dublin of his youth as a place in which everyone Irish said what they liked because the British had final responsibility for social order. The need, therefore, is to discriminate modernisms, as once Arthur Lovejoy called for a necessary discrimination of romanticisms.[46] Irish Modernism has in truth a good deal in common with that of other European peoples, but it also has features peculiar to itself. For one thing, some of its features emerged, as we have seen, astonishingly early, because of the catastrophic onset of modernity after 1600. The broken *filí* were among the first *flâneurs* of Europe, and Stephen Dedalus takes up that tradition, but the cane of the 'youthful bard' is already well-smoothed by the time it is passed down to him.

Village Modernism and the compulsory Bohemia

Is *Ulysses* a novel at all? Novels tend to deal with made societies and Ireland in 1904 was still a society in the making. The short story is calibrated to describe a submerged population group, as Frank O'Connor argued in *The Lonely Voice*, whereas the novel seems more suited to a settled world of differing social classes. *Ulysses* is clearly something more than an exfoliation of short stories and may in fact be written in an evolving Irish genre for which as yet there is no name. That genre seems to feed and celebrate the impulse to tell micro-stories, which are partly linked without ever quite being permitted to join in a seamless narrative.

Joyce's first prose work *Dubliners* had been a collection of stories with sufficient interconnection to suggest to W. B. Yeats the promise of a novelist of a new kind, but *Ulysses* when it came was also caught in the interstices between those forms. Joyce couldn't produce a conventional *bildungsroman* (the Dedalus section is aborted after three episodes) because his youth does not have his hands on the levers of power. Such a *bildungsroman* would typically conclude with a youth who had come in from the provinces, made all the right conquests and now gazes over the rooftops of the capital with a feeling of having arrived at the centre of things. But in *Ulysses* as in *Dubliners*, the city is a place of paralysis. It is less a centrally planned singular entity than a collection of villages that got joined up; and liberation for any protagonist can be imagined only as movement out, away from the centre of paralysis.

The classic novels of Europe written before Joyce were propelled almost invariably by dialogue. Tolstoy (one of Joyce's models) knew how to attribute a sentence or two of interior monologue to his major characters in a given scene, but he saw to it that such brief interludes were well subordinated to the surrounding dialogue. In Joyce's Dublin, however, a place where everyone can talk but few know how to listen, dialogue is ineffectual, thin and does little to advance the plot, whereas the interior monologues are usually so gorgeous in detail as to overwhelm the social world entirely.

These monologues of Stephen, Leopold and Molly are perhaps the greatest technical achievements in Joyce's oeuvre. Taking their cue from Molly Bloom's closing 'yes', most critics see them as an affirmation of everyday life, but there is something suspect and disproportionate about their gorgeousness. Each of these characters is driven back into his or her head as a consequence of frustration and defeat in the outer world. Yeats once said that people are happy only when for every something inside them there is an equivalent something outside; read in that light, the monologues can often seem pathological, a defensive tactic of the marginalised.

This is particularly true of Molly Bloom's closing soliloquy, which may end on a 'yes' but is tragic in its implications. Here is a wakeful woman, beside her sleeping husband, left with nobody to talk to but herself. After an afternoon assignation with her lover, she feels compelled to masturbate repeatedly in the bed, because her visitor came too soon and took all the pleasure for himself. The blank pieces of paper which she posts to herself seem like emblems of her lonely condition, just as her 'yes' seems a desperate tactic to convince herself that life is better than it is. When the Irish actress Fionnuala Flanagan performed the monologue in this way on a US campus in the 1980s, some elderly professors handed back their membership cards to the Joyce Association in disgust at her alleged blasphemy against a sacred text.

Joyce's discovery and development of interior monologue might have been predicted, for long before most other peoples the Irish of the nineteenth century suffered from that most modern of ailments, a homeless mind. After the Great Famine, many who had started life in a windswept village found themselves ending it in baffling and vast conurbations, and even those who stayed at home changed languages with the result that they were living without a key in a suddenly strange environment. They felt removed from the past, from their language and their very setting – which is to say that they were living in a sort of involuntary Bohemia.

The more conventional Bohemia of North America and Western Europe was a voluntary zone, occupied by the impoverished young awaiting employment or by dissident artists. There these groups set out to improvise new forms of art and life, before carrying the revolutionary message back to the wider society. They had entered this special enclave under the pressure of architectural redevelopment or raised rents.

Joyce's Dublin had some things in common with such places, being (as he said himself) 'the last of the intimate cities',[47] i.e. one with a villagey feel wherever you went in it. It was filled with 'ageing youths' of about thirty, such as the character called Lenehan, and broken older men, like Simon Dedalus, hanging around in hopes of a job and filling the time of idleness with bouts of drinking, song and story. But Joyce fled this Dublin in disgust and accordingly showed little interest in moving to the voluntary Bohemia of Montmartre or Montparnasse. Even as a young medical student in Paris, he appalled the visiting J. M. Synge by insisting that they picnic like any bourgeois in the parks at St Cloud. In the later days of his fame, his Parisian neighbours found it hard to reconcile his reputation as a daredevil artist with the uxorious family-man in dapper suits who came and went from his apartment. The famous meeting with Marcel Proust set up by admirers keen for bons mots on 'the ache of the modern' resulted in nothing more than a stiff, uneasy exchange on the merits of dark chocolate truffles.[48]

In Modernist Paris most self-respecting intellectuals despised the bourgeois as a soulless, money-grubbing automaton. It had not been so back in 1789 when writers had celebrated the moment when meritocrats of a new middle class were finally replacing a parasitic aristocracy. Only much later did the intellectuals begin to detach themselves from that class, becoming its first and foremost critics. In Ireland, however, although the old Gaelic aristocracy had fallen after 1600, it had been replaced by English arrivistes who posed as a new gentry. A native middle class was only emerging as a full social formation in the lifetime of James Joyce.

This may be one reason why those intellectuals who led the Irish Renaissance between 1890 and 1921 were so convinced of the link between cultural self-confidence and business success. The Gaelic League, for instance, not only sought to revive the Irish language but to advertise Irish manufactures in parades initiated throughout the world on St Patrick's Day. Joyce's own first published stories were in a farmers' journal, *The Irish Homestead*, edited by George Russell, who believed in connecting 'the dairies of Plunkett' with 'the fairies of Yeats'. Most Irish writers of the time showed a marked talent for business. Wilde edited a woman's magazine and wrote his plays to make a lot of 'gold'. Shaw would complain to a film mogul who wished to buy rights to a play: 'you keep talking about art and all I'm interested in is the money'. Yeats ran two publishing houses and a self-sufficient theatre company.[49]

Joyce was, if anything, the most entrepreneurially inclined of them all. Acting for a continental backer, he set up one of the first cinemas in Dublin in 1909. He won a franchise from the Dublin Woollen Mills to sell Aran sweaters on the continent. His most ambitious project was the setting up of a Dublin broadsheet newspaper to be called *The Goblin*.[50] It never took off, for want of cash, but it could be argued that *Ulysses* is an attempt by art to trump the modern newspaper with an even more detailed account of the life of a city over a single day. Its surreal juxtaposition of clashing styles and topics recalls that of *The Irish Homestead*, in which Joyce's epiphanies appeared alongside the week's manure prices (he was so humiliated by this location in 'The Pigs' Paper' that he took cover under the pseudonym Stephen Dedalus). On more than one occasion the writer of *Ulysses* called himself 'only a scissors-and-paste man'.[51]

If Joyce was impressed by business people, that was because they were, like all artists, brokers in risk, willing to back an initial hunch with long years of hack-work. So it isn't all that surprising that he should have made an ad-canvasser like Bloom the central figure of his modern masterpiece. Throughout that book Bloom is portrayed as someone well aware of the ways in which the advertisement maps the dream world of the unconscious onto everyday settings. Seeing the communicants at All Hallows Church, he remarks on the value of the accompanying slogan: 'Good idea the Latin. Stupefies them first'.[52] Bloom is forever alert to practical business opportunities, whether it be a new tramline to the city docks or a free railway pass to visit his daughter Milly in Mullingar.

Stephen Dedalus has inherited his father's wastrel habits and stands in some need of Bloom's practicality. Stephen's fellow-occupant of the Sandycove Tower, Malachi Mulligan, senses a rival for Stephen's good opinion in the figure of Bloom and warns that he may lust after the youth: 'he is Greeker than the Greeks'.[53] But perhaps it is Mulligan's interest which is more directly sexual, hinted in his early invocation of Wilde. If so, the relationship which develops between Dedalus and Bloom might be seen as a more platonic classical substitute – the willingness of an older man, wise in the ways of the world, to advise a callow but promising youth.

Although Bloom is a surrogate father to Stephen (and one far superior in that parental role than the biological father Simon), his stronger tendency in the later episodes is frankly *maternal*. He haunts the Holles Street Hospital out of sympathy for Mrs Purefoy in her three-day labour. In the 'Circe' episode his fantasy of becoming a mother is realised not just in the dream-play section but more importantly when he rescues Stephen. As May Dedalus's voice-over recalls the ways in which she protected her errant eldest son, it seems as if her ghost is prompting Bloom to take over her vacated role. There is – despite Mulligan – no hint that the relationship might have a sexual dimension. Bloom in fact suspects that Stephen is muttering something about a girl named Ferguson and thinks that this could be the best thing that ever happened to him.[54] At this stage he is simply anxious to protect his friend's son: and the final image in the episode of Bloom's dead son Rudy reading a Jewish text seems a version of Stephen 'lisant au livre de lui-même'.[55]

The Bloom who had earlier mocked the communicants at All Hallows now recreates the sacramental moment in literal earnest by sharing coffee and a bun with the hungry young poet. That communion between bourgeois and bohemian is the true climax of the book in the course of which Bloom worries about cases of early burnout among 'cultured fellows that promised so brilliantly'. When he suggests that Stephen find work, however, he is rudely told, 'Count me out.' Bloom hastens to assure his friend that there is no conflict between their definitions of what such work might be. It would be 'work in the widest possible sense' for 'you have every bit as much right to live by your pen in pursuit of your philosophy as the peasant has'.[56]

Leaving the cabman's shelter, Bloom tells Stephen that if he walks with him he'll 'feel a different man': and, sure enough, linking arms, Stephen 'felt a strange kind of flesh of a different man approach him, sinewless and wobbly and all that'. It is as if a guru has at last got on wavelength with an adept. Bloom's prophetic role with Stephen is not to communicate in words any particular philosophy, but to sacralise the everyday as a way of feeling at home in the world. Joyce pokes tender fun at his own climax, citing lines from a popular song in describing the pair leaving 'in a low backed car' to be married by Father Maher.[57] That undercutting is reinforced by the fact that the cabby's horse shits as they leave. The rapprochement between bohemian and bourgeois is purely temporary: if both were fully sober and less fatigued, how much could they have in common?

The scene in which Bloom shows Dedalus a photograph of a rather younger Molly might be interpreted in various ways. In one sense the picture completes the image of the new 'holy family' Stephen has joined (while also reassuring him that the invitation is not homosexual). Not homosexual – but homosocial perhaps. All through *Ulysses* Bloom has shown a need for the company and ratification of other men. He attended the funeral of a man he scarcely knew, as if anxious to join a ritual with other males on a sacred occasion. In 'Sirens', as he sat next to Richie Goulding, the two men were described as 'married' by the silence of the pub.[58] There may be in Bloom's gesture to Stephen a homosocial desire to share the contemplation of his wife with another man: in

'Ithaca' he appears to be excited by the possibility that many men have actually been lovers of Molly.

In the company of Stephen back at home in Eccles Street, Bloom becomes ever more balanced and androgynous. He is undisturbed by the absence of light in the dark house because of 'the surety of the sense of touch in his firm full masculine feminine passive active hand'.[59] The two men appear to have the polar makings of a whole person, with Stephen epitomising the artistic and Bloom the scientific. Yet their psychic marriage turns out to be a little like the sexual union of Leopold and Molly – a zone of non-intersection and non-friction in which each is haunted by the other, can share the other's solitude, but no more than that.

Bohemian life was often just a means by which failed medical students or lapsed lawyers sought to live artistically. Joyce, however, was a serious worker who fled all that in order to produce a mighty book. He never sought fashionable poverty but rather the money with which to escape it. Far from staging the bohemians' tactical withdrawal from ordinary life, he tried to emphasise the redemptive strangeness of the quotidian. *Ulysses* was published at just that moment in the history of surrealism when Bohemia, through advertising, was about to become an avant-garde form of publicity. In his love of advertising jingles, his openness to art as productive work, his desire to savour Nighttown, Bloom condenses all of these tendencies. In a somewhat similar way, Joyce used the immense resources of money, books and magazines to publicise *Ulysses*, while maintaining a very bourgeois pose (he never used bad language in speech, only in writing) to protect his own privacy.

Indeed by 1922 when *Ulysses* went on sale in the streets of Paris, the war between bohemian and bourgeois in that city was already drawing to an end, as commercial art employed more and more of the techniques of the surrealists. In the decades after that, the bohemians of France, England and the United States broke out of their old confines and helped to create the consumerist lifestyle of the new middle classes (what would later be called 'modernism in the streets').[60] Joyce's own assumption, working out of the special Irish conditions, that there had never been any deep-rooted conflict probably helped to secure his rapid assimilation into the canon. One strange result is that the book which begins by satirising the Oxford student Haines as an example of the English literary tourist now brings thousands of such visitors checking into hotels for Bloomsday celebrations.

Irish Modernism had always been about hard work and serious literary production. Though Yeats liked to talk of *sprezzatura*, he really believed in Adam's Curse and 'the fascination of what's difficult' – as did all of those predecessors from Swift to Shaw, from Goldsmith to Wilde, whom Yeats liked to call Anglo-Irish aristocrats but who were in fact bourgeois Protestants with a strong work ethic.

Joyce, for his part, only seemed French-bohemian on the surface: Stephen's walking-cane is less that of the Parisian *flâneur* than the ceremonial rod carried by the 'youthful bard' of Gaeldom; and Joyce's much-publicised habit of writing while stretched out on a bed drew less on Oblomov than on the traditions of composition of the ancient *filí*. To Joyce the bourgeoisie was something which, like the proletariat itself, had yet to be fully created in Ireland, and so he saw it as glamorous and even mysterious. In Leopold Bloom he created his dream of an absolute Irish bourgeois, one who can enjoy chance encounters with others and feel the streets to be his home.

But that bourgeois figure was already doomed in 1922, to be replaced in a few decades by the middle class. Bloom's was an unplanned, ruralised but civic city. Soon the middle class would urbanise an entire civilisation, whose architecture and shopping-malls would be so completely planned that chance encounters became less and less possible. The seeds of this degeneration are carried, in fact, by Bloom himself, in his ad-man's daydream of a suburban villa in Dundrum ('Bloom Cottage. St Leopold's. Flowerville').[61]

Like all the other characters of *Ulysses*, Bloom is a 'street person', but not in today's degraded sense. As Jane Jacobs has shown, today not only the civic street but also the crowd have been done away with.[62] Dublin's current celebration of Bloomsday is really a lament for lost days when the city still seemed negotiable on foot rather than gridlocked by a hundred thousand private cars. The citizens in Joyce's Dublin circulated in unpredictable ways, and it was that which allowed Joyce to renew his narrative styles in each episode, to keep a sense of possibilities open rather than ousted. What Joyce showed is that growth – the encounter with others – is more a matter of happy accident than deliberate design. It is what happens to the older Leopold as well as the younger Stephen, when the desire for mastery is ablated, when old routines are challenged, and the new practices which might replace them have not yet hardened into system.

It would be hard to imagine any other masterpiece of Euromodernism which climaxes in an act of communion between an artist and a bourgeois. Ireland was indeed a strange place – 'belated' (Joyce's own word) in the emergence of certain art forms and a middle class, but for all that productive of new, unprecedented forms and genres. The crisis at the centre of empire had first manifested itself out on the periphery. There the worlds of modern science and ancient magic coexisted as similar orders of reality – and the need was to find a form adequate to this discrepant experience. The colonial laboratory generated not only new politics but also strange literary forms.

Joyce used interior monologue in ways quite different from previous European artists. From Shakespeare to Tolstoy, soliloquy had often been a prelude to suicide, death or at least the strong possibility of either;[63] but in Joyce's work an unexampled intensity was brought to bear on the ruminations of a person about to brew a pot of tea. Where other European artists during World War I sought out extreme situations, he wished to restore the primacy of everyday life and the middle range of experience. By the start of the twentieth century the old notion of the mob had given way to that of the *masses*, and the ancient fear of the latent instincts of the mob was replaced by panic as to what demons might lurk in the collective unconscious of the masses. Yet Joyce, by minutely documenting the half-articulated thoughts and feelings of ordinary people, showed that, far from fleeing the masses, art might yet engage with them. In a similar style, he celebrated the mass-culture of newspapers and handbills, seriously submitting *Ulysses* as a sort of alternative version of the daily newspaper. This also contrasts utterly with the views of most Modernists, for whom Nietzsche spoke when he jeered that 'the rabble spit forth their bile and they call the results a newspaper'.

The belated bohemians?

If Joyce sought to flee the Irish Bohemia as part of his search for a secure bourgeois lifestyle in which to assemble his masterpiece, the reverse trajectory would be pursued by the Irish-language Modernist Seosamh Mac Grianna just a generation later. By the 1930s a world of civil-service memoranda and bureaucratese seemed to have replaced that of political insurrection and cultural experiment, as radicals who had once said 'revolution or death' now fought the death of their own revolution. The numbing boredom of that life among those who feared the bleakness of freedom is brilliantly captured in a text like *At Swim-Two-Birds* (1939) by Flann O'Brien, but perhaps the definitive account may be found in Mac Grianna's *Mo Bhealach Féin* (My Own Way, 1940), a sad treatise on how the search for a Bohemia is doomed to frustration from the outset.

Yet the ideas and images of Joyce animate that fictional autobiography, even in the famous opening sentence which evokes the image of a roadway:

> Is óg i mo shaol a chonaic mé uaim é, an ród sin a bhí le mo mhian . . . (It was early in my life that I saw it before me, that road which was my desire . . .)[64]

This seems a rather knowing echo of

> Once upon a time and a very good time it was there was a moocow coming down along the road and this moocow that was coming down along the road met a nicens little boy named baby tuckoo . . .[65]

– just as Joyce's own moocow seems a reprise of Gaeldom's 'droimeann donn dílis' (literally 'sweet brown white-backed cow'), the national symbol of old Ireland. That roadway becomes an image of the human mind to both writers. If Joyce wishes 'to forge in the smithy of my soul the uncreated conscience of my race',[66] Mac Grianna has his own way of expressing the aspiration when he closes with the vow 'a fhad agus a mhairfidh mise, beidh mé ag déanamh an eolais chun an tobair seo do Chlanna Gael'[67] (for as long as I live, I shall be providing knowledge from this well for the families of the Gael).

The quest-romance of *Mo Bhealach Féin* is based quite literally on the notion that 'the shortest way to Tara is via Holyhead' – and so the author travels to and across Wales, in hopes of finding at least that Celtic people 'inchurtha lena dhúchas' (compatible with their tradition). Ireland prompts him to toy with despair, being filled only with bourgeois careerists and pen-pushers who never read any books. Mac Grianna believes that the dream of the 1916 rebels has yet to be fulfilled, much as Joyce believes that the conscience of Ireland is yet uncreated:

> Bealach nach bpillfeadh, bealach nach raibh ceangailte idir dhá cheann na himní. Cé a shamhlódh dom nár shiúil mé riamh é, mise ri-éigeas na nGael san fhichiú céad seo, in aimsir na hAiséirí?[68] (A road to which I would not return, a road not suspended between two extremes of anxiety. Who will convince me that I never walked it, I the king poet of the Gaels in this twentieth century, in the era of resurrection?)

One reason for fleeing Ireland is that it is guilty of 'cúnglach' (narrowness), the Mac Grianna word for 'paralysis'. His road can have no place for the paralysed, who merely mock and misunderstand his journeying, unaware that here is a man consciously recreating the deeds of Parthalon in Gaelic tradition. If Joyce centralised the thinking subject in his writings, he did so usually by depicting a figure for whom the act of walking was an analogue for the processes of thought itself. So also does Mac Grianna, whose peregrinations make possible just the sort of episodic structure which allows his book to achieve yet another version of that form of latency which leaves it on the cusp between short-story collection and picaresque novel.

Like Joyce also, he had a fine collection of short stories, *An Grá agus an Ghruaim* (1929), already in print when he attempted this hybrid form; and he followed his model in expecting the sort of reader who, in order to read any of his work, must somehow contrive to know all of it. In the final story of *An Grá agus an Ghruaim*, 'Creach Choinn Uí Dhomhnaill' (The Booty of Conn O'Donnell), a character on the brink of climactic action says 'Ó loisc mé an coinneall loiscfidh mé an torlach'[69] (Since I burnt the candle I'll burn the thumb) – a scene of melodrama mercilessly parodied in *Mo Bhealach Féin*:

> D'iarr mé lóistín agus cuireadh seanleabhar i mo láthair, agus dar leat ar an duilleog nár leagadh peann uirthi ó scríobhadh leabhar na gCeall. 'Ó loisc mé an coinneall loiscfidh mé an torlach', arsa mise liom féin agus scríobh mé 'Cathal Buí Mac Giolla Gunna'. (I sought lodging and an ancient tome was brought to me, and you would have sworn by its leaves that no pen had touched it since the writing of the Book of Kells. 'Since I have burned the candle, I'll burn the thumb', I said to myself and I signed 'Cathal Buí Mac Giolla Gunna'.)[70]

The mockery of a Gaelic literary tradition represented by a famous Ulster poet is exceeded by the sophistication of the self-deflation, which allows the author to disown his cheap, youthful shot, but such a gesture presupposes the sort of intense, Modernist reader who is prepared to devote a good deal of time and effort to decoding the full oeuvre.

Such acts of self-deflation are among the more attractive features of the narrative, as if Mac Grianna fears that he may be found guilty of taking his quest too seriously. Sometimes he achieves his favoured effect by deconstructing the old proverbs which propelled many a Blasket narrative: 'deir siad go bhfuil an fhírinne searbh, ach ní searbh atá sí ach garbh'[71] (they say that truth is bitter, but it's not bitter so much as rough). At other times, the narrator lets the air out of his own high-flown rhetoric, which in a long speech had extolled the virtues of saintly poverty, by a bathetic closing sentence which runs: 'Scar mé uatha, agus d'imigh siadsan ar lorg theach na mBocht agus chuaigh mise isteach i dteach itheacháin'[72] (I left them, and they went looking for the poorhouse while I went into a restaurant).

This is, however, the sort of bathos which led Joyce to contrast the rainbow-pools of seawater on Dollymount Strand in a famous jump-cut in *A Portrait* with the pools of dripping in his mother's kitchen frying-pan, or to juxtapose the soaring aesthetic theorising of Stephen Dedalus with the urgent request for a cigarette from a gasping and bored listener.

Such moments of deflation are a kind of insurance taken out by authors who treat the personality of their authorial selves with an awesome degree of intensity, so much so that everyone else in these narratives seems shadowy, unreal and insubstantial. The quest-romance becomes no more than a pretext for the dramatisation of self; and the world seems to exist solely as a place to be used in the exploration of a self. As Seamus Deane has written of *Mo Bhealach Féin*:

> Mac Grianna sought isolation. He was ready to accept the reputation of being eccentric and unsociable, because he sought a vision of which he could never speak. He could only speak of having sought it.[73]

This autobiography of a super-tramp becomes in the end a thoroughly bohemian sequence of withdrawals, in the attempt to find a meaning – rather than an answer – to the Irish Question. Mac Grianna senses that the act of national revival has been taken away from its exponents, even as they performed it; but he isn't sure when the moment of possibility was lost, and so he can only speak of having lost it. His lament is an expression of the painful old split between fact and value, and his sense is that the wine of the Irish Renaissance has evaporated, leaving only a sordid sediment at the base of the vessel, as nation-making gives way to bourgeois bureaucracy.

If there is for him a 'bearna ró-mhór idir na gníomhartha agus an fhilíocht' (too great a gap between deeds and poetry), that is a sign, perhaps, of a need to go back finally, via Joyce, to a previous generation of the 1890s. Its writers sought out a true Bohemia in which self and art-work were one, in which a life might be the greatest art-work of all. Although the major manoeuvres performed in *Mo Bhealach Féin* recycle and even refine moments in the work of Joyce, there is a sense in which the ghost of Oscar Wilde presides over the entire project. There had been occasional echoes of a similar Wildean bohemianism in the life and work of Pádraic Ó Conaire, but these were never more than hints. Ó Conaire himself had died in a 1920s poorhouse, urging younger writers to acquire a house and secure way of life. The sad truth was that modern writing in the Irish language had come to fruition only just after 1900, and in consequence its bohemianism would always seem forced, belated and out of sync with the emerging new state.

In a Free State?

Irish culture was modern anyway, whether its producers wished it so or not. By the start of the twentieth century, however, the leaders of the national movement devised their own project for alternative forms of modernisation – alternative to the British imperial scheme, that is – and sought the benefits of modernity along with the liquidation of its costs. One sign of that was the Easter Rising, another was *Ulysses*, a third was *A Vision* by W. B. Yeats.

After independence and the ensuing civil war, a certain caution took over. Yet the desire for alternative modernities continued, variously attested in the semi-state bodies set up to promote sugar production, or in the fact that the Abbey Theatre became the first national theatre with a government subsidy in the English-speaking world, or in the use of radio to make the first live European broadcast from a major sporting event in the 1920s.

Inevitably, however, some of the radical intensity of the Renaissance period was lost. Joyce complained to Arthur Power in Paris that the people back home who had shouted what they liked in British days were now running scared of the bleakness of freedom.[74] Writers who had been instrumental in the birth of a nation were often among the first victims of the new nation-state. The censorship acts brought in the 1920s were deeply debilitating, denying artists not just an audience but a livelihood in Ireland. Almost as sapping, perhaps, was the change in the use which large sections of the public had for literature: from once being an element of their daily vision, it was now being degraded to a mere tool for the passing of state examinations.

Yet the paradox underlying all this remained clear. Literature in the eyes of politicians and church leaders was still a force sufficiently powerful and subversive to deserve control and even outright banning. By forbidding so much of the best modern writing, the authorities between the 1930s and 1960s maintained it at the level of a heroic opposition, endowing it with the sort of conspiratorial glamour it had lost in other countries. Both the 'Crazy Jane' poems of Yeats and the casual obscenities of *Finnegans Wake* were cast in a coded language designed to outwit the censors – much as Samuel Beckett in *Murphy*, published in 1938, used the words MUSIC MUSIC MUSIC as a synecdoche for the sexual act.

Exiled writers such as Frank O'Connor liked to joke that they returned every few years simply in order to remind themselves what a terrible place Ireland was. Beckett spoke for more than himself when he had a character remark in *All That Fall* that while it was suicide to be abroad, to stay at home was to court a lingering dissolution.[75] He told his family in 1939 that he preferred to live in France at war than in an Ireland at peace. Yet the agenda of the Irish Renaissance was still upheld, and upheld most notably by this writer, who saw literature as an act of perpetual translation, of necessary translation, as he sought to escape the excesses of wit and wordplay routinely expected of an

Irish author in English. Instead, he burrowed down into his learner's French, seeking not only *le mot juste* but a true point of linguistic underdevelopment: his aim was to use its words with all the literal-minded carefulness of a newly arrived immigrant or guest-worker.

He was just one of many Irish authors who made the strange discovery that they could be truer to themselves in an acquired language. Like Wilde who discovered the meaning of being Irish first in England and later through the writing of *Salomé* in French, Beckett found a similar freedom as a French artist, on the understanding that whenever a man dons a mask his face relaxes sufficiently to reveal some truth. Yet the freedom which Beckett found in French – escape from the pressure of an Anglo-American audience wanting 'blarney' – was found by other artists, such as Brendan Behan and Eoghan Ó Tuairisc, in the Irish language. In it they could express material which might otherwise have been exploited in English. Such writers could indeed forget the whole question of Irishness and Englishness, because writing in Irish meant that they no longer needed to fret as to whether what they wrote was Irish or not. Hence the remarkable pursuit of the 'international theme' in texts as different and exacting as Ó Tuairisc's *Aifreann na Marbh* (The Mass of the Dead) or Caitlín Maude's 'Dán Grá Vietnam'(Vietnam Love-Song).

Ever since the 1960s much – perhaps most – writing in Irish has had a 'counter-cultural' quality, opening itself to influences as diverse as Indian philosophy, African-American music or European fabulism, but always seeking out new forms, unprecedented in its poetic tradition. It is yet another example of how experiment and modernity mask themselves in the rig-out of tradition.

The government was not slow in sensing that the debate was moving on. By 1967 the ban on many books was lifted by 'the youngest government in Europe'; and Fianna Fáil politicians began to be photographed alongside artists whose work and life they had so recently seemed to scorn. In 1969 the authorities announced a tax exemption for writers, as if in an attempt to expiate the guilt of almost four decades spent persecuting the mind. It was in its way yet another attempt to make Ireland an epicentre of good writing. Although the final effects of the measure were to benefit purveyors of potboiler paperbacks more than serious artists (few of whom earned enough to pay much tax), it was a hugely symbolic gesture, to be followed in the 1970s by the founding of *Aosdána* (The Band of Art), a self-electing elite of artists, each of whom is guaranteed a basic annual income. There were some critics who saw in all of this the end of the old Modernist stand-off between artist and establishment and who pointed to the palpable avoidance of social critique in much of the writing that followed, as if the intellectuals were anxious not to bite a hand that yet might feed them. But it is more likely that the change in the character of writing simply reflected the growing privatisation of experience in the later decades of the twentieth century. Even novels and poems dealing with the violence in Northern Ireland tended to see it sourced in the pathology of individuals rather than in a deeply divided and unjust society.

The shadow of that Northern conflict darkened and distorted many a debate. As the Dublin elite integrated the country ever more fully into the European project, some intellectuals – notably those associated with Field Day Theatre Company in Derry – pointed to the colonial element in the Irish past. The economic crisis of the 1980s, when at one stage Ireland owed more per capita to world banks than the Mexicans, seemed to ratify those who argued that the country had much in common with the Third World. However, these analyses were in truth more cultural than economic. For a time, nonetheless, a vibrant debate went on and was even reflected in the differing ways of reading Joyce. While most followed Ellmann in treating him as a European humanist, an increasingly influential group of critics (most of them Irish) began to present him as a type of the postcolonial intellectual. Ireland began to feature, in consequence, in the theoretical writings of such overseas thinkers as Edward Said and Fredric Jameson, although the immense growth in economic prosperity in the late 1990s set a limit to some of the more glib analogies with poorer lands.

If I have emphasised some analogies between Irish art and that of Borges, Rushdie and Márquez, I do not want to suggest that the similarities with the Euromodernism of Proust, Mann or Eliot are less secure. What makes the Irish case interesting is that it is at once post-imperial and postcolonial, a land which contributed to the making of the British empire as well as to its undoing. If the Willy Brandt Commission was correct to suggest that the key relationship of the coming century will be that between North and South in the world, there is a sense in which that confrontation is enacted in many Irish texts of recent times, from *The Commitments* to *Dancing at Lughnasa*, or in those songs which married the technique of the blues to the modes of Gaelic music. This was an overdue reversal of a tendency which, back in the 1920s, had led Langston Hughes and certain artists of the Harlem Renaissance to incorporate the example of Sean O'Casey and J. M. Synge. The use made of the inherited art-forms of western Europe by Irish artists has been reminiscent of that made by those black men and women who picked up the musical instruments of their masters and by sheer audacity of improvisation invented jazz.

Notes

1. James Joyce, *Letters of James Joyce 1*, ed. R. Ellmann (London: Faber, 1966), p. 63; and James Joyce, *A Portrait of the Artist as a Young Man*, ed. S. Deane (London: Penguin, 1991), p. 276.
2. Richard Rose, *Governing Without Consensus* (London: Faber and Faber, 1972), passim.
3. On this see Declan Kiberd, *The Irish Writer and the World* (Cambridge: Cambridge University Press, 2005).
4. James Joyce, *Ulysses* (students annotated edition), ed. D. Kiberd (London: Penguin, 1992), p. 337; and see Lionel Trilling, 'James Joyce in His Letters', in William Chace, ed. *Joyce: A Collection of Critical Essays* (New Jersey: Prentice-Hall, 1974), p. 144.
5. Osborn Bergin, *Irish Bardic Poetry* texts and translation by Bergin, edited and compiled by D. Greene and A. F. Kelly, (Dublin: Institute for Advanced Studies, 1970), pp. 145–6.
6. W. B. Yeats, *Collected Plays* (London: Macmillan, 1952), p. 257.
7. Cainneach Ó Maonaigh, 'Scríbhneoirí Gaeilge an Seachtú hAois Déag', *Studia Hibernica* 2 (1962), pp. 182–208.
8. Samuel Beckett, *Waiting for Godot* (London: Faber and Faber, 1965), p. 12.
9. J. M. Synge, *Letters to Molly: John M. Synge to Maire O'Neill*, ed. A. Saddlemyer (Cambridge, MA: Belknap Press of Harvard University Press, 1971), passim.
10. Samuel Beckett, *Company* (London: Calder, 1982), p. 7.
11. Angela Bourke, *The Burning of Bridget Cleary* (London: Pimlico, 1999), pp. 148ff.
12. John McGahern, 'Change in Ireland', talk at University College Dublin, July 2002.
13. Maria Edgeworth, *Castle Rackrent* (1800; London: Penguin, 1992), pp. 137ff.
14. Quoted in Brian Ó Cuiv, ed. *A View of the Irish Language* (Dublin: Stationery Office, 1969), p. 105.
15. On this see Conor Cruise O'Brien, 'Passion and Cunning: An Essay on the Politics of W. B. Yeats', in A. N. Jeffares and K. G. W. Cross, eds. *In Excited Reverie: A Centenary Tribute* (London: Macmillan, 1965), pp. 221–2.
16. W. B. Yeats, *Collected Poems* (London: Macmillan, 1955), p. 275.
17. F. X. Martin and F. J. Byrne, eds. *Eoin Mac Neill: The Scholar Revolutionary* (Shannon: Irish University Press, 1973), p. 134.
18. Stephen Spender, *World Within World* (London: Hamish Hamilton, 1951), p. 191.
19. Frank O'Connor, *The Backward Look* (London: Macmillan, 1967), pp. 112–13.
20. Ibid., p. 113.
21. Yeats, *Collected Poems*, p. 351.
22. Andrew Carpenter, 'Double Vision in Anglo-Irish Literature', in A. Carpenter, ed. *Place, Personality and the Irish Writer* (Gerrards Cross: Colin Smythe, 1977), pp. 182–3.
23. Horace Walpole, *Letters*, III (London and New Haven: Oxford and Yale University Press, 1952), p. 17.
24. Terry Eagleton, *Heathcliff and the Great Hunger* (London: Verso, 1995), passim.
25. For more on this see Declan Kiberd, *Irish Classics* (London: Granta, 2000).
26. Joyce, *A Portrait of the Artist as a Young Man*, p. 273.
27. Frank O'Connor in conversation reported by Richard Ellmann.
28. Joyce, *Ulysses*, p. 272.
29. John Keats, *Letters*, selected by Frederick Page (London: Oxford, 1954), p. 149.
30. Oscar Wilde, *Table Talk*, ed. T. Wright (London: Cassell, 2000), 77.

31. Benedict Anderson, 'Exodus', *Critical Inquiry* 20, 2 (Winter 1994), p. 316.
32. Yeats, *Collected Poems*, pp. 166–7.
33. On this see Nicholas Mansergh, *The Irish Question 1840–1921* (London: Allen and Unwin, 1968), p. 88ff.
34. Benedict Anderson, *Imagined Communities* (London: Verso, 1983), p. 122.
35. John Montague, *Selected Poems* (Winston-Salem: Wake Forest Press, 1982), p. 108.
36. Samuel Beckett, *Waiting for Godot*, pp. 14–15.
37. Proclamation of the Irish Republic 1916.
38. Salman Rushdie, *Imaginary Homelands* (London: 1992), pp. 124–5ff.
39. Oliver Goldsmith, 'The Deserted Village', in Seamus Deane, gen. ed. *The Field Day Anthology of Irish Writing*, 3 vols. (Derry: Field Day, 1991), I, p. 450.
40. All phrases from *The Playboy of the Western World*.
41. See Malcolm Brown, *The Politics of Irish Literature* (London: Granta, 1972), pp. 35ff.
42. James Joyce, *Finnegans Wake*, ed. S. Deane (London: Penguin, 1992), p. 171.
43. Cited by Bernard Ransom, *Connolly's Marxism* (London: Pluto, 1980), p. 18.
44. Joyce, *Ulysses*, p. 53.
45. See Gilles Deleuze and Felix Guattari, *Kafka: Toward a Minor Literature*, trans. D. Polan (Minneapolis: University of Minnesota Press, 1986), pp. 28ff.
46. Arthur O. Lovejoy, 'On the Discrimination of Romanticisms', in M. H. Abrams, ed. *English Romantic Poets* (Oxford: Oxford University Press, 1966), pp. 3–17.
47. Quoted by Richard Ellmann, *James Joyce* (Oxford: Oxford University Press, 1959), p. 523.
48. For these points see ibid., p. 128.
49. On the business/Bohemia overlap in the Irish Renaissance, see P. J. Mathews, *Revival* (Cork: Cork University Press in association with Field Day, 2003), passim.
50. Mary and Padraic Colum, *Our Friend James Joyce* (New York: Doubleday, 1958), pp. 55–6.
51. Quoted in Ellmann, *James Joyce*, p. 470.
52. Joyce, *Ulysses*, p. 99.
53. Ibid., p. 271.
54. Ibid., p. 702.
55. Ibid., p. 239.
56. Ibid., pp. 747–8.
57. Ibid., pp. 775–6.
58. Ibid, p. 347.
59. Ibid., p. 788.
60. The phrase 'modernism in the streets' is Lionel Trilling's but the underlying concept is spelled out fully in Daniel Bell, *The Cultural Contradictions of Capitalism* (1976; second edn, London: Heinemann, 1979), pp. 1–95. On the evolution and dissolution of Bohemia, see Jerrold Seigel, *Bohemian Paris: Culture Politics and the Boundaries of Bourgeois Life 1830–1930* (Baltimore: Johns Hopkins University Press, 1986), pp. 389–97.
61. Joyce, *Ulysses*, p. 841.
62. Jane Jacobs, *The Death and Life of Great American Cities* (New York: Random House, 1961).
63. Franco Moretti, *Modern Epic: The World System from Goethe to Garcia Marquez*, trans. Quintin Hoare (London: Verso, 1996), pp. 123–82.
64. Seosamh Mac Grianna, *Mo Bhealach Féin* (Dublin: Stationery Office, 1940), p. 5. (Translations are my own.)

65. Joyce, *A Portrait of the Artist as a Young Man*, p. 3.
66. Ibid., p. 276.
67. Mac Grianna, *Mo Bhealach Féin*, p. 173.
68. Ibid. p. 5.
69. Seosamh Mac Grianna, *An Grá agus an Ghruaim* (Dublin: Stationery Office, 1929), p. 107.
70. Mac Grianna, *Mo Bhealach Féin*, p. 19.
71. Ibid., p. 5.
72. Ibid., p. 136.
73. Seamus Deane, *The Pleasures of Gaelic Literature*, ed. J. Jordan (Cork: Mercier, 1977), p. 67.
74. Arthur Power, *Conversations with James Joyce* (London: Millington, 1974), pp. 78ff.
75. Samuel Beckett, *All That Fall* (London: Faber, 1962), p. 24.

2

The Irish Renaissance, 1890–1940: poetry in English

PATRICK CROTTY

Introduction

The fifty years from 1890 to 1940 are at once among the most distinguished and the most problematic in the development of Irish poetry in English. They encompass the steadily incremental and ultimately magisterial career of W. B. Yeats, who, besides being the country's first indisputably great anglophone poet, was a writer of ampler gifts and resourcefulness than any produced by the island's Gaelic tradition since Dáibhí Ó Bruadair. Yeats is as central as Shelley or Tennyson to the history of what used to be called English literature, yet the matter of Ireland is at the core of his themes and figuration, while the manner of Ireland is to varying degrees audible in his idiom. These same years, however, were characterised also by the activities of a range of lesser poets, many of them notably popular in their day, to whose work it is now difficult to respond except in terms of its period interest. One of the problems with Dora Sigerson Shorter, James Stephens, F. R. Higgins and many of the other writers who appear, from our contemporary perspective, to bob in Yeats's wash is that their very success in affecting the manner and/or pursuing the matter of Ireland cut them off from wider concerns. Some of these poets spent more time out of the country than Yeats did, but at best they only intermittently managed to accommodate the broader challenges of modernity in their verse.

Europe underwent tumultuous change in the half-century from the fall of Parnell to the fall of France. A far-reaching realignment of the social classes took place in the West in the aftermath of the Great War, as the nineteenth-century imperial order began to break up, while the triumph of the Bolsheviks in the East inaugurated a period of near apocalyptic intensity in the political divide between Right and Left across the continent: the rise of Fascism in Italy, Germany and Spain issued in due course in an even more barbarous and destructive conflagration than the conflict of 1914–18. In the arts, the first third or so of the new century was marked by the innovative excitements of High Modernism, excitements facilitated by the disturbing and exhilarating insights issuing from psychoanalysis, anthropology, linguistics and the other human sciences that had been emerging over the previous decades. This was a period of convulsive change in Ireland as well, change not without its place in the larger pattern of imperial fragmentation: the long-drawn-out anti-climax of the constitutional movement for Home Rule gave way to the violence of the revolutionary years 1916–23, as the energies represented by the growth of the Gaelic League and the Gaelic Athletic Association, and, to a degree, even of the Literary Revival itself (inaugurated but never quite controlled by Yeats himself) moved decisively from the cultural to the political sphere. From one point of view, the decade or so near the centre of our survey – the years from the signing of the Ulster Covenant in the North (1912) to the cessation of hostilities by anti-Treaty republicans in the South (1923) – makes the period covered by this essay one of the most cataclysmic in the history of the island. These middle years witnessed the formation of the Ulster Volunteers, the National Volunteers and the Irish Citizen Army; the Curragh 'Mutiny'; the Larne and Howth gunrunnings; the Easter Rising; large-scale unionist and nationalist casualties in the Great War; the Anglo-Irish War of 1919–21; the Civil War; and finally the surprisingly rapid consolidation of Northern Ireland and the Irish Free State. From another point of view, however – and the literature of the time attests to the fact almost *ad nauseam* – the period from 1890 to 1940 was one of tranquillity, or, as James Joyce famously put it, paralysis.

The apparent contradiction can be explained by the social continuities underlying the dramatic political disjunctions of the day. The resolution of the land question in a series of parliamentary acts from 1870 to 1903 had ensured the emergence of a large and understandably conservative class of small rural proprietors. Outside the greater Belfast area, the economy of the island remained to a significant degree pre-industrial, and most members of the new Catholic administrative and professional caste of Dublin and other urban centres in the south were removed by no more than a generation or two from the rural hinterland, and were moreover the products of an education system rigidly controlled by the clerical authorities. Despite the role of James Connolly's socialist Citizen Army in the Rising, questions of class and of the ownership of the means of production took a poor second place to the metaphysics of sovereignty in the revolutionary turmoil of 1916–23. Unsurprisingly therefore, the social ethos of the country was much the same in the early decades of independence as it had been at the turn of the century, and the constraints against which the young Joyce kicked in 1901, when he called the Irish 'the most belated race in Europe',[1] were pretty much those that caused Patrick Kavanagh to complain forty years later that 'All Ireland' had 'froze[n] for want of Europe'.[2] The valorisation of the countryside associated with Eamon de Valera's notorious St Patrick's Day broadcast of 1943 was not the sole preserve of nationalist rhetoricians and Catholic priests but was deeply embedded in Irish culture in general, and in Irish literary culture in particular, as the work of the majority of the poets discussed in this chapter makes clear. Indeed the writing of the period as a whole is characterised by a dialectic between idealisation of rural Ireland or of the national past, on the one hand, and aspiration towards a more complex, internationally alert and critical apprehension of Irish experience, on the other. This dialectic is not necessarily a matter of explicit antagonism: while Yeats and Joyce were making the disproportionate contribution to High Modernism that would ensure the continuing interest of the wider world in at least some of the writing issuing from the island for decades to come,[3] they numbered among their friends poets (Oliver St John Gogarty in Yeats's case, Padraic Colum and Stephens in Joyce's) whose lyrics seem radically innocent of the implications of *The Tower*, say, or *Ulysses*, and indeed of the transformed possibilities of early twentieth-century literary utterance generally.

Though the dialectic I have described is to some extent a matter of the perennial tension between talent and genius, the belatedness of the minor poets of the Revival is not to be explained simply by reference to the modesty of their gifts, or, for that matter, to the survival of pre-Modernist poetics deep into the twentieth century throughout the anglophone world. A distinction between modernity and Modernism can be invoked to defend the work of John Masefield and Andrew Young in Britain, or of Edwin Arlington Robinson and Edna St Vincent Millay in the United States. Such a distinction is well nigh meaningless in relation to poets whose adherence to various versions of Irish pastoral (or to a species of old-school-tie classicism in Gogarty's case) seems symptomatic of a culturally induced complacency in the face of contemporaneity. Thus while there have been recent stirrings of critical interest in the 'non-modernist Moderns', as David Goldie has labelled such British and American writers as I have referred to,[4] the stock of the secondary poets of the Revival has fallen very low even in their homeland. Amply represented in anthologies from Kathleen Hoagland's *1000 Years of Irish Poetry* (1947) to Brendan Kennelly's *Penguin Book of Irish Verse* (1970), they are accorded short shrift in more recent compilations like Thomas Kinsella's *New Oxford Book of Irish Verse* (1986) and W. J. McCormack's *Ferocious Humanism: An Anthology of Irish Poetry From Before Swift to Yeats and After* (2000). The latter volumes were assembled in an era of more vigorous poetic production and more stringent criticism than the period under review. (Where poetry is concerned, indeed, the three decades from 1970 have greater claim to the term Renaissance than the three from 1890, at least if the singular figure of W. B. Yeats is removed from the reckoning.) While it is difficult to envisage a future in which the formal conservatism and recurrent (if not quite pervasive) sentimentality of the Revival poets will hold any stronger attraction for readers and critics than it does today, examination of their work throws valuable light on the nature of the cultural matrix from which more lastingly interesting writers, from J. M. Synge and Joyce to Kavanagh and Louis MacNeice, successfully struggled to emerge. It was MacNeice who observed that the productions of minor poets become 'Mere source-books . . . to point or except a rule'.[5] A survey like the present one can perhaps do no more than offer the lesser poets of the Revival a brief reprieve from such a fate, drawing attention to their individuality and incidental successes as well as to their rule-exemplifying failings. If it convinces readers of the merits of the best, anti-idealising verse of Stephens, Colum and Joseph Campbell, it will have achieved much of its purpose. The closing pages of the essay take account of the early work of a number of ultimately more considerable poets – Austin Clarke, Kavanagh and MacNeice – who conducted the greater part of their careers in the period covered by Dillon Johnston and Guinn Batten's chapter, and whose achievement will be more fully documented there.

Yeats

The career of the most versatile and energetic of all poets in Ireland's English-language tradition neatly spans the temporal parameters of the present chapter. Yeats published his first collection of poems in 1889, when he was twenty-four, while his final volume, *Last Poems and Two Plays*, appeared within a few months of his death on 28 January 1939. It is tempting to observe of many of his minor contemporaries that their gifts might have exfoliated more vitally in different cultural circumstances. Yet these were, by and large, circumstances that they shared with Yeats, and that Yeats repeatedly and variously succeeded in turning to advantage over six decades of writing. The sheer force of his creative personality, the acuity of his poetic intelligence and the willpower that propelled his artistic development even in times of trauma and confusion in his personal life, can be cited as crucial in allowing him to do so. It is arguable, however, that some aspects of his cultural situation marked Yeats off from other Irish writers of his time. He was at once more and less Irish – or more

Irish and more English – than most of them. His Irishness was reflected in his first-hand experience of the lore of the countryside, his assiduously acquired knowledge of ancient myths and legends in the (rather questionable) forms in which these had begun to become accessible to English speakers in the late Victorian period, and his systematic command of the work of nineteenth-century predecessors like Thomas Davis, James Clarence Mangan, Sir Samuel Ferguson and William Allingham; he took Ireland as his theme, and sang to sweeten the country's wrong at least as explicitly even as patriot poets like Patrick Pearse and Thomas MacDonagh. His poetic identity also had an English dimension, however, one not to be confused with his Anglo-Irish inheritance as a southern Protestant. He spent crucial phases of his childhood and early manhood in London. It has often been observed that his unhappy experience of school in Hammersmith sharpened his Irish loyalties, giving him a sense of Sligo (where he had passed two uncharacteristically content boyhood years) as a sort of primal, maternal paradise.[6] Yet his intermittent London domicile had directly positive aspects, too, not the least of which was the access to English cultural traditions it offered him. Yeats lived for periods of his teens and twenties in the artist's colony of Bedford Park, where the milieu of his impecunious, portrait-painting father included many writers and artisans from the more respectable reaches of bohemian London. His youthful hero was William Morris, and no less English than Morris were those poets of the past to whom, as he declared two years before his death, he 'owed his soul'[7] – Spenser, Shakespeare, Blake and Shelley. (Working on an edition of Blake's poems as a young man, he convinced himself that the great London radical and spiritualist was in fact Irish, scion of an immigrant family called O'Neal[8] – a self-delusion suggestive of his nationalist bafflement at his failure to register any cultural gulf whatever between himself and Blake.)

Yeats's lifelong faith in poetry as vehicle and guarantor of subjectivity was perhaps the most English thing about him: the concern for the depth and quality of consciousness that led him to theosophy and the occult – to the entire 'southern Californian side' of his enterprise, as W. H. Auden cruelly dubbed it[9] – is best understood in terms of the earnestness of his response to the great Romantics' variously formulated doctrines of the Imagination.[10] He explained in a letter to John O'Leary in 1892 that the reason why the 'mystical life' was at the centre 'of all that I do & all that I think & all that I write' was that he considered himself to be 'a voice of . . . a greater renaissance (*sic*) – the revolt of the soul against the intellect – now beginning in the world'.[11] The poet's Irish patriotism was similarly in the service of that Shelleyan revolt. 'Ireland' and 'England' were for Yeats as much opposing forces in a visionary encounter as they were political and geographical entities. Ireland was his name for spiritual tradition and openness, England for the mercantile modernity that, in perhaps the deepest consistency of his career, he was committed to repudiating. Dislike of the temper of the times was something he shared with his English, Scottish and Welsh 'companions of the Cheshire Cheese' at the Rhymers Club in Fleet Street in the 1890s. What those writers did not have, however, was a country in an inchoate state of possibility, a country moving inexorably, with whatever degree of difficulty, towards a separate, still tantalisingly undefined cultural and political identity. After the death of Parnell, Yeats was intoxicated by the realisation 'that Ireland was to be like soft wax for years to come'.[12] All that was left for the unacknowledged (if not quite unimperious) legislator to do was to impress his seal upon it. His country was thus for Yeats the site of a species of optimism that had been unavailable to poets on the neighbouring island since the high tide of Romanticism almost a century earlier. His reading of the national past and future enabled him to avoid the sense of the irrelevance and diminishing efficacy of the poetic imagination that had so dismayed Tennyson and Arnold, and that was in the process of overwhelming his closest associates among the *poètes maudits* of the nineties. It was enough to keep him from falling to his death off a barstool like Lionel Johnson, or wading into the sea to shoot himself like John Davidson. By the time it was exposed as a misreading – by the time, that is to say, the dominant classes of the new Ireland had revealed themselves to be as little interested as professional and business people elsewhere in Europe in maintaining such links with ancient wisdom as semi-literacy and superstition had granted their forebears – the career was so robustly under way that the poet could make capital even out of the collapse of his dreams and schemes. (Dreaming and scheming were always for him ancillary activities.) Reversing the Catholic–Protestant terms of his rhetoric of the 1890s, he now persuaded himself that as a Protestant he was heir to a distinguished intellectual and imaginative tradition, and that his recoil from the tawdriness of the ambient conditions was proof of the quality of his inherited sensibility. Yeats's mythologizing of history, anti-Protestant in the earlier career, anti-Catholic in the later, is easily discreditable in intellectual terms, but it was not narrowly self-serving. He had to believe these things, or to pretend to himself that he believed them, if he was not to be undone by 'the desolation of reality'.[13] Above all he had to believe them if he was to produce his poems.

And the poems were remarkable from the beginning. The stock account of Yeats's development as a matter of the steady hardening and compression of his lyric idiom is true enough in its way, but it deflects attention from the attained power of his first collection, the most striking debut by any anglophone Irish poet of the last century and a quarter. The title poem, 'The Wanderings of Oisin', retains greater interest than the subsequent (and technically superior) long poems interspersed throughout the career up to 1923. Despite its manifest faults – excessive ornamentation, lack of pace, a preference for description over narration – it sustains a philosophical seriousness that makes Ferguson's Celtic verse-tales seem by contrast mere projections of antiquarian enthusiasm. Like the deceptively simple lyric 'The Stolen Child' (one of the other highlights of the book), the Oisin poem embodies a critique of the urge towards transcendence it at first sight appears to endorse: the fulfilments promised in turn by each of the three enchanted isles prove illusory, and Oisin has to return to Ireland, to live 'in the house of the Fenians, be they in flames or at feast'. The quotidian, this and other poems insist, is the proper haunt of the human, and aspiration towards an ideal perfection, when too freely indulged, can fatally undermine the capacity for everyday living. Yeats acknowledges that the mind is driven by the inadequacies of the world to conceive of otherworlds of one sort or another, but his poetry is too antithetical in procedure and too sceptical in outlook to proclaim either the sufficiency of the familiar or the reliability of the imagined. 'The Wanderings of Oisin' offers the first full expression of the poet's tough-minded and (despite popular misconception) entirely characteristic passion for reality. His one earlier poem with what he called Irish 'scenery',[14] 'The Madness of King Goll', had figured the antithesis between world and otherworld in terms of sanity and madness. While in general it can be said that his recourse to Irish subject matter and settings domesticated Yeats's imagination, affording him a more direct approach to his themes and lending a sensuous particularity to his imagery,[15] the legendary material of the Goll poem served to bring his work perilously 'close to home' in another, more colloquial sense. The lyric appears to have been written less 'out of the common thought of the people',[16] that is to say, than out of the existential miseries of the author's later teens, and it prompts a reading of the lure of Faery throughout the early work as a metaphor for psychological distress. The nature of that distress – if it had a source in the poet's life – is a matter for speculation, though it may have involved anxieties about the mental instabilities that were rife on the Pollexfen side of his inheritance. (The poem was accompanied on its first appearance[17] by a reproduction of a John Butler Yeats portrait of the bearded poet attired as Goll: '[M]y father painted me as King Goll, tearing the strings out [of] a harp, being insane with youth, but looking very desirable', Yeats later told Olivia Shakespear.[18] The painting[19] suggests that the connection between the mad king and the passionate son was not lost on the father.) It is true at least that the otherworlds of most of the subsequent 'Celtic' poems would have something of the character of the woodland through which the deranged Goll dashes, and the poetry charts a struggle to resist the lure of Faery rather than a desire to surrender to it. Considered in terms of a such a struggle, a title like 'The Unappeasable Host' (from *The Wind among the Reeds*, 1899) takes on a considerable charge of dread: the Host may have a purely literary existence, but the force it represents is all too actual and difficult to appease. The most durable of the Celtic and Faery pieces – 'The Man who Dreamed of Faeryland', 'Fergus and the Druid' (both from *The Countess Kathleen and Various Legends and Lyrics*, 1892) – are marked by shrewd diagnostic intelligence rather than wistful melancholy in their treatment of the dangers of 'dreaming'. There may, then, be an urgently intimate sense in which Robert Frost's typification of a poem as a 'momentary stay against confusion'[20] is applicable to Yeats's early lyrics. Indeed the poet himself appears to have thought of his poems in this way – such emblems of art in the early work as Goll's harp and the shells of the protagonists of 'The Song of the Happy Shepherd' and 'The Sad Shepherd' have a conspicuously therapeutic function.

Retrospect allows us to recognise the extent to which the attitudes and procedures of the great poetry of Yeats's maturity – the verse gathered in *The Tower* (1928) and *The Winding Stair and Other Poems* (1933) – were already in place by the end of the 1880s. 'The Stolen Child', for instance, devotes three stanzas to the compulsion to flee the contingencies of the human, imagines a transition from world to otherworld in the gap between its third and fourth stanzas, and ends on a powerful, albeit implicit, acknowledgement of the superior appeal of the quotidian over the eternal. In so doing, it precisely anticipates the structure and argument of 'Sailing to Byzantium', the opening poem of *The Tower*. (The bobbing of the mice 'round and round the oatmeal chest' might even be said to offer, in its rudimentary adumbration of ritual, a prefiguration of the mature poetry's 'ceremony of innocence'.)[21] Also present from the beginning was the esemplastic power that enabled Yeats to combine his varied interests in a unitary poetic discourse and to portray them as aspects of one another – thus 'To the Rose upon the Rood of Time' and 'To Ireland in the Coming Times', that pair of key prospecti to the career, persuasively chart the relations between the poet's patriotism, his spiritualism and his necessary artistic contract with the temporal realm of 'all poor foolish things that live a day'. To that contract can be traced the naturalistic and even earthy impulse that for the most part keeps pace over the decades with the development of its opposite, the spiritual and arcane side of the poetry. When the tension between the two slackens, as it does at a number of points, the work undergoes a loss of power. *The Wind among the Reeds* is perhaps the most problematic of Yeats's collections in this regard. While the volume marks a significant advance on the earlier work in versification, complexity of syntax and subtlety of cadence, its rarefied symbolic landscapes seem troublingly remote both from the intellectual ferment of the later nineteenth century and from the embodied condition of human experience. John Davidson's comment in a review that it was difficult to believe the author had not been dead for many years has a measure of justice, albeit of the rough variety:[22] the poems' putative debt to Mallarmé does little to mitigate their antique and even courtly quality.

From the turn of the twentieth century, however, Yeats's utterance becomes progressively less ethereal and begins to admit a social and historicized dimension. Ever since his meeting in 1889 with the flamboyant (not to say theatrical) nationalist agitator Maud Gonne he had been writing poems of hopeless love, and these now increasingly abandoned plaintiveness in favour of an analytical and even dispassionate tone, a tendency reinforced after Gonne's marriage to John MacBride in 1903. The sacrifice incurred by the struggle for artistic perfection emerges as an explicit concern at this stage of the career, and it is typical of Yeats's success in binding together the diverse strands of his subject matter that 'Adam's Curse', the poem which most fully encompasses the new theme, should also be among the most memorable of his love lyrics. The fall-off in the rate of his lyric production in the first decade of the century is usually attributed to his practical and artistic responsibilities at the Abbey Theatre, which he had founded with Lady Gregory in 1904, and his experiences there – particularly those surrounding the barracking of Synge's *Playboy of the Western World* in 1907 – may be identified also as the main source of his growingly adversarial relationship with his country. The souring of his private and public life is reflected in the dry, disenchanted diction of the poems, and in their cultivation of an attitude hovering between bitterness and hauteur, a foretaste of the aristocratic posturing of his poetry in the 1930s. The process whereby Yeats stripped his idioms and rhythms of ornamentation began with *In the Seven Woods* (1904) and became pronounced in *The Green Helmet and Other Poems* (1910), volumes which pre-date his meeting with Ezra Pound, but the American poet was nonetheless instrumental in bringing the tendency to the fullness of its development in the astonishingly unadorned and immediate poetry of *Responsibilities* (1914), generally recognised as Yeats's first fully modern collection. The dedicatory verses enact a moment of self-recognition at least as terrible (T. S. Eliot's word[23]) as anything in the work of the 'confessional' poets of the mid-century, and the poems record various instances of disappointment in the personal and political spheres, here and there using mythological materials as a measure of the deficiencies of the present rather than as the building blocks of poetic anti-worlds. The overall mood of defiant stoicism is underpinned by the tough, pliant verbal textures. Yeats's disillusionment with Irish politics receives its most forthright expression in 'September 1913' (though the poem's famous refrain about the death of Romantic Ireland is at least partly a self-rebuke for misreading the condition of the country) and in his address to the ghost of Charles Stewart Parnell, 'To a Shade', with its coruscating and perhaps unduly haughty depiction of Dublin's degraded and venal public life.

When Yeats married the young English occultist Georgie Hyde-Lees in 1917 he was fifty-two years old, yet he had produced barely half of his canonical poetry, and the merest handful of the poems on which his claim to consideration as the anglophone world's greatest twentieth-century poet rests. The fulcrum of his career coincided with the revolutionary period in the movement for Irish independence, and with the Great War and its aftermath. He was to become the foremost poetic commentator on the one, and the most articulate medium of the sense of apocalyptic dread generated by the other: in his most powerful work of the decade after 1916, the Irish and European conflicts are conflated in a series of visionary meditations on chaos, order and the ambiguous relationship between civilisation and violence. While Yeats was ultimately to endorse the Dublin rebellion, the poem drafted in its immediate aftermath, 'Easter 1916', is almost inscrutable in its weighing of the single-minded puritanism of the rebel leaders against the heroic grandeur of their actions. (Though 'Easter 1916' has much to say about personal morality, or at least about the impact of individual acts and decisions on the quality of subjectivity, it remains largely silent about the questions of political morality that continue, nine decades after the event, to exercise supporters and opponents of the Rising.) The poet appears to have been astonished that the 'wasteful virtues' attributed to his ancestors in the introductory rhymes to *Responsibilities*, and identified elsewhere in his work with the ancient rather than the modern world, could have been exhibited by the mainly lower-middle-class Catholic insurgents of 1916. The resulting rejuvenation of his faith in Ireland was manifested by his purchase of a Norman tower house at Ballylee, near Lady Gregory's Coole Park estate in south Galway, which he was to use as a summer home after it had been refurbished in 1922. The laconic, embittered manner of *Responsibilities* now began to give way to a new style, magniloquent, compacted and richly symbolic, but the complexities of this later mode would be organic rather than (as in the case of his Celtic poems of the 1890s) merely ornamental. *The Wind among the Reeds* had marked his first success in orchestrating symbols across a range of lyrics, and the poems of the decade and a half leading up to his marriage had effected a similar feat a good deal more accessibly, most notably in their use of the Trojan myth to link erotic and political concerns by identifying Maud Gonne with Helen. (The Homeric resonance of the 'terrible beauty' refrain of 'Easter 1916' is crucial.) From now until the end of his career, however, Yeats sought to elaborate a network of symbols that would integrate his diverse poetic interests and illuminate the underlying unity of his work (early and late) and indeed of the personality that was approaching coherence through that very process of elaboration. One has to look outside the anglophone tradition – to the work of Rainer Maria Rilke, to cite the most obvious example – for a twentieth-century lyric poetry of comparable reach and ambition. Yeats's need to believe that his symbols had an ontological status beyond the poems in which they occur led him to attempt to systematise them in the arcane prose work *A Vision* (1925), a characteristic act of self-persuasion based on the experiments in automatic writing undertaken by his wife to divert him during their initially unhappy honeymoon. (How literally he regarded the book's 'philosophy' is open to question – the second edition includes a prefatory observation to the effect that the 'circuits of sun and moon' described so exhaustively there are mere 'stylistic arrangements of experience'.)[24] The astrological taxonomies of personality types and geometrical illustrations of historical cycles in *A Vision* are not without their fascination, but they are essential to the appreciation only of a small number of atypically gnomic and doctrinal poems. The strongly empirical streak in Yeats's artistic make-up ensured that he grounded his symbols in worldly particulars, and even figures that remain opaque in some poems are, more often than not, elucidated by their recontextualisation in others. Many of the contents of the voluminous and varied *The Wild Swans at Coole* (1919) – a rather shorter version of the collection had been published in Ireland two years earlier – pre-date the occult exhilarations of 1917 that were to transform Yeats's poetic procedures. Though the book includes such major pieces as 'The Fisherman' (very much a pre-Easter Rising, *Responsibilities*-type utterance), 'Upon a Dying Lady', 'In Memory of Major Robert Gregory' (composed in 1918) and the serenely crepuscular title-poem, it marks a deepening rather than an extension of Yeats's gift and is best understood as the last volume of his middle period. The much shorter, more unified collection *Michael Robartes and the Dancer* (1921) features 'The Second Coming', earliest of the great visionary poems on historical process in the packed style Yeats had been evolving to accommodate his 'system', as well as the less vatic but scarcely less panoptic 'A Prayer for My Daughter' – besides finding a place next to a group of frankly republican ballads for 'Easter 1916', which had been held back from publication at the time of composition for fear of further inflaming the political situation.[25]

It was not, however, until the appearance of *The Tower* in 1928 that the full majestic sweep of Yeats's later manner became visible. The most rhetorically potent poetry of the career repeatedly reminds us that it issues from the pen of an ailing and increasingly feeble old man – it takes effort to remember that the poet was under sixty when he wrote many of the poems in the book – and the contrast between the decrepitude of the body and the vigour of the mind provides the controlling antithesis for a series of contemplative sequences and lyrics which range from relative optimism to the darkest pessimism in their posing of the relationship between art and life, suffering and creativity, time and eternity and (to use Arnold's terms) culture and anarchy. No book by Yeats arises with such apparent naturalness out of the particularities of time and place. The poet figures in his public persona – he had been appointed to Seanad Éireann, the upper house of the newly independent Free State's parliament, in 1922, and had been awarded the Nobel Prize for Literature the following year – as well as in his private one as unsuccessful lover of Maud Gonne, whose ageing is not entirely flatteringly depicted. The architecture and furniture of his Galway tower house, the folklore of its locale, the political violence endured by the neighbourhood at the hands of Lloyd George's Black and Tans in the Anglo-Irish War[26] and of the republicans during the Civil War (and that comes literally to the poet's doorstep in the shape of an 'affable Irregular') – all are given emblematic significance and lifted into a meditative discourse at once stately, allusive and colloquial: the power of Yeats's ruminations on the past and future derives from their being written so strongly under stress of the present. The politics of this poetry are unmistakably right-wing: the artistic and intellectual achievements of the past are recognised with equanimity as having been contingent upon the cultivated classes' monopolisation of violence, while the shapelessness and disorder that threaten 'ingenious lovely things' are identified throughout with democracy. (The fact that Yeats's High Modernist contemporaries Eliot and Pound shared such politics can be mentioned for purposes of contextualisation rather than extenuation.) *The Tower* is notable not only for the three 'historical' sequences near the start – the title poem, 'Meditations in Time of Civil War' and 'Nineteen Hundred and Nineteen' – but also for 'Sailing to Byzantium', 'Among School Children' (which reflects on the continuity of the personality from youth to age by way of a dazzlingly unpredictable logic of images) and 'Leda and the Swan'. The latter, surely the century's most compressed and structurally inventive English sonnet, offers a violent reformulation of Yeats's favourite Homeric motif, the catastrophic public consequences of an ill-judged private act. To thus single out individual poems for comment, however, is to detract from the book's consistency of quality and intricacy of design.

The importance Yeats attached to intricacy of design, both within and between volumes, was further illustrated with the publication in 1933 of *The Winding Stair and Other Poems*. (The potentially confusing title – there is no poem called 'The Winding Stair' – acknowledges the appearance of the first five poems as a little collection under that name in 1929.) The half-ruined tower with its spiral staircase is again the major source of figuration in a second series of artfully inter-connected contemplative poems centring on the contrast between extra-temporal perfection and historical fallenness. Some of the poems are more or less explicitly paired with pieces in the previous book – 'Byzantium' with 'Sailing to Byzantium', for instance, or 'Blood and the Moon' with 'The Tower' – while the sequence of eleven lyrics at the end of the volume, 'A Woman Young and Old', answers the similarly structured 'A Man Young and Old' even to the extent of closing with an adaptation of a chorus from Sophocles.[27] Two women young and old – the Gore-Booths of Lissadell – are the subjects of the defiant elegy at the beginning of the book, which functions also as another of those milestone poems on his own ageing with which the witness/survivor who utters 'In Memory of Eva Gore-Booth and Con Markiewicz' had chosen to inaugurate his collections over the previous two decades. The introductory verses to *Responsibilities* had highlighted the poet's age – 'close on forty-nine' – and the opening piece of each subsequent volume, with the arguable exception of *Michael Robartes and the Dancer*, had marked further stages in the process of growing old. The pattern would have been reasserted and brought to completion if the posthumous *Last Poems* had begun, as manuscript evidence suggests it should have, with 'Under Ben Bulben', an address from the grave.[28] Though the style of *The Winding Stair* is less opulent than that of *The Tower*, and sometimes approaches bleakness, the later book has a less embittered air and is generally more at ease with corporeal life. The unrepentant sensuality and songlike simplicity of 'Words for Music Perhaps', the suite of variously voiced lyrics at the centre of the volume, essays a mode that would persist, with increasing raucousness, to the end of the career. (*Words for Music Perhaps* had originally appeared as a separate volume in 1932.)

The poetry of Yeats's last years is marked by an extraordinary formal variety but also by a species of rhetorical overstrain. The period adds a number of masterpieces to the canon: 'The Circus Animals' Desertion', a retrospect on the entire career and a resolution of its long debate between life and art in favour of the former even at its most filthy and reduced; 'Lapis Lazuli', perhaps the most explicit and certainly the most eloquent of the many later poems that promote tragic gaiety as a moral imperative; 'Long-legged Fly', an engrossed yet delicately playful meditation on the quietude that precedes great action; and 'Cuchulain Comforted', written the month Yeats died and depicting the mortally wounded Cuchulain, oldest of all his poetic masks, sewing a shroud that is at once his own and his creator's. A half a dozen or so major pieces, including 'Man and the Echo' and 'Beautiful Lofty Things', reprise incidents or themes from the poet's campaigns of cultural warfare and interrogate his motivation and achievement. A good deal of the later production is problematic, however. The refusal to indulge conventional expectations with regard to the decorum of old age can lead Yeats to the debonair extravagance of 'High Talk', but more frequently it issues in stylistic excess and a shrillness of tone unprecedented in the earlier work. The title poem of *Parnell's Funeral* – as the poetry section of *A Full Moon in March* (1935) is called – communicates a well-nigh sectarian distaste for Catholic Ireland by way of a simplistically schematised historiography and a far-fetched rhetoric of cannibalism. (Other poems similarly seem to have too obvious designs upon the reader's sensitivities in their recourse to images of grotesque bodily violence.) 'The Gyres', which opens *New Poems* (1938), borders on hysteria in its Nietzschean declamation before the spectacle of civilisational collapse, while many of the songs and ballads that dominate the volume bring a too knowing swagger to their patriotism or bawdry. The glorification of the 'indomitable Irishry' in Part V of 'Under Ben Bulben' comes closer to bluster than anything else Yeats wrote and is, moreover, executed in clankingly mechanical couplets. Yet the posthumous collection in which that valedictory sequence appeared is much the strongest of the poet's last three volumes and reveals him at the very end of his life abundantly resourceful and capable of a new serenity alongside a by now familiar rumbustiousness.

Yeats's poetry repeatedly draws attention to the labour that went into its making, and the scale of his success *qua* poet seems all the more extraordinary in the light of the exertions he devoted to other activities – criticism, autobiography, fiction, editorial work, controversy, spiritualism, politics, fund-raising, theatre management and direction and, most remarkably of all, dramatic composition. While his attainment as a playwright is assessed in Adrian Frazier's chapter, no account of his poetry can claim completeness without mention of his status as the English language's pre-eminent practitioner of verse drama in the modern period. In purely poetic terms Yeats's plays are of considerably greater interest than those of T. S. Eliot. Through a wealth of lyrical passages, ranging in manner from the figurative daring of Oona's exhausted speech at the end of *The Countess Cathleen* (1892) to the sober limpidity of the Street-Singer's song that closes *The Death of Cuchulain* (1939), they make a significant addition to the sum of a uniquely capacious twentieth-century poetic achievement.

Ascendancy poets

'After us the Savage God', Yeats wrote in *The Trembling of the Veil*.[29] After him, the timid poet. Yeats so outranks his contemporaries and immediate successors in the scope of his vision and the vigour of his forms that criticism has to scale down its operations in moving from his work to theirs. Yet timidity can be ascribed to the other Irish poets of the period only in the relative sense that their verse lacks the assertive and assimilative energies that distinguish his, and one should be wary of overstating the extent to which, individually or collectively, they were *intimidated* by his example. The compatriot of Yeats whose work from the 1890s is still widely read today, at any rate, had rather more to contend with in that decade than the ambition of his younger contemporary and friend. Almost all the verse composed by Oscar Wilde (1854–1900) belongs to the period before he had found his three-fold *métier* as dramatist, essayist and writer of fiction, a period beyond the scope of the present chapter. The exception is 'The Ballad of Reading Gaol', written mainly at Berneval in north-western France in the summer of 1897, shortly after his flight from England on completion of his sentence of two years' penal servitude for offences against the Criminal Law Amendment Act of 1886. Wilde extended the poem during the following months before publishing it in February 1898 under the signature 'C.3.3'. (The author's name was appended in square brackets after his convict number in the seventh printing of the regular edition in June 1899). The 'Ballad' is unique among Wilde's poems not only in coming from the opposite end of his cruelly foreshortened career but also in sacrificing aestheticism to a utilitarian purpose, propaganda in the cause of penal reform. The faults of the 'Ballad' are manifest and have been enumerated by commentators both in Wilde's time and our own: it is (at 654 lines) too long, too given to personification of concepts such as Sin and Terror, too obviously indebted to 'The Rime of the Ancient Mariner', and too prone to sentimentality. At its worst, it lapses into self-exculpatory theatricality of the kind that vitiates *De Profundis*, Wilde's lengthy prison letter to his *homme fatal*, Lord Alfred Douglas. The rhythm of the poem falters here and there and even the rhyming, at times, lacks assurance. Yet the enduring popularity of 'The Ballad of Reading Gaol' is less a testament to the deficiencies of public taste (as its ever-teasing author might have argued) than to the bleak force of its evocations of prison life and to its success in making both the witness-narrator and the reader appear complicit in the barbarism of judicial murder. Though the poem may, as Wilde himself remarked, 'out-Kipling Henley',[30] its uncertainties of tone and gauche lunges towards the reader's sympathy never quite extinguish the fiercely moral quality of its engagement with the hypocrisies of the penal system.

Seamus Heaney has ingeniously suggested that the tradition of Irish republican prison writing provides one of the literary contexts of the 'Ballad',[31] and much recent work on Wilde's dandyism and on the critique of English social mores offered by his plays has centred on the ambiguities of his position as an Irishman pursuing a career in the English metropolis. Wilde is unusual among Protestant poets[32] of his generation, however, in eschewing explicitly Irish subject matter. In the decades leading up to the Revival, practitioners like Ferguson, Davis, de Vere, Allingham and Wilde's mother 'Speranza' had pressed material drawn from the ancient or recent history of Ireland into the service of an array of political and theological imperatives. John Todhunter (1839–1916), Emily Lawless (1845–1913), William Larminie (1849–1900) and Herbert Trench (1865–1923) seem by virtue of their old-fashioned diction to belong with these and some of the other writers discussed in Matthew Campbell's chapter, rather than with Yeats and his inheritors, even though they were animated to a greater or lesser extent by the Revival ethos and produced much or all of their work in the period under review. Austin Clarke remarked in a radio broadcast in 1971 that 'Ferguson must be regarded as the father of the revival in all its phases',[33] and the Celtic narratives of Todhunter, Larminie and Trench certainly owe a more significant debt to the older poet than to Yeats. Larminie's 'Fand' and 'Moytura' (from *Fand and Other Poems*, 1892) and Todhunter's 'metrical' renderings of 'the Three Sorrows of Story-Telling' (*Three Irish Bardic Tales*, 1896) nonetheless lack the scope and energy of *Congal* and *Lays of the Western Gael*. More notably, though, they lack the metaphorical dimension that makes the business of Yeats's Celtic poems always add up to more than the mere recreation of lost grandeur. Todhunter was a lifelong friend of John Butler Yeats and, for a time, a close associate of his older son. He had published half a dozen books before turning to Irish themes in *The Banshee and Other Poems* (1888); thereafter he produced prose tales and verse in the Celtic manner, along with a mass of other material. (Though his career as a writer for the London stage was markedly unsuccessful, his enthusiasm may have helped direct Yeats's attention towards dramatic composition.)[34] Todhunter's strong tendencies towards the lachrymose are given a persuasive context in his most enduring poem, 'Aghadoe', a ballad of love betrayed to the Yeomen of '98; they are suppressed in the uncharacteristically laconic and powerful 'Under the White-Boy Acts, 1800. An Old Rector's Story', the opening poem of the inaugural Revival anthology, *Poems and Ballads of Young Ireland* (1888). Otherwise they are indulged at tedious length. Larminie was a far less prolific writer than Todhunter, but a more interesting poet. While his language is frequently jaded (and even inexact), his versification is innovative in a way that was to have a considerable influence on the later development of the Revival. In 1894 he published a pioneering essay advocating the replication in English of the assonantal patterns of Gaelic poetry.[35] Two years earlier, in the Epilogue to 'Fand', he had given a foretaste of what he had in mind:

> Ah! 'twas very long ago,
> And the words are now denied her:
> But the purple hillsides know
> Still the tones delightsome,
> And their breasts, impassioned, glow
> As were Fand beside them.

'The Nameless Doon', also from the *Fand* volume, has had a stubborn longevity in anthologies almost up to our own day – and a puzzling one, given its archaisms and the predictably 'Ozymandias'-like attitudes it strikes in response to the spectacle of the ruined fortress of the title. Much more impressive is Larminie's other stock anthology piece, the dramatic lyric 'Consolation' (again from *Fand*), which brings an admirably unhistrionic agnosticism to bear on the favourite Victorian trope of Love and Death. Trench, an exact coeval of Yeats, won few admirers either in his own day or subsequently, and his poems are more often mentioned for their impact on the young Austin Clarke than for their intrinsic interest. *Deirdre Wed* (1901) is busy with action and empirical detail in a way that contrasts with earlier poetic treatments of the Ulster legends, but its blank verse is dutiful to the point of boredom. Trench's lyric poems – some of them on Irish subjects – are similarly well crafted and lacking in distinctiveness.

Emily Lawless, the only one of these ascendancy poets with genuinely aristocratic origins, was, paradoxically perhaps, much the most popular of them. An essayist, naturalist and prominent historical novelist, she was in her late fifties when her first and best-known collection of poems appeared (*With the Wild Geese*, 1902 – the contents had been privately printed as *Atlantic Rhymes and Rhythms* four years previously). Like Richard Murphy, whose *The Battle of Aughrim* (1968) would similarly explore the Williamite period in the west of Ireland from a perspective of mixed inheritance, she was descended in the paternal line from Gaelic stock relatively recently converted to Protestantism. Antecedents of Lawless had for generations up until the period of her own childhood been associated with opposite sides of major Irish historical conflicts. Though she is usually seen as a unionist who repudiated the patrician nationalism of her father, her poetry is not entirely hospitable either to the conservative condescension or the nationalist ardour in (contradictory) terms of which it has been read. The recurrent linking of courage to folly in the historical poems that make up the first half of *With the Wild Geese* may perhaps be said to express a proto-feminist scepticism towards the martial values of patriarchy. These poems dramatise the departure of the defeated Jacobites from late seventeenth-century County Clare, and celebrate incidents from their subsequent European fortunes and from a number of earlier phases in the decline of the Gaelic aristocracy. To what extent their author can be said to be 'with' the Wild Geese and the volume's other protagonists is an intriguing question. The opening poem, 'After Aughrim', went fully into the public domain in the same year as Yeats and Lady Gregory's *Cathleen ni Houlihan*, and it is instructive to compare its chilly, neutral treatment of the figure of the sacrifice-inducing mother country with the romantic iconography of the play:

> She said, 'I never gave them aught,
> Not mine the power, if mine the will;
> I let them starve, I let them bleed, –
> They bled and starved, and loved me still.'
>
> . . .
>
> She said, 'God knows they owe me nought,
> I tossed them to the foaming sea,
> I tossed them to the howling waste,
> *Yet still their love comes home to me.*'

Lawless's next book, *The Point of View (Some Talks and Disputations)*, was privately printed in 1909. Consisting mainly of meditative poems in conventional late Victorian styles, it is remarkable in more or less equal measure for its intelligent exploration of the implications of Darwinism in 'Kinship (An Evolutionary Problem)' and for its mindless recycling of Celtic stereotypes in 'To Teague O'Toole of the Burren'. The title-piece of the posthumous *The Inalienable Heritage and Other Poems* (privately published in 1914) sustains a tribute to the monks of the early Irish church over twenty-seven vivid quatrains only to end on a pointed anti-Catholic flourish:

The tenets of your far-off home
From high-famed land to land you spread,
Nor to the might of mightiest Rome
Bent that shorn head . . .

Women poets of the Revival

The female contemporary of Lawless who displayed the most 'Protestant' work ethic of the period was the decisively Catholic Katharine (sometimes Katherine) Tynan (1861–1931). Tynan bent her unshorn head to produce 18 collections of lyrics, 105 novels, a quartet of autobiographies, 12 volumes of short stories and a mass of journalistic and other material in a career that spanned five commercially rewarding decades. The foremost epistolary confidante of Yeats in the early stages of his development, she corresponded also with Christina Rossetti, and her work bears superficial resemblances to the lyrics of both writers, though it lacks the depth of either. Tynan's professionalism is nevertheless evident in the competence of her versification, and in her steady, understated working of the autobiographical seam that runs from early poems of filial love through poems of domesticity, maternity and – from the perspective of the mother of two British soldiers – concern for the youthful casualties of World War One. While her domestic lyrics assert the centrality of the contribution made by women to civilisation ('I am the pillars of the house', as the opening line of 'Any Woman' puts it), they can hardly be said to convey a feminist awareness, falling short even of the reforming zeal of her early journalism about the exploitation of the female underclass of urban society. Tynan began her career very much as a Pre-Raphaelite with *Louise de la Vallière* (1885). By 1887 she had become a proponent of the Celtic Twilight – *Shamrocks*, published that year, is generally considered the first significant individual collection of the Literary Revival. She is remembered above all, however, as a poet of devotional Catholicism. 'Sheep and Lambs' (from *Ballads and Lyrics*, 1891), an exquisite, childlike pastoral linking Ireland's landscape to the story of the Crucifixion, is one of the most lastingly popular poems from the period under review. Tynan's religious attitudes can be brought to bear on ostensibly secular materials, as the transition from human to divine perspectives in 'Any Wife', a poem of marital relations, demonstrates. That she was not an entirely doctrinaire or predictable poet,[36] however, but one capable of communicating a charge of dread beyond the scope of any belief system, is demonstrated by the remarkable, if not entirely characteristic, 'The Cattle', an uncollected lyric from 1929:

'Who are these coming? A soundless multitude
Swerving away from the light? These are eyes, eyes, eyes,
The eyes of frightened cattle, red as blood
Pass into the night and its mysteries.

. . .

But these that have passed us by; they go, they go,
Driven with curses and goads, unpitied, unstayed
To the slaughter house and the blood and at last the blow –
The ghostly cattle passing have made me afraid.[37]

Introducing *A Treasury of Irish Poetry in the English Tongue* in 1900, Stopford A. Brooke distinguished between concern 'with poetry for its own sake' and 'with poetry in aggression against England'.[38] If his formulation of the second category was over-vigorous, his distinction usefully highlights the difference between women poets like Lawless and Tynan on the one hand, who, though they may have had more or less manifest ideological agendas, nevertheless placed a premium on technical continence; and some of the lesser women writers of the day, on the other, for whom poetry was a tool in the service of a political cause. The *Treasury* is also the source of John O'Leary's observation that Charles J. Kickham was 'a patriot first and a poet after'.[39] The division between aesthetic and political priorities had already by the end of the nineteenth century become a truism of commentary on the poetry of the 1840s, ranging Ferguson and Mangan against Davis and the poets of the original Young Ireland movement. Alert to this, the more *engagé* poets of the 1890s self-consciously modelled their practice on Davis's populist example. (Their nationalist vehemence has its ghostlife in the operations of 'postcolonialist' critics in our own day. Thus Luke Gibbons can discount Brooke's pluralism as anglophilia,[40] and Stephen Regan valorise texts illustrative of a narrative of colonial disengagement even to the extent of including Ethna Carbery's poems at the expense of those of Lawless and Tynan, and Patrick Pearse's at the expense of Austin Clarke's, in his elegant but partisan anthology of Irish writing from the late eighteenth century to the outbreak of World War II.)[41]

The two most prominent patriotic women poets of the turn of the century were Ethna Carbery (1872–1902)[42] and Alice Milligan (1866–1953), Ulsterwomen of respectively Catholic and Methodist backgrounds, who co-edited the Belfast magazine the *Northern Patriot* (October–December 1895) and its successor, the *Shan Van Vocht* (1896–99), and produced poems of a strongly nationalist, Gael-glorifying character. Carbery (Anna MacManus, née Johnston) also wrote love lyrics. Some of the latter rather insinuatingly incorporate phrases from the Irish language (the title and refrain of 'Beannacht Leat', for example, or the vocative 'a ghrádh' in 'A Glen Song'); others, like 'The Love-Talker', put folk materials to reasonably effective use. Carbery is best remembered for the rebel ballad 'Rody McCorley', and for the highly romanticised 'The Passing of the Gael', which Sean O'Casey could not resist burlesquing in Act 1 of *The Shadow of a Gunman*. In rhythm and phrasing Milligan's poems are no less predictable than Carbery's, though they employ a wider variety of forms. They typically adapt incidents from Irish history or mythology to the requirements of republican and Gaelic League ideology. A realistic, particularising twist elevates some of her work above the level of propaganda, however, and it is difficult not to be amused by her much anthologised ballad 'When I was a Little Girl', a narrative of self-discovery as a clandestine Fenian in an Orange household. Thomas MacDonagh's claim in 1914 that Milligan was the greatest living poet in Ireland[43] is nonetheless a depressing reminder of how far aesthetic discrimination was becoming contaminated by ideological enthusiasm in advanced nationalist circles in the years leading up to the Easter Rising.

Eva Gore-Booth (1870–1926), sister of one of the leaders of the Rising and subject, with her, of a great elegy by Yeats already adverted to in this chapter, began her publishing career in 1898 with lyrics combining two recurrent elements of the verse of the Revival, a nationalistically inflected local piety and a mystical sense of the natural world. 'The Little Waves of Breffny' (1903) exemplifies the charms and limitations of the mode. Gore-Booth's subsequent work is less whimsical, however, and manages at its best, despite its fondness for archaisms, to achieve a (class-derived?) terseness uncharacteristic of poetry by Irishwomen of the period. It includes meditative pieces that throw a Christian colouring over her mystical interests, reflections on public events such as the Rising and the execution and vilification of Roger Casement, speculations on the significance of scientific advance, and 'pagan' mythological poems in which Queen Maeve seems valued in equal measure for her Sligo associations and her status as a 'strong' woman. (One of the Maeve lyrics, 'The Vision of Niamh', conflates the Ulster and Fenian cycles to effect a mild lesbian *frisson*.) Gore-Booth spent most of her life as a political activist and social worker in Manchester, where she lived with her partner, the trade-unionist Esther Roper. Her modern, urban, English experience and ancient, rural, Irish imaginings were not without their points of conjunction: Gore-Booth's Maeve poems come closer to an explicitly feminist politics than anything in the Irish verse of the time other than the lyrics of the young James Stephens.

Other women poets associated with the Revival include Dora Sigerson Shorter (1866–1918) and Nora Hopper Chesson (1871–1906). Sigerson Shorter, daughter of the translator George Sigerson (see below, pp. 82–3), is remembered mainly for her swift retellings of folk-tales in rudimentary ballad quatrains, though her voluminous output encompassed a variety of lyric and elegiac modes as well. Hopper Chesson is something of an historical oddity, an Englishwoman who fell under the sway of the Revival and produced poems profoundly, if unintelligently derivative of Yeats's 'Celtic' style; it is only fair to point out that she soon outgrew her quicken boughs and watery isles, abandoning her faery themes and self-conscious hibernicisms almost a decade before her early death. In the specifically Irish lyrics of such emphatically secondary poets as Sigerson Shorter and Hopper Chesson one encounters more clearly than elsewhere the distinctiveness of the Revival, and recognises in it something more than a mere intensification[44] of trends set half a century earlier by Sir Samuel Ferguson. The ethereal, almost vapid verbal textures, the characteristic reliance on euphonious Gaelic proper nouns, and the repeated insistence that the empirical domain has less reality than a dimly apprehended inner realm (associated with a sense of Ireland in its mythological and topographical aspects as a spiritual condition) all point to the influence of Yeats's early poetry and of the poems and discursive writings of AE.

Susan Mitchell (1866–1926), AE's assistant successively on the *Irish Homestead* and the *Irish Statesman*, published in 1908 a book of mainly religious lyrics (*The Living Chalice*) that steer surprisingly clear of the ephemeral tonalities associated with her employer, as well as a volume of satires on the cultural scene of her day (*Aids to the Immortality of Certain Persons in Dublin: Charitably Administered*). The objects of Mitchell's lampoons include Ulster unionists, British imperialists, George Moore (in the pitilessly forensic 'George Moore – A Ballad History') and even Yeats, with whose family the author had close personal connections. While these attacks reveal a pleasing liveliness of mind and yield valuable insights into what the Revival looked like at ground level, their interest is almost exclusively historical: rough-and-ready versification and overly direct parody suggest that the author never intended them as aids to her own immortality. The unionism that so antagonised Mitchell had its own oblique poetic spokeswoman in Moira O'Neill (1865–1955), an Ulsterwoman of landed background whose immensely popular *Songs of the Glens of Antrim* appeared in 1901. O'Neill (Agnes Nestor Skrine, née Higginson) observed in her preface that her poems had been composed 'by a Glenswoman in the dialect of the Glens, and chiefly for the pleasure of other Glens-people', an assertion that is usually read in terms of regionalist and consequently – in the political conditions of the time – anti-nationalist politics. The volume, published by Blackwoods of Edinburgh, suggests that some of the more 'couthy' vices of Scottish Kailyard verse had made their way across the northern channel, though the continuity of O'Neill's writing with the vogue for hiberno-English comic song set by Samuel Lover in the 1820s is not to be over looked. The dialect-speaking protagonists of O'Neill's sentimental monologues are generally poor Catholics suffering the pangs of emigration ('Corrymeela'), grief ('Denny's Daughter') or mere wonder at the ways of the world ('Her Sister'). The poems are written in an idiom influenced as much by Irish as by Scots, and perhaps owing more to Boucicault and Carleton than to the speech of the author's poorer neighbours. O'Neill displays a degree of metrical skill, and her attitude towards her characters here and there goes beyond the patronising to the persuasively empathetic. If there is a degree of class condescension also in the dialect informing many of the poems of *Songs of Leinster* (1913) and *More Songs of Leinster* (1926), two collections by the prolific novelist, memoirist and writer of fiction Winifred M(abel) Letts (1882–1972), the sympathies of these pieces are broader, the political viewpoint more progressive, and the aesthetic self-demands more exacting than the Ulster *Songs* to which they may initially have been designed to reply.

AE, Synge, O'Sullivan, Stephens

Though the achievement of women poets in Ireland in the years from the fall of Parnell to the setting up of the Free State must ultimately be seen as modest in the extreme, the falling off in literary production by their sisters in the remainder of the period covered by this essay may be taken as an indication of the cultural shrinkage that accompanied the settling in of the new institutional structures on either side of the border. The abandonment of Ireland in 1933 by the writer and editor who had inspired and/or facilitated the work of many of the women poets we have been discussing was a more emphatic index – and indictment – of that shrinkage. Dublin had by the early thirties, in the view of the departing AE, succumbed to 'half-crazy Gaeldom'[45] and domination by 'bigoted Catholics and political louts'.[46] If the Revival is read as a project to secure a role for Protestants in the emerging nationalist dispensation, then AE's self-exile can be said to mark its ending in defeat. AE (George William Russell, 1867–1935) has almost as great a claim as Yeats to be seen as the Revival's guiding spirit. His lyrics, with their tremulous rhythms and shimmering, insubstantial landscapes, lent the poetry of the Irish *fin de siècle* its 'Celtic Twilight' signature, while his lifelong and assiduous fostering (the word is Padraic Colum's)[47] of the talents of others benefited writers as diverse as James Joyce, Seamus O'Sullivan and Patrick Kavanagh. A native of Lurgan in County Armagh, Russell had moved to Dublin with his parents at the age of eleven. Some years later he met Yeats at the Metropolitan School of Art: the otherworldly character of poetry in Ireland at the turn of the century reflects the theosophical interests of the two young men. Russell was literally as well as metaphorically a visionary, someone susceptible to 'visions' of what he took to be the spirit world. Many of his poems and paintings attempt to relay his experiences to those with less keen extrasensory receptors. He was also, however, a man of great practical energy whose services to the Irish Agricultural Organisation Society (Sir Horace Plunkett's Co-operative movement) went well beyond his editorship of the periodicals sponsored by the Society, the *Irish Homestead* (1905–23) and the *Irish Statesman* (1923–30). The sardonic portraiture of *Ulysses* notwithstanding, he appears to have had considerable personal charisma. Austin Clarke, one of the many writers to attest to his magnetism, described Russell's as 'the greatest imagination' to 'come out of modern Ireland'.[48] His poetry, however, gives little sense of the quality of that imagination, being strikingly lacking in attention to what Blake called 'minute particulars', and offering no counterpart to the earthiness that does so much to ballast the ethereal strain in Yeats's lyricism. The following quatrain from 'The Great Breath', a poem in AE's first, most popular and influential collection, *Homeward Thoughts by the Way* (1894), is representative. It describes that most 'Celtic' of natural phenomena, twilight:

> Its edges foamed with amethyst and rose,
> Withers once more the old blue flower of day:
> There where the ether like a diamond glows
>   Its petals fade away.

All thoughts are ultimately for AE the homeward thoughts of his volume's title: his mystical philosophy views human life merely as the record of the soul's journey back to the Deity in which it originated. The message of the poetry remained the same throughout the career, as the closing lines of his sonnet address to Terence MacSwiney in September 1920, the second month of the lord mayor of Cork's hunger strike in Brixton Prison, demonstrate:

> The candles of God already are burning row on row:
> Farewell, light-bringer; fly to thy fountain again.
> ('A Prisoner')

(The 'candles of God', in the poem's primary conceit, anticipate the torches that will accompany MacSwiney's funeral procession.) AE can be careless to the point of laziness. Denis Donoghue has condemned his 'appalling facility [that] makes anything change into anything at the drop of a syllable'.[49] When animated by a subject falling outside the bland verities of his philosophy, however, he displays a memorable phrase-making capacity. The angry tetrameter couplets of 'On Behalf of Some Irishmen Not Followers of Tradition', a rebuttal of the narrow nationalism that would force him into exile two decades later, build to a climactic paradox of proverbial force:

The golden heresy of truth.

And at one point in the career at least, in the penultimate stanza of 'Germinal', Russell's phrase-making powers are deployed with sufficient care to facilitate a moment of lyric gravitas unsurpassed by any of his contemporaries other than Yeats:

In ancient shadows and twilights
   Where childhood had strayed
The world's great sorrows were born
   And its heroes were made.
In the lost boyhood of Judas
   Christ was betrayed.

The Revival label can be misleading. Sometimes it is employed as a loose cognate of the phrase used in a number of chapter headings in the present history, the Irish Literary Renaissance. A distinction between the terms might turn on the difference between writers associated with Yeats and interested in rural Ireland and/or the Irish past, on the one hand, and authors primarily concerned with naturalistic portrayal of the present, on the other. Those in the first category belong to both the Revival and the Renaissance, those in the second only to the latter. Thus Joyce might be identified with the Renaissance but not the Revival, while AE might be said to belong to both. Even then some problems of definition remain. As a close associate of Yeats and composer of the Abbey Theatre's most celebrated and influential plays of Irish rural life, John Millington Synge (1871–1909) might seem unproblematically a contributor to the Revival. The aesthetic priorities of Synge's poems, however, are so radically at variance with the 'Celtic Twilight' ethos of AE and his followers that he seems bluntly antagonistic to the Revival, at least in the form it took in its first decade. The antagonism is made explicit in 'The Passing of the Shee', a lyric from 1907 assertively subtitled 'After looking at one of A. E.'s pictures':

Adieu, sweet Angus, Maeve and Fand,
Ye plumed yet skinny Shee,
That poets played with hand in hand
To learn their ecstasy.

We'll search in Red Dan Sally's ditch,
And drink in Tubber fair,
Or poach with Red Dan Philly's bitch
The badger and the hare.

Maeve and Fand have been encountered in these pages; Angus is probably the protagonist of Yeats's 'The Song of Wandering Aengus' (1899), one of the incontestable lyric achievements of the early Revival. Synge had already mentioned Fand in the first of his mature poems, 'Queens', which anticipates the present piece's preference for the contingent and existential over the literary and historical. The coarsely unromantic proper names of the second stanza here, drawn from the actual Gaelic present of the west of Ireland rather than the imagined Celtic past, combine with the commonest of common nouns (that 'ditch'/'bitch' rhyme is exemplary) and three aggressively active verbs to enforce the poet's characteristic insistence that the powers of earth merit more deference than the powers of air.

Of Synge's five dozen surviving lyrics, most very short and few running to more than four stresses per line, only the half or so composed or substantially revised in the last three or four years of his life are of continuing literary interest. These, for all their smallness of compass, are marked by a muscular, robust quality quite untypical of the Irish poetry of the time. 'It may almost be said that before verse can be human again it must learn to be brutal,' observed the author in the Preface to his posthumously published *Poems* (1909). The earthiness of Synge's lyrics is a matter not only of their frank physicality but also of their awareness that the poet will soon share the soil '[w]ith worms eternally' ('To the Oaks of Glencree'). Yeats claimed that Synge 'dying chose the living world for text'.[50] His poems may lack the extravagance of *The Playboy of the Western World* but they share something of its vitality; entirely eschewing the morbidity of *Deirdre of the Sorrows*, they bring the antinomies of Yeats's tribute into brief, memorable dialogue. The most 'brutal' of them, the violent ballads 'Danny' and 'The Mergency Man', postdate the composition of *The Playboy*, as does the bleak narrative 'Patch-Shaneen', an account of a more natural death than befalls the protagonists of the other two pieces:

He was five foot one or two,
Herself was four foot ten,
And he went travelling asking meal
Above through Caragh Glen.

. . .

Till on one windy Samhain night,
When there's stir among the dead,
He found her perished, stiff and stark,
Beside him in the bed.

. . .

And when the grey cocks crow and flap,
And winds are in the sky,
'Oh, Maurya, Maurya, are you dead?'
You'll hear Patch-Shaneen cry.

In their rebuke to the airy gentility of the Revival, these ballads anticipate the characteristic Modernist distaste for abstraction. Synge's more personal poems, too, exhibit greater consonance with trends in the wider literary world than the work of the great majority of his Irish contemporaries. The single sentence of 'In Kerry', the most compressed of his lyrics, encompasses an argument, a narrative and a clearly visualized location, all rendered in terms of a complex dramatic instant that seems not only post-Victorian but post-Georgian:

We heard the thrushes by the shore and sea,
And saw the golden stars' nativity,
Then round we went the lane by Thomas Flynn,
Across the church where bones lie out and in;
And there I asked beneath a lonely cloud
Of strange delight, with one bird singing loud,
What change you'd wrought in graveyard, rock and sea,
This new wild paradise to wake for me . . .
Yet knew no more than knew these merry sins
Had built this stack of thigh-bones, jaws and shins.

Remarkably, this was written more than a decade before Herbert Grierson's recovery of Donne and the Metaphysicals.

Something of the trajectory of Irish poetry from AE to Synge is incorporated in the artistic development of Seamus O'Sullivan (James Sullivan Starkey, 1879–1958). Though O'Sullivan never wrote with Synge's iconoclastic vigour or syntactical command, he progressively left behind the rural plangencies of the poems he contributed to AE's anthology *New Songs* (1902) in favour of a sharply observed urban lyricism alert to the squalor as well as the atmospheric charm of Dublin. Even such an early piece as 'The Twilight People' is – despite its title – distinguished from the generality of early Revival verse by its historicization of landscape and its presentation of dejection as a response to privation and oppression rather than as a mere poetic attitude:

It is a whisper among the hazel bushes;
It is a long low whispering voice that fills
With a sad music the bending and swaying rushes;
It is a heart-beat deep in the quiet hills.

Twilight people, why will you still be crying,
Crying and calling to me out of the trees?
For under the quiet grass the wise are lying,
And all the strong ones are gone over the seas.

O'Sullivan's urban lyrics may be of little formal or rhythmical interest, but they provide memorable vignettes of working-class and lower-middle-class life in Dublin in the early twentieth century. (Their simplicity gave some of them – 'The Piper', the delicately worked 'The Lamplighter' – a home in Irish primary school textbooks for many decades.) At their best they transcend description to articulate a sort of low-pitched *ennui*. 'Nelson Street', for example, begins with a finely realized evocation of a stale kitchen before turning its focus to the street outside:

I see that it's Monday again,
For the man with the organ is there;
Every Monday he comes to the street
(Lest I, or the bird there, should miss
Our count of monotonous days)
With his reed-organ, wheezy and sweet,
And stands by the window and plays
'There's a Land that is Fairer than This.'

O'Sullivan's poetry took on a strongly nationalist character in the revolutionary period. (His overtly political verse tends towards the sentimental.) After the settlement of 1922 he increasingly devoted himself to editorial work rather than composition. His *Dublin Magazine* (monthly 1923–25, quarterly 1926–58) became the leading Irish literary periodical of its time – and arguably of the entire twentieth century. It provided a forum for an impressively comprehensive roll-call of Irish poets, dramatists and writers of fiction, and also for R. S. Thomas, Alun Lewis and other figures from the so-called 'first flowering' of Welsh writing in English. ('Milk-Wort and Bog-Cotton', perhaps the last of

Hugh MacDiarmid's great Scots lyrics, was also first published there in 1932: the poem bears a dedication to O'Sullivan.)

James Stephens (1882–1950)[51] had a stronger, more idiosyncratic gift than O'Sullivan. No less explicitly impatient with the prettifications of Revivalism than Synge's lyrics, the contents of his first collection, *Insurrections* (1909), cultivate a grim and even sour realism in their depictions of the ugliness and deprivation of the poorer quarters of Dublin. 'The Red-haired Man's Wife' (*not* a version of the famous Gaelic song 'Bean an Fhir Rua') shows a radical political imagination in full possession of its outlook and idiom. (The fact that the period's prime poetic instance of feminist indignation is the cross-gendered utterance of a male writer may tell its own story of the inequality of literary opportunity in the early years of the century.) Elsewhere in *Insurrections*, Stephens's material chafes against the restraint of arbitrarily chosen stanza forms, and archaisms and other poeticisms subvert the colloquial grittiness for which pieces such as the disconsolate 'The Street Behind Yours' – one of the very few Irish contributions to the English language's poetry of urban nightmare – are remarkable. In retrospect, it is difficult not to be dismayed by the alacrity with which, perhaps under the joint influence of AE's spiritual optimism and of the tidy metricality of the Georgian movement, Stephens rejected the gloom and spikiness of his early mode.[52] Grotesquery gives way to whimsy, and social and theological scepticism to an ultimately vacuous sonic virtuosity in the finely crafted but anodyne lyrics of *The Hill of Vision* (1912), *Songs from the Clay* (1915) and subsequent volumes. Proletarian Dublin has not been quite left behind in the later poems, but portraits of its inhabitants (e.g. 'Danny Murphy') are now vitiated by sentimentality, or at least by a too-salving geniality. Stephens's mature 'original' verse bears little trace either of the profligate invention of his masterpiece of prose fiction, *The Crock of Gold* (1912), or of the austere moral intelligence of his first-hand account of the events of Easter Week, *The Insurrection in Dublin* (1916). His central achievement in poetry is to be found rather in the adaptations of seventeenth-, eighteenth- and nineteenth-century Gaelic materials that make up the shrewdly titled *Reincarnations* (1918), a volume that may be said to anticipate something of the success of Robert Lowell's *Imitations* in eliciting a critique of contemporary mores from the texts of long-dead writers from outside the anglophone tradition. Stephens's versions and conflations of – and variations upon – some of the more enraged among the poems of Dáibhí Ó Bruadair and Aogán Ó Rathaille do not attempt to recreate either the strict sense or the metrical character of the originals (though Stephens knew Irish); instead they exploit the instincts for the deformed and cacophonous that had been glimpsed in *Insurrections* to reformulate aristocratic Gaelic fury against the supplanting English caste as humanitarian ire towards mercantile philistinism.[53] To say this is not to suggest that they de-historicize the Gaelic texts – composed in the aftermath of the Rising, *Reincarnations* is a product of the most nationalist phase of Stephens's development – but to salute their success in operating simultaneously on two planes of temporal reference. 'The Glass of Beer' ('Righteous Anger' until its appearance in *Collected Poems*) is probably the best-known, and certainly the most grotesque of them, but three or four others achieve an even fiercer dramatic eloquence:

> If you say, if you think, I complain, and have not got a cause,
> Let you come to me here, let you look at the state of my hand!
> Let you say if a goose-quill has calloused these horny old paws,
> Or the spade that I grip on, and dig with, out there on the land?
> ('O Bruadair')

Translators

Stephens's brilliant recastings are not, of course, the only notable points of cross-over between Gaelic and anglophone poetry in a period that was marked alike by enthusiasm for the revival of the Irish language and by an extension of the characteristic nineteenth-century project of translation. As co-founder of the Gaelic League and editor / translator of the hugely influential *Love Songs of Connacht* (1893), Douglas Hyde (1860–1949) exemplified both tendencies at their most vigorous. In envisaging a cultural separatism without political corollary, the programme of re-Gaelicization set out in his celebrated lecture 'The Necessity for De-Anglicizing Ireland' (1892) stayed resolutely innocent of the complications inherent in the ongoing shift of power from the old ascendancy Protestant class to the more indigenous majority community. Hyde's desire to elide the rancours of the time from his linguistic campaigns led him to resign the presidency of the Gaelic League when that body adopted an explicitly republican constitution in 1915. The paucity of reference in the editorial commentaries of *Love Songs of Connacht* to the material conditions of peasant life in the West has been seen as further evidence of his distaste for the political, though in fact he held strongly nationalist views and would in due course serve as the first president of Ireland for seven years from 1938. The impact of Hyde's book, in any case, was based as much upon such factors as the immediacy of the translations and the emotional (and sexual) frankness of the songs themselves as upon a sense of its retrieval of a lost piece of the national cultural jigsaw. The lineated English versions in the volume's dual-language presentation are strikingly successful in replicating the internal, assonantal rhyme patterns of the originals, an effect the best of them achieve without contorting their stately colloquialism of address. The additional prose renditions accompanying many of the texts, which more convincingly suggest the intimacy and directness of the Gaelic, were the particular focus of Yeats's enthusiasm for the book.[54] The graceful, recognisably but un-insistently Hiberno-English style of the verse and the more emphatically Irish manner of the prose constituted two of the major 'finds' of an era much concerned with the need for a national idiom, and it is probable that admiration for Hyde's achievement as a translator contributed significantly to the turn towards conversational modes in the anglophone poetry of Ireland after 1905 or so. It almost certainly contributed also to the development of Lady Augusta Gregory's much derided but supple and powerful 'Kiltartanese', the strongly West-of-Ireland inflected medium of her plays and retellings of ancient myths and legends. Gregory's literary dialect, based on the speech of rural south Galway, may in turn have influenced Synge's dramatic language, as many commentators have suggested. It undoubtedly left its impact upon his prose versions of Villon, Leopardi and Petrarch, which seem overly stylised when read beside the mainly prose translations of Gaelic verse she collected in her *Kiltartan Poetry Book* of 1919. Gregory (1852–1932) also wrote poetry of her own, most notably the twelve sonnets which she sent to her former lover, Wilfrid Scawen Blunt, in 1883 and which appeared in adapted form as 'A Woman's Sonnets' in his *Love Lyrics and Songs of Proteus* nine years later. Though of considerable biographical interest, Gregory's original verse is undistinguished and even clumsy, never approaching the stark dignity of her translations of Gaelic folk-song:

> It is late last night the dog was speaking of you;
> the snipe was speaking of you in her deep marsh.
> It is you are the lonely bird through the woods;
> and that you may be without a mate until you find me.
>
> You promised me, and you said a lie to me
> that you would be before me where the sheep are flocked;
> I gave a whistle and three hundred cries to you,
> and I found nothing there but a bleating lamb.
>
> ('Donal Oge')

There was a crucial relationship between Douglas Hyde's cultural and linguistic agitation, on the one hand, and his literary activities on the other, in that his translations, unlike those of his predecessors earlier in the nineteenth century, were offered less as a compensation for not knowing the Irish language than as an incentive to learn it. The same cannot be said of T(homas) W(illiam) Rolleston's tamely romantic versions of Gaelic poems, which appeared in such publications as *A Treasury of Irish Poetry*, the anthology he edited with his father-in-law Stopford A. Brooke, before being collected in *Sea Spray: Verses and Translations* in 1909. Though Rolleston (1857–1920) corresponded with Walt Whitman, whose poetry he translated into German, there is little trace of aesthetic radicalism either in his lyrics or his translations from the Irish, which are more or less equally conventional in rhythm and diction. 'The Dead at Clonmacnois', deservedly his best-known piece, is something of an exception. Described by Yeats in 1895 as 'purely emotional' (a category of approval for a poet busy with the love-lorn lyricism of *The Wind among the Reeds*) and as 'an example of the Gaelic lyric form come close to perfection',[55] the poem essays what might be thought of as typically 'Celtic' melancholy in subtly assonantal quatrains:

In a quiet-water'd land, a land of roses,
 Stands St Kieran's city fair,
And the warriors of Erinn in their famous generations
 Slumber there.

There beneath the dewy hillside sleep the noblest
 Of the Clan of Conn,
Each below his stone; his name in branching Ogham
 And the sacred knot thereon.

There they laid to rest the Seven Kings of Tara,
 There the sons of Cairbrè sleep –
Battle-banners of the Gael, that in Kieran's plain of crosses
 Now their final hosting keep.

And in Clonmacnois they laid the men of Teffia
 And right many a lord of Breagh;
Deep the sod above Clan Creidè and Clan Connall,
 Kind in hall and fierce in fray.

Many and many a son of Conn the Hundred-Fighter
 In the red earth lies at rest;
Many a blue eye of Clan Colman the turf covers,
 Many a swan-white breast.

Often assumed (though not by Yeats) to be more or less an original work, 'The Dead at Clonmacnois' is in fact a remarkably faithful rendering of the first five quatrains of 'Cathir Chíaráin Cluain mic Nóis', a fourteenth-century poem which has been wrongly attributed to the sixteenth-century scholar Énóg Ó Giolláin.[56] Gregory A. Schirmer sees Rolleston's lines as characteristic of the Revival in their celebration of 'Ireland's pagan past at the expense of its Christian one', identifying in that preference 'a strategy of obvious political advantage to a movement directed for the most part by a class alienated from contemporary Irish Catholicism'.[57] This may be to discern historical obfuscation and political bad faith – axiomatic qualities of southern Protestant writing in the view of some of the wilder proponents of postcolonial theory – where they do not in fact exist. It is at the very least arguable that 'The Dead at Clonmacnois' privileges neither pagan over Christian nor Christian over pagan but rather, like its medieval *ur*-text, celebrates the antiquity of an Irish past in which Christian and pre-Christian elements are mixed. The phrase 'famous generations', that is to say, may encompass not just the dead of distant, legendary times but the more recently deceased as well. Conn of the Hundred Battles was a mythical figure from the pre-Christian era, but, as Rolleston and other enthusiasts of Celtic lore would have known, he was believed to be the ancestor of the historical inhabitants of Connacht, the province to which he gave his name. The 'Clan of Conn' would therefore for the anonymous fourteenth-century poet and his late nineteenth-century translator have included the living as well as the dead, just as the 'noblest' of that clan interred at Clonmacnois would have included Christians as well as pagans. At only one point in the Rolleston version, at the end of the third stanza, is there as much as an implication of ironic contrast (and one can put it no more strongly than that) between the values of Christian and pagan Ireland that is not licensed by the Gaelic poem. The immediate source of 'The Dead at Clonmacnois' was probably not 'Cathir Chíaráin Cluain mic Nóis' itself but the verse translation provided by the poem's first editor, William Hennessy, in 1892. Study of Hennessy's five opening stanzas reveals not only the artistry but the startling fidelity of the Rolleston version.[58] Even the Victorian sounding 'land of roses', it transpires, is a rendering of the editor's literal 'rose-red' (*deargróis*) rather than an invention.

The title of George Sigerson's *Bards of the Gael and Gall* (1897; 2nd edition 1907) offers a less dubious index than 'The Dead at Clonmacnois' of Protestant unease with the increasingly strident nationalist conflation of Irishness, Gaeldom and Catholicism. An anthology of translations designed to display the aesthetic breadth and variety of the Gaelic poetic tradition, on the one hand, and the historical hospitality of that tradition to diverse cultural, political and racial influences, on the other, *Bards of the Gael and Gall* was a key text in the Revival's recovery of the Gaelic past, and one that, by demonstrating the classical hardness and directness of the poetry of the island's older language, presented a powerful corrective to the misty excesses of Celticism. Sigerson

(1836–1925), a physician, neurologist and academic zoologist by profession, had begun his literary career as far back as 1860 with *The Poets and Poetry of Munster*, the second publication in the series inaugurated by James Clarence Mangan's famous volume of translations eleven years earlier (see Matthew Campbell's discussion in chapter 12 of volume I). Though his mature writing lacks the fluidity and colloquial ease of Hyde's, it succeeds at least in communicating something of the formal sophistication of the texts it sets out to serve. The respect in which Sigerson was held by other mediators between the linguistic inheritances of the country is suggested by his status as dedicatee both of *Love Songs of Connacht* and Thomas MacDonagh's *Literature in Ireland*.

Colum, Campbell, Joyce, Gogarty

Bards of the Gael and Gall may have highlighted the inadequacies, in point of historical and literary fact, of the native / stranger dichotomy characteristic of the more extreme forms of separatist discourse, but the divisions between Catholic and Protestant Ireland that lurk in the subtext of Sigerson's title were real enough. Something of their extent becomes evident when one considers that, of the writers discussed in this chapter so far, all but two – Tynan and Carbery – came from the Protestant side of the Reformation divide (which is not to say they were all members of the ascendancy). There is in the work of some of the Catholic poets who achieved prominence in the early years of the new century a suggestion of the speech of the subaltern, or at the very least of a sort of writing back against literary stereotype by inhabitants of landscapes pastoralized out of recognition in the poetry of the Celtic Twilight. The relationship between landscape and inhabitant, indeed, is a central concern of the early verse of Padraic Colum (1881–1972), which insists on the difficulty of eking a living from the soil and the even greater difficulty of surviving in the Irish countryside without the connection to the earth conferred by rights of proprietorship or tenancy. The eponymous plougher of the exclamatory opening poem of *Wild Earth* (1907; 1916)[59] simultaneously masters and serves the 'earth savage, earth broken' that surrounds him. The typical Colum protagonist is a less fortunate figure, kept from fulfilment by economic privation or destined to wander across the landscape dreaming of security. The Romantic formal lineage of Colum's verse to some extent disguises its anti-romantic, materialist understanding of the necessities of rural existence, and poem after poem implicitly rebukes the tendency towards diaphanous idyll in the early Revival's depiction of the countryside. Colum's imagination, like the cattle of his consummate narrative lyric 'A Drover', grazes 'scant croppings': his poetry is haunted by a sense of dispossession which it would be foolish not to link to the catastrophic experience of the Irish rural poor in the nineteenth century. Colum's father was master of the Longford workhouse, and the poet was brought up first in Longford and subsequently in his grandmother's house in County Cavan, from where he visited many farms in the region in the company of his uncle, a poultry merchant and repository of local lore. He was consequently from an early age intimate with both the hardship and the folklife of rural Ireland, and it is perhaps no surprise that some of his most memorable poems have a strong undertow of grief – 'An Old Woman of the Roads', 'A Man Bereaved', 'No Child', 'The Poor Girl's Meditation', 'She Moved Through the Fair' (easily the greatest instance of the vogue for folk-song reconstruction inaugurated at the beginning of the Revival by Yeats's 'Down by the Salley Gardens'). Nor is it a surprise that *Wild Earth* seeks to give voice to a communal rather than an individual awareness: Colum almost never speaks *in propria persona*. Even those poems that to a greater or lesser extent offer a self-reflexive commentary on the predicament of the poet – 'The Tin-Whistle Player', 'A Poor Scholar of the 'Forties', 'A Saint', 'The Toy-Maker', 'A Ballad Maker', 'The Poet' – take as their primary business the extension of the overall project of communal portraiture.

That extension was temporal as well as spatial. It may be worth lingering over 'A Poor Scholar of the 'Forties', one of the best-known of the pieces with a historical setting, to illustrate something of the strengths and limitations of Colum's writing. Vividly located in the decade of the original Young Ireland movement, this monologue constructs a paradigm of the conflict between nationalist commitment and the cultivation of aesthetic and intellectual excellence, a conflict of particular intensity in the lives of young Catholic writers like Francis Ledwidge, Thomas MacDonagh and Colum himself, who combined radical separatist aspirations with poetic ambition. The poem builds impressively over four stanzas to its epiphanic climax, where the scholar's exertions – and by implication the poet's – are promised as their solitary yet ample reward the persistence, 'Years hence, in rustic speech', of

a phrase,
As in wild earth a Grecian vase!

It is perhaps paradoxical that the last line's gleaming simile has become the shard that assures Colum's posterity, the phrase from his work that readers of Irish poetry remember and quote. The poem as a whole falls rather short of the status of a well-wrought urn, however, mainly because of the confusions of the opening stanza, where lines 3–7 cry out for blue-pencilling:

> I know the Æneid now by heart,
> My Virgil read in cold and heat,
> In loneliness and hunger smart.
>   And I know Homer, too, I ween,
>   As Munster poets know Ossian.

The *Æneid and* Virgil? And what of the Munster poets' devotion to Ossian? Certainly, Ossianic tales and ballads survived in the oral literature of the southern province well beyond the 1840s setting of the Poor Scholar's utterance, and Munster place-names feature prominently in them and in the written compilations of the Fionn cycle. Gaelic tradition generally was at its strongest in Munster, and it was there that the last of the language's art-poets wrote their incensed protests against the changing social order before the long silence of the nineteenth century. Those poets could have been expected to possess a sound knowledge of the Fionn cycle, in its written and oral forms, as well as of the rest of the corpus of Gaelic literature. They were already long dead by the 1840s, however, so Colum's use of the present tense 'know' is slightly puzzling. Though Oisín is the main advocate for the lost glories of pagan Ireland in the debates with Patrick that make up so much of the Fionn cycle, the metonymic use of his name in this context is unfortunate, not least because the spelling suggests *Ossian*, the popular title for James Macpherson's controversial eighteenth-century 'translation' of a putative Scots Gaelic epic, than which no text could be less likely to commend itself to the poets of Munster. To make matters worse, the archaic 'I ween' is a mere *cheville*, employed as a rhyming partner for the already problematic 'Ossian'.

Colum in due course followed the example of his Poor Scholar and chose the life of the mind over the life of political action: he left Ireland to live as a professional writer in the United States in 1914, the year of his participation in the Howth gun-running. His departure, however, was not the prelude to a further flowering of his poetic gift. He wrote much in the six remaining decades of his long life, but the later verse fails to add significantly to his achievement as a young man. There are some fine pieces along the way – 'Swift's Pastoral', a brilliant dialogue from *Dramatic Legends and Other Poems* (1922), for instance, or 'Pigeons', formally the most adventurous of the sharply observed animal poems of *Creatures* (1927). He revisited his early, Irish subject matter in 'Old Pastures' (1930) and in the additional materials gathered in

The Poet's Circuits: Collected Poems of Ireland (1960), though with an increasing tendency towards idealisation of the rural scene. Colum nevertheless cannot be accused of being content to recycle the themes that had first brought him notice. He deliberately set himself to respond in verse to the experiences that arose out of his governmental commission to investigate the mythology of Hawaii, to his interest in Welsh and Arabic literature, and to his travels, but he never succeeded in developing a sufficiently distinctive idiom to be remembered, where poetry is concerned, as anything other than the Irish Literary Renaissance's pre-eminent poet of rural hardship. The quality of his best work and the competition offered by the poems of his contemporary and friend Joseph Campbell make that a more enviable sobriquet than it might sound.

Campbell (1879–1944) shared Colum's concern with the wretched of the Irish earth, and rivalled him in his knowledge of folklore. He was a native of Belfast, and an occasional recourse to Ulster Scots and a generalised awareness of Scotland give his work a recognisably northern inflection. Early in his career he wrote the words of 'My Lagan Love' to a tune collected by Herbert Hughes, and the song, assuming the condition of folk anonymity as completely as 'She Moved Through the Fair', has become the anthem of his native city. More overtly political than Colum's, Campbell's poetry is characterised by an ardent and sometimes naive idealism. His sympathies were strongly nationalist and democratic (not necessarily complementary categories in the Ireland of his time) and one of his volumes, *The Gilly of Christ* (1907), is notable for its appropriation of Christ as an avatar of Irish sovereignty. (This sort of thing was in the air in the European poetry of the early twentieth century – a decade later Alexander Blok's 'The Twelve' would place the second person of the Trinity at the head of a Bolshevik gang. While Campbell's transgressive theology has more in common with the overheated pietism of Patrick Pearse than with the anarchistic irony of the great Russian poet, the limpidity and impersonality of his ballad style give it a degree of imaginative authority.) Campbell's poems are various and sometimes even experimental in their forms, though stubbornly old-fashioned in their idioms. *Irishry* (1913) takes its cue from that most English of poems, *Piers Plowman*, to present a field full of folk who are, the introductory tetrameters tell us, 'symbols of the god in man'. The book elevates gleaners, tinkers, pipers, horse-breakers and whelk-gatherers – figures representing the antiquity and resilience of Ireland – over mere creatures of materialism like civil servants, Orangemen ('clay marred in the mixing') and professors ('gownèd fools'). Simplistic though this schema may be, it accommodates poems of the quality of 'The Labourer', a social-realist ballad on drunkenness, and 'The Newspaper-Seller', an empathetic dramatic monologue of the Irish diaspora.

One of Campbell's own diasporic interludes – he lived in London for much of the first decade of the century and in the United States for fourteen years from 1925 – brought him into contact with many of the leading practitioners of Imagism. While such vignettes as 'Darkness' (from *The Mountainy Singer*, 1909) have more in common with the proto-imagism of Walt Whitman's briefer poems than with the work of Ezra Pound or T. E. Hulme, some slightly longer pieces, notably the poised, laconic 'Days' (from *The Earth of Cualann*, 1917), exemplify the movement at close to its fragile best. The enthusiasm of Pound and his friends for *vers libre* appears to have had at least as great an impact on Campbell as their insistence on the primacy of the unmediated image, and *The Earth of Cualann* employs free verse as the vehicle for a poetry of strongly Celticized patriotism. 'Raven's Rock', composed in the interval between the Dublin shootings of the leaders of the Rising and the London hanging of Roger Casement, represents Campbell's nationalism at a peak of visionary intensity. Much of the poetry he produced over the ensuing quarter of a century charts his painful retreat from the rapt optimism of the 1917 volume. Incarcerated during the Civil War and for two years thereafter for his republican sympathies, he wrote powerfully unromantic blank verse annotations of his prison experiences. (These, along with other later works, were first collected in Austin Clarke's selection, *Poems of Joseph Campbell*, in 1963.) His years in America were largely given over to attempts to set up institutes of Irish Studies and – more successfully – to teaching Irish literature at Fordham University. On his return to Ireland and his small farm in Glencree, County Wicklow, in 1939, he devoted himself once again to writing and, in circumstances of almost total obscurity, composed the despondent, chastened poetry that must form the basis of the most serious claim that can be made for his literary stature. While he himself appears to have set greatest store by 'A Vision of Glendalough', his long historical poem in unrhymed octosyllabics, a Victorian *modus operandi* and a prelapsarian view of the national past render it of somewhat limited interest (despite its memorably disdainful portrait of William Wordsworth in Ireland). The shorter among the late poems are another matter, however. Their rueful casting of the poet as a Lear figure, a 'lamb in briar' and a 'sad, bald . . . much-wandering old man' is managed humorously and without self-pity. Some of these lyrics are bolder in conception ('July Moon') or subtler in detail ('Country Sorrow') than anything in the earlier work, while one of them, the gentle, resigned 'Ad Limina', the last poem Campbell wrote, is a minor masterpiece:

The ewes and lambs, loving the far hillplaces,
Cropping by choice the succulent crops of heather,
Drinking the pure water of cloudborn lochlands,
Resting under erratics fostered with Abel –
Come to my haggard gate, my very doorstep.

That is the first stanza. The remaining four handle the 'Come to my haggard gate, my very doorstep' refrain with a skill comparable to that of Yeats or MacNeice.

Innovative, ruthlessly intelligent, breathtakingly ambitious and resourceful, the work of James Joyce (1882–1941) is characterised by a cultural and stylistic self-awareness so extreme that it can be said to represent a higher order of response than the lyricism of Campbell and Colum to post-Parnellite Irish Catholic experience. (The rural poets feature respectively as 'Mountainy Mutton' and 'Patrick What-do-you Colm' in 'Gas from a Burner'). Though his major achievement is in fiction, Joyce wrote verse at almost all stages of his career. Much of it is occasional in nature. Of the considerable body of fugitive pieces, perhaps only the playful lines[60] intended as a blurb for the two-shilling edition (1930) of the *Anna Livia Plurabelle* section of *Finnegans Wake* hint at anything of the genius of the prose. The canonical poetry is made up of the thirty-six lyrics of *Chamber Music* (1907), the thirteen lyrics of *Pomes Penyeach* (1927), and the supplementary lyric (the touchingly autobiographical 'Ecce Puer', 1932) and pair of satires that join the contents of those books in the second edition of *Collected Poems* (1957).[61]

The two satires, committed to tetrameter couplets reminiscent of those favoured by that other great Dublin ironist Jonathan Swift, have a more integral place in the overall oeuvre than the lyrics, even the best half dozen or so of which are very slight. Both satires offer mordant commentaries on the Revival, to which Joyce extended the *non serviam* with which his alter-ego Stephen Dedalus defies faith, family and fatherland in *A Portrait of the Artist as a Young Man*. 'The Holy Office' (1904), the more disciplined, if much the more arch of the two, castigates the airiness of the Revival aesthetic by way of a series of sly portraits of unnamed but easily identifiable writers (including Yeats, AE, Synge, O'Sullivan and Joyce's future friend Colum) and presents the author as an artist who is by contrast sufficiently courageous and honest to acknowledge the bodily foundations of human life and submit to the dictates of rationality. 'Gas from a Burner', written as Joyce travelled by rail across Europe on his way back to Trieste after his final and deeply frustrating visit to Dublin in 1912, is an angrier but also a far funnier poem that easily transcends its occasion (rage at the destruction of the first edition of *Dubliners* by a timorous printer). The Revivalists are ribbed by name this time round, in the course of a grotesquely hypocritical monologue supposedly spoken by George Roberts, manager of Maunsel and Co., the firm that had refused to publish *Dubliners* without textual changes unacceptable to the author. (Maunsel was the Revival's publisher *par excellence*, issuing collections by Tynan, Milligan, Gore-Booth, Sigerson Shorter, Mitchell, O'Sullivan, Stephens, Gregory, Rolleston, Colum, Campbell, Patrick Pearse, Joseph Mary Plunkett and Austin Clarke.) Even the most embittered passages of the poem achieve a sort of rapture of rhetorical excess:

> But I owe a duty to Ireland:
> I hold her honour in my hand,
> This lovely land that always sent
> Her writers and artists to banishment
> And in a spirit of Irish fun
> Betrayed her leaders, one by one.
> 'Twas Irish humour, wet and dry,
> Flung quicklime into Parnell's eye;
> 'Tis Irish brains that save from doom
> The leaky barge of the Bishop of Rome . . .

The recourse of Patrick Kavanagh and Thomas Kinsella to tetrameter couplets for satirical purposes later in the century would yield considerably less vigorous results.

Joyce's shorter canonical poems are rather more problematic. All of them appear to have been composed out of an obstinately narrow and conservative conception of the nature of lyric. The fact that the author left the sequencing of the contents of *Chamber Music* to his brother Stanislaus suggests that he (properly, in the view of the present writer)[62] saw his first book as a piece of journeywork, a stepping stone on the way to *Dubliners* and the mature writing. An exercise in pastiche Elizabethanism, *Chamber Music* is notable for its metrical command and for the consistency with which its self-consciously artificial manner is maintained. Some of the lyrics seem to subvert their delicacy of construction with an indelicacy of implication, though scarcely to the extent claimed by William York Tindall in his introduction to the edition of 1954. Poem xxxi excepted, the language of *Chamber Music* is conspicuously deficient in the geographical and historical specificity which is so marked a feature of Joyce's prose at all stages of its development. The shadowy narratives of love and betrayal that have been discerned behind the book's structure[63] are too dependent on its slenderest lyrics to carry much conviction. Only at the very end of the volume, in the last two poems, does the affectation of lute song give way to more urgent and contemporary tonalities. The last poem ('I hear an army charging upon the land') combines characteristic features of Imagism and of Yeats's Celtic mode memorably to stylise a lover's recognition that he has been forsaken. It is tempting to read the anguished awakening from dream enacted by 'I hear an army' as a repudiation of the enchantment constituted by the rest of the book.

Each of the lyrics in *Pomes Penyeach* is printed with a place-name and date, though these are far from reliable guides to composition, having been subjected to adjustment as Joyce prepared the volume for publication. Most of the poems were written between 1912 and 1916, when the author was in his early thirties, and assembled in their present form more than a decade later in an effort to demonstrate that he had not lost his humanity to the intricacies and extravagances of *Finnegans Wake*. The poems explore moments of heightened feeling – another indication of Joyce's dismayingly conventional attitude to lyric – in a variety of styles and with differing degrees of success. 'Alone' and 'A Prayer' are vitiated by the melodramatic language the author characteristically reserved for the subject of erotic encounter (it does less damage to his prose). The first stanza of 'On the Beach at Fontana' is almost adolescent in its alliterative zeal, while many of the other pieces display a predilection for compound adjectives that would in the case of a lesser writer be taken as the mark of an amateur. The irony that keeps the sentimental tendencies of the fiction in check is generally absent, fatally so where 'A Flower Given to My Daughter' is concerned. And yet there are poems of real quality in the volume. 'Tilly', written as early as 1903, offers a classically cool expression of the young Joyce's martyr complex. 'She weeps over Rahoon' revisits the closing scene of 'The Dead', replicating the famous 'falling' cadence of the final paragraph and envisaging the grave of the young lover from the perspective of Gretta Conway/Nora Barnacle rather than Gabriel/Joyce, and in conditions of rain rather than snow. 'Watching the Needleboats at San Sabba', with its simple but effective rhythmic inversion and its title's connection of Trieste to Galway (where sculling shells are known as needleboats)[64] is a heart-rendingly beautiful lyric of exile and ageing.

Of the two aspirant poets who moved into the Martello tower in Sandycove in the autumn of 1904, the older, Oliver St John Gogarty (1878–1957), was to produce far more verse over the following decades than the younger, James Joyce. Yet there is rather less to be said about Gogarty's poems, despite the fact that they won the admiration of Yeats and Hugh MacDiarmid (writers almost as well known for their eccentricity of judgement as for their mastery of lyric form). Seamus Deane has acknowledged the 'technical elegance'[65] of Gogarty's work, and the famous surgeon and wit was undoubtedly capable of deploying a variety of stanzas and metres with brisk competence. In his hands, however, form becomes a mode of *in*sensitivity, rather as (to some extent) it does later in the century in the hands of James Simmons. Attitude and outcome seem predetermined, and the poems rarely if ever appeal to what T. S. Eliot termed the auditory imagination by departing from the predictable in phrasing or 'melody', as the best of the lyrics of Colum and Joyce and even Tynan characteristically do. 'Leda and the Swan' (one of the new pieces in *Selected Poems*, 1933) is untypical in manifesting an organic relationship between subject matter and treatment, but the joke effected by its 'Goosey-goosey-gander' rhythm wears thin after a few stanzas. The machismo that lurks behind the display of mock concern for the ravished girl accords with the overbearing masculinism of some of the shorter lyrics, where classical references and Latin tags bespeak the clubbable confidence of the professional man rather than any quest for illumination through exploration of ancient and modern parallels and divergences. Of the limericks by Gogarty that circulated as a kind of samizdat in Dublin from the turn of the century, those that have survived[66] are frequently ingenious, if always coarse. To turn from them to a soft-centred lyric like 'Golden Stockings', a poem addressed to the author's young daughter, is to recognise the validity of Wilde's adage that sentimentality is philistinism on its bank holiday.

1916 and the Great War

Gogarty, like Yeats, became a senator of the Irish Free State and thus, arguably at least, a beneficiary of the train of events inaugurated by the occupation of the General Post Office and other buildings in Dublin by republican insurgents on Easter Monday, 1916. Of the four of the seven signatories of the Proclamation of the Republic who had published verses, only one, James Connolly, had restricted himself to overtly political and hortatory subject matter. There is a danger, where Thomas MacDonagh (1878–1916), Patrick Pearse (1879–1916) and Joseph Mary Plunkett (1887–1916) are concerned, of reading their work back from the consummation they so assiduously pursued and missing the depth of commitment shown by each to his literary vocation. None of the three was a mere poetaster. MacDonagh, who between 1902 and 1913 published four books of verse, in addition to a play and a work of criticism (*Thomas Campion and the Art of English Poetry*), had the most conventionally literary career of the three, and became an early example of the poet-academic on being appointed lecturer in English at University College Dublin in 1911. His posthumously published *Literature in Ireland* (a series of reflections rather than an integrated study) is remarkable for the frankness of its acceptance that English had by the early twentieth century become the *de facto* language of Irish life and writing, and for the eagerness with which it promotes the compensatory argument that a distinctive 'Irish Mode' in anglophone poetry would reflect the influence of the country's older language through a plainness and directness of address. (The brow-beating populism of the book's conception of the writer's responsibility to 'the Irish people' is also to be noted, demonstrating as it does that the nationalist project was already infected with the anti-intellectual germ that would cause such devastation in the post-independence period.) MacDonagh's attempts to approximate the character of Gaelic poetry in English issued in a handful of exceptionally accomplished translations, of which 'The Yellow Bittern' and 'The stars stand up in the air' are the best known. If his own poetry is too various and derivative to illustrate the theories elaborated in his criticism, it is not without interest. A number of eloquent lyrics of broken love written around 1910 reflect his unhappy relationship with Mary Maguire, who went on to marry Padraic Colum. The dramatic monologue 'John-John' (from *Songs of Myself*, 1910) is committed to an unforced Hiberno-English, though the poem's adaptation of the 'Holy Fair' stanza suggests that it owes its success as much to the example of Robert Burns as to that of Gaelic poetry. Other impressively colloquial pieces include 'The Man Upright', a parable that bears some resemblance to the work of both James Stephens and Robert Graves, and the intriguing ballad 'The Night Hunt'. Both of these were published in *Lyrical Poems* in 1913, a full three years before the Rising. There appears to be little evidence to support Yeats's contention in 'Easter 1916' that MacDonagh was on the point of literary self-realisation ('coming into his force') when the Rebellion intervened.

Pearse is an altogether more problematic figure than MacDonagh, at least when considered solely in the light of his English verses. His poetic legacy in that language consists mainly of sentimental or declamatory poems in pseudo-biblical rhythms, and of imprecise, romantic lyrics in regular stanzas. Most of the lyrics exist also in Gaelic versions, which are by contrast taut and sparely musical. Both intrinsically and in literary historical terms, Pearse's achievement as a poet and songwriter in Irish is considerable (see Philip O'Leary's chapter on the Gaelic poetry of the period). MacDonagh translated one of his lyrics, 'Fornocht do chonac thú', and the translation not only reads more idiomatically than Pearse's own English version, 'Renunciation', but also renders the tonalities of his Gaelic text more faithfully. Of the poems that exist only in English, 'The Rebel', 'The Fool', 'The Mother' and 'The Wayfarer' achieved wide currency in the decades after the rebellion. Written in late 1915, the first three mark the author's irrevocable commitment to the course of action that would lead to his death, while the fourth is said to have been composed on the night before his execution the following May. All four adapt the devotional language of Catholicism to lend an aura of hushed sanctity to Pearse's self-dramatisations. 'The Rebel' and 'The Fool' also appropriate the symbolism of Christian sacrifice to intimate a special connection between the speaker and the Messiah. Seamus Deane has spoken of these poems' 'fusion of narcissism and nationalism',[67] a formulation that may be taken correctly to identify their primary interest as psychological and political rather than literary.

Plunkett eschewed Pearse's theatricality, though he shared his liking for devotional rhetoric, which until the period immediately prior to the insurrection he generally reserved for devotional contexts. His poems are never less than competent in versification and are frequently (and at times obscurely) apocalyptic in vision. They evince an interest in the mystical dimension of Catholicism and a heightened awareness of the brevity of life. (Plunkett suffered from poor health, and was seriously ill when the Rising began.) 'I See His Blood upon the Rose', an early piece, is atypically uncluttered, if perhaps too directly indebted to Tennyson's 'The Higher Pantheism'.[68] There is no trace in the poem of the political cult of blood sacrifice which would eventually become implicated in Plunkett's iconography of crucifixion. The single, unspooling sentence of another Rose poem, however, the late sonnet 'The Little Black Rose Shall be Red at Last', ecstatically articulates the sacrifice trope and suggests that at least one of the leaders of the Rising was motivated in his actions by a heady conflation of sexual, patriotic and religious impulse.

The most moving poetry elicited by the Rising came not from a rebel participant but from a corporal in the Royal Inniskilling Fusiliers, Francis Ledwidge (1887–1917), who was stationed in Ebrington Barracks in Derry during the summer of 1916. Ledwidge, a native of Slane in County Meath, had served in the Balkans the previous year and would be killed by a stray shell near Ypres in July of the following year as he worked behind the lines at his original civilian profession of road mending. One of the large number of National Volunteers to answer John Redmond's call to join the British war effort in Europe, Ledwidge became deeply self-divided in the aftermath of the insurrection and the execution of his friends Pearse and MacDonagh. His crisis of loyalty helped push his poetry towards simplicity and a much-needed urgency. Ledwidge's distress may have exemplified the cross-purposes of Catholic Ireland in general, as Seamus Heaney implies in his famous elegy for him,[69] but it also revealed, in intensified form, a maladjustment to circumstances all too characteristic of the poet himself. His spur-of-the-moment enlistment in October 1914 appears to have been at least partly motivated by a desire to escape a life that remained stubbornly unrewarding both in economic and emotional terms. The class and educational disadvantages that hampered Ledwidge's attempts to make a living and make love are never confronted in the poems (though they are adverted to, all too euphoniously, in 'A Song'). The early work collected in *Songs of the Fields* (1916) is well crafted if derivative, recalling Keats both in its cadenced lushness and its half-conscious witness to the privations of a sensuous but insufficiently forceful nature. 'The lidless eye of noon shall spray/ Tan on her ankles in the hay,/ Shall kiss her brown the whole day long': these lines from 'August' describe not a girl but a month, and their displacement of sexuality onto landscape is typical. Though impressively various, Ledwidge's verse up until 1916 lacks direction. In addition to lyrics on personal relationships and the natural world, it includes ballads and mythological poems (on Greek and Welsh as well as Irish subjects – 'The Wife of Llew', adapted from the *Mabinogion*, is the most self-aware and successful of Ledwidge's eroticisations of nature). The best of the landscape poetry avoids pastiche through its responsiveness to the actual sights and sounds of the countryside. These tend to be arcadianised as they are registered, however, with the result that Ledwidge country becomes a place of fells and gypsies rather than bogs and tinkers.

Ledwidge's experience of combat, though not given overt thematic expression, appears to have had a steadying impact on his poetry, supplanting its air of generalised nostalgia with a bleaker, fatalistic note that became more pronounced again after the Rising. We might adapt a line from 'My Mother' and say that 'there was that in him which always mourned'; it is clear, at any rate, that the executions of May 1916 focused and vindicated a pre-existent disposition towards sorrow rather as the death of Arthur Henry Hallam had done in the case of Tennyson eight decades earlier. 'The Blackbirds', the interestingly odd 'At Currabwee' and some of the other lyrics in which Pearse, Plunkett and MacDonagh are lamented communicate a sense of lostness as well as of loss that works with the pervasive stress on the rebels' status as poets to suggest that to some degree it is Ledwidge himself who is being elegised in these nine poems. Thus 'Thomas McDonagh' (*sic*), the most famous of them, has come to serve as the author's own epitaph. The extent to which the details of the lyric are particular to the executed leader should not be lost sight of, however. Formally, Ledwidge's poem plays a variation on MacDonagh's somewhat self-aggrandising 'Of a Poet Patriot', pastoralising the redemptive nationalist dawn imagined in the original's clamorous third stanza and dampening its confident future tense with a tentative 'Perhaps'. The living poet pays his dead subject the homage of essaying the Irish Mode with unprecedentedly delicate internal rhyming, and of drawing for the figuration of his poem on two of MacDonagh's most influential translations, 'The Yellow Bittern' and 'Druimfhionn Donn Dílis' (Dear Dark Cow). The contrast with the 'sweeter' birds activates the 'bitter' enclosed in 'bittern', while the glancing allusion to the daffodils that 'fill their cups with tears' in 'Lycidas' opens a level of intertextuality singularly appropriate to an elegy for the rebel intellectual who had devoted much of his critical energy to puzzling out key aspects of the relationship between an identifiably Irish anglophone poetry and the English canonical tradition:

He shall not hear the bittern cry
In the wild sky, where he is lain,
Nor voices of the sweeter birds
Above the wailing of the rain.

Nor shall he know when loud March blows
Thro' slanting snows her fanfare shrill,
Blowing to flame the golden cup
Of many an upset daffodil.

But when the Dark Cow leaves the moor,
And pastures poor with greedy weeds,
Perhaps he'll hear her low at morn
Lifting her horn in pleasant meads.

Ledwidge was not the only Irish poet in British uniform in the Great War. His comrades in arms included his patron Lord Dunsany (1878–1957), Patrick MacGill (1891–1963), Thomas Kettle (1880–1916), Thomas MacGreevy (1893–1967), Monk Gibbon (1896–1987) and C. S. Lewis (1898–1963). Though Dunsany was best known as a writer of novels of social comedy and exotic adventure, his voluminous output across the genres included breezily conventional lyrics and narrative poems that survived in Irish anthologies until a decade or so after the demise of their un-ignorable author. MacGill, the so-called 'Navvy Poet', enjoyed considerable popular success in Ireland and Britain with his angry and impassioned *Songs of the Dead End* (1912). Over-emphatic rhythms and stale phrasing make his verse a rather less compelling vehicle for his radical socialist vision than his celebrated prose works *Children of the Dead End* (1914) and *The Rat Pit* (1915). MacGill's poems are not entirely without interest, however. He spent the war years as a stretcher-bearer with the London Irish

Rifles, and such vivid pieces from *Soldier Songs* (1917) as 'In the Morning' and 'The Guns' powerfully convey a sense of the surreal violence of the Western Front. Thomas Kettle, economist, parliamentarian, political activist and, in his student days, fellow agitator with James Joyce against what both saw as the provincialism of the Revival, is a figure who belongs to history rather than to literary history. As a poet he is remembered less for the contents of his single collection, *Poems and Parodies* (1913), than for the poignantly unconvincing sonnet from the trenches in which he explains his reasons for enlisting to his infant daughter ('To My Daughter Betty, the Gift of God'). Unlike Ledwidge and Kettle, (William) Monk Gibbon survived the war, and in due course began a long literary career in which he produced memoirs, travel books, fiction, criticism and seven volumes of poetry. Resolutely conservative and at times awkward in idiom, the poems are marked by a gentility that works against the at least occasional seriousness of their themes. The first book published by the Belfastman Clive Staples Lewis, who would find fame as a medieval scholar, Christian apologist, fantasy novelist and Oxford don, was a volume of poems, *The Spirit in Bondage* (1919). Though the poems are no more exciting than their collective title, they are notable for their overtly Revivalist tonalities, which they sound even in the context of war experience (there is no direct trace of the author's Irish origins in his subsequent development).[70]

Robert Graves, an officer in the Royal Welch Fusiliers, the regiment of David Jones and Siegfried Sassoon, devoted some of his earlier poetry and the most memorable passages of his autobiography *Goodbye to All That* (1929) to description and analysis of his experiences on the Western Front. Graves was the son of Alfred Perceval Graves (1846–1931), a London-based Irish writer who deserves brief mention in an account of the Revival on the basis of his songs (including 'My Love's an Arbutus' and the merry Samuel Lover-like 'Father O'Flynn'), popularising anthologies (replete with his own confident translations from an Irish he did not know) and increasingly Celticised, if otherwise indifferent, lyrics and reflective pieces. The references to Gaelic mythology and nature poetry in *The White Goddess* (1948) aside, however, his son's life and interests do not appear to any appreciable degree Irish – indeed Robert's postwar tour of duty in Limerick, where his grandfather Charles Graves had been Bishop, along with his hectic round-trip from Rosslare to Sligo in April 1929 in search of Geoffrey Phibbs, gave him his only direct experience of Ireland until his widely publicised visit of 1975.[71] Though some commentators and anthologists have accepted the validity of Graves's self-descriptions as an Anglo-Irish writer,[72] it is perhaps futile to attempt to place him in a narrative of Irish verse. Once he is excluded from the reckoning, however, the crop of the country's Great War poetry becomes very meagre. Perhaps the only Irish World War One poem of lasting interest was composed by a poet who is usually discussed in terms of the critically problematic category of '1930s Irish Modernism', the Kerryman Thomas MacGreevy. Serving as a second lieutenant in the Royal Field Artillery on the Ypres salient in December 1917, MacGreevy witnessed the death of a British airman, an event which he placed at the centre of his *vers libre* meditation 'De Civitate Hominum' ten years later. The poem begins with a depiction of an immaculate, apparently timeless winter landscape where only 'the shell-holes are new' before, by way of a bold figure comparing the glittering scene to a silver-shoed model who is in turn likened to 'our bitch of a world', it casts its gaze upward to the 'fleece-white flowers of death / That unfold themselves prettily' about the airman. The contrast between the painterly beauty alike of the backdrop and of the slow-motion violence enacted before it, and the ugliness of the suffering that denizens of the City of Men actually inflict upon each other, is deftly handled:

> I cannot tell which flower he has accepted
> But suddenly there is a tremor,
> A zigzag of lines against the blue
> And he streams down
> Into the white,
> A delicate flame,
> A stroke of orange in the morning's dress.

Unfortunately, however, the poem itself undergoes something of a fall from the empyrean as it struggles to manoeuvre its narrative towards a conclusion reflecting the perspective of the City of God:

> My sergeant says, very low, 'Holy God!
> 'Tis a fearful death.'
>
> Holy God makes no reply
> Yet.

This is embarrassing not only by virtue of its too direct appeal to divine judgement but because its pairing of 'death' with 'yet' facilitates an aural effect that in many parts of MacGreevy's native Munster would be heard as a full, and in this context deeply bathetic, rhyme.

The great majority of MacGreevy's poems were written in the late 1920s and collected in *Poems* (1934). Though subtle in rhythm and authoritative and even masterful in their handling of line-breaks, they are disarmingly naive in their chauvinistic piety. Like Yeats, MacGreevy was appalled by the behaviour of the British authorities in Ireland in 1920 but unlike him, partly perhaps because he had been a British officer himself, traumatised by it. His verse circles obsessively about the events of the War of Independence, using Eliotic techniques of collage to communicate a sense of outrage and disappointment.[73] Some of the poems occlude their subject matter in over-elaborate figuration, while others are satisfied with the direct expression of simple national pride ('Aodh Ruadh Ó Domhnaill') or anti-British animus ('Homage to Vercingetorix', one of a handful of late works). Two beautiful, short contemplative pieces, 'Recessional' and 'Nocturne of the Self-Evident Presence', suggest that MacGreevy was essentially a lyric poet of solitude who mistook his vocation. His thirty-seven surviving poems read like the brilliant prolegomena to an achievement that never materialised.

In a Free State: Higgins, Lyle Donaghy, Donnelly, Devenport O'Neill, Salkeld, Coffey, Beckett, Devlin

The most significant poets of the period from the settlement of 1922 to the outbreak of the Second World War yet to be dealt with were Austin Clarke and Louis MacNeice, who wrote the greater portion of their poems later in the century. Writers whose careers are largely enclosed by the dates in the chapter's title may be mentioned more briefly. F(rederick) R(obert) Higgins (1896–1941), a close friend of Yeats, Clarke and MacNeice (who elegised him as Reilly in *Autumn Sequel*), extended key Revival practices such as cultivation of assonantal effects and celebration of the landscapes and folklife of the West of Ireland. Born in Foxford, County Mayo and brought up in Meath – both counties figure prominently in his verse – Higgins was a Protestant whose dedication to the idea of Irishness in poetry was witheringly diagnosed as self-delusional insincerity by Patrick Kavanagh.[74] With their high level of technical polish, Higgins's lyrics are of more lasting interest for their open-vowelled metrical procedures than for their open-hearted praise of the sights and sounds of a pastoralised, under-interrogated Ireland. While it can be said in the poet's defence that an empirically grounded understanding of rural society and a first-hand appreciation of Gaelic literature distinguish him from earlier followers of Yeats and AE, his deployment of these qualities in the service of a cheerfully patriotic aesthetic leaves his work open to criticisms such as Kavanagh's. *The Gap of Brightness*, published the year before Higgins's death, incorporates a handful of poems from three earlier, generally less spare volumes. It includes the touching elegies 'Father and Son' and 'Padraic O'Conaire, Gaelic Story-teller', both of which just avoid sentimentality, and the uncharacteristically brusque and macabre 'Song for the Clatter-bones', a lyric which suggests that Higgins's real gifts may have been crushed under the enthusiasms of Revivalism.

The work of John Lyle Donaghy (1902–46), conversely, has little obvious connection with the poetry of his immediate Irish predecessors and contemporaries. A native of County Antrim who abandoned the teaching profession to live in seclusion in Wicklow, Donaghy produced several collections of ambitious and at times rather bookish verse before bringing his career to a close on *Wilderness Sings* (1942), a volume that may reflect something of the mental disturbances of the author's later years in its shapelessness and rhetorical excess. Donaghy at his best is capable of considerable delicacy of feeling and cadence. His recourse to a long, loping free verse line gives a rather American texture to some of his work – indeed his vatic elementalism links him to Robinson Jeffers (whose antecedents, perhaps significantly, came from Antrim), while his tenderness towards wild creatures is to some degree proleptic of the poetry of Theodore Roethke. Though the Tyrone-born Charles Donnelly (1914–37) scarcely lived long enough to be more than an apprentice poet, the handful of laconic verses he wrote in the period leading up to his death at the Battle of Jarama shows how deeply he had internalised the materialist implications of the Marxist philosophy he served as a political agitator in Dublin and London and as a soldier of the Abraham Lincoln Brigade in Spain. Mary Devenport O'Neill (1879–1967) published only one volume of verse during the course of a contribution to Dublin literary life in which she featured as a confidante of Yeats and an author of plays for Clarke's Lyric Theatre Company. *Prometheus and Other Poems* (1929) marries imagist objectivity to rather trite rhyming to offer descriptive pieces which, for all their slightness, impressively eschew the emotional incontinence that vitiates so much of the lyrical writing of the time.

Poets who began publishing in the Free State era but whose most substantial work belongs to a later period include Blanaid Salkeld (1880–1959), Brian Coffey (1905–95), Samuel Beckett (1906–89) and Denis Devlin (1908–59). The latter three were close associates of each other and of MacGreevy, with whom they are often grouped as '1930s Irish Modernists', a label which is unhelpful not merely because it valorises a decade in which none of them did his best or most characteristic work but also because it suggests that they were somehow more progressive and innovative than writers like Clarke, MacNeice and Kavanagh, all three of whom in fact displayed far greater stamina and ingenuity in developing distinctive and fully contemporary poetic idioms. It is true, however, that Coffey, Beckett and Devlin were self-consciously 'Modernist' in their distrust of representational poetics, a distrust they shared with the much older Salkeld, whose debut collection, *Hello, Eternity!*, appeared in 1933. The jerky movement and nervous syntax of Salkeld's obsessive, notably unfluent sonnets dramatise a crisis of confidence about her qualifications for poetic discourse which she traces variously to her Anglo-Irish background, her Anglo-Indian experience and her gender. The long poem *The Fox's Covert* (1935) is even more centrally concerned with problems of articulation and more explicitly feminist in its exploration of the reasons why poetry by women 'tells the truth slant' (to adapt Emily Dickinson's phrase). If Salkeld's work in the 1930s is odd but individual, Brian Coffey's is bland almost to the point of featurelessness. The early 'Yuki-Hira' and 'Dead Season' pastiche Pound and Eliot respectively, while 'Dedication' (from *Third Person*, 1938) essays a minimalist style based on repetition and variation that is interesting insofar as it anticipates the (much more musical) lyric mode that would be developed by Coffey's friend Beckett some years later. The remaining poems in the volume spurn what the author would in a subsequent work ('Advent', 1975) call the 'aeolian flatulence of tail-end rhyme'; in spurning also most of the other traditional props to structure and sensory charm, they remain inert in rhythm and pallid in imagery. Beckett, a major novelist and dramatist, and minor though very good poet, had a long literary apprenticeship, which meant that he was none of these things before 1940. The poems of *Echoes Bones and Other Precipitates* (1935) have their moments of illumination ('Alba') and mordant poise ('Gnome') but for the most part they carry their learning heavily and are flat-footed in their attempts at humour: the knotted, allusion-freighted procedures of 'Whoroscope' and 'Serena I' could not be further from the graceful lucidity of Beckett's mature poetic style. Denis Devlin's debut collection, *Intercessions* (1937), wears its erudition even less lightly than Beckett's early work. Most of the fifteen poems are noisily allusive and gaudily oratorical. One of the great critics of the century was later to note Devlin's 'inveterate, insensate passion for bad rhetorical effects and other people's rhetorical effects',[75] and that passion is at its most pronounced in *Intercessions*. When Devlin tires of ostentation, as in 'Liffey Bridge', a light but effective lyric of urban alienation, he emerges as a competent though not particularly individual poet. 'Bacchanal', perhaps the only other piece in the book to meet its own tonal targets, is very much a standard-issue British 1930s 'impure' poem which shares the attitude, if not the panache, of MacNeice's 'Bagpipe Music'.

Clarke and MacNeice

Outright rejection of the themes and techniques of the Revival was one avenue open to Irish poets in the 1920s and 1930s. Adaptation of them in the interests of a critique of contemporary political and cultural developments was another, and in the event a very rewarding one. The young Beckett's antipathy to the Revival blinded him to Austin Clarke's elaboration of just such a critique in *Pilgrimage and Other Poems* (1929); perceiving only the book's continuity with the poetry of the Celtic Twilight, he accused the author of a 'flight from self-awareness'[76] and compounded this misjudgement with a coarse lampoon of him as Austin Ticklepenny in *Murphy* (1938). Clarke (1896–1974) had begun his career as a composer of epic tales combining a debt to the Celtic manner of Ferguson and Herbert Trench with a naturalistic tendency deriving from his desire to acknowledge the concrete, unromantic qualities of the Gaelic source materials (there is a scholarly, revisionist undercurrent to all Clarke's dealings with the Revival and its nineteenth-century hinterland). While the title-poem of *The Cattledrive in Connaught* (1925) manifests a liveliness and comic realism beyond the reach of *The Vengeance of Fionn* (1917) and other immature works, the number and quality of the short poems included in the volume are suggestive of the author's growing recognition that his true gift was for lyric rather than narrative. One of the briefer pieces, 'The Lost Heifer', announces the arrival of a practitioner capable of greater intricacy and tonal subtlety than any poet of the Revival other than Yeats, and shows Clarke for the first time engaging, albeit obliquely, with the demands of contemporaneity. Virginalising the Dear Dark Cow of Jacobite tradition as a heifer unable to find her way to the pleasant meads promised in Francis Ledwidge's elegy for MacDonagh, the lyric registers dismay at the degeneration of the nationalist idealism of a few years earlier into the squalor of civil war.[77] The relatively hopeful closing lines ('And her voice coming softly over the meadow/ Was the mist becoming rain') may have provided the source of the majestic conclusion of one of the great English poems of the mid-century, Philip Larkin's 'The Whitsun Weddings' (1958, collected 1964), where a climactic 'sense of falling' is compared to an 'arrow shower / Sent out of sight, somewhere becoming rain'.[78]

Clarke's distinctive verbal music, intensively assonantal and based on a preference for internal over end-rhyme, is first heard to sustained effect in the *Pilgrimage* volume. The book extends the stylistic resources of poetic Modernism in a manner analogous to the work of William Carlos Williams and Hugh MacDiarmid, two other poets of the 1920s who employed rhythmic innovation and idiomatic daring in the service of fealty to local and national circumstance. Though the *Pilgrimage* poems have sharply realized historical settings, and play variations on a range of Gaelic *ur*-texts, their ultimate concern is with the anglophone Ireland of Clarke's own time: their dialectic between religious asceticism and erotic freedom had particular relevance in the year of the collection's appearance, when the passing of the Censorship of Publications Act signalled what appeared to many observers to be the southern state's willingness to turn colonial liberation into theocratic slavery. Perhaps the most attractive poems in the book are the brightly melodic lyrics 'The Scholar' and 'The Planter's Daughter'. Some of the other pieces are of greater ambition, however. The title poem, its surface as delicately worked as the medieval artefacts it celebrates, introduces the contrast between 'hail and honey' explored in the volume as a whole. The hail falls in the depiction of privation in the anguished, powerful 'Celibacy', while the honey flows in the lithe evocations of sexual delight for which 'The Young Woman of Beare' is remarkable. By evoking phases from the Irish past – mainly, but not exclusively, the immediately pre-Norman Celtic Romanesque era – in which religious life, private experience and cultural production were harmoniously linked, Clarke lodged an eloquent though indirect protest against 1920s clericalism, philistinism and nationalist complacency.

The poet was himself, to a peculiar degree, a victim of the latter forces. In 1921 he lost his position as lecturer in English at University College – he had succeeded to his mentor MacDonagh's post in 1917 – due to the disapproval of the authorities of that institution of his choice of a civil over a religious marriage ceremony. All but ostracised from his country just as it was about to achieve independence, he struggled to make a living for the next sixteen years as a journalist in London, from where he kept a morose eye on developments in Ireland: the wounded patriotism of *Pilgrimage* was in important respects the product of exile. In the autobiographical writings of the later career, Clarke would attribute the mental breakdown he had suffered in 1919 and the failure of his first, two-week marriage to the effects of Catholic teaching on sexual continence. Psychological and theological aspects of the conflict between libido and conscience are the central concerns of *Night and Morning* (1938), the twelve-poem pamphlet published the year after the poet returned to Ireland with his growing family. While many of the *Night and Morning* pieces hint at the scale and horror of that conflict in the poet's personal history, they can hardly be said to illuminate it, or to find a mode of articulation that makes it interesting to readers brought up in a different dispensation. Two of the poems, however, are of exceptional quality, and must be counted among Clarke's greatest works. The multiply punning quatrain 'Penal Law' anticipates Patrick Kavanagh's *The Great Hunger* in its slyly satirical deployment of a nationalist shibboleth, while 'The Straying Student' belatedly accords the *Pilgrimage* theme (the imagination's quest through Irish history for intellectual scope and erotic freedom) its iconic stylisation. As assertions of the rights of the body in the context of Free State puritanism, both poems compare more than favourably with Yeats's immediately contemporary lyrics of ribald dissent; as an exploration of the structural possibilities of assonantal patterning, 'The Straying Student' is surpassed in the lyric poetry of the English language only by Dylan Thomas's 'Fern Hill'.

No poet discussed in the present chapter was more committed to the idea of an explicitly Irish poetic than Austin Clarke, none less so than Louis MacNeice (1907–1963). MacNeice's absorption into a narrative of English rather than Irish poetry is understandable, given that his influential *Modern Poetry: A Personal Essay* (1938) aligns him with his fellow Oxford graduates W. H. Auden, Stephen Spender and Cecil Day-Lewis (the latter Irish-born but English-raised) as an advocate of an 'impure poetry' that would admit the contingencies and ephemera of twentieth-century living into lyric discourse. Even if he was at least partly responsible for his classification as a component of 'MacSpaunday', however, MacNeice from the beginning of his career drew on perspectives unavailable to poets whose cultural contexts were primarily and unproblematically English. As the son of non-unionist southern Protestants transplanted to Ulster, he grew up at odds with the certainties of both of the province's warring traditions, and his English education introduced him to yet a further orthodoxy of identity running counter to the specifics of his experience. Gloomily aware from childhood of the excesses of Orangeism and republicanism, he appears to have been insusceptible to political abstractions, with the result that he never flirted with Marxist absolutes as did Auden and the two minor members of MacSpaunday. (When the new round of 'troubles' erupted a few years after his death, MacNeice's radical scepticism became a model of comportment for northern poets from both sides of the religious divide.) Since his work is everywhere informed by the instabilities of his mixed, unfixed cultural inheritance, it would be inappropriate to restrict this chapter's consideration of MacNeice's early achievement to those poems with declared Irish themes or settings. To suggest that he is an Irish poet in some areas of his writing and an English one in others, that is to say, would do violence to the fluidity and homogeneity of the substantial body of verse constituted by the four volumes he published from 1929 to 1939. (The poems of *Plant and Phantom*, 1941, are omitted from the present account, though some of them initially appeared in the period 1938–40.)

MacNeice's academic interests – he took a double first in classics and philosophy – left their mark on the formalism and stoic poise of his verse. The stoicism co-exists with a dandyish flamboyance connected to his strong sense of poetry's duty to the multifariousness of the phenomenal world ('The drunkenness of things being various', as 'Snow', perhaps the most famous lyric from *Poems*, 1935, puts it). The commitment to multiplicity is in turn linked to an awareness of transience, so that such bravura lyrics as 'River in Spate' and 'Mayfly' – both from the precocious *Blind Fireworks* (1929) – are at once busy with life and haunted by death. An almost programmatic concern with the spatial and temporal categories underlying appearances leads to a series of meditations on places and on the ineradicable human desire to 'cage the minute' ('The Sunlight on the Garden', from *The Earth Compels*, 1938). Poems about Ireland – 'Belfast', 'Train to Dublin', 'Carrickfergus' and the brilliantly observed, if less than successfully valedictory 'Valediction' – are set beside pieces with English, Scottish and Icelandic locations as the particulars of the author's life and travels are brought under lyric scrutiny. The metaphysical concern with time leads to a political engagement with history, though history understood in terms of the individual's responsibilities to the nexus of energies in which he comes to self-consciousness rather than in terms of Marxist or Hegelian dialectic. If *Autumn Journal* (1939) is more successful even than the best of Auden's poetry of the 1930s in penetrating to the marrow of that depressed and dread-dominated decade, it paradoxically owes its superior historicity to its greater attentiveness to surfaces and impressions. Over almost 3,000 lines of 'rapportage, metaphysics, ethics, lyrical emotion, autobiography, nightmare', the poem's variously chummy, austere and opinionated rhetoric gives expression to what MacNeice described to T. S. Eliot as such 'different parts' of himself as 'the anarchist, the defeatist, the sensual man, the philosopher, the would-be good citizen'.[79] The subjectivity of *Autumn Journal* is ultimately of interest for the way in which it facilitates the poem's subtle registering of the strains of the public sphere in the closing months of 1938, as the Tories' policy of appeasement of Hitler – represented by the triumph of Quentin Hogg in the Oxford by-election in Section XIV – elevated false consciousness into a political principle. Section XVI's caustic commentary on Ireland – identified as an example of spur-of-the-moment exaggeration in the author's nervous March 1939 Note to the poem – brings the stand-alone nationalism of MacNeice's native island into congruence with that of the island of his domicile as a supporting example of the escapist political philosophy that ultimately (if unintentionally) colludes in the extension of Fascist power. To read the section as an anglicised Ulsterman's diatribe against a country he does not fully understand is both to decontextualise it and to misconstrue MacNeice's tortured, contradictory but never less than self-aware relationship with Ireland. Published just after Yeats's death, *Autumn Journal* is in its Irish and English (and even ancient Greek) settings one of the few twentieth-century anglophone poems to emulate the success of the author's great compatriot in playing off public and private experience against each other.

Two of the poets whose work straddles the 1940 barrier pursued their vocation from both sides of the Irish Sea. While L(eonard) A(lfred) G(eorge) Strong (1896–1958) may have greater claim to posterity as a novelist, memoirist and critic than as a poet, he was capable of bringing a tough, unsentimental intelligence to traditional lyric forms at all – but particularly at the later – stages of a career that spanned from 1921 to 1957. Geoffrey Phibbs (later Taylor) (1900–56) made a signal contribution to Irish poetry as an editor and anthologist after his return from a decade-long English sojourn in 1940. The verse he published in four volumes in the period under review, however, is significantly more mannered and showy than the poems he composed in the last decade and a half of his life.[80] It is with the work of a third straddler of the 1940 boundary that I wish to bring this chapter to conclusion. No one could have guessed in 1936 that the already 32-year-old author of the naive and pietistic *Ploughman and Other Poems* would come to dominate Irish poetry at the mid-century and for decades thereafter, securing a position as the tradition's great counterweight to Yeats. Patrick Kavanagh (1904–67) may have made an uncertain debut – 'Inniskeen Road: July Evening' is the only one of the thirty-one lyrics in *Ploughman* to hint at his genius for mythologizing the everyday – but he had already stumbled upon a subject and the rudiments of a method. The subject was whatever was near at hand and contingent, the method an apprehension of the subject in its existential immediacy rather than its historical framework. Kavanagh's actualist vision demanded a poetic language based on the day-to-day speech of the poet and his community rather than on an ideal of compensation for the fractures in his country's linguistic heritage. Installing the present rather than the past as the presiding deity of his poetry, Kavanagh cut the Gordian knot of Irish lyric idiom. His new doctrine of fealty to the here and now would be as liberating for urban poets as for rural, for Protestants as for Catholics, for women[81] as for men, and would spell the end of the Revival aesthetic.

Notes

1. James Joyce, 'The Day of the Rabblement', in *Occasional, Critical and Political Writing*, ed. with an introduction and notes by Kevin Barry (Oxford: Oxford University Press, 2000), p. 50.
2. Patrick Kavanagh, 'Lough Derg', in *Selected Poems*, ed. Antoinette Quinn (London: Penguin, 1996), p. 59.
3. As evidenced, for example, by Wallace Stevens's 1948 poem, 'Our Stars Come from Ireland'. See Stevens, *Collected Poems* (London: Faber and Faber, 1955), p. 454. Stevens's lyric was written in response to the poems of his friend Thomas MacGreevy. See *Letters of Wallace Stevens*, selected and edited by Holly Stevens, with a new foreword by Richard Howard (Berkeley, Los Angeles and London: University of California Press, 1996), p. 608.
4. David Goldie, 'The Non-modernist Modern', in Neil Roberts, ed. *A Companion to Twentieth-Century Poetry* (Malden and Oxford: Blackwell, 2001), pp. 37–50.
5. Louis MacNeice, 'Elegy for Minor Poets', in *Collected Poems*, ed. E. R. Dodds (London: Faber and Faber, 1966), p. 232.
6. A view which receives perhaps its most elegant formulation in the Prologue to Terence Brown's *The Life of W. B. Yeats: A Critical Biography* (Dublin: Gill and Macmillan, 1999).
7. 'A General Introduction for My Work', in W. B. Yeats, *Essays and Introductions* (London: Macmillan, 1961), p. 519.
8. See Brown, *Life of Yeats*, p. 67. See also R. F. Foster, *W. B. Yeats: A Life, Vol. I: The Apprentice Mage, 1865–1914* (Oxford and New York: Oxford University Press, 1997), p. 99.
9. W. H. Auden, 'Yeats as an Example', in John Crowe Ransom, ed. *The Kenyon Critics* (Cleveland and New York: World Publishing Co., 1951), p. 109.
10. In highlighting the English Romantic aspect of Yeats's poetic commitment to subjectivity, I do not seek to deny that his spiritualist interests have a crucial context in the crisis of late nineteenth-century Anglo-Ireland. See R. F. Foster, 'Protestant Magic: W. B. Yeats and the Spell of History', in *Paddy and Mr Punch* (London: Penguin, 1993), pp. 220–2, and Selina Guinness, '"Protestant Magic" Reappraised: Evangelicism, Dissent, and Theosophy', in Margaret Kelleher, ed. *Irish University Review: Special Issue – New Perspectives on the Irish Literary Revival* 33, 1 (Spring/Summer 2003), pp. 14–27.
11. *The Collected Letters of W. B. Yeats, Vol. I: 1865–1895*, ed. John Kelly, associate ed. Eric Domville (Oxford: Clarendon Press, 1986), p. 303.
12. W. B. Yeats, *Autobiographies* (London: Macmillan, 1955), p. 199.
13. W. B. Yeats, 'Meru', in *Yeats's Poems*, edited and annotated by A. Norman Jeffares with an appendix by Warwick Gould (London: Macmillan, 1989), p. 407.
14. 'When I first wrote I went here and there for my subjects as my reading led me, and preferred to all other countries Arcadia and the India of romance, but presently I convinced myself . . . that I should never go for the scenery of a poem to any country but my own, and I think that I shall hold to that conviction to the end.' Note on

the *Ballads and Lyrics* in his 1908 *Collected Works*, reprinted in Peter Allt and Russell K. Alspach, eds. *The Variorum Edition of the Poems of W. B. Yeats* (New York: Macmillan, 1957), pp. 843–4.

15. As becomes vividly apparent, for example, in the contrast between the treatment of the divided self theme in the almost exactly contemporary Indian and Irish poems, 'Anashuya and Vijaya' and 'The Madness of King Goll'.
16. Note on the *Ballads and Lyrics* in 1908 *Collected Works, Variorum Poems*, p. 844.
17. The poem was first published in *The Leisure Hour* in September 1887 as 'King Goll: An Irish Legend'. The superior polish of the canonical version of 1895 occludes the anguished intensity of the original, which appears to have been composed in 1884.
18. *The Letters of W. B. Yeats*, ed. Allan Wade (London: Rupert Hart-Davis, 1954), p. 705.
19. Reproduced in Foster, *Life*, I, plate 9.
20. 'The Figure a Poem Makes', in *Robert Frost: Collected Poems, Prose, and Plays*, eds. Richard Poirier and Mark Richardson (New York: Library of America, 1995), p. 777.
21. 'The Second Coming', *Yeats's Poems*, p. 294.
22. See John Sloan, *John Davidson, First of the Moderns: A Literary Biography* (Oxford: Clarendon Press, 1995), p. 180. Sloan's account of the antagonism between Yeats and Davidson offers a useful corrective to Hibernocentric views of the matter. See also Patrick Crotty, 'Farewell Despair: The Grim Vernacular and Terrifying Visions of John Davidson', *Times Literary Supplement* (2 February 1996), pp. 3–4.
23. T. S. Eliot, 'Yeats', in *On Poetry and Poets* (London: Faber and Faber, 1957), p. 256.
24. W. B. Yeats, *A Vision* (2nd edn, London: Macmillan, 1937), pp. 24–5.
25. See Tom Paulin, 'Yeats's Hunger-Strike Poem', in *Minotaur: Poetry and the Nation State* (London: Faber and Faber, 1992), pp. 133–50, for an account of the circumstances surrounding the appearance of 'Easter 1916' in the *New Statesman* during the 1920 Brixton Prison hunger strike of Terence MacSwiney, lord mayor of Cork. R. F. Foster has suggested that Yeats's decision to defer publication of the poem until then was based not only on directly public considerations but on his fear of antagonising his Ulster Unionist and British allies in the controversy over the Hugh Lane bequest. See Foster, *W. B. Yeats: A Life, Vol. II: The Arch-Poet, 1915–1939* (Oxford and New York: Oxford University Press, 2003), pp. 64–5.
26. Referred to in terms of outraged protest in the fourth stanza of 'Nineteen Hundred and Nineteen' (and also in the posthumously collected 'Reprisals').
27. For an arresting reading of the cross-gendered lyrics of 'A Woman Young and Old' in terms of Yeats's hostility to the authoritarianism and sexual puritanism of the Irish Free State, see Marjorie Howes, *Yeats's Nations: Gender, Class, and Irishness* (Cambridge: Cambridge University Press, 1996), pp. 131–59.
28. Yeats's more recent editors tend to place 'Under Ben Bulben' at the beginning rather than the end of their presentation of material from the posthumously titled *Last Poems and Two Plays*. See, for example, *Yeats's Poems, W. B. Yeats: The Poems*, ed. Daniel Albright (London: J. M. Dent, 1990) and *Collected Poems*, ed. Augustine Martin (London: Vintage, 1992).
29. Yeats, *Autobiographies*, p. 349.
30. Richard Ellmann, *Oscar Wilde* (New York: Alfred A. Knopf, 1988), p. 533. See also pp. 31–4, 551, 559–61.
31. Seamus Heaney, 'Speranza in Reading: On "The Ballad of Reading Gaol"', in *The Redress of Poetry: Oxford Lectures* (London: Faber and Faber, 1995), pp. 83–102.

32. That is, Protestant by background and formation: de Vere's conversion to Catholicism is reflected throughout his work, while Wilde was admitted to the Roman church on his deathbed.
33. Austin Clarke, 'Gaelic Poetry Rediscovered: The Early Period', in Seán Lucy, ed. *Irish Poets in English* (Cork and Dublin: Mercier Press, 1973), p. 31.
34. See Clarke, 'Gaelic Poetry', p. 41; also Robert Hogan, ed.-in-chief. *Dictionary of Irish Literature*, 2 vols. (revised and expanded edn, London: Aldwych Press, 1996), II, p. 1, 190.
35. William Larminie, 'The Development of English Metres', in *Contemporary Review* 66 (November 1894), pp. 717–36.
36. The later, devotional poetry of Emily Henrietta Hickey (1845–1924), a poet who flirted with the Revival before her conversion to Catholicism in 1901, offers a contrasting example of the genuinely doctrinaire.
37. Thomas Moult, ed. *The Best Poems of 1929* (London: Jonathan Cape, 1929), p. 41. The contents page states that the poem first appeared in the *Spectator* in October 1929. Michael Longley has given Tynan's lyric renewed currency by reprinting it in his *20th Century Irish Poems* (London: Faber and Faber, 2002).
38. Stopford A. Brooke and T. W. Rolleston, *A Treasury of Irish Poetry in the English Tongue* (London: Macmillan, 1900), p. xiv.
39. See Matthew Campbell's discussion in volume I, chapter 12.
40. Luke Gibbons, ed. 'Constructing the Canon: Versions of National Identity', in Seamus Deane, gen. ed. *Field Day Anthology of Irish Writing* 3 vols. (Derry: Field Day, 1991), II, p. 969.
41. Stephen Regan, ed. *Irish Writing: An Anthology of Irish Literature in English 1789–1939* (Oxford: Oxford University Press, 2004)
42. There is some confusion about the date of Carbery's / Anna Johnston MacManus's birth. Her death certificate for 2 April 1902 gives her age on her last birthday as twenty-nine, while her birth certificate has not been tracked down. (I am grateful to Claire Peterson for this information.) Biographical references almost universally cite 3 December 1866 as her date of birth.
43. Thomas MacDonagh, 'The Best Living Irish Poet', *Irish Review* 4 (September–November 1914), pp. 287–93.
44. The term is Norman Vance's. For a clear-sighted rehearsal of the debate about the Literary Revival and of the relationship between tradition and innovation in the writing of the period, see his *Irish Literature since 1800* (Harlow: Longman, 2002), pp. 99ff.
45. Quoted in Foster, *Life*, II, p. 438.
46. Quoted in Richard J. Loftus, *Nationalism in Modern Anglo-Irish Poetry* (Madison: University of Wisconsin Press, 1964), p. 100.
47. Colum's *Wild Earth: A Book of Verse* (1907) bore a dedication 'To A. E., who fostered me'.
48. Austin Clarke, 'A. E.', in Gregory A. Schirmer, ed. *Reviews and Essays of Austin Clarke* (Gerrards Cross: Colin Smythe, 1995), p. 80.
49. Denis Donoghue, 'AE', in *We Irish: Essays on Irish Literature and Society* (Berkeley, Los Angeles and London: University of California Press, 1986), p. 200.

50. 'In Memory of Major Robert Gregory'.
51. Hilary Pyle has argued in her *James Stephens: His Work and an Account of his Life* (London: Routledge and Kegan Paul, 1965), p. 5 that Stephens was born on 9 February 1880 rather than 2 February 1882, the date of his friend James Joyce's birth.
52. See Gregory A. Schirmer, *Out of What Began: A History of Irish Poetry in English* (Ithaca: Cornell University Press, 1998), pp. 256–61, for a discussion of the rationale of Stephens's development.
53. The most forceful of these poems are grouped, along with uncharacteristically wrathful materials from other phases of the career, in 'Less Than Daintily', Book V of Stephens's thematically arranged *Collected Poems* (London: Macmillan, 1926; 2nd edn, with later poems added, 1954).
54. See W. B. Yeats, 'Samhain: 1902', in *Explorations* (London: Macmillan, 1962), p. 93.
55. John P. Frayne, ed. *Uncollected Prose of W. B. Yeats*, 2 vols; vol. I: *First Reviews and Articles 1886–1896* (London: Macmillan, 1970), p. 378.
56. The last of the Gaelic poem's nineteen quatrains, which may be read as attributing the poem to Ó Giolláin, appears to be a later addition to the fourteenth-century manuscript (MS Rawlinson B.486 in the Bodleian Library, Oxford). The poem was first edited by William Hennessy for *Christian inscriptions in the Irish Language, chiefly collected and drawn by George Petrie, and edited by M[argaret] Stokes*, 2 vol. (Dublin: 1872 and 1878), I, pp. 5–7. I am grateful to Máirín Ní Dhonnchadha for the information in this note.
57. Schirmer, *Out of What Began*, pp. 185–6.
58.

Ciaran's city is Cluain-mic-Nois,
A place dew-bright, red-rosed:
Of a race of chiefs whose fame is lasting
[Are] hosts under the peaceful clear streamed place.

Nobles of the children of Conn
Are under the flaggy, brown-sloped cemetery;
A knot, or a craebh, over each body,
And a fair, just, Ogham name.

The sons of Cairbre over the eastern territories,
The seven great princes from Tara;
Many a sheltering standard on a field of battle
[Is] with the people of Ciaran's plain of crosses.

The men of Teffia, the tribes of Bregh,
Were buried under Cluain's clay;
The valiant and hospitable are yonder under thy sod;
The race of Creide, and the Clan-Conaill.

Numerous are the sons of Conn of the Battles,
With red clay and turf covering them;
Many a blue eye and white limb
Under the earth of Clann-Colman's tomb.

59. *Wild Earth: A Book of Verse* (Dublin: Maunsel, 1907); expanded as *Wild Earth and Other Poems* (Dublin: Maunsel, 1916, 1922).
60. 'Buy a book in brown paper', in Richard Ellmann, A. Walton Litz and John Whittier-Ferguson, eds. *James Joyce: Poems and Shorter Writings* (London: Faber and Faber, 1991), p. 139.

61. 'Ecce Puer' was the only additional poem printed in the first edition (1936).
62. J. C. C. Mays brings characteristic elegance to his elaboration of a counterview in the introduction to his edition of James Joyce, *Poems and Exiles* (London: Penguin, 1992).
63. See ibid., pp. 268–9, for an account of these.
64. See ibid., pp. 288–9.
65. Seamus Deane, ed. 'Poetry 1890–1930', in *The Field Day Anthology of Irish Writing*, II p. 721.
66. See *The Poems and Plays of Oliver St John Gogarty*, collected, edited and annotated by A. Norman Jeffares (Gerrards Cross: Colin Smythe, 2001), pp. 351–6.
67. Deane, ed. 'Poetry 1890–1930', p. 757.
68. As Austin Clarke intimated in *Poetry in Modern Ireland* (2nd edn, Cork: The Mercier Press, n.d., but 1951), p. 38.
69. Seamus Heaney, 'In Memoriam Francis Ledwidge', in *Field Work* (London: Faber and Faber, 1979), p. 59.
70. See Terence Brown, 'C. S. Lewis: Irishman?', in *Ireland's Literature: Selected Essays* (Mullingar: Lilliput, 1988), pp. 152–65, for an account of Lewis's relationship with Ireland.
71. See Martin Seymour-Smith, *Robert Graves: His Life and Work* (London: Hutchinson, 1982), pp. 70–1, 161–2.
72. See, for example, Fran Brearton, *The Great War in Irish Poetry: W. B. Yeats to Michael Longley* (Oxford: Oxford University Press, 2000), pp. 83–115. Graves is included in both Donagh MacDonagh and Lennox Robinson's *Oxford Book of Irish Verse* (Oxford: Oxford University Press, 1958) and John Montague's *Faber Book of Irish Verse* (London: Faber and Faber, 1974).
73. There seems to me to be no textual basis for Gregory A. Schirmer's argument that these poems ironise stock nationalist attitudes. See *Out of What Began*, pp. 289–92.
74. Patrick Kavanagh, 'The Gallivanting Poet', in *Irish Writing* 3 (November 1947), pp. 62–70. Collected in Patrick Kavanagh, *A Poet's Country: Selected Prose*, ed. Antoinette Quinn (Dublin: Lilliput, 2003), pp. 193–204.
75. Randall Jarrell, *Poetry and the Age* (2nd edn, London: Faber and Faber, 1971), p. 202. Jarrell's critique of Devlin (pp. 201–3) originally appeared in a review of *Lough Derg and Other Poems* (1946), a volume which incorporated some of the contents of *Intercessions*.
76. Beckett lays this charge against all the poets of the Revival tradition, whom he classes as 'antiquarians' and contrasts to Coffey and Devlin, creators of 'the nucleus of a living poetic in Ireland'. He singles out Clarke for particular dispraise on the basis of the strength of his antiquarianism: 'The fully licensed stock-in-trade, from Aisling to Red Branch Bundling, is his to command. Here the need for formal justifications, more acute in Mr Clarke than in Mr Higgins, serves to screen the deeper need that must not be avowed.' See Samuel Beckett, 'Recent Irish Poetry', in *The Lace Curtain* 4 (Summer 1971), pp. 58–63. Beckett's fiercely denunciatory essay originally appeared in *The Bookman* in August 1934.
77. The allusion to the 1916 poem was first noted by Maurice Harmon, who drew attention to Clarke's replication of Ledwidge's 'lain' / 'rain' rhyme. See Maurice Harmon, *Austin Clarke: A Critical Introduction* (Dublin: Wolfhound, 1989), p. 44.

78. The intertext may have been facilitated by Larkin's friend Donald Davie, who developed a passion for Clarke's poetry while on the staff of the English department at Trinity College Dublin from 1950 to 1957.
79. See Edna Longley, *Louis MacNeice: A Study* (London: Faber and Faber, 1988), p. 56.
80. These chastened, observant, intertextually alert pieces have yet to be collected. See Terence Brown, 'Geoffrey Taylor: A Portrait', in *Ireland's Literature: Selected Essays*, pp. 141–51.
81. For some women at least – Eiléan Ní Chuilleanáin and Rita Ann Higgins seem in their different ways indebted to the Kavanagh aesthetic, while Eavan Boland works out of Irish poetry's older, historicizing tradition.

Select bibliography

Allt, Peter and Russell K. Alspach, eds. *The Variorum Edition of the Poems of W. B. Yeats*, New York: Macmillan, 1957.

Bourke, A., Kilfeather, S., Luddy, M., MacCurtain, M., Meaney, G., Ní Dhonnchadha, M., O'Dowd, M. and Wills, C., eds. *The Field Day Anthology of Irish Writing*, vols. IV and V, *Irish Women's Writing and Traditions*, Cork: Cork University Press in association with Field Day, 2002.

Boyd, Ernest, *Ireland's Literary Renaissance*, New York: Alfred Knopf, 1916; revised edn, London: Richards, 1922.

Brooke, Stopford and T. W. Rolleston, *A Treasury of Irish Poetry in the English Tongue*, London: Macmillan, 1900.

Costello, Peter, *The Heart Grown Brutal: The Irish Revolution in Literature from Parnell to the Death of Yeats, 1891–1939*, Dublin: Gill and Macmillan, 1977.

Deane, Seamus, *Celtic Revivals: Essays in Modern Irish Literature, 1880–1980*, London: Faber and Faber, 1985.

gen. ed. *The Field Day Anthology of Irish Writing*, 3 vols., Derry: Field Day, 1991.

Garratt, Robert F., *Modern Irish Poetry: Tradition and Continuity from Yeats to Heaney*, Berkeley: University of California Press, 1986.

Hogan, Robert, ed.-in-chief. *Dictionary of Irish Literature*, Westport, CT: Greenwood Press, 1979; revised and expanded edn, 2 vols., London: Aldwych Press, 1996.

Howarth, Herbert, *The Irish Writers, 1880–1940*, London: Rockliff, 1958.

Innes, C. L., *Woman and Nature in Irish Literature and Society 1880–1935*, Hemel Hempstead: Harvester Wheatsheaf, 1993.

Loftus, Richard, *Nationalism in Modern Anglo-Irish Poetry*, Madison and Milwaukee: University of Wisconsin Press, 1969.

Lucy, Seán, ed. *Irish Poets in English*, Cork and Dublin: Mercier Press, 1973.

McCormack, W. J., *From Burke to Beckett: Ascendancy, Tradition and Betrayal in Literary History*, Cork: Cork University Press, 1994.

Regan, Stephen, ed. *Irish Writing: An Anthology of Irish Literature in English 1789–1939*, Oxford: Oxford University Press, 2004.

Schirmer, Gregory A., *Out of What Began: A History of Irish Poetry in English*, Ithaca: Cornell University Press, 1998.

Skelton, Robin and David R. Clark, *Irish Renaissance: A Gathering of Essays, Memoirs, and Letters from* The Massachusetts Review, Dublin: Dolmen, 1965.

Vance, Norman, *Irish Literature: A Social History*, Oxford: Blackwell, 1990; 2nd edn Dublin: Four Courts Press, 1999.

Irish Literature since 1800, Harlow: Longman, 2002.

Watson, George J., *Irish Identity and the Literary Revival*, London: Croom Helm, 1979; 2nd edn, Washington, DC: Catholic University of America, 1995.

Welch, Robert, ed. *The Oxford Companion to Irish Literature*, Oxford: Oxford University Press, 1996.

3

The Irish Renaissance, 1890–1940: prose in English

JOHN WILSON FOSTER

The Irish Literary Revival defined itself in part as an abstention from the English literary tradition, and this included the 'English novel', using the term in a generic as well as national sense. After all, it was thought by some Irish cultural nationalists that the English novel written by Irish novelists had tended to demean Ireland, perpetuating in the middle and late nineteenth century a view of the island that Yeats acidly referred to as the 'humourist's Arcadia'.[1] In any case, the kinds of stories, characters, themes and literary styles that the Revivalists wished to resuscitate or invent did not suggest the novel as their best vehicle, and so the novel did not fare as well as poetry and drama once the Revival got under way. The Revival thought of itself as returning to the past to achieve a beginning, so its exponents and promoters paid little attention to the Irish Victorian novel which continued through the 1890s and into the Edwardian decade and beyond. In our own day, literary historians of the period have maintained this inattention. The Revival has retained its centrality and while this has permitted consideration of a counter-Revival (see, for example, three sections so titled in the third volume of the *Field Day Anthology of Irish Writing*, 1991), creditable Irish writing that neither promoted nor repudiated the Revival has been neglected. The 'English connection' in literature and society has been ignored. Yet despite the Home Rule movement, the Irish-Ireland movement, the republican movement (and Easter 1916), the setting up of the Free State in 1922 and the later declaration of the Republic, relations between Ireland and Britain continued, with their direct and indirect literary and cultural expressions, but find little or no place in the story of Irish fiction. (The Irish Mail train between Euston and Holyhead speeds through Irish popular novels of our period and this implies what was the case in real life: a steady volume of human traffic – and therefore cultural traffic – between Ireland and Britain.) Nor do works by major Irish writers set outside Ireland normally find a place, since the Revival demanded exclusive engagement with Ireland. And so, for example, a discussion of George Moore in the Revival context will feature *A Drama in Muslin* (1886) and *The Untilled Field* (1903) but not *A Mummer's Wife* (1885) or *The Brook Kerith* (1916), though these are indubitably works by an Irish novelist of the period. Oddly, the critical practice of, in effect, bisecting some writers' oeuvres is not frowned upon. The popular novelists, often taking relations between England and Ireland as their subject, make this practice impossible.

Non-Revival fiction 1890–1920

Popular fiction

The popular novel is entirely missing from standard accounts of Irish fiction between 1890 and 1940. 'Popular' can often connote work that does not outlive fashion and contemporary appetites but in fact, some popular novels were in print or republished over a period of thirty-five years or more. By 1890, the popular novel catered to a complex demographic in Ireland as well as Britain. The Education Act of 1870 set in motion an expansion of literacy and learning in the United Kingdom; by 1890 the regular school attendance rate in Ireland was more than 60 per cent and by 1911 only 12 per cent of the population could not read or write.[2] There were those who blamed this growth of literacy for an inundation of cheap fiction; royalties, it was claimed, were now the test of merit, and sales of the most popular novels resembled the French national debt expressed in francs.[3] Popularity was orchestrated by publishers, and many of the British houses most active between 1830 and 1870 were still going strong in 1890.[4] Irish novelists published with these houses before, and after 1890 with other British houses just as well known. There were Irish publishers who published homegrown fiction, including Maunsel; Sands and Co.; Duffy; Sealy, Bryers and Walker; M. H. Gill. The Irish publishers were motivated by varying degrees of patriotism, or by religion: Catholic writers were assured of a kindly eye in the United States by Benziger Brothers of New York and in England (after 1868) and Ireland (after 1899) by the Catholic Truth Society. The Catholic novelist Katharine Tynan (1861–1931) was published by the CTS but also by the bigger English firms; popular novelists were versatile in their readerships.

And in their settings. Readers of popular novels were unconcerned whether they were set in Britain or Ireland; the same indifference was at work in the novelists who could as readily set their fiction in England as Ireland without surrendering their sense of the Irishness of their work or themselves. Whereas differences between the two islands were a frequent theme, common ground was tacitly asserted by publishers and readers. Numbers of Irish novelists, Catholic or no, lived in England; by doing so they violated what became the tacit 'Residency Requirement' of the Revival most famously invoked by Yeats when he exhorted Synge to abandon Paris and return to Ireland to live and write about it.

Literary developments as well as cultural politics served to marginalise popular fiction among critics, not only in Ireland but also in Britain and America. Modernism encouraged the idea that literature is a taxing and exiguous affair and its proper readership a select one. Beside the notion of the artist inching forward through the complexities of his art and times, the prolificness of late Victorian and Edwardian popular novelists seems vulgar and even alarming. Tynan published roughly 105 novels and twelve story collections. L. T. Meade from Co. Cork is credited with almost 200 novels, many of them written for schoolgirls; in her revised version of Charles A. Read's 1879 *Cabinet of Irish Literature*, Tynan calls Meade 'perhaps the most voluminous of all living writers'.[5] The *British Museum Catalogue pre-1956 Imprints* lists 32 novels under the name of M. E. Francis and 21 under her real name, Mary Blundell. In her brief forty-two years, Mrs Hungerford wrote something like 55 novels and five volumes of stories. The British Library Public Catalogue lists 45 novels by Mrs Alexander, 27 of them published in 1890 or after.[6] Mrs Riddell from Carrickfergus published at least 39 books of fiction, as well as two novels under the *nom de plume* Rainey Hawthorne and eight under the *nom de plume* F. G. Trafford. Women dominated the world of the popular novel in our period and this world included Ireland, but it was easy for male critics to marginalise novels by 'authoresses' or 'literary ladies' writing under their own gender.

Writers published their novels for a potentially huge readership: 200,000 copies of *John Chilcote, M.P.* (1904) by the Cork novelist Katherine Cecil Thurston were sold in the United States alone.[7] By contrast, Yeats (1865–1939) when he finished his novella 'John Sherman' (1891) wrote to Tynan, saying 'I have no desire to gain that kind of passing regard a book wins from the many. To please the folk of few books is one's grand aim.'[8] This suggests the enmity between Revival ideals and popular realities. Together, Revivalism and Modernism sidelined popular fiction which has only recently begun to receive critical attention. Yet into the years of the Revival and beyond, the Irish popular novels often engaged seriously with developments in Ireland; they portray an Ireland overlooked in Revival literature. Many were 'problem' novels (or 'fictional polemics') that depicted specific social ills.[9] While they inevitably cover a range of literary ambition and accomplishment, the best of these Irish novels deserve the category 'mainstream' fiction rather than merely popular fiction, written as they were for the general and informed reader. Looked at collectively, they alter our notion of Irish writing and culture of the period and at the very least provide a new context for the Revival and counter-Revival. They disprove the assumption of some writers and critics of the time that a flight from the English novel was from the 1890s onwards the only alternative to the 'humourist's Arcadia'.

A rare exception to the critical neglect of popular novels is the case of *The Real Charlotte* (1894) by Somerville and Ross (E. Œ. Somerville, 1858–1949, and 'Martin Ross', i.e. Violet Martin, 1861–1915). Because of the popularity of their *Some Experiences of an Irish R.M.* (1899), Somerville and Ross were regarded as superior examples of 'rollicking' Anglo-Irish authors the Revival was wise to discountenance, yet *The Real Charlotte* is a realistic depiction of the western gentry about whom George Moore daydreamed in 1894 of writing a serious novel but concluded that it was too late for that gentry to sustain such steady attention.[10] As realists Somerville and Ross undertake to reveal the real Charlotte behind their title character's deceiving appearance. Moreover, the range of social classes confidently depicted is vast and testifies to the authors' privileged grasp of contemporary social reality in Ireland. True, there is much about politically changing Ireland they ignore and they seek too much to ingratiate themselves with their English readers, but the novel is still a fine achievement in what we might call affirmative realism.

Religion and the novel

In the late nineteenth century several external and internal developments troubled Christianity in the United Kingdom: doctrinal and liturgical controversies in the Church of England and Church of Ireland (for example the rise of Ritualism) and the issue of disestablishment; the challenge of materialism and evolutionism to both Protestantism and Catholicism; the University Question that vexed the Irish Catholic Church. It is in the mainstream novel that we find the large religious issues fictionalised at length. *The Rambling Rector* (1904) by Eleanor Alexander (1857–1939) is a novel about, among other things, the threat posed to a newly appointed and unworldly rector in the Church of Ireland by the seduction of Anglo-Catholicism and Ritualism from one side and rebellion by a vigilant congregation from the other. Ritualism (or Sacerdotalism) was seen by many as an organised movement to undo the Reformation and the issue was still burning in 1900. In *The Rough Way* (1912), the County Wexford writer W. M. Letts (1882–1972) sends her hero Antony Hesketh on a passage through cultural movements that attracted the young intellectual in the late Victorian and Edwardian periods: belated

Pre-Raphaelitism, Ibsenism, feminism, socialism; he horrifies his mother with 'Modernist opinions that he had gathered in hasty glimpses of works beyond his grasp'.[11] The novel anticipates Joyce's *Portrait of the Artist* in several regards but though tempted by journalism, art, love and marriage, Hesketh unlike Stephen Dedalus is captivated by religion; he is influenced by Shorthouse's novel *John Inglesant* (1881) that concerned the suppressed sect of Molinists who originated inside the Jesuits in the late sixteenth century and who attempted to square human freedom with predestination and God's foreknowledge. Both *John Inglesant* and *The Rough Way* connect themselves with the Anglo-Catholic movement that troubled the Anglican church. Ella MacMahon (d.1956?) is said to have converted to Catholicism,[12] and one is tempted to see MacMahon's conversion adumbrated in Magdalen Ponsonby in *A Pitiless Passion* (1895) who leans towards Anglo-Catholicism (or Ritualism). Set in London and the English Midlands, this is a problem novel about alcoholism as well as Anglo-Catholicism. MacMahon uses Magdalen as a means by which to explore many of the repeating themes of the Irish novel of the period: love, marriage, money (riches or poverty), art, religion, types of womanhood. Magdalen, a painter, is a strong woman, whose aim, however, is not the self-realisation of the New Woman. Tempted into an affair with a married man she loves, Magdalen chooses instead his alcoholic wife's need for her ministration; MacMahon attempts to resolve Magdalen's dilemma through her transcendence into a higher spiritual state.

No spiritual dilemmas trouble the fiction of the Evangelical Anglican Deborah Alcock (1835–1913).[13] Alcock occupies a distinctive if peculiar niche, subjecting the genre of church history for children to the blow-torch of her adult fervour. She overheard her father read the account of the burning of John Huss from Emile de Bonnechose's *The Reformers before the Reformation* (trans. 1844) and found her abiding theme: martyrdom suffered by Protestants or those who like Huss could be regarded as proto-Protestants. She fictionalised the life and death of the Bohemian reformer in *Crushed Yet Conquering* (1894). Alcock's fiction has a sinewy toughness; there is little ambiguity of event or character in her fiction. In terms of her overall fictional project, Alcock was doing with Christian material what Standish James O'Grady, Lady Gregory, Eleanor Hull, T. W. Rolleston and other Revivalists were doing with pagan material: recovering heroes from the past in order to tell a cultural story of heroism and noble suffering. Alcock went deeper into her cradle Protestantism to find her heroes, while the Protestant Revivalists abandoned their cradle faith (chiefly the Church of Ireland) and exchanged pre-Christian heroes for the heroes she and they inherited.[14]

A writer as decidedly Catholic in view as Alcock was Protestant was Rosa Mulholland (Lady Gilbert, 1841–1921) from Belfast.[15] The number of social ills Mulholland diagnoses in *Father Tim* (1910) stretches to capacity the term 'problem novel': illegitimacy, emigration, suicide, wife-beating, urban poverty, decline of the rural gentry and, above all, the 'drink plague' which affects the socially exalted as well as the poor. Father Tim Melody works from his church in the slums off St Stephen's Green and Mulholland is unflinching in her depiction of them, proving erroneous the claim that James Stephens's *The Charwoman's Daughter* (1912) 'is the first novel to deal with life in Dublin's slums'.[16] Mulholland's only solutions to these terrible problems are charity and ministration. In a sermon, Father Tim suggests 'it might be God's special loving intention to keep Ireland always poor. Riches might rob us of our inheritance'![17] Change in Mulholland comes as conversion, repentance, self-reform; and it is in the hands of the saintly Father Tim and a legion of lay women: strong selfless women, intensely pious, rather like inversions of feminists.

Many popular Irish novels during the period 1890–1920 are informed by the conservative religious culture of Victorian feminine philanthropy. In this culture femininity and altruism were equated. This philanthropic culture receded in the twentieth century with state schemes of social intervention and with the Land Acts that reduced the power of the town and country houses from which the philanthropy had often radiated. On one side of the religious divide, the culture can be traced back to what has been termed 'the devotional revolution' in mid- and late nineteenth-century Catholic Ireland.[18] Catholicism was to produce its gifted dissenters and apostates, including George Moore and James Joyce, but also its apologists, as in the less gifted but still interesting Canon Joseph Guinan (1863–1932; *Scenes and Sketches in an Irish Parish*, 1903; *The Soggarth Aroon*, 1905) who writes at parochial ground level, as it were, whereas Mulholland writes from a Catholic upper-middle-class vantage point. A different kind of apologist is the intellectual Canon Sheehan (1852–1913); 'Catholic apologetics' would do novels such as *Geoffrey Austin, Student* (1895) and its sequel, *The Triumph of Failure* (1899) scant justice. These follow a young man spiritually astray who must acquaint himself with degradation before finding God and donning the habits of the Carmelite brotherhood. If this sounds not unlike Yeats's contemporaneous 'apocalyptic stories', that is because both writers exploited the *fin-de-siècle* theme of descent into the spiritual abyss. The sequel depicts a 'great religious revival' among Dublin Catholics in the 1870s, a movement led by a charismatic lay reformer of fiery sermons. Geoffrey

Austin is reconverted to his Catholic faith by three consecutive visions as powerful as any in the pages of AE or Yeats. *The Triumph of Failure* is a strenuous and eloquent attack on the nineteenth-century cultural forces that have seduced Austin: paganism, realism, materialism, German metaphysics, liberalism and humanism. Sheehan muses (prophetically) on the desirability of a Catholic theocracy in Ireland and proclaims the superiority of Catholic art and philosophy over their fashionable rivals, a pre-emptive strike, as it were, against the opposing view espoused by Moore in *Hail and Farewell* (1911–14).

In the north of Ireland the rival to Catholicism was not paganism or art but another Christianity; in the north-east corner of the island was an especially heated version of the friction between Protestantism and Catholicism. The Dublin Catholic novelist M. E. Francis (Mary Sweetman, later Blundell, 1859–1930) tackled the theme of sectarianism in *Dark Rosaleen* (1915). Francis's best-known book was *In a North Country Village* (1893), which depicted in twelve sketches life in the northern English village of 'Thornleigh', life far different from that in her native Ireland, with a benign squirearchy and loyal tenants, and with leisure for the rhythms of everyday life interrupted only by the domestic ruptures of births and weddings, illnesses and deaths, partings and homecomings. The more volatile and dangerous settings of *Dark Rosaleen* switch between Connemara and Londonderry; the action takes place between 1890 and 1914 when the chances of a mixed marriage working in Ulster, especially in Derry, are non-existent. The readable and at times unswerving realism of the novel dissolves into tendentious allegory when the painful birth of a new Ireland is the promise of triumph for Catholicism, nationalism and Irishness.

Ulster novelists were less sanguine than Francis and their fiction, where sectarianism was concerned, more realistic. The claim in a *Manchester Guardian* review of E. Rentoul Esler's *A Maid of the Manse* (1895), and appended to the same writer's *'Mid Green Pastures* (1895), that 'Ulster has hitherto been a region which has found little favour in the eyes of the novelist' was true when it was written but no longer true by 1914 and beside the well-known names of Shan F. Bullock, Forrest Reid and St John Ervine, we could add the creditable names of John Heron Lepper, Robert Cromie, Mrs J. H. Riddell, Filson Young, F. E. Crichton, Rosa Mulholland, J. Johnston Abraham, James Douglas, Sarah Grand, Arthur Mason, Andrew James and M. Hamilton. Several novels handle the intractability of sectarianism with intimate knowledge: *Across an Ulster Bog* (1896) by Hamilton (Mary Churchill Luck); *Dan the Dollar* (1906) by Bullock;

The Unpardonable Sin (1907) by Douglas; *The Soundless Tide* (1911) by Crichton; *Mrs Martin's Man* (1914) by Ervine.

The realism of poverty

The condition of Ireland in the late nineteenth and early twentieth centuries was more grievous than England's. For example, Ireland had rural poverty unmatched in the rest of the British Isles. George Moore (1852–1933) showed a moribund countryside in *A Drama in Muslin: A Realistic Novel* (1886) and thought it bad enough to suggest (prophetically) that a revival must be at hand: 'the inevitable decay which must precede an outburst of national energy'.[19] The realistic depiction of rural poverty and priest-induced lethargy that he believed would speed the necessary revival appeared as a volume of stories after the manner of Turgenev's *A Sportsman's Sketches*; the first six appeared in Irish and then the full suite in English in 1903 as *The Untilled Field*. The picture is of rural Ireland's 'slattern life': choked drains, empty cabins, fallen bridges – the untilled fields of Ireland. In one story the feebleness of the west is contrasted by a returned Yank, James Bryden, with 'the modern restlessness and cold energy' of Americans, much as Bullock's *Dan the Dollar* noted the same instructive contrast three years later.

The Untilled Field, a rural precursor of Joyce's *Dubliners* (1914), established a realism uncomfortable for Revivalists who sang the praises of the west and who identified it as the site of inspiration and spiritual centre of the coming Ireland. The once celebrated novels of Patrick MacGill (1891–1963; 'the Navvy Poet') compose a more savage portrait of life on the wilder fringes of Donegal and Derry a century ago; if his stated theme – 'life in all its primordial brutishness' – is a characteristic overstatement, there was undoubtedly colossal penury in the windswept periphery of north-western Ireland. His north-west town is dominated by the police barracks, Catholic chapel and workhouse, images of bondage and oppression in MacGill's fiction which in its socialist sympathies lives entirely outside the culture of philanthropy. Gombeen merchant and gombeen priest drive MacGill's poor to Scotland for seasonal work: movements and experiences that compose the loose narratives of *Children of the Dead End* (1914) and *The Rat-Pit* (1915). MacGill's narratives are picaresque and bristle with ructions; despite shortcomings, they are mysteriously engaging, full of memorable characters and incident. Their world straddles the famine-racked countryside of nineteenth-century Ireland and urban industrial squalor of twentieth-century Britain. MacGill rightly calls his cast of characters and the places they inhabit – from Donegal to Glasgow – 'the underworld' and his novels can be set beside English portraits of the 'sinking classes' in documentary revelations such as Charles Masterman's *From the Abyss* (1902) and fictional explorations of the urban deeps such as Jack London's *The People of the Abyss* (1903).

MacGill, Letts (in *The Rough Way*) and Mulholland depicted urban destitution. Set in the Dublin slums even earlier than Mulholland's *Father Tim* is an arresting short novel, *The Moneylender* (1908), by Joseph Edelstein that depicts Jewish life in Dublin fourteen years before the appearance of *Ulysses* and written with a knowledge of that life Joyce did not have. It belongs also in the category of religious fiction. Its peculiar stridency at times suggests the work of an anti-Semitic *agent provocateur* but the novella is prefaced with this caveat: 'The author confidently commends his work to the impartial judgment of the public, his object being rather to expose the causes of usury for eradication than the effects for vituperation. J. E.'. If he paints the Jew in a bad light it is to exculpate him by laying bare the reasons for his usuriousness, chief among which is rabid anti-Semitism, in Ireland as in everywhere else. The story opens in Russia in 1900 where an impoverished Moses Levenstein, the victim of anti-Semitism, decides to emigrate, fetching up in Dublin's Jewish quarter: the respectable area around South Circular Road and Leinster Road. But when he becomes a packman (or pedlar) and then a moneylender in his own right, Levenstein works the 'Coombe', a slum west of Mulholland's Cuffe Street south of the Liffey. Moses is no peacemaking Leopold Bloom: the narrative is punctuated by Moses's vengeful mental excursions on the theme of the *Judenhetz* and they are his self-justification for his uncharitable treatment of Gentiles, exclusively the poor of south Dublin. Moses has a Dickensian deathbed change of heart and when he leaves most of his money to Dublin charities (mainly Gentile), the novel assumes the context of Irish philanthropic culture. But it is not a religious conversion; rather, Moses becomes a good Jew at the end, true to his faith. Beneath the gritty details of Jewish moneylending and Dublin slums, *The Moneylender* shares the impersonality of oral tradition. It has more in common with the stories of Isaac Bashevis Singer than any Irish fiction writers, and thus enacts its own theme of the curious estrangement of the Jew.

Poverty of another order – the sinking economic fortunes of the gentry – is a theme in what we might call the country house novel, which draws its plots, settings and characters from what MacMahon called 'Society – spelt big' that consorted in elegant townhouses in London or Dublin and country houses in England or Ireland. The Irish gentry were not exclusively Protestant and it is the Catholic gentry whom Moore targets in *A Drama in Muslin*. But country house novels easily survived Moore's onslaught; a short list of them between 1894 and the Second World War would include novels by MacMahon, Katherine Cecil Thurston, Eleanor Alexander, Filson Young, George H. Jessop, Barlow, Crichton, Croker, Conyers, Douglas Goldring, Duffin, M. J. Farrell (Molly Keane), Constance Malleson, Kathleen Coyle, Elizabeth Bowen, Kate O'Brien. The disproportionate importance of the country house in Irish life was a function of the structure of Irish society until the Land Acts, the Great War and the creation of the Free State. The novels are always, in a sense, problem novels, the chief problem being the decline of the country house. That decline had its political coordinates in the series of Coercion Bills and Land Acts, culminating in the Wyndham Land Act of 1903. House burnings in the south of Ireland by the IRA up until the 1920s completed the transfiguration of the literal and metaphoric landscape. After that, country house fiction was only possible largely in retrospect. But the attempts to save the country house, recorded by the novelists above, are various and resourceful.

For example, *Lismoyle: An Experiment in Ireland* (1914) by B. M. Croker from Roscommon depicts the decline of a country house due to the Land Acts. As in many of the country house novels, there is a nostalgic depiction of country house life before the Acts – the horse racing, riding, hunting and dancing. A visiting relation from England decides to save Lismoyle. (Here are two country house novel motifs in one: most visitors to Ireland fall under Ireland's spell; and there is often a figure who functions as a *deus ex machina* to rescue the house from bankruptcy.) As it turns out, a genuine Romney is found during the rummaging among household effects for a debt-reducing auction and so the Anglo-Irish cultural past of the country house redeems the penurious Irish economic present. English help and Irish self-help could turn the situation around, and for Croker and other novelists, the revival of the country house is the key to Irish betterment: its centrality is assumed.

New Woman fiction

Love is the daydream element of the romance novel, often little more than the genre's assumed furniture and trivially treated as a prelude to the marriages that often ended the novels. Some novels, though, subjected love and marriage to a serious scrutiny that intensified for various reasons in the decade on either side of 1900. In *A Pitiless Passion*, Ella MacMahon in her own voice refers to 'the relationship between the sexes, as we like to call it now,' suggesting a changing contemporary perception of an old theme in human nature (and in fiction).[20] One aspect of the change was the wish to distinguish love from marriage and to scrutinise the identities and dynamics of both. This meant seeing marriage in its fuller contexts – economic, social, psychological, sexual – and the ways in which it could be regarded as the natural terminus for love or a sensible counterweight to reckless or romantic love that threatened the family, which was society writ small.

The latter was the subject of *The Fly on the Wheel* (1908) by Katherine Cecil Thurston (1875–1911), set in the town of Waterford amidst the Catholic middle class. Stephen Carey, thirty-eight, a lawyer, has quashed his earlier desire to flee the stagnation of Waterford and has accepted his slavery to a 'big machine called expediency'. His well-oiled machine grinds to a halt when he meets the orphaned Isabel, twenty, back from her convent schooling in Paris. Headstrong and in battle with convention, she is a double threat by falling in love with the married Carey. He explains the incompatibility of impulsiveness of the heart with the economic welfare of the family (i.e. the Irish middle-class marriage) before he himself falls for Isabel. But he returns to his naive wife Daisy and repents. Isabel's position had always been precarious: 'upon the stage of middle-class Irish life the godmother's wand has lost its cunning, the rags remain merely rags, and the lean mice gnaw the pumpkin. To girls such as Isabel, the future is cruelly stereotyped . . . in no country in the world does the feminine mind shrink more sensitively from the stigma of old maid than in Ireland, where the woman-worker – the woman of broad interests – exists only as a rare type.'[21] Isabel has only a glimmering of the culture that produces her own tragedy.

Love is, in the ordinary way, defeated but not in Thurston's next novel, *Max* (1909), in which a Russian princess and artist flees her imminent marriage and goes to Paris as a boy, Max. There, Maxine strikes up a friendship with Edward Blake, a Clare man with whom she tastes bohemian life. Her resolution to avoid love and marriage weakens in her deepening love for Blake, to whom she reveals herself but as Max's sister. However, Max and Maxine alternate and it is a conflict larger than one between love and marriage on one side, independence on the other. She exclaims: 'We have all of us the two natures – the brother and the sister! Not one of us is quite woman – not one of us is all man! . . . It is war, . . . a relentless, eternal war; for one nature must conquer, and one must fail. There cannot be two rulers in the same city.'[22] Maxine wills the man in her to triumph because as a man it is easier to escape the snares of love and marriage. The modernity of the novel lies in Thurston's notion of self-fashioning as an expression of individuality. Impersonation had been the major plot device in Thurston's best-selling *John Chilcote M. P.* (1904), a novel that exhibits the contemporary interest in the *Doppelgänger* and the 'Other' that we find in Stevenson's *Dr Jekyll and Mr Hyde* (1885), Wilde's *Dorian*

Gray (1890), Stoker's *Dracula* (1897) and Conrad's 'The Secret Sharer' (1912). But if nature tragically loses in *The Fly on the Wheel*, it wins out in *Max*, and self-fashioning as an expression of will fails in the end, while love succeeds, and this is Thurston's conservatism behind her daring: Max returns to Blake as the beautiful Maxine.

Sarah Grand (1854–1943) took a sterner line on the Marriage Question, as befitted the coiner of the term New Woman. Behind both love and marriage she saw the alteration taking place in women's sense of themselves. Women had lost their faith in men; marriage was not working, damaged by divorce, the double standard and male immorality. Evadne, Grand's heroine in *The Heavenly Twins* (1893), expels her husband from the marriage bed because of his prior dissoluteness, and declares: 'I see that the world is not a bit the better for centuries of self-sacrifice on the woman's part and therefore I think it is time we tried a more effectual plan. And I propose now to sacrifice the man instead of the woman.'[23] Grand became a strenuous advocate of the proper education of women and the scandalous deprivation of it became a feminist theme in her fiction, placing her alongside novelist Hannah Lynch in this regard. Appropriately, an autodidacticism pervades Grand's fiction and gives it its bristling manner, frequent clumsiness and its quirky changes of narrative focus and direction; her polemical long-windedness threatened the integrity even of the baggy three-decker novel which in a pioneering move she later abandoned. Nonetheless, through *The Heavenly Twins* Grand became a formidable figure in the feminist landscape of the 1890s and a leader in the Social Purity campaign. It was described soon after its publication as 'a work more widely discussed and sold than any book of the day'.[24] Her first novel, *Ideala* (1888), and *The Beth Book* (1897) – the first ninety pages of which recreate Grand's childhood in Ireland – completed her trilogy on the Woman Question.

Fin de siècle: Oscar Wilde

George Egerton (b. Mary Chavelita Dunne, 1859–1945) expressed the New Woman's suspicion of marriage while rejecting Grand's virtual exclusion of healthy, passionate sexuality from her ideal world and her sexist attribution of impurity to men and purity to women.[25] In 'A Cross Line,' a story set in Ireland from Egerton's landmark volume, *Keynotes* (1893), it is the wife who suffers from thwarted sexual and romantic desires.[26] Sexuality is affirmed but not marriage, and even imminent maternity seems not to lessen the self-sufficiency of the heroine, who in this respect is not unlike Grand's heroines. Egerton followed *Keynotes* with *Discords* (1894), the long first story of which,

'A Psychological Moment at Three Periods', charts the development of Isabel as a child in rural Ireland, a schoolgirl in Dublin and a woman in London, and finally a mistress in Paris. Discarded by her paramour, she declines the offer extended by the wife of her paramour's solicitor of a place in an Irish convent 'where they receive Magdalens of a better class'. She refuses to accept charity, apologises to no one, scorns 'the mangy idols of respectability, social distinctions, mediocre talent', and, fortified in her suffering, takes 'the first step of her new life's journey'.

Keynotes appeared with a cover by Beardsley, which suited the musical and painterly analogies which play through her stories. Sarah Grand as a New Woman writer was opposed to the aims and practices of Art for Art's sake. The New Woman was not yet an artist, as one intriguing Grand story, 'The Undefinable: A Fantasia' (1894, collected in *Emotional Moments*, 1908), claims. But Hannah Lynch and Ella MacMahon believed the woman both as professional and as artist had already arrived, and make her respectively the heroine in their novels *Daughters of Men* (1892) and *A New Note* (1894). The conflict in Victoria Leathley, MacMahon's young violinist determined to turn professional, is between love and marriage on one hand, art and career on the other. She refuses marriage to an Irish aristocrat, achieves success in London as a violinist and fame as a composer of a one-act opera. She is then snared by love for a fellow musician until betrayed, and closes the novel in a room of her own in which she lives, sleeps and composes. The novel is an attack on the promotion of marriage as a safe haven for women and a summons to female self-reliance.

MacMahon's *A Pitiless Passion* is likewise a study of 'the artistic temperament', thereby reflecting contemporary interest in the influence of heredity and the role of predisposition in character and behaviour. Oscar Wilde (1856–1900) was deeply interested in environment and heredity; in this he was very much of his time, and *The Picture of Dorian Gray*, despite its unique Wildean qualities (the dandified tone of voice, the epigrammatic conversations, the opulent descriptions), inhabits the world of the mainstream Irish novel. Dorian Gray is a specimen of blemished heredity, as well as a specimen of Lord Henry Wotton's malign nurture. He has inherited his mother's beauty and the character poverty of his male forebears. Gray suffers from an inherited sickness and the novel is a late Victorian study in pathology, in degeneration and monstrosity. A refrain in *De Profundis* (1897) is the flawed heredity of the Douglases which Wilde thought partly explained Lord Alfred's degenerate behaviour. The decadence displayed in *Dorian Gray* and alleged to be displayed in Wilde's life was variously interpreted at the time as mental, moral or artistic. Wilde toyed with the very impurity Grand and others inveighed against and came to represent all that the Social Purity campaigners fought.

Wilde sported too in the social abyss other writers either avoided or earnestly investigated; the pairing of city slum and elegant town house (or artist's studio) was a Decadent ploy, a more extreme form of the country house/peasant hovel dichotomy in Irish Society fiction. The decline of the country house takes the form in *Dorian Gray* of the alleged moral deterioration at Gray's Selby Royal about which Basil Hallward has heard disturbing rumours. When in search of adventure Gray wanders eastwards in London (and discovers Sibyl Vane), he enters the London equivalent of the Dublin slums of Mulholland, Edelstein and Stephens. Gray's friends, Hallward charges, have under Gray's influence 'gone down into the depths'. Other swells have slummed, but for purposes of charity. Lord Henry first hears Dorian's name at the home of his own aunt, Lady Agatha, who wishes Dorian to help in her charitable efforts in the East End. Lord Henry is naturally cynical about philanthropy; the nineteenth century has gone bankrupt 'through an overexpenditure of sympathy'; the philanthropic are the tedious trying to improve the hopeless failures and 'interfere with scientific laws'.[27] Wilde's knowledge of Darwinism informs the latter dictum.

Lord Henry repudiates the self-denial the charitable were required to practise. 'The real tragedy of the poor is that they can afford nothing but self-denial', but for the rest of us, the aim of life is 'self-development. To realize one's nature perfectly – that is what each of us is here for.' Time and again in his writing, Wilde returns to the necessity for self-realisation. Charity and self-denial impede the race while sin – here Wilde upends Sarah Grand and other Social Purity campaigners – is an extreme expression of the individual and increases 'the experience of the race'. About love and marriage, those other staples of mainstream fiction, Lord Henry is equally cynical. The charm of marriage is that it makes deception necessary, its drawback that it makes one unselfish. Hallward tells Gray that 'Love is a more wonderful thing than art' but Lord Henry calls love an illusion in which one begins by deceiving oneself and ends by deceiving others: 'that is what the world calls a romance' and it is what happens to Dorian and Sybil and makes of *Dorian Gray* a romance novel wrapped inside its brilliantly cynical inversion. It is love that destroys Sibyl's acting, her engagement to Dorian and her life. That love is inimical to life, art and marriage is a proposition to which the New Woman novelist would have returned an echo, but it plays havoc with the more romantic of the country house novels.[28]

Aestheticism did not expire with the death of Wilde as the once scandalous *The Sands of Pleasure* (1905) by the County Down writer Filson Young (1876–1938) demonstrates.[29] A youthful fling with Aestheticism animates some other Irish novels of the period, including Young's *When the Tide Turns* (1908), W. M. Letts's *The Rough Way* (1912) and Douglas Goldring's *The Fortune* (1917).

Category fiction

Wilde had a great interest in science and at times *Dorian Gray* reads like science fiction.[30] In 'The Critic as Artist', Gilbert claimed that science like art stands outside the reach of morality. This coupling was a feature of *fin-de-siècle* culture and allows Bernard Bergonzi to see the scientific romances of the young H. G. Wells as expressions of this culture.[31] He detects in Wells's scientific romances the feeling of *fin du globe*, the feeling of fatigue the Duchess of Monmouth expresses in response to Lord Henry's murmured '*Fin de siècle*'. This is a context inhabited also by the County Down novelist Robert Cromie (1856–1907), whose scientific romance *A Plunge into Space* (1890) appeared five years before Wells's *The Time Machine*.[32] All the big questions of Cromie's time have been answered on Mars (which is Earth's possible future) – the Woman Question, the Race Question, the Nationalism Question, the Empire Question. The Martians – who play the role England plays in Cromie's time – have passed through the capitalist and colonialist stages and have reached the end of history and are on the cusp of initial decay. Like Wells's Eloi, they have lost curiosity; action has given way to contemplation, as though in realisation of Wilde's recipe for the ideal society. The novel is a readable performance in a genre that was in its infancy and still to be designated science fiction.

Cromie tried his hand at ghost stories, as did many writers of the 1890s, including Wilde, author of 'The Canterville Ghost'. Cromie was not in the same league, however, as Mrs J. H. (Charlotte) Riddell (1832–1906), who has been described as 'the best distaff writer of ghost stories'.[33] There is only apparent discrepancy between her realistic and supernatural fiction, for her ghost stories are businesslike, operating narratively as far from the supernatural as possible, to render its possibility more convincing. Riddell was still writing ghost stories after 1890 and in 'Conn Kilrea', for example (from *Handsome Phil and Other Stories*, 1899), she recruits the decline of the country house for service in the supernatural genre.[34]

Science fiction and supernatural fiction can overlap, as in *Dorian Gray*. Among the educated, and even the scientific, the branch of supernaturalism called spiritualism began a long period of popularity in Britain after 1850, and it may have served as substitute religion for deserters from Christianity in the late nineteenth and early twentieth centuries. The Irish Revival drew in part on this interest in supernaturalism, as the careers of Yeats and AE illustrate, and Yeats's occult societies were British and European rather than Irish; the major Revivalists were themselves refugees from Christianity. Bram Stoker (1847–1912), too, availed himself of the supernatural for his novels, though not in the service of national Revival and without necessarily implicating his own private beliefs; like Riddell's, his fiction combined business with the paranormal, which in his case took the form of horror.

In *Dracula* (1897), the decline of the country house has been trajected into utter moral degradation; Dracula inhabits a deeper moral abyss than even Dorian Gray. In one of the many inversions, indeed perversions, of the country house genre, the title villain is his own heir to Castle Dracula, he being in theory immortal. Stoker's adoption of the theme of heredity out-Wildes Wilde; when Dracula sucks your blood, you become kin. Despite the gothic furniture of the novel and the resemblances between Dracula and Milton's Satan, Dracula is a strikingly late Victorian, *fin-de-siècle* monster. Dorian Gray's unfortunate forebears and Lord Henry's unfortunate influence are conjoined and intensified in Dracula, wicked ancestor and seducer combined. Dracula infects by sucking blood, but such extraction is also a poisonous infusion, made obvious when he causes Mina Harker to drink *his* blood. 'Poison-infection-contagion-malign influence-destructive inheritance-hereditary bad blood' formed a thematic syndrome in *fin-de-siècle* writing, working mischievously against the background of the widespread Social Purity consciousness, but a milder version of the syndrome can be found in many mainstream Irish novels of the time.

Dracula carefully plans a crusading invasion of England (with a one-ship armada); *Dracula* is among other things an invasion story and as such takes its place beside science fiction works of the day, including *The War of the Worlds*. Dracula intends to recruit his army inside fortress England from those he turns into 'renegades' and 'irregulars' through vampirism, an army that sleeps by day and conducts its guerrilla warfare by night. It is not far-fetched to see shadowed out in *Dracula* the invasion scare that simmered in Britain from the late nineteenth century until the Great War and that took the imagined forms of space-invasion and German invasion, and invasion by the swarthy races that were on the move, and assumed to be hostile and alien; and then too there was the fear of 'internal' invasion by the native Morlocks, the restive underclass and working class. Dracula is described as 'a monster of the nether world', chief denizen of the Abyss that writers and early sociologists were both fascinated and frightened by in Stoker's time.[35]

Against the power of the supernatural Van Helsing pits scientific method and applied science. The anti-Dracula posse deploys telegrams, the Underground, the typewriter, the Winchester repeating rifle, field-glasses and the phonograph (a dictation machine using wax cylinders). Although Jonathan Harker reminds himself that 'the old centuries had, and have, powers of their own which mere "modernity" cannot kill', nevertheless modernity in the end vanquishes Dracula and the Middle Ages.[36] Part of modernity's success is revealed in the efficiency of the business firms Stoker is careful to list through the novel. Efficiency, as Jonathan Rose has shown, was a dominant motif in Edwardian socio-literary culture in Britain and Ireland.[37] Some promoted it as the answer to Ireland's problems, but, as we know, other answers prevailed.

Equally of its time is *Dracula*'s exploration of the nature of manhood and womanhood, a familiar theme in the Irish novel of the time. The men pursuing Dracula are all 'brave' and in their chivalry are the heroes of the country house romances. The women are more complicated. They are motherly as well as attractive, self-sacrificial, weaker than men (Dracula like Milton's Satan goes after the weaker vessel), man's helpmate, emotionally open. Dracula is a pressing sexual threat to the men's ability to protect and keep their women, which they fail to do in the case of Lucy Westenra and almost do in the case of Mina Harker. Stoker's dark variations on the themes of love and marriage are extended in the curious polyandrous situation in which Lucy and Mina are placed. Lucy is proposed to by Quincey Morris, Arthur Holmwood and John Seward and she wonders in a letter to Mina why a girl can't marry three fellows. Van Helsing calls Lucy a 'polyandrist' and himself a 'bigamist'. Mina reverses Lucy's 'polyandry' when she comforts in turn Arthur, Quincey and Jonathan; it is still a male harem but the woman is in charge. Yet Mina is no New Woman, and she talks slightingly of New Woman writers.[38] We have already met her in the Irish novel: strong and competent and without the need of ideology or politics to emancipate her. This is one element of the popular novel not written by the New Woman writers that Stoker does not invert. Unselfishness to the point of self-sacrifice is part of her strength, whereas Dracula's selflessness (a very different thing: he has no self to relinquish) is the inverse of the charity principle. Stoker like Wilde turns the popular novel inside out for effect but unlike Wilde upholds its values.

According to Van Helsing, Dracula resembles a criminal and Mina Harker puts Van Helsing's fumbling attempts at explanation of the criminal mind into the context of contemporary thinking and she cites Cesare Lombroso and Max Nordau on the criminal type. As the story of the pursuit and capture of a 'murderer', *Dracula* is a detective or crime novel, and the Holmesian figure of Van Helsing has as sidekick Mina Harker, the lady detective. *Dora Myrl, The Lady Detective* (1900) is the title of one of several volumes of more familiar detective stories written by M. McDonnell Bodkin (1849–1933) from Galway, whose primary detective was Paul Beck, introduced in *Paul Beck, The Rule-of-Thumb Detective* (1898). These stories frequently have an English country house setting with titled characters and fit perfectly the bill of what we regard as the classic English whodunnit, a formulaic subgenre of the country house novel, though behind the polite formulas of the genre lay popular fascination with the criminal mind.[39] Although Bodkin insists Myrl is no New Woman, he created a character who is at loose ends because her talents and her status as a young woman are at odds, as they were in many real-life cases.[40] Myrl gate-crashes a profession synonymous with masculinity and feels at home in the world of technical advance – telephones, the telegraph, motor-cabs, trains, electric cars, bicycles and fingerprints.

Fiction of the Great War

In *The Riddle of the Sands* (1903), Erskine Childers (1870–1922) wrote a subgenre of the detective novel we might call spy fiction, and because it combines detection with high adventure we might also call it a thriller. It is also an invasion story and 'coming war' story, and like that other invasion story, *Dracula*, it has rarely if ever been out of print. Carruthers (a bored Foreign Office employee) accepts an invitation from his friend Davies to yacht in the Baltic but finds he has been invited to join 'a perilous quest' to discover if there are grounds for Davies's suspicions that the rich German Dollmann, whom Davies is convinced is a renegade English lieutenant in the Royal Navy (Lieutenant X), is a spy aiding Germany to devise some plan to the detriment of England. There are, and the plan is the invasion of England from the obscurity of the Frisian Islands. By the time of the novel's action – 1901 or 1902 – suspicion about German intentions was growing in Britain. The novel's epilogue is written by the 'editor' ('E.C.') and is the novel's non-fiction version of itself, explicating the possible invasion of Britain by Germany.[41] The novel is written by an English patriot exercised by what Carruthers calls 'the burning question of Germany'.[42]

There is an implied resemblance between the initial unpreparedness of Carruthers and Davies to carry out their dangerous mission and the current unpreparedness of England to resist German aggression or even see it as a threat. Germany is the professional, England the muddling amateur; Dollmann too is a professional, the two friends amateurs who must take him on. What Childers championed, like Kipling, Conrad, Stoker and other

'Efficiency men' who denounced muddle, was *inspired* amateurism – enterprise and initiative that generated their own efficiency and could under the right circumstances defeat the professionals. Carruthers is sure that naval guerrilla warfare will come, just as he is sure that the next war will be primarily a maritime one. The origin of Childers's admiration for irregular warfare lay in his South African experience. *In the Ranks of the C.I.V.* (1900) is an engrossing, novel-like account of his experiences as a driver of field artillery for the City of London Imperial Volunteers during the Boer War. He was impressed by the cavalry methods of the Boers, who comported themselves as irregulars, inspired amateurs.[43] When the Irish decided to fight for independence, Childers joined them. In this altered context, England became the professional opponent, Ireland the amateur protagonist. It was less a case of a substitution of loyalty than a *superimposition* of loyalties, a graphic version of the dual or multiple identity exhibited by many Irish, and Irish writers, of the time. Childers ran arms for the pro-Home Rule, pro-neutrality Irish Volunteers in his yacht in July 1914 and *then*, when war broke out between Germany and England, was summoned to the Admiralty and set the task of planning for the occupation of the German Frisian Islands! He became a Lieutenant in the Royal Naval Volunteer Reserve, served throughout the Great War and was awarded the DSO in 1916. But back in Ireland he had already become the renegade Lieutenant X.

Expectation of a coming war for forty years before it happened created a tradition of fiction imagining that war in detail.[44] To that tradition, Robert Cromie contributed *For England's Sake* (1889) then *The Next Crusade* (1896), a pre-play of the Great War. Then the war so often imagined broke out. The maritime war Childers envisaged in *The Riddle of the Sands* became chiefly a land war, and the cavalry war he envisaged in his imperial trilogy became static trench war, when cavalries were stymied in virtually frozen fronts after the early neutralising clashes of infantries. But he was right to claim that England would have to turn its amateurism into professionalism to have a chance at victory, and quickly, and this speeded-up transformation is acted out for us in the first volume of Patrick MacGill's Great War 'trilogy', *The Amateur Army* (1915). MacGill did not conceive his three books as a trilogy, for the first started life as a series of articles dashed off in his spare time while he underwent military training with the London Irish Regiment in England in order to become part of the British Expeditionary Force. Thereafter his experiences as a rifleman and then stretcher-bearer provided the material for two more books, *The Red Horizon* (1915) and *The Great Push: An Episode of the Great War* (1916) which take his story from embarkation for France to action at Loos. Full of characters, incidents and easy transitions like his fiction, these volumes have the readability and momentum of his popular novels; they are by turns painful realism, casual comedy even as they capture war, and at length a kind of war romance, to set beside the other kinds of romance we have encountered in Irish fiction.

The literary impulse in MacGill's Great War trilogy is the absorption of its otherwise realistic events and characters into an impersonality that derives as much from literature, and the author's own writings, as from personal experience. This literary impulse is there too in Lord Dunsany's *Tales of War* (1918), thirty-two short narratives that incline towards folk legend and romance because those were Dunsany's proven genres. This does not prevent moving work – witness 'Last Scene of All', the death of a soldier convincingly imagined from his own point of view. But the tales compose a generalised portrait of a Waste Land with the Kaiser as a malevolent and sick Fisher King and British pilots as questing heroes. It was not only Dunsany, of course, whose vision of a waste land was generated out of the devastated French landscapes of the Great War.

It would have been impossible for Royal Inniskilling Fusilier Dunsany to have transferred his allegiance from the British Army to Sinn Féin, but this is what Harold Firbank does in *The Fortune* (1917) by Douglas Goldring. Firbank's conversion loosely resembles Goldring's own experience.[45] *The Fortune* is a sprawling *Künstlerroman* and Aldous Huxley, who supplied a Preface to the 1931 edition, claimed that it is 'the earliest, indeed the only contemporary, fictional account of War-time pacifism'.[46] Firbank enlists on the outbreak of war, sees action, is wounded and sent to England to convalesce, becoming a CO while doing so. Mended, Firbank arrives in Ireland in 1916 to take up a War Office posting in the Curragh. His heart is not in the suppression of the Easter Rising and in what is not entirely a tragic irony, he is shot dead by one of his own men as a rebel spy. The last chapter includes references to 'the saintly Pearse, poor Joseph Plunkett', while Firbank's widow rediscovers the depth of her own Irishness, so that Firbank's conversion to the Irish cause is posthumously completed.

The panoramic, if not untidy, nature of *The Fortune* accords with the instability of its political angle but it is unmistakably a post-Victorian novel, like the novels of Filson Young. *Changing Winds* (1917) by St John Ervine (1883–1971) is also a post-Victorian novel, despite its essentially three-decker structure, and crosses some of the same turbulent terrain as *The Fortune*. A group of young talented friends are buffeted by the cross-winds of public events, ideas and movements, which have their violent double-headed apotheosis in the Great

War and the Easter Rebellion. Henry Quinn, an Ulster Protestant, makes three close friends at an English public school, and after attending Trinity College Dublin resumes their friendship in London where like Firbank he becomes a successful writer; since Quinn writes a novel entitled *The Wayward Man* (the title of an Ervine novel published ten years later) we are tempted to see a good deal of personal fact in *Changing Winds*. Clouds gather in Ireland: the resistance to Home Rule by the drilling UVF, the Curragh Mutiny, the rise of Sinn Féin and National Volunteers.

Ervine has captured in Quinn the waywardness of the Ulster Protestant, who loves England and Ireland, but does not always love either, yet whose love of Ireland can nonetheless become support for Home Rule. But the Home Rule Quinn envisages is very different from that of his old tutor, a Sinn Féin republican and Gaelic revivalist. Quinn admires Belfast's industrial genius and believes practical reforms along with freedom from the bondages of religion, drink, history and romance are the way forward; it is a kind of Home Rule that does not entirely nullify Irish unionism and it was a common position of the time, if now forgotten. But all is pre-empted by the Easter Rising, which Quinn witnesses in Dublin. All along, Quinn's ideas and resolutions are dogged by his fear of cowardice; in contrast is his tutor, who is killed as a leader of the rebellion, deluded but brave. Then there are Quinn's friends who enlisted when the larger war broke out and are killed. Returning from Dublin to England, he resolves to marry and then enlist and is sure he will be killed.

The action of *The Fire of Green Boughs* (1918) by Mrs Victor (Jesse Louise) Rickard (1878–1963), like that of *The Fortune*, crosses from England to Ireland in order to seek the emotional and psychological – and less directly the political – resolution of the novel's crises exacerbated by both the Great War and the smaller yet closer Sinn Féin war in Ireland. Despite the bitter harvest of the young reaped by a war led by old men, and though the 'ruling classes' do not realise it, the old order has ended. Dominic Roydon (invalided home from the war), Willie Kent (a Kerry MP) and Sylvia Tracy (Dominic's orphaned cousin) are described as 'moderns who owed nothing to the past', moving about with blank misgivings in a world not yet realised. Tracy wants to join the vast home-front army of workers engaged in helping their country; the novel depicts women's war work originating with the organisational prowess in female Victorian philanthropy.[47] Unfulfilled, Tracy drifts over to Ireland and becomes 'the visitor to Ireland' and there communes with the spirit of the original native owners of Roydon Lodge.[48] But she has landed amidst Sinn Féin menace though it is collusion with Germany that lands her in trouble when she harbours a dying submariner; she is considered a traitor and a probable Sinn Féin sympathiser. She is spirited away to England by Kent, whom she has come to love. To the 'moderns', love had seemed improbable but the novel ends by redeeming both love and marriage, which will survive the wars and the new dispensation.

Revival fiction 1890–1924

The Irish Literary Revival was to provide the literature of the new Ireland, and the culture of Anglo-Ireland was to subsume itself in an expanded and rejuvenated native culture. What W. B. Yeats referred to in 1913 as 'the present intellectual movement'[49] was meant to sweep away demeaning views of Ireland and any credence still given to contemporary Anglo-Irish values and behaviour. There is an irony, then, attached to the role in that Revival played by the country house in which Standish James O'Grady happened upon O'Halloran's *Antiquities*; by Edward Martyn's Tulira castle, in which Yeats arranged the introduction of Martyn to Lady Gregory; and by Lady Gregory's own seat, Coole Park. However, O'Grady and Yeats wished to restore to a refurbished aristocracy the semblance of an older, more cultivated feudalism spatially binding a compliant peasantry (with its rich oral culture) and a guild or class of craftsmanly artists, the whole bound through time by a consciousness of lineage and tradition. The actual contemporary life of the country house bore no interest for Yeats; nor, then, did the country house novel; indeed, the genre of the novel, as it was being practised by the English and Irish, held little interest for him. The Revival canon excels in drama, poetry and varieties of literary prose but did not produce an impressive body of short stories and novels. Rather, the Revival required building on unique national foundations which preceded and precluded the literature of cities (to which the novel was a generous contributor), distinctive Irish culture being anciently rooted in the countryside, especially in the Irish-speaking far west of the island.[50] The novel's inclination to social analysis and implied remedial prescription was to be avoided; Ireland was at base a healthy society merely overlaid by an alien modern culture that was to be peeled back.

Several kinds of long fiction remained that could make a contribution to the Revival. There was an upsurge in the historical novel, and among the undeservedly neglected, most popular or less obscure novels are those by M. McD. Bodkin, Julia M. Crottie, H. A. Hinkson, Mrs Stacpoole Kenny, Sir Samuel Keightley, Justin McCarthy, Katharine Tynan, Rosa Mulholland, George A. Birmingham (Canon J. O. Hannay), Emily Lawless, John Heron Lepper,

F. Frankfort Moore and Frank Mathew. Although some of these novels are essentially pre-Revival or have loyalists, unionists or planters as their sympathetic foreground figures, many of them have a national, if not nationalist perspective (dating as they do before partition) and the best and most popular of them could raise Irish consciousness among American and English as well as Irish readers.

Another kind of narrative that could swell the young Revival canon was the fictional adaptation of scholarly or popular translations and redactions of sagas and heroic romances in Irish manuscripts.[51] Among the most influential of these translations (usually looser versions of scholarly translations) – and which were attempts to provide the Irish Revival with founding epic narratives – were those by Lady Gregory, Eleanor Hull and T. W. Rolleston. The scholarly recovery of neglected or untranslated narratives sponsored the rewriting of these narratives as, in effect, historical fiction, history now being pushed back before the Middle Ages to the legendary events of pre-historic Ireland. Standish James O'Grady (1846–1928) began this Revival genre with *Cuculain: An Epic* (1882) and continued with his trilogy, *The Coming of Cuculain* (1894), *In the Gates of the North* (1901) and *The Triumph and Passing of Cuculain* (1917). O'Grady also published modern historical novels.

Although his writing often has a cartoonish sprightliness of event that could be mistaken for 'children's literature', and although there is a mock-heroic strain in his work that undercut the heroism the Revival fostered, James Stephens (1882–1950) was seriously attempting to render the old narratives into modern fiction, his main project being to adapt the *Táin Bó Cúailgne* (composed perhaps in the eighth century and part of the Ulster Cycle) in five novels. Only two were published and the project languished. *Deirdre* (1923) exhibits a fascination with the heroine of *Longes mac n-Uislenn* (a tale translated as 'The Fate of the Sons of Uisneach') shared with numerous writers of the Revival (including Synge), and milks its heroism, romance and pathos with Stephens's characteristically swift prose. But there is danger in his supplying his characters with the inner lives they do not enjoy in the original versions, for they can appear uncomfortable inside epic. Beneath the heroic self-sacrifice and stoic surrender to fate the characters of the old stories display (an aspect of the self-reliance that appealed to the Revivalists as cultural nationalists), Stephens chooses to detect in his heroes an ungovernable egotism and power hunger that prevent self-mastery, particularly among women, be it Deirdre, or Mary, the heroine of *The Demi-Gods* (1914). Stephens was not by nature orthodox or nationalistic; in his work energetic individuality is always warring with caste or category or the inevitabilities of stories already told, and his gift for parody and ventriloquism with the demands of a literary programme and the serious redaction of texts meant to be founding literature.

Stephens was not merely a psychologist of sorts, but also a Modernist of sorts. His internal references to the original narratives, as well as his occasional footnote, can read like Modernist devices. He plays self-consciously with the bardic material and if his drollery and irony threaten to 'humorise' it, a more respectful adaptation of the old narratives resides in his fictional experimentation with them in a direction in which they themselves already excelled: narrative involution; this, with its reflexive interest in the dynamics of storytelling, is the most notable element of *In the Land of Youth* (1924). *Irish Fairy Tales* (1920) had been an even more brilliant excursion in forms. It had nothing to do with fairies and was not really a creative collection of fairy tales in the Grimms' sense. But although it was instead a coruscating adaptation of tales from the Mythological and Fenian cycles, the early modern Fionn tales he drew upon had folk origins and Stephens's own writing exhibited likeness to European fairy tales in their comedy, darkness, violence and impersonal contraction of event. The marvellous plays a larger role in the Fionn than in the Ulster Cycle and this suited Stephens's comic genius; he followed the heroic and tragic into comedy and cosmic laughter. Yet *Irish Fairy Tales* is the purest and least didactic of his books, and has a *faux-naïf* spirit best captured in the formula-like comment in one of the tales: 'Nor is there any reason to complain or to be astonished at these things, for it is a mutual world we live in, a give-and-take world, and there is no great harm in it.'[52] The mutuality is enacted in the reappearance of characters and resumptions of storylines, in the use of in-tales and in the theme and episodes of metamorphoses. It is arguable that Stephens is displaying in disguise Ireland as an ancient culture keeping its identity and purity through repeated invasions and changes to which it adapted with the bright comic energy Stephens as a writer wishes to emulate.

It was thought at first that Stephens was the author of *The Return of the Hero* (1923) by 'Michael Ireland' in part because of the brisk epigrammatic purplish prose, in part because the book drew on a modern Fionn tale about Oisin and the contest for supremacy in Ireland between paganism and Christianity, but the author turned out to be the novelist and political activist Darrell Figgis (1882–1925). Oisin returns from the Land of Youth to find Ireland in the grip of Patrick and his bishops and there ensues a tale-telling contest in which Figgis's sympathies are clearly with Fenian Ireland; in the end Oisin returns to the heroic past – forever young but damned by the bishops – preferring Hell with the Fianna to Ireland with the sub-heroic Christians.

In the year *The Return of the Hero* was published, Eimar O'Duffy (1893–1935) began the first volume of the Cuandine trilogy, *King Goshawk and the Birds* (1926), which casts a cold eye on Oisin's preference. In the novel Cuchulain returns from Tír na nÓg to redeem man from wickedness and folly. But O'Duffy's novel is not in the Revival vein of updating ancient Irish matter to educate an emerging, re-heroized Ireland. The trilogy is more properly described as counter-Revivalist satire, even if the satire stems like Swift's out of frustrated idealism, exploits the material that so inspired the Revival and bears a passing resemblance to some fiction of Stephens. Cuchulain is so disgusted by what he finds that he returns whence he came, though not before taking a mortal wife and producing a son (Cuandine, the Hound of Man) who has the stomach for the work of redemption. Scorned in Ireland, Cuandine proceeds to England, where he is celebrated and then reviled. He intervenes in a one-sided dispute between a powerful dictatorship and a small nation after the League of Nations has abjectly failed to confront the erring big power: 'Thus far the account of the Wolfo-Lambian war; and here endeth the first part of the ancient epic tale of the deeds of Cuandine.' The novel is set in the future, the 1950s, and narrated from an even remoter future, but O'Duffy is actually writing about squalid post-Civil War Ireland and an unequal post-Great War world dominated by American capitalism. His socialism has many targets in the novel and in its Irish context may have been exercised by what O'Duffy regarded as the failure of nationalism; his disillusionment with the Easter Rising is chronicled in an earlier and very different novel, *The Wasted Island* (1919). *King Goshawk and the Birds* demonstrates an innovative use of the old material; the internal forms of saga are here – the pillow-talk, the runs, the in-tales, the catalogues – but as in Stephens are sometimes difficult to distinguish from the internal forms of Modernist encyclopedic fiction: tables, lists, newspaper extracts and even the entire act of a Shavian comedy of manners and ideas. It is less his Modernism than his dark satire that puts O'Duffy beyond the Revival pale.

Many of the oral narratives of the native Irish were thought to have originated in pre-Christian Ireland or at least to have preserved in their retellings the elder pagan faiths of Ireland. As such, they were regarded as intrinsically important to the cultural renaissance as founding fictions, like the sagas preserved in the manuscripts, and matter for inspiration and adaptation for contemporary writers. There was overlap between the manuscript and oral tales, to which Edmund Leamy's *Irish Fairy Tales* (1890), Alice Furlong's *Tales of Fairy Folks, Queens and Heroes* (1907) and Ella Young's *Celtic Wonder Tales* (1910) testify. The collecting of folk-tales in the field and their interpretation in the study marginally preceded literary use of them.[53] The serious folklore contributions to the Revival included Jeremiah Curtin's *Myths and Folk-Lore of Ireland* (1889) and *Hero-Tales of Ireland* (1894), Douglas Hyde's *Beside the Fire: A Collection of Irish Gaelic Folk Stories* (1890) and *Legends of Saints and Sinners* (1915) and William Larminie's *West Irish Folk-Tales and Romances* (1893). These were assemblies of elder narratives re-presented at the court of the new literary revival.

Yeats showed an early interest in Irish folk-tales, less for their narrative structures than for their testaments to an enduring Irish peasant belief in the supernatural. His anthologies *Fairy and Folk Tales of the Irish Peasantry* (1888) and *Irish Fairy Tales* (1892) retrieved folk-tales with supernatural content from the rollicking nineteenth-century Anglo-Irish fictions in which they had been embedded. *The Celtic Twilight* (1893) – a work of various editions – shared the miscellaneousness of the anthologies, comprising the folk testimonies and traditions Yeats had heard, the visions he had experienced himself and the interpretations he makes of visions and Otherworld experiences. But the volume is more creative and fictional than its predecessors, though not as shapely and fictional as the pseudo-folklore of *Stories of Red Hanrahan* (1908) with its complicated history of composition and revision (1892–1905) and which indulged Yeats's lifelong inclination to legend (that narrative interpretation of the world and people midway between history and myth, fact and fiction) and partiality to rogues and rapparees. Yeats's exaltation of the *tale* functioned to divert attention from both the short story and the novel; Yeats did not write short stories in the modern way while *The Speckled Bird*, the only novel he attempted (between 1896 and 1902), remained unfinished.

Stephens was inspired by folk-tales as he was inspired by epic romances and sagas. *The Charwoman's Daughter* (1912) registers the tension implicit in Revival fiction, exhibiting as it does both the gloomy realism of some of the urban problem novels discussed above and fairy-tale-like romance that works easily as Revival writing. The elements of *Märchen* in the novel are many and obvious, and its plot includes the Oedipal drama of Cinderella, but the psychology and setting are modern and realistic. The cross-purpose is established in the very first sentence: the opening fairy-tale clause – 'Mary Makebelieve lived with her mother' – is followed by a realist qualification – 'in a small room at the very top of a big, dingy house in a Dublin back street'. Stephens's proffered resolution to all the oppositions in this and other works is achieved apocalyptically: a golden age is reached after the first golden age has been lost, to be followed by an age of conflict and division. Many of Stephens's fictions can be read as allegories for the progress of Ireland from an ancient unity through ruptures caused by Christianity and then conquest to the eve of independence and reunification, allegories that owe as much to Blake as to the Revival (though we recall Yeats was a pioneer Blake admirer). *The Crock of Gold* (1912), Stephens's most famous fiction, and a philosophical fantasy, is a plethora of oppositions, and it offers characters as fractions of Man (sensuality, emotion, intellect, convention, law, innocence, etc.), all of which must be rejoined at novel's end; it also offers varieties of prose styles and narrative genres, old and modern and often in parody form. The search for wholeness achieves success in apocalypse; the last scene is a hosting of the *sidhe*, on Kilmasheogue, the hill of the fairies, but a second journey there is promised, to fulfil the return of Heroic Ireland. This masterpiece had an odd sequel. Four years after it appeared, Stephens was an eye-witness to the events in Easter week, 1916, and recorded his observations impressively but without fanfare in *The Insurrection in Dublin* (1916). What he saw was no hosting of the *sidhe* or crock of gold but a brutal farce turning into tragedy. His diary of observations records incongruities, rumour, silence and query – the opposite of war commentary or chronicle and the opposite of tale or epic. The style is in service to the developing theme: the absence of revelation. At the end of the book he wrote of the need not of new Cuchulains or Irish aggrandisement but of local politics and Irish self-counsel. Stephens had at least to suspend his Revival preoccupation with visionary freedom.

In terms of narrative design, the most brilliant use made of folk-tales may be found in *The King of Ireland's Son* (1916) by Padraic Colum (1881–1972), a work closest in the Irish canon to Stephens's *Irish Fairy Tales*, ostensibly for children but a structural masterwork that involves two major tales with a score of tales within and across them, ravelled and unravelled, the whole marvellously wrought. It is difficult to tell which tales came from storytellers, which from story collections, and which were invented, but it is likely Colum benefited from the collections of Curtin, Larminie, Hyde and Gregory and the work of Standish Hayes O'Grady and P. W. Joyce. The debts are less important than the book's design and its secret nationalist impulse. Colum's Gilly (one of his two major characters) is an Irish peasant who turns out to be in reality Flann, a king's son: here is the Revival motif of the hidden and usurped nobility of the Irish peasant. Colum is attracted to the folk-tale as a form depicting freedom of times and places (and its 'masterless men') but also to its structural constraints, its themes and formulas of capture, disguise and mistaken identity, all coded and perhaps attractive to a national mind conspiring for independence. In the veritable 'conspiracy' of tales that compose his book, Colum was in pursuit of a new national self. In *The King of Ireland's Son*, true national and personal identity is revealed only when the 'Unique Tale' is completed; Colum's story is the Story of Ireland, one that can be brought to fulfilment only when Ireland achieves independence.

The leading Protestant Revivalists abandoned their cradle Christianity for varieties of heterodox or heretical belief systems, from theosophy through Rosicrucianism to spiritualism. Yeats was drawn to all of these, even to magic and séances, and from the late 1880s until 1904 he experimented with fiction that would embody his abstruser musings. The result was *The Secret Rose* (1897) and stories meant at first to be a part of that volume – the Red Hanrahan stories (published separately in 1904) and the three so-called 'apocalyptic' stories, 'Rosa Alchemica' (included in *The Secret Rose*), 'The Tables of the Law' and 'The Adoration of the Magi' (the latter two privately printed in 1897). A recurring theme in these fictions is the war between the spiritual and natural orders and between Christianity and both Celtic mysticism and the Eleusian mysteries. Spiritual experiment in, and pursuit of, the occult is presented as dangerous, as Owen Aherne, Michael Robartes and the narrator of 'Rosa Alchemica' discover and which provides the apocalyptic stories with their plots. Yeats claimed to despise 'the pale victims of modern fiction' who passed for heroes and preferred those who were placed by their creators 'where life is at tension'.[54] Another theme is the imminence of a new post-Christian, post-material, post-Enlightenment dispensation to which Yeats regarded the Irish Revival as a pioneering contribution. Yeats described 'Rosa Alchemica' as an attempt at an 'aristocratic esoteric Irish literature . . . for the few', while we might regard *Stories of Red Hanrahan* as his attempt at 'literature for the people'.[55] The latter was inspired by the beliefs, tales and visions of the folk and the former by the techniques and concerns of literary symbolism.

We can relate this cultural millenarianism and mystical impulse to the social conditions of the Anglo-Irish.[56] The Revival's chief mystic, despite his hard-headed interest in economic cooperatives, was AE (George Russell, 1867–1935). Poet, painter, editor and agricultural thinker, AE thought his best prose effort was a curious later work, *The Interpreters* (1922), a symposium conducted in the unusual venue of a gaol cell occupied by rebels captured after an abortive insurrection loosely based on Easter 1916. It is also a species of science fiction, for the events are happening in an undetermined future of winged airships. The major participants in the debate resemble aspects of AE's contemporaries, including Pearse, Yeats, O'Grady, Gogarty, Stephens, Eglinton, Connolly or Larkin, William Martin Murphy; these advance the various philosophical and political positions associated with the Revival and counter-Revival. *The Interpreters* is not really a novel; as AE admitted in the Preface, 'I was not interested in the creation of characters but in tracking political moods back to spiritual origins'.[57] It is the spiritual origin of our diverse politics and social philosophy that allows AE to achieve unity and resolution, a consummation devoutly to be wished in a country racked with divisions. But a destiny of spiritual unity has not been Ireland's, and AE was one of those Revivalists who left the island when their hopes were dashed during what he saw as the emerging Catholicism and materialism of the Free State which came into being the year *The Interpreters* was published.

Counter-Revival fiction 1903–1922

George Moore

In 1899 George Moore announced his intention to join the cause of the Revival; he returned to Ireland from Paris and London in 1901, contemplated learning the Irish language, took an interest in the country's folk-tales and devised contributions to the literary renaissance. Quite soon after his arrival in Ireland a rift with Yeats opened and his 'self-consciousness' (his own word) and antipathy to Ireland's demand that one sacrifice oneself to her, his anti-transcendentalism and anti-Irishness reasserted themselves. His defection from the Revival was a return to earlier modes of thinking and expression. The realism of *A Drama in Muslin* (1886) had been followed by *Esther Waters* (1894) which brought him literary eminence. The innovative nature of this novel has been pointed out – the occupation of the foreground by a member of the servant class; the absence of a judgmental narrative voice; the refusal to dignify the heroine with Hardyesque tragic infusions and devices; authorial detachment tinged with 'carefully restrained sympathy'[58] – all of which distinguish the novel from most of the Irish novels so far discussed. However, the decline of the country house Woodview that closes the novel would be familiar to readers of those novels, likewise some of the scenes of penury. *A Drama in Muslin* had already used this motif, Brookfield being a shadow of its cultivated eighteenth-century self; Brookfield reappears in *The Untilled Field*, further sunk in a narrow Catholic nationalism.

In *Esther Waters* there is a naturalistic emphasis on environment (life in the country house and in London; the subculture of horse breeding, racing and betting) but above that is a controlling analytic realism. Skilton quotes a character in Moore's first novel, *A Modern Lover* (1883): 'the basis of life being material and not spiritual, the analyst inevitably finds himself, sooner or later, handling what this sentimental age calls coarse . . . The novel if it be anything, is contemporary history, an exact and complete reproduction of social surroundings of the age we live in.'[59] This required a realistic rendering of surfaces which in turn on occasion required a special kind of realism. Much has been made of the resemblance of the novel's Derby scenes to Frith's famous canvas, 'Derby Day', but certain descriptive scenes, for example those in chapter 23, display an impressionism more reminiscent of Edgar Degas's race scenes. Nor did Moore withhold from his armoury of styles what we might call lyrical realism, of which the prose arias on Esther's discovery of a country evening (opening of chapter 6), the pouring of gold into Shoreham (chapter 9), Esther's new-born baby (chapter 16) and the 'Cockney pilgrimage' (chapter 22) are superior examples.

Even if Moore's prose styles were in theory recruitable by the Revival, his promotion of the self and his scathing anti-Catholicism were not. Revival opposition to the Catholic church was generally muted (Yeats was guarded in his opposition) because the chief Revivalists were Protestant and functioned within the boundaries of courtesy and minority status; to be strenuously anti-Catholic was construable as being anti-Irish. As a Catholic, Moore, like Joyce, had licence for his anti-clericalism. His abandonment of Catholicism was announced in *Confessions of a Young Man* (1888), which Stephen J. Brown S. J. regretted.[60] Moore claimed soon after arriving back in Ireland that if Gaelicisation was the first order of Revival business, anti-clericalism was the second. What dominates in *The Untilled Field* (1903) is not any philosophical objection to religious doctrine but the unacceptable observable results of clericalism in ordinary lives. The anti-clerical note got more insistent as composition of the stories progressed; the priests are inimical to sensuality and, for related reasons, to art. Few characters resist the power of the priests; five stories concern those who do: 'Home Sickness', 'Some Parishioners', 'The Wedding Feast', 'Julia Cahill's Curse' and 'Fugitives'. These rebels have an instinct for self-realisation and are surrounded by 'dupes of convention', as Father MacTurnan terms cardinals and government officials. Fr MacTurnan is one of Moore's good priests, modestly (and ineffectually) proposing to the Vatican a married priesthood to counter the depopulating effects of emigration; informing 'A Letter to Rome' is Moore's belief that the deplorable Romanization of the Irish church was completed in the nineteenth century. Father MacTurnan appears to subscribe to the reforming philosophy of Catholic Modernism, a movement which the 1907 papal encyclical *Pascendi Dominici Gregis* crushed. The encyclical deplored the advocacy of some Modernists of 'the suppression of ecclesiastical celibacy'.

'The Wild Goose' is the major story in *The Untilled Field* (playing a role comparable to that of 'The Dead' in *Dubliners*) and the trajectory of the main character resembles that of Moore as an Irish Revivalist. Ned Carmady returns to Ireland from abroad and sees grounds for optimism in Ireland's future; he meets a nationalist whom he is drawn to, though he dislikes the Catholicism that has repressed her sensuality and is an element of her nationality, whereas he wishes to annex nationality to sexuality. They marry and he throws himself into the enthusiasms of the new cultural revivalism. But he grows restive under clericalism and increasingly resents the 'religious submission' of his wife. (Yet she is also something of a New Woman oppressed by male clericalism and male chauvinism.) Carmady begins a journal called *The Heretic*, then leaves his wife, and soon Ireland, becoming a wild goose in service not to a foreign army but to himself. The three stages of Ned's involvement with Ireland are those Moore later entitled 'Ave', 'Salve' and 'Vale' (the three volumes of the autobiographical *Hail and Farewell*, 1911–14) and the three stages of marriage as Carmady sees them: mystery and passion; passion alone; then resignation. They are stages on the road to self-realization, an end incompatible with the Revival project.

The Lake (1905) treats the theme of self-realisation (the novel's own word) in an appropriately unpreening prose style. The hero of *The Lake* is a priest who seeks self-realisation at the expense of his vocation. The bulk of the novel is set between Fr Gogarty's fatigue with Ireland's sad beauty and his secret departure to America, and much of the intervening time in the novel is filled by letters between Fr Gogarty and the schoolmistress whose sexual vitality he once championed but whom he denounced from the altar when she got pregnant. Now, hearing that she is alive and well in London (he had assumed she drowned in the nearby lake), he writes to her and receives a reply and so begins a correspondence that furthers his progress towards leaving the church and Ireland. He comes to believe the mass 'to be but a mummery' and he is replacing Catholicism with belief in nature; he emerges out of hypocrisy, realising he denounced Nora not out of piety but out of jealousy and realising more slowly that he wants to have her body, not save her soul. This realising of himself (becoming self-aware) is a prerequisite to self-realisation (self-fulfilment); he comes to see that 'there is no moral law except one's own conscience';[61] he is becoming a 'Protestant', though Protestantism for Moore was merely a stage between Catholicism and a cultivated neopaganism. Moore's 'halcyon days' in Ireland were the seventh and eighth centuries, when appreciation of nature, art and woman prevailed and true Christianity had not been perverted by its clerical custodians; this Ireland is celebrated in *A Story-Teller's Holiday* (1918). Gogarty in the end fakes his own suicide by swimming the lake in moonlight with his clerical habits on the bank behind him, like the cast of his previous self abandoned while his new and genuine self is 'baptised' in the freeing waters. They will assume him drowned as he assumed Nora drowned.

It has been suggested that the original for Fr Gogarty was the writer Gerald O'Donovan (1871–1942), previously Fr Jeremiah O'Donovan, a Galway priest who ran afoul of church dogma and his superiors and who left the priesthood in 1904, went to Dublin, then England, changed his name and became a novelist and editor.[62] O'Donovan like the Moore of 1901–11 offers the ostensibly puzzling case of a writer who supported Irish cultural renewal while in Ireland (through, in O'Donovan's case, the Gaelic League, the agricultural co-op movement, the Literary Revival and collaboration with Yeats) but whose anti-church views in social philosophy, and realism in literary philosophy, placed him outside the Revival and inside a British literary milieu more generally. O'Donovan in his strongly autobiographical first novel, *Father Ralph* (1913), is a realist in the senses both of rendering surfaces with succinct fidelity and revealing hidden or unacknowledged and uncongenial motives and forces, and a realist too in Moore's sense of having his main character pursue self-realisation, however painful that proves to be.

The life of the priest in O'Donovan's novel is one of repression, of the self and others; *Father Ralph* joins 'The Wild Goose', *The Lake* and *A Portrait of the Artist as a Young Man* (1916) – which Joyce was writing as O'Donovan was writing *Father Ralph* – in depicting the lonely cultured self besieged within a Catholic conscience and compelled to become apostate or wither. Young Ralph O'Brien survives the benightedness of the seminary and when he is ordained, against the tide of his real being, he ministers in a western parish not far from the country house of his family, who are Catholic gentry. Like his creator, the new young priest is enthusiastic about the emerging new Ireland but is dismayed to find an authoritarian and gluttonous priesthood in cahoots with the gombeen men. He starts a proto-union and civic organisation and sees it swiftly crushed by the clergy bowing the knee to Rome. For the new Catholic Modernist encouragement of social action is to be condemned along with other Modernist tenets and practices. O'Brien comes to detest Rome's absolutism, and the last straws are Pope Pius X's 1907 encyclicals *Lamentabili Sane* and *Pascendi Dominici Gregis*. The latter stated that Modernism was the second grave error in religious truth after Protestantism, the third, Atheism, lying in ambush were Modernism not extirpated. Ordered to engage in a public act of self-criticism, O'Brien refuses and goes into exile, a kind of Protestant by default.

Authoritarian and gluttonous priests reappear in O'Donovan's second novel, *Waiting* (1914). As *Father Ralph* focused on the church's hostility to Modernism as a local adjunct to Irish revival, *Waiting* focuses on the church's implacable opposition to other adjuncts to Irish revival: secular participation in education for Catholics and marriages between Catholics and Protestants. O'Donovan's young Catholic teacher, Maurice Blake, falls foul of the local parish priest on both counts, by refusing to boycott a young agricultural consultant and by wishing to marry her (having fallen in love with her). The young Protestant woman is called Alice Barton, O'Donovan's tribute to George Moore whose heroine in *A Drama in Muslin* bore that name. The church refuses Blake a dispensation to marry and on the heels of Blake's marriage in a Dublin registry office comes word of the church's new *Ne Temere* decree (issued 1907), invalidating marriages between Catholics and non-Catholics, and which is energetically embraced by the Irish hierarchy. The decree, which overnight labels Blake an adulterer and his wife a whore, destroys Blake's candidacy in 1910 as a Revivalist and west of Ireland Home Rule MP. The church's leadership in the opposition to Blake carries echoes of the Parnell affair – one of Blake's enemies is one Healy.

James Joyce

James Joyce (1882–1941) joined Moore and O'Donovan as lapsed Catholics who wrote realism, but unlike them Joyce from the start opposed what he regarded as the self-deluding romanticism of the Revival. The slice of Dublin (and Irish) life served up in *Dubliners* (1914) was one neglected by the Revivalists because of no use to them. The majority of the stories in this volume depict the lower middle class ('After the Race' is a notable exception), substantially framed by a descending middle class in the final story, 'The Dead', and in the first three stories an embryo bohemian intelligence in attempted flight from the lower middle class. The idleness of the lower middle class suggests the moribund economy of late Victorian Dublin.[63] When there is motion in *Dubliners* it is usually ineffectual, the characters circulating through the Dublin streets like fitful winds (as they will do even more busily but just as ineffectually in *Ulysses*). Joyce's lower middle class is without coherence or integrity, its culture scrappy, half-English, half-Irish, inherited from above or below. Joyce, whose own family descended to the bottom of the middle class, made himself at home with the rich but piecemeal culture of his Dubliners, their jokes, anecdotes, gossip, songs, half-baked knowledge – like a parody of the wisdom Yeats and others sought among the peasantry. Dublin itself is the ghost of a metropolis, wearing in 'After the Race' 'the mask of a capital'.

Joyce's *Dubliners* proved intractable material for the Revival. What order their culture displays is that of routine and empty ritual, and those who daydream of remedying matters (such as Mr Duffy in 'A Painful Case' or Gabriel Conroy in 'The Dead') are set at naught. For the most part Joyce like the Moore of *The Untilled Field* avoids analysis and is content to foreground the observable results of what ails his Dubliners. One could argue that the Irish malaise is traceable back between Joyce's lines to the two empires Stephen Dedalus cocks a snook at, the Roman and British; the volume opens with the boy in 'The Sisters' prematurely oppressed by the weight of liturgical mystery (and, less gravely, by family) and closes with the boy's grown-up counterpart, Gabriel Conroy, laid under obligation to family and gazing out towards the snow-capped Wellington monument. However, what most distinguishes the stories in *Dubliners* is the eloquently established mundane ineffectively lit by the chief characters' guttering and pseudo-romantic daydreams. Joyce claimed – though it might have been special pleading as he sought to find a publisher – that his realism was compulsory and had a higher purpose: 'in composing my chapter of moral history in exactly the way I have composed it I have taken the first step towards the spiritual liberation of my country'.[64] If so, such preparative realism overstepped itself, given the ubiquity in *Dubliners* not just of idleness but of paralysis and death, from the first page of the volume to the last: 'I call the series *Dubliners* to betray the soul of that hemiplegia or paralysis which many consider a city,' Joyce wrote in a letter.[65] He depicts a city, and by extension a nation, without transcendence. Joyce's realism is deeper than ground-clearing; like Moore's in *The Untilled Field* it implies a moral and spiritual rot too entrenched to be reversed. The first page of *Dubliners* introduces the reader to the idea of aimlessness with '*paralysis*', spiritual corruption with '*simony*' and absence with '*gnomon*' and the ensuing pages provide examples of all three with the surgical precision of a coroner.

That precision had the impassive fidelity of a 'nicely polished looking-glass', which was Joyce's own metaphor when writing to Grant Richards to encourage him to publish, though as in his earlier letter to Richards he claimed purpose in his holding up of a mirror. One can see neutrality of presentation in Joyce's naturalistic slices of life, but not randomness, for Joyce's own description of his way of writing – 'scrupulous meanness' – suggested a nicety of selection in incident and character and a studied avoidance of purple in execution, in other words a punctilious thrift throughout.[66] But Joyce relaxed his scruples in his last story, 'The Dead', which, whatever else it does to the discredit of Ireland, celebrates Dublin hospitality and thaws to some extent the frost of the preceding stories, though death is ever-present and minatory. At long last an element of the transcendent is admitted into the world of *Dubliners*. And Joyce allowed himself a fuller, even opulent prose at story's end. Widening spirals of generosity, i.e. of abundance and kindliness ('Generous tears filled Gabriel's eyes') that become generality ('snow was general all over Ireland') and thence universality ('he heard the snow falling faintly through the universe') gesture towards the supreme neutrality Joyce was to come closer to in *Ulysses* and *Finnegans Wake* and that in the Ithaca episode of *Ulysses* he calls 'the apathy of the stars'.

Because he early thought of himself as an advanced urban writer, Joyce's artistic priorities were beyond the remit of the Revival. (He turned his back on the Irish countryside and its inhabitants.) They also proved in time to be beyond the remit of late Victorian and Edwardian urban fiction. But at first, his ambitions as a fiction writer placed him amidst the circumstances of that fiction. *A Portrait of the Artist* in its beginnings recreates the ambience and even ethos of the English public school; it might even be described as an *imperial* feel and Joyce, when justifying his exclusive interest in Dublin for a volume of stories, reminded Grant Richards that the Irish city was the second city of the British Empire.[67] Moreover, against the tide of the Revival, *A Portrait* does not depict, as a patriotic Irish reader might have expected in 1916, a young man who sheds Britishness and dons his rediscovered Irishness. But neither does he embrace Britishness; he will leave Ireland but not for England, just as Joyce, unlike O'Donovan, when he judged Ireland impossible, declined to head for England except as a staging post on his way to the continent in December 1902 and again in October 1904. Joyce's is a third way; in a reaction to Ireland more like Moore's, but more single-minded, Joyce went where he thought his art might flourish best: the alternative to Ireland need not be Britain but rather a Europe outside the Empire that spoke new languages.

But Joyce could not yet escape what we know to be the familiar preoccupations of the late Victorian and Edwardian Irish novel, though we will look in vain for any interest in the country house novel or the Irish gentry. The Irish Question is asked throughout *A Portrait* – and provoked the famous Christmas dinner scene – even if the student Dedalus reflects Joyce's own reluctance to forge a political position. The importance in the novel of religion and spiritual crisis is neither unusual nor especially Catholic in the light of mainstream Irish novels; the novel's unusualness lay in the conclusiveness of Stephen Dedalus's apostasy, for in most Irish novels concerning spiritual life some orthodox religious faith is embraced by the hero at novel's end. The thematic refrain of heresy, which is heard through both *A Portrait* and *Ulysses*, was a product of the doctrinal wars of the late nineteenth century. If Joyce retained a Catholic theological perception of the world (one feature of which was a pedantic scholasticism he passed to Stephen), he was at the very least guilty of the contemporary heresy of Modernism in that religion, which according to *Pascendi Dominici Gregis* held that knowledge was confined within two limits, 'the one external, namely, the visible world, the other internal, which is consciousness', all else being unknowable. Joyce made his fiction wholeheartedly out of the visible (requiring the 'ineluctable modality' of exact and proliferating empirical detail) and the conscious (requiring a deepening interiority, best conveyed through the stream-of-consciousness method that developed throughout his fiction). In both regards Joyce, who began as a late Victorian writer, became (in both senses) a Modernist writer.

The importance of sin in *A Portrait* was inevitable if the novel were to show the effects of an Irish Catholic upbringing and the struggle of a budding artist to escape its snares. But the wider quandary is of its time. For example, when he yields to temptation of the flesh, Stephen visits the city's brothel area in 'a maze of narrow and dirty streets' and 'foul lanes' in an adventure and setting (the nether world of the slums) familiar from Victorian and Edwardian novels, in both their realist and *fin-de-siècle* forms.[68] In plot, the Victorian orthodoxy of *A Portrait* is superseded really only towards the end (its most didactic and pedantic portion) when Dedalus tries to fashion an aesthetic entirely separate from, and opposed to, Roman Catholic theology. And even then Joyce borrows heavily from that theology. The 'call of life' Stephen hears on Dollymount strand in the fourth chapter of *A Portrait*, and the call to art he hears (answering which he will become a priest of the imagination) is still a version of the 'joys of faith' to which the future Cardinal Manning refers in *Sin and Its Consequences* (1876). And the 'profane joy' Stephen experiences in the fourth chapter of *A Portrait*, when he sees the girl, is still a version of the 'joys of vision' Manning describes as flowing from the 'joy of the Resurrection' and personal rebirth.[69] Dedalus's conversion to a faith in art might align him with Wilde and Yeats but the impress of Christianity remained deeper with Joyce than with those two Protestants.

As a portrait of a young man in struggle with his heritage and in passage through the tempting advanced movements of his day, *A Portrait* has resemblances to some contemporary Irish *bildungsromans*, including those by W. M. Letts and Filson Young. As a portrait of a young Irish Catholic boy, it has a female precursor in *Autobiography of a Child* by Dublin-born novelist and travel writer Hannah Lynch (1862–1904), published in *Blackwood's Edinburgh Magazine* 1898–1899 and in book form in 1899. Lynch's work is an alarming testimony of girlhood suffering and martyrdom. If it is fiction, it reads with the unflagging honesty of autobiography. The narrator, the grown-up Angela, regards herself as now 'resting in the equable tones of middle life' and as having achieved a 'drab-robed content', but her story is one of nearly surrealistic suffering at the hands of her mother, sisters, uncle and, later, nuns in a convent school. Her life has charted three phases: the passive and suffering phase; the rebellious phase; and the present phase of contentedness.[70] The settings for these phases are, respectively, Kildare, an English convent school and Ireland again in her maturity.

Growing up in Ireland, Angela would 'warble' her 'strange symphonies' and a friend would recall her stepfather's prediction that 'She'll be a Catherine Hayes yet . . . or maybe she'll compose illigant operas.' (Catherine Hayes was the nineteenth-century Limerick-born diva.) The grown-up Angela remarks sadly: 'Alas! I neither sing nor compose, and listen to the singing and music of others with unemotional quietude. So many different achievements have been fondly expected of me, that I have preferred the alternative of achieving nothing. Better demolish a multitude of expectations than build one's house of the perishable bricks of a single one.' The *Autobiography* is a reverse *Portrait of the Artist as a Young Man*: the artistic ambition has been killed not roused by adversity, for Angela is a girl and thus already labours under disability; it is a *Portrait of the Artist Manquée as a Young Girl*. 'On the stage, whether actress or dancer, my fortune would long ago have been made, and as an acrobat I should have won glory in my teens. But old-fashioned parents never think of these things. If you are a girl, and fortune forsakes the domestic hearth, they tell you to go and be a governess, and bless your stars that, thanks to their good sense, you are enabled to earn a miserable crust in the path of respectability'.[71]

Whereas Lynch's membership of the Ladies' Land League and her publishing of *United Ireland* from Paris on its suppression would suggest familiar Irish nationalism[72] of the distaff auxiliary variety, the Europeanised Lynch's field of view was far wider than Irish nationalism's. Fifteen years or so before Joyce, she travelled in Europe, lectured in Paris on English literature, published a book on George Meredith, and had influence at *Le Figaro*. She was much concerned with the education of girls and devotes a great deal of space to the subject in her study *French Life in Town and Country* (1901), during which she examines (clearly with deep personal interest) convent education.

Joyce did not in his fiction foreground social problems, as did Lynch and others, and instead promoted the fictional self, as did Moore; in post-Victorian fiction with affinities to Modernism, literary psychology superseded literary sociology, which still dominated the mainstream Edwardian novel. Joyce is complicit with Stephen's pride, will and intellect (respectively the agency, motive and instrument of sin, according to Manning). Stephen's defiant 'I will not serve', originating in Lucifer's rebellion, means that in secular terms, beyond his withdrawal from the Catholic communion, he will look first to his own interests, take part in no campaign of social reform, entertain no self-sacrifice or perform no philanthropy. 'Dedalus', MacCann says, 'I believe you're a good fellow but you have yet to learn the dignity of altruism and the responsibility of the human individual.'[73] Joyce did not simply have Dedalus refuse to serve; he also demonstrated that refusal through perspective, an increasing reliance on the sense-impressions and cognition of individual minds. It is the sustained prose equivalence of Dedalus's thoughts that constituted Joyce's break with the contemporary Victorian and Edwardian novel. For his next novel he added the consciousness of Leopold Bloom and Molly Bloom. The intellectually well-stocked mind of the first, the unintellectual but nevertheless curious mind of the second, and the relentlessly gossipy thoughts of the last meant that Joyce was sacrificing nothing by this shrinking purview, and when he sent the first and second on journeys around Dublin, that meant a wealth of empirical detail. The result was a busier canvas than that of almost any other fiction writer, before or since.

However, in *Ulysses* (1922), subjectivity does not necessarily mean Dedalian self-centredness, for though Joyce deepens the interiority of Stephen Dedalus, the novel is ostensibly dominated by Bloom's consciousness. We are privy to a host of Bloom's private thoughts over one day, yet he counterbalances Stephen's self-preoccupation. He has a social conscience Stephen lacks: 'he desired to amend many social conditions, the product of inequality and avarice and international animosity'.[74] He refers to 'drink, the curse of Ireland' and he is himself temperate and sober, in his behaviour and his judgements; he is moderate, tolerant, and 'the prudent member' (as he is referred to in scornful innuendo by a drinker); he inhabits a society that resembles the one depicted in the mainstream Irish novel. While he and Stephen are in the cab shelter, a streetwalker appears and then disappears when she is told to take herself off. Bloom wonders aloud to his indifferent companion how a prostitute reeking with disease has the effrontery to solicit customers and says he is a 'stalwart advocate' of the system whereby such women are licensed and medically inspected. He is alluding to the Contagious Diseases Acts of 1864, 1866 and 1869. This is Bloom's concern for social health. But Bloom admits that 'some man is ultimately responsible for [the prostitute's] condition'.[75] As usual, Bloom sees both sides of the coin. Here is the issue in essence, for whereas the Acts blamed loose women for infecting men, this was seen as a double standard by opponents of the Acts who waged the 'Social Purity' campaign aimed at repeal of the Acts and at persuading men to cease their recourse to prostitutes.

There is possibly a wider significance in Bloom's thoughts on prostitution. A recent critic has claimed that Joyce actively sought to provoke the Social Purity advocates and that much of his fiction is in conscious reaction against them as he sought notoriety for his depictions of impurity.[76] Despite his concern for Social Purity of the Contagious Diseases Acts sort, Bloom thinks many impure thoughts during his day. He ponders the 'sweets of sin' as often as he does their penalty (it is Stephen who in *A Portrait* receives the wages of sin for a while). *The Sweets of Sin* is the novel Bloom buys for Molly, but he himself daydreams of living the arousing excerpt he reads (and that comes back to him during the day), either as the cuckolder (in the case of Martha Clifford) or cuckold (in the case of Molly). Bloom after all, out of empathy or prurience, lives others' lives and this includes the lives of characters in popular fiction. It is fitting that the first half of the Nausicaa episode (which got Joyce into hot water with the American authorities) is written in parody of popular romances for women (while the second half is in a soberer prose, approximating Bloom's post-ejaculation realism), even though the first half is conducted through the eyes and mind of Gerty MacDowell.

Gerty daydreams of herself as a heroine of the sort she has met in popular fiction for women, and the encouragement of extra-textual daydreaming was presumably a calculated effect of such fiction. Gerty has read Maria Susanna Cummins' *The Lamplighter* (1854) which sold 40,000 copies in a week and was reprinted as late as 1906. The name of the heroine of this novel, Gerty, would have stimulated Gerty MacDowell's daydreaming. Not only does Gerty recruit the bystanding Bloom (a foreign-looking figure) as hero of her daydream but Joyce chooses both to utter her thoughts (indirectly through third person narration) and describe her (also in the third person) in the emollient sentimental-romantic language of such fiction, contrasting sharply with the harsh contentious male language of the preceding Cyclops episode. Joyce has injected into the Nausicaa episode several staple elements of popular fiction. Gerty (already a fiction), like her fictional namesake, is (or daydreams she is) a girl abused but willing to be self-sacrificial (she is identified with the Virgin Mary in the episode), emulating the paramount female virtue in many popular novels. As victim heroine, she recalls her father's drunken violence and thinks how 'that vile concoction which has ruined so many hearths and homes had cast its shadow over her childhood days'.[77] Her thoughts (given to us by Joyce in the language of problem fiction) have been provoked by her hearing the litany of Our Lady of Loreto recited during the men's temperance retreat being conducted by a Jesuit missioner in a nearby Catholic church. Joyce is exploiting the Irish genre of the 'Temperance' story, so categorised by Stephen J. Brown in *Ireland in Fiction*. But he is also subverting it; not only is it ironically fitting that the hope of Ireland's being sober be couched in the language of degraded romantic wish-fulfilment, but Joyce fuses the mass with Gerty's profane day-dreams and Bloom's sexual arousal throughout the episode, sometimes even in the same sentence.

The language of low-end popular romance perseveres even after the sexual climax (conveyed in the notorious Roman candle passage) and after we appear to shift to Bloom's point of view, one shaped and primed by *The Sweets of Sin*. 'What a brute he had been! At it again? . . . An utter cad he had been. He of all men!'[78] The style changes decisively only when Gerty gets up and Bloom sees the reality of her lameness. But soon he imagines writing a story for *Titbits* about the scene, 'The Mystery Man on the Beach', which oddly is to see himself from Gerty's point of view, though typically on settling the title he thinks immediately of remuneration: 'Payment at the rate of one guinea per column';[79] all day he has fitfully thought of himself as a potential popular author.

But in the sheer diversity of his thoughts and their occasional impurity Bloom violates the genre of popular fiction that frequently he seems, unlike Stephen, to be at home in. Moreover, if Bloom is in many ways a Victorian figure, he is also alive to large changes and the emerging features of modernity; he thinks about 'the velocity of modern life' and the unexploited possibilities of 'the modern art of advertisement'; he is post-Victorian Man as well as Victorian Man, convinced, for example, of the futility of war and nationalism, as though he knew of the Great War (which had been waged before Joyce completed *Ulysses*).[80] The modernity of *Ulysses* itself, beyond the thoughts of its two main characters, is its revolutionary structural representation of the inadequacy and even obsolescence of partial views and uncomplicated verities, and this included the novel as it had been written by most novelists up until then. Above all, Joyce had to achieve multiplicity to represent that primary feature of the world: multiplicity of character, thought, feeling, event; multiplicity of prose styles and even genres; multiplicity of meaning in language (the novel is a feast of puns, repeated motifs, double entendres); multiplicity of points of view; multiplicity of problems and of solutions; multiplicity in virtual time, multiplicity in virtual space. Multiplicity, then – but also glimpses of unity and meaning; happily, Joyce was pedant enough to plant some of the big words that hint at what he is doing: *parallax*, *metempsychosis*, *omphalos*, *entelechy*.

There was a price to be paid in novelistic terms for this astonishing essay in encyclopedic presentation of the world, past and present. For all the interiority, the narrating voices refuse to relinquish control to the characters. Joyce often but not always is forced silently to detach character from speech (and the language of the character's rendered thoughts) in order to carry out a design he believed more important than any plausibility of character. For example, Bloom's speech in Cyclops is presumably meant to be 'his own' but not, or not always, in Eumaeus. This supersession of plausibility and primacy of character by architectural design that flouts realism and flags the artifice of the whole, is the Modernism of *Ulysses*. It carries the obvious danger that the character is but a mouthpiece for a narrative technique; for all Bloom's vividness, he is in the ordinary terms of the novel form, utterly implausible. What Bloom imparts to Stephen about the Jews and the Spanish Inquisition is in a tired but formal sophistication of language that cannot be that of the man we listened to in Barney Kiernan's pub. This is the design of *Ulysses* speaking, not Bloom (the plan calls for the episode to be told in 'narrative (old)'. The catechism technique of Ithaca requires Joyce to lend Bloom ideas and vocabulary entirely beyond his capacity, for example on the subject of the admirable qualities of water. Whereas Stephen is an educated and sophisticated man whom we tend to think of as Joyce himself, and therefore capable of framing any idea in the novel, Bloom is made to be himself but also Everyman and indeed a vehicle for Joyce's vast bookish learning as well as his brilliant insights into human nature. It is the severance of point of view from character and the schematic abandonment of *parole* that threatens the identity of *Ulysses* as a novel (while enhancing it as an encyclopedia and anatomy) and results in some mechanical stretches in one of the most stunning works of literature ever written.

Attempted realisms

The affirmative realism of Daniel Corkery (1878–1964) is often contrasted with Joyce's dissenting realism, but the Joyce of *Dubliners* has things in common with the author of the novel *The Threshold of Quiet* (1917) beyond the quietly observant eyesight of the realist. Like Joyce, Corkery knows best the lower middle class, though his clerks and commercial travellers are more upright than Joyce's idlers. Both writers are Catholic, one lapsed. One's Cork is even more provincial than the other's Dublin and like Joyce's city has seen better days: 'the way there used to be great sport and life in Cork City'.[81] Like Joyce's, Corkery's characters live in a kind of limbo, living lives of quiet desperation and languishing without resemblance to the heroes and dramatic incorrigibles of Revival literature. The death of Frank Bresnan brings to light the thwarted ambitions, bridled emotions, unfulfilled loves or unsatisfied wanderlusts of his surviving friends. Corkery shares with the author of *Dubliners* the paralysis of his characters, their privatised lives, the imagery of light and dark in which they stand at times as though in *tableaux vivants*.

Corkery's realism can occasionally melt into wistful reverie and even twilit epiphanies that do not resemble the striking visions of AE, Synge and Yeats. A defeated wish for personal and political autonomy surely lies back of the novel's world though the Irish Revival and militant nationalism are wholly out of sight and sound. It as if Corkery is absenting himself from the brilliance and centrality of Revival writing, which as a critic Corkery judged to be a disguised Ascendancy literature at best, at worst an exotic branch of English literature. He repudiated the Revival's claim to be a national literature because it was written by those he considered 'alien-minded'. His local realism, like Joyce's in *Dubliners*, took him into narrow crevices of Irish life where the Revivalist could not follow him. Munster was not just a province in which Corkery took local pride, but symbolically the real Ireland herself; one character in *The Threshold of Quiet* is 'so much a piece of Ireland in his genial quietness, in his lack of ambition'.[82] The repression suggested in this – and which is the undeclared dimension of the novel's theme – was righted by Corkery after the Revival when its implication of Catholic nationalism was made explicit in his influential and controversial work of criticism *Synge and Anglo-Irish Literature* (1931). Joyce shared Corkery's disbelief in Revival authenticity, but could not have followed the Cork writer into a literary nationalism; in aiming for a limitless perspective, Joyce worked by comprehension and absorption (the names and spirits of Wilde, AE and Yeats recur in *Ulysses*), not by exclusion.

The Gael (1919), which Corkery praised in his critical volume, is also an affirmative nationalist realism, the author of which, Edward E. Lysaght (later MacLysaght, 1887–1986), believed Ireland could be revived through a resuscitation of Gaelic culture. The Gael is Con O'Hickie, who is raised in England and returns in 1905 to the house of his ancestors, members of the Catholic gentry in Galway. He discovers Hyde's Gaelic League, Horace Plunkett's co-operative movement and D. P. Moran's Irish Ireland movement, and wishes to see a 'godly' industrialism monitored by a liberal Catholicism and lent its values by a revived pre-Conquest Gaelic social and legal code. He wants to see his country house spearhead a 'Gaelic-speaking co-operative commonwealth'; in this way Lysaght hijacked the country house novel for radical Ireland. But O'Hickie's ideal programme is interrupted by the Easter Rising, the guerrilla warfare against Britain and British reprisals. He who deplored armed insurrection and wanted like Father Ralph gradual evolution of social and political conditions, makes common cause with the physical-force philosophy (as did James Connolly) and the novel ends with him in gaol, his utopia indefinitely deferred. A Gaelic idealism subverts the realism of this interesting novel and makes unconvincing its explanation of O'Hickie's conversion to militant republicanism.

As a reader for Maunsel, Lysaght recommended for publication the first novel by Brinsley MacNamara (1890–1963). Like Corkery, the author of this novel made the Revival project seem problematic; whereas Corkery strove quietly for a literary revival more native to Catholic Ireland MacNamara (b. John Weldon), like Joyce, thought genuine revival out of the question in the part of Ireland he knew well. One inhabitant of the fictional valley of Tullahanogue that gave its name to *The Valley of the Squinting Windows* (1918) shows a volume of poems by Masefield to another character and says, 'no poet at all could imagine any tale of love and passion springing from the life about us here. The people of the valley seem to have died before they were born.'[83] MacNamara portrayed provincial reality so shockingly that he was driven from his native Westmeath and his novel publicly burned.[84] MacNamara's indomitable Irishry are an astounding throng of drunkards, liars, thieves, eavesdroppers and blackmailers and to depict them the author requires what he calls a 'sickening realism' that borders on surrealism. The selfishness of MacNamara's characters mocks the selfless philosophy (if not reality) of both the philanthropic culture of the popular novel and the selfless culture of the revivalist nationalists (from AE to Pearse). Reality is so offensive in MacNamara's village that we might call his method avenging realism; the feverish energy of the writing derives from a frustrated romantic nationalism.

Readers of MacNamara's first novel could persuade themselves that only the Midlands of Ireland was being savagely indicted. *The Irishman* (1920), published under the pseudonym of Oliver Blyth, swiftly removed that illusion, since this novel satirised Dublin's literary revival. In *The Clanking of Chains* (1920), MacNamara, having subverted the woolly notions of the Irish countryman and the Irish literary Revivalist, chose as victim the sturdy Irish patriot whose hypocritical idealism is belied by the 'dismal reality . . . the hopeless, dead, empty years which followed the death of Parnell';[85] in this respect, MacNamara's patriots resemble Joyce's in 'Ivy Day in the Committee Room'. MacNamara's hero Michael Dempsey, alongside Ulick Shannon, Moore's Oliver Gogarty and Ned Carmady, O'Donovan's Ralph O'Brien and Joyce's Stephen Dedalus and Gabriel Conroy, is the besieged and disabused hero of much twentieth-century Irish Catholic fiction, in retreat from hollow nationalist idealisms and the philistine and shoneen Irelands that gave such idealisms the lie. MacNamara's savage indignation swamps any hope he might cherish for a change of heart in Ireland. In response to the 'cruel realism' of life in Ballycullen, Dempsey goes into exile and knows that he will have to be 'a realist dealing only with facts in whatever country he might go to'.[86] MacNamara's realism is consolation for its own impossibility.

The fiction of three Irelands 1922–1940

Writing of the Free State

Liam O'Flaherty (1896–1984) was in some ways a child of the Revival: he wrote about the west of Ireland (including the Aran islands, where he was born), and was, in Revival terms, a peasant. But like MacNamara, he is a writer of vindictive realism, of savage naturalism. Reaching for the same metaphor as Joyce, he insisted: 'In my work I have been forced in honesty to hold a mirror to life as I found it in my country.'[87] If unlike MacNamara he is also a writer of overcharged romantic transcendence, this makes of him a prodigal son of the Revival. There is, of course, a great deal of quiet observation of country life in O'Flaherty's short stories. But the insight into animals can lapse into anthropomorphism and pathetic fallacy which return to vitiate his observation in the forms of suicidal cows, cannibalistic cormorants and arrogant blackbirds.

If in the stories animals are given the virtues and vices of men, in his novels men are given the virtues and vices of animals. In O'Flaherty, Nature and human nature alike can go to the bad, as they do in *The Black Soul* (1924). Nature's indifference poses as great a threat to life as the 'civilisation' that has spawned the Great War, the slum and the nationalist struggle. It is possible to read *The Black Soul* (set on Inverara, a fictional Aran island), like that other island novel *Skerrett* (1932), as a bitter parody of Revival island-worship. But the realist reaction against Revival romanticism is so excessive as to become its own wayward romanticism. If Nature and those close to Nature can go to the bad so can those cut off from Nature, be they rural exiles like Gypo Nolan in *The Informer* (1925) and McDara in *The Assassin* (1928) or urban exiles such as the Stranger in *The Black Soul*. Then there are those imprisoned in Dublin's slum district, 'that foetid morass on the north bank of the Liffey'.[88] His fanatics, revolutionaries and informers symbolise a broken and imbalanced world, yet appear elemental, mythic, would-be tragic heroes – Gypo Nolan is Laocoon, an Ethiopian god, Manannán; but in O'Flaherty's zoomorphic vision Nolan returns to Katie Fox's (sic) like an animal returning to its lair; more extravagantly he is the Minotaur slain by Gallagher's Theseus. The influence of D. H. Lawrence rather than the Revival is unmistakable,[89] though nowhere is there Lawrence's view of the ideal selfhood and society; but if O'Flaherty is artistically inferior, he at least inherited a mythopoeia that Lawrence had to contrive at great pains.

Critics have noted resemblances between O'Flaherty and the Donegal novelist Peadar O'Donnell (1893–1986), as unblinking rural naturalists and disabused laureates of the rugged west coast. It was O'Flaherty who encouraged his English publisher to publish O'Donnell's *Adrigoole* (1929).[90] As this novel and *The Knife* (1930) show, O'Donnell was the more politicised of the two: he was a socialist and also a propagandist for the IRA and served time in a Free State prison for his activities. But he shared O'Flaherty's intimacy with peasantry and poverty. Indeed, the documentary likeness between O'Donnell's novel *Islanders* (1927) and the now classic 'peasant' autobiography by the Blasket islander Tomás O'Crohan, *The Islandman* (published in Irish in 1929 and in English in 1934), is striking. However, the themes of rural decline and individual dissatisfaction with island life are foreground in O'Donnell's novel where they are potential foreground only in O'Crohan's majestic proto-novel.

In the 1940s O'Donnell took over editorship of the influential journal *The Bell* from the Cork writer Sean O'Faolain. O'Faolain (b. John Whelan, 1900–1991) chose to see the Irish as Celts who were forever seeking a synthesis 'between dream and reality, aspiration and experience, a shrewd knowledge of the world and a strange reluctance to cope with it' and failing to find a synthesis in favour of a perpetual oscillation.[91] This would seem to fit O'Flaherty if not O'Donnell, but O'Faolain was purporting to explain the general absence in Ireland of realistic fiction. He claimed in 1947 that only eight realistic Irish novels had been written since 1900: The *Lake* (1905) and *Muslin* (1915) by Moore; *A Portrait of the Artist* (1916) and *Ulysses* (1922) by Joyce; *The Loughsiders* (1924) by Shan F. Bullock; *The Informer* (1925) by Liam O'Flaherty; *Adrigoole* (1929) by O'Donnell; *The Last September* (1929) by Elizabeth Bowen.[92] This was clearly to ignore novels by Irish writers set outside Ireland, as were some of Moore's, Bullock's and Bowen's. Bullock's *Robert Thorne: The Story of a London Clerk* (1907), for example, is an interesting sortie into Edwardian realism. Broaden the Irish canon and the realist novel is not the *rara avis* it has seemed.

Yet Catholic novelists remaining in the Irish Free State (1922–1949) indeed faced formidable obstacles, the Revival's hostility to realist prose being followed by the hostility of the new state.[93] A civil war, a powerful and unsophisticated Catholic church, an understandable official chauvinism and isolationism, censorship by both church and state, a new 'flight of the earls' (i.e. of the gentry,

Catholic and Protestant), leaving in prominence an uncultivated petty bourgeoisie – these represented a deadening rather than enlivening adversity.[94] The Cork writer Frank O'Connor (b. Michael O'Donovan, 1903–66) referred to 'a new Establishment of Church and State in which imagination would play no part, and young men and women would emigrate to the ends of the earth, not because the country was poor, but because it was mediocre'.[95] In 1936 O'Faolain published 'A Broken World', a short story that saw Ireland with the passing of the gentry as an incomplete society, a train carriage from which the story's 'three bits of separateness' – priest, farmer and writer – are 'flung off . . . like bits of the *disjecta membra* of the wheel of life'.[96] Around the same time, O'Connor similarly claimed that 'the forces that had made for national dignity, that had united Catholic and Protestant, aristocrats like Constance Markiewicz, Labour revolutionists like Connolly and writers like AE, began to disintegrate rapidly, and Ireland became more than ever sectarian, utilitarian (the two nearly always go together), vulgar and provincial'.[97]

Also in 1936 O'Faolain published his novel *Bird Alone* (promptly banned by the Irish Censorship Board), written as though to fill the prescription its author had made out for the Irish writer: in the impossibility of realism, he must turn inward; 'for there alone in his own dark cave of self can he hope to find certainty of reality'.[98] This was a significant contribution to the notion of the besieged Irish self (the figurative 'only child', to borrow O'Connor) that since Joyce and his contemporaries has dominated canonical Irish novels. O'Faolain and O'Connor both thought that the dismal state of Irish society encouraged the short story writer but discouraged the novelist.[99] This was to overlook many Irish novels and overestimate the importance of social integrity to the success of a novel; it was paradoxical therefore for O'Faolain to write the novel *Bird Alone* to demonstrate thematically his thesis. On one level it succeeds in depicting the pathology of Free State society which originated in the divisions and setbacks following the downfall of Parnell. *Bird Alone* is set in a darkness relieved only by tantalising lights of decaying possibility and the mocking daylight of ordinariness and disappointment. This imagery (its dim origins possibly in Catholic liturgy), along with that of windows, derives from *Dubliners* and can be found in O'Connor's *Dutch Interior* (1940) and later novels by John McGahern and Edna O'Brien. After the clamorous and divisive politics of Parnellite Ireland had disturbed his childhood, Corney Crone decides not to leave 'the darkness of self' or 'the cave of loneliness'; he decidedly will *not* go forth to forge the conscience of the race. But *Bird Alone* is also in part a saga of a disintegrating family which is the stuff of long fiction even as it seeks to prove O'Faolain's point; Ireland, especially Cork, from around 1886 until around 1933 is realistically drawn. In a specific but telling paradox, the more O'Faolain wishes to tell us about Ireland, here and in his stories, the more subjective he becomes. 'But that is the misfortune of my nature,' says Crone, 'that all things end by becoming me until, now, nothing exists that is not me'.[100] On this level *Bird Alone* functions as a kind of epitaph for the Irish novel as O'Faolain conceived it.

Corney Crone becomes at the end of *Bird Alone* 'what they call, in Cork, a *character*', while it could be said of *Dutch Interior* (banned by the Irish Censorship Board) that its theme is character, defined in the novel by Peter Devane as 'personality gone to seed . . . When 'tis all shaped and limited by circumstances, and there isn't a kick left in it.'[101] This definition could apply to many of Joyce's Dubliners but somehow the Irish forces of oppression got more intimate and more officially pervasive once De Valera's Ireland took hold; MacNamara's Ireland became, as it were, constitutional; aspects of Catholic Irish life that had once been boltholes or saving graces under the dispensation of British Ireland were now hostile to native self-realisation. *Dutch Interior* is about furniture and people who have the passive repose of furniture; it is about rooms and stairways, about windows and doorways, about streets, lanes and roads, and light and shade. Objects and spaces are arranged and lighted in a series of painterly, sculptural and architectural tableaux. Characters and surroundings are caught in the paralysed gestures of portraiture: they are equal components in a curious poetics of space. On almost every page, shape and lighting define the hopelessness of life in O'Connor's Ireland for his two heroes, Peter Devane and Stevie Dalton. Deadening forces of family, religion and nationalism bear in upon the sensitive self and the novel creates interlocking spaces of captivity.

The first part of *Dutch Interior* seems to be set in the years before the Troubles (1916–23) and the second part some time in the 1930s. Rebellion, the break with Britain and the Civil War (not to speak of the Great War) all take place during the novel's time-span but only in the silent corridor of time between the novel's two parts, for they are never mentioned. They do not need to be, for paralysis and unfulfilment have survived the Troubles intact. There are possibilities only for those who, like the returned American Gus Devane, are at home with the inward-looking patriotism and political opportunism of post-revolutionary Ireland. The others are caught in slow and barren decay in which only gestures towards real life are possible. It is arguable that like *Bird Alone*, *Dutch Interior* creates its spaces too intimately for it to be a realist novel. Yet both novels are at pains to demonstrate why self-fulfilment is not possible in post-1916 Ireland. They are cases of 'meta-realism', representations of what prevents their own realisation.

The European settings and mobile heroes of the novels of Francis Stuart (1902–2000) are very different from the sedentary figures and captive spaces of *Dutch Interior*. As well as having been born in Australia and educated in England, he was of Ulster Protestant stock and lived for long years in Europe. In his early novels he offers his characters choices of ideals and ways of life that ought to be liberating but are in fact urgent and bewildering. Nevertheless, Stuart delights in celebrating the practical, unintellectual sides of life: car-racing, horse-racing, gambling, poultry-farming. Viewed as a reaction against the Revival that he saw as a young, privileged, yet detached insider (he married Maud Gonne's daughter, Iseult), Stuart's realism is deflationary. Yet, like O'Flaherty, he is after larger and more various game, though O'Faolain's broken Irish world is backdrop in his novels. The church, mysticism, nature, the city, love, sex, Ireland, Europe: all issue their summons and form a spectrum of possibility the poles of which are in the title, *Women and God* (1931). Stuart's married and entangled couples are, like Lawrence's, survivors of social and psychic upheavals and the consoling idea of the commune fitfully attracts them. They are vanguards of 'the modern spirit', as one character calls it in *Women and God*: 'They are afraid of having to come to some conclusion about everything. They know it would be such an awful one.'[102]

The 'Ladies' Road'

The cultural malaise of the Free State appeared to affect male Catholic writers more than it did female Catholic writers, perhaps because for one reason or another male writers took internal Irish politics and culture more to heart than their female colleagues. Moreover, the apparent lack of fuss with which women writers left Ireland emulated that of their female predecessors; *exile* as a post-Joycean or post-1922 theme and course of action would be melodramatic if applied in their cases, so some other cultural explanation should be sought for the fact that Elizabeth Bowen, Pamela Hinkson, Kate O'Brien, Helen Waddell, Constance Malleson and Margaret Barrington all lived in England for lengthy periods (O'Brien lived also in Spain and Hinkson in Germany; Kathleen Coyle lived in Paris before leaving for the United States). Perhaps they were at ease in the old pre-1922 dispensation; their fiction is not of the Free State but of another Ireland, part Anglo-Irish, part English, part upper-middle-class (or even upper-class) expatriate. This generation of Irish women novelists (born between 1886 and 1904, their first novels appearing with one exception between 1923 and 1933) disproved the O'Connor-O'Faolain thesis that contemporary Irish society could not produce novels in the English manner. However, they wrote the kind of novel that Modernism and Irish nationalism had induced critics to neglect. Whereas the Irish novel of the period is often talked about as having a fractured history, these female novelists maintain continuity in style and theme with their predecessors. On the whole, they depict a social world more elevated than their male counterparts and several of them, moreover, have an international perspective through education and travel rather than the agenda of exile. Perhaps they inherited a traditional subtlety for the intricacies of social relationship (Jane Austen rather than Joyce or Moore is their ancestor) and if this reflects the marginal political role women have traditionally played in Ireland, it also permits a social objectivity missing in so much male Irish fiction.

Several of them contribute to the country house novel; Bowen and Malleson knew the country house from the inside, as did D. G. Waring and M. J. Farrell (Molly Keane). The Irish country house was always a convenient venue in which to write variations on the themes of love and marriage and to examine English and Irish cultural differences, often via the plot-formula of the visitor-to-Ireland. Certainly war sharpened those differences and lent them a political colouring. If Ireland was pulled between loyalty to England and to herself, then the Great War increased the tension, and Sinn Féin activity during the war even more, and that tension was felt particularly in the country houses: plot conflict was ready at hand. The sons of those houses may have felt no compunction in fighting for England but they still regarded themselves as Irishmen, and the other Ireland was on the fringes of the demesne or even inside it and so tension was increased by the proximity of hostility.

Behind the screen of trees around their demesne, the Anglo-Irish in the stories of Elizabeth Bowen (1899–1973) feel safe from the vulgar drama being played out in Ireland, but they are a community in denial, distracted, in part by their own obsession with right behaviour, and increasingly vulnerable to the emboldened native Irish. Bowen's characters, remnants of the Protestant Nation, live in a maroon world 'the colour of valediction'[103] and when the danger intrudes upon them, they turn bleakly but gracefully to face the consequences. *The Last September* (1929) gives us life at Danielstown, a country house in County Cork whose days are numbered during the 'war of independence'. It is 1920 and only a few sense danger or the incongruity of dances while British soldiers are ambushed and neighbouring Big Houses are put to the torch. Only the young nephew and niece of Sir Richard and Lady Naylor are aware of a central emptiness and an irrelevance to the 'violent realness' beyond the demesne. Lois Farquar and Lawrence a have 'a sense of detention, of a prologue being played out too lengthily, with unnecessary stresses, a wasteful attention to detail',[104] and this could be said of the doomed life at

Danielstown. The IRA, a shadowy reality throughout the novel, fire Danielstown in February 1921, the door of which, while the 'executioners' depart, 'stood open hospitably upon a furnace'.

The adverb has been carefully chosen, reminding us, beyond the cruel irony, of 'the social idea' embodied in the country house. Bowen thought that ideally the country house enabled its inhabitants and visitors to escape from egotism, instability and greed into impersonality and the 'steady behaviour' she saw etched into every line of her own ancestral home.[105] Yet it was Bowen's belief too that from a broader perspective the lives of the Anglo-Irish, 'like those of only children, are singular, independent and secretive'.[106] This is Lois Farquar's profile and the implication is that she represents the last and lost childhood of the Ascendancy and when she leaves for Europe she enacts the small diaspora that accompanied the passing of that childhood. That young Easter Chevington in *Mad Puppetstown* (1931) by M. J. Farrell (born Molly Keane; 1904–96) is an only child and is, moreover, motherless entirely fits the genre of the country house novel set during the Great War and Irish Troubles. Set in county 'Westcommon' between 1908 and the early years of the Free State, it offers for its first eighty pages Easter's idyllic childhood years in a family devoted to horse-riding and fox-hunting; these girlhood years re-create symbolically the heyday of the Ascendancy. Then 'the Great War in Europe and the little bitter, forgotten war in Ireland' obtrude.[107] Easter's family decamps to England when the Troubles hot up and only Aunt Dicksie's refusal to leave Puppetstown prevents it from going the fiery way of many country houses. When young Easter, more Irish than English and heir to the house, returns at her age of majority in 1921 with Basil her cousin to claim Puppetstown, times have changed. The efforts of Easter and Basil to restore life to the house, despite the contempt of the newly empowered native Irish, is a disguised form of accommodation to the new dispensation. Easter and Basil, who love each other only as kin, need not wed as long as Aunt Dicksie is alive, so it is an uncertain future they (like their class) have: temporary, reduced and doubtless infertile but happy in its individual homecoming and triumph of the spirit.[108]

The Ladies' Road (1932) by Pamela Hinkson (1900–82), daughter of Katharine Tynan, ends like *The Last September* with the burning of a country house that had always been surrounded by the mysterious, protective and in the end dangerous woods – 'That night Cappagh lit a torch for the countryside'.[109] Together, the Troubles and the Great War bring the decline of the country house to a climactic end. This is one of the larger themes of the novel, another being the remoteness of the world 'before the War', a world remembered for us in the novel chiefly by young Stella Mannering from England who recalls Cappagh, where she spent her childhood summers, as set in a magical land of uncertainty and adventure (rather too adventurous by novel's end). The artistic equal of *The Last September*, Hinkson's is the best novel about the effects of the Great War at home in Ireland and one of the best Irish novels of its day. The insulation of the characters' lives, the emotional reticence of their class, the subjective blurring of sharp distinctions between the recent and the more distant past in the memories of the characters – these are fused with that pathos and sentimentality that the Great War sanctioned and the highly politicised Troubles were reluctant to. Finally, the pathos in both *The Last September* and *The Ladies' Road* is the irrelevance of the attitudes of the Big House inhabitants to their tenants, to Ireland, to politics; history was overtaking them and they were powerless. An elegiac note, the sense of an ending, sounds through many of the novels by these women writers.

The Ladies' Road explores the suffering of women too attentive to others, and of those who are forced to wait too long for the return of a loved one, causing loyalty to warp love and love to fall victim to estrangement. (Both of Stella's brothers are killed in the War.) It explores too the way war sponsors at home a kind of self-absorption and an exclusiveness of grief: there are innumerable descriptions of characters feeling shut out or standing in doorways looking in. Among the roads that thread their way through the novel the most important is the imaginary, hardly consoling 'Ladies' Road' of the title down which Stella might yet go, retracing her brother David's steps into France and the nameless villages he passed through and the nameless wood where he lay since May 1918.

Because the inhabitants of the country house primarily constituted a caste rather than a religious minority, deep cultural and political changes that threatened the Protestant inhabitants threatened likewise Catholic inhabitants, as the superb novels of the Limerick writer Kate O'Brien (1897–1974) demonstrate. The malaise of the Mulqueens of *The Anteroom* (1934) hardly differs from what afflicts the Ascendancy. Like other country house novels, O'Brien's exploit the immense convenience of having various characters under one roof with the story pleasingly punctuated by arrivals and departures. The highest common thematic factor of the tradition remained love. Expatriation may in O'Brien's novels solve some problems but not the abiding problem of love, as O'Brien's *The Land of Spices* (1941) shows. This is a rich, meditative novel of two women's flight from love, warmth and emotional attachment into *la pudeur et la politesse* of religious vocation. Life in the Belgian convent is meticulously rendered, and though it is a kind of illusory retreat from Irish and European upheavals of O'Brien's girlhood (Home Rule agitation, the Gaelic revival, the suffragette movement, European nationalism and an imminent Great War), it also permits the growth into womanhood of Anna and Helen, both intellectually inclined and both psychologically wounded by early emotional experiences.

War and woman's love: these are the supreme realities in O'Brien's novels. But the latter surprisingly invites, as in Bowen and Hinkson, compunction, detachment, loneliness. This is due in part to the 'chauvinism' of the ineffectual men, whose patronising attentions O'Brien's women have to endure, as the unmarried Agnes must in *The Anteroom*. Incomplete women by the standards of love, Agnes and the other heroines nevertheless are fuller human beings, and inhabit a real and honest world from which the would-be lovers recoil. Agnes finally rejects the love of her brother-in-law Vincent, not because he wishes merely to avoid the reality of his marriage, or even because of her Catholic conscience, but because of her sisterly devotion. Rejected, Vincent turns a shotgun on himself, one of the uncommon instances of suicide in an Irish Catholic novel. There is infatuation in O'Brien's novels, but lasting passion is impossible because of 'the fatuous egotism of love . . . the final impenetrability of one mind by another'.[110]

In the fiction of Bowen and O'Brien, expectations in love have risen unfulfillably as the society that once kept them in check has collapsed. Moreover, to the extent that they accept a final subjectivity, these women novelists are realists in a special sense, making necessity into some kind of virtue, turning anteroom into living-room. In *My Cousin Justin* (1939) by Margaret Barrington (1896–1982), the familiar theme of the collapse of society around the inhabitants of the country house is offered with an equally familiar obliqueness deriving from the female apolitical point of view, in this case that of Loulie (Anne-Louise Delahaie), the novel's narrator. She is brought up in her grandfather's Donegal house with her aunt and cousin Justin Thorauld (the 'orphan' perspective to match the 'only child' perspective). The Thoraulds (of continental extraction) made their money from linen in the Lagan Valley, in which the second part is set (during the activities of the Ulster Volunteer Force), before the novel returns after the grandfather's death to the neglected big house, Loulie and Justin reclaiming it after the civil war but in a state of emotional isolation and siege. In the first part of the novel about the childhood of Justin and Loulie, Justin is a proud, unmoored boy whose life seems already inscribed with tragedy or unfulfilment. His solo war with the local Catholic boys is repaid when his chief opponent, who like Justin goes off in time to the Great War, becomes an IRA activist who arranges the murder of a British officer and his girlfriend, Justin's estranged English wife. Loulie, who has fallen for Justin's enemy and marries him, is abandoned by her husband and she and Justin come together again by default. Whereas she tries to adapt to changed personal and social circumstances, Justin is a proud realist and tells her that the Irish will not allow their kind to put their shoulder to the wheel of the new Free State. The love of Loulie and Justin exists midway between cousinage and desire and implies the withdrawal, infertility and endurance of the Anglo-Irish after the series of blows to their esteem and position delivered by the Land Acts, Great War, War of Independence, creation of the Free State, and Civil War; in their state of siege they suggest faintly a Faulknerian neo-gothic isolation.

Fiction from Northern Ireland

There were eminent Northern Irish novelists writing after 1922 and even into the 1930s who had made their names before partition, including Shan Bullock, Forrest Reid and St John Ervine. But the generation of Ulster fiction writers who came of literary age in the 1930s, with only an abbreviated memory of pre-partition Ireland, were mainly women. These were later neglected by Irish critics on grounds of their being female, Northern Irish and (most of them) internationalist like their southern counterparts.

The title heroine of *Liv* (1929) by Derry-born Kathleen Coyle (1886–1952) is a young, restless woman who leaves her Norwegian village and her fiancé and travels to Paris, where she fetches up among a community of bohemian artists. There she finds 'Love' with Per Malom, a half-Norwegian, half-Spanish painter against whom Liv is warned and for whom she falls like all the other women who have met him. Their love is true but he is married, and answering a drive as unignorable as that which brought her through the mountains, Liv returns to Norway. Her aunt Sonja tells her they are 'the daughters of Ibsen' but also 'the daughters of the Vikings', restless when young but drawn back to the white country: 'Here we . . . we preserve our pride. When we go south, into warmer lands, we lose something of ourselves.'[111] Rebecca West, who predicted Coyle's emergence as 'an extremely distinguished writer', praised Coyle's earlier novels but thought they displayed a shadowy quality that *Liv* escaped, yet the startling brightness of the Norwegian landscape in *Liv* is still overshadowed by the emotional interiority of Coyle's heroines that is her hallmark as a novelist, though West may have wished it otherwise.[112]

That interiority we see again in *A Flock of Birds* (1930) in which the Ladies' Road is travelled single-mindedly by Catherine Munster, the widowed mother of a boy condemned to death for murder during an IRA ambush. The Munsters are wealthy and travelled Protestants who live outside Dublin in a country house called Gorabbey, and the novel registers the collision between the

Protestant wealthy and two realities, the Great War and the Catholic populace mobilising for freedom. However, the collision is muffled almost beyond our hearing by the Nietzsche-reading Catherine's intense introspections; the gaoling and sentencing of Christy is the occasion for Munster's painful examination of her life, the emotional meanings of motherhood, marriage, love, the profound differences between men and women. Coyle achieves deep, almost Woolfian interiority without stylistic innovation beyond a distinctive obliquity of presentation.

The novel explores psychologically Pearse's contention that ''tis women that keep all the great vigils' and tries to reconcile it with Joyce's contention, quoted by Catherine's Europeanised daughter, Kathleen, that Ireland is a sow that eats its own farrow, Christy being one of its farrow in this case. Catherine is a rival of her daughter and Christy's fiancée for her son's affections. But she is also a self-sacrificial woman who belongs 'to that communion of mothers who have given their sons; whose sons have been taken'; she discovers that what she feels for her son is 'something greater than love'.[113] It is as if Cathleen Ni Houlihan were subjected to genuine psychological scrutiny. Her son's doom is a catalyst for her own pilgrimage to the grace that lies the far side of love. Despite the rather heavy-handedness by which Christy Munster is Christ and Catherine is Mary, *A Flock of Birds* is a fine achievement in emotional realism that only occasionally cloys. The chief success of the novel lies in Coyle's depiction of the tense courteous maintenance of outward composure by Catherine – related to her social class – behind which is her internal turmoil.

(Lady) Constance Malleson (1895–1975) remains entirely overlooked as an Irish artist, though she was of the well-known Annesley family of Castlewellan House in County Down; she described her girlhood there in her autobiography, *After Ten Years* (1931), and mentions her family's involvement in the unionist cause during the gunrunning days of the final Home Rule crisis. She was, however, famous in Britain as the actress Colette O'Niel (sic) and was friend and mistress of Bertrand Russell and was active in Labour party politics and conscientious objection during the Great War.[114] In Malleson's hands, it is as though the country house genre has gone feral. The advanced crowd ('our lot') – intellectual bohemians and on the whole, a wealthy set – makes up the cast of *The Coming Back* (1933), set in Cambridge, Devonshire, London and Dublin and which depicts the emotional life of Konradin Waring, an Irish-Finnish would-be novelist. From the beginning she wishes for passionate love with freedom, for intensity without marriage. The time of the novel is unclear and presumably it is just after the Great War but there is a very 1930s' *fin du globe* assumption at work that supports no political discussion in the novel; it is as if the multiple political positions of the 1920s and 1930s have been transposed into emotional positions, with Waring's freedom representing political egalitarianism but never spelled out beyond a vague idealism.

In *Fear in the Heart* (1936), Auriel, Lady Mallory becomes involved with Hilary Barnes, a married artist, and discovers fearlessness again. Hilary and Auriel are in search of an ideal love with freedom and Hilary early associates her with Heloise, while her surname Mallory combines that of the novelist with that of the author of *Morte d'Arthur*. Auriel lends Hilary the story of Abelard and Heloise. 'He looked at the spine of the book to read the lettering. *Peter Abelard. A Novel. Helen Waddell. Constable.*' She sees herself as Waddell's heroine and quotes: 'I would rather be called your harlot than be empress of Christendom', echoing Heloise.[115] The popular and superbly written *Peter Abelard* (1933) by the Tokyo-born Belfast writer Waddell (1889–1965) followed her brief scholarly ruminations on Abelard in *The Wandering Scholars* (1927), a work of prose brilliance. She called Abelard 'the scholar for scholarship's sake . . . one of the makers of life, and perhaps the most powerful, in twelfth-century Europe' and declared that 'His personality, no less than his claim for reason against authority, was an enfranchisement of the human mind.'[116] This dimension of Abelard provides one strand of the novel: the conflicts between the mundane and the cloistered, between heresy and dogma, reason and faith, authority and individuality. The other dimension, Abelard's capacity for a fateful passion and the lyric gift his passion wrung from him, must have appealed to the hidden romantic novelist in Waddell; the 37-year-old Abelard neglected scholarship 'for a windflower of seventeen growing in the shadow of Notre Dame'. By the time the story had played itself out, 'Their love had been a street-song in Paris; the outrageous vengeance of the girl's uncle on her love and tardily made husband had been a blazoned scandal.'[117] The terrible revenge of castration by Fulbert, Heloise's uncle, and the later years of Heloise and Abelard, are *sui generis* yet *Peter Abelard* takes its place among those novels by Irish women whose concern is love and marriage and what Heloise calls 'this spider's web of woman's life, with its small panic fears and caution and obsequiousness' and whose heroines are sometimes those who fly above these nets, on principle in the New Woman novels, through character in other novels.

Two markedly different Northern Irish novelists (and markedly different from each other) published novels during the 1930s. D. G. Waring (1891?–1977) published at least eleven novels between 1936 and 1942. One of the better is *Fortune Must Follow* (1937) which concerns life and affairs at two country houses in Northern Ireland during the political thirties and involving a Northern

Irish ex-British spy who, his cover having been blown, returns from Germany to Ulster and there becomes involved in cracking a cross-border smuggling ring. The novel is politically unstable (perhaps like the thirties themselves, including thirties Northern Ireland), but Waring shakes down as a Kipling admirer and a sympathiser with early National Socialist aims, in short as a kind of internationalised upper-class Ulster unionist.

If Waring is happiest with large-scale background developments, Olga Fielden (1903?–?) in *Island Story* (1933) and *Stress* (1936) writes in the airless dimension of foreground and dispenses with subplots, the better to subject her characters to her full narrative glare. Fielden is a rural naturalist sharing nothing with the country house novelists; her Irish affines are MacNamara and O'Flaherty, but her more immediate Ulster kin in fiction are M. Hamilton (Mary Churchill Luck), author of the sombre *Across an Ulster Bog* (1896), and the later novels of Sam Hanna Bell, Anthony G. West and Maurice Leitch. But Fielden has an unflinching narrative address all her own, though *Island Story*, which concerns struggles to the death among members of a family on an Ulster island, has some of the power of the early scenes in Lawrence's *Sons and Lovers* and the narrative is tense with sexual and physical hostility. The story opens in 1921 and proceeds after an extended flashback to the years between 1885 and the novel's present. Easter 1916, the Irish War of Independence and partition are remote from the lives of Fielden's semi-primitives, though they sometimes get as far as the railway stations of Belfast. Even the Great War is an irrelevance. Not so in *Stress*, for in this novel Fielden chose as major characters those on the same island who came to maturity just after the Great War and were a lost generation. The title is apt: Fielden's world is full of personal rather than social *Sturm und Drang*. As in *Island Story*, violence, degeneration, animal desires and greed battle with the gentler aspirations to refinement, cultivation, decency.

New directions

The health of the Irish novel at the end of the 1930s was obscured by its critically challenging diversity. 1938 saw the publication of *Castle Corner* by Joyce Cary, *The Green Fool* by Patrick Kavanagh, *Murphy* by Samuel Beckett, *Antidote to Venom* by Freeman Wills Crofts, *Julie* by Francis Stuart, *Death of the Heart* by Elizabeth Bowen, *Out of the Silent Planet* by C. S. Lewis and *Pray for a Wanderer* by Kate O'Brien. Despite his birth and early education in Belfast, Lewis (1898–1963) is overlooked as an Irish writer. *Out of the Silent Planet* owes an acknowledged debt to Wells's scientific romances (like *A Plunge into Space* by Cromie, it involves an expedition to Mars) and to *Gulliver's Travels* in its allegorical dimension and mild misanthropy, while in its combination of adventure and scholarship it has affinities with the work of Lewis's friend J. R. R. Tolkien.[118] 1939 saw *Finnegans Wake* by Joyce, *Call My Brother Back* by Michael McLaverty, *At Swim-Two-Birds* by Flann O'Brien, *Fatal Venture* by Crofts, *My Cousin Justin* by Margaret Barrington and *The Great Squire* by Stuart. Crofts (1879–1957) joined Bodkin and Conyers as an Irish detective writer, and was thought by many to be the best living practitioner of the genre. He published *The Cask* in 1920 and was prolific thereafter (at least a dozen novels appeared in the 1930s, heyday decade both of Crofts and the genre), establishing his reputation through his invention, Inspector French. At least two of Crofts's novels were translated into Irish.[119]

Of the works published at the close of the decade, it was those by Beckett and Flann O'Brien that seemed to be taking the novel – not just the Irish novel – in a new direction, and at the time largely unapplauded save by the literary avant-garde in Paris and London. With *Finnegans Wake* Joyce seemed to have settled for himself the matter of the genre by recreating, renovating and ransacking it out of all recognition, publishing a masterpiece that signalled not a direction but a terminus that most writers and critics avoided by returning to the main line of fictional development. The writers influenced by Joyce, including Beckett and O'Brien, were influenced by *Ulysses* rather than the master's last work.

Where Beckett (1906–1989) was concerned, it was a case of emulation by inversion of the Joycean method. In *Murphy* (1938), a lugubrious philosophical tragicomedy, we find Joyce's love of the abstruse, Joyce's cultivation of interiority and Joyce's text-consciousness, but in reduced or specialised forms. Amongst the obscure words that pock-mark the text, there is a predominance of physiological-anatomical and psychological argot. The salience of these words is a form of mock-erudition (Joyce did not appear to mock erudition), but as in the case of Joyce, the erudition works against the expectations of the novel reader. Beckett's words play their part, of course, in both the self-consciousness of the text and what we might strive to regard as a 'theme' of *Murphy* – the notion of life as a pathological condition: '"I greatly fear," said Wylie, "that the syndrome known as life is too diffuse to admit of palliation. For every symptom that is eased, another is made worse."' His friend Neary comes to see the wisdom of this.[120] This idea, pursued through plays and novels after *Murphy*, supported the popular idea of Beckett as an incurable pessimist.

Whatever the disease it is a form of wasting, and whereas Joyce's abstruseness, interiority and textual self-referentiality amplify his fiction, in Beckett we see a process of reduction in theme and form that was to continue throughout his canon. The reluctant employee Murphy finds work in a London mental hospital in which he witnesses – and rejoices in – varieties of mental and physical degeneration and progressive circumscription. Murphy, after all, is on a quest to find 'the Belacqua bliss'. His 'Belacqua fantasy' is of an 'embryonal repose', a limbo devoid of desire, a Dantean Antepurgatory for which he rehearses by withdrawing as much as possible from the world (including its labour, he being a 'chronic emeritus'), whose goods he has reduced to a rocking chair on which he, a 'seedy solipsist', binds himself naked, a position in which he opens and closes the novel, at first unhappily alive though imagining himself free (but at least doing his own restraining and rocking to his chosen rhythm), and then dead, free at last.[121] Murphy's is not O'Faolain's and O'Connor's cave of self, to which Irish society drives their heroes, but a reduction of self ('whom he hated') as well as a withdrawal from society, to which mere existence drives him. Murphy has an equal disdain for the world ('a colossal fiasco') and the self that is obliged to inhabit it; indeed, the world itself is bound, the sun having no alternative but to shine, the moon compelled to set, the leaves complaining and the pond panicking.[122]

This anthropomorphism we find in plenty in Flann O'Brien and it has the effect of parodying and neutralising Romantic attitudes to and depictions of nature, which in the hands of these writers becomes a variety of stage properties to be arranged at will by the authors. Yet O'Brien and Beckett, like Joyce (and to a lesser degree Wilde), can be sensed chafing even under the freedom of manipulation, as though impatient with the finite stock of props associated with fiction, indeed literature. These Irish writers exhibit a surplus of energy and imagination that causes them to have the appearance of condescending to their own work, let alone that of others. 'Manipulation' is the advised word, for the impersonalised narrator of *Murphy* admits (or boasts) that all the characters in the book are 'puppets', all save Murphy.[123] Just as Murphy rejects the notion that those who are deemed to have been 'cut off' from life – hence their mental disorder – should be reconnected with the world, so Beckett implicitly rejects the notion that fiction should be obviously and organically connected to the world; his fiction is a more mechanical affair.

There is of course the skeleton of a realistic plot in *Murphy*. The novel is set in September and October 1935. Murphy has travelled from Cork to London in flight from the self of which he is tired, meets an Irish prostitute, Celia Kelly, who wants him to find work, support her and make an honest woman out of her; they set up house together and he does find work in the mental hospital, but leaves one night, divests himself and returns to his rocking chair to die.

He has been sought by Neary, his Cork mentor, and Miss Counihan, who loves Murphy, and who, with Neary's friend Wylie (Miss Counihan's second suitor after Neary) and a private eye-cum-minder (Cooper), travel to Dublin and then London in pursuit of him, because Miss Counihan will countenance Neary's suit only when evidence is found that Murphy has not been preparing for marriage with her but is dead. On this second quest, the material quest that balances Murphy's philosophical quest, Neary substitutes as his goal friendship with Murphy for marriage with Miss Counihan. Both quests are successful but to no avail, success and failure being identical in the novel. In any case, the submerged realism is likewise set at naught. Murphy is an anti-hero, who takes only 'courses of inaction' and he has to quell any feelings of love for Celia or anyone else, though Celia believes he could not go on without her, and the narrator adds: 'So love is wont to end, in protasis, if it be love.'[124] The pathetic Celia is our link with the familiar novel form, not Murphy, who, despite the narrator's claim, is the novel's most prominent puppet. He is after all the medium of Beckett's interest in closed systems and the search for order amid life's 'big blooming buzzing confusion' (a refrain in the novel that Tindall attributes to William James), and for an 'indifference to the contingencies of the contingent world'.[125] Murphy's success would end the mind-body cleft, which is an aspect of the disunity of being which is the chief philosophical subject of the novel.

Beckett by his inspired puppetry succeeds in suspending our empathy for his characters, though the stringency of his anti-humanism sometimes falters or relaxes, as does the deliberate severity of his prose into a residual poetry. There is the use of repetition like the response in liturgy, a trope Beckett was to make peculiarly his own in his later work. And there is familiar description, like that of kite-flying in chapter 8, that is, in Beckett fashion, almost more poetic for its apparent desire to avoid poetry. Kite-flying ends the novel and reverses the clever rigor mortis of earlier passages; the cry of the park-keeper that closes the book, '*All out*', suggests also the end of an innings (defeat in Beckett's beloved cricket), including perhaps all the philosophies and fictions of system, and poignantly rejoins Beckett's novel to traditions he would appear to wish to flee.

At Swim-Two-Birds (1939) by Flann O'Brien (1910–1966) is more closely inspired by *Ulysses* than is *Murphy*. Like *Ulysses*, *At Swim-Two-Birds* is full of demotic humour and demonstrates the author's impeccable ear for lower-class Dublin speech. And like Joyce's novel it is written on the principle of amplification rather than reduction, *At Swim-Two-Birds* exhibiting with Joycean *brio* the master's encyclopedic love of learning and lore – there are catalogues and set-pieces galore in the novel. One form of amplification is the manufacture of multiple plot-lines. O'Brien's variation on this is the clever development of one plot-line inside another. The novel is about an unnamed University College Dublin undergraduate who is chided for his sloth by his uncle with whom he lives but who in his spare time from idleness is writing a novel about an author (Dermot Trellis) who is writing a novel, one of the characters of which writes his own novel. Further, O'Brien leaves the flaps of these plot envelopes open, as it were: Trellis is a character in his own novel and he rapes his heroine Sheila Lamont, who gives birth to the novel's third character, Orlick. Orlick Trellis is writing his own novel to exact revenge on his creator-father Dermot, who is set upon by other characters, many of them borrowed by Dermot from Irish mythology and the pages of an Irish western novelist, William Tracy. Where Ireland is concerned, this is a case of the farrow eating their dam![126] These characters – according to the artistic principle the undergraduate author grandly calls 'aestho-autogamy' – are emancipated from Dermot's imagination while he is asleep. Joyce's (and Beckett's and Modernism's) text-consciousness, a wholesale defamiliarisation process, is made literal and explicit in O'Brien's novel and pages are devoted to the student narrator's theory of an ideal novel that would be 'a self-evident sham to which the reader could regulate at will the degree of his credulity'. Characters in existing literature could be regarded as puppets (cf. Beckett's *Murphy*) which could be employed when required by a novelist, original creation being a last resort. In this way, 'the modern novel should be largely a work of reference'.[127] Certainly it is a fabrication, and *At Swim-Two-Birds* opens and closes variously in the spirit of readerly choice.

The narrator's friend Brinsley on hearing the theory, replies: 'That is all my bum' and one feels that O'Brien agrees, that he is writing a novel parodying the theory, as well as Modernism, for which reason we can call *At Swim-Two-Birds* a post-modern novel. The parody derives from the literalising of the theory, a form of *reductio ad absurdum*. The novel is indeed a nest of burlesques of various literary forms, fictional and non-fictional alike, and pastiches of specific works or styles. Irish sagas, tipsters' circulars, newspapers, biographical dictionaries, the Bible, folk-tales are among the humorously imitated forms; Yeats, O'Casey, Stephens and Joyce among the humorously imitated authors. In the novel, the Irish Literary Revival is immersed in the solvent of O'Brien's wit and Finn MacCool, the folk figure of the Pooka, and Suibhne (mad Sweeny) are let loose in the asylum of the novel's world. The plot-lines gradually and cleverly become tributaries that become a confluence, with characters joining and swelling a communal quest narrative of a kind we find in certain Irish folk-tales and in *The Crock of Gold* and *The King of Ireland's Son*. O'Brien's mock-erudition is more sustained than in *Murphy* and resembles that in the latter pages of *Ulysses* or that in Swift, who like O'Brien was a satirist of abstruse learning, where Joyce was a genuine admirer of it.

Despite all the humorous mockery, there is, as with *Murphy*, a seemingly serious and eloquent 'ultimate' conclusion involving suicide and 'the serial enigma of the dark', which gestures towards O'Brien's second and far more genuinely disturbing novel, *The Third Policeman*, composed and put away by O'Brien in 1940 and published posthumously in 1967, by which time the Ireland of his early creativity was embarking on what would prove to be a sea-change.

As good a work as any to end this survey of the 1890–1940 period is Lord Dunsany's *My Ireland* (1937), which embeds current Irish issues inside another kind of quest narrative. The question prompting the long answer of the book is 'Do the Irish like their new form of government?' and the knight Dunsany goes in search of an answer, rather like Chaucer's bachelor knight, who is sent in search of an answer to the question 'What do women want?' The question is topical: in the year of the book's publication, Eamon de Valera with a new constitution put paid to the hopes of a tolerant, diverse Ireland with living room for the remnants of the Ascendancy. The answer is deferred until the end of the book and even then is not unambiguously declared. The knowledgeable chapters on Irish field sports recreate an Anglo-Irish world under threat at the time of Dunsany's writing while imitating the episodic nature of Dunsany's own fictional mock legends and fairy tales, be they his short tales or such a longer one as his popular *The King of Elfland's Daughter* (1924). But the deferment of the answer is not only formulaic but substantive; if the answer is 'yes', that need not be good news to someone of Lord Dunsany's background, but in fact, out of courtesy to the quester, the fount of wisdom (or oracle), 'Old Mickey', to whom the author keeps returning, hedges the answer. There is a murder of a Protestant (perhaps a 'turned' Catholic) disturbing the story and a darkness on the edge of Dunsany's Ireland. This clever, whimsical book functions as an oblique adieu to a long era now ended.

Notes

1. W. B. Yeats, *Fairy and Folk Tales of the Irish Peasantry* (1888), introduction; quoted by Seamus Deane, *A Short History of Irish Literature* (London: Hutchinson, 1986), p. 114.
2. F. S. L. Lyons, *Ireland since the Famine* (London: Fontana, 1973), pp. 87–8.
3. See Editor, 'Penny Fiction', *Blackwood's Edinburgh Magazine* 164 (1898) and 'Fashion in Fiction', *Blackwood's Edinburgh Magazine* 166 (1899).

4. J. A. Sutherland, *Victorian Novelists and Publishers* (Chicago: University of Chicago Press, 1976), pp. 4–5.
5. Charles A. Read, *Cabinet of Irish Literature* (1879–80); revised and expanded edn, ed. Katharine Tynan, 4 vols. (London: Gresham Publishing Company, 1902–3), IV, p. 193. L. T. Meade was the pseudonym of Elizabeth Thomasina Toulmin Smith.
6. Mrs Alexander (1825–1902) from Dublin is not to be confused with the novelist Eleanor Alexander from County Tyrone (daughter of Mrs Cecil Alexander the hymnist and William Alexander, archbishop of Armagh), nor with the (chiefly historical) novelist Miriam Alexander (later Mrs Harold Stokes).
7. According to Stephen J. Brown, *Ireland in Fiction: A Guide to the Irish Novels, Tales, Romances and Folklore* (1915; 1919; New York: Barnes and Noble, 1969), p. 293. By the middle of 1916, *Dubliners* (1914) had sold about 550 copies: Richard Ellmann, *James Joyce* (Oxford: Oxford University Press, 1983), p. 400.
8. Yeats, quoted by Tynan, *The Middle Years* (London: Constable, 1916), p. 71. Some Revivalists did court popularity but in the hope that the peasantry would assimilate Revival poems into their anonymous repertoire.
9. 'Fictional polemics' is David Trotter's term and he discusses Sarah Grand (born in Donaghadee, County Down) under the section of this title in *The English Novel in History 1895–1920* (London: Routledge, 1993), pp. 116–17.
10. George Moore, *Hail and Farewell* (1911–14; Gerrards Cross: Colin Smythe, 1976), pp. 58–74.
11. Letts, *The Rough Way* (Milwaukee: The Young Churchman Co., 1912), p. 140.
12. Princess Grace Irish Library biographical notes: www.pgil-eirdata.org. Library catalogues do not furnish MacMahon's birthdate. She published between 1884 and 1928 (or 1949, if her last few titles, published by Mellifont Library, appeared during her lifetime). COPAC lists twenty-seven titles by her. She was born in Dublin and was domiciled in London.
13. Born in Kilkenny, Alcock was the daughter of Rev. John Alcock, who thereafter was a Church of Ireland curate in Tralee, Cork, the Isle of Man and Dublin, finally becoming archdeacon of Waterford. Some of her novels have been recently republished by religious publishing houses in Canada and the United States.
14. See Vivian Mercier on the Church of Ireland background of many of the Revivalists and on Evangelicalism as a root-strand of the Revival project: 'Victorian Evangelicalism and the Anglo-Irish Literary Revival', in Peter Connolly, ed. *Literature and the Changing Ireland* (Gerrards Cross: Colin Smythe, 1982), pp. 59–101.
15. Other Catholic women fiction writers included Tynan, Julia M. Crottie, Clara Mulholland, Mary Maher, M. E. Francis, Hannah Lynch, Charlotte Dease, Helena Walsh (Mrs Concannon), Katherine Cecil Thurston and Gertrude M. O'Reilly. Most of these were educated at convent schools, often in Europe or England. Their Protestant equivalents included Alcock, Letts, Eleanor Alexander, Helen Duffin, M. Hamilton (Mary Churchill Luck), B. M. Croker, Dorothea Conyers, Jane Barlow, Emily Lawless, Riddell, Erminda Rentoul Esler, F. E. Crichton, L. T. Meade and Eleanor Hull. Many were daughters of clergy: Alexander, Barlow, Croker, Esler, Catherine J. Hamilton, Frances Craig Houston, Maggie J. Houston, Mrs Hungerford, Rosamond Langbridge, Mabel S. Madden, Meade, MacMahon, Lydia M. Foster. An impressive number of

Protestant women writers were educated at Alexandra College (founded 1866) with which the Irish Clergy Daughters' School (founded 1843) merged in 1888.

16. Augustine Martin, introduction to *The Charwoman's Daughter* (Dublin: Gill and Macmillan, 1972), p. 4.
17. Rosa Mulholland, *Father Tim* (London: Sands and Company, 1910), p. 160.
18. In *Catholic Fiction and Social Reality in Ireland, 1873–1922* (Westport: Greenwood Press, 1997), James H. Murphy credits the historian Emmet Larkin with the phrase 'devotional revolution'.
19. Moore, *A Drama in Muslin: A Realistic Novel* (1886; London: Walter Scott, 1918), p. 325.
20. Ella MacMahon, *A Pitiless Passion* (London: Hutchinson, 1895), p. 285. Edward Westermarck published his *History of Human Marriage* in 1889 (a third edition appeared in 1901), which was influential.
21. Katherine Cecil Thurston, *The Fly on the Wheel* (1908; London: Virago, 1987), pp. 82, 223–4.
22. Katherine Cecil Thurston, *Max: A Novel* (New York: Harper and Brothers, 1910), pp. 183.
23. Madame Sarah Grand, *The Heavenly Twins* (New York: Cassell, 1893), p. 80.
24. Helen C. Black, *Notable Women Authors of the Day* (1893; Freeport: Books for Libraries, 1972), p. 324. Five of the thirty novelists Black profiles are Irish: Riddell, Mrs Alexander, Mrs Hungerford, May Crommelin and Grand.
25. See Carolyn Christensen Nelson, *British Women Writers of the 1890s* (New York: Twayne, 1996), p. 22.
26. I am using texts of the stories from *Keynotes* and *Discords* in an omnibus volume entitled *Keynotes* (London: Virago, 1983). Egerton was born in Australia of an Irish father and Welsh mother, was raised in New Zealand, Chile, Wales, Ireland and Germany. In Ireland she was educated at a convent school. She eloped in 1887 to Norway with a married man, met Knut Hamsen and read Ibsen. She left her lover the following year and moved back to London, where she married a Canadian writer, George Egerton Clairmonte, and moved to County Cork. She divorced Clairmonte but kept his forenames and married a theatrical agent. She died in Sussex.
27. Oscar Wilde, *The Picture of Dorian Gray*, in Richard Aldington and Stanley Weintraub, eds. *The Portable Oscar Wilde* (New York: Penguin Books, 1981), pp. 310, 184, 251.
28. Ibid., pp. 227, 158, 143, 222, 233, 197.
29. 74,000 copies of the 1905 edition of Young's novel were printed; it was reprinted by Grant Richards in 1919. Young had strong Portaferry, County Down connections.
30. See my article 'Against Nature? Science and Oscar Wilde', *University of Toronto Quarterly* 63, 2 (1993/4), pp. 329–47, reprinted in Jerusha MacCormack, ed. *Wilde the Irishman* (New Haven: Yale University Press, 1998), pp. 113–24.
31. Bernard Bergonzi, *The Early H. G. Wells: A Study of the Scientific Romances* (Toronto: University of Toronto Press, 1961).
32. Born in Clough, Cromie was on the staff of the *Northern Whig* newspaper in Belfast, a city that datelines the prefaces or dedicatory notes of the three novels I have read. *A Plunge into Space*, dedicated to Jules Verne, was reprinted in 1976 by Hyperion Press.
33. E. F. Bleiler, introduction to *The Collected Ghost Stories of Mrs J. H. Riddell* (New York: Dover, 1977), p. ix.

34. Helen Duffin did the same thing in *Over Here* (1918).
35. Bram Stoker, *Dracula* (1897; London: Penguin Books, 1979), p. 303.
36. Ibid., p. 49. Yeats opposed modernity and promoted a creative medievalism.
37. Jonathan Rose, 'The Efficiency Men', in *The Edwardian Temperament, 1895–1919* (Athens: Ohio University Press, 1986), pp. 117–62.
38. Stoker, *Dracula*, pp. 110–11.
39. Julian Symons pays tribute to Bodkin in his history of the genre and laments his neglect: *Bloody Murder: From the Detective Story to the Crime Novel: A History* (London: Faber and Faber, 1972), p. 89. Bodkin was a County Court judge, Nationalist MP, Catholic hagiographer and acting editor of *United Ireland*.
40. See Grand, 'The Modern Girl,' *North American Review* 158 (1894), pp. 706–14.
41. Erskine Childers, *The Riddle of the Sands: A Record of Secret Service* (1903; London: Sidgwick and Jackson, 1927), p. 89. Apparently Childers disliked his book being promoted as a novel and thought of it more like an extended Foreign Office memorandum, cast in fictional form to enhance its effectiveness as a serious warning. See T. J. Binyon, review of Jim Ring's *Erskine Childers* (1996), *Times Literary Supplement*, May 24 1996, p. 32. See also Preface to *The Riddle of the Sands*, pp. vii–viii.
42. Born in England, Childers went to live with his uncle in Glendalough House, a county house in County Wicklow when his parents died young. Two biographers write: 'Anglo-Irish he was, Irish he was later to claim to be; yet, in many ways, he was English to the bone': Hugh and Robin Popham, eds. *A Thirst for the Sea: The Sailing Adventures of Erskine Childers* (London: Stanford Maritime, 1979), p. 7.
43. Childers wrote *War and the Arme Blanche* (London: Edward Arnold, 1910), in which he recommends substituting mounted riflemen for cavalrymen armed with steel, and *German Influence on British Cavalry* (1911), in which he discourages any dependence on German models. Chapter 10 of the first book is devoted to 'The Guerilla War'. The two books are coming war writings and might be said to constitute with *In the Ranks of the C.I.V.*, Childers' imperial trilogy.
44. See I. F. Clarke, ed. *The Tale of the Next Great War, 1871–1914: Fictions of Future Warfare and of Battles Still to Come* (Liverpool: Liverpool University Press, 1995).
45. Goldring was born in 1887 in Greenwich and was educated at Oxford before going to London, where he became sub-editor under Ford Madox Ford at the *English Review*. He enlisted in 1914 but was invalided out, and became a conscientious objector. He travelled to Dublin to investigate the events of Easter Week. He met his future Irish wife and wrote *The Fortune*, which was published by Maunsel. Goldring traced his Irish connection in *Odd Man Out: The Autobiography of a 'Propaganda Novelist'* (London: Chapman and Hall, 1935) and in a chapter, 'Irish Influences,' in *The Nineteen Twenties: A General Survey and Some Personal Memories* (London: Nicholson and Watson, 1945).
46. Aldous Huxley, preface to *The Fortune* (1917; London: Desmond Harmsworth, 1931), p. viii.
47. Mrs Victor Rickard, *The Fire of Green Boughs* (1918; New York: Dodd, Mead, 1919), p. 238.
48. The visitor to Ireland plot component typically provides dramatic potential for difference, for misunderstanding and clash; it also offers the possibility of romantic attraction

across a cultural divide; it can also serve to educate the English reader about Ireland should the visitor be from England. The country house had a tradition of long and frequent stays by visitors. The visitor-to-Ireland device in fiction goes back at least as far as the national tale of the early nineteenth century.

49. See A. Norman Jeffares, ed. *Yeats's Poems* (London: Macmillan, 1989), p. 543.
50. However, despite the insistence on Irish uniqueness, the Irish Revival can be charted in an atlas of nineteenth-century European romantic and nationalist cultural revivals.
51. I discuss fictional adaptations both of sagas and folk-tales in *Fictions of the Irish Literary Revival: A Changeling Art* (Dublin: Gill and Macmillan, 1987).
52. James Stephens, *Irish Fairy Tales* (1920; New York: Macmillan, 1968), p. 218.
53. Just as the study of Old and Middle Irish manuscript material was part of a study of Celtic languages by European philologists, so Irish folk-collecting and study was part of the surge of British interest in folklore from the 1880s.
54. For the reference to pale victims, see Peter Faulkner, *William Morris and W. B. Yeats* (Dublin: Dolmen Press, 1962), p. 22. The phrase 'where life is at tension' is from John Aherne's description of the wanderings of his brother Owen and Michael Robartes in Ireland: 'Stories of Michael Robartes and his Friends' (1931), in *A Vision* (1937; New York: Collier Books, 1966), p. 52.
55. Allan Wade, ed. *The Letters of W. B. Yeats* (London: Rupert Hart-Davis, 1954), p. 286.
56. I discuss such prophecies among the Anglo-Irish in *Fictions of the Irish Literary Revival*, pp. 59–61.
57. AE, Preface to *The Interpreters* (London: Macmillan, 1922).
58. See David Skilton, introduction to George Moore, *Esther Waters*, ed. Skilton (1886; Oxford: Oxford University Press, 1983), pp. x–xv.
59. Ibid. p. x.
60. Brown, *Ireland in Fiction*, p. 215.
61. George Moore, *The Lake* (1921; Gerrards Cross: Colin Smythe, 1980), p. 173. This edition reprints the 1921 revision of Moore's earlier 1905 revision of his story begun in 1903.
62. Peter Costello, *The Heart Grown Brutal: The Irish Revolution in Literature, from Parnell to the Death of Yeats, 1891–1939* (Dublin: Gill and Macmillan, 1977), pp. 59–61.
63. In the year *Dubliners* appeared, a government Housing Commission classified half of the population of Dublin under the heading of 'Indefinite and unproductive class': see David Krause, *Sean O'Casey: The Man and his Work* (New York: Macmillan, 1975), pp. 5–6.
64. Letter to Grant Richards (13 May 1906), quoted in Ellmann, *James Joyce*, p. 221. I have silently amended (I hope with justification) the phrase 'in my country' in this 1983 edition of Ellmann's biography in favour of 'of my country', which is how it appears in the 1965 edition.
65. Letter to C. P. Curran in 1904, quoted in ibid., p. 163. I have silently corrected the spelling of 'hemiplegia' in Ellmann's 1983 revision.
66. 'I seriously believe that you will retard the course of civilisation in Ireland by preventing the Irish people from having one good look at themselves in my nicely polished looking-glass': letter of 23 June 1906, quoted in ibid., p. 222. 'Scrupulous meanness' occurs in a letter to Grant Richards (5 May 1906), quoted by Ellmann, p. 210. Joyce in a letter to his

brother Stanislaus (18 September 1905) uses the word 'scrupulous' twice in identifying qualities of Russian writing: quoted by Ellmann, p. 209. In 'The Dead', Gabriel has a chastening glimpse of himself in the (presumably nicely polished) cheval-glass in the bedroom of the Gresham Hotel.

67. Letter of 15 October 1905, quoted in ibid., p. 208n.
68. Dedalus walks through the slum streets, 'wondering whether he had strayed into the quarter of the jews': *A Portrait of the Artist as a Young Man* (1916; New York: Penguin Books USA, 1992), p. 107. This would be the area in which Edelstein's Jewish tickmen ply their trade and live until they achieve success like Moses Levenstein and move up in the city.
69. Henry Edward Manning, *Sin and Its Consequences* (New York: D. and J. Sadlier, 1876), pp. 238, 243, 237.
70. Hannah Lynch, *Autobiography of a Child* (New York: Dodd, Mead and Company, 1899), pp. 269, 270.
71. Ibid., pp. 96, 162, 224.
72. According to the entry for Lynch in the Princess Grace Irish Library eirdata bibliography.
73. Joyce, *A Portrait*, p. 215.
74. James Joyce, *Ulysses* (1922; Harmondsworth: Penguin Books, 1969), p. 617. This is written in the tired pomposity Joyce's stylistic scheme called for.
75. Ibid., pp. 309, 296, 553.
76. Katherine Mullin, *James Joyce, Sexuality and Social Purity* (Cambridge: Cambridge University Press, 2003).
77. Joyce, *Ulysses*, p. 352.
78. Ibid., p. 364.
79. Ibid., p. 373.
80. Ibid., pp. 641, 604.
81. Daniel Corkery, *The Threshold of Quiet* (Dublin and Cork: Talbot Press, 1917), p. 53.
82. Ibid., p. 168.
83. Brinsley MacNamara, *The Valley of the Squinting Windows* (1918; New York: Brentano's, 1919), p. 95.
84. See Padraic O'Farrell, *The Burning of Brinsley MacNamara* (Dublin: Lilliput, 1990).
85. Brinsley MacNamara, *The Clanking of Chains* (Dublin: Maunsel, 1920), p. 35.
86. Ibid., pp. 145, 236.
87. Liam O'Flaherty, 'The Irish Censorship' (1932), reprinted in Julia Carlson, ed. *Banned in Ireland: Censorship and the Irish Writer* (Athens: University of Georgia Press, for Article 19, 1990), p. 140. In the same article, O'Flaherty again echoes Joyce when, thinking of how Ireland had recently been intellectually respected, he describes Free State Ireland as a 'sick bitch biting the hand that fed her,' p. 140.
88. Liam O'Flaherty, *The Informer* (New York: Knopf, 1925), p. 279.
89. Edward Garnett, to whom *The Black Soul* was dedicated, was an encourager of both Lawrence and O'Flaherty.
90. Richard Fallis, *The Irish Renaissance: An Introduction to Anglo-Irish Literature* (Dublin: Gill and Macmillan, 1978), p. 207.
91. Sean O'Faolain, *The Irish* (1947; Harmondsworth: Penguin, 1969), p. 22.

92. Ibid., p. 130.
93. The 1937 constitution of the Irish Free State that superseded the more liberal constitution of 1922 (drawn up by Darrell Figgis and others) made official what had been happening in the Free State since 1922. In 1949 the Free State was declared a Republic.
94. For censorship in the new state, see Carlson, *Banned in Ireland*. This book includes articles or statements by AE, Yeats, Shaw, O'Flaherty, O'Faolain, O'Connor and Beckett.
95. Frank O'Connor, *An Only Child* (London: Macmillan, 1962), p. 147.
96. Sean O'Faolain, *Stories of Sean O'Faolain* (Harmondsworth: Penguin Books, 1970), p. 95.
97. The claim appears in a 1942 article in *Horizon*, quoted by Terence Brown, 'After the Revival: The Problem of Adequacy and Genre', *Genre* 12 (1979), p. 571.
98. Quoted by John Nemo, *Patrick Kavanagh* (Boston: Twayne Publishers, 1979), p. 57. Kavanagh himself as a writer faced the same dilemma as O'Faolain describes.
99. O'Faolain is quoted to this effect from a 1949 article in *The Month* by Brown, 'After the Revival', p. 573. O'Connor is summarised to this effect by Benedict Kiely in *Kenyon Review* 30 (1968), p. 464.
100. Sean O'Faolain, *Bird Alone* (1936; Dublin: Millington, 1973), 119. Compare Gabriel Josipovici: 'A complete realism is indistinguishable from a complete solipsism, since I am not an object in the world but the limits of my world', *The World and the Book: A Study of Modern Fiction* (St Albans: Granada, 1973), p. 312.
101. Frank O'Connor, *Dutch Interior* (1940; Dublin: Millington, 1973), p. 205.
102. Francis Stuart, *Women and God* (London: Jonathan Cape, 1931), p. 189.
103. The phrase occurs in 'The Happy Autumn Fields', reprinted in Elizabeth Bowen, *Elizabeth Bowen's Irish Stories* (Dublin: Poolbeg Press, 1978), p. 96.
104. Bowen, *The Last September* (1929; London: Jonathan Cape, 1960), p. 163.
105. See Bowen's 1940 essay, 'The Big House', reprinted in Hermione Lee, ed. *The Mulberry Tree: Writings of Elizabeth Bowen* (London: Virago, 1986), pp. 25–30. See also Bowen's account of the house she grew up in: *Bowen's Court* (London: Longman, 1964), p. 26.
106. Quoted by Victoria Glendinning, *Elizabeth Bowen* (New York: Avon Books, 1979), p. 10.
107. M. J. Farrell (Molly Keane), *Mad Puppetstown* (1931; London: Virago, 1985), p. 23.
108. Farrell's first novel, *The Knight of Cheerful Countenance* (1926) is in the tradition of Conyers, Somerville and Ross, Croker and Mrs Hungerford: the 'open-air' branch of the country house novel and verges on the Irish sporting novel to which reference is made. The Civil War remains too firmly in the background for the novel to escape into seriousness.
109. Pamela Hinkson, *The Ladies' Road* (London: Gollancz, 1932), p. 319.
110. Kate O'Brien, *The Anteroom* (New York: Doubleday, Doran and Co., 1934), p. 265.
111. Kathleen Coyle, *Liv* (London: Jonathan Cape, 1929), pp. 216, 101–2, 252.
112. Rebecca West, introduction to *Liv*.
113. Katherine Coyle, *A Flock of Birds* (New York: E. P. Dutton, 1930), pp. 242, 39.
114. Malleson appears at length in Ronald W. Clark's *The Life of Bertrand Russell* (London: Weidenfeld and Nicolson, 1975).
115. Constance Malleson, *Fear in the Heart: A Novel* (London: Collins, 1936), pp. 200, 245.
116. Helen Waddell, *The Wandering Scholars* (1927; Harmondsworth: Pelican Books, 1954), pp. 129–30.

117. Ibid., pp. 130–1.
118. Lewis was a scholar of medieval and Renaissance allegory. A more explicit allegorical fable is his *The Pilgrim's Regress* (London: Dent, 1933), subtitled *An Allegorical Apology for Christianity, Reason and Romanticism*. The allegorical journey and the explicit pilgrimage can share invented geographies with the sci-fi voyage.
119. *The Pit-Prop Syndicate* (1922) appeared in Irish in 1933, *Sir John Magill's Last Journey* (1930) in 1935.
120. Samuel Beckett, *Murphy* (1938; New York: Grove Press, 1957), pp. 57, 200.
121. Ibid., pp. 78–9, 21, 82.
122. Ibid., pp. 194, 178, 1, 250–1, 278.
123. Ibid., p. 122.
124. Ibid., pp. 38, 234.
125. Ibid., pp. 4, 29, 245. For James, see William York Tindall, *Samuel Beckett* (New York: Columbia University Press, 1964), p. 16. See also *Murphy*, p. 168.
126. Flann O'Brien, *At Swim-Two-Birds* (1939; Harmondsworth: Penguin Books, 1967), p. 217.
127. Ibid., pp. 11, 25.

Select bibliography

Brown, Stephen J., *Ireland in Fiction: A Guide to Irish Novels, Tales, Romances and Folklore*, 1919; New York: Barnes and Noble, 1969.

Brown, Terence, *Ireland's Literature: Selected Essays*, Mullingar: Lilliput, 1988.

Cahalan, James, *The Irish Novel: A Critical History*, Dublin: Gill and Macmillan, 1988.

Costello, Peter, *The Heart Grown Brutal: The Irish Revolution in Literature, from Parnell to the Death of Yeats, 1891–1939*, Dublin: Gill and Macmillan, 1977.

Deane, Seamus, gen. ed. *The Field Day Anthology of Irish Writing*, 3 vols., Derry: Field Day, 1991.

Fallis, Richard, *The Irish Renaissance: An Introduction to Anglo-Irish Literature*, Dublin: Gill and Macmillan, 1978.

Foster, John Wilson, *Fictions of the Irish Literary Revival: A Changeling Art*, Dublin: Gill and Macmillan, 1987.

Lyons, F. S. L., *Ireland since the Famine*, London: Fontana, 1973.

Murphy, James H., *Catholic Fiction and Social Reality in Ireland, 1873–1922*, Westport: Greenwood Press, 1997.

Weekes, Ann Owens, *Irish Women Writers: An Uncharted Tradition*, Lexington: University Press of Kentucky, 1990.

4

The Irish Renaissance, 1890–1940: drama in English

ADRIAN FRAZIER

Myths of origin

Histories of the drama of the 'Irish Renaissance' usually do not begin in 1890; they begin instead in the summer of 1897. Following signposts in memoirs by W. B. Yeats and Augusta Gregory,[1] scholars often date the conception of modern Irish drama to a conversation between these two held in a land agent's office on the seaside Galway property of a landlord with the storybook name, Count Florimande de Basterot. As the rain fell outside, 32-year-old Yeats spoke to 45-year-old widowed Lady Gregory of his long-held wish for an Irish theatre in which the plays he and her neighbour Edward Martyn had written could be performed. But what was the use? No professional theatre in Dublin would take them; a sufficient audience could not be found for them; and who would subsidise such unpopular performances? Lady Gregory took the bait, and asked how much was needed. £300 for one week of performances. She thought that such a sum might be raised by a public-spirited appeal to people of wealth and position in Ireland, many of whom she herself knew. To start the fund, she donated £25 of her own money.

By the middle of July, having moved into Lady Gregory's 'Big House' called Coole Park, Yeats had written up a prospectus for a 'Celtic Theatre' – later called 'The Irish Independent Theatre Society', and finally 'The Irish Literary Theatre':[2]

> We propose to have performed in Dublin in the spring of every year certain Celtic and Irish plays, which whatever be their degree of excellence, will be written with a high ambition; and to make beginning next spring with two plays, a play of modern Ireland and in prose by Mr Edward Martyn and a play of legendary Ireland and in verse by Mr W. B. Yeats . . . Dramatic journalism has had full possession of the stage in England for a century, and it is perhaps impossible for audiences, who are delighted by dramatic journalism, however brilliant, to delight in the simplicity and naivety of literature

> unless it is old enough to be a superstition. We hope to find in Ireland an uncorrupted and imaginative audience trained to listen by its passion for oratory, and believe that our desire to bring upon the stage the deeper thoughts and emotions of Ireland will ensure for us a tolerant welcome, and that freedom to experiment which is not found in theatres of England, and without which no new movement in art or literature can succeed. We will show that Ireland is not the home of buffoonery and of easy sentiment, as it has been represented, but the home of an ancient idealism, and we are confident of the support of all Irish people, who are weary of misrepresentation, in carrying out a work that is outside all the political questions which divide us.
>
> We have asked for a guarantee fund of £300 for our first attempt . . .

This statement is often taken for what it means to be, a founding constitution for a certain sort of modern Irish drama: one clearly set apart from English theatre, commercial theatre, un-literary theatre, non-idealistic theatre, politically one-sided theatre, and all former representations of Ireland and its people on the stage. However, like all myths of origin, this one is false and misleading.

Irish national theatre before the Irish National Theatre Society

Certainly, the long partnership of Lady Gregory and Yeats first formed in the summer of 1897 was important to the Abbey Theatre (which opened 27 December 1904). And the 1897 prospectus is indeed a link in a chain of events leading to a week of Irish Literary Theatre performances in 1899, 1900, and 1901, when the chain was briefly broken, before being reforged by W. G. Fay and his brother Frank, with the production of plays by Yeats and Gregory (*Cathleen ni Houlihan*) and AE (*Deirdre*) by the Irish National Dramatic Society in April 1902. The Fays' society is the hereditary parent of the National Theatre Society, which still does business on Abbey Street in Dublin. However, the history of an expressive form like theatre is not a single chain of causation, and the massive variety of theatrical activity in a country cannot have been the doing of one or two people.

At the time of publication of the prospectus for the Irish Literary Theatre, there had been regular productions for twenty years of plays by Irish authors about Irish subjects performed to large audiences in Dublin theatres. The trope of rebel martyr and fair colleen, done down by a pack of double-dealing informers and well-armed redcoats, was exploited time and again by J. W.

Whitbread (1847–1916). Quite a number of such plays were founded on folklore history of the 1798 rebellion – such as Whitbread's *Lord Edward, Or '98* (1894) and *Theobald Wolfe Tone* (1898), staged at the Queen's Theatre and subsequently taken on tour to Cork, Belfast, and the cities of Britain.[3] Born and laid to rest in England, playwright, actor and theatre-manager Whitbread was proprietor of the Queen's from 1884 to 1907, working in a tradition that took its inspiration from the great Dion Boucicault (1820–1890) and was continued by Hubert O'Grady (1841–1899).[4] Queens' had a right to call itself the Irish National Theatre, both before and after the registration of the society by that name on 9 August 1902.[5] It was nationalist, Irish in setting and characters, and, in terms of spectacle and action, truly theatrical. But it was not a literary theatre.

The plays of the 'Revival' are best understood not as separate from the Irish plays at the Queens' Theatre, but as written and enjoyed in a dialectical relation to those of this popular tradition. *Cathleen ni Houlihan* (1902), for instance, the first and most popular play of the early Irish National Theatre Society, is a boiled-down motif consonant with the 1898 plays of Whitbread. In the famous photograph of Maud Gonne as Cathleen ni Houlihan (Mother Ireland herself), her outlandish make-up, wig, cloak, lines from rebel songs, and stagey gaze are all properties of Whitbread's melodramas that have been artistically recycled into a more succinct form of agitprop. The first play staged by J. M. Synge, greatest of the Revival playwrights, was *In the Shadow of the Glen* (1903). The playacting by the old man who pretends to be dead is conceived very broadly and almost farcically, that is, after the manner of the Star of Erin music-hall. Afterwards, *The Shadow* rapidly grows dark, lyrical and ultimately shocking – an 'evil compound of Boucicault and Ibsen', as it was seen to be at the time.[6]

By 1897 Dublin audiences were hardly 'uncorrupted' or altogether 'tired of misrepresentation', as claimed in Yeats's prospectus. They had seen at the Gaiety the best and worst of the global entertainment market: blackface 'coon' shows from the USA, the American star Edwin Booth and the English star Henry Irving play Shakespeare, Sarah Bernhardt in *La Dame aux Camélias* (1881) and Mrs Patrick Campbell in *The Second Mrs Tanqueray* (1893).[7] Frank Fay modelled his Abbey acting on that of the Paris great Coquelin, seen at the Gaiety. Of course, readers of Joyce know of this variety of theatrical entertainments. *The Dead* includes sophisticated conversation about nineteenth-century European *virtuosi*, and *Ulysses* owes more to Dan Lowrey's entertainments at the Olympia (originally 'Star of Erin Music Hall') than to the Irish dramatic revival.

1890 turns out to be a reasonable starting date for a revised history of modern Irish theatre.[8] The fall of Charles Stewart Parnell, following the publicity given to his adultery with Katherine O'Shea, coincided with the impact of Ibsen's plays on London audiences, so that 'Irish politics operated in tandem with European theatre'.[9] George Bernard Shaw saw the connection, and *The Quintessence of Ibsenism* (1891) 'pushed the play to the front of social change',[10] seizing a piece of the leadership from parliamentarians in a Fabian move to penetrate the public with new ideas. The notoriety heaped on those found to have shattered the dead ideals of the middle class (Ibsen, Parnell or Shaw himself) was accepted by leading practitioners as a sign of progress and education.

The benefit of this framework for modern Irish drama is that it includes within its limits crucial factors deliberately excluded by Yeats's descriptions of Revival theatre: the major impact of Ibsen, the centrality of London as a sphere of Irish display (thus reintegrating Shaw and Wilde into Irish literary history) and the deliberate participation of writers in an iconoclastic movement for social change. The Irish dramatists of this period were all Home Rulers, so a chief aspiration of the writers, and expectation of Dublin audiences, was a drama that tended to support, or at least not to undermine, the chances of independence. To show how a people lived – how they dressed, talked, courted, fought, forged family relations, all in their own way – was a kind of proof that they were a people unto themselves, and thus deserving of nationhood.

However, in addition to Home Rule, other forms of social change were advanced on stage, and not just by the socialist Shaw. Themes of urban renewal, the labour movement and the position of women were little noticed by early historians. Now it can be seen that Irish dramas are a major tributary of the 'New Woman' plays inaugurated by Ibsen's *A Doll's House* (1879). Two of the best examples of the type are Shaw's *Mrs Warren's Profession* (1893) and Oscar Wilde's *An Ideal Husband* (1895).[11] The tradition was continued on the Irish National Theatre stage. Synge's Nora, like Ibsen's, walks out on her husband at the play's end (*Shadow of the Glen*, 1903); the door of the model farm is locked on the heroine of Lennox Robinson's anti-romance *The Cross Roads* (1910), while she awaits the return of her wife-battering husband.[12] Even *Cathleen ni Houlihan* copied the *coup de théâtre* at the end of Ibsen's play, but in this case it is a young man who walks out the door, leaving behind the banalities of marriage and family for the liberation of death in battle. The play crystallized a link between feminism and terrorism: in both cases, all politics becomes personal. Everywhere, following Ibsen, writers praised depth, freedom and 'the great world' over family, convention and religion.[13]

One play by Ibsen was even more formative than *A Doll's House*: that was *The Enemy of the People*.[14] Dr Stockman, an obstinate, arrogant truth-seeker, is charged with inspecting the public baths on which the prosperity of his town depends. He declares the baths to be polluted, though the town officials and townspeople break his windows, threaten his family and declare him an 'enemy of the people'. The Fay brothers were delighted with this play at the Gaiety Theatre, Dublin, on 28 September 1894. Six years later, the righteous intellectual who stands alone – thought wrong by the liberal majority, but proved right in time by progress – became the prototype for the missing hero of George Moore and Edward Martyn's *The Bending of the Bough* (1900), during the second season of the Irish Literary Theatre (another title for this play might have been, 'Ireland Without Parnell'). Indeed, Shaw's habit of ridiculing majority opinion in his plays, and Yeats's concept of artists as a vanguard of society who cherished integrity of vision over popularity, were both deeply structured by the modern European role of the artist-intellectual, as dramatised in Ibsen's play, and most fully embodied in the writing life of J. M. Synge.

The nationalist schemata of colonialism, liberation and postcolonialism has illuminated one side of Irish drama, while throwing others into the shadows. Everything has been interpreted with respect to England or the 'English in Ireland'. But modern Irish drama is not just Irish, but modern drama, and part of an international movement, in which London, Stockholm, Christiana, Paris and Bayreuth are all centres of origin and places of destination.

Paris, Bayreuth and Dublin

One place of origin for modern Irish drama was the Théâtre-Libre in Paris, 20 May 1890. On the bill was yet another play by Ibsen, *Ghosts* – the story of a family destroyed by hereditary syphilis, and more importantly, by genteel lies and Protestant hypocrisy. It was staged in a naturalist manner by André Antoine (1858–1943), who would later become the self-conscious model of the Fay brothers in Dublin. In the Théâtre-Libre audience that night were George Moore (1852–1933) and Arthur Symons (1865–1945). 'Nothing but the play existed for me,' Moore reported the next month. 'The remorseless web that life had spun, and the poor boy entangled in it, I watched . . . I saw life represented as blind, senseless, insatiate . . . [N]ature was shown working out her own ends, deaf to our appeal.'[15] In the same article, Moore asked why London had no Théâtre-Libre: 'Surely there should be no difficulty in finding a thousand persons interested in art and letters willing to subscribe five pounds a year for . . . twelve interesting plays.' An interesting play would be one by a great writer – poet, novelist, or whatever, but not a stage hack. It would be a play without a happy ending forced on it, or comic scenes in a serious story, or blameless heroes and virginal heroines; it would have a logical relationship from incident to incident, and between character and environment. Within a short time, Moore made common cause with like-minded people – such as William Archer, J. T. Grein and George Bernard Shaw – and the Independent Theatre Society was formed on a subscription basis. It opened with *Ghosts* (1891), followed by Shaw's first play, *Widowers' Houses* (1892), and Moore's sceptical drama about the labour movement, *The Strike at Arlingford* (1893).

After the withering away in the mid-1890s of the Independent Theatre, Moore was recruited by Yeats to the executive of his new venture. The Irish Literary Theatre became the Independent Theatre relocated to Dublin, and with a patriotic refit.[16] The continuity with European Modernism was strengthened by Frank and W. G. Fay, who had come to idolise André Antoine. Working men like him, they made the Irish National Theatre Society into the Théâtre-Libre of Dublin, imitating as best they could its ensemble playing, natural acting and anti-commercialism.

Still another place of origin of Dublin drama was Germany, the small town of Bayreuth, site of summer festivals of Wagner's dramatic operas. There gathered in the 1890s – drawn by the 'Wagner madness' – many of those who would play key parts a few years later in the Irish dramatic revival. One was the tea heiress Annie Horniman, a truly devout Wagnerian who bankrolled plays of what she hoped would be a comparable aestheticism. First, she paid the bills for Florence Farr's productions at the Avenue Theatre, London, of Yeats's *The Land of Heart's Desire* and Shaw's *Arms and the Man* (21 April 1894). She later invested on a much grander scale in the Irish National Theatre Society and bought the Abbey Theatre in Dublin. Fundamentally, she aimed to enable Yeats to become a second Wagner with his laboriously costumed, poetic sagas of ancient Ireland, such as *The King's Threshold* (8 October 1903), *The Shadowy Waters* (4 January 1904) and *On Baile's Strand* (27 December 1904).[17]

Edward Martyn (1859–1923), a convinced disciple of Wagner, brought his friend George Moore to Bayreuth in August 1894 (the first of five visits).[18] Like Moore, Martyn was a Catholic landlord of the west – his estate Tillyra (or Tulira) bordered Lady Gregory's Coole in County Galway; like Moore he was a long-term resident of the Temple in London trying to make a name for himself; and unlike Moore, he had been unsuccessful. Travelling through

Germany, the two worked on the draft of *The Heather Field*, performed by the Irish Literary Theatre in 1899. Upon their return, Moore began to experiment with Wagnerian opera stars, Wagnerian composers, and Wagnerian themes as constituent elements of a novel, *Evelyn Innes* (1898). His long-term ambition was to become an artist in words as Wagner was in music, structuring works by means of literary leitmotifs, and in tale cycles. *Evelyn Innes* includes a major portrait of W. B. Yeats ('Ulick Dean') as a Wagnerian composer building his Modernist operas on the framework of Celtic myths. Indeed, one of Dean's compositions is a *Tristan and Isolde*-style libretto startlingly similar to the play Moore and Yeats would soon write together for the Irish Literary Theatre – *Diarmuid and Grania* (21 October 1901).

Shaw, of course, was one of Wagner's first apostles in London. When William Archer struck up an acquaintance in the British Library with the young writer in 1883, Shaw was reading Marx's *Capital* and the scores of Wagner.[19] When he turned to writing plays in the 1890s, Shaw orchestrated relationships between cast members as if they were soloists in an opera – an alto, a tenor, soprano, bass, etc.[20]

Yeats himself seems to have been deaf to orchestral influence, but if he was not affected by Wagner's operas (no trip to Bayreuth for him), he was swept along by Wagnerianism through its offshoot, French Symbolism.[21] The poet's first visit to Paris in 1894 climaxed when he attended with Maud Gonne a performance of Villiers d'Isle Adam's *Axël*, a hyper-Wagnerian *Liebestod* without the music. Yeats was delighted with *Axël*'s anti-realism: 'all the characters are symbols and all the events allegories'.[22] At the Irish National Theatre, the drama that did not follow the Ibsen line offered a Wagnerian alternative, in heroic, legendary, poetic and symbolic costume dramas. In spite of Yeats's one remove from the Wagnerian experience, he would become the most ardent disciple of a theatricalist 'total theatre' of the type first conceived by the German genius.[23]

The difficult case of Oscar Wilde

There is one unsolved problem that embarrasses any historian of modern Irish drama. The plays of Oscar Wilde do not fit into the available narratives. Still, those plays are written by a person certainly Irish, and they are among the best comedies written in English. Unlike almost all the plays of the period, including many famous works by Shaw, they have not aged. Newly each decade on television, and recently, over and again in Hollywood films, *Lady*

Windemere's Fan (1892), *A Woman of No Importance* (1893), *An Ideal Husband* (1895), *The Importance of Being Earnest* (1895) and even the symbolist *Salomé* (1893) prove to be crowd-pleasers around the world.

Obviously, the plays come out of a certain Irish tradition, social life and subject position. No modern drama is so like the Restoration tradition of William Congreve. The most famous plays of the two Trinity College Dublin students, *The Way of the World* (1700) and *The Importance of Being Earnest* (1895), share superior intelligence, buccaneering cynicism, brilliance of epigram and, like the skull beneath the skin, animality showing itself through hyper-civility. The genius lavished on witty conversation may well, as Davis Coakley says, derive from the culture of table-talk in Merrion Square, home of the playwright's famous Dublin parents, Dr William Wilde and his wife Speranza.[24] The wholly amused and disenchanted viewpoint on all things English – marriage, class, property, patriotism – is rather like that of other turn-of-the-century Irish writers in London, such as Moore, Yeats and Shaw. It is a resident-alien viewpoint, when that alien is professionally dependent on entertaining the natives.[25] So one can explain where it was Wilde came from (Ireland), but not where his influence went right after his death in Paris, 30 November 1900. Not, certainly, to put its stamp on the Abbey playwrights of the first two generations, except in so far as Yeats, Synge, and Moore ranked beauty above morality, and individuality over everything, and thus were, along with Wilde, part of the School of Walter Pater.[26]

At least four aspects of Wilde's life and work made him, if an artist and thinker to be admired, not an example that could be followed. First, genius is inimitable, and genius of phrase and insight is much of what Wilde's plays have to offer. Second, his character-set is composed of the class of wealth, education, and power:

> GERALD: I suppose society is wonderfully delightful!
> LORD ILLINGWORTH: To be in it is merely a bore. But to be out of it simply a tragedy. Society is a necessary thing.
>
> (*A Woman of No Importance* [1893], act 3)

Yet this 'necessary thing' was little to be found in Ireland at the turn of the century except among the diminishing Ascendancy. A theatre determined to put Irish people on stage would have to look beyond the sophisticates. Third, the anti-morality of Wilde – that perfume of sin that pervades his plays – even if emanating from a certain European sort of Catholic sensibility, was intolerably offensive to the alarmist, puritanical sort of Irish Catholic sensibility in Dublin. Fourth, and finally, on 25 May 1895, once the judge pronounced sentence on

Wilde for gross immorality, and he was taken off to Pentonville prison, the playwright and all his doings were wiped off the slate, unmentionable, unproducible, for many years to come. Not until 1928 did Micheál Mac Liammóir and Hilton Edwards risk Wilde's *Salomé* (published 1893) on the stage of the Peacock; surprisingly, no scandal then arose.

It is a pity that multiple factors stood in the way of Wilde's work having an earlier and more profound impact on the Irish dramatic Revival. *An Ideal Husband* (1895) is one of the earliest and best plays about the Parnell problem, staged just four years after the leader's death. It is also a powerful critique of the sentimentalities of feminist drama. Lady Chiltern is a high-minded Christian with an ideal conception of her husband, Robert Chiltern. A government minister, he is being blackmailed by a woman with a past, Mrs Cheveley. Her edge is that she knows that long ago he sold state secrets to a financier. The deal gave Chiltern the wealth he required to get into politics. At heart, he accepts 'the most terrible of all philosophies', the Nietzschean 'philosophy of power' and 'the gospel of gold'.[27] Wealth and power have given him 'freedom, and freedom is everything'. But his wife's love depends on her concept of him as a man of integrity. His political position hangs in the balance too: 'In England a man who can't talk morality twice a week to a large, popular, immoral audience is quite over as a serious politician.' Remarkably, the *deus ex machina* – here, the Wildean dandy Lord Goring – enters the action not to punish the less-than-perfect politician, but to save him, and to instruct Lady Chiltern that her concepts of consistent principle and chaste integrity are false ideals.

Not even Ibsen was this Nietzschean. In relation to the Parnell scandal, the moral was obvious: the Irish Party should never have followed the lead of the Non-Conformist and hypocritical Liberal Party in condemning Parnell just because he sought pleasure and used power. Those are natural to the male of the species. Manifest even within such conduct, the play implies, is the fact Parnell was a great man.

Irish theatre as Lady Gregory's theatre

The Irish Literary Theatre (1899–1901) was a subscription theatre society using English actors hired for the one week of performances once a year; thus its work was seen by a relatively small section of the public. Even this limited public gave a mixed welcome to the plays. Catholic descendants of famine survivors took insult at Yeats's *Countess Cathleen* (8 May 1899), due to the characterisation of the Catholic peasantry as having been eager to sell their souls during the famine, while the landowner was depicted as self-sacrificingly charitable. The very same audience had only praise for Edward Martyn's *The Heather Field*, although the hero whose mental breakdown constitutes the play's subject is an Irish landlord with contempt for his tenants; he also hates women and has a fondness for men. Evidently, no one raised an eyebrow at any of these potentially objectionable features. The following year, the naturally offensive Moore shocked Yeats by turning *The Bending of the Bough* into an unpredictably popular play (20 February 1900),[28] while Alice Milligan, the Belfast nationalist, got little reaction with her romantically heroic *The Last Feast of the Fianna*. The patriotic audience succeeded in reading a rebellious message into Edward Martyn's *Maeve*, but it was only that message they applauded; the play itself failed. In the final season of the Irish Literary Theatre, the ambitious three-act *Diarmuid and Grania* by two of the most celebrated Irish writers of the era, Yeats and Moore, was upstaged at the Gaiety Theatre by a ten-minute comedy in Irish, credited to Douglas Hyde, founder of the Gaelic League.

This was *Casadh an tSúgáin* (The Twisting of the Rope, 23 October–3 November 1901). It was the first play by the Irish Literary Theatre that did not feature landlords or ancient heroes, but ordinary cottiers speaking the native language. Yeats had in fact written the scenario, and Lady Gregory furnished information about its hero, wandering Connaught poet Anthony Raftery (*c.*1784–1835). It was Hyde, however, who put Irish on it, removed the taint of Anglo-Irish literariness and took the lead role on stage. *Casadh an tSúgáin* turns on the way a wandering poet is treated by the local community, which admires his genius and deplores his life. This 'artist-disturber' hero became the template of later plays by Yeats, Gregory and Synge.[29]

Following the last season of the Irish Literary Theatre, others agreed with Yeats that something native-grown and day-to-day in its operations was called for.[30] In April 1902, from the 2nd to the 4th, the Fay brothers' Irish National Dramatic Society started this new initiative, using costumes, scenery and some players from Maud Gonne's feminist-nationalist society, the Daughters of Erin. They staged two plays in a Catholic temperance hall on Clarendon Street in Dublin: *Cathleen ni Houlihan* – starring Maud Gonne, signed by Yeats and secretly co-authored by Lady Gregory – and AE's *Deirdre*. The performances, though amateur and very much so, were received by their young nationalist audiences with genuine excitement. The Fays made plans to capitalize on this excitement by means of regular performances. But first they had to get some Irish plays to perform that were suitable to the company's capacities: short, high-impact, uncomplex psychologically, with small casts and inexpensive sets.

Who would write them? Many had a try. Right after the performances, on 5 April, the young and baby-faced Padraic Colum, an actor in the company, came round to Yeats's hotel and read him a draft of *Broken Soil*, a problem-play about land-hunger, ultimately produced in December 1903.[31] The Fays asked another actor, James Cousins, to write a play, and within a week he gave them *The Racing Lug*, the best one-act Frank Fay had seen in fifteen years.[32] Maud Gonne herself would write a propaganda play on the model of *Cathleen ni Houlihan*, called *Dawn*. Lady Gregory had in mind a 'sketch' to make up one in 'possibly a week of little plays'; this would become a play about return migration, *Twenty-Five*.[33] Yeats set his sights on a mystery play about how someone who knows everything but doesn't know belief is no better than a fool; he thought it would get him out of the doghouse with Roman Catholics, still offended by the politics and theology of *The Countess Cathleen*. As *The Hour-Glass* (1903), that play was staged along with Lady Gregory's *Twenty-Five* on 14 March 1903.

Out of this welter of play-writing, Lady Gregory emerged as a central shaper of modern Irish theatre. As mentioned above, she brought to life Yeats's vision of the 1898 *aisling* play, *Cathleen ni Houlihan*. That play, like Hyde's, takes place in a peasant cottage, a stage set that became so common at the Abbey that practically no work other than repair and repainting was required of the stage carpenter from play to play, year in and year out. Lady Gregory, far more than Hyde, Moore, Martyn or Yeats, had visited the originals of such cottages, whether on mercy-missions around her estate or collecting folklore on behalf of Yeats. She observed manners carefully and picked up turns of phrase common in the west. Out of the local 'Kiltartan' speech-forms, she confected an original, comic and poetic stage dialect; it is also, less winningly, condescending, cute and syrupy. From a childhood fascination with romantic Irish felons as glorified in ballads, Lady Gregory arrived at an Irish patriotism in harmony with that of the people across the footlights. She was a dab hand at turning a plot, though she found it difficult to resist a denouement that made all difficulties vanish. With a kind of Christian magic, in her plays this world becomes a better world just as the lights go out. The Irish dramatic Revival simply could not have done without Lady Gregory. She came up with its typical stage set, stage speech, folk-tale plots and plays people enjoyed.

Quite a number of the works in *The Collected Plays of W. B. Yeats* would not exist had it not been for Lady Gregory's direct assistance in writing dialogue, sometimes nearly all of the dialogue. These include *Cathleen ni Houlihan* (1902), *A Pot of Broth* (1902), *The Unicorn from the Stars* (1908), *The Cat and the Moon* (an excellent play, 1926), and the Blind Man-Fool underplot of *On Baile's Strand* (1904). She was an essential stepping stone for Synge. He was galvanised by her use of a poetic peasant dialogue; he borrowed the artist-disturber situation; he seized upon the peasant-cabin set; and, James Pethica suggests, her wild-talking figure of 'Christie' in *The Losing Game* (1903) may have influenced Synge's conception of his heroes.[34]

Gregory appears to have had a particular genius for the plot that could be imitated. As much as any other, she must be credited with originating the popular *mise en scène* 'the stranger in the house'.[35] Another germ of many later Irish shows is at the heart of *The Rising of the Moon* (1903). Little but a barrel, with a wanted poster pasted on its side, is needed for a set. A Fenian on the run awaits a signal from a boat at the Galway quays; he encounters a police sergeant on the watch. Through tricky talk and sappy songs, appealing to common patriotism, he brings the sergeant round, so, when the wanted man's identity becomes known at the play's conclusion, the sergeant lets him escape. The docks, the policeman, the vagrant and a common culture of sentimental opposition have made up, and still make up, successful Irish plays – witness Joe O'Byrne's *It Come Up Sun* (Passion Machine, 2000).

Gregory's biggest impact may be in her fashioning of a myth that became a state ideology. Colm Tóibín's *Lady Gregory's Toothbrush* (2002) makes a case that out of Ascendancy guilt and trauma, Gregory became a key figure in the invention of a romantically glorified Ireland. For her, the most Irish of Irish people were the good souls in the west who could tell stories of fairies, people who were humble, imaginative, wise and Irish-speaking. Those in dirty Dublin, middle-class or worse, were evidently less Irish. Gregory's rosy, glorified view of the Irishman of the west became Eamon de Valera's view, a kind of state ideology, in an independent Ireland that no longer had room for the class of people that dreamed it up.

J. M. Synge

When Yeats and Gregory, Moore and Martyn, the Fays and Maud Gonne were bringing into being a new Irish theatre in Dublin, John Millington Synge (1871–1909) was no part of it at all, even though he would be the only one to write truly immortal plays. In April 1902, Synge was in Paris, the only student who came to class at the Sorbonne to hear Professor de Jubainville lecture about Old Irish. He had little money, and little prospect of making any by means of his articles in French on Irish culture. For a great writer, his letters are surprisingly quotidian, incoherent and suffocatingly polite, without self-expression.

At the end of April, he received in Paris a book that gave him, he later told its author, 'intense delight', and he read it again and again; he almost threw his friend Richard Best downstairs for criticising it.[36] The book was *Cuchulain of Muirthemne* by Lady Gregory. Nearly two years later, he was still reading it.[37] Such force of feeling, such pertinacity, is unusual in Synge's correspondence up to this time. Certain questions lay on his mind: how could he himself make further use of his notebooks, with their transcriptions of stories told on the Aran Islands? Would his studies of Gaelic syntax and idiom be of any advantage to him as a beginning author?

Everything came together for Synge when he began *In the Shadow of the Glen* in June 1902. As he stayed with his mother in County Wicklow, the details of setting were all about him: the glens, the fogs, the sheep, the vagrants.[38] Other things came not from without, but from within. The metaphysical loneliness of place, in the *long nights, bad nights, wild nights,*[39] is also, quite obviously, an intensely personal loneliness, that of a man who had come to the age of thirty-one without a woman in his life. Death is throughout the play as a waiting presence for everyone – it might come upon a woman, who'd be stretched like a dead sheep with the frost on her, in the butt of a ditch, or upon an old man, getting his death by a cold from going about in his nightshirt. That omnipresence of death came from the mind of the writer, one with a large lump in his throat, a susceptibility to coughs, and no belief in an afterlife. (In less than seven years, Synge would die of the disease that caused the tumour.)

As the play opens, there is an almost comical introduction to the audience of Synge's persona, and that of his heroine, as well as the first note of a melody of phrase he will play out through the entire dialogue, as a fiddler might to the dancing of others:[40]

> Good evening to you, lady of the house.
> Good evening, kindly, stranger; it's a wild night, God help you, to be out in the rain falling.

The audience is shown a re-creation of an authentic Irish wake, with pipes, though not new pipes, and whiskey, though few drinkers of it. In fact, it soon becomes apparent that nothing's quite what the guidebooks say it should be. Each turn in the story, as John Butler Yeats observed, is a surprise.[41] This strangeness of everything – people and customs – the surprising particularity of life, is the mark of authenticity of witness, the inside of a way of life seen from without, as arbitrary, not as natural.

The plot of the play within the play Synge took from a folk-tale Pat Dirane told on Aran: a stranger coming from afar stops in a lonely cottage, where a man is pretending to be dead in order to catch his wife in an act of unfaithfulness. When she lies down in bed with a young fellow, the old husband arises and beats her with a stick till the blood leaps up and hits the gallery. 'That is my story.' But Synge had in mind something other than a folk Irish bloody *Taming of the Shrew*. Lonely, full of longing for the lusty shrew, he dreamed of pulling a romantic rabbit out of a moralistic hat. When Nora Burke walks out with the Tramp, it is a beautiful wish-fulfilment for the author, and a private curse on marriage, property and propriety.

As such, it seemed a deliberate outrage on the audience of an Irish national theatre, which believed its men were good and its women pure. Under Maud Gonne, the Irish feminist movement was utterly subordinated to the nationalist one. So when chauvinist journalists declared, 'An Irish woman would never leave her husband for a fine-talking rambler,' no free-thinking suffragette said, 'Wait a minute . . . I might. It depends on the husband, and the rambler.'[42]

Synge, a nationalist rebel in an old Wicklow Protestant family, was uncomfortable with many of his new-found co-patriots. The party line was never his line. The sometimes ridiculous objections to *In the Shadow of the Glen* got up his nose. Suspicion went both ways. The critics, the Gaelic Leaguers, and the nationalist clubs would not leave him be. They even disliked *Riders to the Sea* (25 February 1904), the shortest fully developed tragedy in dramatic literature, a real classic. George Moore was one of the only ones in the audience for *The Well of the Saints* (4 February 1905) to see it as a masterpiece; according to the more typical Joseph Holloway, this Modernist miracle play (once their sight is restored, a blind couple wish to be blind again) gave a nasty and depressing vision of life. In a letter to a friend built on the they-haven't-seen-anything-yet trope, Synge promised in the future to write a play really to 'make them hop'.[43] On 26 January 1907, that play was performed: *The Playboy of the Western World*.

During its debut, the Widow Quin was trying to coax the supposedly father-killing hero to make himself safe, and to leave off his pursuit of the barmaid heroine, Pegeen Mike, 'a girl you'd see itching and scratching, and she with a stale stink of poteen on her from selling in the shop'.[44] In place of Pegeen, the Widow offers Christy herself, a dowry, an escape route and 'finer sweethearts at every waning moon', but he refuses:

> It's Pegeen I'm seeking only, and what'd I care if you brought me a drift of chosen females, standing in their shifts itself maybe, from this place to the Eastern World –

The crowds hopped out of their seats and cried out, 'That's not the west!'[45] According to Lady Gregory's telegram to Yeats (then in Scotland), the outbreak occurred precisely at the word 'shifts'. From then on, the play caused a week of nightly riots, so that the actors could not be heard. Police were brought in to arrest those who disturbed the peace. If it was indeed the fact that one word in one sentence triggered the uproar on opening night, why it did so will always be a question both fascinating and mysterious.[46]

But a speculative depth analysis of this particular sentence may be beside the point. Nearly every sentence in *The Playboy of the Western World* will sustain a depth analysis of its elegant power to perturb. Pegeen Mike, for instance, when she aims to discredit her rival for Christy, the Widow Quin, declares, 'Doesn't the world know you reared a black ram at your own breast, so that the Lord Bishop of Connaught felt the elements of a Christian, and he eating it in a kidney stew?'[47] Each phrase tops the next in its fantastical, lyrical grotesquerie. It evokes a picture of a woman nursing, so that feelings about sex and motherhood make mischief together; to that it adds a reference to interspecies sexuality; on top of that comes a kind of black mass parody of communion, using the accurately theological word for the host – 'elements'; and finally it trumps even this by an insinuation that the princes of the church are pampered, gluttonous and unconsciously sacrilegious. The speed with which disturbing conjunctions stream out made it impossible for the audience to settle into a familiar mode of comprehension. They must have wondered – audiences still do – is this realism, satire, black humour, poetry, tragedy? Where are we and what am I? *The Playboy* is not a one-night wonder, caused by one weirdly outrageous line. The whole play is an astonishing work of genius. It deserves to be the classic of world theatre that it has become.

The larger structures of *The Playboy* ring the changes on the great 'mythemes' of European culture. Christy Mahon is Christ the Man, to whom like the Magi Susan, Sara and Honor bring gifts in act 2. He is Narcissus looking into the mirror. He is Oedipus who killed his father. He is Achilles winning the games in the *Iliad*, before the battle at Troy. He is Caesar marching off at the end with a heathen slave. He is, to give him his due, as Pegeen at the curtain finally does, 'the only Playboy of the Western World'.[48]

The Playboy, even measured against other masterpieces, is with unusual intensity both for all times and of its time and place (26 January 1907, Abbey Theatre, Dublin). Synge did nothing to avoid, and a good deal to bring about, the disturbances on that night. The following day, he wrote to his beloved Molly Allgood (who starred as Pegeen Mike): 'It is better to have the row we had last night, than to have your play fizzling out in half-hearted applause.' 'Now,' he accurately prophesied, 'we'll be talked about. We're an event in the history of the Irish stage'.[49] In fact, *The Playboy*'s first night is *the* event in the history of Irish stage. Earlier theatre riots are compared with that one.[50] Later plays measure their genius and volatility against the response created by *The Playboy*. It was a remarkable feat to make the audience part of the drama, so that in the final act a 'brutal riotous scene takes place' both on stage and in the audience, as, in the words of Ben Levitas, high-minded spectators 'shout down the action that they themselves perform'.[51]

Yeats's disappointment in Yeats's theatre

In the immediate aftermath of the *Playboy* riots, W. B. Yeats took over the authorship of the meaning of the event. During a debate at the Abbey, Yeats held that the play itself was simply a beautiful work of art; the disturbances were organized by political clubs hostile to the freedom of the individual and, like the weakling in the play, Shawn Keogh of Killikeen, 'docile to Father Reilly'.[52] After the death of Synge in 1909, Yeats developed this sectarian theme of the great (Protestant) artist done down by a Catholic nationalist mob in 'J. M. Synge and the Ireland of his Time'.[53] The essay sizzles with disillusionment, caused not only by the death of his friend (which after all was as a result of disease not public persecution), but by the disappointment of his own hopes with the Abbey Theatre.

The greatest poet to write in English for centuries, Yeats nonetheless lacked the abilities of an ordinary popular playwright. He could not imitate common speech or allow a scene to develop naturally from conversation. He was not good at inventing suspenseful plots that evoke deep contemporary conflicts within the public psyche. He was at odds with modern urban democratic life and longed to replace it with images of noble, heroic creatures, activated by loftier passions and displaying more splendid gestures. Unless set to music, or sensationally melodramatised, such stage conduct is not much enjoyed by modern audiences.

On top of these defects (from the point of view of theatrical success), Yeats wanted to write verse plays. Shakespeare and his contemporaries had done so; eighteenth-century verse tragedies were sometimes successful in the eighteenth century; but at the time Yeats was writing, verse drama had been dead for 100 years. To succeed where Wordsworth, Byron, Shelley, Browning and Tennyson had all failed in the nineteenth century, Yeats had to tap into a still-living twentieth-century appreciation for Shakespeare or start from scratch a wholly new tradition. In the decade after the founding of the Irish National Theatre, Yeats looked for an alternative to the methods of production appropriate to prose realism or to popular Shakespeare revivals, but he did not find what he was looking for. His insistence on rhythmical declamation must have struck contemporaries as not an innovation, but a reversion to the worn-out elocutionary acting. His decorative – as opposed to either spectacular or realistic – stage sets were again a mix-up of the avant-garde with the superseded painted backdrops of the eighteenth- and nineteenth-century theatres.

So the Abbey Theatre in which Annie Horniman hoped that Yeats might achieve fame gave the poet only failures (*The Unicorn from the Stars*, 21 November 1907; *The Golden Helmet*, 19 March 1908) and half-successes (*On Baile's Strand*, 27 December 1904). The one Yeats play of the period that came closest to contemporary success – though it is not often acted today – is *Deirdre*.

On 9 November 1908, the most celebrated actress of the London stage, Mrs Patrick Campbell, took the lead role in an Abbey revival of Yeats's play based on the Red Branch cycle of Irish heroic tales. At the play's conclusion, the poet at last heard the sweet sound of ovations and calls for the author. This time he took the stage not to denounce the audience, but to accept gracefully its admiration.

In *Deirdre*, the *mise-en-scène* had been perfectly chosen: a torchlit table on which chessmen sit. The exposition by the Musicians in crystal-clear verse lays out the situation: a young Naoise carried off the long-intended girl bride of King Conchubar, and fled to Scotland. Lured by promises of forgiveness, Deirdre and Naoise have returned to the King's palace. But everyone knows the old story: no welcome is planned, but a murder of Naoise and rape of Deirdre. Now, amid great tension, the lovers play chess. Yeats's characterisation of Deirdre is as 'actressy' as a star could wish.[54] She begs, pleads, lies, charms, seduces, rages – 'moment by moment [she] changes'. For a tragedy, the play is admittedly very short, but Yeats had to accept that his own gift for lyrical intensity meant that a play had to be nearly all climax, no sloping upward to a high point, with a quiet fall toward resolution. After the beautiful, high-strung Mrs Patrick Campbell's performance in *Deirdre*, he could boast, 'I am now accepted as a dramatist in Dublin'.[55] It would, however, be a long time before he had a second Abbey success. More and more, the stage would belong to that rival school of drama he had from the beginning aimed to supplant, the school of prose realism.

Holding the door against George Bernard Shaw

In the English-speaking world, the greatest advocate of modern realistic drama was George Bernard Shaw (1856–1950). In spite of his Dublin birth and education, Shaw's Irishness was sometimes questioned in Ireland. Indeed, the familiar witticism could be quoted on the subject: 'Just because a man is born in a stable doesn't make him a horse.' But more generous and telling is another Shaw adage from 1948, near the end of his long life: 'Eternal is the fact that the human creature born in Ireland and brought up in its air is Irish.'[56] Shaw was part of the declining Ascendancy in late-nineteenth-century Ireland, 'a downstart and the son of a downstart'.[57] Shaw's father expected a sinecure, drank disgracefully and saw his wife form a ménage with an operatic voice coach. His son was left with a poor education (no Trinity College for GBS) and went to work at age sixteen in a land agent's office.

From aversion to his family's snobbery, his father's idleness and the landlord system of profit without labour, Shaw derived elements of a lifelong philosophy. All men should be treated equally; all should be compelled to labour; property should be publicly owned. There is also something of a secularised version of the Irish Protestant's righteousness and thorny independence in Shaw's manner of evangelising for these beliefs. He is certainly Irish (no one in England thought of him as anything else), but he never desired to confine himself or his attentions to Ireland, much less Dublin:[58]

> To this day my sentimental regard for Ireland does not include the capital. I am not enamoured of failure, of poverty, of obscurity, and of the ostracism and contempt which these imply; and these were all that Dublin offered to the enormity of my unconscious ambition.

So in 1876, Shaw took up residence in London, where the business of writing in the English language was mainly transacted. Rarely did he return to Ireland. Of Shaw's fifty-odd plays, only one is directly about Ireland, *John Bull's Other Island*, undertaken at the request of W. B. Yeats and Lady Gregory, with a view toward a Dublin première. Strangely, it turned out to be the end of his efforts to write for the Irish theatre, and the beginning of his massive celebrity in England.

It is tempting to see Yeats's rejection of *John Bull's Other Island* as a negative means by which he sought to secure the Abbey against a rival school of drama. The play was finished by September, in good time for the Abbey Theatre opening in December. On 4 October 1904, the director W. G. Fay wrote to Yeats that he thought it 'a wonderful piece of work', though difficult to cast in Dublin. This does not seem an insuperable problem.[59] The cast required only one Englishman to play the lead; the rest of the parts were for Irish actors. A leading man could have been hired in on contract, just as Mrs Patrick Campbell was for *Deirdre*. On 5 October, Yeats wrote the author a holding letter, mostly complimentary, and not very sincere (to Gregory he gave his opinion that *John Bull* was 'fundamentally ugly').[60] Seven months passed. Then Yeats dropped altogether plans to stage one of the classics of modern Irish theatre. It was first produced at the Court Theatre, London, on 1 November 1904. Prime Minister Balfour attended five of the six performances, bringing leaders of the Opposition parties with him. The king – a fat man – came, and laughed so hard he broke his chair. It became Shaw's biggest success yet.[61]

John Bull's Other Island straightforwardly dramatises a typical Englishman in relationship to many representative types of Irishmen: the brilliant emigrant engineer, the drunken London Paddy, the patriarchal priest, the mad saint, the land-hungry farmer, the pale colleen, the servant boy, the man of business, the merry, bigoted and obscene shopkeeper, and the good, honest woman. Through a brilliant comedy of disillusionment, driven by cynical stage interpreter Larry Doyle, the play traces the real causes of stereotyped false impressions.[62] For instance, Nora Reilly is not pale because she is spiritual, as Broadbent thinks, but because she is undernourished. Irish people are not inclined toward melancholy because of their 'Celtic' temperament, but because they live in an impoverished, colonised island where it rains all the time. The former tenant has not been liberalised by getting ownership of his fields, but made more mean, grasping and callous towards his unpropertied neighbour. For once, Shaw turned out to be admirably clairvoyant about the direction of progress: his double-heroes, Larry Doyle and Father Keegan, project an Ireland in which nationalism is simply a transitional stage toward interpretive centres, suburban land development, golf links, hotels and the global economy; towards, that is, internationalism, in which Ireland would for all intents and purposes be absorbed into the Commonwealth and Europe. In the foreseeable future, the nation-state would not matter much, but it would matter whether all forms of life on the planet – from the grasshopper to the poet – might be headed toward a damnation of human design.[63]

As it turned out, the first play by Shaw to appear on the Abbey stage was not one of his best, but one of his worst. *The Shewing-Up of Blanco Posnet* was written simply as a provocation of the Lord Chamberlain, during parliamentary hearings on stage censorship. It was a melodrama about religious salvation, with one or two merely technical violations of the ban on blasphemy and immorality on stage. Ridiculously, the Lord Chamberlain censored it. As the censor's writ did not apply in Ireland, Lady Gregory was eager to produce *Blanco Posnet* at the Abbey. It would help with both the box office and the directors' street cred with republicans.[64] She baited and defied the undersecretary at Dublin Castle with the same courage, cynicism and savvy that Shaw had used to manipulate the Lord Chamberlain.[65] But the play, performed on 25 August 1909, is a poor example of Shavian drama.

Realists and Catholics enter by the back

Even at a distance Shaw drew the younger Abbey playwrights into his orbit. In 1909, Yeats came to believe he had found in the young Lennox Robinson (1886–1958) a successor to Synge as Abbey playwright and to the Fays as stage manager. Robinson's two plays up to that time had successfully irritated the Dublin critics. Produced exactly five years after *In the Shadow of the Glen*, Robinson's *The Clancy Name* (8 October 1908) ridiculed the efforts of a county family to keep up appearances. It was ridiculously complained in the *Freeman's Journal* (9 October) that the play was an insult to the honour of all those in Ireland named Clancy. *The Crossroads* (1 April 1909), Robinson's second play, was an unpoetic, realist re-examination of the subject of Synge's *Shadow of the Glen*: the loveless marriage among Irish cottiers, in which this time the woman of the house chooses *not* to walk out with the young man at the end. Cheered by Robinson's daring, Yeats invited the tall, effeminate and self-educated young man to become director of the theatre in 1910.

As Robinson knew absolutely nothing about how to direct a play, Yeats sent him to learn his craft from Shaw and Harley Granville Barker at the Court Theatre in London. Perhaps Yeats accepted the fact that the work of Robinson's generation would be motivated by a rebellion against the idealism of the cultural nationalists. Yeats's own age-mates had seen Ireland as 'A young girl with the walk of a queen', to quote the ending of *Cathleen ni Houlihan*; Robinson admitted that 'We young men, a generation later . . . , didn't see her as a queen, didn't see her all fair in purple and gold . . . Just because we loved her so deeply her faults were clear to us.'[66] The work of Robinson and the other 'Cork Realists', R. J. Ray, Daniel Corkery and T. C. Murray, was anti-idealist and anti-poetic. Its method of representation owed far more to Ibsen and Shaw than to Wagner and Yeats.

In over twenty-five plays and forty years of association with the Abbey, Robinson would experiment with many dramatic trends, sometimes successfully (e.g., *The Whiteheaded Boy*, 1916, a comedy; *The Big House*, 1926, an atmospheric tragedy; and the Pirandello-influenced *Church Street*, 1934). An excellent example of Robinson's early realistic work and of the mood of the time is *Patriots* (11 April 1912). The play exposes the reality of political culture in an Irish town twenty years after the death of Parnell. It centres on the family of James Nugent, a man just getting out of prison after an eighteen years' sentence for political crimes. He is fired up to call a mass meeting and kick into life the dormant republican movement. But his wife feels exploited, his followers are feckless, and he can make no headway against the 'mean, huckstering spirit' of the new Ireland.[67] In some ways, the play is a dramatic version of Yeats's poem 'September 1913', with its disgust at Paudeen the shopkeeper and bitter nostalgia for the 'delirium of the brave'. Again like the poem, Robinson's play showed little awareness of the growing strength of Sinn Féin and the Irish Republican Brotherhood in the lead-up to Easter 1916.

The house for *Patriots* 'listened with rapt attention like a class of well-behaved schoolchildren eager to be taught and willing to hear all their faults with meekness . . . there was lots of laughter where there should be, and choking sobs the next moment'.[68] The Abbey had found an able playwright who wrote both seriously and in growing harmony with the audience. Robinson would serve in this capacity for decades to come.

A second of the 'Cork Realists' was that long-needed figure, a reliable playwright who was truly Catholic. T. C. Murray (1873–1959) was the seventh of eleven children. Born in Macroom, he taught school for nearly forty years at Rathouff in County Cork. A shy, retiring man, wholly unable to imitate, or else willfully renouncing, the poetic colour of Synge, Murray made his characters – 'all honest, decent folk' – speak an austere, concentrated version of common speech in his thirteen plays.[69] Murray was evidently kept on a leash by the clerical administrator of his school; this both annoyed and intimidated him.[70] Regarding one of his best plays, *Maurice Harte*, Murray wrote to a friend, 'I read an article by Reverend George O'Neill in which he states that the Abbey plays were either non-Catholic or anti-Catholic. This is a notable exception. Four priests – three of them on the Dublin mission – have read the Mss and have it as their opinion that it is elevating.'[71] The hyper-Catholic Edward Martyn had the Irish Literary Theatre plays passed by not one priest, but four priests! The sense of the hierarchy keeping watch is acute.

Astonishingly, *Maurice Harte* (premièred 20 June 1912) appears to explode altogether the concept of a vocation for the priesthood. Set in a 'bright, comfortable farmhouse kitchen', the play dramatises the tragedy of one of the sons of Michael Harte and his strong-willed wife, Ellen. The 'backstory' to the plot is complex and crucial. The mother's ambition – a common one at the time – was that her brightest son should become a priest. It required money to fulfil this ambition, so the Hartes had mortgaged the family farm. However, Maurice's brother, partly on the strength of the new status the family would have once Maurice became a priest, arranged a favourable match with a neighbour girl. Her dowry would restore the family fortune.

Here the action of the play begins. In his last year before ordination, Maurice returns home, pale, fat, hollow-eyed, with his nerves shattered. There surely must be such a thing as a call from God, and he has not to his knowledge heard one. The local priest advises Maurice that his troubles are over 'some absurd scruples . . . that are easily got over'.[72] His mother declares she'd rather be dead than shamed in front of the neighbours and bankrupted by her son not being 'priested'. Overborne, Maurice agrees to return to the seminary. Mrs Harte kneels and gives thanks to 'God and the Blessed Mother this day', as ironical an oath as anything in Synge.[73] From Maynooth Maurice Harte is finally sent home shattered to his ruined family.

Weirdly, this most Catholic of plays manages to raise the question of whether other priests had heard any more of a call from God than Maurice had done. Wasn't it all 'only talk about a vocation'? Yet the special authority of the clergy rested on a literal interpretation of the metaphor of 'a call from God'. A sincere invigilation of an article of Catholic faith thus resulted in an unconsciously ironical indictment of a theocratic society.

It was Murray's view – given out in his 1922 paper to the Catholic Truth Conference – that an Irish playwright has to be a Catholic playwright. Yeats's best plays were those in which 'his mind was absorbed in Catholic thought'; Synge's *Playboy* was poor because 'alien in faith to the people he describes'.[74] One of Murray's fellow 'Cork Realists', Daniel Corkery (1878–1964), advanced a similarly bald argument in *Synge and Anglo-Irish Literature* (1931). Corkery helped found the Cork Dramatic Society in 1908. His plays – such as *King and Hermit* (1909) and *The Yellow Bittern* (1917) – nonetheless draw heavily upon his Anglo-Irish forerunners for their models of dialogue and plot.

More naturally gifted was Padraic Colum (1881–1972). Born in a workhouse (his father was the master), he had a national school education before starting work at seventeen for the railways. In 1902, he acted in the first plays of the Irish National Theatre Society, and then straightaway began to write plays. *Broken Soil* (1903; revised as *The Fiddler's House*) was good enough to arouse Synge's jealousy. The young audience felt their concerns were truly represented by Colum on stage, neither sugar-candied nor steeped in acid. *The Land* (1905) gave voice to young Dublin's weariness of the old parliamentary nationalist obsessions. Yet Yeats's prophecy to Synge when the young playwright seceded from the Abbey in 1906 – 'Colum will be chaos without us' – proved correct.[75] Afterwards, he wrote plays less frequently and less well.

Another from T. C. Murray's long list of truly Irish because truly Catholic playwrights was William Boyle (1853–1923). Boyle's early good-humoured satires were the most successful plays at the Abbey in its first decade, though they did not become part of the enduring repertoire of Irish theatre. *The Building Fund* (1905) and *The Eloquent Dempsy* (1906) targeted new forms of vice on the Irish scene, sneaky greed in the first case, and slippery politicking in the second. In a modernising and democratising Ireland, these were the vices the audience thought worth public ridicule, as opposed to the characteristics that Synge marked out for comedy. When Boyle seceded in protest at *The Playboy of the Western World*, the Abbey lost a capable playwright in tune with its audience.

Murray oddly lumps George Fitzmaurice (1877–1963) together with the group of Irish Catholic playwrights. Fitzmaurice's mother was a Catholic of the tenant class in Kerry, but his father was a Church of Ireland clergyman. The playwright chose to be buried in Mt Jerome, the Protestant cemetery in Dublin. Perhaps the fact that Fitzmaurice's satiric fantasies caused no trouble in the theatre suggested to Murray that he was, like Colum, Boyle and Murray himself, in tune with the public's religious sensibility. His first play, *The Country Dressmaker* (1907), seemed to herald a playwright with both phrase-making genius and acquaintance with country customs. *The Pie-Dish* (1908) and *The Magic Glasses* (1913) further suggested a playwright willing to explore types of theatre – symbolist, idiosyncratic, writerly – Yeats alone had exhibited before. But though Fitzmaurice went on to write fourteen more plays, they were not equal to his first three, and they were not to appear on the Abbey stage. Like Colum, Fitzmaurice was a gifted playwright whose early promise was not completely realised.

Out of Belfast

The Irish National Theatre Society that had for home the Abbey Theatre was not the only patriotic theatre society in the country. Those who hated the Abbey, or seceded from it, started competing theatre societies in Dublin (such as the Theatre of Ireland, 1906), and those who admired the Abbey's work started comparable groups in other cities, such as the Cork Dramatic Society, already mentioned, and the Ulster Literary Theatre (1902–1934). Initially, this group put on plays in Belfast that the Irish National Theatre Society had premièred in Dublin. Subsequently, Lewis Purcell, Gerald MacNamara and Rutherford Mayne wrote light satires for the Ulster Literary Theatre on issues of Belfast concern. For instance, MacNamara's *Thompson in Tir na nÓg* (9 December 1912) farcically transports one of King William's generals into the Irish Land of the Ever-Young, where the bewildered Protestant converses in Orange idiom with Cuchulain, Maeve, Finn MacCool and other legendary heroes. They put the Orangeman on trial for false entry into this Irish Elysium: he doesn't have an Irish name; he knows no Irish history before the Battle of the Boyne; he cannot speak Irish; he has not killed anyone. This slapabout burlesque was a means of engaging with a tensely sectarian situation. While the Ulster Literary Theatre had talented actors and writers, and the sense of what was right for Belfast, they did not own a venue, much less a lovely little theatre with a big subsidy like the Abbey. This houselessness was a serious impediment for them, as it was for the other patriotic theatre companies around the country.

In the years after the departure of the Fay brothers (driven out of the Abbey Theatre on 13 February 1908, effectively by Annie Horniman's hatred and Yeats's aesthetic ambitions)[76] Yeats and Gregory were the company's executives, but they employed a stage manager to manage the daily operations and direct the plays. Many people were hired for, then fired from, this position: Ben Iden Payne (1907), Norreys Connell (1909), Lennox Robinson (1910), Nugent Monck (1911), A. Patrick Wilson (1914), St John Ervine (1915), J. Augustus Keogh (1916), Fred O'Donovan (1917), Michael J. Dolan (1924) and Hugh Hunt (1935).[77] Of all these appointments, the strangest Yeats made was that of St John Ervine (1883–1971).

A loud, loquacious child of Belfast deaf-mutes, St John Ervine had lived in London since 1900, where he met his lifelong hero Shaw and joined the Fabian Society (1911). Ervine did not like Lady Gregory, or Yeats, or their plays.[78] Evidently, as author of a movement, Yeats believed that by means of St John Ervine he could broaden the dramatic representation of Irish life from peasant cabins to urban tenements and from Dublin and Cork to Belfast.[79]

In *Mixed Marriage* (30 March 1911) – Ervine's first Irish play – he dived into a subject that still causes bloodshed in Northern Ireland: love matches between Protestants and Catholics. The main character is a Protestant shipyard worker. He agrees to speak in favour of a labour union uniting Protestants and Catholics, until he finds out his son wants to marry a 'Papish wumman' (yet another Nora). Sensationally but illogically, the house is attacked by rioters and Nora is the one who is shot. While ugly, unconstructed and melodramatic, the importance of Ervine's subject, whether from a Protestant or a Catholic viewpoint, made the play a hit on opening night.[80] Reviewers knew what it was saying, and agreed: in Ireland, 'Prejudice [was] Deeper than Reason', and religion often wasn't morality.[81]

Dublin's love affair with a playwright critical of Belfast Protestants came to a quick end with the 10 October 1912 production of Ervine's 'New Woman' play, *The Magnanimous Lover*. Critics were shocked by the theme (child out of wedlock) and language (whore, bastard, etc.).[82] Infuriated, Ervine wrote a letter to the *Irish Times* (22 October): 'Dublin dramatic critics are symbols of the decadence of Dublin; they are exhausted men . . . You have a hundred years to make up in Ireland . . . You need to learn common sense and to cease to play the fool . . . No wonder that my [Ulster] friends refuse to be governed by you; nor will they ever be governed by you.'

Still, after that 'corker' of a letter,[83] St John Ervine was appointed by Yeats and Gregory as manager of the Abbey in October 1915. Right away, he introduced 'Ulster discipline' and drove the idle actors out of the green room. His 'Orange blood' was quick to boil.[84] In January, he gave a lecture describing Ireland as 'a sick nation', 'very nearly a lunatic nation'.[85] After the Easter Rebellion, in which past and present Abbey actors saw action, Ervine was outspoken in his contempt for nationalism. He drove the actors hard in rehearsal and on tour and, when they complained, put them all on notice of dismissal.[86] On 29 May 1916, Joseph Holloway came as he always did to see the play at the Abbey. The doors were locked. A boy gave him a handbill, 'The Players will NOT APPEAR at the Theatre under the present Manager, MR. ST. JOHN ERVINE'.[87] On a small scale, this rebellion reprised the Easter Rising of the April just past. To Yeats's relief, Ervine gave up the fight in July, in an adumbration of Ulster's partition from the Irish Free State.

St John Ervine was not long enough at the Abbey to produce plays by Shaw, but his successor, J. Augustus Keogh, an Irishman trained in English theatres, rapidly carried out that intention. He put on *John Bull's Other Island* (25 September 1916), *Widowers' Houses* (9 October 1916), *Arms and the Man* (16 October 1916), *Man and Superman* (26 February 1917) and *The Doctor's Dilemma* (26 March 1917). He made Yeats and Gregory's Abbey Theatre, as Joseph Holloway complained, into 'a sort of Shaw playhouse'.[88] The movement from literary drama to realism, from Yeats to Shaw, was complete.

Sean O'Casey's masterpieces

The Shaw excitement caused one Dublin labouring man to read *John Bull's Other Island*: Sean O'Casey. He did not see its performance because he could not afford Abbey prices. Later, a friend took him to Lennox Robinson's production of *Androcles and the Lion* (4 November 1919).[89] In this wild experiment, Shaw gave a music-hall treatment to a fable by Aesop, as part of a send-up of the Christians and Romans melodrama, Wilson Barrett's *The Sign of the Cross* (1895).[90] (The strangeness of the play was captured by Howard Hughes of RKO films when he originally cast Harpo Marx as Androcles, to play opposite Jean Simmons and Victor Mature.) *Androcles* can hardly have triggered O'Casey to become a playwright, but the reading of *John Bull*, and perhaps other works like *Widowers' Houses*, may well have been formative.

When O'Casey submitted his third play, 'The Crimson in the Tri-colour', to the Abbey directorate, Yeats evidently recognized with dismay that the future of the Abbey was not going to be a Yeatsian future. He moaned to Lady Gregory, 'If [Lennox] Robinson wants to produce it let him do so by all means & be damned to him. My fashion has gone out.' It was, he correctly stated, 'Queens melodrama brought up to date', with some red socialism in the Tricolour.[91]

Sean O'Casey (1880–1964) was the youngest of thirteen children of a poor Dublin Protestant family. Largely self-schooled, the young O'Casey seems to have developed by lurches, fanatacism following fanatacism. The Protestant Church was followed by an Orange Lodge, then in fairly rapid order the Gaelic League, the Irish Republican Brotherhood, Larkin's Irish Transport and General Workers' Union and finally James Connolly's Citizen Army. By the time he began to write plays, he had experienced all the enthusiasms of his native city, and been a witness in 1916 to what he took to be the wrong revolution (not nationalism but socialism was needed).

In 1923, the Abbey received an O'Casey play they could produce: *The Shadow of a Gunman* (12 April). The comedy, the Dublinese, the humour, the pathos all came easily to the ensemble of Abbey actors. No one could do such a play so well as they could, and no play could get so much out of Arthur Shields, Barry Fitzgerald, F. J. McCormick, May Craig and the other greats of 1920s Irish theatre.

Within three years, O'Casey would write three masterpieces. Each captures and comments on a major phase of recent Irish history. *The Shadow of a Gunman* deals with the Anglo-Irish War (1919–21); *Juno and the Paycock* with the Civil War (1922–3), and *The Plough and the Stars* with the Easter Rising of 1916. O'Casey did not have to wait for success. The Abbey did better business with his first two plays than it had ever done before.

From 1923 to the present day, when the theatre's bookings would fall off, management could revive any one of these three O'Casey plays to fill the house.[92]

In view of O'Casey's radical opinions, this massive popularity in Dublin might appear to be surprising. In *Juno* (3 March 1924), he puts a tenement family on stage in which the son, Johnny, is a republican, a martyr and an informer all rolled into one – by Catholic nationalist ideology, an impossible combination. The daughter, Mary, is a labour unionist and a 'New Woman' who has been reading Ibsen. Her fiancé is, like Yeats and AE, a gentleman theosophist. Nationalism is put into the mouths of the father of the family, Captain Boyle, and his sidekick Joxer, both lazy, drunken blowhards. O'Casey manages to get away with this display of feminism, anti-nationalism and pacifism partly because he makes the normative voice of the play that of Juno, a realistic, 'salt of the earth' mother. She takes the air out of her husband and children. For instance, when Johnny proclaims the republican ideals which got him shot in both the Rising and the Civil War, because 'a principle's a principle', she retorts, 'Ah, you lost your best principle, me boy, when you lost your arm; them's the only sort o' principles that's any good to a workin' man.'[93]

Yet the reasons why O'Casey's plays are popular are obvious to those who have seen one on stage. In the Dublin trilogy, O'Casey creates unforgettable characters, laugh-out-loud situations, and beautifully phrased, gut-wrenching conclusions. At the close of *Juno*, the daughter, pregnant, has been ditched by the theosophist, who has also ruined the family's chances of a windfall inheritance (Captain Boyle: 'The boyo that's afther doin' it to Mary done it to me as well. The thick made out the Will wrong . . .').[94] Mournful that her poor child will have no father, Mary is comforted by Juno: 'It'll have what's far better – it'll have two mothers.'[95] Cue the handkerchiefs out. As the blindly drunk Joxer and Captain Boyle stumble on stage, the curtain closes to tremendous applause.

The same Dublin audience, however, rose up against its favourite playwright when *The Plough and the Stars* was put on (8 February 1926), a year, as Nicholas Grene points out, when the Easter Rising was near enough in time for participants, or their widows, to be present, and 'far enough away to be hallowed in memory'.[96] Thus it was not the right time to construct a parodic revision of the new nation's sacred drama. At the end of act 2, soldiers from the Citizens' Army conduct a catechism that reads like a parody of *Cathleen ni Houlihan*, the favourite of all republican plays:[97]

CLITHEROE: You have a mother, Langon.
LIEUT. LANGON: Ireland is greater than a mother.
CAPT. BRENNAN: You have a wife, Clitheroe.
CLITHEROE: Ireland is greater than a wife.
LIEUT. LANGON: Th' time for Ireland's battle is now – th' place for Ireland's battle is here.

It was greatly objected to by the widows of republican leaders that, while a speech by Patrick Pearse is heard offstage in act 2, onstage is a pub into which stroll both a prostitute and men carrying national flags, then felt to be an obscene and sacrilegious conjunction. Furthermore, two middle-aged mothers from the same tenement, one a Catholic and the other a Protestant loyalist, neither with a husband, get into a fistfight in the pub. They are thrown out by the barman, leaving one baby behind. By means of such knockabout comedy, a society was represented in which the national question seemed the least of its problems, and one in which the the people were hardly saints, even in 1916.

The Plough and the Stars, however, had too many great characters, and a plot too important to the country's life, to long stay under a ban. Fluther Good, the Covey, Bessie Burgess, Mrs Grogan and even Rosie Redmond the whore became the most beloved characters of the Abbey stage, as this play by O'Casey came to be revived more than any other in the national repertoire. A 1937 film directed by John Ford enables one to see performances by Barry Fitzgerald, F. J. McCormick, Eileen Crowe and other Abbey greats, in support of Barbara Stanwyck as Nora Clitheroe.

The question about O'Casey has always been: having written the great Dublin trilogy, why did he stop writing in the same manner, at the same level, about similar subjects? He went on to write many more plays, but they are not tragi-comedies of the tenements dealing with national issues.

Partly, the answer must be that after *The Plough and the Stars*, O'Casey could rest neither on his laurel crown nor his crown of thorns. He was still moving, as he had done in his youth, from one fascination to the next. In the 1920s, several Dublin playwrights felt that Abbey realism was old hat. Pirandello, Chekhov, Eugene O'Neill, Georg Kaiser and Ernst Toller had been produced on Monday nights at the Abbey by the Dublin Drama League, led by Lennox Robinson and Mrs W. B. Yeats.[98] Robinson tried, unsuccessfully, to bring elements of German Expressionism into his work; Denis Johnston had the same ambition; and O'Casey would have a go as well.

When he submitted *The Silver Tassie* to the Abbey directors in early 1928, it included an expressionist second act, to go with his customary tragi-comic

Dublin elements in the other parts. Robinson and Gregory thought the play jumbled and inferior to his past works, and failed to reflect that *The Silver Tassie* could be worse than those masterpieces and still be better than anything either of them had ever written. What is this thing, 'Impressionism [sic]', Yeats wanted to know from Lady Gregory. She was unable to enlighten him on the subject. Without due consideration, Yeats sent O'Casey a letter of rejection that happened to arrive on the morning the playwright's first child was born. The tone of the letter was schoolmasterly and presumptuous: 'You are not interested in the Great War; you never stood on its battlefields, never walked its hospitals, and so write out of your opinions.'[99] It may be true that Yeats did not like anti-war propaganda, but to some extent all O'Casey's plays up to that time had been anti-war propaganda. This one was just about war in Europe, rather than in Ireland. The insinuation was that non-Irish politics were not for the Irish national theatre.

The misjudged and mishandled refusal of O'Casey's play – and the bitter newspaper controversy that followed it – turned out to be harmful both to its author and to the Irish stage. Much too late, 1935, the directors reconsidered their decision (Lady Gregory: 'We were wrong and I fully confess it'),[100] and decided to produce *The Silver Tassie* at the Abbey. By then a church-dominated, Fascist-leaning public life was united against free expression of minority opinion. One Father M. H. Gaffney wrote to the press warning about *The Silver Tassie* and insinuating a threat against the Abbey's state subsidy for daring to stage a play.[101] The image of a Crucifix on the battlefield in act 2, and what was seen as 'the travesty of the Sacred Office' in the same scene, were singled out for opprobrium. Yeats's own resignation was called for – 'no literary leader for a Catholic country'.[102] Reviewers then fell into line and condemned the play – O'Casey never after wrote a better one – as 'cold blooded obscenity and blasphemy'.[103] The management took the play off after a week, in spite of the fact that it was doing very good business. Cut off from his audience in Dublin for the rest of his life (his next play, *Within the Gates* (1934) was a moral allegory set in London), O'Casey became both self-righteous and artistically chaotic.

Dublin Expressionism at the Gate

While O'Casey's experiment with new dramatic trends had this sad result, another of the Dublin Expressionists enjoyed a triumph that was both unpredictable and unrepeatable. Denis Johnston (1901–84) was a Dublin Protestant lawyer who had been educated at Cambridge and Harvard. As a young man in Dublin, Johnston became more interested in avant-garde theatre than in the courtroom. Still talent-spotting, Yeats soon had his eye on Johnston as a possible future director for the Abbey. Johnston was invited to direct *King Lear* at the Abbey (26 November 1928). However, when he submitted a manuscript entitled 'Rhapsody in Green', it was returned to him with – Johnston claimed – the following words scrawled on the cover: 'The Old Lady says, "No"', the old lady being Lady Gregory.[104] Under that title, it was produced in 1929 by the new Gate Theatre Company, still without its own venue, at the Peacock, a studio theatre adjunct to the Abbey. The Gate gave *The Old Lady* a production so brilliant that it made all current Abbey productions look both amateurish and antiquated. Hilton Edwards's direction and Micheál Mac Liammóir's grandstanding performance style had found a perfect vehicle.

The Old Lady Says 'No!' wears on its sleeve the influences of Joyce's Modernism, the dream quests of Strindberg, the Pirandellian play with reality and illusion and the Expressionism of Toller and Kaiser. The language is an associated frenzy of allusions, parodically interactive. Scenes shift with the shifting thoughts of the leading character, an actor cast as Robert Emmet in a play within the play. He suffers a concussion at the outset, and the rest of the action is his hallucination. Some characters are types, such as Flower Woman and Flapper; others are take-offs on known public figures – O'Cooney, for instance, is an unfriendly portrait of O'Casey.

Irish Modernism would not go farther until Beckett wrote *Waiting for Godot* (1952). There is, of course, a significant difference in nature and quality between the two plays. Beckett's play, originally baffling to its audiences, has grown familiar as a pleasurably rendered myth for end-of-the-world, god-starved humanity. *Godot* is endlessly revived in different languages, in different theatrical treatments. *The Old Lady Says 'No!'* has followed an opposite course. It cannot be successfully translated from its language, time or even original leading man and director. Many of the songs, slogans and plays to which Johnston parodically alluded were well known – as clichés, all too well known – but have now been forgotten. Thus, the sting of the allusions is lost in a contemporary revival. *The Old Lady Says 'No!'* gives expression to the viewpoint of a liberal Dublin Protestant, fed up with the provincial culture, chauvinism, and defunct heroism of the new Catholic Gaelic Free State, but even that sense of alienation floats obscurely through this unique work of Irish dramatic literature. The disparate influences that came together in *The Old Lady Says 'No!'* fell apart again afterwards. Johnston rapidly moved toward the Shavian play of ideas with *The Moon in the Yellow River* (1931).[105]

Denis Johnston is often wrongly identified as the Gate playwright par excellence. His next play was produced at the Abbey, and the Gate found no other literary extravaganzas quite like *The Old Lady*. Indeed, while 'Abbey playwrights' are a very large and distinguished class of writers, Gate playwrights are neither, at least until the 1980s and 1990s.

Mary Manning (1906–99) like Johnston declined from a brilliant beginning.[106] She too was liberal, intelligent, educated, Anglo-Irish and passionate about theatre (she had been in Sarah Allgood's acting classes at the Abbey). Joining the Gate when it was organised, she became its publicity manager and editor of *Motley*, the house magazine. On 8 December 1931, at its impressive premises in the 1764 concert rooms of the Rotunda in Parnell Square, the Gate staged a three-act comedy by Manning, entitled *Youth's the Season . . .* Its splendid cast included Denis Johnston, Cyril Cusack, Meriel Moore, Coralie Carmichael and Mac Liammóir. The Gate's leading man played Desmond Millington, 'a youthful invert in a cyclamen polo jumper'. Manning and Mac Liammóir made common cause in characterising Desmond as homosexual through and through. Here is Mac Liammóir's summary of his part: Desmond 'painted lampshades of a rather dubious Greek origin, got tight at a party and slapped a boyfriend's face, wept and said how hard it was to be called Flossie at school, and ended up with a lament for a young suicide'.[107] Denis Johnston was also typecast. He played an overly serious poet called Terence Killigrew, who apparently has been reading too much of Eliot's *The Waste Land* and, as he admits, 'too much Proust. Too much Joyce', so he cannot find himself as a writer.[108]

The men and women who come together and fall apart at the twenty-first birthday party of Desmond Millington are from a generation troubled by alcoholism, depression, sexual frustration and terror about 'what is to be done'. Is there anything but marriage for the girls and a desk in father's firm for the boys? In dreary Free State Dublin, they cannot even feel tragic. 'My dear Toots, if I felt tragic I'd do the thing properly. I'd grow a black tangled beard and live on an island with three raging miles of sea between myself and the mainland. An uncle of mine did that. They called him Timon of Athens. He died mad. No, the truth is that I'm a bloody farce.'[109] This Chekhovian sense of one's own ridiculousness, and of the futility of one's personal desires, is blended with a witty social comedy in the manner of Oscar Wilde. The cast has three strongly individualised parts for modern intelligent women, an unheard-of abundance in the drama of the period. Manning's combination of Wilde with Chekhov was original, entertaining and unrepeated for decades to come. Subsequently, Gate revivals of the plays of Oscar Wilde did duty for a successor to Wilde.

While the Gate had a splendid theatre building, it did not have, as the Abbey did, a government subsidy. Mac Liammóir and Edwards soon had to be rescued by patrons, Lord and Lady Longford, both of whom wished to see their own works performed. After an artistic falling-out, from 1936 two separate companies divided the year at the Gate premises. For six months, Longford Productions put on works such as *Mr Jiggins of Jigginstown* by Lady Christine Longford (1900–80) and *The Armlet of Jade* by Lord Edward Longford (1902–61), while the Mac Liammóir-Edwards Gate company went on tour; for the other six months, the Gate Company was again resident at the Gate Theatre. A certain accommodation to the taste of the upper-middle-class public was required. Seasons of Shakespeare, other classics, samples from the current New York or London stages, and the occasional original play – all stylishly produced – became the trademark of Mac Liammóir and Edwards.

The late, great Yeats and Anglo-Irish drama

For nearly two decades up to the late 1920s, Yeats had effectively abstracted himself as a playwright from the theatre he managed. He sought his players and audience elsewhere for a new sort of play, a mixture of closet drama, magical rite, and séance. Inspired by the translations of Japanese Noh plays Ezra Pound had shown him, Yeats began to write intensely lyrical, short dance plays, opening and closing with songs. This form gave him the quality of ritual he sought, while isolating him from the demands of realism, plausibility and intelligibility. One of his first and most impressive essays in the form was *At the Hawk's Well*, like several other successes (*The Only Jealousy of Emer* (1919) and *Death of Cuchulain* (1939)), based on the life of Cuchulain from the Irish heroic sagas. These are great plays, poetry both in the theatre and of the theatre.

The Hawk's Well was first performed in Lady Islington's drawing room, London, on 4 April 1916. The plot is like a parable. A Young Man is on a quest for the waters of youth and immortality. He comes to a well guarded by an Old Man, who has waited years for one of those moments when water bubbles up into the dry leaves of the well. Just as the waters rise, a Woman of the Sidhe (a faery bride) who guards the well performs a hawklike dance. The Old Man falls asleep, and the Young Hero shows his courage – and unwisdom – by chasing after the hawk woman, thus missing his chance to drink from the fountain of youth. Thus neither man will become immortal, but the courageous hero will become famous. He has at once passed and failed the great test.

Only nineteen days after the performance of this play, other young men, perhaps 'cursed by gazing into her unmoistened eyes', would go out in search of Cathleen ni Houlihan, and 'lose what may not be found Till men heap his burial-mound And history ends'.[110] Yeats became vividly aware – both proud of, and haunted by – this foreshadowing in his plays of what would both befall and uplift his country: 'When Pearse summoned Cuchulain to his side, What stalked through the Post Office?' he asks in a late poem, and affirming that life imitates art, answers the question: 'The lineaments of a plummet-measured face' ('The Statues').

The Only Jealousy of Emer can be even more beautiful if given performers who are able to deliver verse, play appropriate string and wind music and consummate the action with a frightening and sexually alluring dance. At the beginning of this play, the figure of Cuchulain lies on an empty stage as if dead after his spellbound battle with the sea. His wife Emer and mistress Eithne Inguba attend his body. At the urging of Emer, Eithne kisses his lips, and the body stirs – but it is not Cuchulain's spirit that stirs it. Bricriu, a man of the Sidhe, has taken his place, in order to tempt Emer. If she renounces his love, he will come back to life; if she doesn't, he will spend eternity in the arms of a beautiful woman of the Sidhe. A further condition is that, if returned to life, Bricriu warns, Cuchulain will 'never sit beside you at the hearth Or make old bones, but die of wounds and toil On some far shore or mountain, a strange woman Beside his mattress'.[111] (The great Patrick Magee's rendering of these lines in a Caedmon recording is seductively spine-tingling.) At first, the Ghost of Cuchulain – Emer can see him, but he can't see her – is torn between regret for his lost wife and the temptations of the Woman of the Sidhe. At last, however, he is about to give in to his faery temptress when Emer renounces his love forever. Cuchulain then wakes in the arms of Eithne Inguba. The Musicians close the play with a song whose opening question the audience, however moved, might be helpless to answer: 'Why does your heart beat thus?' The action is intense – a double drama of life and death, and of love and betrayal – but what does it mean?

Like some other verse-plays by Yeats, *The Only Jealousy of Emer* is compacted of Yeats's beliefs about the afterlife, his sense of the place of the individual in history, and his struggle to order his personal life (at the time of composition, he was romantically entangled with George Hyde-Lees, Maud Gonne and Iseult Gonne). Ordinary theatre-goers often cannot make head or tail of the imposing mysteries of Yeats's Noh plays, but readers of his poetry and admirers of dance theatre find there what cannot be found anywhere else. One of those appreciative spectators was Samuel Beckett, who acknowledged that he would give up all of Shaw for 'a sup at the Hawk's Well, or the Saint's'.[112] The barren stage, the dry well, the philosophical weight, the perfection of phrase, the waiting for something that never arrives, or arrives and is somehow missed, the otherworldly view of this world . . . to Beckett, all these elements were worthy of emulation. Certainly, even if the Noh plays of Yeats have never and will never sell many tickets, it is no mean thing to have written the best twentieth-century verse plays in the English language, and opened the way for its greatest prose playwright.

In 1930, a former senator of the Free State, and wholly at odds with it, Yeats re-engaged as a dramatist with the Abbey Theatre. *Words upon the Window Pane* (17 November), *The Cat and the Moon* (21 September) and *The Dreaming of the Bones* (6 December) were all performed in that year. All three are good work, especially the first. This play provides a splendid vehicle for a star actress. It dramatises a Dublin séance in which the medium – a simple, dowdy woman named Mrs Henderson – becomes possessed with first one spirit, then another, until Jonathan Swift takes over, driving out others, except for the voices of his two lovers, Stella and Vanessa, the latter of whom asks Swift to place his hands on her breasts ('white, ivory dice') and begs him to reproduce. But Swift tears himself away. He refuses to 'add another to the healthy rascaldom and knavery of the world'.[113] 'Perish the day that I was born!' is the play's last line. The re-creation of the voice of Swift is flawless: tormented, majestic and great-hearted. He leaps frighteningly into contemporary life and curses its democracy, low-mindedness and envy of greatness. Those in the Abbey audience must truly have felt that they had seen a ghost.

The last Yeats play staged at the Abbey during his lifetime was his masterpiece, *Purgatory* (10 August 1938), appropriately as part of a two-week festival celebrating the theatre's achievements over the previous forty years. In the play, an Old Man and his Son return to the Big House, now burned out. It was in that house, he tells the boy, that he was conceived, begot upon the daughter of the house by a drunken jockey; she died in childbirth. Once he had grown to be a man, the Old Man stabbed to death his own father because the drunk had set the house on fire; 'to kill a house' is 'a capital offence'.[114]

After this exposition, the ghost of his mother reappears in an upstairs window of the floorless house; the hoofbeats of his father's horse can be heard approaching; she prepares to re-enact the night of conception. Son and grandson are about to watch the primal scene. She has to do it over and over, the Old Man thinks, because the consequences of her sin continue, and will always continue so long as she has descendants. Perhaps if she had no descendants, she would be free. With sick consistency, the Old Man opens his pocket-knife and, on stage, kills his own son, just then grovelling on the ground for some pennies. This desperate effort to affect in this life the outcome of the next life is unavailing even for a minute. The sound of hoofbeats can be heard again as the curtain drops.

As Robert Welch points out, a play with this story and the title *Purgatory* must have seemed downright blasphemous to an Irish audience that had clearly defined ideas about Hell, Purgatory and Heaven – Roman Catholic ideas to put it plainly.[115] A director of the Abbey and friend of Yeats, F. R. Higgins, was asked the next day by a priest what the play was about. Higgins said he was not sure. Lennox Robinson, next pressed for an answer, replied that only Yeats knew. Yeats at first offered little help: the play contained, he said, his beliefs about this world and the next.[116] Then he wrote to the papers to say that *Purgatory* was a 'plea for the ancient sanctities'.[117] Perhaps these were the sanctities that Protestants are married to Protestants, Catholics to Catholics, Big Houses and their dynasties are held in reverence and money-grubbing rascals are executed, as in the grand old days. Given that hundreds of Big Houses had been burned or knocked by the IRA in the Civil War and afterwards, including Moore Hall and Coole Park, and a leader of the IRA from that time was now Taoiseach, Eamon de Valera, to declare it a capital offence to kill such a house was implicitly to threaten war on the people and state of Ireland. But the play's nightmarish depiction of a nihilistic cyclicity goes beyond even Yeats's great rage at modernity and especially modern Irish democracy in a Catholic, Gaelic state.

When *Purgatory* opens, there is a ruined house and a bare tree in the background. 'Study that tree,' the old man orders. 'What is it like?' Surely, given the play's obsession with family and genealogy, the tree is like a family tree, in particular, the dynastic tree of the Anglo-Irish. Fifty years ago, it was full of 'green leaves, ripe leaves'. Then decadence, it is insinuated, began: the tree became like a fruit overripe, full of 'leaves thick as butter, Fat greasy life'. Finally, a 'thunderbolt' struck it, and now it's 'stripped bare'.[118] What was that thunderbolt? Interbreeding? Sex, drink, and general self-indulgence? Easter 1916? It was at any rate something deserving of punishment from Heaven. The play as a whole doesn't simply rage at modern Ireland; it is more obviously tormented with guilt that the race and culture symbolized by tree and house brought destruction upon themselves. The guilt gives way to a violent impulse: given how much is lost, let everything be destroyed, let all things pass away. No doubt, *Purgatory* has something in it of the misery of marginalised Irish Protestants, but one must remain aware that while Yeats was an old man, he was not the truly wild and wicked Old Man of *Purgatory*.

Purgatory is a fitting swan-song for fifty years of modern Irish drama. The best of that drama is to a large extent the work of Anglo-Irish authors. Not many were raised in Big Houses with avenues and parks – only Martyn, Moore and Gregory, among those discussed here. Others were the children or grandchildren of clergymen, whose financial maintenance was stopped in Ireland by the Disestablishment Act of 1867. That group includes Yeats, Synge, Fitzmaurice and Robinson. Still, these downwardly mobile members of the Cork or Dublin middle class came to be lumped together by the politics of the new century with the landlords and the English garrison in Ireland. After 1923, exile was about the only place for them to call home. AE, Moore, St John Ervine, O'Casey, Mary Manning, Denis Johnston and Samuel Beckett all left for residence elsewhere.

A last spell of excellence

In the period of this study, 1890 to 1940, there was one last spell of quality Irish theatre at the Abbey from 1936 to 1938. This followed the appointment of a 24-year-old English director with an Oxford education, Hugh Hunt. He then hired a talented set-designer, also English, Tanya Moiseiwitsch. Hunt put on new, stylishly designed and not very successful interpretations of Yeats, Synge, Shaw and non-Irish classics, but he also premièred strong and more popular work by young Irish writers, such as Frank O'Connor (*In the Train*, 31 May 1937), George Shiels (*The Passing Day*, April 1936), Paul Vincent Carroll (*Shadow and Substance*, 25 January 1937), and Teresa Deevy (*Katie Roche*, 16 March 1936).

Paul Vincent Carroll's *Shadow and Substance*, starring Arthur Shields and Phyllis Ryan, received a Broadway production and won the Drama Critics Circle award for best foreign play; it is still performed in Ireland by amateur groups. Rather daringly for its time, *Shadow and Substance* put a cast of clergymen on stage. A well-educated canon is the protagonist; his antagonists are two under-educated curates and a self-righteous schoolmaster; the female part belongs to their housekeeper, a young girl of unstable mind who sees visions of St Brigid. An ugly and hysterical society is represented, not wholly unlike the one in Arthur Miller's Salem witchcraft play, *The Crucible* (1953). It certainly took courage for Carroll to dramatise the message that rural Irish Catholicism was the shadow, not the substance, of true Christianity.

The most interesting of these young playwrights of the 1930s is Teresa Deevy (1903–63). A Waterford girl, Deevy had seven sisters and five brothers.[119] None of the Deevy girls married; two became nuns. Strangely, the theme of Deevy's twenty-five plays is typically a rebellious woman who must accept that her fate is to be married.[120] The way in which she is confronted with this necessity is, time and again, that she is beaten with a stick by her husband or father or both. The stick is often a big, solid one; with it, she's knocked to the ground, weeping.[121] There is never a question that it is a man's right to batter a woman, if she forgot to make his tea, walked out to a dance or invited a passing man into the cabin. In fact, the Deevy heroine sexually craves a suitor who will treat her as badly as her father has done.

For instance, in *The King of Spain's Daughter* (29 April 1925), Jim is a sweet-natured road labourer who has courted Annie for four years without any success. A neighbour woman, Mrs Marks, kindly advises him to try his success with rough treatment: 'Don't be moved to any foolish compassion. The hard man wins.'[122] In the end, this turns out to be an accurate profile of the heroine's psychology. Once Annie sees from Jim's notebook that he has put by two shillings a week for 200 weeks, she concludes he would therefore be the right husband for her, not because he's well fixed, but because he's fierce:

> ANNIE: . . . he is a man that – supposin' he was jealous – might cut your throat. (*Quiet, – exultant: she goes.*)

Given that Deevy was deaf (from her early twenties, as a result of Meniere's disease), it is surprising that her dialogue is pitch perfect. It is lyrical but idiomatic, not thesis-driven and always in character. Her specific gifts as a playwright – unstereotyped characterisation, surprising plot turns, subtly interpretive stage directions, expressive use of pauses – were greater than those of Gregory, Robinson, Murray, Johnston, Shiels or Carroll.[123] Here is a scene from *Katie Roche*, a play revived at the Abbey in 1975 and 1994. Katie Roche is a young woman born out of wedlock now employed as a house-servant. In the following scene, she has just received a proposal from Stanislaus, old enough to have courted her mother, and now an architect. He wants, he says, 'her heart and her mind':[124]

> KATIE (*flaming*): My heart and my mind! A queer way to love! . . . Taking a body to pieces!
>
> STAN: Very well, whatever you like . . . (*takes this as a refusal, moves a little away*). At any rate, *I* wouldn't have let you go to this dance.
>
> KATIE: It wouldn't be grand enough for you? (*Thrilled.*)
>
> STAN: It wouldn't be grand enough. (*Pause: looks at her.*) Perhaps I should have told you, my desire to get married was partly because that might benefit my work. But I'd have liked it very much. I know that was true (*as one who fears to say a word more than he feels*).
>
> KATIE (*goes to him*): Is it me to be the woman behind you? A help at your work? Is that what you want? (*Eager.*)

STAN: You might indeed: you very well might (*so condescending that she is repulsed*).
KATIE: I might!

For all her gifts, Deevy was condemned to rewrite a single story: marriage as the death of the maiden. In Ibsen's play, the woman walks out of the doll's house at the end; in Deevy's plays, the woman is driven into it, and the door closed forever. Her plays are depressing rewritings of Synge's *In the Shadow of the Glen* in which the old man does beat the wife, and the wife does not get out of the door with the tramp. Wifehood is treated as both virtuous and deadly. Deevy does not protest this state of affairs; she just represents it. Her characters enact as women what became Deevy's own fate as a playwright – the repression of female identity. After the departure of Hugh Hunt from the Abbey (he joined the British army at the outset of World War II), she was cast aside by the sterile patriarchy established under new artistic director Ernest Blythe. He rejected her three-act *Wife to James Whelan* in 1942, adding coldly he had no further use for her plays.

The patriarchal, woman-sacrificing world of Deevy's plays is often seen in relation to the Irish Constitution of 1937, which stipulated that a woman's place was in the home, as a mother, subservient to her husband. Once married, women were prohibited by law from continuing to work as doctors, teachers or any other profession ('the marriage bar'). Yet it must be added that long before the 1937 Constitution, marriage is often a tragedy for the heroine of an Irish play. Consider *Deirdre*, whether by AE, Synge or Yeats; *Grania*, whether by Moore and Yeats or Gregory; *Dervogilla* by Gregory; the marriage-that-was for Juno and the-marriage-that-wasn't for Mary in *Juno and the Paycock*; and, in *The Plough and the Stars*, pregnant Nora Clitheroe is thrown to the street by her brave captain, Jack Clitheroe, causing a miscarriage. Synge got brickbats fired at him for breaking this convention of female submission in *In the Shadow of the Glen*. Cathleen ni Houlihan had 'the walk of a queen' at the end of the play, and that was because men died for her, not she for them.

Conclusion

From 1901 to 1906, when the Irish National Theatre Society was being established, W. B. Yeats articulated its goals in an occasional magazine, *Samhain*. Again and again, he asserted that the theatre's priority would be soliciting dramatic literature of the highest order. Morality, politics, popularity, spectacular sets and star-quality acting all mattered much less than literature for the stage:

- [National literature] is the work of writers who are moulded by the influences that are moulding their country, and who write out of so deep a life that they are accepted there in the end. [1904][125]
- *First*. Our plays must be literature or written in the spirit of literature. The modern theatre has died away to what it is because the writers have thought of their audiences instead of their subject. [1904][126]
- Our opportunity in Ireland is not that our playwrights have more talent – it is possible that they have less than the workers in an old tradition – but that the necessity of putting a life that has not hitherto been dramatised into their plays excludes all these [old stereo-]types which have their origin in a different social order. [1905][127]
- All good art is extravagant, vehement, impetuous, shaking the dust of time from its feet, as it were, and beating against the walls of the world. [1905][128]

In line with these ideals of the great impresario, the Abbey Theatre invited and responded to unsolicited manuscripts. By the 1930s, it was receiving over 300 each year. From 1910 to 1930, Lennox Robinson and Lady Gregory would read these scripts, and pass the best along to W. B. Yeats. Young authors would get criticism, sometimes detailed criticism from Yeats himself. Thereafter, the tradition continued. At the Abbey, writers came first, new writers were taken seriously, and they were expected to express their own personal visions of life, as life had shown itself in Ireland to an Irish person. The fact that the Abbey Theatre was a repertory theatre in which plays had short runs had two benefits: first, prospective writers had a chance to see the Irish canon in revivals; second, new writers had a chance to have their plays staged. Certainly, Yeats deserves significant credit for making dramatic literature flourish in Ireland. A tiny country with little precedent for plays by Irish people for Irish people rapidly became famous the world over for great drama, with distinctive emphases on fine language and the soul of the nation.

Notes

1. Lady Gregory, *Our Irish Theatre* (Gerrards Cross: Colin Smythe, 1972), p. 18; W. B. Yeats, *Autobiographies* (London: Macmillan, 1955), pp. 383–458.
2. See Warwick Gould, ed. *The Collected Letters of WB Yeats, Vol. II: 1896–1900* (Oxford: Clarendon Press, 1997), pp. 123–4. Hereafter cited as LWBY2.
3. Cheryl Herr, *For the Land They Loved: Irish Political Melodramas, 1890–1925* (Syracuse: Syracuse University Press, 1991).
4. Stephen Watt, 'Boucicault and Whitbread: The Dublin Stage at the End of the Nineteenth Century', *Éire-Ireland* 18 (Fall 1983), p. 24; Herr, *Land*, p. 10.

5. For a concise history of the Irish Literary Theatre, Irish National Dramatic Society and the Irish National Theatre Society, see John Kelly and Ronald Schuchard, eds. *The Collected Letters of W. B. Yeats, Vol. III: 1901–1904* (Oxford: Clarendon Press, 1994), pp. 713–18. Hereafter cited as LWBY3.
6. *Leader* (17 October 1903), pp. 124–5.
7. Christopher Morash's *A History of Irish Theatre 1601–2000* is likely to put paid once and for all to the idea that Irish drama began in the summer of 1897. His story of Irish drama begins in the seventeenth century and in its account of causes and effects spreads across Europe.
8. In *The Theatre of Nation: Irish Drama and Cultural Nationalism 1890–1916* (Oxford: Oxford University Press, 2002), an account of theatre and the 'new nationalism', Ben Levitas takes as his terminal points 1890 and 1916.
9. Ibid., p. 11.
10. Ibid.
11. See Kerry Powell, *Oscar Wilde and the Theatre of the 1890s* (Cambridge: Cambridge University Press, 1990), for the relationship between Wilde's plays and the 'New Woman' dramas in London.
12. A connection drawn by Levitas, *The Theatre of Nation*, p. 164.
13. Naomi Lebowitz, *Ibsen and the Great World* (Baton Rouge and London: Louisiana State University Press, 1990).
14. A discovery made by Levitas; see *The Theatre of Nation*, pp. 10, 27, 57, 108, and especially p. 237.
15. *'Le Théâtre-Libre'*, *The Hawk* (17 June 1890), pp. 695–6.
16. George Moore traces this lineage of the Irish Literary Theatre in his preface to Edward Martyn's *The Heather Field and Maeve* (London: Duckworth, 1899), p. vii.
17. Adrian Frazier, *Behind the Scenes: Yeats, Horniman, and the Struggle for the Abbey Theatre* (Berkeley and Los Angeles: University of California Press, 1990), p. 114.
18. Adrian Frazier, *George Moore 1852–1933* (London and New Haven: Yale University Press, 2000), pp. 244–5.
19. A. M. Gibbs, *A Shaw Chronology* (London: Palgrave, 2001), pp. 48–9. Shaw's first visit to Bayreuth was in 1889 (p. 89).
20. For a fuller account, see Martin Meisel, *Shaw and the Nineteenth-Century Theater* (Princeton: Princeton University Press, 1963), pp. 47–61.
21. Ulrich Müller and Peter Wapnewski, eds. *Wagner Handbook* (Cambridge, MA and London: Harvard University Press, 1992), pp. 376–7.
22. Roy Foster, *W. B. Yeats: A Life, Vol. I: The Apprentice Mage* (Oxford: Oxford University Press, 1997), p. 139.
23. James Flannery, *W. B. Yeats and the Idea of a Theatre* (Toronto: Macmillan, 1976).
24. Davis Coakley, *Oscar Wilde: The Importance of Being Irish* (Dublin: Town House and Country House, 1994), pp. 48–75.
25. Declan Kiberd, *Inventing Ireland* (Cambridge, MA: Harvard University Press, 1995), pp. 29–66.
26. Adrian Frazier, 'The Power of the Moment: Ireland's Literary Revivals', *Bullán* 6, 1 (Summer/Fall 2001), pp. 20–1.
27. The quotations from *An Ideal Husband* are from act 2.
28. Frazier, *George Moore*, pp. 286–8.

29. James Pethica, 'Ireland Real and Ideal: Lady Gregory's Abbey Theatre Drama', unpublished manuscript. My thanks to the author for giving me the essay prior to its publication.
30. W. B. Yeats, *Explorations* (London: Macmillan, 1962), pp. 77–8.
31. Yeats to Henry Newbolt; 5 April [1902]; LWBY3, p. 169.
32. Frank Fay to Yeats; 15 April 1902; LWBY3, p. 174n.
33. Lady Gregory, *Seventy Years: Being the Autobiography of Lady Gregory* (Gerrards Cross: Colin Smythe, 1974), p. 413.
34. Pethica, 'Ireland Real and Ideal'.
35. It must be acknowledged that Yeats's *The Land of Heart's Desire* (1894) and *The Countess Cathleen* (1899) earlier employed versions of a similar *mise en scène*. See Nicholas Grene, *The Politics of Irish Drama: Plays in Context from Boucicault to Friel* (Cambridge: Cambridge University Press, 1999).
36. Ann Saddlemyer, ed. *The Collected Letters of J. M. Synge*, 2 vols. (Oxford: Oxford University Press, 1983–4), I, p. 55.
37. Ibid., p. 55 n. 1.
38. Nicholas Grene, ed. *Interpreting Synge* (Dublin: Lilliput, 2000), p. 33.
39. J. M. Synge, *The Complete Plays*, ed. T. R. Henn (London: Methuen, 1981; new edn, 1993), p. 90.
40. Ibid., p. 82.
41. John Butler Yeats, 'Ireland in the Dock', *United Irishman* (10 October 1903); reprinted by Robert Hogan and James Kilroy, *Laying the Foundations 1902–1904, The Modern Irish Drama, a Documentary History, Vol. II* (Dublin: Dolmen Press, 1976), pp. 76–7.
42. For feminist subordination to nationalism, see Levitas, *The Theatre of Nation*, p. 86.
43. J. M. Synge, *Collected Works*, 4 vols. (Oxford: Oxford University Press, 1962–8), II, p. 283.
44. Ibid., IV, p. 127.
45. James F. Kilroy, *The 'Playboy' Riots* (Dublin: Dolmen Press, 1971), p. 43.
46. For a plausible recent explanation, see Grene, *The Politics of Irish Drama*, pp. 77–109.
47. Synge, *Collected Works*, IV, p. 89.
48. Ibid., IV, p. 173.
49. Saddlemyer, ed. *The Collected Letters of J. M. Synge*, I, p. 285.
50. See index under 'riots' in Morash, *A History of Irish Theatre*.
51. Levitas, *The Theatre of Nation*, p. 124.
52. 'Parricide and Public: Discussion and the Abbey Theatre,' *Freeman's Journal* (5 February 1907); quoted by Levitas, *The Theatre of Nation*, p. 133.
53. W. B. Yeats, *Essays and Introductions* (London: Macmillan, 1961), pp. 311–42.
54. Peter Ure, *Yeats the Playwright* (London: Routledge and Kegan Paul, 1963), p. 57.
55. Foster, *Apprentice Mage*, p. 392; Allan Wade, ed. *Letters of W. B. Yeats* (London: Rupert Hart-Davis, 1954), p. 512.
56. Bernard Shaw, *The Matter with Ireland*, ed. David H. Greene and Dan H. Lawrence (London: Rupert Hart-Davis, 1962), p. 248.
57. Ibid., p. 1.
58. Ibid., p. 9.
59. BL Ms Add. 50553, fols. 144–5; quoted in Gibbs, *Shaw Chronology*.
60. This quotation and other details in Foster, *Apprentice Mage*, pp. 325–6.

61. Michael Holroyd, *Bernard Shaw*, 5 vols. (London: Chatto and Windus, 1988–92), II, p. 350.
62. Grene, *The Politics of Irish Drama*, pp. 18–34.
63. G. B. Shaw, *John Bull's Other Island, with How He Lied to Her Husband, and Major Barbara* (London: Constable, 1931), pp. 168–77.
64. Foster, *Apprentice Mage*, pp. 409–11.
65. See Lucy McDiarmid, 'Augusta Gregory, Bernard Shaw, and the Shewing-Up of Dublin Castle', *PMLA* 109, 1 (January 1994), pp. 25–44; and Foster, *Apprentice Mage*, pp. 409–11.
66. Lennox Robinson, *Ireland's Abbey Theatre* (1951; reprint, Port Washington: Kennikat Press, 1968), p. 84.
67. Lennox Robinson, *Curtain Up!* p. 104; quoted by Christopher Murray, 'Lennox Robinson: The Abbey's Anti-Hero', in Masuru Skeine (ed.) *Irish Writers and the Theatre*, Irish Literary Studies 23 (Gerrards Cross: Colin Smyth, 1987), pp. 120–1.
68. Miss Byrne to Yeats, 15 April 1912; Robert Hogan, Richard Burnham and Daniel P. Poteet, eds. *The Modern Irish Drama, a Documentary History, Vol. IV: The Rise of the Realists 1910–1915* (Dublin: Dolmen Press, 1979), p. 185.
69. Richard Allen Cave, introduction, *Selected Plays of T. C. Murray* (Gerrards Cross: Colin Smythe; Washington, DC: Catholic University of America Press, 1998), p. x.
70. Robert Hogan, 'The Brave Timidity of T. C. Murray', *Irish University Review* 26, 1 (Spring/Summer 1996), pp. 155–62.
71. Robert Hogan and Michael J. O'Neill, eds. *Joseph Holloway's Abbey Theatre: A Selection from his Unpublished Journal, 'Impressions of a Dublin Playgoer'* (Carbondale and Edwardsville: Southern Illinois University Press; London and Amsterdam: Feffer and Simons, 1967), pp. 153–5.
72. *Selected Plays of T. C. Murray*, p. 71.
73. Ibid., p. 84.
74. Robert Hogan, 'The Brave Timidity of T. C. Murray', p. 156.
75. Yeats to Synge, [?4 January 1906]; Ann Saddlemyer, ed. *Theatre Business: The Correspondence of the First Abbey Theatre Directors: William Butler Yeats, Lady Gregory, and J. M. Synge* (Gerrards Cross: Colin Smythe, 1982), p. 91.
76. Frazier, *Behind the Scenes*, pp. 176–9.
77. During many intervals between other managers, Lennox Robinson took over, and served at length in the 1920s. See the records of casts and directors in his *Ireland's Abbey Theatre*.
78. John Cronin, ed. *Selected Plays of St John Ervine* (Gerrards Cross: Colin Smythe; Washington, DC: Catholic University of America Press, 1988), pp. 7–8.
79. Robert Welch, *The Abbey Theatre 1899–1999* (Oxford: Oxford University Press, 1999), p. 58.
80. Hogan and O'Neill, *Joseph Holloway's Abbey Theatre*, p. 149.
81. J. H. Cox, 'Prejudice Deeper Than Reason', *Irish Independent* (31 March 1911), p. 5.
82. Quotations from newspapers reprinted in Hogan et al., *The Rise of the Realists*, pp. 200–2.
83. William Boyle's description of Ervine's letter, quoted in ibid., p. 202.
84. St John Ervine, *Some Impressions of My Elders* (London: Allen and Unwin, 1923), p. 24.
85. Cronin, *Selected Plays of St John Ervine*, p. 8.

86. Welch, *Abbey Theatre*, pp. 69, 72.
87. Hogan and O'Neill, *Joseph Holloway's Abbey Theatre*, p. 187.
88. Ibid., p. 193.
89. David Krause, *Sean O'Casey: The Man and His Work* (London: MacGibbon and Kee, 1960), p. 36.
90. See Shaw's hilarious review of this crowd-pleaser in *The Saturday Review* (11 January 1896); reprinted in George Rowell, ed. *Victorian Dramatic Criticism* (London: Methuen, 1971), pp. 214–15.
91. Quoted in David Krause, ed. *The Letters of Sean O'Casey*, 2 vols. (Cassell: London, 1975), I, p. 90.
92. In December 2002, *The Plough and the Stars* ran at the Abbey Theatre, Dublin, and did good business at the end of what had been a lean year at the box office.
93. Sean O'Casey, *Three Plays* (New York: St Martin's Press, 1957), p. 27.
94. Ibid., p. 62.
95. Ibid., p. 71.
96. Grene, *The Politics of Irish Drama*, p. 141. Grene points out that objections did not begin right away; they arose because of the outrage of mothers and wives of republican martyrs who were in the audience (pp. 139–50).
97. O'Casey, *Three Plays*, p. 178.
98. Ann Saddlemyer, *Becoming George: The Life of Mrs W. B. Yeats* (Oxford: Oxford University Press, 2002), pp. 354–8, and Brenna Katz Clarke and Harold Ferrar, *The Dublin Drama League 1918–1941* (Dublin: Dolmen Press, 1979).
99. Quoted by Welch, *Abbey Theatre*, pp. 106–7.
100. Quoted by Hugh Hunt, *The Abbey: Ireland's National Theatre 1904–1978* (New York: Columbia University Press, 1979), p. 132.
101. After a three-and-a-half-year campaign for government support by Gregory and Yeats, in August 1925 the Abbey was awarded an annual subsidy of £850 by the Cumann na nGaedheal government. For details, see Lionel Pilkington, *Theatre and the State in Twentieth-Century Ireland: Cultivating the People* (London: Routledge, 2001), pp. 88–90.
102. *Standard* (30 August 1935), quoted by Hunt, *Abbey*, 151.
103. Quoted by Christopher Murray, *Twentieth-Century Irish Drama: Mirror Up to Nation* (Manchester: Manchester University Press, 1997), p. 135.
104. According to Grene, this oft-told story was fabricated by Johnston; *Politics of Irish Drama*, p. 150.
105. *The Moon in the Yellow River* resembles not just Shaw's discussion plays but AE's allegorical symposium on the new Ireland, *The Interpreters* (New York: Macmillan, 1923).
106. Manning moved to Boston in 1935 and married a Harvard law professor. Manning published several successful novels and collections of stories, including *Lovely People* (1953) and *Chronicles of Ballyfungus* (1978).
107. Mac Liammóir's summary of the part, as quoted by Christopher Fitz-Simon, *The Boys: A Biography of Michael MacLiammoir and Hilton Edwards* (London: Nick Hern Books, 1994), p. 79.
108. Mary Manning, 'Youth's the Season . . .', in Curtis Canfield, ed. *Plays of a Changing Ireland* (New York: Macmillan, 1936), p. 366.

109. Ibid., p. 332.
110. W. B. Yeats, *The Collected Plays* (London: Macmillan, 1952), pp. 215–17.
111. Ibid., p. 289.
112. Anthony Cronin, *Samuel Beckett: The Last Modernist* (London: HarperCollins, 1997), p. 57. *The Well of the Saints* is a 1905 play by Synge that in retrospect appears very Beckettian.
113. Yeats, *Collected Plays*, p. 610.
114. Ibid., p. 683.
115. Welch, *The Abbey Theatre*, p. 133.
116. Wade, *Letters of W. B. Yeats*, p. 913.
117. Quoted by Terence Brown, *The Life of W. B. Yeats: A Critical Biography* (Dublin: Gill and Macmillan, 1999), p. 373.
118. Yeats, *Collected Plays*, pp. 681–2.
119. Judy Friel, 'Rehearsing *Katie Roche*', *Irish University Review* 25, 1 (Spring/Summer 1995), p. 117.
120. Six of Deevy's plays were produced at the Abbey in the 1930s. For a bibliography, see Martina Ann O'Doherty, 'Deevy, A Bibliography', *Irish University Review* 25, 1 (Spring/Summer 1995), pp. 163–70.
121. Instances enumerated by Eibhear Walshe in 'Lost Dominions: European Catholicism and Irish Nationalism in the Plays of Teresa Deevy', *Irish University Review* 25, 1 (Spring/Summer 1995), p. 133.
122. Teresa Deevy, *The King of Spain's Daughter and Other One-act Plays* (Dublin: New Frontiers Press, 1947), p. 30.
123. Christopher Murray has an excellent analysis of Deevy's stagecraft in 'Introduction: The Stifled Voice', *Irish University Review* 25, 1 (Spring/Summer 1995), pp. 8–9.
124. Teresa Deevy, *Three Plays* (London: Macmillan, 1939), pp. 39–41.
125. Yeats, *Explorations*, p. 156.
126. Ibid., p. 164.
127. Ibid., p. 185.
128. Ibid., p. 193.

Select bibliography

Flannery, James, *W. B. Yeats and the Idea of a Theatre*, Toronto: Macmillan, 1976.

Frazier, Adrian, *Behind the Scenes: Yeats, Horniman, and the Struggle for the Abbey Theatre*, Berkeley and Los Angeles: University of California Press, 1990.

George Moore 1852–1933, London and New Haven: Yale University Press, 2000.

Gregory, Lady, *Our Irish Theatre*, Gerrards Cross: Colin Smythe, 1972.

Grene, Nicholas, *The Politics of Irish Drama: Plays in Context from Boucicault to Friel*, Cambridge: Cambridge University Press, 1999.

Herr, Cheryl, *For the Land They Loved: Irish Political Melodramas, 1890–1925*, Syracuse: Syracuse University Press, 1991.

Hogan, Robert, gen. ed. *The Modern Irish Drama*, a *Documentary History*, vols. I–VI, Dublin: Dolmen Press; Newark: University of Delaware Press; Gerrards Cross: Colin Smythe, 1976–92.

Hogan, Robert, and Michael J. O'Neill, eds. *Joseph Holloway's Abbey Theatre: A Selection from his Unpublished Journal, 'Impressions of a Dublin Playgoer'*, Carbondale and Edwardsville: Southern Illinois University Press; Edwardsville: London and Amsterdam: Feffer and Simons, 1967.

Hunt, Hugh, *The Abbey: Ireland's National Theatre 1904–1978*, New York: Columbia University Press, 1979.

Kilroy, James. F., *The 'Playboy' Riots*, Dublin: Dolmen Press, 1971.

Levitas, Ben, *The Theatre of Nation: Irish Drama and Cultural Nationalism 1890–1916*, Oxford: Oxford University Press, 2002.

Meisel, Martin, *Shaw and the Nineteenth-Century Theater*, Princeton: Princeton University Press, 1963.

Morash, Christopher, *A History of Irish Theatre*, Cambridge: Cambridge University Press, 2002.

Murray, Christopher, *Twentieth-Century Irish Drama: Mirror up to Nation*, Manchester: Manchester University Press, 1997.

Pilkington, Lionel, *Theatre and the State in Twentieth-Century Ireland: Cultivating the People*, London: Routledge, 2001.

Powell, Kerry, *Oscar Wilde and the Theatre of the 1890s*, Cambridge: Cambridge University Press, 1990.

Robinson, Lennox, *Ireland's Abbey Theatre*, 1951; reprint, Port Washington, NY: Kennikat Press, 1968.

Saddlemyer, Ann, ed. *Theatre Business: The Correspondence of the First Abbey Theatre Directors: William Butler Yeats, Lady Gregory, and J. M. Synge*, Gerrards Cross: Colin Smythe, 1982.

Welch, Robert, *The Abbey Theatre 1899–1999*, Oxford: Oxford University Press, 1999.

5

The Irish Renaissance, 1880–1940: literature in Irish

PHILIP O'LEARY

Introduction

Just three years after its foundation, the Society for the Preservation of the Irish Language (SPIL) proclaimed in its annual report for 1879 that its object was 'the Preservation and Extension of the Irish as a Spoken Language', and that in order to achieve this end it would, among other things, encourage 'the production of a Modern Irish Literature – original or translated'.[1] By 1882, the Gaelic Union, a dissenting offshoot of SPIL, had taken a significant initial step in this ambitious direction by founding the bilingual journal *Irisleabhar na Gaedhilge* (The Gaelic Journal), a periodical that would appear, somewhat sporadically, until 1909, after 1893 under the management of the Gaelic League. The audacity of SPIL's commitment to fostering a modern literature in Irish – as opposed to the safer and more obvious goal of collecting and preserving manuscript materials from the distant and recent past – was underscored in 1909 by the poet and scholar Tadhg Ó Donnchadha ('Torna') (1874–1949), who, looking back on the Gaelic literary landscape of 1882, wondered whether there had then been more than fifty people in the whole country who could read, much less write, Irish in the native script.[2] While it should be evident from the chapter by Gearóid Denvir in volume 1 of this history that Ó Donnchadha was exaggerating for effect to pay tribute to the courage of those who founded *Irisleabhar na Gaedhilge* in such inauspicious circumstances, there can be no doubt that the focus on original literature so early in the Revival was an act of faith and hope as much as it was a rational decision based on an objective assessment of the contemporary linguistic and cultural climate. That such faith was in no short supply among those dedicated to the language is evident from the fact that virtually from its foundation in 1893, the populist, popular, and, at the time, eminently pragmatic Gaelic League also declared as one of its two principal goals 'the study and publication of existing Irish literature, and the cultivation of a modern literature in Irish'.[3]

In retrospect, this foregrounding of written literature by a movement struggling against formidable odds to arrest the precipitous decline of a language virtually all of whose native speakers were illiterate may well have been a major tactical mistake – premature at best, misguided and dreadfully wasteful of scarce material and intellectual resources at worst. But however questionable the decision to emphasise the need for a new literature in Irish, it was entirely understandable. In the wake of the Macpherson controversies of the later eighteenth and early nineteenth centuries, Irish cultural nationalists had become ever more aware of the nation's rich literary inheritance – among other things as the possessor of the oldest vernacular literature in Europe north of the Alps. From this point of view, the paucity of Gaelic literary achievement in the modern language was a standing reproach to those who stressed the cultural continuity of the Gaelic nation, a reproach that had to be addressed at once. From a quite different but equally compelling perspective in the cultural and political climate of the time, many in the language movement suffered consciously or otherwise from a colonial inferiority complex that demanded that a resurgent, Gaelicizing Ireland possess, indeed excel in, all of the cultural modes of expression that characterized contemporary European – above all, English – civilisation. On the playing fields, this impulse was to give birth to hurling and Gaelic football; in fashion, it was to put (albeit not very many) Irishmen in kilts; in literature, it inspired writers of Irish, many of them recent learners or still students of the language, to create – largely *ex nihilo* – a native tradition in the short story, the novel and the drama, and to expand into new forms and radically new sensibilities the rich and in some areas still fairly vital native heritage of poetry. For a generation of Irish intellectuals trained to see writers like Shakespeare, Milton, Scott, Dickens and Tennyson as the pinnacle of literary achievement, it must have been painful to have nothing recent to boast of in reply but the pleasantly unambitious verse of Robert Weldon (*c.*1835–1914) and Colm de Bhailís (1796–1906).

Building on the past: poetry

At least, as Denvir has shown in the previous volume, there were such poets in Irish, figures who continued to cultivate and develop traditional genres, metres and stylistic devices in painfully diminished circumstances while continuing to embody an ancient tradition that saw poets as significant arbiters of public opinion across a wide range of topics central to the lives of their audiences. Those of literary bent in the language movement were aware and appreciative – perhaps overly so – of this poetic inheritance. The most valuable expression of this appreciation took the form of the collecting, editing and publishing of the work of earlier writers and of still-surviving and active folk poets. The most prolific of the workers in this area were the lexicographer Father Patrick Dinneen (Pádraig Ua Duinnín) (1860–1934), Risteárd Ó Foghludha ('Fiachra Éilgeach') (1871–1957) and Tadhg Ó Donnchadha. As for more contemporary work by folk or local community poets, the Gaelic League issued the collected works of the Connemara centenarian Colm de Bhailís in 1904, and of the Waterford poet Robert Weldon (Roibeárd Bheldon) in 1925. *Duanaire Dúithch' Ealla*, Seán Ua Cadhla's collection of poems by the Kerry poet Domhnall Ó Conchubhair (1872–1935) appeared in 1930, while *Duanaire Duibhneach*, an anthology of verse compositions from the Dingle Peninsula spanning the previous century or so, was edited by Seán Ó Dubhda and published in 1933. Among the poets whose work is anthologised in the *Duanaire* is Seán Ó Duinnshléibhe (1812–1889), the Blasket Island poet who so tormented Tomás Ó Criomhthain in *An tOileánach*.

This editorial work was an impressive accomplishment, making available to readers and writers alike a significant body of the work of their ancestors and folk contemporaries for study and possible emulation. Its appearance must, however, have often been a very mixed blessing, for when we turn to new work by the Gaelic poets of the early Revival we find little of lasting value. Some writers may well have been awed (though not into silence) by the achievements of their predecessors. Too often even the more gifted among them seem to have contented themselves with mastering, to varying degrees of proficiency, the linguistic and technical resources of the past. Doubtless this approach was for many motivated by a justifiable desire to preserve and cultivate a threatened literary continuity. But all too often, in the absence of any real individual technique and/or voice, the result was literary taxidermy, yielding stiff, soulless and largely irrelevant replicas of once vibrant exemplars.

This fixation with a mechanical mastery of outmoded forms and themes is seen quite clearly in the work of the scholarly poets who established Árd-Chúirt Shochaide na Suadh in 1903. Modelled on the poetic courts of eighteenth-century Munster that Daniel Corkery was later to extol in *The Hidden Ireland* (1924), they would meet every year at the Munster Feis for a *dáil* or conference at which lectures would be given on poetic topics, thorny questions of traditional metrics, diction and other aspects of verse craft would be discussed, and new poems would be read, often verse epistles on intramural topics exchanged among the poets themselves, again in the fashion of their eighteenth-century predecessors. In 1908, the group published their first anthology, *Saothar na Suadh*, to be followed by another volume of the same title in 1912, by which time the organisation had changed its name to Árd-Chúirt na hÉigse. Among the active members of the Cúirt were Dinneen, Ó Foghludha, Piaras Béaslaí (1883–1965), Ó Donnchadha and Pádruig Ó Cruadhlaoich ('Gaedheal na nGaedheal') (*c.*1861–1949). Many of these poets took leading roles again when the direct descendant of the Cúirt, Dámh-Sgoil Mhúsgraighe Uí Fhloinn, based in Ballyvourney in the Cork Gaeltacht, was founded in 1925. This group published their first and only anthology, *Saothar Dhámh-Sgoile Mhúsgraighe*, in 1933, a work containing poems by, among others Dinneen, Ó Donnchadha and Tomás Ó Criomhthain, but dominated by the work of Ó Cruadhlaoich, who was later to publish his collected works in the two volumes of *Filidheacht Phádruig Uí Chruadhlaoich* (1936, 1942).

This antiquarian approach may have been unintentionally fostered by the Gaelic League's annual national festival An tOireachtas from its inception in 1897 to its suspension after the financial failure of the 1924 gathering. While An tOireachtas did sponsor competitions for original verse of various kinds, including poems on history (1897, 1920), original humorous songs (1910, 1911), new lyrics for traditional airs (1900, 1901, 1902, 1903, and regularly thereafter), as well as for 'lyric poems' (1897) and, frequently, for 'new poems on any topic' (1900, 1901, 1902, 1903, etc.), the most prestigious poems at the festival, read publicly with considerable fanfare, were the Oireachtas 'Odes', and these tended to be formulaic works on predictable propaganda topics. To be fair, however, some of these poems were technically quite polished, and one of the most famous of them, 'An Préachán Mór' (The Great Crow) by Douglas Hyde ('An Craoibhín Aoibhinn') (1860–1949), was an engaging and accessible piece in which the obnoxious, grating and ravenous bird is the symbol for Anglicisation.[4]

Other poets of the early Revival, in an attempt to break new ground and avail themselves of the previously unavailable opportunity for publication offered by Brooklyn's *An Gaodhal* (The Gael, founded 1881) and *Irisleabhar na Gaedhilge*, turned to translation, cultivating a creative option with a long and honourable history in the language, but one that was to be a source of ongoing contention in the first half-century of the modern Revival. Largely ignorant of languages other than Irish and English (and not always in full command of both of those) and with little if any experience in the art of translation itself, writers produced Gaelic versions of things they and their audiences knew and liked, favourites like 'The Bells of Shandon', 'God Save Ireland' and even 'The Star-Spangled Banner'! Most of these translations are now mere linguistic curiosities, but some of them probably did serve a purpose for the more ambitious poets of the time, allowing them, through direct engagement with the work of writers outside their own tradition, to grapple with contemporary subject matter and challenging new settings like the cities from which Irish had long been excluded. At any rate, writers like Tadhg Ó Donnchadha, Dinneen, Béaslaí, or Liam S. Gógan (1891–1979), all of whom, as we will see, consciously attempted to expand the range of poetry in Irish, included translations as a matter of course in their books.

The first such book of original poetry in Irish was Douglas Hyde's *Úlla de'n Chraobh* (1901), his only published collection, though he wrote far more poems that appeared in contemporary periodicals but were not collected until long after his death. It is hard if not impossible to determine why he chose the poems that make up the book over the ones he omitted, for there is little or no difference among them with regard to theme, style or quality. In jingly, sing-song rhythms and rhyme schemes and occasionally flawed Irish, hackneyed poems of lost or rejected love, of exile and of the beauties of the Irish landscape share the pages with propaganda pieces on the dire threat to the Irish language from its mongrel and unlovely English rival and formulaic denunciations of the perfidy of the English and their Irish lackeys. Indeed, if anything stands out in these poems, it is the virulent Anglophobia of many of the political pieces, an emotion doubtless more strategic than real, and one out of character for the diplomatic, non-sectarian and non-political president of the Gaelic League, who in 1915 resigned when the organisation declared national independence one of its chief objectives.

A more accomplished first volume of original verse was Tadhg Ó Donnchadha's *Leoithne Andeas* (1905). The scholarly Ó Donnchadha (he was eventually to be named professor of Irish at University College Cork) did not actually have all that much more to say than did Hyde, but he said it more elegantly in impeccably native metres, explained in his preface to the book. In some ways, Ó Donnchadha was the poet laureate of the early revival, and in this volume we see him conscientiously fulfilling his duties, in particular by keening the movement's illustrious dead in unexceptionably orthodox clichés. *Leoithne Andeas* contains five sections. Along with the keens and translations, there are *amhráin náisiúnta* (national songs) of a conventional nature, songs on the beauty of the country and miscellaneous songs of love, sport and fun. Ó Donnchadha's second and final original collection, *Caitheamh Aimsire* (1918), is characterised by the same linguistic mastery, but shows little meaningful development. Some of Ó Donnchadha's most impressive poetic efforts are to be found in his translations in contemporary journals and in *Guth ón mBreatain* (1912), a selection of his versions of Welsh poems, and *Fíon Gearmánach* (1930), a collection of his translations from the German.

Another scholarly poet, who only published a single volume of original verse, was Osborn Bergin (1873–1950), a linguist and authority on Irish bardic poetry. His *Maidin i mBéarra agus Dánta Eile* (1918) is a predictable enough product of its time with its laments, poems on the language and orthodox nationalist idealism, but the title poem, a song to the tune of 'The Londonderry Air', became popular among Irish-speakers at the time. There is also a welcome touch of satire in 'File na Gall-Ghaedhilge' (The Poet with Anglicised Irish), a parody of a poem written by a learner with high ambition and a shaky command of the language. The volume concludes with translations of 'Mary Had a Little Lamb' into both Modern and Old Irish!

Piaras Béaslaí was one of the most thoughtful and versatile literary figures of the first decades of the Revival, and one who made a special study of the eighteenth-century poets in his two-volume *Éigse na Nua-Ghaedhilge* (1933). Yet despite his devotion to his eighteenth-century predecessors and his active involvement with Cúirt na hÉigse and to a lesser extent Dámh-Sgoil Mhúsgraighe, his only published volume of poems, *Bealtaine 1916 agus Dánta Eile* (1920), is, while undistinguished and predictable in its patriotic fervour, remarkably free of affected antiquarianism.

Every bit as patriotic and even more predictable was Peadar Ó hAnnracháin (1873–1965), a veteran language activist and a volunteer in the War of Independence, who published two collections during these years: *An Chaise Gharbh* (1918) and *An Chaise Riabhach* (1937). Ó hAnnracháin, who had learned the language in adolescence, was unapologetic in his admission that he had not taken up poetry from inspiration or for literary reasons, writing in his preface to *An Chaise Gharbh*: 'Grádh don Ghaedhilg do mheall i dtosach mé chun tabhairt fé ranna Gaedhilge do scríobhadh' (It is love for the Irish language that first led me to attempt to write verses in Irish).

Patriotic verses also appeared in Micheál Ó Murchú's *Tuaim Inbheir agus Dánta Eile* (1923) and dominated Séamus Ó Maoildhia's (1881–1928) only collection, *Dánta agus Amhráin* (1940). The former could serve as a handy sampler of the kinds of poetry being written in Irish at the time. Ó Murchú includes laments for Cathal Brugha and Tomás Mac Curtain, pious verses, poems celebrating the beauty of rural places, seasonal lyrics and translations from French, Scots Gaelic and earlier forms of Irish. Several poems in the latter collection, published posthumously twelve years after the poet's death, were written decades earlier for League occasions like the Galway Feis of 1900 or the Oireachtas of 1902.

There were several surprisingly ambitious poetic ventures in our period. Father Dinneen retold incidents from the gospels in verse in *Startha as an*

Soiscéal i bhFilidheacht (1911) and used the traditional form of the *aisling* or vision to pay tribute to the men of Easter Week in the more than 100 pages of *Spioraid na Saoirse: Aisling Draoidheachta ar an mBliadhain 1916* (1919). Donnchadh Ó Liatháin ('An Rí Liath') (1869–1950) also turned to the Bible for inspiration, offering poetic versions of various stories from the Old and New Testaments in *An Tiomna Naofa agus Dánta Eile* (1931), a book that included a few other religious lyrics. His later collection, *Ceol Abhann agus Gleann* (1938), was a more conventional mix of patriotic, religious and landscape poems, although the laments for his two sons who died of influenza in the great post-World War I epidemic are genuinely touching. In Pádraig Ó Miléadha's (1877–1947) long narrative poem *An Fiannaidhe Fáin* (1934), the poet meets the spirit of the wandering soldier of the title, who had been deceived into joining the British Army under the pretence of fighting for small nations in World War I. After condemning British duplicity and describing at some length the horrors of the trenches, the soldier tells of his conversion to the cause of Irish freedom and his death as an IRA volunteer in the War of Independence.

The first Gaelic poems of the Revival marked by a personal, and recognisably modern, voice were the few short lyrics of Patrick Pearse (Pádraig Mac Piarais) (1879–1916), most of which were collected in *Suantraidhe agus Goltraidhe* (1914). Pearse's reputation as an artist has been unfairly overshadowed by his status as a patriotic icon, with his literary works analysed for clues to his nationalist ideology or to the psychology that led him to embrace what he believed to be redemptive martyrdom. Certainly, his best-known poems in either English or Irish are overtly patriotic works like 'The Rebel', 'The Fool', 'Mise Éire', 'An Dord Féinne' or a poem like 'Fornocht do Chonac Thú', which can be read as a prophecy of his own upcoming sacrifice. But Pearse was a complicated human being with a genuine literary gift he never allowed himself the time to adequately explore or develop in any of the genres in which he wrote with skill and sensitivity. Modern readers troubled by a messianic nationalism whose Irish and European context they do not fully understand may nonetheless still be moved by the emotional turmoil and honesty in well-crafted lyrics like 'A Mhic Bhig na gCleas' or 'Cad Chuige Díbh Dom' Chiapadh?'.

Unlike Pearse, Liam S. Gógan was able to devote himself to his poetry over a lengthy lifetime in which he produced six collections. The first of these was *Nua-Dhánta* (1919), to be followed before 1940 by *Dánta agus Duanóga* (1929) and *Dánta an Lae Indiu* (1936). While Gógan was, like several of his contemporaries, a scholar as well as a creative writer – he wrote learned articles on antiquities in both Irish and English and worked with Father Dinneen on his revised and expanded dictionary of 1927 – he used his scholarship in the service of his poetry to develop the resources of Irish as a modern literary language. For example, while poets like Ó Donnchadha apologised for their occasional recourse to glossaries and notes explaining idioms, etc., Gógan saw such linguistic aids as a means to revive obscure words or technical terms and to explore their potential in new contexts. Some of Gógan's work is predictable enough – patriotic pieces, poems on the Dublin Eucharistic Congress of 1932, verses addressed to Dámh-Sgoil Mhúsgraighe – but he also experimented with a range of styles, with the sonnet (*duanóg*) a particular favourite. His most lasting contribution was that he wrote some of the few poems from the period worthy of his own title *dánta an lae indiu* (modern poems), poems that can still engage and move the reader.

Among the handful of other poets at the time attempting the personal lyric were Séamus Ó hAodha (1886–1967) and Áine Ní Fhoghludha (1880–1932). Most of the short poems in Ó hAodha's *Uaigneas* (1928) and *Caoineadh na Mná agus Duanta Eile* (1939) celebrate nature or the Roman Catholic faith, although a few of the best deal with the lives of the poor – fisherfolk or the evicted woman of the title poem of the 1939 collection. All are appealing in their straightforward sincerity, as are the brief lyrics in Ní Fhoghludha's *Idir na Fleadhanna* (1930), a volume of additional interest as the single collection of verse published by a woman during our period. It would, however, be difficult to make too much of her gender. Her poems, in some of which she speaks through a male persona, are every bit as conventional as those of most of her male contemporaries.

Breaking new ground: prose

Prose had, of course, a long and distinguished history in the Gaelic literary tradition, from the time of *Táin Bó Cúailnge* and the prosimetric *Acallamh na Senórach*, through *Pairlement Chloinne Tomáis* and the classic works of Aodh Mac Aingil and Geoffrey Keating in the seventeenth century, and Seán Ó Neachtain's *Stair Éamoinn Uí Chléire* and other proto-novels in the eighteenth century.[5] While this tradition of sophisticated and highly crafted prose did not, as Denvir has shown in the previous volume, die out in the nineteenth century, it never gained all-important access to the printing press in Ireland, and became increasingly marginalized even among the scribes dedicated to the literary cultivation of the language. By the time *Irisleabhar na Gaedhilge* published its first issue in 1882, the dominant prose form in the language was the folk-tale, of which there was an extraordinarily rich and varied corpus in the repertoires of skilled storytellers in all Irish-speaking areas. Some critics at the time saw these tales as a treasure-trove that preserved quintessentially

Gaelic narrative patterns and therefore provided impeccable native models for the evolution of a new prose literature in Irish that would be true to its own heritage. The most forceful and articulate spokesman for this position was the Waterford-born and German-trained scholar Father Richard Henebry (Risteárd de hIndeberg) (1863–1916). Henebry is now best known for championing a form of the language based on seventeenth-century Irish (*'Gaeilge Chéitinn'* or 'Keating's Irish') over the everyday speech of the contemporary Gaeltacht (*caint na ndaoine*) as the medium for the new Irish literature. He was, however, impressed by the literary potential of the narrative patterns he felt the oral folk-tales had preserved from the earlier literary tradition. In a polemic series of 1908 essays in *The Leader* under the title 'Revival Irish', he went so far as to posit the form of the oral narrative as the best native model for short fiction in the language. Henebry's campaign to impose his understanding of the folk standard on writers of a new prose literature in Irish was, as we will see below, vigorously and successfully contested by Pearse. But his views also won, to varying degrees, the support of such influential Revivalists as Fathers Peter O'Leary (Peadar Ó Laoghaire) (1839–1920) and Patrick Dinneen, and Pádraig Ó Siochfhradha ('An Seabhac') (1883–1964), and they should not be dismissed out of hand. After all, when he was writing, the oral folk-tale *was* the most popular, vital and potentially generative prose genre in the native tradition, and the subsequent explorations of its literary possibilities by prose writers like Seosamh Mac Grianna, Máirtín Ó Cadhain, Pádraig Ua Maoileoin and Angela Bourke show how an informed and sensitive openness to folk narrative could enrich contemporary prose in Irish.

The 'speech of the people'

Henebry was an advocate of what I have called elsewhere the 'nativist' position within Gaelic cultural debates of the early Revival.[6] Many of the issues raised by the nativists – in particular the threat to 'Gaelic' Catholic Ireland from foreign contamination in the form of 'bad' books, immodest female fashions, jazz and the like – are extraneous to any discussion of literature *per se*.[7] But the central insight motivating those who shared to whatever extent and in whatever contexts the nativist position in any of its often reactionary and distasteful manifestations did have a basis and justification in fact. Native Irish culture was under threat at the time, and some, like Henebry, saw the threat menacing the very essence of that culture, the Irish language itself.

For those who agreed with Henebry – the best-known of whom were Thomas O'Neill Russell (1826–1908) and Father John M. O'Reilly (1864–1941), whose *The Native Speaker Examined Home: Two Stalking Fallacies Anatomized* ruffled quite a few Gaelic feathers on its publication in 1909 and again on its reissue in 1925 – the state of the Irish language at the dawn of the Revival was the unfortunate and unnatural result of historical developments that had driven it into isolated, largely impoverished rural areas far from the European intellectual and cultural mainstream in which it had long functioned, even flourished. Henebry and those who shared his views felt that as a result of this imposed isolation, a language long known for its literary homogeneity across all of Ireland and Gaelic Scotland had degenerated into several dialects, two of which, Manx and Scots Gaelic, had evolved – or devolved! – into separate languages. Henebry and his allies were not alone in their sensitivity about the dialecticised state and rural isolation of the language. The charge that 'Irish' was little more than a generic term for a group of rustic *patois* was one that all Revivalists felt deeply and were eager to refute.[8]

Henebry was, however, exceptional for the vigour, clarity and consistency with which he advanced his solution for this lamentable state of linguistic impoverishment. If the past two centuries had seen the steady degradation of Irish as a literary medium, the effects of those two centuries would have to be cancelled out and the link re-established between the spoken language of 1900 and the cultivated literary language of 1700 and before, what was often called 'classical Irish' or 'the Irish of Keating', after the great seventeenth-century prose stylist. Once again, we should not caricature Henebry's position here. He never suggested that speakers of Irish should try to return to some artificial standard from the past. His focus in this argument was on literature. Nor did he imagine – or want – any artificial and absolute distinction between the language as spoken by articulate native speakers and the language as written by competent writers. In his condemnation of what he saw as the debased 'Revival Irish' in most of what little fiction was being produced by his contemporaries, he specifically commented that not only was it 'not in continuity with any Irish literature that ever went before it', but that it was also not 'in agreement with the idiom of those who still speak Irish to-day'.[9] Rather, he insisted that any new Irish prose style worthy of the name had to be continuous with its own tradition, and since that tradition had largely ceased to evolve by the eighteenth century, would-be Irish writers, however fluent their command of the spoken language, would have to immerse themselves in the prose classics of the past. All of this is, of course, simple common sense, and the problem with Henebry's core argument was not with its self-evident central premise, but with his own zealous and often extreme application of that principle, as when in his 'Revival Irish' series he scrupulously and maliciously analysed prose excerpts from several of his contemporaries and then rewrote them in an idiosyncratic and anachronistic form of 'modern' Irish that won no converts and alienated the impartial.

For those who rejected the arguments of Henebry and the small band who shared his views, the battle cry was *caint na ndaoine* (the speech of the people). For these writers, any new prose that was to have a chance of gaining an audience among either native speakers or learners of the language had to be rooted in the language as spoken by those for whom it was their first language. The triumph of *caint na ndaoine* is often simplistically attributed to the example of the prolific Father Peter O'Leary, and in particular of his novel *Séadna*, serialised in part, with accompanying English translation, in *Irisleabhar na Gaedhilge* between 1894 and 1897, and published in book form in 1904.[10] O'Leary was, however, a forceful, relentless and effective advocate of the position he spelled out in a 1900 letter to his friend and ally in the cause, the writer Séamus Ó Dubhghaill ('Beirt Fhear') (1855–1929):

> Abradh na scoláirí a rogha rud, is í caint na ndaoine a bhéarfaidh bua sa deire. To build up a literature without laying its foundations on the actual living speech of the people is like building your house commencing at the chimney.
>
> Let the scholars say what they want, the speech of the people will triumph in the end. (The rest of the quote is in English in the original).[11]

But in retrospect, the ultimate – and quite rapid and total – victory of *caint na ndaoine* can never have been in serious doubt. Virtually all writers and critics of the time, whether native speakers or learners of the language, turned to *caint na ndaoine* without the slightest hesitation. Hyde, Dinneen, Ó Donnchadha, Pearse, Pádraic Ó Conaire, Béaslaí, Ó Siochfhradha, W. P. Ryan (1867–1942), Liam Ó Rinn (1886–1943) – all wrote in the language – and the dialect – they had learned at the hearth or in the classroom. Nor did they really have a choice. There was no other Irish being spoken by anybody. Even Henebry seems never to have developed a literary language of which he himself would have approved. The vast majority of what he wrote, including his most effective polemical pieces, appeared in English.

The role of the native speaker

Nevertheless, if *caint na ndaoine* won an overwhelming and inevitable victory early in the Revival, that victory was to be the source of one of the most virulent and largely sterile controversies of the first fifty years of the language and literary movement. To speak or write *caint na ndaoine* was of necessity to speak or write dialect. From the moment one opened one's mouth or soon after one put pen to paper, one was speaking or writing not just Irish, but Munster Irish, Connacht Irish, or Ulster Irish. At first, when the writing or speaking of any kind of Irish outside any of the *Gaeltachtaí* was both a novelty and a source of pride and accomplishment, dialect seemed a secondary issue. With the rapid growth of the Gaelic League throughout the country from 1901 on, and particularly with the expansion of the movement in Dublin, where native speakers and enthusiastic learners of the various dialects met on a regular basis, tensions began to arise as legitimate provincial or parochial pride in one's own form of Irish on occasion led to suspicion about the undue status and influence of other forms within the inner circles of the League bureaucracy. One positive effect of these rivalries was the creation of journals devoted to the cultivation of individual dialects. As we will see below, a good number of journals were founded in the first thirty or so years of the Revival to meet the new and growing interest in the language generated by the Gaelic League. Dialect was one of the principal *raisons d'être* for the launching of a new periodical. Thus Munster Irish was at various times to be catered for by *Banba, Loch Léin, Glór na Ly, An Lóchrann, An Muimhneach* and *An Birín Beo*. Those who wanted to read the Irish of Connacht could turn at one time or another to *An Connachtach, An Chearnóg, An Stoc* or *Ar Aghaidh*. Ulster readers were served by *An Crann* and *An t-Ultach* (the latter, founded in 1924 and still published monthly, by far the longest lived of this generally ephemeral list).

As time went on, however, this benign and even constructive rivalry soured. Two factors played leading roles in this change. First of all, earlier battles between nativists and progressives within the movement were now overshadowed by a growing division between native speakers and those who had learned the language. Second, national independence had made the language an important qualification for service – and reward – under the new state. The first battle in this war was fought out in 1921 in the pages of the League's official organ *Misneach* between the native speaker of Donegal Irish Séamus Ó Grianna ('Máire') (1889–1969) and Piaras Béaslaí, a fluent learner who, to make matters worse, favoured Munster Irish. Ó Grianna was to fight a lifelong and increasingly bitter campaign for the primacy of the native speaker, ending up a marginal and rather embarrassing fanatic. In 1921, he was just coming into his own, and was to make himself as novelist, short-story writer, satirist, polemicist and editor of the official organ of the Gaelic League, one of the language movement's most ubiquitous and influential writers of the two decades following Irish independence. One can only surmise how many dedicated learners of the language he and his ilk turned away from writing the language in that crucial time.

Ó Grianna began as the spokesman of a new generation of native speakers eager to take what they saw as their rightful position at the head of the language and cultural revival. From early in the movement, native speakers had heard themselves apotheosised as the most authentic – if not the sole – heirs of the genuine Irish tradition. At first, few had the education and/or experience to actively claim this birthright, but largely as a result of the work of the League, many now were, like Ó Grianna, graduates of third-level educational institutions and veterans of the struggle against the English. Why, then, should they now take orders from those to whom they had taught the language not that long ago? Unfortunately, this legitimate ambition was too often linked with suspicion (and worse) of those who had learned the language. Even more disastrously, native speakers of the various dialects frequently turned on each other even more savagely than they did on the learners. The Ulster speakers, outraged by the 1921 Anglo-Irish treaty that allowed six of Ulster's nine counties to remain under British rule, and feeling isolated and marginalised in the new Free State, were downright paranoid in their attitude to the other dialects. They were particularly suspicious of the Munster dialect, whose adherents, whether native speakers or learners, occupied many key positions in the new order and were seen as copper-fastening the unjust dominance their dialect had enjoyed from the start of the Revival, when many of the most influential writers were from Cork, Kerry and Waterford. All too often it was Ó Grianna who set the vitriolic tone of the debate, turning his formidable powers of sarcasm and abuse on opponents unable, or unwilling, to answer him with the same vigour. In the process, he must have convinced many of his compatriots that the language movement was a refuge for embittered cranks while at the same time alienating even potential allies with comments like the following from a 1925 letter to the editor of *Fáinne an Lae*:

> Fosgail 'Fáinne an Lae' do na canamhaintí go dtroididh an cath i n-ainm Dé. Níl acht amaidigh dúinn a rádh nach bhfuil an cath seo romhainn, nó nach bhfuil adhbhar troda ar bith againn. Tá daoiní ann adeir nach bhfuil difear ar bith eadar na canamhaintí. Ní h-amhlaidh. Ní aon chineál amháin Gaedhilce atá ó Chonamara go Rosa Tír Chonaill agus atá i gCúige Mumhan. Ní aon teanga amháin iad. Agus is amaideach an té a déarfas gurb eadh.

> Open 'Fáinne an Lae' to the dialects so they can fight the battle in God's name. It is nothing but foolishness for us to say that this battle is not ahead of us, or that we have nothing at all to fight over. There are people who say that there is not any difference at all among the dialects. Not so. The Irish from Conamara to the Rosses of Donegal is not the same kind as there is in the province of Munster. They are not a single language. And the person who says they are is a fool.[12]

Revival institutions and publications

The writer wanting to try his hand at prose was, then, entering an uncharted minefield, supported by little consensus concerning appropriate subject matter, style, or language. What kept him going? A major inspiration, in addition to in most cases a deep and genuine sense of patriotic mission and in a few cases at least a modest literary talent, was the possibility of prizes, publication and, sometimes, payment. From its inception in 1897, An tOireachtas followed the lead of local League *feiseanna* (festivals) in sponsoring competitions to encourage cultural activity of all kinds, including literature, rewarding winners with cash prizes and perhaps more important for the committed, recognition and even a limited fame. In the early years – though less frequently as time went on – An tOireachtas also published and promoted winning literary efforts. Moreover, for the first time ever, writers of Irish actually had a choice of journals to which they could submit their work, and, thanks to the Gaelic League, a growing audience able to read and appreciate it.

From 1881 to 1898, Michael Logan's (1836–1889) *An Gaodhal* was published more or less monthly in Brooklyn, New York. From 1882 to 1909, *Irisleabhar na Gaedhilge* appeared, at first monthly and then less regularly. 1898 saw the birth of Brian Doyle's weekly newspaper *Fáinne an Lae*, to be followed in 1900 by the League's own paper *An Claidheamh Soluis* (later called *Fáinne an Lae* and *Misneach*), which quickly absorbed Doyle's paper under League sponsorship. The first decade of the twentieth century also saw the appearance of *Banba*, *An Muimhneach Óg*, *Loch Léin*, *An Lóchrann* and *An Connachtach*, and however transient most of these were, they were to have successors throughout our period, like the journals promoting specific dialects mentioned above, and other periodicals like *An Branar*, *An t-Éireannach*, *An Sguab* and *An Tír*. In addition, various national and provincial papers, religious journals and school and university magazines began to publish contributions in Irish with some regularity. On a more ambitious level, the League itself was actively engaged in publishing from 1899 on, and quickly issued an impressive list of titles, though most of them were propaganda pamphlets and language textbooks of various kinds rather than literary works. Unfortunately, however, the glory days of the League as a press were short-lived, and by the late 1910s, angry complaints about its failure in this area were being heard, notably from Pádraic Ó Conaire (1882–1928). The most important private companies engaged in the publication of literature at the time were M. H. Gill and Sons and The Irish Book Company, which published the work of Father O'Leary, after he took his books away from the League as a result of a series of disputes about editorial policy with regard to language and orthography.

The creation of a native state, many of whose leaders were alumni of the League and one of whose main goals was claimed to be the re-Gaelicisation of the nation, increased the options for Gaelic authors. Virtually no publications of whatever kind – a predictable exception here was the *Irish Times* – did not pay at least lip service to the language in the years of the Free State. Most did considerably more, with both the *Irish Independent* and the *Irish Press* publishing material in Irish every day, the *Press* a whole page's worth. Moreover, the foundation in 1926 of An Gúm as the state's Irish-language publishing agency filled the enormous void left by the League's virtual abandonment of its role as publisher. An Gúm was to become a lightning rod for controversy, but there can be no doubt that with its creation, an even braver new world seemed to open before writers of Irish in the new native state.

Short fiction

What the editors of most of these journals wanted in the early years of the Revival were short, engaging and linguistically accessible prose works geared to the needs, and limitations, of an audience new to the reading of Irish. Of course, this demand for short, simple pieces also suited many of the would-be authors, themselves new to writing, Irish or both. Predictably enough, both editors and contributors saw the folk-tale as an ideal model right at hand – brief, entertaining and believed to be impeccably native. Indeed, it is often difficult in the absence of explicit attribution to an oral informant to tell the difference between more or less genuine folk narratives and 'original' stories modelled on them. Three of the earliest practitioners of the Gaelic short story, Séamus Ó Dubhghaill, 'Gruagach an Tobair' (Pádraig Ó Séaghdha) (1864–1955) and 'Conán Maol' (another Pádraig Ó Séaghdha) (1855–1928), established themselves with collections of such short and light rural tales, Ó Dubhghaill with *Tadhg Gabha* (1901) and *Prátaí Mhichíl Thaidhg* (1904), 'Gruagach' with the three booklets of *Annála na Tuatha* (1905–1907) and 'Conán' with *An Buaiceas*

(1903). The last is the best of this undistinguished lot, having won an Oireachtas prize in 1898 and been praised, excessively, by Pearse in a 1903 review in which he stated that '"Conán Maol" is one of the few who have fashioned for themselves a distinctive style in Irish.'[13] Harmless stories of rural hijinks would continue to be a staple of Gaelic fiction throughout our period and beyond.

Whatever he felt about the sort of *caint na ndaoine* he found in works like *Annála na Tuatha* and *An Buaiceas*, Henebry would have approved of their fidelity to traditional narrative patterns. It was Pearse's rejection of those patterns in his 1907 story 'Íosagán' that provoked the sharpest of Henebry's critical diatribes in his 1908 'Revival Irish' series. Henebry blasted Pearse for what he called the 'explosive opening' of the story, his failure to carefully set the scene for his audience in the time-tested manner of the *seanchaí* (storyteller). Pearse responded to Henebry's charge that the story was written to 'the standard of revolt which is called Impressionism' with one of the language movement's first literary manifestos:

> It was meant as a standard of revolt, but my critic must pardon me if I say that the standard is not the standard of impressionism. It is the standard of definite art form as opposed to the folk form.[14]

This was no new argument for Pearse, himself an urban learner of the language, who had written in 1906:

> This week we lay down the proposition that a living modern literature *cannot* (and if it could, should not) be built up on the folktale . . . In point of form the folktale is bound by a convention, which, by the way, is not a distinctively Irish convention but rather a distinctively folk convention, – that is to say, a convention which, in essentials, obtains amongst the folk universally . . . Why impose the folk attitude of mind, the folk convention of form on the makers of a literature?

With regard to subject matter, Pearse was equally iconoclastic:

> This is the twentieth century; and no literature can take root in the twentieth century which is not of the twentieth century. We want no Gothic revival. We would have the problems of to-day fearlessly dealt with in Irish . . .[15]

For all the confidence with which he defended these controversial positions, Pearse had an appropriately modest sense of his own achievement as a writer of short stories. In his response to Henebry quoted above, Pearse continued: 'I may or may not be a good standard bearer, but at any rate the standard is raised and writers of Irish are flocking to it.' He was not the best standard bearer, for however sensitively crafted were the short stories in his two collections,

Íosagán agus Sgéalta Eile (1907) and *An Mháthair agus Sgéalta Eile* (1916), the stylistic innovation that made them important in their own time is now of chiefly historical interest and few modern readers will appreciate the often saccharine sentimentality of these stories of innocent children and stoically suffering women. But Pearse was right when he said that writers of Irish were flocking to his standard, and some of them blessed with greater creative gifts would win the day for the literary principles he espoused.

The most significant of Pearse's progressive allies was Pádraic Ó Conaire. Raised in the Gaeltacht, if not a native speaker in the strictest sense of the term, Ó Conaire was a novelist, playwright, and essayist, but it was as a writer of short stories that he made his greatest contribution to literature in Irish. After leaving Ireland for a civil service position in London, Ó Conaire began his writing career and did by far his best work in the English capital before his return to a wandering life in Ireland in 1914. Recalling the thrill readers like himself felt when they first encountered Ó Conaire's stories, Liam Ó Briain wrote in 1936:

> Cé gur thosaigh an Piarsach ar a scéalta féin díreach an tráth céanna agus cé gur mhaith iad agus gur álainn, níor thug sé an croitheadh sin as ré na seanscéalaíochta isteach i réaltacht lom, ghránna an tsaoil mar a bhí thart timpeall ar lucht na Gaeltachta agus na Galltachta, a bhí ag teastáil san am, má bhí i ndán dár ngluaiseacht aon dáiríreacht a thaispeáint. Ní féidir a thuiscint inniu cén misneach mór ba ghá a bheith ag an té a scríobhfadh leithéid 'Nóra Mharcuis Bhig' an uair úd.
>
> Although Pearse began his stories at the same time, and although they are fine and beautiful, he did not provide the same jolt out of the age of traditional storytelling and into the twentieth century, into the bare ugly reality of life as it was around the people of the Gaeltacht and of English-speaking Ireland, the jolt that was necessary if our movement was to show any seriousness. It is not possible today to understand the courage it took to write something like 'Nóra Mharcuis Bhig' at that time.[16]

'Nóra Mharcuis Bhig,' a stark story of a Connemara father's disowning his daughter when he realizes the life of impoverished dissipation she has lived when away in London, won an Oireachtas prize for short fiction in 1906. The author's depiction of the city as a soulless and debasing place here and elsewhere is fairly stereotypical. It is his treatment of rural Ireland, particularly the Gaeltacht, that sets his work at its best apart. In the finest stories in *Nóra Mharcuis Bhig agus Sgéalta Eile* (1909), *An Sgoláire Bocht agus Sgéalta Eile* (1913) and *Síol Éabha* (1922), he offers a pioneering honest confrontation with the social problems and human tragedies behind the myth of a rural, Irish-speaking utopia in the West, a myth born in the early Revival, fostered by the stories of Pearse and achieving its classic expression in Éamon de Valera's famous 1943 speech about Ireland as a cheerful countryside full of 'athletic youths and comely maidens'.

Ó Conaire's range is apparent in *An Chéad Chloch agus Sgéalta Eile* (1914), his re-creations of stories from the New Testament, including those of Salomé and Lazarus; in *Seacht mBuaidh an Éirghe Amach* (1917), dealing with the Easter Rising of 1916 from a series of original perspectives; and in the light, largely forgettable comic pieces of *Fearfeasa Mac Feasa* (1930) and *Scéalta an tSáirsint Rua* (1941). Ultimately, his greatest sin as a writer was that he wrote too much, with too little quality control, often recycling plotlines or even shamelessly publishing the same story twice with only minor revisions or merely under a different title. He was also probably responsible for introducing into Gaelic short fiction its greatest and most baneful influence, that of O. Henry, whose 'surprise' endings quickly became an unavoidable feature of the literary landscape in Irish. We should, however, be forgiving. Ó Conaire was attempting to become the first writer of Irish in centuries to make a living by his pen alone. He died in abject poverty in 1928.

In an important 1936 essay on Ó Conaire, Seosamh Mac Grianna (1900–90), a Donegal native speaker and the brother of Séamus Ó Grianna, wrote that it was his reading of Ó Conaire's *An Chéad Chloch* that turned him to literature in Irish. If so, this decision has to be seen as another of Ó Conaire's major contributions to that literature. Mac Grianna's masterpiece was his spiritual autobiography *Mo Bhealach Féin* (1940), but he was also a skilled writer of short stories. Although he published just one collection dedicated entirely to this genre, *An Grádh agus an Ghruaim* (1929), there are also stories in *Dochartach Dhuibhlionna agus Sgéaltaí Eile* (1925) (the title piece is a novella to be discussed below) and in *Pádraic Ó Conaire agus Aistí Eile* (1936). Mac Grianna's best work deals in a rich native Irish with the plight of great (*éifeachtach*) individuals trapped in sharply diminished times and restrictive places, including the contemporary Gaeltacht. But he could also draw on a consciously elevated style influenced by his reading of earlier literature to give an added resonance and dignity to both his own brand of *caint na ndaoine* and to characters who lived and acted in what he saw as the more vital and expansive times when Ireland was fully Gaelic. The best examples of this carefully crafted prose appear in his historical story set in the fifteenth century, 'Creach Chuinn Uí Dhomhnaill' and in his Famine story 'Ar a' Tráigh Fhoilimh' (both in *An Grádh agus an Ghruaim*); in *Eoghan Rua Ó Néill* (1929), about the seventeenth-century leader of the Gaelic Irish against the Cromwellians; in *Na Lochlannaigh* (1938), dealing with the Vikings in Ireland; and, with great effect, in passages throughout *Mo Bhealach Féin*.

Séamus Ó Grianna was to write far too much before he put down his pen and bitterly declared that he wished he had never written a word of Irish.[17] But in our period, he was still deeply, if not always generously, committed to the revival of the language and the development of its literature. His two novels from this time will be discussed below, but in 1926 he also published *Cioth is Dealán*, the first and finest of his thirteen collections of stories. Unfortunately, Ó Grianna's short fiction was to show no growth or development over time, and as he fell back again and again on the same setting in the Donegal Rosses of his youth, the same repetitive plots, stylistic mannerisms and linguistic clichés, not even his marvellously rich and – to use a term favored by Revivalist critics – racy Donegal Irish could redeem the later stories as literary fiction, although they always attracted a loyal readership, especially, of course, in Ulster.

One of Ó Grianna's staunchest and most unyielding allies in the cause of both the native speaker and the Ulster dialect was Seán Bán Mac Meanman (1886–1962), of whom Nollaig Mac Congáil has written 'go gcuireann sé an t-eolas faoi [an "Hidden Ireland" dá chuid scéalta] inár láthair ar an dóigh chéanna a bhfuair sé é óna chuid oidí múinte, mar atá, na seanchaithe, oidhrí dlisteanacha an traidisiúin bhéil' (that he puts knowledge about it [i.e. the 'Hidden Ireland' of his stories] before us in the same way he got it from his teachers, namely the storytellers, the legitimate heirs of the oral tradition).[18] Certainly in the three story collections he published during this period – *Sgéalta Goiride Geimhridh* (1915), *Fear Siubhail a's a Chuid Comharsanach agus Daoine Eile* (1924) and *Indé agus Indiu* (1929) – Mac Meanman insisted that he had only written 'mám sgeulta as mála fir siubhail' (a handful of stories from the bag of a travelling man), all of which had some basis in fact.[19]

Another pair of native-speaking brothers, the Kerry-born Pádraig and Micheál Ó Siochfhradha (1883–1964, 1900–86), published important story collections in our period. Both were also high-profile figures in the revival, Pádraig as an essayist, author of popular books like *Jimín Mháire Thaidhg* (1921) for children and young readers, folklorist and League official, Micheál as an author of history textbooks and one of the language's more accomplished and ambitious playwrights. Pádraig's collection of comic stories about the people of the Dingle Peninsula, *An Baile Seo 'Gainne*, was enthusiastically received on its publication in 1913, and its idiomatic Kerry Irish, satirical humour and distinct, forceful and consistent narrative voice have kept it in print over most of the past century. Micheál has not been so lucky. His 1930 collection *Seo mar Bhí* is now forgotten, but is well worth revisiting, especially for its satirical take on some of the national pieties of the time in stories like 'An Turus' and 'An Corp', dealing with the collection of folklore, or 'Glóire Bhaile an Phludaigh', set during the War of Independence.

While Liam O'Flaherty (1896–1984), a native speaker from the Aran Islands, did not publish a collection of short fiction in Irish until 1953, several of his stories in the language did appear pre-1940. Pádhraic Ó Domhnalláin (1884–1960), the editor of the League journal *Fáinne an Lae*, doubtless spoke for many when he introduced O'Flaherty's story 'Bás na Bó' to his readers in July, 1925:

> Muna bhfuil dul amudha mór orainn atá sgríobhnóir úr againn a árdóchas an Ghaedhilg go hárd i gcúrsaí litridheachta.
>
> If we are not greatly mistaken, we have a new writer who will bring Irish to new heights in literary affairs.[20]

Unfortunately for the cause if not for his own well-being, O'Flaherty did not follow the lead of his friend Pádraic Ó Conaire by devoting himself exclusively, or even significantly, to Irish and published only five stories in Irish in our period, all of them among the finest of the time.

Although he lacked O'Flaherty's real genius in short fiction, Tomás Bairéad (1893–1973), a native speaker from Connemara, published five collections, three – *An Geall a Briseadh* (1932), *Cumhacht na Cinneamhna* (1936) and *Cruithneacht agus Ceannabhán* (1940) – in our period. The first in particular became a popular school text, going through four editions in twenty years. To see Bairéad as a school writer is, however, a real injustice. While most of his stories treat with sometimes surprising honesty life in the Galway Gaeltacht, he also wrote historical stories like 'Ciarán Cathach', set during the Cromwellian period; 'An Crochadóir nár hÍocadh', a tale of graverobbing in nineteenth-century Dublin; 'Teach Ósta na dTans' and 'An Dath a d'Athraigh', stories of the War of Independence, the latter an unidealised account in which the heads of suspected female collaborators are shaved; and 'Mná Chaointe na Linnseach', a rare story in Irish dealing with the Big House Ascendancy. About a quarter of his stories have urban settings, among them 'Saibhreas na gCon', in which working-class men in Belfast seem to treat their greyhounds better than they do their children; and 'Cáit a' Mheadhoin Oidhche', a stark tale of urban poverty that An Gúm omitted from later editions of *An Geall a Briseadh* and that even Liam O'Flaherty apparently found offensive.[21]

Life as lived in his home place of Caherea, County Clare, was the subject of the stories in *Cathair Aeidh* (1937) by Micheál Ó Gríobhtha (1869–1946), who also wrote *Lorgaireacht* (1927), a volume of detective stories to be considered below. Pádhraic Ó Domhnalláin was to publish three collections before 1940: *Ar Lorg an Ríogh agus Sgéalta Eile* (1925), *Na Spiadóirí agus Sgéalta Eile* (1934) and *Oidhre an Léighinn agus Aistí Eile* (1935). The majority of his stories deal with either Gaeltacht life or Irish history, a subject on which he also wrote a good deal in his many essays at the time, some of which were collected in *Dréachta* (1935). The stirring history of the recent past also provided the subject matter for Ó Conaire's Easter Rising collection *Seacht mBuaidh an Eirghe Amach* (1917), for *An Cogadh Dearg agus Sgéalta Eile* (1924) by Peadar Mac Fhionnlaoich ('Cú Uladh') (1856–1942), and for Máiréad Ní Ghráda's (1896–1971) *An Bheirt Dearbhráthar agus Scéalta Eile* (1939), the only Gaelic collection to attempt to come to terms with the tragedy of the Irish Civil War.

Town- and city-bred learners of the language wanting to write of the life they knew best and in the process to bring a whole new world into the language faced a daunting challenge, one that some critics feel has yet to be overcome. Pádraic Ó Conaire created a memorably disturbing London in his 1910 novel *Deoraidheacht* and wrote effectively of the same city in stories like 'Nóra Mharcuis Bhig' and 'An Ceol agus an Chuimhne'; of Dublin in 'M'Fhile Caol Dubh'; and of Galway, in 'Neill'. But in other stories, and especially in his essays, he too often fell back on the kind of anti-urban clichés popular among many of his rural and Gaeltacht contemporaries. He did, however, indirectly make possible the publication of the first collection of Gaelic stories that treated urban life with an unselfconscious and natural honesty. Ó Conaire was one of the leading advocates for the creation of a Gaelic book club to be called An Ridireacht Liteartha, believing that such an initiative would foster the development of literature in Irish by guaranteeing a decent and predictable audience for new books. The scheme, launched during the political turmoil that followed the Easter Rising of 1916, never got off the ground, wrapping up after publishing a single 59-page book. That book was, however, Liam Ó Rinn's *Cad Ba Dhóbair Dó agus Sgeulta Eile* (1920). A Dubliner by birth and rearing, Ó Rinn took a genuine and perceptive pleasure in his home city, and unlike so many of his fellow Revivalists depicted it as a comfortable and secure home in which his characters could structure their lives around routines as stable and reassuring as those available to their country cousins. Ó Rinn went on to become a prominent Gaelic critic, but apart from one or two stories in periodicals, he never returned to the form in which he had showed so much early promise.

He did, however, have several worthy successors in his attempt to make Irish at home in the city and vice versa. Dublin is the setting for the majority of the stories in León Ó Broin's (1902–90) four collections from our period – *Árus na nGábhadh agus Sgéalta Eile* (1923), *Béal na hUaighe agus Sgéalta Eile* (1927), *Ag Stracadh leis an Saol agus Scéalta Eile* (1929) and *An Rún agus Scéalta Eile* (1932). Like Ó Rinn – and unlike some of his colleagues who confined their occasional urban stories to language movement settings – Ó Broin took the city for granted in his work, using Irish naturally and successfully to deal with a world where it was in fact little spoken in everyday life. He had a fine comic sense and was willing to poke fun at Free State politics and pieties in stories like 'Troid na gComharsan' and 'Mairg a Phósfadh', but his most memorable stories are darker. Three of the stories in *Ag Stracadh leis an Saol*, including the title piece, involve suicide, a subject at least one contemporary critic felt was inappropriate for fiction in Irish. In 'Is Fearr le Dia na Mná', he tells the tale of an unwed pregnant woman driven by intolerance to give birth alone in a wintry field.

The stories in Micheál Mac Liammóir's (1899–1978) *Lá agus Oidhche* (1929) with their cosmopolitan sensibility, frequently exotic settings and esoteric subject matter must have startled many readers of Irish at the time. His characters move easily through Dublin, Paris and Sicily, discuss spiritualism, Freud and Joyce, speak French or Italian, and enjoy fine art, classical music and café society. Readers may have felt less at sea with the work of Seán Mac Maoláin (1884–1973), a learner from County Antrim of whose Irish even Ó Grianna approved. Praising the urban stories in his collection *Ceannracháin Cathrach* (1935), the Capuchin priest An tAthair Micheál wrote 'gur thuit fallaing Phádruig [Uí Chonaire] ar Sheán má thuit sé ar aoinne ameasc sgríobhnóiri Gaedhilge' (the mantle of Pádraic [Ó Conaire] has fallen on Seán if it has fallen on anyone among writers of Irish).[22] Mac Maoláin's most Ó Conairesque story is 'Maighréad na Milseán,' in which the owner of a sweet shop in Dublin, having been swindled out of her life savings by a con-man with whom she has fallen in love, loses her mind and has to be committed to an asylum. In 'Cor de Chuid na Cinneamhna', the author depicts the almost ant-like quality of tenement life in the slums, but even here he transcends the usual anti-urban stereotype through his recognition of the humanity and vitality of the poor, a recognition that enables him to see the loving side of a mother given to drink.

Most of the stories in Seán Ó Ciosáin's (*c.*1896–1982) *Sgéalta Cois Laoi* are, as the title indicates, set in Cork City. The most engaging work in the collection is 'An Bheirt Intleachtóirí,' in which two provincial pseudo-intellectuals, clearly modelled on Corkmen Frank O'Connor and Seán Ó Faoláin, are satirised. Also of interest, however, are 'An Fear do Bhuail Umam i Montréal', an Ó Conairesque tale about a character who claims to have met Trotsky in

Canada; 'An Múinteoir Gaedhilge', a comic story about a greedy and hypocritical teacher of Irish; 'Móna', another of the rare Gaelic stories involving the Ascendancy; and 'Eachtra an Mhála', in which Irish-speaking friends go to the movies and enjoy listening to Negro spirituals as well as that bugbear of the time, jazz. There are only four stories in *Cois Life* by Seosamh Ó Torna ('Seán Sabháiste') (1888–1967), but all have Dublin settings. The influence of Ó Conaire is evident in 'Spré Ghráinne Ní Aichir', in which an increasingly deranged woman tries to kill the man she believes jilted her.

Roibeárd Ó Faracháin's (1909–1984) *Fíon gan Mhoirt* (1938) is an entertaining if uneven collection about middle-class life in Dublin by a writer who would, as Robert Farren, make a name for himself in English as a poet, playwright, critic and broadcaster. Three of the stories, 'An Mhúscailt', 'Pilib an Cheoil', and 'Urlabhra', have as protagonists professional musicians; the main character of 'Imtheachta Chlub na gCleasaidhthe' is an Irishman with a passion for American gangster films, a passion that has led him to assume a rather startling would-be Chicago accent with accompanying underworld lingo from a country he has never visited. Ó Faracháin's most original and effective work is 'An Feall Gránna', a frame story in which the author gently satirises the fixation of Gaelic short story writers with O. Henry gimmickery. Among other writers who published occasional stories with town or urban settings in our period were Seán Ó Caomhánaigh (1885–1947),[23] Piaras Béaslaí, Peadar Ó Dubhda (1881–1971), Séamus Ó Néill (1910–1981) and Máighréad Nic Mhaicín (1899–1983), the last two writing of Belfast.

As our period ended in 1939, the man who was to become the finest writer of fiction in Irish in the twentieth century published his first collection of stories. *Idir Shúgradh agus Dáiríre* by the Connemara native speaker Máirtín Ó Cadhain (1905–70) was, in light of what he went on to accomplish, an apprentice effort. As a result of the author's profound knowledge of, and sympathy with, the people of the Gaeltacht and his unparalleled mastery of his linguistic medium, it was also, with the possible exceptions of Ó Conaire's *Nóra Mharcuis Bhig* or *An Chéad Chloch*, the finest book of stories produced to date. Ó Cadhain later wrote some of the most challenging urban fiction ever written in Irish, but the stories in *Idir Shúgradh agus Dáiríre* are all set in his home place.

The novel

Writers of short fiction had, then, accomplished much in the first half-century or so of the Revival. Taking advantage of at least rudimentary native models and a small but relatively predictable audience in the periodicals, they had won the modern literary short story for the language, a success evident in Máirtín Ó Flaithbheartaigh's 1934 anthology *An Craobh Chumhra*, and especially in Máighréad Nic Mhaicín's 1938 anthology *As na Ceithre hÁirdibh: Cnuasach Gearr-Scéal*. Writers working with the novel were nowhere near so fortunate, or successful. In his essay 'An tÚrscéal nár Tháinig' (The novel that did not come), Cathal Ó Háinle has argued that some of the prose narratives written in Irish in the sixteenth and seventeenth centuries showed signs of evolving into novels just as similar narratives did elsewhere in Europe. The salient fact, however, is that they did not, as in Ireland this evolutionary process was aborted by the political and cultural turmoil that, among many other things, denied the language access to print technology. Early Revivalists with the ambition to become novelists would have to make do without native models. They would also have to make do without much of an audience. It was one thing for a recent learner to read a few pages of Irish prose. It was quite a different thing to make his or her way through – much less write – a novel-length work. Agnes O'Farrelly (Úna Ní Fhaircheallaigh) (1874–1951) found one solution to this problem. Her *Grádh agus Crádh* (1901), subtitled 'úirscéilín' (a novelette) has just twenty-four pages, while *An Cneamhaire* (1903), which she calls 'úrscéal' (a novel – literally 'a new story') has a hefty thirty-two!

It was, however, unthinkable for most literary Revivalists that this most popular of all contemporary genres should be ceded to English without a fight. Lacking traditional exemplars in the language or any real hope for an immediate audience, writers would have to generate the genre in Irish one way or another. Despite his own contempt for what he called 'navvils', Father O'Leary was the first to answer the call with *Séadna*, although the entire text was not published in book form until 1904. O'Leary drew his inspiration from an Irish version of the Faust story, which he then set within the framework of a storytelling session in his native West Cork Gaeltacht. *Séadna* has been called a number of things since it first appeared – '*sui generis*' (Hyde), a *Novelle* (Norah Meade), 'a country story' (*sgéal tuaithe*) ('Maol Muire'), 'a sort of folk-novel' (Aodh de Blácam), a *Sage* (Pádraig A. Breatnach), 'a modern, experimental, self-referential novel' (*úrscéal nua-aimseartha turgnamhach féinthagarthach*) (Alan Titley).[24] In many ways, its central narrative is a folk-tale super-sized, but with a more flexible modern understanding of the genre, 'novel' seems as good a label as any. It certainly provided its eager first readers the kind of long, satisfying read those in other cultures sought in the novel.

The first Gaelic novel to appear as a book was Father Dinneen's *Cormac Ua Conaill* (1901), an episodic tale that is far more a patriotic adventure story than a perceptive recreation of the late sixteenth century and its tangled politics. The book also began the long Gaelic tradition of novels that tried to simultaneously provide serious literature for adults and escapist yarns for the young, succeeding in full at neither. This problem was compounded when An Gúm was established within the Department of Education and when its seal of approval certified a book's appropriateness, and marketability, as a text in secondary schools. Dinneen was both widely read in and respectful of the English literary tradition, and *Cormac Ua Conaill* reads like a (very) poor man's Walter Scott. Scott could also be blamed, in part, for O'Leary's novel of the court of Brian Boru, *Niamh* (1907), by far the longest novel of the first fifty years of the Revival, a book of which Pearse wrote that it was marred by 'the cardinal fault of being untrue – not merely to history . . . but to historical vraisemblance'.[25] It was marred by far more than that – a simplistic reading of Brian's reign and military campaigns as a straightforward tale of conflict between good and evil, a saccharine romantic sub-plot and several anachronistic howlers.

History was to remain the single most popular topic for Irish-language novelists throughout our period, particularly after the creation of the new state and the foundation of An Gúm, when few writers could resist the temptation to offer their fictional perspective on the recent struggle against the English, a struggle in which some of them had fought and suffered. In addition to a flood of short stories dealing with the post-1916 period, we have Ó Grianna's novel of the Easter Rising *Mo Dhá Róisín* (1920); Maoghnas ('Fionn') Mac Cumhaill's (1885–1965) *Tusa a Mhaicín* (1922) and *Maicín* (1924), the latter a novella really; Seán Ó Ruadháin's (1883–1966) *Pádhraic Mháire Bhán, nó An Gol agus an Gáire* (1932); *Toil Dé* (1933) by Éamonn Mac Giolla Iasachta (Edward MacLysaght) (1887–1986); Alín de Paor's *Paidí Ó Dálaigh* (1933); Peadar Ó Dubhda's *Brian* (1937); and Seán Mac Maoláin's *Éan Corr* (1937).

We can gain a fascinating insight into the enormous shift in Irish popular opinion following the Easter Rising by comparing Ó Grianna's stirringly patriotic *Mo Dhá Róisín* with his first published effort at a novel, *Castar na Daoine ar a Chéile 's ní Chastar na Cnuic nó na Sléibhte*, serialized in the *Irish Weekly and Ulster Examiner* in 1915.[26] In the earlier work, the author's idealistic protagonists are passionate supporters of Home Rule. By the time *Mo Dhá Róisín* appeared five years later, their equally committed counterparts are ready to die in arms for the Republic.

Other historical novels from the time were O'Farrelly's *Grádh agus Crádh* (1901), set in County Cavan in 1798; Tomás Ó hAodha's (1866–1935) *An Gioblachán* (1903), an outlandish adventure story set during Fenian times; *Mac*

Fínghín Dubh (1903) by Pádraig Ó Séaghdha ('Conán Maol'), about the activities of patriotic rapparees in the Ireland of the Penal Laws; Seán Ó Ruaidhrí's (*c.*1840–1926) *Bliadhain na bhFranncach*, dealing with County Mayo during and after the rising of 1798; 'Fionn' Mac Cumhaill's *An Dochartach* (n.d., early 1920s?), a far-fetched sea yarn involving the white slave trade in the West Indies; Nioclás Tóibín's (1890–1966) *Róisín Bán an tSléibhe* (1923) and *An Rábaire Bán* (1928) and Micheál Ó Gríobhtha's *Buaidh na Treise, 'Cogadh Gaedheal re Gallaibh'* (1928), all three dealing with landlord oppression in the nineteenth century. There were also Seosamh Mac Grianna's *Eoghan Rua Ó Néill* (1931), a cross between a novel and a biography of the seventeenth-century leader; Seán Ó Ciarghusa's (1873–1956) *Bun an Dá Abhann* (1933), a rambling Kickhamesque tale of eviction and tenant resistance in the nineteenth century; Diarmuid Ua Laoghaire's (1871–1942) *An Bhruinneall Bhán* (1934), dealing with the same topic; Diarmuid Ó hÉigeartaigh's (1892–1958) *Tadhg Ciallmhar* (1934), an account of the life and triumphs of the insufferably sensible and smug nineteenth-century protagonist of the title; Niall Ó Domhnaill's (*c.*1907–1995) *Ar Scáth na Croiche* (in *Bruighean Feille*, 1934), a novella about the 'Invincibles' who murdered the British Chief Secretary in Phoenix Park in 1882; and *An Seod Do-Fhághala* (1936) by Úna Bean Uí Dhíocsa ('Bláth Aitinne') (1880–1958), a novel in which national resistance and Christian pacifism come into conflict on the Shannon in the early nineteenth century. Seán Mac Maoláin's *Iolar agus Sionnach* (1938) deals with the 1798 Rising in Ulster; while Aindrias Ó Baoighill's (1888–1972) *An t-Airidheach* (1939) offers another take on the injustices of landlordism. 'Fionn' Mac Cumhaill's *Na Rosa go Bráthach* (1939), classified by Alan Titley as a novel in his authoritative *An tÚrscéal Gaeilge* (1991), seems more a lightly fictionalised local history.

In 1929, An Gúm announced it was sponsoring a competition for a new novel in Irish. The competition was to create an interesting and revealing problem for its judges. The two finalists, however similar they may have been felt to be in quality, had little else in common. Seán Ó Ruadháin's *Pádhraic Mháire Bhán* was the safe and predictable Gaelic novel *par excellence*, written in the vivid Irish of the native speaker and full of proverbs, references to folk beliefs and customs, noble Irish-speaking 'peasants', and self-sacrificing republican freedom fighters, rounded off with a chaste love story. *Lucht Ceoil* by Art Ó Riain ('Barra Ó Caochlaigh') (1893–1968), a middle-class Dubliner, was a mystery tale of sorts set for the most part in Dublin and London – part takes place in a countercultural commune outside the English capital! – among protagonists with a love for European classical music. Clearly baffled as to how to respond, the judges compromised by awarding a full first prize to both novels.

Their decision points to a core ambiguity at the time about what the Gaelic novel should be and do. Particularly among native speakers, it was felt the novel should chronicle and celebrate the life of the Gaeltacht, and as time passed, for many this idea took on an added urgency as traditional ways died out in the face of modernisation and the English language. For other Revivalists, mostly town- and city-bred learners, the novel in Irish should, as a thoroughly modern European genre, confront contemporary Irish life in all its complexities as it was actually lived by the majority of Irish people while waiting for, and hastening, the day when all of Ireland could be considered a Gaeltacht of a new kind.

Apart from the historical works considered above – and many if not most of those are as much and more about the Gaeltacht as they are about the past – virtually all novels in Irish before 1939 fall into one of these two categories. The most prolific author of Gaeltacht fiction at the time was Connemara-born Pádhraic Óg Ó Conaire (1893–1971), distantly, if at all, related to his famous namesake. Pádhraic Óg published six novels between 1922 and 1939: *Mian a Croidhe* (1922), *Solus an Ghrádha* (1923), *An Fraoch Bán* (1924), *Seóid ó'n Iarthar Órdha* (1926), *Éan Cuideáin* (1936), and *Ceol na nGiolcach* (1939). None of these will appeal to a modern reader, but *Ceol na nGiolcach* won a major prize from the Irish government in 1937, and *Éan Cuideáin*, the best of them, offers an honest critique of hide-bound Gaeltacht conservatism in a tale of intergenerational conflict. He returned to this theme in the posthumously published *Déirc an Díomhaointis* (1974). It is this ongoing engagement with the life and future of the Gaeltacht, his love for its people and its traditions tempered by his awareness of its serious faults and fear for its future, that gives his fiction an importance that transcends its aesthetic mediocrity.

The most popular and acclaimed Gaeltacht novel of the time was Ó Grianna's *Caisleáin Óir* (1924), written in the author's customarily superb Irish and driven by an action-packed and engaging story that moves between the Rosses of Donegal and the goldfields of the Yukon. Although the author was eventually to publish seven more novels, the next one did not appear until 1958. A similarly lengthy delay denied readers access to his brother Seosamh's *An Druma Mór*, a powerful tale of personal and political rivalries in Irish-speaking Donegal in the wake of the Easter Rising. Timidity in the face of possible libel suits apparently kept the book under wraps at An Gúm until 1969. The pity here is that this was the most artistically crafted and challenging Gaeltacht novel of its time, one that with timely publication could have had a real influence on the development of fiction in the language. In the radically changed linguistic and cultural climate of the late 1960s it was in many ways reduced to the status of an historical artifact.[27]

Ó Grianna's prolific friend Seán Mac Maoláin published no fewer than three novels with rural settings in 1940: *Mallacht na Máthara, Slios den tSaoghal* and *File Callánach*. The third is by far the most interesting today as one of the first novels in Irish, or indeed in Ireland, to cast a jaundiced eye on the heritage industry. Set twenty years in the future, in 1960, it tells of how the residents of an Ulster Gaeltacht village set out with predictably comic results to create and then cash in on the 'fame' of a local Gaelic rhymester.

Given the centrality of the Gaeltacht in Revivalist ideology and the leading role played by writers who were native speakers, it is actually surprising how many novels of our period did attempt to claim new territory of various kinds for the language. The first, finest and bravest of those efforts was Pádraic Ó Conaire's *Deoraidheacht* (1910). Winner of a 1909 Oireachtas prize for a novel (*finnscéal* as it was then called), *Deoraidheacht* is the tale of an Irish emigrant in London who is horribly injured in an automobile accident, squanders his compensation money, joins a circus freak show, and goes on to live a nightmarish marginal life in England and on tour in Ireland before he is murdered in a London park. The novel remains powerful and disturbing today, and was an extraordinary and unique accomplishment for its own time, the single Gaelic novel of this period worth serious consideration as a successful work of creative fiction.

Liam P. Ó Riain (William P. Ryan), who also wrote a novel in English, *The Plough and the Cross* (1910), published two important novels in Irish in our period: *Caoimhghin Ó Cearnaigh* (1913) and *An Bhóinn agus an Bhóchna* (serialised in *An Claidheamh Soluis* in 1915 and 1916). Both were inspired by the author's interest in Eastern and what today would be called Celtic spirituality and deal with how an educated, committed and pragmatic nationalist mystic could best serve Ireland. What is most interesting here is that the two works arrive at diametrically opposite conclusions, with the former arguing for full involvement in the world in an attempt to awaken the Irish people to their true spiritual identity and mission, and the latter suggesting withdrawal in a personal quest for the absolute. This question clearly obsessed Ó Riain, for he returned to it yet again in his long narrative poem *Inghean Mhanannáin* (1917) and in his verse play *Feilm an Tobair Bheannuighthe* (1936), in both of which he espoused the position advanced in *Caoimhghin Ó Cearnaigh*.

Mac Grianna's novella *Dochartach Dhuibhlionna* (1926) explores the overwrought psyche of a parricide as he talks with a priest on the eve of his execution. Surprisingly, the novella provoked virtually no negative reaction among Gaelic critics. Seán Ó Caomhánaigh ('Seán a' Chóta') was not so lucky. His *Fánaí* (1927), the story of the adventures of an Irish emigrant living on the Minnesota–North Dakota border, was the only novel in Irish to run afoul of state censorship at the time, having provoked a detailed attack by the Dublin diocesan censor for its treatment of the protagonist's courtship of his fiancée. The offending scenes, not all of which An Gúm deleted or changed, were entirely innocuous, though that in which the young woman is sexually assaulted by the protagonist's rival is still disturbing today.[28]

Éamonn Mac Giolla Iasachta's *Cúrsaí Thomáis* (1927) also drew some criticism for its frank treatment of sexual topics. Prostitution, illegitimacy and, in veiled fashion, abortion are all mentioned. The book is really a companion piece to his English-language novel *The Gael* (1919). As in *The Gael*, Mac Giolla Iasachta uses the novel to preach his gospel that the small farmer must be the true backbone of the nation, and while he devotes a good deal of space to the accurate and sensitive depiction of rural customs, social patterns and labour practices, he also discusses subject matter quite alien to most of the Gaelic fiction of his time. Moreover, despite the narrator's explicit denial that he is in any way an intellectual or a philosopher, he regularly raises weighty issues like ethnic identity and religion, as well as sexuality. Of particular interest is Mac Giolla Iasachta's unconventional approach to Catholicism and the Catholic clergy in the novel. The narrator's friend and employer, Stiofán Mac Conmara, attributes his own heterodox Catholicism to his long residence in America, where he saw few priests and stopped attending mass. He does not, however, feel any shame about having lapsed from formal practice of his faith, and he is even willing to engage the parish priest in debate on the subject. In a more traditional work of Gaelic fiction, that debate could only end with the triumph of the priest and the repentance of the sinner. Mac Conmara does not yield an inch.

Mac Giolla Iasachta, who served in the Senate of the Free State, explored the political and social ramifications of his ruralist philosophy in the changed circumstances of independence in *Toil Dé*. A rather schizophrenic novel, *Toil Dé* is primarily concerned with political and cultural ideas in the chapters leading up to the Irish Civil War, but then focuses on personal and romantic concerns thereafter. Among the important issues addressed in the novel are several familiar from *The Gael* and *Cúrsaí Thomáis*. For example, once again Mac Giolla Iasachta affirms his belief that a productive and enlightened rural population should be the foundation for the new state and that that population required leadership from those more prosperous and better educated. A major blind spot for Mac Giolla Iasachta was his apparent inability to imagine a constructive leadership role for women in the new order. His son's fiancée, an articulate and committed anti-Treaty republican, meekly subordinates her opinions to those of her Free State husband-to-be, just as the young man's New Zealand-born mother had earlier yielded to the views of his father.

Women were marginal figures on the Gaelic literary scene in the 1920s and 1930s with the exception of Ní Ghráda at the end of the period, and Úna Bean Uí Dhíocsa (Elizabeth Rachel Dix), whose historical novel *An Seod Do-Fhághala* has already been mentioned. The fact that Dix is now all but forgotten is a real and great injustice, for her 1932 novel *Cailín na Gruaige Duinne*, written under the pen-name 'Breanda', is the most iconoclastic book written in Irish in the first fifty years of the Revival. Dix's commitment to non-violence was both lifelong and unwavering. In a 1925 letter to the editor of *Fáinne an Lae*, she asserted her repudiation of violence and her belief in 'cómhacht na fírinne' (the power of truth), arguing that by shedding blood the IRA had brought 'mallacht' (a curse) on the country.[29] In *Cailín na Gruaige Duinne*, she explores the whole question of violence as an appropriate means to a laudable end. Her protagonist, a young Protestant woman of unionist stock, becomes an Irish nationalist, but retains her commitment to the pacificism that led her to oppose World War I. Indeed she is every bit as discouraged by the Irish recourse to violence to achieve freedom as she was by the mass slaughter engaged in by the major world powers in the trenches of Europe. Simultaneously inspired and dismayed by the actions of Pearse in Easter Week – and both Pearse and the Rising were by 1932 seen by the vast majority of language revivalists and their fellow citizens in the Free State as subjects too sacred for criticism – she concludes that had Pearse and his comrades sacrificed themselves through Ghandian non-violence rather than taking up arms, 'ní bheimís in iomar na haimléise mar atá muid i láthair na huaire' (we would not be in the slough of despond as we are at present). Her belief was that there was 'fás nádúrtha planda faoi'n saoirse náisiúnta' (a natural organic growth to national independence) that would come to fruition in time without armed intervention. By the novel's end, she has followed her political rebirth with a religious conversion to Catholicism, but remains unwavering in her commitment to non-violence, able to forgive the Free State soldiers who kill her husband after he is betrayed by his own brother. Nor does Dix's courage and willingness to violate contemporary taboos stop with politics. She deals honestly and forthrightly in this novel with the sensitive subject of marital breakdown, fifteen years before Séamus Ó Néill made it a central theme in his much better known novel *Tonn Tuile*

(1947). Dix portrayed an incipient if inchoate feminist awareness behind her protagonist's decision to leave her brutish Gaeltacht husband and go to live in a YWCA hostel in Belfast. Equally honest is her depiction of the woman's post-partum depression, a mental state that causes her to ignore her baby and to even consider killing the infant.

Piaras Béaslaí's *Astronár* was serialized in the *Weekly Freeman* in 1921, but not published as a book until 1928. (Indeed, in his preface to the novel, the author insists that he had begun the work as early as 1899 and had finished it by 1912.) The novel recounts the attempt of the eponymous protagonist and his fellow nationalists to liberate 'Amora', his fictional eastern European homeland, from the colonial oppression of 'Kratónia'. The novel's subject and theme explain Béaslaí's insistence on dating its evolution so precisely. No Irish reader taking up the work in either 1921 or 1928 could avoid reading it as an allegory of the Irish struggle or even as a *roman à clef* giving the author's impressions of his own republican comrades. Pádraig Ó Siadhail has expressed reservations about Béaslaí's claim that the novel as we have it is largely unchanged from the text supposedly completed in 1912, but even if *Astronár* is not a retrospective assessment of the recent past, it offers a fascinating insight into the internal ideological and tactical debates affecting the advanced nationalist movement in the decade before the Easter Rising of 1916.[30]

Unfortunately, Béaslaí was never to write another novel, devoting his subsequent literary career for the most part to the theatre. Séamus Mac Conmara (1909–1936) also left us just a single novel, but in his case, a career that showed early promise was cut off by his untimely death. *An Coimhthigheach*, published posthumously three years later in 1939, is by far the most substantial work of the time in Irish dealing with a subject that might have been expected to attract more interest: the challenges and rewards of a priestly vocation. While one could wish that Mac Conmara, himself a seminarian, had further humanised his protagonist, a suspended priest who has been unjustly imprisoned in England and is now living incognito in the north of Ireland, by giving him more of the self-doubts and failings that might well trouble even someone who has suffered in stoic silence as he has, *An Coimhthigheach* is a landmark in Gaelic fiction for its willingness to at least raise, in a serious and sustained manner, the question of the potential isolation and loneliness of priests ministering to a population that could only with great difficulty understand the nature and challenges of their vocation.

Ciarán Ua Nualláin (1910–1983) was the brother of Brian ('Flann O'Brien', 'Myles na gCopaleen') (1911–1966), himself just then beginning his career as a writer of Irish with comic sketches in his self-published humour magazine

Blather, in the University College Dublin journal *Comhthrom Féinne*, and in the *Irish Press*. But Ciarán was an important and prolific figure in his own right. In 1939, he published the first full-length mystery novel in Irish, *Oidhche i nGleann na Gealt*, a rather dark study of rural greed and arranged marriage as a source of economic strife within families. His detective, Parthalán Mac Mórna, manages to thwart a man's intricate and long meditated plot to kill his own brother to prevent being ousted from the family homestead on that brother's marriage. His was not, however, by any means the first attempt to cultivate in Irish the subgenres of popular light fiction. Micheál Ó Gríobhtha's *Lorgaireacht* contains three stories about a Holmesean detective working for the Garda Síochána, the Irish national police force. Others writing detective fiction in Irish for periodicals at the time were Father Seoirse Mac Clúin (1894–1949); Father Gearóid Ó Nualláin (1874–1942), the uncle of Ciarán and Brian; and Art Ó Riain. The most satisfying Gaelic work in this subgenre to emerge from our period was Seoirse Mac Liam's novel *An Doras do Plabadh* (1940).

There was very little science fiction written at the time, and it is interesting that very little of what there was relies on fantasies of scientific or technological progress, focusing instead on questions of cultural and social evolution, as in Seosamh Ó Torna's 'Duinneall' and 'Cheithre Bhuille an Chluig', or Ó Riain's 'Aisling'. An exception here is Ó Riain's 1927 novella *An Tost*. The narrative is divided into five sections, set in 1914, 1916, 1921, 1938 and 1975. In the final two sections set in the future, the protagonist is the Irish government's 'Aire um Aer-Thaisdeal' (Minister for Air Travel) to whose lot it falls to defend the nation against the combined threat of England and Japan, eager to occupy the country for strategic purposes. In the period just before hostilities erupt, the Irish president declares neutrality, but soon Ireland is driven to surrender that neutrality for an alliance with 'an dá America' (the two Americas), a move that fails to stave off an invasion by the English and Japanese. After the occupation of the country and the torture of the heroic protagonist with a laser-like device, the nation is liberated by a joint Irish and American rescue operation flown in in enormous American aircraft ('oll-longa Ponncánacha'). Ó Riain's tale is noteworthy for its creation of the kind of futuristic devices that are the stock-in-trade of so much science fiction – the laser gun, the huge aircraft and coin-operated pay radios on the street. Fantastic machines also featured in Máiréad Ní Ghráda's *Manannán* (1940), a science-fiction thriller for young readers in which an Irish astronomer discovers a mysterious new planet and names it after the Irish sea god. The first full-length sci-fi novel in Irish would not appear until Seán Mac Maoláin's *Algoland* (1947), a work vaguely reminiscent of Edward Bellamy's 1888 classic *Looking Backward, or 2000–1887*.

Other works of light escapist fiction from the time were *Eoghan Paor* (1910) by 'Conán Maol', the story of a patriotic millionaire's scheme to free Ireland; Peadar Ó Dubhda's *Ar Lorg an t-Seanchaidhe* (1915), a work that introduced the airplane into Gaelic fiction; Micheál Ó Gríobhtha's *Go mBeannuighthear Dia dhuit* (1925), an improbable blend of Catholic religiosity and gun-toting adventure that takes its protagonist from Ireland to New York to the gold fields of the Wild West and the mean streets of Rio de Janeiro; and his *Briathar Mná* (1928), a tale of patriotic smugglers on the coast of Clare in the early nineteenth century. 'Fionn' Mac Cumhaill's *Is É Dia an Fear is Fearr* (1928) is another amalgam of Catholic piety and adventure in the American West, while Seán Ó Ciarghusa's *Onncail Seárlaí* (1930) takes its hero to the North Pole, where he encounters terrifying polar bears, villainous sailors and folk-singing Eskimos. Tadhg Ó Murchadha's (1899–1978) *An Cliathán Clé* (1932) is a school story whose rugby-mad characters would have scandalised members of the Gaelic Athletic Association.

Gaeltacht autobiography

No novel from this period, of whatever kind, was to have and hold such a fascination for readers of Irish as did – and still to some extent do – the three so-called Blasket Island autobiographies: Tomás Ó Criomhthain's (1855–1937) *An t-Oileánach* (1929), Muiris Ó Súileabháin's (1904–1950) *Fiche Blian ag Fás* (1933) and Peig Sayers's (1873–1958) *Peig. i. A Scéal Féin* (1936). And to these one should add Ó Criomhthain's *Allagar na h-Inise* (1928) and Sayers's *Machtnamh Seanmhná* (1939). Moreover, it is important to note that translations into English of *An t-Oileánach* and *Fiche Blian ag Fás* were also published in our period, that of the former in 1937, that of the latter the same year the book appeared in Irish. As a result, almost immediately the Gaeltacht autobiography became the keystone of the evolving canon of writing in Irish. In fact, the literary production of this tiny island off the Kerry coast was so startling in both its quantity and quality that it led Thomas Barrington to a hyperbolic dismissal of the literary work of all the rest of the country in a 1936 essay in the *Irish Rosary* entitled 'Fishermen and Literature': 'The output of this island of poverty-stricken fishermen only serves to underline the fact that Gaelic letters in the rest of Ireland is dead, dead as a doornail.'[31] The satirical monthly *Dublin Opinion* paid a more light-hearted tribute to the islanders' literary triumphs on the cover of the June 1933 issue with a cartoon labelled 'The Literary Wave Hits the Islands', a drawing that showed every nook, cranny and cave of the Great Blasket filled with people furiously scribbling or typing while a curragh pulls away laden with rolled manuscripts.

All of these books were very much Revival projects, inspired, midwived, critiqued and edited by enthusiastic outsiders. Brian Ó Ceallaigh and Pádraig Ó Siochfhradha encouraged and worked with Ó Criomhthain, George Thomson with Ó Súileabháin, and Peig's son Micheál Ó Gaoithín and Máire Ní Chinnéide with Sayers, who was herself illiterate. It is hard to criticize these people since without them it is unlikely we would have had all – even any – of these books. Their involvement could, however, have a significant effect on what the authors included and how that material was organised and treated. Ó Criomhthain had the most powerful original voice of the three, but the text of *An tOileánach* as it first appeared in print after having been edited by Pádraig Ó Siochfhradha is quite different from the text Ó Criomhthain himself produced. Ó Siochfhradha intervened in the text most intrusively by cutting entirely Ó Criomhthain's occasionally earthy treatment of sexual matters, and removing some of his references to the islanders' fondness for strong drink.[32] With the publication in 2002 of Ó Criomhthain's original text as edited by Seán Ó Coileáin of University College Cork, we can now better assess the author's own genuine and considerable artistry. Thomson's involvement with Ó Súileabháin's text seems to have been of a higher order, as beginning with its Greek epigraph, *Fiche Blian ag Fás* is a more consciously polished text than one might expect from the author. Doubtless her collaborators, and particularly her son Micheál, who had literary aspirations and wrote an autobiography and poetry, influenced Peig's narrative as well. But what is most clear now is that this book, long maligned and ridiculed because of its mandatory inclusion on school curricula and all too often unimaginatively taught, represents the thoughts of a strong, independent and intelligent woman of profound and vital spirituality. Other, far less accomplished and influential Gaeltacht autobiographies from the period were the Donegal native Niall Mac Giolla Bhrighde's (1861–1942) *Dírbheathaisnéis Néill Mhic Ghiolla Bhrighde* (1938), dictated to Liam Ó Connacháin; and, perhaps the first of them, the schoolmaster and novelist Diarmuid Ó hÉigeartaigh's *Is Uasal Céird*, apparently written in 1926, though not published until 1968.[33]

Drama

If autobiography turned out to be the most comfortable and adaptable genre for some writers of Irish, drama was the most exotic and challenging. It was also one that literary Revivalists felt had to be developed at once to counter the argument that their compatriots writing plays in English and gaining an appreciative international audience were creating the foundations of a legitimate national theatre. Drama was not, however, a genre indigenous to Irish, so the search for appropriate models required considerable flexibility. Those of nativist bent saw the best such models implicit in the Gaelic tradition, in the dialogues between Oisín and Saint Patrick from the medieval Fenian Cycle of tales, and in the histrionic performance style of the traditional *seanchaí*, whose repertoire, moreover, often included some of the Ossianic dialogues. It was, in fact, just such a dialogue, Pádraic Ó Beirne's translation of the 'Saint Patrick at Tara' section from Father Eugene O'Growney's *The Passing of Conall*, performed at the Gaelic League's Aonach Thír Chonaill in 1898, that is often named as the first 'play' produced in Irish. That honour actually belongs to Paul McSwiney's (1859–1889) *An Bárd 'gus an Fó*, staged in Brooklyn's Steinway Hall in November 1884, and serialized in *An Gaodhal* beginning the following month. A play published even earlier, though never performed, was Father John O'Carroll's (1837–1889) *Amharca Cleasacha / Dramatic Scenes in Irish*, a bombastic and unwieldy work dealing with Brian Boru that commenced serialisation in the very first issue of *Irisleabhar na Gaedhilge* in November, 1882.[34]

In 1904, one 'E.' though eager to see a flourishing drama movement in Irish, was honest enough to admit that 'perhaps we are still at the *Ralph Royster Doyster* or the *Gammer Gurton's Needle* Stage'.[35] Some of the early Gaelic dramatists, however, wanted all the colour and scope of Shakespeare or Boucicault, probably the two playwrights most of them knew best, in the one-act skits that were the most League branches were able to mount at the time. In particular, authors of many of the early history plays – and history was from the beginning one of the most popular subjects for plays in Irish – had startlingly high ambitions. For example, *An Bealach Buidhe* (1906), Father O'Leary's one-act play on Hugh O'Neill, the late-sixteenth-century earl of Tyrone, has eight scenes, all with different settings, and nine speaking parts, plus extras; while *Aodh Ó Néill* (1902), a one-acter by 'Conán Maol' about the same leader, has seven scenes with six sets and more than twenty characters! When dramatists were offered more scope, the result could be frightening. In December 1906, what must still be the most extravagant play ever produced in Irish was performed by the seminarians at Maynooth. Written by an anonymous Maynooth student, the five-act *Eoghan Ruadh Ua Neill, nó Ar Son Tíre agus Creidimh* kept its cast of more than twenty on stage for over five hours. Other full-length plays from the early Revival inspired by Irish history or medieval heroic literature were O'Leary's

Bás Dhalláin (1901); his closet drama *Táin Bó Cuailnge 'na Dhráma* (serialised 1900–1, published 1915); Séamus Ó Duirinne's (1876–1946) *Ar Son Baile agus Tíre* (1905); Tomás Ó hAodha's *Seabhac na Ceathramhan Caoile* (1906); *Mac Cárthaigh Mór* (1908) by 'Pádraig na Léime' (a third Pádraig Ó Séaghdha) (1880–1921); Father Tomás Ó Ceallaigh's (1879–1924) *An Foghmhar* (1908), *Deirdre* (1909) and *Eithne, nó Éan an Cheoil Bhinn* (1909), the last an operetta; Béaslaí's *Coramac na Cuile* (sic) (1909); and Seán Ó Ceallaigh's (1872–1957) *Cú Roí* (1913). Writers who published one-act plays of this kind included Pearse, Hyde, Peadar Mac Fhionnlaoich and Father Dinneen, whose *Creideamh agus Gorta* (1901) is interesting as an early play on the Famine, about which he was to later write another short play entitled *Teachtaire ó Dhia* (1922).

While there was some humour in a few of these plays, most of them were serious, even ponderous, and their authors may well have felt that in writing them they were helping give substance and dignity to a language still derided by some of their opponents as a rustic *patois*. For audiences, however – and particularly for that elusive ideal audience in the Gaeltacht – it was comic plays set among those who actually spoke the language that were most popular. Once again, Father O'Leary was a pioneer in this regard. His farce *Tadhg Saor* opened eyes when it was successfully produced at a League *feis* in Macroom in 1900, the year before the more famous performance of Hyde's *Casadh an tSúgáin* by the Irish Literary Theatre in Dublin. In 1902, Father Dinneen's *An Tobar Draoidheachta* and Peadar Mac Fhionnlaoich's *Eilís agus an Bhean Déirce* entered the Gaelic repertoire. These playwrights inspired a host of others to write short, simple, humorous plays or knockabout farces to draw and hold audiences new to the theatre or the language, or both. Hyde was particularly adept at producing plays of this kind, many of which, in the translation of Lady Gregory, were to win audiences in English as well. Pádraic Ó Conaire also tried his hand at drama at this time, although predictably he explored the darker side of Gaeltacht life in plays like *An Droighneán Donn* (1905), *Bairbre Ruadh* (1908), and *An tUdhacht* (published in *An Claidheamh Soluis*, 1915).

Also popular among Gaelic League audiences of the early Revival were propaganda plays for the movement, some of them, such as Felix Partridge's *An tAthrughadh Mór* (1906), Séamus Ó Beirne's *Obair!* and *An Dochtúir* (both 1909), and McShane and Johnson's *Toradh na Troda* (n.d.), were bilingual. Lorcán Ua Tuathail's anti-emigration melodrama *An Deoraidhe* (1907) also quickly became and remained a favourite of groups throughout the country interested in staging a play in Irish.

One of the main problems impeding the growth of Gaelic drama was the fact that production was entirely reliant on such dedicated amateurs, usually from the Gaelic League. It was, therefore, a giant step forward when Piaras Béaslaí's group Na hAisteoirí took the stage for the first time in 1913 and in their first year not only performed at the Abbey, but also toured the Gaeltacht. With a regular, albeit still amateur, company active in Dublin, playwrights working in Irish could for the first time hope for competent production of their work in decently equipped theatres in the national capital. The finest playwright Na hAisteoirí produced was Béaslaí himself, who in the years before independence provided the company with successful comedies like the following (dates are for first performance, all were published in our period) *Cluiche Cártaí* (1913), *Fear na Milliún Punt* (1915) and *An Sgaothaire* (1915). He was to sharpen his comic sense in later plays like *Cúigeachas* (1927), *An Fear as Buenos Ayres* (1928), *An Fear Fógraidheachta* (1934) and *Blúire Páipéir* (1936). He also wrote two of the most ambitious tragedies of the time, the history plays *An Danar* (1929) and *An Bhean Chródha* (1931).

After independence, Na hAisteoirí evolved into An Comhar Drámaidheachta, with Béaslaí, Gearóid Ó Lochlainn, Pádraig Ó Siochfhradha, Risteárd Ó Foghludha and Liam Gógan on its board of directors. The group, like the Abbey, was granted a state subsidy in 1924, and for two decades was to perform regularly in the Abbey, the Peacock and the Gate, before itself being absorbed into the Abbey company in 1942 under a plan developed by Ernest Blythe. In Galway, Taibhdhearc na Gaillimhe was founded in 1929 as a theatre devoted exclusively to the production of plays in Irish. The 1920s, and especially the 1930s, were to be the glory days of drama in Irish. Both An Comhar and An Taibhdhearc ran full seasons of plays in their respective home cities, creating an unprecedented demand for scripts.

While translation understandably played a significant role in meeting this demand, there were also a fair number of competent original plays, not all of them rural farces or historical costume dramas. Along with Béaslaí, two of the most interesting playwrights of the period were Gearóid Ó Lochlainn, like Béaslaí an actor, director and translator as well as a dramatist, and Séamus de Bhilmot (Wilmot). The former was the more versatile of the two, the latter the more ambitious and experimental. Among Ó Lochlainn's plays produced in our period were comedies like *Na Gaduithe* (1935), plays of the national struggle like *An tÉirighe Amach* (produced 1937, published 1944) and *Na Fear-achoin* (produced 1938, published 1946), and a social problem play like *Bean an Mhilliúnaí* (1923). Along with his Famine play *Baintighearna an Ghorta* (produced 1938, published 1944), de Bhilmot wrote the rural tragedies *An Casán* and *Múchadh an tSolais* (both 1931); *'San Am Soin–* (performed 1936, published 1944), a play about Barabbas; and *'Grádh Níos Mó'* (performed 1938, published

1947), a still-provocative drama about the morality of using weapons of mass destruction.

Ó Lochlainn and de Bhilmot were, however, by no means alone in their creation of competent and stageworthy scripts at the time. Micheál Mac Liammóir's *Diarmuid agus Gráinne*, the premier production of Taibhdhearc na Gaillimhe in August 1928, remains one of the finest plays ever written in Irish. Séamus Ó Néill, later a prominent Gaelic novelist and playwright, based his *Buaidh an Ultaigh* (1936) on another story about Fionn Mac Cumhaill and his Fianna, while Micheál Ó Siochfhradha turned to the Ulster Cycle for inspiration in his *Aon Mhac Aoife Alban* (1938), a stageworthy tragedy about Cú Chulainn's killing of his own son. The versatile Ó Siochfhradha also produced historical dramas about the Fenians in *An Ball Dubh* (1929) and about the War of Independence in *Deire an Chunntais* (1932). The latter was one of two Gaelic plays at the time, the other being Ó Lochlainn's *Na Fearachoin*, that used a plot-line involving the execution of prisoners better known from Frank O'Connor's story 'Guests of the Nation'. In his play *An Mhallacht* (1931), León Ó Broin explored the dreadful consequences of recent violence, however politically or militarily justified, on the Irish psyche. Ó Broin also had a gift for stage comedy, as is evident in plays like *Siamsa Gaedheal*, *An Sgríbhinn ar an mBalla* (both 1931) and *An Clósgríobhaí* (1936). And in *An Oíche Úd i mBeithil* (performed 1939, published 1949), he offered a modern, anti-colonial perspective on the events surrounding the birth of Christ. The Donegal native speaker Eoghan Mac Giolla Bhrighde wrote two history plays, *In Aimsir an Mháirtínigh* (1937) and *An Fealltóir* (1939) that became staples in the repertoire of Aisteoirí Ghaoth Dobhair, the local theatre company founded in the Donegal Gaeltacht in 1931. Máiréad Ní Ghráda, later to become one of the most original and accomplished playwrights in the language, was just beginning her career at this time with apprentice pieces like the comedies *An Udhacht* (1935) and *An Grádh agus an Gárda* (1937). Liam O'Flaherty's only play in Irish, *Dorchadas*, staged at the Abbey in 1926, was never published in the original, though an English translation did appear the same year in the summer issue of the English magazine *New Coterie* and in a limited edition of 100 copies.

Literary criticism

Among the many challenges facing writers of Irish at the time was the absence of virtually any, much less an informed and insightful, literary criticism, a situation neatly lampooned by Donn Piatt in 1931:

> Caidé mar ghníthear léirmheas i n-Oileán na Naomh? Tá sin furasd a innse. Caitheann tú suas pighinn. Má thuiteann sí agus an chearc ar uachtar cáinfidh tú an leabhar. Anois, foscail an leabhar seo áit ar bith is léigh leat go bhfágha tú (a) dearmad cló (b) dearmad 'sa litriú (c) canamhaint nach dtaitneann leat (d) droch-Ghaedhilg cheart (e) 'droch-Ghaedhilg' do réir baramhla atá agat féin. Scríobh léirmheas ar na lochtaí annsin, is tá leat. Má thig an chláirseach ar uachtar mol an leabhar is cuir i gcomórtas í le Dante nó le rud ínteacht eile nár léigh tú ariamh. MÁ'S CARA DUIT A SCRÍOBH AN LEABHAR FAN AG CAITHEAMH PIGHNEACH GO dTARAIDH AN CHEARC AR UACHTAR.

> How is criticism done in the Island of the Saints? That is easily told. You throw up a penny. If it lands with the hen up, you will find fault with the book. Now, open this book anywhere and read on until you find (a) a typographical error (b) a mistake in spelling (c) a dialect you don't like (d) genuinely bad Irish (e) 'bad Irish' according to your own opinion. Write a review on the faults then, and there you have it. If the harp comes up, praise the book and compare it to Dante or something else you've never read. IF IT IS A FRIEND OF YOURS WHO WROTE THE BOOK, KEEP THROWING PENNIES UNTIL THE HEN COMES OUT ON TOP.[36]

There were, however, a few promising signs of change. A handful of critical articles of some sophistication appeared in the various Gaelic journals, particularly in the short-lived *Humanitas*, founded by Father Pádraig de Brún in 1930. More important, in 1926, there appeared Father Seoirse Mac Clúin's *An Litríocht: Infhiúcha ar Phrionnsabail, Fuirmeacha agus Léirmheastóireacht na Litríochta*. Throughout, Mac Clúin asserts an Arnoldian view of literature as criticism of life and shows a clear distaste for propaganda or for writing that focuses on the ugly, morbid or immoral, an aberration that he sees far too much of in the work of modern authors. For his contemporaries, the most controversial aspect of Mac Clúin's work was the degree to which he relied on English literature for his illustrative examples. Críostóir Ó Raghallaigh's *An Léirmheastóir* (1931) is a textbook consisting of passages from seventeen authors followed by a general and pedestrian discussion of each. The target audience for Séamus Ó Searcaigh's *Nua-Sgríbhneoirí na Gaedhilge* (1933) was again secondary school students. Ó Searcaigh also devoted a significant amount of attention to the literary work of Pearse in his biography *Pádraig Mac Piarais* (1938), which included a lengthy chapter on 'An tUghdar'. Pearse's work was also discussed in Séamus Ó hAodha's brief bilingual monograph *Pádraic Mac Piarais, Sgéaluidhe / Patrick H. Pearse: Storyteller* (1919). A longer study of the work of a single author was *An tAthair Peadar Ó Laoghaire agus a Shaothar* (1939) by 'Maol Muire' (Sister Mary Vincent). *Prós na hAoise Seo* (1934) by Shán Ó Cuív (1875–1940) is a study of fifteen contemporary Gaelic writers. Ó Cuív's approach is strongly biographical and throughout he stresses the central significance of those writers who were native speakers. More substantial than Ó Cuív's booklet was Muiris Ó Droighneáin's *Taighde i gComhair Stair Litridheachta na Nua-Ghaedhilge ó 1882 anuas* (1936), a history of modern literature in Irish from the foundation of *Irisleabhar na Gaedhilge* on, with separate discussions of poetry, prose and drama. Ó Droighneáin was, however, emphatic that he wrote as a historian and not as a critic. One Gaelic writer never reluctant to express a critical opinion on any subject literary or otherwise was Seosamh Mac Grianna, whose lengthy essay on Pádraic Ó Conaire gave its title to his 1936 collection *Pádraic Ó Conaire agus Aistí Eile*.

There was a fair amount of writing in Irish on the Gaelic tradition in poetry, in particular poetry written in the eighteenth century. Some of this interest was inspired by Daniel Corkery's seminal classic *The Hidden Ireland: A Study of Gaelic Munster in the Eighteenth Century*. It was, for example, to correct what he saw as Corkery's ignorant and unjust neglect of Ulster poetry that Mac Grianna wrote for *Fáinne an Lae* in 1925 the essays that were published as a booklet the following year under the title *Filí gan Iomrádh*. Mac Grianna also delivered a series of lectures on Ulster poets at Coláiste Bhríde in Omeath in the summer of 1925, lectures that were subsequently published in *Pádraic Ó Conaire agus Aistí Eile*. Others who wrote on this poetry at the time were Toirdhealbhach Ó Raithbheartaigh (1905–1984) in his *Máighistrí san Fhilidheacht: Láimh-Leabhar ar na Filí Móra ó Chéitinn anuas* (1932) and Piaras Béaslaí in the two volumes of *Éigse Nua-Ghaedhilge* (1933).

The most erudite, versatile and enterprising critic writing in Irish at this time was Liam Ó Rinn. In addition to his many insightful reviews and essays on literary matters, in particular those he wrote for the weekly papers *The United Irishman* and *United Ireland* in the early 1930s, in 1939 he published, to a unanimously laudatory reception, *Mo Chara Stiofán*, the memoir of his friendship with the Irish classicist Stephen McKenna (1872–1934). His summaries of conversations and correspondence with the polyglot and urbane McKenna both in Ireland and after the latter's emigration to England range over literary and cultural topics as diverse as Negro spirituals, Yoga, Buddhism, the work of James Joyce and the role of translation in the language revival. To help would-be writers of Irish, Ó Rinn published *Peann agus Pár* (1940), a practical manual of the writer's craft modelled on similar books in English and French.

Conclusion

As our period ended, those in the language and literary movement had much to celebrate. Who could have believed sixty years earlier that there would be a small but growing literature in the language encompassing all modern genres? There had even been a film released in 1935, the ten-minute *Oidhche Sheanchais*, produced by none other than Robert Flaherty. And while it did little more than provide a visual record of a *seanchaí* telling a story and failed to entertain even committed activists, it did exist and offered a new possibility to be explored.[37]

Furthermore, by 1938, An Gúm had in its twelve years of existence put more than 500 titles on the market, selling over 300,000 copies of them.[38] Many at the time and since have criticized the quality of a good number of those titles, and particularly An Gúm's heavy reliance on translation of mediocre English books – about 80 per cent of the novels published by An Gúm in our period were translations, mostly from English. It is, however, hard to see how An Gúm could have avoided such a reliance if it were to have had any hope of achieving its goal of providing even a modicum of reading matter for the potential new Irish readership being produced by the schools.

Most of the literature discussed above is now of almost purely historical interest, far more important for its mere existence and quantity than its quality. Nevertheless, even if the literary side of the language revival still had a long way to go in 1940, any objective observer would have to agree with 'An Sagart' when he boasted of his own day in 1937: 'Gaelic has never been flung so broadly on the waters of the world during even our Golden Age.'[39]

Notes

1. See Máirtín Ó Murchú, *Cumann Buan-Choimeádta na Gaeilge: Tús an Athréimnithe* (Dublin: Cois Life, 2001), pp. 324–5.
2. Tadhg Ó Donnchadha, 'Réamhrádh', in E. M. Ní Chiaragáin, ed. *Index to 'Irisleabhar na Gaedhilge' 1882–1909* (Dublin: Three Candles Press, 1935), p. vii.
3. See Pádraig Ó Fearaíl, *The Story of Conradh na Gaeilge: A History of the Gaelic League* (Dublin: Conradh na Gaeilge, 1975), p. 6.
4. Hyde, 'An Préachán Mór,' in Tadhg Ó Donnchadha, ed. *Imtheachta an Oireachtais 1901 (Leabhar a hAon)* (Dublin: Connradh na Gaedhilge, 1903), pp. 2–3.
5. For a discussion of these works and their significance, see Cathal Ó Háinle, 'An tÚrscéal nár Tháinig', in *Promhadh Pinn* (Maynooth: An Sagart, 1978), pp. 74–98.
6. See Philip O'Leary, *The Prose Literature of the Gaelic Revival 1881–1921: Ideology and Innovation* (University Park: Penn State Press, 1994), pp. 14–16.
7. For more detailed discussions of this subject, see O'Leary, *Prose Literature*, pp. 19–27, 32–45; and O'Leary, *Gaelic Prose in the Irish Free State 1922–1939* (Dublin: University College Dublin Press, 2004), pp. 48–65.

8. To refute the charge of the Trinity College professor Robert Atkinson that Irish was an 'out-of-the-way and troublesome language', Douglas Hyde lined up an all-star cast of Irish and European scholars to testify before the British Government's Vice-Regal Inquiry into Intermediate Education in 1899. See P. J. Mathews, 'Hyde's First Stand: The Irish Language Controversy of 1899', *Éire-Ireland: Special Issue – Translation*, ed. Philip O'Leary, 35, 1–2 (Spring–Summer, 2000), pp. 173–87.
9. Richard Henebry, 'Revival Irish', *The Leader* (5 December 1908).
10. In a recent, as yet unpublished essay, Brian Ó Conchubhair argues convincingly that the situation was more complex, and that the theories of Max Müller on dialect had a significant influence on the views of many in the language movement with regard to *caint na ndaoine*.
11. Peter O'Leary, Letter to Séamus Ó Dubhghaill, 17 November, 1900, quoted by An tAthair Pádraig Ó Fiannachta in 'Ag Cogarnaíl le Cara', *Irisleabhar Mhá Nuad*, 1991, p. 114.
12. Séamus Ó Grianna, Letter, *Fáinne an Lae*, 21 February 1925.
13. Patrick Pearse, review of *An Buaiceas* by 'Conán Maol', *An Claidheamh Soluis* (14 March 1903).
14. Pearse, 'By Way of Comment', *An Macaomh* (December 1909), p. 18.
15. Pearse, 'About Literature', editorial, *An Claidheamh Soluis* (26 May 1906).
16. Liam Ó Briain, 'Pádraic Ó Conaire', *Comhar* (December 1956), p. 14.
17. See his letter to the editor in *Comhar* (December 1969), p. 4.
18. Nollaig Mac Congáil, 'An Traidisiún Béil i Saothar Sheagháin Mhic Mheanman,' in Séamus Ó Cnáimhsí, ed. *Éigse 1988: Seán Bán Mac Meanman* (Dublin: Coiscéim, 1988), p. 17.
19. See Seán Mac Meanman, 'Réamhrádh', in *Fear Siubhail a's a Chuid Comharsanach agus Daoine Eile* (Dublin: An Gúm, 1937), n.p., and Mac Meanman, 'Réamhrádh', in *Indé agus Indiu* (Dublin: An Gúm, 1929), n.p.
20. Pádhraic Ó Domhnalláin, 'I mBaile is i gCéin', *Fáinne an Lae* (18 July 1925).
21. See Tomás Bairéad, *Gan Baisteadh* (Dublin: Sáirséal agus Dill, 1972), p. 240.
22. An tAthair Micheál, 'Ceannracháin Cathrach', review, *The Father Mathew Record* (August–September 1935), p. 411. In 1942, An Gúm published Mac Maoláin's *I mBéal Feirste Dom*, a book rooted in his considerable personal experience of the northern capital, *terra incognita* for many in the language movement.
23. In 1911–12, Ó Caomhánaigh published a series of pieces on urban topics in *Sinn Féin* under the title 'Catharach Nuadh'. In 1913–14, he published in the same journal the serialised story 'An Truaghán Mná', an Ó Conairesque look at the seamy underside of Dublin.
24. See Norah Meade, 'The Contemporary Irish National Movement in Literature', *Weekly Freeman* (12 March 1910); 'Maol Muire' (Sister Mary Vincent), *An tAthair Peadar Ó Laoghaire agus a Shaothar* (Dublin: Browne and Nolan, 1939), p. 39; Aodh de Blacam, *Gaelic Literature Surveyed* (Dublin: Browne and Nolan, 1929), p. 379; Pádraig A. Breatnach, '*Séadna*: Saothar Ealaíne,' *Studia Hibernica* 9 (1969), p. 112; Alan Titley, *An tÚrscéal Gaeilge* (Dublin: An Clóchomhar, 1991), pp. 535, 574.
25. Patrick Pearse, 'History and Romance', review of *Niamh* by Peter O'Leary, *An Claidheamh Soluis* (7 September 1907).
26. The full text of this novel has now been edited and published by Nollaig Mac Congáil in Ó Grianna, *Castar na Daoine ar a Chéile (Scríbhinní Mháire I)* (Dublin: Coiscéim, 2002).

27. See Nollaig Mac Congáil, 'Réamhrá', in *Seosamh Mac Grianna / Iolann Fionn: Clár Saothair* (Dublin: Coiscéim, 1990), p. 37.
28. See Tadhg Ó Dúshláine, 'Scéal Úrscéil: *Fánaí*, Seán Óg Ó Caomhánaigh, 1927', *Léachtaí Cholm Cille* 19 (1989), pp. 93–128.
29. Úna Bean Uí Dhíocsa, letter, *Fáinne an Lae* (26 December 1925).
30. See Pádraig Ó Siadhail, 'Gaiscígh, Gaigí agus Guamóga: Téama an Laochais i Scríbhinní Cruthaitheacha Phiarais Bhéaslaí', *Irisleabhar Mhá Nuad* (1990), pp. 137–54.
31. Thomas Barrington, 'Fisherman and Literature', *The Irish Rosary* (July 1936), p. 521.
32. See James Stewart, '*An tOileánach* – More or Less', *Zeitschrift für celtische Philologie* 35 (1976), pp. 234–83.
33. See Stiofán Ó hAnnracháin, 'Réamhrá', in Diarmuid Ó hÉigeartaigh, *Is Uasal Ceird* (Dublin: Foilseacháin Náisiúnta Teoranta, 1968), p. 8.
34. In December 1915, a brief dramatic fragment entitled 'Dúnlaing Óg agus a Leannán Sidhe' was performed on the same bill with two of Pearse's plays by the Theatre of Ireland in Dublin's Hardwicke Street. The programme for the evening noted that the piece had been 'enacted among the people up to sixty or seventy years ago'. 'Dúnlaing Óg' was little more than a dialogue between the title character and his otherworld lover on the eve of the battle of Clontarf. See the programme in the collection of the Pearse Museum, Rathfarnham, Dublin. In the journal *An Lóchrann* (December 1909 to January 1910; April–August 1918; and November–December 1918), Fionán Mac Coluim published three dramatic fragments he had collected from the narration of Tadhg Ó Conchubhair of Lispole, County Kerry. Ó Conchubhair attributed two of these to Muiris Ó Gríbhghín, who had lived in the neighbourhood eighty years earlier. All three of these little sketches have multiple characters and simple stage directions.
35. 'E.', 'Recent Plays', *An Claidheamh Soluis* (1 October 1904).
36. Donn Piatt, 'Aistriú agus Rudaí Eile', *An tUltach* (July 1931), pp. 2–3.
37. The text of the story in the film was published by the Free State's Department of Education in 1934.
38. See León Ó Broin, 'A State-Fostered Literature', *Irish Monthly* (February 1938), p. 126.
39. 'An Sagart', 'Towards the Irish Revival', *An Ráitheachán* (March 1937), p. 11.

Select bibliography

Breathnach, Diarmuid, and Máire Ní Mhurchú, *1882–1982: Beathaisnéis*, vols. I–V (Dublin: An Clóchomhar, 1986–97).

1983–2002: Beathaisnéis (Dublin: An Clóchomhar, 2003).

Delap, Breandán, *Úrscéalta Stairiúla na Gaeilge* (Dublin: An Clóchomhar, 1993).

Greene, David, *Writing in Irish Today* (Cork: Mercier Press, 1972).

Nic Eoin, Máirín, *An Litríocht Réigiúnach* (Dublin: An Clóchomhar, 1982).

Ní Dhonnchadha, Aisling, *An Gearrscéal sa Ghaeilge 1898–1940* (Dublin: An Clóchomhar, 1981).

O'Brien, Frank, *Filíocht Ghaeilge na Linne Seo* (Dublin: An Clóchomhar, 1968).

Ó Cadhain, Máirtín, 'Conradh na Gaeilge agus an Litríocht', in Seán Ó Tuama, ed. *The Gaelic League Idea* (Cork: Mercier Press, 1972), pp. 52–62.

'Irish Prose in the Twentieth Century', in J. E. Caerwyn Williams, ed. *Literature in Celtic Countries* (Cardiff: University of Wales Press, 1971), pp. 139–51.

Ó Cuív, Shán, *Prós na hAoise Seo* (Dublin: Browne and Nolan, 1934).

Ó Droighneáin, Muiris, *Taighde i gComhair Stair Litridheachta na Nua-Ghaedhilge ó 1882 Anuas* (Dublin: An Gúm, 1936).

Ó Glaisne, Risteárd, *Ceannródaithe: Scríbhneoirí na Nua-Ré* (Dublin: Foilseacháin Náisiúnta Teoranta, 1974).

O'Leary, Philip, *Gaelic Prose in the Irish Free State 1922–1939* (Dublin: University College Dublin Press, 2004).

The Prose Literature of the Gaelic Revival 1881–1921: Ideology and Innovation (University Park: Penn State Press, 1994).

Ó Siadhail, Pádraig, *Stair Dhrámaíocht na Gaeilge 1900–1970* (Indreabhán: Cló Iar-Chonnachta, 1993).

Ó Súilleabháin, Donncha, *Scéal an Oireachtais, 1897–1924* (Dublin: An Clóchomhar, 1984).

Ó Tuama, Seán, 'Úrscéalta agus Faisnéisí Beatha na Gaeilge: Na Buaicphointí', *Scríobh* 5 (1981), pp. 148–60.

Titley, Alan, *An tÚrscéal Gaeilge* (Dublin: An Clóchomhar, 1991).

'Litríocht na Gaeilge, Litríocht an Bhéarla, agus Irish Literature', *Scríobh* 5 (1981), pp. 116–39.

6

Contemporary prose and drama in Irish 1940–2000

MÁIRÍN NIC EOIN

Introduction

The years 1940–2000 have been a period of uneven growth and development for Irish-language prose and drama. The most significant development of all during these decades was the emergence of a great diversity of literary forms as many writers gradually distanced themselves from the more restricting aspects of Revivalist ideology and began to experiment more with language, structure and subject matter. Critical perspectives also evolved and it was recognised that the cultural context in which the Irish language had survived now demanded expression in a manner which often defied the strictures imposed by genre or particular aesthetic paradigms. Linguistic norms are challenged in many works, both by Gaeltacht and non-Gaeltacht writers, and questions of cultural change and cultural hybridity become stylistic concerns as much as themes in much of the prose literature of the period. During this time Máirtín Ó Cadhain was to gain prominence as a major prose writer, and a host of other new and distinct voices emerged such as those of novelists and short story writers Diarmaid Ó Súilleabháin, Alan Titley, Micheál Ó Conghaile and Pádraig Ó Siadhail. These years also witnessed a continuation of a strong Gaeltacht tradition of autobiography and auto-ethnography, side by side with an unprecedented amount of experimental prose writing. The publishing house Sáirséal agus Dill, which was established in 1946, was responsible for the publication of much of the most original and innovative fiction of the period, while in the 1980s the newly established Coiscéim and Cló Iar-Chonnachta were to play a prominent role in the encouragement of many new and younger writers. The re-establishment of the Oireachtas literary competitions in 1939 provided motivation for many new and practising writers, while the monthly reviews *Comhar* (1942–) and *Feasta* (1948–) provided a platform for writers and a regular forum for literary criticism and debate. The post-1940 period also saw a number of attempts to establish an Irish-language theatre in an urban context, with the work of writers such as Eoghan Ó Tuairisc, Seán Ó Tuama and Críostóir Ó Floinn providing for a time the core of a new contemporary theatrical repertoire. It witnessed the continuation of a lively tradition of amateur drama particularly in the Gaeltacht, and the seemingly effortless movement of the work of authors such as Johnny Chóil Mhaidhc Ó Coisdealbha and Joe Steve Ó Neachtain from local community halls to the context of the new Irish-language broadcast media.

The decades from 1960 onwards saw the emergence of literary biography and literary criticism as distinct forms of prose writing. The journal *Irisleabhar Mhá Nuad* was to play an important role in the development of new critical perspectives, while specialised literary journals like *Scríobh* (1974–1984), *Oghma* (1989–1998), *Bliainiris* (2000–) and *An Aimsir Óg* (1999–) encouraged regular critical dialogue between creative writers and their readers. If much of the literature of the period 1880 to 1940 is now of almost purely historical interest, as argued by Philip O'Leary in chapter 5 of this volume, this is far from being the case for the period under discussion here. This chapter will provide a survey of Irish-language prose literature and drama written since 1940, and by focusing on key texts and movements, will identify areas of continuity as well as dealing with the most significant emerging trends.

Prose fiction and autobiography

New voices, new directions: 1940s and 1950s

The 1940s opened with the publication of two of the most distinctive of twentieth-century prose works in Irish: Seosamh Mac Grianna's autobiographical study in paranoia *Mo Bhealach Féin* (1940) and Myles na gCopaleen's hilarious parody of early twentieth-century Irish-language literature *An Béal Bocht* (1941). In stark contrast to the emphasis on external reality and on the individual as part of a community to be found in Gaeltacht autobiography of the 1920s and 1930s, Mac Grianna's account, which he sets in the 1932–3 period, is a psychological study of a Gaeltacht writer astray in what he perceives as an alien, and alienating, urban environment. While the voice may be interpreted as that of a modern artist frustrated by the materialism and absurdity of contemporary life, a sense of antipathy towards others pervades the work and the narrator's sense of unease and displacement is revealed as fundamentally pathological and ultimately disabling. The publication branch of the Department of Education, An Gúm – who published the book and with whom Mac Grianna worked regularly as a translator – comes in for particular criticism. One reason for his disillusionment with An Gúm was their treatment of his earlier novel of Gaeltacht life *An Druma Mór* which was deemed unpublishable for legal reasons when submitted in the late 1920s or early 1930s. Though the novel was significantly edited and revised in the 1930s and prepared for publication in 1935, it was not actually published until 1969,[1] at which time its appeal to readers was limited in comparison to the interest being shown in new works by a younger generation of prose writers.

Appended to the original edition of *Mo Bhealach Féin* was Mac Grianna's unfinished and final work *Dá mBíodh Ruball ar an Éan . . .*,[2] whose title alone is symbolic of the exasperating incompleteness of his creative enterprise. In contrast to the bleak pessimism of *Mo Bhealach Féin*, the pseudo-autobiography *An Béal Bocht* provides a hilarious antidote to the seriousness with which cultural positions can be adopted and defended. The image of a prison occurs at the beginning and the end of *An Béal Bocht*, where the central character Bónapart Ó Cúnasa – a parody of the heroic subject of Gaeltacht autobiography – is brought in to the same prison in which his father before him was incarcerated. Though often read as a satire of Tomás Ó Criomhthain's *An tOileánach* (1929), which it parodies, the book is rather a scathing attack on those language revivalists who would idealise the life of poverty portrayed in such accounts. Its aim was to expose and to critique notions of Gaelic culture where poverty, ignorance and squalor are deemed to be positive cultural markers. As literary satire, it owes much of its plot and character details to the work of Donegal authors, in particular Séamus Ó Grianna's *Caisleáin Óir* (1924).[3] Another amusing and highly readable satirical novel which has received surprisingly little critical acclaim is Séamus Wilmot's *Mise Méara* (1946)[4], which examines the position of Irish in independent Ireland through the eyes of a disillusioned native speaker.

One would imagine that the publication of a work such as *An Béal Bocht* would radically alter the course of Irish-language writing, and yet this was far from being the case. Instead, one finds evidence of two dominant and quite different strands in the prose writing of the period 1940 to 1980: a traditional, regional strand on the one hand (a strand associated most often, though not exclusively, with Gaeltacht writers) and an innovative, Modernist strand, where linguistic and stylistic innovation are coupled with formal and generic experimentalism. The work of Séamus Ó Grianna (1889–1969) is indicative of the first of these strands. As Philip O'Leary has demonstrated in his discussion in chapter 5 of Ó Grianna's early work, he was already an established author by 1942 when he published a memoir of his Donegal childhood in *Nuair a Bhí Mé Óg* (1942). Here the mixture of dramatic style and gritty social realism presents Gaeltacht life in a manner which introduces an element of socio-cultural criticism into the narrative. This was followed by another autobiographical work, *Saoghal Corrach* (1945), dealing with the period 1907 to 1931 and covering Ó Grianna's experiences as a student, as a young primary school teacher and eventually as a translator with An Gúm. As a short story writer, Ó Grianna continued to produce popular collections throughout the 1940s and 1950s. He published twelve collections between 1940 and 1968 – three collections in 1955 alone – and his success was based on his fidelity to the style and subject matter of his celebrated early collection *Cioth is Dealán* (1926).[5] There he created a formula for the highly sentimentalised depictions of Donegal Gaeltacht life which proved popular in particular with northern readers familiar with the dialect. Writing in 1956, Proinsias Mac Cana claimed that this positive reader response ensured a consistency of style which would later be seen by critics as a lack of creative development.[6] As a novelist Ó Grianna continued to be a central figure in the development of a distinctive form of literary regionalism in Irish. Like Pádhraic Óg Ó Conaire and Connemara, imaginatively Ó Grianna never left his native Rann na Feirste and the bulk of his work eventually came to be valued primarily as a linguistic corpus and as a valuable source for the social historian.[7]

A number of significant non-Gaeltacht writers were to emerge in the 1940s and 1950s. Born in London in 1917 (d. 1990) and with a unionist background, Tarlach Ó hUid's fictional and autobiographical writings provide an interesting perspective on questions of identity and belonging. His first novel *An Bealach chun a' Bhearnais* (1949) recounts the story of a black North American descended from the Irish transported by Cromwell to the West Indies. This was followed by an exploration of the divided community in the north of Ireland in the decades after partition in *An Dá Thrá* (1952), a theme which is followed through in his third novel *Adios* (1975), where he takes a mixed marriage as focus, and the responsibilities of political affiliation and military activism as theme. Ó hUid's fiction is marred by an intrusive authorial presence and a didactic style, using fiction to explore issues which are central to his autobiographical accounts *Ar Thóir mo Shealbha* (1960) and *Faoi Ghlas* (1985). He is best known in his role as editor (1979–84) of the weekly newspaper *Inniu*, where he was responsible for implementing rigorous linguistic and literary standards. Antrim author Seán Mac Maoláin (1884–1973) was one of the most prolific fiction writers of the period. His work was published by An Gúm, whose dilatory schedule resulted in four novels of his appearing in 1940 alone. While his literary output was impressive, and his work did attract an audience (mainly northern and of similar linguistic background to himself), his fiction lacked the creative edge which would make it endure.[8] The work of

County Down writer Séamus Ó Néill (1910–1981) was to attract more critical attention, especially for his first novel *Tonn Tuile* (1947), which has often been hailed as the first attempt at urban social realism in an Irish-language novel. Set in wartime Dublin, it depicts the life of a middle-class Irish speaker, cut off both from his own east Ulster rural background and from the western Gaeltacht region which he tends to idealise. Ó Néill's 1959 novel *Máire Nic Artáin*, dealing as it does with the effect of sectarian tensions on interpersonal relationships in Belfast in the 1920s, was to have greater long-term appeal for readers, especially as the issues it addressed became more critical in subsequent decades.

The 1950s produced a number of exceptional individual works by authors who did not follow through with more of the same. Liam O'Flaherty's (Ó Flaithearta's) only Irish-language publication, the collection of short stories *Dúil* (1953), is arguably his most accomplished literary work. The collection includes a wide range of stories, including lyrical studies of nature and animals, dramatic sketches of life on the Aran islands and sensitive explorations of critical events and relationships in the life cycle of individuals and family groups. Sean O'Faolain identifies the central quality of the collection when he says: 'I know very few instances in Irish writing, in either language, that weld the tender and the tough as consistently as O'Flaherty does.'[9] Published two years later, the collection of stories by brother and sister Donncha Ó Céileachair (1918–60) and Síle Ní Chéileachair (1924–85) from Cúil Aodha in West Cork, *Bullaí Mhártain* (1955), contains vivid depictions of rural and urban Ireland and the cultural uncertainties underlying social interactions between the two. Donncha later co-authored, with Proinsias Ó Conluain, an important biography of lexicographer, editor and language activist Pádraig Ó Duinnín, the first literary biography of its kind to appear in Irish.[10]

Nóra Ní Shéaghdha (1905–75) was one of the few women prose writers of this period. Ní Shéaghdha's autobiographical account of her experience as a young teacher on the Great Blasket in the late 1920s, *Thar Bealach Isteach* (1940), provides a female mainlander's perspective on island life which supplements the Peig Sayers story, another version of which was to be published from the pen of Peig's son Micheál Ó Gaoithín (1904–74) in *Beatha Pheig Sayers* (1970). Nóra Ní Shéaghdha also turned her hand to romantic fiction in *Peats na Baintreabhaighe* (1945), a tall tale which departs from the plot of Gaeltacht marriage and matchmaking lore to recount the misfortunes and fortunes of a penniless lad from West Kerry who finally gets to marry his own true love while inheriting a fortune from his rich paramour.

Connemara-born Máirtín Ó Cadhain (1905–1970) was undoubtedly the major prose voice to emerge in the postwar period. His short-story collection *An Braon Broghach* (1948) marked his early departure from the folk structures and idioms of his first collection *Idir Shúgradh agus Dáiríre* (1939). With such classic depictions of the hardship and cruelties of Irish life on the western seaboard as 'An Taoille Tuile', 'An Bhearna Mhíl', 'An Bóthar go dtí an Ghealchathair' and 'An Bhliain 1912', Ó Cadhain's mature work was set to expose the abject poverty and physical deprivation of a community whose cultural richness – of which Ó Cadhain's own linguistic skill and versatility is a palpable illustration – was to become a stigmatising social marker. Ó Cadhain's most important prose works, the episodic novel *Cré na Cille* (which appeared in serial form in the *Irish Press* before its publication as a book by Sáirséal agus Dill in 1949) and the collection of stories *Cois Caoláire* (1953), demonstrate his mastery of both the comic and the tragic literary modes. *Cré na Cille*, though faulted for its failure to adhere to the conventions of literary realism and particularly for its preoccupation with the depiction of negative human traits, was hailed from the outset as a linguistic tour de force and as a comic classic which succeeded in subverting forever any idealised notions of Gaeltacht community life.[11] Set in a graveyard, and presented as a series of conversations between the dead, the story revolves around the lifelong and all-consuming conflict between the central character Caitríona Pháidín and her sister Neil. *Cré na Cille* criticism has been divided on the issue of whether the work seeks to address fundamental existential issues in the tradition of Beckett or Sartre, or whether its primary function is that of blistering social satire.[12] The answer is that the work may function for readers on both levels. The novel provides a profound and detailed insight into class and cultural affiliation in an impoverished rural community where relationships with the land and with language are the most significant social determinants. At the same time, the existential issues are also central to the structure of the novel. Not only are the speaking characters dead and buried and therefore incapable of agency, but they are also presented consciously as subjects incapable of self-analysis and self-transformation. In this context it is only the medium in which they are inscribed – the physical medium of the soil and the human medium of language – which is subject to dramatic metamorphosis.

In contrast to the non-realistic setting and structure of the novel, most of the stories in *Cois Caoláire* adhere to the conventions of social realism. This collection includes two of Ó Cadhain's most celebrated short stories, 'Ciumhais an Chriathraigh' and 'An Strainséara', which, like the stories in *An*

Braon Broghach mentioned above, deal with the unarticulated sufferings of rural women. 'An Strainséara' explores the unspoken and recurring trauma of the mother of stillborn children in a society where childlessness is punished both psychologically and economically, while in 'Ciumhais an Chriathraigh' we are presented with an image of a middle-aged unmarried woman struggling alone to make fertile the rough mountain land which – like Kavanagh's 'stony grey soil of Monaghan' – has eroded her youth and vitality.

Critics and readers of Ó Cadhain generally differentiate between his earlier and later work, with *Cois Caoláire* marking a departure from the depictions of Gaeltacht community and culture in his early work to a more existential examination of individual character and motivation in the later collections. One could argue, however, that the vision elaborated in many of the stories in his later collections *An tSraith ar Lár* (1967), *An tSraith dhá Tógáil* (1970) and *An tSraith Tógtha* (1977) – a pessimistic interpretation of human nature and of human power to effect change – was very much present in Ó Cadhain's earlier work. Thus stories such as 'An tSraith ar Lár' and 'Úr agus Críon' in the 1967 collection take up the themes of stasis and metamorphosis which are central preoccupations in his early stories. One could argue also that in the depiction of the bereaved civil servant N. in 'Fuíoll Fuine' in *An tSraith dhá Tógáil* – with its emphasis on his niggardliness, on his limited and negative range of emotional response and on his obsessive and ritualistic behaviour – Ó Cadhain is merely restaging in an urban context the study of human limitations that is *Cré na Cille*. The most significant aspect of Ó Cadhain's progression towards the absurd surrealism of stories such as 'An Eochair' (*An tSraith ar Lár*) and 'Ag Déanamh Páipéir' (*An tSraith Tógtha*) is the gradual paring back of plot and narrative action, and their replacement with a central preoccupation with being and process. In stories such as 'An sean agus an nua' and 'Gorta' in *An tSraith ar Lár*, for example, social and political events such as war and famine are presented in terms of elemental physical and biological processes. As plot is dispensed with, the referential function of language is replaced in many of the stories by a largely performative one. Ó Cadhain's linguistic virtuosity combines with his deep familiarity with Irish literary tradition to subvert the conventions of traditional heroic narrative in stories such as 'Fuíoll' (*An tSraith dhá Tógáil*), just as he successfully subverted narratives of rural neighbourliness in *Cré na Cille*. Ultimately it is the tension between the social/historical, the physical/biological and the metaphysical/existential in Ó Cadhain's work which accounts for the pressure he exerts on narrative form, and on the strictures of conventional genre.[13]

As a committed nationalist and Gaeltacht activist for whom the survival of the language was central to his cultural vision, Ó Cadhain's political writings reflect a growing pessimism and frustration with Irish political life and with what he saw as the more bourgeois aspects of the language movement itself.[14] The issue of cultural change, and the dynamics of language shift, are central preoccupations in his work and are reflected also in his active interest in the fate of the Welsh and Scottish Gaelic languages.[15] His sense that he was writing in a rapidly eroding language was articulated most strongly in the lecture and pamphlet *Páipéir Bhána agus Páipéir Bhreaca* (1969), where the situation of Irish is seen ultimately as a challenge to the creative writer. The language itself had become a central theme in his later collections in stories of miscommunication and cultural confusion such as 'Aisling agus Aisling Eile' in *An tSraith dhá Tógáil*. Here Ó Cadhain takes two categories of language user – a middle-aged native Connemara woman and a scholarly visitor to the area – and demonstrates how an authentic encounter between them is made impossible by their attitudes to language. For the scholar, referred to throughout as 'the stranger', the Irish language is of academic interest, something to be collected, studied, described, its use a matter of measurement and accurate mapping. For him, the Gaeltacht people are necessary as informants, as cultural sources which he relies upon as the *raison d'être* for his own existence. For the woman, however, the language is something to be dispensed with, particularly if one is to impress a stranger, which she attempts to do with the inevitable negative outcome. If interpersonal communication provides the central focus of much of Ó Cadhain's writing, this particular story represents his deep understanding of the kinds of distorted communication which the sociolinguistic realities of Irish can induce. Surprisingly very little of Ó Cadhain's work has been made available to a larger audience through translation, though this may be explained in the context of the general dearth of contemporary prose translation from the Irish where – with the exception of works such as the Blasket Island autobiographies – there has been remarkably little translation activity. The difficulties of translating Ó Cadhain's work must also be taken into account, however, as a number of attempted translations to English of *Cré na Cille* have been rejected to date as being inadequate.

A number of works by Ó Cadhain which remained unpublished when he died in 1970 have subsequently been edited and made available. These include his second novel *Athnuachan* (1995), which won a major Oireachtas award in 1951, but which was considered unready for publication by Ó Cadhain himself. *Athnuachan* shares many characteristics with *Cré na Cille*, especially its dramatic structure, its mastery of direct speech and its relentless comic power. The plot centres around an elderly man's fear of death and the propensity of youth to play on such fears. The negative aspects of human interactions are again to the fore in what is a richly Rabelaisian depiction of human cruelty and vulnerability. Unlike *Cré na Cille*, however, there is an element of redemption in *Athnuachan* when the central character Beartla ultimately comes to terms with his own mortality and the novel ends on a more lyric and elegiac note. In the context of Ó Cadhain's development as a prose writer, the novel shows clearly his preoccupation with themes of communication, stasis and metamorphosis, and his ability to employ raucous humour to explore the deepest of human concerns about life and mortality. Another extended prose work written in the 1960s, *Barbed Wire* (2002),[16] illustrates Ó Cadhain's anarchic and vitriolic satirical style and may be related to earlier works such as 'A Simple Lesson'[17] and 'Do na Fíréin',[18] where linguistic virtuosity is used as a powerful satirical weapon. While these posthumous publications will be of great interest to linguistic scholars and literary detectives, one senses that Ó Cadhain's literary reputation will rest, however, on those earlier works such as *Cré na Cille* which proved so immensely popular also among his native community in Connemara.

Most 1940s writers continued to publish into the fifties, with new novels by Seán Mac Maoláin, Tarlach Ó hUid, Séamus Ó Néill, Fionn Mac Cumhaill (1885–1965) and Séamus Ó Grianna. Of the new authors to appear at this time – such as Tadhg Ó Rabhartaigh (with his novel set in the Arigna coal mine *Thiar i nGleann Ceo* (1953) and his sentimental account of a rural childhood *Gasúr de Chuid Bhaile na nGrág* (1955)), Liam Ó Catháin (with his novel of Irish heroism in the face of Black and Tan brutality *Eibhlín a' Ghleanna* (1954)) and Críostóir Ó Floinn (with his more successful novel of conflict and relationship set in the Corca Dhuibhne Gaeltacht in *Lá dá bhFaca Thú* (1955)) – Ó Floinn (b. 1927) was to prove the most prolific in the years to come, though his work as a dramatist was to attract more critical attention than his works of prose fiction, most of which were adventure stories aimed at a young readership.[19] Both Sáirséal agus Dill and An Gúm were keen to attract younger readers, and both publishing houses initiated series specifically targeted at such an audience. Throughout the 1940s and 1950s An Gúm published dozens of adventure stories by Dublin-based author Cathal Ó Sándair (1922–1996), for example. Though most renowned for his popular detective series 'Eachtraí Réics Carlo' (The Adventures of Rex Carlo), Ó Sándair also wrote a Wild West series 'Leabhar-Chlub an Iarthair Fhiáin' (The Wild West Book Club), science fiction and many more adventure and mystery stories (some of which were published as part of another series 'An Club-Leabhar Nua-Éireann' (The New Ireland Book Club). The facility with which Ó Sándair's books presented Irish and non-Irish characters, and urban, rural and extra-terrestrial settings, was quite remarkable and without parallel in the work of any subsequent Irish-language author writing either for young readers or for adults. Much of the fiction aimed at a young and popular market in Irish tended to be in the form of historical adventure, with a strong didactic strand. Typical examples of the genre are Annraoi Ó Liatháin's *Laochra na Machairí: Scéal Indiaigh Dhearga Mheiriceá* (1958) and *Claíomh an Díoltais* (1961), both published in Sáirséal agus Dill's 'Scéalta Gaisce' (Adventure Stories) series. *Laochra na Machairí* depicts the war against the Sioux and the Cheyenne Indians from a native American perspective, while *Claíomh an Díoltais* is a tale of heroism, romance and exile set in seventeenth-century Ireland. During the 1960s Ó Liatháin (1917–81) wrote a series of historical novels, all of which portrayed Irish characters in heroic conflict with foreign injustice and brutality. These works may have been the necessary background for the writing of his best-known and most successful work, the popular novel *Nead na gCreabhar* (1977), where English–Irish relations are mediated through the conventions of the political thriller and the didactic element is occluded in the process. Historical novels and murder mysteries proved popular choices also for Máirtín Ó Corrbuí (b. 1912), another writer whose work was targeted mainly at young readers. Other categories of prose writing encouraged by publishers in the 1950s and 1960s were travel writing and memoirs. Among the most accomplished of these are Liam Ó Briain's memoir of the 1916 Rebellion *Cuimhní Cinn* (1951), Micheál Mac Liammóir's theatre memoirs in *Ceo Meala Lá Seaca* (1952) and his Mediterranean diary *Aisteoirí faoi Dhá Sholas* (1956), though other authors to produce such works of discursive non-fiction include Annraoi Ó Liatháin, Earnán de Blaghd (1889–1975), Seosamh Ó Duibhginn (1914–94), Tarlach Ó hUid and Risteard de Paor (1928–70).

The 1950s saw a renewal of Irish emigration to Britain. The work of Dónall Mac Amhlaigh (1926–1989) – firmly rooted in the experiences of the 1950s generation of emigrants to Britain – was to become a distinctive voice for the working-class Irish in Britain. His own experience as an Irish navvy is documented in great detail in his first book *Dialann Deoraí* (1960), and later works, such as the short-story collections *Sweeney agus Scéalta Eile* (1970) and *Beoir Bhaile* (1981) and the novel *Deoraithe* (1986), draw on the same social and historical contexts. With his distinctive form of realism – both social and socialist – and fluent narrative style, Mac Amhlaigh successfully represents the social and economic challenges as well as the psychological stresses experienced by the Irish community in Britain and at home in that period. A preoccupation with questions of affiliation and identity is palpable throughout. This is most marked in *Deoraithe*, where three separate life stories are recounted simultaneously and one is given an insight into the diversity of Irish working-class experience and the different models of acculturation available to Irish emigrants in Britain. Mac Amhlaigh is best known for his early *Dialann Deoraí*, and this was followed by two other works of an autobiographical nature, *Saol Saighdiúra* (1962), which is a humorous depiction of his period in the Irish army in the late 1940s, and the *bildungsroman Diarmaid Ó Dónaill* (1965), which recounts the coming of age of a young man in Kilkenny, where Mac Amhlaigh lived from 1940 to 1947. While his preoccupation with the Irish emigrant experience may have limited the scope of Mac Amhlaigh's work, his writing is a valuable contribution to an understanding of what was a defining experience for a generation of Irish working-class people. As Mac Amhlaigh himself commented in 1989: 'When we consider that an estimated million plus Irish people came to Britain to make a living since the founding of the Irish Free State in the early 1920s it is surprising to say the least that the experience of this emigration has not found more expression in literature.'[20] His creative writing should ideally be considered together with his large journalistic output, which offered a socialist perspective on a broad range of social, political and economic issues, not all of which related to the Irish community. His stinging satire directed against various forms of literary and cultural pretentiousness *Schnitzer Ó Sé* (1974)[21] demonstrates his versatility as a prose writer, as well as being indicative of an overriding commitment to a literature of working-class experience.

Autobiography remained an important literary genre in Irish throughout the decades, so much so that Seán Ó Tuama included autobiographical accounts in his important 1976 survey of fiction in Irish.[22] Most of the autobiographies were by Gaeltacht people and many of them – like the first generation of Blasket autobiographies – were the result of a collaboration between a native 'author' and an external editor, redactor or mentor, often a priest, a teacher or a folklore collector. In many cases, the life was dictated to a second party and later edited for publication. *Scéal Hiúdaí Sheáinín* (1940), an account of life in the Rosses by Hiúdaí Sheáinín Ó Domhnaill, for example, was written down by Eoghan Ó Domhnaill, who later published his own account of his youth in the same area in *Na Laetha a Bhí* (1953). The author's children wrote down different sections of Cúil Aodha (County Cork) storyteller Dómhnall Bán Ó Céileachair's *Sgéal mo Bheatha* (1940), and a number of individuals were involved in the editing process. *Beatha Mhichíl Turraoin* (1956), an account of life in Ring, County Waterford, was compiled by Micheul Ó Cionnfhaolaidh; while

Donegal author Micí Mac Gabhann's celebrated *Rotha Mór an tSaoil* (1959) was dictated to his son-in-law, the folklore collector Seán Ó hEochaidh, and later edited by Proinsias Ó Conluain. The encouragement of outside parties was significant even in the work of authors with a high degree of literacy such as Nóra Ní Shéaghdha and Micheál Ó Gaoithín. Ní Shéaghdha was encouraged and assisted by local priests in the writing of *Thar Bealach Isteach* (1940), while Micheál Ó Gaoithín, like the aforementioned Eoghan Ó Domhnaill, moved with ease from the position of redactor (with *Peig* (1936) and *Beatha Pheig Sayers* (1970, written *c*.1940), written down from the mouth of his mother Peig Sayers) to that of author (in *Is Truagh ná Fanann an Óige* (1953)). The popularity of the autobiographical mode can result in some strange literary creations also. *An Gleann agus a Raibh ann* (1963) by south Tipperary author Séamus Ó Maolchathaigh (1884–1968) is the life story of an imaginary individual who would – if he lived – be a contemporary of the author's parents. This individual recounts how life was lived when the region was still an Irish-speaking district! Though the Galway Gaeltacht significantly produced fewer autobiographical accounts than any other Gaeltacht region, *Mise* (1943) by Colm Ó Gaora (1887–1954), modelled on John Mitchel's *Jail Journal*, was a significant contribution to the genre and one of the few accounts of the independence movement by a native Irish speaker.

While they tend to be almost formulaic in structure and content, these autobiographical accounts provide a fascinating insight into Irish-speaking Ireland during the late nineteenth and early twentieth centuries, revealing many interesting aspects of rural social, economic and cultural life. They also reveal regional attitudes to national events and have been justly hailed as invaluable sources for the social historian. The Donegal accounts, for example, provide detailed accounts of the practice of seasonal migration, including some graphic descriptions of the experiences of child labourers. *Rotha Mór an tSaoil* (1959) by Micí Mac Gabhann (1865–1948) stands out in that, as well as providing insights into such local aspects of the west Donegal experience, it also documents the author's exploits in North America, including his work in the iron and steel industry in Pennsylvania and in the silver and copper mines in Montana and finally his adventures as he travelled up the Yukon during the Klondyke gold rush. This form of Gaeltacht autobiography was to continue in works such as Fionn Mac Cumhaill's *Gura Slán le m'Óige* (1967), though the genre took a different turn from the 1960s onwards as the Irish language came under greater pressure both in the Gaeltacht itself and nationally.

Reacting to social and cultural change: 1960s and 1970s

Both emigration and language shift resulted in a redefinition of the Official Gaeltacht boundaries in 1956, and the maps produced under the Gaeltacht Areas Order of 1956 – while they were to define the geographical context for the formulation of Gaeltacht policy by the newly formed government department Roinn na Gaeltachta – were graphic representations of the decline of the language in its core regions since 1925. The 1960s saw a major review and redirection of state language policy, all of which were to have a profound impact on Irish-language writing. Ironically, perhaps, the decade saw a minor renaissance in Irish-language publication, facilitated by the by now well-established and progressive publishing house Sáirséal agus Dill.

Despite – or perhaps because of – increased economic prosperity, themes of social change, rupture and displacement become central to 1960s and 1970s prose writing. Much of the tension fuelling Gaeltacht literature of this period arises from the sense that socio-economic change cannot be achieved without cultural loss. Pádraig Ua Maoileoin's documentary *Na hAird ó Thuaidh* (1960) – originally a series of radio talks – depicts a community and a culture experiencing a process of modernisation over which it has no control. A grandson of Tomás Ó Criomhthain, Ua Maoileoin (1913–2002) is motivated less by a sense that 'our likes will never be seen again' than by an urge to warn his Gaeltacht community about the ongoing and accelerating nature of social and cultural change. The crisis of modernity involved is also the main theme of *Lá dár Saol* (1969) by Tomás's son, Seán Ó Criomhthain (1898–1975). From his new home on the mainland, Ó Criomhthain laments the desertion of the Great Blasket Island while simultaneously embracing the economic values which made such desertion inevitable. His account deals with issues such as social-welfare dependence, also the subject of Pádhraic Óg Ó Conaire's novel *Déirc an Díomhaointis* (1972), and the inter-relationship between changing consumer patterns and traditional rural agricultural practices.

Even a writer such as Séamus Ó Grianna breaks away at this period from the sentimental depictions of Donegal Gaeltacht life still to be found in his novels of the 1950s to create a more radical voice in *Bean Ruadh de Dhálach* (1966), a novel which introduces an element of socio-cultural critique totally absent from most of Ó Grianna's fiction. Here the central character, the independent-minded Róise, is depicted as a liberating influence who has set herself the mission of freeing the young women of her generation from the hardships experienced by their mothers, especially those associated with the highly gendered system of seasonal migration in operation in west Donegal when Ó Grianna was growing up. Much of the novel centres around issues of mobility and personal choice. Not for Róise the existence of her mother walking shoeless to the nearest town to deliver her homeknit stockings to a cruel gombeenman while her menfolk are away in Scotland. In contrast to the acceptance of hardship to be found in works like *Peig*, or the depiction of stoic resistance to physical and emotional pain in Ó Cadhain's representations of Connemara women, *Bean Ruadh de Dhálach* presents us with a young woman who willingly turns her back on community norms and values, choosing instead the economic prosperity and social freedoms associated with emigration.[23]

Two years after the publication of *Bean Ruadh de Dhálach*, Pádraig Ua Maoileoin published his most celebrated novel *Bríde Bhán* (1968). Here the main character is again a rebellious young woman who rejects the fatalism of older generations of Gaeltacht women and seeks new social and sexual freedoms. In a plot which draws on the material of folk legend, Bríde Bhán is depicted as someone who hopes to realise her desires at home. The cowed response of the local young men, when the mysterious character Tadhg an Bhodaigh attempts to abduct her, prevents her from achieving her aim, however. Though rightly hailed as a fresh depiction of Gaeltacht life and social values, the novel's social vision contains an underlying conservatism.[24] This is apparent in particular in the depiction of an ostensibly modern and modernising woman as one who will only be satisfied with a man capable of traditional male heroics. Stigmatised by her own community, the heroine's only option at the end of the novel is to emigrate. A similar difficulty with female characterisation mars the comic potential of Ua Maoileoin's later novel *Ó Thuaidh!* (1983), a work which turns the images of island life associated with Blasket Island literature into a comic farce and provides an antidote to the nostalgia and sentimentality of the autobiographical accounts of pining ex-islanders. The book is a farcical account of how an American visitor to the area attempts to turn 'Oileán Ban' (the Great Blasket Island) into a sex-holiday camp called Paradise Island. The ex-islanders, now living on the mainland, are only too willing to sell their island and its heritage to the highest bidder, but the scheme is eventually thwarted by language Revivalists (from Cork) and by Micheál the Poet, son of Peig Sayers (who appears anachronistically – she died in 1958 – under the name of Meig in the book). Though interesting as an illustration of a Gaeltacht writer's perception of his own people's response to cultural change, its effectiveness as a form of social satire is reduced, however, by its denigratory depictions of female characters, who are invariably presented as socially subservient and sexually exploitable. Ua Maoileoin's short novel *Fonn a Níos Fiach* (1978) – based on an event during the Famine, recorded in folk legend from the Joyce Country – is arguably his most successful fictional work. It has been compared to Hemingway's *The Old Man and the Sea*, depicting as it does the heroic feats of endurance possible when an individual is under pressure of the most elemental kind.

Pádraig Ua Maoileoin's work should be seen against the backdrop of contemporary Gaeltacht and island narratives. Though the last inhabitants were to leave the Great Blasket Island in 1953, the community there having dwindled to a handful of households, the mystique of the island was to continue, aided by the publication throughout the 1970s and 1980s of fresh accounts by Blasket 'exiles' on the mainland such as Seán Sheáin Í Chearnaigh's autobiographical works *An tOileán a Tréigeadh* (1974) and *Iarbhlascaodach ina Dheoraí* (1978) and Máire Ní Ghuithín's auto-ethnographic depictions of island life in *An tOileán a Bhí* (1978) and *Bean an Oileáin* (1986). Island narratives were also to appear from the Donegal Gaeltacht, with island priest Eoghan Ó Colm's account of life on Tory in *Toraigh na dTonn* (1971), ex-islander Seán Mac Fhionnlaoich's depiction of life on Gola up to its desertion in 1967 in *Ó Rabharta go Mallmhuir* (1975) and Pádraig Ua Cnáimhsí's telling, in autobiographical form, of the life of Róise Rua Mhic Grianna on Aran Island (County Donegal) in *Róise Rua* (1988).[25] Despite differences of perspective, all of these accounts acknowledge the vulnerability of island life and culture. Neither were such accounts limited solely to depictions of, or elegies for, island life. Seán Ó Conghaile's *Cois Fharraige le mo Linnse* (1974), as well as his later autobiographical *Saol Scolóige* (1993), both deal with social change in the Connemara Gaeltacht, while the Corca Dhuibhne mainland has produced a steady stream of such publications.[26] The main difference between more recent examples and earlier writing of this kind is the incorporation into the narrative of the experiences of Gaeltacht people outside of their native regions. Tomás Ó Cinnéide's *Ar Seachrán* (1981), for example, takes the reader to Cork, Dublin and San Francisco, while the intercultural contact between Irish missionaries and the native communities in Nigeria and Korea is explored with great honesty and sensitivity in Pádraig Ó Máille's *Dúdhúchas* (1973) and Pádraig Ó Murchú's *Idir Dhá Shaol* (1989) respectively. While most publications of this kind to appear in recent decades are the work of educated authors literate in the Irish language, nevertheless the encouragement and collaboration of academic mentors or editors has been essential in most cases. As a literary trend, this kind of Gaeltacht writing has always been supported by Irish-language publishers, and has received particular support in recent years from the publishing houses Coiscéim and Cló Iar-Chonnachta, with their regional ties to the Corca Dhuibhne and Connemara Gaeltacht areas respectively.

While narratives of social change and mobility dominate the work of Gaeltacht writers from the 1960s onwards, non-Gaeltacht writers begin increasingly to use the novel as medium for a new form of socio-cultural critique. The 1960s saw a major reappraisal of the state's Irish-language revival policy, and this process continued into the 1970s, when new strategies were devised to drive a less strident state language policy. The sense of frustration, marginalisation and increasing helplessness experienced within the Irish-language community as certain state supports for the language were removed and the policy of Revival was replaced by more ambiguous cultural objectives is reflected in literary work which becomes increasingly politically *engagé*. Contemplative and polemic novels – of the *roman à thèse* variety – replace the more realist social commentary of earlier generations. Three writers in particular are indicative of this development: Breandán Ó Doibhlin, Diarmaid Ó Súilleabháin and Eoghan Ó Tuairisc.

Breandán Ó Doibhlin (b. 1931) – a critic and translator whose influence on the St Patrick's College, Maynooth journal *Irisleabhar Mhá Nuad* was to have an enduring influence on the development of Irish-language criticism – made a unique and significant contribution to the development of the novel form in Irish. Influenced by a host of continental writers, his first novel *Néal Maidine agus Tine Oíche* (1964) introduced a meditative note into Irish-language prose writing which was to manifest itself also in the work of Diarmaid Ó Súilleabháin and of younger writers such as Ciarán Ó Coigligh and Pádraig Ó Cíobháin. Drawing self-consciously on Judaeo-Christian and classical images of exodus, odyssey and return, the novel is simultaneously an allegory of repossession and an affirmation of the importance of cultural continuity, even in the face of historical rupture and social fragmentation. Written in an almost hypnotic lyrical style, the richly intertextual use of language and idiom serves in itself as an illustration of the process of recuperation which the novel suggests is necessary if a dispossessed community is to survive, to thrive and to develop a vision for the future. The main body of the novel is devoid of actual historical reference and the political allegory could be applied in any number of historical situations, yet the dedication – 'Do Róisín Dubh – ar ndóigh!' ('For Róisín Dubh – of course!) – and the vindicatory preface where the author addresses the dilemma of the Irish-language writer who feels devoid of community, adrift in a language with no clear terms of cultural reference, locate the vision being expressed clearly in the context of postcolonial Ireland. Ó Doibhlin's borrowing from the Old Testament Exodus – the book was initially entitled 'Eacsodas' and the 'Morning Star and Night-time Fire' of the published title derives from the Book of Exodus – is a reworking of a seventeenth- and eighteenth-century theme in Irish-language political poetry where the plight and the hopes of the dispossessed Irish are compared to those of the Israelites.[27]

If *Néal Maidine agus Tine Oíche* was an attempt at mapping out the course of cultural repossession in allegorical terms, Ó Doibhlin's second novel *An Branar gan Cur* (1979) deals with the dilemmas posed for an individual by the social, cultural and political implications of the personal choices he must make. Set in the 1950s, the novel's central character Fearghus Mac Giolla Chalma embarks on a train journey north, travelling first on the Dublin–Belfast train to Portadown and onward to his native Derry. The journey – which is structurally and thematically central to the narrative – is both a journey home from the middle-class urban environment of Dublin (where he has settled) to the alienated environment of the nationalist community in Northern Ireland and a meditation on the direction his life should take in the future. Though the book ostensibly charts the dilemma of a young college lecturer who has broken off an engagement to be married in favour of a religious vocation (previously contemplated and rejected), the main theme of the book is a political one, as Fearghus analyses his situation in terms of his ability to adapt to different social, cultural and political environments. Central to his meditation are questions relating to language and culture, and specifically the relationship between the two in modern Ireland, both north and south of the border. As critic Mícheál Mac Craith perceptively points out, the train journey in this novel functions as a liminal zone of representation in which personal uncertainties are reflected in the constant movement between different states of consciousness, between political states whose border is palpable though invisible, between counties with historical but physically imperceptible borders, between the past and the present, memory and anticipation, all occurring significantly on that most liminal of calender dates, Hallowe'en.[28] The novel takes the form of an internal monologue, a meditation where the 'double consciousness' of the Irish speaker is examined in personal and socio-political terms. Fearghus's decision at the end of the novel – to return to his upper-middle-class sweetheart Laura – involves an acceptance both of the complexity of contemporary cultural realities and of his own responsibility as mediator and translator of a perspective which is no longer that of mainstream Irish culture.

The employment of internal monologue as narrative technique is a distinctive feature in the work of Diarmaid Ó Súilleabháin (1932–85), where it may be used to launch a searing critique of contemporary Irish culture or to explore issues of personal identity and conscience. While these thematic preoccupations are very much to the fore in his first novel *Dianmhuilte Dé* (1964) – where conventional realist techniques are employed and interpersonal relationships are used as a stage for an exploration of social and ideological conflict – a more meditative note is introduced in his second novel *Caoin Tú Féin* (1967), which takes up the same themes but in a more contemporary context. The focus of the narrative in *Caoin Tú Féin* is Ian, whose wife Bea and two children have left him and who is now reflecting on his past life, his recent behaviour and his future prospects. A sense of entrapment pervades the novel, and a sense of deep dissatisfaction with the limitations of the role of a teacher in an educational system where class divisions are preserved and where the intellectual becomes an unquestioning automaton. Marital conflict is depicted in terms of class and ideology, and Ian is used by the author to voice opinions on many topics, particularly on the predictability and claustrophobia of small-town Irish life. Ó Súilleabháin's narrative style attracted attention from the outset, in particular his non-conventional sentence structure, his use of lexical compounds and neologisms and his distinctive use of punctuation and capitalisation. After the publication of his third novel *An Uain Bheo* (1968), these came to be accepted as characteristic features of his style, part of his attempt to 'startle the Irish language' by extending the scope of expression in new directions.[29] A major motivation for such innovation was Ó Súilleabháin's attempt to depict through Irish social situations and relationships which would not normally be associated with the language. The central character in *An Uain Bheo*, Louis Stein, is a well-off medical student of Jewish background and much of the novel revolves around his interactions with the Irish social elite, with their horses, their designer labels, their expensive cars and their interest in art and literature. Though Louis Stein's dilemma centres around his own crisis of identity – the death of his sweetheart Orla a central event in a narrative of loss and recuperation – social commentary is implicit throughout and, as Alan Titley points out in his subtle reading of the novel, the character drawn most sympathetically is that of Darach, a republican schoolteacher who is teaching Louis Irish.[30] Himself a committed nationalist who was imprisoned in 1972 for his involvement with Provisional Sinn Féin, Diarmaid Ó Suilleabháin's politics pervades most of his work. One of the narrative strands in his fourth novel *Maeldún* (1972) portrays a distain for the new political elite to emerge in the Republic in the 1960s and 1970s. In focusing on the political and business set who descend on the fictional east coast resort of Bailethaca ('the town of Taca', a play on the name of the fundraising organisation established by political party Fianna Fáil in the 1960s), Ó Súilleabháin mercilessly attacks the culture of materialism, consumerism, hedonism and corruption which he saw replacing the republican idealism of previous generations. The novel is arguably his most successful work, mainly because he manages to sustain three major narrative themes, which challenge the reader while avoiding the dangers of a monologic story line. The narrative foci are provided by the characters Rónán, Súilí and 'an Mairnéalach'. Rónán is a student working in the hostelry which is the main focus of social interaction in the novel. It is through his eyes that Ó Súilleabháin explores the behaviour and attitudes of the political jet set. Súilí, an elderly voyeur who spends the summer lurking around the caravan park and peeping at the young people on the beach, acts as a silent and pathetic overseer of tourist culture, and 'an Mairnéalach' (loosely based on the image of Maeldún in the medieval tale *Immram Maíle Dúin*) is a sailor whose voyage of transformation as he exchanges his physical existence for an otherworldly life of the spirit provides a metaphysical backdrop to the sensory experiences of the population of Bailethaca. Issues such as teenage sexuality are openly discussed, and a sustained meditation on place and sense of place is conducted in a manner which complements the depiction of a tourist landscape and its summer inhabitants in the novel.

Ó Súilleabháin's collection of short stories *Muintir* (1971) confirmed his growing reputation as an experimentalist. The collection contains a range of short pieces, some of which are impressionistic reconstructions of symbolic images where plot is dispensed with totally, others more sustained studies of transformative experiences. The moment of death, which provides the theme of transformation in one of the stories in the collection 'Trasna', is the subject of Ó Súilleabháin's novel *Aistear* (1982), a work which builds on the metaphysical dimension of his earlier works, and takes it in the direction of speculation about the experience of death and life after death. Existence itself, and the relationship of living beings and non-living things with the passing of time, were explored in an earlier work, *Lá Breá Gréine Buí*, which remained unpublished in book form until 1994, when it appeared together with another work of the 1960s, *Oighear Geimhridh*. *Lá Breá Gréine Buí* takes the multifocality of *Maeldún* a few steps further to produce a more complex interweaving of narrative elements, all centred around the passing of one day. The influence of French existentialist writing, modern painting and cinematography on Ó Suilleabháin's prose style have all been commented on by critics.[31] These dimensions of his work were often occluded by the political content of his work, however. While his critique of contemporary Ireland underpins in different ways the novels *Caoin Tú Féin, An Uain Bheo* and *Maeldún*, his most overtly political novel *Ciontach* (1982) interweaves an account of his imprisonment in 1972 with a sustained attack on the cultural values of post-independence Ireland. He reserves particular odium in all his work for the comfortable middle classes, whom he saw as reaping the benefits of independent statehood at the expense of the working classes and Northern Irish nationalists. The limitations of his political analysis are discernible, however, in the treatment of class and gender in his work, and particularly in the manner in which political affiliation is presented in terms of patrimony and class position.[32]

If Ó Súilleabháin's work from the 1960s onwards opened up new possibilities for representing contemporary Ireland in the Irish-language novel, a new kind of historical novel was also to emerge in the same period. The romantic heroic view of Irish history to be found in earlier examples of the genre was to be replaced in the work of Eoghan Ó Tuairisc (1919–82) by a more nuanced critical perspective on key historical events. His first novel *L'Attaque* (1962) anticipated revisionist historical scholarship of the 1980s in its sophisticated exploration of the various political, social, economic and religious motivations behind the 1798 rebellion.[33] By placing centre stage a newly married and illiterate young countryman, a recent recruit to the United Irishmen in County Leitrim, and by using a range of narrative techniques to represent the huge class and ideological divides between the soldiers and the revolutionary leaders who mobilised them into action, the novel dramatically exposes the complex reality of this particular period in Irish history. The novel deals with a sequence of events leading up to a successful moment in the 1798 campaign – the routing of English forces from Castlebar in August 1798 by the United Irishmen and a force of French troops led by General Humbert.[34] By focusing on the tragic fate of one particular footsoldier, Ó Tuairisc makes a powerful statement about the ironies of victory and the dehumanising effect of all wars, in particular a war where primitive means and weapons face new more powerful military technologies. The technological divide underpins a conflict between pre-modern and modern notions not only of warfare, but also of heroic narrative itself. A key moment in the novel occurs when Humbert looks down upon a bedraggled Irish army, untrained and un-uniformed, with farm implements as weapons, and is reminded of a former mission in La Vendée. The irony of his situation, however, is that on this occasion these are the revolutionaries and he and they are on the same side.[35]

Ó Tuairisc's second historical novel, *Dé Luain* (1966), was written to mark the fiftieth anniversary of the 1916 Rising. The novel is far from being a eulogy of the heroes of the uprising, however, providing instead a sustained meditation on the ideals of Pearse and Connolly. Unlike *L'Attaque*, *Dé Luain* focuses on the central players and – by employing internal monologue as narrative device throughout – presents Pearse's predicament in the 24-hour period leading up to the reading of the Proclamation of the Republic at noon on Easter Monday. What we see in the novel is not a heroic character certain of his convictions, but a sensitive human being who must steel himself for the lead role he is to play in a tragic drama whose outcome is by no means certain. The depiction of Eoin Mac Néill is an important aspect of the novel. Though his pragmatism and his historian's sense of inevitable defeat were responsible for the countermanding order which ultimately ensured that the rising was a military failure, he is presented as the revolutionary leader with the clearest vision, a vision of cultural repossession which was the single most important motivating force behind the events of 1916. In its preoccupation with what was lost in 1916, the novel can be read as much as an interrogation of post-independence cultural values as a psychological exploration of Pearse. Completed in circumstances of great pressure after the untimely death of Ó Tuairisc's wife, the artist Una McDonnell, in 1964, a sense of incompleteness mars the novel's overall effect. As critic Proinsias Ó Drisceoil points out, however, one of the most important aspects of the work is as an illustration of Ó Tuairisc's adherence to a Platonic vision, and to his interpretation of the city as site on which human actions are not only enacted but also inscribed and embodied in the architectural fabric itself.[36]

Ó Tuairisc was one of the most significant non-Gaeltacht writers in Irish throughout the 1960s, publishing poetry, fiction and drama, as well as contributing to the development of literary criticism in Irish. A bilingual writer, his prose writing helped to stretch the possibilities of Irish-language literature in many new directions. His third novel, the autobiographical *An Lomnochtán* (1977), came as such a surprise to Irish-language readers at the time that critical responses were few, while admirers were numerous. Here, the creative potential of the Irish language is used to great dramatic effect as the world is seen through the eyes of a young English-speaking boy depicted through the medium of an Irish which is self-consciously not the Irish of the Gaeltacht. As the psychological development of the child is plotted along a trajectory of dramatic episodes, language use itself becomes a central theme as it is employed to mark class, education, age and geographical background. Play with language occurs at various levels within the novel, and codemixing is employed both for comic effect and as an illustration of actual language use.[37]

If Ó Tuairisc's *An Lomnochtán* demonstrated the rich possibilities of Irish as a medium to depict English-speaking small-town Ireland in the 1920s, Alan Titley's second novel (though the first to be published) *Méirscrí na Treibhe* (1978) introduced a prose voice which would challenge any claim that the Irish-language writer would inevitably be restricted by the sociolinguistic realities of contemporary Ireland. The novel boldly depicts a postcolonial African state (based on Nigeria during the Biafran war) through the eyes of a young native recently returned from college in Europe. While the novel explores the process whereby Paul Lodabo sheds his layers of Western-inculcated values to come to an understanding of the tragedy of his people, the dense style of the writing demands a reading process which mirrors the efforts required if western Europeans are to comprehend adequately the complexities of African colonial history. Titley (b. 1947) set his earlier novel *Stiall Fhial Feola* (1980) in Dublin, where a hilarious black comedy is staged, involving a frustrated agony aunt, her unfaithful husband and their children, conservative primary school teachers and their innocent pupils, a trendy priest and his flock, a spoilt priest and his macabre cannibalistic take on transubstantiation. This novel established Titley's reputation as a comic writer in whose work language itself becomes a powerful medium of play, and social satire is tempered by an anarchic sense of the absurd in the ordinary. Remarking on Alan Titley's style in a review of his first collection of short stories *Eiriceachtaí agus Scéalta Eile* (1987), critic Seán Ó Tuama claimed that Titley was writing as if he had millions of readers.[38] In his work the sociolinguistic situation in which the Irish language finds itself becomes irrelevant as the creative writer claims total freedom of expression and refuses to be constricted by realist expectations. This sense of boldness and celebratory defiance is a distinctive feature of all Titley's work, and the linguistic dexterity is matched only by his ability to flout formal and generic convention, much as Ó Cadhain and (less successfully) Diarmaid Ó Súilleabháin did before him. As the story 'Scéal Bleachtaireachta' proclaims, no narrative has special claim to truth value. All storytelling is a form of heresy. Familiarity with Irish literary tradition is assumed in many of the stories in *Eiriceachtaí agus Scéalta Eile*, where intertextuality is employed to great dramatic and comic effect. Intertextuality is also an integral part of the narrative technique in *An Fear Dána* (1993), a novel based on the poetry and the scattered biographical evidence surrounding thirteenth-century Irish poet Muireadhach Albanach Ó Dálaigh. In this novel, Titley employs his remarkable linguistic skill to construct a biographical narrative which succeeds in simultaneously linking Ó Dálaigh as subject with contemporary literature in Irish, and creating an idiom which evokes a sense of the utter strangeness – to modern sensibilities – of the period in which he lived. The short fables in *Fabhalscéalta* (1995) and the collection *Leabhar Nóra Ní Anluain* (1998), classified into subsections as a collection of folk-tales would be, illustrate once again that in Titley's work we are dealing with a comic sensibility which is ready always to pull the rug from under any preconceived literary or critical notions.[39]

The short story in Irish had been experiencing a lean period when Alan Titley's *Eiriceachtaí agus Scéalta Eile* was published in 1987. One of the most accomplished practitioners was Pádraic Breathnach (b. 1942), whose first collection, *Bean Aonair agus Scéalta Eile* (1974), showed an assuredness of style which was repeated in regular subsequent volumes. His best short stories are well-wrought character studies with an important dramatic dimension, and he has also published two less successful novels. Unlike the prolific Breathnach, the immensely talented Seán Mac Mathúna (b. 1937) had only published two short-story collections by 2000, the highly popular collection *Ding agus Scéalta Eile* (1983) and a second collection *Banana* (1999). Both collections contain superb comic stories, as well as sensitive explorations of intergenerational communication and sociocultural conflict.

A search for form: 1980s and 1990s

The 1980s and 1990s saw the emergence of a host of new prose writers, and the publication of a large volume of creative fiction. The period is most marked for the sense of experimentation in prose works which defy classification and which reflect a freedom of expression which may be only available to writers writing from the margin, independent of market forces. While short story writers and novelists such as Gearailt Mac Eoin, Joe Steve Ó Neachtain, Aodh Ó Canainn and Ciarán Ó Coigligh successfully adhere to the conventions of literary realism, much of the prose writing of the period tends to eschew social realism and its formal conventions in favour of non-mimetic and contemplative creative strands. One of these strands is that of magic realism, where conventional plot is dispensed with in favour of dramatic special effects and metafictional interventions; the other is a form of contemplative, meditative or lyric prose, where subjectivity itself is explored, often by subverting the centred subject of classic realism. Critics Caoimhín Mac Giolla Léith and Máire Ní Annracháin have explored these anti-realist strands in Irish-language fiction in the context of Irish literary history and contemporary sociolinguistic realities.[40] Mac Giolla Léith traces a self-reflexive non-realist strand in the Irish-language novel from *Séadna* onwards, while Ní Annracháin applies linguistic, psychoanalytic and Marxist perspectives to an examination of the decentred subject in a range of contemporary prose texts. While both critics acknowledge the ideological basis of the Revivalist preoccupation with the establishment of a tradition of realist prose, and concur in exposing the limitations of nineteenth-century realism as an appropriate critical paradigm for twentieth-century prose writing in Irish, questions of readability and reader expectation also need to be taken into account, as does the ongoing concern of Irish-language publishers about the creation of a regular reading public.[41] The preponderance of unclassifiable prose works to be published in recent years reflects, in my view, what amounts to a crisis of communication, resulting in a desperate search for adequate form. The notion of a community of readers may be discounted in the process, however, as the creative act becomes a celebratory or an anarchic declaration of authorial autonomy.

One of the first Gaeltacht authors to break away from the social realism so dominant in Gaeltacht fiction was Inis Oírr writer Dara Ó Conaola. Greatly indebted to the oral storytelling tradition, the magic realism of the stories in his collections *Mo Chathair Ghríobháin agus Scéalta Eile* (1981) and *Amuigh Liom Féin* (1988) is achieved by the dramatic use of a first-person narrator, and the employment of a seductively simplistic and lyric narrative style. Style and narrative structure become more problematic in the work of Dublin-born writer Lorcán S. Ó Treasaigh (b. 1956). His short novel *Sracfhéachaint* (1985) is an experimental work where a series of unrelated narrative episodes – some of which were originally published as short stories – are used to create a world of the imagination which challenges the reader to create connections and generate meaning. His second novel, *An Dealbhóir sa nGairdín* (1991), explores personal relationships in a simple episodic narrative where physical descriptions become visual and dramatic details, rather than being an integral part of plot development. Ó Treasaigh's third novel, *Bás san Oirthear* (1992), opens with a direct address to his audience 'Litir ón nGalltacht' (A letter from the Galltacht) and then moves to a lyric allegorical exploration of the psychological pressures associated with an Irish-speaking upbringing in a non-Gaeltacht environment. *Bás san Oirthear* is an unusual work in that it deals head-on with a theme which manifests itself indirectly in much contemporary fiction in Irish.

The most successful non-realist fiction of the 1980s and 1990s was undoubtedly the trilogy by Dublin-born Séamus Mac Annaidh (b. 1961): *Cuaifeach mo Londubh Buí* (1983), *Mo Dhá Mhicí* (1986) and *Rubble na Mickies* (1990). Usefully interpreted as a work of 'metafiction' by critic Mícheál Mac Craith, this series of novels – where a realist preoccupation with plot and story-line is dispensed with – is the most dramatic illustration of the kinds of self-reflexivity identified by Caoimhín Mac Giolla Léith in modern Irish-language fiction.[42] The authorial presence is palpable throughout, intruding directly in *Cuaifeach mo Londubh Buí* with: 'Is cuma faoin scéal. / Amharc sna súile agam. Déanaimis caidreamh' (The story doesn't matter. Look into my eyes. Let's relate to each other). A multi-layered and richly intertextual work, the novels in the trilogy play with plot and characterisation in a manner which is, nevertheless, highly structured. Themes of intergenerational tension, teenage culture and identity politics are explored through a surreal central narrative, presented against the backdrop of Northern Irish sectarianism and violence. The first novel in the trilogy was Mac Annaidh's most audacious and most successful work. It was difficult for him to reproduce the hilarity of *Cuaifeach mo Londubh Buí* in the later works. The Northern Irish conflict manifests itself in the more macabre and restrained tone of *Mo Dhá Mhicí*, while the play with the author–reader relationship becomes a source of tedium in *Rubble na Mickies*, as if, as Alan Titley suggests, the author had by then imbibed too much post-structuralist literary theory.[43] Mac Annaidh has continued to experiment with literary form, publishing a collection of humorous short pieces, *Féirín, Scéalta agus Eile* (1992), and the whodunnit, written in diary form, *An Deireadh* (1996).

The response to *Cuaifeach mo Londubh Buí* both by critics and readers may have encouraged other writers to experiment with various forms of non-mimetic fiction. Among the most successful are Dáibhí Ó Cróinín with his novel *An Cúigiú Díochlaonadh* (1994) and short-story writer Daithí Ó Muirí who published his first collection *Seacht Lá na Díleann* in 1998. *An Cúigiú Díochlaonadh* (1994) is one of those unclassifiable novels which reads like a folk-tale, until the narrator is brought to an otherworldly location where his encounter with a community of Irish-language revivalists becomes a hilarious send-up of Irish literary and scholarly activity. As in Alan Titley's *Fabhalscéalta*, in this novel the fabulist mode allows the author total freedom of expression. Ó Muirí's stories – many of which are very short dramatic pieces – are likewise written in a masterly style where the real and the super-real, the material and the imaginative are interwoven in a highly seductive form of magic realism. Angela Bourke has also produced a number of short stories in a magic realist mode, weaving fantastic dramatic plots around the themes and structures of folk narrative.[44]

If magic realism is a rich strand in contemporary fiction, the meditative strand has also produced some striking works of prose writing in recent years. Central themes in this kind of work are questions of individual and community identity, cultural representation and language itself. *Kinderszenen* (1987), written by *nom de plume* 'Robert Schumann', uses the structure of the music sequence 'Kinderszenen' by the composer Schumann to explore the elusive borders of individual identity. The reader is challenged throughout the book to adopt an active creative role, to treat the words as a musician would a musical score, to fill in the interstices left by the (absent) author. The novel is as much about the process of reading itself as it is the story of a young man's attempt at self-definition. It is fuelled by the same kind of critical awareness as is Liam Mac Cóil's novel *An Dr Áthas* (1994), a dramatic fictional exploration of Freudian theory, in particular the question of the role of narrative in personal identity. *An Dr Áthas* (or Dr Freud) presents a series of texts to be interpreted, together with a commentary on the process of interpretation itself. The relationship between theory and experience is a central theme of the novel, providing the subject for one of the most hilarious scenes towards the end of the novel where Freudian concepts are presented as a series of articles of faith which may be accepted or rejected, but not ignored.[45] Mac Cóil (b. 1952) set his later novel *An Claíomh Solais* (1998) around the activities of a new Irish-language television channel, and the novel is a dramatic multifocal exploration of the complex process of cultural representation. The question of how the media mediate is central to the story's plot, as a resolution is sought between the romantic idealism of the television editor and the cultural confidence of his young female companion.

The work of Tipperary-born author Liam Prút (b. 1940) should also be considered here. His first novel *Désirée* (1989), though it lacks the theoretical dimension of novels like *Kinderszenen*, is nevertheless similar in mood and theme.[46] The boundaries between the self and the other are explored in this lyric meditation on the role of desire in identity formation. In seeking the other, ego boundaries collapse, but the search for the desired one becomes ultimately a search for the self. A published poet, Prút had already produced a collection of short stories,[47] and went on to publish a disturbingly stark exploration of the inner world of a speechless disabled individual in *Geineasas* (1991). His latest prose work *An Leanbh sa Lamborghini* (1996) builds on the strengths of his earlier work to produce a mystery story which is also a subtle psychological study of human attachment and detachment. Another master of the contemplative style is Kerry writer Pádraig Ó Cíobháin (b. 1951), author, by 2000, of three novels and three collections of short stories.[48] His work is notable for its preoccupation with language and meaning, its attention to details of place and character and its dramatic exploration of themes of identity and belonging. While his first novel, the *bildungsroman An Gealas i Lár na Léithe* (1992), was firmly grounded in his native Corca Dhuibhne, his later works move back and forth between rural and urban, Irish and foreign settings. He has developed a highly literary prose style – eschewing the conversational styles of Gaeltacht speech in favour of a scholarly etymological approach to language – which is in tune with the philosophical musings of his central characters. Another recent novel to explore questions of identity and belonging is Liam Ó Muirthile's *Ar Bhruach na Laoi* (1995). By placing a character suffering from the psychological state of amnesia centre stage, Ó Muirthile (b. 1950) enacts a drama of recovery and self-discovery which has an important cultural dimension. While much of the novel records a journey west along the banks of the river Lee, the lives of Cork City's marginalised underclass are also realistically and dramatically depicted.

Certain contemporary writers stand out for the range and versatility of their work. The fictional writings of Micheál Ó Conghaile (b. 1962), for example, range in style from the realist to the absurd and explore various aspects of contemporary Gaeltacht and urban life. His short-story collections *Mac an tSagairt* (1986) and *An Fear a Phléasc* (1997) demonstrate a mastery of the real and the fantastic, while his novel of homosexual youth *Sna Fir* (1999) moves with ease between rural and urban environments and social situations. Other writers have also successfully taken on the challenges posed by literary realism and produced accomplished works where the Irish language is competently translated into a wide range of social situations. The success of these works depends, in large part, on the strength of the characterisation. Dramatic character portrayal makes Pádraig Ó Siadhail's first novel, *Parthas na gCleas* (1991), an engaging study of marital strife, and it is the realist accuracy with which he portrays relationships in his second novel, *Éagnairc* (1994), which sustains reader interest and provides a focus for the development of the novel's central theme of political responsibility. With narrative strands set in Dublin in 1988, and Derry in 1972, the dialogue is realistic throughout and the tension between the principle characters palpable. The third novel by Ó Siadhail (b. 1958), *Peaca an tSinsir* (1996), is a more ambitious, but less successful, attempt to portray someone whose past is coming back to haunt him. Set in Canada and in Ireland, with a plot centring around a retired university professor's more than academic interest in murder, the novel becomes a thriller with an ironic satirical dimension. Other Northern writers who have successfully employed realist modes include Aodh Ó Canainn (b. 1934), whose novels explore historical and political themes, and Déirdre Ní Ghrianna, whose first collection of short stories, *An Gnáthrud* (1999), contains powerful depictions of contemporary Belfast life, including some very moving and disturbing depictions of the lives of women and children.

Ciarán Ó Coigligh (b. 1952) employs a more introspective realist style in his novels *Duibhlinn* (1991) and *Slán le Luimneach* (1998), both of which document a personal journey where cultural repossession is linked with a deep-felt need for moral and ethical certainty. Ó Coigligh's accomplished use of language – urban and rural environments and social interactions are translated into an idiomatic Irish which disguises the historical process of Anglicisation – ironically belies the sense of cultural loss and cultural betrayal often expressed by his central narrators. An authoritative authorial presence is apparent throughout, and the overall monological effect is seldom broken, despite the use of direct speech and a multivocal narrative style. This is even more marked in the collection of stories *An Troigh ar an Tairne agus Scéalta Eile* (1991), most of which are short satirical sketches.

The depiction of non-Gaeltacht environments in realist fiction is closely linked to the question of creating Irish-language popular fiction. The problem of promoting fiction which would attract a large popular readership has always been a vexed one for Irish-language publishers, not least because of the linguistic challenges posed for many readers by any Irish-language literary text. Much of the creative literature to appear in the language has been the work of writers with a strong academic background and colleges and universities have in turn been the main market for such writing. Works such as the highly successful *bildungsroman Lig Sinn i gCathú* (1976) by Breandán Ó hEithir (1930–1990) – which was read avidly by Gaeltacht and non-Gaeltacht readers alike – have been scarce. Critical response to Ó hEithir's novel was surprising, however, as instead of assessing its success as a racy best-seller centred on the activities of a disgruntled young man in Galway in 1949, reviewers emphasised its literary attributes, comparing it to Ó Cadhain's *Cré na Cille*, Ó Conaire's *Deoraíocht*, Mac Grianna's *Mo Bhealach Féin*, the English novels of Liam O'Flaherty, Myles na gCopaleen's *An Béal Bocht*, the work of Spanish novelist Pérez Galdós, the twelfth-century century *Buile Shuibhne*, the seventeenth-century *Pairlement Chloinne Tomáis*, the eighteenth-century 'Cúirt an Mheán Oíche', James Joyce's *A Portrait of the Artist as a Young Man* and the work of a host of other modern and contemporary writers.[49] Only one reviewer assessed it as a work of popular fiction, a light read,[50] but that review attracted a large volume of negative critical comment. The main difficulty here centred on the concept of popular fiction and an unwillingness to give critical recognition to such a literary categorisation. Though Annraoi Ó Liatháin's thriller *Nead na gCreabhar* (1977) was recognised as a popular success, it was only with the work of Pádraig Standún (b. 1946) from the 1980s onwards that the category of popular fiction was admitted into Irish-language critical discourse and such books assessed on their actual merits. Standún's first novel, *Súil le Breith* (1983), was written with the intention of raising the issue of clerical celibacy, while grappling also with the cultural and economic issues affecting disadvantaged Gaeltacht regions. Since then he has published eight novels, each of which deals in different ways with social and personal issues related to sexuality, family relationships and the changes affecting west of Ireland communities.[51] Standún's success is based on the contemporariness of his themes, his easy style and his vivid use of language. Other authors producing novels involving similar themes and situations (such as Micheál Ó Ciosóig and Liam Mac Uistín, and Gaeltacht writers Colm Ó Ceallaigh, Diarmaid Ó Gráinne and Micheál Ó Ráighne) have been less successful, though Maidhc Dainín Ó Sé, from the Corca Dhuibhne Gaeltacht and Máirtín Ó Muilleoir from Belfast have attracted considerable attention, Ó Sé for his humorous anecdotal style and the familiarity of his Gaeltacht subject matter, Ó Muilleoir for his irreverent depictions of life and politics as experienced by self-aware young Northern Irish Catholics.

The difficulty of writing a successful best-seller was apparent when Breandán Ó hEithir's second novel, the picaresque *Sionnach ar mo Dhuán* (1988), failed to live up to the promise of his first book. On this occasion, a harsh review by Proinsias Ó Drisceoil published in the *Irish Times* on 14 January 1989 sparked off a lively critical debate about realism in the Irish-language novel. Ó Drisceoil used the novel as ground for his view that it is 'virtually impossible for a writer in Irish to set realist fiction in modern urban society'. The heated discussion which followed, where Ó hEithir's supporters sought to refute such claims by alluding to works in Irish set in non-Irish-speaking settings, ignored the conclusion reached by critic Seán Ó Tuama in his 1976 article on modern Irish fiction, where he stated: 'Máirtín Ó Cadhain will continue to be the main model for writers of fiction in Irish, in particular for short-story writers, for the foreseeable future. It may also be that, with the success of *Cré na Cille*, the fantasy or non-realistic novel will continue to be seen for a long time as the most viable novel-genre for the writer of Irish in modern Ireland.'[52] Ó Drisceoil reiterated this view when he made the following assertion: 'None of the artistically sustained novels in the language is wholly realist: Máirtín Ó Cadhain's great *Cré na Cille* is set among the dead, and the only really successful novel of recent years is Séamus Mac Annaidh's *Cuaifeach mo Londubh Buí*, a highly experimental work in the manner of B. S. Johnson. The novelist in Irish must, like Mac Annaidh, look to genres which make a strength of what appear to be disabilities.' As the millennium drew to a close, Ó Drisceoil's analysis seemed to be borne out as prose writing in Irish could now be seen to be evolving in two distinct directions – an art literature (whose dominant strands are fabulist/magic realist on the one hand and lyrical/philosophical/contemplative on the other and whose core audience is highly educated and academic); and fiction of a more popular nature (with a social realist thrust, with Gaeltacht and non-Gaeltacht strands and directed at a larger, younger and less academic audience).

With a steady output of art literature, and a regular market for such writing within the university communities, the last decade of the twentieth century saw fresh attempts to promote popular fiction and popular literacy in a less formally academic context. Both the Gaelic League, through its annual Oireachtas literary competitions, and Bord na Leabhar Gaeilge, the state-sponsored board responsible for Irish-language publishing, initiated schemes to promote popular fiction, teenage fiction and fiction suitable for adult learners of Irish. This has resulted in a growing body of literature which may be looked upon as part of a continuum which includes popular adult fiction (such as is to be found in the work of Pádraig Standún and Máirtín Ó Muilleoir, and including the work of new female authors of romantic fiction Nóirín Uí Mhaolaoi and Tina Nic Éinrí); fiction for adult learners (provided by authors such as Pól Ó Muirí, Colmán Ó Drisceoil and Éilís Ní Dhuibhne); teenage fiction (exemplified in the work of Muireann Ní Bhrolcháin and Siobhán Ní Shúilleabháin) and hybrid forms (such as is to be found particularly in the work of Dublin author Ré Ó Laighléis), which may attract teenage or young adult readers. The main difference between such popular forms in recent years and the light fiction published in the 1950s and 1960s is the preoccupation with contemporary social issues and social problems in the later material. Where the easy reading of an earlier generation included historical novels, adventure and detective stories, thrillers and romantic narratives, examples from the 1990s tend to deal with contemporary issues in texts where youthful heroism is replaced by teenage angst, romance by sex, and history by politics.

Drama and theatre: in search of an audience

While the period 1940–2000 was a period of consolidation and unprecedented growth for prose literature, the fate of Irish-language theatre was less fortunate. The predicament of Irish-language drama during the period is best summed up in the titles of two critical articles published in 1969 and 1971 respectively – 'Drámadóir gan phobal?' (A dramatist without a community?), a study of the work of Eoghan Ó Tuairisc by Oilibhéar Ó Croiligh,[53] and 'Drámadóir gan traidisiún' (A dramatist without a tradition), a study of three Seán Ó Tuama plays by Tadhg Ó Dúshláine.[54] In focusing on the work of urban-based playwrights, these articles identify the challenges posed by the absence, both historically and in a contemporary context, of an urban, Irish-speaking, theatre-going bourgeoisie. While early twentieth-century Irish-language drama may be situated in the context of the role envisaged for it in language revival, developments from the 1940s onwards have moved in two main directions. One has been an urban-based movement, whose objective was the establishment of a professional Irish-language theatre and the development of a modern dramatic repertoire; the other a more organic Gaeltacht-based folk drama movement, where theatrical performance is seen as an extension of oral community art forms such as the highly popular 'agallamh beirte' (dramatic dialogue). Amateur drama draws its energy from both sources, and the best of such drama results from the creative collaboration of Gaeltacht and non-Gaeltacht participants.

Dublin and Galway are the centres where most efforts have been made to establish a permanent Irish-language theatre. In 1940 the drama association An Comhar Drámaíochta was still in existence and occasional Irish-language plays were staged in the Abbey, the Peacock and the Gate Theatres by various affiliated amateur companies. While most of these were translations, some new plays, including three by a member of An Comhar, Séamus Wilmot, were staged at that time. Suffering from lack of funding and a permanent location, low audience support and sparsity of new Irish-language material, the operations of An Comhar Drámaíochta were effectively wound up in 1942 when the director of the Abbey Theatre, Ernest Blythe, arranged for the incorporation of An Comhar's state subsidy into the Abbey's annual grant. While Blythe's commitment to making the Abbey a truly bilingual national theatre cannot be denied, some of the strategies he employed to promote and to create audiences for Irish-language drama have been widely criticised, in particular his strategy, initiated in 1946, of presenting short one-act plays in Irish as an unadvertised supplement to English-language productions. Blythe was responsible for the introduction of bilingual Christmas pantomimes at the Abbey, on the model of the successful bilingual variety shows staged by An Compántas Amharclainne, a new group founded in 1944 by those members of An Comhar Drámaíochta who were unhappy with what they saw as an Abbey Theatre takeover of Irish-language drama. The pantomimes – which were to be an annual feature from 1945 to 1966 – were to prove highly popular, mainly due to their use of song, dance and lavish theatrical effects, which made them attractive to audiences with a limited understanding of Irish. This kind of production suited Tomás Mac Anna, who was responsible for most of the Irish-language productions in the Abbey from his appointment in 1947 through to the 1980s. Mac Anna's vision for Irish-language drama was that it should create a truly alternative kind of theatrical experience. This sometimes led to experimentation with bilingualism and variety show techniques which did not always satisfy the core Irish-language audiences. Ironically, perhaps, many of the Abbey's most successful Irish-language productions were stage adaptations of familiar literary texts, such as Pádraig Ó Siochfhradha's *An Baile Seo Againne*, adapted and produced by Michael Judge in 1968, and Peadar Ua Laoghaire's *Séadna*, produced by Mac Anna in 1969. After the opening of the new Abbey and Peacock Theatres in 1966 and 1967, Irish-language productions were removed to the smaller, more intimate venue. While the Peacock was envisaged as a forum for new and more experimental drama, the size and layout of the theatre placed limitations on the type of production possible. Nevertheless, in its early years the new Peacock staged important works by Máiréad Ní Ghráda (1896–1971) and Críostóir Ó Floinn, and has subsequently staged the work of a younger generation, including Antaine Ó Flatharta (b. 1953), Alan Titley and Éilís Ní Dhuibhne (b. 1954).

By 1967 other developments had taken place to indicate that the dream of establishing a distinctly Irish-language theatre space and professional company in the capital was still very much alive. Former members of An Comhar Drámaíochta began to regroup in the early 1950s, and new formations such as An Chomhairle Náisiúnta Amharclainne led to the establishment in 1955 of An Damer, under the auspices of Irish-language organisation Gael Linn. While the objective of establishing a permanent professional company was never realised, An Damer did for a period provide a regular venue which enabled the emergence of a small contemporary repertoire, centred around the work of playwrights Máiréad Ní Ghráda, Críostóir Ó Floinn, Seán Ó Tuama and Eoghan Ó Tuairisc. The role of Frank Dermody, who was employed in the role of theatrical director from 1957 to 1961, was important, and during his period with An Damer a group of highly talented young actors came together who could have formed the kernel of a professional company.

Highlights of the Damer years were Frank Dermody's production of Brendan Behan's *An Giall*[55] in June 1958, and Tomás Mac Anna's production of Máiréad Ní Ghráda's *An Triail*[56] in September 1964. *An Giall* was specially commissioned by Gael Linn for the Damer stage and was Behan's only Irish-language play. A moving tragedy about a young English soldier held as a hostage in a Dublin boarding house for an IRA prisoner who is to be executed in Belfast, the play has attracted attention over the years, not least for its caricature of puritanical nationalism. It was later rewritten as *The Hostage* for Joan Littlewood's theatre in London, but, as Anthony Roche explains in chapter 10 of this volume, it is unclear whether Behan himself collaborated in the process of cultural translation which dramatically transformed his sombre Irish-language original into an English music-hall comedy. Máiréad Ní Ghráda was one of the most important figures in Irish-language drama in the 1950s and 1960s. A prolific dramatist, her comic one-act plays were produced regularly by the Abbey from 1953 to 1961, as part of Blythe's policy of including short works in Irish after the main feature. *An Triail* is her best-known work, though the satirical *Breithiúnas*, which was first produced in the Abbey in February

1968, has also been widely acclaimed. Both works eschew naturalism in favour of Brechtian techniques, forcing the audience to actively engage with the moral dilemmas they pose. *An Triail* is a powerful exposition of contemporary Irish society's responses to pregnancy and motherhood outside of marriage. The play is presented as a trial, and the viewer must assess the evidence and decide who is responsible for a young mother's desperate act of infanticide and suicide. *Breithiúnas* again draws the audience into the narrative, by exposing and submitting to audience judgement the affairs and motivations of a public representative.[57]

Despite the enthusiasm and promise of actors, directors and playwrights associated with An Damer, the much-sought permanent professional company never materialised. By the end of the 1960s, the golden days of An Damer were over. Though Bord na Gaeilge established Aisteoirí an Damer in 1979 in a renewed attempt to establish a regular Irish-language theatre in the capital, the attempt failed and the group was disbanded in 1981. Meanwhile in Galway, the progress of An Taibhdhearc mirrored the difficulties experienced in Dublin. An Taibhdhearc was also struggling to maintain a regular programme of Irish-language plays. Like An Damer, it had failed to develop a professional company, becoming instead the venue for amateur productions by Gaeltacht dramatic societies, and various variety shows and musical productions by non-professional and school drama groups. Anxious to counteract the overdependence of amateur groups on translations, An Taibhdhearc co-sponsored an Oireachtas drama competition which was to provide much-needed encouragement in the early 1960s to writers such as Ó Tuairisc and Ó Tuama.

The most important dramatists to come to the fore in the 1960s were undoubtedly Ó Tuama, Críostóir Ó Floinn and Eoghan Ó Tuairisc. Poet, playwright and academic Seán Ó Tuama (b. 1928) was a founder member of the amateur theatre company Compántas Chorcaí, established in the early 1950s for the promotion and production of Irish-language plays in Cork City. He remained closely involved with the company until 1964, providing them with a regular output of plays, some of which were later produced at the Damer and at other venues. Ó Tuama's work as a dramatist is accomplished and ambitious. It is marked by a conscious sense of experimentation, as each play attempts to portray a new perspective on issues of personal responsibility and individual freedom. *Gunna Cam agus Slabhra Óir*, first produced in the Abbey Theatre in October 1956 (publ. 1964), is arguably his most successful play. Here, a sixteenth-century Irish chieftain's response to the Tudor policy of assimilation is used to explore the conflict between politics and violence in a manner which also evokes Civil War and subsequent Irish political conflicts. His more experimental works, such as *Corp Eoghain Uí Shúilleabháin* (perf. 1963, publ. 1966), are less effective, because, as critic Pádraig Ó Siadhail points out, while the influence of Beckett, Harold Pinter and N. F. Simpson may be discernible, the absurdist techniques employed are often simply stylistic features, unlinked to the central philosophical concerns of the work.[58]

In the work of Críostóir Ó Floinn a range of styles and dramatic situations is employed to explore the tensions between individual or group ideals, ambitions and aspirations and the power structures which impose limits on individual or group action.[59] Social and political critique permeates works such as *Is É a Dúirt Polonius* (publ. 1973), where an individual employee is seen to be at the mercy of an anonymous official apparatus where procedure takes precedence over natural justice. Ó Floinn's sense of irony often takes an overtly satirical turn, and this is especially marked in the documentary-style *Mise Raifteaí an File* (perf. 1973, publ. 1974) which explores the cultural politics of the nineteenth-century Revival in the context of twentieth-century cultural debates. Ó Floinn's dramatic work could be compared thematically and stylistically to that of Eoghan Ó Tuairisc. Ó Tuairisc's early comedies *De Réir na Rúibricí* (perf. 1961) and *Cúirt an Mheán Oíche* (perf. 1962, publ. 1988)[60] contain a social satirical element which proved popular with audiences in the Damer and the Taibhdhearc in the 1960s and 1970s. Ó Tuairisc's dramatic style is less naturalistic, however; the dialogue ranges from the lyrical to the tendentious, and the characterisation often tends towards the symbolic and archetypal. The latter tendency is apparent in his Civil War tragedy *Lá Fhéile Míchíl* (perf. 1963, publ. 1967), for example, where the political tensions of the period are depicted in terms of fundamentally irreconcilable categories. Using the garden of a convent, where the 'republican' Pacaí has sought refuge, as scene, a primal drama is played out among a small group of intimate acquaintances. Despite the true republicanism and the intellectual understanding of the conflict of the reverend mother La Mère Michelle, she is shown to be blind to the passions which fuel the actions of the other characters. Idealism and pragmatism struggle heroically for supremacy, with the inevitable tragic outcome. Though *Lá Fhéile Míchíl* is arguably Ó Tuairisc's finest play, much of his subsequent work reflects his understanding of the need to develop theatrical techniques which would attract larger audiences to Irish-language theatre. The element of farce apparent in *De Réir na Rúibricí* and *Cúirt an Mheán Oíche* – where Ó Tuairisc was building on his experience as a scriptwriter for Abbey pantomimes in the 1950s[61] – comes to the fore again in the later comedies *An Hairyfella in Ifreann* (perf. 1974) and *Aisling Mhic Artáin* (perf. 1977, publ. 1978), where, especially in the latter, attempts at dramatic naturalism are dispensed with in favour of highly stylised visual and musical effects. His musical depiction of the life of eighteenth-century composer *Carolan* was staged very successfully in the Damer in 1979, and his final play, the prize-winning *Fornocht do Chonac* (perf. 1979, publ. 1981) also employs non-mimetic special effects to conjure up a vision of Patrick Pearse and his legacy.

While Ní Ghráda, Ó Tuama, Ó Floinn and Ó Tuairisc were central figures, the work of playwrights such as Pádraig Ó Giollagáin and Máirtín Ó Diomasaigh should also be acknowledged, particularly for their contribution to Irish-language drama in Dublin. The work of amateur drama groups in the Gaeltacht has also been important, not least as a means of training actors who might later participate in professional productions. Though largely dependent on translations, some important original work has emerged from the activities of these Gaeltacht groups. The work of Connemara author Johnny Chóil Mhaidhc Ó Coisdealbha (b. 1930), himself an accomplished actor, for example, is typical of the kind of play popular with Gaeltacht audiences. A master of oral poetry, he is the author of comic plays that display a fine mixture of poetic idiom and colloquial Gaeltacht speech. His black comedy, *An Mhéar Fhada* (perf. 1992, publ. 1995),[62] is like an extended 'agallamh beirte', that genre of poetic dialogue still highly popular as an oral art form in Gaeltacht regions. The influence of the 'agallamh beirte' is also discernible in the work of Siobhán Ní Shúilleabháin (b. 1928), whose play *Cití* (publ. 1975) was first produced as a radio play in 1975. Like Ó Coisdealbha, Ní Shúilleabháin has produced scripts for amateur groups in her native Corca Dhuibhne, and the dramatic output of both writers cannot be adequately assessed without taking the implied producers of their work, as well as their implied audiences, into account.

Developments in Irish-language drama since the 1980s have not altered fundamentally the pattern established in the 1950s. In 1992 Bord na Gaeilge, the state board responsible for Irish-language policy implementation, established Amharclann de hÍde, which was to be responsible for the commissioning and regular production of new Irish-language drama. In contrast to previous attempts to establish a professional company in a permanent location, the new body's function was based on a production process which acknowledged the occasional nature, and the impermanent and nomadic position, of contemporary Irish-language theatre. Amharclann de hÍde's work resulted in the production at various venues in Dublin and elsewhere of exciting new plays by Antaine Ó Flatharta, Liam Ó Muirthile, Tom MacIntyre, Éilís Ní Dhuibhne and Alan Titley. Despite some excellent productions, the task of attracting urban audiences is still a major challenge, however. The difficulty lies in the high standards required by the core target audience, who may be critical of actors with sub-standard Irish, of plays with macaronic scripts, or of productions which smack of jaded experimentalism. An underlying concern is that the dominant theatrical form may become a kind of burlesque presentation where the language itself may all too easily become part of the farce. A key issue in audience reception of Irish-language drama has been the question of bilingual scripts. The work of Connemara-born dramatist Antaine Ó Flatharta has been criticised for its depiction of contemporary language patterns in the Gaeltacht.[63] Though Ó Flatharta does employ symbolist techniques in certain plays, he is fundamentally a dramatist in the realist mode who uses strong characterisation to depict communities and individuals with a confused sense of cultural identity. Linguistic code-mixing and code-changing in his plays are both realist depictions of actual language use (examples of late twentieth-century 'caint na ndaoine') and methods of exploring the communication difficulties experienced by communities in transition. Whether the focus is on the relationships associated with a summer Irish-language college, as in *Gaeilgeoirí* (perf. 1981, publ. 1986), or the challenges associated with creativity and entrepreneurship in a demoralised rural community, as in *Imeachtaí na Saoirse* (perf. 1983, publ. 1986), or the difficulties for minority languages posed by the new electronic media, as in *An Solas Dearg* (perf. 1995, publ. 1998), questions of communication and miscommunication are central. Ó Flatharta's success lies in his ability to interweave different forms of cultural media – from *sean-nós* singing to contemporary popular music; from community ritual to film technology; from traditional storytelling to the politician's soundbite – in a manner which forces audience attention on individual and group conflicts and vulnerabilities. The result is often a disturbingly realistic depiction of individuals for whom the community can no longer provide adequate understanding or support. His play *Grásta i Meiriceá* (perf. 1990, publ. 1990), which depicts the odyssey of two young Connemara men on a pilgrimage to Graceland in quest of the spirit of Elvis, presents a world of music and the imagination where confused identities are reflected both in the elusive plot and the macaronic script.

The plays of Liam Ó Muirthile are also concerned with the problems of the individual, and deal in particular with the drama of particular psychological states. His first play, *Fear an Tae* (perf. 1995, publ. 1999), is a subtle attempt at depicting the mind-set of an alcoholic. Set in a psychiatric hospital, the play explores the internal conflict between intellect and instinct, logic and desire. His second play, *Liodán na hAbhann* (perf. 1999, publ. 1999), takes up some of the themes of his novel *Ar Bhruach na Laoi*, where psychological wellbeing is imagined in terms of the individual's attachment to physical place. Tom MacIntyre has turned to earlier literary works in Irish as the basis of his plays *Caoineadh Airt Uí Laoghaire* (perf. 1998, publ. 1999) and *Cúirt an Mheán Oíche* (perf. and publ. 1999). Though interesting as examples of the work of a playwright better known for his work in English, neither of these plays manages to develop the dramatic or poetic potential of the original works which are themselves dramatic masterpieces. Éilís Ní Dhuibhne's employment of folk narrative in *Dún na mBan trí Thine* (perf. 1994, pub. 1997)[64] was much more successful, and comparable in dramatic terms to poet Nuala Ní Dhomhnaill's highly evocative reworkings of folk legend material. Alan Titley has also turned to literary sources in his work for theatre. His first play *Tagann Godot* (perf. 1990, publ. 1991) is a hilarious sequel to Beckett's tragicomedy, while his later *An Ghráin agus an Ghruaim* (perf. 1999) can be read either as an inversion of the rural idyll or an exaggeration of the rural squalor to be found in certain kinds of popular Irish autobiographical writing.

One of the most significant developments for Irish-language drama in recent years has been the opportunity provided by Irish-language television since the establishment of TG4 (originally TnaG) in 1996. The emergence of Irish-language television drama, such as the highly successful Connemara-based soap 'Ros na Rún' or the hilarious Donegal-based comic series 'CU Burn' and 'Gleann Ceo', offers a whole new context for Gaeltacht drama. Here, teams of scriptwriters must work collaboratively with actors, some of whom have come to television after years of experience of amateur acting in parish halls. The ease with which Gaeltacht writers have taken to the new media is evidenced in the work of actor/writer Joe Steve Ó Neachtain (b. 1942). Author of the popular radio soap *Baile an Droichid*, which ran for ten years (1987–97) on Raidió na Gaeltachta, his play *Níor Mhaith linn do Thrioblóid* played to packed audiences in Taibhdhearc na Gaillimhe in 2000. As in the case of Johnny Chóil Mhaidhc Ó Coisdealbha, the success of Ó Neachtain's work lies in audience familiarity with the situations and themes explored. Just as the 'agallamh beirte,' of which both authors are masters, has proved a medium adaptable to contemporary concerns, so can certain aspects of traditional Gaeltacht oral art – topicality, linguistic playfulness, referentiality – be adapted to create a theatrical experience which is a natural organic development of folk art forms.

Literary criticism and literary biography

Roibeárd Ó Faracháin, in a 1940 article entitled 'Teastuigheann léirmheast-óireacht uainn' (We need criticism),[65] made an urgent plea for an informed and understanding literary critical practice. Nine years later, Máirtín Ó Cadhain drew attention to the lack of objective critical analysis of literary works in his celebrated lecture 'Tuige nach bhfuil litríocht na Gaeilge ag fás?' (Why isn't Irish-language literature developing?).[66] This need for a more sophisticated literary criticism was responded to in the work of critics writing for the literary magazines *Comhar* and *Feasta*, which, together with the more regional *An t-Ultach*, did provide platforms for literary and cultural criticism and debate.[67] Tomás Ó Floinn (1910–1997), who wrote under the pseudonym 'Flann Mac an tSaoir,' was a regular reviewer of new books in Irish, and a collection of his critical essays published in *Comhar* between 1942 and 1987 reveals a sustained engagement with the problems of literary creativity in a marginalised and minoritised language, including the particular difficulties associated with writing in one's second language.[68] It was not until the 1960s, however, that concerted efforts were made to develop critical writing as an important literary field in its own right. Two developments were central to the process of developing a more rigorous and sustained critical discourse in Irish: the work of Breandán Ó Doibhlin and his colleagues and their students in St Patrick's College, Maynooth, and the editorial policies of the Irish-language publishing house An Clóchomhar. While professor in the Department of French in Maynooth, Ó Doibhlin saw to it that the college Irish-language annual *Irisleabhar Mhá Nuad* became a literary journal, devoted to the promotion of a rigorous literary critical practice, based on the kind of close reading and detailed textual analysis then common in the teaching of French literature. The journal was devoted entirely to literary criticism during the period 1966–78, during which time many seminal critical studies of modern and contemporary writing in Irish were published.[69] The journal continued to publish high-quality critical work throughout the 1980s, though in recent years it has reverted to the theological and spiritual concerns which were to the fore in the period prior to Ó Doibhlin's interventions. Maynooth also publishes *Léachtaí Cholm Cille*, an annual collection of scholarly lectures based on a conference hosted each year by the Faculty of Celtic Studies in St Patrick's College and its successor NUI Maynooth. Initiated in 1970 by Professor of Irish Pádraig Ó Fiannachta and based on a different theme each year, the Léachtaí have provided an invaluable platform for critical discussion and analysis, complementing and expanding in many instances the achievement of *Irisleabhar Mhá Nuad*. The most significant achievement of the Maynooth-based critics was their avoidance of the prescriptive approaches of earlier practitioners such as Seoirse Mac Clúin and Liam Ó Rinn. Instead of seeking to advise writers about genre and technique, a new emphasis was placed on the reading process itself, on textual description and analysis, and on the relationship between literary works and the social contexts which shaped them.

The work of academic publishing house An Clóchomhar has been central to the development of Irish-language literary and cultural criticism. Established in 1954 at a time when academic publication in Irish was very limited, An Clóchomhar soon moved into the field, initiating in 1958 its prestigious 'Leabhair Thaighde' (Research Publications) series. Running to eighty-eight titles by the year 2000, this series has become the core of a new corpus of literary critical studies, and reflects the movement in literary study from the predominantly historical and philological approaches of the 1950s and 1960s to a more diverse range of socio-cultural and critical perspectives from the 1980s onwards.[70] Among the early path-breaking contributions are Seán Ó Tuama's seminal work on the love song tradition[71] and Frank O'Brien's critical analysis of contemporary poetry in Irish,[72] the first ever full-length study of contemporary literary production in Irish. Among the many highly original studies to be published in the series are the first substantial literary history ever to be published in Irish,[73] Angela (Bourke) Partridge's literary and ethnographic study of 'Caoineadh na dTrí Muire',[74] Aisling Ní Dhonnchadha's monograph on the short story,[75] Alan Titley's major survey of the novel in Irish[76] and Breandán Ó Buachalla's monumental study of Jacobite literature.[77] An important feature of the series has been the publication of careful studies of particular authors or works, such as Breandán Ó Conaire's close examination of Myles na gCopaleen's Irish-language sources,[78] or Pádraig de Paor's detailed textual analysis of the work of poet Nuala Ní Dhomhnaill,[79] the first large-scale critical work on Ní Dhomhnaill's poetry to be published in Irish. An Clóchomhar also published six volumes of *Scríobh*, an influential forum for cultural and intellectual debate in Irish in the ten-year period 1974–84, and one where creative writers and academic critics were encouraged to engage in active dialogue.

The role of literary biography has been important in establishing a body of information and source material for critics and readers. With Ó Conluain and Ó Céileachair's *An Duinníneach* as an early example, in the 1980s Bord na Gaeilge and the Oireachtas literary competition co-sponsored a commissioning scheme to encourage authors to undertake similar biographical research. The scheme resulted in the publication of a series of literary and biographical studies of writers Seán Ó Ríordáin, Eoghan Ó Tuairisc, Máirtín Ó Cadhain, Samuel Ferguson, Pádraic Ó Conaire, Seán Ó Ruadháin and Breandán Ó hEithir. As a form of cultural history, these literary biographies are particularly interesting in their approach to questions of sociolinguistic context and in the manner in which they account for the linguistic and literary paths chosen by their subjects in the course of their careers. In documenting the critical response to their subjects' work, they also serve as useful chapters in the history of Irish-language criticism itself. The publication of collections of literary and critical essays by creative writers and scholarly critics alike has also helped to chart the course of twentieth-century Irish-language critical writing. Indeed, the literary essay in Irish is itself worthy of particular attention, especially in the hands of masters of the genre, such as Seán Ó Ríordáin.[80] Certain essays, such as Máirtín Ó Cadhain's brilliant 'Béaloideas'[81] (originally a lecture), which deals with the perceived mummification and museumification of a living Gaeltacht culture by the folklore movement, or Eoghan Ó Tuairisc's literary testament 'Religio Poetae'[82], have gained particular status as powerful cultural and creative statements.

A greater interest in the theoretical aspects of contemporary literary criticism led to the publication in 1984 of a special supplement of *Comhar* devoted to literary critical theory[83], while the work of Ó Doibhlin and the Maynooth critics was the subject of Antain Mag Shamhráin's study *Litríocht, Léitheoireacht agus Critic* (1986). A more sophisticated theoretical awareness marks much of the critical writing to appear in new journals of the 1980s and 1990s, such as *Oghma* (1989–1998), *Bliainiris* (2000–) and *An Aimsir Óg* (1999–), where an attempt is also made to broaden the range of Irish-language cultural critique to include visual art and media criticism, philosophy and politics. The role of theory in literary criticism itself became a matter of lively debate among certain Irish-language writers and critics,[84] leading to the publication of the important collection of critical essays *Téacs agus Comhthéacs: Gnéithe de Chritic na Gaeilge* (1998), edited by Máire Ní Annracháin and Bríona Nic Dhiarmada. Not surprisingly, perhaps, questions of language and literary form are central to critical debates in Irish, as appropriate paradigms are sought which will place literary developments in Irish in the context of historical and contemporary sociolinguistic realities. The value of postcolonial critical perspectives should be obvious to Irish-language critics,[85] though such perspectives need to be deepened if the complexities of societal and literary language use are to be adequately dealt with. The role of the aforementioned literary journals is crucial in encouraging a younger generation of critics to break new ground, while the publication of works of a literary critical nature by new publishing houses such as Cois Life will also be very important in the years ahead. Caoilfhionn Nic Pháidín, herself a founding member and director of Cois Life, is one of those critics most keenly aware of the need to incorporate sociolinguistic categories and concepts more closely into Irish-language literary analysis.[86] What is clear at present is that the groundwork has been done; a critical idiom has been established and a corpus of high-quality analytical writing is now available to be built on in the years ahead as the literature itself makes new demands on its readers.

Conclusion

Few writers or readers in the 1940s could have predicted the developments in Irish-language writing which have occurred in the last sixty years. The sheer volume of material being published each year has increased tenfold, while the number of publishing houses involved, and the range and quality of the material being produced, has expanded apace. The huge challenge to contemporary Irish-language prose literature and drama is, as always, the status of the language itself and the strength of the Irish-language community which will inevitably be its core audience. The fragile position of the language may function as an incentive to some writers, but may discourage others, or force them into forms of literary introspection or in the direction of literary forms where communication with a recognisable interpretative community is no longer a central concern. Prose writing in Irish can be seen to reflect social and cultural change, and also to speak out against homogenising forces both in Irish society and globally. In so far as writing in Irish can never be fully considered without taking into account its ability to create its own reading public, it must be read also as a form of critique, as a statement of protest against the perceived inevitability of cultural and linguistic loss, as a manifestation of what critic Neil Lazarus described in an African context as 'Pessimism of the Intellect, Optimism of the Will'.[87] If literature can thrive on the tensions involved in what has become a constant struggle for cultural survival, then the new millennium may well see a further flowering of creative activity in Irish. The challenge for Irish-language writers now is to define and develop creative roles for their chosen medium in a cultural environment where identity is no longer seen as foundational but as fluid, performative and hybrid.

Notes

1. See Cathal Ó Háinle, '*An Druma Mór:* Athléamh', *Léachtaí Cholm Cille* 19 (1989), pp. 129–69, esp. pp. 129–37.
2. Published separately by An Gúm in 1992. See Antain Mag Shamhráin, 'Portráid den Stoirm: Úrscéal Deireanach Sheosaimh Mhic Grianna', *Oghma* 2 (1990), pp. 41–6. For a perceptive reading of *Mo Bhealach Féin*, see Seamus Deane, '*Mo Bhealach Féin* Seosamh

Mac Grianna', in John Jordan, ed. *The Pleasures of Gaelic Literature* (Dublin/Cork: RTÉ/Mercier, 1977), pp. 52–61.

3. For a definitive treatment of Myles na gCopaleen's sources and motivation, see Breandán Ó Conaire, *Myles na Gaeilge: Lámhleabhar ar Shaothar Gaeilge Bhrian Ó Nualláin* (Dublin: An Clóchomhar, 1986).
4. An English version followed, entitled *And So Began* (Cork: Mercier Press, 1972).
5. For bibliography, see Nollaig Mac Congáil, *Máire: Clár Saothair* (Dublin: Coiscéim, 1990). For discussion of Ó Grianna's novels, see Máirín Nic Eoin, *An Litríocht Réigiúnach* (Dublin: An Clóchomhar, 1982), pp. 179–205.
6. Proinsias Mac Cana, 'Stracfhéachaint ar nualitríocht Ghaeilge Uladh', *Fearsaid* (1956), pp. 47–53.
7. Ailbhe Ó Corráin, *A Concordance of Idiomatic Expressions in the Writings of Séamus Ó Grianna* (Belfast: Institute of Irish Studies, The Queen's University of Belfast, 1989); Tomás Ó Fiaich, 'Saothar Mháire mar Fhoinse don Stair Shóisialta', *Léachtaí Cholm Cille* 5 (1974), pp. 5–30.
8. Gearóidín Uí Laighléis, *Seán Mac Maoláin* (Dublin: Cois Life, 2003), pp. 87–126. For an insightful critique of Mac Maoláin as novelist, see Alan Titley, *An tÚrscéal Gaeilge* (Dublin: An Clóchomhar, 1991), pp. 347–50.
9. Seán Ó Faoláin, '*Dúil* Liam Ó Flaithearta', in Jordan, *The Pleasures of Gaelic Literature*, p. 116. For a study of Ó Flaithearta's exploration of human instincts and elemental emotions in *Dúil*, see Gearóid Denvir, *An Dúil is Dual* (Inverin: Cló Iar-Chonnachta, 1991).
10. Proinsias Ó Conluain and Donncha Ó Céileachair, *An Duinníneach* (Dublin: Sáirséal agus Dill, 1958).
11. See the important early reviews: Domhnall Ó Corcora, '*Cré na Cille*', *Feasta* (May 1950), pp. 14–15; Flann Mac an tSaoir (Tomás Ó Floinn), '*Cré na Cille*', *Comhar* (April 1950), pp. 7–8, 30, republished in Tomás Ó Floinn, *Cion Fir: Aistí Thomáis Uí Fhloinn in Comhar*, ed. Liam Prút (Dublin: Comhar, 1997), pp. 47–53; Seán Ó Tuama, '*Cré na Cille* agus *Séadna*', *Comhar* (February 1955), pp. 7–8, 29.
12. For the terms of this debate, see Breandán Ó Doibhlin, 'Athléamh ar *Cré na Cille*', in *Léachtaí Cholm Cille* 5 (1974), pp. 40–53, republished in *Aistí Critice agus Cultúir* 2 (Belfast: Lagan Press, 1997), pp. 36–50; Caoilfhionn Nic Pháidín, '*Cré na Cille* agus Ealaín na Maireachtála', *Comhar* (October 1980), pp. 43–8; Gearóid Ó Crualaoich, 'Domhan na Cille agus Domhan na Bréige', *Scríobh* 5 (1981), pp. 80–6; Seosamh Ó Murchú, 'An Chill agus a Cré', *Irisleabhar Mhá Nuad* (1982), pp. 5–20; and Declan Kiberd, '*Cré na Cille*: Ó Cadhain agus Beckett', in *Idir Dhá Chultúr* (Dublin: Coiscéim, 1993), pp. 241–60. The satirical and comic features of the novel are to the fore in much of the criticism. See, for example, Breandán Ó hEithir, '*Cré na Cille* Máirtín Ó Cadhain', in Jordan, *Pleasures of Gaelic Literature*, pp. 72–84; Caoilfhionn Nic Pháidín, '*Cré na Cille* mar Úrscéal Grinn', *Comhar* (July 1978), pp. 21–2; Ailbhe Ó Corráin, 'Grave Comedy: A Study of *Cré na Cille* by Máirtín Ó Cadhain', in International Congress of the International Association for the Study of Anglo-Irish Literature (9th: 1986: Uppsala University), *Anglo-Irish and Irish Literature: Aspects of Language and Culture*, II (Stockholm: Almqvist and Wiksell, 1988), pp. 143–8; Verona Ní Bhroin, '*Cré na Cille* mar Aoir', *Léachtaí Cholm Cille* 18 (1988), pp. 137–61.

13. For detailed discussion of Ó Cadhain's development and narrative style, see Gearóid Denvir, *Cadhan Aonair: Saothar Liteartha Mháirtín Uí Chadhain* (Dublin: An Clóchomhar, 1987); Louis de Paor, *Faoin mBlaoisc Bheag Sin* (Dublin: Coiscéim, 1991). For new critical perspectives, see also Liam Mac Cóil, Máire Ní Annracháin and Cathal Ó Háinle in Cathal Ó Háinle, ed. *Criostalú: Aistí ar Shaothar Mháirtín Uí Chadhain* (Dublin: Coiscéim, 1998); and Liam Mac Cóil, 'An Chritic Shíocanailíseach', in Máire Ní Annracháin and Bríona Nic Dhiarmada, eds. *Téacs agus Comhthéacs: Gnéithe de Chritic na Gaeilge* (Cork: Cork University Press, 1998), pp. 94–112.
14. See Máirtín Ó Cadhain, *Irish Above Politics* (Dublin: Press Cuchulainn, 1964); *Gluaiseacht na Gaeilge: Gluaiseacht ar Strae* (Dublin: Misneach, 1970); *An Ghaeilge Bheo – Destined to Pass*, ed. Seán Ó Laighin (Dublin: Coiscéim, 2002).
15. See Máirtín Ó Cadhain, *Bás Nó Beatha*, trans. of *Tynged yr Iaith* by Saunders Lewis (Dublin: Sáirséal agus Dill, 1963).
16. Máirtín Ó Cadhain, *Barbed Wire*, ed. Cathal Ó Háinle (Dublin: Coiscéim, 2002).
17. In *An tSraith ar Lár* (Dublin: Sáirséal agus Dill, 1967), pp. 187–204.
18. In *Comhar* (March 1962), 8–26, republished in *Caithfear Éisteacht: Aistí Mháirtín Uí Chadhain in Comhar*, ed. Liam Prút (Dublin: Comhar, 1999), pp. 97–144.
19. For example: *An Claíomh Geal* (Dublin: Sáirséal agus Dill, 1953); *An tIolar Dubh* (Dublin: Sáirséal agus Dill, 1956); *An tIolar Dubh agus Long na Marbh* (Dublin: Sáirséal agus Dill, 1958).
20. Dónall Mac Amhlaigh, 'Documenting the Fifties', *Irish Studies in Britain* 14 (Spring/Summer 1989), p. 7. For discussion of Mac Amhlaigh as a working-class writer, see Máirín Nic Eoin, 'An Scríbhneoir agus an Imirce Éigeantach', *Oghma* 2 (1990), pp. 92–104.
21. For critical commentary, see Tadhg Ó Dúshláine, 'Schnitzer Ó Sé', *Léachtaí Cholm Cille* 18 (1988), pp. 61–88.
22. Seán Ó Tuama, 'The Other Tradition', in Patrick Rafroidi and Maurice Harmon, eds. *The Irish Novel in Our Time* (Lille: Publications de l'Université de Lille, 1976), pp. 31–47. An Irish version of this article was published as 'Úrscéalta agus Faisnéisí Beatha na Gaeilge: Na Buaicphointí', in *Scríobh* 5 (1981), pp. 148–60; another version was published as 'Some Highlights of Modern Fiction in Irish', in *Repossessions: Selected Essays in the Irish Literary Heritage* (Cork: Cork University Press, 1995), pp. 199–211.
23. For a discussion of this novel, see Nic Eoin, *An Litríocht Réigiúnach*, pp. 199–202; Damien Ó Muirí, 'Saoirse na mBan in "Bean Ruadh de Dhálach"', *Léachtaí Cholm Cille* 12 (1982), pp. 112–44.
24. For an insightful reading of Ua Maoileoin's depiction of female characters, see Antain Mag Shamhráin, 'Íde na Leabhar is na mBan', *Oghma* 3 (1991), pp. 72–7.
25. For an interesting discussion of this particular account, see Breandán Ó Conaire, 'Nótaí ar Fhaisnéis Bheatha as Árainn Mhór', *Studia Hibernica* 31 (2000–2001), pp. 147–67.
26. For example: An tSiúr M. de Lourdes, *Thar Balla Isteach* (Maynooth: An Sagart, 1982); Neilí Uí Bheaglaoich, *Carraig a' Dúin* (Dublin: Coiscéim, 1989); Caitlín P. Mhic Gearailt, *Nach aon Saol mar a Thagann sé* (Dublin: Coiscéim, 1992); Maidhc Dainín Ó Sé, *Chicago Driver* (Dublin: Coiscéim, 1992); *A Thig ná Tit orm* (Dublin: C. J. Fallon, 1995); Muiris Ó Bric, *Spotsholas na nDaoine* (Dublin: Coiscéim, 1995).

27. See Breandán Ó Buachalla, *Aisling Ghéar: na Stíobhartaigh agus an t Aos Léinn* (Dublin: An Clóchomhar, 1996), pp. 178–9; 566–7. For discussion of the biblical and literary sources employed in the novel, see Nóra Ní Laidhigh, 'An Duine Fuascailte: "Néal Maidine agus Tine Oíche" i gComhthéacs Fhealsúnacht Chríostaí an Eisithe', *Irisleabhar Mhá Nuad* (1970), pp. 12–28; Mícheál Mac Craith, 'Léitheoir Cruthaitheach', *Irisleabhar Mhá Nuad* (1971), pp. 56–72.
28. For a discussion of the novel, see Mícheál Mac Craith, 'Fearann Coimirce an Scríbhneora: Úrscéalta Bhreandáin Uí Dhoibhlin', *Irisleabhar Mhá Nuad* (1996–7), pp. 66–78.
29. See Diarmaid Ó Súilleabháin, 'Bí tú féin, a Úrscéalaí', *Comhar* (July 1965), pp. 19–22; 'An Uain Bheo: Focal ón Údar', *Irisleabhar Mhá Nuad* (1972), pp. 65–9; Éamon Ó Ciosáin, 'Diarmaid Ó Súilleabháin – Geit as an nGaeilge?', *Nua-Aois* (1978–1979), pp. 25–36.
30. Titley, *An tÚrscéal Gaeilge*, pp. 542–3.
31. For critical commentary, see Éamon Ó Ciosáin, '"Ganaonscéal", "Lá Breá Gréine Buí" agus Cúrsaí Eile', *Comhar* (Nollaig 1986), pp. 15–20; Seosamh Ó Murchú, 'I dTreo an tSolais', ibid., pp. 36–41; Iarla Mac Aodha Bhuí, *Diarmaid Ó Súilleabháin: Saothar Próis* (Dublin: An Clóchomhar, 1992).
32. See: Máirín Nic Eoin, 'An Pholaitíocht Faoi Cheilt', *Comhar* (December 1986), pp. 24–8.
33. For example, see Marianne Elliott, *Partners in Revolution: The United Irishmen and France* (New Haven: Yale University Press, 1982). For discussion of Ó Tuairisc as a literary revisionist, see Máirín Nic Eoin, 'An Litríocht mar Athscríobh na Staire: *L'Attaque* agus *Dé Luain* le hEoghan Ó Tuairisc', *Léachtaí Cholm Cille* 21 (1991), pp. 27–76, esp. pp. 32–50.
34. For a discussion of the Leitrim involvement in this campaign, see Liam Kelly, *A Flame Now Quenched: Rebels and Frenchmen in Leitrim 1793–1798* (Dublin: The Lilliput Press, 1998).
35. For critical commentary, see Mícheál Mac Craith, '*L'Attaque*: Úrscéal faoi Stiúir', *Macalla* (1985), pp. 15–36; Breandán Delap, *Úrscéalta Stairiúla na Gaeilge* (Dublin: An Clóchomhar, 1993), pp. 71–86.
36. See Proinsias Ó Drisceoil, '"Ní Áit í an Caisleán ach Íomhá a Leanann Dínn": Athléamh ar *Dé Luain* le hEoghan Ó Tuairisc', *Oghma* 10 (1998), pp. 31–40; Nic Eoin, 'An Litríocht mar Athscríobh na Staire', pp. 50–73.
37. For one of the rare critical discussions of the novel, see Martin Nugent, 'An Lomnochtán', *Comhar* (October 1985), pp. 9–13.
38. Seán Ó Tuama, 'An Domhan a Chruthaigh Titley', *Comhar* (December 1987), pp. 17–19.
39. For important critical response to Titley's work, see Tadhg Ó Dúshláine, 'Beckett ag Borradh Aníos: Léirmheas ar "Stiall Fhial Feola"', *Irisleabhar Mhá Nuad* (1982), pp. 63–73; Éamon Ó Ciosáin, 'Eiriceachtaí', *Graph* 5 (Autumn 1988), p. 7; Bríona Nic Dhiarmada, 'Smulcairí, Fiosracht agus Eile: Cás na Critice sa Ghaeilge', *Léachtaí Cholm Cille* 26 (1996), pp. 159–77.
40. See Máire Ní Annracháin, 'An tSuibiacht Abú, an tSuibiacht Amú', *Oghma* 6 (1994), pp. 11–22; Caoimhín Mac Giolla Léith, '"Is cuma faoin scéal": Gné d'Úrscéalaíocht na Gaeilge', *Léachtaí Cholm Cille* 21 (1991), pp. 6–26.

41. For a discussion of patterns of literacy and reading in Irish, see the essays in Róisín Ní Mheachair, ed. *Idir Lúibíní: Aistí ar an Léitheoireacht agus ar an Litearthacht* (Dublin: Cois Life, 2003).
42. See Mac Giolla Léith, '"Is cuma faoin scéal"'.
43. See Titley, *An tÚrscéal Gaeilge*, pp. 584–6.
44. See 'Iníon Rí an Oileáin Dhorcha', *Oghma* 3 (1991), pp. 17–23; 'Iníon Rí na Cathrach Deirge', in Eoghan Ó hAnluain, ed. *Leath na Spéire* (Dublin: An Clóchomhar, 1992), 108–14.
45. For a further insight into Mac Cóil's interest in Freudian theory, see Mac Cóil, 'An Chritic Shíocanailíseach'.
46. Máire Ní Annracháin alludes to *Kinderszenen* and *Désirée* in her discussion of the decentred subject in 'An tSuibiacht Abú, an tSuibiacht Amú'.
47. Liam Prút, *Sean-Dair agus Scéalta Eile* (Dublin: Coiscéim, 1985).
48. Pádraig Ó Cíobháin, *Le Gealaigh* (Dublin: Coiscéim, 1991); *An Gealas i Lár na Léithe* (Dublin: Coiscéim, 1992); *An Grá faoi Cheilt* (Dublin: Coiscéim, 1992); *Desiderius a dó* (Dublin: Coiscéim, 1995); *Ar Gach Maoilinn tá Síocháin* (Dublin: Coiscéim, 1998); *Tá Solas ná hÉagann Choíche* (Dublin: Coiscéim, 1999).
49. See Liam Mac an Iomaire, '*Lig Sinn i gCathú* – i nGaillimh', in *Breandán Ó hEithir: Iomramh Aonair* (Inverin: Cló Iar-Chonnachta, 2000), pp. 387–422.
50. Rita Kelly, 'Leabhar Éadrom', *Feasta* (July 1976), pp. 11–4.
51. Pádraig Standún, *A.D. 2016* (Inverin: Cló Chonamara, 1988); *Cíocras* (Inverin: Cló Iar-Chonnachta, 1991); *An tAinmhí* (Inverin: Cló Iar-Chonnachta, 1992); *Cion Mná* (Inverin: Cló Iar-Chonnachta, 1993); *Na hAntraipeologicals* (Inverin: Cló Iar-Chonnachta, 1993); *Stigmata* (Inverin: Cló Iar-Chonnachta, 1994); *Saoire* (Inverin: Cló Iar-Chonnachta, 1997).
52. Seán Ó Tuama, 'Some Highlights of Modern Fiction in Irish', p. 211.
53. Oilibhéar Ó Croiligh, 'Drámadóir gan Phobal? Drámaí Uí Thuairisc', *Irisleabhar Mhá Nuad* (1969), pp. 31–43.
54. Tadhg Ó Dúshláine, 'Drámadóir gan Traidisiún', *Irisleabhar Mhá Nuad* (1971), pp. 42–51.
55. Brendan Behan, *Poems and a Play in Irish* (Dublin: Gallery Books, 1981).
56. Máiréad Ní Ghráda, *An Triail – Breithiúnas* (Dublin: An Gúm, 1978).
57. For discussion of Ní Ghráda's work, see Siobhán Ní Bhrádaigh, *Máiréad Ní Ghráda: Ceannródaí Drámaíochta* (Inverin: Cló Iar-Chonnachta, 1996).
58. Pádraig Ó Siadhail, 'Drámaí Sheáin Uí Thuama', *Irisleabhar Mhá Nuad* (1986), pp. 7–41, esp. p. 32.
59. This central structural aspect of his work is discussed in Damien Ó Muirí, 'Drámaí Chríostóra Uí Fhloinn', *Léachtaí Cholm Cille* 18 (1979), pp. 92–130.
60. Published as *Cúirt na Gealaí* (Dublin: An Gúm, 1988).
61. Ó Tuairisc collaborated with Tomás Mac Anna on a number of pantomimes, commencing with 'Ulyssés agus Penelopé' in 1955. For his own description of his experience as a scriptwriter, see 'Oiliúint Dhrámadóra', *Comhar* (October 1977), pp. 5–6, 20. For detailed discussion of Ó Tuairisc as a playwright, see Martin Nugent, *Drámaí Eoghain Uí Thuairisc* (Maynooth: An Sagart, 1984).
62. Johnny Chóil Mhaidhc Ó Coisdealbha, *An Cruastóir/An Mhéar Fhada* (Indreabhán: Cló Iar-Chonnachta, 1995).

63. For a discussion of this, and other aspects of Ó Flatharta's work, see Muireann Ní Bhrolcháin, 'Antoine Ó Flatharta mar Dhrámadóir Gaeltachta', *Léachtaí Cholm Cille* 19 (1989), pp. 42–92.
64. Éilís Ní Dhuibhne, *Milseog an tSamhraidh agus Dún na mBan trí Thine* (Dublin: Cois Life, 1997).
65. Roibeárd Ó Faracháin, 'Teastuigheann Léirmheastóireacht Uainn', *Éire* (1940), pp. 70–3.
66. Máirtín Ó Cadhain, 'Tuige nach bhfuil Litríocht na Gaeilge ag Fás?', *Feasta* (November 1949), pp. 9–12, 20–2. Also in Seán Ó Laighin, ed. *Ó Cadhain i bhFeasta* (Dublin: Clódhanna Teo, 1990), pp. 85–109.
67. See Tomás Ó Floinn, '"Comhar" agus an Léirmheastóireacht', in Stiofán Ó hAnnracháin, ed. *An Comhchaidreamh* (Dublin: An Clóchomhar, 1985), pp. 55–61; Aisling Ní Dhonnchadha, 'Is sa Duine atá ár Spéis: Sracfhéachaint ar Roinnt Aistí Léirmheasa ar Phrós na Gaeilge sna Caogaidí', *Léachtaí Cholm Cille* (1998), pp. 48–73.
68. Tomás Ó Floinn, *Cion Fir*.
69. See Antain Mag Shamhráin, *Litríocht, Léitheoireacht, Critic* (Dublin: An Clóchomhar, 1986).
70. For a full list of An Clóchomhar's academic publications 1958–2000, see Máirín Nic Eoin, 'An Clóchomhar agus léann na Gaeilge', *Studia Hibernica* 31 (2000–1), pp. 105–117.
71. Seán Ó Tuama, *An Grá in Amhráin na nDaoine* (Dublin: An Clóchomhar, 1960).
72. Frank O'Brien, *Filíocht Ghaeilge na Linne seo* (Dublin: An Clóchomhar, 1968).
73. J. E. Caerwyn Williams and Máirín Ní Mhuiríosa, *Traidisiún Liteartha na nGael* (Dublin: An Clóchomhar, 1979).
74. Angela Partridge, *Caoineadh na dTrí Muire* (Dublin: An Clóchomhar, 1983).
75. Aisling Ní Dhonnchadha, *An Gearrscéal sa Ghaeilge: 1898–1940* (Dublin: An Clóchomhar, 1981).
76. Titley, *An tÚrsceal Gaeilge*.
77. Ó Buachalla, *Aisling Ghéar*.
78. Ó Conaire, *Myles na Gaeilge*.
79. Pádraig de Paor, *Tionscnamh Filíochta Nuala Ní Dhomhnaill* (Dublin: An Clóchomhar, 1997).
80. For a discussion of Ó Ríordáin's essays as an example of postcolonial cultural criticism, see Stiofán Ó Cadhla, *Cá bhFuil Éire?: Guth an Ghaisce i bPrós Sheáin Uí Ríordáin* (Dublin: An Clóchomhar, 1998).
81. Máirtín Ó Cadhain, 'Béaloideas', *Feasta* (March 1950), pp. 9–12, 19–25, republished in Ó Laighin, *Ó Cadhain i bhFeasta*, pp. 129–69.
82. Eoghan Ó Tuairisc, 'Religio Poetae', *Comhar* (January 1963), pp. 6–12, republished in Máirín Nic Eoin, ed. *Religio Poetae agus Aistí Eile* (Dublin: An Clóchomhar, 1987), pp. 11–21.
83. *Comhar* (December 1984). *Comhar* was edited at the time by Micheál Ó Cearúil, who was subsequently co-editor (with Seosamh Ó Murchú agus Antain Mag Shamhráin) of *Oghma* and later editor of *An Aimsir Óg*.
84. See, in particular Alan Titley, 'An Cogadh in Aghaidh na Critice', in *Chun Doirne: Rogha Aistí* (Belfast: Lagan Press, 1996), pp. 1–32; Nic Dhiarmada, 'Smulcairí, Fiosracht agus Eile'.

85. See Declan Kiberd, *Idir Dhá Chultúr* (Dublin: Coiscéim, 1993).
86. See, in particular chapter 8 'An Traidisiún Liteartha' in her *Fáinne an Lae agus an Athbheochan (1898–1900)* (Dublin: Cois Life, 1998), pp. 153–70.
87. Neil Lazarus, *Resistance in Postcolonial African Fiction* (New Haven and London: Yale University Press, 1990), p. 46.

Select bibliography

Breathnach, Diarmuid and Máire Ní Mhurchú, *Beathaisnéis a hAon: 1882–1982*, Dublin: An Clóchomhar, 1986.

Beathaisnéis a Dó: 1882–1982, Dublin: An Clóchomhar, 1990.

Beathaisnéis a Trí: 1882–1982, Dublin: An Clóchomhar, 1992.

Beathaisnéis a Ceathair: 1882–1982, Dublin: An Clóchomhar, 1994.

Beathaisnéis a Cúig: 1882–1982, Dublin: An Clóchomhar, 1997.

Delap, Breandán, *Úrscéalta Stairiúla na Gaeilge*, Dublin: An Clóchomhar, 1993.

Denvir, Gearóid, *Cadhan Aonair: Saothar Liteartha Mháirtín Uí Chadhain*, Dublin: An Clóchomhar, 1987.

Kiberd, Declan, *Idir Dhá Chultúr*, Dublin: Coiscéim, 1993.

Mag Shamhráin, Antain, *Litríocht, Léitheoireacht, Critic*, Dublin: An Clóchomhar, 1986.

Ní Annracháin, Máire and Bríona Nic Dhiarmada, eds. *Téacs agus Comhthéacs: Gnéithe de Chritic na Gaeilge*, Cork: Cork University Press, 1998.

Ní Bhaoighill, Caoimhe, 'An Drámaíocht Ghaeilge 1954–89: Stair agus Ceacht', *Irisleabhar Mhá Nuad* (1991), pp. 131–61.

Nic Eoin, Máirín, *An Litríocht Réigiúnach*, Dublin: An Clóchomhar, 1982.

'An Clóchomhar agus Léann na Gaeilge', *Studia Hibernica* 31 (2000–2001), pp. 105–17.

Trén bhFearann Breac: An Díláithriú Cultúir agus Nualitríocht na Gaeilge, Dublin: Cois Life, 2005.

Ó Conaire, Breandán, *Myles na Gaeilge: Lámhleabhar ar Shaothar Gaeilge Bhrian Ó Nualláin*, Dublin: An Clóchomhar, 1986.

Ó Conghaile, Micheál, 'Coisméigeacha Beaga agus Coisméigeacha Móra', *Bliainiris* (2001), pp. 279–318.

Ó Doibhlin, Breandán, *Aistí Critice agus Cultúir*, Dublin: Foilseacháin Náisiúnta Teoranta, n.d.

Aistí Critice agus Cultúir II, Belfast: Lagan Press, 1997.

Ó Fiannachta, Pádraig, ed. *An tÚrscéal sa Ghaeilge: Léachtaí Cholm Cille* 21 (1991).

Litríocht na Gaeltachta: Léachtaí Cholm Cille 19 (1989).

Ó hAnluain, Eoghan, ed. *Léachtaí Uí Chadhain I*, Dublin: An Clóchomhar, 1989.

Ó hUiginn, Ruairí, ed. *Iriseoireacht na Gaeilge: Léachtaí Cholm Cille* 28 (1998).

Ó Siadhail, Pádraig, *Stair Dhrámaíocht na Gaeilge 1900–1970*, Inverin: Cló Iar-Chonnachta, 1993.

Ó Tuama, Seán, *Cúirt, Tuath agus Bruachbhaile: Aistí agus Dréachtaí Liteartha*, Dublin: An Clóchomhar, n.d.

Repossessions: Selected Essays on the Irish Literary Heritage, Cork: Cork University Press, 1995.

Titley, Alan, *An tÚrscéal Gaeilge*, Dublin: An Clóchomhar, 1991.

7

Contemporary poetry in Irish: 1940–2000

LOUIS DE PAOR

The excitement generated by Seán Ó Tuama's 1950 anthology *Nuabhéarsaíocht* is evident in the publishers' claim that the collection would vindicate those who believed any worthwhile literature Ireland might produce in the future would be written in Irish. The advertisement for the book in advance of its publication goes on to declare, with enthusiasm bordering on the belligerent, that Ó Tuama's selection of poems from the previous decade should silence those who believe the term 'Irish' to be nothing more than a useful geographical definition.[1] The idea that the emergence of a Modernist poetics confidently articulated in Irish corresponds to a more widespread sense of national renewal during and following the Second World War is further articulated in Ó Tuama's considered, but nonetheless polemical, introduction and reiterated enthusiastically by contemporary reviewers. In a review published in *Feasta* in February 1951, Criostóir Mac Aonghusa, a careful and scrupulous critic, suggests the achievement of the poets whose work is included in *Nuabhéarsaíocht* is such that a revival in the fortunes of Irish is imminent, that if Irish people have sufficient courage to commit themselves to learning the language, 'níl sé beo an té chuirfeadh gobán ina mbéal' (no one could silence them).

Nuabhéarsaíocht contains poems by twenty-one poets published between 1939 and 1949. That most of those included were not native speakers of Irish anticipates the accelerated development of the modern lyric mode in Irish away from the vigorous tradition of folk or community poetry that continues to be the dominant form of poetry in Gaeltacht areas.[2] A number of older poets of established reputation are acknowledged by a single poem, an indication of their waning reputation as their achievements have been outpaced and, in some cases, outdated by the radical innovations of their juniors. A single poem by An Suibhneach Meann (Pádraig Mac Suibhne), the sole representative of the formally and thematically conservative Dámhscoil Mhúscraighe,[3] indicates the major realignment that had taken place since the publication of Éamonn Cuirtéis's 1920 anthology, *Cuisle na hÉigse*, thirty years previously. Interestingly, more traditional forms are also favoured by two younger poets, Tomás Tóibín and Eoghan Ó Tuairisc, whose subsequent work would be characterised by greater experiment and innovation. The importance of translation in the modernising process is acknowledged by the inclusion of adaptations from French by Monsignor Pádraig de Brún and Tomás Ó Floinn, whose work incorporates the influence of contemporary and classical European literature. Other notable contributions include the exotic voice of Micheál Mac Liammóir, the historical sense and public engagement of Séamus Ó hAodha, the formal conviction and political awareness of Séamus Ó Neill as well as the tenderness of his more domestic poems, and the surprising gentleness of Brendan Behan, the youngest contributor, whose early poems in Irish seemed at the time an earnest of more substantial work to come.

In its inclusions and exclusions, then, *Nuabhéarsaíocht* was unusually alert to the contemporary moment and astute in its critical judgement, its careful discrimination between the achievements of a previous generation whose reputations have subsequently diminished and a number of emerging voices whose work now provides the standard by which modern poetry in Irish is judged. The precedence given to the work of Máirtín Ó Direáin, Seán Ó Ríordáin and Máire Mhac an tSaoi in Ó Tuama's anthology has been vindicated by the passage of time, but in 1950 it was an audacious piece of literary revisionism, pre-empting the deliberations of future critics in its estimation of the three most outstanding younger poets, two of whom had yet to publish a full collection in their own right.

Despite the enthusiasm of contemporary critics for Ó Tuama's anthology, the persistence of a more conservative poetics is evident in the work of an earlier generation of poets who continued to publish work in the 1950s and 1960s apparently undisturbed by the achievements of their Modernist successors. In her review of Fionnán Mac Cártha's *Amhráin ó Dheireadh an Domhain* (1953) and Pádraig Ó Miléadha's *Trí Glúine Gaedhal*, (1953), Máire Mhac an tSaoi applauded the senior poets' unerring use of language while deploring the complete absence of innovation in their work (*Feasta*, September 1954). In an illuminating preface to his own 1956 anthology, *Nua-Fhilí 1 1942–1952*, Séamus Ó Céilleachair insisted on religious faith as a necessary ingredient in the production of poetry and went on to counsel his contemporaries on the necessity for strict allegiance to the Gaelic tradition and the rigorous exclusion of all influence emanating from English. Although a much less discriminating selection than Ó Tuama's, the continued popularity of Ó Céilleachair's book suggests a continuity of literary and moral values shared by the editor and a considerable readership as well as by a great many of the poets included.

Máirtín Ó Direáin and Liam S. Gógan

There is general consensus as to the groundbreaking significance of *Coinnle Geala*, the first collection of Máirtín Ó Direáin (1910–88), published at his own expense in 1942. In that initial volume and two subsequent collections, *Dánta Aniar* (1943) and *Rogha Dánta* (1950), the Aran poet is credited with introducing a Modernist sensibility to poetry in Irish, fulfilling Pearse's prediction that a new poetry in Irish would be grounded in a detailed knowledge of earlier phases of the Irish tradition but equally familiar with contemporary European practice. The sense of alienation, of spiritual and emotional dislocation which is characteristic of the Modernist imagination is evident throughout Ó Direáin's work, where the concerns of his European contemporaries are modified by the poet's personal circumstances in the context of extraordinarily rapid change in Ireland in the 1940s and subsequent decades. The disruption of traditional certainties, of a human identity founded on a secure relationship with God, family and community, and the crisis of confidence in man apparently made in God's image but nonetheless capable of obscene atrocities against his fellow man, inform the work of Ó Direáin and his contemporaries in Irish as they do the work of writers in English and other European languages, albeit in a more oblique manner. 'All this and the Hydrogen Bomb too,' is Ó Direáin's rebuke to those who cite with naive approval the benefits of 'progress'.[4]

Ó Direáin's abiding theme is the spiritual and moral decay he associates with the disintegration of traditional rural communities under the pressure of urbanisation and increasing modernisation. His own experience of dislocation on leaving Inishmore at the age of seventeen to work in the post office in Galway and eventually to a lifelong career of clerical work in Dublin can be seen as representative of his generation during a period of rapid demographic change which saw the gradual collapse of many rural communities as more and more young people relocated to the cities and towns in search of employment and greater economic opportunity. The sense of doubt and despair that accompanied this disruption of community, the bitterness and nostalgia of the uprooted, is articulated in Ó Direáin's poetry in language culled from the argot of peasant farmers and fishermen in his native Aran and enhanced by echoes of Ó Bruadair, Ó Rathaille and others among his predecessors in the annals of Irish literature. As Frank O'Brien has pointed out in *Filíocht*

Ghaeilge na Linne Seo (1968), the first sustained critique of modern poetry in Irish, the literary resonances gleaned from his extensive reading in earlier Irish literature are supplemented in Ó Direáin's work by familiarity with poetry in English with Yeats, Eliot and Pound among the more obvious and abiding influences.[5]

Ó Direáin's poetic diction is capable of extraordinary dignity, a grandeur that rarely compromises its colloquial clarity. A footnote appended to 'Scéal an Tí Mhóir' on its initial publication in *Feasta* (May 1951) provides an insight into his poetic method. The footnote provides a gloss on the term 'trá-ghaoithe', which is used in preference to more clichéd images such as 'cúr na habhann' (river-froth) and 'sneachta aon oíche' (overnight snow) to indicate the transience of temporal human achievement. Ó Direáin elaborates on the unfamiliar image, a technical term used in gathering seaweed to refer to a harvest cut at ebbtide but not gathered immediately as it will be brought ashore by the imminent flood-tide. It is a measure of Ó Direáin's achievement that the technical language of work among peasant farmers and fishermen can be developed beyond the context that originally lent it meaning to impress itself on a readership largely unaware of its practical function among the remnants of the poet's own community. With the further disintegration of that community, there is a valedictory element to Ó Direáin's poems, where a language whose purchase on empirical reality has become more and more attenuated maintains, nonetheless, its grip on the imagination.

Ó Direáin has been criticised for his failure to develop beyond the primary contradiction articulated in his work between the communal values of traditional rural society and the deracinated individualism of the modern urban industrial world.[6] It might be argued that there is a similar stagnation in the language of his poetry as his constant evocation of life in Aran during his own childhood gradually deteriorates into cliché. In the earlier work, the details of everyday life in Inishmore are remembered with great clarity and expressed in a language of deceptive simplicity. In the later poems, the link with the remembered Eden of childhood and the subsequent fall from grace becomes frayed and the language, at times, appears bankrupt of any meaningful connection with the actual. In the shorter lyric poems however, such as 'Cuireadh do Mhuire', 'An tEarrach Thiar', 'Dínit an Bhróin', 'Ealabhean', 'Mí an Mheithimh', and many more besides, Ó Direáin achieves a rare integrity of language and feeling, a confident manipulation of form and style unmatched in modern Irish. There is a similar assurance and craft at work in 'Cranna Foirtil', 'Blianta an Chogaidh', 'Stoite' and 'Fuaire', which give vent to a growing bitterness at the moral degeneration of the modern world. In the longer poems, 'Ó Mórna' and 'Ár Ré Dhearóil', the narrative structure allows the poet to extend his lyric ability over a broader range with little diminution of the linguistic grace and emotional conviction of the shorter poems. Even in his least memorable writing, Ó Direáin remains the consummate stylist, the master craftsman. His renovation of traditional usage to articulate his own Modernist sensibility remains the watermark by which subsequent experiments in language, form and style are judged.

The extent to which Ó Direáin's achievement has influenced the critical reception of modern poetry in Irish is evident as early as Tomás Ó Floinn's perceptive review of *Coinnle Geala*, published in *Comhar* (June 1942), where he applauds the primacy of demotic speech and emotional sincerity over artifice in his work. Interestingly, by the time he came to review Ó Direáin's second collection, *Dánta Aniar* (1943), Ó Floinn had moderated his approval, regretting the absence of 'the deep undertones, the organ notes', the lack of turmoil and conflict which, he argued, were necessary to the formation of poetic sensibility (*Comhar*, October 1943). While such criticism of a poet in the early stages of development may seem unduly harsh, Ó Floinn anticipates the reservations subsequently expressed by Seán Ó Tuama and others who have argued that Ó Direáin's work remains in a state of arrested development, compromised by a refusal or inability to allow any deeper disturbance to disrupt the formal and linguistic stability which are hallmarks of his writing.

In terms of literary reputation, the work of Liam S. Gógan (1891–1979) has, perhaps, been the greatest casualty of Ó Direáin's success and the consequent preoccupation with the vernacular *caint na ndaoine* (the speech of the people) as the touchstone of linguistic and artistic integrity. His work is characterised by a dynamic archaism, a radical departure from the prescriptive limitations of the demotic in an attempt to move Irish beyond the boundaries of historical precedent. Given his own work as a scholar of early Irish and a principal contributor to Dinneen's dictionary, Gógan was ideally placed for the kind of literary archaeology he advocates in his critical writing, where he reminds a largely unsympathetic readership of the recuperative function of poetry in giving currency again to forgotten coinage. In his introduction to *Dánta agus Duanta* (1952), Gógan elaborates on his own metrical experiments and the possibility of effecting a new accommodation between native and European models through translation. His own familiarity with and enthusiasm for German poetry, first encountered during his time as a prisoner of war at the Welsh prison camp of Frongoch following the 1916 Rising, is given as an exemplar. While applauding the achievement of his juniors, Máirtín Ó Direáin and Seán Ó Ríordáin, who have made the preoccupation with the personal a literary aesthetic, he confesses himself wary of the restrictions imposed by 'miseachas' (me-ism) on the production of poetry. In reviewing *Dánta Eile* (1946) for *Comhar* in March 1947, Tomás Ó Floinn had earlier abandoned his usual circumspection to bestow upon Gógan the title of 'an té is cumasaí atá ag scríobhadh filíochta i nua-ré seo na Gaeilge' (the most accomplished of those now writing poetry in modern Irish).

The critical neglect of Gógan, already evident at the height of his achievement, is particularly unfortunate as much of his work anticipates innovations usually credited to his successors. From his earliest work, he demonstrates many of the characteristics associated with the modern period: scholarly familiarity with precedents in the Irish literary tradition, receptivity to European influence, formal experiment and the extension of the semantic capacity of Irish to include the modern urban industrial world as subject matter and as a legitimate linguistic resource. The urban setting of a train station, for instance, is easily manipulated in 'An Ceileabhradh Deireannach' where the train provides a metaphoric vehicle for the poem's preoccupation with the passage of time. The use of metaphor as a structural principle and, indeed, as a strategy for the consideration of abstract concepts given concrete expression in the course of a poem, an innovation usually credited to Ó Ríordáin, is as characteristic of Gógan as it is of the younger poet. His refusal to accept the limitations imposed on Irish by its wretched colonial history is, for the most part, justified by his own achievement in developing an alternative diction replete with classical allusion to Greek, Latin and early Irish literature and an informed knowledge of contemporary European history, art and literature. At his best, in poems such as 'Eachtra Criosaintéimeach', 'Fantais Choille', 'Liobharn Stáit', 'Tré-Líneach' and perhaps his best-known and most frequently anthologised poem, 'Na Coisithe', Gógan's individual voice, in all its strange impersonality, is unhampered by its weight of erudition. In these and a handful of other poems, the difficulty of language is an integral part of the poetic process rather than a vain and inessential embellishment, a necessary strategy in the approach to a psychological or emotional truth gradually revealed.

While the crisis of the war years is mentioned by critics and poets alike as a crucial influence in the emergence of a Modernist poetics in Irish in the 1940s and early 1950s, there is little overt reference in the poems themselves to the fraught international context in which they were written. If the preoccupation with the private and the personal is itself a reaction against the public atrocity of war, the exclusion of any direct reference to the international conflict is nonetheless remarkable. The stable pieties of Ó Direáin's 'Coinnle ar Lasadh' gain a peculiar poignancy from the date appended to the poem (6 January 1939, the Feast of the Epiphany), but the contrast between the gentle sanctity of the candlelit welcome for the infant Saviour and the turmoil of European war is not explicitly a part of the domestic drama enacted within the poem itself. A handful of poems by Séamus Ó Néill (1910–81) provide a rare and worthy exception to the rule of the blind eye. The political commitment and international awareness evident in 'Aoileach' (*Comhar*, July 1942), 'Abschied' (*Comhar*, April 1943), 'Do'n Ghréig' (*Comhar*, May 1943) and 'Stalingrad' (*Comhar*, July 1943) are at odds with Ó Néill's own reputation as formally and thematically conservative. 'Aoileach', a contemporary gloss on the war in Russia, achieves its effect by an unexpected subversion of apparently traditional clichés. 'Abschied' remembers the contribution of German scholarship to the study of Irish literature and language and contrasts the physical beauty of the German countryside with the Rhine in wartime 'ag brúchtadh le fuil' (overflowing with blood). 'Do'n Ghréig' celebrates individual heroism over the anti-human technologies of war. Another poem worthy of mention is 'Clog an Chlochair' (*Comhar*, November 1943), where the consolation of Christian belief assuages the ontological terror confronted in the poem. The comforting image of the church bells, suggestive of stability and devotion, anticipates a much more subversive treatment of the same image in Ó Ríordáin's 'Siollabadh'.

In an essay on the uneasy relationship between writers and critics, Máirtín Ó Direáin cites the acerbic observation of Liam Ó Rinn: 'dá gcaiteá méaróg ó bharr Cholún Nelson go dtitfeadh sé ar chinsire éigin' (if you threw a stone from the top of Nelson's Pillar, it would hit a censor).[7] A trawl through the principal literary journals of the period confirms the moral conservatism of poetry in Irish in the 1940s and early 1950s, the conformity of progressives and traditionalists alike to received values.[8] The poets' allegiance to the moral guidance of the Catholic church is apparently unforced and there is, for the most part, little evidence of any subterranean current of resistance or dissent. The literary expression of unquestioned faith is, with very few exceptions, heartfelt and unproblematic, uncomplicated by the sense of religious doubt generally associated with European Modernism. The spiritual despair following a momentary lapse of faith articulated in Eithne Ní Chonaill's 'Caillte' (*Comhar*, April 1943) is quite exceptional in this regard. Although ultimately unsuccessful, her innovative use of compound words to contain the strain of emotional and metaphysical conflict is a foretaste of a technique subsequently employed to the same end but to much greater effect by Seán Ó Ríordáin. Significantly, Ó Ríordáin's earliest published work is more remarkable for its linguistic strangeness and technical innovation than for any sustained questioning of received values.

Despite the innovations of his early work, Máirtín Ó Direáin is the laureate of this moral consensus. The almost aristocratic dignity of peasant endurance and the stability of traditional community values articulated in his poetry are an extension of the idealism of early cultural nationalism, an affirmation of the heroic aspirations of those involved in the project of state formation in the 1920s and 1930s. The bitterness and disillusion which later come to dominate his poetry speak of a more general disappointment at the failure to achieve or sustain those ideals. The deteriorating behaviour of women in particular is seen as symptomatic of the moral decline of the war years, when the constant threat of imminent death led to all kinds of indulgence: 'ragús aisteoireachta agus ragús péintéireachta, ragús óil, agus ragúis eile nach luafar' (a flurry of acting, painting and drinking, and other unmentionable urges).[9] Not unusually, the destiny of Ireland is confused with the fate of individual women, who are denigrated for failing to realise the imagined national ideal in the actuality of their everyday lives. Ó Direáin's treatment of such material is occasionally vicious as the reprehensible sexual mores of modern urban women, in thrall to Dior and Max Factor, are contrasted with the incorruptibile piety of the shawled women of Aran. In 'Girseach Mná', the poet senses a premature awareness of sexual power with all its destructive possibilities in the young girl who blushes when he looks at her. In this and a number of other poems, the destructive potential of female beauty is innate, its exploitation inevitable. The gentle regret at the physical disintegration of a lover who has died in 'Leannán dá ghrádh a fuair bás' is replaced by a barely restrained gloating at the destruction of female sexual power in 'Éiric an Ghrádha' as time punishes the vanity of irresponsible beauty. 'Do bhaoth-mhaighdin ar bith' reiterates the resentment with apparent satisfaction that age has left the everywoman of the title thrown aside 'mar sheanbhalcais éadaigh' (like old clothes). These poems are unremarkable in terms of the sentiments expressed and distinguished only from many others in this period by Ó Direáin's superior manipulation of language and form which adds considerably to their emotional and psychological power. Interestingly, the most negative of these poems are not included in any of Ó Direáin's collections and no mention is made of them in his collected poems.[10]

Brendan Behan

Brendan Behan's (1923–64) 'Do Bhev', which applauds the materialism of a young woman who finds comfort in marriage to a wealthy older man and physical satisfaction elsewhere, provides welcome, if very light, relief. As against that, 'Aithrighe' articulates a surprisingly gentle but entirely orthodox religious devotion. That the poem was written in Strangeways Jail, Manchester, during a four-month sojourn there for travelling on a false passport, lends it a degree of poignancy otherwise unachieved in the writing itself. The same might be said of 'Jackeen ag Caoineadh na mBlascaod', which laments the depopulation of the Great Blasket while celebrating its natural beauty in the expected manner; the emotional impact of the poem is strengthened by advertising the fact that it was written in Mountjoy Jail, Dublin in July 1947, where Behan had been sentenced to a month's imprisonment on charges of being drunk and disorderly and assaulting a Garda.[11] If the prison context is an incidental effect in the earlier poems, it is integral to the emotional drama of 'Uaigneas', where the remembered taste of blackberries and the whistle of a passing train accentuate the loneliness of the prisoner. While poems in celebration of James Joyce and Oscar Wilde flirt with moral transgression by acknowledging figures of dubious repute, there is, nonetheless, an acknowledgement of prevailing standards as the moral subversion of Joyce and Wilde is suggested obliquely rather than declared openly. Wilde's deathbed conversion provokes the cheerful conclusion of 'Do Sheán Ó Súilleabháin' that Oscar had it both ways. The muted interrogation of conventional morality is more a momentary indulgence than a corrective as the not so subtle *double entendre* defuses the threat that might have been posed by a more overt declaration of Wilde's bisexuality. The humour of 'Do Bhev' and of the closing lines of 'Do Sheán Ó Súilleabháin' may have disarmed contemporary readers but it also rendered more or less harmless the challenge which a more forthright treatment of the material might have presented to standard morality.[12]

Máire Mhac an tSaoi

The most consistent challenge to the prevailing moral consensus is contained in the work of Máire Mhac an tSaoi (b. 1922), which, on occasion, admits the absolute nature of female desire as a threat to the prevailing social and moral order. While the women whose subversive integrity is invoked in 'AthDheirdre' and 'Gan Réiteach' appear careless of the consequences of their unappeasable desire, the author's dedication of her first collection, *Margadh na Saoire* (1956), 'don té a léifidh le fabhar' (to the well-disposed reader) indicates a certain apprehension as to the sanction her work might provoke. The need for discretion is further evident in the organisation of the poems into different categories under the headings of 'Liricí' (lyrics), 'Eachtraíocht agus amhráin tíre' (tales and folk songs) and 'Aistriúcháin' (translations). That this is not merely a scholarly convenience or a hangover from her academic work is evident in the progress of the work itself from one section to another. While the lyric poems are more or less orthodox in form and sentiment, the personae through which her poetic voice articulates itself in the imitations of traditional folk models allow a more subversive ethic to gradually assert and distinguish itself from the anonymity of pastiche. The transgression is most clearly voiced in the final section of the book in her translation of Lorca's 'An Bhean Mhídhílis' (The Unfaithful Wife), as though such immorality might be tolerated only at a cultural and geographical remove.

While Mac an tSaoi's imitation of the forms and poetic diction of earlier phases of Irish poetry from the bardic period through to the folk songs familiar to her from extended childhood visits to Dún Chaoin has been criticised as pastiche, the almost classical rigour of her language also provides a cover for a more subversive enterprise, deflecting attention from the challenge posed to standard morality in her most achieved work. The ventriloquism that allows an alternative morality to be articulated through a mask may be a necessary subterfuge, a strategy which allows otherwise prohibited emotions to be expressed discreetly. The near anonymity of the initial 'M', the signature to her earliest published work in *Comhar*, which conceals her gender as well as her personal identity, is another form of subterfuge that allows the otherwise unspeakable its say. Her work, in any case, is more conflicted than is immediately apparent. That her most famous poem, 'Ceathrúintí Mháire Ní Ógáin',[13] should be attributed to a persona whose name is synonymous with the folly of young women is, to some extent, a corrective to the transgression enacted in the course of the poem where the world extends no further than the edge of the bed and the woman abused in love declares herself careless of people's suspicion and of clerical prohibition. Although she prays to God to liberate her in the opening lines of the poem and declares her desire to conform to the established moral order, she reiterates in the closing verses her willingness to repeat the transgression even as she repents her original sin.

That tension between individual desire and conventional values is central to Máire Mhac an tSaoi's poetic method. The orthodox sentiments expressed in many of her poems are less a genuflection to the prevailing moral codes than an indication of the ambivalence and confusion dramatised in her best work. The nationalist sentiment of her elegy for an executed sixteenth-century Irish chieftain, 'Inquisitio 1584', is moderated in the later 'An Fuath (1967)', where she reminds herself and the reader that hatred which blooms in conflict might also sustain a garden built on sand-dunes between two tides 'mar a maireann ár mná 's ár bpáistí' (where our wives and children live). The conflict in the North provokes an even more fundamental realignment in 'Fód an Imris: Ard-Oifig an Phoist, 1986'. The reverence of 'Oíche Nollag' and 'Amhrán Céad Chomaoine' is countered by a fundamental doubt and half-belief in 'Bás mo Mháthar', while an uneasy reconciliation is effected in 'Moment of Truth', when the ultimate question as to God's existence, posed by a dying woman, is answered with less than wholehearted conviction: 'Am briathar ná feadar / Ach nach mór dom creideamh na gcomharsan / mar mhapa chun go mbreacfainn marc air' (I honestly don't know / only that I need the neighbours' faith / as a map I can leave a mark on).

The powerful female antecedents whose exemplary courage she is incapable of or unwilling to follow in 'AthDheirdre' and 'Gan Réiteach' provide the heroic model for 'Adhlacadh Iníon an Fhile', where death is preferable to old age and, indeed, for a poem of homage to Nuala Ní Dhomhnaill, 'Do Nuala Ní Dhomhnaill', whose achievement might be seen as a vindication of some of the more transgressive elements in her own work. The emergence of a subsequent generation of women poets in Irish may account, in part, for the growing conviction of the dramatised 'I' in Máire Mhac an tSaoi's later collections, where she flouts the standard conventions of authorial discretion by exploiting the overlap between her public and private personae. In addressing by their proper names members of her immediate and extended family and others, she provokes the reader to relate her poems to the known details of her intimate but nonetheless public life. Despite the conventions of contemporary critical practice, which would disallow such a conflation of biography and poetry, her later work exploits common knowledge of the domestic details of her private life to produce work that allows the intimate to infiltrate the public, to reorder and rewrite it from within.

Although her work has been sporadic, a measure, perhaps, of the difficulty of sustained innovation, the most persistent aspect of her achievement is the precedence given to the intimate and the domestic in her poems. Long before the publication of Eavan Boland's groundbreaking volume in English, *Nightfeed* (1982), which placed the nursing mother and her infant child in a nighttime suburban kitchen at the heart of a poetic universe, Máire Mhac an tSaoi had effected a similar revolution in the language and thematics of poetry in poems such as 'Do Shíle', 'An Chéad Bhróg' and 'Comhrá ar Shráid'. The same reversal of values informs later poems such as 'Do Mháiréad sa tSiopa Cóirithe Gruaige' and 'Codladh an Ghaiscígh', where the baroque language is matched by unusual intensity and intricacy of feeling. The central ambivalences of her work and the integrity of her own refusal to effect a facile reconciliation between them is still evident in her most recent poems where she continues, despite her own stated religious convictions, to celebrate the independence of women who refuse to be intimidated by the authority of the Church and its moral sanctions. There is a further emotional complication in the more intimate poems as the passage of time causes a deepening tenderness in filial relationships on the one hand and a growing horror on the other at the imminence of physical disintegration, barely assuaged by the consolation of Christian belief. The integrity of her achievement, her subtle interrogation and gradual subversion of prevailing orthodoxies, and her influence on the generation of women poets who emerged in the 1980s have been considerable although understated and, perhaps, insufficiently acknowledged.

Seán Ó Ríordáin

In the years preceding the publication of his first volume of poems, *Eireaball Spideoige* (1952), the work of Seán Ó Ríordáin (1916–77) was the subject of extraordinary critical attention based on a handful of published poems. The remarkable claims made for a poet without a full collection to his name indicates the profound disturbance occasioned by his earliest work, a *frisson* comparable to that created by Baudelaire in French literature according to his most formidable supporter.[14] The extent of that shock, and the difficulty of effecting a less than quiet revolution in critical and poetic practice, might equally be gauged from the vehemence and longevity of the debate that raged in Irish and English in the pages of *Comhar*, *Feasta*, *Studies*, *Inniu* and the *Irish Times* following the publication of his debut collection.[15] The controversy, which eventually brought Patrick Kavanagh and Brendan Behan into the fray, on opposite sides, brought charges of illegitimacy and incompetence in language and metre as well as unorthodoxy in philosophical and religious matters against a poet whose work is characterised by doubt and uncertainty and a rigorous self-questioning.

Ó Ríordáin's work is more in keeping with the prevailing spirit of European Modernism than that of any of his contemporaries. Born into the *Breac-Ghaeltacht*[16] of Baile Mhúirne (Ballyvourney), County Cork, he grew up in a bilingual community where the traditional authority of Irish was rapidly giving way to the encroachments of English. The sense of cultural unease arising from the confusion of two languages was further complicated by illness and the threat of imminent mortality from the time of his first diagnosis with tuberculosis at the age of twenty. In an interview recorded some weeks before his death, he remarked that the degree of TB had proved a greater resource for the production of poetry than that of BA.[17] The isolation from family and community which was part of the prescribed treatment for tuberculosis confirmed his sense of alienation and led to a profound and tormented questioning of identity out of which Ó Ríordáin elaborated his own poetic technique based on the unremitting quest for authenticity. The extended preface to *Eireaball Spideoige* is as much an elaboration of a personal morality as it is a literary manifesto. Ó Ríordáin argues for surrender to the otherness of the world as a way of discovering an authentic self which would be the arbiter of personal and literary integrity. He proposes that poetry take the impression of the otherness of the world in language sensitive to the essence of the subject considered, the thingness of things. He cites Hopkins's theory of inscape in support of his own aspiration towards a poetry that would register the inalienable and irreducible 'haeccitas' of each and every aspect of the animate and inanimate world.

It is a philosophy and literary technique familiar from the writings of St Thomas Aquinas through to the fiction of James Joyce and is, perhaps, the most useful strategy for a sympathetic reading of Ó Ríordáin's poetry. In poems such as 'An Lacha', 'An Gealt', 'Cúl an Tí', 'Siollabadh', 'An Dall sa Studio' and a great many more of his shorter poems, a particular register of language is developed to take the impression of the poem's subject, whether it be the ungainly dignity of the living aberration that is a duck, the accelerated tension and subsequent blunting of feeling that characterise mental breakdown, the orderly chaos of a backgarden, the dehumanising of the infirm that reduces existence to a pulse rate, or the undiminished personal vanity of a blind man. The poet's approach to his material is, perhaps, most evident in 'Malairt', where the character Turnbull's empathy for the essential sadness of the horse is such that he inhabits that sadness, and by a reciprocal act of fellow-feeling, the horse shares the burden of the man's suffering. In Ó Ríordáin's work empathy is a technique that admits the otherness of the world and allows its articulation in language attuned to its essential difference.

Aside from an insignificant number of grammatical and syntactical errors and a handful of mistakes in the use of idiomatic expressions which he subsequently remedied,[18] criticism of Ó Ríordáin's (ab)use of language is based on a profound misunderstanding of the function of disordered language in his work. The debate over the presence of English influence is a distraction as the source of the alleged contamination of Irish is almost immaterial when set against the reordering of language that is a crucial element of his poetic signature. Ó Ríordáin's deliberate disordering of language is deeply subversive in flouting the notion that, in a broken tradition, a complete reconciliation is possible or, indeed, desirable between an individual writer and the inherited patterns of language that survive in the apparently undisturbed speech of the Gaeltacht and in earlier phases of the literary and oral tradition. He is acutely aware of the dissonance between the authority of such precedents and the disruptive needs of his own imagination. While acknowledging the coherence and facility of the tradition, he insists on keeping his distance and refuses to be consumed by it. He addresses Irish as 'a theanga seo leath-liom' (language that is half-mine) and struggles to effect an accommodation with the received patterns of the language without compromising the separate integrity of his own voice.

The term he coins for reordering language according to his own needs is 'Ríordánú', and that Riordanising of Irish with its consequent estrangement of the reader schooled in conventional habits is, perhaps, the most distinctive and challenging feature of his work. Contrary to the advice offered in 'Fill Arís', which recommends a complete alignment with the tradition as it has survived in the Gaeltacht community of Dún Chaoin and a rejection of the dislocations of colonial history since the Battle of Kinsale, Ó Ríordáin's work is a profound challenge to the notion that such a tradition exists and that an unproblematic relationship is possible between the received patterns of Irish and the individual poet. The surprising juxtapositions barely contained in the metaphoric language of his poems are acts of creative violence made necessary by a discontinuity of imagination and language, the cultural inheritance of a divided tradition. The compound words, which are as characteristic of his work as the strange metaphors, carry the imprint of psychological strain and emotional pressure in a fragmented diction whose very instability and strangeness is a necessary and authentic response to the deformation of the Irish tradition. The incongruous extended metaphors are developed as metaphysical conceits that allow sustained interrogation of the most basic dichotomies of human existence, of a life lived under the shadow of death. The attempt to reconcile language and reality, to insist that words establish some purchase on the empirical, is a function of profound insecurity with received structures of meaning. 'Pound' is a fine example of the scrupulous effort to make language accord with empirical reality as the word 'feairín' (a diminutive man), in this instance, incorporates the essential presence in the world of the poem's subject.

While the longer poems made a considerable impression on contemporary readers, subsequent criticism has revised that judgement in favour of the shorter lyrics. That revision may in turn require further reconsideration as the longer poems, despite occasional lapses, represent the most sustained attempt in modern Irish at a poetry capable of extended consideration of the most fundamental questions of human existence. In 'Oileán agus Oileán Eile', 'Na hÓinmhidí', 'Saoirse', 'Cnoc Mellerí' and 'Adhlacadh mo Mháthar', Ó Ríordáin forged a flexible and highly effective rhetoric, grounded in the empirical, which allows rigorous and extended investigation of the metaphysical dimension of human existence. He challenges the ethical and categorical distinction between the carnal and the spiritual, between the terror of existential freedom and the consolation of orthodox belief, between the temporal world and the unassuaged nostalgia for eternity. The final section of 'Saoirse', the only poem Ó Ríordáin himself claimed as entirely successful in fulfilling his original ambition,[19] is reminiscent of Hopkins in its dramatisation of the ontological terror and awesome responsibility of absolute human freedom. What Máire Mhac an tSaoi referred to in her review of *Eireaball Spideoige* (*Feasta*, March 1953) as 'gnáthscrupaill choinsiasa an ghnáthChaitlicigh óig sa tír agus san aois seo' (the usual scruples of conscience common to young Catholics in this country in this era) is also a persistent theme as the conflict between sexual desire and the abstinence advocated as the supreme human achievement by the Catholic church is dramatised to great effect in 'Cnoc Mellerí' and other poems. Despite his considerable influence, no subsequent poet in Irish has achieved, or, indeed, attempted the kind of philosophical inquiry and the reordering of language necessary to sustain that inquiry, negotiated by Ó Ríordáin in these remarkable poems.

There is a dramatic reduction in his poetic output following the publication of *Eireaball Spideoige*, the most substantial of his four volumes of poetry. The exhilarating iconoclasm of the earlier volume is less in evidence in the thirty pages of poems that comprise *Brosna*, published in 1964 after a twelve-year hiatus. In its place, there is a sustained intensity of language and feeling, an integrity of tone unmatched in any other single collection in modern Irish. Ó Ríordáin's poetic voice speaks with uncompromised authority and rare conviction as he achieves finally a dynamic realignment between the urgent needs of his own imagination and the stabilities of traditional usage. In the intervening years since the publication of *Eireaball Spideoige* in 1952, Ó Ríordáin had continued the relentless search for 'an mise ceart' (the correct me), an authentic self and a poetic voice capable of articulating that self in all its uncompromised individuality. In *Brosna*, he achieved a temporary reconciliation between his own voice and the reassuring stability of the vernacular as spoken in the Gaeltacht community of Dún Chaoin, a dynamic realignment which allowed his poetic voice to speak with the accumulated authority of tradition.

There is a considerable waning of achievement in Ó Ríordáin's work following *Brosna*. The pressure to conform and the distress of isolation are evident throughout as he attempts to acknowledge the tradition without disowning his own poetic voice. He is equally aware of the dangers of suffocation within the limits of a prescribed language and of his own exclusion from the authority available to those who reconcile themselves to the dictates of convention. As his later work moves ever closer to such a reconciliation, an accommodation which has all the appearance of capitulation, he acknowledges with regret the waning of inspiration that has accompanied the resolution of his differences with community, religion, language and tradition.[20] *Línte Liombó*, published in 1971, is the least substantial of the three volumes published during his lifetime. Although poems such as 'Súile Donna', 'Solas' and 'Tá Pearsa Imithe as an Saol' contain the unmistakeable inflections of Ó Ríordáin's poetic voice, there is a sense of growing exhaustion and little sustained engagement with the major preoccupations of the earlier work. In the posthumous collection, *Tar Éis mo Bháis* (1978), it seems as though the gradual acceptance of established authority has resolved the existential struggle towards meaning into an exhausted silence. If his confidence in his own abilities as a poet are shaken, his confidence in the creative capacity of Irish remains overwhelming: 'creidim go raibh riamh agus go bhfuil fós agus go mbeidh an fhilíocht is doimhne ar chumas an Éireannaigh lonnaithe sa Ghaeilge' (I believe the deepest poetry of which an Irish person is capable has always been, is now, and will continue to be, in Irish).[21]

Poetry in the 1960s

In the course of a useful, if occasionally ill-tempered debate, the bilingual poet and critic Conleth Ellis challenged the prevailing notion that there had been a lull in the development of poetry in Irish between the emergence of Ó Ríordáin, Ó Direáin and Máire Mhac an tSaoi in the 1940s and early 1950s and the precocious innovations of the *Innti* generation, who began to assert themselves in a recognisably different approach to language, form and subject matter from 1970 onwards.[22] Rejecting the notion that those born in the 1920s and 30s had somehow reneged on their responsibilities, leaving Michael Davitt and his *Innti* associates facing into a silence 'which resembled nothing so much as the great poetry hunger of the 19th century', Ellis railed against the perception of a 'lacuna' or 'hiatus' in Irish-language poetry 'hereinafter referred to as the L&H theory'. In support of his argument, he cited Art Ó Maolfabhail's 1964 collection *Aistí Dána*, 'a book that duly nodded in the direction of things past and then hurried off in its own modern way', and Pearse Hutchinson's 'excitingly iconoclastic and outward-looking' *Faoistin Bhacach* (1968). He also mentioned Tomás Tóibín, Seán Ó Leocháin, Seán Ó hÉigeartaigh and Pádraig Ó Croiligh, all of whom published interesting work during the 1960s and early 1970s, and Caitlín Maude, an accomplished actress and *sean-nós* singer whose published work, prior to her untimely death in 1980, shows a highly idiosyncratic voice of rare conviction taking liberties with language and form to considerable dramatic effect. While 'Amhrán Grá Vietnam' and 'Géibheann' are, perhaps, her best-known poems, 'Le Criathrach atá mo Dháimh' has more of the uncompromised intensity that characterises her remarkable singing. The list of neglected voices from the 1960s might be further extended to include the understated achievement of Caoimhín Ó Conghaile, whose work delivers its modest effects through a careful manipulation of language and form, and Réamonn Ó Muireadhaigh, whose two collections, *Athphreabadh na hÓige* (1964) and *Arán ar an Tábla* (1970), attempt the integration of a French impressionist technique into poetry in Irish. Of the remaining 'Ulster' poets whose contribution to the 'maintenance of continuity' had, according to Ellis, been underestimated, only Gréagóir Ó Dúill continued to produce substantial new work through the 1980s and 1990s.

Of all the poets mentioned by Ellis, the most substantial reputations are those of Eoghan Ó Tuairisc (1919–82) and Seán Ó Tuama (b. 1926). Published on the same day as his remarkable long poem in English, 'The Weekend of Dermot and Grace', Ó Tuairisc's 1964 volume *Lux Aeterna* contains an unusual degree of formal and linguistic variation, from the gentle devotion of 'Amhrán Nollag' and the nationalist ballad 'An Gunnadóir Mag Aoidh' to the bardic imitation of 'Deibhí don Dreancaid'. The most extraordinary poem in a distinguished collection is his angry and anguished response to the atrocity of Hiroshima, 'Aifreann na Marbh', the single most ambitious long poem in modern Irish. The structure of the poem follows the liturgical pattern of the Mass for the Dead as it reflects on heroic aspects of Irish history and the achievements of European civilisation, all of which are compromised by 'lá blaisféime na gréine' (the day of the sun's blasphemy). The ghosts of Eriugena, Dante, Pearse and O'Connell are invoked to no avail as the scientific abomination of a new sun obliterates the former glories of human and divine creation. From the 'blooming buzzing confusion' of war,[23] Ó Tuairisc, the former soldier, returning from his honeymoon to news of nuclear destruction, was forced to re-evaluate the totality of Christian heritage and values, of European and Irish literature and civilisation reduced to meaninglessness by 'ainmhian eolaíochta' (scientific lust). While Ó Tuairisc's contributions to the 1981 collection *Dialann sa Díseart*, co-authored with Rita E. Kelly, reveal an acute sensibility adapting language to articulate a moment of heightened sensory perception, his collected poems show a prodigious ability which does not sustain itself through an extended body of work. Given his difficult economic circumstances and his prolific production in other genres in Irish and in English, his work is, nonetheless, an extraordinary testament to a writer who lived his life in the republic of language with an almost religious devotion to the exigencies of the word.[24]

There is a similar sense of incompleteness in Seán Ó Tuama's poetry considered in isolation from his prodigious achievement as dramatist, scholar and critic. The 1964 collection *Faoileán na Beatha* is, however, one of the most significant works by an emerging poet published in a year which produced substantial work by a number of his contemporaries as well as Ó Ríordáin's crowning achievement in *Brosna*.[25] From the opening lament for a young man who drowned, through a poem in dedication to St Gobnait which regrets the contemporary lack of faith in the miraculous among 'críostaithe seo na droch-réasúnaíochta nach eol / Dóibh riamh aon taibhreamh' (these unreasoning Christians who know nothing of dreams), to the long poem 'Baoithín', which dramatises the imagined return of an early Irish saint to Ireland and concludes with the advice of Colm Cille that suffering and tolerance must now replace the heroics of Cú Chulainn, the poems are infused with a profound sense of Christian devotion. By the time *Saol Fó Thoinn* was published in 1978, the Christian sensibility which had been a structural principle in the earlier work had apparently collapsed to be replaced by an agnostic humanism foreshadowed in 'Amhrán na Geilte Mná' in the 1964 volume. Empathy with unnecessary but inevitable suffering and the unassuagable trauma of human mortality replace the consolation of Christian belief in *Saol Fó Thoinn* and in the 1988 collection *An Bás i dTír na nÓg*. The sensual animal pleasure of the flesh provides momentary relief from the unavoidable barbarism of God, which afflicts the helpless and children to the extent that the poet can no longer grieve for deceased friends or, indeed, for his own death. He could sooner forgive the Black and Tans than a God who provoked fear in his father, despite his faith, at the approach of death. As against the flawed creation of a careless God, there is some comfort in the notion of a shared humanity that mitigates the horror of oblivion and is best expressed by 'the poet' in 'Rousseau na Gaeltachta' who insists that a young girl be let grow without impediment 'go dtína hairde cheapaithe: / tá an t-aer fós bog os a cionn' (to whatever height she is meant for: the air is still soft above her head). The respite is momentary, however, as nothing can assuage the torment of the 78-year-old widow on the death of her 84-year-old husband, a prince whose death she laments with shrieks and 'méireanna págánacha' (pagan fingers) while the Christians in attendance pray the 'sruth bolcánach' (volcanic flow) of her grief subside. Even the consolation of human empathy is undermined in *An Bás i dTír na nÓg* as the incontinent old man silences those who were wont to believe in the dignity of human life. In 'The White-Cheeked Gibbon (Washington 1985)', some miles from the Pentagon, the speaker regrets that most of the human race will never be as human or as trustworthy in their affections as the monkeys.

While his achievement is impressive, there is, nonetheless, a sense of incompletion in Ó Tuama's collected poems as though the profound change of sensibility that has occurred between the publication of *Faoileán na Beatha* (1964) and his re-emergence as a poet of substance with *Saol Fó Thoinn* (1978) has taken place off the page, that the struggle between competing values has not been articulated in the poetry itself to the extent it might have been. As with Ó Tuairisc, it may be that other forms of writing provided a more suitable arena for consideration of such matters and a proper appreciation of Ó Tuama's achievement would require a detailed investigation of his entire works as poet, dramatist and critic. His later poems have much in common with those of the *Innti* poets who emerged at University College Cork in the early 1970s. While Nuala Ní Dhomhnaill, Michael Davitt, Liam Ó Muirthile and others have cited Ó Tuama as an enabling presence and critical influence on their early work, their innovations in turn may have proved a liberating influence for their teacher. The relaxed tone and unobtrusive craft of his later poems, wrought but never overwrought, are, in any case, more characteristic of the contemporary than of the modern period.

Despite the useful corrective of Conleth Ellis's quibble then, there is a sense of marking time in much of the poetry in Irish published in the 1960s. As early as 1961, Máirtín Ó Direáin had chastised the younger poets for their failure to follow the radical innovations of Ó Ríordáin and his frustration seems justified in retrospect.[26] While Ó Ríordáin's is the most pervasive influence among the younger poets, there is a corresponding retreat to the security of more traditional techniques also evident in the literary journals of the period. Even among Ó Ríordáin's imitators, there is a certain timidity which mitigates their achievement. Despite the flurry of publications in the earlier part of the decade, the defining moments of the 1960s are provided by Ó Direáin and Ó Ríordáin, whose earlier achievements are consolidated and extended by the publication of some of their most significant work during this period. Ó Ríordáin's *Brosna* (1964) and Ó Direáin's *Ár Ré Dhearóil* (1962) and *Cloch Choirnéil* (1966) remain the landmark achievements of the 1960s, with Ó Tuama and Ó Tuairisc representing the only significant challenge to the pre-eminence of their seniors. The only notable successors to Máire Mhac an tSaoi during this period are Máire Áine Nic Gearailt and Caitlín Maude, whose poems were not collected during her lifetime. There is a regrettable hiatus in Mac an tSaoi's own work which further diminishes the collective achievement of poets in Irish in the 1960s.

The *Innti* poets

It would be difficult to overstate the importance of *Innti* in the development of poetry in Irish since its initial publication as a student broadsheet in 1970 to its demise in 1996. During that time, it provided several generations of Irish-language poets with access to a substantial audience and editorial guidance which exercised both discretion and discrimination in its regulation of submissions, a generous discernment which benefited emerging poets and readers alike. The extent of Michael Davitt's ambition as founding editor is evident from the outset with 4,000 copies of the second edition printed and circulated. It is equally evident in the production values of the later issues, which included artwork from some of Ireland's leading artists and maintained an unusually high standard in layout and design. *Innti* is as much a response to the changing Ireland of the late 1960s as the work of an earlier generation is to the changes of the postwar period. Liam Ó Muirthile has pointed out that many of the early contributors to *Innti* would never have made it to university had it not been for a new system of scholarships made possible by recent economic prosperity.[27] Equally important was the sense of cultural confidence and experimentation which led to the revival of Irish traditional music and a renewed interest in indigenous culture. The curiosity about alternative lifestyles and older cultures which sent a generation in revolt on the road to India and elsewhere led at least some of the non-conformists in Ireland to the Gaeltacht in search of liberation. The violent trauma of the North has also been cited as a contributing factor, although its impact on the first generation of *Innti* poets at least is, for the most part, subterranean. More recently, the Troubles have been a formative element in the work of two younger poets from Belfast, Pól Ó Muirí and, more particularly, Gearóid Mac Lochlainn, who has given literary currency to the street-talk and jailtalk of his own community in the Irish-speaking areas of West Belfast.

The coincidence of three major figures in the cultural revival of the late 1960s and early 1970s at University College Cork is also crucial to the emergence there of a new literary movement, although agglomeration might be a more appropriate term, given the eclecticism of the group subsequently referred to without discrimination as the *Innti* generation. Seán Ó Riada, chief architect of the music revival, was joined at UCC by Seán Ó Ríordáin, whose attempt to reconcile European Modernism with the inherited patterns of Irish paralleled Ó Riada's own efforts to forge a dynamic relationship between European classical music and Irish traditional music. Seán Ó Tuama's innovative approach to the critical appreciation of poetry in Irish and his controversial plays, denounced from the altar and applauded by critics and audiences, completed the triumvirate whose influence on Michael Davitt, Nuala Ní Dhomhnaill, Liam Ó Muirthile, Gabriel Rosenstock and their colleagues provided a catalyst for their early development. That virtually all of those associated with the *Innti* group were native speakers of English who rejected the possibilities of a world-language for one which, in the words of Máirtín Ó Cadhain, might predecease them, gives some idea of the buoyant optimism of the 1960s and early 1970s in Ireland.[28]

The cacophony of competing voices on the pages of *Innti* is in marked contrast to the isolated voices of the modern period ever mindful of the possibility of their imminent extinction. There is a further reaction against the solemnity of the Modernists in the 'hymn to devil-may-care'[29] and the celebration of the everyday that characterise much of the work of the *Innti* poets. The expansive approach to influences from beyond the Irish tradition is even more open and less contentious than among the Modernists, although the influence is more likely to be American, Asian or Eastern European than any of the major cultures and languages of western Europe favoured by their predecessors. The impact of the women's movement is confirmed by the presence and, it might even be argued, the pre-eminence of women's voices, which emerge in greater numbers and with greater authority as the *Innti* bandwagon gains momentum.

Although the early promise shown by the poets chiefly associated with *Innti* since its inception has been largely fulfilled, it took longer than they themselves might have imagined for the voices of Davitt, Ó Muirthile and Ní Dhomhnaill to assert themselves. Gabriel Rosenstock (b. 1949) was the first of the core group to publish a full collection and his debut volume, *Susanne sa Seomra Folctha* (1973), continues the assault on convention already evident in Mícheál Ó hUanacháin's *Go dTaga Léas* (1971) and subsequently extended in Tomás Mac Síomóin's *Damhna* (1974). While Ó Direáin, Ó Ríordáin, Mac an tSaoi and Ó Tuairisc are among the thirty-two poets who contributed to the first three editions of *Innti*, the most challenging and, indeed, some of the most achieved work in those early editions is provided by Rosenstock, Ó hUanacháin and Mac Síomóin, whose assurance suggested, for a time at least, that their radical experiments might prove the dominant note in the emerging poetry of the late twentieth century. While the experiment with eastern and other influences has continued in Rosenstock's work, most notably in his adaptation of the haiku and in his prodigious work as a translator, the radical assimilation of exotic influences is at its most impressive in the work of Tomás Mac Síomóin (b. 1938), which shows equal facility with the inherited forms of poetry in Irish and with a wide array of European literatures and philosophies. The conviction and flexibility of style evident in *Damhna* (1974) are further developed in *Codarsnaí* (1981) and in his single most impressive collection, *Cré agus Cláirseach* (1983). The longer poems in that third volume justify and are, in turn, sustained by the virtuouso technique whose uncompromised authority is more usually associated with an unadventurous traditionalism. The surreal pastiche of 'Ar Leathmhás Gan' and the travesty of scientific method in 'Brúdlann Thomáis' come closest to achieving Mac Síomóin's aspiration towards 'an fhís' (vision / insight) that would grow 'as iomarbhá na bhfocal' (from the contention of words) but might equally emerge through prayer or lovemaking or, indeed, from a cup of tea or a game of snooker.[30] The shorter poems, although less ambitious, retain much of the stylistic accomplishment of Mac Síomóin's chosen master, Ó Direáin.[31] His deference to the Aran poet as the one most at home in the language is a useful reminder that, for all its innovation, the conviction of Mac Síomóin's own work is grounded in a detailed knowledge of the historical and contemporary possibilities of Irish, an understanding that the limits of the language must be identified and recognised before they can be extended or, indeed, transgressed. Regrettably, Mac Síomóin announced that the publication of *Cré agus Cláirseach* marked the end of an era in his own work and he has maintained a more or less scrupulous silence ever since.[32]

Michael Hartnett / Mícheál Ó hAirtnéide

The disappearance of *Innti* from 1973 until 1981 is as noteworthy as its original appearance and its absence the more troubling given the early promise shown by its principal contributors. The silence is hardly relieved by the 'premature' publication of two collections by Cathal Ó Searcaigh (b. 1956)[33] or the sturdy well-made poems of Mícheál Ó Siadhail before his conversion to English,[34] or even by the work of Conleth Ellis,[35] whose restless voice occasionally achieves an uneasy and momentary equilibrium between language, form and subject matter. With the apparent abdication of some of the more precocious among the early *Innti* poets, the surprising shift of sensibility in Ó Tuama's *Saol Fó Thoinn* (1978) and the dramatic intervention of Michael Hartnett / Mícheál Ó hAirtnéide (1941–99) with *Adharca Broic* (1978) following his farewell to English mark the high points of poetry in Irish in the late 1970s. If Hartnett's subsequent output in the language is uneven and compromised on occasion by a lack of facility with the language, particularly in its spoken idioms, there are, nonetheless, unmistakeable traces of a formidable lyric voice throughout his work in Irish.[36] While his translations of Ó Bruadair and Ó Rathaille have been applauded by critics and his adaptation of work by Nuala Ní Dhomhnaill provides a working model for the kind of close collaboration based on bilingual competence and detailed knowledge of writing in Irish required by such an enterprise, Hartnett's greatest achievement in Irish is the handful of poems where his reconstructed voice fully inhabits the lyric possibilities of the language. The poems in which he most successfully courts 'the language of my people' include 'Fís Dheireanach Eoghain Rua Uí Shúilleabháin', 'Domhan Fliuch', 'Gné na Gaeltachta' and, perhaps, 'Dán do Rosemary', 'Dán do Lara', 'An Giorria' and 'An Dobharchú Gonta'. If his extended exasperated meditation on the function of poetry and imagination in 'An Phurgóid' and 'An Lia Nocht' is marred by infelicities of style and language, the sustained intellectual inquiry is leavened by memorable lines that come close to aphorism in their precision and wit.

Nuala Ní Dhomhnaill

Nuala Ní Dhomhnaill's (b. 1952) first collection, *An Dealg Droighin* (1981), confirmed the promise noted as early as 1973 by Seán Ó Ríordáin[37] and provoked Tomás Ó Floinn to remark that there were aeons rather than generations between her and her kinsman, the hereditary Blasket poet Seán Ó Duinnshléibhe.[38] What distinguishes Ní Dhomhnaill's work from that of virtually all her contemporaries is its unmitigated ambition, the determination of a major poet to rewrite the world in her own words. In two early poems, 'An Cuairteoir' and 'Scéala', she revises some of the most powerful and oppressive stories in Christian mythology, restoring Christ and his Mother to a fuller humanity by acknowledging the sexual element of their divine, but nonetheless human, being. In 'Na Súile Uaine' she imagines the Garden of Eden before the Fall as a world where physical intimacy is celebrated without shame or remorse. Her love poems, which draw heavily on the folk songs of an earlier period, are forthright and unabashed in their explicit treatment of sexual encounters. The emphasis on integrity in sexual relations is part of a larger project which insists on integration or 'conjugation'[39] as the defining principle of the world as she would have it, as opposed to the mistaken and tyrannical order of the rational mind that sees chaos in place of profusion and anarchy where a dynamic stability is sustained by the reconciliation of opposites. The redemptive power of human love, however fraught and contingent, is the single most cohesive force in this project and it is the love poems which provide the greatest vindication both of her ability as a poet and of her vision of reconciliation and complementarity.

The 'sexual embrace' is crucial to this aspect of her work as it is in early and medieval Irish literature where the symbolic significance of *feis*, the legitimate and equal union of opposites in the sexual act, confirms the temporary suspension and ultimate reconciliation of contraries on which the precarious equilibrium of the world depends. The same expansive accommodation of otherness is evident in 'Fáilte Bhéal na Sionna don Iasc', 'Leaba Shíoda' and 'Blodeuwedd', where the categorical distinctions between the human and the natural worlds are blurred and the lovers' bodies become an extension of the landscape. In 'Venio ex Oriente', her physical presence in the world takes its character from an intimate relationship with the landscape: 'tá mus eile ar mo cholainnse / boladh na meala ó Imleacht Shlat / go mbíonn blas mismín is móna uirthi / is gur dorcha a dath' (my body has another smell, / of honey from Imleacht Shlat / that tastes of mint and turf / and is dark in colour). In 'I mBaile an tSléibhe' she reaffirms her sense of belonging in a particular location by naming the places and people to which and among whom she belongs, rehearsing the local names of flowers and plants and the shared stories that establish her connection to the landscape that has been home to her ancestors for seven generations.[40]

There is little evidence of the Modernist or post-modernist insecurity with language in Ní Dhomhnaill's work as she attempts to reconcile words and the world they would make present. In 'Greidhlic', for instance, the official names for a plant that grew on cliff-faces on the Great Blasket are supplanted by the vernacular 'greidhlic' (samphire), whose connotative power is such that just thinking about it, she says, was enough to make an islander's mouth water. Her deference to the variousness of the world past and present is further evident in the integration of her own voice(s) with those of the tradition so that her Irish, according to Máire Mhac an tSaoi, 'is like that of children brought up by their grandmothers, a hundred years old, a kind of miracle of survival'.[41]

Her project of integration is further extended through recuperation of a hidden discourse from the world of mythology and folklore, and particularly women's lore, which allows her to confront the more vindictive aspects of human nature. While the power of the loving mother is acknowledged in the reassuring traditional lullabies of 'Ag Cothú Linbh', the 'suppressed evil in the female principle'[42] is voiced in 'Breith Anabaí Thar Lear' where the woman who has miscarried will not visit her best friend's new-born child 'ar eagla mo shúil mhillte / do luí air le formad' (for fear my evil eye would ruin him with envy). As is frequently the case in her best poems, the dynamic potential of traditional folk-belief is activated by a recognition of its continuing psychological validity. The horrific element which critics have noted from her earliest published work becomes more pronounced in the later collections as the figures of the demon lover, the hag and *bean an leasa* challenge the precarious order of a world apparently built on quicksand. It is most pronounced in *Féar Suaithinseach* (1984), which is dominated by misogynist male characters and predatory images of 'the terrible mother'. The nightmare *bean an leasa*, the sinister otherworldly presence that infiltrates the everyday world of the besieged *bean an tí* (woman of the house), is articulated in language that leans heavily on the Irish folk tradition while admitting the contemporary world of Black and Deckers, duty free and kitchen devils.

While some of her critics have expressed a concern that the metaphysical superstructure has, on occasion, threatened to overwhelm her work, it is equally acknowledged that this is a necessary element of her poetic project. If the narrative is flawed in many of the longer and more derivative poems and the exploitation of Jungian archetypes in *Féar Suaithinseach* (1984) and *Feis* (1991) seems overdetermined and contrived at times, it is these same structures that provide the groundwork for poems such as 'Aubade', 'Gaineamh Shúraic', 'Dán do Mhelissa', 'An Rás', 'Titim i nGrá', 'Fear', 'An Bhábóg Bhriste', 'Máthair', 'An Mhaighdean Mhara', 'Gan do Chuid Éadaigh', 'Éirigh a Éinín' and more besides that emerge in the course of writing through the particular preoccupation which provides the unifying element in each of the later collections. Many of the poems in her most recent collection, *Cead Aighnis* (1998), contain moments of doubt occasionally, but not always, redeemed by a reaffirmation of belief. If 'Dubh – ar thitim Shrebrenice, 11ú Iúil 1995' proves the almost limitless capacity of human destruction, the intolerance of difference that would obliterate all polarities so that even the word 'bán' (white) is implicated in the baleful destruction of its opposite, 'dubh' (black), then 'Daphne agus Apollo' is a reminder that the power of the sun is not necessarily a harbinger of violence but can heal the divisions between the human, the natural and the supernatural. The submerged narrative of the amphibious merpeople who navigate between two elements provides the organising principle of her most ambitious project to date, the extended sequence 'Na Murúcha a Thriomaigh' that concludes *Cead Aighnis*. The image of the stranded seapeople in this instance serves as an extended conceit for the plight of those who make the traumatic journey from the wor(l)d of one language and culture to another. Although the enterprise seems excessively programmatic at times and the narrative ultimately fails to sustain itself, the extravagance of her ambition is nonetheless remarkable, as indeed are the number of poems of the first order in this as in each of her four substantial collections which confirm her status as one of the major Irish poets of the twentieth century.

It is difficult to assess the extent to which Nuala Ní Dhomhnaill's achievement has precipitated the work of other women whose poetry has developed along parallel lines to her own. That Máire Mhac an tSaoi's re-emergence after a prolonged silence is partly a response to the younger woman's work might be inferred from her critical endorsement of Ní Dhomhnaill and the dedication of a remarkable poem to her.[43] Likewise, Máire Áine Nic Gearailt, whose poetic voice seems more confident and relaxed in her later work from the 1990s than in the earlier *Éiric Uachta* (1971), and Eithne Strong (1923–99), whose work in both Irish and English is noticeably more prolific following the publication of her debut collection in Irish (*Cirt Oibre*, 1980).[44] Equally, the presence of a formidable precedent for their own work as an enabling influence on Biddy Jenkinson (b. 1949), Áine Ní Ghlinn (b. 1955) and Deirdre Brennan (b. 1934) should not be discounted. In the sophisticated interior world of Brennan's poems, the domestic protocols of the quotidian conceal trapdoors into profound emotional and psychological disturbances. In Ní Ghlinn's work, language teeters on the brink of the unsayable as words skirt the irredeemable hurt that lurks at the heart of her best poems. Her first collection, *An Chéim Bhriste* (1984), reprinted within six months of its publication, is one of the outstanding poetry collections of the 1980s.

Biddy Jenkinson

In a letter to the editor of the *Irish Review* (Spring / Summer 1991), the pseudonymous Biddy Jenkinson outlined her view of the poet as 'a troublemaker by profession, one who looks under carpets, one who notices that the emperor is wearing designer clothes'.[45] She goes on to argue that poetry 'is a way of loving whatever there may be by exploring to the driven limits of capacity and opportunity everything that can be reached'. Her preference that her work not be translated into English in Ireland is entirely in keeping with the 'delight that things are as they are' which is the animating principle of her work. In 'Mo Ghrása mo Dhia', she addresses God 'nach móide gur ann dó ach idir dhá b'fhéidir mo dhóchais' (who probably only exists between the two maybes of my hope) as a chancer, a botcher, a trickster, while she delights in the accidental miracle of the world as it is. The insubordination to the divine or, indeed, to any other form of ordered tyranny, is further extended in 'Éiceolaí', where the natural world in all its carelessness proves resistant to human improvement. In 'Cáitheadh' and 'Crannchur' the metaphoric connection between the lovers' bodies and the physical world gradually collapses to the point where they have become virtually indistinguishable. The unity possible through 'conjugation' is also at the heart of 'Aubade', where the woman's body is an extension of her lover's, and in 'Truslóga', where a flea could not fit between them and yet eternity is no wider than 'an bhearna seo eatarthu nach mbeadh spás sceite tríd ag deora' (this gap between them that is too small for tears to pour through).

Her deference to the unreconstructed natural order includes an acceptance of the violence necessary to its continued survival. The overwhelming pleasure of human sexuality is articulated through the metaphor of nuclear destruction and endorsed without misgiving in 'Crann na Tubaiste', while in 'Alabama. Samhradh '98' she watches with horrified wonder as the female mantis decapitates the male, whose ardour and reproductive power is thereby increased. The same appalled love is evident in the Chinese mother's lullaby for her daughter as she binds her feet in 'Suantraí na Máthar Síní'. The erotic mischief of many of the poems only barely conceals the threat of violence as humour both allows and assuages the latent aggression, permitting the otherwise inadmissable with an uneasy smile. While 'Iníon Léinn i bPáras' celebrates the overthrow of an oppressive morality, the woman who stalks her sleeping lover in 'Codail a Laoich' advises him that she is not to be trusted. As in the early Irish sagas, which are a sustaining presence in her work, it is the women characters who take the initiative in prosecuting affairs of the heart and flesh with the same subversive intent and potentially destructive consequences. Occasionally, it seems as though the formal exigencies of regular metre provide the only restraint on such willfully chaotic and potentially destructive impulses. That tension between formal precision and an overwhelming emotion inimical to such order is as characteristic of her work as the sustained and mischievous subversion of ideology. The authority of authorship itself, made problematic in the first instance by her use of a pseudonym, is further challenged in many of her poems.

The linguistic and literary archaeology evident in Jenkinson's retrieval of material from the early Irish literary tradition is a continuous element in her fiction and drama as much as in her poetry and may account for a certain hesitancy in the use of language as she attempts to resuscitate the older material. There is a greater degree of assurance in the manipulation of that source material in her later work, particularly in the long poem 'Gleann Maoiliúra', which tells the story of Róis Ní Thuathail from the time of her marriage to Fiach Mac Aoidh Ó Broin to his execution by Elizabeth I in 1597, and in certain passages in the extended sequence 'Mis'. The narrative and dramatic elements are particularly successful in 'Gleann Maoiliúra', a love poem of considerable violence executed with a high degree of emotional and psychological conviction. The dramatic juxtaposition of love and destruction is extended in 'Eanáir 1991' as the lovers stand 'gan phóg gan dóchas / in áit na marbh / faoi gach buama a thiteann / mar fhianaise / nach dár ndeoin iad' (without a kiss, without hope, in the place of the dead, under each bomb that falls, as evidence that this is not done with our consent).

Michael Davitt

While Michael Davitt's (1950–2005) achievement was enthusiastically endorsed by his peers through the various stages of its development, the critical response to his work was more querulous, and occasionally vindictive.[46] Seán Ó Ríordáin's hesitation in deciding between gimmickry and poetry in the early poems is echoed by the exasperation of subsequent critics who saw Davitt's playful transgression of convention as a meaningless and ultimately trivial pursuit. Although he suspended any final judgment, Ó Ríordáin identified the qualities he associated with poetry in some of Davitt's earliest work, which reminded him of Japanese poetry 'mar is eol dom í tríd an mBéarla' (what I know of it through English).[47] That element of hybridity is crucial to Davitt's achievement as an innovator whose work continues to open up new possibilities for his contemporaries. Seán Ó Tuama, despite some misgivings, has argued persuasively that the flexibility of style and confident manipulation of different registers of language in Davitt's best work are the ultimate dividend from his playful exploration of the available resources of Irish.[48] It should also be pointed out that the travesty of traditional grammar that aroused critical suspicion of early poems such as 'Ar an gCaorán Mór' and 'Poker' reflects and, in some cases, anticipates developments in the vernacular, where such usage is now customary, if not yet standard, among the younger inhabitants of the Gaeltacht. In this, and in the more orthodox elements of his work, Davitt was more attuned than any other poet in Irish to the full range of *caint na ndaoine*, from the unexhausted resources of traditional usage to the less reverential coinages of a younger generation of native speakers and the unofficial Gaorla[49] of the Gaelscoileanna (Irish-medium schools) and Coláistí Samhraidh (Irish-language summer colleges) where Irish cheerfully adapts itself to the deep structure of English. It is difficult to imagine any other poet in Irish who could incorporate the multiple registers of language that are carefully interwoven in 'An Scáthán', 'Máistir Scoile', 'Ciorrú Bóthair', 'Lúnasa', 'Do Phound ó Dhia', 'Meirg agus Lios Luachra', 'Urnaí Maidne', 'I gClochar na Trócaire' and 'Bean' so that the spoken dialects of several Gaeltachtaí are merged with literary usages from an earlier period, neglected words recovered from the dictionary, new terminologies which do not, as yet, have the sanction of the vernacular and inventions of his own making. It is the ability to adapt language to the precise requirements of each momentary shift of mood and feeling within the individual poem that finally vindicates the experiment. The integrity of tone in poems as diverse as 'Hiraeth' and 'Chugat' from his debut collection through to 'Voyeur', 'Cloigíní' and 'Shoktin' in his later work indicates not only the range of Davitt's own ability but also the alternative possibilities that can be generated by a language which, like any other living language, is in a constant state of unarrested development. Davitt's role as 'pied piper' to his peers should not distract from his own singular achievement as one of the outstanding poets of his generation.[50]

Cathal Ó Searcaigh

By the time *Innti* re-emerged from its extended sabbatical in 1980, Cathal Ó Searcaigh (b. 1956) had published two collections of poems, *Miontragóid Chathrach* (1975) and *Tuirlingt* (1978), a joint publication with Gabriel Rosenstock, which confirmed an affinity of sensibility with his UCC contemporaries. Although both collections are compromised by a certain technical inadequacy and have been dismissed as 'premature' by the poet himself, the publication of *Súile Shuibhne* (1983) is a vindication of the experiment of the earlier volumes, introducing a confident and distinctive poetic voice to a large and enthusiastic readership. The sense of place which is a continuous and defining feature of poetry in Irish from the earliest period is reiterated in a contemporary idiom in 'Cor Úr', where the landscape is eroticised, and 'Níl aon Ní', where surprising images reveal the landscape in a new light. The delighted wonder at the renewability of the natural world is sustained through the later work in poems such as 'Lá de na Laethanta', where a stream, dying of thirst, is renewed by tears and the wind returns its cap of fog to a hitch-hiking hill which had left it in the back of the poet's car. Ó Searcaigh's interest in the Beat poets and in eastern forms of poetry, further developed through extended stays in Nepal, is evident in the free-form of his longer poems and in his adaptation of the haiku to articulate a momentary perception of intimate communion between the human and the natural worlds. The experiment is most successful in 'speal mo sheanathar', and a similar effect is achieved in the slightly more extended format of 'Marbhna' and 'Séasúir'. If the eastern influence is most evident in these and other shorter poems, they are equally reminiscent of the Old Irish monastic lyrics, which provide similar glosses on reality and imagination.

While the celebration of homosexual love has become the most readily identified feature of Ó Searcaigh's work, it was only with the publication of *Suibhne* (1987) and, more particularly, *Na Buachaillí Bána* (1996) that the homoerotic element of his voice asserted itself unequivocally. In contrast with the poems of Pearse Hutchinson or, indeed, the tender and discreet intimacies of Seán Hutton, the homoerotic element of Ó Searcaigh's earlier work is muted or, at least, confused. Although there may be more exemplars than are generally allowed in the Irish tradition, the strain of innovation is evident in his efforts to find a form and language suitable to the material. Free adaptations from Cavafy are used as well as rewritings of the formulae of Irish folk song, the most successful of which, 'Ceann Dubh Dílis', is a subversive rewriting of one of the most beautiful love songs in the Irish tradition and among Ó Searcaigh's finest poems. The experiment with looser and longer forms evident in an early poem, 'Do Jack Kerouac', is continued in 'An Lilí Bhándearg', 'An Duibheagán', 'Gort na gCnámh' and 'Cré na Cuimhne', which confront the misery of incest, isolation and repressed sexuality. As in the case of Davitt and Ní Dhomhnaill, the performative and oral element is crucial to Ó Searcaigh's enterprise. His status as one of the most popular contemporary Irish poets is confirmed by translation of his work into several languages and the continued demand for the bilingual selected poems, *An Bealach 'na Bhaile*, since its initial publication in 1993.

Poetry from the Gaeltacht

Unusually among the more prominent *Innti* poets, Ó Searcaigh is a native speaker of Irish and continues to live in the Donegal Gaeltacht of Gort a'

Choirce. While there is a strong sense of place, community and tradition in his poems, his work is in marked contrast to that of the community poets whose work maintains its profile and popularity among Gaeltacht audiences, particularly in Connemara, more or less untouched by the formal innovations of the second half of the twentieth century. In the introduction to the single published collection of his poems, *Buille Faoi Thuairim Gabha* (1987), the most accomplished of these oral poets, Johnny Chóil Mhaidhc Ó Coisdealbha (b. 1930), indicates his disdain for a poetry that would make a virtue of incomprehensibility, arguing that poetry is redundant if it fails to reach an appreciative audience. While his own work has the ribald humour, the immediate connection with local politics and the dramatic technique associated with the best folk poetry, there is unusual pathos in his finest individual poem, 'Raifthearaí agus an File', a poetic debate between past and present in which he promises the dead eighteenth- and early nineteenth-century poet that he will resume his argument with him in the graveyard after elegies have been composed to give him due honour by Ó Direáin, Ó Ríordáin, Mac Liammóir and himself. Two other Connemara poets of distinction, Mícheál Ó Cuaig (b. 1950) and Seán Ó Curraoin (b. 1942), have found their separate ways of negotiating between the literary traditions of the Gaeltacht and the innovations of the moderns. The language of Ó Cuaig's poems is austere and meticulous, avoiding any linguistic flourish or excess in its articulation of a carefully realised emotional drama. Seán Ó Curraoin's long poem 'Beairtle' is a swaggering portrayal of 'Everyman na hÉireann', equally at home among the gladioli on Grafton Street or the existential philosophies of the Parisian Left Bank, in a currach hunting basking sharks or cutting turnips and mangels at home in Cois Fharraige. Again, for all its exaggeration and flamboyance, the language has the rhetorical conviction of a recognisable and geographically specific dialect.

Liam Ó Muirthile

Liam Ó Muirthile (b. 1950) was the last of the original *Innti* poets to publish a full collection, and the 1984 volume *Tine Chnámh* shows the extent of his progress from the early poems – in which, according to Ó Ríordáin, nothing is said, unforgettably – to the 'bachannalian' title-poem, a verse-play which dramatises the sexual high-jinks associated with the bonfires of St John's Eve in a synthetic dialect that casts the impression of inner-city Cork English in the mould of Irish. The collection also contains love poems of blunt and sometimes brutal emotional realism including 'Riastaí na Fola' and 'Codladh na hOíche' and a series of poems in which the dead are remembered in language that contains the accents of their own speech and behaviour. The empathy of these early poems, which admit the irregular patterns of actual human speech in Irish, English or an amalgam of both, is further developed in two subsequent volumes, *Dialann Bóthair* (1992) and *Walking Time agus Dánta Eile* (2000). Ó Muirthile's stubborn insistence on linguistic realism acknowledges that a modern (sub)urban poetry in Irish does not and cannot, in good conscience, draw on the full resources of the vernacular as spoken in the rural Gaeltacht without compromising its own fractured inheritance. His work is not, however, a naive celebration of hybridity as the recognition of rupture and discontinuity is paralleled by a persistent attempt at reintegration. In *Dialann Bóthair* (1992), the connection between language and reality is gradually restored as the urban poet begins his apprenticeship in unaccustomed physical labour familiar to his rural forebears. In unearthing the meaning of words, he discovers their application and, perhaps, their genesis in the working interaction between generations of Irish-speakers and the rural landscape. Digging, planting, mowing all have their specific register of language which the poet recovers through physical work and reinhabits in the course of writing. The project is extended in *Walking Time agus Dánta Eile* in a series of poems which re-establish the relationship between father and son through the acquired language of carpentry. The sense of awe associated with ritual and the intimidating burden of history in an early poem such as 'An Parlús' is replaced in the later collection by an almost oriental sense of surrender to the present moment as the less forbidding everyday rituals of hospitality celebrated in 'An Searmanas Tae' and 'Country Relish' offer momentary consolation. The persistent interrogation of technique and the restlessness of form that characterise all of Ó Muirthile's work are evident again as the collection opens with a series of short poems reminiscent of the compression and clarity of early Irish monastic lyrics, followed by a series of long sprawling poems towards the close of the book where the submerged narrative is barely sustained through the circumlocutions of an unusually extended syntax. By contrast, one of his finest poems, 'Cad é', achieves its effect through a scrupulous simplicity of language and form.

Poetry since 1980

The re-emergence of *Innti* in 1980 as the primary forum for poetry in Irish and, perhaps, the most significant literary journal in Ireland throughout the following decade, followed by the publication of groundbreaking individual volumes by Davitt, Ní Dhomhnaill, Ó Muirthile and Ó Searcaigh, confirmed the extent of their separate and collective achievements, initially with readers of Irish but increasingly, through translation, with a bilingual and Anglophone readership. Throughout the 1980s and early 1990s, *Innti* also presided over the (re)emergence of an unusually diverse group of poets whose development can be traced through its pages. A shortlist of the most notable among the (re)emergent voices might include Biddy Jenkinson, Deirdre Brennan, Conleth Ellis, Áine Ní Ghlinn, Louis de Paor,[51] Colm Breathnach, Seán Ó Leocháin, Pádraig Mac Fhearghusa, Rita E. Kelly, Seán Ó Curraoin, Mícheál Ó Cuaig, Seán Hutton, Pól Ó Muirí, Eithne Strong, Gréagóir Ó Dúill and Derry O'Sullivan. O'Sullivan's technical ingenuity and agitated intelligence are such that they constantly threaten to outrun his linguistic ability; his elegy for a stillborn child, 'Marbhghin: Glaoch Ó Liombó', is one of the most achingly beautiful Irish poems of the twentieth century.

Of the generation of poets to emerge in the 1980s and 1990s, the most substantial achievement is that of Colm Breathnach (b. 1961), whose five collections to date show a rare command of language and form. While the poems draw heavily on earlier phases of literature, there is little sense of transgression in their ready accommodation of the modern urban world nor indeed of any disruption to traditional precedent. The language in Breathnach's poetry is equally at ease in a nightclub or in the world of mythology and the effect in each case is neither subversive nor obviously conventional. His technical accomplishment is evident in *Croí agus Carraig* (1995), where the extended conceits of heart and stone provide the unifying principle, and in *An Fear Marbh* (1998), which explores the relationship between a son and his dead father in language informed by the father's knowledge and love of music. The earlier volume, *Scáthach* (1994), is even more ambitious, drawing on the resources of early Irish literature and on the figure of the female warrior who inducted Cú Chulainn into the martial arts to sustain the investigation of human relationships, and particularly the intimacies shared between men and women, through a substantial collection of some ninety poems. It is his finest achievement to date as the ragged format of the poems and the blurred lines between them match the psychological pressure that is maintained unresolved throughout. Many of the poems speak in the voices of female characters from Irish mythology, a risky but ultimately successful technique. The extended format and the inconclusivity of many of the individual poems taken in isolation from each other are in contrast to much of the earlier work, where the poet's unusual facility with form often results in premature closure as though the pressures which provoked the poem to begin with were contained and diverted before being fully articulated. As against that, it might be argued that a great many of the poems in *Cantaic an Bhalbháin* (1991) and *An Fearann Breac* (1992) are as much about the reflexive pleasure of language itself and its legitimate indulgence as they are about their apparent subject matter. In other poems, there is a refined sensibility at work, a grand tenderness and awareness of the transitory consolation of a momentary intimacy or empathy.

The question of translation

For better and for worse, the anxiety with regard to legitimacy of language and form that characterised poetry in Irish throughout much of the twentieth century is almost entirely absent from the contemporary situation. In its place, there is a consensus among poets and critics, a new orthodoxy, that would dismiss the arguments of previous generations as reactionary and disabling. And yet, the anguished struggle to identify enabling precedents from within and without the Irish tradition and the attempt to reconcile those disparate and sometimes conflicting elements provided the dynamic for the most impressive work produced in the modern period. The hesitancy and uncertainty of Ó Ríordáin in particular is born of an acute appreciation of the difficulty involved in reconciling a Modernist sensibility with the authority of an age-old tradition that must be challenged and regenerated but cannot be rejected out of hand. The oppressive burden of the past which threatened to silence an earlier generation weighs very lightly if at all on the work of most contemporary poets.

For all that poetry in Irish is more visible now than it has been for several centuries through increased opportunities for publication, through readings on radio and television and at literary festivals in Ireland and internationally, there is considerable anxiety as to the actual or potential audience for such poetry. The situation is complicated by the increasing popularity of translation and the publication of poetry in a dual-language format with English versions facing up to the original poems in Irish across the page. In public readings likewise, English has become a password or b(u)y word which promises access to an audience but only at a remove from the poems as originally written. The game of Chinese whispers that ensues once the English version becomes the basis for critique of a poet's work and for subsequent translations into other languages further complicates the relationship between poems in Irish and their audience.

If translation aggravates the situation, it is not the root cause of the uncertain relationship between poetry in Irish and its intended or imagined audience.

The absence of a sufficient number of competent speakers and readers of the language is a concern even for a poet as apparently secure in his relationship with an immediate and identifiable local audience as Johnny Chóil Mhaidhc, who asks, in exasperation, what use is a poem if it is not read or understood?[52] In that respect, at least, little has changed since the revival of Irish was first attempted in the late nineteenth century as the production of poetry continues to be overdetermined by the critical state of the language itself. While the confidence of contemporary poets in their own ability and in the creative possibilities of Irish is, to some extent, a vindication of the painstaking endeavours of their predecessors, their work is nonetheless fraught with continuing uncertainty as to the future of the language, and with a lingering insecurity with regard to their actual audience here and now. As Liam Ó Muirthile asks, with customary candour, in 'Éinne amuigh thar tairseacha?' (Is there anyone out there past the thresholds?)

> deonaigh dúinn nach macallaí
> fuaimthoinne amháin ár nguí
> ag luasghéarú trí shaol na saol
> ar ais amach i gcrith mo scairte.[53]

(grant that our prayer is more than echoes of a soundwave accelerating back out through eternity in the trembling of my raised voice)

Notes

1. *Feasta* (November 1950), p. 2.
2. See Gearóid Denvir, *Litríocht agus Pobal* (Inverin: Cló Iar-Chonnachta, 1997), pp. 239–45, 263–93.
3. Dámhscoil Mhúscraighe was established in the Cork Gaeltacht of Baile Mhúirne in 1925 as a forum for the performance and circulation of more traditional forms of verse. See Philip O'Leary's discussion in chapter 5 of this volume.
4. Máirtín Ó Direáin, *Feamainn Bhealtaine* (Dublin: An Clóchomhar, 1961).
5. Frank O'Brien, *Filíocht Ghaeilge na Linne Seo*, trans. Aodh Mac Dhubháin (Dublin: An Clóchomhar, 1968). While O'Brien's analysis of individual poems and his judgement of the respective merits of Ó Direáin, Ó Ríordáin and Mac an tSaoi have been vigorously disputed by subsequent critics, his application of the principles of New Criticism to poetry in Irish is the first sustained application of a particular literary theory and methodology to the subject. His general discussion of developments in poetry from the Revival through to the modern period and his survey of material from the principal literary journals is rigorous, informative and perceptive.
6. See for example Seán Ó Tuama's introduction to Ó Tuama and Louis de Paor, eds. *Coiscéim na hAoise Seo* (Dublin: Coiscéim, 1991), pp. ix–x (English translation by Aodán Mac Póilín in *Krino* 11 (1991), p. 27), and Frank Sewell, *Modern Irish Poetry: A New Alhambra* (Oxford: Oxford University Press, 2000), pp. 142–4.

7. Ó Direáin, *Feamainn Bhealtaine*, p. 146.
8. The two most important outlets for poetry during this period were *Comhar*, founded in 1942 by An Comhchaidreamh, the university students' organisation, and *Feasta*, the official publication of Conradh na Gaeilge, a publication established in 1948. Other publications included *An Síol*, published by An Chuallacht, the Irish students' society at UCC, and *An tUltach*. Many of Liam S. Gógan's more public poems were first published in the *Irish Press/Scéala Éireann* during Cearbhall Ó Dalaigh's time as literary editor of the paper.
9. Ó Direáin, *Feamainn Bhealtaine*, p. 152.
10. 'Éiric an Ghrádha' and 'Do bhaoth-mhaighdin ar bith' were published in *Comhar* in August 1944 (p. 3) while 'Girseach Mná' appeared in the same journal in September 1945 (p. 5).
11. Ulick O'Connor, *Brendan Behan* (London: Hamish Hamilton, 1970; Abacus edition 1993; reprinted 1995, 1997, 1998), pp. 135–41.
12. For detailed discussion of Behan's poems in Irish, see Colbert Kearney, *The Writings of Brendan Behan* (Dublin: Gill and Macmillan, 1977) pp. 46–61, and 'Filíocht Bhreandáin Uí Bheacháin', in Seán Ó Mórdha, ed. *Scríobh* 3 (Dublin: An Clóchomhar, 1978), pp. 44–57.
13. According to tradition, Máire Ní Ógáin was the mistress of poet Donnchadh Ruadh Mac Conmara (1715–1810).
14. Seán Ó Tuama, *Filí faoi Sceimhle* (Dublin: An Gúm, 1978; second edn 1984), p. 5.
15. See Seán Ó Coileáin, *Seán Ó Ríordáin: Beatha agus Saothar* (Dublin: An Clóchomhar, 1982; reprinted 1985), pp. 234–66.
16. An area where Irish is gradually giving way to English.
17. 'Seán Ó Ríordáin ag Caint le Seán Ó Mórdha', in Ó Mórdha, ed. *Scríobh* 3, p. 169.
18. Ó Coileáin, *Beatha agus Saothar*, pp. 245–6.
19. Ibid., p. 176.
20. Ó Mórdha, *Scríobh* 3, pp. 170–1.
21. Seán Ó Ríordáin, 'Scríobh na Filíochta', in Seán Ó Mórdha, ed. *Scríobh* 2 (Dublin: An Clóchomhar, 1975), p. 73.
22. Conleth Ellis, 'The Creature from the Black Lacuna', *Poetry Ireland Review* 17 (Autumn 1986), pp. 13–15. The debate began with a review by Peter Denman in *PIR* 14 (Autumn 1985), pp. 40–6, in which he posed the question: 'What happened to the generation of poets born between the late twenties and the early forties?' and continued in a highly engaging and provocative manner through *PIR* 15, 16 and 17.
23. Dáithí Ó Coileáin, 'Fíodóir na bhFocal (Agallamh le hEoghan Ó Tuairisc)', *Comhar* (October 1974), pp. 8, 20, cited by Mícheál Mac Craith, 'Aifreann na Marbh: Oidhe Chlainne Hiroshima', in Pádraig Ó Fiannachta, ed. *Léachtaí Cholm Cille*, XVII (Maynooth: An Sagart, 1986), pp. 61–94.
24. See Eoghan Ó Tuairisc, *Religio Poetae agus Aistí Eile*, ed. Máirín Nic Eoin (Dublin: An Clóchomhar, 1987).
25. A shortlist of other noteworthy publications in that year would include Eoghan Ó Tuairisc, *Lux Aeterna* (Dublin: Allen Figgis, 1964); Caoimhín Ó Conghaile, *Dánta* (Dublin: An Clóchomhar, 1964); Micheál Mac Liammóir, *Bláth agus Taibhse* (Dublin: Sáirséal agus Dill, 1964); and Seán Ó hÉigeartaigh, *Cama-Shiúlta* (Dublin: An Clóchomhar, 1964).
26. Máirtín Ó Direáin, 'An Nua-fhilíocht', *Comhar* (February 1961), pp. 20–6.

27. Liam Ó Muirthile, *Irish Times* (21 April 1977), cited in Eoghan Ó hAnluain, 'Nuafhilíocht na Gaeilge 1966–1986: Úire agus Buaine', *Léachtaí Cholm Cille*, XVII, pp. 15–17.
28. Máirtín Ó Cadhain, *Páipéir Bhána agus Páipéir Bhreaca* (Dublin: An Clóchomhar, 1969), p. 40.
29. Alan Titley, *The Bright Wave / An Tonn Gheal* (Dublin: Raven Arts Press, 1986), p. 15.
30. Mac Síomóin outlines his poetic manifesto thus on the cover of *Cré agus Cláirseach* (Dublin: Sáirséal-Ó Marcaigh, 1983).
31. See interview with Proinsias Ní Dhorchaí and Gabriel Rosenstock in *Innti* 5, ed. Michael Davitt (Dublin, 1980), pp. 25–37.
32. Mac Síomóin, however, published two novels: *Ag Altóir an Diabhail: Striptease Spioradálta Bheartla B /* (Dublin: Coiscéim 2003) and *In Inimhe* (Dublin: Coiscéim, 2004), as well as a polemical pamphlet entitled *Tuairisc ón bPluais* (Dublin: Coiscéim, 2004).
33. Cathal Ó Searcaigh, *Miontragóid Chathrach* (Falcara: Cló Uí Chuireáin, 1975) and *Tuirlingt*, co-authored with Gabriel Rosenstock with photographs by Bill Doyle (Dublin: Carbad, 1978). Frank Sewell's description of these volumes as 'premature' (*A New Alhambra*, p. 59) is confirmed by Ó Searcaigh in an interview recorded for the Centre for Irish Studies, National University of Ireland, Galway, 29 November 2002.
34. Mícheál Ó Siadhail, *An Bhliain Bhisigh* (Dublin: An Clóchomhar, 1978); *Runga* (Dublin: An Clóchomhar, 1980); and *Cumann* (Dublin: An Clóchomhar, 1982).
35. Conleth Ellis, *Fómhar na nGéanna* (Dublin and Cork: Clódhanna Teoranta, 1975); *Aimsir Fháistineach* (Dublin and Cork: Clódhanna Teoranta, 1981); *Nead Lán Sneachta* (Dublin: Coiscéim, 1982); *Táin* (Dublin: Coiscéim, 1983); *Seabhac ar Guairdeall* (Dublin: Coiscéim, 1985). Ellis also published several collections in English including *Poems*, with Colm O'Neill and others (Carlow: Nationalist and Leinster Times, 1961); *Under the Stone*, (Dublin: Gill and Macmillan, 1971); *After Doomsday* (Dublin: Raven Arts, 1982); and *The Age of Exploration* (Dublin: Dedalus, 1985).
36. Mícheál Ó hAirtnéide, *Adharca Broic* (Dublin: Gallery Press, 1978). Hartnett's first full collection in Irish was preceded by the bilingual publication of *Cúlú Íde / The Retreat of Ita Cagney* (Kildare: Goldsmith Press, 1975). Subsequent volumes include *An Phurgóid* (Dublin: Coiscéim, 1982); *Do Nuala: Foighne Chrainn* (Dublin: Coiscéim, 1984); *An Lia Nocht* (Dublin: Coiscéim, 1985).
37. Seán Ó Ríordáin, 'Nuafhilíocht', review of *Innti* 3, *Irish Times* (28 April 1973), cited by Ó hAnluain in 'Nuafhilíocht na Gaeilge 1966–1986', pp. 7–23.
38. Tomás Ó Floinn, 'Sappho a thuirling ag geataí na glóire', *Comhar* (November 1981), pp. 27–9.
39. The terms 'sexual embrace' and 'conjugation' are paraphrased by Frank Sewell from the work of sculptor Lloyd Gibson and applied to Ní Dhomhnaill's poetry in *A New Alhambra*, p. 183. See also Louis de Paor, 'A Feminine Voice: The Poems of Nuala Ní Dhomhnaill', in Rebecca Pelan, ed. *Irish-Australian Studies: Papers Delivered at the Seventh Irish-Australian Conference July 1993* (Sydney: Crossing Press, 1994), pp. 93–110.
40. See Seán Ó Tuama, 'Celebration of Place in Irish Writing', in *Repossessions: Selected Essays on the Irish Literary Heritage* (Cork: Cork University Press, 1995), pp. 248–66.
41. Máire Mhac an tSaoi, introduction to *Nuala Ní Dhomhnaill: Selected Poems*, trans. Michael Hartnett (Dublin: Raven Arts Press, 1986), p. 7.
42. Seán Ó Tuama discusses the presence of Jungian archetypes of the 'loving' and 'terrible' mother in Ní Dhomhnaill's early work in 'Filíocht Nuala Ní Dhomhnaill: "An Mháthair

Ghrámhar is an Mháthair Ghránna" ina Cuid Filíochta', in *Léachtaí Cholm Cille* 18 (1986), pp. 95–116, and in '"The Loving and Terrible Mother" in the Early Poetry of Nuala Ní Dhomhnaill', *Repossessions*, pp. 35–53.

43. Máire Mhac an tSaoi, 'Do Nuala Ní Dhomhnaill', *An Cion go dtí Seo* (Dublin: Sáirséal-Ó Marcaigh, 1987), p. 118.
44. Eithne Strong, *Cirt Oibre* (Dublin: Coiscéim, 1980); *Fuil agus Fallaí* (Dublin: Coiscéim, 1983); *Aoife fé Ghlas* (Dublin: Coiscéim, 1990); *An Sagart Pinc* (Dublin: Coiscéim, 1990), and *Nobel* (Dublin: Coiscéim, 1998).
45. Biddy Jenkinson, 'Letter to an Editor', in Peter Denman, ed. *Irish University Review* 21, 1 (Spring/Summer 1991), pp. 27–34.
46. See, for example, Liam Ó Muirthile's review of *Bligeard Sráide* (1983) in Aingeal Ní Chualáin and Gearóid Denvir, eds. *Macalla* (Galway: An Cumann Éigse agus Seanchais, Coláiste na hOllscoile, Gaillimh, 1984), pp. 191–7, and Pól Ó Muirí's endorsement of *Scuais* (1998), *Irish Times*, 27 May 2000, p. 11.
47. Seán Ó Ríordáin, review of *Scríobh* 2 in *Irish Times* (11 January 1975), cited in Ó hAnluain, 'Nuafhilíocht na Gaeilge 1966–1986'.
48. Seán Ó Tuama, 'Michael Davitt: File Séimh Foréigneach', in Louis de Paor, ed. *Innti* 12, pp. 25–32. See also introduction to Michael Davitt, *Freacnairc Mhearcair/The Oomph of Quicksilver: Rogha Dánta/Selected Poems 1970–1988*, ed. Louis de Paor (Cork: Cork University Press, 2000).
49. A conflation of the word 'Béarla' (English) and 'Gaeilge' (Irish) to indicate the hybrid sub-dialect of Irish common among younger speakers and particularly among those whose primary contact with the language is at Irish-medium schools and summer colleges.
50. Ó Tuama, 'Filíocht Nuala Ní Dhomhnaill, p. 95.
51. Philip O'Leary writes: 'De Paor (b. 1961) published five collections in Irish between 1988 and 2002, and three bilingual volumes including *Aimsir Bhreicneach / Freckled Weather* (Canberra: Leros Press, 1993) and *Gobán Cré is Cloch / Sentences of Earth and Stone* (Melbourne: Black Pepper Press, 1996). De Paor lived in Australia for nine years before his return to Ireland in 1996, and his experience of emigration there opened new perspectives on his own geographic, cultural, and linguistic allegiances, bringing a striking if subtle political dimension to the lyric sensibility of his first collection *Próca Solais is Luatha* (Dublin: Coiscéim, 1988).'
52. Johnny Chóil Mhaidhc Ó Coisdealbha, *Buille Faoi Thuairim Gabha* (Inverin: Cló Iar-Chonnachta, 1987), pp. 9–10.
53. Liam Ó Muirthile, 'Tairseacha', in *Walking Time agus Dánta Eile* (Inverin: Cló Iar-Chonnachta, 2000), p. 76.

Select bibliography

de Paor, Louis, 'Disappearing Language: Translations from the Irish', in Pierce, David, ed. *Irish Writing in the Twentieth Century: A Reader*, Cork: Cork University Press, 2000, pp. 1,139–1,142.

de Paor, Pádraig, *Tionscnamh Filíochta Nuala Ní Dhomhnaill*, Dublin: An Clóchomhar, 1997.

Doan, James and Frank Sewell, eds. *On the Side of Light: Critical Essays on the Poetry of Cathal Ó Searcaigh*, Galway: Arlen House, 2002.

Dorgan, Theo, ed. *Irish Poetry Since Kavanagh*, Dublin: Four Courts Press, 1996.

Ellis, Conleth and Rita E. Kelly, eds. *Poetry Ireland Review: Special Eugene Watters Issue* 13 (Spring 1985).

Fallon, Brian, *An Age of Innocence: Irish Culture 1930–1960*, Dublin: Gill and Macmillan Ltd, 1998.

Mac Craith, Mícheál, *An tOileán Rúin agus Muir an Dáin: Staidéar ar Fhilíocht Mháirtín Uí Dhireáin*, Dublin: Comhar, 1993.

Mac Giolla Léith, Caoimhín, ed. *Cime Mar Chách: Aistí ar Mháirtín Ó Direáin*, Dublin: Coiscéim, 1993.

'Metaphor and Metamorphosis in the Poetry of Nuala Ní Dhomhnaill', *Éire-Ireland* 35, 1–2 (Spring/Summer 2000), pp. 150–72.

Nic Dhiarmada, Bríona, 'Téacs Baineann, Téacs Mná: Gnéithe d'Fhilíocht Nuala Ní Dhomhnaill', unpublished Ph.D thesis, National University of Ireland, 1995.

Nic Eoin, Máirín, *Eoghan Ó Tuairisc: Beatha agus Saothar*, Dublin: An Clóchomhar, 1988.

Trén bhFearann Breac: An Díláithriú Cultúir agus Nualitríocht na Gaeilge, Dublin: Cois Life, 2005.

Nic Ghearailt, Eibhlín, *Seán Ó Ríordáin agus 'An Striapach Allúrach'*, Dublin: An Clóchomhar, 1988.

Ní Fhrighil, Ríóna, 'Coileach Ban ar Chearcaibh nó File Mná i mBaile – Comórtas idir Filíocht Nuala Ní Dhomhnaill agus Filíocht Eavan Boland', unpublished Ph.D thesis, National University of Ireland, 2001.

'Faitíos Imní an Scáthaithe: Eavan Boland agus Nuala Ní Dhomhnaill', *New Hibernia Review* 6, 4 (Winter 2002), pp. 136–49.

Ní Ghairbhí, Róisín, 'An tSiobairne idir Dhá Theanga i Saothar Michael Hartnett agus Eoghain Uí Thuairisc', unpublished Ph.D thesis, National University of Ireland, 2004.

'Cuimhne na nDaoine agus Aistear an Aistriúcháin i Saothar Michael Hartnett: "Gósta Garbh-Bhéarla"', in Micheál Ó Cearúil, ed. *Aimsir Óg*, 2 vols., Dublin: Coiscéim, 2000, ii, pp. 141–59.

O'Brien, Frank, *Filíocht Ghaeilge na Linne Seo*, trans. Aodh Mac Dhubháin, Dublin: An Clóchomhar, 1968.

ed. *Duanaire Nuafhilíochta*, Dublin: An Clóchomhar, 1969.

Ó Cadhla, Stiofán *Cá bhFuil Éire? Guth an Ghaisce i bPrós Sheáin Uí Ríordáin*, Dublin: An Clóchomhar, 1998.

Ó Coileáin, Seán, *Seán Ó Ríordáin: Beatha agus Saothar*, Dublin: An Clóchomhar, 1982.

Ó Croiligh, Pádraig, ed. *Irisleabhar Mhá Nuad: Téamaí as Litríocht na NuaGhaeilge*, Maynooth: An Sagart, 1967.

Ó Direáin, Máirtín, *Feamainn Bhealtaine*, Dublin: An Clóchomhar, 1961.

Ó Dúshláine, Tadhg, *Paidir File: Filíocht Sheáin Uí Ríordáin*, Inverin: Cló Iar-Chonnachta, 1993.

Ó Fiannachta, Pádraig, ed. *Léachtaí Cholm Cille XVII: An Nua-Fhilíocht*, Maynooth: An Sagart, 1986.

Ó hAnluain, Eoghan, ed. *An Duine is Dual: Aistí ar Sheán Ó Ríordáin*, Dublin: An Clóchomhar, 1980.

Ón Ulán Ramhar Siar: Máirtín Ó Direáin ag Caint ar Chúlra Saoil Cuid dá Dhánta, Dublin: An Clóchomhar, 2002.

Ó Mórdha, Seán, *Scríobh* 1–6, (1974–1984) Dublin: An Clóchomhar, 1991.

Ó Tuairisc, Eoghan, *Religio Poetae agus Aistí Eile*, ed. Máirín Nic Eoin, Dublin: An Clóchomhar, 1987.

Ó Tuama, Seán, *Cúirt, Tuath agus Bruachbhaile*, Dublin: An Clóchomhar, 1991.

Filí Faoi Sceimhle, Dublin: An Gúm, 1978.

Repossessions: Selected Essays on the Irish Literary Heritage, Cork: Cork University Press, 1995.

'Twentieth Century Poetry in Irish', in Aodán Mac Póilín, ed. *Krino* 11 (1991), pp. 26–31.

Sewell, Frank, *Modern Irish Poetry: A New Alhambra*, Oxford: Oxford University Press, 2000.

8

Contemporary poetry in English: 1940–2000

DILLON JOHNSTON AND GUINN BATTEN

Introduction

Any consideration of Irish poets as a collective, much less a coherent, body of study may be skewed by two misconceptions of the 'Irish' 'poet'. First, there is a popular tendency to think of that poet as a heroic individual who represents or embodies 'Irishness', standing in for the other and – according to this view – lesser poets of his (we use the gender deliberately) generation. Yeats served this purpose during the first Irish literary Renaissance until the year of his death, just before this chapter begins; likewise Seamus Heaney is misconstrued as the single and singularly gifted poet for the second such Renaissance in Ireland. Yet if this misconception needlessly narrows two rich and broadly various periods in Irish literary history, so does its corollary: that the 'Irish poet' is a faceless figure carried forward from the bardic past, his or her individual strengths or even eccentricities effaced by the relentless march of tradition.

In the *Anthology of Irish Writing* produced by Field Day, itself a literary collective, Seamus Deane argues that most nineteenth-century Irish poets 'survived by clinging on to an organized grouping' and that 'this structural organization of Irish writing was to persist into the twentieth century, with the Irish Revival and the northern poets as the dominant groups'.[1] While such groupings can be convenient to critics, in actuality Irish poetic movements have been incoherent and short-lived after and, partially, because of William Butler Yeats. A history of Irish poetry over the last six decades of the twentieth century begins with a handful of poets struggling not to succeed the great poet and *chef d'école* Yeats but to gain independence from his dominant influence. The sixty years that are the focus of this section contain some collaborative factions that are short-lived, hollow annunciations of the second Renaissance, and some individual poets foreswearing all poetic collaboration.[2]

Critics have further fragmented the cracked looking-glass of Irish poetry. Early in our six decades, most serious early scholars of Yeats were Americans, such as Thomas Parkinson and Richard Ellmann, but their interest rarely carried over to other Irish poets. With the close of Irish journals such as *The Bell*, which were mostly preoccupied with fiction, Irish criticism became shadowy and even, arguably, ineffectual. And, in Britain, until the emergence of Heaney, reviewers hardly noticed Irish poetry. Over the last three decades, American critics have been preoccupied with Eavan Boland, often with a stronger interest in her feminist polemics than in her poetry, or with other poets resident in American academia such as Heaney, Paul Muldoon and, to a much lesser extent, Eamon Grennan. For British critics, the poetic map usually locates Irish poetry in Belfast, and the blank spaces to the south might as well be marked 'Here be lions!'[3] in the manner of medieval maps registering the cartographer's warning to avoid the unknown.

Irish literary anthologies or anthologies of Irish poetry cannot pretend to shape the canon nor even to mark the tidal extremes in a uniform alternation of opinion. Rather, each tends to represent one side over another in various antitheses present in Irish poetry. For example, recent Irish or British poetry anthologists have preferred the dead over the living, the North over the South, the South over the North, or regionalists over Modernists.[4] While Patrick Crotty's *Modern Irish Poetry* may be the least unsatisfactory recent anthology, it nevertheless includes only seven women among its nearly four dozen poets.[5] When the third volume of *The Field Day Anthology* virtually ignored women writers, representing women poets as only 5 per cent of a post-Yeatsian poetic hierarchy, enterprising women critics and scholars countered by burying the canon under eleven pounds of paper and 3,300 pages of women's writing, with the gathering of nearly five dozen women poets over the last fifty years making volume III's mostly male canon look diminutive.[6]

Just after Yeats

If Yeats's immediate Irish successors could manoeuvre fairly easily around his occult and spiritualist interests, they had to move more deliberately to escape the legacy he laid down in 'Under Ben Bulben' of scrupulous craft, agrarian topics and heroic nationalism, not to mention his lofty standards and international reputation. One of Yeats's most promising but most spancelled successors, Austin Clarke, said that for the younger generation Yeats was 'rather like an enormous oak-tree which . . . kept us in the shade'.[7] Through deconstructive or evasive measures, the younger poets pioneered their own independent space and strategies of voice. By most estimates, the best of those poets for whom Irish issues were inescapable – Louis MacNeice, Patrick Kavanagh, Clarke himself, Padraic Fallon, W. R. Rodgers and John Hewitt – achieved success that was partial or only partially recognised. Influenced in great part by Joyce, another handful of poets – Denis Devlin and Samuel Beckett and their friends Thomas MacGreevy, Brian Coffey and George Reavey – turned from matters peculiar to Ireland to more global topics and more international models such as European Modernism. Because of their absence from Ireland and delayed and scattered publishing, a few of these 'Irish Modernists' only recently achieved subsidiary positions in the canon of modern Irish poetry. Eventually, many younger poets would find in the urban, democratic, multi-voiced Joyce an alternative or supplement to Yeats.

The assumption of most critics that Ireland's first post-Yeatsian decade was culturally depressed – isolated by neutrality in World War II, by rationing and a stagnant economy, and by censorship – is supported by anecdote and evidence. In *The Bell* of 1943 – a journal which, from 1940 to 1952, was the leading voice against cultural isolation – founding editor Sean O'Faolain wrote: 'We have become . . . alienated from Europe to such an extent that we sometimes seem less to belong to it than barely to adhere to it.'[8] Ireland's neutrality made Irish productions, including literature, unpopular and neglected abroad, while censorship, enacted in 1929, banned the work of many Irish writers at home and interdicted much important writing from elsewhere. While economic and social conditions, combined with the Emergency, as the Irish called World War II, pressed down on these writers, Yeats's prescribed heroic topics and grand style corseted their verse.

Just after Yeats and Joyce: the 1940s and 1950s in the North

The Belfast-born poet Louis MacNeice, who published seventeen volumes of poetry between 1929 and his death in 1963, hardly seems stunted or constrained by Yeats's influence. On the contrary, Yeats may have helped liberate MacNeice to accept the intense ambivalence of his Anglo-Irish heritage. The son of an Anglican clergyman who preached Home Rule to his unionist parishioners, MacNeice (b. 1907) spent his school years at Marlborough, the English public school, and later studied at Merton College, Oxford, thus (as Patrick Crotty has noted in his discussion of the early MacNeice in chapter 2) encountering in his early years various orthodoxies that ran counter to his specific experience.

At Oxford he fell into an association with W. H. Auden, Stephen Spender and C. Day-Lewis that would locate him on the poetry map as an English poet until a rescue mission, begun in the 1980s, by Michael and Edna Longley, Peter McDonald, Tom Paulin and other Ulster critics, recovered him as an Irish poet, or at least a dual citizen of English and Irish poetry.

MacNeice's conflict of identities, which was exacerbated by Ireland's neutrality during the Emergency, found expression, and a partial model for resolution, in the first full study of W. B. Yeats, which MacNeice published in 1941. Although his view of any poet as 'an ordinary man with specialized gifts'[9] differed sharply from Yeats's visionary Romantic view of the artist, in his study MacNeice plays down this difference and makes of Yeats a sort of Irish godparent; this, along with MacNeice's own identification with the west of Ireland, can be seen as establishing a basis for the younger poet's Irish affiliation. The two poets would seem to differ most in their views of history. In 'Lapis Lazuli' Yeats saw the mid-1930s approach of a European war as part of a determined recurrence ('All things fall and are built again') whereas in *Autumn Journal*, as his title implies, MacNeice distills from the anxiety of the material moment – 'Hitler yells on the wireless, / The night is damp and still' – today's news and weather.[10] In the insistence on the historical moment in *Autumn Journal* ('I wonder what the morning / Paper will say, / . . . / . . . the day is to-day'),[11] MacNeice can echo other poems of the 1930s, such as Auden's near-sloganeering in 'Spain 1937' ('To-morrow the bicycle races / Through the suburbs on summer evenings: but to-day the struggle').[12] Yet, even this difference with Yeats MacNeice softens, asserting that Yeats 'has recognized the necessity of the descent into time', although the biographer concedes that this descent was one strophe in Yeats's 'philosophy of antinomies'.[13]

Concerning his commitment to living in one's moment while imagining other times and places, MacNeice wrote enduring poems throughout his thirty-odd-year career, although his first creative decade, which closes with *Autumn Journal* (1939), contains a greater density of such poems, including anthology pieces such as 'Snow', 'The Sunlight on the Garden' and 'Bagpipe Music'. Such poems become a form of memoir in that the seemingly ordinary moment is made historically momentous and is shared by MacNeice's audience. His career as a producer with the BBC, the nation's hearth during wartime, must have focused his sense of audience. His confidential tone, however, at times masked secrets, especially in the allegorical substitutions he called 'parables'.

The Heraclitean thrust of the poetic moment is often represented by modern conveyances – escalators, fast cars, trains: 'The train's rhythm never relents, the telephone posts / Go striding backwards like the legs of time' ('Train to Dublin').[14] The train's momentum and its enclosure also represent MacNeice's phenomenological concerns in these miniatures of man's journey: '. . . why does your reflection seem / So lonely in the moving night?' ('Corner Seat').[15] This ensphered self, which finds expression in a variety of MacNeice's poems, is stated most simply and profoundly in 'House on a Cliff' (1955): 'Indoors the sound of the wind. Outdoors the wind'.[16]

One need only compare *Autumn Journal* to *Autumn Sequel* (1953) or look into the formulaic sequences of the 1950s, such as 'A Hand of Snapshots' or 'Dark Age Glosses', to recognise MacNeice's middle-age decline. In the 1960s, however, a new love relationship he describes as 'Blain and dazzle together' ('Spring Cleaning')[17] quickened his poetic pulse and produced nearly a dozen poignant but complexly private poems in *The Burning Perch* (1963). In September of 1963, while taping underground and outdoors his last radio play (a genre which, like his non-fictional prose, complemented his poetry), he contracted viral pneumonia and died soon after.

In a memorial service a month later, his wife Hedli spoke of the 'House that Louis Built' where among various rooms for various friends and purposes was located 'a very small one, just space for two: himself and a Welsh poet Dylan Thomas or an Irish W. R. Rodgers' with whom he would discuss 'the making of poetry, but only with them'.[18] This small posthumous colloquy suggests the placement of MacNeice in a Celtic fringe of Welsh and Ulster poetry but also a Northern Irish line of descent. Compared to MacNeice, both Rodgers and Thomas were loose craftsmen, Rodgers the more so for a tendency to imitate Thomas. He had been a Presbyterian minister in Armagh from 1934 to 1946 before resigning to become a writer for the BBC and a frequent courier of ideas and conversation between London and Belfast or Dublin. One can imagine a reader of Rodgers's first book of poetry *Awake! and Other Poems* (1941) opening to the title poem where echoes of Shelley and Hopkins and Thomas collide in the 'Wind . . . that claps and batters / The bent-backed and running roaring waters, / That squats and squints and squeals evilly in trees', and then closing the book to silence the clatter. Rodgers's other volume, *Europa and the Bull and Other Poems* (1952), suffers from the same shunting of sounds, but occasionally poems achieve the quieter balance of a MacNeice-like parable, as in 'The Harvest Field', where the poet cautions his entrapped self to listen to 'the hiss / Of the scythe in the long grasses of your laughter . . . / . . . this / Is Time's swathe, and you are the one that he's after.'[19] The awkward over-extended last line is symptomatic of a milieu in which poems are not scrutinised and improved.

In an interview published in 1999, Roy McFadden, who from his initial publication in 1943 was a part of that first generation of Ulster poets, recalls that John Hewitt named Northern Ireland of the late 1940s 'a Sahara of the arts', presumably for its aridity but perhaps also for its poets' nomadic lives. McFadden writes that 'the dominant poets here [Belfast] in 1946 would have been Hewitt and Rodgers and both were largely concerned with landscape whereas in England the New Apocalypse poets often attempted . . . neo-Surrealism'.[20] The esteem paid to Rodgers by his contemporaries has since been largely forgotten, but at the time his energised poetry provided a significant antidote to the nostalgic Georgian landscape poetry that still persisted and which the Dionysian poetry of early Thomas, Vernon Watkins and other New Apocalypse poetry also opposed.

Although Rodgers (1909–69) and Hewitt (1907–87) were both Ulster Protestants who became, respectively, a lapsed Methodist and lapsed Presbyterian, Hewitt's influence on contemporary and subsequent poets from the North has been established while Rodgers's readership has dwindled. Although Seamus Heaney found in Hewitt 'the kind of music I was after',[21] Hewitt's influence is chiefly political, in his forthright proclamation of his own identity as both Irishman and Protestant. Born of planter-stock and candidly suspicious of Catholicism, he writes, 'I fear their creed as we have always feared / the lifted hand against unfettered thought' ('The Glens').[22] Freethinking, agnostic, selectively Marxist, Hewitt was influenced in his youth by the Victorian poet William Morris, who espoused in poetry and prose a pre-industrial individualism and a return to handicraft. Hewitt's poetry was often indistinguishable from second-best Victorian verse, especially when he became polemical, as in the long poem 'Freehold', where he denounced 'the mad engines thumping through the night'.[23] Morris had employed the same iambic couplets and Jeremiad urgency eighty years earlier: 'Forget six counties overhung with smoke, / Forget the snorting steam and piston stroke'.[24] As Hewitt's evangelical socialism intensifies, he becomes deaf to the Victorian quaintness of his own verse.

Whereas Morris would return to an earlier time, Hewitt sought a pre-industrial space which he found in the west of Ireland ('The Swathe Uncut') or more often in the Glens of Antrim. In developing his concept of 'Regionalism', he collected and published verse by pre-industrial 'rhyming weavers', craftsmen who, down to the introduction of power-looms in 1843, wrote in Ulster-Scots vernacular (see Andrew Carpenter's discussion in chapter 7 of volume I). In the late eighteenth century, many of these poets were United Irishmen, members of the movement to free Ireland that bound Dissenters and Catholics in a common love of region, as Hewitt interpreted their history. He challenged the few poets in Belfast in the 1940s and 1950s – McFadden, Rodgers, Robert Greacen (all of whom left, at least for a time), Padraic Fiacc (over for a few years from New York), and George Buchanan (whose poetry career began years later) – to liberalise their views on sectarianism, the City and the Region, and globalism. Greacen has said, 'If I had stayed in Belfast I would have been influenced even more by Hewitt than I was. I might have become a disciple – as McFadden did for a time.'[25]

Yet, the mentor himself departed Ireland when, as a reflection of the tightening unionist control in the North, Hewitt was passed over in 1953 for directorship of the Belfast Museum. He became, instead, from 1957 to 1972, director of the Herbert Art Gallery and Museum in Coventry. By the time he returned to Belfast on his retirement, the political and poetic landscape had altered drastically, and globalism, the Troubles and the appearance of superior poets had rendered regionalism and his poetry outdated. Finally, Hewitt's best poems may be his late autobiographical sonnets and other lyrics, nostalgic for the past and circling the lonely center of an isolated self.

Looking back, we can now recognize Hewitt's extensive extrapoetic influence over his peers. Edna Longley calls his regionalism the 'ideological engine'[26]of the Belfast literary journal *Lagan* (1943–6) which otherwise was modelled on *The Bell*. From 1948 to 1953, much persuaded by Hewitt's ideas, Roy McFadden co-edited with Barbara Hunter Belfast's first poetry journal, *Rann*. From his Coventry base, Hewitt himself served for five years as poetry editor of *Threshold*, a journal of Belfast's Lyric Theatre, which was founded by Mary O'Malley in 1951 on the model of Austin Clarke's verse-speaking theatre in Dublin. It seems likely that Hewitt's extrapoetic influence – his exemplary integrity and his belief that regional loyalties might supercede sectarian allegiances – may have contributed more than his own poetry to the remarkable flowering of Ulster poetry in the 1960s.

Just after Yeats and Joyce: emigrant poetry

We do know that in the 1940s, North and South, Irish poetry's infrastructure – the journals, reviewers, publishers and funding agencies – that might have conducted poetic traffic in the generation after Yeats had developed too slowly to serve these poets' trade. Chafing under the weight of Irish theocracy and enchanted by Joyce's example, a remarkable number of writers emigrated from Ireland or otherwise lived abroad, either finding some audience as an international writer or writing, largely, in neglect. One group who graduated from UCD and Trinity College, Dublin in the early 1930s – Denis Devlin, Samuel Beckett and Brian Coffey (who are in turn associated with older writers such as Thomas MacGreevy and George Reavey) – has even acquired the name 'the Thirties Writers' as if acknowledging that their careers ceased with their emigration in the middle of that decade. After publishing *Intercessions* (1937), the most accomplished poet in this group, Denis Devlin, by some estimates a major poet, would publish only one other volume of poetry, and that with a North American publisher. Following Devlin's death from leukemia in 1959, publication in the US of poems selected by Allen Tate and Robert Penn Warren (1963) and of two volumes by the Dolmen Press in 1964 and 1967 would somewhat boost his reputation.

In 1935 Devlin departed from Ireland to develop a successful career in the Irish Foreign Office, assuming posts in Geneva, Rome and the US. His deep involvement with French poetry, both as scholar and translator, may have given rise to an association in readers' minds of Devlin's poetry with that of French surrealist verse of the 1930s. Perhaps this, as much as his absence from Ireland and from British or Irish publication, has limited Devlin's English-speaking audience. Devlin's complexities, however, derive from an older European rhetoric that serves poetic fluidity. In his poetry Devlin often substitutes for anticipated words surprising surrogates; ambiguous diction or phrasing delivers multiple conflicting meanings; paradox and circular references and definitions proliferate. Perhaps most basic to his poetry are anacoluthon (where a sentence shifts from, or otherwise fails to complete, an anticipated grammatical structure) and antistasis (where the same word is repeated with differing meanings) because they challenge our process of reading and render poetic language self-conscious.

In 'Farewell and Good', a poem from *Lough Derg* (1946), he grieves for Edenic love, a beloved in her first remembered form, and asks, 'What use my hermit grief to a world bitten in self, / . . . ?'[27] The substitution of *world* and *self* for the more familiar *apple* and *half* introduces the theme of this poem, that the self is born from our loss of paradisal love. Through desire, however, she emerges in waking glimpses and dreams: 'struck by a wind-flash / In snood of leaves or in phantasms of sleep assembling her form, / I restore my kingdom in her, the real that deepened the dreamed-on'. The poem concludes: 'Still the complaint, still no comfort to her and me split / Like a glass, like life spilt by some Sistine hand, / Our life that brimmed over like diamonds in our light'. The anagrams – *split* and *spilt* – guide the reader from the lover's separation from God to the creation of humanity, from shattered glass to faceted diamonds, and from wasteful spillage to a radiant effluence, that like the fortunate fall is both 'farewell' and 'good'.

The rhetorical term antistasis might be generalised to characterise Devlin's poetry as a whole or, particularly, his masterpiece *The Heavenly Foreigner*, where the ideal is reflected not in static images but within the flux of real time, where the rapidity and fluidity of perception can be approximated only in a poetic, fluid language. Published piecemeal in journals between 1949 and 1951 and as an entire poem posthumously in 1967, *The Heavenly Foreigner* pursues divine love as it was glimpsed in one supreme lover – 'an instant precognising eternity' – and refracted through memory both of her and of encounters with other women.[28] These encounters were restricted to a particular moment as actual as, and even conditioned by, the cathedral towns or other architectural sites which become the titles of the poem's eleven sections. This unified divine love may be the essence of that supreme lover or a projection from the poet himself, or nothingness, death or God, but while the poet remains within time, he cannot know: 'Time virtual is what keeps me in Time: / Leave me in abeyance'.[29]

If Devlin's interest in the relation between the ideal and the real borrows from courtly love poetry, in his experimental, destabilising techniques, Devlin like Samuel Beckett resembles European Modernists. Although they share with Yeats's Modernism a refusal to assign causality to a linear history, they reject Yeats's use of Irish myth, his association of myth with the unconscious and his nationalism. Devlin and Beckett ally themselves with European, more specifically French, Modernists in decentring the self. Concerning Beckett's value as a poet, particularly his poetry after the 1930s, which is uncollected from periodicals and often in French, the jury is still out and demanding further evidence such as a complete poems in French and English and bibliographical notes.

For this handful of émigré Irish writers, Europe becomes another location where Irish poetry fails to take place in the 1940s and 1950s, where no substantial publishers gather their scattered poems, where readerships dwindle, and the poets themselves lose heart. Those facts hardly improve our picture of Irish poetry in the first decades after Yeats.

Just after Yeats and Joyce in Éire

Back in Ireland, those poets who lived south of the border, a few with real talent such as Padraic Fallon, Valentin Iremonger, Donagh MacDonagh, Anthony Cronin and Patrick MacDonogh, could not sustain a significant poetic career or overcome an isolation from an insular readership which was itself isolated from Britain and Europe. Among the victims of this torpid era who deserve reappraisal, Padraic Fallon (1905–74) has received quickening attention from critics such as Dennis O'Driscoll, Eamon Grennan and Seamus Heaney.[30] Born in Athenry near Yeats's Thoor Ballylee, 'as the crow flies fifteen miles away',[31] Fallon discloses the most explicit traces of an Oedipal struggle with Yeats. After secondary school in Roslea he worked as a customs official, in Dublin initially and then Wexford. He lived much of his adult life on a small farm outside Wexford with his wife and six sons. Although he published poems in *The Dublin Review* and other journals, he did not gather poems into a book until the year of his death, and so he was known as much for his verse plays heard on Radio Éireann as for his poetry. While these plays may have curtailed his production of lyrics, as they did Austin Clarke's during the 1940s, the radio reached a wider audience than published poetry could have provided in mid-century Ireland.

Although from the beginning Fallon disclosed a gift for memorable phrasing, he often evoked the Celtic Twilight where shadows of Yeats played across his poetry (e.g. 'horsemen go / To guesting-house and beer'; 'For there's no glory in a house, / Where the master's absent, if his son's a mouse').[32] His early and persistent theme is the relation of the mythic to the real, the typological to the particular, often denying the archetype only to have it reassert itself 'within where all the underworld / Is turning into myth'.[33] From mid-century, but particularly in the 1960s, he turns directly to address Yeats as if to exorcise his heroic phrasing and reliance on myth. In 'Yeats At Athenry Perhaps' Fallon speculates on the possibility that, as a youth, he crossed paths with Yeats ('But I'd never heard of him, the famous poet').[34] The poem succeeds unevenly, moving between vivid accounts of his own Gaelic and Catholic alterity to Yeats, appropriately surreal, and representations of Yeats through images which do not escape the pastiche. 'The Head', a long poem written in association with his radio play *The Vision of Mac Conglinne*, represents an essential dialectic in Fallon's work of take and give. The head of Orpheus, on whose lyricism Thracian civilisation was founded, floats seaward, after being decapitated by lustful and jealous Thracian women. Reduced by the elements to its hollow core, the head sings of irreducible desire: 'And from the still centre / . . . came the tiny whimper / Of some unhouselled thing; / The head's first cry'. Unheard by nature and the woman, the cry remains 'What happens and the happening / That will never come to pass'.[35] Fallon here is unlike other confident Irish advocates of less-is-more – Beckett, Mahon, sometimes Montague and Kinsella. As the seaward head loses its scalp and bone, its song fading and essentialising, the poem that cradles it enhances symphonically: 'While the coracle under it of sally withes / Dried, withered in sunlight, salt sealight / . . . / . . . sprung the spent lashings'. It seems symptomatic of Fallon's uncertain, attenuated relation to audience and his underrated career that this extraordinary poem was lost in a drawer for over a decade.[36]

In that post-Yeatsian generation isolated within Ireland, the purest lyrical talent, Patrick Kavanagh, became triply isolated, remaining at odds with and a curiosity within the circle of writers in Dublin who were themselves isolated from readers. 'The audience is as important as the poet. There is no audience in Ireland,' Kavanagh said later in his career.[37]

After a brilliant start in his native Monaghan and in Dublin, which reached a climax in 1942, and before a recovery in the last decade of his life, Kavanagh endured a less creative stretch which was reinforced by the wasteland of post-Yeatsian Irish poetry. Born in County Monaghan in 1904 to a cobbler/small farmer and, in Kavanagh's words, 'a simple peasant woman, twenty years younger than father',[38] he was as close as modern Ireland could produce to the nationalists' stereotype of the peasant or to Robert Burns or the rhyming weavers whom Hewitt celebrated. When Kavanagh moved to Dublin in the year of Yeats's death, he might have been mistaken for the pure, pre-industrial peasant or the stage Irishman, but it would become his principal intention as reviewer and essayist to oppose identity politics generally and, specifically, Celtic-Twilight Irishness, which he saw as 'a form of anti-art. A way of posing as a poet without actually being one.'[39]

Kavanagh's own representation of his life as 'two kinds of simplicity, the simplicity of going away and the simplicity of return' with a middle period of acrimony[40] has led several critics to arrange Kavanagh's career into three stages. Although he had written some of his most accomplished poems such as 'Inniskeen Road: July Evening', 'Shancoduff' and 'Art McCooey' before and just after his move to Dublin in 1939, his most productive year was 1942, when he completed and published his masterful anti-pastoral *The Great Hunger* and the long pilgrimage poem *Lough Derg*, which remained unpublished until after his death in 1967.

When writing *The Great Hunger* in the fall of 1941, Kavanagh was heavily influenced by Sean O'Faolain, editor of *The Bell*, who intended to supplant the myth and legend of Yeats's generation with a new realism, principally a fictional mode. Although O'Faolain paid homage 'to an imagined poet whose lamp "will, in the end, light far more than we can ever do"'[41] prose remained his medium of social criticism, and *The Bell*, at least during the tenure of its long-time poetry editor Geoffrey Taylor, never really rose beyond the mediocrity of English Georgian poetry.[42] Kavanagh's biographer and leading scholar Antoinette Quinn writes that 'it was not until autumn 1941 that he succeeded in refashioning himself as a writer in the disenchanted, socio-analytic *Bell* mode'.[43] The sociological issues *The Great Hunger* addresses – rural stagnation, depopulation and late and loveless marriages, all expressing the deep psychological wound of the Famine – had been mostly background to plot in prior Irish literature, such as Synge's *In the Shadow of the Glen*. In Quinn's words, Kavanagh saw 'with eyes *The Bell* had unsealed', with a resulting 'intense visionary clarity'.[44] Yet, beyond the social realism *The Bell* advocated, *The Great Hunger* undertakes an experimental point of view to win sympathy for and dramatize his hero Maguire's plight. No longer the autobiographical 'I' of the earlier poetry, the narrator invites a *we* into what is as much a documentary film as what he calls 'the tragedy'.[45] Once our perspective as sympathetic observer is established, the *we* can divide into the narrator and his 'Imagination' who are summoned to empathize – 'O let us kneel where the blind ploughman kneels / And learn to live without despairing'.[46] Although our viewpoint is often local and myopic, contained within Maguire's speech and viewpoint, even that viewpoint opens on the broad perspective of neighbours on adjoining hills and on broad meteorological perspectives: 'the winds / That blew through Brannagan's Gap on their way from Siberia'. Fading shots diminish Maguire against a widening landscape: 'that man on a hill whose spirit / Is a wet sack flapping about the knees of time',[47] a panning analogous to the movement from the individual day to the full span of human life.

The influence of cinema in *The Great Hunger* may be seen in shifts in 'camera angles' early in section III: 'Two black cats peeped between the banisters / And gloated over the bacon-fizzling pan. / Outside the window showed tin canisters. / The snipe of Dawn fell like a whirring stone / And Patrick on a headland stood alone'.[48] Later, in a 1946 column, Kavanagh advocated documentaries on the ordinary and quotidian, citing images from *The Great Hunger* 'to show the kind of material that should be recorded on film'.[49] Yet Kavanagh the director is not always certain in his jump-cuts and camera-angles, sometimes merging characters and sometimes assuming a false distance from his subject – 'An ignorant peasant deep in dung. / What can the passers-by think otherwise?'[50] – while in section XIII, the narrator assumes a scholarly remoteness from his subject as 'The world looks on / And talks of the peasant'.[51] Both of these distancings seem *provincial* in Kavanagh's terms of not trusting 'what his eyes see until he has heard what the metropolis . . . has to say on the subject'. The 'parochial mentality on the other hand . . .' never doubts 'the social and artistic validity of his parish'.[52] Nevertheless, in its socio-psychological probing, its vivid imagery, and its formal variety, *The Great Hunger* must be, with MacNeice's *Autumn Journal*, the most significant Irish long poem published in the two decades after Yeats's death.

During the second, middle, stretch of his career, Kavanagh remains mostly a prose writer: author of the novel *Tarry Flynn*, of columns and reviews for the *Irish Press* and the *Standard*, of a 'Diary' for John Ryan's journal *Envoy*, and, finally, of vituperative essays in *Kavanagh's Weekly*, which lasted for three months in 1952. Eventually, he would see that 'satire is unfruitful prayer'[53] and that his adversarial existence was ploughing 'my way through complexities and anger, hatred and ill-will towards the faults of man'.[54]

Kavanagh speaks of the third stage of his career as a rebirth, 'As a poet, I was born in or about nineteen-fifty-five', after a humiliating, failed libel suit and a medical operation which removed his cancerous lung. Confronting both a loss of dignity and his own mortality, he learned 'how not to care' and tuned his poetry accordingly 'to play a true note on a dead slack string'.[55] The instrument so tuned during this third phase is often the sonnet, as in 'The Hospital', 'Come Dance with Kitty Stobling', 'October', 'Dear Folks', 'Lines Written on a Seat on the Grand Canal . . .' and 'Canal Bank Walk'. This last poem weaves a form – nest, web, and 'a new dress woven' – for the incarnate Word. Balanced against this evident form are surprising enjambments – 'that I do / The will of God' and 'the breeze adding a third / Party to the couple kissing' – and off-rhyme: web / ad lib; woven / proven.[56] They contribute to a poem that seems aleatory and open to Grace. Through such signal achievements in the sonnet form that Yeats had mastered, Kavanagh, more than any of his successors, blazes for others the truant's path from Yeats's self-proclaimed school of perfectionist poetry.[57] Kavanagh's unheroic subject matter and his slack-string rendering of 'the true note', which Heaney would call 'prospector's luck',[58] seemed liberating to many of his successors.

Kavanagh shared the space of Dublin and of literary agorae such as The Palace Bar with his chief rival Austin Clarke, with whom he differed in numerous ways: the autodidact Kavanagh left school at thirteen whereas the scholarly Clarke obtained an MA and lectured, briefly, at UCD; Kavanagh dismissed literary uses of Irish myth while Clarke had undertaken as a legacy from Yeats portions of *The Táin* and of Irish legends; Kavanagh was peasant stock, and Clarke was from an urban middle-class family; Kavanagh was mercurial and hyperbolic in prose and poetic satire whereas a 'sense of honesty and truth-telling on the one hand and . . . painstaking attention to technical excellence on the other', in Hugh Maxton's estimate, make Clarke 'a figure of singular integrity'.[59] Although Kavanagh recognised that his relations with women were in 'childhood perverted by Christian moralists' ('One Wet Summer'),[60] for the most part his Catholicism expresses itself as praise of nature or of the everyday, recording 'love's mystery without claptrap'('The Hospital').[61] In sharp contrast, Clarke was imbued with a nearly crippling sense of shame, particularly as it arose from sexuality. These qualities – his integrity and his guilt – were definitive for Clarke.

Like Joyce, Clarke (1896–1974) was born into a large Dublin Catholic middle-class family, and attended Belvedere College and UCD; also like Joyce, he suffered a repressive Jansenist Catholicism, girded by Victorian prudishness and sealed in post-famine guilt. In 1919 Clarke experienced a severe breakdown which required nearly a year's confinement and electric-shock treatment in St Patrick's Hospital (founded on Jonathan Swift's patrimony), an experience not fully disclosed until publication of his powerful account in *Mnemosyne Lay in Dust* (1966). After a short-lived marriage at the beginning of 1921, Clarke emigrated to London for seventeen years. At his return to Dublin in 1938, he had published five volumes of poetry based mostly on Irish legend or set well before the Counter-Reformation in early Christian Ireland.

Having studied under Thomas MacDonagh and read his mentor's book on Irish prosody, *Literature in Ireland*, as well as having succeeded to his teaching position when MacDonagh was executed as a leader of the Easter Rising, Clarke was, in his own words, 'tempted to experiment in forgotten forms . . . in partial rhyming and muting'.[62] He discovered a menu of prosodic devices carried over from the Irish: 'we can have rhyme or assonance, on or off accent, stopped rhyme (e.g. *ring, kingdom; breath, method*), harmonic rhyme (e.g. *hero, window*), cross-rhyme'.[63] Preoccupied with poetic drama and the Lyric Theatre, which he founded with Robert Farren, the repatriated Clarke did not publish poetry for seventeen years. As Thomas Kinsella says of this period, 'In those flat years in Ireland at the beginning of the nineteen fifties, depressed so thoroughly that one scarcely noticed it, the uneasy silence of Austin Clarke added a certain emphasis.'[64]

Clarke re-emerged powerfully in 1955 with *Ancient Lights*, of which the title poem retains some unsolved but undismissable secrets. The autobiographical poem recalls the pious youth on an urban excursion when 'Nature read in a flutter / An evening lesson above my head', the vespers message being, first, that Darwinian nature is 'red in tooth and claw'. Secondly, nature is no longer an ancillary scripture to be read but a space in which man can intercede, act morally and adopt reason over irrational fear and guilt. Apparently, the child frightens away sparrows who were mugging an escaped cage-bird, as a result of which 'my fears / Were solved. I had absolved myself',[65] an absolution which he would extend to all humanity in 'A Sermon on Swift' (1968).

Between *Ancient Lights* in 1955 and his death in 1974, Clarke outproduced his younger rivals by publishing eight complete volumes of poetry which included topical satires against the theocratic state and the worldly church, some often erotic lyrics and long or longish poems – *Mnemosyne Lay in Dust*, 'The Healing of Mis', *Tiresias* and 'The Wooing of Becfola' – which address psychological, political or celebratory aspects of sexuality. Although many of his satires respond to daily news, such as a dedication of a statue or a funeral, some arise from more personal situations, such as the death of 'Martha Blake at Fifty-One', based on the death of Clarke's own sister. Enrolled in a lay order of the Carmelites, Martha Blake experiences not the ecstasies of the flesh recounted by her heroine St Theresa, but a renegade body: 'Ill-natured flesh / Despised her soul.' As she drains toward death, 'Wasted by colitis, refused / The daily sacrament / By regulation', her physical setting also turns against her: 'The Nuns had let the field in front / As an Amusement Park / . . . / Mechanical music, dipper, hold-tights, / Rifle-crack, crash of dodgems. / The ward, godless with shadow, lights, / How could she pray to God?'[66] The final question seems answered by the cacophony of overstressed lines and a conclusion in which *God* stop-rhymes evasively with *dodgems*.

Published in 1963, 'Martha Blake at Fifty-One' stands on the threshold of Clarke's remarkable last decade, a period which saw the publication of his self-healing *Mnemosyne Lay in Dust* and 'A Sermon on Swift', his poetic disclosure of Jonathan Swift's 'secret belief', proclaimed in turn many centuries earlier by the Irish scholar Eriugena as universal and 'Eternal Absolution'. He also published three celebrations of unbridled eroticism – 'The Healing of Mis,' 'The Wooing of Becfola' and *Tiresias* (1971). Pointedly, in the last poem sex is not the cause of sterility, as in Eliot's *The Waste Land*, but the cure of these social ills. Toward the end of this long poem, Clarke's blind seer foresees a new religion in which Christ's 'priests will wear the toga / At new altars, sacrifice the invisible' – a vision which sounds more like Protestant abstraction than the lusty incarnations Tiresias celebrates.[67] At the poem's ending, when the seer's wife calls her husband indoors, we witness this surrogate for the poet at peace with his day's close: 'Come in, dear / Friend, for the purple-robed hours pass by. Luna has led her / Star-flocks home – and your cup of hot milk waits on the table.'[68] Because of the longevity of his career, his exemplary honesty, his courage in taking on major adversaries, and perhaps even his belief that the music of a dead literature can be revived, all of which are receiving more respectful critical notice recently, Clarke's place in future canons of Irish poetry seems assured.

The 1960s and after: Murphy, Kinsella, Montague and the Dolmen Press

Clarke's re-emergence in the 1960s and 1970s results largely from his collaboration with Liam Miller, who founded the Dolmen Press in Dublin in 1951, and with younger poets associated with Dolmen who featured him in readings and publications. Before Dolmen emerged, the Irish Republic offered its poets very few book publishers beyond the chapbook publishing of Cuala Press. The tradition of periodical publication was better established – from *The Dublin Magazine* through such journals as *The Bell*, *Envoy*, *Poetry Ireland* and *The Kilkenny Magazine*, all of which published or reviewed Clarke and some, such as *Lace Curtain* and *Atlantis*, which did not. For book publication Clarke submitted to London publishers – Allen and Unwin, Macmillan – eventually for rejection and then published himself for a time with Bridge Press. Liam Miller assisted Clarke by typesetting these volumes of 1955, 1957 and 1960 before becoming Clarke's principal publisher over the poet's last dozen years.

Trained as an architect, Miller devoted many of his after-hours to drama (perhaps inspired in part by Clarke's commitment to his Lyric Theatre), enlisted with the Earlsfort Players, and began Dolmen Press publication with a book of four tinkers' ballads collected by one of the players, Sigerson Clifford.[69] Although totally dependent on the special gifts of Liam Miller, the Dolmen Press often elicited the sort of collaborative efforts that enriched the lives of participants and readers alike and that, in retrospect, we might call a poetic movement. Among the writers and artists who participated in Liam and Jo Miller's kitchen project was Thomas Kinsella, whose first publication, *The Starlit Eye* (1952), was set by Kinsella and published as the Dolmen's fourth publication. In its first eight years, Miller published Richard Murphy's *The Archaeology of Love* (1955), Kinsella's *Poems* (1956) and *Another September* (1958), and John Montague's *Forms of Exile* (1959), and altogether some three dozen books and broadsides in this short span. First to publish a full verse volume with Dolmen, Murphy (b. 1927) entrusted to Miller the broadside publication of three long poems which were collected in a Faber and Faber publication, *Sailing to an Island*, in 1963. Murphy was included in one of the events that signalled the arrival of this new generation – a reading with Kinsella and Montague organised by Miller in the ballroom of the Royal Hibernian Hotel in February of 1961 – and was barred from the second, the *Dolmen Miscellany*, published in 1962. In his autobiography *The Kick*, Murphy recalls being invited to edit this anthology with Kinsella and Montague, only to find during an absence in Galway that he had been 'excluded as an editor',[70] despite the fact that his long poem 'The Cleggan Disaster' was one of the outstanding offerings of the anthology.

Murphy writes that this exclusion confirmed him in his attachment to the west coast, where 'the sea chastened my resentment',[71] although it is difficult to imagine him as a collaborative poet or editor. In spite of his many friends among poets, he appears to be the only major Irish poet, perhaps with Boland, who has not edited an anthology or a journal's special issue of Irish writing, and his poems reinforce the sense that he is an isolated figure, the last Anglo-Irish poet of the planter caste whose poems focus from a controlled distance on the lives of Galway fishermen, tinkers, colonial subjects in Rhodesia or Ceylon or other participants in Ireland's colonial history. Murphy's historical poem *The Battle of Aughrim* (1964), which retells from various viewpoints this decisive 1691 battle, would join Montague's *The Rough Field* (1972), which it may have influenced, on most critics' lists of the best modern narrative poems. Often, in the cool clarity of Murphy's narration, sympathy is withheld or displaced, as onto a wolfhound, an Irish emblem but also an actual dog faithfully guarding the body of her master, an ensign in the Irish Jacobite army.[72] When a British soldier tries to detach the faithful dog from her master's corpse, 'She springs: in self-defence he fires his gun. / People remember this. // By turf embers she gives tongue / When the choirs are silenced in wood and stone'.[73]

In Murphy's next volume, *High Island* (1974), the equivocal calibration of poetic distance becomes a poetic subject, as when the poet-voyeur witnesses seals mating: 'But I must remember / How far their feelings are from mine marooned' ('Seals At High Island').[74] When a seal bull is killed by a rival, the poet projects onto the remaining seals the anthropomorphic feelings he has previously withheld: 'At nightfall they haul out, and mourn the drowned, / Playing to the sea sadly their last quartet, / An improvised requiem that . . . / . . . / Brings pity trembling down the rocky spine / Of headlands, till the bitter ocean's tongue / Swells in their cove, and smothers their sweet song'.[75]

That Murphy's restrained sympathy for victims and marginalised figures was reinforced by his own vulnerability as a bisexual poet has become explicit in his writing only with the obliquely confessional sonnets of *The Price of Stone* (1985) and his autobiography *The Kick* (2002). That publication on the heels of his *Collected Poems* (2001) has allowed reviewers to reassess in light of his remarkable integrity this slender, but hardly slight, poetic career.

Among the important collaborative efforts of the Dolmen Press, one project succeeded in transforming the most important poetic career of the last half-century in Ireland. In so doing, Dolmen also transformed Irish poetry generally, down to the present. With the important participation of Miller and the artist Louis le Brocquy, Thomas Kinsella (b. 1928) published in 1969 a translation of Ireland's major epic, the *Táin Bó Cúailnge*. During the fifteen-year gestation of *The Tain*, beginning with *The Sons of Usnech* (1954), Kinsella strengthened his skills as a scholar, linguist, translator and poet, and, at least to some extent, altered his concept of poetry.

Although he had studied the Irish language and legends in school and in summer courses, his upbringing within an urban working-class Catholic family inclined Kinsella away from Yeats and the Anglo-Irish Renaissance and toward Joyce's urban topics and English poetic models. In the poetry of W. H. Auden he found examples of form as dandyism, an ironic, slightly overdressed elegance. Over the first twelve years of his career – *Poems* (1956), *Another September* (1958), *Moralities* (1960), *Downstream* (1962), *Wormwood* (1966), *Nightwalker and Other Poems* (1968) – he sometimes wrote, as in 'Soft, To Your Places' ('Soft, to your places, love; I kiss / Because it is, because it is'),[76] what Eavan Boland identifies as 'the trenchant, ironic and musical send-up of accepted attitudes to poetry'.[77] Kinsella's first major publication, *Another September* (1958), a Poetry Book Society 'Choice' for the season, received laudatory reviews that Kavanagh and Clarke might have envied.

This achievement did not, however, prepare readers for the darkening and deepening of Kinsella's poetry, which, in part, resulted from the translation of the *Táin*, a rich medieval epic concerning war between Ulster and Connacht over the theft of a prize bull. From short cryptic poems embedded in the *Táin* called *rocs(ad)a* or *retoiric*, Kinsella may have assumed permission for dark, even secret passages in his own poetry.[78] As a consequence, his poetry would become more dramatic, multivocal, inclusive of various time-frames within the present moments of the poem, and resistant to closure.

Although the lessons learned over the twelve-year translation would help transform his poetry, *The Tain* itself would not be Kinsella's central myth. Rather, a closer analogue to Kinsella's own psychic voyages of discovery was found in the *Lebor Gabála Érenn*, the twelfth-century pseudo-history of the six successive settlements of Ireland, translated by R. A. Stewart Macalister as *The Book of Invasions* (1938–41).[79] In its recurrences, this legend could be made to represent not only a collective but also a personal history, the individual's necessity in love or social formation to return to, repossess and renew the same ground. This concern for renewal in love arises in 'Phoenix Park' and earlier poems before Kinsella had made any overt use of *The Book of Invasions*.

In *New Poems 1973* and after, Kinsella presents episodes from *The Book of Invasions*, fragmentary and uncontextualized, or permits mythic fragments to emerge within accounts of his own family or national history. As Kinsella has said, 'In rooting back into my own identity and finding Irish fathers and grandfathers, Irish history, . . . my model of the emergence of the psyche . . . necessarily take[s] Irish forms.'[80] For an example of Kinsella's use of multiple layers of history, we might consider *One*, where Amergin recalls embarking from 'Finistère': 'Where the last sunken ray withdrew. / A point of light. // A maggot of the possible / wriggled out of the spine / into the brain.'[81] A few pages on, the autobiographical 'Minstrel' extends the young poet's imagination toward the limits of his understanding as he experiences a moment of creation: 'A distant point of light / winked at the edge of nothing'. This creative moment ends in a startling division of the self: 'A knock on the window / and everything in fantasy fright / flurried and disappeared. / My father looked in from the dark, / my face black-mirrored beside his'.[82] In the previous poem '38 Phoenix Street', we encounter a similar mirroring when the boy is lifted above his garden wall only to meet the face of the neighbour's child held up on the other side. In 'Minstrel', coming of age creatively divides Kinsella's poet between the unconscious self and the self-conscious creative observer.

One also exhibits the unusual synchronous quality of Kinsella's poetry, with 'His Father's Hands' tracing the family succession. His grandfather – a fiddler and cobbler as well as an employee of Guinness – encourages children who visit his shoe-maker's shop to register their presence by knocking into a large block of wood shining shoe-sprigs, 'bright points among hundreds gone black'.[83] The poem recedes in time to the 1798 rebellion and in stages to a pre-historic account of dolmen makers, with images suggestive of *The Book of Invasions*: 'First, a prow of land / . . . / then boulders chosen / and sloped together, stabilized in menace'.[84] When the poet returns in the recent past to his grandfather's yard and recovers the cobbler's block, artifacts of the past become larval and uncannily generative: '[I] . . . stood it up, wet and black: / it turned under my hands, an axis / of light flashing down its length, / and the wood's soft flesh broke open, / countless little nails / squirming and dropping out of it'.[85]

The endings of these three poems – '38 Phoenix Street', 'Minstrel' and 'His Father's Hands' – startle us into a living moment, the poem's present tense. Kinsella's clear images and unblinking view of his own experience fulfil F. R. Leavis's prescription for successful poetry, which occurs when a poet is 'more alive than other people, more alive in his own age'.[86] We recognise from the poems cited above, however, that Kinsella's 'own age' embodies coded strata of various ages – genetic, biographical, historical and mythic – and that, consequently, the proprietary poetic self to which *his* refers remains unstable, dissolving and reforming within the poem.

From 1972, for a time with Liam Miller's assistance, Kinsella published his sequences of poems under his own Peppercanister imprint. The series was initiated with a broadside-ballad response, in the spirit of Swift's 'Drapier', written within a week of the Widgery Tribunal's report exonerating the British Army in the killing of thirteen civil-rights marchers in Derry. Kinsella contends that the savage indignation of his poem, rather than the increasing difficulty of his style, cost him his British readers.[87] The Peppercanister series gave Kinsella control, initially, to respond quickly to these political events but also to continue to publish poems of different lengths, various modes, and different degrees of seriousness, with the possibility of later revision or resituation within sequences.

Although these slender volumes lend themselves to sequences, they rarely narrate or dramatise a conventional linear story. Frequently they rearrange time, as in the very accessible tribute to Kinsella's father, *The Messenger*, where time moves backward in stages from the nightmare image of the father's maggoty corpse to arrive at the father as child setting out on his first job as a telegram messenger, 'all excitement . . . / shoes polished, and a way to make in the world'.[88]

However, as Kinsella implies in another reprise, even the most consoling poetry cannot undo the past or locate its beginnings. In 'Morning Coffee', an image of a foetus from the 1960s poem 'Ballydavid Pier' ('Lost in self-search / – A swollen blind brow / Humbly crumpled over / Budding limbs, unshaken / By the spasms of birth or death')[89] marks a tidal return in the Peppercanister volume *Madonna and Other Poems* (1991) to the survivors Kinsella had adapted from *The Book of Invasions*: 'We thought at first it was a body / rolling up with a blank belly onto the beach / the year our first-born babies died. // A big white earthenware vessel / settled staring up / open mouthed at us'. A survivor concludes: 'Soon we were making up stories / about the first People / and telling them to our second born'.[90] The 'blank belly' suggests the post-Darwin controversy concerning Eve's origination, to which Stephen Dedalus refers in the Proteus episode of *Ulysses* and which calls into question the folly of seeking an origin outside or within a cyclical history.

More recently, *The Familiar* (1999) returns to the poet's Baggot Street flat, the setting for earlier poems about poetic creations, such as 'Baggot Street

Deserta', and about early stages in his affair with his future wife and muse. Following the *Book of Invasions*' pattern of recurrence, repossession and renewal, and eschewing finality and closure, *The Familiar* reprises and revises the lovers' quarrel, separation, return and reconciliation, like those recorded in a half-dozen earlier poems and sequences, such as 'Phoenix Park', 'Wedding Morning' and *Madonna*. This familiar setting becomes a setting for mostly feminised familiars – 'demons over the door', the lover as muse, 'three graces' on a poster with one 'holding the mirror', an *aisling* 'nymph' appearing in dream, the household cat, two crows, 'Three women from the North side' and the poet and lover returning as 'Her shade' and with 'ghost hands' respectively.[91] 'The Familiar' sequence closes with a morning repast, as in earlier volumes, a breakfast ritual that conveys layers of memory, prepared by the poet-priest and blessed by the woman as 'shade': 'You are very good. / You always made it nice.'[92] As postscript to 'The Familiar', the volume ends with two poems, 'St John's', which returns to the setting of 'Another September', and 'Iris', which recycles from *The Messenger* the image of the dragonfly, attendant at the moment of the poet's conception in the earlier poem where 'The wings // close up like palms. The body, a glass worm, / is pulsing. The tail-tip winces and quivers: / I *think* there is where I come in.'[93] This 'gossamer ghost' carries the code of its past, whether as larva, cocoon and imago, or as a sperm-like go-between, wedding the parents and their centuries of genetic but also human history. In concluding this later volume, the generative 'maiden messenger' – 'Her frail tail / uplifted, leaving / a virginal drop' – is feminised, as are all of the poets' 'familiars' in this revision. The poem's title identifies her as Iris, employed in the *Iliad* in Hermes' role as messenger to the gods, but also in some accounts the mother of Eros, who addresses the poet in the epilogue to this volume: 'Love bent the sinewy bow / against His knee, / saying: *Husband, here is a friend / beseeming thee.*'[94]

Such recycling and revising, within works and from earlier volumes, reduces our sense of linearity, of closure, and of a single self existing within history as it redefines our relation to the past as a complex balance of memory, history and poetic traces. One may argue plausibly that the most complex and multi-layered of the Peppercanister poems – including *Vertical Man*, *One*, *A Technical Supplement*, *The Messenger*, *Songs of the Psyche*, *Out of Ireland*, *St Catherine's Clock* and *The Pen Shop* – taken with the 1968 and 1973 volumes and some of the earlier poems – comprise the most challenging, most achieved, and therefore most rewarding body of poems from the British Isles over this past half-century.

While Peppercanister gave Kinsella interim control of his own publication, the death of Miller in 1987, his move with Eleanor Kinsella from Percy

Place in Dublin to Laragh in Wicklow in the mid-1980s and his eventual move to Philadelphia in 2000 (with a part-time base soon after in Wicklow town) severely attenuated his active participation in the Irish literary scene.

In contrast, neither ageing nor displacements has diminished John Montague's fervour for literary collaboration. Three years after graduation from UCD, Montague (b. 1929) travelled to the US for what became a three-year apprenticeship in American poetry at Yale, Indiana, the Iowa Workshop and the University of California at Berkeley. With friends and acquaintances such as Berryman, Dickey, Snodgrass, Bly, Snyder and Duncan, Montague, in his own words, 'felt a strong sense of kinship, the shared adventure of modern literature to which Ireland has contributed much as well'.[95] Upon his return to Dublin in 1956, he moved to the centre of collaboration: 'I finally found, with Kinsella and Liam Miller of the Dolmen Press, a working relationship based on the thrust of common ideals. Liam especially had a rich generosity which transformed work into adventure.'[96]

Adding Richard Murphy's name to his and Kinsella's gave some plausibility to Montague's exhortative assertion, frequent in his letters of that time, that they were the emerging generation or, indeed, the 'Second Anglo-Irish Renaissance'![97] Joint activities over the period of the late 1950s and early 1960s began, as mentioned earlier, with a public reading by these three poets at the Royal Hibernian Hotel in 1961, orchestrated by Miller. With Kinsella and Miller, Montague edited the *Dolmen Miscellany*, a one-off anthology (1962), and, with Miller, he organised the Dolmen Editions readings in Dublin, *A Tribute to Austin Clarke on His Seventieth Birthday* (1966) and the poetic sequence of *The Rough Field*. This latter work was enhanced by Miller's design, juxtaposing sixteenth-century woodcuts from John Derricke to emphasize the sequence's autobiographical and historical bi-focalism. Montague served as advisory editor with Tim O'Keeffe to bring into print for the London publisher MacGibbon and Kee selections of Kavanagh's poetry, fiction of Francis Stuart and poems of Hewitt. Montague guided Garech Brown in the founding of Claddagh Records, which recorded readings by Kavanagh, Clarke, Kinsella, Heaney, Graves and others. At Michael Longley's invitation, Montague joined the 1970 and 1971 reading tours in Northern Ireland with Hewitt – billed as 'The Planter and the Gael'. Finally, he supervised a dramatic reading of *The Rough Field*, with the Chieftains and well-known readers, in the Peacock Theatre, Dublin, and then the Roundhouse in London. During this period he published as major collections *Forms of Exile* (1958) with Dolmen, *Poisoned Lands* (1961), *A Chosen Light* (1967) and a collection of stories with MacGibbon and Kee, and *Tides* (1970) and *The Rough Field* (1972) with Dolmen.

Montague's sense of the writer's life as an adventure to be shared by the family of writers may have been compensation for his childhood exclusion from his parents, when at age five he was shipped back from his birthplace in Brooklyn to the fosterage of his father's two sisters in Northern Ireland. When his mother returned three years later to live nearby, she left her son in the care of his aunts. This wound of maternal rejection surfaces throughout his poetry – 'All roads wind backwards to it. / An unwanted child, a primal hurt'.[98] In his need for collaborative work, a sharing of rituals, a breaking of bread, we witness what Montague calls 'Company', the title of his autobiography, the first instalment of which was published in 2002.

Montague has earned a place in the contemporary canon in part by fulfilling the poet's lonely eremitical functions. From his earliest poetry he enters the page with restraint, as in 'The Water Carrier', a poem that must have influenced Heaney's 'Personal Helicon'. In Montague's poem the boy draws spring water that 'ran so pure and cold, it fell / Like manacles of ice on the wrists'.[99] That startling freshness Montague recovers often, following the prescription of Wordsworth for 'the real language of men in a state of vivid sensation'. The unusual but appropriate word 'manacles' suggests that restraint is part of this experience, as it is in much of Montague's poetry. The poems usually understate, often gesturing toward the unspoken, the silent and the white of the page, as in his love poem 'Tracks', which recalls a hotel rendezvous: 'The vast bedroom / a hall of air, / our linked bodies / lying there'.[100] The poem concludes: '*I shall miss you* / creaks the mirror / into which the scene / shortly disappears: / the vast bedroom / a hall of air, the / tracks of our bodies / fading there, while / giggling maids push / a trolley of fresh / linen down the corridor'. The lucid details ironically record transience where the mirror, a conventional image for art, speaks of absence as it absorbs and erases. In brief accelerated lines, body and trolley tracks fade as the coupling *air* and *there* from the opening stanza also fade into lines that enjamb. 'Maids' and 'fresh linen' prepare for this erasure and others' beginning.

'Tracks' found its place in *The Great Cloak* (1978), the powerful lyric sequence, as poignant as Meredith's *Modern Love* or Graves's love poetry, that recounts the breakdown of Montague's marriage and the renewal of love in a second marriage. In 1971 he moved to Cork to lecture at UCC, to raise two daughters with his wife Evelyn, and eventually to publish four books of poetry – *A Slow Dance* (1972), *The Great Cloak, The Dead Kingdom* (1984) and *Mount Eagle* (1988). Prior to Montague's move to Cork, with the exception of Seán Ó Ríordáin (writing in Irish) and perhaps Patrick Galvin (whose witty ballad-like poetry anticipated Durcan), Cork had not been fertile ground for poetry. During his sixteen-year residence in Cork, his longest stay to date in one place, he and the poets Sean Lucy and Seán Ó Tuama influenced a circle of young writers who included Thomas McCarthy, a poet of great skill but restricted somewhat by his topic of Irish political history, Sean Dunne, a very promising poet who died at age thirty-nine, Theo Dorgan, Maurice Riordan, Gregory O'Donoghue, Greg Delanty, Nuala Ní Dhomhnaill, Michael Davitt, Liam Ó Muirthile and Gabriel Rosenstock.

John and Evelyn Montague's first home in Cork, Roche's Point, becomes the setting for the opening of *The Dead Kingdom*: 'my wife, from the shore / at Roche's Point, calls, / "John, come in, come home, / your mother is dead"'.[101] So, as in *The Rough Field*, Montague begins another journey north, where family matters mesh inextricably with sectarian politics. Montague intersperses photographs and drawings with his own poems – *dinnshenchas* (narratives that explain a place-name), accounts of sectarian violence, and memories of his mother's neglect for which he finds solace in 'A new love, a new / litany of place names; / the hill city of Cork / lambent under rain'.[102]

Montague left Cork in 1988 for a Distinguished Chair in the New York State Writers' Institute in Albany, New York, from which he retired in the late 1990s. In 1993 he published the autobiographical poems about his school days *Time in Armagh* and, two years later, his *Collected Poems*, which contains 'Border Sick Call', an impressive new long poem about an emergency home visit with his brother, a medical doctor, through a heavy trace-effacing snowstorm along the boundary between the North and the Republic: 'where demarcations disappear, / landmarks, forms, and farms vanish / into the ultimate coldness of an ice age, / as we march towards Lettercran, / in steelblue, shadowless light, / The Ridge of the Tree, the heart of whiteness'.[103] In 1998 Montague returned to Ireland, to take up the first three-year appointment as the Irish Professor of Poetry at Queen's, Trinity and UCD. In the next year, he published *Smashing the Piano*, which contains some startling candid poems and others that suggest that, in spite of his relative isolation, living with his third wife the novelist Elizabeth Wassell in southern France and west Cork, the adventure of this major writer's life goes forward.

To remain current with readers and reviews, however, Montague feels obliged to accept readings in, or otherwise call on, Dublin, which, over the last two decades, retained its centrality in the Irish literary life. Poetry readings in Dublin have been a better indicator of popular reception than book sales. Ireland may be fortunate in that its recent popular poets evolve out of a mixture of the oral tradition and visionary, iconoclastic poetry with Kavanagh as a model. In the mid 1980s and 1990s, Brendan Kennelly (b. 1936) and Paul

Durcan (b. 1944), who began publishing in the 1960s and who have developed dramatic, even charismatic reading styles, acquired a popular audience available to Heaney but perhaps to no other Irish poet. From his first publication in 1963, Kennelly published nearly a book a year for the two decades that led to his most popular work *Cromwell* (1983). Questions of when prolificacy becomes mere prolixity may be muted by this long poem's energetic rush of dramatic statements by various contemporary and seventeenth-century characters whose savage bluntness and historical quaintness become riveting in a public reading. From his first full volume in 1975, Durcan's very real lyric gift became increasingly drawn out and conversational, refrains becoming semi-sensical punctuation in a reading modelled as much on Theatre of the Absurd as on Irish storytelling. *The Berlin Wall Café* (1985) and *Daddy, Daddy* (1990), which enlarged his British audience as well, mixed lyrics with very effective satires. Sometimes directed against the Catholic hierarchy, monocular nationalists, or party hacks, Durcan's satirical verse would have been the envy of Kavanagh in his middle period.

If some poets can draw crowds in Dublin, poets can also live privately there, remaining eccentric to poetic circles. After the success of two early books, *Windfalls* (1977) and *Minding Ruth* (1983), Aidan Mathews (b. 1956) published his third book of poetry fifteen years later after devoting time and talents to fiction and drama. Intricate and precise, *According to the Small Hours* (1998) conveys its spiritual concerns in long lines, often overfreighted with ideas and slightly overwritten, yet too richly intelligent to be dismissed. Of less brilliance than Mathews, John F. Deane also writes what might be called Christian existential or even Counter-Reformational poetry, which returns to spiritual themes and the body–soul cohabitation. As with Peter Fallon, Deane's role as a publisher (of Dedalus Press) overshadows his role as a poet.

Another group of poets based with a Dublin publisher proclaims its own eccentricity, not simply as one type of poetry among many but as a Modernist, avant-garde alternative to what it sees as a mainstream Irish poetry. With the help of critics such as Alex Davis, J. C. C. Mays and Patricia Coughlan, the editor and poet Michael Smith has found in the work of 1930s Modernists such as Coffey, Devlin and Beckett a patrilineage for Trevor Joyce, Augustus Young, Gerard Smyth, Geoffrey Squires and other contemporary poets associated with his New Writers Press, which, in turn, may have given heart to new presses such as Black Mountain, Abbey and Wild Honey Press, which publish formerly inaudible but potentially important poets such as Maurice Scully and, especially, Randolph Healy. In making the case for this late-Modernist writing, Smith and other revisionists tend to 'ride a little roughshod over the complexities of the Irish cultural landscape, postulating a poetic uniformity and, pitted against it, an avant-garde, that are equally paper tigers'.[104] Yet, without accepting these writers as the experimental alternative to Medbh McGuckian, Eiléan Ní Chuilleanáin, Paul Muldoon and other truly experimental poets, we can recognise the merit of Trevor Joyce and others in this group.

Seamus Heaney's career

Of the various shifting assemblies of Irish poetry in the last half-century – Cork, Dublin, Galway and Belfast – perhaps the most unlikely and certainly the most publicised has been the Northern Irish capital of the 1970s and early 1980s. Certainly, since the 1968 rekindling of the Troubles, British journalists have projected images and voices of Belfast into both British and US homes and brought extraliterary attention to Northern Irish poets. Yet, before the initial brick was hurled at Burntollet, Seamus Heaney (b. 1939) had published his first, well-acclaimed book, *Death of A Naturalist*, in 1966, and before that – as we follow the normal backward course of Ireland's Sisyphean history – the existence of a 'Belfast Group' and the centrality of the Derry poet Heaney to this group were acknowledged in Dublin by Liam Miller and Montague.[105]

In 1963 the elder British critic and poet Philip Hobsbaum arrived at Queen's University to teach and with his wife to host poets regularly at his home for readings and stringent critiques of their poetry. Although Mahon and Longley have raised questions about the importance of the Group to the improvement of poetry in Belfast,[106] clearly it was helpful to Heaney, Simmons and some younger poets. Earlier yet, in 1961, Heaney had researched his meagre Ulster poetic legacy as represented in old issues of *Lagan* and *Rann*, journals which may have also influenced James Simmons in founding the long-lived *Honest Ulsterman*. And even earlier, when Heaney had left his eight younger siblings on a forty-acre farm in County Derry to attend on scholarship St Columb's College in Derry and then Queen's University, Belfast, he found in the poetry of Hewitt clues for representing his own amphibian landscape. He later quotes a passage in which Hewitt's tactile imagery reinforces sound effects which Hewitt centres in primal diction, in this case an elongation of Stephen Dedalus's word *suck*: 'for we have rights drawn from the soil and sky; / . . . / the rain against the lips, the changing light, / the heavy clay-sucked stride, have altered us'.[107]

From Heaney's earliest poetry, certainly from 'Personal Helicon' onward, his labile and tactile imagery is reinforced by an Irish vertical geometry in which the speaker's direction is downward, through digging, the 'dark drop', soundings, or 'striking inward and downwards'. Such probings are part of the poet's effort to define the self, in great part by characterising what is not-self and part of the unconscious, both personal and collective. In Heaney's fourth book, *North*, his psychological intentions are obscured by the accidental conjunction of history – his personal discovery of the uncanny photographs of ancient corpses in P. V. Glob's *The Bog People*, the foundation of the People's Democracy movement (joined by many of Heaney's students) and the resumption of the Troubles. Although Heaney participated in at least one march, for many months of the first years of the Troubles he was away from the North, travelling in Spain on a fellowship, teaching in Berkeley, before moving to Wicklow in 1972, and later to a permanent residence in Dublin.

Heaney's departure from the North hardly eased the pressure on the poet to address issues of the Troubles and to affirm, in Seamus Deane's words, 'the fidelity of the poet to his community'.[108] His third volume, *Wintering Out*, portrays a continuity between his chosen craft and those of his community's pre-industrial artisans. In a half-dozen other poems he grounds the poet's language in the wet and rocky aspects of his landscape, as he proclaims himself 'lobe and larynx / of the mossy places' ('Oracle').[109] In 'The Tollund Man' he initiates the association between ancient sacrificial victims, whose corpses he had studied in Glob's *The Bog People*, and victims of the Troubles.

Of course, Heaney was not the first Catholic poet from Ulster to write about his community and the Troubles, and from the model of John Montague's *Poisoned Lands*, which Heaney read in 1963, but especially *The Rough Field* in 1972, he could find both encouragement and the basis for his own independent approach to the Troubles. Because Montague composed most of *The Rough Field* before the re-eruption of the Troubles, he used history and autobiography – the return to a homeland from which he is permanently separated – to give his multivoiced narrative greater coolness and distance. In contrast, Heaney in his next volume, *North* (1975), employs myth – images of the bog burials that are detailed and obsessive – and his own composed voice to give warmth and immediacy to his more current account of the Troubles. *North* quickly became, and has remained, Heaney's most celebrated and controversial volume. It opens with two prefatory poems, which are followed by part I – a long section on the Antaeus myth, bog-burials, Viking myth and art – and a briefer part II, in which the poet comments more personally on the Troubles. Most critics focus on part I, many interpreting it to be a myth of Northern violence as a response and tribute to an earth goddess for whom the bog-burials, no less than the current sectarian homicides, provide sacrificial victims.

Certain poems do posit a kinship between Cathleen ni Houlihan and the goddess Nerthus, and between the victims of each: 'report us fairly, / how we slaughter / for the common good // . . . / how the goddess swallows / our love and terror' ('Kinship').[110] However, Heaney's suggestions in these few poems and in *Preoccupations*[111] that the violence in Northern Ireland and ancient Denmark are cognate and determined by psychological forces present in ancient Northern rituals of sacrifice are supported by neither argument nor real evidence. Finally, other poems in section I such as 'The Bog Queen', 'The Grauballe Man' and 'Punishment', valuable in themselves, are too exploratory, tentative and dialectical to compose a coherent myth.

In *Field Work* (1979), the volume that followed *North*, Heaney included three elegies to friends who had died in the Troubles, explicit in their gory details but also aestheticising and memorialising beyond the mere obituary. In the subsequent volume *Station Island* (1984), he dramatised his dilemma not only as a self-appointed but popularly acclaimed witness-bearer to the plight of a colonised people but also as a poet reluctant either to exploit sensational history or to have it both ways by including appalling details in elegies that 'whitewash [. . .] ugliness'. In volumes after *Station Island* – *The Haw Lantern* (1987), *Seeing Things* (1991) and *The Spirit Level* (1996) – Heaney enlarged the question of how art accommodates violence and horror to the question of where art and the imaginary life are situated in relation to our 'shared' life. From early in his poetry Heaney's poems have all carried as subtexts, explored or unexplored, questions about the relation of art to life, about those spaces where poetry impinges on political reality and vice versa.[112]

Heaney's locations of the imaginative world and the world we think we share find full expression in *The Redress of Poetry*, published in 1995 from lectures delivered at Oxford University between 1989 and 1994, when Heaney was Professor of Poetry. He concludes this volume with a simplified version of these two worlds:

> Within our individual selves we can reconcile two orders of knowledge which we might call the practical and the poetic; . . . each form of knowledge redresses the other and . . . the frontier between them is there for the crossing.[113]

He then cites a poem from *Seeing Things* (1991) based on a meeting of these two worlds. A ship from the Otherworld gets its anchor accidentally entangled in the altar rail of an oratory. The poem concludes with an appeal to release the ship into its own sphere: '"This man can't bear our life here and will drown," // The abbot said, "unless we help him." So / They did, the freed ship sailed, and the man climbed back. / Out of the marvellous as he had known it'.[114] Heaney opens *The Redress of Poetry* by speaking about 'crossing from the domain of the matter-of-fact into the domain of the imagined',[115] but as we see from the *Annals* poem, traffic sails both ways.

Seeing Things contains so many reflective surfaces that we move the stress from the title's second word, where it resided in the earlier, palpable verse, to its first word and an emphasis on shifting perspective and startling perception. The epilogue from Virgil and part I, the length of a book in themselves, prepare us for 'Squarings', four groups of a dozen twelve-line stanzas in which the form frames new vistas. For example, preparatory to the poem from the *Annals*, mentioned above, the first part of the title poem 'Seeing Things' recounts a crowded boat trip to Inishbofin: 'One by one we were being handed down / Into a boat that slipped and shilly-shallied / Scaresomely . . .'[116] The poem's emphasis on precise trim so close to the water's surface may keep us from recognising this is the Psychopomp or Charon, and we are moving through time as well as space toward the Otherworld, until the perspective suddenly plumbs 'The deep, still, seeable-down-into water'. As if looking down from an airborne boat, he 'could see / How riskily we fared into the morning, / And loved in vain our bare, bowed, numbered heads'. As 'in vain' indicates, these poems maintain another sort of trim between recognition of an 'old truth . . . there is no next-time-round' and the intention – in an allusive colloquy with Philip Larkin, Thomas Hardy, Derek Mahon and other famous unbelievers – to elegise his recently dead father and humanity generally.[117]

Although *Seeing Things* invests in a different form and mode and what Heaney called 'a whimsicality, almost, of invention',[118] it retains his familiar voice. Heaney's popularity has continued to grow through the reception of his last six poetic volumes and his four major collections of essays, in part because readers were reassured by a recognizable personal voice. Even in his least lyrical poems, such as the dramatic monologues of *Station Island* (1984), the voice in the poem remains familiar and the persona congenial and trustworthy. In a 1974 lecture, Heaney offers his popular poem 'Digging' to illustrate what he calls 'finding a voice', meaning 'you can get your own feeling into your own words. . . . A voice is like a fingerprint, possessing a constant and unique signature.'[119] The critic Ian Gregson credits Heaney with such 'voice': 'One of his most remarkable achievements has been to construct a version of himself as a poet which his readers recognise. This is partly a matter of his public persona, the 50-ish year old public smiling man . . . old-fashioned as a poet should be, and above all actually a very nice man.'[120] Poets discussed in this chapter, including Kinsella, Ciaran Carson, Paul Muldoon and Eiléan Ní Chuilleanáin, who deflect personality and offer readers multi-layered or fragmented selves, may lead readers to question such a consistently recognisable voice. David Lloyd, perhaps Heaney's harshest critic, identifies this 'strong sense of the implied author' with conservatism: 'The cautious limits which Heaney's poetry sets round any potential for disruptive, immanent questioning may be the reason for the extraordinary inflation of his current reputation.'[121] We should recognise, however, that readers' trust in Heaney must have been grounded, in part, on frank rebukes to English audiences and critics who were honouring him. For example, in 1983 he reminded editors who had made him the keystone in an anthology of 'British' poetry that 'No glass of ours was ever raised / To toast *The Queen*',[122] and in 1988 upon receiving the *Sunday Times* Award he candidly told an admiring English audience that 'policies which Downing Street presumably regards as a hard line against terrorism can feel like a high-handed disregard for the self-respect of the Irish people in general'.[123]

In what had come to seem an inevitable selection, Heaney won the Nobel Prize in 1995. A few months before that award, the esteemed English critic Donald Davie, shortly before his death, declared that among English-language poets, Heaney held 'a position of unchallenged authority' which he had 'earned by solid accomplishment'. Davie then expresses relief that Heaney had 'consistently refused, in the face of tempting offers, to be either outlandish or partisan'.[124]

Without denying Heaney's extraordinary accomplishment – his translations from Anglo-Saxon, Irish, Greek, Italian and Romanian, his collections of lectures and essays, his editing of anthologies and his own poems – we might wonder if other Irish poets might not also have 'solid accomplishment' but fail Davie's tests of prudency for the laureateship: Montague's self-confessed 'vomit surge of race hatred', Muldoon's affrontive kinkiness and his poetic hectoring of Heaney, Mahon's Achillean withdrawal, Ní Chuilleanáin's respect for the hidden, and Kinsella's savage indignation, expressed in *Butcher's Dozen*. In *Songs of the Psyche* (1985), Kinsella asks critics and readers, 'Possibly you would rather I stopped / – uttering guttural Christ curses / . . . / . . . / in a fury beside your head?' and prescribes a self-service lobotomy 'until there is / glaze and numbness in "that" area' which would have the effect of making him more suitable to Davie's standard, less 'outlandish or partisan': 'Then you would see how charming / it is possible to be, / how fluent and fascinating, / a startlement to all, / internationally, and beyond.'[125]

The North: *The Honest Ulsterman*, Simmons, Mahon, and Longley

Heaney's self-declared journalistic bridges – *Lagan, Rann* – to the scarce Ulster poetic tradition may have been less necessary for Michael Longley and Derek Mahon, who had sustaining Anglo-Irish models in Yeats and MacNeice. All of Heaney's contemporaries and even their successors, nevertheless, have been bolstered by *The Honest Ulsterman*, the long-lived journal founded by the balladeer, songwriter and serious poet James Simmons (1933–2001) in 1968. The journal often mirrored the unpretentious non-sectatian and anti-elitist spirit of its founder, whose considerable body of poetry often spoke hard truths candidly, as in the ironically titled 'From the Irish': 'Familiar things you might brush against or tread / upon in the daily round, were glistening red / with the slaughter the hero caused, though he had gone. / By proxy his bomb exploded, his valour shone'.[126] In another poem Simmons imagines a censorious bookshop owner objecting to his journal's sexual frankness: '"This is pure dirt," he says.'[127] Seizing the man by 'his private parts', the poet forces the shopkeeper at last to testify on behalf of poetry: '"It's true. It's urgent. What else could I say?" // "That's how the poet feels," I smile. "Good day."'

After nineteen monthly issues Simmons passed on the editorship to Frank Ormsby, who edited it with Michael Foley, then by himself, and then with Robert Johnstone; eventually Ruth Hooley and then Tom Clyde served as sustaining editors. Simmons's monthly editorial 'Revolutionary Advice' lacked the gravity of Sean O'Faolain's columns for *The Bell*, but, months before the Burntollet confrontations and the resumption of the Troubles, it spoke out against sectarian narrowness and conveyed a cheeky nudge to staid thinkers to move over for this younger generation of Heaney, Mahon, Longley, Carson, McGuckian, Ormsby, Simmons himself and others even as the journal was restoring the voices of Hewitt, Sam Hanna Bell, George Buchanan and other older writers and importing poets from the Irish Republic and Great Britain.

Meanwhile, Derek Mahon (b. 1941) and Michael Longley (b. 1939) were beginning their careers away from Northern Ireland. While usually characterised as Belfast poets, they were in fact contemporaries at Trinity College, Dublin, in the 1960s and part of a literary circle that included Brendan Kennelly, Eavan Boland, Eamon Grennan, Rudi Holzapfel, Richard Eckersley and Edna Longley (neé Broderick). While Mahon and Longley were subsequently recognised as part of the fore-mentioned 'Belfast Group', which gathered weekly with Seamus Heaney (and later, Paul Muldoon and Frank Ormsby) under the sponsorship of the English scholar and poet Philip Hobsbaum, Mahon has denied his participation: 'I was a member of my own group in Dublin,' he has written.[128] There he developed a lifelong attraction not only to such apostles of the existential self as Beckett (widely admired by his teachers), Camus and the contemporary French poets whom he would translate and imitate, but also to the very notion of a group of writers and artists who shoulder together against a world that no longer has a place for them.

If Mahon has been perhaps the most peripatetic participant in either Dublin or Belfast poetic circles, that fact might have been anticipated from his earliest volume, *Night-Crossings*, published in 1968 when Mahon was twenty-six. Praised in *TLS* and *Poetry*, it includes 'In Carrowdore Churchyard', a tribute to Louis MacNeice, another expatriate poet who, with Auden, was a major influence. Already in these poems the speaker identifies with what he will call the 'mute phenomena' ejected from the homeplaces of humanity, 'pits, slag-heaps, beetroot fields', a bleak landscape in which, in 'the dying light of truth', 'God gutters down to metaphor' ('Van Gogh among the Miners').[129] Perhaps related to that sympathy for the uprooted is a predilection for poetic revision, a linguistic precision that will, for example, lead Mahon a decade later to revise in these lines 'truth' to 'faith' ('A Portrait of the Artist').[130] While Mahon's early poems are often rhetorically extravagant, they are self-mockingly so, acknowledging that they emerge belatedly in an age in which forms have outlived their life or meaning. 'I am not important and I have to die,' the speaker offers in 'Exit Molloy'. 'Strictly speaking,' he continues, 'I am already dead, / But still I can hear the birds sing on over my head'.[131] Mahon writes in 'Rage for Order' four years later in *Lives*, that 'poetry' is 'a dying art / An eddy of semantic scruple / In an unstructurable sea'.[132] Yet he increasingly succeeds in finding within the disorder of the age – particularly within his own Ulster, where, as in his 1975 *The Snow Party*, death is 'In the service / Of barbarous kings' – the civility and even hope of the marginal.[133] 'God is alive and lives under a stone,' Mahon writes in 'After Nerval': 'Already in a lost hub-cap is conceived / The ideal society which will replace our own'.[134]

The impulse to imitate the 'banished gods' by effacing the self, identifying with whatever detritus or weed 'will be left / After the twilight of metals, / the flowers of fire'[135] is a trait Mahon shares with Longley (see below, 'The White Garden'). Both poets recognise that whatever integrity persists beyond the madness of war or ecological ignorance manifests itself in the objects of the world taken for granted by the 'brute hegemony' of a majority, whether of a religious denomination or simply those whose privilege causes them to ignore in the garbage heap 'the terminal democracy of hatbox and crab, of hock and Windowlene' ('The Apotheosis of Tins').[136] Mahon's most celebrated poem on that persistence, 'A Disused Shed in Co. Wexford', is post-apocalyptic not only in its identification with what survives (read allegorically, the mushrooms who are its subject could be survivors of the concentration camps) but more remarkably in its insistent focus on an unallegorical reading, one in which what is truly alien – fungal life, the brute phenomena – clamours for our attention. 'Even now there are places where a thought might grow,' he writes, identifying *as* thought the sentient mushrooms of a 'burnt-out hotel' from the Troubles that 'have learnt patience and silence'.[137]

Questioning the value of poetic distance, from local as from global catastrophe, Mahon writes in his poem 'Afterlives' of his departure from Belfast and dedicates the poem to James Simmons, a poet who stayed: 'Perhaps if I'd stayed behind / And lived it bomb by bomb / I might have grown up at last / And learnt what is meant by home'.[138] But what does 'home' mean? The poems in *The Hunt by Night* (1982) suggest that Mahon was moving increasingly toward the perspective of cosmic exile, a theoptic view taken in the title poem in which human endeavour dwindles before the vastness of history and the larger universe. Over a decade later in *The Hudson Letter* (begun when Mahon was residing in New York), he makes clear that his politics lie, as ever, with the homeless. In vigorous hexameters, Mahon's facility with form matched here by an ear for the demotic, he writes in 'Alien Nation' of the depression and alcoholism that kept him from writing poetry for much of his middle age, even while he continued to be a successful journalist, screenplay writer and translator of French and classical drama: 'I too have been homeless and in detox' ('Alien Nation').[139] Mocking his own previous rhetorical success by gesturing to earlier poems, Mahon in this confident, creative comeback now openly expresses his outrage at the spectacles of global poverty, located as ever in the particular locale, where 'even the inert contribute to the universe', and 'even perceived losers have often won / for there, of course, a different truth is known'. The poem continues: 'Blown here like particles from an exploding sun, / we are all far from home, be our home still / a Chicago slum, a house under the Cave Hill / or a caravan parked in a field above Cushendun'. Humour does not hide the biting irony: 'Clutching our bits and pieces, arrogant in dereliction, / we are all "out there", filling the parks and streets / with our harsh demand: "Sleep faster, we need the sheets!"' Yet irony itself is not, Mahon suggests, the end of civilisation or the ultimate perspective. *The Yellow Book* (1998) transforms Mahon, a Dublin resident once again, into 'a decadent who lived to tell the story' ('Remembering the 90s'), 'surviving even beyond the age of irony'.[140] Of the Irish poetry written at the end of the twentieth century, the poems of Derek Mahon are among those most likely to survive to the end of the twenty-first.

Michael Longley, a nearly lifelong resident of Belfast, has written what are perhaps the most moving, and by now the most often quoted, lines on the Troubles. In 'Ceasefire', Achilles and Priam momentarily put aside the masculine roles of the battlefield 'to stare at each other's beauty as lovers might, / Achilles built like a god, Priam good-looking still / And full of conversation'.[141] But the resolve that will make ceasefire effective depends on the ineffaceable bitterness, and honesty, of Priam's words: 'I get down on my knees and do what must be done / And kiss Achilles' hand, the killer of my son'. 'Ceasefire' appeared in *The Irish Times* just two days after the IRA did in fact declare a ceasefire in 1994. It features Longley's signature strength since his first major publication, *No Continuing City* (1969), twenty-five years earlier: an ability to condense epic themes into the personal and immediate scope of the lyric. Complementary to this gift are what Michael Allen has identified as two later resources that are inseparable from one another: a mastery of the long line (in part because of Longley's Latin scholarship) and an uneasy but powerful conjoining of the private and particularly the erotic with political themes.[142] The result is a poetry in which the tone is confiding and understated, a particular achievement given Longley's refusal to flinch before such subjects as war-time – and peace-time – brutality.

Those qualities in his professional and personal life as in his poetry were acquired by Longley, the son of English parents who relocated in Belfast, through such public commitments as directing the Northern Irish Arts Council and assisting his wife, the noted critic Edna Longley, with the leadership of the John Hewitt Summer School. An admirer and an editor of Louis MacNeice, a predecessor who also made the public event personal, Longley has written that 'in the context of political violence the deployment of words at their most precise and most suggestive remains one of the few antidotes to death-dealing dishonesty'.[143] Such strengths have enabled Longley to write some of the most successful love poems of his generation. Poems such as 'The Linen Industry' are also implicitly political and even socioeconomic, yet he has also written fairly explicitly on the subject of sexuality, perhaps most memorably in 'Mr 10 1/2': 'I find myself considering his first months in the womb / As a wee girl, and I substitute for his two plums / Plum-blossom, for his cucumber a yellowy flower'. As Neil Corcoran has observed, Longley uses his considerable gifts as a nature poet (and, indeed, as an accomplished amateur naturalist) on behalf of such seemingly incongruous subjects, in effect botanising the body.[144] In

'The Butchers', which moves between the revenge of Odysseus and sectarian killing in contemporary Belfast, we witness in the poem's conclusion the transformation of the victims' souls to batsqueaks and the bog asphodels of an Irish *sheugh*.[145] With poetic tact, through the telling object, Longley palpably evokes the dead or, indeed, whatever is tellingly absent: the murdered workers and his dead father through a set of dentures in 'The Linen Workers' or the effaced poet in 'The White Garden,' where 'So white are the white flowers in the white garden that I / Disappear in no time at all among lace and veils'.[146] He concludes: 'For whom do I scribble the few words that come to me / From beyond the arch of white roses as from nowhere / My memorandum to posterity? Listen. "The saw / Is under the garden bench and the gate is unlatched."'

Poems that, like this one, confront the meaning of absence in the elegiac mode are among the most successful in Longley's recent volumes. *The Weather in Japan* (2000) features a number of strong poems written specifically to commemorate lost friends, including the intensely observed poems of unabashed bereavement, 'Daffodils' and 'The Mustard Tin'. Both concern the approaching death of the poet's mother-in-law. In the latter, the speaker seeks a memory from childhood of some object, any object, with which he might, as she slips into death, 'close' her 'terrible yawn': 'I focus on the mustard tin propping your jaw, / On the total absence of the oval mustard tin' ('The Mustard Tin').[147]

Growing up in the Troubles: Muldoon, Carson, McGuckian, Paulin

In the fifteen years between the New Ireland Forum of 1983 and the Good Friday Agreement of 1998, a second and in many ways different generation of distinguished poets from Northern Ireland came into its strength. Like Heaney, these poets – Paul Muldoon (b. 1951), Ciaran Carson (b. 1948), and Medbh McGuckian (b. 1950) – were Catholics, and like him they attended Queen's University, Belfast. Tom Paulin (b. 1949), while educated at Hull and Oxford, shares with these poets the definitive experience of the Civil Rights movement of 1968 that began in their early adulthood (and the years of ensuing violence that escalated into the 1980s). Indeed, whether in rural or urban Northern Ireland, they grew up in communities that witnessed acts of violence executed by rival sectarian groups and, just as important, those of a state that openly protected majority (Protestant) interests. The official response to terrorism, from the British Army to the courts, led to such seemingly arbitrary threats to individual liberties as the renewal of the Special Powers Act (suspending the normal processes of law) and censorship (alleged terrorists could not be simultaneously seen and heard on television). These contexts, in which the mundane may be punctuated by the macabre, may help to explain one quality that characterises the poems emerging from this second generation of Northern Irish writers: a fragmentation of narratives in which no centre holds and in which no stable central consciousness emerges. While these poets are, like Heaney, Mahon and Longley, quite capable of writing with skill and even panache the so-called well-made poem – and like them are drawn to such conventional English forms as the sonnet – they devise in their different ways strategies in which a visibly contrived and even imposed form betrays the ambivalences and tensions behind its construction.

Like Longley before them, Muldoon, Carson, McGuckian and Paulin have in their own ways participated in and, in some cases, even shaped the infrastructures of culture in Northern Ireland: the BBC (Muldoon), the Northern Irish Arts Council (Carson), poetry workshops for interned political prisoners (McGuckian). Paulin is the most public of these poets. The author of such widely read collections of poetry as *Liberty Tree* (1983), *Fivemiletown* (1987), *The Wind Dog* (1999) and, most recently, an epic concerning World War II, *The Invasion Handbook* (2002), Paulin is better known as a founder of Field Day and as an outspoken television panelist and journalist than as a poet. As a polemicist and as a scholar, he advocates the legacy of the Protestant Enlightenment in Ireland, calling attention to the debts of contemporary Irish republicanism to the 1798 United Irishmen. As a poet and an academic, he has promoted the importance of the Ulster vernacular.

Complementary to the Protestant Paulin is an equally prominent literary presence in Northern politics, the poet-scholar and Catholic nationalist Seamus Deane. Both are founders and active members of Field Day; both look back to the eighteenth century in France and Ireland; both have academic responsibilities that limit poetic production. Deane has been professor of English at UCD and, over the last decade, at Notre Dame in the US, and while he is a successful novelist as well as one of the three or four most influential scholars of modern Irish literature, the promise of *Gradual Wars* (1972) and *History Lessons* (1983) remains unfulfilled. If the Troubles have drawn attention to writers from the North, the number of radiant poets who are the focus of this chapter have cast talented poets, such as Robert Johnstone, Gerald Dawe, Martin Mooney, Peter MacDonald, Colette Bryce and even the deft understated poet Frank Ormsby into the shade.

For the poets who are the focus of this section – Muldoon, Carson and McGuckian – the public events of their era are treated obliquely, and the legacy of the Enlightenment (see especially Muldoon's *Madoc*) is challenged rather than unthinkingly affirmed. More particularly, the Troubles enter into their poetry only as they intrude into the intimacy of domestic space or the security of personal belief or individual identity. Indeed, the element that is often most elusive in the poetry of McGuckian, Carson and Muldoon is the 'poet'. As if in contradiction to the relatively public and representative roles for the poet being claimed by Montague in *The Rough Field* and more widely by Seamus Heaney and Eavan Boland, these younger poets question whether any writer may speak on behalf of his or her community. As Muldoon memorably writes in *To Ireland, I* (2000), the Clarendon lectures he delivered at Oxford in 1998, 'One way or another, it does seem that Irish writers again and again find themselves challenged by the violent juxtaposition of the concepts of "Ireland" and "I". . . . It's as if they feel obliged to extend the notion of being a "medium" to becoming a "mediator".'[148] Muldoon, Carson and McGuckian all share a scepticism toward such mediation and a preoccupation with the condition of being caught in between two states, two selves, even between the word and the world toward which it gestures.

Paul Muldoon's innovativeness and intellectual breadth would alone distinguish him from most English-language poets of his generation. But two other qualities established early his international reputation: a capacity to stay at least a few steps ahead of critical theory, so that his readers can almost feel the imprints of his heels in the post-structuralist texts by which they might wish to read him, and to risk losing those readers not fleet enough to follow. While this might suggest that his poetic persona is aloof or that his poetry is cold, in fact Muldoon succeeds in writing poems that are at once formally austere and powerful in their emotional impact. The Muldoon 'voice' is distinctive (even as it insists on such quotation marks).

The sly, shady and sinister qualities of the shape-changing Hermes particularly came to characterise Muldoon's work in the 1980s, where the poet is often a 'go-between' or medium (even a trickster figure) between the daylight world of the living and the dark forces of the underworld. Throughout his thirty-year career Muldoon has eschewed the straight line of narrative, preferring variations on such repetitive forms as the sestina and villanelle, forms which he has proven capable of expanding across vast sequences of lines and even pages of his longer poems. As Muldoon wryly hints in his poem 'Errata', 'For "ludic" read "lucid"'.[149]

Muldoon may be playful, but he shares with the famously ludic Romantic poet Lord Byron (about whom Muldoon has himself written avidly) a taste for the irregular and even perverse as well as for the regular rhymes of 'traditional' verse. Witness Muldoon's venereal 'Aisling', which deromanticises a visionary genre in which Ireland, personified as a beautiful woman, seduces the poet to her cause. Linking such seduction to a sexually transmitted disease, the poem is central to a volume in which other exchanges (including the smuggling of arms and drugs) are made more effective in a global economy where sex, like illegal substances, travels. In that world, *Quoof* (1983) suggests, the designations and interconnections of cartels (from the Esso sign to drug lingo to the sectarian pronunciation of a word such as *sheugh* or the family word for the hot-water bottle 'quoof') are as unstable as the atom, or as the mind-blown self.

But also like Byron, Muldoon is a poet deeply insistent that politics – indeed, history – cannot be kept from poetry. As he writes through the voice of 'Wystan' Auden in '7, Middagh Street', 'For history's a twisted root / with art its small, translucent fruit // and never the other way round'.[150] While Muldoon has refused to commit himself to the obvious *yeas* or *nays* of local and national Irish politics, the very hermeticism of his mysterious, closed, even claustrophobic, worlds ensures that Muldoon's reader will feel there is no escape, in art or any other contrivance, from consequence. Yet he sometimes adopts a voice that seeks to cut through word play, even as that voice acknowledges that it cannot escape its own homonymic wavering, as it seeks to reclaim 'reality': 'Enough of Colette and Céline, Céline and Paul Celan: / enough of whether Nabokov / taught at Wellesley or Wesleyan. // Now let us talk of slaughter and the slain, / the helicopter gun-ship, the mighty Kalashnikov: / let's rest for a while in a place where a cow has lain'.[151] Muldoon makes uncertainty, ambivalence and even slip-ups or slips of speech a wedge into alterity, politically but also metaphysically, which he more explicitly defines in *To Ireland, I* as an Irish attraction to the otherworld: 'This idea of there being a contiguous world, a world coterminal with our own' offered 'a kind of psychological trapdoor, to a people from under whose feet the rug is constantly being pulled, often quite literally so'.[152]

Even alternative worlds (less typically associated with poetry than with science fiction) have figured in Muldoon's audacious experiments with narrative, allowing the poet to foreground the surreal violence that irrupts when two cultures collide. *Madoc: A Mystery* (1991) continues an interest in native (specifically, Native American) culture expressed in *Quoof* (the trickster cycle) and *Meeting the British* (1987). In the title poem for the latter volume, Muldoon writes of the exchanges that occurred with white traders: 'They gave us six fishhooks / and two blankets embroidered with smallpox.'[153] *Madoc* is dominated by a long poetic sequence that imagines what might have happened had Coleridge and Southey founded (as they in fact had planned) a utopian community in America. It explores two impulses in the Eurocentric imagination that have led to the settlements of New Worlds, settlements that prove, invariably, to carry with them the contaminations of the Old. The first is the drive to know, emblematised in 'Madoc' by the names of philosophers that provide the intriguing titles of the sub-sections in the sequence. The second is idealism, the hope that westward expansion might lead humankind into a kind of *Tír na nÓg*: the ideal land of the forever young to which Muldoon refers in *To Ireland, I*, itself associated with the west. In that sense the poem 'Madoc', with its alternative world of Romantic idealism gone awry, repeats a theme inaugurated over a decade earlier in the long poem at the end of *Why Brownlee Left* (1980): 'Immram'. In this mock-heroic version of the 'Voyage of Máel Dúin' (which Muldoon has playfully taken as a family name), the narrator discovers that Los Angeles (or, more broadly, the West Coast) can stand in for *Tír na nÓg*, 'So long as there's an "if" in California'.[154]

The Annals of Chile (1994) confirmed that Muldoon rarely abandons themes and tropes, including most obviously those (exploited even in his prose works) that involve circles, spirals and mirrors. In this volume the circling devices and images of *Why Brownlee Left* and *Quoof* combine with a more outspoken ambivalence toward the dead – and toward their political causes – returning like bad memories. These preoccupations find figuration in the rewindings and fast forwards of a VCR and in the counterclockwise gyres of the sacrilegious, the sinister 'left', hurricanes, tornadoes and sink drains. Poetic form itself in this volume is modelled on such spirals: Tim Kendall has observed that the long poem 'Yarrow' is a series of intercut sestinas.[155] Continuing to locate in the New World both the daydreams and nightmares of the Old, the political swerves left and right, Muldoon offers in 'Yarrow' an anti-elegy for the 1980s and, more explicitly, for the drugs, sex and rock and roll whose promises of liberation are portrayed here (as one would now expect from Muldoon) with the same ambivalence that his more personal poems of mourning express, with almost terrifying honesty, toward the dead. The volume's unabashed elegy 'Incantata', written in memory of the visual artist Mary Farl Powers who died of cancer in 1992, was quickly identified by critics as one of Muldoon's most accessible and successful long poems.

If the poems are less pointedly bleak in *Hay*, the 1998 volume in which one long poetic sequence, 'Sleeve Notes', is explicitly about the revival of rock and roll has-beens, that may in part be because since 1987 Muldoon, with his wife the novelist Jean Hanff Korelitz, has lived outside Northern Ireland. Currently he is the Howard G. B. Clark Professor in the Humanities at Princeton, and in 2002 he won a major American prize, the Pulitzer, for his 2002 collection *Moy*

Sand and Gravel. A more likely reason, however, for *Hay*'s relative good cheer (as 'The Mudroom' would suggest) might be the discovery of yet another coterminous world to that of the Moy, and one no less rich and strange: the Hebraic traditions of his wife's ancestors, parallel tracks to those of Irish émigrés in the New World. The hunger of these exiles contrasts with and yet also sustains the cosmopolitan tastes of urban America, a culture that, as the deservedly acclaimed *Moy Sand and Gravel* intimates, cannot satisfy the demands of the dead.

Among this generation of poets from Northern Ireland, Ciaran Carson has made a career of thinking across the narrow categories of high and traditional cultures, of genre and of the musical and verbal arts. Drawing from his knowledge of traditional music, his poetry readings interweave poems, songs, flute or whistle tunes, even jokes rendered as traditional tales. But Carson's commitment to the practice, study and preservation of Ireland's traditional arts, illuminated briefly and brilliantly in his 1996 prose volume *Last Night's Fun*, is neither nostalgic nor conventional. Rather, he is attuned to the innovative ways in which the most traditional forms have represented history by reshaping the very notion of time, and how as a consequence practitioners and audiences have over time reconceived what seem to be the ineluctable trajectories of the past into the present and thence the future. As he writes in the 1989 poem 'Hamlet', each time a story is retold such events as the ships from the Armada that failed to arrive in 1588 appear on the horizon 400 years later: 'For the voice from the grave reverberates in others' mouths, as the sails / Of the whitethorn hedge swell up in a little breeze, and tremble / Like the spiral blossom of Andromeda'. Such retellings transform loss into victory: 'so suddenly are shrouds and branches / Hung with street-lights, celebrating all that's lost, as fields are reclaimed / By the Starry Plough'.[156] Just as important for this Belfast native is the capacity of the traditional tale, and the storyteller, to evolve with the radical displacements of a modern city under daily siege, a destabilising of the self and of its spaces that Carson has, since his highly acclaimed first book *The New Estate* (1976), figured in terms of actual and imaginary maps.

In *The Irish for No* (1987), which emerged after a decade-long hiatus, the poet writes 'as the charred beams hissed and flickered, I glimpsed a map of Belfast / In the ruins: obliterated streets, the faint impression of a key'.[157] A native Irish speaker, Carson in these poems exploits the fact that there is in fact no Irish word for 'no', suggesting that narrative, like syntax, accommodates itself to that absence of absolute negation through deviation, indirection, reconstruction. In a city where sectarian identity continues to be at once omnipresent and uncertain, the presiding metaphors of this poem are the interrogation site and the trash dump. More hopeful are the motifs of the junkyard and the patchwork quilt that appear in two of the eight long poems ('Dresden' and 'Patchwork'), each powerfully evoking how memory may be fragmentary while also providing a self-renewing source for fresh linkages, new connections and resources.

These motifs are enlarged and extended in *Belfast Confetti* (1989), where in 'Question Time', one of the volume's short essays, Carson writes, 'don't trust maps. . . . Though if there is an ideal map, which shows this city as it is, it may exist in the eye of that helicopter ratcheting overhead'.[158] Under interrogation, 'I am this map which they examine, checking it for error, hesitation, accuracy; a map which no longer refers to the present world, but to a history, these vanished streets; a map which is this moment, this interrogation, my replies.'[159] Yet memory elsewhere nevertheless offers a moment of reclamation, of poetic creation or the storyteller's yarn, that connects the alphabet, the basis of language, to things.

The prose contributions to *Belfast Confetti* proved to be a point of departure for Carson, who, while continuing to write strong volumes of poetry up to the present (*First Language* [1993], *Opera Et Cetera*, [1996], *The Twelfth of Never* [1998], *Breaking News* [2003]), left his position with the Arts Council in 1998. That act inaugurated a prolific decade in which Carson produced four volumes that combine memoir, history, metaphysics and occasionally fiction: *Last Night's Fun* (1996), *The Star Factory* (1997), *Fishing for Amber* (1999) and *Shamrock Tea* (2001). In the *Twelfth of Never* (1998), a series of sonnets explores the recurring nightmares of 1798 (cast in the ballads of the day), the laudanum-induced dreams of the Romantics and the Hibernian fantasies of 'the Celtic Tiger'. Included are surreal encounters with aislings, cluricaunes and pookas: 'I knew it was a faery trick to take me from / The imminent republic of the future, / For the ballot-box contained a condom time-bomb, / And the red hand still remained without a suture' ('Fairground Music').[160] From this dark volume Carson embarked on his award-winning translation of *The Inferno* (2002) that employs the Ulster idiom even as it conforms to tradition by using the form of the *terza rima*.

Like Carson, Medbh McGuckian in 1998 offered a poetic response to the 1798 bicentenary. Titled *Shelmalier* (from a group of Wexford fowlers who participated in the rebellion), this volume surprised readers who had come to expect since her 1982 *The Flower Master* poems preoccupied with domestic, and particularly feminine, interiors. While her peers Muldoon and Carson had by the early 1980s already established themselves as public figures (in, respectively, the BBC and the Arts Council), McGuckian wrote poems in the hours she could spare from motherhood. Although she has said that her poetic self is a core nourished by family, in the same statement she contradicts herself, calling each poem that she writes 'a whirlpool around me to protect the inner inwardness', even though 'there always must be some part of it that cannot be penetrated'.[161]

That statement both characterises and is characteristic of McGuckian's poetry, in which the protective borders between self, word and world are not only threatened but also, productively, elided. The very title of 'Journal Intime' captures McGuckian's gift for portraying the inner shadows that haunt the language of our dailiness. As is typical of her poetry, in this poem's conclusion a proposition – 'As if, what is lifelike, could be true' – would seem to lead the reader out of the mirror of art into something like 'reality'.[162] 'Realism' might seem to offer escape and even empowerment to this poem's deliberately hesitant, feminine speaker who in the poem's opening stanza confronts a world dominated by 'the death-devoted colour of masculinity', a world that consigns women to 'artfully-placed mirrors'. Yet in the final line we must hear the hinge of that 'as if' as it hesitates between the identity and the difference of the 'lifelike' (poetic representational realism) and the 'true', the subjunctive predication of 'reality' as, precisely, whatever lies *beyond* the scope of the 'lifelike'.

Like Muldoon, McGuckian is drawn to mirrors as an image of claustrophobic, self-duplicating interiors within which one may glimpse a fleeting otherness that is a secret withheld even from the self, a secret that is the very point but also the very process of 'poetry'. In 'The Time Before You' she writes, 'The secret of movement / Is not the secret itself / But the movement / Of there being a secret'. The processes of language are foregrounded in her work: 'Every hour the voices of nouns / Wind me up from their scattered rooms, / Where they sit for years, unable to meet, / Like pearls that have lost their clasp, // Or boards snapped by sea-water / That slither towards a shore'.[163] Characterized by elusive referents, by similes that compound until their ground is effaced, and sometimes by such skilful manipulations of syntax that the reader may feel shipwrecked between subject and predicate, McGuckian's poems disturb our expectations of a mimetic, one-to-one correspondence between word and object (precisely the expectation that guarantees our agency as subjects). In poems where the poet requires the reader to map her own transit across a landscape of figures that are introduced without transition, the reader's ability to connect those figures with one another is crucial to the poem's communication of meaning. That connection may require, particularly in the poems in *On Ballycastle Beach* (1988) and in *Marconi's Cottage* (1991), interpretation of the figural presence of water, the sound waves that enabled Marconi to deploy the transatlantic cable. (McGuckian now owns and lives much of the time in Marconi's cottage in Ballycastle.)

The sensual in McGuckian's poetry is more often than not transcendental, requiring that the reader move without preparation between abstract statements of process and literalisations of the same abstractions that can be starkly compelling. In one of her most often discussed (perhaps because most accessible) poems 'The Dream-Language of Fergus', (mis)communication is figured in the following: 'As if an aeroplane in full flight / Launched a second plane, / The sky is stabbed by their exits / And the mistaken meaning of each'.[164] In other poems the sea – the medium of sound and meaning – at once shapes thought and is, itself, inseparable from reception. Exploring how such mediation may confound the delivery of meaning and its arrival, in 'Lighthouse with Dead Leaves' the poet opens the borders between ship, sea and lighthouse: 'As if a ship that opened her planks / To the carpentry of the sea, / Became a thinking fog in which / All wounds began to glow, / And lighthouses sprang to mind'.[165] Often literalising 'metaphor' as the passage of meaning across the sea of language, such poems carry the hermeneutic freight defined by Freud as the dream language of displacement and condensation.

In subsequent volumes, without abandoning these themes McGuckian's poems also become more explicitly political. *Captain Lavender* (1995) was written while the poet worked with political prisoners, even as she mourned the death of her father. As if in announcement of her subsequent volumes, she writes in a poem for him, 'The Albert Chain', 'I am going back into war, / like a house I knew when I was young'. An affirmation of intention, in uncharacteristically direct language, the poem continues, 'I am learning my country all over again, / how every inch of the soil has been paid for / by the life of a man, the funerals of the poor'.[166] In the poems of *Shelmalier* (1998), a collection written explicitly in response to McGuckian's adult realization that she had grown up knowing little about the events of 1798 that had taken place on that soil, the speaker finds herself inhabited by the dead martyrs of a newly familiar history. Images of trees in this volume, symbolic of liberty but also used for summary execution in that historical moment, become as prevalent as those of water had been in previous volumes. Like water, trees are associated with thoughts and words ('some part of my pine-wooded / mind sleeping or dead' ('Dream in a Train'),[167] but often, as in this example, they emblematise repressed speech. They are versions of the dead who in rooting themselves in the speaker give her their words, but do so by uprooting her sense of self, of the boundary between private and public: 'No place in the room is safe enough / to close itself back / over those still unused voices, / that slide from music / to soon-to-be-living words'.[168] While the body itself may be a shared prison for the speaker as for the ghosts she houses in her recent poems (a theme that McGuckian continues in the poems of her 2001 collection *Drawing Ballerinas* and 2002 volume *The Soldiers of Year II*), nevertheless these most recent poems suggest that we may find in language, if not release, then at least the consequences of words that must be fought for, and won: 'I am forced by sound alone to learn / from that afflicting language // with its busy words, never to use / a word that has not first been won, / nor write your name till it becomes the man' ('Oration').[169]

To understand how McGuckian's own development as a poet paralleled but also departed from that of her peers Muldoon and Carson, we must also locate it within the contexts of the international movement for women's rights that gained momentum in tandem with the civil rights movement in Northern Ireland. To do so, however, we must also recognise that McGuckian's situation as a Northern poet is not fully comparable to that of those women poets, to be discussed now, who emerged a decade before her in the Republic.

New models for the Irish woman writer

In the same year that the People's Democracy movement was organised in Belfast (1968), the Council for the Status of Women was founded in the Republic, representing a quarter of a million women in the thirty groups participating.[170] Just a year before, Eavan Boland (b. 1944), the Irish poet who would become internationally celebrated for her representation of women's issues, published her first volume, *New Territory*. Four years later, in 1972, that same Council for women's issues had become a Commission and, in a year which began in January with the British Army's violent reaction against the Northern Irish civil rights movement that came to be called Bloody Sunday, this women's rights organisation produced a document with forty-nine recommendations to eliminate discrimination against women.[171] In that year Eiléan Ní Chuilleanáin (b. 1942), a Cork poet who by then was teaching at Trinity College, Dublin, published her first volume, *Acts and Monuments*. It would be ten years before McGuckian, in the year she graduated from Queen's, published her own first full collection of poems, *The Flower Master*.

Yet, as Anne Fogarty has persuasively argued, it would be mistaken to assume that the rise or fall of the fortunes of Irish women's poetry depends on those of feminism.[172] She reminds us that while such activist publications as *The Bell*, for example, virtually ignored women's poetry, *The Dublin Magazine*

(1923–72) welcomed such women writers of the 1940s and 1950s as Rhoda Coghill, Temple Lane, Winifred Letts, Blanaid Salkeld, Sheila Wingfield and Mary Devenport O'Neill. Later, in the 1960s and 1970s, poets beyond Boland and Ní Chuilleanáin were introduced in that same journal, including Anne Cluysenaar, Leland Bardwell and Eithne Strong.

The publication and favourable reception of Boland's pamphlet *A Kind of Scar: The Woman Poet in a National Tradition* (1990) was followed by *Object Lessons: The Life of the Woman and the Poet in Our Time* (1995), Boland's essays on gender discrimination and forms of masculinity misshaped by nationalism in the Republic. Both volumes represent the degree to which the rights of women remained politically to the fore in that part of Ireland even as the Troubles in the North fuelled an Irish cultural criticism increasingly marked by postcolonial theory. By 1991, when Field Day published its three-volume anthology of Irish writing, one of its most powerful critics, Edna Longley, was able to call on the principles of feminism, buttressed by revisionism's parallel track in cultural history, to chastise what she called 'old whines in new bottles', noting as did other critics the anthology's relative inattentiveness to women writers. (In 2002 Field Day published the fourth and fifth volumes devoted to writing on and by Irish women).

During those fifteen years between *New Territory* and *The Flower Master*, both feminism and a critique of postcolonial culture and politics in Ireland empowered to a greater or lesser degree each of these quite different poets, in each of whose work critics have sought (and found) what are typically called women's themes: the home, children, tending the sick. But in tone, temperament and form any such resemblance among these poets ends. In part, this may have to do with the quite different circumstances out of which they emerged as writers. For example, while Boland and Ní Chuilleanáin both became published writers while living as contemporaries in Dublin, already in 1972 they moved in different intellectual circles. By her own account Boland's sometimes alienating experience as a housewife and mother in a Dublin suburb had to be forcefully claimed as a subject, as she does in the succinct and powerful description that concludes 'Woman in Kitchen': 'The wash done, the kettle boiled, the sheets / spun and clean, the dryer stops dead. / The silence is a death. It starts to bury / the room in white spaces. She turns to spread / a cloth on the board and irons sheets / in a room white and quiet as a mortuary.'[173] Eiléan Ní Chuilleanáin moved in the quite different sphere of bohemian intellectual Dublin, a circle which included Pearse Hutchinson, Leland Bardwell and Ní Chuilleanáin's future husband, the undervalued poet Macdara Woods.[174] To promote this cosmopolitan group's shared commitment to the literature and culture of other European nations, Ní Chuilleanáin in 1975 co-founded the journal *Cyphers*. Boland, to the contrary, was sceptical of any community and cultural tradition that failed explicitly to support what, in *Object Lessons*, she calls 'the life of the woman and the poet in her times' and of that woman writer within Irish culture in particular.

By 1975 Boland had published a second volume, *The War Horse*, in which she discovers, as she later wrote in 'Subject Matters', that 'in Ireland, with its national tradition and its bardic past, the confusion between the political poem and the public poem was a dangerous and inviting motif. It encouraged the subject of the poem to be representative'. In such poetry 'private registers of feeling . . . would be truly lost',[175] particularly the private, often ordinary, experiences of wives and mothers. Ní Chuilleanáin in 1975 produced a quite different volume, *Site of Ambush*, the title poem of which responds to contemporary events in the North and to Irish republican history more generally by returning to the Irish Civil War. Concerning a historical moment marked by particular violence in Ní Chuilleanáin's native Cork, this long poem based on history reflects as well Ní Chuilleanáin's less hostile attitude toward the male and bardic tradition (and to other 'male' histories, Irish and European) that Boland will increasingly write against. As Ní Chuilleanáin has asserted, 'The modern Irish poet is not a man in the foreground, silhouetted against a place . . . Like a Gaelic bard the creature can be male or female, nomadic without losing tribal identity.'[176] Her capacity, as a poet and as an intellectual, to navigate the currents that cross feminism, postcolonialism, nationalism and (in the broadest sense) European history, have made Ní Chuilleanáin one of the major poets writing in English at the end of the century. In conversation Ní Chuilleanáin has noted just how crucial to her poetry has been her own attraction to travel, particularly her regular visits to a family home in Italy, and to such Irish exiles as nuns and priests. It is no small achievement that, while writing as a European (sometimes from the perspective of those exiles), she has remained cosmopolitan but without dismissing as provincial the persistence of Ireland's nationalist past into the international present.

Boland, of all the Irish women writing today, has most forcefully reacted against a nationalist 'Irish' and tribal identity that she argues can only be male; indeed, she has become internationally known for her representation of the woman writer who must cease, in her words, being the 'object' of male (particularly nationalist and Romantic) poets and become 'that image come to life', a living woman who may speak without shame 'with the ordinary and fractured speech of a woman living in a Dublin suburb, whose claims to the visionary experience would be sooner made on behalf of a child or a tree than a century of struggle'.[177] While she recognises that her poetic themes may seem 'private and obsessive', they are 'simultaneously political'. On behalf of all women who have been excluded from the writing of poetry by being, as she claims, poetic objects, she has seized, she says, 'an authority which, in my view, could be guaranteed only by an identity – and this included a sexual identity – which the poetic tradition, and the structure of the Irish poem, had almost stifled'.[178] For example, in one of her most celebrated poems, 'The Journey', the poet has a vision in which Sappho leads her into the underworld of women who have lost their children to disease. 'I whispered, "Let me be / let me at least be their witness," but she said / "What you have seen is beyond speech, / beyond song, only not beyond love"'.[179] Of the women witnessed, Sappho tells the poet, 'Do not define these women by their work: / not as washerwomen trussed in dust and sweating', because, as Sappho continues, they share with the poet a more important identity: the sensuous and the domestic experiences which define them as individuals – 'these are women who went out like you / when dusk became a dark sweet with leaves, / recovering the day, stooping, picking up / teddy bears and rag dolls and tricycles and buckets'. While a few critics have noted that such individual experiences (indeed, the very possession of a 'private life') are in fact available only to the woman who is also middle-class, so persuasive has been Boland's voice on behalf not only of Irish women but also, more generally, of the woman writer in the West that she has the measurable success of having held a chair in poetry in a major American university.

Boland has lowered the fence between the private and the public in part by making her poetry uncluttered by qualifiers, evasions, ambiguities, her lines sometimes short and usually direct, syntax repetitive and pithy, her persona drawing on such conventions of verisimilitude as 'I whispered'. These distinctive traits may be seen as early as 'The Black Lace Fan My Mother Gave Me', where endstopped lines, straightforward syntax and direct verbs bring the past into the present so that a memory of her mother in a particularly feminine, flirtatious moment may be witnessed as though through a reporter's camera: 'She ordered more coffee. She stood up.'[180] Even a short-line poem, such as the polemical and often cited 'Mise Éire', rarely breaks lines in the middle of a phrase. Taking its title ('I am Ireland') from the identification of 'Ireland' with a woman who appeals to male warriors to redeem her, the poem overturns both the older convention of the *aisling* poem and its more recent incarnation in Patrick Pearse's poem. In Boland's poem, the speaker speaks for the 'real' Irishwoman strong enough to survive the particular sufferings inflicted on women in two centuries of male struggle for the body of the nation: the prostitute 'in the precincts of the garrison', the emigrant woman 'holding her half-dead baby to her'.[181] The speaker is direct and to the point – 'I won't go back to it – // my nation displaced / into old dactyls, / oaths made.' Already in these opening lines language is a male tool complicit with a nationalism that displaces, in speaking for, the 'real' Ireland, a reality falsified as it is romanticised by poets in the third stanza: 'the scalded memory/the songs/that bandage up the history, the words/that make a rhythm of the crime'. A central irony emerges: if poetry tells only lies, then how might this poet herself be able to rely on 'words', 'dactyls' and poetic 'rhythm' to speak on behalf of the women who have been victims of that crime?

There is a further irony: haunting this poem's ambivalence toward language is the voice of a male poet, Seamus Heaney, in the poem's final, and most aurally rich, stanza: 'mingling the immigrant / guttural with the vowels / of homesickness'. In this penultimate stanza the speaker seems about to offer, with her riskier enjambment across phrases and even one across a stanza break, a more complex model for how language at once limits and may free the oppressed, empowering even the powerless. Certainly, the effectiveness of the three lines just quoted derives in part from the disappearance of the speaker's 'I' from the description of an immigrant woman whose own power may lie (as the poet / speaker's does not) in a liberating indifference to the shackles of speech. Yet the final stanza, returning to line breaks after the completion of clauses, perpetuates in its own self-referential knowingness, a resigned, confining conclusiveness that keeps the immigrant woman (whether in the New World or, we might conjecture, even in a feminist poem) ignorant and therefore in her place: 'a new language / is a kind of scar / and heals after a while / into a passable imitation / of what went before'.[182] Language will change, but it will remain the same. It will touch the female poet but not the consciousness of her female subject.

Yet elsewhere in her writing Boland has more optimistically suggested the liberating possibilities for poetry of a change in subject matter that, she believes, will necessarily come about with a change in the poet's gender. 'My muse must be better than those of men,' Boland writes in 'Envoi', 'who made theirs in the image of their myth.'[183] 'I have the truth and I need the faith. / It is time I put my hand in her side', an allusion to Thomas, the doubting disciple of Jesus. While that sceptical view – that words, like faith, must be true to a 'reality' a woman poet best knows for herself – has found Boland a wide and international following among feminists, younger women poets in Ireland (as we will see in a subsequent section) have not uniformly followed Boland's model.

Unlike Boland, Ní Chuilleanáin in her chosen subjects prefers acceptance of the quiet miracle of the body to the hand thrust in its side. In her approach to such matters, she chooses indirection, exploiting the possibilities of sinuous, long lines, in part because of her familiarity as a scholar with the Baroque and, formally, with Alexandrines and hexameters. As a professor of Renaissance literature at Trinity College, Dublin, she relishes, as she calls it, 'excess, the absence of restraint', 'the idea that every way of saying something has an alternative, that there's a kind of virtue in copiousness'.[184] But if Ní Chuilleanáin draws skilfully on a polyglot's word-hoard, her poems are marked by restraint and indirection. Like pearls, they draw from and around the grit that they protect, histories which are hidden (and thereby remain powerful) within 'Ireland' as well as within individuals. The very possibility of witnessing the sufferings of others, even other women, she suggests in her poem 'Vierge Ouvrante', may be obtrusive. Stating in an interview that much of her poetry responds to pain and death, whether experienced at hand or from a distance, she says that *The Magdalene Sermon* (1989) 'was unified by disasters and by – I felt quite strongly – the way people speak about disasters, about things which are in some ways unspeakable, which are resistant to speech'.[185] Ní Chuilleanáin acknowledges that a series of personal deaths drew her, as she argues that they must, 'into the question of how does one think about very large and terrible events'.[186] For example, in her poem 'The Informant', 'I was actually writing about – which I've never done, and I don't usually identify with – a particular death in the north, the deaths of the soldiers who were dragged out of a car at a funeral and shot.'[187] What is impossible to witness, what remains talismanic or even forbidden, locked up and 'out of reach', may in fact, she suggests, be like the saint's relic 'the real thing': 'True stories wind and hang like this, / Shuddering loop wreathed on a lapis lazuli / Frame' ('The Real Thing').[188] As for Sister Custos, who is custodian of the narrative, 'Her history is a blank sheet, / Her vows a folded paper locked like a well. / The torn end of the serpent / Tilts the lace edge of the veil. / The real thing, the one free foot kicking / Under the white sheet of history'. Reality is not what language veils, what words on folded paper withhold, but rather what we know only because it survives under surfaces at once unreadable and replete with meaning. It is female, powerful and 'free', all the more so for appearing here in a spondee that ends in a feminine syllable before an energising, even ecstatic, act of enjambment.

Nuns have often served as subjects in Ní Chuilleanáin's poems (see especially *The Magdalene Sermon* [1989]), for, as she writes in 'Nuns: A Subject for a Woman Writer' it is not 'language or image but subject that really defined me as a poet; I wished to look at the feminine condition through the equal glass of the common language, making it my subject on my own terms'.[189] She found in nuns 'a living subject': 'Was a female subject one which came merely from an assemblage of concerns that have been brushed into the corner labeled "women"? . . . Then I saw in memory a nun working, sewing, polishing, writing, looking after altar and relics, loading patients on lorries in a war.' While for Boland description typically becomes most elaborate in presenting female clothing, for Ní Chuilleanáin the 'physical ideal of femininity' is the nun's body that 'unself-consciously clothed itself in full plain cloth and moved as intently as a fish in water'.[190]

Water is indeed Ní Chuilleanáin's poetic element, from her early poem 'The Second Voyage' in the 1977 eponymous volume to the poem 'Gloss / Clós / Glas' in her volume *The Girl Who Married the Reindeer* (2001). Here, Ní Chuilleanáin plays on the fluidity of the sounds and meanings of these words across English, French and Irish (the Irish *glas* means both 'green' and 'lock'), suggesting that language, far from being ineluctably restrictive (as in 'Mise Éire') in fact contains in its roots an embedded bodiliness, even as the object we would hold through words slips from their grasp. In 'Gloss / Clós / Glas' through restriction itself a scholar seeks 'the price of his release: / Two words, as opposite as *his* and *hers* / . . . / Two words / Closer to the bone than the words I was so proud of, / *Embrace* and *strict* to describe the twining of flesh and bone'.[191] 'Embrace', we note, derives from the Old French *embracer*, 'in the two arms'; 'strict' from the Latin *stringere*, 'to draw tight', but the scholar has in his arms ('up to his oxter') not flesh but texts as he unpicks the locks of language, restless 'Until he reaches the language that has no word for *his*, / No word for *hers*'. Ironically, what he believes to be locked is in fact already, without him, loosening: 'The rags of language are streaming like weathervanes, / Like weeds in water they turn with the tide'. In approaching this ideal language without possessives or gender – an objective to be reached, importantly, only *through* the discipline of language – what the scholar has sought is already slipping from his embrace, already beyond his cell rusting with her (note the feminine possessive) damp, living breath the locks that he would pick: 'Who is that he can hear panting on the other side? / The steam of her breath is turning the locked lock green'.

Whatever the degree to which Boland's polemics have swept her own path, undeniably they have been enabling for many younger women. In readings and interviews Paula Meehan (b. 1955) has thanked Boland for her trail-blazing. From the volume *The Man Who Was Marked by Winter* (1991) to *Dharmakaya* (2000), Meehan's gift is sizable – wit, sympathy, precision, an easy demotic line, intellectual complexity – and fragile. She often writes about the injuriousness of words – 'words can pluck you, / leave you naked' – and implicitly her own words defend, as well.[192] Among the small sub-genre of poems about the male gaze (including Boland's 'Degas's Laundresses' and Ní Chuilleanáin's 'Man Watching a Woman'), Meehan's 'Zugzwang' must be the wittiest. In servitude as wife-and-model – 'He imagines Dutch paintings, bourgeois / interiors, *Woman Washing, Woman Setting / a Table, Woman Bending over a Child'* – the woman changes perspective by shattering 'into smithereens': 'Each shard will reflect the room, the flowers / the chessboard, and her beloved sky beyond / like a calm ocean lapping at the mountain'.[193]

A number of other women poets, including Kerry Hardie (b. 1951), published by The Gallery Press, and Mary O'Malley (b. 1954), Moya Cannon (b. 1956) and Rita Ann Higgins (b. 1955), published by Salmon Publishing, are distinctive, accomplished poets who have entered the middle stretch still pursuing the fulfilment of their earlier promise. Vona Groarke's third book *Flight* (2002), published by Gallery, may be just such an achievement, a stepping over the gap between promise and maturity. In her first book *Shale* (1994), behind the lovers' totems and tokens, such as these clouds – 'We cup our hands around them, / passing them between us like small gifts' – which as here can seem coy, resides a preoccupation with exchange.[194] If in her second book, *Other People's Houses* (1999), this idea is diminished by a domestic formula, it finds a rich expression in this third volume, where the topic is often the materials and process of writing in transaction with desire. To express meaningful action the right verb is sought, and, in the title poem, poetry compensates for the impossibility of flight.

Bilingualism: Irish and cosmopolitan

Polyglot fluency has characterised an Irish culture notable for its cosmopolitanism since at least the ninth century, offering perhaps most notably in this century the examples of Joyce and Beckett. Such poets as Devlin, Mahon, Montague and Carson have made the translation of French poetry and prose central to their oeuvre. Eiléan Ní Chuilleanáin and Ciaran Carson have written macaronic poems in French and English. Homer, Virgil, Ovid and Dante have found able translators among contemporary Irish poets; indeed, the Ulster idiom of Carson's 2002 translation of *The Inferno* restores for English-language readers the original's grittiness. Similarly, but as an act of postcolonial appropriation, Heaney translated the English foundational epic *Beowulf* into his own Ulster English.

Irish poets who write largely in English have increasingly exploited resourcefully the opportunities of the Irish language. As Bernard O'Donoghue has argued, syntax, rhythm and sound effects that are distinctively Irish enabled Yeats and his successors to emerge from the confinement of late Victorianism.[195] If Hiberno-English was a liberating medium for Joyce, Clarke, Beckett and Flann O'Brien, the next generation, including Montague (*The Faber Book of Irish Verse*), Kinsella (*The Tain* and *An Duanaire*, with Seán Ó Tuama) and Heaney (*Sweeney Astray*) undertook translations of central texts from the Irish. Through translations by more than a dozen Irish poets, and especially book-length projects by Michael Hartnett (1941–99), Paul Muldoon, Medbh McGuckian and Eiléan Ní Chuilleanáin, Nuala Ní Dhomhnaill (b. 1952) has emerged as an internationally known poet who has encouraged translation by her fellow writers as a popular poetic avocation.

By contrast, Hartnett's own remarkable poetry seems undervalued in English, if not in Irish, excepting perhaps his controversial *A Farewell to English* (1975). In this work, he drew up the bridge between Ireland's two languages by foreswearing English, with the intention of writing thereafter only in Irish. Although his abandonment of English, which lasted for a decade, first seemed a Rimbaud-like rejection of our common civilisation, gradually he conveyed the notion that much Irish poetry is a translation of motifs, ways of saying, and habits of mind from the older culture. Like the dispossessed poets in Irish of the seventeenth and eighteenth centuries, he can write bitterly of the iron hand in the velvet glove of Anglo-Irish dominance. In an account of his visit to a Big House, he sees this showcase for Georgian bad taste and musical culture as built on sinister colonial practices: 'I went into the calmer, gentler hall / In the wineglassed, chattering interval: . . . And heard the crack of ligaments being torn / And smelled the clinging blood upon the stones.'[196] He can also celebrate the timeless and still fruitful Irish nature: 'You've felt the rack. Lie back, relax / And let the venom gargle in their throats – / Watch your children walk the western rocks / Gold and full of grain, like stooks of oats'.[197]

Learning from poets in Irish such as Hartnett and Michael Davitt, Paul Muldoon has come to see Irish language and poetry as emerging into Irish poetry like a sub-cutaneous wound or haemorrhage that lies beneath the surface of English.[198] Perhaps the macaronic poem in Irish and English confirms most clearly that Irish remains a formidable presence within Irish poetry in

English. One could point to the poetry of Ní Chuilleanáin, studded with references known to Irish-language readers, or to that of Muldoon himself, who in perhaps his most demanding long poem, 'Yarrow', has taken the macaronic possibilities of Irish and English to a new degree of complexity, writing lines that may offer more words in Irish than in English.

The acquisition of a second language in early childhood – Irish in the Republic's primary schools, a curriculum of classical languages in the North – encouraged multilingualism among Irish poets, and, from Ireland's relative isolation, the intellectually curious were attracted like Stephen Dedalus by Europe's 'spell of arms and voices'.[199] Aside from acquiring languages, expatriate poets and those who have sojourned abroad have enriched the domestic readership and promoted new European or American poets and poetics to their peers. Just as an earlier generation of poets such as Pearse Hutchinson (b. 1927) and Desmond O'Grady (b. 1935) introduced Ireland to Spanish and Greek poetry, respectively, so, more recently, Peter Sirr (b. 1960), Harry Clifton (b. 1952), Michael O'Loughlin (b. 1958), Mary O'Malley, Desmond Egan (b. 1936) and others have provided Irish journals with reliable insights into European poetry. Poets such as Bernard O'Donoghue (b. 1945) and Matthew Sweeney (b. 1952), working in England, and Eamon Grennan (b. 1941), Eamonn Wall (b. 1955) and Greg Delanty (b. 1958) living in the US, are better known in their host countries than in Ireland. Grennan, for example, appears more than twice as frequently in American journals, including regularly the *New Yorker*, than he does in Irish publications. His principal subjects – landscape, still-lives, acute observations of nature: 'The whole chorus saying only one thing: look / at what goes, where we stand in the midst of it' – have remained the same over his five books.[200] At the same time, his reflection on mortality (that, paradoxically, we cannot stand but 'must travel at the speed of light') deepens in his most recent work, as captured in his last book's title, *Still Life with Waterfall*.[201] Younger and less accomplished, Wall and Delanty write a hybrid poetry, in Wall's case cool and understated in the manner of James Schuyler or Frank O'Hara, and in Delanty's, truly lyrical descants that lift out of the sometimes ponderous body of the poem.

Remarkably, the poet-critic who keeps the most accurate account of expatriate poetry and poetry translated from European languages remains tethered to his post within Irish governmental bureaucracy. Dennis O'Driscoll (b. 1954) has been for some decades Ireland's most informed critic of imported poetry, as well as a very good, although somewhat specialised, poet in his own right. As an official in Irish Customs, O'Driscoll's six volumes of poetry are frequently caustic satires that apply bureaucratic language literally, if ironically. As his book titles suggest – *Hidden Extras* (1987), *The Bottom Line* (1994), *Exemplary Damages* (2002) – his poems strip-search the legal or bureaucratic clichés in which we clothe our intentions. The topics and targets of his poems are the destructiveness of global capitalism, the suicidal pace of our lives, the lost luggage of sceptical liberalism, as in 'Missing God': 'Miss him when the TV scientist / explains the cosmos through equations, / leaving our planet to revolve on its axis / aimlessly, a wheel skidding in snow'.[202]

Yeats could regret 'the day's war with every knave and dolt, / Theatre business, management of men',[203] but he hardly could have imagined O'Driscoll's poetry of the Common Market, Thomas McCarthy's lyrical critiques of post-independence politics, or the cosmopolitan poetry of Michael O'Loughlin, Peter Sirr or other urban Irish poets who prefer the 'sidewalks gray' of cityscapes. These poets of the Republic who began publishing after the return of the Troubles have all suffered the neglect of critics and anthologists. McCarthy (b. 1954) is the admired but relatively undervalued laureate of Fianna Fáil politics and keeper of parochial memory. Author of five books of poetry gathered with new poems in *Mr Dineen's Careful Parade* (2001), his attention to local politics may make him the most European, or East European, of Irish poets. On the other hand, Peter Sirr's setting in European cities shifts towards Dublin in his most recent volume, *Bring Everything*, with poems confected of desire and memory. 'Sometimes it's the whole population of want, / a furious traffic // – at the pawnshop auction / a hair-dryer, an identity bracelet / a saxophone'.[204] A rooftop view renders 'ingredients for The City / which is not the city / but the grocery of an eye' ('The Domes of the City').[205] He recognises that the guarantor of the city is not any one citizen's memory but a collective ongoingness: 'The routes don't remember us, / the language doesn't pine for our mouths // but a solid city still roots in the bone / and not a brick is missed, not a scent, not a shimmer // nothing's lost, the map's already drawn' ('Going Back'), lines that evoke both Joyce's reconstruction of Dublin and Ciaran Carson's Belfast cartography.[206] Although the working-class districts of north Dublin have found voice or music in Roddy Doyle's novels or the poetry of Paula Meehan, Michael O'Loughlin, who now lives in Amsterdam, links his childhood borough to Europe's drab 'postwar suburbs / where nothing has ever happened' and which maintain a surly silence, wilful, 'obmustescent'.[207]

The surest sign of a hopeful future for Irish poetry has been the growth of the poetic infrastructure of publishers, reviews and journals, prizes and government funding. An accomplished poet himself, Peter Fallon of the Gallery Press has developed a poetic list that in length and quality is unmatched in the British Isles. Through skilful editing, imaginative projects and dependable schedules, Fallon has surpassed the Dolmen Press as the financially stable and reliable publisher in this past century. Other publishers, especially Blackstaff under Anne Tannahill, Goldsmith Press founded by the poet Desmond Egan, Dedalus led by poet John F. Deane, New Writers' Press led by Michael Smith, Ravens Arts Press by novelist, poet and dramatist Dermot Bolger, and Jessie Lendennie's Salmon Publishers have offered valuable, but more limited, lists. With this diverse range of poetry presses, English publishers such as Faber, Bloodaxe, Carcanet and Anvil, who publish Irish poets, simply offer competition rather than the mercantile market that existed in Yeats's day and for some time after. The Arts Councils, North and South, have invested their money wisely. Regular bursaries from Aosdána offer some degree of security to poets. Among subsidised journals that primarily serve poetry – *Poetry Ireland Review* (renewed under the editorship of Peter Sirr), *Cyphers*, *The Honest Ulsterman*, *Irish Pages* and others – the most promising must be *Metre*, edited by young poets David Wheatley (b. 1970) and Justin Quinn (b. 1968) and loosely associated with a new generation of poets including Vona Groarke (b. 1964), Conor O'Callaghan (b. 1968) – author of two books of assured and accomplished poetry, Caitríona O'Reilly (b. 1973) and Sinéad Morrissey (b. 1972), as well as Wheatley and Quinn. In a recent issue of London's *Poetry Review*, Quinn has labelled these writers 'post-national poets', a phrase that also suits poetry on the 'fringe' such as the work of Trevor Joyce and Randolph Healy. Institutions such as Poetry Ireland, particularly under the guidance of the poet Theo Dorgan, have supported poetry effectively. Under Conor O'Callaghan's direction, the Poetry Now festival in Dun Laoghaire took on the dimension of London's Poetry International. Awards day for the *Irish Times* Literature Prize for Poetry is starred on the calendar. With such support, in greater numbers than in Yeats's day, Irish poets rise to renew language, dissolve dogmas, blur boundaries, defamiliarise dailiness and otherwise carry on the work of poetry. If like Yeats they should be tempted to address Ireland, their verse may be directed more to the future than to the past, sounding less like 'To Ireland in the Coming Times' than like 'Come as You Are', the quiet invitation of the true Belfast poet Frank Ormsby:

> You are nobody's bid for perfection.
> Come as you are.
> Not as a promise,
> not as hope and heir
> of the new century
> or trammeled with any care.

No weight of expectation.
Come as you are
when your day and hour beckon.
We'll take it from there.[208]

Notes

1. Seamus Deane, gen. ed. *The Field Day Anthology of Irish Writing*, 3 vols. (Derry: Field Day, 1991), II, p. 2.
2. Michael Smith, 'Interview with Thomas Kinsella', *Poetry Ireland Review* 75 (Winter 2002/3), pp. 108–19. In Kinsella's words, 'The only encounter that matters is between the individual and the significant ordeal' (p. 117).
3. This information on medieval map-makers comes from Yeats's essay 'Village Ghosts' in *The Celtic Twilight* (1893), quoted by Joyce in 'The Literary Influence of the Renaissance', in Kevin Barry, ed. *Occasional, Critical, and Political Writing* (Oxford: Oxford University Press, 2000), p. 189.
4. The respective editions follow: Thomas Kinsella, ed. and trans. *The New Oxford Book of Irish Verse* (Oxford and New York: Oxford University Press, 1986); Paul Muldoon, ed. *The Faber Book of Contemporary Irish Poetry* (London: Faber and Faber, 1986); Anthony Bradley, ed. *Contemporary Irish Poetry* (Berkeley and Los Angeles: University of California Press, 1980; new and revised edn, 1988); Derek Mahon and Peter Fallon, eds. *The Penguin Book of Contemporary Irish Poetry* (New York and London: Penguin, 1990); Edna Longley, ed. *The Bloodaxe Book of Twentieth Century Poetry from Britain and Ireland* (Tarset: Bloodaxe, 2000).
5. Patrick Crotty, ed. *Modern Irish Poetry: An Anthology* (Belfast: Blackstaff, 1995).
6. Angela Bourke, et al., eds. *The Field Day Anthology of Irish Writing*, vols IV and V: *Irish Women's Writing and Traditions* (Cork: Cork University Press in association with Field Day, 2002).
7. W. R. Rodgers, ed. *Irish Literary Portraits* (New York: Taplinger, 1973), p. 19.
8. *The Bell* 5, 6 (March 1943), p. 423. Yet, younger writers recall an adolescence made more colourful by the war, at least in the North, where Allied troops were based. James Simmons remembers that in Derry the war 'brought money and work and glamorous sailors with English and American accents and smart uniforms into our homes and dance halls' (John Brown, *In the Chair: Interviews with Poets from the North of Ireland* [Cliffs of Moher, Clare: Salmon, 2002], p. 61). John Montague recalls his own Ulster childhood: 'I loved the War', which 'was a spectacular background to my small existence from the age of ten to sixteen' (*The Figure in the Cave and Other Essays* [Dublin: Lilliput, 1989], p. 27).
9. Louis MacNeice, *Modern Poetry*, 2nd edn (London: Oxford University Press, 1968), p. 24.
10. Louis MacNeice, *The Collected Poems*, ed. E. R. Dodds (London: Faber and Faber, 1966), p. 113.
11. Ibid., p. 110.
12. Edward Mendelson, ed. *The English Auden: Poems, Essays and Dramatic Writings, 1927–1939* (London: Faber and Faber, 1977), p. 212.

13. MacNeice, *Modern Poetry*, pp. 128, 126.
14. MacNeice, *The Collected Poems*, pp. 27–8.
15. Ibid., p. 218.
16. Ibid., p. 462.
17. Ibid., p. 525.
18. Jon Stallworthy, *Louis MacNeice: A Biography* (New York: W. W. Norton, 1995), p. 482.
19. W. R. Rodgers, *Poems*, ed. Michael Longley (Oldcastle: Gallery Press, 1993), p. 81.
20. Brown, *In the Chair*, pp. 24–5.
21. Ibid., p. 81.
22. John Hewitt, *The Collected Poems of John Hewitt*, ed. Frank Ormsby (Belfast: Blackstaff, 1991), p. 310.
23. Ibid., p. 370.
24. Cecil Lang, ed. *The Pre-Raphaelites and Their Circle*, 2nd edn (Chicago and London: University of Chicago Press, 1975), p. 280.
25. Brown, *In the Chair*, p. 13.
26. Edna Longley, *The Living Stream: Literature and Revisionism in Ireland* (Newcastle upon Tyne: Bloodaxe, 1994), p. 123.
27. Denis Devlin, *Collected Poems of Denis Devlin*, ed. J. C. C. Mays (Dublin: Dedalus Press; Winston-Salem: Wake Forest University Press, 1989), p. 213.
28. Ibid., p. 262.
29. Ibid., p. 261.
30. 'Fallon's *oeuvre* can now be seen to stand in secure and complementary relation to the achievements of Austin Clarke and Patrick Kavanagh': Seanus Heaney, introduction to Padraic Fallon, *Padraic Fallon: Collected Poems*, ed. Brian Fallon (Manchester: Carcanet; Oldcastle, Meath: The Gallery Press, 1990), p. 11.
31. Fallon, *Collected Poems*, p. 112.
32. Ibid., pp. 23, 27.
33. Ibid., p. 46.
34. Ibid., p. 112.
35. Ibid., pp. 67–70.
36. Ibid., notes, p. 274.
37. Patrick Kavanagh, *Collected Pruse* (1967; London: Martin Brian and O'Keeffe, 1973), p. 16.
38. Alan Warner, *Clay Is the Word* (Dublin: Dolmen, 1973), p. 12.
39. Kavanagh, *Collected Pruse*, p. 16.
40. Ibid., p. 20.
41. Ben Howard, *The Pressed Melodean: Essays in Modern Irish Writing* (Brownsville: Story Line Press, 1996), p. 75.
42. Ibid., p. 78.
43. Antoinette Quinn, *Patrick Kavanagh: A Biography* (Dublin: Gill and Macmillan; Syracuse: Syracuse University Press, 1991), p. 169.
44. Ibid., 169.
45. Patrick Kavanagh, *Collected Poems* (1964; London: Martin Brian and O'Keeffe, 1972), p. 34.
46. Ibid., p. 48.

47. Ibid., pp. 35, 50.
48. Ibid., p. 37.
49. Quinn, *Patrick Kavanagh*, p. 245.
50. Kavanagh, *Collected Poems*, p. 44.
51. Ibid., p. 52.
52. Kavanagh, *Collected Pruse*, p. 282.
53. Kavanagh, *Collected Poems*, p. 132.
54. Kavanagh, *Collected Pruse*, pp. 21–2.
55. Ibid., pp. 20, 22.
56. Kavanagh, *Collected Poems*, p. 150.
57. Of course, Yeats's admonition to his successors to 'sing whatever is well made' he himself violated, when the poet admitted into poems such as 'High Talk' and 'Lapis Lazuli' images of violence and desolation and found broken rhythms suitable to his subject.
58. When Kavanagh applies this phrase to Auden, he praises the English poet's ability to recover poetic gold from 'a world we all thought bankrupt', whereas Heaney converts it to qualified praise for Kavanagh's intuitive, aleatory and chance-taking tendencies. See Kavanagh, *Collected Pruse*, p. 251 and Seamus Heaney, *Preoccupations: Selected Prose, 1968–1978* (London and Boston: Faber and Faber, 1980), p. 118.
59. Austin Clarke, *Selected Poems*, ed. Hugh Maxton (Winston-Salem: Wake Forest University Press; Dublin: Lilliput, 1991), p. 17.
60. Kavanagh, *Collected Poems*, p. 174.
61. Ibid., p. 153.
62. Austin Clarke, *Poetry in Modern Ireland* (Cork: Mercier Press, 1962), p. 43.
63. Clarke, *Selected Poems*, p. 50. In the opening two lines of his often anthologised 1938 lyric 'The Straying Student' we see what Clarke calls this 'Gaelic linear pattern of assonance and consonance, ABBAC': 'On a holy day when sails were blowing southward, / A bishop sang the mass at Inishmore.' This poem appeared in *Night and Morning* (1938) among poems that are conscience-stricken and partially obscure, but that convey some of the intense sincerity of the reason/faith struggle as in Hopkins's 'Terrible Sonnets'.
64. Thomas Kinsella, 'The Poetic Career of Austin Clarke', *Irish University Review* 4, 1 (Spring 1974), pp. 128–36, p. 128.
65. Clarke, *Selected Poems*, p. 85.
66. Ibid., p. 92.
67. Ibid., p. 187.
68. Ibid., p. 188.
69. Interview with Jo Miller, Fitzwilliam Square, Dublin, 29 June 1991.
70. Richard Murphy, *The Kick: A Memoir* (London: Granta, 2002), p. 209.
71. Ibid.
72. Richard Murphy, *Collected Poems 1952–2000* (Oldcastle: Gallery Press, 2000; Winston-Salem: Wake Forest University Press, 2001), pp. 67–8.
73. Ibid., p. 60.
74. Ibid., p. 83.
75. Ibid, pp. 83–4.

76. Thomas Kinsella, *Collected Poems 1956–2001* (Manchester: Carcanet Press, 2001), p. 6.
77. Eavan Boland, 'Downstream', in *Tracks* (special Thomas Kinsella issue, ed. John F. Deane) 7 (1987), pp. 19–23, p. 20.
78. See chapter 15 of volume 1, 'Literature and the Oral Tradition', for a detailed discussion of Kinsella's translation.
79. R. A. Stewart Macalister, ed. and trans., *The Book of Invasions*, 4 sections (Dublin: Irish Texts Society, 1938–41).
80. Daniel O'Hara, 'An Interview with Thomas Kinsella', *Contemporary Poetry* 4, 1 (1981), pp. 1–18, pp. 3–4.
81. Kinsella, *Collected Poems 1956–2001*, p. 162.
82. Ibid., p. 170.
83. Ibid, p. 171.
84. Ibid., p. 173.
85. Ibid.
86. F. R. Leavis, *New Bearings in English Poetry* (1932; new edn. London: Chatto and Windus, 1950), p. 13.
87. Personal discussions with Kinsella at his home in Laragh, 1998 and 1999. A recent British judicial review seems to have confirmed details of Kinsella's poem.
88. Kinsella, *Collected Poems*, p. 218.
89. Ibid., p. 57.
90. Ibid., p. 307.
91. Ibid., pp. 329–34.
92. Ibid., p. 332.
93. Ibid., p. 215.
94. Ibid., p. 329.
95. John Montague, "The Figure in the Cave: A Chapter of Autobiography', *Irish University Review: Special John Montague Issue* 19, 1 (Spring 1989), pp. 73–88, p. 87.
96. Ibid., p. 79.
97. Dillon Johnston, *The Poetic Economies of England and Ireland* (Basingstoke: Palgrave, 2001), p. 139.
98. John Montague, *Collected Poems* (Oldcastle: The Gallery Press; Winston-Salem: Wake Forest University Press, 1995), p. 181.
99. Ibid., p. 189.
100. Ibid., p. 88.
101. Ibid., p. 128.
102. Ibid., pp. 181, 184.
103. Ibid., p. 348.
104. Patricia Coughlan and Alex Davis, *Modernism and Ireland: The Poetry of the 1930s* (Cork: Cork University Press, 1995), p. 9. With the publication in 2001 of a collected poems *With the First Dream of Fire They Hunt the Cold* (Dublin: New Writers' Press/ Shearsman Books), Joyce offers a full basis for reassessment.
105. Montague to Miller, 18 November and 24 November 1965, Wake Forest University Archive.
106. See 'The Belfast Group: A Symposium' in *The Honest Ulsterman* 53 (November/December 1976), pp. 53–63 for such a discussion.

107. Hewitt, *Collected Poems*, p. 79.
108. Seamus Deane, 'Unhappy and at Home: Interview with Seamus Heaney,' *The Crane Bag* 1, 1 (Spring 1977), pp. 61–7, p. 61.
109. Seamus Heaney, *Opened Ground: Selected Poems 1966–1996* (New York: Farrar, Straus and Giroux, 1998), p. 56.
110. Ibid., p. 119.
111. Seamus Heaney, *Preoccupations: Selected Prose, 1968–1978* (London: Faber and Faber; New York: Farrar, Straus, Giroux, 1980), p. 57.
112. Conor Cruise O'Brien, in calling those impingements an 'unhealthy intersection', voices the fears of several scholars who have found the relationship of poetry and politics in Heaney's works troubling. See 'An Unhealthy Intersection', *The New Review* 2, 16 (1975), pp. 3–8.
113. Seamus Heaney, *The Redress of Poetry* (New York: Farrar, Straus and Giroux, 1995), p. 203.
114. Heaney, *Opened Ground*, p. 338.
115. Heaney, *The Redress of Poetry*, p. xiii.
116. Heaney, *Opened Ground*, p. 316.
117. Ibid., 'Lightenings (i)', p. 332.
118. Steven Ratiner, ed. *Giving Their Word* (Amherst: University of Massachusetts Press, 2002), pp. 101–2
119. Heaney, *Preoccupations*, p. 43.
120. Ian Gregson, *The Male Image: Representations of Masculinity in Postwar Poetry* (Basingstoke: Macmillan, 1999), p. 130.
121. David Lloyd, *Anomalous States: Irish Writing and the Post-Colonial Moment* (Dublin: Lilliput, 1993), p. 35.
122. Seamus Heaney, 'An Open Letter,' A Field Day Pamphlet, 2 (Derry: Field Day, 1983), p. 9.
123. Seamus Heaney, 'Anglo-Irish Occasions,' *London Review of Books* (5 May 1988), p. 9.
124. Donald Davie, 'Donald Davie on Critics and Essayists', *Poetry Review* 85, 3 (Autumn 1995), p. 38.
125. Kinsella, *Collected Poems*, p. 244.
126. James Simmons, *Poems 1956–1986* (Oldcastle: Gallery Press; Newcastle upon Tyne: Bloodaxe, 1986), p. 169.
127. Ibid., p. 94.
128. James Murphy, Lucy McDiarmid and Michael J. Durkan, 'Q. & A. with Derek Mahon', in James T. Myers Jr., ed. *Writing Irish: Selected Interviews with Irish Writers from the Irish Literary Supplement* (Syracuse: Syracuse University Press, 1999), p. 193.
129. Derek Mahon, *Night-Crossing* (London: Oxford University Press, 1968), p. 19.
130. Derek Mahon, *Collected Poems* (Oldcastle: Gallery Press, 1999), p. 23.
131. Mahon, *Night-Crossing*, p. 18.
132. Derek Mahon, *Lives* (Oxford: Oxford University Press, 1972), p. 22.
133. Derek Mahon, *The Snow Party* (Oxford: Oxford University Press, 1975), p. 8.
134. Ibid., p. 23.
135. 'What Will Remain', Mahon, *Lives*, p. 26.
136. Mahon, *The Snow Party*, p. 27.

137. Ibid., p. 36.
138. Ibid., p. 2.
139. Derek Mahon, *The Hudson Letter* (Oldcastle: Gallery Press, 1995; Winston–Salem: Wake Forest University Press, 1996), p. 62.
140. Derek Mahon, *The Yellow Book* (Oldcastle: Gallery Press, 1997; Winston-Salem: Wake Forest University Press, 1998), p. 28.
141. Michael Longley, *The Ghost Orchid* (Winston-Salem: Wake Forest University Press; London: Jonathan Cape, 1995), p. 39.
142. Michael Allen, 'Longley's Long Line: Looking Back from *The Ghost Orchid*', in Alan J. Peacock and Kathleen Devine, eds. *The Poetry of Michael Longley* (Gerrards Cross: Colin Smythe, 2000), pp. 121–41.
143. Neil Corcoran, 'My Botanical Studies: The Poetry of Natural History in Michael Longley', in Peacock and Devine, *The Poetry of Michael Longley*, pp. 101–19, p. 111.
144. Longley, *The Ghost Orchid*, p. 16; Corcoran, 'My Botanical Studies'.
145. Longley, *Gorse Fires*, p. 51.
146. Longley, *The Ghost Orchid*, p. 52.
147. Michael Longley, *The Weather in Japan* (Winston–Salem: Wake Forest University Press; London: Jonathan Cape, 2000), p. 37.
148. Paul Muldoon, *To Ireland, I* (Oxford and New York: Oxford University Press, 2000), p. 49.
149. Paul Muldoon, *Poems 1968–1998* (London: Faber and Faber, 2001), p. 445.
150. Ibid., p. 178.
151. Ibid., p. 346.
152. Muldoon, *To Ireland, I*, p. 7.
153. Muldoon, *Poems 1968–1998*, p. 161.
154. Ibid., p. 95.
155. Tim Kendall, *Paul Muldoon* (Chester Springs: Dufour, 1996), p. 228.
156. Ciaran Carson, *Belfast Confetti* (Oldcastle: Gallery Press; Winston-Salem: Wake Forest University Press, 1989), p. 107.
157. Ciaran Carson, 'Smithfield Market', in *The Irish for No* (Oldcastle: Gallery Press; Winston-Salem: Wake Forest University Press, 1987), p. 37.
158. Carson, *Belfast Confetti*, p. 58.
159. Ibid., p. 63.
160. Ciaran Carson, *Twelfth of Never* (Oldcastle: Gallery Press; Winston–Salem: Wake Forest University Press, 1998), p. 21.
161. Medbh McGuckian and Nuala Ní Dhomhnail, 'Comhrá', with an afterword by Laura O'Connor, *Southern Review* 31, 3 (July 1995), pp. 581–614, p. 606.
162. Medbh McGuckian, *Marconi's Cottage* (Oldcastle: Gallery Press, 1991; Winston-Salem: Wake Forest University Press; Newcastle upon Tyne: Bloodaxe, 1992), p. 26.
163. Medbh McGuckian, *On Ballycastle Beach* (Winston-Salem: Wake Forest University Press; Oxford: Oxford University Press, 1988; Oldcastle: Gallery Press, 1995), pp. 45, 44.
164. Ibid., p. 57.
165. Ibid., p. 32.
166. Medbh Mc Guckian, *Captain Lavender* (Oldcastle: Gallery Press; Winston–Salem: Wake Forest University Press, 1995), p. 68.

167. Medbh McGuckian, 'Dream in a Train', in *Shelmalier* (Oldcastle: Gallery Press; Winston-Salem: Wake Forest University Press, 1998), p. 17.
168. Medbh McGuckian, 'The Rose-Trellis', in *Shelmalier*, p. 24.
169. Medbh McGuckian, *The Soldiers of Year II* (Winston-Salem: Wake Forest University Press, 2002), p. 123. This poem also appears in *Drawing Ballerinas* (Oldcastle: Gallery Press, 2001), pp. 25–26, p. 26.
170. James M. Cahalan, *Modern Irish Literature and Culture: A Chronology* (New York: G. K. Hall, 1993), p. 283.
171. Ibid, p. 293.
172. Anne Fogarty, 'The Influence of Absences': Eavan Boland and the Silenced History of Irish Women's Poetry', *Colby Quarterly*, 35, 4 (December 1999), pp. 256–74.
173. Eavan Boland, *Outside History: Selected Poems 1980–1990* (New York: W. W. Norton, 1990), p. 121.
174. In an *Irish Times* (7 April 2001) review of two of Macdara Woods's volumes, his collected poems *Knowledge in the Blood* (Dublin: Dedalus, 2000) and *The Nightingale Water* (Dublin: Dedalus, 2001), Bernard O'Donoghue has called him 'an absorbing and relatively unplaceable presence in Irish writing', in part because of 'the internationalising tendency of his poems to push the boundaries of Irish poetry outwards'.
175. Eavan Boland, *Object Lessons: The Life of the Woman and the Poet in Our Time* (Manchester: Carcanet, 1995), p. 179.
176. John Kerrigan, 'Hidden Ireland: Eiléan Ní Chuilleanáin and Munster Poetry', *Critical Quarterly* 40, 4 (Winter 1998), pp. 76–100, p. 86. Kerrigan has identified this poet's abiding interest in the 'Hidden Ireland' celebrated by Daniel Corkery.
177. Boland, *Object Lessons*, pp. 184–5.
178. Ibid., p. 185.
179. Boland, *Outside History*, p. 95.
180. Ibid., p. 19.
181. Ibid., pp. 78–9.
182. Ibid., p. 79.
183. Ibid., p. 97.
184. Kevin Ray, 'Interview with Eiléan Ní Chuilleanáin', *Éire-Ireland* 32, 2–3 (Summer–Fall 1997), pp. 62–73, pp. 66–67.
185. Ibid., p. 63.
186. Ibid., p. 64.
187. Ibid., p. 64.
188. Eiléan Ní Chuilleanáin, *The Brazen Serpent* (Oldcastle: Gallery Press, 1994; Winston-Salem: Wake Forest University Press, 1995), p. 16.
189. Eiléan Ní Chuilleanáin, 'Nuns: A Subject for a Woman Writer', in Patricia Boyle Haberstroh ed. *My Self, My Muse* (Syracuse: Syracuse University Press, 2001), pp. 17–31, p. 23.
190. Ibid., p. 21.
191. Eiléan Ní Chuilleanáin, *The Girl Who Married the Reindeer* (Oldcastle: Gallery Press, 2001; Winston-Salem: Wake Forest University Press, 2002), p. 40.
192. Paula Meehan, 'The Exact Moment I Became a Poet', in *Dharmakaya* (Manchester: Carcanet, 2000; Winston-Salem: Wake Forest University Press, 2002), p. 14.

193. Paula Meehan, *The Man Who Was Marked by Winter* (Oldcastle: Gallery Press, 1991), p. 14.
194. Vona Groarke, 'Rain Bearers', in *Shale* (Oldcastle: Gallery Press, 1994), p. 57.
195. Bernard O'Donoghue, 'The Translators' Voice: Irish Poetry before Yeats', *Princeton University Library Quarterly* 59, 3 (Spring 1998), pp. 299–320.
196. Michael Hartnett, 'A Visit to Castletown House', in *A Farewell to English*, enlarged edn (Dublin: Gallery Press, 1975, 1978), p. 58.
197. Michael Hartnett, 'Mother Earth', in *Poems to Younger Women* (Dublin: Gallery Press, 1988), p. 17.
198. Paul Muldoon, 'Getting Round: Notes Towards an *Ars Poetica*', *Essays in Criticism* 48, 2 (April 1998), p. 109.
199. James Joyce, *A Portrait of the Artist as a Young Man*, ed. Seamus Deane (London and New York: Penguin, 1992), p. 275.
200. Eamon Grennan, 'Art', in *Relations: New and Selected Poems* (St Paul: Graywolf Press, 1998), p. 220.
201. Eamon Grennan, 'Itinerary', in ibid., p. 221.
202. Dennis O'Driscoll, *Exemplary Damages* (London: Anvil, 2002), p. 29.
203. William Butler Yeats, 'The Fascination of What's Difficult', in Richard Finneran ed. *Collected Poems* (New York: Macmillan, 1983), p. 93.
204. Peter Sirr, 'A Gent's Watch', in *Bring Everything* (Oldcastle: Gallery Press, 2000), p. 31.
205. Ibid., p. 32.
206. Ibid., p. 25.
207. Michael O'Loughlin, *Another Nation: New and Selected Poems* (Dublin: New Island Books, 1996) p. 96; p. 45.
208. Frank Ormsby, *The Ghost Train* (Oldcastle: Gallery Press, 1995), p. 50.

Select bibliography

Bourke, A., Kilfeather, S., Luddy, M., MacCurtain, M., Meaney, G., Ní Dhonnchadha, M., O'Dowd, M. and Wills, C., eds. *The Field Day Anthology of Irish Writing, Vols. IV and V: Irish Women's Writing and Traditions*, Cork: Cork University Press in association with Field Day, 2002.

Brown, John, *In the Chair: Interviews with Poets from the North of Ireland*, Cliffs of Moher, Clare: Salmon, 2002.

Cahalan, James M., *Modern Irish Literature and Culture: A Chronology*, New York: G. K. Hall, 1993.

Clarke, Austin, *Poetry in Modern Ireland*, Cork: Mercier Press, 1961.

Coughlan, Patricia and Alex Davis, *Modernism and Ireland: The Poetry of the 1930s*, Cork: Cork University Press, 1995.

Davis, Alex, *A Broken Line: Denis Devlin and Irish Poetic Modernism*, Dublin: University College Dublin Press, 2000.

Deane, Seamus, gen. ed. *The Field Day Anthology of Irish Writing*, 3 vols., Derry: Field Day, 1991.

Fogarty, Anne, 'The Influence of Absences': Eavan Boland and the Silenced History of Irish Women's Poetry', *Colby Quarterly* 35, 4 (December 1999), pp. 256–74.

Foster, John Wilson, 'The Dissidence of Dissent: John Hewitt and W. R. Rodgers', in *Colonial Consequences: Essays in Irish Literature and Culture*, Dublin: Lilliput Press, 1991, pp. 114–32.

Garratt, Robert F., *Modern Irish Poetry: Tradition and Continuity from Yeats to Heaney*, Berkeley: University of California Press, 1986.

Grant, Patrick, *Breaking Enmities: Religion, Literature and Culture in Northern Ireland, 1967–97*, Basingstoke: Macmillan, 1999.

Haberstroh, Patricia, *Women Creating Women: Contemporary Irish Women Poets*, Dublin: Attic Press, 1996.

Johnston, Dillon, *Irish Poetry after Joyce*, 1985; revised edn Syracuse: Syracuse University Press, 1997.

Harmon, Maurice, *Austin Clarke: A Critical Introduction*, Totowa: Barnes and Noble, 1989.

Howard, Ben, *The Pressed Melodeon: Essays on Modern Irish Writing*, Brownsville: Storyline Press, 1996.

Kendall, Tim, *Paul Muldoon*, Chester Springs: Dufour, 1996.

Kerrigan, John, 'Hidden Ireland: Eiléan Ní Chuilleanáin and Munster Poetry', *Critical Quarterly* 40, 4 (December 1998), pp. 76–100.

Kiberd, Declan, *Inventing Ireland: The Literature of the Modern Nation*, London: Jonathan Cape, 1995.

Kinsella, Thomas, ed. with Seán Ó Tuama, *An Duanaire: 1600–1900: Poems of the Dispossessed*, Portlaoise: Dolmen, 1981.

The Dual Tradition: An Essay on Poetry and Politics in Ireland, Manchester: Carcanet, 1995.

ed. and trans. *The New Oxford Book of Irish Verse*, Oxford: Oxford University Press, 1986.

Lloyd, David, *Anomalous States: Irish Writing and the Post-Colonial Moment*, Dublin: Lilliput, 1993.

Longley, Edna, *The Living Stream: Literature and Revisionism in Ireland*, Newcastle upon Tyne: Bloodaxe, 1994.

Poetry and Posterity, Tarset: Bloodaxe, 2000.

Poetry in the Wars, Newcastle upon Tyne: Bloodaxe, 1986.

McDonald, Peter, *Mistaken Identities: Poetry and Northern Ireland*, Oxford: Clarendon Press, 1997.

Muldoon, Paul, *To Ireland, I*, Oxford and New York: Oxford University Press, 2000.

Peacock, Alan J. and Kathleen Devine, eds. *The Poetry of Michael Longley*, Gerrards Cross: Colin Smythe, 2000.

Quinn, Antoinette, *Patrick Kavanagh: A Biography*, Dublin: Gill and Macmillan; Syracuse: Syracuse University Press, 1991.

Stallworthy, Jon, *Louis MacNeice: A Biography*, New York: W. W. Norton, 1995.

Warner, Alan, *Clay Is the Word: Patrick Kavanagh 1904–1967*, Dublin: Dolmen, 1973.

Wills, Clair, *Improprieties: Politics and Sexuality in Northern Irish Poetry*, Oxford: Oxford University Press, 1993.

9

Contemporary prose in English: 1940–2000

GEORGE O'BRIEN

Introduction

At first glance, the outlook for literary work in the Ireland of 1940 was not propitious. The international situation's constriction of the English publishing industry, on which most Irish writers depended for a living, together with the constraints placed on domestic literary activity, created an environment that was unpromising, to say the least. In the case of imaginative prose, the prospects appeared to be particularly gloomy, with silence and exile the ostensible order of the day. The departure into exile of Samuel Beckett, in 1939, and Francis Stuart, in 1940, was accompanied by the silence created by Joyce's death in 1941. And the self-imposed silence and internal exile of Flann O'Brien following the 1941 rejection of his second novel, *The Third Policeman* (published posthumously in 1967), also made it difficult for the Irish novel to sustain the international reputation it enjoyed in the inter-war period. For Irish novelists the absence of such figures, and of the possibility of a genuinely independent Irish novel their innovative work exemplified, gave rise to problems of continuity and change both conceptually and thematically.

In addition to World War II threatening the loss of audiences outside Ireland, the rigorous enforcement of the Censorship of Publications Act – mainly directed against prose works – ensured that much new writing failed to reach an Irish audience (the 1941 banning of novels by Frank O'Connor (*Dutch Interior*) and Kate O'Brien (*The Land of Spices*) are cases in point).[1] Novelistic productivity in the 1940s was generally low, and novelists in the Irish Free State proved reluctant to engage imaginatively with what was known as the Emergency (this was not true of either Northern Ireland novelists or of short-story writers in the Free State). Yet if, as Frank O'Connor, a leading writer of the day observed, 'the year 1940 is the crucial year for any study of modern Irish literature',[2] the year is as much a departure as a terminus. Prevailing conditions should not be exaggerated. Even in a not notably fertile decade like the 1940s,

Irish imaginative prose produced a number of initiatives ensuring both new departures and a commitment to continuity. In the case of the latter, the short stories of Sean O'Faolain and Frank O'Connor sustained a view of the variety and incorrigibility of human experience, a welcome perspective at an ideologically dark time at home and abroad. The adaptation by women novelists of arguably the most important genre of the Irish novel, the *Bildungsroman* – in the 1940s novels of Kate O'Brien, Maura Laverty's *No More than Human* (1943) and Mary Lavin's *The House in Clewe Street* (1945) – contributed to a sense of both recurring preoccupations and an emerging formal tradition. And Elizabeth Bowen's *The Heat of the Day* (1949) and Molly Keane's *Loving Without Tears* (1951) place women novelists among the first authors dealing explicitly with war's impact on Irish conditions.

The founding of *The Bell* in 1940 under the editorship of Sean O'Faolain stimulated fresh possibilities for Irish writing generally, offering a much-needed outlet for emerging authors such as Mary Lavin, James Plunkett and Bryan MacMahon as well as a forum for criticism. In addition, *The Bell* proposed new orientations for Irish writing. Instead of the nation, the local was suggested as the writer's most useful concern; instead of writing as an elite activity, it had a value which the citizenry at large could create and benefit from; and setting and subject matter were more likely to be rural and personal than metropolitan and general: 'All over Ireland . . . there are men and women with things itching them like a grain stuck in a tooth. You who read this know intimately some corner of life that nobody else can know . . . something that means Ireland to you. It means the whole world.'[3] Thus forms such as the essay, autobiography and travel writing were encouraged as worthwhile contributions to Irish imaginative prose.

Other, more prominent developments during the period under review include the growth and diversity of women's writing; a rethinking of genre, not only in the case of the Big House novel but also in that of historical, anti-realist and popular fiction; and a sustained critique of what were perceived to be the ideological sterilities and imaginative stultifications of standard-issue nationalism and Catholicism, expressed in terms of the travails of family life or – increasingly – in the representation of international *milieux* as lenses and filters through which fresh alignments of identity and affiliation might be seen.

In addition, the postwar period saw the rise of the novel in Northern Ireland; the rapid expansion of the Irish publishing sector; the establishment of the *New Irish Writing* page in the *Irish Press* newspaper, under the editorship of David Marcus, which gave new impetus to the short story; and the increasing toothlessness of the Censorship of Publications Act, which enabled works previously banned to be republished, thereby not only giving them a new lease of cultural life but also broadening the basis for a more comprehensive awareness of Irish imaginative prose in the second half of the twentieth century.

The novel

Samuel Beckett and Francis Stuart

Although it had comparatively little effect on the Irish novel, generally speaking, World War II made a decisive impact on the two most noted Irish novelists of the postwar period, Samuel Beckett (1906–89) and Francis Stuart (1902–2000). Difficulties abound in linking these two names, but these are not strictly of a literary-historical nature and in any case it is the polar opposite character of their artistic strategies in breaking the silence of their exile that concerns us here. In both cases, those strategies address problems of continuity. Such a preoccupation might be expected from authors resuming their careers. For Beckett and Stuart, however, continuity is no mere resumption. Both authors consider continuity problematically, and treat it with a considerable degree of intellectual and rhetorical energy.

Beckett's postwar trilogy – *Molloy* (1951 (1955)), *Malone Dies* (1951 (1956)) and *The Unnamable* (1953 (1958))[4] – constitutes the most comprehensive engagement with the war's legacy of exhaustion, loss and displacement. The notoriously bleak setting of these works, a country of aftermath as poorly served by signposts and landmarks as it is by representations of home and rest, suggests the superannuation of such activities as cultivation, building and similar constructive undertakings – Malone's recollections of rural life reveal its unremitting brutality and ignorance. And just as the terrain deteriorates throughout the trilogy, so does the ability of the novels' hapless and disabled eponyms to traverse it. This inability culminates in crawling through mud in *The Unnamable*, a fate rich in philosophical and religious connotations in addition to being a highly charged allusion to twentieth-century combat.

Beckett's representation of these post-humanist and non-natural landscapes is conveyed in terms of a critique of the novel form itself. In particular, the trilogy subverts the idea of the novel as an expression of quest and desire. This critique is conveyed most explicitly in part 2 of *Molloy*, where it is harnessed to a satirical discourse on method. Moran, the narrator, has a systematic code of practices and usages, and intends to carry out his search for Molloy in the letter and spirit of his system. His search's failure exposes the limitations of the man who thinks therefore he is. Moran's inability to go on confirms limit, terminus and crisis as the coordinates of the map of the Beckett world.

Misgivings regarding the viability of narrative, together with an aesthetic which radicalises still further the calculated misalignments of time and space characteristic of Modernism, have made Beckett's trilogy a work of European significance. But these novels also echo Irish themes, in their unproductive landscapes and moribund sense of agency. The trilogy also discloses an arguably Anglo-Irish sensitivity to decline and fall, concealed within which is an implicit challenge to history as either a prototype of narrative or a context aiding understanding.

In addition, Beckett's ability to represent 'the principle of disintegration in even the most complacent solidities'[5] gives his work a distinctive place in the Irish comic tradition, as does his deflationary use of Hiberno-English, an idiom whose deployment is also consistent with his non-standard imaginative premises. The idiom also mediates the trilogy's important oral dimension. If all else is lost in Beckett's world, the voice persists. Thus, the narrative focus is not on the fact of loss but on awareness of the fact. The trilogy's multiple occasions of loss present obvious challenges to continuity. But the articulation of loss at least relies on persistence, a precondition of continuity. Deprived of the contexts and civilities which would attach them to the human family, Beckett's protagonists can only speak their minds. Yet to be conscious evidently counts for something. As *The Unnamable* has it, 'You must go on, I can't go on, I'll go on.'[6]

Although to a certain extent postwar Irish fiction shares in different ways the dislocation, restlessness, linguistic self-consciousness, uneasiness regarding the status of the subject and the representation of home as a problematical location which are part of Beckett's thematic repertoire, this author's direct influence on the Irish novel is small. In contrast, one of the most prominent cultural events in late twentieth-century Ireland was the emergence of Francis Stuart as something of a literary father figure.[7] The novel to which Stuart's late significance is largely due is the autobiographical *Black List, Section H* (1970). This work draws on his earlier trilogy – *The Pillar of Cloud* (1948), *Redemption* (1949) and *The Flowering Cross* (1950) – which deals with Stuart's wartime sojourn in Berlin. Rather than representing the subject as embattled in his subjectivity as Beckett does, these works valorise subjectivity. Stuart privileges his subject's access to consciousness through feeling, whereas the source of consciousness for Beckett's subjects is invariably the intellect, or rather its imperfections. (Beckett's vision of the limitations and compulsions of intellection receives its ultimate expression in the disembodied voices of *Company* (1979 [1980]), *Ill Seen Ill Said* (1981) and *Worstward Ho* (1983), a trilogy whose minimalist method condenses and critiques the earlier one.)

Stuart's heavily sexualised, masochistically inclined and neuraesthenic protagonists go where their irrational faculties lead them. They become subjects through their complicated dependence on agencies such as fate, chance, impulse and omen, which they cannot control. Soldiers of fortune of a very specialised, Modernist variety, their main battle is to find a place in the world commensurate with their own uniqueness. Yet following one's wayward star is not an end in itself but rather a precondition for a new beginning, the essential elements of which are return, rehabilitation and restitution. Ezra Arrigho, the protagonist of *Redemption*, having survived wartime Berlin, returns to a provincial Ireland where he is at odds with local values. The novel asks if Ezra's experiences can be the basis for a new ethos. Various locals are enlisted in Ezra's quest, including a saintly and independent-minded priest, a typically provocative Stuart characterisation. The living-room wedding of the virginal Romilly to the murderer Kavanagh is one illustration of the sought-after revision of conventional mores.

Stuart's emphasis on subjectivity highlights its psychological reality rather than its usefulness as an ideological resource. In *Redemption* this emphasis is personified by Margareta, Ezra's Berlin companion, whom he had left for dead. Emblematic of resurrection, Margareta's reappearance is an inspirational instance of the ability to rise above historical contingency and local conditions. The unlikelihood of her survival – her continuity – affirms other new departures consistent with Margareta's exemplary spirit. The way forward for Ezra thus entails sacrifice, suffering, purification and resurrection, enabling events which also resonate with central aspects of Irish religious, political and historical traditions. Returning to a renovated version of these aspects is Ezra's way forward, an outcome which also enables Stuart to keep the faith with the 'concrete romanticism' of his pre-war work.[8] If Beckett's narratives seem directed to a point of no return, thereby indicating a problematic conception of continuity, Stuart's are preoccupied by going back, which is an alternative version of the same problematic conception.

A New Generation: McGahern, O'Brien and Higgins

The works of many other Irish novelists of the immediate postwar period were also preoccupied by questions regarding direction and development. The rural as an image of Irish authenticity is presented in a troubled light in the Drombridge trilogy of Francis MacManus (1909–65) – *This House Was Mine* (1937), *Flow On, Lovely River* (1941) and *Watergate* (1942). Set in the Nore valley of the author's native County Kilkenny, these novels are muted but knowing critiques of the codes of patriarchy, class and religion whereby rural family and community – the most salient *topoi* of a newly-liberated nation – maintain the *status quo*. And whether the border country of poet Patrick Kavanagh can be a country for young men is the central question of *Tarry Flynn* (1948), his novel of rural dreams and country mores. The fate of the folk is the main concern of *Children of the Rainbow* (1952) by Bryan MacMahon (1909–98). Drawing on the Gaelic ethos of the author's north Kerry, the action is set in 1926, but more clearly reflects contemporary anxieties about the continuing viability of traditional lifestyles.

Attempts to offset the cultural claustrophobia of the immediate postwar years by maintaining the satirical vein pioneered by an earlier generation are made in Mervyn Wall's adventures of a medieval monk, *The Unfortunate Fursey* (1946) and *The Return of Fursey* (1948), both devoted, in part, to risible exposés of institutional orthodoxies.[9] Turning to a contemporary setting in *Leaves for the Burning* (1952), however, Wall (1908–97) is not quite so playful as he depicts the inglorious peregrinations of a group of friends who become increasingly lost, distracted and inebriated on their way to Yeats's reburial. And losing his way is the protagonist's fate in Michael Farrell's *Thy Tears Might Cease* (1963), whose culmination is the 1916 rebellion.

Individual destinies are generally difficult to deal with in the novels of the late 1940s and early 1950s. Those which do deal with them – Kiely's *Honey Seems Bitter* (1952) and Francis MacManus's *The Fire in the Dust* (1950), for example – see the individual as a pretext for moral reflection, with particular emphasis on sexual morality. Typically dwelling on the conflict between conscience and passion, such works address the creative possibility of the novel of Catholic ideas, the dramatic interest of which would rely on the individual trapped between instinct and training, and divided between the neighbour and the self.[10] The possibility was not realised. Kiely's *There Was an Ancient House* (1955) is a disillusioned valedictory to clerical regimes.

What makes the immediate postwar years an interim period for the Irish novel is the emergence in the late 1950s of a new generation of novelists, much of whose work deals with personal history, private realities and breaking away. Such concerns suggest a movement away from narratives pertaining to the sovereignty of the nation towards the narrative of individual sovereignty. The works of John McGahern (b. 1934), Edna O'Brien (b. 1930), Aidan Higgins (b. 1927) and John Broderick (1927–89) (the last more debatably) – together with the early Northern Ireland novels of Brian Moore (1921–99) – represent important shifts of focus in the Irish novel's themes and techniques. These shifts include a broader formal, stylistic and linguistic diversity; an emphasis on character rather than on plot; more detailed observation of the secular and material realities of daily life; the depiction of locales previously overlooked by the somewhat reductive geography of Irish literary culture; and a widespread and self-conscious repudiation of inherited moral codes and other structures of derivative thought.

The younger novelists take the concerns of their older contemporaries to greater diagnostic and expressive lengths. Thus, for instance, McGahern's *The Barracks* (1963) not only signals in its title the claustrophobia and constraint of provincial Irish life but also is set in the rather anonymous Upper Shannon region. In addition, these conditions are given unexpected psychological depth and symbolic force from the novel's focus on a dying mother, whose life neither church nor state is able to preserve. Similarly, if salvation from the even more oppressive, and equally little-known, social confines of mid-century, middle-class Catholic Belfast is an option in Brian Moore's *The Lonely Passion of Judith Hearne* (1956; first published as *Judith Hearne*, 1955), it is Judith herself who must bring it about, since the Catholicism in which she has sought peace of mind fails to do so. And these women's frailty also indicates the counter-heroic turn the novel has taken.

Related adjustments in thought, theme and focus are found in Edna O'Brien's *The Country Girls Trilogy*, where the protagonist Cait Brady moves continually towards relationships utterly at odds with those expected from a young woman of the rural middle-class background and boarding-school education depicted in *The Country Girls* (1960). Naive and painful Cait's pursuit of romance and passion may be, but she does not go back on it. In this respect, the escape from paternal control which constitutes the dramatic turning-point in the second volume of the trilogy, *The Lonely Girl* (1962; retitled *Girl with Green Eyes*, 1964), is an image of a generation going its own way. This way leads to the replacement of *The Country Girl*'s rural East Clare setting by, first, Dublin and then, in *Girls in Their Married Bliss* (1964), London. But it also leads to overcoming the borders and restrictions of the hereditary definitions of Cait Brady's gender role, even if doing so leads to her unhappy end in the trilogy's *Epilogue* (1986).

Arguably this generation's most comprehensive new departure is Aidan Higgins's *Langrishe, Go Down* (1966). Although its *leitmotif* is breakdown without the promise of breakthrough envisaged by Moore and O'Brien, the pursuit of passion and the location of agency (however temporarily) relates this novel to theirs. Set in the author's native County Kildare, another fictional *terra incognita*, and among a family of sisters who are minor Catholic gentry, this account of failing fortunes gains additional weight from having late 1930s Europe as a backdrop, with a predatory Germany represented by the feral and exploitative Otto, a student of Celtic culture, by whom Imogen Langrishe is seduced and abandoned. The European context and an overall tonality of terminus place the novel close to Beckett's imaginative terrain.[11]

Higgins's depiction of the amenities of civilisation's failure to mask the irrationalities of passion and power also brings a greater range to the Irish novel. In contrast, John Broderick's diagnoses of provincial bourgeois consciences attempt to extend and develop the moral interests of MacManus and Kiely. Set around a market town resembling the author's native Athlone, County Westmeath, Broderick's novels such as *The Pilgrimage* (1961) and *An Apology for Roses* (1973) pass unsparing judgement on prominent citizens' weak bodies and callow souls. Although Broderick's work reiterates problems in writing the postwar Irish Catholic novel, it also addresses tensions between sexuality and social convention that align it with that of McGahern and O'Brien. Treatment of these tensions is of particular note in *The Waking of Willie Ryan* (1965), which deals with the hidden subject of homosexuality.

Increased emphases on sexuality, passion and emotional life; on the existence of an autonomous, distinctive, conditioning-resistant inner life; on the presence of the spirit, not understood in religious or sectarian terms but more humanistically as a matter of energies, hungers and drives are features shared with striking consistency by the early novels of McGahern, Moore, Higgins and O'Brien. These features are embodied in female protagonists. The distaff side of Irish social life, the social status of which has traditionally been thought of as marginal, secondary and irrelevant to the conception of the nation state, becomes creatively co-opted as typical and representative.

Use of the feminine also recognises the woman's body as a site of crisis, where her socially weak and emotionally powerful realities attain critical mass. Moreover, the women characters tend to be neither entirely at home with themselves or fully integrated into the life around them. Thus, their stories go beyond 'inherited dissent' towards narratives dealing with whatever lies underneath political, confessional and ideological heritage.[12] In Richard Power's *The Land of Youth* (1964), for example, the representation of Aran Islands folk life is more trenchant than that of MacMahon's *Children of the Rainbow* (1952) because the career of Power's female protagonist lies along the fault lines created by the conflict between individual and community, which contains within it larger and more disintegrative tensions between tradition and modernity.

Women's needs and experiences can also subvert the patriarchal structure of traditional family life, as *The Country Girls Trilogy* indicates, although challenges to the power of the father generally take place in the context of more general issues pertaining to the refashioning of male identity. Both challenge and context are exemplified in the second novels of both John McGahern and Brian Moore – *The Dark* (1965) and *The Feast of Lupercal* (1957), respectively. These works share a sense of the institutional and emotional barriers placed in the path of self-realisation. The primary architect of these barriers is the father – biological in *The Dark*, clerical in *The Feast of Lupercal*. One enactment of development, then, is an Oedipal one. This drama recurs in McGahern's third novel, *The Leavetaking* (1974), where the clerical father must be overcome, and in Moore's *The Emperor of Ice-Cream* (1965), in which the biological father becomes redundant. In the cumulative cultural impact of these works there are unmistakable signs of what has been called 'the age of inhibitions' coming to an end.[13]

While struggles with the biological father and with the family context which he sustains are difficult, the priest, the primary authority figure from outside the home, is rejected much more readily. Some of the cultural implications of the diminution of priestly power may be assessed by comparing the depiction of the clergy in Francis MacManus's *The Greatest of These* (1943) with Thomas Kilroy's *The Big Chapel* (1971), both dealing with the same nineteenth-century County Kilkenny clerical controversy. The bad faith which John Broderick attributes to his numerous clerical characters is also part of this development, while the most sympathetic portrait of a priest in the postwar Irish novel – Richard Power's *The Hungry Grass* (1969) – dwells not on his authority but on his isolation.

The effective repudiation of the clergy, or at least the local priest, is not matched by a novelistic confrontation with the founding fathers of the state. Many novels by the younger generation do, however, direct hostile asides towards the secular powers that be, so that a general sense emerges of hand-me-down nationalism being rejected in the same way as knee-jerk Catholicism. Thus, a comparison between Farrell's *Thy Tears Might Cease* and James Plunkett's *Strumpet City* (1969) – the latter being a Dublin perspective on working-class realities in the years immediately preceding the 1916 Rebellion – highlights the not merely nationalist colouration of the historical scene. An important dimension of *Strumpet City* is its emphasis on the political meaning and social expression of charity. Other attempts to produce new imaginative configurations of a viable moral economy – though not necessarily in Plunkett's communal terms – result in charity replacing faith and, as a corollary, psyche replacing conscience.

Arguably it is only with John McGahern's *Amongst Women* (1990) that a sufficiently flexible framework is found within which to contain the interactions between gender, generation, politics and cultural values. The death of the patriarch Moran not only has historical and social significance, it is also in keeping with the larger existential rhythms of time and nature, the variable rhythms of 'the living stream' which contrast so powerfully with Moran's rocklike totemic presence.[14] As the novel's title indicates, these rhythms are connoted by the feminine, which enacts the accommodation of the monolithic and overbearing past by the present's fluid contingencies. Freed from land and history, the women go on. Such an outcome conveys an understanding of not only the indeterminate nature of this new, post-historical freedom but also – thanks to *Amongst Women*'s sense of loss – of its ambivalent quality.

The Big House novel

The story of how to get beyond the dominating influence of land and freedom is also central to the postwar Big House novel, particularly since the houses themselves were emblematic of social and political eclipse. Instead, however, the Big House novel continues to rely on its generic enactments of decline and fall, now updated to include recent Irish history and the fate of the Protestant minority in that history's aftermath. And on the basis of such updating, both Aidan Higgins in *Langrishe, Go Down* and John Banville in *Birchwood* (1973) could further adapt the genre to pursue, among other concerns, more wide-ranging interrogations of historical experience.[15]

Yet the genre initially signalled its postwar significance with representations of renewal and development. These signals were given both in Elizabeth Bowen's (1899–1973) *The Heat of the Day* (1949) and Molly Keane's (1904–96) *Loving without Tears* (1951). And although the Bowen novel is too complex to belong to any genre, pastoral and property collaborate in it to represent an alternative of war-torn London, a place of peace and recovery, for which a use may yet be found. Similarly, but much more explicitly, *Loving without Tears* projects the return of the son and heir from serving in the Royal Air Force as most auspicious for the renovation, along modern lines, of the *ancien régime*. Both novels' sense of triumphal return, their hope of translating military victory into social renewal and their acknowledgment of the primacy of the male reverse the status of the Big House as a site of social decline and family anomie.

The note of renewal is temporary, however. After *The Heat of the Day* Bowen effectively abandoned the Big House novel, while Keane, after a prolonged silence, returned to the genre with works – particularly *Good Behaviour* (1981) – which use its gothic register to subversively comic effect. Instead of showing how return and renewal enable the Big House to become economically integrated into postwar Irish society – a possibility rehearsed in *Loving without Tears* – the genre shows the house to be an insupportable structure because of the hyphenated nature of its Anglo-Irish foundations. Thus, the house lends itself to stories of sectarianism, division and political violence.

Social relations in Jennifer Johnston's *The Captains and the Kings* (1972), *How Many Miles to Babylon?* (1974) and *The Old Jest* (1979) are doomed largely due to the Anglo-Irish divide. Johnston (b. 1930) employs a variety of settings, including contemporary Ireland, World War I and the Irish War of Independence, but regardless of time and place – Northern Ireland of the Troubles in *Shadows on Our Skin* (1977) being another example – the contact which might override class or religious difference is attempted only to succumb to historically conditioned reflexes. The friendship between aging Protestant Charles Prendergast of the Big House and young Catholic lower-class villager Diarmuid Toorish in *The Captains and the Kings* cannot possibly be innocent in Diarmuid's parents' eyes. In *How Many Miles to Babylon?* Alex Moore and Jerry Crowe are friends and World War I comrades, but their friendship cannot withstand the army's hierarchy. Johnston's works are parables about borders and cordons and taboos. In addition, their scenarios have no place for the feminine, not necessarily because of men but because of the historically determined world to which the author's male couples stand in innocent and unconscious opposition. And the culmination of this deficiency is the unavailability of young blood to ensure the Big House's continuity.

Issues of male adequacy, historical trauma and feminine agency are also significant in *Troubles* (1970), J. G. Farrell's ambitious mutation of the Big House novel. In this inaugural work of the author's Empire trilogy, the Big House now is an hotel, a structure where service and shelter are illusory. Internal architectural flaws are counterpointed by the presence of republican militants in the grounds. Less an Irish novel than a novel dealing with the entropy of systems set in Ireland, *Troubles* nevertheless tellingly peels away an image of Anglo-Irish hegemony to reveal modern anxieties and displacements.

Its conceptual interests lend *Troubles* an air of detachment, a feature which also distinguishes William Trevor's Anglo-Irish novels, although in Trevor's case detachment seems less the product of the history of ideas than of a carefully disciplined rhetoric. Prior to his Big House novels, Trevor

(b. 1928) produced a number of works – among them *The Old Boys* (1964), *The Boarding-House* (1965) and *The Love Department* (1966) – tacitly articulating a view of Anglo-Irishness which derives not from a sense of historical collapse but from a perception of cultural difference. Set in London, these works dwell on the presuppositions and misprisions of a picaresque cast of lower-middle-class native English in their efforts to feel at home. The independence from but engagement with the Anglo homeland by a native of Mitchelstown, County Cork, imparts to Anglo-Irishness a literal reality, unburdened by historical baggage, with the works in question being not a case of speaking back to empire but of simply speaking to it.

For Trevor, the burden of history exists not in the metropolis but in rural Ireland, where the natural attractions of the good earth are vividly at odds with the violent depredations of man. Trevor's most extensive treatment of this violence's historical genesis and protracted effects is in *Fools of Fortune* (1983). Spanning a number of generations and a broad class spectrum, the story tells of the physical and the moral destruction of the Quintons resulting from the burning by Crown forces of the family home during the War of Independence, a loss eventually avenged by Willy Quinton, heir to the ruin. Vengeance, in turn, brings about Willy's exile and the breakup of family. But his return to Kilneagh – return and renewal also generate the narrative dynamic of Trevor's other Big House novel, *The Silence in the Garden* (1988) – cleanses the house of its violent heritage, relieves it of its historical symbolism and restores it to appropriately life-sized dimensions.

In both *Fools of Fortune* and *The Silence in the Garden* women characters are custodians of the rehabilitative domestic space which counterpoints history's temporal attrition. The feminised *genius loci* represents openness, possibility and suffering redeemed. And Trevor's relocation of this iconic presence from a broad historical canvas to a more limited communal setting in the novella 'Reading Turgenev' (in *Two Lives* (1991)) – a work in which there is no Big House available – is a means of focusing on decline and abjection in the minority community.

The eponymous protagonist of *Felicia's Journey* (1994) offers a further perspective on Trevor's use of the feminine. This novel is built around Irish Felicia's homelessness and the English home where she is held captive and which is her would-be murderer's castle – a dangerously parodic Big House. Taken in by the monstrous Mr Hilditch, who intends her to be his next victim, Felicia overcomes both Irish and Anglo attempts to brutalise and efface her identity. Although this success leads to further homelessness, she embraces the openness of her condition, finding in it a space and latitude beyond the binaries of Irishness and Englishness. Such concerns of the Big House novel as deracination and loss of structure recur here, but *Felicia's Journey* is also a further illustration of the postwar Irish novel's troubled engagement with forward movement.

'The nightmare of history': O'Brien and Banville

Mixed results notwithstanding, the postwar Big House novel desires to transcend its historical pretexts. In this way it shares an ambition to awake from the nightmare of history expressed in other ways by other Irish novelists. The two most substantial of Flann O'Brien's (Brian O'Nolan (1911–66)) postwar novels experiment with the implications of this ambition, and in both *The Dalkey Archive* (1964) and *The Third Policeman* (1967) a considerable amount of comic invention is devoted to the proposition that progress may be more conceit than concept. Thus, James Joyce, who appears as a character in *The Dalkey Archive*, seems to embody a nightmarish version of his own history, disowning much of his own work and wishing to become a Jesuit. In contrast, the savant De Selby, who claims among his accomplishments his mastery of time, has created Omnium (the neologism's totalitarian echoes can hardly be coincidental) and intends to blow the world to smithereens with the stuff. Mick, the average citizen, is caught between Joycean paralysis and De Selbian change. But the novel ends with neither a bang nor a whimper, rather with the pregnancy of Mick's girl-friend. Life does go on – or rather, repeats itself – by means of natural and ahistorical sequences and processes.

This serious comedy of the vanity of human wishes is a diluted version of *The Third Policeman*. In that novel, the full scale and consequences of consciousness's capacity for self-generated nightmare is developed. The murder which launches the story is carried out in the name of De Selby scholarship, an expression of the lust for power concealed within the quest for knowledge. The murder's aftermath takes place in a realm where space, time, proportion, judgement, physical dimensions, sense perception and molecular stability are entirely unreliable, causing the narrator much mental suffering. Release merely restarts this hell of circularity, which shows that epistemology, chronology and linear narrative contain the seeds of their own undoing, and which is the opposite of the liberating progress the narrator believed the murder would underwrite.

The complex intellectual vision underlying Flann O'Brien's work may make the concerns of other novelists with family difficulties and the unavailability of a usable past seem parochial and prosaic. Yet his work's deep scepticism of ideas, traditions, belief systems and culturally conditioned habits of thought does have a bearing on many fundamental preoccupations of other novelists – including, for example, their grasp of method and subject matter. And O'Brien's comment on Joyce – 'With laughs he palliates the sense of doom that is the heritage of the Irish Catholic'[16] – applies equally well to his own writings.

O'Brien's inimitable intellectual distinctiveness, stylistic flair and tonal control make him commonly thought of as a significant contributor to the Irish comic tradition. Yet this is perhaps the thinnest of the various formal and generic strands which make up Irish imaginative prose in the second half of the twentieth century. Even O'Brien's own *The Hard Life* (1961), a satirical take on both faith and good works, does not greatly enhance the tradition. On the other hand, *The Poor Mouth* (1973, a translation from the Irish of the author's *An Béal Bocht*, 1941), is an excoriation of Irish language policy so stinging as to be impossible to match. Comic novels that stand out include *The Life of Riley* (1964), poet and critic Anthony Cronin's chronicle of picaresque adventures in bohemian Dublin, and Benedict Kiely's romp *Dogs Enjoy the Morning* (1968). Poet and playwright Sebastian Barry's polyphonic *The Engine of Owl Light* (1987), which combines elements of fantasy with those of the American road novel, and which is set in America, contains much light-hearted exuberance. Irish-American Timothy O'Grady's *Motherland* (1989) also unites various fictional forms and discourses to produce a haunting and high-spirited fantasy-meditation on Irish historical and mythological themes. Broadly speaking, however, the connection proposed by Modernist Irish fiction between comic vision and formal experimentation lapses in the postwar period.

A perhaps less obvious but more significant sign of Flann O'Brien's influence may be seen by considering the place of ideas in postwar Irish fiction. For although O'Brien is not responsible for a renewed interest in the novel of ideas on the part of Irish novelists, the consolidation of his artistic reputation with the publication of *The Third Policeman* coincides with such a renewal. Thomas Kilroy's *The Big Chapel* (1971), set in the Parnell era, questions the idea of a stable historical record by showing concept, perception and interpretation to be as fundamental to it as events. Carlo Gébler's exploration of the concept of violence in nineteenth-century Ireland in *The Cure* (1994) is also apropos. And historical change as an entropic heart of darkness is the subject of Vincent Lawrence's *An End to Flight* (1973), whose protagonist is an Irish teacher caught in the war in Biafra. These novels' consideration of history place in eclipse the historical romance. The work of Walter Macken (1915–67) – *Seek the Fair Land* (1959), set in Cromwellian Ireland, and *The Silent People* (1962), a novel of the Great Famine are representative – constituted a virtual swan song for the genre among Irish authors.

O'Brien's familiar mixture of the ludic and the menacing features in the novels of Patrick McGinley (b. 1937). Set for the most part in the author's native Donegal, these works also elaborate on such O'Brien tropes as the futility of knowledge and the relativity of perception, most notably in *The Trick of the Ga Bolga* (1985). O'Brien's perceptual games, minus the menace, are also at play in Alf MacLochlainn's *Out of Focus* (1978).

It is in the novels of John Banville (b. 1945), however, that the idea is most comprehensively proposed as an alternative to conventional history. The first two novels by the Wexford-born author, *Nightspawn* (1971) and *Birchwood* (1973), subverted the genres of the international thriller and the Big House novel, respectively – *Nightspawn* is set in a Greece on the eve of the Colonels' coup of 1967; *Birchwood* alludes unsystematically to various Irish historical turning points. Rather than a deconstruction of the Big House, *Birchwood*, because of its narrator's self-conscious role of writer, is more interested in dismantling the structures of historically determined narratives, of which the Big House novel is the distinctive Irish example.

The possibility that narratives do not derive from, or owe allegiance to, the world as found is explored most fully in Banville's next three novels, *Doctor Copernicus* (1976), *Kepler* (1981) and *The Newton Letter* (1982). As their titles suggest, these are Irish novels with a difference, and their chief concern is to articulate their difference, in the spirit of their eponymous protagonists. In the first two novels, difference arises in a Europe whose humanism is constantly in crisis, whose Christian ethos is manifestly found wanting, whose authority is administered pettily and arbitrarily, and whose consciousness is fuelled by a reflexive reliance on tradition. Both Copernicus and Kepler are materially dependent on this ramshackle imperium. Given the vicissitudes and contingencies of the historical moment in which the two protagonists find themselves, the appeal of other worlds and a new start is clear; and eirenic, intellectually rewarding, heretical thought underscores the importance of the heterodox and the cultural potential of imaginative power and daring. The publication of these novels during the height of Northern Ireland's civil strife gives them additional resonance.

Representations of imagination and difference form the core of Banville's second trilogy, consisting of *The Book of Evidence* (1989), *Ghosts* (1993) and *Athena* (1995). In these novels, the focus is on the work of art, specifically painting, and the storylines deal not with the constitutive agency of the imagination but with the disorder which failure of imagination creates. Betrayal and inauthenticity in various forms recur throughout these works, and it is in the light of such human failings that the work of art – because of its technical reliance on, and expressive transmutation of, artifice – exerts its forceful humanistic appeal. Freddie Montgomery, who commits murder in the course of stealing a painting in *The Book of Evidence*, is to some degree rehabilitated in *Ghosts*, having served his jail sentence. In *Athena*, love's uncertainties are viewed in the light of descriptions of pictures by the anagramatically named Jean Vaublin. Yet, as *The Untouchable* (1997) – a pendant to the art trilogy, as *Mefisto* (1986) is to the science trilogy – makes clear, the work of art is much frailer than the cosmologist's vision, is more readily misunderstood and misappropriated. But such vulnerability also makes the work of art all the more necessary in a world (the setting for the art trilogy is contemporary Ireland) where resources to counteract the bad faith and random violence of the day are so scarce.

The European reach of *The Untouchable* – including its ambitious foray into the upper echelons of English politics and society from the 1930s to the 1970s – lifts it beyond, even as it obliquely reflects upon, the parochial and the contemporaneous. In doing so, the novel acknowledges the nightmare of history while proposing the energies of intellection – thought, imagination, ideas – as one of the few dimensions of the human capable of allaying the nightmare.

The novel in Northern Ireland

The uncertainties of progress and individuation which recur in various ways in the postwar novel in the Irish Republic indicate that its typical form is the spoiled *Bildungsroman*. Analogously, preoccupations in the Northern Irish novel with settlement and demography, and with the relationship between territory and community, make spoiled pastoral its typical form. If time is the problematic of the novel in the Republic, space is in the Northern novel. The novel in the Republic has devoted comparatively little attention to the Troubles, despite the influence the Troubles have had on the impetus in the Republic to revise and authenticate the national narrative. And in treating its local concerns, the Northern novel has evolved its own distinctive set of tropes and tones.

The problematical nature of space, and the particular ways in which it is culturally coded, may be seen in *Lost Fields* (1941) by Michael McLaverty (1904–92) and *Land without Stars* (1946) by Benedict Kiely (b. 1919), both of which draw on their authors' provincial backgrounds to deal with questions of habitat and affiliation. Divisive family problems colour *Lost Fields*, and political tensions overshadow notions of home in the Kiely novel, while their titles signal deprivation and the difficulty of charting a course. The unchanging nature of such conditions is reflected in the avoidance of Northern settings in all of Kiely's subsequent novels, the satirical anathema of *Nothing Happens in Carmincross* (1985) being the one exception. And later McLaverty novels such as *The Three Brothers* (1948), *School for Hope* (1954) and *The Choice* (1958) focus on the moral life of the minority population rather than on its overall social context with a view to creating a Northern Catholic novel.

It is not only the minority who experience the constraints of group loyalty and sense of limits, borders and taboos which those constraints impose. Sam Hanna Bell's (1909–90) *December Bride* (1951), whose action takes place in the pre-Northern Ireland twentieth century and is set in the Ards peninsula, one of the foundational landscapes in the cultural imagination of the majority, deals with the moral constrictions which a group ethos enjoins. Sarah Gomartin has an affair with both of the sons on whose farm she is a servant, becomes pregnant, refuses to name the child's father and is ostracised. The local minister eventually prevails on her to marry for the child's sake, which both saves the community's moral face and sharply contrasts with Sarah's sense of personal loyalty. Difficulties of individuation, of breaking patterns and entering into new territory, are the subject of the same author's *The Hollow Ball* (1961), while his two historical novels – *A Man Flourishing* (1973) and *Across the Narrow Sea* (1987) – adopt a wider canvas on which to depict issues of solidarity and settlement.

These two works, however, have not stimulated many other contributions to the genre. *Dream* (1986) by David Martin (b. 1937, later McCart Martin), which depicts the effects of late nineteenth-century history and politics on personal loyalties in rural County Antrim, and *Death and Nightingales* (1992), by playwright Eugene McCabe (b. 1930), in which public unrest from the same period in the border country of County Fermanagh is paralleled by traumatic personal events, are two exceptions. Carlo Gébler – strictly speaking, not a Northern novelist – traces militancy and violence to nineteenth-century County Monaghan in *How to Murder a Man* (1998).

The novels of Janet McNeill (1907–94) also deal with entrapment by the force of social appearances by showing how the personal behaviour of her Belfast Protestant middle-class characters belies the ostensible solidity of their public front. In such novels as *As Strangers Here* (1960), *The Maiden Dinosaur* (1964) and *The Small Widow* (1967), this vulnerability is seen in terms of loss of male power, a loss which has less to do with sexuality as such than with caution and inexpressiveness. Thus the male-made world which Sarah Vincent haplessly inherits at the conclusion of *The Maiden Dinosaur* makes problematical her capacity to inherit her own gender.

Brian Moore's early works – *The Feast of Lupercal* (1957) and *The Emperor of Ice-Cream* (1965) – attempt to go beyond the well-established lines of communal demarcation and personal constraint. Moore's later career ostensibly stands at a distance from the Northern Irish novel, a distance initiated by his two emigrant novels, *The Luck of Ginger Coffey* (1960), set in Montreal, and *An Answer from Limbo* (1962), set in New York. Yet, this distance can be deceptive, and in any case is not consistently maintained. Thus, *The Doctor's Wife* (1976) centres on an escape scenario set in the south of France replete with sexual liberation for the wife in question. The novel ends, however, questioning whether a new start away from home can become permanent, a question which recurs more dramatically in Moore's final Belfast novel, *Lies of Silence* (1990). Moreover, despite their international settings, Moore's later novels contain such familiar concerns as identity problems (in *I Am Mary Dunne* (1968) and *Fergus* (1970)), border crossings of various kinds – political (*The Revolution Script* (1971)), temporal (*The Great Victorian Collection* (1975)) and cultural (*Black Robe* (1985)) – and states of violent upheaval (*Lies of Silence, No Other Life* (1993) and *The Statement* (1995)).

In addition, beginning with *Catholics* (1972), Moore focuses on the matters of faith and doubt first raised in *The Lonely Passion of Judith Hearne*. These matters are examined in a variety of ways – clerical and ideological in *The Colour of Blood* (1987), visionary experiences in *Cold Heaven* (1983) and *The Temptation of Eileen Hughes* (1981), and as accessories to imperial ambition in *Black Robe* and *The Magician's Wife* (1997). The unchanging continuity of faith offers an objectively immutable sense of purpose and source of agency to the protagonist who believes. Yet, even for these men (typically), the contingency of circumstance elicits powerful subjective responses which threaten faith, making doubt an equally plausible ground for action and conduct. It is not difficult to imagine the protagonists of these works casting, like Banville's scientists, an oblique reflection on recent Northern developments.

Later Northern novelists have not shown the same interest as Moore in religion, but other themes introduced in his novels have been taken up, in particular sexual identity and historical violence. The first of these is addressed from within the majority community by Antrim novelist Maurice Leitch (b. 1933) in such works as *The Liberty Lad* (1965) and *Poor Lazarus* (1969). Sexual dysfunction in the latter finds a counterpart in the former's depiction of hypocrisy and repression apropos homosexuality. Leitch's *Stamping Ground* (1975) unmasks the pathologies of the Northern psyche as expressed through sexuality and violence in a rural setting. Subsequent Leitch novels bring the same potent combination of themes to explore the Belfast of Protestant paramilitarism in *Silver's City* (1981), the career of a country-and-western singer in *Burning Bridges* (1989) and the mind of a renegade Protestant clergyman in *Gilchrist* (1994). To a certain extent, Leitch's novels, particularly his early ones, can be seen as both a development and critique of subject matter broached by Anthony C. West (b. 1910) in such novels as *The Native Moment* (1959) and more particularly *The Ferret Fancier* (1963), in which the narrowness of local mores is shown as the enemy of the natural and of human nature.

Leitch has also contributed to the canon of Northern World War II fiction with *The Smoke King* (1998), in which the presence of Black American troops stationed in the North during World War II is used as a context for probing racism. Besides this novel and Brian Moore's *The Emperor of Ice-Cream*, other World War II works include Anthony C. West's *As Towns with Fire* (1968), whose fighter-pilot protagonist in part memorialises official and unofficial Irish participation in the war. David Martin's *The Ceremony of Innocence* (1977) deals with personal and communal relations in the context of the 1941 Belfast blitz. These novels underline both the North's membership of the United Kingdom and the physical and psychological effects of historical violence.

As the Troubles exacerbated the reality of being socially vulnerable and also demonstrated the instability of the prevailing hegemony, so victimisation and psychological breakdown became increasingly familiar plot strategies, even if breakdown predates the Troubles, as Joseph Tomelty's *Red Is the Port Light* (1948) illustrates. But in the novels of Ian Cochrane (b. 1942), the first three of which – *A Streak of Madness* (1973), *Gone in the Head* (1974) and *Jesus on a Stick* (1975) – are set among the Protestant working class of mid-Antrim's so-called Bible Belt, breakdown is endemic and systemic. The protagonists' painfully comedic self-destructive behaviour effectively corroborates the Northern polity's historically induced pathologies. Inner-city Belfast is treated in a similar, though more broadly satirical, vein by John Morrow (b. 1930) in *Confessions of Proinsias O'Toole* (1977) and *The Essex Factor* (1982), two knowing farces whose denouement is implosion.

Breakdown as a result of direct involvement in the Troubles is the outcome of the revenge plot of David Martin's *The Task* (1975). But it is also the upshot of the reparation plot of Bernard MacLaverty's *Cal* (1983). Cal MacCrystal's love for the widow of a policeman in whose murder he has been involved may be a prototypical enactment of the Christian ethos (in the sacrificial and salvific dimensions of which MacLaverty (b. 1942) had already written in *Lamb* (1980), set outside Northern Ireland). But Cal's embodiment of both *eros* and *agape* is not enough to save him. In *The Task* and *Cal* the focus is on the aftermath of violence. An alternative approach is taken in the novels of Eoin McNamee (b. 1961), where the narrative interest is in the representation of the mind-set of perpetrators. In particular *Resurrection Man* (1994), based on the notorious Shankill Butchers murders and drawing on both their sexualised fetishism and ritualised aspects, details a decadent inversion of subjective agency. The first two novels of Belfast novelist Ronan Bennett (b. 1956) – *The Second Prison* (1991) and *Overthrown by Strangers* (1992) – find their focus in membership of the Provisional IRA, while his third novel, *The Catastrophist* (1998), deals with revolutionary violence in an international context.

From one point of view, breakdown may be regarded as representing a victim's oppositional identity. Representing opposition by means other than breakdown has been a challenge which the novelists who emerged towards the end of the twentieth century – among them Glenn Patterson (b. 1961), Deirdre Madden (b. 1960) and Robert McLiam Wilson (b. 1964) – have taken up. To their works, two novels by a pair of older authors may be added: *Reading in the Dark* (1996) by poet and critic Seamus Deane (b. 1940) and Bernard MacLaverty's *Grace Notes* (1997). Deane's semi-autobiographical novel is suffused with varieties of border crossings and trespass which vividly convey the haunted history of the narrator's nationalist family and his struggle to lay its ghosts. In *Grace Notes*, the move beyond the family, while fraught with tension, is depicted as the struggle for, and eventual triumph of, harmony on the part of its unusual protagonist, a female composer. The inventive latitude mapped in Belfast poet Ciaran Carson's *Fishing for Amber* (1999) also speaks for new departures.

The note of breakthrough sounded in *Grace Notes* echoes similar tones of recovery and onward movement in, for instance, Deirdre Madden's *Hidden Symptoms* (1986; 1988), where the protagonist's struggle to carry on after her brother's murder constitutes the main narrative interest. In Madden's *The Birds of the Innocent Wood* (1988), the internalisation of some symptomatic Northern social and cultural practices is the subtext of a portrait of an emotionally distant family. And the sense of relief and possibility felt by the young Northern woman's Italian sojourn in *Remembering Light and Stone* (1992) is further highlighted by the rather glum lives of the group of Donegal-based women detailed in *Nothing is Black* (1994).

A comparable trajectory of growth, emergence and potential autonomy is provided by the novels of Glenn Patterson. In *Burning Your Own* (1988) the trials and tensions of a Protestant suburban Belfast boyhood are depicted. The elaborate story of returning to a physically renovated Belfast which remains an emotionally fraught fatherland is told in *Fat Lad* (1992), a title which is an acronym of the initials of Northern Ireland's six counties. The difficulty of relocating both sets of formative Northern structures – physical and emotional – is elaborated upon in *Black Night at Big Thunder Mountain* (1995), set in the building site of Euro Disney. Place, displacement, physical structure and return also form the nexus of *The International* (1999), set in the eponymous bar on the eve of the Troubles.

The tension in *Black Night at Big Thunder Mountain* between the ease of breaking new ground geographically and the challenge of doing so in the realm of consciousness is also central to Robert McLiam Wilson's *Ripley Bogle* (1989). One of this novel's many layers is a satire on the idea of stable identity, in which the eponymous tramp-narrator represents himself as having been no less at home growing up in his native Belfast than he now is in his marginal London existence. The penchant of Wilson's fiction for boundary crossing, transgression and provocative realignments is given full play in *Eureka Street* (1996). Set in – but not confined by – Belfast, this novel's inclusive cast of characters and geographical range articulate effectively the outward-reaching, forward-looking tendencies of the novel in Northern Ireland at the close of the twentieth century.

Writing the Irish Republic

If border and other demarcations of troubled and contested space have an explicit structural role in the Northern Ireland novel, their place is also thematically important in the novel in the Republic, particularly since the 1970s. In the course of the Republic's postwar evolution from nationalist to Christian Democrat state, and given a certain European cultural turn within that evolution, there has been an inclination to consider baggage from the nationalist era, such as the border, to be passé. Nevertheless, even if novelistic representations of the historical border – in novelistic terms, at least – are relatively uncommon, habits of thinking in terms of borders, limits, constraints and fixed social strata persist.

An influential model of the cultural and imaginative implications of border-crossing is Francis Stuart's *Black List, Section H* (1971). Indeed, Stuart stands as something of an *éminence grise* behind a certain amount of Irish fiction written in the 1980s and 1990s, most influentially, perhaps because of the embrace of insecurity in his work.[17] This aspect is very much in evidence in *Black List*, a confessional work in which Stuart, behind his persona H, recounts his life on the margins of Irish society and European history, from which he emerges with the enhanced moral standing of the witness, the survivor, the outcast who, having suffered more than those who would judge him, knows more and has greater authority than they. H's story demonstrates that the fears endemic to the Irish condition from independence until perhaps the economic boom of the 1990s – fear of exile, poverty, homelessness, risk, as well as fear of outspokenness and non-conformity – can be the basis of a new beginning grounded in spiritual insight and psychological integrity.

Though there is no explicit link between Stuart and the authors in question, the appeal of and struggle for new bases for identity may be found in the works of the Irish Writers Co-operative of the mid-1970s. The novels of Neil Jordan (b. 1950, founder of the Co-operative and subsequently a noted film-maker) and Desmond Hogan (b. 1950) depict the pressure felt by young male protagonists to remain oneself by breaking away. Identity as an index of difference informs much of this work, with difference being represented in terms of class, sexuality and family history. The tensions between mothers and sons in Hogan's *The Ikon Maker* (1976) and *The Leaves on Grey* (1980) are one indication of how uncertain a domicile home has become. Having nowhere to go but their own way, Hogan's protagonists embody an indeterminacy which finds them desiring to mediate between self and world but without the emotional or spiritual resources to do so. Indeterminacy as, in effect, a synonym for identity is the subject of *A Curious Street* (1984), narrated by a British soldier of Anglo-Irish origins stationed in Belfast, while the tensions between sexual and political identity are dealt with in *A New Shirt* (1986). Hogan's work is often concerned with the destruction of innocence, and the same theme may be found in the most sustained novelistic attempt to confront conditions in Northern Ireland, the *Children of the North* trilogy of Dublin-born M. S. Power (b. 1935). The trilogy consists of *The Killing of Yesterday's Children* (1985), *Lonely the Man without Heroes* (1986) and *A Darkness in the Eye* (1987).

A sense of the uncertainty contained within the quest for identity is also central to Jordan's *The Past* (1980). Indeterminacy here arises with the protagonist's realisation that the past is two-faced, possessing both a continuing presence and an irrecoverable actuality. With little to go on, the protagonist seeks his own true story as one which disentangles his family roots from the history of the country, a project which leaves him with incomplete versions of both. The power of the father is prominent here, and recurs again in the renegotiation of the father's history in *Sunrise with Sea Monster* (1994).

Among other Irish Writers Co-operative writers, both Sebastian Barry (b. 1955) and Ronan Sheehan (b. 1953) deal with Dublin middle-class suburbia. Sheehan's *Tennis Players* (1977) exposes the mores of the children of the city's *nouveaux riches*, while Barry's *Macker's Garden* (1982) portrays the shifting moral and emotional ground of adolescence. These novels contrast instructively with the picture of the pre-World War II capital detailed by James Plunkett (b. 1920) in his *Farewell Companions* (1977), and also with the clergy-dominated early postwar period of his *The Circus Animals* (1990). These works' patient narrative also contrasts with the tonal and syntactical departures typical of Irish Writers Co-operative authors.

Changing novelistic representations of Dublin make their most noticeable cultural impact through the novels of Roddy Doyle (b. 1958) and Dermot Bolger (b. 1959), although the Dublin which both these authors depict owes little or nothing to the city's inner, Joycean core.[18] Instead, the citizens represented are tied to their immediate locales, the peripheral communities of Bolger's Finglas and Doyle's Barrytown. Displacement and relocation are crucial experiences of both novelists' characters. In his Barrytown trilogy – *The Commitments* (1987), *The Snapper* (1990) and *The Van* (1991) – Doyle conceives of such experiences in terms which ostensibly reconstitute the nuclear family, with Jimmy Rabbitte as the family's head. But the headship is merely titular, resulting in a less hierarchical family structure. Thus, solidarity, support and resilience replace patriarchy, judgement and demoralisation.

An instance of the Rabbitte ethos is her parents' support of unmarried Sharon's pregnancy in *The Snapper*. The indifference to church and state implicit in the Rabbittes' attitude indicates that their survival is in nobody's hands but their own, and although such a declaration of independence is treated more problematically in *Paddy Clarke Ha Ha Ha* (1993) its value remains intact. This novel's action begins in 1966 with the creation of Barrytown, a new domicile located between the rural and the metropolitan. Paddy Clarke is one of the founding children of this tradition-free place. His father's rejection of Barrytown results in marital breakdown. In contrast, young Paddy Clarke withstands the social and emotional deficiencies of the only world he knows, and in doing so is a striking instance of the breaking-away theme. Paddy's spirit of survival is also fundamentally important to Paula, the battered-wife narrator of Doyle's fifth novel, *The Woman Who Walked into Doors* (1996), while a more elaborate and typically heterodox version of Doyle-style 'indomitable Irishry' is expressed by the picaresque adventures in nation-building of Henry Smart, star of the subversive historical novel *A Star Called Henry* (1999).

Survival is also a primary concern in the novels of Dermot Bolger, though Finglas is a much less genial terrain than Barrytown and the chances of realising a distinctive identity within it are correspondingly diminished. Bolger conveys as tragedy what Doyle treats as farce. In novels such as *Night Shift*

(1985), *The Woman's Daughter* (1987; revised 1991) and *The Journey Home* (1990), the city is more obviously modernisation's casualty than its beneficiary.[19] And in their abject characters, depleted communities and need for some redemptive possibility these works echo the critical notes of Francis Stuart's novels, particularly *The Journey Home*'s story of love, hope and breaking away. Later Bolger novels – *Emily's Shoes* (1992), *A Second Life* (1994) and *Temptation* (2000) – focus on individual case histories in which desire and damnation act out a tense struggle within ostensibly commonplace circumstances, while *Father's Music* (1997) stages this struggle in more explicit psycho-cultural terms, represented by a missing father and a visceral attachment to Irish traditional music.

Marginalised Irish citizens are also typical of representation of the international scene. In Aidan Higgins's *Balcony of Europe* (1972), set in a colony of expatriates in southern Spain, Dan Ruttle, an Irish painter, has an extramarital affair with an American. The affair, rendered in terms of unpredictable moments of intensity, is set against a backdrop of Cold War anxiety and fellow residents' transience. Similar representations of transgressive love as a life-line in a sea of historical and cultural futility inform Higgins's two later novels, *Bornholm Night-Ferry* (1983) and *Lions of the Grunewald* (1993).

Crossing international borders into terrains where self-realisation is synonymous with desire is also the subject of Colm Tóibín's *The South* (1990), the story of a woman who leaves her loveless marriage for Barcelona and the Pyrenees. In contrast, Tóibín's *The Heather Blazing* (1992), drawing on the County Wexford roots of its author (b. 1955), examines the life of Judge Eamon Redmond, in whose life and career there has never been a hint of transgression, and who has lived a life of spiritually numbing fidelity to the letter of the law. The result is a man for whom desire seems an alien concept, and who is almost terminally hampered by an inability to conceive of a life different from his own.[20] In *The Story of the Night* (1996), non-Irish characters and an Argentinian setting establish a realm where gay identity and its social and familial negotiation may have its say. Tóibín's revision of hierarchical, paternalistic family structures in the light of desire also forms the subject of *The Blackwater Lightship* (1999), where Declan, a successful European functionary now fatally ill with AIDS, visits his Wexford origins. Here he is cared for not only by his immediate family, consisting of three generations of women, but by a surrogate family of gay friends. Secure in his identity, Declan exemplifies how his blood relatives might accept their own and be tolerant of each other's. Similarly, homosexuality may be the least challenging of the family conflicts in Keith Ridgway's *The Long Falling* (1998), in which generational and country–city tensions are sexually inflected and where Dublin has a fully functional gay culture.

Relocation and identity play a decisive role in the novels of Carlo Gébler (b. 1954) and Joseph O'Connor (b. 1963). Gébler, following in the footsteps of his mother, Edna O'Brien, focuses on the emigrant experience's moral corrosiveness in *Work and Play* (1987) and *Life of a Drum* (1991), dealing with problems of vulnerability and choice. In both works, social controls and self-control enter into increasingly destructive conflict, and the same territory and concerns are dealt with in darker tonalities by J. M. O'Neill (1921–99) in *Open Cut* (1986) and *Duffy is Dead* (1987). For the protagonists of Dublin novelist O'Connor, getting away from their native city is a central experience. Whether it takes the form of a comic revision of emigration in *Cowboys and Indians* (1991), a broken family's search in *Desperadoes* (1994) for a son presumed missing in Nicaragua, or the closer-to-home retreats and pilgrimages in *The Salesman* (1998) and *Inishowen* (2000), leaving the city is an essential overture to finding a way forward. The character in greatest need of moving on in these works is a conflicted father, whose emotional limitations find revealing parallels in the confinements of his class status.

Leaving, and having left, are also fundamental to *Surrogate City* (1990) by Hugo Hamilton (b. 1953), although the Berlin of the protagonist's landfall turns out to reproduce Dublin, reversing departure on itself. Crossing back into Germany from the Sudentenland at the end of World War II is the subject of Hamilton's second novel, *The Last Shot* (1991), while *The Love Test* (1995) deals with East and West Germans' encounters with each other across, through and after the Berlin Wall. In these works, the force of individual need renders permeable the most solidly entrenched of social and historical structures, appearances and lines of demarcation.

Surrogacy is also a feature of two works by Dublin-born Colum McCann (b. 1965): *Songdogs* (1995), in which rural Mayo is a counterpart of rural Mexico, and *This Side of Brightness* (1998), which associates the history of the New York Irish with the destiny of the city's African-Americans. Following in another's footsteps is a storyline common to both these novels. The figure of a wayward and transgressive father is the point of departure in *Songdogs*. In *This Side of Brightness* the labour of a previous generation is adapted for cultural and social purposes which that generation could not have foreseen. Thus, inheritance becomes a resource once its burden is lifted.

The risks and challenges of seeking release from history's impersonal and oppressive bequest may be gathered from those novels dealing with the border between Northern Ireland and the Republic. Rather than confront the politics of the actual jurisdictional divide, these works use its presence obliquely and critically. Dermot Healy's (b. 1947) familiarity with the north-west of the country, for example, has given his two novels set there a strong sense of unconscious emotional division and psychological misgiving. The effect of such fissures on a family in the border country is depicted in *Fighting with Shadows* (1984), while the couple in *A Goat's Song* (1994) wish to adapt for productive private ends terms such as loyalty and independence which had long been thought to be confined to the language of political and cultural exclusivity.

The representation of border country as a distinct psycho-cultural zone is a prominent feature of the novels of Patrick McCabe (b. 1955), notably *Carn* (1989), *The Butcher Boy* (1992) and *Breakfast on Pluto* (1998). The hallmarks of this geographically undefined but sociologically recognisable area include emotional malnourishment and social transgression, paternal neglect and institutional failure, abandonment and betrayal, mindlessness and murder. Such a landscape of incoherence and insecurity is obviously not the direct result of the historical border. But the border's existence, at once metastatic and irrelevant, does have an influence as an officially sanctioned marker of imbalance, arbitrariness and rupture whose metaphorical potential McCabe inventively develops. Attempts to find the same potential in the national picture presented in *The Dead School* (1995) show how specific to McCabe's border country it is.

Francie Brady, the protagonist of *The Butcher Boy*, is the poster child of the divisions and incompatibilities writ large by the historical border. Son of dysfunctional Northern parents and eventually a ward of an incompetent Southern state, his transgressive behaviour articulates the absence of a reasoned alternative to social and institutional inadequacies. His presence denotes failure to observe boundaries of any kind – geographical, class or gender (gender transgression is further developed in *Breakfast on Pluto*). Set in the 1960s in order to highlight the backwardness of old pieties and rigidities in the light of a looser, populist, youth-oriented American culture, and, furthermore, to suggest the irrelevance of inherited constraints in view of America's nuclear arsenal, *The Butcher Boy* dramatises issues of individual sovereignty, and interrogates the nature and consequences of a form of citizenship which has no ground other than indeterminacy. Its closing lines represent the convicted and incarcerated Francie as still free to entertain the image of not being alone, of moving forward, 'tracking in the mountains . . . and me with the tears streaming down my face'.[21]

Women novelists

Of all the developments in the postwar Irish novel, none has been as comprehensive as that carried out in novels by women.[22] Yet, the nature and quality of these developments are somewhat disguised, not only by virtue of being subsumed under the overall history of the form but because of their unobtrusiveness. In contrast to the diffuse sense of recommencement detectable in the works of male writers in the immediate postwar period, the consistent productivity of women novelists can be charted from the 1940s novels of Kate O'Brien (1897–1974), Elizabeth Bowen (1899–1973) and others to those of younger authors.

This continuity is due, in part, to the fact that their productivity was not constrained during World War II. Kate O'Brien's war-years novels – *The Land of Spices* (1941), *The Last of Summer* (1943) and *That Lady* (1946) – maintain her thematic concerns with the distinctive qualities of female consciousness and the highlighting of spirituality and sexuality. O'Brien's protagonists possess a certain readiness to face the world as they find it, even when attempting to efface themselves and their history, as the Reverend Mother in *The Land of Spices* tries, but fails, to do. They also legitimately aspire to power and to its judicious use, as the struggle between Ana de Mendoza and King Philip II of Spain in *That Lady* shows. Similar themes recur in the two works which conclude O'Brien's career, *The Flower of May* (1953) and *As Music and Splendour* (1958).

The pioneering work of women writers in children's literature is also an aspect of their distinctive presence in the immediate postwar period. The career of Patricia Lynch (1898–1972), the pre-eminent children's author of the day, developed apace during the 1950s when she produced her Turf-Cutter's Donkey and her Brogeen series, as well as *The Bookshop on the Quay* (1956), among many other works. Other writers of children's literature in this period include Eilís Dillon (1920–94), whose *The Island of Horses* (1956) and *The Singing Cave* (1959) broadened the genre's scope, and Eileen O'Faolain (1900–88), whose *Irish Sagas and Folk-Tales* (1954) and *Children of the Salmon and other Irish Folktales* (1965) adapt for young readers the Celtic material once considered the keystone of an Irish national literature.

New novelists who emerged during the 1940s include Maura Laverty (1907–66) and Mary Lavin (1912–96). The first two of Laverty's three most noteworthy novels strike an autobiographical note, at the time a departure in itself for novels by women, with *Never No More* (1942) drawing on the rural County Kildare community of her childhood, while *No More than Human* (1944) is based on her sojourn as a governess in Madrid. Community is also the central focus in *Lift up Your Gates* (1946; published as *Liffey Lane*, 1947), with the protagonist, young Chrissy Doyle, exemplifying the economic strains and emotional tensions of inner-city Dublin life. Girlhood in Dublin at a higher-class level is the subject of *A Time Outworn* (1951) by Val Mulkerns (b. 1925). The formative effects of provincial life are conveyed by Mary Lavin – more widely known as a short-story writer – in *The House in Clewe Street* (1945), whose story of Gabriel Galloway contributes to the Irish *Bildungsroman*. In *Mary O'Grady* (1950), Lavin deals with motherhood, though not in a way which seems fully attuned to the subject's rich cultural resonances.

In Bowen's *The Heat of the Day* (1949) – which marked the postwar resumption of her career as a novelist – Stella is the target of desertion and betrayal and risks being disenfranchised of her distinctively feminine worldliness. Committed but independent, loyal but for that reason vulnerable, Stella is a prototype of the postwar woman protagonist in whom self and world are unwittingly at odds. What Stella embodies proves difficult to sustain, however, and Bowen's three other postwar novels – *A World of Love* (1955), *The Little Girls* (1964) and *Eva Trout* (1968) – seem minor works in comparison to *The Heat of the Day*, although their variations on the theme of renewal are of thematic interest.

Female sexuality comes to the fore in the post-*Country Girls* novels of Edna O'Brien, where it is represented in terms of a dynamic of repression and transgression. In works such as *August is a Wicked Month* (1965) and *Casualties of Peace* (1966) sexual exploitation is a precondition for self-assertion, while revisiting the home ground of the *Trilogy* in *A Pagan Place* (1970) produces a story of emotional hunger and sexual abuse. Both *Night* (1972) and *The High Road* (1988) highlight their female protagonists' willingness to cross the sexual boundaries imposed by the conventions of gender roles. Most of these works have English settings and the immigrant's alienation, loneliness and defencelessness are subsumed under the depiction of women's emotional lot, sometimes resulting in pathological emotional scenarios – the lover's murder in *Johnny, I Hardly Knew You* (1977), for example. In later works, O'Brien tends to draw on the headlines of the day to underline women's continuing vulnerability, whether as mothers in *Time and Tide* (1992) or as victims of child sexual abuse in *Down by the River* (1996) or as prisoners of rural Ireland's atavistic social and family life in *Wild Decembers* (1999). These treatments of controversial aspects of late twentieth-century Ireland include dealing with the IRA in *House of Splendid Isolation* (1994).

The sensibility of expatriation running through O'Brien's oeuvre also informs, in different ways, the works of Olivia Manning (1908–90) and Iris

Murdoch (1919–99). Drawing on the deracination and displacement of her Anglo-Irish upbringing, Manning's Balkan and Levant trilogies display a sharp awareness of the contingent factors governing identity. These works also show Harriet, wife of the protagonist Guy Pringle, to be an equal partner in his undertakings without compromising her own distinctive insights and sensitivities.[23] The two Iris Murdoch novels set in Ireland, *The Unicorn* (1963) and *The Red and the Green* (1965), are more concerned to articulate the author's philosophical interests than in Irish conditions as such. But expatriate Irish characters recur throughout Murdoch's novels, from Finn in *Under the Net* (1954) to Emma in *The Philosopher's Pupil* (1983). Their self-possession, independent-mindedness and sexual confidence have an obvious bearing on an empowered Irishness.

Worldliness and expatriation form a central theme in the novels of Julia O'Faolain (b. 1932). Beginning with *Godded and Codded* (1970), the story of a young Irishwoman's adventures in Paris, O'Faolain's female characters find means of either empowering themselves or of withstanding male power. The consequences of failing to do the latter are graphically depicted in *Women in the Wall* (1975), the title of which describes the fate of Radegunda, a nun in sixth-century Gaul. In *No Country for Young Men* (1980), however, O'Faolain dismantles the stereotype of the virginal, supposedly ineffectual, female by installing passion as the keystone to her female characters' makeup. Other novels such as *The Obedient Wife* (1982), set in California, and *The Irish Signorina* (1984), set in Italy, also dwell on passion and empowerment. And power is the subject of O'Faolain's ambitious historical novel, *The Judas Cloth* (1992), set in nineteenth-century Rome during the papacy of Pius IX.

Both *Women in the Wall* and *No Country for Young Men* show that the place occupied by women in the overall historical scheme of things is a basis for their own alternative history as a gender – hence the satirical revision in *No Country for Young Men* of an exemplary episode in the national struggle. These perceptions and understanding can be those of the author regarding historical subject matter, as shown in *The Red and the Green*, Murdoch's novel of Easter 1916, where the misogyny of Pat Dumay, the revolutionary leader, raises questions about the quality and objectives of his leadership. And Eilís Dillon's treatment of the birth of the nation in *Bold John Henebry* (1965), *Across the Bitter Sea* (1973) and *Blood Relations* (1977) is alert to its patriarchal dimension.

Alternatively, a female protagonist can also embody a specific sense of women's history. Such an approach is the basis of novels such as Clare Boylan's (b. 1948) *Holy Pictures* (1983) and *Home Rule* (1992), with the latter providing historical background for the earlier novel's lower-middle-class Dublin. Other similar works of retrieval and reorientation include two novels by Leland Bardwell (b. 1928), *Girl on a Bicycle* (1977), set in the unpromising Dublin of the war years, and *That London Winter* (1981), set in 1959, in which problems of personal freedom persist despite the ostensible openness of London life. And in *Mother of Pearl* (1996), by Mary Morrissy (b. 1957), the prevalence of tuberculosis as an historical marker and the power of the protagonist's imagination combine to show intersections between recovery, desire and the conventions of gender destiny. A tonally and formally more relaxed sense of where the Irish have come from in the postwar period is provided in the novels of Maeve Binchy (b. 1940), though the inviting surfaces of such well-known works as *Light a Penny Candle* (1982) and *Circle of Friends* (1990) mask a good deal of shrewd observation about Irish women's recent past.

The history recuperated in such novels domesticates, physicalises and in certain instances – the emphasis on disease in *Mother of Pearl*, for example – pathologises such key elements of national, male-generated history as violence, difference and moral imperatives. This is a history of the body rather than of the idea, and the conditions it documents bear a striking resemblance to the colonial apparatus whose overthrow public history records. How national policy becomes implicated in women's history is dramatised in *The Killeen* (1985), a novel by Mary Leland (b. 1941), in which Mother Ireland and literal motherhood oppose each other during the politically tense 1930s. And how such mainstays of Irishness as the Irish language, folk tradition, rural ancestry and native landscape, much of it represented in matrilinear terms, can have a beneficial influence on a generation of schoolgirls coming to maturity in modern Dublin is explored by Éilís Ní Dhuibhne (b. 1954) in her novel *The Dancers Dancing* (1999). In contrast, the problems faced by a young man returning to his much-changed native Dublin are depicted in Val Mulkerns's *Very Like a Whale* (1986).

The two-histories concept is given a European dimension in *Unholy Ghosts* (1996) by Ita Daly (b. 1944), the Nazi backdrop of which the protagonist has to reckon with, and in Mary Morrissy's *The Pretender* (2000), based on the fate of the Romanovs. In both works, public events are alienating and repressive, making the history of their women characters a retreat into worlds of their own. Two quite different works by Northern women novelists Mary Beckett (b. 1926) and Caroline Blackwood (b. 1931) show a similar tendency. Maintaining dignity and integrity are central in Beckett's *Give Them Stones* (1987), the fifty-year saga of a woman from the nationalist community of inner-city Belfast, a member of a minority within a minority. In contrast, Blackwood's *Great*

Granny Webster (1977) is a darkly comic subversion of the landed majority's revealingly tribal mores, the author herself being a daughter of the Big House. Despite the achievements of Janet McNeill and Deirdre Madden, however, the novel has not been the form preferred by Northern women writers, although in *The Railway Station Man* (1984) and *Fool's Sanctuary* (1987) Jennifer Johnston deals with love and violence in the context of the Troubles. The imaginative possibilities exhibited by Frances Molloy (b. 1947) in her novel *No Mate for the Magpie* (1985), with its unique use of dialect and border-crossing narrative, await further development.

The difficulties of life in a world of one's own are addressed in Ita Daly's *Ellen* (1986) and *A Singular Attraction* (1987), both of which are alert to the vicissitudes of personal freedom while endorsing the protagonists' desire to seek it. The same difficulties in a rural Irish context receive an emotionally blunter treatment in Evelyn Conlon's (b. 1952) *Stars in the Daytime* (1989). And novels such as the formally and stylistically inventive *The Wig My Father Wore* (1995) and *What Are You Like?* (2000) by Anne Enright (b. 1962) feature protagonists who are the equal of the unpredictabilities which accompany inhabiting one's own identity. A note of play and adventurousness is also shown in Anne Haverty's (b. 1959) *One Day as a Tiger* (1997), while her *The Far Side of a Kiss* (2000), based on the life of Sarah Walker, William Hazlitt's rejected mistress, extends the range of dual-history works, as does Emma Donoghue's *Slammerkin* (2000), the story of an urchin teenage servant set in eighteenth-century London and Wales.

The representation of women's sexuality draws attention to that area of their existence which Irish society officially regarded as women's most marginal property, the one over which they had least freedom of choice; such representations also entail a critique of male sexuality, typified in terms of an oppressive sense of entitlement supported by brute force. This critique has produced a number of disturbing works, among them *In Night's City* (1982) by Dorothy Nelson (b. 1952), the experimental language of which mimics the confused consciousness of the abused and dependent protagonist. And even in the bourgeois setting of Jennifer Johnston's *The Invisible Worm* (1991), the protagonist's discovery of a capacity to love requires not only facing a failed marriage but confronting her incestuous past.

Greater candour about sexuality in novels by women has coincided with greater visibility for the gay woman's Irish novel, with Emma Donoghue's *Stir-fry* (1994) and *Hood* (1995), and also *Biography of Desire* (1997) by poet and novelist Mary Dorcey (b. 1950), among the principal works. Donoghue (b. 1969) locates her lesbian protagonists in daily life, ensuring that their status is neither elite nor marginal. In *Stir-fry*, it is just as likely that a young girl coming up to university in Dublin from a narrow, provincial Catholic background, would discover and affirm her lesbian body as she would make any other discovery about herself. And what's notable about Pen, the protagonist of *Hood*, is her fidelity. These portrayals of lesbianism show it to be an achieved realisation of a world of one's own, reflecting thereby the overall sense of breakthrough – in subject matter, sense of audience, self-consciousness and the interplay between autonomy and authenticity – characteristic of the postwar Irish novel.

Short fiction

Continuities

The short story is another means by which continuity of fictional production was maintained throughout the war years and immediately afterwards, not only because this period was the heyday of two of its most noted practitioners, Sean O'Faolain (1900–91) and Frank O'Connor (1903–66), but also because a new generation of short-story writers emerged at the same time, beginning with Mary Lavin's *Tales from Bective Bridge* (1942). In addition, this new generation found an outlet for its work in *The Bell* and also in such journals as *Irish Writing* (1946–57) and *Envoy* (1949–51). The regular appearance of anthologies – ranging, to take two representative instances, from Valentin Iremonger's *Irish Short Stories* (1960) to David Marcus's *State of the Art* (1992) – has also helped to maintain the form's public presence. And the short story's success in international – largely American – markets effectively made it the public face of Irish fiction.[24] In addition, O'Connor and O'Faolain also shared a fundamental preoccupation with the nature and viability of independence, with O'Connor treating it from an emotional and psychological perspective, and O'Faolain bringing an intellectual and cultural orientation to bear, although obviously neither approach is made at the expense of the other.

Frank O'Connor's standpoint can be seen evolving from the publication of his third collection, *Crab Apple Jelly* (1944). Here, although 'The Long Road to Ummera' honours the dignity and self-possession which abiding by tradition can provide, stories such as 'Uprooted' and 'The Mad Lomasneys' deal, respectively, with having taken the road away from one's native landscape and with the difficulty of emotional agency. These and stories like 'Darcy in the Land of Youth' (in *Traveller's Samples* (1951)) and 'Fish for Friday' (in *Domestic Relations* (1957)), portray protagonists coming to terms with their limited temperaments – or failing to. These stories' focus is largely private, not only in their concentration on the expression of uncertainty and indecisiveness in relations between the sexes, but in their unconscious abandonment of familiar structures of Irishness, with the place of Catholicism as a moral arbiter or emotional tutor evaluated at length. O'Connor's stories portray a generation which has come of age between the end of the Irish Civil War and the beginning of World War II, and which is making the surprising discovery that life is both more shapeless and more nuanced than it had been led to believe.

A collective loss of innocence typifies O'Connor's oeuvre, a condition underlined by his child narrators, most notably in the Larry Delaney stories in *Domestic Relations*, but also in the depiction of childhood conditions in such stories as 'Babes in the Wood' (in *The Common Chord* (1947)), one of a number in which O'Connor draws attention to illegitimacy and women's sexuality. Such stories also economically consolidate thematic interests such as energy, desire, autonomy and commitment. Mapping a familiar conflict between romance and reality, the stories see it as a new aspect of Irish life, bringing with it an unforeseen dilemma. Now that independence exists in the body politic, how may it be affirmed in the body personal, the body sexual, the body spiritual and all the other manifestations of selfhood whose sovereignty still belatedly await ratification?

Frank O'Connor's stories portray the Irish people becoming individuated, while those of Sean O'Faolain test the limits of individuation. As a result, O'Faolain's stories tend to be more detached, more intellectual in their thematic development, and more critical in perspective. In such stories as 'The Man Who Invented Sin' (in *Teresa, and Other Stories* (1947)) and 'No Country for Old Men' (in *I Remember! I Remember!* (1962)), his critique of Irish social and cultural conditions is acute, and in the latter story, satirical. Yet the critique is never entirely circumstantial, but is also used to reveal the limits of self-knowledge, the power of illusion and the inevitability of mistakes. Thus, the eponymous meddler who imputes harm where none existed, thereby inventing sin, embodies not only an oppressive moral climate but also highlights the unworldly innocence of the 'sinners'. Newcomers to the ranks of the Irish bourgeoisie are portrayed in 'The Fur Coat' (in *The Finest Stories of Sean O'Faolain* (1957)), but the story also suggests the difficulty of changing one's identity. The imaginative potential and cultural resources of rural, or indeed hidden, Ireland are enshrined in 'The Silence of the Valley' (in *Teresa*), but the story deals with how the different characters view the place and its tutelary spirit, the local cobbler, when death breaks the spell that united the disparate group. This story, with its distinctive representations of the land and its traditions, and 'Lovers of the Lake' (in *The Finest Stories of Sean O'Faolain*), with its treatment of penance and passion, align representations of important structures of Irish experience with the characters' fitful acknowledgment of those structures' adequacy and significance.

O'Faolain's oeuvre migrates from a concern with obviously Irish themes to dealing with human behaviour more broadly considered, expressed through an increasing number of non-Irish settings and characters, though also found in works set in his native Cork. In the latter, movement and modulation take place from 'Up the Bare Stairs' (in *The Finest Stories of Sean O'Faolain*) through 'One Man, One Boat, One Girl' (in *The Heat of the Sun: Stories and Tales* (1966)) to 'The Kitchen' (in *The Talking Trees and Other Stories* (1970)). But the typical late O'Faolain story goes beyond local contexts to casting a worldly eye on characters' preconceived ideas, unexamined assumptions, groundless expectations and a whole repertoire of quixotry. A case in point is 'The Faithless Wife' (in *Foreign Affairs and Other Stories* (1976)), where the reversal of gender roles is of equal significance as the reversal of national stereotypes. The perspective is that of a liberal moralist, one who permits his characters their illusions even as he knows where illusions lead. Seen in this light, O'Faolain's short fiction may be viewed as a consistent exemplification of the alternatives to narrow-mindedness.

A third contributor to the continuity of Irish short fiction is Elizabeth Bowen, whose postwar stories show no falling off from the high level of artistry and insight in her pre-war work. Although a connection exists between Bowen's and O'Faolain's stories in their shared interest in personality and in the politics of intimacy, and in their eye for the materialistic sign-language of class, Bowen's sensitivity to atmosphere and the fear and cruelty she finds in her scenarios ultimately locate her short fiction in an emotionally charged realm far removed from that of O'Faolain's intellectual connoisseurship. Bowen displays these aspects of her work to arresting effect in two war-time London stories, 'Mysterious Kôr' and 'The Demon Lover' (both in *The Demon Lover and Other Stories* (1945)). Their haunted landscapes of ruin and loss find compensation in those postwar stories Bowen sets in Ireland such as 'The Happy Autumn Fields' (in *The Demon Lover*) and 'Hand in Glove' (in *A Day in the Dark and Other Stories* (1965)). No indication of an Irish setting is explicitly given in 'The Happy Autumn Fields', but there is in that story, and in others with an Irish setting such as 'Summer Night' (in *Look at All Those Roses* (1941)) and 'A Day in the Dark' (in *A Day in the Dark*), a vibrant sense of home.

As well as being noted for their short stories, O'Connor, O'Faolain and Bowen each wrote a good deal in a variety of other forms. With the exception of Maeve Brennan, whose stories are only now being thought canonical, Mary Lavin is the only Irish writer of the postwar period whose reputation rests exclusively on her short fiction. Moreover, hers is an oeuvre which for the first time stakes out the Irish short story as a formally appropriate means of representing women's roles and the effect these roles have on their inner lives.

In general, Lavin's stories may be described as postwar not merely in chronological terms or because they share in the tendency noted among Irish novelists to think of the feminine as the repository of spirit but also because of the emotional cold-wars – the stand-offs, breaches, tensions, frustrations and isolation – to which her characters are vulnerable. Such conditions generate questions of good faith and bad faith, with the latter given a sectarian reading in both 'The Convert' (in *A Single Lady and Other Stories* (1951)) and 'An Akoulina of the Irish Midlands' (in *The Patriot Son and Other Stories* (1956)). Located largely in unparticularised villages and other non-urban locales, Lavin's stories chart the inner life of provincialism. This focus by-passes, without ignoring, historically divided, factional Ireland to dwell on the more commonplace and disturbing disconnections and excesses within individuals – women, particularly – in their pre-social roles as parent, spouse, widow and girl.

Yet Lavin does not take a critical position from outside her material. Though hardly indifferent to the stifling moral atmosphere her characters must breathe, she is not a moralist, choosing instead to observe in a tone of impassioned neutrality their attempts to be true to their natures. Not all Lavin characters are able to sustain such an attempt, however, as Flora in 'The Becker Wives' (in *The Becker Wives and Other Stories* (1946)) demonstrates. This story inaugurates Lavin's pioneering work in the novella, and she is also an exponent of the story sequence, the most elaborate of which is the Grimes series – 'A Visit to the Cemetery' (in *A Single Lady*), 'An Old Boot', 'Frail Vessel' and 'The Little Prince' (in *The Patriot Son*) and 'Loving Memory' (in *The Great Wave and Other Stories* (1961)). Lavin's typical rejection of town mores and a preference for locating her protagonists, as the title of one of her collections has it, *In the Middle of the Fields* (1967) – a place distinguished by its fertility and other pastoral qualities – associates them with not only cycles of repetition and renewal but also makes them aware of the continuing and ineffaceable features of their own natures.

Extending the tradition

Much more characteristic of postwar fiction than Lavin's career is authors' successful production of both novels and short stories. This is the pattern of not only James Plunkett's and Bryan MacMahon's output, authors whose short fiction rehearses, in the case of the former, the Dublin of his novels (in *The Trusting and the Maimed and Other Irish Stories* (1955)), and, in the latter's case, stages the colourful folk (in both *The Lion-tamer and Other Stories* (1948) and *The Red Petticoat and Other Stories* (1955)) familiar from his novels. The practice is also true of the new generation of Irish writers, as the outputs of John McGahern, Edna O'Brien and William Trevor indicate, though their stories are more closely related to their novels.

McGahern's interest in the Moran family of *Amongst Women* dates from 'Wheels' (in *Nightlines* (1970)) and is taken up again in his 'Gold Watch' (in *High Ground* (1985)). A story like Edna O'Brien's 'Cords' (in *The Love Object* (1968)) depicts intricate attachments to home which recur in the title story of *Returning* (1982). And in William Trevor's short fiction the dual focus on Irish and English settings and characters which make him an Anglo-Irish writer in the literal sense is more sharply evident, not only in the historical perspective of the title story of *The News from Ireland and Other Stories* (1986), but from a concern with the shared consequences for both nationalities of cruelty, ignorance, betrayal and related failings, of which neither culture is shown to have a monopoly.

These authors' stories extend the tradition of the Irish short story, not by following the example of O'Faolain, O'Connor and Lavin but by their acute readings of Joyce's *Dubliners* – Trevor has even written a story entitled 'Two More Gallants' (in *The News from Ireland*).[25] The main effect of their readings has been an increased sensitivity to the short story's verbal potential than was shown in their predecessors' theme-driven work. The typical short story of this new generation also displays a heightened sense of the symbolic, an increased interest in the resources of the epiphany and a broader conception of pattern. This preoccupation with structure and method has also had thematic repercussions.

Instead of writing, as they do in their novels, from within the family, as it were, McGahern, O'Brien and Trevor adopt in their stories the point of view of a character who may be of the family but no longer in it. Motifs of departure, separation, return, rejection and various other negotiations of insecurity and disruption are prominent. Foreign locales are frequently deployed as the counterpart of personal unsettlement. But whether these are the Spain of McGahern's 'Peaches' (in *Nightlines*) or 'The Beginning of an Idea' (in *Getting Through* (1978)), or the Italy of Trevor's novella 'My House in Umbria' (in *Two Lives* (1991)) or 'The Smoke Trees of San Pietro' (in *Collected Stories* (1992)), or the unnamed Mediterranean resort of O'Brien's 'Paradise' (in *The Love Object*) or 'Forgetting' (in *Mrs Reinhardt and Other Stories* (1978)), the characters remain in the grip of what they intended to leave behind.

Stories of provincial Ireland and of its relation to modernity – such as 'The Ballroom of Romance' (in *The Ballroom of Romance and Other Stories* (1972)) or 'The Distant Past' (in *Angels at the Ritz and Other Stories* (1975)) – are counterbalanced in Trevor's oeuvre by stories with an English setting in which the modern is all too corrosively present, as in 'Access to the Children' (in *The Ballroom of Romance*) or the three-story sequence comprising 'Matilda's England' (in *Lovers of their Time and Other Stories* (1978)). An especially painful intersection of ancient history and modern conditions in Trevor's stories is to be found in his treatment of Northern Ireland, as in the title story of *Beyond the Pale and Other Stories* (1981) or, more unusually, the portrait of the visionary Milton, a youth from the fringe of fundamentalist Protestantism in 'Lost Ground' (in *After Rain* (1996)). And throughout Trevor's stories there are dynamics of estrangement and belonging, alienation and attachment, misprision and exaggeration.

Home as a place that can neither be entirely forsaken or completely accommodated is a prominent motif in Edna O'Brien's stories also – in 'The House of My Dreams' (in *A Scandalous Woman and Other Stories* (1974)), for example, and 'The Connor Girls' (in *Returning*). And just as unsatisfactory as O'Brien's townlands and villages are her hotel rooms and other anonymous sites of assignation. John McGahern's three collections express a sense of home not merely in terms of domicile but also in terms of territory. Strengthening and counterpointing this fidelity to a notion of native ground is a marked anti-metropolitan strain, particularly where Dublin is concerned, whether the capital is portrayed as an unsatisfactory trysting place in 'My Love, My Umbrella' (in *Nightlines*), or a habitat in 'Doorways' (in *Getting Through*) or a cultural centre in 'Parachutes' (in *High Ground*). In *High Ground*, also, the possibility is rehearsed that the local, intimately known territory contains a prototype of civil coexistence. The title story's rejection of the clientilism of local politics is one means of expressing that possibility, as is the enactment of cultural affiliation in both 'Old Fashioned' and 'The Conversation of William Kirkwood'.

The modern turn

At the same time as the Joycean short story was firmly establishing itself, a more experimental use of the form was also emerging. The main instances are Aidan Higgins's *Felo de Se* (1960; subsequently published as *Asylum and Other Stories* (1978) and partly reprinted with revisions in *Flotsam and Jetsam* (1996)) and John Banville's *Long Lankin* (1970). Banville's collection also contains a novella, 'The Possessed' (not reprinted in the revised 1984 edition), and the recurrence of this form in the works of a large number of postwar short-story writers is one obvious indication of the Irish short story's changing character.

The modern turn continues in such collections as Neil Jordan's *Night in Tunisia and Other Stories* (1976), Desmond Hogan's *The Diamonds at the Bottom of the Sea and Other Stories* (1979), Niall Quinn's (b. 1943) *Voyovic and Other Stories* (1980), Dermot Healy's *Banished Misfortune* (1982) and Ronan Sheehan's *Boy with an Injured Eye* (1983). The musical allusions in the Jordan and Healy titles (the former to a number by jazz musician Dizzy Gillespie, the latter to a traditional Irish tune) signal release of potential through body language – in dance, for example. Both collections, however, are fully aware of how difficult it is to realise this potential, an awareness presented with particular starkness in Jordan's 'Last Rites'. Like this story, some of those in *Banished Misfortune* deal with the emigrant mentality, and like Jordan, Healy deals with this quite unsentimentally, with his characters' unpredictability their saving grace.

Desmond Hogan, his generation's most prolific short-story writer, also deals with emigrant experiences, in 'Memories of Swinging London' (in *Children of Lir: Stories from Ireland* (1981)), for instance, or in 'Miles' (in *Lebanon Lodge* (1988)), and his work in general reveals a taste for the international. But Hogan is also concerned with tensions between the world's openness and the claims of home. His protagonists' realisation of their identity, particularly their sexual identity, frequently runs aground on their return to Ireland – 'Jimmy' (in *The Diamonds at the Bottom of the Sea*) is an example. The continued negotiation of these tensions gives Hogan's stories a marked transitional quality. And being unsettled also manifests its strain in the brutal underworlds, foreign and domestic, of Quinn's stories. Though not quite a sequence, Sheehan's *Boy with an Injured Eye* features a variety of pieces coordinated around vision. Stories range from a view of the panopticon in 'Universitatis' to 'The Death of Petronious', set in Ancient Rome. Both the form and content of this collection suggest fresh perspectives, and in terms of content these have been taken up by David M. Kiely (b. 1949) in the historical reconstructions of his *A Night in the Catacombs* (1995).

Adventurous subject matter is also characteristic of both *Getting It in the Head* (1996) by Mike McCormack (b. 1965) and Blánaid McKinney's (b. 1961) *Big Mouth* (2000), the former containing forays into the new gothic while the latter collection has a number of stories drawing on arcane information and others that venture into the American Deep South. America is also the setting for some stories in Colum McCann's *Fishing the Sloe-Black River*

(1994), while Hugo Hamilton's *Dublin Where the Palm Trees Grow* (1996) deals with intimations of *Weltschmerz* in Dublin (scene of 'Nazi Christmas'), Berlin and Morocco. *The Inside Story* (1989), written by poet Michael O'Loughlin (b. 1958), moves between Dublin and Europe as well, though here the point of origin is Dublin's Northside and the destinations are less than exotic. Emigration is irreverently revamped in some of the stories of Joseph O'Connor's *True Believers* (1991). The revisionist impetus evident in the late twentieth-century Irish novel is also to the fore in the short story of the same period.

The greater discursive resources of the novella are availed of in a diverse group of texts including Neil Jordan's Dublin dystopia, *The Dream of a Beast* (1983), Sebastian Barry's *Time Out of Mind* and *Strappado Square* (1983) and the title story of Colum McCann's *Everything in this Country Must* (2000), a comparatively rare instance of an Irish writer from outside Northern Ireland addressing conditions there – screenwriter Shane Connaughton's collection *A Border Station* (1989) is, to stretch a point, perhaps, in the same category.

The short fiction of poet and playwright Tom MacIntyre (b. 1931) in *The Word for Yes: New and Selected Stories* (1991) relies on brevity to arresting dramatic effect, as in 'Left of the Door', and also features redactions of folkloric and mythological materials in 'The Mankeeper' and 'Rise Up, Lovely Sweeney'. The capacity of language to edge away from its naturalistic effect is a feature of 'Above and Beyond' in *Dublin where the Palm Trees Grow*, while the title story of *Fishing the Sloe-Black River* is an extended metaphor for the outlook of parents left behind by their emigrant children. The more condensed and elusive language in recent short fiction derives in part from poets' interest in the form, as is clear from the stories of O'Loughlin and McIntyre, and is particularly striking in the short fiction of poet Aidan Carl Mathews (b. 1956), who, in both *Adventures in a Bathyscope* (1988) and *Lipstick on the Host* (1992), ranges freely over time and space in works like the title novella of the latter collection and 'Moonlight and the Chambermaid' in the same volume, in both of which fresh thematic openness is articulated in terms of its aesthetic potential.

Short fiction in Northern Ireland

Short fiction has a more muted presence in the postwar literature of Northern Ireland, without either a counterpart to the tradition-bearing phase the form went through with O'Connor and O'Faolain or a commitment to new formal and thematic departures. Nor are Northern novelists, as a rule, also short-story writers. But the Northern short story has provided an opportunity for the minority community to register its presence, and perhaps the typical location of that presence in ex-urban settings parallels the short story's interplay of constraint and disclosure. Despite the example of Sam Hanna Bell's slightly ethnographic *Summer Loanen and Other Stories* (1943), the Northern short story has largely been written by writers from the minority.

The characteristic tone and thematic scope of the early postwar Northern Irish short story is established in the works of Michael McLaverty and Brian Friel (b. 1929). Both authors seem dedicated to relieving the anonymous lives they depict and to showing that there is more human substance to the existence of the minority population than other discourses – political, for example – might allow. In contrast to O'Connor and O'Faolain, McLaverty and Friel submerge their authorial presence within the lives of their characters, their objectivity sympathetic but not untroubled. McLaverty's story 'Pigeons' (in *The Game Cock and Other Stories* (1947)) contrasts the heroism attributed to the brother of Frankie, killed in the nationalist cause, with the protagonist himself, whose more modest claim to attention is the care he devotes to his dead brother's pigeons. Not only does the story keep faith with the living, but it sets that faith within the quietism of a hobby.

The short stories of Benedict Kiely and Patrick Boyle (1905–82), on the other hand, are much less soft-spoken and fastidious than those of McLaverty and Friel. Although a certain number of Kiely stories – 'The Dogs in the Great Glen' (in *A Journey to the Seven Streams* (1963); revised edition (1977)), 'A Room in Linden' (in *A Ball of Malt and Madame Butterfly* (1973)), and 'Your Left Foot is Crazy' (in *A Letter to Peachtree and Nine Other Stories* (1987)), to take a representative sample – are set in the Republic, and in general Kiely may be thought of as an all-Ireland writer, most of his stories are set in and around his native Omagh, County Tyrone. This imaginative landscape is free from many of the restrictions and inhibitions which have traditionally been associated with Northern life, and the stories' digressive oral narrative style, incorporating mythological lore and snatches of popular songs and various other embellishments, transmits a sense of idiosyncracy and non-conformity. This is an environment where innocence and desire may enjoy their natural expression – 'Down Then by Derry' (in *A Ball of Malt and Madame Butterfly*) and 'Near Banbridge Town' (in *A Cow in the House* (1978)) are elaborate meditations on their doing so. And the power of political violence to usurp a natural way of life is the great affront dealt with in the novella *Proxopera* (1977).

The natural in the stories of Patrick Boyle is a darker affair, partly because Boyle is less interested in landscapes of childhood than any other Irish short-story writer of his generation. Instead, the salient site of his stories is the adult male body, its sexual blunders and its physical and moral frailty. Such stories as 'Meles Vulgaris' (in *At Night All Cats are Grey and Other Stories* (1966)) add a sexual dimension which is otherwise missing from the work of Boyle's peers, an absence which has the possibly unwitting implication that McLaverty's and Friel's characters are virginal. Even the sexual high jinks in Kiely's stories are fundamentally harmless, confirming that his characters too inhabit a realm not of spoiled pastoral, as in the Northern novel, but of illusory pastoral.

A preoccupation with versions of pastoral which characterises early postwar Northern short fiction persists in Anthony C. West's *River's End and Other Stories* (1958), to the extent of finding itself applied to Welsh farm labourers in a Canadian prairie summer in the collection's concluding novella, 'The Monocrats'. But a formally comprehensive move away from pastoral is made by poet John Montague (b. 1929) in his collection *Death of a Chieftain and Other Stories* (1964). The move is accomplished by transferring the site of pastoral to institutional settings – church, in the case of the boarding-school story 'The Dark Accomplice', and state in 'The Cry', where lack of social, administrative and juridical protection in the North can no longer be suffered in silence. This subject matter is dealt with in the dissident tonalities and Oedipal animus of Southern fiction, as well as in some of its internal and international border-crossings.

The altered perspectives and broader range of subject matter in *Death of a Chieftain* were almost immediately made more resonant by the challenge to identity, citizenship and affiliation brought on by the Troubles. Yet, although the urban dimension of the Troubles, with its well-demarcated enclaves and habitats, structures the title story of David Park's *Oranges from Spain* (1990), broadly speaking, this terrain has not appealed to short-story writers. Instead, the availability of the Troubles as subject matter has resulted in Northern short fiction treating them circumspectly. The music lessons in Bernard MacLaverty's 'My Dear Palestrina' (in *A Time to Dance and Other Stories* (1982)) or the Spain of 'Happy Hours' in Maurice Leitch's *The Hands of Cheryl Boyd and Other Stories* (1987) are instances of distancing the Troubles. The Leitch collection also ventures into areas to which not very much imaginative attention tends to be paid, with evangelical Protestantism providing the setting of the title story and 'The Green Mile' dealing with the conditioning of a British soldier serving in Northern Ireland. The skits, burlesques and satirical romps of John Morrow's *Northern Myths* (1979) and *Sects and Other Stories* (1987) exemplify what a change in tone can accomplish, not only through use of Belfast demotic but by sheer irreverence, as in 'Colon' (in *Northern Myths*), which casts a subversive eye on Northern military service in the British army.

Changes in orientation and attitude have also to some extent been expressed by changes in form, with the novella emerging as a resource in such works as David Martin's *The Road to Ballyshannon* (1981), Maurice Leitch's *Chinese Whispers* (1987) and Eoin McNamee's *The Last of Deeds* (1989; republished 1992) and *Love in History* (1992). In general, however, innovation has not been to the fore, Philip MacCann's (b. 1963) collection of experimental stories *The Miracle Shed* (1995) being an exception, while Bernard MacLaverty amplifies his *Walking the Dog and Other Stories* (1994) by interpolating wry sketches and anecdotes between the actual stories, a comedic variation on Ernest Hemingway's innovation in *In Our Time*.

A more representative treatment of the Troubles has been to show them disrupting a *modus vivendi*, that of an ex-urban community, typically. The border country is a particularly receptive terrain to such considerations, as the stories of Eugene McCabe demonstrate. Here, the approach tends to be indirect, as in 'Music at Annahullion' (in *Heritage and Other Stories* (1978)), which harks back to the ostensible simplicity of earlier Northern stories in its account of a countrywoman's dream to own a piano, while at the same time invoking the present's oppressiveness in the futility that follows acquiring the instrument. The story's trajectory from dream to destruction typifies how unattainable peace of mind is in McCabe's remote, nominally self-supporting rural areas.

Though by no means overlooking the Troubles, the stories of Bernard MacLaverty are arguably of greater interest for their tacit commitment to normalising Northern life. In its focus on coming-of-age incidents of various kinds, *Secrets and Other Stories* (1977), for instance, seems to be offering the short story's standard fare. Yet fidelity to the norm also means exploring areas which are, as the volume's title indicates, often kept hidden. Among these are issues of class and second-class citizenship in 'The Exercise'; the destructive force of conventional moralising in the title story; and the consequences of an emigrant's sexual infidelity in 'Between Two Shores'. The eminent ordinariness of the characters' human frailty retrieves them from the larger categories in whose name the Troubles exist.

Short fiction by women, never a prominent feature of Northern writing, has also come somewhat to the fore with material dealing with the Troubles. This material has largely appeared in anthologies – *The Female Line: Northern Ireland Women Writers* (ed. Ruth Hooley, 1985), for instance; *The Wall Reader* (1979) also contains several stories by Northern women writers. The title story of Mary Beckett's *A Belfast Woman* (1980) features a narrator who associates the present violence with that of her girlhood in 1921 in tones combining endurance with resilience. And many of Beckett's stories are quietly but unmistakably critical of, and resistant to, the essentially male embodiment of militancy and active operations, a perspective also revealed by some of the stories in *The Way-paver* (1986) by playwright Anne Devlin (b. 1951).

Women's short fiction

The growth and diversification of women's short fiction in the Republic, in contrast, have contributed to developments in the form already noted. But although there are certain formal and thematic overlaps between men and women's short fiction in such areas as sexuality and internationalism, the corpus of women's short fiction also contains features which give it its own distinctive repertoire of concerns and effects. And as in so many areas of Irish literary activity, here again the anthology is a primary resource, with *Wildish Things* (ed. Ailbhe Smyth, 1989) and *If Only: Short Stories of Love and Divorce by Irish Women Writers* (eds. Kate Cruise O'Brien and Mary Maher, 1997) among numerous instances. The latter title's representation of love in conjunction with and in opposition to divorce formulates a broader spectrum of domestic and emotional destinies than that conventionally allotted to Irish women. And it also suggests itself as a metaphor for the tensions between attachment and separation, quiescence and agency, and tradition and modernity which, ever-present though they may be throughout postwar Irish fiction, enact some of their most illustrative occasions in short fiction by Irish women.

The title story of Éilís Ní Dhuibhne's *Blood and Water* (1988), for instance, deals with strains between rural Donegal and suburban Dublin, between an aunt redolent of memory and origins and folklore and her niece, who is a modern professional woman. Tradition, variously considered, has a prominent place in other Ní Dhuibhne collections, as is illustrated by the formal innovation of dispersing the folk-tale 'The Search for the Lost Husband' amongst the stories of *The Inland Ice and Other Stories* (1997). The title story of *The Pale Gold of Alaska and Other Stories* (2000), which deals with an emigrant woman's physical and emotional travail in the Arctic, also focuses on the artistic resources of traditional perspectives.

Julia O'Faolain's short stories, on the other hand, are thoroughly modern in their concern with the inescapable vagaries of sexuality. Both *We Might See Sights and Other Stories* (1968) and *Man in the Cellar* (1974) juxtapose love and divorce in ways which generate a dynamic relationship between them, often metaphorically. The central circumstance in the title story of *Man in the Cellar* depicts a wife's imprisonment of a brutalising husband. In 'The Knight', a sexless lay associate of a religious order runs over his wife's English lover. In

O'Faolain's stories, a *buffo* quality eases their sting, and makes them seem like updates of a much more long-lasting battle of the sexes than the one currently joined.

Clare Boylan's short stories – in *A Nail on the Head* (1983), *Concerning Virgins* (1989) and *That Bad Woman* (1995), as well as *Collected Stories* (2000) – cultivate some of the same terrain as Julia O'Faolain's. A keen eye for nuances of class and a satirical tone show Boylan's sense of the performative moments and ritualistic occasions of social life. A number of her stories depict the collapse of frameworks or the inversion of norms, ranging from unsuspected homosexuality in 'Black Ice' (*A Nail on the Head*) to the repercussions of an exploitative mother-and-child scandal in 'The Little Madonna' (in *Concerning Virgins*). Comparably observant views of family life with a Dublin focus are contained in Val Mulkerns's story sequence, *Antiquities* (1978), and *An Idle Woman and Other Stories* (1980). And the capital is central to stories from an earlier period by Maeve Brennan (1917–93). These rediscovered works – reissued in *The Springs of Affection: Stories of Dublin* (1997) and *The Rose Garden* (2000) – are unsparing in their anatomy of Catholic bourgeois family life. Brennan, a noted *New Yorker* journalist, is particularly alert to all that is friable and fissionable in family emotional bonds. Her work belatedly establishes her as a significant founding mother for Irish women short-story writers.

The focus on gay women's experience in Mary Dorcey's *A Noise from the Woodshed* (1989) also represents a tonal as well as a thematic breakthrough. Dorcey's stories reflect new aspects of women's presence in late twentieth-century Ireland, particularly regarding body consciousness and minority rights. Her 'A Sense of Humour' conveys a strong repudiation of, and breaking away from, men's emotional immaturity. Women's issues in their own right – abandonment, sexual exploitation, emotional deprivation – are also featured in the work of Maeve Kelly (b. 1930), including *A Life of Her Own and Other Stories* (1976) and *Orange Horses and Other Stories* (1991) and in such collections by Moy McCrory (b. 1953) as *The Water's Edge and Other Stories* (1985) and *Those Sailing Ships of his Boyhood Dreams* (1991). These volumes introduce a sharp sense of women's experience of mind-body problems, which also plays a substantial role in the short stories of Evelyn Conlon. Her work – *My Head is Opening* (1987), *Taking Scarlet as a Real Colour* (1993) and *Telling: New and Selected Stories* (2000) – conveys a stark sense of the turmoil of women in the conventional roles of wives and mothers for whom neither love nor divorce is possible.

The experience of branching out recurs in poet Sara Berkeley's (b. 1967) *The Swimmer in the Deep Blue Dream* (1991), enhanced by the London and San

Francisco settings of some of the stories. Here, however, motifs of pursuit and estrangement also lurk, and questions of agency and self-affirmation persist. A similar disturbing confluence of release and doubt figures in the emotionally far-reaching stories of *By Salt Water* (1996) by Angela Bourke (b. 1952), stories which also focus on another emerging aspect of Irish women's writing, namely a pronounced element of risk. This development has been expressed in a number of different ways. In Mary Morrissy's *A Lazy Eye* (1993), for example, its effect is thematic. The characters in these stories are typically shorn of romance, and instead possess a deviant agency. The narrator of 'Divided Attention' makes contact with the man making obscene phone calls to her, and in 'Rosa' an unwanted baby is left in the Christmas crib of a department store. The risk of a socially barbarous future is faced in Leland Bardwell's *Different Kinds of Love* (1987). In Anne Enright's *The Portable Virgin* (1991) the expression of risk is in the stories' narrative innovations. Technique highlights the collection's portraits of women going their own way, even if the direction is not always one they can control. In '(She Owns) Every Thing', for example, a protagonist who in the command she exercises over her handbag counter virtually becomes an accessory to accessories, encounters her opposite, which leads to the collapse of her system. And the title story of *Antarctica* (1999) by Claire Keegan (b. 1968) is an engagement with and critique of the protagonist's sexual risk-taking set in a picture-postcard English market town. Other Keegan stories have American settings. But perhaps the greater risk is suggested by stories such as 'The Ginger Rogers Sermon' and 'Men and Women', where the familiar, rural, familial male-focused preserve of the Irish short story is acknowledged but also asked to find room for the difference which women's experience can make to it.

Memoir, travel and miscellaneous

Travel writing

Economic factors and cultural commitment both ensured that Irish writers during the first half of the postwar period wrote in a wide variety of forms. One distinctive sub-genre to emerge from this activity might be entitled internal travel writing. This subgenre was inaugurated by Sean O'Faolain's *An Irish Journey* (1940), when international travel was obviously out of the question – when it was restored, O'Faolain furthered his European interests with *A Summer in Italy* (1949) and *South to Sicily* (1953). Because of the extent of their authors' background knowledge, works such as *An Irish Journey* cannot be regarded as mere travelogues – they also have a marked autobiographical dimension, for instance. Yet their narrators function as outsiders, regarding their material without being either independent of it or feeling entirely at home with it.

The tension between author and subject resulting from this stance is clear in Frank O'Connor's Irish journeys, recounted in *Irish Miles* (1947) and *Leinster, Munster and Connaught* (1950). In these works, the shabbiness and neglect of the social and cultural environment – particularly the dilapidated state of the country's architectural heritage – enable the author to register the distance between himself and society's cultural standards. Another early contribution to this subgenre is *Mind You, I've Said Nothing!* (1953) by Honor Tracy (1913–89).

Even when a note of cultural critique is not present, the sense persists of Irish writers of the 1950s and 1960s evidently needing to pay court to their native country. In these works – Kate O'Brien's *My Ireland* (1962), Brendan Behan's *Brendan Behan's Island* (1962), Bryan MacMahon's *Here's Ireland* (1971; revised edition, 1982), James Plunkett's *The Gems She Wore* (1972) and Benedict Kiely's *All the Way to Bantry Bay and Other Irish Journeys* (1978) – there is the continuing implication of discovery. Elizabeth Bowen's *The Shelbourne* (1951) suggests the subgenre's flexibility. These writings, culminating in Kiely's ballad-based tour, *And as I Rode Out by Granard Moat* (1996), disclose a more diverse country than more formal documentation reveals. And they also project a depoliticised view of the whole island. The subgenre has evolved through such works as Colm Tóibín's *A Walk Along the Border* (1987; reissued as *Bad Blood*, 1994), Rosita Boland's *Sea Legs: Hitchhiking around the Coast of Ireland* (1992) and Tim Robinson's various works of cultural and scientific cartography devoted to the Aran Islands and Connemara, notably *Stones of Aran: Pilgrimage* (1986) and *Stones of Aran: Labyrinth* (1995).[26] But books such as Northern author Sam McAughtry's *Down in the Free State* (1987) are rare, with works exploring Northern Ireland only slightly less so – exceptions being Cathal O'Byrne's Belfast survey, *As I Roved Out* (1946), Sam Hanna Bell's *Erin's Orange Lily* (1956) and *Sam McAughtry's Belfast* (1981).

Partly because of their tone and subject matter, and partly because the best-known Irish writers of the day produced them, works in this subgenre overshadow international travel writing. Distinctive contributions to this genre include playwright Denis Johnston's *Nine Rivers from Jordan* (1953), which brings the war home in the author's account of being among the first to enter Buchenwald concentration camp, and Conor Cruise O'Brien's *To Katanga and Back* (1962), which is also a mixture of record-keeping, travel and autobiography. The dual, fitfully connected presences of self and world are contemplated in Aidan Higgins's travel writings, from *Images of Africa* (1971) to *Ronda Gorge and other Precipices* (1989). The author's eye for detail notwithstanding, travel here is ultimately the record of certain states of mind, as though travel confirms that everything can be left behind but the self.

Duality supplies the point of departure and point of arrival in Joseph O'Connor's *Sweet Liberty: Travels in Irish America* (1996), a journey between the various Dublins of the United States. The careful research of Colm Tóibín's *Homage to Barcelona* (1990) underlines, even as it seems to ignore, a sense of that city as an alternative Dublin. The centrepiece of the same author's *The Sign of the Cross: Travels in Catholic Europe* (1994) somewhat belies its title, being a Dublin-based, non-Catholic inner journey. The numerous travel works of Dervla Murphy (b. 1931) seem to belong to an earlier mode of doughty, dangerous treks, but there is also an emphatic personal dimension to her conception of travel as work and witness, as the links between her first book, *Full Tilt* (1965) and her autobiography, *Wheels within Wheels* (1979), indicate.

Travel writing is not one of the most highly developed genres in postwar Northern Irish writing, although Robin Bryans (1928–2005), better known as the autobiographer Robert Harbison, is a prolific exponent of the form, with books on, among other places, *Crete* (1965). And Robert McLiam Wilson's account of homelessness in Britain, *The Dispossessed* (1992), counts as at least constituting a moral journey.

Memoir and autobiography

A further instance of diversifying representations of Irishness is the proliferation of autobiography, which seemingly coincides with the decline of the autobiographical novel. This decline may be dated from Aidan Higgins's *Scenes from a Receding Past* (1977), which transposes autobiographical materials to a fictional setting, resulting in both an affirmation and critique of the complementarity of memory and invention. A transposition along related lines is carried out in Desmond Hogan's *A Farewell to Prague* (1995). And the location of the true record of events in either narrative or memory is a central preoccupation of Seamus Deane's *Reading in the Dark*. Fiction has either implied or combined the coexistence of the local and the national, or post-national, leaving autobiography to be the main preserve of regional interests, as in the representations of Kerry in John O'Donoghue's *In a Quiet Land* (1957) and Rory O'Connor's *Gander at the Gate* (2000). And regarding withdrawal from the national, perhaps autobiography's backward look and childhood focus reflects an unconscious aversion to the rapid recent changes in Irish society.

An example of autobiography conveying an unfamiliar inside story is provided by works about the Big House – for instance, Elizabeth Bowen's *Bowen's*

Court (1942), David Thompson's *Woodbrook* (1974) and Annabel Davis-Goff's *Walled Gardens* (1989). These works counterpoint the novelistic view of the Big House as an image of decline. A broader perspective on Anglo-Irish life and its historical destiny is provided in Brian Inglis's *West Briton* (1962).

Autobiography also makes other types of houses accessible – carceral in the case of Brendan Behan's *Borstal Boy* (1958) and Brian Keenan's *An Evil Cradling* (1992), governmental in Noël Browne's *Against the Tide* (1986) and custodial in Paddy Doyle's *The God Squad* (1988). Each of these works exemplifies autobiography's interest in raising awkward questions. Behan's fluid and subjective rendering of identity casts a critical light on the die-hard mentality of his earlier Republicanism. Doyle's narrative is an exposé of the institutional regime to which outcast children were subjected by religious care-givers. Keenan's Middle-Eastern captivity narrative has unexpected resonances with domestic outlaw activities. Browne's recollections not only discuss the political and cultural difficulties encountered by Irish social reformers but also recall striking notes of dissidence and principle. But there is a relative paucity of memoirs by public figures, though exceptions include C. S. Andrews's *Dublin Made Me* (1979) and *Man of No Property* (1982) and former Taoiseach Garret FitzGerald's *All in a Life* (1991).

Many of these works portray poverty as a major formative fact of life, and other Irish autobiographies, particularly those conceived of in terms of broad popular appeal, also highlight impoverishment. Some of these – Dominic Behan's *Teems of Times and Happy Returns* (1961) and Éamonn Mac Thomáis's *Gur Cakes and Coal Blocks* (1976) and *The Labour and the Royal* (1979) – focus on community life in mid-century Dublin and earlier, thereby contributing to a more textured view of Irish social history. An artistically more expressive work in the same vein is Patrick Galvin's *The Raggy Boy Trilogy* (2002), consisting of *Song for a Poor Boy* (1990), *Song for a Raggy Boy* (1991) and *Song for a Fly Boy* (2002), works which span the author's formative years from a Cork city tenement childhood through custody in a reformatory to serving in the RAF during World War II.

In Frank McCourt's *Angela's Ashes* (1996), strictly speaking a work of Irish-American literature, poverty is counteracted by personality. And an Irish-American son's account of his mother's emigration is given in historian Richard White's *Remembering Ahanagran* (1998). Yet there remains a dearth of emigrant memoirs, particularly ones dealing with the Irish in England, with John O'Donoghue's *In a Strange Land* (1958), Brian Behan's *With Breast Expanded* (1964), Dónall Mac Amhlaigh's *A Navvy's Journal* (1964; first Irish language edition, 1960) and George O'Brien's *Out of Our Minds* (1994) among the few, while

John Walsh's *The Falling Angels* (1999) offers a rare glimpse into the upbringing of an Englishman of Irish emigrant parents.

Other established writers besides Elizabeth Bowen – Frank O'Connor and Sean O'Faolain – have also produced autobiographies. Both O'Connor's *An Only Child* (1961) and O'Faolain's *Vive Moi!* (1964; revised edition, 1993) place the authors' emerging selfhood in the context of the emerging nation. The problems arising from the end of that symbiosis is the subject of O'Connor's *My Father's Son* (1968). The shifts of emphasis from national service and 'rebel Cork' to personal expression and a wider world, which provide the narrative trajectory of these three autobiographies, reiterate one of the persistent themes in postwar Irish writing. Among other novelists' autobiographies, Aidan Higgins's trilogy – *Donkey's Years* (1995), *Dog Days* (1998) and *The Whole Hog* (2000) – chronicles the historical, class and cultural displacements which underlie his geographical restlessness. Dermot Healy's *The Bend for Home* (1996) is a superficially conventional reminiscence which somewhat subversively reveals desire to be at odds with memory, particularly when the occasion of memory is mourning. And mourning forms the basis of poet Seán Dunne's *In My Father's House* (1991), the Waterford city setting of which gives rare glimpses of and insights into provincial Irish working-class life. Dunne's later *The Road to Silence* (1994) is a quest for spiritual recuperation.

Literary reminiscences of the early postwar years in Dublin are provided both by editor John Ryan's *Remembering How We Stood* (1975) and Anthony Cronin's *Dead as Doornails* (1976), both of which make the prefatory point that they are not autobiographies. Bryan MacMahon's *The Master* (1992) is revealingly alert to differences between the oral and the written. Non-literary artists' autobiographies include sculptor Seamus Murphy's *Stone Mad* (1950), actor and playwright Micheál Mac Liammóir's *All for Hecuba* (1946) and *Enter a Goldfish* (1977), and actor Eamon Kelly's *The Apprentice* (1995) and *The Journeyman* (1998).

The life and culture of the Protestant middle-class minority are dwelt on in some of the essays in William Trevor's *Excursions in the Real World* (1993). And similar territory is covered with interrogative acuity in literary scholar W. J. McCormack's (Hugh Maxton) *Waking: An Irish Protestant Upbringing* (1997). Catholic middle-class business life in Dublin is portrayed in Adrian Kenny's *Before the Wax Hardened* (1991) and *The Family Business* (1999), while lower-middle-class life in south County Dublin is recalled by playwright Hugh Leonard in *Home before Night* (1979) and *Out after Dark* (1989), works which show how not to turn personal vicissitudes to exploitative account. The capacity of autobiography to reclaim lives which, through handicap, might otherwise receive inadequate representation is exemplified in Christy Brown's *My Left Foot* (1954) and Christopher Nolan's *Under the Eye of the Clock* (1987).

Surprisingly, perhaps, the number of memoirs by Irish women is small, with the best known of them – Alice Taylor's *To School through the Fields* (1988) – belonging as much to the subgenre of childhood memoir as to women's autobiography. Elaine Crowley's *Cowslips and Chainies* (1996) and *Technical Virgins* (1998) recall an inter-war Dublin girlhood. Set in postwar Dublin, Nuala O'Faolain's *Are You Somebody? The Accidental Memoir of a Dublin Woman* (1996; revised edition, 1998) places itself in a rather different category by focusing on the troublingly asymmetrical relationship between freedom and fulfilment.

Northern autobiography has not attained the same cultural and commercial prominence as that by Southern authors. Yet the most sustained commitment to Irish autobiography in the postwar period is Robert Harbison's tetralogy, *No Surrender: An Ulster Childhood* (1960), *Song of Erne* (1960), *Up Spake the Cabin Boy* (1961) and *The Protégé* (1963). Additions to the subgenre of prison autobiography are made by Bobby Sands's *One Day in My Life* (1983) and Gerry Adams's *Cage Eleven* (1990), while the rebel memoir subgenre now includes Adams's *Falls Memories* (1982) and *Before the Dawn* (1996) as well as Bernadette Devlin's *The Price of My Soul* (1969) and, more provocatively, Eamonn Collins's *Killing Rage* (1997) and Malachi O'Doherty's *The Trouble with Guns* (1998). Seamus Deane's *Reading in the Dark*, though generally considered a novel, sharply highlights issues concerning memory and invention which have a particular bearing on the transmission of not only historical truth but an agreed and publicly accepted past. There are also more memoirs of Northern public life, especially success stories by members of the minority community such as Patrick Shea's *Voices and the Sound of Drums* (1981), Paddy Devlin's *Straight Left* (1993) and Maurice Hayes's *Minority Verdict* (1995).

Maurice Hayes's two memoirs of a County Down childhood – *Sweet Killough Let Go Your Anchor* (1994) and *Black Pudding with Slim* (1996) – depict physical and material well-being and economic progress, which not only contrast with Southern poverty but which also convey a resonant subtext of self-sufficiency. A comparable state of autonomy is depicted in Polly Devlin's *All of Us There* (1983). These memoirs attest to cultural sturdiness and *savoir faire* in recalling a reality which was not wholly determined by Northern Ireland's social and political conditions. A more complicated narrative of cultural positioning – complications which persist during student life in the South – is Denis Donoghue's *Warrenpoint* (1990), named for the author's boyhood County Down home, which is not far geographically from Maurice Hayes's home, though in other ways quite distant. In contrast, there is a lack of autobiographical material focusing on the life of the minority in urban settings, Mary Costello's *Titanic Town* (1993) being one exception, and another being the limitless fascination and involvement with Belfast conveyed in Ciaran Carson's *The Star Factory* (1997). Carson's *Last Night's Fun* (1996) has Irish traditional music as its subject, but it also suggests links between autobiography and the multiplicity of tradition. Memoirs of a time before Northern Ireland was created are provided in Florence Mary McDowell's *Other Days Around Me* (1966) and *Roses and Rainbows* (1972).

Harbison's tetralogy deals not only with his urban origins and upbringing in rural County Fermanagh but in its two final volumes enters into more recondite territory, particularly in its insider's view of fundamentalist Protestantism, including episodes from the training of a preacher in *The Protégé*. The same confessional realm is also the subject of Max Wright's *Told in Gath* (1990). Harbison's general sensitivity to social context, notably class, is also reflected in other autobiographies by Northern writers, such as playwright John Boyd's *Out of My Class* (1985) and *The Middle of My Journey* (1990). The first volume is the story of a scholarship boy; the second is an account of his early work experiences. Both volumes draw attention to social mobility, again in contrast to Southern autobiography. The poet Michael Longley's *Tuppenny Stung* (1994) contains memories of early days in Belfast and a view of the postwar literary history of Northern Ireland, while poet John Hewitt's *Kites in Spring: A Belfast Boyhood* (1980) draws on the flavours and fixtures of the pre-war city. The earlier period is also part of the background of Louis MacNeice's unfinished *The Strings are False* (1966), though his poetic career is quite dissimilar to Longley's and Hewitt's. Attachment to origins is the subject of Benedict Kiely's childhood memoir, *Drink to the Bird* (1991), while a second volume, *The Waves Behind Us* (1999), reminisces about Dublin literary life. Largely urban in setting and for the most part representing selves in search of a future and who seem to assume that they have a world to gain, Northern Irish autobiography provides a fascinating and arguably challenging counterpoint to typical usages of the form in the Republic.

Cultural commentary

Irish writers also contribute to, and intervene in, Irish public debate, although their commitment to doing so has given way in the later part of the postwar period to the development of a commentariat on the one hand, and on the other a greater willingness on the part of other branches of the intelligentsia – academics, in particular – to write cultural commentary. Only material appearing in book form can be dealt with here, with one exception – 'Cruiskeen Lawn', the newspaper column of Myles na gCopaleen, the pseudonym used by Brian O'Nolan in addition to Flann O'Brien. This column ran with few breaks in the *Irish Times* from 1939 until the author's death in 1966. Subsequent book-length selections of this material – *The Best of Myles* (ed. Kevin O'Nolan, 1968), for example – highlight its formal variety, mordant perspective and range of content. The column's success was such that Irish comic writing seems not to have quite recovered, its successors being largely confined to Brendan Behan's *Hold Your Hour and Have Another* (1963), a collection of newspaper sketches, and Joseph O'Connor's three-volume lampooning of the Irish male, beginning with *The Secret World of the Irish Male* (1994).

A counterpoint to Myles na gCopaleen's satirical outlook is contained in the writings of Hubert Butler (1900–90), the publication of whose works in book form – *Escape from the Anthill* (1985), *The Children of Drancy* (1988), *Grandmother and Wolfe Tone* (1990) and *In the Land of Nod* (1996) – has been taken as something of a cultural landmark. Working in the minor form of the essay and writing from the minority standpoint of a liberal Protestant, Butler's work combines travel writing, autobiography and cultural critique. His subjects evince complex gestures of solidarity and witness, and his work exemplifies the cultural value of a measured individual voice.

The inaugural work of commentary in the postwar period is Benedict Kiely's *Counties of Contention* (1945), focusing on Northern life under partition. This addition to the historically voluminous genre of 'condition of Ireland' literature was followed by Sean O'Faolain's *The Irish* (1947), a meditation on origins and identity and on the cultural behaviour through which they are mediated. This work may also be seen as initiating a greater degree of self-critical awareness about nation and identity. Other works of this kind are Conor Cruise O'Brien's *States of Ireland* (1972) and *Ancestral Voices* (1994), the latter's apocalyptic tone a virtual refutation of the former's engagement. The ostensible subject of Breandán Ó hEithir's *Over the Bar: A Personal Relationship with the GAA* (1984) is Gaelic games, a subject which also provides a lens through which to survey the state of the nation.

The commentary provided by intellectuals such as Cruise O'Brien largely devolved to journalists during the 1980s and 1990s, years which saw a large increase in books written from a journalist's perspective and few contributions to public debate in book form by academics and intellectuals. There are exceptions, however, a cross-section of which includes Anthony Cronin's *An Irish Eye* (1982), Desmond Fennell's *Heresy: The Battle of Ideas in Modern Ireland* (1993) and Liam de Paor's *Landscape with Figures* (1998). These works discern and assess social developments, cultural epiphanies and ideological trends, in commentary not of the news-oriented journalistic variety. Some overlap exists between such works and those of the main practitioners of media-based viewpoints, a list of whose books includes Fintan O'Toole's *A Mass for Jesse James* (1990), *Black Hole, Green Card* (1994) and *The Ex-Isle of Erin* (1997), Colm Tóibín's *The Trial of the Generals* (1990) and John Waters's *Jiving at the Crossroads* (1991) and *Every Day like Sunday?* (1995). Debate has also been amplified by compilations of essays, among them *16 on 16* (ed. Dermot Bolger, 1988), *Letters from the New Island* (ed. Dermot Bolger, 1991), *Revising the Rising* (eds. Máirín Ní Dhonnchadha and Theo Dorgan, 1991) and *Arguing at the Crossroads: Essays on a Changing Ireland* (eds. Paul Brennan and Catherine de Saint Phalle, 1997). Contributions by women journalists to cultural self-awareness have not been widely published in book form, with the pamphlets collected in *A Dozen Lips* (1994) an important exception.[27]

Single-authored commentaries are also of interest from a generic point of view, being adaptations to Irish conditions of what has become known internationally as 'the new journalism'. Among its generic attributes is the representation of the author as participant-observer, resulting in a number of works – the Tóibín collection and the title essay in *A Mass for Jesse James*, for instance – that contain a mixture of analysis and autobiography. Writings of this kind also give first impressions of and initial reactions to the emergence of a new and unfamiliar Ireland. This modernising country is one in which the power of inherited historical, ideological and confessional narratives has been greatly diminished, where a sense of collective identity has been challenged by class consciousness and identity politics, and where the demands of participating in the global economy have highlighted the complexities of the evolution from nation to society. And such works of commentary also function as pendants to the pronounced and diversified engagement with the possibilities and principles of change which has supplied Irish imaginative prose between 1940 and 2000 with its moral landscape, its cultural resonance, its narrative objectives and its artistic versatility.

Notes

1. For censorship see Julia Carlson, ed. *Banned in Ireland: Censorship and the Irish Writer* (London: Routledge, 1990), Donal Ó Drisceoil, *Censorship in Ireland 1939–1945: Neutrality, Politics and Society* (Cork: Cork University Press, 1996), and, more generally, Michael Adams, *Censorship: The Irish Experience* (Dublin: Scepter, 1968).
2. Frank O'Connor, *The Backward Look: A Survey of Irish Literature* (London: Macmillan, 1967), p. 224.

3. Sean O'Faolain, 'This is Your Magazine,' *The Bell* 1, 1 (October 1940), p. 2. This editorial is reprinted in Sean McMahon, ed. *The Best from* The Bell (Dublin: O'Brien, 1978), pp. 13–16.
4. Dates in square brackets refer to first English translation from the original French.
5. Samuel Beckett, 'The Essential and the Incidental', review of Sean O'Casey's *Windfalls*, in Ruby Cohn, ed. *Disjecta: Miscellaneous Writings and a Dramatic Fragment by Samuel Beckett*, (New York: Grove Press, 1984), p. 82. The comic in Beckett is discussed by Vivian Mercier in both *The Irish Comic Tradition* (Oxford: Clarendon Press, 1962) and *Beckett/Beckett* (Oxford: Oxford University Press, 1977).
6. Samuel Beckett, *Molloy, Malone Dies, The Unnameable* (London: Calder, 1959), p. 418.
7. For some sense of Stuart's impact, see *Writing Ulster* 4 (1996): 'A Francis Stuart Special Issue'; 'Introduction' by Paul Durcan to Francis Stuart, *Redemption* (Dublin: New Island, 1994), and 'Introduction' by Hugo Hamilton to Francis Stuart, *The Pillar of Cloud* (Dublin: New Island, 1994); Robert Welsh, 'Francis Stuart: "We Are All One Flesh" ', in *Changing States: Transformations in Modern Irish Writing* (London: Routledge, 1993), pp. 138–61; and Colm Tóibín, 'Issues of Truth and Invention', *London Review of Books* 23, 1 (4 January 2001).
8. The phrase is Stuart's, cited in W. J. McCormack, 'An Introduction to Francis Stuart's Novels', in McCormack, ed. *A Festschrift for Francis Stuart on his Seventieth Birthday* (Dublin: Dolmen, 1972).
9. José Lanters, *Unauthorized Versions: Irish Menippean Satire 1919–1952* (Washington, DC: Catholic University of America Press, 2000) is a study of this satirical tradition.
10. Interest in this conception of the novel and in adapting it to Irish conditions may have received additional impetus from Donat O'Donnell's *Maria Cross: Imaginative Patterns in a Group of Catholic Writers* (London: Chatto and Windus, 1953). Much of this book originally appeared in *The Bell*.
11. For Higgins and Beckett see the letter from Beckett in *The Review of Contemporary Fiction* 3, 1 (Spring 1983), pp. 156–8.
12. See Augustine Martin, 'Inherited Dissent: The Dilemma of the Irish Writer', *Studies* 54, 213 (Spring 1965), pp. 1–20.
13. See Maurice Harmon, 'The Age of Inhibitions: Irish Literature 1920–1960', in Masaru Sekine, ed. *Irish Writers and Society at Large* (Gerrards Cross: Colin Smythe, 1985), pp. 31–41.
14. This point is indebted to the discussion of McGahern's use of imagery from Yeats's 'Easter 1916' in Denis Sampson's *Outstaring Nature's Eye: The Fiction of John McGahern* (Washington, DC: Catholic University of America Press, 1993), pp. 215ff.
15. A case for considering these works as Big House novels is presented in Vera Kreilkamp, *The Anglo-Irish Novel and the Big House* (Syracuse: Syracuse University Press, 1998), pp. 234–60.
16. Flann O'Brien, 'A Bash in the Tunnel', in *Flann O'Brien: Stories and Plays* (Harmondsworth: Penguin, 1977), p. 208.
17. For an expression of Stuart's artistic outlook, see, for example, his 'The Soft Centre of Irish Writing', in William Vorm, ed. *Paddy No More* (Dublin: Wolfhound, 1978), pp. 5–9.
18. The changing face of Dublin is recorded in Dermot Bolger, ed. *Invisible Cities. The New Dubliners: Travels Through Unofficial Dublin* (Dublin: Raven Arts, 1988) and Ronan Sheehan and Brendan Walsh, *The Heart of the City* (Dingle: Brandon, 1988).

19. Almost uniquely, Bolger's work has drawn hostile critical attention. See Declan Kiberd, 'The Children of Modernity,' *Irish Times* (22 June 1991). The argument is paraphrased in Kiberd's *Inventing Ireland* (Cambridge, MA: Harvard University Press, 1995), pp. 609–10. See also Ray Ryan, *Ireland and Scotland: Literature and Culture, State and Nation 1966–2000* (Oxford: Clarendon Press, 2002), pp. 141–98.
20. Ibid., pp. 267–75.
21. Patrick McCabe, *The Butcher Boy* (London: Picador, 1992), p. 215.
22. For an indication of the range of fictional production generally, see Fintan O'Toole, 'Everybody's Doing It', *Irish Times*, 12 May 1990.
23. Manning's Balkan trilogy consists of *The Great Fortune* (1960), *The Spoilt City* (1962) and *Friends and Heroes* (1965); *The Danger Tree* (1977), *The Battle Lost and Won* (1978) and *The Sum of Things* (1980) make up the Levant trilogy.
24. For a sense of the cultural and artistic implications of the Irish story in the American market-place, see Michael Steinman, ed. *The Happiness of Getting it Down Right: Letters of Frank O'Connor and William Maxwell 1945–1966* (New York: Knopf, 1996).
25. See also John McGahern, '*Dubliners*', in Augustine Martin, ed. *James Joyce: The Artist and the Labyrinth* (London: Ryan, 1990). Edna O'Brien has long identified herself with Joyce, as her *James Joyce* (London: Weidenfeld and Nicolson, 1999) testifies.
26. See also 'Sean O'Faolain: A Journey', in Desmond Hogan, *The Edge of the City: A Scrapbook 1976–1991* (Dublin: Lilliput, 1993), pp. 172–5.
27. See also Elgy Gillespie, ed. *Changing the Times: Irish Women Journalists 1969–1981* (Dublin: Lilliput, 2003).

Select bibliography

Acheson, James, ed. *The British and Irish Novel since 1960*, New York: St Martin's Press, 1991.

Bolger, Dermot, 'Introduction', *The Picador Book of Contemporary Irish Fiction*, London: Picador, 1993; 2nd edn, 2000.

Brown, Terence, *Ireland: A Social and Cultural History 1922–1985*, London: Fontana, 1981; expanded edn, 2004.

and Patrick Rafroidi, eds. *The Irish Short Story*, Villeneuve-d'Ascq: Publications de l'Université de Lille III, 1979.

Bourke, Angela, *Maeve Brennan: Homesick at* The New Yorker, London: Jonathan Cape, 2004.

Cahalan, James M., *Great Hatred, Little Room: The Irish Historical Novel*, Syracuse: Syracuse University Press, 1983.

The Irish Novel: A Critical History, Boston: G. K. Hall, 1988.

Connolly, Peter, ed. *Literature and the Changing Ireland*, Gerrards Cross: Colin Smythe, 1982.

Cronin, Anthony, *A Question of Modernity*, London: Secker and Warburg, 1966.

Heritage Now, Dingle: Brandon, 1982.

No Laughing Matter: The Life and Times of Flann O'Brien, London: Grafton, 1989.

Samuel Beckett: The Last Modernist, London: HarperCollins, 1996.

Donoghue, Emma, 'Noises from the Woodsheds: Tales of Irish Lesbians, 1886–1989', in Í. O'Carroll and E. Collins, eds. *Lesbian and Gay Visions of Ireland*, London: Cassell, 1995, pp. 158–70.

Elborn, Geoffrey, *Francis Stuart: A Life*, Dublin: Raven Arts, 1990.

Ellmann, Maud, *Elizabeth Bowen: The Shadow Across the Page*, Edinburgh: Edinburgh University Press, 2003.

Foster, John Wilson, *Forces and Themes in Ulster Fiction*, Dublin: Gill and Macmillan, 1974.

'Irish Fiction 1965–1990', in Seamus Deane, gen. ed. *The Field Day Anthology of Irish Writing*, 3 vols. (Derry: Field Day, 1991), III, pp. 937–43.

Garfitt, Roger, 'Constants in Contemporary Irish Fiction', in Douglas Dunn, ed. *Two Decades of Irish Writing*, Cheadle Hulme: Carcanet, 1975, pp. 207–41.

Genet, Jacqueline, ed. *The Big House in Ireland: Reality and Representation*, Dingle, Brandon: 1991.

Glendinning, Victoria, *Elizabeth Bowen: Portrait of a Writer*, London: Weidenfeld and Nicolson, 1977.

Grubgeld, Elizabeth, *Anglo-Irish Autobiography: Class, Gender and the Forms of Narrative*, Syracuse: Syracuse University Press, 2004.

Harmon, Maurice, *Sean O'Faolain: A Critical Introduction*, Dublin: Wolfhound, 1984 (2nd edn).

Sean O'Faolain: A Life, London: Constable, 1994.

and Patrick Rafroidi, eds. *The Irish Novel in Our Time*, Villeneuve-d'Ascq: Publications de l'Université de Lille III, 1976.

Harrington, John P., *The Irish Beckett*, Syracuse: Syracuse University Press, 1991.

Harte, Liam, ed. *Modern Irish Autobiography: Self, Nation and Society*, Basingstoke: Palgrave, 2005.

Harte, Liam and Michael Parker, eds. *Contemporary Irish Fiction: Themes, Tropes, Theories*, Basingstoke: Macmillan, 2000.

Higgins, Aidan, 'The Heroe's [sic] Portion: Chaos or Anarchy in the Cultic Twoilet', *The Review of Contemporary Fiction* 3, 1 (Spring 1983), pp. 108–14.

'Tired Lines, or Tales My Mother Told Me', in John Ryan, ed. *A Bash in the Tunnel: James Joyce by the Irish*, Brighton: Clifton Books, 1970, pp. 55–60.

Imhof, Rüdiger, *John Banville*, Dublin: Wolfhound, 1989.

The Modern Irish Novel: Irish Novelists since 1945, Dublin: Wolfhound, 2002.

ed. *Contemporary Irish Novelists*, Tübingen: Narr, 1990.

Jeffers, Jennifer M., *The Irish Novel at the End of the Twentieth Century: Gender, Bodies and Power*, New York: Palgrave, 2002.

Kearney, Richard, 'A Crisis of Imagination: An Analysis of a Counter-Tradition in the Irish Novel', *The Crane Bag* 3, 1 (1979), pp. 390–402.

Kelly, A. A., *Mary Lavin: Quiet Rebel. A Study of Her Short Stories*, Dublin: Wolfhound, 1980.

Kenny, John, 'After the News: Critiquing the Irish Novel since the Sixties', *The Irish Review* 25 (Winter/Spring 1999–2000), pp. 62–74.

Kilroy, James F., *The Irish Short Story: A Critical History*, Boston: Twayne, 1984.

Kilroy, Thomas, 'Teller of Tales', *Times Literary Supplement* (17 March 1972), pp. 301–2.

Kirkland, Richard, *Literature and Culture in Northern Ireland since 1965: Moments of Danger*, Harlow: Longman, 1996.

Knowlson, James, *Damned to Fame: The Life of Samuel Beckett*, London: Bloomsbury,1996.
Kreilkamp, Vera, *The Anglo-Irish Novel and the Big House*, Syracuse: Syracuse University Press, 1998.
McCartney, Anne, *Francis Stuart: Face to Face. A Critical Study*, Belfast: Institute of Irish Studies, 2000.
McMinn, Joseph, *The Supreme Fictions of John Banville*, Manchester: Manchester University Press, 1999.
Magee, Patrick, *Gangsters or Guerrillas? Representations of Irish Republicans in 'Troubles Fiction'*, Belfast: Beyond the Pale, 2001.
Mahony, Christina Hunt, *Contemporary Irish Literature: Transforming Tradition*, New York: St Martin's Press, 1998.
Matthews, James, *Voices: A Life of Frank O'Connor*, New York: Athenaeum, 1983.
Ní Anluain, Clíodhna, ed. *Reading the Future: Irish Writers in Conversation with Mike Murphy*, Dublin: Lilliput, 2000.
O'Brien, George, ed. *Colby Library Quarterly* 31, 1 (March 1995), Contemporary Irish Fiction Number.
O'Keeffe, Timothy, ed. *Myles: Portraits of Brian O'Nolan*, London: Martin Brian and O'Keeffe, 1973.
Peach, Linden, *Contemporary Irish Novel: Critical Readings*, Basingstoke: Palgrave, 2004.
Pelaschiar, Laura, *Writing the North: The Contemporary Novel in Northern Ireland*, Trieste: Edizioni Parnaso, 1998.
Reynolds, Lorna, *Kate O'Brien: A Literary Portrait*, Gerrards Cross: Colin Smythe, 1987.
Roche, Anthony, ed. *Irish University Review* 30, 1 (Spring/Summer 2000), Contemporary Novel Number.
Ryan, Ray, ed. *Writing in the Irish Republic: Literature, Culture and Politics 1949–1999*, Basingstoke: Macmillan, 2000.
St Peter, Christine, *Changing Ireland: Strategies in Contemporary Women's Fiction*, New York: Palgrave, 2000.
Sampson, Denis, *Brian Moore*, Toronto: Doubleday, 1998.
Outstaring Nature's Eye, Washington, DC: Catholic University of America Press, 1993.
Sheehan, Ronan, 'Novelists on the Novel: Interview with John Banville and Francis Stuart', *The Crane Bag* 3, 1 (1979), pp. 408–16.
Sheehy, Maurice, ed. *Michael/Frank: Studies on Frank O'Connor*, London: Macmillan, 1969.
Smyth, Gerry, *The Novel and the Nation*, London: Pluto, 1997.
Storey, Michael L., *Representing the Troubles in Irish Short Fiction*, Washington DC: Catholic University of America Press, 2004.
Tóibín, Colm, introduction, *The Penguin Book of Irish Fiction*, London: Viking, 1999, pp. ix–xxxiv.
Trevor, William, *A Writer's Ireland: Landscape in Literature*, London: Thames and Hudson, 1984.
Walsh, Éibhear, ed. *Ordinary People Dancing: Essays on Kate O'Brien*, Cork: Cork University Press, 1993.
ed. *Sex, Nation and Dissent in Irish Writing*, Cork: Cork University Press, 1997.
Weekes, Ann Owens, *Irish Women Writers*, Lexington: University Press of Kentucky, 1990.

10

Contemporary drama in English: 1940–2000

ANTHONY ROCHE

The years 1940 to 2000 saw Ireland undergo an unprecedented and accelerating degree of social change. The impact of modernisation on a traditionally conservative society had a huge influence on initiating the revival of Irish drama which began in the late 1950s and which witnessed the emergence, development and consolidation of an extraordinary level of dramatic achievement by such playwrights as Brian Friel, Tom Murphy, Hugh Leonard, John B. Keane and Thomas Kilroy, a second Renaissance to set beside the first. Many of their plays dramatise that abrupt, rapid and dizzying transformation, as long-established social practices are broken up by the shock of the new. All of these writers have focused on the forces of change operating upon and within Irish society, drawing on a wide variety of forms. John B. Keane has written of the people of Kerry with the intimate knowledge and ambivalence of an insider. Hugh Leonard has trained his mordant satire on the suburbs of South County Dublin and on the troubled conscience beneath the glossy veneer of his suburbanites. Tom Murphy and Thomas Kilroy are the most restless and experimental of contemporary Irish playwrights, diagnosing a stark existential quandary at the heart of the society. But it is Brian Friel who has become increasingly recognised as the pre-eminent living Irish playwright, managing to present an uncompromising vision of the competing claims of tradition and modernity while securing a wide national and international following.

The period is marked by an influx of new theatrical ideas, from England, the US and the Continent. The result is a greater degree of technical sophistication and theatrical innovation in the handling of familiar situations. The source of many of these ideas turned out to be Samuel Beckett, an expatriate Irishman domiciled in Paris and writing in French, who transmitted his theatrical revolution back to the country he had left through his own translation of *En Attendant Godot* as *Waiting for Godot*[1] and who continued to exercise considerable influence on more obviously 'Irish' playwrights. The 1970s and 1980s registered the impact of the Northern 'Troubles' in bringing newer playwrights to the fore, notably Donegal's Frank McGuinness and Belfast's Stewart Parker, whose darker visions were accompanied by a strong vein of anarchic humour. The 1990s saw the internationalisation of Irish drama through the worldwide success of Brian Friel's *Dancing at Lughnasa* and the emergence of a new group of young playwrights whose work took a more savage and unforgiving view of Irish society.

The chapter will adopt a decade-by-decade approach to the sixty years of crowded dramatic activity under review. This structure facilitates a more detailed socio-political focus on the plays at any given historic moment, whether it be those representing emigration in the 1960s or the impact of events in Northern Ireland from the 1970s on. The juxtaposition of better-known, canonical plays with lesser-known, neglected works will not only restore a sense of context, especially in relation to their reception, but will also chart the highs and lows within the oeuvres of each of the major playwrights of this second wave of Irish drama. A decade-by-decade breakdown of careers, such as that of Brian Friel which spans over forty years, will give a more complex sense of their achievement. The overall shaping of this chapter will also counter the automatic centring of the history of Irish drama on Dublin. It will look at the development of the All-Ireland amateur drama movement in the 1950s; the opening of Galway's Druid Theatre in the 1970s as the first of a series of companies operating outside Dublin; and two important theatre movements from the North of Ireland in the 1980s, the Derry-based Field Day Theatre company co-founded by Brian Friel and actor Stephen Rea and the Belfast-based women's collective Charabanc, which fostered Marie Jones's emergence as a world playwright. The final decade will centre on the extent to which the prominence of Irish plays on London stages – by Martin McDonagh, Marina Carr, Conor McPherson and Sebastian Barry – has a bearing on how Irish drama views itself. In relation to the development of Irish drama, this chapter will emphasise the tension and necessary balancing between radical innovation and an inherent conservatism. Irish theatre practices, however experimental, are rooted in the act of storytelling. They manifest a felt desire to keep a connection with audience and maintain a continuity of social practice while striving to find new ways to tell stories that threaten to remain untold.

The 1940s: conservation and continuity

In the 1940s the emphasis is squarely on the conservative. The death of Yeats in 1939 removed the last of the original directorate from a role in the running of the theatre; and such younger writers as Sean O'Faolain and Frank O'Connor appointed by Yeats to the Abbey Board in 1930s withdrew because their primary literary interests lay elsewhere than in drama. Yeats's chosen successor, the poet F. R. Higgins, took over as managing director but died of a heart attack just under two years later, on 8 January 1941, at the age of forty-four. His untimely death ushered in the appointment of Ernest Blythe / Earnán de Blaghd (1889–1975) as 'temporary manager' in 1941, an appointment which lasted for twenty-six years and which was seen as ushering in a period of stagnation. But some of the problems preceded Blythe's appointment and should not be laid at his door. The Abbey in general, and Yeats in particular, had set their face against the National Theatre as a place of experiment in the year 1929, with the double rejection of two plays in the Expressionist mode, Sean O'Casey's *The Silver Tassie* and Denis Johnston's *The Old Lady Says 'No!'*. The rift with the Abbey meant that the theatre for much of its subsequent history steered clear of staging any of O'Casey's later plays and concentrated to a lamentably predictable degree on revivals of the three plays of the so-called 'Dublin trilogy'. At a 1947 revival of *The Plough* a walkout was staged by the poet Valentin Iremonger and the UCD academic Roger McHugh in protest at the low level reached in the standards of production; Iremonger described the current Abbey directorate as being characterised by 'utter incompetence'.[2] *The Silver Tassie* was occasionally produced at the Abbey (in 1935 and in 1951); but O'Casey's subsequent dramatic career, if it found no place at the National Theatre, still found unexpected expression on Dublin stages. Shelagh Richards directed the world première of his dramatisation of the Dublin Lock Out, *Red Roses For Me*, in March 1943 at the Olympia Theatre; and three years later Ria Mooney restaged her London production of the same play in the Gaiety Theatre (this was the production O'Casey preferred and to which he always referred as its première). The staging of world premières of new O'Casey plays in Dublin continued into the 1950s. In February 1955 Tyrone Guthrie directed the first production of *The Bishop's Bonfire* at the Gaiety with Cyril Cusack; and in 1958 plans to have *The Drums of Father Ned* staged at the Dublin International Theatre Festival drew down the wrath of the Catholic Archbishop of Dublin, John Charles McQuaid. As a result O'Casey banned all professional productions of his plays in Ireland, a decision only rescinded some months before his death in 1964. Until the very end of his long and productive life, therefore, Sean O'Casey retained a vital and controversial link with the staging (and sometimes the premièring) of his later plays in Dublin, a relationship which the Abbey's earlier rejection of the *Tassie* is inclined to obscure. That these plays were in a markedly different style from the original three, requiring a much greater degree of stylisation in movement, speech and costuming, drew attention to the limitations of the Abbey style and underscored the necessity to look elsewhere in Irish theatre for a commitment to experiment and innovation.

The realistic style of drama that predominated in the Abbey Theatre during the 1930s and 1940s is best represented by the plays of George Shiels (1881–1949). Born in Ballymoney, county Antrim, Shiels's early plays were written for the Ulster theatre but after the Abbey Theatre accepted *Bedmates* in 1921, he had a play staged there every year until 1948, the year before his death at the age of sixty-three. His early plays, like the hugely popular *Professor Tim* (1925), were comedies of character, with a series of well-known types offering expressive possibilities not just to the Abbey players but to the burgeoning amateur theatre groups around the country, particularly the north-west. What Shiels's dramatic career as it unfolded made clear was how carefully informed by close observation of Irish country life all of his plays were, whatever their chosen theatrical mode.[3] The centenary revival in 1981 of his *Passing Day* (1936) revealed an unsentimental yet moving portrayal of the miserly shopkeeper at its centre, especially as played by the Donegal-born Ray McAnally. But it was *The Rugged Path* of 1940 and its sequel *The Summit* that showed what Shiels dramatically was capable of; and made impossible any direct equation between a playing for easy laughs and greater popularity. For *The Rugged Path* had its run at the Abbey extended to twelve weeks, well beyond the usual two, and this for a play which was Shiels's most serious and complex to date. As with many of the plays of the period, there is a contrast between an older generation, set in their ways, opposing themselves to a younger generation anxious for change. The more interesting conflict is between two families, the Dolises, the wild mountainy men who intimidate and live off the surrounding community, and the Tanseys, a more settled family who eventually decide to break with tradition and inform on the Dolises for their brutal murder of an old man. Peter Dolis is arrested and charged, but released when intimidation makes the jury reluctant to convict. The play ends with a bullet coming through the Tanseys's window. Any accusation that the National Theatre was peddling a rural idyll during this period can be countered by the evidence of such plays as *The Rugged Path* and Louis D'Alton's *Lovers' Meeting* (1941), whose tragic portrait of a young woman forced to marry a much older wealthy man had an influence on later playwrights like John B. Keane. The relative freedom from censorship enjoyed by the stage in Ireland, even during this conservative period, became clear when Una Troy (1910–93), writing under the pseudonym of 'Elizabeth Connor', adapted her banned 1936 novel *Mount Prospect* as a play which was staged at the Abbey in 1940. The stage version of *Mount Prospect* went on to win the Shaw Prize for Best Play and three more plays by Troy were produced at the Abbey over the decade: *Swans and Geese* (1941); *Apple a Day* (1942) and *Dark Road* (1947), which was based on her 1938 novel *Dead Star's Light*. After the staging of plays by Teresa Deevy in the 1930s and by Una Troy in the 1940s, the theatre co-founded by Lady Gregory was to be an almost exclusively male preserve until the arrival of Marina Carr in the 1990s.

Shiels's *The Rugged Path* was produced in 1940 during F. R. Higgins's brief tenure as managing director. But Ernest Blythe was happy to continue the Abbey's association with George Shiels, not least because they were both Northerners. Blythe further developed contacts with the Ulster Theatre when the work of one of their leading playwrights, Joseph Tomelty (1911–95), was staged at the Abbey. What occurred in the Abbey's collaboration with Tomelty, who was born at Portaferry near Belfast, was a dual development across the border whereby his plays were restaged in Dublin after first productions in Belfast. For example, the Ulster Group Theatre (of which Tomelty was a board member) first produced his play *All Souls' Night* in Belfast in September 1948; it was then produced at the Abbey the following year. Tomelty's most powerful work of the 1940s was *The End House*, first produced in 1944.[4] Set in the Falls Road in Belfast, it centred on a conflict between the father, a house painter with radical but anti-republican sympathies, and the son, who had been in prison for IRA involvement. *The End House* was the first stage representation at the Abbey of the Northern situation since St John Ervine's *Mixed Marriage* in 1911. But where the household shown in Ervine's was Protestant, that in Tomelty's was Catholic; and the Catholic emphasis of Tomelty's plays only increased as he opted for less challenging fare, culminating in his most successful play, *Is the Priest At Home?*, produced by the Group Theatre in Belfast in 1954 and that Christmas at the Abbey. It was to be several decades and the renewed flaring of 'the Troubles' before the Northern Protestant experience would be represented on the Abbey and Peacock stages.

Ernest Blythe's greatest interest lay in the restoration of the Irish language. This idealistic imperative determined most of his artistic and dramatic decisions. It had a bearing on both the Abbey actors and the repertoire. In 1942 it became the policy to accept only actors who could perform in Irish as well as English; and while this brought to the fore talented players like Siobhán McKenna and Ray McAnally it also put off many interested actors from even applying, narrowing the range of those who trod the boards of the National Theatre. Blythe also wished to see more plays performed in Irish at the Abbey and kickstarted the policy in February 1942 by translating the medieval morality play *Everyman* into an Irish-language version, *Cách*. The policy was in line with the cultural views of the then-Taoiseach Eamon de Valera and had also been part of the original theatre movement's policy in its founding years. In practice the plays staged by the Abbey Theatre in the four decades since had practically all been written in English and thus in so single-mindedly pursuing this policy Blythe was putting aside a large measure of the theatre's achievement. The shortage of plays in Irish (particularly original plays, rather than translations) and the small numbers of those who would attend such productions militated against any great success. The expedient then devised was the Abbey pantomime. The first of these was presented in 1945, an adaptation by Mícheál Ó hAodha of Lady Gregory's *The Golden Apple* as *Muireann agus an Prionnsa*, and met with great success. It set the template for several decades, with the traditional story used as a peg on which to hang political satire, translations of popular songs and a medley of theatrical styles. Although they have made no lasting imprint on literary history and were a mixed aesthetic experience, the Abbey Irish panto was to provide many Irish school children with their first live theatrical experience. As Máirín Nic Eoin shows in chapter 6 of this volume, it also demonstrated some of the less obvious possibilities for a theatre in Irish and provided considerable latitude for a young man of the theatre brought in by Blythe, Tomás Mac Anna (b. 1926), for whom he predicted great things. Mac Anna would come into his own when the new Abbey opened in 1966 but the theatrical skills he had honed were in part perfected on the Abbey panto.

If most of the plays performed at the Abbey since its founding were in English, the greatest dramatist of the early movement – Synge – had shown the linguistic and dramatic possibilities for a spoken English closely modelled on Irish syntax and phrasing. Most of those who followed after him, from the 'Cork Realists' on, chose to develop the more realistic side of Synge's art. Only the Kerry dramatist George Fitzmaurice had really followed in the wake of Synge's more poetic and fantastic side, writing dialogue in which 'every speech should be as fully flavoured as a nut or apple'.[5] If the playwrights of the 1940s so far considered might be seen as realists, the greatest of those to emerge – Galway-born M. J. Molloy (1913–94) – was the most evidently Synge's inheritor[6] and showed that, even under Blythe, the Abbey Theatre had not completely lost touch with the aims and examples of its founders. All of his early plays were staged at the Abbey in the 1940s, *The Old Road* (1943), *The Visiting House* (1946) and the first of his two great works, *The King of Friday's Men* (1948). The language of this play is as rich and distinctive as Synge's and has the same Hiberno-English flavour; but the syntax is more straightforward and the tone more formal. The scenario of *The King of Friday's Men* has recognisable links to *The Playboy of the Western World*, with the stranger falling in love with the local girl and being persuaded that he is not condemned to a lifetime of loneliness. What complicates this scenario is the play's eighteenth-century setting on the Anglo-Irish estate of Caesar French and the colonial theme explicitly identified and addressed by Molloy. For what the heroine Una is seeking to avoid in her love for young Owen is the *droit du seigneur* exercised by the landlord French on the most beautiful daughters of his tenants. Molloy's play reveals in almost all of the characters an acquiescence and complicity in their master's rapaciousness. Into this society steps Bartley Dowd, the man from Tyrawley, who has been summoned to support the locals in a faction fight. In order to get Bartley to defend her, Una pretends to be in love with him; and for much of the play her feelings oscillate between her untried young lover and this battle-scarred veteran for whom she conceives a growing affection. When Una is forced to confess her stratagem and returns to her original lover, Bartley is left to the isolated fate he always felt was his and finds a curious mirror image in the landlord Caesar French, who would have married his most recent tally woman Maura did not the decrees of his class forbid it. Molloy's play has more than a dash of Boucicault; but it resists the temptation to cast the landlord as villain. Instead it shows French's own entrapment by the colonial system, which envelops all the characters save the marginalised Bartley.

Molloy's second great work, *The Wood of the Whispering*, was produced at the Abbey in January 1953 and was among the first to tackle the theme of emigration. It was an issue of which Molloy, living in Galway, was only too acutely aware and he made an unsolicited and heartfelt deposition to the government board of inquiry into the effects of emigration in the west.[7] In this play, his taste for the grotesque is even more developed than in *The King of Friday's Men*. The central character, Sanbatch Daly – a man in his mid-sixties who is rather 'crazy and absurd and wild'[8] – feigns madness at the close to gain admission to the mental hospital but is not far from madness itself. The carnivalesque extreme of the ending is of a piece with the alternative society sketched out in *The Wood of the Whispering*.[9] Its hope for the renewal of society is mitigated by its even more profound sense of the psychic suffering which all of its people have experienced. Part of the project of renewal for the west of Ireland Molloy envisages is cultural and, while he was no doubt glad to have his plays staged at the Abbey Theatre, he claims they will only rightly be understood and have their most authentic representation through the work of the amateur drama societies:

> Country people know all about it, and they know the background of this play, the comedy of the eccentric old bachelors, and the tragedy, too. So it was no coincidence that its first two amateur performances were by two tiny rural villages: Inchovea in County Clare and Killeedy in County Limerick, which between them won half a dozen drama festivals with it – before their dramatic societies were shattered by emigration. Every activity is hit by a falling population; and every activity is helped by an expanding population.[10]

The 1950s: innovation and breakthrough

The work of dramatists like George Shiels, Joseph Tomelty and M. J. Molloy makes the period of the 1940s at the Abbey Theatre more vital and interesting than has generally been conceded. But an event occurred in 1951 that reduced the theatre to a shell of its former self and threatened its achievement with extinction. At one a.m. on the morning of Wednesday 18 July 1951, after the curtain had fallen on yet another revival of *The Plough and the Stars*, flames were seen coming from the theatre and five sections of Dublin's Fire Brigade called. But in less than an hour the backstage was destroyed, the stage badly damaged, the auditorium roof had collapsed, while much of the contents of the theatre went up in smoke. The Abbey Theatre having burned to the ground, Blythe's resourcefulness met its greatest challenge. In the long run – and it took a full fifteen years – he would see and see through the building of a new Abbey Theatre on the site of the old. In the immediate term, Blythe leased the old home of melodrama, the Queen's Theatre, as the new (temporary) home for the National Theatre. The Queen's, a barn-like structure which seated 760 (approximately 50 per cent more than the old Abbey), was in a considerable state of disrepair. The move across the Liffey to Pearse Street led to the acquisition of a double staff and the loss of the experimental space of the Peacock Theatre. The net effect of increased seat capacity and the dire economics was predictable: long runs for familiar favourites. The occasional outstanding new Irish play was performed, as with Molloy's *Wood of the Whispering* in 1953. But the main staple of the Abbey in the 1950s was provided by John McCann, with plays like *Twenty Years A-Wooing* (1954) and its stock characterisation, local references and happy endings. The few theatrical successes for the Abbey at the Queen's in the 1950s tended to be with Irish productions of foreign classics, where the actors relished the opportunity to tackle more challenging parts. Two outstanding examples would be Tomás Mac Anna's production of his beloved Brecht's *Life of Galileo* in 1956 and Frank Dermody's production of Eugene O'Neill's *Long Day's Journey into Night* in April 1959. But for most of this decade the Abbey was not the place to seek for developments in Irish theatre. And while it might seem reasonable for a young aspiring playwright to send his or her manuscripts to the National Theatre, a combination of artistic and economic factors decreed that they were just as automatically being rejected.

The need for a new theatre in Dublin in the early 1950s gained momentum with postwar developments in world drama. And so Alan Simpson (1920–80), by day a captain in the Irish army and former apprentice to director Hilton Edwards, decided in 1953 to open a small theatre in Dublin with the intention of presenting 'plays of all countries on all subjects . . . which, for various reasons, would not be seen on either the larger or smaller commercial stages'.[11] The aim of the Pike Theatre, according to the manifesto of founders Simpson and his wife Carolyn Swift (1923–2002), was a resolutely contemporary one: 'We hope to give theatregoers [in Dublin] opportunities to see more of the struggle going on at present in world theatre, to introduce new techniques and new subjects in play writing.'[12] This struggle to introduce new techniques was one that equally engaged Irish playwrights frustrated by the lack of an outlet other than the Abbey. While the Pike Theatre during its nine-year existence made a particular cause of producing the plays of Tennessee Williams, and inaugurated a late-night cabaret slot, it won its greatest acclaim and made a profound contribution to the development of contemporary Irish drama with its two productions of first plays by Dublin-born playwrights: the world première of *The Quare Fellow* by Brendan Behan (1923–64) on 19 November 1954 and the Irish première of *Waiting for Godot* by Samuel Beckett (1906–89) on 28 October 1955. The first drew the attention of Joan Littlewood at Stratford East in London and subsequently enabled an Irish playwright like Behan to go international; the second enabled an international play like *Godot* to come home, to find a large Irish audience in a remarkably short time.

The Quare Fellow, though not produced until 1954, had been on Behan's mind since the 1940s and his four years in Mountjoy Prison for republican activities. Mountjoy served Behan as the urban equivalent of a hedge school; his fellow republican prisoner Seán Ó Briain taught him Irish. It was there he wrote his first play, *The Landlady*, where it was staged by the prisoners, some of whose cellmates in the audience objected to portions of it as blasphemous or obscene. While in prison, Behan subjected Ernest Blythe to a barrage of letters. One of these, dated 18 May 1946, reveals that the writing of *The Quare Fellow* was already under way (under its original title of *The Twisting of Another Rope*):

> I enclose the first Act of my play – The Landlady . . . I have written one Act of another play. The Twisting of Another Rope I call it, because everything is shown in the black cell in some prison. Two men are condemned to death and waiting for the Rope – I would send it with this but better not scare the Department of Justice before we have anything done. There is nothing political in it, of course. I'll send it to you if you like.
>
> Every thanks to yourself, Ernest Blythe
> for your kindness to
> Brendan Behan
>
> P. S. You know I have no chance of typing the M. S.[13]

Both on this occasion and eight years later, when he once more submitted his play to the Abbey, it is ironic that it should have been rejected, given Behan's impeccable republican and Irish-language credentials. Indeed, the original version sent to Blythe was in Irish (and in its original title chose to refer explicitly and mordantly to Hyde's one-act play of 1901). The version sent to Blythe in the early 1950s was translated into English and had been extended to three acts. It was also submitted to and rejected by the Gate, as having no suitable part for Micheál Mac Liammóir; but it was noticed by Mac Liammóir's niece, Sally Travers, who was friendly with Simpson and Swift and passed it on to them.[14]

The staging of *The Quare Fellow* at the Pike made the cramped, intimate quarters of the small theatre work for the producers by reproducing the claustrophobia of prison life. The physical intimacy brought the audience closer to sharing the condition of the prisoners, abolishing the distance usually separating them and forcing them into close proximity. The play required an all-male cast of thirty, over half the number the Pike could seat; this was reduced to twenty-two by doubling. Alan Simpson got Behan himself to record 'The Old Triangle', the song sung throughout by an off-stage prisoner whose verses punctuate or rather orchestrate and help to compose the action of the play. Simpson and Swift and most of the critics failed to realise the extent to which Brendan Behan was the most formally innovative Irish-based playwright to have appeared in well over a decade, much more an accomplished international playwright and much less the inspired local amateur he has often been taken for. The play, in a curious parallel with Beckett's *Godot*, has no leading man. The title character, the condemned prisoner whose imminent hanging generates the activity of the play, never appears. The case against capital punishment can equally be made in his absence but, more to the theatrical point, what is central to the play is the effect of the quare fellow's death on the other characters, especially his fellow prisoners. It becomes increasingly clear not only that the title character is never going to appear on stage but that the quare fellow will not be returned to the stage of life, as the slender thread of hope for a last-minute reprieve is definitively snapped.

The play's form is of a continuous alternating ensemble with various fluid groupings occurring on stage, and with little dramatic continuity from one prisoner or warder to the next. Much of Behan's approach may be seen as deliberately Brechtian: to acknowledge the spectacle of the hanging as a theatrical event and to penetrate through this façade to the social practices that authorise its continuance. *The Quare Fellow* was recognised as hearkening back to O'Casey, through its dramatic use of Dublin speech and its potent theatrical fusion of music-hall and politics. The mixture of high and low art which the socialist playwrights O'Casey, Brecht and Behan favour has always offended equally the caretakers of high culture, the bourgeois middle-class audience who see it as 'vulgar' and the cultural nationalists whose view of an Irish theatre prefers a narrow and unified consistency of style. Even Alan Simpson objected to the presence of old jokes in *The Quare Fellow* and instanced this as a sign both of Behan's laziness and a lack of technical competence, which is to miss the point almost entirely. In a play where the rituals and routines of prison life determine so much of the action, critics objected to its lack of plot; and Simpson and Swift edited much of the original script with a view to eliminating many of its repetitions and producing something more linear.

The dramatic emphasis is instead thrown on talk, on the orality of speech as a site of potential freedom and self-realisation. The delight in talk for its own sake, so prominent a feature throughout Irish drama, gains particular prominence from the threat of silence, enforced externally by the warders and threatened internally by the depersonalising conditions in which the prisoners have to exist. The prisoners' speech is a linguistic hybrid, crammed with local Dublin idiom and reference, mixed in with cockney slang. They have their own internal means of communicating and defeating the 'officialese' of the authorities. One of these alternative languages or counter-codes is their tapping on the pipes, which readily converts to 'yapping'. The Irish language also serves the same function. For if private communication between the prisoners shuts out the authorities, Irish goes even further by breaking down the absolute separation and distinction between warder and prisoner. In a scene reminiscent of Lady Gregory's *Rising of the Moon*, the play switches to Irish for a necessarily brief dialogue between Warder Crimmin and Prisoner C, a young man from the Kerry Gaeltacht. The 'sir' of the English switches to first-name address in the Irish ('a Thomáis'); but the English public titles of 'Governor', 'Chief' and

'Principal' stubbornly refuse to be translated. Rather than saying that Behan began writing *The Quare Fellow* in Irish and then switched to English, it would be truer to say that this is a play of two languages with one text haunted by its ghostly double.

The same is true of the other important play given its Irish première the following year, Samuel Beckett's *Waiting for Godot*, though here the two languages are French and English rather than Irish and English. Having moved from Ireland to France in the 1930s, Beckett made the radical decision while working for the French Resistance during the war years to move from writing in English to writing in French. He carried through on this decision with the major works he produced in the late 1940s, the prose trilogy of *Molloy*, *Malone meurt* and *L'Innommable* and his dramatic debut, *En Attendant Godot*. The huge acclaim which greeted the first staging of this play at the Théâtre du Babylone in Paris in January 1953 established Beckett's world reputation and led to instant demands for a translation of *Godot* into English. Beckett insisted on providing his own English translation of the play, and proved notoriously slow at doing so. The translated pages were fed to Alan Simpson and Caroline Swift in Dublin as they went about preparing an Irish production. The term 'translation' scarcely covers the process of rewriting in which Beckett was engaged. In the opening lines of the French, Estragon halts Vladimir's verbal flow with 'Assez' ('Enough'); in the translated version, this becomes 'Ah, stop blathering'.[15] It soon became clear to Simpson that there was a vein of Hiberno-English in Beckett's translation, something he augmented freely in the staged version, altering 'It'd be amusing' to 'It'd be gas', for instance.[16] It is also evident from Beckett's English text that the incidence of Hiberno-English spoken by the two tramps increases significantly when they are in the intimidating presence of Pozzo, whom they repeatedly address as 'mister'; and that Beckett has substituted explicit Irish references in Lucky's speech, not least the reiteration of 'Connemara' (in place of 'Normandie'). Simpson built on these Irish suggestions to give the play what it conspicuously lacked, a local social and historical context. In the Pike interpretation, the two tramps were played as markedly Irish, whereas Pozzo became an Anglo-Irishman dominating one native (Lucky) and objecting to the presence of two others (Vladimir and Estragon) on his lands. It became standard practice after this for the actor playing Pozzo to be Anglo-Irish or English, with Alan Stanford taking the role in the Gate production of the 1990s.

The première of *Godot* at the Pike on 28 October 1955 had two important consequences for the decolonisation of theatre in Ireland. Firstly, the English production of *Godot* still came under the scrutiny of the Lord Chamberlain and had a number of lines excised (e.g. 'What about hanging ourselves?/Hmm. It'd give us an erection').[17] Simpson made good on a promise to Beckett by delivering a more textually complete production (albeit corrupted by his own additions) than the London production, a further example to set with Shaw's *Blanco Posnet* at the Abbey in 1909 of the Irish theatre's independence from English censorship. The Pike also stood up to the London producers of the play, who sought to stop the Dublin production on the basis that they held the sole UK rights. Alan Simpson was able to point out in return that in 1948 Ireland had left the Commonwealth and since 1949 had been an independent Republic. Therefore, the gentleman's agreement with the author still held and, though delaying a number of weeks in deference to the author (and benefiting from the London publicity), the Pike's near-simultaneous presentation of the play in Dublin gave it a more independent status.

The placing of *Godot* on a Dublin stage and in an Irish theatrical context brought a dimension to the play which was not apparent in either Paris or London. The Irish playwright who had most promoted the tramp from the social margins to centre stage was Synge. When asked in the last six months of his life who 'had influenced his own theatre most of all, [Beckett] suggested only the name of Synge';[18] and *Godot*'s original director Roger Blin had earlier staged a production of Synge's *In the Shadow of the Glen*, in which a tramp figures prominently. Two tramps sitting on an almost bare stage waiting for a quasi-miracle to occur directly conjures up the two blind beggars in Synge's *The Well of the Saints*, who have their sight restored by a saint but have to cope with the subsequent disillusionment. The psychological and physical interdependence of the two tramps also has its roots in Irish theatre. The physical interaction of Didi and Gogo draws on a Yeats play like *On Baile's Strand*, where the Fool and the Blind Man make one; and their verbal interchanges recall the male double act of Captain Boyle and Joxer in O'Casey's *The Plough and the Stars*, with 'chassis' as an initially comic, ultimately tragic form of chaos. The Irish play that *Godot* most immediately recalled was Yeats's *Purgatory*, staged during August 1938, the one month of that year which Beckett spent in Ireland. Both plays feature an almost bare stage, except for a stone on which one of the characters sits and a tree stripped of leaves. Its two characters are vagrants, wanderers, men of the roads, who have come to this spot to wait for a miracle; instead, a legacy of murder repeats itself and the play itself dramatises a structure of cyclical recurrence, as *Godot* notoriously was to do, with its second act mirroring its first. But the Second World War had intervened and there is in Beckett's play no consoling, albeit jaundiced, nostalgia for the past.

Waiting for Godot had as profound and far-reaching an influence on an Ireland emerging from the self-imposed isolationism of several decades as it had on contemporary drama elsewhere. But Samuel Beckett also has a particular and distinctive significance for contemporary Irish drama which puts him in the position of ghostly founding father. It is only in part a question of direct influence (though that is there, in many cases). More important is the fact that the critical act of placing Beckett in the context of contemporary Irish theatre reveals preoccupations that he shares with more clearly 'rooted' Irish playwrights: translation; exile; estrangement and dispossession in their language and stage situations. The people in Beckett's plays frequently find themselves in an imposed situation which is none of their making and which they seek to disguise or subvert through rituals of gesture and play and through a relentless verbal undercutting. This proves no less the case for Behan's prisoners or (to take a much later instance) for Frank McGuinness's First World War Northern Irish Protestant recruits in *Observe the Sons of Ulster Marching towards the Somme* (1985).

Behan's subsequent career brought him increasingly towards a world stage but, it is often thought, at the expense of his Irish roots. His second play, *An Giall*, was a commissioned work in the Irish language, premièred in Dublin's Damer Hall on 16 June 1958. It told the story of an English soldier held prisoner by the IRA and killed in reprisal for the hanging of one of their men. There is a chaste love affair between the English prisoner and a young Irish woman, Teresa; and a bawdy context in the brothel where the play is set. In this instance, the cultural process of translation operated in the reverse direction from *Godot*. A play first of all written in Irish was translated into English (as *The Hostage*) and a play first staged in Dublin was transferred to a London stage. But its English director Joan Littlewood was renowned for her workshop techniques and collaborative style of production; and *The Hostage* underwent a considerable change, more in the direction of a comedy, with added songs, topical references and several homosexuals. A debate has raged since then concerning the degree to which Behan authorised or consented to these changes. One view has it that the English translation diluted and travestied the cultural linguistic purity of the original, producing an exercise in stage Irishry for cultural export; the other argues that Behan willingly collaborated in the process, welcoming the move away from a narrow Abbey Theatre naturalism into a more formally experimental and culturally hybrid form of socialist theatre.[19] Behan followed the success of *The Hostage* from London to New York, and the free flow of alcohol that ensued took a lethal toll on his diabetes. But even after his tragically early death in 1964, he continued to have a direct as well as an indirect influence on contemporary Irish theatre, with Tomás Mac Anna's Brechtian staging of Behan's prose work *Borstal Boy* (in a version by Frank McMahon) triumphantly taking the new Abbey stage in October 1967.

The main theatrical development outside of Dublin in the 1950s was the consolidation and expansion of the amateur theatre movement. This was bolstered by the establishment in 1953 of a national amateur theatre festival, the All-Ireland drama finals in Athlone. Local theatre groups were now stimulated by a competitive edge which had a national dimension. Interest and involvement both expanded, and local acting and directing talent now had a larger stage on which to perform. The plays of Molloy, Shiels and others had a life beyond the capital, with amateur groups giving them countrywide circulation.[20] It should be no surprise, therefore, that several of the important contemporary playwrights who first emerged in this decade did so with the help of the amateur drama movement. John B. Keane (1928–2002), who had reversed the trend of one-way emigration from his native Listowel in Kerry by returning from England to run a local pub, had his first play *Sive* staged in the town on 2 February 1959 by the Listowel Drama Group. The play was a rich mix of Boucicaultian melodrama, with the sacrifice of its virginal young heroine, of the folk drama of Synge and Molloy in its two visiting tramps who act as a kind of tragic chorus, and of the Abbey realism of D'Alton in the harsh economics which have soured the central relations in the household. Although Keane had one early play staged by the Abbey (*Hut 42* in 1962), the other plays he submitted – including *Sive* – were returned to him, he believed unread.[21] It was to be many years before the Abbey was to make amends; in the 1980s, artistic director Joe Dowling appointed director Ben Barnes to direct productions of Keane's major plays on the Abbey stage, one of which (*The Field*) was to be the flagship of the theatre's visit to Russia. But by then Keane's reputation had been made and it was made initially by the amateur theatre tradition and by people who had graduated from its ranks. In 1959 *Sive* won the All-Ireland trophy, the first original play to do so, and as a result of which ironically was given a one-night performance at the Abbey Theatre.

In the same year, Tom Murphy (b. 1935), a young man who had acted in several amateur productions in his native town of Tuam, County Galway, submitted a one-act play he had co-authored with his friend Noel O'Donoghue to the Festival's New Play competition. They won the fifteen-guinea prize for *On the Outside*, a play they had first conceived of standing around in the Tuam Square after mass one Sunday. 'One thing's for sure,' O'Donoghue had remarked, 'it won't be set in a cottage.' Instead, the play took place outside a local dance-hall, a setting which reflected Ireland's growing modernisation; but as the title indicates, the two young male protagonists have not the money to gain admission and try to cadge their way in. Here, as later, Murphy would show a keen eye for details of class and economic differences operating in Irish life. In 1960, his full-length play *The Iron Men* won the All-Ireland script competition. Ernest Blythe rejected it and stormed out of its first Dublin production with the comment: 'I never saw such rubbish in my life.'[22] The play, retitled *A Whistle in the Dark*, was taken up by Joan Littlewood at Stratford East in 1961. The sense of exclusion faced by Murphy's two characters outside the dance-hall was also experienced by the playwright himself in relation to the Irish stage. Murphy emigrated to England in the early 1960s, where he would continue to write plays which remained unproduced in England.

By the end of the 1950s most of the major playwrights had emerged. Brian Friel was writing short stories and having his early plays produced on radio. John Keyes Byrne had a play produced at the Abbey (*The Big Birthday* in 1956) but when subsequent works were rejected there, took the name of a psychopath in one of them – Hugh Leonard – as a playwriting pseudonym. Leonard would benefit from the development of the Dublin Theatre Festival which, after its bumpy start with the removal of O'Casey's *Drums of Father Ned*, soon became a meeting ground between the modernising impulse in Irish drama and imported work. Leonard would contribute both original work and adaptations to the Festival virtually every year. Tom Murphy and John B. Keane were launched on their very different careers by the amateur drama movement. Both Behan and Beckett had made direct contributions. In the furore over the O'Casey ban, Beckett withdrew his work from Irish performance, thus foreclosing on Simpson's planned production of *Endgame*. The Pike itself was closed in the wake of a financially injurious trial, when the police shut down their production of Tennessee Williams's *The Rose Tattoo*.[23] What the 1950s shows then is fitful fire, but fire nonetheless that would blaze in subsequent decades.

The 1960s: change and development

A decade that was to see an unprecedented degree of social change got off to a dramatic start with the staging of Sam Thompson's play about the Belfast shipyards, *Over the Bridge*, at the Empire Theatre on 26 January 1960. The play had first been submitted to the Group Theatre two years earlier where it was ultimately rejected on the grounds that its depiction of sectarianism would stir unrest; but some of the younger bloods resigned and founded

Ulster Bridge Productions in order to have it staged. The Belfast production ran for an unprecedented six weeks and then for a further four in Dublin. Sam Thompson wrote little more of interest; nothing more was heard of the group that produced his play; and the Group dissolved a few years later. But as Stewart Parker indicated in his introduction to the 1970 printing of the play, the example of Thompson became an important one for aspiring playwrights from Northern Ireland.[24] And in the same year as *Over the Bridge* the Group produced a play called *The Francophile* by an aspiring young playwright, a teacher from Derry called Brian Friel (b. 1929). At the time, Friel was more widely recognised as a writer of short stories; a number had been published in *The New Yorker* and he was to publish two collections during the 1960s. But Friel had also made a few tentative forays into the medium of drama, primarily by contributing radio plays for broadcast on BBC Northern Ireland. His first staged play, *The Francophile*, details the social pretensions of a postal worker in Derry, Willie Logue, and has not been adjudged a success by those who have read or seen it. (Friel has not allowed the piece to be published.) It does indicate the extent to which the major source of inspiration for aspiring Irish playwrights was postwar American drama, given that Friel's Willie Logue is clearly a version of Arthur Miller's Willie Loman in his 1949 play *Death of a Salesman*. It also serves to indicate Friel's ambition in the drama, even if he had a distance to travel and his development would involve progressing beyond the uneasy social comedy of his first staged play. Friel's dramatisation of the exile of St Columba on Iona, *The Enemy Within*, was staged by the Abbey at the Queen's on 6 August 1962; and showed a marked development in thematic and linguistic confidence. But it was with the 1964 staging of his breakthrough play, *Philadelphia, Here I Come!* at Dublin's Gaiety Theatre in a production by the Gate Theatre under Hilton Edwards's direction that Friel's career and contemporary Irish drama achieved its first major breakthrough.

In 1960 Friel had given up his teaching career for full-time writing and with the success of this play decided to abandon the short story and to concentrate wholeheartedly on the theatre. A major influence in arriving at these decisions was the director Tyrone Guthrie, who invited Friel to attend rehearsals at a custom-built theatre (the Guthrie) in Minneapolis in 1964. This gave the playwright what he later described as 'my first parole from inbred claustrophobic Ireland'.[25] The plays he saw in rehearsal there were to prove influential on his later career, particularly Chekhov's *Three Sisters*. On his return Friel immediately sat down and wrote *Philadelphia, Here I Come!*. The question of where to have it staged was by no means an obvious one. The play in certain respects resembles an Abbey play of the 1950s: a young Donegal man, on the eve of emigration to the USA, weighs up the pros and cons of his decision and has encounters in turn with each of the key figures in his life, staples both of small-town life in Ireland and the dramatis personae of Irish drama: the schoolteacher; the canon; the other young fellas who are staying behind; the woman he loved but lost to another man; the housekeeper (mother surrogate); and above all the taciturn, emotionally reticent father with whom he shares a lonely house and a family business. But the play went beyond such traditional fare because of its innovative staging demands. And the increase in theatricality paradoxically serves only to increase the play's emotional effectiveness. It does so by going beyond the limitations of social realism. Above all this is achieved through Friel's decision to reflect and dramatise the competing and contradictory urges in Gar O'Donnell by having him represented in two roles and hence by two actors. As the stage directions to the play put it: 'The two Gars, PUBLIC GAR and PRIVATE GAR, are two views of the one man. PUBLIC GAR is the Gar that people see, talk to, talk about. PRIVATE GAR is the unseen man, the man within, the conscience, the *alter ego*, the secret thoughts, the id. PRIVATE GAR, the spirit, is invisible to everybody, always.'[26] This male psychological double act is crucial to the success of *Philadelphia, Here I Come!*, the dynamism on which it runs. It ventilates and gives light, colour, humour and a variety of perspectives to the human dilemma at its core, freeing the representation of that dilemma from a no-longer-adequate form. In particular the verbal extravagance and physical mime which go into the enactment of Gar's fantasies make a more serious point about the society Friel was representing. The two Gars encourage and inspire each other to a greater degree of self-expression than is possible in the family or public domain, where silence is the norm. And the revised version of the popular song 'California, Here I Come!' which gives the play its title and which Gar sings snatches of throughout indicates the extent to which Gar O'Donnell does not need to emigrate, because by the end of the 1950s – with the Fianna Fáil government now reversing its earlier insulation to encourage the investment of foreign capital – the USA had already come to Ireland, as the play's proliferating movie and music references make clear.

Throughout his long and distinguished career, Friel has always continued to live in the North, moving back and forth across the border between the two Irelands. He has had plays staged in Belfast and Dublin and (with his co-founding of the Field Day Theatre Company in 1980) in his native Derry. But in 1964 he had the good fortune to gain the lengthy theatrical expertise of Hilton Edwards (1903–82) to direct the world première of *Philadelphia*. Edwards had co-founded Dublin's Gate Theatre with Micheál Mac Liammóir (1899–1978) in 1928, but though they had made their debut with Denis Johnston's experimental *The Old Lady Says 'No!'* the Gate had contributed little in the intervening thirty-six years to the canon of contemporary Irish drama. An exception should be made for the important and under-recognised role the Gate played in the staging of plays by living Irish women playwrights. In the 1930s, the Gate staged the satiric comedies of Mary Manning (1906–99) (such as 1931's *Youth's the Season*) and later the historical plays of Christine Lady Longford (1900–80) (such as the 1941 *Lord Edward*), thus proving itself one of the few Irish theatrical spaces hospitable to women playwrights. When the novelist Maura Laverty (1907–66) had four of her novels in a row banned by the Censorship Board in the 1940s, the Gate staged several of her plays (as the Abbey had done with Una Troy a decade earlier). The most successful of Laverty's stage plays was *Tolka Row* (1951),[27] which depicted the lives of a working-class family moved from the inner city to one of the new housing estates on the city periphery. Mac Liammóir essayed a rare character role in this production. But most of the plays staged at the Gate were by continental rather than Irish authors, since it saw the latter as the Abbey's domain, and most required a leading role for the flamboyant acting of Mac Liammóir, which favoured the classic over the contemporary. With the latter's ongoing success in 1962 with his one-man show based on the life and works of Oscar Wilde, *The Importance of Being Oscar*, Edwards was freed up to consider directing contemporary Irish plays with younger men (like Donal Donnelly and Patrick Bedford as the two Gars) in the lead. The unparalleled theatrical demands of *Philadelphia* required the sophistication (in regard to lighting, movement, stage space, etc.) of Edwards's experience in world drama, in particular his skill at transforming a fixed conventional setting (the bedroom and kitchen of the O'Donnell household) into a fluid psychological space. Edwards went on after the success of *Philadelphia* to direct Friel's next three plays, two of them on Broadway: *The Loves of Cass Maguire* (1966) with Siobhán McKenna as the aged returned émigré from the US; *Lovers* (1967), Friel's thematically linked tales of young and old couples; and *Crystal and Fox* (1968), with Cyril Cusack and Maureen Toal as the eponymous owners of a tatty travelling theatre, Friel's dark parable on his own art and a precursor to *Faith Healer* (1980), but not a success at the time.

The 1960s saw other important plays staged on the subject of emigration. Tom Murphy's *The Fooleen* (rechristened *A Crucial Week in the Life of a Grocer's Assistant*) was first written in 1962 but not staged until later in the decade. It featured a wonderfully acerbic depiction of the returned émigré, back to flash his (alleged) fortune at the locals. He was one of the large cast surrounding the titular grocer's assistant John Joe, who finally decides not to emigrate and stands in the town square in the middle of the night broadcasting home truths to all and sundry. John B. Keane's *Many Young Men of Twenty* (1961) was first staged by the Southern Theatre Group at the Father Mathew Hall in Cork and was much produced around the country, where it was seen by a young Garry Hynes as her first theatrical encounter.[28] The play is based on the popular song 'Many Young Men of Twenty', and its pub setting provides a natural site for the singing and dancing which permeate the play and which so impressed themselves on the young Hynes. Another powerful example would be Eugene McCabe's *King of the Castle* (1963), where the older farmer unable to have a child uses a surrogate in the form of a virile young worker to impregnate his younger bride. John B. Keane wrote of the atavistic hold of the land on the race memory of Irish people in *The Field* (1965). In his portrait of the play's central character, 'The Bull' McCabe, Keane emphasised the brutal nature of the deed through which the Bull and his son Tadhg retained control of their land; but also brought out a stronger vein of mythic realism through his portrayal of a man who sought to hold on to what he saw as a sacred bond in the face of encroaching capitalism.[29] Keane's *Big Maggie* (1966) installed a fierce matriarch at the centre of its family drama, but it was only in the context of the play's 1980s Abbey staging that Keane felt free to add a lengthy monologue in which Maggie spoke of the frustration of her sexual desires. The increasing liberalisation in the 1960s only served Keane up to a point. Increasingly, in plays like *The Chastitute* (1980), his sensitivity to character and idiom was sacrificed to easy laughter at the supposedly ribald.

The key theatrical event of the 1960s was the long-promised (and much-deferred) opening of the new Abbey Theatre, in a design by Michael Scott and Ronald Tallon. The more visionary designs which had been contemplated were scaled down by Ernest Blythe's insistence that the new theatre remain on the old site of the Mechanics' Institute and by economic considerations in terms of what the government would be prepared to finance. The new Abbey had a fan-shaped auditorium and a seating capacity of 628. The stage was wide but shallow, 72 feet (21.5 metres) across, only 28 feet (8.4 metres) deep, though the forestage could be further extended.[30] The new stage space militated against the intimacy which had so much marked the earlier Abbey, and is one reason why O'Casey's *Juno and the Paycock* could be staged at the Gate Theatre so successfully in the 1980s, since the scale and design of the Gate more closely resembles that of the old Abbey. On the other hand, the greater technical flexibility of the new Abbey stage – with the stage floor adaptable to various levels and a more flexible lighting rig – made possible a more radical staging of an O'Casey play, such as Garry Hynes's neo-Brechtian production of *The Plough and the Stars* in 1991, where the human characters were reduced by the sheer scale of the war going on around them. In general, the more Expressionist aspects of O'Casey's playwriting, which developed in his writing from *The Plough* on, have been best served by the features of the new Abbey stage. Ironically, these were the very elements which had led to O'Casey being banished from the old Abbey; a point made magnificently clear by Hugh Hunt's staging of *The Silver Tassie* at the new Abbey in 1972, where Bronwen Casson's apocalyptic design for the notorious second act at the Somme made full use of the stage's scenic potential.

The new Abbey Theatre was opened on 18 July 1966 by the aged President, Eamon de Valera, in the same year as the upbeat celebration of the fiftieth anniversary of the Easter Rising, including a commemorative pageant staged by Tomás Mac Anna in the Phoenix Park. The new Peacock was opened the following year, 23 July 1967, by the then Minister for Finance, Charles J. Haughey. In a way the two events, though close together in time, vividly dramatise the shift from the old to the new Ireland, tensions which would be increasingly present in the idea of a National Theatre. For its first few years the Abbey and the Peacock managed to do honour both to its repertoire and to bringing an increasing number of the important new playwrights on to its two stages. The Peacock had 157 seats and a flexible staging arrangement which meant that plays could either be staged in a traditional if intimate proscenium manner; or as a sunken stage with seats heavily raked on both sides. While it tended to be the case that the plays from the repertoire were placed on the main stage, while new plays went on at the Peacock, the possibilities for theatrical experimentation were felt right across the National Theatre. Paradoxically, some of these possibilities stemmed from stage adaptations of popular Irish novels, notably Patrick Kavanagh's *Tarry Flynn* (1966) and Brendan Behan's *Borstal Boy* (1967). Tomás Mac Anna directed both and, far from finding the origins in a novel to be restrictive, gained access to a greater area of innovative staging, especially in the group movements which found an expressive idiom for life in a borstal, or in the barnyard scenes in *Tarry Flynn* which allowed for a greater degree of actorly innovation. The Peacock also became an important venue for plays in the Irish language, with its opening production in July 1967 a stage adaptation (again!) of Flann O'Brien/Myles na gCopaleen's satiric novel *An Béal Bocht/The Poor Mouth*. Beckett also was taken on by the National Theatre, in acknowledgement both of his Irishness and his 1969 Nobel Prize for Literature. *Waiting for Godot* was produced on the main stage in December of that year, with Peter O'Toole and Donal McCann as the two tramps, and the

Peacock followed its 1967 production of Beckett's *Play* with the world première of *Come and Go* the following year.

This Beckettian context, of an Irish playwright who simultaneously inhabited a milieu of European theatre, set a precedent for another important act of cultural reappropriation by the National Theatre in the late 1960s: the staging of two plays by Tom Murphy, *Famine* at the Peacock in 1968 and *A Crucial Week* at the Abbey in November 1969. Murphy had been living in England since 1962 and, though continuing to write plays, had had only one play staged in either country during that time. The cultural confidence betokened by the opening of the new Abbey and Peacock is nowhere better exemplified than in this support for a talented young contemporary playwright in exile. *A Crucial Week* had lost some of its newness by 1969 but still followed on from *Tarry Flynn* to present a less misty-eyed and more deliberately demythologising look at contemporary country life. Murphy's historical play *Famine*, written in London in the early 1960s, still retained its power to shock when staged at the Peacock in March 1968 by Tomás Mac Anna. With its titles before each scene, its large and shifting cast of characters, its use of different registers of speech and fragments of song and folklore, and above all the intimacy with an audience which the new Peacock enabled, *Famine* was an extraordinary translation of Brecht into an Irish context. What impinged negatively on the first few years of success at the new Abbey was the rapid turnover in artistic personnel. Blythe insisted he remain in control, only permitting the title 'artistic adviser' rather than 'artistic director' and that on a strict one-year contract. When Hugh Hunt found himself rapidly succeeding first Tomás Mac Anna and then Alan Simpson in this role, he insisted that the post be retitled 'artistic director' and that whoever occupied the position be given a greater measure of independence from the board.[31]

As the 1960s came to a close, the social optimism that had powered so many developments began to founder, nowhere more than in Northern Ireland. The civil rights movement began to seem naive in a context where it was being met with armed repression; and the British Army became a familiar sight on the streets. Brian Friel's plays began to register these changes. If the focus of his early plays had been primarily on familial relationships, a more complex aspect of that emerged in 1968's *Crystal and Fox*, when the theatrical couple's prodigal son returned from England. Welcomed home and given shelter, he is soon followed by two detectives who are looking for him on a charge of armed robbery. After Gabriel is arrested, Fox tries to raise money for his release but finally drives Crystal away by saying he has handed in their son. The IRA are never mentioned in the play, but the issues of loyalty and betrayal it dramatises are worked out in terms which the developments in the North would serve to illuminate. The subordinate criticism of the Southern state in *Philadelphia* is foregrounded by Friel in his 1969 political satire *The Mundy Scheme*, where a mendacious Taoiseach, while making high-minded noises about his nationalist credentials, plans to sell unprofitable boggy real estate in the west of Ireland to sentimental Irish-Americans. The play had been rejected by the Abbey as too controversial and was staged at the Olympia Theatre by the Dublin Theatre Festival in that year. The play is only a mixed success; but it is fuelled by a sense of unease and outrage, of a betrayal of idealism, of a sense that everything on the surface is not as comfortable as it may appear. As such, it seems an appropriate dramatic endnote to the 1960s.

The 1970s: tragic and comic disillusion

From the early 1970s, drama from and about Northern Ireland develops in significance. There is an important two-way process. The 'Troubles' play (as it came to be known) is a reflex of the intensely politicised and frequently violent events in the North that developed across twenty-five years. On the other hand, the playwrights and all of those involved in the act of theatre are attempting to create a space in which some kind of meaningful dialogue can be enacted, in which indeed the limitations of language can be both demonstrated and gone beyond. The Northern Irish play has marked dramaturgic features which may collectively constitute a new genre. Its particular stage procedures have developed in relation to the complex political and social order out of which they have emerged. For the most part, no single character dominates; instead, there is a protean ensemble as characters are displaced from their original affiliations into potentially new groupings and proto-communities. Structurally, Northern Irish drama moves in opposition to the well-made play, emphasising instead discontinuity, fragmentation and juxtaposition. The Northern Irish play is extremely sceptical with regard to language and language's claim to validate reality. Initially, the models were Shavian and in particular O'Caseyan, generating a good deal of talk to demonstrate its practical and political inefficacy. But the terms increasingly become Beckettian, recapitulated in a key of heightened realism, with the living confronted by the dead, speech challenged by silence.

The first Northern play to deal with the post-1969 violence was John Boyd's *The Flats*, staged in Belfast in March 1971. Boyd (b. 1912) was born in Ballymacarrett, a Protestant working-class neighbourhood in East Belfast. After completing a degree at Queen's University and some time as a teacher, he spent twenty-five years as a radio producer of plays at BBC Northern Ireland. *The Flats*, his second play, began Boyd's long and fruitful association with the Lyric Theatre, founded in 1967 by Mary O'Malley. While it always made a special place for staging Yeats's plays, which had their own ways of representing and responding to politically motivated acts of violence, the Lyric also sponsored the low-key realism of Boyd's playwriting, which offered a more immediate and graphic response to political events. The theatrical model for *The Flats* is clearly O'Casey.[32] The emphasis is on one particular working-class Catholic family, the Donnelans, in the midst of a tumultuous Belfast. But there are different inflections when this Junoesque O'Caseyan ensemble is moved to 1970 Northern Ireland. The daughter now throws over the local suitor, not for a wealthier man from outside her class, but for a British soldier. The trope of an exogamous relationship between the local Irish girl and the British soldier posted to Ireland was to prove remarkably durable. Tragedy is inevitable and the play ends with the soldier bringing on the dead body of Monica Donnelan. The interest of *The Flats* is primarily historic. It captures the moment when the British Army, which had been called in to protect the Catholics from the Protestants, gave way to an insurgent defence movement from within the Catholic community; the play vividly demonstrates the forces which made this inevitable.

The most politically engaged piece of theatre about Northern Ireland in the early 1970s came, surprisingly and uncharacteristically, from Brian Friel. His 1973 play *The Freedom of the City* was staged simultaneously on 20 February at the Abbey Theatre in Dublin, in a production directed by Tomás Mac Anna, and at the Royal Court Theatre in London, where the director was the stage and film actor Albert Finney. Although the play is distanced in time to 1970, its most immediate provocation was the death by shooting of thirteen members of a civil rights protest march in Derry on 30 January 1972, what soon became known as 'Bloody Sunday'. More precisely, the play takes one of its primary dramatic bearings from the Widgery Tribunal, which subsequently investigated the event and exonerated the British Army from all blame. *Freedom of the City* is framed as a dramatic investigation into the series of events by which three civil rights marchers who occupied the mayor's Guild Hall parlour in Derry came to be shot by the Army. The key question in both cases is whether they were armed or not. A series of witnesses from the army, the police and the medical profession give testimony in a dry, empirical fashion. The judge says early on that he wishes to 'make abundantly clear . . . that this tribunal of inquiry, appointed by her Majesty's Government, is in no sense a court of justice . . . It is essentially a fact-finding exercise.'[33] Other commentators also fill the stage:

a Catholic priest addressing his congregation; an RTE commentator covering the funerals; a republican balladeer who adds the dead trio to the pantheon of republican martyrs; an American sociologist who represents them as victims of a 'culture of poverty'. Where, then, is justice to be found? The play itself has opened with the shooting dead of Michael, Lily and Skinner; and as it unfolds we see them come to life again as the play presents its own version of what occurred in the Guild Hall. *Freedom* presses beyond the limits of realism since those limits serve only to prop up the status quo. It offers drama as an alternative discourse to the procedures by which official history is recorded. In its furthest break with realism, the three protestors at the moment of their death articulate an objective assessment of their lives. Lily, the working-class Catholic mother of a large family, whose humour and resilience are the life force of the play, is pierced not only by the bullets but by the recognition that

> life had eluded me because never once in my forty-three years had an experience, an event, even a small unimportant happening been isolated, and assessed, and articulated. And the fact that this, my last experience, was defined by this perception, this was the culmination of sorrow. In a way I died of grief.[34]

The two most important of the younger generation of Northern Irish playwrights who emerged in the 1970s were Stewart Parker (1941–88) and Graham Reid (b. 1945). Parker was born in East Belfast and attended Queen's University there. Having spent some time studying and teaching in the US, Parker returned to his native Belfast shortly after the outbreak of the Troubles; he subsequently lived in Edinburgh and London. Tragically, he died of cancer on 7 November 1988. Like Synge and Behan before him, here was a major Irish playwright cut off in his prime; but the sense with Parker was that he still had much more to contribute. Nevertheless, between 1975 and 1988, he produced nine stage plays, nine radio plays, seven television plays and a six-part television series, *Lost Belongings*, which updated the legend of Deirdre and the Sons of Usna to 1980s Belfast. Stewart Parker's unique sense of play enabled him to treat of that most deadly and potentially deadening of subjects, the contemporary crisis in Northern Ireland, with an unrivalled wit and lightness of touch. Music made a central contribution to his drama. His first play, *Spokesong*, staged during the Dublin Theatre Festival of 1975, was a Flann O'Brien-like history of a Belfast bicycle shop which amounted virtually to a musical. The lyrics were by Parker and the music by fellow Northerner Jimmy Kennedy, composer of 'Red Sails in the Sunset' and 'South of the Border (Down Mexico

Way)'. In his second play, *Catchpenny Twist* (1977), the two male leads Roy and Martyn are archetypal Parker dreamers. They earn a living writing ballads for opposed sets of paramilitaries while dreaming of success in the Eurovision Song contest. The songwriters offend both factions and leave town, failing to win the contest and opening a parcel that explodes in their faces.[35] In his first two plays, the Protestant Parker broke the mould by bringing a colourful imagination to bear on a community often characterised as dour and grey and showing it had a culture worth celebrating.

The plays of Graham Reid are at the opposite end of the spectrum from Parker's, their humour of a more acrid kind and their engagement with violence and its trauma unflinching in its directness. Reid was born in Belfast and having left school at fifteen returned to full-time studies when he was twenty-six, graduating from Queen's University in 1976. His first play, *The Death of Humpty Dumpty* (1979), remains in ways his most powerful. Set in a Belfast hospital, it deals with someone who is not centrally involved in the conflict but has been a victim of one of its many acts of random violence. His Humpty Dumpty is George Sampson, a school-teacher; Reid's 1983 play *The Hidden Curriculum* was to be set in a Belfast school. But Sampson is neither a role model nor a complaisant victim. The play's flashbacks show his abusive relationship with his family, that he is repeatedly unfaithful to his wife and tyrannises his children. In the play's present, he is in turn brutalised by a sadistic orderly and the play's violent end has his two children smothering him in his bed. But the play's greatest violence is verbal, an astonishing torrent of invective and rage that pours out of Sampson in relation to his being paralysed from the neck down. There is again a link to O'Casey, in this case to the disabled WWI soldier and former soccer player Harry Heegan in *The Silver Tassie*. Both plays make the point that the most uncomfortable presences in a time of violent conflict are not those who survive and can resume their lives, nor those who die and can be martyrised or sentimentalised; but the living dead, the walking wounded, who refuse to lie down and be quiet.

The changing political climate brought a more cynical attitude in the South, in contrast with the innocent acceptance that had greeted the 1966 celebrations of the Easter Rising. And the unprecedented affluence which became the hallmark of the new Catholic bourgeoisie lent itself to satire. Hugh Leonard duly obliged with his play *The Patrick Pearse Motel*, produced in March 1971 for the Dublin Theatre Festival. The Festival had been an important platform for Leonard in the 1960s, staging his technically sophisticated stage adaptation of Joyce's *A Portrait of the Artist* (as *Stephen D*) and of John McGahern's *The Barracks*. Leonard had spent most of the 1960s in London, writing stage and television adaptations of prose fiction by English and Irish authors. But the decision by finance minister Charles Haughey to grant tax-free status to creative writers for money earned from their writings enabled Leonard to return to live in Dublin and to devote himself full-time to original plays for the stage. In one sense, *The Patrick Pearse Motel* is another adaptation, since it is clearly indebted to Feydeau farce. But the characters, the settings and the issues are so fully translated to suburban south Dublin in the early 1970s that the result is an original work. The setting is Foxrock, 'a suburb in Dublin's vodka-and-bitter-lemon belt',[36] where the younger of the two couples, Dermod and Gráinne, live. Their names recall the two legendary lovers, with the direction of the proposed sexual betrayal altered. This ironic mismatch between past and present will reoccur in the motel of the title, named after the executed 1916 leader and with rooms appropriately devoted to many of Ireland's martyred dead. Leonard followed this contemporary farce with a succession of plays throughout the 1970s, all of which hinged on a double time scheme, a juxtaposition of the same characters in the present and the past. The most outstanding was his play of 1973, *Da*, an autobiographical work which went on to Broadway and a Tony Award for the dramatist. It dealt with the biographical circumstances by which John Keyes Byrne, an orphan, was adopted by an older working-class couple as a child. Now a well-to-do writer living in London, Charlie is summoned home for the funeral of his cantankerous and opinionated old father. The play opens with his return from the graveyard to what he presumes is the now deserted family home. But the big chair is occupied as it always has been by his da, who may be dead but refuses to go away, even when his son enjoins him to 'piss off'.[37] The older Charlie is than treated to a Dickensian succession of scenes from his childhood and adolescence, with his idiosyncratic father, his socially minded mother and the spectacle of his younger self. The play is a brilliant dissection of the issue of class in a changing Ireland, and the embarrassment of the nouveau riche writer at a past that will not let him alone. In his 1979 play *A Life* Leonard elevated a minor figure from *Da*, his civil service employer Drumm, to central-character status and subjected this desiccated, dying man to a series of flashbacks to his youth to see where his life had taken a wrong turning. 1979 also saw the stage debut of Bernard Farrell (b. 1939), who has proved in many ways Leonard's successor as satirist of the south Dublin, nouveau riche bourgeoisie. His debut play, *I Do Not Like Thee, Dr. Fell,* set the template with its couples submitting themselves to self-help therapy and having more than they bargained for revealed in the process. Farrell has written a series of successful comedies over the decades, the best of which – 1993's *Last Apache Reunion* – reveal a darker, less accommodating facet of his talent.

This play, focusing on a school reunion, resurrects the tormenting of a gay classmate in ways that go beyond the stereotypes to which Farrell's plays can succumb.

Another major playwright brought back from London to Dublin by Haughey's tax concessions was Tom Murphy. No doubt encouraged by the Abbey's staging of two of the plays he had written in London, he now offered them a third, *The Morning After Optimism*, which was given a sumptuous staging by Hugh Hunt on the main stage for the 1971 Theatre Festival. Into the enchanting otherworld forest setting of Bronwen Casson's design run two incongruous figures, the ageing whore Rosie and her pimp James. The play and its production managed to bring together the poetic drama of the theatre's founders with the realism and greater freedom of expression of the 1960s. The play is linguistically adventurous, even more so than Murphy's norm. It juxtaposes the tough-guy idiom of Rosie and James with the archaic patter of the young lovers, only to expose a vein of hidden lyricism in the former and to show up the latter as banal and studied. But the play's remoteness from the everyday is too extreme and the plays Murphy subsequently wrote show a greater engagement with the realities of contemporary Irish life, as Leonard's also did. *The White House* (1972) contrasted the idealism of the 1960s with the increasing disillusionment of the 1970s. This was originally reflected in its two-act structure: the 1960s act showed a group of young people gathering around a charismatic older man who bore an uncanny resemblance to John F. Kennedy; the 1970s act saw them reassembling years later to welcome back one of their number who had emigrated. The relation between the two acts was always problematic and the running order was switched during the run. In the 1980s Murphy revisited the play and brilliantly solved the problem by cutting the chronologically earlier act. In its revised one-act version, *Conversations on a Homecoming*, the 1960s is now never directly represented. The charismatic JJ is now an offstage presence, like Beckett's Godot, endlessly invoked but never seen. Only one of the characters has been a 'success', Liam; and it is towards him that the pub owner, Missus, is steering her young daughter. Liam and the values he represents are memorably denounced by the school teacher Tom: 'This eejit, this bollocks, with his auctioneering and tax-collecting and travel-agenting and property dealing and general greedy unprincipled poncing, and Sunday night dancing – Mr. Successful swinging-Ireland-in-the-Seventies.'[38] Murphy's third Abbey main stage play of the 1970s, *The Sanctuary Lamp*, staged a full frontal assault on the Catholic Church which provoked walkouts from the theatre on a scale not seen since the days of Synge and O'Casey. Murphy's attack was an informed one, since he worked in the 1970s as a lay member of the International Commission on the Use of English in the liturgy. The place of refuge is now a church, both an actual and a symbolic place, already occupied by the waif-like figure of Maudie, entered into by the circus strongman Harry, and subsequently joined by the vengeance-minded Francisco, threatening to kill Harry for an imagined affair with his wife Olga. The three social misfits form an alternative (holy) family; but the true dialogue is with the absent or absconded God.

At the Abbey Theatre in the 1970s, the old order was changing. Ernest Blythe finally stepped down from the board in 1972. Figures associated with the earlier development of Irish theatre – like Hugh Hunt and Alan Simpson – had returned for important productions and their wealth of experience lent real quality to the new Abbey's first five years. But they could not be expected to continue forever; and the 1970s saw a necessary and welcome changing of the guard. Tomás Mac Anna, the most important link at the Abbey throughout these decades and with much still to contribute, was always a keen-eyed encourager of young talent; and never more so than when he promoted the young actor-turned-director Joe Dowling to artistic directorship of the Peacock Theatre, where a conscious effort was made to attract younger audiences, most notably through stylish productions of Shakespearean comedy. When he in turn became artistic director of the National Theatre in the late 1970s, Dowling and script editor Sean McCarthy (another significant development) actively encouraged a developmental approach to playwriting which brought new talent to light. Dowling also kept a very important space on the Abbey main stage for the work Brian Friel was doing through the 1970s, whatever the reception of any one production. In this decade the Abbey premièred three major new Friel plays in succession: *Volunteers* (1975), which brought together the internment of republican prisoners with the protests in Dublin overturning the excavated Viking village into a car park; *Living Quarters* (1977), a reworking of *Phèdre* in its story of the tragic liaison between the stepmother and son of an acclaimed Irish military hero; and *Aristocrats* (1979), which declares Friel's burgeoning interest in Chekhov in this study of the fate of a Catholic Big House. These plays reveal how the pressures of the decade drove Friel to develop as a dramatist by finding theatrical resources to mediate and provide perspective on the insistent topicality of the daily news bulletins.

The other important arrival at the Abbey in the 1970s was a protégé of Hunt's from England, Patrick Mason, who was to become, like Dowling, an artistic director at the theatre and an important director of productions by contemporary playwrights. Virtually Mason's first assignment as director was a 1977 production of Thomas Kilroy's *Talbot's Box* at the Peacock. Kilroy (b. 1934) had started life as an academic, lecturing in English at University College, Dublin, and going on to become Professor of English at NUI Galway. He has always been one of the foremost critics of Irish drama, with a particularly keen insight into the work of the Protestant Anglo-Irish tradition. Kilroy's deepest instincts were creative and he has contributed some of the most theatrically innovative and thematically challenging works to the contemporary canon. His first play, *The Death and Resurrection of Mr Roche*, was staged at the Dublin Theatre Festival in 1969 and memorably depicted an all-night drinking party in which the young men eventually scapegoat a middle-aged homosexual, the Mr Roche of the title. *Talbot's Box* in 1977 confirmed the extent to which Kilroy is attracted to the marginalised or eccentric figure whose radical individuality threatens the social norm. In the case of the Dublin working-class mystic Matt Talbot (1856–1925), Kilroy had to overcome an initial difficulty of identification with such a figure of devout belief. But in a way the author's unease mirrors the doubts of many in Irish society in the 1970s with regard to its traditional religious allegiances. *Talbot's Box* makes more clear than Kilroy's debut how theatrically adventurous his work is. In Mason's production and Wendy Shea's design the entire stage was framed with '*a huge box*',[39] designed to suggest in turn a coffin, a confession box, a witness stand, a wooden bulwark constructed by Talbot the carpenter against the encroaching chaos. It is also Thomas Kilroy's own box of theatrical tricks, the props and stratagems of the playwright's trade openly on display. The play begins with Talbot's corpse being brought to the morgue, where the stripping and revealing of the emaciated body, hunger increased by fasting, reveals it to be wrapped in chains. The play is from the start a consciously theatrical re-enactment of Talbot's life, which runs parallel with the turbulent founding of the Irish state. *Talbot's Box* pairs up with Murphy's *Sanctuary Lamp* in the extent to which a questioning of traditional Catholicism in contemporary Irish drama led to more radical but not necessarily less spiritual ends.

Outside of Dublin and Northern Ireland, the key theatrical development in 1970s theatre had a modest beginning in the west of Ireland. There, two students who had met and worked together in college productions at University College, Galway – director Gearóidín (Garry) Hynes (b. 1953) and actress Marie Mullen – decided when they graduated that they wanted to form their own company and lead a life in the theatre. Having approached and won the interest of Mick Lally, an established actor at Galway's Irish-language theatre An Taibhdhearc, the three founded the Druid Theatre Company in 1975. Like so much of the work done in universities and by the newer companies of the time, many of the plays chosen were by non-Irish, particularly continental, playwrights. But Druid had an awareness that they were from the west of Ireland, a region which, while it had been the symbolic locus for much Irish drama, had had little in the way of professional theatres. An important element of their artistic programme was reclaiming plays that had had their origins in the west – such as a landmark production of M. J. Molloy's *The Wood of the Whispering* in 1983. Druid first made its mark with their innovative staging of Synge's *Playboy of the Western World*. The peasants presented in their version were far removed from the romanticised versions that had long held Dublin stages. This was a Pegeen Mike who did indeed stink of poteen. And the Widow Quin, traditionally cast as a much older woman and hence grotesque in her desire for Christy Mahon, was now played by Marie Mullen as a still sexually attractive young woman in her twenties, and hence real competition for Pegeen. The violence of the play, in particular the climactic fight between father and son, was rendered more graphic and immediate by the intimacy of the staging at Druid's tiny theatre in Chapel Lane. The confidence of their production of Synge was also grounded on a thorough knowledge of the Irish language, syntax and structures that underlay Synge's speech and gave it its radical authenticity. The company's policy of touring meant that their production of Synge was seen all over Ireland, including on the Aran Islands. By the end of the 1970s the emergence of Druid set the pattern for other important theatre companies to develop outside Dublin and Belfast.

The 1980s: transcendence and achievement

The 1980s was the decade of greatest achievement as far as the period under review is concerned. Brian Friel topped and tailed it with two of his most culturally resonant and widely acclaimed plays, *Translations* (1980) and *Dancing at Lughnasa* (1990). Tom Murphy re-emerged with a vengeance with his two greatest plays, *The Gigli Concert* (1983) and *Bailegangaire* (1985), both of which received productions and performances to match. Thomas Kilroy only managed one new play in the decade, but *Double Cross* (1986) surpassed even his high standards. The decade was marked by the emergence of a number of important new playwrights, none more so than Frank McGuinness, whose second play, *Observe the Sons of Ulster Marching Towards the Somme* (1985), achieved the same status of instant classic as Friel's *Translations*. An important experiment to move Irish theatre away from its fixation on the verbal towards a greater emphasis on the image emerged in the three-way collaboration between director Patrick Mason, actor Tom Hickey and playwright Tom MacIntyre. And women playwrights, who had been so conspicuous an absence on the Irish scene, emerged from Northern Ireland, with such figures as Anne Devlin, Christina Reid and Marie Jones's collaboration with Eleanor Methven and Carol Scanlon in the Charabanc Theatre Company.

Friel's *Translations* was the inaugurating production of the Field Day Theatre Company. Co-founded by playwright Friel and actor Stephen Rea, it was soon augmented by a board comprising writer and academic Seamus Deane, poet Seamus Heaney, musicologist David Hammond, poet and critic Tom Paulin and (some years later) by playwright Thomas Kilroy, the only Southerner in the group. In terms of theatre, Field Day arose from Rea's wish to act in productions in his own place (his career was largely London-based) and from Friel's to have the plays staged initially in the place where they had been written and which they represented. In this act, they did much to reverse the trend whereby the sources of Irish drama were often in remote, rural areas but were written to be staged in and for the metropolitan centre, whether Dublin, Belfast or London. Field Day did not intend for the productions to remain local. Instead, after the initial week's run in Derry, the company toured the production around a number of venues in the two Irelands, at one level recreating the fit-up companies of old, at another helping to develop a taste for cutting edge new plays in rural areas. And for Field Day their enterprise was cultural and political in its scope and energies. Even the choice of venue in a town like Derry which had no proper theatre and which had been denied a proper university was symbolically apt: the mayoral Guild Hall with its legacy for the Catholics of gerrymandering and second-class citizenship. Since then, all these features have changed; but the need for such change was highlighted by Field Day's activities. The first nights in the Guild Hall saw Sinn Féin, SDLP and Unionists of various shades within the same social and political space. Under Deane's direction, Field Day also undertook a series of pamphlets on Irish writing. This soon grew into the mammoth *Field Day Anthology* project, which sought to found a canon from works which had either 'disappeared' into the English canon (like the plays of Wilde and Shaw) or which had enjoyed very little prominence. In the political vacuum that was Northern Ireland in the 1980s, Field Day wished to make the same kind of cultural intervention, to conjure a 'fifth province' as they put it, as the founders of the Irish Literary Revival had a century earlier. The enduring importance and continuing influence of the work they did during the decade justifies the comparison.[40]

Like the first theatre movement, they engaged with the issue of language, in particular what language is appropriate to an Irish theatre that works through the medium of English. Friel's *Translations* approached the subject philosophically by drawing on George Steiner's *After Babel: Aspects of Language and Translation* and historically by looking at the period in nineteenth-century Ireland when the English language began to establish its hegemony. The play centres on the visit of the Ordnance Survey Commission to a remote area of Donegal to map the area and in particular to translate the place names from Irish to English. The play's setting is a hedge school where the locals are educated (principally in Greek and Latin) by schoolmaster Hugh, one of whose sons teaches with him, the other of whom arrives as translator. The setting may seem idyllic; certainly it seems so to Lieutentant Yolland, when he watches rural people spouting the Classical languages as if time had passed them by and particularly when he meets Maire Chatach (Maire of the curly hair). But the appearance is deceptive. For this is a society on its last legs, with pressure for change coming not only from outside but from within, as when Maire challenges Hugh to teach her English rather than Latin or Greek, saying that is what she'll need when she emigrates to Brooklyn. Hugh finally agrees: 'Yes, I will teach you English, Maire Chatach. . . . But don't expect too much. I will provide you with the available words and the available grammar. But will that help you to interpret between privacies? I have no idea. But it's all we have.'[41] The only Irish words heard in the play are the place-names: Bun na hAbhann, Tobair Vree, etc. The central dramatic conceit is that the Irish characters within the play are speaking Irish but that we hear them as English. Thus, when Owen translates what Captain Lancey is saying to his family and father's pupils, everything we hear is in English and the air of mutual mis-comprehension between the two cultures is fully conveyed. The effect in act 1 verges on farce; but the tragic aspect emerges in act 3, when Yolland disappears and Lancey threatens an eviction; on this occasion the act of translation is brutally direct. Friel has spoken of the fact that all four of his grandparents were Gaelic-speaking and yet within two generations almost all of that has been lost. The play struck a chord in its Irish audience, allowing them to reimagine a crucial event in the development of Irish consciousness from the perspective of the present. But criticism was subsequently voiced about the issue of historical accuracy in the play, in such details as the British soldiers anachronistically employing bayonets. And there was a sense that Friel had loaded the dice dramatically in his presentation of the English commanding officer who not only did not know any Irish but knew none of the Classical languages, either. Friel's 1988 Field Day play *Making History* counters these criticisms by arguing that the writing of history, no less than the writing of a play, involves the construction of a narrative; that every chronicle of the past is also a literary construct whose facts are shaped and selected by the model it chooses to follow (comic or tragic, praise or blame) and by the pressures of the present.

Friel's second annual play for Field Day in 1981 was a version of Anton Chekhov's *Three Sisters*. The play itself remained set in Russia but the language spoken was designed to sit easier on the tongues of Irish actors than the standard translations which came via London. Friel's version of the Chekhov needs to be set in the context of the cultural confidence which in 1980s Ireland saw an increasing popularity of adaptations of Greek tragedy and versions of Russian and Scandinavian drama. Some of these were sponsored by Field Day – for example, Tom Paulin's 1984 version of Sophocles' *Antigone*, *The Riot Act*. The characters and setting in the Paulin version remained the struggle between Antigone and her uncle Creon over the burial rites of her dead brother; but the language moved closer to that of Northern Ireland: 'You're talking wild.'[42] And a clear parallel emerged between the characters and recognisable figures from the Northern political landscape. But events in the South saw two versions of *Antigone* written there in the same year (1984) by poets Aidan Carl Mathews and Brendan Kennelly. Mathews was provoked by the series of repressive legal measures, the curbing of individual liberties carried out ostensibly as a response to the crisis in the North; Kennelly's was overtly feminist, in a decade which saw measures to introduce abortion and divorce into Ireland overthrown. But the fullest linguistic and geographic translation of a foreign classic was Thomas Kilroy's 1981 version of Chekhov's *The Seagull* (originally for London's Royal Court Theatre) where the characters, events and setting were transposed from Russia at the end of the nineteenth century to the west of Ireland, with the actress-mother as a star on the London stage and her idealistic poet-son a Yeats figure who wishes to bring a Celtic theatre into existence. All of these versions brought about what has been called a 'benign colonisation'.[43] They reversed the trend by which Irish stagings of the foreign classical repertoire were merely provincial replications of the London style and idiom of production. Instead, they drew on the strengths of the native tradition to forge a distinctly Irish version of the classics, while also placing them in the context of European and world theatre.

The two most important original works created by Field Day, after *Translations*, were Kilroy's *Double Cross* (1986) and Stewart Parker's *Pentecost* (1987). Kilroy's two roughly contemporary Irish protagonists both undergo a process of self-reinvention. Brendan Bracken became an Englishman, Churchill's Minister for Information in World War II, while William Joyce adopted the persona of Lord Haw Haw in his notorious radio broadcasts from Nazi Germany.

Both parts were performed in a stunning *tour de force* by Field Day co-founder Stephen Rea, and a clever use of video enabled them to appear in the same scene. Both relied uniquely on the projection of voice to establish their identity and this gives a certain ironic appropriateness to their fates, one killed by cancer of the throat, the other hanged as a traitor. The play was originally intended by Kilroy as a Field Day pamphlet and then it evolved to dramatise issues central to Field Day's debates: the relation between language and identity; the hazardous crossing over of established boundaries; the inevitability of betraying self and others in any movement beyond the tribe. Bracken and Joyce both become, not free individuals who have shed their Irish past, but men who have traded in the role of historical victim for the mirror image of oppressor and placed all their faith in the symbols of the culturally dominant race. *Pentecost* was produced by Field Day in 1987, ironically giving Parker his greatest success just before he died and rebutting the notion that Field Day was some sort of nationalist cabal. The play sets a personal drama – the deteriorating marriage of solicitor Marian and itinerant musician Lenny – against the political backdrop of the Ulster Workers' Strike of 1974. Lenny's relationship with Marian – they cannot live together, they cannot live apart – has certain features in common with Northern Ireland itself; but they are reluctant to declare their marriage a failed entity. Holed up in a house with another damaged couple during the siege, they are joined by the ghost of the dead woman Lily Mathews who has lived in the house all her life and wants them gone. The characters largely have to work out their own salvation. But that the term 'salvation' is justified is indicated by the play's setting on Pentecost Sunday and the injunction to 'speak with other tongues, as the Spirit gave them utterance'.[44] And the presence of Lily's ghost adds an earlier generation's experience to the process of reconciliation. Lenny fuses spirituality and sexuality through the music he plays on his beloved trombone; Marian discovers her buried self through taking on Lily's suppressed history and the shared loss of a child. The characters' personal politics speak to the politics of the province, reminding everyone who cares about the North that, in Parker's words, 'there is a whole culture to be achieved'.[45]

If Field Day's achievement comprehended both Catholic and Protestant, its exclusions are also revealing. When the three-volume *Field Day Anthology of Irish Writing* was published in 1991, there was an outcry at the paucity of women's writing represented by the all-male members of the editorial board. A similar observation might be made about the exclusively male membership of the board of the Field Day Theatre Company and of the playwrights they sponsored. But Northern Irish women playwrights were not waiting on Field

Day for an invitation to contribute. The situation in the North, through its questioning of inherited norms of identity, has brought several significant women playwrights to the fore. This development is all the more striking in contrast to the Republic of Ireland where (with the exception of Marina Carr) women playwrights have been markedly absent from the main stages. Theatre, more than the other forms of literature, is a social praxis; and as such remains bound up in and replicates the power structures of the society in which it is produced. While Irish theatre has been happy to present a succession of actresses onstage, the key roles of writer and director remained for many decades in men's hands. All the evidence suggests that women in the Republic have been writing plays, but that these plays have not been staged. For example, when the *Irish Times* sponsored a women playwrights' competition in 1982, 188 plays were submitted for the prize of £1,000. The winner, Mary Halpin's *Semi-Private*, received a production in that year's Dublin Theatre Festival and has been successfully revived many times since.[46] But such initiatives were rare and were not matched by any pro-active move from the theatres themselves. Since politically it still remains part of the United Kingdom, Northern Ireland retains close cultural and economic ties with London; and so a Northern Irish woman playwright like Anne Devlin (b. 1951) can look to the Royal Court Theatre there, and its fostering of feminist playwrights like Caryl Churchill, to encourage her emergence as a dramatist. Her first play, *Ourselves Alone* (1986), was commissioned by the Royal Court; her second, *After Easter* (1996), by the Royal Shakespeare Company. Both plays are striking for their staging of the fraught relationship between Ireland and England in terms of gender politics and for their reimagining of relationships through a radical experimentation with dramatic form.

Christina Reid (b. 1942), from a Protestant working-class background in Belfast, is one of the few contemporary Irish women playwrights to have had a continuous working career in theatre. The feminist emphasis of her play *Tea in a China Cup*, staged in Belfast at the Lyric in 1983, is on the supportive interaction of working-class Protestant women. The story is laced with sardonic humour and is told through the mother–daughter relationship of Sarah and Beth, one dying, the other struggling to come to terms with her own identity. Like Parker's *Pentecost*, the play is set in 1970s Belfast and reaches back to the past to represent the experiences of its Belfast family in the two world wars and in the contemporary Troubles. Unlike Friel's memory plays, the memories dramatised in *Tea in a China Cup* are more than personal; they extend beyond their teller into the lives and material conditions of those women among and by whom she was reared.

A major development in women's theatre in Northern Ireland was the founding of the Charabanc Theatre Company in 1983. It was a collaborative venture proceeding from five actresses who were stung by the absence of strong roles for women in Irish theatre. As one of them remarked: 'I played nothing but Noras and Cathleens.'[47] Three went on to form the nucleus of the company: Marie (Sarah) Jones, Carol Scanlon Moore and Eleanor Methven. The writing and the performing (but not the directing) were collaborative. For their first project, the company decided to research the lives of Belfast women working in the linen mills early in the century, and to focus a play around the mill workers' strike of 1911. Belfast playwright Martin Lynch, whom they initially approached, encouraged them to write it themselves 'and I'll help' and the result was *Lay Up Your Ends*, which established Charabanc's combination of social acuity and satiric comedy. In the subsequent years of the 1980s, they divided the year into six months of researching and writing the plays and six months of extensive touring in Northern and Southern Ireland. Their touring venues were designed to cross traditional class divides, in venues ranging from conventional theatres to community centres and church halls. Belfast's Divis Flats was the setting of the 1988 Charabanc production, *Somewhere Over the Balcony*, which takes place on the eve of internment. The women left behind are potentially more subversive, since they remain on the outside. As such, they are continuously under surveillance. We become aware as audience of (and are implicated in) the presence of offstage anonymous forces watching the women on the balcony of their flats. This Beckettian set-up provokes great resistance in terms of the verbal defiance the women hurl at their observers and even more by the surrealistic verve with which they reimagine the terms of their daily lives. When these verbal resources and the women's mutual support fail, there are moments of isolation and an underlying sadness. *Balcony* was the last collaborative Charabanc venture. After *The Hamster Wheel* in 1990, which Marie Jones singly authored, she left the group to pursue a solo writing career; the group disbanded in 1995. Jones broke through in the 1990s to an unprecedented level of success for a contemporary Irish woman playwright, with *Women on the Verge of HRT*, *A Night in November* and *Stones in their Pockets* all enjoying long runs in London and New York.

If there was one play in the 1980s that got away from Field Day, it was Frank McGuinness's *Observe the Sons of Ulster Marching Towards the Somme* (1985). Northern Protestant writers like Derek Mahon, Tom Paulin and Stewart Parker who contributed plays to Field Day were generally in reaction against the perceived character of Ulster unionism as dour, humourless and generally without culture. So perhaps it is appropriate that it took a Catholic from

Buncrana, County Donegal, to write a powerful and moving drama about eight representatives of the 6,000 members of the thirty-sixth Ulster Division who were slaughtered at the Battle of the Somme on 1 July 1916. The play takes the form of an old man, Kenneth Pyper, forced to relive yet again the trauma of the war, the death of his friends in the regiment and in particular of the man he loved, David Craig. The presence of Pyper in the midst of the Ulster Volunteers complicates the political issue by raising sexuality and manhood as a challenge to all of the characters. That the audience is drawn into the collective fates of the hard men from Ulster and into the doomed love affair between Pyper and Craig is a tribute to the lengths McGuinness will go, in particular the extremes of humour and despair which are negotiated. The eight sons of Ulster learn to endure through the most modest of means, a handful of words, some simple gestures, to improvise a mode of going on when their own fears tell them they cannot. McGuinness proved astonishingly prolific in the years after *Sons of Ulster*. His life of Caravaggio, *Innocence*, was produced at the Gate in Dublin in 1986. In 1988, *Carthaginians* was staged during the Dublin Theatre Festival at the Peacock. Originally, it had been intended for production by Field Day in 1987 along with Parker's *Pentecost*. But McGuinness became unhappy with the demands that two full-length plays were putting on the company's resources and withdrew his. A Catholic counterpart to the Protestant emphasis of the earlier play, *Carthaginians* shows its characters struggling with the trauma surrounding Bloody Sunday as they gather in a Derry graveyard to await the resurrection of the dead. By the end of the 1980s such works as these had established Frank McGuinness as the strongest new Irish dramatist to emerge.

The 1980s in the South saw the decentralisation of Irish theatre and an increasingly dynamic regional theatre: in Waterford, Red Kettle, with local playwright Jim Nolan, who had already enjoyed an Abbey main stage production with *Moonshine*; in Limerick, Island, where Mike Finn moved from directing to writing; in Clonmel, Gallowglass; and in Ennis, Theatre Omnibus. The most important development in this respect in the mid-1980s were the two years Tom Murphy spent as writer-in-association with Druid. It brought the Tuam native back from Dublin to theatrical developments in Galway; and it forged an important link between the company and a contemporary Irish playwright, one of the very best, which enabled them to build on what had been accomplished with their Synge and M. J. Molloy productions. For Druid, Murphy revised his earlier play *White House* as the one-act *Conversations on a Homecoming*. But on 5 December 1985 Druid premiered a masterpiece, Murphy's *Bailegangaire* (from the Irish, 'town without laughter'), in which – unusually for the playwright and the Irish stage – all three of the characters were women (as was the director, Garry Hynes).[48] The play brings two worlds into creative conflict. It presents the mythic timelessness of an old woman sitting in a bed reciting a folk-tale to her two granddaughters, Mary and Dolly, in a thatched cottage setting; but the time is 1984, as the text and the off-stage sounds reminds us, with cars and helicopters passing and references to computers and Japanese factories in the locality. What renders the context grotesque is that the old woman is senile and rambling and the two granddaughters in their early forties. Mommo's oft-told and never completed story hinges around the fateful death of the third grandchild, Tom; the concern in the present is with Dolly's unwanted pregnancy. As so often in his plays, Murphy is proving himself the most incisive commentator on the Southern (rather than the Northern) crisis and social change in the Republic over these decades. The character Dolly's declared intent to bury the baby in a field resonated off the legal and constitutional debates surrounding the control of women's fertility in the Republic of Ireland during the 1980s and in particular two key events in 1984: as Nicholas Grene puts it, 'the death in labour of a fifteen-year-old schoolgirl at the end of a pregnancy completely concealed from her family, and the notorious "Kerry Babies" case in which not one but two murdered infants were found in a single area of Kerry'.[49] The part of Mommo was memorably performed by Siobhán McKenna (also a homecoming for her, since she started her career at the Taibhdhearc); it proved to be her swansong when she died a year later. If Murphy's Mommo recalled the tragic heroines in *Cathleen ni Houlihan* and *Riders to the Sea*, a more post-modern association was with Beckett's Mouth in *Not I*. Persistently refusing to relinquish the third person, Mommo and Mouth are also alike in the stuttering, fragmented, terrified and repetitious quality of their verbal outpourings.

Two years earlier, Murphy had re-emerged from the doldrums with *The Gigli Concert* at the Abbey. Like so many of the most important plays of the 1980s, it was directed by Patrick Mason, whose experience of directing opera helped him to tackle an epic play which could be seen as a contemporary version of Faust. As so often in Murphy, the apparently realistic setting – here, of a psychiatrist's dingy office – works as a kind of refuge for a character running from the oppressive conditions of his life. Here, the symbolically named Irish Man represents both the material success brought to him by his life as a building developer and the spiritual anomie that accompanies it. His mad desire to sing like Gigli speaks both to his vaunting ambition and to his self-disgust.

Since the quack doctor the Irish Man seeks out is an Englishman, Murphy can make the play at one level a Shavian debate about Irishness and Englishness. But *The Gigli Concert* also acknowledges an increasingly post-Catholic society which can no longer go to the priest for confession and absolution; and a postcolonial society where language serves more to hinder than to aid self-expression. The actor Tom Hickey (who played the Englishman King) was responsible, along with director Mason and the playwright Tom MacIntyre (b. 1931), for a series of important dramatic experiments at the Peacock Theatre, inaugurated by their production of *The Great Hunger* in 1983. These collaborative productions between actor, director and playwright made for an important break with a predominantly verbal, naturalistic theatre and a movement towards a more mime-based and avant-garde style. The production was based on Patrick Kavanagh's long poem *The Great Hunger* and marked the changes in theatrical style since the new Abbey's staging of Kavanagh's *Tarry Flynn* in the 1960s. The improvisation techniques which Hickey had studied in the Stanislavski training of Deirdre O'Connell at Dublin's tiny Focus Theatre were drawn on to develop the character of the middle-aged, sexually repressed farmer, Patrick Maguire; and the scenes between himself and the young women were a choreographed mating ritual rather than a realistic encounter. But these experiments did not exist in isolation from the mainstream. Rather, they fed right in to the work Mason and Hickey did on new plays like *Gigli Concert*. The difference was one of degree rather than of kind.

The cultural self-confidence that marked this decade in Irish theatre was also reflected by the Irish success, after the Broadway failure, of Brian Friel's most radical and challenging work, *Faith Healer*. When staged in New York with James Mason in the title role, it closed in a number of days; the following year, 1980, it was staged at the Abbey by Joe Dowling with Donal McCann and was not only a commercial success but profoundly influenced developments in Irish theatre in the following two decades. It did so by helping to create an audience for spare, demanding plays of emotional and spiritual crisis (in this regard, it pairs up with Murphy's *Gigli Concert*) and it proved hugely influential in terms of its development of a drama exclusively by means of monologue. For the intertwined life stories of Faith Healer Frank Hardy, his wife / mistress Grace and his cockney business manager Teddy are not told through the conventional means of chronological scenes and an interchange of dialogue but through a series of competing monologues. Each of the characters takes the stage alone to present the audience with her or his version of their lives together on the road in England and Scotland and of the events leading to Frank's death on their return to his home town, Friel's archetypal Ballybeg (from the Irish 'baile beag', small town) in County Donegal. The play is distinctly Beckettian in that these three characters are narrating a retrospect of their lives from beyond the grave. Many of the significant details do not match up. In Frank's version, Grace is his mistress, in hers, she's his wife. Grace claims she bore him a stillborn child; Frank does not mention this and claims she was barren. *Faith Healer* thus brings to an extreme the themes of loneliness, isolation and defiant subjectivity, and the absence of a meaningful political or religious context, which had concerned Friel's plays from the start. It also inaugurated a debate on whether the monologue form could properly be considered dramatic, which continued into the 1990s and Friel's return to the form in 1994's *Molly Sweeney*. The negative view holds that such a form is inherently lacking in drama, that it calls on narrational skills more suited to the novel or short story; and that it denies most of the traditional pleasures of the dramatic experience. The positive view sees the monologue as allowing for a direct, unmediated exchange between the actor/character and the audience; as suited to the Irish context in being related to the traditional role of the storyteller or *seanchaí* in Irish culture; and as being post-modern in its explicit acknowledgement that we are in a theatre and that the audience has a central role in the process. More than any other of his plays, *Faith Healer* related Friel to the more radical developments in Irish theatre.

Other companies developed in Dublin in the 1980s to offer alternative theatre. Prominent among these were Rough Magic, which favoured a sophisticated urban middle-class in the plays they either imported or wrote themselves; initially, the directing was shared by Lynne Parker (Stewart's niece) and Declan Hughes; but Parker eventually took over the directing while Hughes developed as a playwright, the laureate of South County Dublin in plays like *Digging for Fire* (1991). Passion Machine, under director/writer Paul Mercier, saw the distinctive emergence of a Northside working-class idiom in plays by Mercier himself and by Roddy Doyle, honing that talent for dialogue which proved so distinctive a feature of his first novel, *The Commitments* (1988). In 1989 Glasshouse Productions was founded in Dublin as a feminist collective by a producer (Caroline Williams), a director (Katy Hayes), an actress (Sian Quill) and a writer (Clare Dowling). During their five years of existence they produced new plays by Dowling, Trudy Hayes and Emma Donoghue (her lesbian dramas, *I Know My Own Heart* and *Ladies and Gentleman*) and stage anthologies of work done by earlier Irish women playwrights.[50]

The 1990s: the Celtic Tiger and the marketing of the 'Irish' play

The Irish play in the 1990s became, in Nicholas Grene's words, a 'distinct and distinctly marketable phenomenon . . . a commodity of international currency',[51] with notable London productions of work by such new playwrights as Billy Roche, Sebastian Barry, Marina Carr, Martin McDonagh and Conor McPherson and Broadway productions of McDonagh's Leenane trilogy, McPherson's *The Weir* and Barry's *The Steward of Christendom*. What might be termed the internationalisation of Irish drama was begun in 1990 by the phenomenal success of Brian Friel's *Dancing at Lughnasa* at the Abbey Theatre. With this play, Friel broke his association with Field Day[52] and sought the greater resources of producer Noel Pearson, who staged it first at the Abbey in May 1990 in a production by Patrick Mason and the memorable 'field of wheat' design by Joe Vanek, before taking it on to even greater acclaim in London and New York, where it was awarded a Tony for Best Play in 1991. *Lughnasa* opened to mixed notices and reasonable houses at the Abbey, but then began to build and build as audiences responded to the dramatisation of the plight of these five Donegal women from the 1930s. The dedication in the published text, 'In memory of those five brave Glenties women', suggested a basis in autobiography. (Friel's mother was from Glenties in County Donegal.)

Lughnasa was also a step away from Field Day in that it moved the energies of women from the margins to centre stage. By distributing the dramatic weight equally amongst his five female characters, Friel is writing against the symbolisation of woman so central to the nationalist tradition. There are some men in the play: the women's older brother Jack, a missionary priest who has returned from Africa converted from the Catholicism he went to preach to a faith in the goddess-centred rituals of the Ryangan people; and Gerry Evans, the father of Chrissie's son Michael, who pays two brief visits to mother and son during the play. Michael narrates *Lughnasa* from his adult perspective and is like Gar O'Donnell in occupying a double role as both witness to and participant in the events he narrates. But the other self is so much younger here that *Lughnasa* ceases to be about him and becomes instead about the shared lives of the five women among and by whom he was jointly reared. As the narrator, Michael occupies the sidelines of the play and yet is central to its construction, since he is the one actively remembering all the other characters into existence. Michael's ambivalent position could be read as Friel's acknowledgement that, for all the play's emphasis on women, it is being authored by a man. What is so striking in any viewing of *Lughnasa* is the extent to which these memories elude their narrator, the extent to which they possess a range and meaning beyond his conscious control. The unity-in-difference of the women is most memorably expressed through the dancing that became *Lughnasa's* defining moment and most memorable theatrical image. (This was only a few years before the *Riverdance* phenomenon and no doubt contributed to it.) Begun by the wild card Maggie, the dance moves like a live current through all of the others until even the strait-laced Kate joins in. If this passionate outbreak is liberating, it occurs early on in the play and is followed by the depression of its fizzling out. Dancing is the play's most potent and memorable metaphor; as Michael's closing monologue intimates, dancing suggests that there is another way to speak, a non-verbal way 'to whisper private and sacred things, to be in touch with some otherness'.[53] It harmonises with the close of *Translations* on the limits of expression for any Irish dramatist writing in the English, and by extension any, language.

Both *Faith Healer* and *Dancing at Lughnasa* found their first success in Dublin. But the contrasting trajectories of the two plays in production does much to illuminate the difference between Irish theatre in the 1980s and in the 1990s. Where the first period saw a burgeoning of cultural self-confidence, with Irish audiences being the first to acknowledge and acclaim the important Irish plays, the 1990s saw the axis of decision-making shift significantly to London (in particular) and New York; the Noel Pearson-produced documentary *From Ballybeg to Broadway* (1994) suggested the latter as the inevitable destination and ultimate point of validation for Irish plays. Where *Faith Healer* failed abroad and then succeeded at home, *Lughnasa* went on to even greater success in London and New York and helped to create a fashionable trend for Irish plays in those two capitals throughout the decade. The axis of power and influence shifted accordingly and the net effect was this: where throughout the 1980s new Irish plays established their reputations and meaning in their country of origin, increasingly Irish plays in the 1990s were first staged and acclaimed in London before coming to Ireland to have that process replicated.

The Bush Theatre staged a trilogy of plays by Wexford-born Billy Roche (b. 1949), focusing on the lives of characters from a small-town background who are in various ways rebelling against its confines: *A Handful of Stars* (1988); *Poor Beast in the Rain* (1989); and *Belfry* (1991). Frank McGuinness's 1992 play *Someone Who'll Watch over Me* about three prisoners being held hostage in Beirut, was first staged at London's Hampstead Theatre in 1992, with Stephen Rea as the Irishman and Alec McCowen as the Englishman; its success led to subsequent productions in New York and Dublin (at the Abbey, with a different cast). Conor McPherson's *The Weir* (1997) was commissioned by the Royal Court and played in London for over a year, before travelling to Dublin (and the Gate) and to New York. Dublin-born Conor McPherson (b. 1970) was one of the most important young playwrights to emerge during the decade and foremost among those who worked with the monologue as their central dramatic device, as Friel had done in *Faith Healer*. The monologue play enabled a more direct engagement with the audience and liberated the drama from the visual clichés of the 'Irish' play. McPherson in such works as *This Lime-Tree Bower* (1995) and Mark O'Rowe (b. 1970) in his groundbreaking *Howie the Rookie* (1999) also forged a distinctive Dublin idiom, tough yet with a vein of lyricism, for plays of contemporary urban experience represented in monologue form. And Eugene O'Brien (b. 1967) made the transition from acting to writing with the acclaimed *Eden* (2000) at the Peacock and the Abbey, where the alternating monologues of his estranged young married couple allowed for multiple gendered perspectives on a single situation.

The Royal Court made it a condition of their commission of *The Weir* that McPherson's not be a monologue play; but although he gathered three men and one woman in a pub, the monologue persisted in the foregrounding and interweaving of their individual narratives. It was disturbing to see this most urban of contemporary Irish playwrights opt for the most traditional and recognisably 'Irish' dramatic ingredients: old men sitting in a rural pub telling stories of ghosts and fairies, albeit in wonderful and compelling language. But the success garnered by *The Weir* has in turn enabled McPherson to follow his own path since, and at a much higher degree of international attention.

Sebastian Barry (b. 1955) since 1988 had been presenting a series of plays at the Peacock on members of his family whose historic experiences had been marginalised and silenced by the dominant nationalist narrative of Irish history. In 1990's *Prayers of Sherkin*, for example, Fanny Hawke ends the play by leaving forever the Quaker community on Sherkin Island (of which hers is the sole surviving family) to enter into a mixed marriage with a Cork lithographer on the mainland, and by so doing enables the birth of the playwright many decades later. Barry's plays confer dramatic life on people from his family's past about whom little or nothing was said because they had in some way transgressed the taboos defining Catholic nationalist Ireland and so they were consigned to oblivion, written out of both family and public history. 1995's *The Only True History of Lizzie Finn* on the Abbey main stage displays Lizzie as a dancer on an English music-hall stage in the early 1900s. 1995's *The Steward of Christendom*, premièred in London, centres on another family member,

Thomas Dunne, a loyal Southern unionist who has been an officer in the Dublin Metropolitan Police and who resides in an asylum of the play's present, a casualty of history. The play was a very good one, and provided Donal McCann with a last memorable role before his untimely death from cancer; it was seen by a great many more Irish people than any Barry play up till then. Where most of Barry's Dublin-premièred plays had modest runs at the Peacock, the fact that *Steward* was commissioned and premièred in London to much acclaim by Max Stafford Clarke's UK company Out of Joint before an English and Irish tour had a great deal to do with the thronging of audiences to see it when it arrived at Dublin's Gate Theatre.

The figure who most raises all of the issues regarding the 1990s development of the Irish play in London is Martin McDonagh. He does so in part because his own background throws into question any easy assumptions about national origins. The son of émigré Irish parents, McDonagh was born and raised in London. It has been argued that his plays of the 1990s are less to do with the history of Irish theatre but are best understood as part of the British 'in yer face' theatre movement associated with Sara Kane and characterised by stark language and brutal physical violence. McDonagh himself denies any great knowledge of or interest in theatre, claiming movies as his great interest. Yet the evidence of his plays suggests a deep knowledge of theatre and of classic Irish theatre at that, bearing as they do unmistakeable and frequent traces of one J. M. Synge.[54] The title of the third play in McDonagh's Leenane trilogy, *The Lonesome West* (1997), directly quotes Pegeen's father from *The Playboy*: 'Oh, there's sainted glory this day in the lonesome west.'[55] And when a character in the second play, *A Skull in Connemara* (1997), has a spade driven into his skull and then returns to say he's not dead yet, we are clearly in the vicinity of Synge's father-and-son parricidal conflict. The title of this McDonagh play is itself a quote from the closing lines of Lucky's lengthy speech in Beckett's *Godot*. But part of McDonagh's plays' unsettling, post-modernist effect is that they fuse these elements from the classical canon of Irish drama with popular elements from American television and cinema. The mother and daughter in *The Beauty Queen of Leenane* (1996) may recall Tom Murphy's *Bailegangaire*; but in the grotesque pouring of the burning cooking oil on one by the other we are also close to the camp melodrama of Hollywood's *Whatever Happened to Baby Jane* (1962). And if the endlessly feuding brothers in *The Lonesome West* are close kin to their equivalents in Lady Gregory's *Workhouse Ward*, the prissiness of the one and slobbishness of the other are straight out of Neil Simon's *The Odd Couple*, in its widely disseminated TV rather than its prior stage or cinematic representations.

The staging of *The Beauty Queen of Leenane* by Garry Hynes at Druid, before it toured the country and transferred to London and New York, led to objections of misrepresentation that echoed those which had been launched at Synge a century earlier. The argument ran that what was being dished up here, primarily for non-Irish consumption, was stage Irish stereotype, a reliance on characters of limited intelligence and psychopathic tendencies. The involvement of respected theatre professionals like director Hynes and of actors like Marie Mullen, Anna Manahan, Mick Lally and Maelíosa Stafford served only to give a gloss of authenticity to plays which were not Irish. If Irish audiences responded by turning out in great numbers and responding with laughter to what they saw, then it only served to show how thoroughly colonised they were.[56] What was so striking a feature of the Irish audiences McDonagh drew was that many of them were young and few of them could be characterised as 'regular theatregoers'. The plays work with a calculated cunning and an utter lack of sentimentality, towards the Irish theatrical canon as much as anything else. My own feeling is that the smash-and-grab theatrics of Martin McDonagh have, in their phenomenal impact in Ireland and throughout the world, changed the Irish landscape irrevocably. They have done so in particular because they have dispensed with nostalgia and any evocation of a consoling Irish past. There is no clear time frame for McDonagh's plays: they draw on images from traditional Irish plays of decades past, particularly the rural cottage setting, but their younger characters endlessly discuss characters from popular 1970s American television series; and other references indicate a more contemporary provenance. Their cultural references are no more secure and prove equally free-floating; and they suggest that what Irish theatre now has to offer is a range of signifiers which may be played with at random rather than anything which has direct relation to social reality or historical continuity. In this sense, McDonagh has had a discernible impact and effect on many Irish playwrights, no doubt envious of the trail McDonagh's plays have blazed around the world.

The other playwright whose career came to prominence in the 1990s is Marina Carr (b. 1964). Her earliest work in the late 1980s showed a heavy debt to Beckett as she applied gender politics to the theatre of the absurd in plays like *Low in the Dark* (1989) and *Ullaloo* (1991). With the two plays at the Peacock in the mid-1990s with which she gained widespread recognition, *The Mai* (1994) and *Portia Coughlan* (1996), Carr found her own voice and created a distinctive dramatic world. Its setting is the Irish midlands and she has found a dialect to match. The first printed version of *Portia Coughlan* (1996) has lines like the following; 'ya mus' be ouha yar mine',[57] which she rendered as 'ya must be out of your mind'[58] in the 1999 Faber *Plays One*. As much as Synge and Gregory, Marina Carr is fashioning a dramatic speech of her own, bending and shaping the forms of Standard English, disrupting the linguistic present by the Irish past and evolving a flexible linguistic medium to address her plays' concerns with the living and the dead, the real and the mythic. This is particularly the case with *Portia Coughlan*, where the heroine only half occupies her unhappy marriage and is repeatedly drawn to the liminal space of the Belmont river and a psychic encounter with her drowned twin Gabriel. In her 1998 play *By the Bog of Cats* Marina Carr made an important transition to the Abbey main stage and extended the range of her drama into the Greek tragedy of a Medea. *On Raftery's Hill* (2000) seemed like a misstep, a brutal representation of incest in an Irish family which went for the broad strokes of a McDonagh rather than the sensitive treatment the subject demanded. Carr's plays are noteworthy for their wide range of female characters: the forty-year-old Mai is in a line from her hundred-year-old Grandmother Fraochlain, her two visiting aunts and a grown-up daughter Millie. But while Carr's plays adopt no Manichean line on gender stereotypes (some of the women characters can be just as destructive of the heroine's desire as the men) they are centred on women's experience and provide both a challenge and alternative to the male-dominated world of Irish playwriting. *Portia Coughlan* remains her most impressive and achieved work. Carr's more recent plays, in aiming for an Irish version of Greek tragedy, have increasingly toppled over into melodramatic excess, particularly in the onstage representation of violence.

A variant on the monologue play was inaugurated in the early 1990s by the success of the stage version of Patrick McCabe's award-winning novel *The Butcher Boy* (1992). Entitled *Frankie Pig Says Hello*, what was dramatically innovative about the piece was that, although the stage was crowded with characters from McCabe's novel, only two actors appeared in it. One (David Gorry) played the damaged young man at its centre, living in a fantasy world made out of comics and science-fiction movies; all of the other parts – the mother who breaks up his friendship with Francis Nugent and calls his family 'pigs', the alcoholic father and depressed mother, the local gossips, etc. – were played by the other actor (Sean Rocks). The stage version of *Butcher Boy*, directed by Joe O'Byrne of the experimental Commotion Theatre Company, got closer than either McCabe's novel or Neil Jordan's movie version to the poignancy at the heart of the narrative. Marie Jones used the same format – of two male actors taking on a wide range of characters – in her 1999 play *Stones in his Pockets*, with its tale of two Irish extras on location in Kerry for a Hollywood 'Oirish' movie. A great success in Dublin, London and New

York, the play for all its humour raised the question of the exploitation of 'Irishness' for foreign consumption both as an issue within the play and as a factor in its worldwide success. A combination of monologue and mime fuelled the actor Donal O'Kelly's one-man piece *Catalpa* (1997), which told of an Irish escape from a convict ship in the last century. Two companies which used mime as the basis of their theatre came to the fore during the decade: Barrabas in Dublin and Blue Raincoat in Sligo. Both did original pieces, for the most part, but also produced stunning reinterpretations of two classics from the Irish repertoire – Blue Raincoat with a version of Synge's *Playboy of the Western World* and Barrabas with Lennox Robinson's *The White-Headed Boy*. Completely freed from the usual restraints of realistic casting and setting, these mime-based interpretations cast a 35-year-old actress as Pegeen Mike and the clown-faced Mikel Murfi as the youngest daughter in the Robinson play. Directors Niall Henry and Gerard Stembridge showed possibilities for investigating and reinvigorating the repertoire that the National Theatre itself only rarely attempted.

The changing political landscape in the 1990s was registered in the theatre. In 1994 first the IRA and then the loyalist paramilitaries declared a cease-fire; the Abbey, in the first year of Patrick Mason's tenure as artistic director, mounted a main stage revival of Frank McGuinness's *Observe the Sons of Ulster Marching Towards the Somme* to mark the breakthrough. Both Field Day and Charabanc Theatre Companies, who had done so much for Irish theatre in the 1980s, came to an end; but their impact was registered by the younger companies and new playwrights who came to the fore in the North. The actor Tim Loane has written of the impact the Field Day production of Thomas Kilroy's *Double Cross* had on him when he was a student at Queen's University in Belfast in the 1980s. In 1988 he and fellow actor Lalor Roddy co-founded Belfast's Tinderbox Theatre Company with the declared intention of developing and producing new work that would interrogate and explore life in Northern Ireland. In 1998 there was a symbolic passing of the torch when Tinderbox joined with Field Day (in its last ever production) to co-present Stewart Parker's *Northern Star*, on Belfast-born Henry Joy McCracken and his participation in the 1798 Rebellion, in a Presbyterian church. In 1993 they premièred the first stage play by the most important Northern Irish playwright to emerge during the decade, Gary Mitchell's *Independent Voice*. Mitchell (b. 1965) was born in Rathcoole, north Belfast, and began (as so many other Northern playwrights, including Friel, had done) by writing plays for BBC radio. In 1994 he was the first playwright from Northern Ireland to win the Stewart Parker award, set up in the late playwright's memory to honour the best new first play staged in the preceding year. Mitchell came to wider attention with his two plays of the late 1990s, *In a Little World of Our Own* (1997) and *As the Beast Sleeps* (1998), staged first at the Peacock in Dublin with subsequent productions at Belfast's Lyric and London's Donmar Warehouse. Both plays seemed designed to discomfit any cosy notions that the advent of the peace process in Northern Ireland would transform hardened traditional attitudes and patterns of behaviour overnight. Their heavily male casts feature members of the Ulster Defence Association, who register a sense of betrayal and confusion that the cause to which they have committed themselves for so many years must now be pursued by other means. Both plays powerfully dramatise a self-incarcerating logic in which the violence so long doled out to the other side is now turned in on itself and brother betrays brother, wife betrays husband. The plays recognise that a change has had to come but also show the pressure on those for whom an inch is a very long way indeed.

By the 1990s the outstanding contemporary playwrights could be (and were) celebrated with festivals of their work. The Beckett Festival at the Gate in 1991 had the imprimatur of the Paris exile before his death in 1989; and staged all nineteen of his stage productions within the same time frame. The Gate Festival seriously advanced the claims for Beckett as an Irish dramatist in the immediate aftermath of his death. On the occasion of Brian Friel's seventy-fifth birthday in 1999, the Abbey and the Peacock staged a retrospective of six of his plays, from often seen (*Lughnasa*) to rarely seen plays, like *Living Quarters* (1977) and *Making History* (1988). The celebration of Friel made one wonder if a contemporary Irish play would ever again receive such a uniformly positive and united a reception as *Lughnasa* had. In particular, its international success suggested that a play of pronounced rurality set in the Irish past would provide a more identifiably 'Irish' play for a foreign audience than works which grappled with a less certain and defined Irish present. When Friel sought to do the latter in 1993's *Wonderful Tennessee* its stay on Broadway was a short one.

In the country itself a singular Ireland and hence a single Irish audience can no longer be assumed or identified now that the Catholic nationalist consensus no longer holds sway. The great conflict which fuelled so many of the plays by the canonical contemporary playwrights, the clash between tradition and modernity, has now been definitively decided in favour of the latter. Irish plays can no longer be set in rural cottages other than for the purposes of a McDonagh parody. What Irish theatre now has to contend with is a series of micro-Irelands, all widely differing from each other in terms of the social reality they represent. But even in the first theatre movement there was never an agreed and unified identity of purpose in the writing and reception of Irish plays. As Christopher Morash puts it, writing of the year 2000, 'there is no such thing as *the* Irish theatre; there are Irish *theatres*, whose forms continue to multiply as they leave behind the fantasy of a single unifying image, origin or destiny.'[59] From the start of Ireland's national theatre a century earlier, the staging of a new play that implicitly claimed to represent Irish experience was immediately met with vociferous claims that it failed to do so. Then, the issue was likely to be one of Protestant versus Catholic ideology or of arguments between differing strands of nationalism. Now, the areas of exclusion are likelier to be those of women (certainly in plays authored by women themselves), gays or, in an Ireland that now has a significant multi-racial population, of plays which reflect the immigrant experience in anything but a tokenistic way. What has always marked the vitality of the Irish stage is a strong element of creative contradiction, the generation of potentially endless plays by one playwright reacting to another and challenging his or her claim to represent Irish experience. There is no reason why this process should not continue well into the new century.

Notes

1. For Beckett in relation to contemporary Irish drama in English, see Anthony Roche, *Contemporary Irish Drama: From Beckett to McGuinness* (Dublin: Gill and Macmillan, 1994; New York: St Martin's Press, 1995), passim.
2. Hugh Hunt, *The Abbey Theatre: Ireland's National Theatre 1904–1978* (Dublin: Gill and Macmillan; New York: Columbia University Press, 1979), p. 173.
3. Robert Hogan, *After the Irish Renaissance: A Critical History of the Irish Drama Since* The Plough and the Stars (London and Melbourne: Macmillan, 1968), p. 33.
4. Robert Welch, *The Abbey Theatre 1899–1999: Form and Pressure* (Oxford: Oxford University Press, 1999), pp. 146–7.
5. J. M. Synge, preface to *The Playboy of the Western World*, in *Collected Works*, IV (Oxford: Oxford University Press, 1968), p. 54.
6. Welch, *The Abbey Theatre 1899–1999*, p. 148.
7. Arnold Marsh papers, Manuscript Room, Trinity College, Dublin.
8. *Selected Plays of M. J. Molloy*, chosen and introduced by Robert O'Driscoll (Gerrards Cross: Colin Smythe; Washington, DC: Catholic University of America Press, 1998), p. 115.
9. Vic Merriman, 'Staging Contemporary Ireland: Heartsickness and Hopes Deferred', in Shaun Richards, ed. *The Cambridge Companion to Twentieth-Century Irish Drama* (Cambridge: Cambridge University Press, 2004), pp. 246–8.
10. *Selected Plays of M. J. Molloy*, p. 112.
11. Alan Simpson, *Beckett and Behan and a Theatre in Dublin* (London: Routledge and Kegan Paul, 1962), p. 2.
12. Ibid.

13. Ulick O'Connor, *Brendan Behan* (London: Black Swan, 1985), pp. 87–8.
14. For the full complicated story see John Brannigan, *Brendan Behan: Cultural Nationalism and the Revisionist Writer* (Dublin: Four Courts Press, 2002), p. 80. One source cited by Brannigan argues that Blythe claimed never to have received the three-act manuscript.
15. Samuel Beckett, *En Attendant Godot*, ed. Colin Duckworth (London: Harrap, 1966), p. 4; Samuel Beckett, *Waiting for Godot* (London and Boston: Faber and Faber, 1956), p. 10.
16. For details of Simpson's additions to Beckett's script, see Christopher Morash, *A History of Irish Theatre 1601–2000* (Cambridge: Cambridge University Press, 2002), p. 199.
17. Beckett, *Waiting for Godot*, p. 17.
18. James Knowlson, *Damned To Fame: The Life of Samuel Beckett* (London: Bloomsbury, 1996), pp. 56–7.
19. On this controversy, see Nicholas Grene, *The Politics of Irish Drama: Plays in Context from Boucicault to Friel* (Cambridge: Cambridge University Press, 1999), pp. 157–65.
20. See Morash, *A History of Irish Theatre 1601–2000*, pp. 210–11.
21. See Anthony Roche, 'John B. Keane: Respectability at Last!', *Theatre Ireland* 18 (April-June 1989), pp. 30–2.
22. Fintan O'Toole, *The Politics of Magic: The Work and Times of Tom Murphy* (Dublin: Raven Arts Press, 1987; rev. edn Dublin: New Island Books; London: Nick Hern Books, 1994), p. 7.
23. For a full account of the controversy, see Gerard Whelan with Caroline Swift, *Spiked: Church-State Intrigue and* The Rose Tattoo (Dublin: New Island Books, 2002).
24. Sam Thompson, *Over the Bridge*, ed. Stewart Parker (Dublin: Gill and Macmillan, 1970).
25. Cited in Ulf Dantanus, *Brian Friel: A Study* (London: Faber and Faber, 1988), p. 51.
26. Brian Friel, *Plays One* (London: Faber and Faber, 1996), p. 27.
27. See Christopher Fitz-Simon, *The Irish Theatre* (London: Thames and Hudson, 1983), p. 179.
28. Cathy Leeney, Interview with Garry Hynes, in Lilian Chambers et al., eds. *Theatre Talk: Voices of Irish Theatre Practitioners* (Dublin: Carysfort Press, 2001), p. 195.
29. For Keane's identification with 'The Bull' McCabe, see Roche, 'John B. Keane: Respectability at Last!', p. 32.
30. See Hunt, *The Abbey*, p. 196, and Morash, *A History of Irish Theatre 1601–2000*, pp. 226–7.
31. See Hunt, *The Abbey*, p. 207.
32. For O'Casey as influence on contemporary Northern Irish drama, see Christopher Murray, *Twentieth-Century Irish Drama: Mirror up to Nation* (Manchester: Manchester University Press, 1997), pp. 189–91.
33. Friel, *Plays One*, p. 109.
34. Ibid., p. 150.
35. On Parker, see D. E. S. Maxwell, *A Critical History of Modern Irish Drama 1891–1980* (Cambridge: Cambridge University Press, 1984), pp. 181–3.
36. *Selected Plays of Hugh Leonard*, chosen and introduced by S. F. Gallagher (Gerrards Cross: Colin Smythe; Washington, DC: Catholic University of America Press, 1992), p. 88.
37. Ibid., p. 172.
38. Tom Murphy, *After Tragedy: Three Irish Plays* (London: Methuen, 1988), p. 108.
39. Thomas Kilroy, *Talbot's Box* (Dublin: Gallery Press, 1979), p. 11.

40. For a detailed account of Field Day's early years, see Marilynn J. Richtarik, *Acting Between The Lines: The Field Day Theatre Company and Irish Cultural Politics 1980–1984* (Oxford: Clarendon Press, 1994).
41. Friel, *Plays One*, p. 446.
42. Tom Paulin, *The Riot Act: A Version of Sophocles's* Antigone (London: Faber and Faber, 1985), p. 11.
43. Fintan O'Toole, 'Judged by its Peers: Frank McGuinness's Translation of Ibsen's *Peer Gynt*', *Theatre Ireland* 17 (December 1988/March 1989), p. 28.
44. Stewart Parker, *Three Plays for Ireland*: Northern Star, Heavenly Bodies *and* Pentecost (Birmingham: Oberon Books, 1989), p. 204.
45. Stewart Parker, *Dramatis Personae*, John Malone Memorial Lecture (Belfast: Queen's University, 1986), p. 18.
46. See Eileen Kearney, 'Current Women's Voices in the Irish Theatre: New Dramatic Visions', *Colby Quarterly* 27, 4 (1991), pp. 225–32, ed. Anthony Roche, special issue on Contemporary Irish Drama.
47. Eleanor Methven; quoted in Claudia W. Harris, 'Reinventing Women: Charabanc Theatre Company', in Eberhard Bort, ed. *State of Play: Irish Theatre in the Nineties* (Trier: Wissenschaftlicher Verlag, 1996), p. 111.
48. For Murphy's comments on this, see Roche, *Contemporary Irish Drama*, p. 147.
49. Grene, *The Politics of Irish Drama*, p. 226.
50. See Caroline Williams, Katy Hayes, Sian Quill and Clare Dowling, 'People in Glasshouse: An Anecdotal History of an Independent Theatre Company', in Dermot Bolger, ed. *Druids, Dudes and Beauty Queens: The Changing Face of Irish Theatre* (Dublin: New Island Books, 2001), pp. 132–47.
51. Grene, *The Politics of Irish Drama*, p. 262.
52. Under Stephen Rea, three more plays were produced: Kilroy's *The Madame MacAdam Travelling Theatre* (1991); a version of Chekhov's *Uncle Vanya* by Frank McGuinness (1995); and a co-production of Parker's *Northern Star* (1998) with Belfast's Tinderbox.
53. Brian Friel, *Dancing at Lughnasa* (London and Boston: Faber and Faber, 1990), p. 71.
54. See Shaun Richards, '"The Outpouring of a Morbid, Unhealthy Mind": The Critical Condition of Synge and McDonagh', *Irish University Review* 33, 1 (Spring/Summer 2003), pp. 201–14, ed. Margaret Kelleher, special issue on the Irish Literary Revival.
55. J. M. Synge, *Collected Works*, IV, p. 65.
56. On the latter, see Vic Merriman, 'Decolonisation Postponed: The Theatre of Tiger Trash', *Irish University Review* 29, 2 (Autumn/Winter 1999), pp. 305–17.
57. Marina Carr, *Portia Couglan*, in Frank McGuinness, ed. *The Dazzling Dark: New Irish Plays* (London and Boston: Faber and Faber, 1996), p. 240.
58. Marina Carr, *Plays One* (London: Faber and Faber, 1999), p. 194.
59. Morash, *A History of Irish Theatre 1601–2000*, p. 271.

Select bibliography

Bolger, Dermot, ed. *Druids, Dudes and Beauty Queens: The Changing Face of Irish Theatre*, Dublin: New Island Books, 2001.

Bort, Eberhard, ed. *State of Play: Irish Theatre in the Nineties*, Trier: Wissenschaftlicher Verlag, 1996.

Chambers, Lilian, Ger FitzGibbon, Eamonn Jordan, Dan Farrelly and Cathy Leeney, eds. *Theatre Talk: Voices of Irish Theatre Practitioners*, Dublin: Carysfort Press, 2001.

Fitz-Simon, Christopher, *The Irish Theatre*, London: Thames and Hudson, 1983.

Grene, Nicholas, *The Politics of Irish Drama: Plays in Context from Boucicault to Friel*, Cambridge: Cambridge University Press, 1999.

Hadfield, Paul, and Lynda Henderson, eds. *Theatre Ireland* 1–31 (1981–93).

Hogan, Robert, *After the Irish Renaissance: A Critical History of the Irish Drama Since* The Plough and the Stars, London and Melbourne: Macmillan, 1968.

Hunt, Hugh, *The Abbey Theatre: Ireland's National Theatre 1904–1978*, Dublin: Gill and Macmillan; New York: Columbia University Press, 1979.

Maxwell, D. E. S., *A Critical History of Modern Irish Drama 1890–1980*, Cambridge: Cambridge University Press, 1984.

Morash, Christopher, *A History of Irish Theatre 1601–2000*, Cambridge: Cambridge University Press, 2002.

Murray, Christopher, *Twentieth-Century Irish Drama: Mirror up to Nation*, Manchester: Manchester University Press, 1997; Syracuse: Syracuse University Press, 2000.

Richards, Shaun, ed. *The Cambridge Companion to Twentieth-Century Irish Drama*, Cambridge: Cambridge University Press, 2004.

Richtarik, Marilynn J., *Acting Between the Lines: The Field Day Theatre Company and Irish Cultural Politics 1980–1984*, Oxford: Clarendon Press, 1994.

Roche, Anthony, *Contemporary Irish Drama: From Beckett to McGuinness*, Dublin: Gill and Macmillan, 1994; New York: St Martin's Press, 1995.

Welch, Robert, *The Abbey Theatre 1899–1999: Pressure and Form*, Oxford: Oxford University Press, 1999.

11

Cinema and Irish literature

KEVIN ROCKETT

So extensive has been the range of adaptations of Irish literary works for the screen that it is difficult to find a version of a major play or book that has not been seen in the cinema (or on television, an area largely outside of this discussion). Unsurprisingly, those works with a narrative thrust, which allow them to transcend their stage-bound or literary origins, have been favoured.

For our purposes, the range of adaptations discussed is confined to Irish-subject plays and novels (and short stories). Thus, Oscar Wilde does not feature, even though many of his most famous plays, such as *Lady Windermere's Fan* (including a version directed by Ernest Lubitsch in 1925), and novel *The Picture of Dorian Gray*, have been adapted for screen. Indeed, two film versions of his notorious *Salomé* were produced in 1908 alone, while three adaptations of *Dorian Gray* were made before 1915. Similarly, Bernard Shaw is omitted even though many of his plays were filmed, including his *Arms and the Man*, which was made into *The Chocolate Soldier* in 1914, and *Pygmalion*, which won an Oscar in 1938 (there were also German and Dutch filmed versions in the 1930s); but his key 'Irish' play, *John Bull's Other Island* (1904), has yet to be made into a feature film. While all Samuel Beckett's stage works have been adapted for the (small) screen, as has his one 'screenplay', *Film*, made as a 22-minute cinema film in 1964, and featuring Buster Keaton,[1] these are not discussed here. Other omissions reflect the course of cinematic history. With the exception of the one-act play *Words upon the Window Pane* (Mary McGuckian, 1996), W. B. Yeats has been excluded from the cinema. And the chronicler of the Aran Islands, J. M. Synge, has been given only slight cinematic recognition through two versions of *Riders to the Sea* (in 1936 by Brian Desmond Hurst and in 1987 by Ronan O'Leary), and a 1962 version of *The Playboy of the Western World* (Brian Desmond Hurst).

Adaptation has been widely discussed in critical literature. Too often it has been used by literary critics to denigrate cinema as a medium incapable of producing or responding to the 'quality' of literary texts, rather than recognising cinema as a profoundly different form of expression which through its synergy of image, sound and movement produces a unique cultural experience. This failure to celebrate on its own terms cinema's particular aesthetic, for example, allowed Edward Murray to declare after viewing Joseph Strick's 1967 version of James Joyce's *Ulysses* that the attempt was 'doomed to failure' because the verbalisation and 'linguistic-intellectual level' of Joyce's text was 'beyond the capacity of the movie camera to record'. In a backhanded compliment to the cinema, he added that though cinema is 'unsurpassed at rendering the surface of things', when it comes to rendering the 'complex psyche' of a character, it is 'sadly inferior' to what can be done by the stream-of-consciousness novelist. Ironically, as Luke Gibbons[2] points out in this context, it is Joyce's stream-of-consciousness which draws the text close to the cinema, a fact acknowledged by other Joyceans. Though *Ulysses* occupies a unique place in Irish literature, nevertheless the ease with which critics of all forms of literature choose to contrast an adaptation unfavourably with its literary origins remains all-pervasive in Irish (and other) cultures. Until it is acknowledged that films are made under particular conditions, with their own critical and historical contexts, then the framework for discussing these texts will remain limited.

Early cinema and Irish literature

Cinema did not emerge from bourgeois literature or theatre, but from popular forms of scientific, magical and visual exhibition and entertainment, postcard and comic or cartoon culture, slapstick and increasingly, and most especially, variety and theatre, predominantly the nineteenth-century melodramatic tradition. Later, bourgeois literary and theatrical conventions were 'imposed' on the cinema as it sought both to develop new narrative strategies and to attract the middle classes to this popular entertainment, particularly through the adaptation of well-known literary and dramatic works. In Irish terms, at least before the 'literary' became all pervasive, such early cinema, anchored in the popular, necessarily drew on the plays of Dion Boucicault.

It is no surprise that when the American company Kalem[3] came to Ireland during the summers of 1910–12 to produce a range of Irish fiction films that adaptations of Boucicault featured amongst their first films. Indeed, 1911 is a milestone in the sense that not only did Kalem adapt Boucicault's *The Colleen Bawn* as their first film that year, but elsewhere two other filmed versions of the play were made. One of these was a one-reel (approximately ten minutes) version produced in America by Yankee and released in August 1911, two months before Kalem's three-reel version was screened there. An Australian filmed version of the play, which seems to have been even longer than Kalem's, was also released before Kalem's adaptation – in this case, September 1911 – and featured well-known actress Louise Cabasse as the Colleen Bawn and James Martin as Danny Mann. During its Melbourne screening the film was accompanied by the not uncommon practice in early cinema of having a 'lecturer' interpret the film for the audience, while songs by John McCormack, Clara Butt and Melba were played.[4] In all, up to twenty adaptations of Boucicault's plays, or films inspired by, or which plagiarised elements of, his writings, were produced before 1930; thereafter, such plays fell into (cinematic) disuse during the sound era. Perhaps, as had happened in both Ireland and the USA in the early sound era, strenuous objections were made to dialogue which was perceived to be stage-Irish, or worse, and thus producers who may not have had the subtlety or sophistication to appreciate Boucicault's subversive nuances, were wary of his dialogue. This issue was brought into sharp relief in 1930 when the American film *Smiling Irish Eyes* (William A. Seiter, 1929) was released in Dublin. Set in Ireland and America, this migration story contrasted Irish backwardness (Irish heroine playing with pigs, crude stage Irish stereotypes, endless fighting Irish, etc.) with American modernity and opportunity. Writing in the *Irish Statesman*, Mary Manning, later a playwright and novelist, commented that 'Boucicault stands as a stern and uncompromising realist' beside this film,[5] and following a protest by cultural activists during its screening at Dublin's Savoy cinema, the film was withdrawn from Irish distribution.[6] No further public protests occurred as Hollywood responded to both Irish and Irish-American objections to such representations.

While Kalem's thirty-minute version of *The Colleen Bawn* (the only one of the three 1911 films of which a copy exists) is a conventional adaptation, other Boucicault adaptations, such as *Arrah-na-Pogue* (from the 1864 play; also made in 1911) and *The Shaughraun* (first performed in 1874; and made as a film in 1912), can only be assessed from written records as they have not survived. The British trade publication *Bioscope*[7] regarded *Arrah-na-Pogue* as Kalem's 'finest' Irish film, while *The Shaughraun* was enthusiastically received in the USA. Writing in the film trade publication *Moving Picture World*, influential critic W. Stephen Bush commented that when Kalem 'began filming Irish plays on Irish soil it entered a new field of cinematographic endeavour', and demonstrated that film 'is vastly more than a mere vehicle of cheap dramatic composition'. His enthusiasm notwithstanding, Bush also promoted landscape over the word, such as in his suggestion that Kalem 'well-nigh touched perfection in the use they made of outdoor scenery'. When Bush got around to talking about the play *The Shaughraun* itself, he praised the use of the film's intertitles because 'wherever possible' they were taken from the text of the play.[8] Of course, Boucicault himself had used in his stagecraft techniques which would later be interpreted as (crude or primitive) early cinematic montage or editing devices.[9]

The elevation of landscape was not confined to Boucicault's work; even historical dramas such as *Rory O'More* (1911) interrupt the narrative flow to cast an eye on the splendid Kerry landscape,[10] but such 'real' pauses disappeared from fiction film-making by the mid-1910s as classical cinema's 'illusionism' took a firm grip over narrative cinema. Thus, cinema's extension of the literary or dramatic work in the early silent period was twofold. While the text itself was often cut down to conform to the ten to thirty minutes of fiction film-making predominant during (roughly) 1905–15, what was ultimately championed was cinema's ability to film in 'real' locations, or at least outdoors, together with its ability to draw on 'sublime' elements of the 'romantic' landscape to articulate a character's personality – something more difficult, or 'artificial', within the theatre itself.

While no other Irish playwright received the degree of attention in the American cinema as did Boucicault, the British film industry of this period largely confined itself to an exploration of eighteenth-century theatre in the person of the Irish-born star of the London stage Peg Woffington. Although the British films *Murphy's Wake* (1903 and 1906) were short (perhaps one to three minute) versions of the famous wake scene from *The Shaughraun*, a scene also filmed in America, *Peg Woffington* (1912) was an adaptation of the popular play *Masks and Faces* (1852) by Tom Taylor and Charles Reade, two versions of which were made in the USA (in 1910 and 1914), as well as a British full-length adaptation that used the play's title in 1917. In spite of the historical reputation of the fiery (and promiscuous) Dublin actress as foil to upper-class English society, Peg's Irishness was of secondary consideration in these films. A sound-era version of the story, *Peg of Old Drury,* was produced in Britain in 1935, again with the emphasis on London society rather than on Dublin.

It was left to (belated) developments in Ireland to tackle Irish novels. The Film Company of Ireland (FCOI), the first indigenous Irish production company, established in 1916, quickly made its mark with a range of short dramas and comedies. Though most of the early FCOI films were directed for the screen by the Abbey Theatre's J. M. Kerrigan – later a Hollywood character actor – and utilised the Abbey players, for example in a 1917 adaptation of the stage comedy *The Rise of Constable Rafferty* by Nicholas Hayes, it was the company's adaptations of two popular historical novels, Charles Kickham's

Knocknagow (1873; dir. Fred O'Donovan, 1918) and William Carleton's *Willy Reilly and His Colleen Bawn* (1855; dir. John MacDonagh, 1920), which would prove its greatest cinematic legacy.

While the novel *Knocknagow* is not time-specific (it could be set in the 1840s, the 1850s, or even the 1860s), the film is set in 1848 (it is announced in the film's opening title that the events occurred 'seventy years ago'), at the height of the Famine (a point also emphasised in the film's publicity booklet) and in the year of the Young Ireland Rising, with which Kickham was associated. Much of the narrative, especially in the novel, is taken up with a series of meandering love stories, but it is the relationship to the land, rather than personal relationships, which dominates the film. Directed by the Abbey Theatre's Fred O'Donovan, the film also places greater emphasis on the role of the land agent Pender (J. M. Carre), 'the one black cloud' in the community, who is seeking on behalf of the landlord to clear the land of tenants in order to make way for the more profitable enterprise of cattle grazing. His opponent is the 'freeman' Mat the Thrasher (Brian Magowan), who defends the rights of small farmers and the dispossessed, some of whom are evicted from their homes. Deciding to emigrate himself, Mat is wrongly arrested in Liverpool for the theft of the landlord's rents, but eventually he succeeds in exposing Pender as the culprit. By then, the benign landlord has arrived in Ireland and castigates Pender for his anti-social behaviour, so that, unlike the book, the film succeeds in creating a grand alliance of landlord with large and smaller tenant farmers in a display of unity. Of course, such a sense of communal well-being neatly dovetailed with, or responded to, the search for a united front being sought by the Irish nationalist leadership by 1918. Rather than seeing, as Kickham had done, the large (Catholic) tenant farmer Kearney as lacking sympathy for the small farmer and the landless labourer, here Irish unity demanded that all landed classes be brought together to face the common enemy (in the present), England's colonial might.[11]

If *Knocknagow* was clearly linked to the (ideological) struggle during the post-1916 period, reflected in the film's release on the second anniversary of the Rising, this is no less the case with *Willy Reilly*, which was released on the fourth anniversary of the Rising. Its director John MacDonagh, brother of executed 1916 leader Thomas MacDonagh, and himself imprisoned for his part in the Rising, was also one of the founders of the Irish Theatre Company, the innovative and politically radical alternative to the Abbey Theatre. Both novel and film focus on gentleman Catholic farmer Willy Reilly, who is helped to maintain ownership of his lands with the aid of sympathetic Protestants during the penal laws of the 1840s. He falls in love with the Colleen Bawn, the daughter of bigoted Protestant Squire Folliard, who will only allow Willy to marry her if he converts to Protestantism. They decide to elope, but are apprehended with Willy sentenced to seven years' exile for abducting a minor, the Colleen Bawn. She sinks into a deep depression and only recovers when Willy returns to Ireland, whereupon the squire accepts their relationship. The film ends with an image of (religious) harmony and family bliss as the couple, their baby and the squire all smile for the camera. Such family unity was easily read by contemporary audiences as carrying a parallel to the deep sectarian divisions within Ireland and, released in 1920, when partition was introduced, the film unambiguously resonated with the broader thrust of nationalist politics. As Ireland's first film trade publication, *Irish Limelight*, put it when commenting on the film's 'remarkable' commercial success, it was perhaps not so remarkable because 'in the hearts of most of the Irish people is a yearning to have buried forever the mean wicked head of bigotry wherever it rises'.[12] It was not until a cycle of films dealing with the 1916–23 period reached the screen in the 1930s that a similar engagement with Irish politics and history would become evident.

History on film, in the post-independence period

It is hardly surprising that the work of two of the most prominent writers on the 1916–23 period in Ireland, Sean O'Casey and Liam O'Flaherty, should have been chosen for big screen treatment. In both cases, the film-makers were not Irish, a factor that reflects the post-independence paucity of indigenous Irish fiction films on the screen, while exposing the dominant role British and American cinemas had in producing cinematic images of the Irish from the 1920s to the 1970s.

For his second sound film, Alfred Hitchcock adapted O'Casey's *Juno and the Paycock*, the first Abbey Theatre play to be filmed. However, Hitchcock was embarrassed by the project, feeling that he had neither done justice to the play, nor created a film which had anything to do with cinema.[13] O'Casey was similarly despondent with the film, regarding it 'as timid as hell',[14] and complaining that of the original cast Sara Allgood was the only one retained. Barry Fitzgerald, who played the Paycock / Captain Boyle in the original production, was replaced by the inexperienced British actor Edward Chapman, while Fitzgerald's brother, Arthur Shields, was replaced in the role of Johnny Boyle by John Laurie. (Fitzgerald does appear, but in the newly written role of 'Orator'.) As the film's American title – *The Shame of Mary Boyle* – indicates, the film played on the role of pregnant and unmarried Mary Boyle. However, given the censorship regime in Ireland whereby anything deemed contrary to public morality[15] was forbidden, it is most likely that such sexually 'deviant' scenes were cut in the Irish version. Despite such censorship, two reels of the film were taken from a Limerick cinema and destroyed in the street, because, as the *Limerick Chronicle*[16] commented, it 'contained scenes which were considered objectionable'. Further screenings of the film were cancelled, as was the case also in Waterford and Derry.[17]

O'Casey fared slightly better with John Ford's adaptation of *The Plough and the Stars* (1936), though he, too, made bizarre casting choices: American actor Preston Foster appeared as Jack Clitheroe with Barbara Stanwyck as his wife Nora. The Irish press complimented the Irish actors, especially Arthur Shields as Patrick Pearse and Barry Fitzgerald as Fluther Good, for saving the film from the often grating tones of Stanwyck's accent. However, the issue of Dublin tenement speech or working-class *patois* cannot be separated from sound cinema's adaptations of Irish plays and novels. With the demands of the British and American film industries requiring that lead roles be played by their own nationals so as to maximise return on investment through audience recognition of their own star, the ability of such actors to deliver the rhythm and cadences of Irish literary and dramatic speech is always doubtful. An extreme example of this is Gary Raymond's failure to register the subtlety inherent in J. M. Synge's words in the 1962 adaptation of *The Playboy of the Western World*. Thus, Stanwyck and Foster's American-accented Clitheroes, while readily identifiable to Californians, left a gap between O'Casey's words and the Irish audience's ears, a primitive distancing device not planned for by the realist playwright! 'What a sorry job they made of it!', wrote O'Casey.[18] *Ireland Today* agreed. In a truculent attack on the film, especially its depictions of Pearse and James Connolly, this short-lived but radical journal commented that 'it looks as if the Irish subject [film] had better be left for someone other than John Ford'.[19]

Another aspect of this production, and of other films dealing with the 1916–23 period, was the hostile responses such projects received from the British Board of Film Censors (BBFC), which in the 1930s included, as a key figure, Colonel J. C. Hanna, who had served in the British military in Ireland during the War of Independence. Seeking to discourage producers from employing such narratives, though he never banned one, he wrote in an internal memo prior to *The Plough and the Stars* being made, that O'Casey's 'language is impossible from a film standard. It is very coarse, full of swearwords and most of the political speeches would be prohibitive from our point of view.' He went on to reveal his real objection to such films. The 1916 Rebellion, he wrote, 'evokes many sad and painful recollections and will always prove highly controversial . . . it is undesirable to rouse these feelings through . . . Cinema'.[20] After the film's release, Britain's *Monthly Film Bulletin*[21] noted that two 'problems' presented themselves in the adaptation which led to 'a toning down of high lights'. One was 'the censorship of O'Casey's virulent dialogue', while the second was 'the difficulty of reproducing typical Dublin tenement speech *so as to be understandable*' (emphasis added). It was not just the British censor who had difficulty with such 'realist' representations of the period: Hanna's Irish counterpart, James Montgomery, the Official Irish Film Censor, also took a stern approach when it came to adaptations of Liam O'Flaherty's work, especially his *The Informer*.

Two film versions of *The Informer* were released within a six-year period: the first was a silent film by Chicago-born director Arthur Robison in 1929 (and later released in a sound version), and in 1935 John Ford also adapted the novel. In neither case were Irish locations used. Robison's film concentrated less on the political activities during the civil war than on, as the film's tag line had it, 'Romance and Tragedy in the Dublin Underworld'. Notwithstanding this, the studio-based film, much of which is beautifully composed and features wonderfully stylised acting from British and continental European actors, includes an introductory scene at Party headquarters, 'where politics were often punctuated by gunfire', indicating the Hollywood crime genre focus of the film. As a result, the opposing sides during the Civil War are represented as two gangs (though it may be recalled that O'Flaherty's novel was influenced by an agricultural labour strike in the early 1920s and not by the military events in Ireland). Gypo's betrayal of Francis is not in his delusional attempt to emigrate to the USA (the central focus of Ford's adaptation of the novel), but is motivated by his misreading of the relationship Francis has with his girlfriend Katie. Otherwise, the narrative follows the trajectory of both the novel and Ford's later film, in which Gypo gets shot while escaping, and collapses and dies after pleading for forgiveness from Francis's mother in a church.

Irish audiences were denied the opportunity of seeing Robison's film, as censor James Montgomery banned it. Commenting on the adaptation, Montgomery said that it was a

> sordid show of Chicago gunmen, armed police and prostitutes at gunplay and soliciting in the standard slum of movieland. It is offered as a realistic picture of the underworld of Dublin. It is a pity that the citizens cannot take an action against the producers for a libel on our city.[22]

The dubbed sound version of the film was, however, seen in London by the *Irish Statesman*'s Mary Manning. Following the screening, she wrote that 'the cultural accents of Dublin's underworld, the cardboard inanities of the studio Dublin and the naivete of the captions were vastly entertaining. No Dubliner must miss this film.'[23] *Bioscope* took a more positive view, regarding it as almost a great British film, but, like Manning, questioned its failure to take expert advice on Irish customs, such as the normally unarmed Irish police carrying guns, and on dialect. The reviewer noted that the talking sequences with European actress Lyn de Putti, who plays Katie Fox, were dubbed with 'a voice without a trace of an Irish accent', while Irish patriots speak 'in distinguished Oxfordian tones, which all but break down the illusion and turn drama into farce'.[24]

Ford's *The Informer* was also banned by Montgomery, though the Films Appeal Board passed it uncut, while the BBFC made 129 cuts to the film, including all references to violence, the IRA, and the Black and Tans. It is often regarded as not just one of Ford's finest films, but regularly features on top ten lists of best American films. Winner of four Academy awards in 1936 (Ford as director, Victor McLaglen as Best Actor in the role of Gypo, Dudley Nichols for Best Screenplay, and Max Steiner for Best Sound), this is perhaps surprising, not least because the film refuses the conventions of classical American cinema, and instead draws on the 1920s German Expressionist legacy, especially that of F. W. Murnau and his *Sunrise* (1927). Consequently, the film, which recreates Dublin in a Hollywood studio, makes the city 'unreal', and emphasises that the urban fog is really a metaphoric projection of Gypo's confused mind.[25] A third adaptation of O'Flaherty's book *Up Tight* (Jules Dassin, 1968) is set in Cleveland, Ohio, in the context of the struggle for African-American civil rights.

A more modest War of Independence project was the 1935 adaptation by playwright Denis Johnston of Frank O'Connor's seminal short story 'Guests of the Nation' (1931). In this silent film (though made well into the sound era), two British soldiers, Belcher and Hawkins, are held captive by the IRA in the hope of their being exchanged for IRA prisoners about to be executed. When the British authorities refuse an exchange of prisoners, the soldiers' IRA guards reluctantly take the men to their deaths. Johnston's film dramatised the main scenes in the story, but added events not depicted by O'Connor, including a column of IRA men, an ambush of a military convoy during which two IRA men are captured, people praying outside Kilmainham jail as the IRA men are about to be executed, and a woman courier (Shelah Richards) who passes on news of the execution. The film was assessed at the time in the context of how the humanistic empathy between the two opposing armies might overcome centuries of bitterness, but the British characters can be viewed also within the tradition of how the 'good' English are more Irish than the Irish themselves.[26] *Guests of the Nation* also features a range of well-known stage actors who went on to appear in primarily British and American feature films, including Barry Fitzgerald, Denis O'Dea, Hilton Edwards and Cyril Cusack, and in the process created considerable difficulties for both the artistic and financial policies of the National Theatre.

While the 1930s had been a prolific time for cinematic adaptations of the 1916–23 period, such films fell out of favour during the following decades. An exception is the popular version of Reardon Conner's 1934 novel *Shake Hands with the Devil*, adapted for the screen by Michael Anderson in 1959 and featuring James Cagney as an IRA leader during the War of Independence.[27] It was not until the 1980s that a number of War of Independence adaptations were produced again and these, in part, paralleled a series of novels dealing with contemporary Northern Ireland. Of those set during the 1919–21 period, most focused on the declining fortunes (politically and materially) of the Anglo-Irish Big House. In this regard, Pat O'Connor's adaptation of William Trevor's 1983 novel *Fools of Fortune* exposes how the focus on the world of the Anglo-Irish gentry during the War of Independence ends up emulating its British 'heritage' film counterparts. As *Monthly Film Bulletin* commented, there was nothing distinctly Irish about the film, 'which emerges as a piece of classically British filmmaking in the television style: restrained, elliptical, curiously reticent in its commitment to the passion inherent in the story of love thwarted by family trauma'.[28] The adaptation of Elizabeth Bowen's *The Last September* (Deborah Warner, 2000) also was more concerned with family matters, in this case its coming-of-age narrative focusing on the doomed relationships of Anglo-Irish teenager Lois (Keeley Hawes) with a lower-class British captain, a narrative line matched by a similar trajectory in her fascination and interrupted love affair with the leader of the local IRA unit.

The post-independence world is conveyed through the surreal writings of Spike Milligan's *Puckoon*, which was made into a feature film by Terence Ryan in 2002. In this film, set in 1924, the joint Irish-British Boundary Commission is deciding on the new border between Northern Ireland and the Irish Free State. After months of haggling over every inch of territory, the commissioners are forced to finish the job by hand when a bicycle accident destroys the surveyors' equipment. The result for the village of Puckoon is that the border is drawn down the middle of the village, dividing house from outhouse, husband from wife, pub chairs from the bar, the church from the cemetery. Dan Madigan

(Sean Hughes) wakes up to find the beer cheaper on the wrong side of the pub and a border patrol demanding passports. A more serious assessment of the independence struggle and its civil war aftermath is to be found in Cathal Black's 1995 feature film adaptation (or development) of 'Korea', a short story by John McGahern. In this film, set in 1952 in a County Cavan village, teenager Eamon Doyle (Andrew Scott) seeks, with the help of his girlfriend Una (Fiona Molony), to overcome the bitter legacy of civil war between their respective fathers (Donal Donnelly, Vass Anderson). Migration to the USA is Eamon's father's preferred option for his son as a means of detaching him from Una, but at this time such a journey is fraught with extreme danger as witnessed by Una's brother who has been killed fighting for the American army during the Korean War. When his stars and stripes-draped coffin is brought by boat to an island cemetery it produced one of Irish cinema's most poignant images. However, the film sides with Eamon, as ultimately it does with Irish modernisation: the Rural Electrification Scheme is being extended to the village, while tourism is signalled as a new source of income in rural Ireland, even if it displaces Eamon's father's traditional eel fishing on the lakes.

Such an engagement with the broken legacy of republican idealism during the War of Independence and its shattering afterwards in civil war has rarely been explored by Irish cinema, an explanation for such artistic retardation being the often confused response in the Republic of Ireland to the outbreak of war in Northern Ireland in 1969. In that regard, many of the literary texts, and certainly their cinematic adaptations, have, in the main, concerned themselves with the debilitating effects of violence on the individual. Whether it is Kieran Hickey's 1983 adaptation of William Trevor's short story 'Attracta', Bernard MacLaverty's *Cal* (Pat O'Connor, 1984), Daniel Morrin's *All Our Fault* (made by Thaddeus O'Sullivan as *Nothing Personal*, 1995), or Eoin McNamee's depiction of the Shankill Butchers in *Resurrection Man* (Marc Evans, 1998), Northern Ireland in the 1970s and 1980s has been represented as a place lacking hope, a future and even rationality. By concentrating (metaphorically) on Northern Ireland as a form of abattoir (where the third scene in O'Connor's *Cal* is set) there appears to be no future, only slaughter.

It was not until the advent of the Peace Process in the mid-1990s that such po-faced, regressive and backward-looking films gave way to a new generation of film-makers who, while not seeking to engage with the world of rational politics any more than their predecessors, at least envisaged Northern Ireland as containing hope, and also utilised political irreverence and satire, whereby republicans and loyalists, no more contextualised than in the past, at least were ridiculed, thus providing a form of cathartic release from the province's decades-long tensions. While the exemplary film here is the adaptation of Colin Bateman's novel *Divorcing Jack* (David Caffrey, 1998), these films are almost certainly only a transition stage with the most likely developments in representations of Northern Ireland being towards the cinematic norms already established in the Republic: the emergence of genre cinema (romantic comedy, 'ordinary' crime) as a means of finding a global market for the 'new look' Northern Ireland, and focusing on apolitical personal relationships. However, as two original films dealing with the 1980–1 hunger strikes, *H3* (Les Blair, 2001) and *Silent Grace* (Maeve Murphy, 2001), show, there are those who recognise that the past is very much part of the present and is likely to erupt into it at any time.

The Abbey Theatre and film

With many Abbey and Gate actors getting a taste of film production and its relatively well-paid employment, it is not surprising that one of the major crises which faced the Abbey Theatre, in particular from the 1930s onwards, was the drain of talent to cinema. While in the 1930s such high-profile actors as Sara Allgood and Barry Fitzgerald migrated to Hollywood, the following two decades saw a haemorrhaging of talent to the British film industry. A comparison of annual wages tells its own story. Whereas a full-time Abbey actor would receive less than £300 per annum in the mid-1940s (a rate which had been more or less static for fifteen years), remuneration in the British film industry could be eight times that amount. Furthermore, under British income tax law, an actor could work there for up to six months tax-free, allowing many actors to return to Ireland just for those roles they wished to take, rather than accept the dictat of the Abbey's autocratic artistic director, Ernest Blythe. The problem of such migration led Blythe desperately to seek in 1946 an increase in the Abbey's paltry annual government subsidy of £1,000, the same amount received in 1927 (though cut to £750 in 1933 and later gradually restored to £1,000), as a means of stemming the flow to Britain. Eventually, the subsidy was increased to £3,000 in 1947. An additional problem for the Abbey was that many writers were also being lured to film and television work, in part because of the Abbey's conservative artistic policy evident in the paucity of new plays being staged.

With the increasing inroads film producers were making with Irish subject films, such as the 1947 adaptations of Daphne de Maurier's Irish historical novel *Hungry Hill* (Brian Desmond Hurst) and Philip Rooney's Irish Land War drama *Captain Boycott* (Frank Launder), the appetite, especially within the British film industry, for both Irish actors and Irish-theme films continued unabated. Such was the extent of this following the release of Carol Reed's *Odd Man Out* (1947) – for which Abbey stalwarts such as F. J. McCormick, Denis O'Dea, Maureen Delany, Dan O'Herlihy and Cyril Cusack were singled out for praise – that one reviewer noted the following:

> It is an old joke in Dublin that the only members of the Abbey Theatre staff who have never been offered film contracts are the Irish wolfhound and his mistress who have appeared for over forty years on the programme.[29]

Thus, when the inevitable requests came for help in the screen adaptation of Abbey Theatre plays as well as for support for an Irish film studio, the Abbey management was forced to act or be marginalised. While the success of the Abbey's American tours in the 1930s encouraged interest in such developments, it was not until the 1950s that these were fully realised. Although Irish plays and novels continued to be adapted for the screen in the 1950s with exteriors sometimes shot in Ireland, interiors were filmed in Britain because of the lack of an Irish film studio. These films included Louis D'Alton's successful 1947 Abbey comedy *They Got What They Wanted*, which was reworked for the cinema and released under the title *Talk of a Million* (John Paddy Carstairs, 1951); M. J. Farrell's (Molly Keane) play *Treasure Hunt* (John Paddy Carstairs, 1952); novels such as Catherine Cookson's Belfast drama *Jacqueline* (1956) and her Dublin novel *Rooney* (1958), both directed by George H. Brown; and Una Troy's *We Are Seven* (adapted by Cyril Frankel as *She Didn't Say No!*, 1958).

The agent for major film developments in Ireland in the 1950s was the unlikely Emmet Dalton, whose varied career during the Irish War of Independence and Civil War included being with Michael Collins when he was assassinated in west Cork. Dalton entered the British film industry after World War II and, seeking to produce Irish-subject films, he, along with local partners, theatre impresario Louis Elliman and the Gate Theatre's Hilton Edwards, met with Blythe. The outcome of this collaboration was the establishment of a production company to adapt Abbey Theatre plays for the screen, especially television, and of which Blythe was a director.

The first play adapted, George Shiels's 1925 *Professor Tim*, concerns a 'professor' of zoology (Tim Kavanagh) who returns to an Irish village after an absence of twenty years. Though apparently poor, he purchases the estate of his niece's (Marie O'Donnell) once-wealthy fiancé Hugh (Ray McAnally) to stop it falling into the hands of a local gombeen landlord (Geoffrey Golden), and eventually gives it to the couple as a wedding present. Despite the presence of McAnally, one of the Abbey's rising stars, the film was overshadowed by the release the same year of John Ford's three-part *The Rising of the Moon*, its title story being taken from Lady Gregory's 1907 play. Undaunted, Dalton and Elliman expanded their plans to build film studios which were realised with the opening in 1958 of Ardmore Studios, a three sound stage facility at Bray, County Wicklow. If this finally allowed Irish film production to become integrated with the international film industry it was also intended to facilitate the production of Abbey play adaptations. As film producer Tom Hayes, commenting twenty years after Ardmore's establishment, remarked, the 'basic aim was to build an Irish film industry powered by the Abbey Theatre'.[30] Indeed, as early as 1917, as noted above, the Abbey was seen as the natural means through which film in Ireland would emerge: 'Any company starting in Ireland without representation from the group of actors who have developed Irish drama would have lacked an essential element in striving for high artistic and general acceptable success.'[31] In the opinion of a reviewer writing over thirty years later, this position remained. Writing on Paul Rotha's *No Resting Place* (1951), a feature film set in Wicklow about Irish travellers (adapted from the novel by Ian Niall), and in which many Abbey actors appeared, the *Guardian* critic deemed it 'the best effort [so far] to establish what might be called the Abbey school of filming – filming which would display the real-life integrity of the best Continental models'.[32] Even though such a view held limited currency in the 1950s commercial cinema, nevertheless there were few alternatives for a professional mainstream Irish film practice at the time.

Fittingly, another George Shiels play, *The New Gosoon*, retitled for the screen as *Sally's Irish Rogue* (George Pollock, 1958), was the first of the Ardmore Studios' adaptations to be released. Set in Wicklow, it concerns the relationship between Sally (Julie Harris) and Luke Casey (Tim Seely), who temporarily rejects his marriage commitment to her because of his overbearing mother, and takes up with another girl. Reviewers raised an issue already alluded to, namely the miscasting of even minor foreign actors, such as the British Tim Seely, instead of the use of an Irish actor. The second of the Abbey plays adapted at Ardmore was Walter Macken's *Home is the Hero*, in which Macken himself received widespread praise for his role as Paddo, 'the Goliath of Galway', who, in a drunken rage, kills the father of Maura (Marie O'Donnell), childhood sweetheart of his son Willie (Arthur Kenendy). During his five years in prison Paddo's patriarchal role in the family has been taken by Willie, but he resumes his previous oppressive role upon his release. Opposing Willie and Maura's relationship, as well as his daughter Josie's (Joan O'Hara) involvement with a local playboy, he is eventually subdued by Willie.

In spite of the praise for Macken's performance, doubts were raised about this and other adaptations being able to transcend their stage origins,[33] a factor not confined to the 1950s but still current in the late 1990s with such films as *Disco Pigs* (Kirsten Sheridan, 2001) from the play by Enda Walsh, and *Saltwater* (2000), directed by Conor McPherson from his own play. Perhaps what all of these adaptations have in common is that the literary or dramatic text takes precedence over the image. In a society anchored in the culture of the word (whether oral tradition or the obsession with James Joyce's texts) recourse to the image is often deemed an unfortunate by-product of cinema. With very few exceptions, the failure to imagine *visually* a play, novel or even original script remains *the* most serious limitation to the development of a dynamic Irish cinema.

Another 1959 release was an adaptation of Hugh Leonard's first play, *The Big Birthday* (released in Britain as *Broth of a Boy*). In this film, a British television reporter Tony (Tony Wright) seeks out 110-year-old Patrick Farrell (Barry Fitzgerald), who is thought to be the oldest man in the world. Having falsified his age in order to get a pension, he refuses the publicity. However, his granddaughter Silin (Julie Thornton), who falls in love with Tony, convinces Patrick to co-operate, whereupon it transpires that he is, after all, the oldest man in the world. Although this was regarded as the weakest of the Abbey adaptations, another two were produced: a 1960 film version of St John Ervine's 1936 play *Boyd's Shop*, in which the professionalism of the Abbey Players was wasted on 'a naïve and self-consciously charming story',[34] and what is perhaps the most interesting, and amusing, of the adaptations, director Muriel Box's 1959 version of Louis D'Alton's play *This Other Eden* (first staged posthumously in 1953).

A prologue set during the War of Independence shows an IRA leader, Carberry, driving to a rendezvous with his friend Devereaux (Niall MacGinnis) to discuss the end of the war with a British officer. Carberry is shot by the Black and Tans and it is presumed that the British officer betrayed him. The film proper is set twenty years later, when a statue is about to be unveiled in Carberry's honour in his home village. During the course of the film a range of themes is explored, such as the memory of the dead patriots, wealthy nuns, political opportunism, emigration, illegitimacy, Irish/English relationships and the Irish language, not to mention modern art, the idiom in which the (despised) statue of Carberry has been rendered. The catalyst for many of these issues is Englishman Brown (Leslie Phillips), the son of the wrongly accused British officer, who falls in love with local girl Maire (Audrey Dalton), a representative of a younger generation which is not so tied to the memory of the struggle with the old enemy, England.

Three of *This Other Eden*'s most reviled characters are Clannery (Harry Brogan), who is xenophobically anti-English, local T. D. McNeely (Paul Farrell) and Maire's father (Geoffrey Golden), the ultimate gombeen man, who is a hotelier, garage owner and auctioneer. It is through Devereaux, now the village's newspaper owner, that post-independence hypocrisy is exposed. Indeed, the resonance of Devereaux to Emmet Dalton's own life – that he was somehow responsible for the death of Carberry / Collins – hovers over the film. When the crude modern sculpture is blown up, a village mob blames Brown, but it is revealed that the real culprit is aspiring cleric Conor Heaphy (Norman Rodway), who turns out to be Carberry's illegitimate son. He was conceived while Carberry was on the run and had no opportunity to marry the girl, who was Devereaux's sister, and who subsequently died in childbirth.[35]

While such a potent mix indicated the potential for a critical Irish cinema, sadly neither in the Abbey Theatre adaptations, nor in the broader film culture, was there support for such a cinema of ideas. Instead, after this initial and brief phase of Abbey adaptations, Ardmore Studios converted to a more international cinema. A few key films, certainly, were produced there, most particularly the adaptations of *Shake Hands with the Devil*, as noted, and of Arthur Roth's 1958 novel dealing with IRA activity in Northern Ireland during World War II, *A Terrible Beauty* (Tay Garnett, 1960). However, most of the subsequent films made at Ardmore simply used Ireland as another location and were unconcerned with the cultural impact their films might have. Consequently, it was not until the 1970s and after that a significant range of films was made which drew on the Irish literary and dramatic traditions, and in doing so produced some of the most culturally incisive screen adaptations of Irish literature.

Breakthroughs in Irish cinema

It is now widely accepted that the pioneering film for Irish cinema was Bob Quinn's *Caoineadh Airt Uí Laoire* (1975), a reworking of the last great lament in the Irish language written by Eileen, wife of Art O'Leary, killed in 1773. Unlike most of the other 'Wild Geese', he returned to Ireland in 1767 to assert his ownership of his family's ancestral lands, but was killed by English soldiers six years later. The film is structured around the members of an amateur drama group in Irish-speaking Connemara who are putting on a play about O'Leary under the direction of an Englishman, played by playwright John Arden, during which both representation and realism are questioned. Interspersed within this formally complex film are excerpts from the poem; filmed inserts set in the eighteenth century; modern-day rehearsal and debate around the play's direction; and 'real' interviews on current politics. The interweaving of present and past is further reinforced by the play's director playing the eighteenth-century landowner, while the actor playing Art also doubles for his 'historical' role, and, like Arden, seems to (over-) identify with the role.

This complex periodisation, together with its meditation on the nature of the cinematic process, places the film firmly within a Modernist sensibility. Indeed, the widespread notion that the Irish literary tradition could be used only for 'realist' short stories or classical narratives has ignored the alternative tradition within Irish literature (notwithstanding the limitations in the adaptation by Strick of Joyce's Modernist novel, as already mentioned). The case of writer and film-maker Neil Jordan illustrates the dilemma. In a piece of film criticism entitled 'Word and Image' (1978),[36] Jordan wrote of the relationship between the different strains of the Irish literary tradition and the cinema while reviewing Irish film director Cathal Black's first film, his 1976 adaptation of a John McGahern short story, 'Wheels'. The context in which he was writing was one where only a handful of Irish films were being made, but these were initiating what would become within little over a decade an internationally acclaimed cinema, ironically with Jordan at the forefront.

In this article, Jordan noted that while the most prominent screen images about Ireland had concerned the Northern Ireland Troubles, other images of Irish experience remained unexplored, having found expression only in the written word. In common with many Irish commentators he suggested that in anticipation of what form Irish cinema might take, it would necessarily rely on an examination of the literary medium through which Irish experience has been 'most thoroughly and brilliantly drawn'. Acknowledging that comparisons and marriages between the written word and visual images were unfashionable in the 1970s, he added that it was in areas of visual achievement, especially the decorative calligraphy and monumental sculpture of Early Irish Christianity, that 'the visual image performs a function that is uncannily close to the verbal concept'. Moreover, he noted that the 'best achievements' of indigenous Irish cinema to date, *Caoineadh Airt Uí Laoire* and *Wheels*, both took their impetus from literary works.

While Jordan praised the literary 'realist' tradition, it was the Irish Modernist (as well as the 'surreal' and gothic) legacy which he chose to highlight in 1978. Thus, while *Wheels* explored 'the tacts and contours' portrayed in the Irish short story, there remained another Irish 'imaginative' landscape, mapped out by Joyce, Yeats, Swift and Beckett, whose work, if not as easily analysed as the short story, offers in 'its myths, its obsessions and its metaphysics' an equally and no less concrete part of our heritage. Though such an 'attempt by film to depict [this latter] world would be infinitely more difficult', in Jordan's words, it would also be 'infinitely more rewarding'. This call for a cinema informed on the one hand by a Modernist engagement with the past, and on the other, by the literary 'realist' tradition, highlights the tension which is at the core of Jordan's own film work, but which is also apparent in the work of other Irish film-makers. In Jordan's case his films usually have a 'realist' beginning and then go somewhere else, as he himself put it, to a realm which may be the non-rational or the supernatural.

In setting such a challenge for Irish film-makers just as Irish cinema was coming into being, it was clear that the literary adaptation would continue to play a significant role. Jordan himself has adapted three Irish literary works. The first of these was his reworking of his own short story 'Night in Tunisia' (1976) in *The Miracle* (1990); the second, his acclaimed 1997 version of Patrick McCabe's novel *The Butcher Boy*, for many the key Irish feature film of the 1990s; while four years later, he directed Samuel Beckett's fourteen-minute *Not I* as part of the *Beckett on Film* project. Of course, other Irish writings have cast creative shadows on his work, notably the adaptation of Bernard McLaverty's novel *Cal*; and Frank O'Connor's 'Guests of the Nation' and Brendan Behan's *The Hostage* in *The Crying Game* (1992).[37]

Jordan nevertheless also appreciates the limitations that the literary tradition imposes on visual culture. Commenting on his decision to forego (temporarily, as it has emerged) his own writing career as short-story writer and novelist, he said that he had exhausted the medium, his first novel *The Past* (1980) having been largely made up of description with the effect that he was 'writing himself out of [the] form entirely'. In fact, on numerous occasions Jordan himself (and reviewers of his literary fiction) have laid stress not so much on the narrative drive of his writing, but on its visual power. *The Past*, for example, is largely devoid of dialogue. Furthermore, Jordan has highlighted the difficulty in maintaining the different forms of expression which seem to struggle against one another. Jordan did not abandon prose fiction: three further novels, *The Dream of a Beast* (1983), *Sunrise with Sea Monster* (1994) and *Shade* (2004), have been published to date. Additionally, interest in the Irish literary tradition, especially its gothic elements, remains an influence on his film output. After all, it is as a film-maker that his reputation largely rests even if some reviewers regarded this as a great loss to literature; 'fiction's loss', the *Irish Times* literary critic Eileen Battersby wrote in 1994, 'was film-making's gain'.[38] Another reason cited by Jordan for his shift from literature to film has been his belief that Irish writing had gone over the same territory time and again. Yet, ironically, he himself, at least in his early film work, revisited aspects of that dominant literary tradition. His first script 'Travellers' reworked, at least in part, J. M. Synge's *The Playboy of the Western World* (1907), even if this element did not find its way into the final film, *Traveller* (1981), directed by Joe Comerford.[39] Thus, although many of the most innovative films, such as those by Jordan, were from original scripts, the strength of the literary heritage has always been seen as a major marketing advantage for Irish cinema.

The breakthrough film for Irish cinema as regards the international marketplace was unquestionably Jim Sheridan's 1989 adaptation of Christy Brown's 1954 autobiographical novel *My Left Foot*. Nominated for five Academy awards, it won two, for Daniel Day-Lewis as the adult Christy and Brenda Fricker as his mother. The film was in sharp contrast – industrially, formally and narratively – to the smaller-scale indigenous films of the 1970s and 1980s from the independent film sector, which were made on limited budgets, and were influenced by European 'art' cinema and its Modernist sensibility. Moreover, these films were often based on original scripts which were anchored within a social, political or historical discourse, and often carried a critique of the dominant British or American cinematic representations of the Irish, such as Quinn's *Caoineadh Airt Uí Laoire* and his *Poitín* (1978), Thaddeus O'Sullivan's *On a Paving Stone Mounted* (1978), Joe Comerford's *Down the Corner* (1978) and his *Traveller*, Cathal Black's *Our Boys* (1981) and his *Pigs* (1984), Pat Murphy and John Davies's *Maeve* (1981) and Pat Murphy's *Anne Devlin* (1984); nor did these films seek to engage a mainstream commercial cinema audience. Most importantly, *My Left Foot* mapped the way for a new more commercially and entertainment-driven cinema more akin to Hollywood than the European model.

'Bookended' by a visit by Christy and his family to a Big House of the Anglo-Irish gentry of another era, in the first instance the film is a very conventional three-act drama with a decisive trajectory: it depicts in the first act the relative deprivations of Dublin working-class family life in the 1940s and 1950s; in a second act our hero suffers setbacks, yet through these develops adult awareness; and in the third act he achieves not only success as an artist and writer, but in the film's climax, finds a wife. Such an uplifting individualist and ultimately Oedipal tale of the cerebral palsy victim overcoming physical adversity and finding a lover / wife (or another mother) is a familiar one, at least in narrative structural terms within mainstream commercial cinema, especially its American variety. As a result, its endorsement by the Academy Awards and its hailing as an Irish national event by, amongst others, the man who closed the Irish Film Board in 1987, Taoiseach Charles Haughey – who chose, like most others, to ignore the fact that *My Left Foot* was largely funded from British and American sources – suggests that Irish commercial cinema had come of age. With the adaptation of this book, not only was the central role of Ireland's literary output confirmed for Irish cinema, but in sweeping aside Irish 'art' cinema it elevated traditional narrative cinema as the form most favoured for a new international Irish cinema, a process which would be consolidated in the 1990s with the re-establishment of the Film Board and the advent of 'Celtic Tiger' cinema.[40]

Jim Sheridan, originally a playwright and theatre director before embarking on a film career, chose as his second project an adaptation of John B. Keane's play *The Field* (1990, from the 1965 stage play). In this case, Richard Harris, who plays the film's main protagonist, Bull McCabe, was nominated for an Academy award, but unlike Day-Lewis and Fricker, he was unsuccessful. While *My Left Foot* was generally true to the periodisation of Brown's book, this is not the case with *The Field*. While adaptations come in many forms, even the most conventional or artistically lazy necessarily make departures, such as dropping or transforming (minor) characters or events or, as is the case with the adaptation of Brian Moore's 1955 novel *The Lonely Passion of Judith Hearne* (Jack Clayton, 1987), changing the setting (from Belfast to Dublin). The differences between Keane's play and Sheridan's film are so significant, however, that it is worthwhile pointing out some of the more important ones as it helps illustrate how the demands of the international film industry can often alter a text so completely that its original cultural dynamic may be lost. This is also arguably the case in Pat O'Connor's 1998 adaptation of Brian Friel's play *Dancing at Lughnasa*, which loses much of the play's poignancy and subtlety as it descends into a cinematic and touristic celebration of the Irish landscape.

While many minor scenes, characterisations and even gender relations were modified in *The Field*, perhaps the two most glaring changes were the film's periodisation and the role of the Bull's nemesis, William Dee. The original events upon which Keane's play are based occurred in the late 1950s, and the play, first performed in 1965, was able to explore the issue of modernity and tradition within the framework of Ireland's social and economic transformation in the 1960s. The film, by contrast, is set in the 1930s, in fact 1939, and thus loses such resonances. It is in part because of this that the Yank (Tom Berenger) appears so incongruous and his desire to pave over such a remote field appears absurd within that period. The Yank, of course, is not in the play, as he replaces the character of William Dee. Dee, in contrast to the Yank, is an Irish-born interloper who is returning from England with his wife, not from the politically (though not culturally) neutral United States. As a result, the play's powerful theme of the English-influenced Irishman seeking to take land from the 'native' Irish was diluted by the introduction of the Yank, a character effectively imposed on the production because, while the film was funded by British television, the crucial distribution deal was with the American company Miramax (also distributors of *My Left Foot*), which required American audience recognition of one of their own (even if minor) film stars. Similarly, the change of period was within the realm of non-Irish audience familiarity with locations being set in a pre-modern, even primitive, and, arguably, given the Bull's increasingly 'unreal' behaviour, mythological time.[41] Consequently, the attempt by the socially, culturally and politically committed Irish cinema sector in the 1970s and 1980s to break the cycle of foreign-influenced cinema images can be said, at least in this context, to have suffered a setback. The evidence of the 1990s is that while such blatant regression was generally not repeated, and a great many of the films made, both adaptations and original scripts, were anchored within contemporary Ireland, yet the form of cinematic narrative was clearly established. Having said that, many films have been produced which provide complex insights and juxtapositions often unavailable to the novelist or scriptwriter. The case of *December Bride* helps to illustrate this.

Sam Hanna Bell's novel *December Bride*, first published in 1951, was adapted for the stage as *That Woman from Rathard* in 1955, while in 1963 another version was produced for Northern Ireland radio, all of which points to the text's germinal importance in Northern Ireland culture. Additionally, novelist Maurice Leitch adapted the novel for the screen (though this project was not realised), but it was David Rudkin's script which was made into a feature film by director Thaddeus O'Sullivan and released in 1990. Set in the early twentieth century, both novel and film were able to explore issues which might have been more difficult to examine in a contemporary film set in Northern Ireland. While it can be argued that the film downplays the novel's religious sectarianism, its focus on a rural Protestant (Presbyterian) community in which a servant, Sarah (Saskia Reeves), moves into the farmhouse of two brothers (Donal McCann, Ciaran Hinds) and has sexual relations with both of them, producing two children in the process, the paternity of whom remains a mystery, is not the kind of story one normally associates with such a community. Yet this triangular relationship throws into relief the narrow-mindedness, hypocrisy and superficiality of the local clergyman and his parishioners, who not only are outraged at the trio's behaviour but respond violently to it. Though shown as outcasts from their own community, their depiction allows for a meditation not just on such bigotry, but on the very land which they occupy. If the Lambeg drum reminds all, especially Catholics, that the planters have taken over this part of Ulster, Sarah's placement at the center of the narrative, and her positioning within the physical landscape, radically alters the tradition of male-dominated representations of the land. In this latter sense, too, the tradition within Irish cinematic (and more broadly visual culture) of representing the land as a place for playfulness and leisure, or as a sublime and awesome environment against which man must heroically struggle to tame, is subverted here, with human inscription continually reinforced, especially through unromanticised agricultural labour. Thus, the film, which follows on from the independent cinema's reimagining of landscape during the 1970s and 1980s – in films such as Quinn's *Poitín*, *Budawanny* (1987), and its reworking as *The Bishop's Story* (1994), Kieran Hickey's *Exposure* (1978) and *Maeve*, amongst others – succeeds in presenting a new version of the Irish landscape, one in which the visual tradition of the Catholic-nationalist association with the rural landscape is problematised through the insertion not just of a Protestant community, but of a strong woman character within it.[42] This is most effectively conveyed in the film's opening and closing scenes when it is Sarah's gaze on the landscape which is balanced in the frame with a gnarled tree, representative of (sublime) nature, and a reminder of the precariousness of all human settlements and their communities.

Such a complex positioning of women (and men) within the Irish landscape has a singularly important predecessor in John Ford's *The Quiet Man* (1952). Adapted from Maurice Walsh's original 1933 short story and its subsequent incorporation into his novel *Green Rushes* (1935), the film is unquestionably the most influential and most analysed film about Ireland ever produced. Luke Gibbons has very ably shown how Walsh's original (and slight) short story was transformed into the Ford film, with its mediations on the following complex range of themes: reverse migration (from the USA to Ireland, which together with more generalised migration to Ireland was to become an increasing trope within Irish cinema from the 1990s onwards), violence (communal symbolic and, in the background, political), independent women and, most of all, the issue of representation itself.[43] So influential has this film been that not only did it become the paradigm for Irish tourist films, but also it is the one film against which almost any aspect of Irish film culture is measured, both positively and negatively. It is testimony to Ford's film and Walsh's texts that it has allowed for a mature revisiting of that endlessly circulating dichotomy of realism and romanticism[44] and where the former is not, at least in the Irish context, seen to be necessarily the most critically or culturally productive. Gibbons's incisive analysis, in part, has reformulated the critical focus on the film away from Ireland to suggest its influential role in American cinema itself. Thus Irish cinema, too, at its most critically and culturally engaging, is also exporting its own cinematic representations as a means of problematising diasporic Irish cinema and culture.

The emergence of a new Irish cinema

Having argued that, in the main, literary and theatrical adaptations of Irish literature have had a debilitating effect on the emergence of Irish visual culture, it remains to scrutinise more closely the shift in Irish cultural activity towards the personal from the late 1980s onwards. In this post-modern preoccupation with the self and the body in the context of (relative) material prosperity of Irish people, the rupture into society of issues such as institutional abuse and migration indicated that the repressed had returned at the moment of celebratory capitalism in Celtic Tiger Ireland. In this regard, adaptations of Irish literary work continued to play a vital but often conservative cultural role.

While the focus on the personal may have served a cult of consumption (of sex, food, property, etc.), it is often through the personal that people can develop connections between their 'real' subject position and the state, or between the private and the public spheres. By relaying in graphic detail such abuse through personal testimony, television played a central role in exposing decades of child sexual abuse in institutions run by religious orders with state support. Additionally, two cinematic adaptations in particular scutinise the religious institutions where tens of thousands of young boys and girls were detained during the post-independence decades. Set in 1939, Patrick Galvin's *Song for a Raggy Boy* (Aisling Walsh, 2003) focuses on how a lay teacher (Aidan Quinn) responds to the verbal and physical abuse doled out by the Christian Brothers in a reformatory school, while a more modern version of such an institution is depicted in the adaptation of Bernard MacLaverty's 1980 novel *Lamb* (Colin Gregg, 1985), in which a Brother (Liam Neeson) takes one of the boys away from its harsh environment, but such a relationship is doomed to failure. Something of this abrasive world even filters through the blackly nostalgic realist style narrative of *Angela's Ashes* (Alan Parker, 1999) from Frank McCourt's best-selling autobiographical novel, and also appears in McCabe and Jordan's *The Butcher Boy*. This focus on religious institutions and the dysfunctional Irish family reminds us that the idealised family, as represented in the 1937 Constitution, was built on a legal and cultural lie whereby issues of gender and social class were suppressed, and in the context of post-1960s liberalisation is now seen as part of a social and cultural crisis in Irish society. However, that which is replacing the 'traditional' Irish family may not be the panacea for Irish social ills, but like much of the literature and cinematic representations of Irish-American culture for many decades, the dysfunctional family is now at the centre of Irish national discourse.

With the family emerging as a site of cultural engagement, the long-standing issue of migration had never gone away, but was only reoriented into a new complexity. In tandem with the demographic shift from country to city from the 1960s onwards, cinema brought its own inimitable focus to the topic, even if the treatment was more concerned with the family than the broader social and economic forces at work in Ireland. In John McGahern's 'Wheels', as adapted by Cathal Black in 1976, a migrant from rural Ireland who has settled in Dublin returns to visit his father and stepmother on the family farm. He is gruffly treated by his father, who realises not only that the farm will probably pass out of the family with his generation, but that the relative luxury, freedom and economic independence experienced by his son is one which he would have envied as a young man. This was a prescient vision of how internal migration would accelerate, but also how centuries-old rhythms of farming would give way to the accelerated dynamics of urban Ireland. For many 'modernisers' the leaving of such a patriarch could only be viewed positively, especially by women, as was the case with another tyrannical father who is at the centre of McGahern's *Amongst Women*. In this 1998 television series the iron-grip of the father in 1950s rural Ireland is only loosened by his daughters and sons as they leave for Dublin or London, and by their stepmother. Similarly, in Brian Friel's *Philadelphia Here I Come!*, adapted for the screen in 1970 by John Quested, Gar (Donal McCann as the public persona) debates with his alter ego (Des Cave as the private persona) as to whether he should leave the depressing home town and migrate to Philadelphia, where his aunt lives. Like Gar, for many men and women in 1950s and 1960s Ireland, the answer was in the affirmative, a decision also taken by jobless Ginger Coffey in the adaptation of Brian Moore's 1960 novel *The Luck of Ginger Coffey* (Irvin Kreshner, 1964), who migrates from Ireland with his wife and fourteen year-old daughter to Canada.

The 1990s also saw a new social and cultural dynamic emerge, namely immigration, and with it a series of filmic texts focusing on both reverse migration and the new phenomenon of political and economic refugees. While the feature film *The Nephew* (Eugene Brady, 1986), from an original script, made comic relief of the African/Irish-American 'return of the native' to the west of Ireland, the traditional paternalistic Irish attitude to non-westerners, Africans in particular, reinforced the (neo-)colonial stereotype of the infantalising of the colonised, a condition with which the Irish ought to be familiar. The discomfort felt in these circumstances by Irish people enjoying a new privileged material reality is a subject explored in just a few films. While Irish prejudice is satirised in Gerard Stembridge's television film *Black Day at Black Rock* (2001), and an African is the subject of deportation in Roddy Doyle's *When Brendan Met Trudy* (Kieron J. Walsh, 2001), the most poignant exploration of the relationship between Irish and African cultures, and religious practices, comes from a dramatic source.

In Pat O'Connor's adaptation of Brian Friel's popular play *Dancing at Lughnasa*, while concerned in part with reverse migration (and at the end of the play, emigration), the outsiders throw into relief both the oppressive conditions under which local people lived – in this case five sisters in rural Donegal in the 1930s – and the nature of belief. When their older brother, a priest (Michael Gambon), comes home from the African 'missions', he appears to have 'regressed' to a pagan state, and his 'going native' takes on a quite different connotation to its normal Irish pejorative meaning as his sympathies for African 'pagan' beliefs are expressed, much to the distress of his sister (Meryl Streep) who is employed as a primary schoolteacher by the local Catholic priest. The appearance of another outsider, the feckless though charming boyfriend of one of the sisters who has fathered her boy, and who gives them a glimpse of love, desire and freedom, throws into stark relief the blighted emotional lives of women in particular in rural Ireland of this period. Overarching these elements is a subtlety of language which is transcended only by the sisters' emotional and carefree dancing to music on the radio during the pagan festival of Lughnasa, elements which did not always translate so readily to the screen.[45]

As Irish writing emerged from the stranglehold of both Modernist and realist male writers, and women became more central to Irish writing, it was often in the devalued genre of popular romantic fiction that such voices were heard. When the post-World War II generation of women writers emerged in the 1960s, their texts were filled with depictions of backwardness in rural Ireland, while celebrating the economic and sexual freedom which the 1960s economic boom allowed. Thus, representations of apparently independent women fill the 'popular' novels of Edna O'Brien and Maeve Binchy, both of whom explore the oppressive environment for women living in conservative Catholic rural or small-town Irish society in the 1950s and 1960s, and their decision to move to Dublin. The three adaptations of O'Brien's work directed by Desmond Davis – *Girl with Green Eyes* (1964) from her 1962 novel *The Lonely Girl*; *I Was Happy Here* (1965), which reworks her short story 'A Woman by the Seaside'; and *The Country Girls* (1983) from the 1960 novel of the same name – focus on women brought up in County Clare in the 1950s and their subsequent migration to Dublin or London, involvement with men and becoming pregnant. Happiness is generally not the outcome for many of these women, a generic condition which also afflicts some of Maeve Binchy's characters. In her case, the three girls at the centre of *Circle of Friends*, adapted by Pat O'Connor for the screen in 1995, become exposed to the exciting temptations and dangers of city and student life in the late 1950s, including unwanted pregnancy and inevitable migration to England, though the sexually 'good', rational and independent Benny (Minnie Driver) determines her own happy future.[46]

As discussed earlier, the rural has dominated Irish cultural discourse, and it was not until the social and cultural transformations of the post-1960s decades that the cultural focus shifted more fully to urban Ireland. Representations of Dublin itself, though rare in the history of Irish cinema both in terms of adaptations and original scripts, emerged in the 1980s and 1990s as major elements of Irish cinematic output. In part this was a response by a new generation of film-makers to the changes in Irish society, most notably increased urbanisation and its cultural expression, which made it apparently quite different to its rural literary predecessors. 1970s and 1980s film-makers such as Joe Comerford (*Down the Corner* (1978), *Withdrawal* (1982)) and Cathal Black (*Pigs* (1984)) produced films based on original scripts which focused on working-class and marginal Dubliners; Kieran Hickey (*Criminal Conversation* (1980)) examined middle-class suburbia; and, in the 1990s, such diverse directors as Paddy Breathnach (*I Went Down* (1997)) and Gerard Stembridge (*About Adam* (2001)) drew, respectively, on contemporary criminal and middle-class Dublin life. It is, however, two very different authors, James Joyce and Roddy Doyle, who perhaps require the most attention.

As noted, Strick's *Ulysses* was a disappointing attempt to produce a 'realist' film which failed to draw on Modernist or avant-garde film practices in order to engage the viewer in the production of meaning which is such a central feature of Joyce's aesthetic. Here simple recitation of Joyce's words is often deemed sufficient to convey their visual qualities. Such linguistic dexterity (and explicitness) was enough for the Irish Film Censor to ban the film in both 1967 and 1977, a ban only rescinded when Strick resubmitted the film in 2001.

Strick was more successful with his adaptation of Joyce's *Portrait of the Artist as a Young Man* (1977), perhaps because the original's 'realist' aesthetic was largely maintained. An altogether more adventurous and successful adaptation of a Joyce text is Mary Ellen Bute's *Passages from James Joyce's Finnegans Wake* (1967). In this film, adapted by Mary Manning from her 1955 stage play *Finnegans Wake, a Dramatisation in Six Scenes from the Book of James Joyce*, Dublin publican Finnegan dreams he is present at his own wake, and experiences being part of the universe, embracing the whole of history and all of humanity. Using contemporary experimental film techniques, it seeks to give a sense of the radical nature of Joyce's text.

Perhaps because of the accessibility of its source – the most appreciated of the short stories in *Dubliners* – John Huston's *The Dead* (1987) is, of all Joyce's adaptations, the one which has received the most critical attention. In a special 2002 issue of the *Yale Journal of Criticism* on Ireland, four of the contributors write on 'The Dead' as short story and film. In the contributions by Luke Gibbons[47] and Kevin Whelan,[48] and elsewhere by Kevin Barry,[49] the extensive textual excavation undertaken is designed in particular to uncover the latent Irish historical memory in both texts. In that regard, the story's and film's anchorage in 1904 Dublin seems less important than, after Frederic Jameson, the national allegory which the texts (perhaps unconsciously) explore. Most extensively, the social and political conditions of colonialism are examined, often from the point of view of the servant Lily.[50]

The adaptation of Roddy Doyle's novel *The Commitments* (Alan Parker, 1991) signalled a very different type of Irish urban sensibility either from that seen in Joyce or even that of the earlier working-class writer Christy Brown. Here was a cosmopolitan Dublin where northside Dubliners could envisage themselves as being the hip interpreters of African-American soul music. Whatever the problematics of appropriating such a culturally specific music for white western Europeans, the vibrancy of Parker's film overcame for many its cultural hybridity and dubious references to the Irish being the blacks of Europe and northside Dubliners being the blacks of Ireland. Doyle's novels and their screen adaptations are marked by a modern secular humanism and display a sense of exuberance and pleasure, and delight in their Irishness, if not through place, then through language.[51] While Doyle, amongst other writers, shifted the focus from rural to urban Ireland, authentic Irish experience in the city is seen to reside in working-class communities. Indeed, many literary, cinematic and television representations of urban Ireland in recent decades have sought to contrast working-class culture and community with middle-class materialism and social alienation. In this regard, the lack of 'tangible imagery', to use Colm Lincoln's phrase,[52] makes Dublin look like any other place. Thus, Roddy Doyle's 'Barrytown', as seen in the adaptations of *The Commitments*, *The Snapper* (Stephen Frears, 1993) and *The Van* (Stephen Frears, 1996), lacks 'particularity', with his suburbia devoid of history or memory, an unremarkable place which has the sameness of other nameless working-class estates anywhere else in the world. But, by concentrating on community and family, the *real* Ireland, at least at the visual or cinematic level, continues to be located in the rural. In that sense, the image has proven to be more powerful than the word, whether the films are literary adaptations or not.

Conclusion

Irish literature has provided cinema with many of its most incisive productions, but literary critics often have failed to acknowledge the differences between the two media, preferring to highlight the deviations from, rather than developments of, the original text. As a result, the nuances of cinema, not to mention its visual and aural richness, have been neglected in favour of an analysis of literary narrative form. Nevertheless, the production of cinematic texts at a time different to the original novel, play or short story throws into relief contemporary cultural and social conditions. In these adaptations, the faithfulness is not necessarily to the original text but to the environment in which the film is produced. Thus, MacDonagh's *Knocknagow*, Johnston's *Guests of the Nation*, or Box's *This Other Eden* are film texts which need to be explored on their own terms and within their own milieux. Whatever the merits of these films, until Irish cinema transcends its dependence on Irish literature, it will fail to become the (relatively) independent art form of which it is capable and the consequent imbalance between the literary and the visual in Irish culture will remain.

Notes

1. See Samuel Beckett, *Film: Complete Scenario*, with essay 'On Directing *Film*' by Alan Schneider (London: Faber and Faber, 1972); and Enoch Brater, 'The Thinking Eye in Beckett's *Film*', *Modern Language Quarterly* 36 (1975), pp. 166–76.
2. Luke Gibbons, '"The Cracked Looking Glass" of Cinema: James Joyce, John Huston, and the Memory of "The Dead"', *Yale Journal of Criticism* 15, 1 (2002), p. 127.
3. For a general account of Kalem's visit to Ireland, see Kevin Rockett, 'The Silent Period', in Kevin Rockett, Luke Gibbons and John Hill, *Cinema and Ireland* (London: Croom Helm, 1987), pp. 7–12.
4. *Age* (25 September 1911), p. 11.
5. Mary Manning, *Irish Statesman* 13, 25 (22 February 1930), p. 497.

6. See Rockett et al., *Cinema and Ireland*, pp. 53–5.
7. *Bioscope* (21 December 1911), p. 829.
8. W. Stephen Bush, *Moving Picture World* (14 December 1912), p. 1,065.
9. See A. Nicholas Vardac, *Stage to Screen: Theatrical Method from Garrick to Griffith* (Cambridge, MA: Harvard University Press, 1949), pp. 41ff; and Luke Gibbons, 'Romanticism, Realism and Irish Cinema', in Rockett et al., *Cinema and Ireland*, pp. 213ff.
10. See Kevin Rockett, 'Representations of Irish History in Fiction Films made before the 1916 Rising', in Laurence Geary, ed. *Rebellion and Remembrance in Modern Ireland* (Dublin: Four Courts Press, 2001), pp. 214–28; and Gibbons, 'Romanticism, Realism and Irish Cinema', p. 223.
11. See Rockett, 'The Silent Period', pp. 18–23.
12. *Irish Limelight* 4, 1 (1920); see also Rockett, 'The Silent Period', pp. 23–30.
13. Alfred Hitchcock, quoted in François Truffaut with the collaboration of Helen G. Scott, *Hitchcock* (1967; London: Panther Books, 1969), p. 48.
14. Sean O'Casey, in a letter to Frank McCarthy, 27 March 1949, cited in David Krause, ed. *The Letters of Sean O'Casey, Vol. XI: 1942–1954* (New York: Macmillan, 1980), p. 603.
15. See Kevin Rockett, *Irish Film Censorship: A Cultural Journey from Silent Cinema to Internet Pornography* (Dublin: Four Courts Press, 2004); and Kevin Rockett, 'Protecting the Family and the Nation: the Official Censorship of American Cinema in Ireland, 1923–1954', *Historical Journal of Film, Radio and Television* 20, 3 (2000), pp. 283–300.
16. *Limerick Chronicle* (12 November 1930), p. 5.
17. *Limerick Chronicle* (25 November 1930).
18. Sean O'Casey in a letter to Lovat Dickson at publishers Macmillan, 11 May 1945, cited in Krause, ed. *The Letters of Sean O'Casey*, p. 240.
19. *Ireland Today* (September 1937), pp. 69–70.
20. Colonel J. C. Hanna's report for the British Board of Film Censors on the proposal to make an adaptation of *The Plough and the Stars*, dated 7 May 1935. The following day, Hanna met with representatives of the film production company, who wished to establish whether a film version of the play was likely to be banned in Britain, and they were told that while the 'theme could not be considered prohibitive', the language 'went far beyond what has been allowed'. See Rockett, *Irish Film Censorship*, pp. 328–9.
21. *Monthly Film Bulletin* 3, 35 (December 1936), p. 220.
22. Reject 284, Censor's decision, 18 March 1930. There was no appeal.
23. *Irish Statesman* (30 November 1929), pp. 255–6.
24. *Bioscope* (23 October 1929), p. 37.
25. For a detailed exposition of the film, see Patrick F. Sheeran, *The Informer* (Cork: Cork University Press, 2002).
26. For a discussion of *Guests of the Nation*, see Kevin Rockett, '1930s Fictions', in Rockett et al., *Cinema and Ireland*, 1987, pp. 60–2.
27. For a discussion of *Shake Hands with the Devil*, see John Hill, 'Images of Violence', in Rockett et al., *Cinema and Ireland*, 1987, pp. 164–7.
28. *Monthly Film Bulletin* 57, 678 (July 1990), p. 195.
29. *Manchester Guardian* (7 February 1947).

30. *Irish Times* (13 June 1978), p. 8.
31. *Irish Limelight* (January 1917), p. 3.
32. *Manchester Guardian* (8 January 1959).
33. *Sunday Independent* (26 April 1959), p. 23.
34. *Monthly Film Bulletin* 27, 318 (July 1960), p. 97.
35. See Kevin Rockett, 'An Irish Film Studio', in Rockett et al., *Cinema and Ireland*, 1987, pp. 108–10; and Fidelma Farley, *This Other Eden* (Cork: Cork University Press, 2001).
36. *Film Directions* 1, 2 (1978), pp. 10–11.
37. See Emer Rockett and Kevin Rockett, *Neil Jordan: Exploring Boundaries* (Dublin: The Liffey Press, 2003), pp. 128–30. Behan's prison drama and plea against capital punishment, *The Quare Fellow*, was adapted for the screen in 1962 by Arthur Dreifuss, while his semi-autobiographical novel *Borstal Boy* was directed for the screen by Peter Sheridan, 2000. Neil Jordan's adaptation of Patrick McCabe's *Breakfast on Pluto* (2005) was first publicly shown in September 2005 at the Toronto Film Festival.
38. Eileen Battersby, *Irish Times* (31 December 1994), weekend supplement, p. 8.
39. See Rockett and Rockett, *Neil Jordan*, pp. 9–13.
40. See Kevin Rockett, *Ten Years After: The Irish Film Board, 1993–2003* (Galway: Bord Scannán na hÉireann, 2003), and Martin McLoone, *Irish Film: The Emergence of a Contemporary Cinema* (London: British Film Institute, 2000).
41. For a more sympathetic reading of *The Field*, see Ruth Barton, *Jim Sheridan: Framing the Nation* (Dublin: The Liffey Press, 2002), and Cheryl Herr, *The Field* (Cork: Cork University Press, 2002).
42. See Lance Pettitt, *December Bride* (Cork: Cork University Press, 2001); and Martin McLoone, '*December Bride:* A Landscape Peopled Differently', in James MacKillop, ed. *Contemporary Irish Cinema: From The Quiet Man to Dancing at Lughnasa* (Syracuse: Syracuse University Press, 1999), pp. 40–53.
43. Luke Gibbons, *The Quiet Man* (Cork: Cork University Press, 2002).
44. This is extensively explored by Luke Gibbons in 'Romanticism, Realism and Irish Cinema', pp. 194ff.
45. Another reverse migration narrative is *Moondance* (Dagmar Hirtz, 1994), a contemporary setting for Francis Stuart's novel The *White Hare*, in which a German teenager becomes lover to two brothers in rural Ireland, while a more traditional migration story, set amongst 1980s / 1990s Irish in New York, is found in *Gold in the Streets* (Elizabeth Gill, 1996) from the play *Away Alone* by Janet Noble, though this film, like others mentioned above, fails to transcend its stage-bound origins.
46. A later, male-point-of-view coming-of-age film is *The Last of the High Kings* (David Keating, 1996), which is taken from Ferdia Mac Anna's novel of the same name and is set in 1977.
47. Gibbons, '"The Cracked Looking Glass" of Cinema', pp. 127–48.
48. Kevin Whelan, 'The Memories of "The Dead"', *Yale Journal of Criticism* 15, 1 (2002), pp. 59–97.
49. Kevin Barry, *The Dead* (Cork: Cork University Press, 2000).
50. See Gibbons, '"The Cracked Looking Glass" of Cinema'; Whelan, 'The Memories of "The Dead"'. Though not from a literary source, but from the biography by Brenda Maddox, Pat Murphy's *Nora* (2000), evokes the period during which *Dubliners* was

written and, more broadly, the passionate relationship between Nora Barnacle and Joyce. See Gerardine Meaney, *Nora* (Cork: Cork University Press, 2004).

51. See Kevin Rockett, '(Mis) Representing the Irish Urban Landscape', in Mark Shiel and Tony Fitzmaurice, eds. *Cinema and the City* (Oxford: Blackwell, 2001), pp. 223–4.
52. Colm Lincoln, 'City of Culture: Dublin and the Discovery of Urban Heritage', in Barbara O'Connor and Michael Cronin, eds. *Tourism in Ireland: A Critical Analysis* (Cork: Cork University Press, 1993), p. 219.

Select bibliography

Barry, Kevin, *The Dead*, Cork: Cork University Press, 2000.

Barton, Ruth, *Jim Sheridan: Framing the Nation*, Dublin: The Liffey Press, 2002.

Farley, Fidelma, *This Other Eden*, Cork: Cork University Press, 2001.

Frazier, Adrian, 'Hollywood and the Abbey', *Dublin Review* 15 (Summer 2004), pp. 68–86.

Gibbons, Luke, '"The Cracked Looking Glass" of Cinema: James Joyce, John Huston, and the Memory of "The Dead"', *Yale Journal of Criticism* 15, 1 (2002), pp. 127–48.

The Quiet Man, Cork: Cork University Press, 2002.

Herr, Cheryl, *The Field*, Cork: Cork University Press, 2002.

McLoone, Martin, '*December Bride*: A Landscape Peopled Differently', in James MacKillop, ed. *Contemporary Irish Cinema: From the Quiet Man to Dancing at Lughnasa*, Syracuse: Syracuse University Press, 1999.

Irish Film: The Emergence of a Contemporary Cinema, London: British Film Institute, 2000.

Pettitt, Lance, *December Bride*, Cork: Cork University Press, 2001.

Screening Ireland: Film and Television, Manchester: Manchester University Press; New York: St Martin's Press, 2000.

Rockett, Emer and Kevin Rockett, *Neil Jordan: Exploring Boundaries*, Dublin: The Liffey Press, 2003.

Rockett, Kevin, *Irish Film Censorship: A Cultural Journey from Silent Cinema to Internet Pornography*, Dublin: Four Courts Press, 2004.

The Irish Filmography: Fiction Films 1896–1996, Dublin: Red Mountain Media, 1996.

'(Mis) Representing the Irish Urban Landscape', in Mark Shiel and Tony Fitzmaurice, eds. *Cinema and the City*, Oxford: Blackwell, 2001.

Rockett, Kevin, Luke Gibbons, John Hill, *Cinema and Ireland*, London: Croom Helm, 1987; London: Routledge, 1988.

Sheeran, Patrick F., *The Informer*, Cork: Cork University Press, 2002.

12

Literary historiography, 1890–2000

COLIN GRAHAM

Making readers

In 1906 D. J. O'Donoghue published *The Geographical Distribution of Irish Ability*.[1] O'Donoghue was one of the first, and also one of the most energetically patriotic, Irish literary critics of the twentieth century. He is best remembered now, if at all, as editor of the pioneering *The Poets of Ireland: A Biographical Dictionary*,[2] and for the ease with which Yeats dismissed him as, for example, a man who 'spoke the most Cockney dialect imaginable'.[3] O'Donoghue's *The Geographical Distribution of Irish Ability* is the critical impulse of the Irish Literary Revival run rampant. Using indices and figures, O'Donoghue, as if in deadpan parody of Victorian blue-book statistics, tries to prove that Ireland has more geniuses per head of population than 'mainland' Britain. O'Donoghue's 'ardour'[4] in cataloguing and proving Ireland's literary and cultural worth is the exaggerated epitome of an Irish Revival literary historiography, which was trying to put its foundations in place while the rest of the building was being constructed around it. Perhaps more than any other single critic of the Revival period, O'Donoghue reflects a pervasive anxiety that the weight of the tradition of 'English' literature will suppress a nascent Irish writing before it can become fully established. His *Poets of Ireland* was an argument for an historical and living tradition of writing in Ireland; *The Geographical Distribution of Irish Ability* tips the scales further towards Ireland by reclaiming Irish roots for many 'English' or 'British' cultural achievements (Sheridan's plays, for example). Such cultural politics are understandable in their context – Robert Crawford's *Devolving English Literature* (1992), arguing that the idea of 'English' literature has Scottish intellectual origins, could be said to stand in the same conceptual relationship to late twentieth-century Scottish devolution as O'Donoghue's book does to the early twentieth-century cultural-nationalist argument for Irish independence.[5] O'Donoghue's career is, then, over-symptomatic of the difficulties faced by the beginnings of Irish 'literary historiography' and criticism during the early years of the Literary Revival. The problems which he and those writing Irish criticism at the time faced are, in the main, the same problems which Irish critical writing has gone on confronting in the 100 years or so since.

This chapter concentrates primarily on describing the ways in which Irish literary history has been constructed from the Revival period to the present day, and focuses initially on how the Revival formulated its sense of the literary past. The chapter will attempt to outline the shape of Revival, and then subsequent versions of Irish literary historiography, by concentrating on key critical texts, histories and anthologies. While, for reasons of space, this is by no means a fully comprehensive survey of every intervention in the field, the chapter will endeavour to encompass the major developments over the century, a period in which attempts to define Irish literature through its historical development have been legion. Literary historiography is undoubtedly reflective of the moment in which it occurs – an eccentric but admirable figure such as O'Donoghue can be explained in few other ways. However, literary history and criticism are also ways in which polemic and dissent are articulated, and where future literary agendas are set. As David Trotter suggests, 'the making of readers has often involved the making of moral and political dissidents',[6] and Irish literary criticism, including Irish literary history, has been about the 'making of readers' as much as it has been concerned with the making of literature. A national literature, which, simply put, is what the object of Irish literary historiography is, needs a national and international readership which recognises its nationality, in the same way as a nation's integrity must be consciously recognised by its citizens and by the international community of which it is part. Creating what is then thought of as 'natural', or convincing itself and others that a national literature, and therefore literary history, has always existed, has often been the fragile foundational paradox on which Irish criticism has leant its weight.

Running through the quest for a convincingly 'national' literature there are, of course, many fissures, some ideological, some more practical in origin. Like all nations, the 'Ireland' of Irish literary history has looked both within itself for affirmation of its existence, and, with some wariness, to outside validation. In the nineteenth century, cultural nationalism found an expression through antiquarianism (itself an early version of literary historiography), often citing the mere interest of European scholars in Irish writing as a validation of certain literary traditions.[7] This persists even into Douglas Hyde's famous 'De-Anglicisation' (1892) speech, in which Hyde notes that linguistic and literary scholars who are 'dispassionate foreigner[s]', place literary and linguistic knowledge of Ireland on a higher plane than that of, say, political science ('whether Mr Redmond or Mr MacCarthy lead the largest wing of the Irish party').[8] Similarly, in the twentieth century an international, 'non-Irish' interest in Irish literature was often used to give credence to one particular view or other of how Irish literary history should be understood. There is little better example of this than W. B. Yeats's 'A Lecture Delivered to the Royal Academy of Sweden' after he had received the Nobel Prize for Literature (1923). 'The modern literature of Ireland, and indeed all that stir of thought which prepared for the Anglo-Irish war, began when Parnell fell from power in 1891,' Yeats told the assembled dignitaries,[9] using this moment of international honour to promote a far from self-evident narrative of the Revival (and as we'll see below, Yeats had a capacity throughout his life to spot how important international critical judgement was in constructing an orthodox interpretation of his Revival narrative). Later in the twentieth century, larger shifts in the world of Western literary criticism create a backwash effect in Irish criticism. The 'arrival' of New Criticism in Ireland in the 1950s (discussed further below) is one such instance. Similarly, from the mid-1980s on, the rise of what is now lumped together under that cumbersome nomenclature 'postcolonial criticism' is further evidence of an often uncomfortable relationship in Irish literary historiography between the indigenous and the international.

Other forces have also been at work to complicate the apparently obvious perception that Irish literary history is tied to the fortunes of the idea of Ireland itself. From the time of the early days of the Revival it was clear that there would be a tension between the metropolitan centres where the Revival was fostered (London and then, predominantly, Dublin) and more provincial Irish energies and narratives. Given the political power dynamics of the island, and in literary terms the obvious ways in which Yeats, Synge and the Revival in general turned specific areas of rural Ireland into competing sites of authentic Irishness, it is not surprising that there have periodically been reactions against metropolitan constructions of Irish traditions and histories of Irish literature. Most famous and influential amongst these was undoubtedly Daniel Corkery's *The Hidden Ireland* (1924),[10] which, like any such polemic in favour of a readjustment of the national tradition, exposes as many contradictions as it covers.

However it is the partitioning of the island in 1921 (the year of the opening of the Northern parliament)[11] which most clearly splinters the possibility of any consensual national story of literature in Ireland. In the period with which we are concerned, this literary partition has its roots in the early days of the Revival and the now infamous visit of Bulmer Hobson and David Parkhill to

Yeats in 1902, when Yeats's refusal of permission for an Ulster Branch of the Literary Theatre lead Hobson to famously declare 'Damn Yeats! We'll write our own plays!' The setting up of the literary journal *Uladh* in 1904, with its aims of being 'more satiric than poetic', signalled that a different sensibility was at work in Ulster Revivalists of the first years of the century.[12] However, even before this 'split' in the Revival, there were signs of a possible alternative 'Northern' or Ulster history of literary production, visible faintly, for example, in the historical writings and poetry of Sir Samuel Ferguson. Later, the same impulses, in a post-partition context, are to be found in the 'regionalism' of John Hewitt, and most specifically in his edited collection of the Rhyming Weaver poets.[13] The rise of a newly prominent Northern Irish literary scene during the early years of the Troubles raised again the problem of how the relatively recent historical fact of the border could be read backwards through literary history, the 'separateness' of Northern writing being just one of the ways in which any stability which 'Irish literature' had attained was shaken by the Northern 'Troubles'.

All of this suggests that each time 'Irish literature' has tried to define itself some complicating factor has beset the apparent consensus, usually and inevitably long before it has been agreed on. Most of these disturbances to the possible equilibrium simply replicate the way the 'nation' is argued over, or is socially or politically divided. New literary histories seem to have to arise, as David Trotter suggests they should, from places of 'dissent', pitted against the trend towards an all-encompassing nation-narrative. This is partly the case for feminist literary historiography in Ireland, which has recently reached its zenith with the publication of *The Field Day Anthology of Irish Writing, Vols. IV and V: Irish Women's Writing and Traditions* (2002). This most recent reinvention and realignment of Irish literary history has an unresolvable conceptual relationship to a male-dominated mainstream of Irish criticism, which imagines both the canon and the ways in which it should be read in self-endorsingly masculine terms.

In the case of Irish literature, as we will see below, canonicity has often been a battle fought out through the publication of anthologies, and the space between the first three volumes of *The Field Day Anthology of Irish Writing* (1991)[14] and its succeeding two volumes of women's writing is the most fascinatingly complex arena in which the nature of not only Irish sexuality but Irish textuality is under scrutiny. The Field Day anthologies as a whole opened out the type of text which was considered part of the canon, and the definition of 'writing' widened under Field Day's remit to include the 'non-literary'. This flexibility in thinking about what constitutes Irish writing still leaves problematic, as it has been throughout the period, the relative placing of Irish-language and English-language literatures within any definition of 'Irish literature' and its history. The obvious dominance of English language literature in the canon of 'Irish writing' has both occluded the texture of Irish language literature and drawn it continually into debates which place it in the context of the better-known English language tradition. Reactions to this shadow which is cast over the language and its literature have been understandably varied – in recent years, for example, Declan Kiberd's *Irish Classics* (2000)[15] posits a story of the development of Irish literature in which Irish and English texts react to each other. On the other hand, Frank Sewell's *Modern Irish Poetry: A New Alhambra* (2000) is an example of a literary history of Irish-language poetry which draws its lines of tradition from within the resources of the language, tackling the relative neglect of Irish language poetry, and revealing the poetry's depth and quality through Sewell's finely honed literary criticism.[16]

These, then, are the kinds of intense debates, historical fractures and productive tendencies underlying the multiple versions of Irish literary history which have appeared in the period since the Irish Literary Revival's beginnings. Such metacritical issues are at times played out in direct debate, polemic and theorisation. Equally, the arguments which constitute the ebb and flow of literary historiography can be seen in more subtle manifestations. We may be tempted to see the construction of Irish literary history carried out in critical projects which seek to define the entirety of Irish literature, but seemingly small-scale interventions also play a potentially crucial role. In his *After Yeats and Joyce* (1997) Neil Corcoran points out, as Terence Brown had previously, that Joyce and Yeats dominate not only the literature of the twentieth century but its critical trends too. So those writing on Joyce and Yeats may seem to be focused on one writer only, but the slightest alteration in how we read Joyce or Yeats can, because of their stature, have more seismic effects on how we understand Irish literature.[17] Seamus Deane's comparison of Joyce and Yeats in his well-known pamphlet 'Heroic Styles' is an example of exactly this – here Deane deliberately lets the gloom of the Troubles fall upon the legacy of these two iconic figures of twentieth-century Irish literature; and by the end of his essay it appears that Irish literature is not only implicated in the Troubles but that in its subtle sectarianism the divisions of Irish literary tradition may hold some key to the future of Northern Ireland, as seen from the mid-1980s.[18] Decades before Deane's critique, Richard Ellmann's biographical criticism of Yeats and Joyce produced a very particular and influential pattern of reading Irish literature which emphasised individual genius, and the ability, not to reflect history, but to rise above it, as the characteristic of the great Irish writer. Ellmann's canon and literary history had a geometry with Joyce and Yeats at its high points – by the time of Seamus Deane's version of Joyce and Yeats, history had swamped these dizzy heights.

Literary history is also constantly changed in minor ways by what is taught, both within and outside Ireland, especially in second-and third-level education. The popularity of Seamus Heaney's poetry as a 'set text', for example, not only adds to the canon but brings other writing traditions back into focus (the poetry of Patrick Kavanagh may well have benefited internationally in this regard from Heaney's championing of his work and the influence which Heaney avows Kavanagh to have had on his own creativity). Caution is needed here too though, and some resistances to inclusion, despite popularity, are still in place; many schoolchildren in Northern Ireland have read or been taught Joan Lingard's *Across the Barricades* (1972),[19] and the other books in the 'Kevin and Sadie' series, but there is little evidence of Lingard's work appearing as part of the canon of Irish writing.[20] Similarly, contemporary Ireland has produced a whole series of popular women novelists, writing mainly for a female audience, yet Marian Keyes, Cathy Kelly, Patricia Scanlan and Sheila O'Flanagan have so far made little impact on how Irish criticism regards Irish literature.[21]

The development of Irish literary historiography from the Revival to the present day has never been given any full or serious treatment nor been put into a coherent narrative. There is, it is clear, a basic sense in which Irish critical assumptions reflect the debates which exist at the moment of writing. But the cross-hatched influences on that story, arising from the difficulties of 'knowing' Ireland and its literature, and from co-existing trends in taste and critical practice (which are not, thankfully, always in harmony with political thinking), remain unaccounted for. In the rest of this chapter I attempt to show some of the major patterns of thought which have critically shaped 'Irish writing' since the Revival.

Revival projects: 'men have begun to co-ordinate their scattered impressions'

As is well known, and as we saw above with Yeats's 'Bounty of Sweden', it was something of a commonplace during the time of the Revival to encourage the notion that the fall of Charles Stewart Parnell had left a political vacuum which was filled by the cultural activity of the Revival and its most public manifestation in the Abbey Theatre, along with, in different cultural arenas, the GAA and the Gaelic League.[22] The viability of the post-Parnell myth has been questioned in recent years, but it does have the benefit of support both from the Yeatsian side of the Irish literary house and, of course, in a different way from Joyce, since Stephen Dedalus's coming to consciousness is tied to the same historical narrative. Here then, in this imagined chasm of politics, begins the twentieth-century dictum that Irish nationality can be gauged by the strength and coherence of Ireland's literary heritage, which rises with the political nation. And here too the Revival begins as a sometimes reluctant but ever-persistent reproach to the perceived paucity of Irish literature preceding the Revival.

The Irish Literary Revival was intellectually based on a premise about literary historiography. The Revival assumed, *de facto*, that Irish literature was in need of 'revival', and therefore that Irish literature was, at best, in decline, at worst, non-existent, by the end of the 1880s. The patchy literary historiography undertaken during the Revival was never entirely able to fill in, for itself, the narrative of Irish literature that led to the founding moments of the Revival. A tension between the Revival's identification of the very need for revival, and the pride in national literature which this presumed, put paid even to the simple possibility of finding a way to view the history of Irish literature which could see it as, for example, a progressive development, or, as might be imagined, an increasingly full storehouse for the history of Irish oppression. The Revival had to be its own point of origin. In being a revival it had not quite done away with literary history, but it had started from the assumption that almost nothing was in place. Revival anthologies and criticism thus deal with the history of Irish writing by understanding it as a story which explains the moment of Revival. And so in the Revival there is also a tendency for history to be incomplete or even shattered (as we will see in the discussion of Thomas MacDonagh and Daniel Corkery to follow). Throughout the Revival there were arguments over what Irish literature was, who was part of it, and why. But during such debates two common, stable points in literary history emerged which have to do the work of supporting the Revival. One was the myth of its own founding. The other was the myth of myth. In other words, having undermined the history of Irish literature as it led up to the Revival, so that the Revival could happen, the only absolute history which could be agreed on was the history which came before history – that is, the world of a mythological Ireland.

In his book *Standish O'Grady, AE and Yeats*, Michael McAteer notes that for O'Grady, often regarded as 'father' of the Literary Revival, 'historiography' was 'the most crucial problem'. In his *History of Ireland*, according to McAteer, 'O'Grady struggled to articulate a concept of history appropriate to the kind of relationship between history and imagination he wished to promote',[23] and it is, in the broadest terms, this post-Hegelian 'struggle' with history which plays itself out in the literary historiography of the Revival period. O'Grady's fight to rescue Irish mythology from the assumption that it was merely 'poetic fancy'[24] is far from an isolated nineteenth-century instance of the re-evaluation of the play of myth and history in Irish literary culture. Samuel Ferguson's *Congal* (1872) is but one other example.[25] But O'Grady's attempt to find a pattern which could hold myth and history together, described so well by McAteer, is the fundamental reason why his work is central to the Revival's view of literary history. Among other things, O'Grady's work shows that the popularising of myth during and after the 1890s must be viewed on the same interpretative plane as more conventional literary history. In the absence of an agreed literary-historical story, Irish myth had to be both kept at its ahistorical distance and made to do the work of filling the gap between its 'time' and the present moment. So Lady Gregory's *Cuchulain of Muirthemne* (1902), for example, has an importance which stretches well beyond the fact that it makes available in popular, Revival form the legend of Cuchulain. *Cuchulain of Muirthemne* works to reassure the Revival that the gap between the 'then' of Cuchulain and the 'now' of the Revival is not a trauma which collapses historiography.[26] In his preface to *Cuchulain of Muirthemne* Yeats writes that '[poets] have taken their themes more often from stories that are all, or half, mythological'.[27] While this may look like an all-too-familiar piece of self-justifying Yeatsiana, Yeats is primarily intent on holding the impossible past together with the nascent present. 'We Irish,' he writes, 'should keep these personages much in our hearts, for they lived in places where we ride and go marketing, and sometimes they have met one another on the hills that cast their shadows upon our doors at evening.'[28]

The evocation of an Irish landscape alive with a hidden 'history' was to become a common trope,[29] arising directly from the historical strain which the Revival put upon Irish literary historiography, and, whatever other ideological differences are evident, it is a trope most obviously repeated later in the sometimes ghostly Munster landscape of Daniel Corkery's 'Hidden Ireland'. T. W. Rolleston's *Myths and Legends of the Celtic Race* (1911) similarly worries that Irish cultural history is haunted by 'transitory phantoms', and Rolleston uses his retelling of Celtic mythology to conceive of 'a vast historic stream of national life [which] is passing from its distant and mysterious origin towards a future'.[30] Rolleston's version of the legends ends appropriately enough with a barely disguised manifesto for his own literary historical moment:

> Mythology, in the proper sense of the word, appears only where the intellect and the imagination have reached a point of development above that which is ordinarily possible to the peasant mind – when men have begun to co-ordinate their scattered impressions and have felt the impulse to shape them into poetic creations embodying universal ideas.[31]

The dialectic which held pre-history and the present moment together undoubtedly adapted, shifted and changed during the Revival. But its importance remained because, as Rolleston suggests, it supplied the co-ordinates to an otherwise 'scattered' history.

This form of literary historiography, which involved filling out mythological time in lieu of a progressive and complete historical narrative, had within it, of course, a political conviction that Irish culture, like the nation, had been made incomplete and empty through the suppression of the literary culture which might have flowed were it not for the contaminated history which followed Irish mythological time. This in-between time may have been potentially 'empty', but it was certainly not, to complete Walter Benjamin's phrase, 'homogeneous'.[32] Mythological versions of Irish literary history were able to subsume starkly varying micro-narratives, refracting the politics of Ireland in the early twentieth century (Rolleston's 'Celtic' myth, for example, does not stop at the Irish Sea, and moves towards its conclusion by pointing, with apparent political innocence, to the overlap in Irish myths with Arthurian legends). Nevertheless, the fundamental 'co-ordinates' were set. What lay between the absolute past and the evolving present was altogether more contentious, and as the Revival developed, so stones were discovered in the 'vast historic stream of national life' as it passed 'from its distant and mysterious origin'.

The twin pillars of Irish myth and the Revival moment were an awkward foundational structure, and were themselves something of a myth. If the use of Irish mythology was a strained exercise in giving some kind of agreed past for the Revival to contextualise itself as Irish literature, then the freshness of the Revival's arrival in history is equally open to question. The Revival was not the clean break which, using its broadest brush strokes, it came to see itself as, and this has meant that alternative forms of literary history, both during and after the Revival, have been neglected. The nineteenth century preceding the Revival had, of course, an active literary and critical culture exemplified as far back as the early nineteenth-century debates over Lady Morgan's *The Wild Irish Girl*,[33] or later the long-term, if slapdash and contingent, politico-cultural canon-forming series 'Our Portrait Gallery' which ran in the *Dublin University Magazine*.[34] Later, in 1885, the *Freeman's Journal* debate on the best 100 books sits on the cusp of the Revival (as Margaret Kelleher notes in chapter 11 of volume 1). Yeats, anthologising the nineteenth century in *Representative Irish Tales* (1891), managed to hold in place the Revival's self-narrative through a mixture of faint praise and a prophecy of a better literature to come, in his generation: 'Meanwhile a true literary consciousness – national to the centre – seems gradually forming out of all this disguising and prettifying, this penumbra of half-culture'.[35] And throughout the period of the Revival whole realms of Irish literary activity, and their attendant critical enterprises, were occluded by the Revival's presence. Much as popular theatre continued to exist healthily beside the commercially small-scale venture of the Abbey,[36] and Somerville and Ross or George Bernard Shaw wrote an 'Irish' literature which was barely in contact with Revival aesthetics or practice, so critical enterprises went on at a tangent to the Revival's aura. *Uladh*, mentioned above, is one example which is explicitly a reaction to the Revival. Emily Lawless's *Maria Edgeworth* (1904), meanwhile, was a book which was as much part of a sudden interest in Edgeworth as a highly achieved and intellectually subtle woman as it was a celebration of Edgeworth's Irishness, and this critical interest in Edgeworth stretched back beyond the earliest days of the Revival to E. Owens Blackburne's *Illustrious Irishwomen* (1877) and then forwards to Constance Hill's *Maria Edgeworth and Her Circle* (1910).[37] Moreover, a lively reviewing culture existed throughout the period, in journals and magazines of varying political significance and quality, and the literary culture which they supported has been long neglected by Irish literary historians, a phenomenon which is symbolised by the crippling uncertainty felt by poor Gabriel Conroy in Joyce's 'The Dead', when he feels challenged about his journalism in *The Daily Express*.[38]

The Revival, and its ways of understanding literary history and tradition, did not come into the world in quite the state of innocence which its initial self-conception implied. Among the many influences on Revival literary historiography were the nineteenth-century critical, journalistic and antiquarian activities already mentioned. Other ways of shaping the Revival's notion of the existence of and continuity with previous Irish literature would include the superficially less significant role of book collectors, such as John O'Leary;[39] the confidence to imagine that an Irish literature existed without thriving came from such small beginnings and is echoed in important early Revival enterprises such as the 'Library of Ireland' series, published by Fisher Unwin, and the subject of a spat between Yeats and Charles Gavan Duffy.[40]

One final influence on these origins of twentieth-century literary historiography, and one that is rarely acknowledged, is that the Irish Literary Revival was in many way a distinctly Victorian affair. Marshalling its energies in London, and specifically the Southwark Irish Literary Club, the Revival overlaps with a variety of strands of literary thought and taste that were becoming visible in late nineteenth-century literary England. A reinvigorated interest in the peripheries of the British Isles was certainly one factor which gave the Revival its currency, as was a reaction against the tightly controlled poetics and narratives of the high Victorian age. The Revival then was at least partly a struggle against an English aesthetic; but a struggle which was also being undertaken in England, as Yeats, for example, or William Allingham before him, were aware. Robert Browning and the Pre-Raphaelites, it might be argued, were as influential on the Revival as Cuchulain, and the sense of literary history which the Revival broadly adopted was in tune with an English literary tradition which was splintering in anticipation of Modernism. At the same time, English critical voices were bemoaning the malaise created by contemporary industrialism, the death of romanticism and the chaos of high culture in an age of mass production; and both their arguments and indeed tone of voice are echoed in the despair at the current state of Ireland in Douglas Hyde's 'De-Anglicisation' lecture. So, when Walter Bagehot, comparing Tennyson and Browning, expresses his disgust at the 'ornate art, and grotesque art' which is Browning's poems and sees them as symptomatic of the awful vista of a rising but 'headless' middle class, he is reluctantly identifying debates over the aesthetics of the literary text and its place in an industrialised society which would soon produce the stirrings of symbolism, Swinburne, art for art's sake and eventually full-blown Modernism.[41] The Revival, too, is of this time and, in a refracted way, participates in these debates, which, in their deep-seated reaction against a previous generation and era, encourage a literary historiography characterised by a dramatic break with the immediate past.

More practically, we might occasionally wonder where the idea of an Irish literary society came from, in Southwark, and while it is tempting to cast our minds back to the coffee-shop culture of the eighteenth century, there was in fact a much more contemporary cosmopolitan model available. The literary society had a particular currency in the 1880s, since it was in 1881 that the Browning Society began, devoted 'to gather together . . . the admirers of Robert Browning, for the study and discussion of his works'.[42] The effect of Browning's poetry on Yeats has been well documented – most recently R. F. Foster has noted that Yeats's early poem 'How Ferencz Renyi Kept Silent' (published in the *Boston Pilot*) 'echoed Davis as well as Browning',[43] and it is exactly this mixture of the bohemian, 'grotesque' literature which signals the end of Victorianism, on the one hand, and a nationalist literature, on the other, which explains the origins of the Revival in London, and gives context to its particularly cataclysmic view of literary historiography.[44]

The forces which gather around the Revival, then, have a tendency to make solid and substantial an emergent present, to celebrate the mythical past, and then to leave the literary history in between open to the elements of Irish ideological storms. Not surprisingly, the anthologising urge becomes strong in this period; the anthology, standing superficially as a kind of self-evident and undisputable literary history, offers a reassuring density of tradition. What is most fascinating about the kinds of cataloguing and anthologising activities which arise around the Revival period is that, while they are generally acts of literary patriotism, insisting on the depth and richness of Ireland's literary heritage, they also serve to propel Irish literature towards some kind of future. D. J. O'Donoghue's *The Poets of Ireland* (1892) is a solidly forceful reference book, less crankily convinced of Irish genius than *The Geographical Distribution of Irish Ability*. As a reference book it was undoubtedly of great value, practically and ideologically, to the Revival. Most interesting from our perspective is the apparent confidence, in what is effectively a literary dictionary, O'Donoghue has in the literature which is emerging during the compilation of the book. Yeats and Wilde (an occasional participant in the Southwark Irish Literary Club), are included despite their relative youth. In looking back now at O'Donoghue's *Poets of Ireland* there is a lost sense that the poetic tradition which he outlines, with relative impartiality, was meant to become a known and acknowledged part of Irish literary culture. Yet in many ways little has changed until now; Denis Florence MacCarthy is still unread, Thomas Moore is probably even less read than he was, and Irish critics still tend to think as if Irish poetry began with Yeats, the very point at which O'Donoghue finishes. Yeats's own interactions with his poetic tradition mark the realisation that O'Donoghue's project of bringing pre-1880s poetry into the living canon of Irish writing had largely fallen flat, and so Yeats's early, oft-cited enthusiasm for 'Davis, Mangan, Ferguson' petered out, and turned to slight disdain.

At the centre of Revival activities aimed at producing a literary historiography stand those vast acts of anthologisation *The Cabinet of Irish Literature* (1879–1880) and *Irish Literature* (10 vols., 1904), and more minor works such as *Pearson's Irish Reader and Reciter* (1904).[45] *The Cabinet of Irish Literature*, edited by Charles A. Read and T. P. O'Connor, was advertised, as Margaret Kelleher's work shows, both as a Revival project and as a continuation of a Victorian fad for such handy compilations as the *Casquet of Literary Gems*, published, like the *Cabinet*, by Blackie and Son. As Kelleher notes, the 'publisher's announcement . . . explained the origins of the project' thus:

> The conviction has been gradually growing that the literary wealth of Ireland is being scattered broadcast, while yet no standard Work can be produced in which the genius, the fire, the pathos, the humour and the eloquence of Irish literature are adequately represented.
>
> The aim of the Publishers is to supply this want, and from the wide acquaintance of the Editor with the literature of his native land, it is hoped that a Work will be produced thoroughly NATIONAL in character, interesting to readers in general, and valuable as a book of reference.[46]

Gathering up those 'scattered' impressions, and anticipating a 'gradually growing' sense of the worth of Irish literature, the *Cabinet*, even more than O'Donoghue's *Dictionary*, is a signal of the mustering of forces leading into the Revival. In its revised, four-volume edition, edited and 'greatly Extended' by Katharine Tynan (in 1903),[47] a more literary and frankly more confidently Revivalist version of Irish literature is present. The original *Cabinet* has a distinctive shape, beginning with the seventeenth century and moving on towards the present day (leaving sacrosanct the Gaelic heritage), and in that sense insisting always that, in a post-Reformation context, the Irish literature contained in the somewhat quaintly termed 'Cabinet' would have to be imagined across sectarian lines in Ireland. By the time of Tynan's edition this had become a conviction which seems to have been slightly less pressing, and some of the original editors' selections, which include imperial speech-making, for example, are excised, and partly replaced by a more aesthetic take on the literary.[48] Even so, Tynan's edition preserves the main critical breadth of the original and intrudes Irish writing into the English tradition in a way that was to be repeated by the *Field Day Anthology* in our own time.

The slightly later, and even more expansive, *Irish Literature*, with editor-in-chief Justin McCarthy, was a more obviously Revival affair, its editorial board and contributors being the great and the good of the increasingly secure literary establishment of the Revival: W. B. Yeats, Lady Gregory, Douglas Hyde, Standish O'Grady, D. J. O'Donoghue, T. W. Rolleston and Stephen Gwynn were all involved. The final result, in ten extensive volumes solely for the Irish-American market, attests to the power which was vested in the anthology's ability to shape whatever new consensus on Irish culture might emerge from a period of renewal. The tenth volume, edited by Douglas Hyde, which includes 'folk tales and folk songs', along with prose, poetry and drama by 'modern Irish authors', all in Gaelic script with facing English translation, is a landmark in the study and promotion of Irish language literature.

The Library of Ireland series, O'Donoghue's *Dictionary*, the *Cabinet* and McCarthy's *Irish Literature* form the bedrock of the Revival's knowledge of the literature that preceded it and how it was to be assessed. The Revival was caught between an assertion of the wealth and significance of Irish literature over the centuries and the impulse for the new, which was never entirely specific about what exactly was being 'revived'. As I have suggested, this meant that literary history was to become an ideological battleground. The first edition of the *Cabinet* is already an anticipation of that war. Anthologies were forever drawn into such conflicts. Stopford A. Brooke and T. W. Rolleston found themselves in the midst of an unusually frank and fierce version of this warfare after publication of their 1900 anthology *A Treasury of Irish Poetry in the English Tongue*.[49] Brooke and Rolleston, for all that they occasionally succumb to whimsy, detect a modern, pluralistic and 'English' line of influence in Irish poetry which runs alongside the Irish line, 'like two lines of a railway'.[50] Naively or otherwise, this was asking for trouble, and D. P. Moran duly took up the challenge. 'It has a Trinity College liver'[51] wrote Moran of their *Treasury*, and from there the sectarian grounds for argument were set, in the starkest of terms. Inevitably, Yeats became a focus: 'Even Mr. Yeats does not understand us, and he has yet to write even one line that will strike a chord of the Irish heart. He dreams dreams. They may be very beautiful and "Celtic", but they are not ours.'[52] Such divisions, visible more deeply here than usual, were also the stuff of the controversies at the Abbey in later years, especially around J. M. Synge's *Playboy of the Western World*. They emerge out of the pangs of a changing Irish nationalism, the increasing power of the Catholic bourgeoisie, and the need such a class felt for a literature and a culture of its own.[53] Literary historiography, like history, was never going to be a neutral ground for Irish literary critics – and such potentially extreme ways of reading the literary past always hung over both the critical and the anthologising work of Irish literary scholarship and journalism, from the Revival to the present day.

Revival criticism: 'no alien element'

The sweeping gesture which is an anthology or literary dictionary is understandable at a time when the new is perceived as coming into being. But anthologies tend to let us know what to read, not necessarily how to read. The Revival and post-Revival periods are now mainly and rightly admired for the literature which they produced. This has, however, meant that some of the acute and energetic critical activity of the period has been overlooked. Critics such as Thomas MacDonagh, Stephen Gwynn, John Eglinton, Ernest Boyd, Hugh Law and Daniel Corkery all attempted to take the historicising impetus of the anthologist to a more refined height through their criticism, and in doing so each of them tried to justify a way of reading Irish literature *as* Irish literature. While individually imagined contours of Irish literary historiography emerge from these critics, they all effectively engage in debates structurally similar to those which disturb the solidity of the anthologies (there is a constant return to quiet forms of sectarian thinking; to the relative merits of Irish language and English language literatures and whether both are 'Irish' in the same way; and, more widely, a granting or withholding of a kind of literary citizenship to individual writers).

In the best of these critics, such as Thomas MacDonagh, there is a genuine intellectual effort to confront the paradoxes which the new Irish literature is raising. MacDonagh was perhaps the most ideologically alert and intellectually agile critic of this generation, and his *Literature in Ireland* (1916) is a melancholy book if only for the fact of its publication after his death at the hands of a firing squad following the 1916 Rising.[54] *Literature in Ireland* is a far from complete book, but it signals a lost potential in many ways, in that MacDonagh's openness to a concept of the interweaving of English and Irish language literatures leads to a criticism which is provisional and 'experimental', as MacDonagh himself writes.[55] And yet MacDonagh, for all that he breaks down certain linguistic barriers, does not escape from the pressures of literary history. When he effects the substitution of Yeats's 'Celtic Note' with his 'Irish Mode' he is moving towards a more confident statement of nationality (his is a more benign version of Moran's sneer at Yeats's 'Celtic' poetry);[56] indeed MacDonagh's fascinatingly tentative 'Irish' is not only a pointer to a national literature which he wants to see confident and creative. MacDonagh is also envisioning, through his criticism, a new Ireland moving towards statehood, and in this, in his relative acceptance of two linguistic pathways for Irish writing, and in his aversion to pugilistic rhetoric, MacDonagh is a genuinely visionary literary critic.[57]

However, that troublesome span between mythic time and the present, which eats away at attempts at a comprehensive literary history, cuts through even MacDonagh's writing. For MacDonagh the new era looks like a partial recuperation of a medieval tradition, an ascetic and aesthetic form of poetics, which is the bridge between a lost and pure Ireland and the present day. When MacDonagh writes, with solemn enthusiasm, that '[in] Ireland some literature has kept the old way familiar to the Middle Ages'[58] then there is clearly a different ideal literary history at work here than in, say, the *Cabinet*. Indeed, where MacDonagh's 'Irish Mode' can be found from the Middle Ages *backwards*, the *Cabinet* looks from the end of the Middle Ages *forwards*.

They are not entirely mutually exclusive views, but MacDonagh's is a more discriminatory vision, one that sees Irish literature not as the totality of what's been written by those who might be called Irish, but as the constant historic embodiment of some essential 'mode', concentrated and exemplified at particular moments in history. That the 'intellectualism' of the Renaissance, in MacDonagh's view, should bring about the 'decay' of literature is the one point at which his discriminatory powers are used in a less liberal sense; and when the Renaissance is thought to extinguish 'spiritual intuitions' then it seems again that the spectre of sectarian division is circling around this discourse of literary history, confusing the Renaissance with the Reformation, and seeing the realest of real Ireland in a Gaelic past.

Of all literary critics from the early part of the twentieth century, Daniel Corkery has been the most influential. As W. J. McCormack writes: 'For over sixty years Corkery . . . has been a powerful influence in the debates surrounding Irish nationalism, its relation to the Gaelic language and to literature generally'.[59] Corkery's sometimes trenchant and bullish rejection of the Anglo-Irish as a class in *The Hidden Ireland* (1924), and of the Revival (except Synge) in *Synge and Anglo-Irish Literature* (1931),[60] has obvious connotations for the canon of Irish literature, and would effectively rip to shreds the sturdy first edition of the *Cabinet*. Corkery's 'Hidden Ireland' is the bewilderingly tricksy essence of nationality, expressed in his book in literary form by the Munster poets. What remains unanswered in Corkery's schema is whether the 'Hidden Ireland' to be found in Munster is the sole repository of the Ireland which Corkery searches for. If so, then Corkery offers something of a dead-end for Irish literary historiography, since he sets in place firm (partially ethnographic, partly geographic) borders, and narrows Irish literature to a time-bound and dead or dying tradition. If Corkery's 'Hidden Ireland' is taken to be a sign of many other possible 'revivals' to come, better and more 'Irish' than that which began in the 1880s, then Irish literary historiography could, in his terms anyway, have some life breathed back into it. Above all, Corkery's 'Hidden Ireland' is allergic to the internationalism to which other critics and literary historians in Ireland have been periodically drawn. Thomas MacDonagh had insisted that the best Irish critics were familiar with 'the finest critics in the world'.[61] Corkery is, to say the least, an unenthusiastic internationalist, believing that culture only flourishes when it is truly national and that the weakening of cultures occurs when internationalism of any kind, but particularly colonialism, takes place. In this Corkery is close to some strands of postcolonial thinking, but it takes a liberal stretch of the imagination to see Corkery as the Fanon of his time. Corkery's insistence that Ireland throw off 'borrowed alien modes'[62] is radical enough, until it is followed by his inward-looking future-vision.

Those 'alien modes' were, of course, the inherent problem all post-Revival critics writing just before or after independence would confront. Sectarianism, or more properly, the division of Irish identity along confessional lines, was most usually implicit in criticism and literary historiography during the period. The dominant Protestantism of the Revival was always apparent, always just below the surface at best. As we have seen with the debate over Brooke and Rolleston's *Treasury*, there were times when sectarian divisions could come more clearly to the surface. But Irish criticism, like Irish society, has often been more comfortable speaking of the tensions between Irish Catholicism and Irish Protestantism in a coded language. It is just possible to hear these tensions passing to and fro in literary historiography, most often when the debate gets to the point of who should be included in the rapidly developing contemporary canon. So while, as I have noted elsewhere,[63] MacDonagh adapts Yeats's terms 'Celtic Element' and replaces it with 'Irish Mode', Corkery could be seen to continue this terminological switching with his 'alien mode'. The process then continues with Stephen Gwynn, who attempts to swing the debate back to the Yeatsian position in *Irish Literature and Drama in the English Language: A Short History* (1936). With typical tact (though arguably some ignorance of the difficulties faced by Scottish critics), Gwynn notes that 'Scottish national literature . . . brings in no alien element', a phrase which reintroduces into Corkery's language the original Yeatsian 'element' which MacDonagh had excised.[64] 'In Ireland the case is very different,' writes Gwynn, and his book is an argument for the vitality brought to Irish literature, to use the euphemism, by 'that alien element'. Hugh Law catches the same bug in his book *Anglo-Irish Literature* (1926), his refreshing scepticism expressed in *faux* Syngian language: 'It is easy to be talking of the Celtic note or the Irish mode; not quite so easy to define it or even detect it. Who has it, who lacks it?'[65] And yet for all his apparent common sense here, Law does call the bluff of the politics which lie behind the 'mode', 'note', 'element', 'Celtic' and 'Irish' labels which trammel and contain Irish literary history during this time.

Elsewhere the Revival produced notable commentators and literary historians in Ernest Boyd and John Eglinton, who were, in their way, concerned with documenting and comprehending the Revival as it happened. Eglinton was honest enough to doubt whether the Revival had 'brought forth a Book', by which he meant 'a masterpiece'.[66] If such an idea is not now thoroughly outdated, then it is useful to measure the Revival's own historiographical self-fashioning against the break in its epistemology which is James Joyce, and in particular to see how Joyce was included in the up-to-date critical histories undertaken by Gwynn and Boyd. Gwynn has some trouble placing Joyce, and lumps him in with James Stephens and 'the Ulster Writers'.[67] Boyd, in his *Ireland's Literary Renaissance* (revised edition, 1923; previous edition 1916) is admirably open to keeping Joyce, *Ulysses* and all (within a year or so of its publication) inside the fold of Irish writing, and yet Boyd does not reduce Joyce to a status which would make him yet another product of the Revival. Rather, Joyce is treated with intellectual seriousness, in the context of German Expressionism, Zola and Flaubert. Like any critic talking about new work, Boyd on *Ulysses* flounders a little for context. But in seeing that Joyce's work moved between experimentalism and being embedded in locality, Boyd did manage to capture the 'Irish Joyce' early on.[68]

The anomalous place of Joyce in Irish critical debates is a story in itself, since Joyce's reputation has long been torn between a broadly international, Modernist reading of his work and an Irish reading which finds it difficult, even now, to situate Joyce in an Irish tradition and equally awkward to find a way in which to bring Modernism to bear with precision on the Irish context.[69] Joyce is, however, not just a pawn in these critical manoeuvres. In *Ulysses* Joyce himself shows a keen awareness of the literary history that was gathering pace around him in early twentieth-century Dublin. The Scylla and Charybdis episode of *Ulysses*, set appropriately in the National Library, is the novel's conflation of a myriad of sometimes playful and fond, and sometimes vicious pokes at the Revival establishment. If Irish literary criticism is ever to suffer that perennial accusation that it is parasitic on Irish literature, then a reminder of this episode of *Ulysses* should drag to a halt the simple notion that literary criticism, or literary history, stands apart from literature. Irish literature proves again and again how central a sense of literary tradition is to the writer, as well as to the critic or academic.[70] In more recent times the dense intertextuality of Northern Irish poetry has again produced both the poet-critic (Seamus Heaney or Tom Paulin for example) who places herself or himself in a literary heritage, or in literary works which do the same. Heaney's 'meetings' with Joyce and Carleton in 'Station Island', or Paul Muldoon's fictionalising of the Auden generation (and most significantly Louis MacNeice) in '7 Middagh Street', are further examples of the porous boundary between the literary text and criticism of it, and of how Irish literature, constructed around the remnants of the Revival idea of a once-lost tradition, clings closely to its predecessors.[71] In a different way, the desire to become part of the canon of Irish poetry, while feeling excluded as a female poet, leads to an intensely close relationship between Eavan Boland's poetry and her literary criticism.

When critical histories of Irish literature are interwoven into the Irish literary text the primary effect is to position the author inside or outside a perceived literary lineage. A singular example of the creation of a strand of Irish critical orthodoxy can be seen in the way in which W. B. Yeats, sometimes personally, sometimes more distantly, was able to preside over early critical assessments of the achievements of the Irish Revival.[72] An example from the 'middle' years of the Revival is Francis Bickley's *John Millington Synge and the Irish Dramatic Movement* (1912), which was one of a series of slightly off-beat 'Modern Biographies' published by Constable (other subjects for treatment included Lafcadio Hearn, Tolstoy, Sainte-Beuve and Mahommed – a curious selection, with wayward genius something of a linking theme, if such a thing can be said of Mahommed). In his 'Note' at the beginning of his 'biography', Bickley thanks 'Mr. Yeats for his kindness in reading proofs and in giving me some valuable hints', an acknowledgement which strikes an ominous tone for the contemporary reader.[73] Sure enough Bickley's enjoyable book has at its centre a long, Yeats-inflected account of the rise of the Irish Literary Theatre and the Abbey (typified by the way in which the potentially embarrassing episode of the failure to produce Shaw's *John Bull's Other Island* is diplomatically glossed over – 'the society . . . did not feel itself capable of producing so elaborate a work').[74] And, while the book argues for Synge's genius as playwright, it includes Yeats's own insistence that it was his idea that Synge go to the Aran Islands. Cornelius Weygandt's *Irish Plays and Playwrights* (1913) repeats, if in less ventriloquised fashion, the same meeting of Yeats and Synge in Paris as the turning point in Synge's career. And Weygandt, then Professor at the University of Pennsylvania, also expresses his thanks to Yeats, among others, for help with his book. Overall, though, Weygandt's is a wider vision of the Revival than Bickley's, and is perhaps less closely under the critical guidance of Yeats. Weygandt's study of what is effectively the Abbey stage is put inside the parentheses of chapters on the Celtic Renaissance and 'Fiona MacLeod', reminding the Irish Revival of its Celtic Revival roots, though the pan-Celtic notion of the Revival had by then lost its impetus.

Yeats was a purveyor of a literary history which included himself, in narratives that were obviously difficult to resist. Even by the time of Una Ellis-Fermor's *The Irish Dramatic Movement*, published in 1939, the year of Yeats's death, there is still evidence that Yeats's version of the Revival is the primary way in which perceptions of its details are shaped. Ellis-Fermor describes Edward Martyn as 'economical, tongue-tied Martyn',[75] a less than charitable view which echoes Yeats's description of Martyn in *Dramatis Personae* as 'not at heart cosmopolitan enough' (George Moore's view of his cousin, Martyn, as expressed in *Hail and Farewell*, is also an influence).[76] Ellis-Fermor's book, which has an explicitly English engagement with the Revival (using English Elizabethan and Jacobean theatre as a continuous and disingenuous point of comparison), is unusual in that it is strongly averse to Irish nationalism, and as a result sees Revival drama in a thoroughly international context. Ellis-Fermor's book in some ways signals, though is not part of, a new phase for Irish literary historiography and criticism. The deaths of Yeats and Joyce meant that an era looked to have reached its end. The Second World War (and this despite Ireland's neutrality) would mean that literature would not be read in quite the same way again. The Revival, in all its forms of 'counter-Revival', dissent and hagiography, was definitively over and new critical contexts would emerge, some directly, some tangentially, from the global conflict and its aftershocks. Written on the cusp of this time is Louis MacNeice's wonderful book *The Poetry of W. B. Yeats*.[77] Yeats, for MacNeice, is both influence and an increasingly distant past, a romantic Ireland that is dead and gone. Having hollowed out literary history to make a case for itself, the Revival had effectively become the restart moment for Irish literature. Irish literature written before 1880 had, as a result, fallen into critical neglect. The stature of the major figures of the Revival would, however, continue to grow.

Postwar histories: 'things of order'

During and after the Second World War, Irish critical energies are usually thought to be taken up most vigorously in the journal culture of *The Bell* or, later, *Kavanagh's Weekly*.[78] Important as these journals were for signalling a dissatisfaction with the intellectual climate of post-independence Ireland, they were not the kind of publication which would change the way that Ireland's literary history was considered. In some ways, this postwar, post-independence, post-Revival period is most notable for its status as a kind of hiatus in Irish criticism, as if a sense of political and literary exhaustion had taken hold.

While the Revival had left a somewhat unwelcome legacy of neglect for pre-1880 literature, there still flourished an interest in Irish-language literature, persisting somewhat outside the vacuum created by the Revival's end. So just after the war Robin Flower's seminal *The Irish Tradition* (1947) and Myles Dillon's *Early Irish Literature* (1948) added to a constant flow of historical assessments beginning with Douglas Hyde's *A Literary History of Ireland* (1899), through Eleanor Hull's *A Textbook of Irish Literature* (1906), the even more technical Eleanor Knott's *An Introduction to Irish Syllabic Poetry of the Period*

1200–1600 (1928), Aodh de Blacam's *Gaelic Literature Surveyed* (1929), followed by his *A First Book of Irish Literature* in 1934, and then Shán Ó Cuív's *Prós na hAoise Seo* (1934) and Muiris Ó Droighneáin's *Taighde i gComhair Stair Litridheachta na Nua-Ghaedhilge ó 1882 Anuas* (1936). However, as Philip O'Leary and Máirín Nic Eoin point out in their chapters in this volume, critical writing in Irish was often criticised during the century for its lack of vigour, at least until the 1960s.[79] Luke Gibbons argues that de Blacam 'insisted on the multi-faceted character of Irish identity' throughout his writings.[80] It was to be that term and concept of 'identity' which would dominate how Irish criticism, and, in turn, Irish literary historiography, would be shaped in the post-Second World War period.

The success of the Revival, and most obviously of Yeats and Joyce, had the strange critical effect of moving both Yeats and Joyce away from Irish literary history. Emer Nolan has argued that Modernism, both in its writerly and then, later, critical manifestations, pitted Joyce's apparent internationalism against a parochial Ireland which Joyce was thought to loathe:

> Joyceans, then, read their sacred texts in a spirit of benign multiculturalism, which they imagine to be identical to Joyce's own. They are, in fact, impatient only with Irish culture, simply because Joyce (in their understanding of him) informs them that Irish culture is essentially intolerant.[81]

As Nolan shows, this critical separation of Joyce and Ireland began within High Modernism (Ezra Pound being the biggest culprit) and continued with critical readings which aped the tenets of Modernist writing. The tendency was, then, to view Joyce as anti-nationalist, or anti-Irish, and to justify this by evidencing the way in which Joyce's writings were either disregarded or disdained in Ireland (though as the example of Boyd, discussed above, shows, this is by no means a straightforward rejection of Joyce – Boyd, incidentally, was writing from the USA). However as the decades progressed after the war, the political climate changed, and Joyce, like Yeats, was brought back into the fold of Irish literature, in keeping with the swing towards identity politics which has come to dominate the underlying discourse of Irish studies.[82]

Yeats's reputation, which had always been high, was also under pressures which would shift it away from the politics of Irishness towards more 'internationalist' forms of literary tradition, though in Yeats's case this was more towards what MacNeice calls the 'mumbo-jumboism'[83] sometimes associated with Yeats's 'mysticism' rather than with the aesthetics of Modernist poetry. Most famously, Kathleen Raine, but also earlier major Yeats critics such as T. R. Henn (*The Lonely Tower: Studies in the Poetry of Yeats*, 1950)[84] and F. A. C.

Wilson (*Yeats's Iconography*, 1960) had placed Yeats in that mystical line which includes, at its most lucid, William Blake, and at its least appealing a search for what Wilson describes as 'Yeats's ultimate symbolic intentions'.[85]

If Modernism threatened to internationalise Yeats and Joyce, and draw the lifeblood out of a newly established 'tradition' in Ireland, then other kinds of internationalism were moving in ways which would eventually reinforce the Irishness of Irish literature, and bring the pendulum back to a position much more like that at the high points of the Literary Revival. The first signs were in the well-known debate in *Studies* (1955–6), the Jesuit journal, on the subject of the New Criticism and involving Denis Donoghue, Donald Davie and Vivian Mercier. Donoghue's 'Notes Towards a Critical Method: Language as Order' (1955) is a piece of youthfully orthodox criticism, peddling the tenets of American New Criticism with the zeal of a convert: 'poems are made out of the poet's desire to create forms, entities, things of order with which to oppose the continued flux, change, transience of life'.[86] Despite the fact that this is a definitively, almost plangently postwar set of imperatives, Donoghue, following the New Critical line, refuses to historicise Yeats when he reads that most historically exacting of Yeats's poems, 'Blood and the Moon'. Yeats's Irishness is only barely implicit in Donoghue's essay; what is much more to the fore is a conviction of Yeats's greatness as a poet opposing flux, than a poet expressing his nation. For Donoghue, as the years passed, this conviction was to alter, somewhat reluctantly, and as the 1960s and then the Troubles came along, so Donoghue fell into the kind of literary identity politics for which he avows a dislike. In this way Donoghue is a recalcitrant barometer of the ways in which Irish literary history has, since the war, been reinvigorated by the rise, globally, or at least in the western world, of identity politics as a significant mode of cultural understanding.

The other participants in the *Studies* debate, Donald Davie and Vivian Mercier, give a progressively more historical view both of Irish writing and of Irish criticism, though that said, Davie's main, and not entirely politic, point is that Ireland has no critical tradition worth discussing.[87] It is left then to Mercier to argue for the depth and historical density of Irish literature, while suggesting that many critical paths remain uncharted. For Mercier, Ireland has the ready potential for a fully fledged and researched literary history, it is simply that the resources (especially the publishers) are not available.[88] Mercier's vision is in retrospect the most convincing of these three important interventions. Mercier recognises that a curiously curtailed version of Irish literature has become convinced of the worth of only a few writers. Mercier's own *The Irish Comic Tradition* (1962) did much to liberate a stultified postwar canon.

The postwar period was, then, one in which the study of Irish literature was initially impoverished, hampered both by a lack of publications (or publication opportunities according to Mercier) and by the extended focus on Yeats and Joyce. While there was much literary activity in Ireland, little changed by way of notions of literary history or canonicity. It was, however, the case that the building blocks of larger changes to come were being put in place. Mercier's historicisation of Irish literature was one such preparation. Richard Ellmann's biographical writings on Yeats, Joyce and Wilde were equally important, since Ellmann's sense of the worth of the individual literary genius was always an 'identity' rooted in the life, and the life was in turn rooted in a greater identity. So, despite Ellmann's conviction that literature should rise above history, his work kept strong the bonds between Yeats, Wilde and Joyce and their Irish background. In later years Ellmann's eloquent books would feed into the rise of what became a critical paradigm dominated by 'identitarian' concerns.

After the 1960s: 'every mark of cultural identity'

In 1967 Frank O'Connor's *The Backward Look: A Survey of Irish Literature* was full of bleak pronouncements on the state of Irish literary studies:

> The abandonment of every mark of cultural identity by the Irish people during the nineteenth century has left a historical gap that is hard to span. Ours is probably the only civilized country which has no such thing as a chair of national literature.[89]

O'Connor's despair is clear enough, but it is even more heightened if we realise that he is deploying, more explicitly than ever, that Revival trope of the dead nineteenth century and its logical follow-on, that is, the need for national literary renewal. In their own way, the Troubles, already stirring in Northern Ireland when O'Connor's book was published, were to raise the energies of Irish literary history again, to the point where it could certainly not be argued that 'cultural identity' had been 'abandoned'. Indeed, it was 'cultural identity' which would become the factor that would reinvigorate both Irish literature and the way in which it was thought of historically.

The Troubles were initially remarkable for the literature rather than the criticism, or literary historiography, which they produced. And much of the debate about canonicity and criticism in the post-1960s era has flowed from the literature of the Troubles. If literary texts, from Heaney's poetry to popular fiction, were quick to respond to the civil disturbances of late 1960s Northern Ireland, then criticism, in ways which are not always commented on, was not far behind. A case in point is the recuperation of Louis MacNeice by Irish poetry criticism. In 1971, for example, MacNeice's poetry was the subject of William T. McKinnon's painstaking book *Apollo's Blended Dream: A Study of the Poetry of Louis MacNeice.*[90] McKinnon, in chapters which are interested in things such as 'Metaphysical Image', 'Prosody' and 'Image and Structure', makes little mention of MacNeice's Irish background, as his reading of MacNeice skims the surface of the elusive philosophy of MacNeice's verse. By the time of Terence Brown's *Louis MacNeice: Sceptical Vision* in 1975, the sceptical-liberal version of MacNeice which Brown is interested in is entwined with MacNeice's often sardonic but affectionate relationship with Ireland.[91] In reading MacNeice as something of a stranger in his own land, and as a man of personal and individualist integrity at a time of ideological extremity (in the 1930s in Britain), Brown's book claims a role for literary heritage in the maintenance of a neutral or, at least, 'sceptical' vision when regarding the conflict in the North. Because it is one of the first substantial pieces of literary criticism in Ireland to undertake a rewriting of 'Northern' literature of the period immediately preceding the Troubles, Brown's book is absolutely crucial to the development of literary historiography from the 1970s on. Through its quiet polemic about the role of the writer (which effectively argues – by exemplary reading – that literature will always be political yet rise above dogma because it is literature), Brown's book marks out some of the key concepts by which both contemporary and past Irish writers are now understood. Brown's arguments about MacNeice are given further context by his *Northern Voices: Poets from Ulster* (1975) and are clearly similar to those developed by Edna Longley in *Poetry in the Wars* (1986).[92] While Longley's writing is usually regarded as a mixture of strong polemic and subtle close reading, what is often neglected about her work is its argument for new canonicities. Longley's arguments with the Field Day anthologies are well known, and her work has always sought to break out of the nationalised containments of the twentieth-century poetry canon.[93] Hence *Poetry in the Wars* contains essays on Edward Thomas, Robert Frost and Philip Larkin, and her *Bloodaxe Book of 20th Century Poetry* (2000) contains within its selection an example of what Longley might describe as archipelagic anthologising.[94] Longley also completed the process of saving MacNeice for Ireland with her *Louis MacNeice: A Study* (1988), a book which makes even more explicit the kind of MacNeice which Brown was edging towards.[95]

Given that the Troubles emerged out of the discourse and practice of the civil rights movement in the southern states of the US, and that these roots coincided with the intellectual and social revolutions taking place across the western world in the 1960s, it might be expected that the Northern conflict specifically, and Ireland in general, would come to be discussed in the context of the theory wars raging in humanities departments in the western academy in the 1970s, 1980s and 1990s.[96] That it took 'theory' so long to arrive in Ireland is something of an oddity, then (though there are of course many exceptions to this rule – *The Crane Bag* (1977–1985) and the literary and cultural criticism of Richard Kearney are some).[97] Perhaps the fact that much of Ireland's intellectual traffic still passed through mainland Britain is one reason for this. Shaun Richards has pointed out that at the Essex Sociology of Literature conferences (1976–), the breeding ground for British literary 'theory', only a handful of the hundreds of papers given were on Ireland – this despite the fact that the Troubles, then at their worst, were on the very doorstep, indeed in the same jurisdiction as the Essex conferences. As Richards notes, most of this handful of papers were given by W. J. McCormack, and it is no accident that McCormack is the most sophisticated 'theoriser' of Irish literary history in recent years – his *Ascendancy and Tradition* (later revised as *From Burke to Beckett*) still stands as a model of how to rethink the detail and the broad sweep of the Irish literary canon.[98] Shaun Richards himself was co-author, with David Cairns, of *Writing Ireland* (1988), one of the most important books of Irish literary criticism in the last decades of the twentieth century for the way in which it gave an alternative, and then entirely novel, narrative to Irish literature, a narrative seen through Edward Said, Althusser and Gramsci, rather than Gaelic Ireland, the Revival or orthodox nationalism.[99]

As is well known, and unnecessary to rehearse here, the theoretical awakenings signalled by Cairns and Richards, Seamus Deane and the Field Day project led to the emergence of a postcolonial critique of Irish literature and culture, a reading which is sometimes pitched, rather unconvincingly, against a 'revisionist' mode of reading. How easily this translates into merely reinvigorated forms of nationalist/liberal, or even nationalist/unionist, debate is an open question. We might however expect the canon of Irish writing to have been shaken severely by such angry exchanges, yet overall the outcome seems to have been largely an expansion rather than a complete splitting of the canon. The partial exception here is a 'revisionist' micro-history which recurs throughout the Troubles, arguing for a specifically Protestant or just Northern literary history. This can be seen in the critical volume *Across a Roaring Hill*, edited by Gerald Dawe and Edna Longely (1985), or in John Wilson Foster's *Forces and Themes in Ulster Fiction* (1974). It also arguably spawns its own literary version of anthology culture, going back to the 1974 edition of the work of the Rhyming Weavers by John Hewitt.[100]

If such micro-histories need some over-arching grand narrative to pit themselves against, then that is now, no doubt, provided by the *Field Day Anthology of Irish Writing* (1991), volumes I–III, and the subsequent two volumes of *Irish Women's Writing and Traditions*. The first three volumes, as Seamus Deane makes clear in his general introduction, were compiled in the knowledge that they repeated the Revivalist projects of the *Cabinet* and *Irish Literature*.[101] *Field Day*, in the first three volumes, is self-consciously a smash and grab raid on 'English literature', and, as mentioned above, it is important to recall that Robert Crawford was undertaking a similar reclamation process for Scottish literature at more or less the same time. In as much as the *Field Day Anthology*, I–III, is a product of a colonial diagnosis of Irish cultural history, it straddles an awkward line between an assertion that Irish culture has been annexed and lost, and the resultant anthology's belief that a 'meta-narrative' is filled out by the 'tradition' selected by the anthologists. One practical and theoretical outcome of the *Field Day Anthology* is that the broad shift from 'literature' to 'writing' takes us back to a tradition more like that of the *Cabinet* in its first edition. Texts are chosen from across many genres of writing, and, while certain hierarchies are assumed (preserving, in part, the literary as a transcendent genre), there is an overall 'new historicisation' of Irish literature in *Field Day*. Literary texts are seen as (a perhaps special) part of a greater discourse which reveals the 'achievement of Irish people of many centuries'.[102] At times, though, Deane seems to disavow the 'meta-narrative' which he elsewhere proclaims:

> The anthology does not propose that we have here an exemplary instance of either a 'national' or a 'colonial' literature or body of writing. It does propose that the interchange between these conceptions of writing, more violently and frequently effected in Ireland than in most European cultures, demonstrates the configurations of power within a society that consistently has refused to accept their force or yield to their allure. What is exemplary, then, is the extent to which, in Irish conditions, canonical forms have not been established and, because of that, how clearly the purpose of such canonical forms is exposed.[103]

These effectively anti-anthology sentiments make for odd reading at the beginning of such an enormous, sweeping and agenda-setting anthology. The *Field Day Anthology* justifies itself here by suggesting that there is no canon of Irish writing, that this anthology is not itself a canon of Irish writing, and that what the anthology will do will be to show the inherent resistence in Irish culture to the encompassing cultural hubris of canonicity. Whether this is contradictory or not, it is symptomatic of the way in which the belief that Irish culture is a 'colonial condition' altered Irish critical discourse, and in that sense, Irish literary historiography. Deane's assertion that Ireland is 'more violently and frequently' affected than most of the rest of Europe by the cultural collisions and outcomes of colonialism may or may not be historically true, but it is here a more benign form of a sometimes blinkered particularism in Irish postcolonial thinking, an assertion that Ireland is the first and last European colony and therefore like others, but more so.[104] This drains any comparative critique of its energies before they have begun, and tends to draw the critical eye to the centre of Irishness rather than its boundaries. More profoundly, Deane recognises here the difficult imperative at the heart of postcolonial thought, at least as it has been taken up in Irish criticism. When Irish culture is imagined as oppressed it has a radicality written into it. When it is properly postcolonial that oppression can still be seen, either in the continuing cultural or economic influence of Britain, or in a kind of cultural cringe effect. But to imagine Irish culture, or literature, as powerfully replete, by itself, would be to give it an orthodox, canonical position in which that inherent radicality and recalcitrance would be nearly impossible to find. For this reason Deane remains sceptical of the very idea of the canon while carrying out the most significant canon-forming act in Irish culture since the Revival. And so the advent of postcolonialism has meant less activity in interrogating literary history than might be expected. Joyce and Yeats have been read in new ways. Occasionally lost figures have reappeared, and, arguably, the nineteenth century and the eighteenth century have to some extent been saved from ignominy.[105] But postcolonial criticism in Ireland has not charged itself with undoing the Irish canon.

The most profound sign of real change in Irish literary historiography is undoubtedly the publication of *The Field Day Anthology of Irish Writing*, volumes IV and V. While it was arguably trammelled by appearing under the 'Field Day' imprint as a riposte to the first three volumes' forgetfulness about women writers, volumes IV and V (*Irish Women's Writing and Traditions*) extend the range of Irish writing in ways that stretch the lineage of Irish culture more fully than the first three volumes, to the point where the containment of all issues under the collective banner 'Irish' can look at times like something of a misnomer. *Field Day* volumes IV and V try to perform fully that hope that Deane had in 1991 that Irish writing would expose the nature of canonicity and the lines that literary history likes to draw. In her general introduction to the 'Women and Writing, 1700–1960' section of volumes IV and V, Gerardine Meaney carefully situates the paradoxical nature of the project as both anti-canonical and canon-forming:

> To some extent, all feminist literary history is a reaction formation. If there were no argument about women's representation within traditional canons, if that representation had been equitable to begin with, there would be no function for anthologies of women's writing and no feminist literary history. In this case, the relationship between Volumes IV and V and the previous three dramatizes precisely that reactive element with the postulation of a women's canon. For no matter how insistent on postmodern values of diversity or difference, no matter how reluctant to postulate any one narrative, the grouping together of material in this way is an exercise in canon formation.[106]

Taken together, the five volumes of *The Field Day Anthology of Irish Writing* are both a nostalgically nineteenth-century cultural gesture and an embodiment, in their split nature, of the paradoxes of postcolonial identity, that notion which has quietly taken a firm grip of the discourse of Irish criticism.

One of the outcomes of an identitarian orthodoxy is that the very feminist arguments about the nature of Irish literary canons which brought about *Field Day* IV and V suffer through a continuing and containing tokenism. As Moynagh Sullivan puts it: 'The insistence on woman's discursive position as categorically separate means that women's studies can function as an object through which Irish studies can be validated.'[107] And so the work of feminist literary historians, from as far back as Emily Lawless, is still in need of a way of asserting an independent existence.[108] The massive achievement of volumes IV and V of the *Field Day Anthology* may well be the change that is needed, but it will take some time for literary history to catch up with the work of the editors of those volumes, and with the implications of the vast amounts of material published in volumes IV and V. The signs of change, both in terms of literary history and critical theory, are apparent over the past few years of Irish criticism.[109] But the Irish canon is stubborn, and it remains to be seen whether Irish literary studies will always treat feminism as the representations made by 'The Mad Women in the Annex'.[110]

Conclusions

The end of the twentieth century looks like the Revival period, in terms of Irish literary historiography. Any comparison of the Troubles in the North, from the late 1960s on, with the political machinations and violence of the years leading up to and then coming after the Revival would be strained, if thought of purely through political science. However, what is shared across these two time periods is a sense of Irish identities of various kinds as central to culture; in both identity is presumed to be what gives culture its shape, its existence, its essence.

In recent years this has produced what is close to an agreed set of assumptions in Irish criticism. Despite the bitterness of the differences occasioned by nationalist-revisionist or postcolonial controversies, both 'sides' (or all sides) have rarely questioned that an historical identity is the core of what Irish literature is. The kinds of cultural histories which this idea (an academically global, not just Irish idea) produces are often richly textured in the way they move from literary text to political history. Terence Brown's *Ireland: A Social and Cultural History, 1922–1979* (1981; revised 1985, 1990 and 2004), Norman Vance's *Irish Literature since 1800* and James H. Murphy's recreation of the cultural density of nineteenth-century Ireland are good examples.[111] And Joep Leerssen's *Mere Irish and Fíor-Ghael* (1986) and *Remembrance and Imagination* (1996) stand as simply monumental achievements in literary and cultural history.[112]

As we have seen, anthologies and dictionaries formed the early staple of Revival self-conceptions, providing bourgeois nationalism with the literary substance of a newly heightened cultural position. Anthologies and dictionaries abound in post-1960s Ireland, creating something of a revival feel to the period.[113] There is a certain, sometimes unconsidered, surface pluralism to the literary identities enclosed within these anthologies' boundaries, but the most striking thing about contemporary anthologies, signified by their sheer number, is that they imagine a different kind of readership. The *Field Day Anthology*, volumes I–V, while they might represent the moment of the 1990s and early twenty-first century in the way they shape the canon of 'Irish Writing', nevertheless, as books, are extraordinarily old-fashioned ventures. Most anthologies of Irish literature in the last few decades have been shaped, yes, by ideological considerations, but also by the professionalisation of the study (and criticism) of Irish writing. The increasing popularity of studying Irish literature at university level seems to have brought out a mania for the encyclopedic in its practitioners. And that professionalisation process means that particular kinds of literature are read in particular ways. The reading of current anthologies for North–South, feminist or anti-feminist bias is a real and proper concern, but it is also reflective of the extent to which cultural politics of a specific kind have come to dominate readings of Irish writing. It is not necessarily to be mourned that Irish literary studies should understand the recent and more distant history of Irish literature in this way, but it is important to know that such shapings are taking place and that they are reinforced by the academy's demands for ideological neatness and pedagogic standardisation. The most obvious outcome of this is that claims for newness in the canon are often assimilated quickly and efficiently as subsidiary parts of the Irish story, keeping the story, the metanarrative, intact. This is certainly the case with feminist literary historiography. Equally, the fate of the argument about the quality of Irish 'Modernist' poetry is a case in point.[114]

If the end of the twentieth century was curiously like the end of the previous century, then this too has been registered on the barometer of Irish literary history. In other words, in reading the Revival now, critics tend to recognise its similarity to our own recent literary past (a time of renewed literary energy) but also to search out those plural identities by which we wish to understand our current cultural climate – hence there is an interest in the Northern version of the Revival, and in slivers of Revival history which were hidden in the grander narrative the Revival told about itself.[115]

Irish literary historiography in the (long) twentieth century, as we have seen, is given shape by the strength of its beginnings and the upheavals of its endings. The Revival, while a complex phenomenon, had the effect of sweeping away any continuously imaginable Irish literary history. The best it could do was see recent literary history as a glorious failure, its positive qualities merely the embers from which greater things would catch fire. The all-pervasive nature of the language and thought of identity politics is perhaps the reason why *Field Day*, for example, seems to have overcome those historical gaps which open in every Revivalist's notion of history (MacDonagh and Corkery's Renaissance-less Ireland, or the *Cabinet*'s solely post-seventeenth-century literature). Early twenty-first-century Irish criticism finds identity everywhere, constantly, going back as far as the critical eye can see, and stretching across all texts. The resultant breadth of what constitutes Irish writing may be newly liberal and free from the contusions of the early part of the century – or it may simply attest to the way in which thinking primarily through an uncritical identity politics has blunted the critical faculties which give a shape to Irish literature.[116]

Notes

1. D. J. O'Donoghue, *The Geographical Distribution of Irish Ability* (Dublin: O'Donoghue / Gill; London: Simpkin, Marshall, 1906).
2. *The Poets of Ireland: A Biographical Dictionary* (Dublin: Hodges Figgis and Co, 1906).
3. W. B. Yeats, 'Ireland After Parnell', in *Autobiographies: Reveries over Childhood and Youth and The Trembling of the Veil* (New York: Macmillan, 1927), p. 256.
4. The word is Yeats's. See John Kelly and Eric Domville, eds. *The Collected Letters of W. B. Yeats, Volume I: 1865–1895* (Oxford: Oxford University Press, 1986), p. 201.
5. Robert Crawford, *Devolving English Literature* (Oxford: Clarendon, 1992).
6. David Trotter, *The Making of the Reader: Language and Subjectivity in Modern American, English and Irish Poetry* (London: Macmillan, 1984), p. 14.

7. See Joep Leerssen, *Remembrance and Imagination: Patterns in the Historical and Literary Representation of Ireland in the Nineteenth Century* (Cork: Field Day/Cork University Press, 1996) and Clare O'Halloran, *Golden Ages and Barbarous Nations: Antiquarian Debate and Cultural Politics in Ireland, c.1750–1800* (Cork: Field Day/Cork University Press, 2004).
8. Douglas Hyde, 'The Necessity for De-Anglicizing Ireland', in David Pierce, ed. *Irish Writing in the Twentieth Century* (Cork: Cork University Press, 2000), p. 6.
9. W. B. Yeats, 'The Irish Dramatic Movement', from 'The Bounty of Sweden' in *Autobiographies* (London: Macmillan, 1970), p. 559.
10. Daniel Corkery, *The Hidden Ireland: A Study of Gaelic Munster in the Eighteenth Century* (1924; Dublin: Gill and Macmillan, 1989).
11. The Boundary Commission nominally set up to decide on the final status and/or place of the border collapsed in 1925, confirming the current border as 'permanent'.
12. See Marnie Hay, 'Explaining *Uladh*: Cultural Nationalism in Ulster', in Betsey Taylor FitzSimon and James H. Murphy, eds. *The Irish Revival Reappraised* (Dublin: Four Courts Press, 2004), pp. 119–31.
13. John Hewitt, ed. *Rhyming Weavers: And Other Country Poets of Antrim and Down* (1974; Belfast: Blackstaff, 2004).
14. Seamus Deane, gen. ed. *The Field Day Anthology of Irish Writing*, 3 vols. (Derry: Field Day, 1991).
15. Declan Kiberd, *Irish Classics* (London: Granta, 2000).
16. Frank Sewell, *Modern Irish Poetry: A New Alhambra* (Oxford: Oxford University Press, 2000).
17. Neil Corcoran, *After Yeats and Joyce: Reading Modern Irish Literature* (Oxford: Oxford University Press, 1997); Terence Brown, 'Yeats, Joyce and the Irish Critical Debate', in *Ireland's Literature: Selected Essays* (Mullingar: Lilliput, 1988), pp. 77–90.
18. Seamus Deane, 'Heroic Styles', in Field Day Theatre Company, ed. *Ireland's Field Day* (1972; London: Hutchinson, 1985), pp. 45–58.
19. Joan Lingard, *Across the Barricades* (London: Penguin, 1989).
20. Lingard's novel is discussed in Joe Cleary, *Literature, Partition and the Nation State: Culture and Conflict in Ireland, Israel and Palestine* (Cambridge: Cambridge University Press, 2002), pp. 112–19 and passim.
21. See Kathy Cremin, 'Satisfaction Gauranteed? Reading Irish Women's Popular Fiction', in P. J. Mathews, ed. *New Voices in Irish Criticism* (Dublin: Four Courts Press, 2000), pp. 77–83.
22. The 'vacuum' narrative of post-Parnell Ireland was of course promoted by Yeats, and largely, though not entirely, replicated by historians, most prominently F. S. L. Lyons in *Culture and Anarchy in Ireland, 1890–1939* (1979; Oxford: Oxford University Press, 1982). It continues to have currency in both literary history and history. See, for example, D. George Boyce, *Nineteenth-Century Ireland: The Search for Stability* (Dublin: Gill and Macmillan, 1990).
23. Michael McAteer, *Standish O'Grady, AE and Yeats: History, Politics, Culture* (Dublin: Irish Academic Press, 2002), pp. 3, 4.
24. Ed Hagan quoted in McAteer, *Standish O'Grady*, p. 38.
25. Samuel Ferguson, *Congal: A Poem in Five Books* (London: Bell and Daldy, 1872).

26. See also Sinéad Garrigan Mattar, *Primitivism, Science, and the Irish Revival* (Oxford: Clarendon, 2004) and Michael McAteer, '"Kindness in Your Unkindness": Lady Gregory and History', *Irish University Review: Special Issue*–Lady Gregory, 34, 1 (2004), pp. 94–108.
27. Yeats, 'Preface' to Lady Gregory, *Cuchulain of Muirthemne* (1902; Gerrards Cross: Colin Smythe, 1990), p. 15.
28. Ibid., p. 16.
29. And it also had a history reaching back beyond the Revival. Daniel O'Connell's sense of the political sublime, which could be accessed through the landscape during his 'Monster Meetings', is one example.
30. T. W. Rolleston, *Myths and Legends of the Celtic Races* (London: George G. Harrap, 1917), p. vii.
31. Ibid., p. 418.
32. Walter Benjamin, 'Theses on the Philosophy of History', in *Illuminations* (1968; London: Pimlico, 1999), p. 252.
33. See Sydney Owenson (Lady Morgan), *The Wild Irish Girl*, ed. Claire Connolly (1806; London: Pickering and Chatto, 2000).
34. See Wayne A. Hall, *Dialogues in the Margin: A Study of the* Dublin University Magazine (Gerrards Cross: Colin Smythe, 2000).
35. W. B.Yeats, *Representative Irish Tales* (1891; Gerrards Cross: Colin Smythe, 1979), p. 32.
36. See for example Ben Levitas, *The Theatre of the Nation: Irish Drama and Cultural Nationalism, 1890–1916* (Oxford: Clarendon Press, 2002), and Philip B. Ryan, *The Lost Theatres of Dublin* (Westbury: Badger, 1998).
37. Emily Lawless, *Maria Edgeworth* (New York: Macmillan, 1904); E. Owens Blackburne, *Illustrious Irishwomen*, 2 vols. (London: Tinsley, 1877); Constance Hill, *Maria Edgeworth and Her Circle in the Days of Buonaparte and Bourbon* (London: John Lane, 1910).
38. Recent scholarship on magazine culture includes Tom Clyde, *Irish Literary Magazines* (Dublin: Irish Academic Press, 2002) and Frank Shovlin, *The Irish Literary Periodical, 1923–1958* (Oxford: Oxford University Press, 2004).
39. Booksellers were arguably just as important. For a lively account, which includes a meeting with John O'Leary, see Seamas O'Sullivan, *The Rose and the Bottle and Other Essays* (Dublin: Talbot, 1946).
40. See R. F. Foster, *W. B. Yeats: A Life, Vol. I: The Apprentice Mage* (Oxford: Oxford University Press, 1997), pp. 118–20 and passim.
41. Walter Bagehot, 'Wordsworth, Tennyson and Browning; or, Pure, Ornate, and Grotesque Art in English Poetry', in Edmund Jones, ed. *English Critical Essays: Nineteenth Century* (1916; London: Oxford University Press, 1947), p. 419.
42. 'Prospectus of the Browning Society', *Browning Society's Papers* (London: Browning Society, 1881–4), part 1, p. 19.
43. R. F. Foster, *W. B. Yeats: A Life*, 1, p. 56.
44. For Yeats involvement in any coterie hinted at the possibility of a more mystic form of 'brotherhood'. This partially explains Yeats's odd reading of Browning as a 'mystic' in the memorial notice he wrote for *The Boston Pilot*, cited in George Bornstein, 'Last Romantic or Last Victorian: Yeats, Tennyson, and Browning', in Richard J. Finneran, ed. *The Yeats Annual* (Dublin: Gill and Macmillan, 1982), p. 122.

45. Charles A. Read and T. P. O'Connor eds., *The Cabinet of Irish Literature: Selections from the Works of the Chief Poets, Orators and Prose Writers of Ireland*, 4 vols. (London, Glasgow, Edinburgh and Dublin: Blackie, 1879–80); Justin McCarthy, gen. ed., *Irish Literature*, 10 vols. (New York: Bigelow, Smith for the Catholic University of America 1904); *Pearson's Irish Reader and Reciter* (London: C. Arthur Pearson Ltd, 1904).
46. Margaret Kelleher, '*The Cabinet of Irish Literature*: A Historical Perspective on Irish Anthologies', *Éire-Ireland* 38, 3 and 4 (2003), pp. 68–89, p. 72.
47. Charles A. Read, ed. *The Cabinet of Irish Literature: Selections from the Works of the Chief Poets, Orators, and Prose Writers of Ireland* , revised by Katharine Tynan Hinkson, 4 vols. (London: Gresham, 1903).
48. Kelleher, '*The Cabinet of Irish Literature*', p. 84.
49. Stopford A. Brooke and T. W. Rolleston, eds. *A Treasury of Irish Poetry in the English Tongue* (London: Smith and Elder, 1900).
50. Stopford A. Brooke, 'From *A Treasury of Irish Poetry in the English Tongue*', in *The Field Day Anthology of Irish Writing*, II, p. 969.
51. D. P. Moran, 'From *The Leader*: "More Muddle"', in *The Field Day Anthology of Irish Writing*, II, p. 970.
52. Ibid., p. 971.
53. On this broad context see Senia Paseta, *Before the Revolution: Nationalism, Social Change and Ireland's Catholic Elite, 1879–1922* (Cork: Cork University Press, 1999).
54. Thomas MacDonagh, *Literature in Ireland: Studies Irish and Anglo-Irish* (Dublin: Talbot, 1916).
55. Ibid., p. vii.
56. Ibid., p. vii.
57. See Johann A. Norstedt, *Thomas MacDonagh: A Critical Biography* (Charlottesville: University Press of Virginia, 1980). Norstedt (p. 117) cites, as an influence on MacDonagh, William Rooney's essay 'A Recent Irish Literature' in *Prose Writings* (Dublin: Gill and Son, [1909?]). The uncertainty over the date of publication is also in Norstedt's account.
58. MacDonagh, *Literature in Ireland*, p. 6.
59. W. J. McCormack, 'Editor's Preface' to Louis M. Cullen, *The Hidden Ireland: Reassessment of a Concept* (Mullingar: Lilliput Press, 1988), p. vii.
60. Daniel Corkery, *Synge and Anglo-Irish Literature* (Cork: Cork University Press, 1931). The best critical account of Corkery's life and works is Patrick Maume, *'Life that is Exile': Daniel Corkery and the Search for Irish Ireland* (Belfast: Institute of Irish Studies, 1993). For an alternative reading of Corkery see Conor Carville, 'Becoming Minor: Daniel Corkery and the Expatriated Nation', *Irish Studies Review* 6, 2 (1998), pp. 139–48.
61. MacDonagh, quoted in Norstedt, *Thomas MacDonagh*, p. 114.
62. Corkery, *The Hidden Ireland*, p. 14.
63. Colin Graham, *Deconstructing Ireland: Identity, Theory, Culture* (Edinburgh: Edinburgh University Press, 2001).
64. Stephen Gwynn, *Irish Literature and Drama in the English Language: A Short History* (London: Thomas Nelson, 1936), p. 2.
65. Hugh Alexander Law, *Anglo-Irish Literature* (1926; Folcroft: Folcroft Library Editions, 1974), p. ix.
66. John Eglinton (William Kirkpatrick Magee), *Anglo-Irish Essays* (1918; New York: Books for Libraries Press, 1968), p. 87.

67. See Stephen Gwynn, *Irish Literature and Drama in the English Language*.
68. Ernest Boyd, *Ireland's Literary Renaissance* (1916; London: Grant Richards, 1923).
69. See, for example, Gregory Castle, *Modernism and the Celtic Revival* (Cambridge: Cambridge University Press, 2001), and Emer Nolan, 'Modernism and the Irish Revival', in Joe Cleary and Claire Connolly, eds. *The Cambridge Companion to Modern Irish Culture* (Cambridge: Cambridge University Press, 2005), pp. 157–72.
70. On Joyce and the Revival see Len Platt, *Joyce and the Anglo-Irish: A Study of Joyce and the Literary Revival* (Amsterdam: Rodopi, 1998), and Clare Hutton, 'Joyce and the Institutions of Revivalism', *Irish University Review* 33, 1 (2003), pp. 117–32.
71. Seamus Heaney, *Station Island* (London: Faber and Faber, 1984); Paul Muldoon, *Poems, 1968–1998* (London: Faber and Faber, 2001).
72. Of more minor interest here is Dorothy M. Hoare, *The Works of Morris and of Yeats in Relation to Early Saga Literature* (Cambridge: Cambridge University Press, 1937).
73. Francis Bickley, *J. M. Synge and the Irish Dramatic Movement* (London: Constable, 1912), p. 5. Another early account of Synge is Maurice Bourgeois, *John Millington Synge and the Irish Theatre* (London: Constable, 1913).
74. Ibid., p. 78.
75. W. B. Yeats, *Dramatis Personae* (London: Macmillan, 1936), p. 35.
76. Una Ellis-Fermor, *The Irish Dramatic Movement* (1934; London: Methuen, 1967), p. 14.
77. Louis MacNeice, *The Poetry of W. B. Yeats* (1941; London: Faber and Faber, 1967).
78. On *The Bell* see Terence Brown, *Ireland: A Social and Cultural History, 1922–1985* (London: Fontana, 1985), pp. 199–206, and Richard Kearney, *Transitions: Narratives in Modern Irish Culture* (Manchester: Manchester University Press, 1988). On *Kavanagh's Weekly* see Gerry Smyth, *Decolonisation and Criticism: The Construction of Irish Literature* (London: Pluto, 1998).
79. Robin Flower, *The Irish Tradition* (Oxford: Oxford University Press, 1947); Myles Dillon, *Early Irish Literature* (1948; Dublin: Four Courts Press, 1994); Douglas Hyde, *A Literary History of Ireland* (London: Fisher Unwin, 1899); Eleanor Hull, *A Textbook of Irish Literature* (Dublin: Gill, 1906); Eleanor Knott, *An Introduction to Irish Syllabic Poetry of the Period 1200–1600* (Cork: Cork University Press, 1928); Aodh de Blacam, *Gaelic Literature Surveyed* (Dublin: Talbot, 1929), *A First Book of Irish Literature* (Dublin: Talbot, 1934).
80. Luke Gibbons, 'Constructing the Canon: Versions of National Identity', in *The Field Day Anthology of Irish Writing*, II, p. 955.
81. Emer Nolan, *James Joyce and Nationalism* (London: Routledge, 1995), p. 3.
82. See, for example, Vincent J. Cheng, *Joyce, Race and Empire* (Cambridge: Cambridge University Press, 1995).
83. MacNeice, *The Poetry of W. B. Yeats*, p. 25.
84. T. R. Henn, *The Lonely Tower: Studies in the Poetry of Yeats* (London: Methuen 1950).
85. F. A. C. Wilson, *Yeats and Iconography* (1960; London: Methuen, 1969). See also the essays collected in Kathleen Raine, *Yeats the Initiate: Essays on Certain Themes in the Writings of W. B. Yeats* (London: George Allen and Unwin; Dublin: Dolmen, 1986).
86. Denis Donoghue, 'Notes Towards a Critical Method: Language as Order', *Studies* 44 (1955), p. 181.
87. Donald Davie, 'Reflections of an English Writer in Ireland', *Studies* 44 (1955), pp. 439–445.
88. Vivian Mercier, *The Irish Comic Tradition* (Oxford: Clarendon Press, 1962).

89. Frank O'Connor, *The Backward Look: A Survey of Irish Literature* (London: Macmillan, 1967), p. 1.
90. William T. McKinnon, *Apollo's Blended Dream: A Study of the Poetry of Louis MacNeice* (London: Oxford University Press, 1971).
91. Terence Brown, *Louis MacNeice: Sceptical Vision* (Dublin: Gill and Macmillan, 1975).
92. Terence Brown, *Northern Voices: Poets from Ulster* (Dublin: Gill and Macmillan, 1975); Edna Longley, *Poetry in the Wars* (Newcastle upon Tyne: Bloodaxe, 1986).
93. For Longley's most sustained criticism of the *Field Day Anthology* see Edna Longley, *The Living Stream: Literature and Revisionism in Ireland* (Newcastle upon Tyne: Bloodaxe, 1994).
94. Edna Longley, ed. *The Bloodaxe Book of Twentieth Century Poetry form Britain and Ireland* (Tarset: Bloodaxe, 2000).
95. Edna Longley, *Louis MacNeice: A Study* (London: Faber and Faber, 1988). See also Peter McDonald, *Louis MacNeice: The Poet in His Contexts* (Oxford: Clarendon Press, 1991).
96. Amongst many accounts see Bernard Bergonzi, *Exploding English: Criticism, Theory, Culture* (Oxford: Clarendon Press, 1990).
97. See, for example, Richard Kearney, *Transitions*.
98. Shaun Richards discussed these origins of recent Irish theory in a plenary lecture at the symposium, 'Speaking of the Nation', Princess Grace Irish Library, Monaco, October 2004. A volume of proceedings is forthcoming, edited by Bruce Stewart. Among the papers by W. J. McCormack which Richards refers to are 'The Genesis of the Protestant Ascendancy' which was delivered at the 1981 Essex Sociology of Literature conference '1789: Reading Writing Revolution'; and 'J. Sheridan Le Fanu's "Richard Marston" (1848): The History of an Anglo-Irish Text', delivered at the 1977 conference '1848: The Sociology of Literature'. See W. J. McCormack, *Ascendancy and Tradition in Anglo-Irish Literary History from 1789 to 1939* (Oxford: Clarendon, 1985), revised and enlarged in *From Burke to Beckett: Ascendancy, Tradition and Betrayal in Literary History* (Cork: Cork University Press, 1994).
99. David Cairns and Shaun Richards, *Writing Ireland: Colonialism, Nationalism and Culture* (Manchester: Manchester University Press, 1988).
100. Gerald Dawe and Edna Longley, eds. *Across a Roaring Hill: The Protestant Imagination in Modern Ireland* (Belfast: Blackstaff, 1985); John Wilson Foster, *Forces and Themes in Ulster Fiction* (Dublin: Gill and Macmillan, 1974); Hewitt, ed. *The Rhyming Weavers*.
101. Seamus Deane, general introduction in *The Field Day Anthology of Irish Writing*, i, p. xix.
102. Ibid., p. xxvi.
103. Ibid., pp. xx–xxi.
104. Ibid., p. xx.
105. There is still a paucity of available texts, in print, from both centuries. Andrew Carpenter's anthologising work has renewed our sense of pre-nineteenth-century Irish poetry; Andrew Carpenter (ed.), *Verse in English from Eighteenth-Century Ireland* (Cork: Cork University Press, 1998), and *Verse in English from Tudor and Stuart Ireland* (Cork: Cork University Press, 2003).
106. Gerardine Meaney, 'Women and Writing, 1700–1960', in Angela Bourke et. al. eds. *The Field Day Anthology of Irish Writing, Volumes IV and V: Irish Women's Writing and Traditions* (Cork: Cork University Press in association with Field Day, 2002), v, p. 766.

107. Moynagh Sullivan, 'Feminism, Postmodernism and the Subjects of Irish and Women's Studies', in P. J. Mathews, ed. *New Voices in Irish Criticism* (Dublin: Four Courts Press, 2000), p. 250.
108. For some other notable contributions see Ann Owens Weekes, *Unveiling Treasures: The Attic Guide to the Published Works of Irish Women Literary Writers* (Dublin: Attic Press, 1993), and *Irish Women Writers: An Uncharted Tradition* (Lexington: University Press of Kentucky, 1990); Siobhán Kilfeather, 'Feminism', in Cleary and Connolly, eds. *Cambridge Companion to Modern Irish Culture*, pp. 96–116 and Margaret Kelleher, 'Writing Irish Women's Literary History', *Irish Studies Review* 9, 1 (2001), pp. 5–14.
109. See, for example, Elizabeth Butler Cullingford, *Ireland's Others: Gender and Ethnicity in Irish Literature and Popular Culture* (Cork: Field Day/Cork University Press, 2001); Peggy O'Brien (ed.), *The Wake Forest Book of Irish Women's Poetry, 1967–2000* (Winston-Salem: Wake Forest University Press, 1999); Katie Donovan, A. Norman Jeffares and Brendan Kennelly, eds. *Ireland's Women: Writings Past and Present* (London: Kyle Cathie, 1994).
110. The phrase is Edna Longley's, referring to the then proposed additional women's writing volume to the *Field Day Anthology*. Edna Longley, *The Living Stream*, p. 35.
111. Terence Brown, *Ireland: A Social and Cultural History*; Norman Vance, *Irish Literature since 1800* (London: Longman, 2002); James H. Murphy, *Ireland: A Social and Cultural History, 1791–1891* (Dublin: Four Courts Press, 2003).
112. Joep Leerssen, *Mere Irish and Fíor-Ghael: Studies in the Idea of Irish Nationality, Its Development and Literary Expression Prior to the Nineteenth Century* (1986; Cork: Field Day: Cork University Press, 1996) and Leerssen, *Remembrance and Imagination*.
113. For example, Robert Welch, ed. *The Oxford Companion to Irish Literature*, assistant ed. Bruce Stewart (Oxford: Clarendon Press, 1996). The vast resources of the EIRDATA project could not be matched by any printed volume (http://www.pgil-eirdata.org/). Of the many anthologies the most ambitious, and the anthology most explicitly intended for the student market, has been Pierce, ed. *Irish Writing in the Twentieth Century*.
114. See Patricia Coughlan and Alex Davis, eds. *Modernism and the Poetry of the 1930s* (Cork: Cork University Press, 1995).
115. See FitzSimon and Murphy, eds. *The Irish Revival Reappraised*, and *Irish University Review: Special Issue–New Perspectives on the Irish Literary Revival* 33, 1 (2003) for new scholarship on the Revival.
116. For a genuinely alternative way of reading the period see Joe Cleary, 'Toward a Materialist-Formalist History of Twentieth-Century Irish Literature', *Boundary 2* 31, 1 (2004), pp. 207–42.

Select bibliography

Blackburne, E. Owens, *Illustrious Irishwomen*, 2 vols., London: Tinsley, 1877.

Bourke, A., Kilfeather, S., Luddy, M., MacCurtain, M., Meaney, G., Ní Dhonnchadha, M., O'Dowd, M. and, Wills, C. eds. *The Field Day Anthology of Irish Writing, Vols. IV and V: Irish Women's Writing and Traditions*, Cork: Cork University Press in association with Field Day, 2002.

Brown, Terence, *Ireland: A Social and Cultural History, 1922–1979*, 1981; revised edition (to 1985), 1985, new and expanded edition (to 2002), London: Harper, 2004.

Boyd, Ernest, *Ireland's Literary Renaissance*, 1916; London: Grant Richards, 1923.

Cairns, David and Shaun Richards, *Writing Ireland: Colonialism, Nationalism and Culture*, Manchester: Manchester University Press, 1988.

Cleary, Joe and Claire Connolly, eds. *The Cambridge Companion to Modern Irish Culture*, Cambridge: Cambridge University Press, 2005.

Corkery, Daniel *The Hidden Ireland: A Study of Gaelic Munster in the Eighteenth Century*, 1924; Dublin: Gill and Macmillan, 1989.

Synge and Anglo-Irish Literature, Cork: Cork University Press, 1931.

Deane, Seamus, gen. ed. *The Field Day Anthology of Irish Writing*, 3 vols., Derry: Field Day, 1991.

Graham, Colin, *Deconstructing Ireland: Identity, Theory, Culture*, Edinburgh: Edinburgh University Press, 2001.

Gwynn, Stephen, *Irish Literature and Drama in the English Language: A Short History*, London: Thomas Nelson, 1936.

Kearney, Richard, *Transitions: Narratives in Modern Irish Culture*, Manchester: Manchester University Press, 1988.

Kiberd, Declan, *Irish Classics*, London: Granta, 2000.

Law, Hugh Alexander, *Anglo-Irish Literature*, 1926; Folcroft: Folcroft Library Editions, 1974.

Lawless, Emily, *Maria Edgeworth*, New York: Macmillan, 1904.

Longley, Edna, *The Living Stream: Literature and Revisionism in Ireland*, Newcastle upon Tyne: Bloodaxe, 1994.

MacDonagh, Thomas, *Literature in Ireland: Studies Irish and Anglo-Irish*, Dublin: Talbot, 1916.

McCarthy, Justin, gen. ed. *Irish Literature*, 10 vols., New York: Bigelow, Smith for the Catholic University of America, 1904.

McCormack, W. J., *From Burke to Beckett: Ascendancy, Tradition and Betrayal in Literary History*, Cork: Cork University Press, 1994.

Mercier, Vivian, *The Irish Comic Tradition*, Oxford: Clarendon Press, 1962.

O'Connor, Frank, *The Backward Look: A Survey of Irish Literature*, London: Macmillan, 1967.

Pierce, David, ed. *Irish Writing in the Twentieth Century*, Cork: Cork University Press, 2000.

Read, Charles A. and T. P. O'Connor, eds. *The Cabinet of Irish Literature: Selections from the Works of the Chief Poets, Orators and Prose Writers of Ireland*, London, Glasgow, Edinburgh and Dublin: Blackie, 1879–80.

Vance, Norman, *Irish Literature since 1800*, London: Longman, 2002.

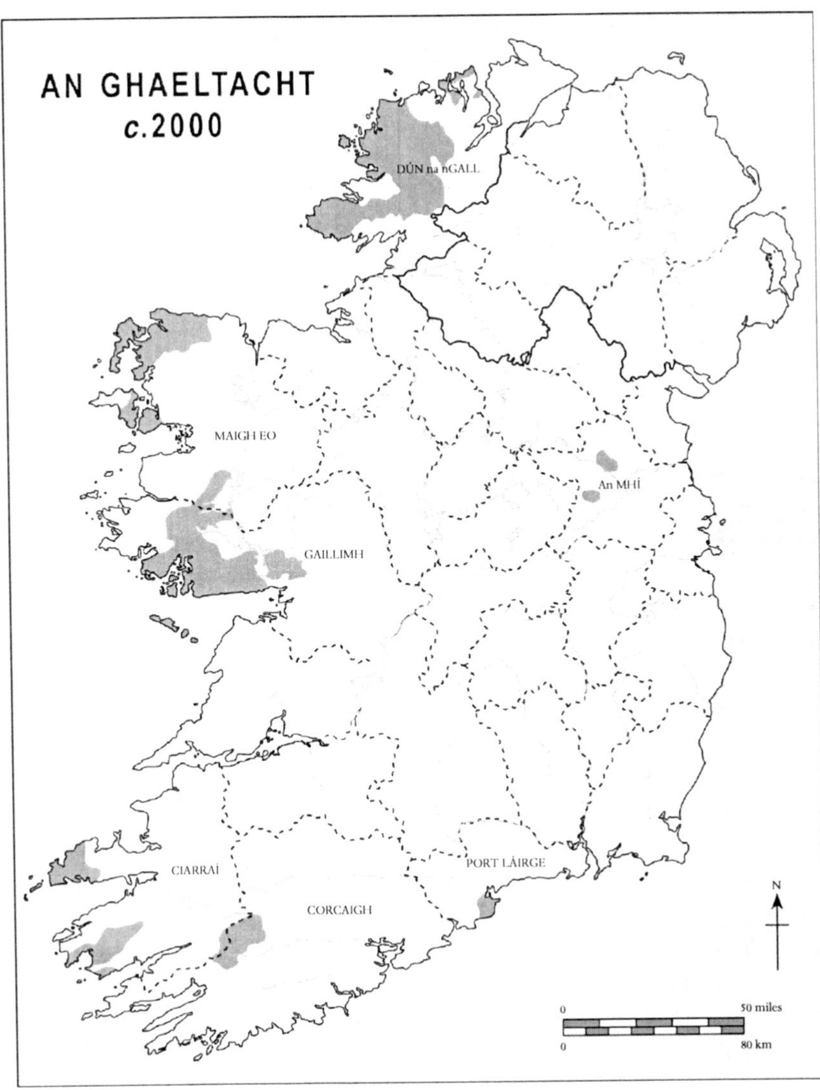

After Frank J. Convery, Sheila Flanagan, Michael Keane, Mícheál Ó Cinnéide, *Ón Bhonn Aníos: Straitéis Turasóireachta don Ghaeltacht* (An Daingean: An Sagart, 1994), p. 250. Map by Matthew Stout.

Afterword: Irish-language literature in the new millennium

BRÍONA NIC DHIARMADA

Who would be a soothsayer? In tales of yore Cassandra was fated to be ignored, her warnings spurned, before eventually being put to death. Prophecy is always a dangerous business. In 1991 Reg Hindley, an English geographer, proclaimed 'The Death of the Irish Language'.[1] He was following a long, if not exactly glorious, tradition in his declaration of doom. The demise of the Irish language has been much prophesied over the past hundred years and yet the language has managed to stumble on, sometimes with an energising burst of verve and vigour such as was seen with the explosion of the *Innti* generation on to the poetic scene,[2] or post-Hindley, with the burst of creativity occasioned by the establishment in 1996 of the first Irish-language television station, *Teilifís na Gaeilge*, now known as TG4. The continued growth and success of *Gaelscoileanna*, Irish-language medium primary schools, situated in the main in urban centres outside the traditional *Gaeltachtaí* (official Irish-speaking areas), might also be mentioned in this context.

In a further rebuttal to Hindley's view, more recent linguistic scholarship into language death would dispute that Irish be included in the astonishing and alarming number of world languages already moribund or in imminent danger of extinction. Writing in 1997, the linguist James McCloskey stated that contrary to all the harbingers of doom, Irish, according to the criteria established in the latest linguistic studies, was in the 10 per cent of world languages considered to be 'safe': 'there is little chance that Irish will become moribund (at least in the technical sense) in the next hundred years. Claims occasionally and casually made that Irish is already dead border on the irrational.'[3] And yet . . . Cassandra's ghost hovers.

In the case of the trajectory of literature in the Irish language, prophecy has proven itself no less treacherous. In the late 1960s Máirtín Ó Cadhain,[4] the foremost prose writer in Irish in the twentieth century, was highly critical of the fact that poetry was the preferred form for most creative writers in the language.[5] Ó Cadhain's pessimistic and perhaps deliberately inflammatory views were posited on what he saw as the privileging of poetry over prose in Irish-language writing and in minority languages generally – he mentions Scottish Gaelic as a further example. This was an inversion of the contemporaneous position in the anglophone world and one perceived by Ó Cadhain to be a parlous one and an extremely bad omen. He mentions, in particular, that comparatively speaking, more poetry was being written in Ireland in Irish than in English. He also stated *inter alia* that poetry in the Irish language would henceforth produce only short lyrics – the implication of this being a pejorative one. If prose were the cement, concrete and building blocks of life – 'Sé an prós tathán, coincréad, clocha saoirsinne an tsaoil'[6] – poetry was associated with a laziness and lack of rigour, with resulting consequences for the language and literature in which it occupied a premier place.

Ó Cadhain's words, published later in pamphlet form as *Páipéir Bhána agus Páipéir Bhreaca*, were first delivered at the inaugural Scoil Gheimhridh (winter school) of Cumann Merriman in 1969. In the audience was one of the major poets of the postwar period, Seán Ó Ríordáin.[7] He was to give 'a stunning impromptu response . . . to Ó Cadhain',[8] as Nuala Ní Dhomhnaill, also in the audience on that occasion, later remembered. Ní Dhomhnaill, undisputedly the foremost contemporary Irish-language poet, and the most visible Irish-language writer, was then a teenage schoolgirl. She returned to her boarding school with Ó Ríordáin's response 'ringing in her ears', her vocation as a poet affirmed and embraced.

Whatever about the impact of Ó Ríordáin's memorable extempore defence of poetry on the night, the passage of time, although confirming Ó Cadhain's own reputation as the master of modern prose, has given the lie to many of his predictions concerning the future of poetry as a literary form and its range in Irish. There is no doubt that poetry still continues to be pre-eminent. One only needs to rehearse the rollcall of contemporary poets who have achieved and continue to achieve due recognition from an Irish-language audience as well as on a wider scale nationally and internationally – Nuala Ní Dhomhnaill, Michael Davitt, Máire Mhac an tSaoi, Louis de Paor, Biddy Jenkinson, Liam Ó Muirthile, Gearóid Mac Lochlainn, for example – to acknowledge that fact. With notable exceptions – Micheál Ó Conghaile, Alan Titley, Seán Mac Mathúna and Pádraig Ó Cíobháin would count among these – it would be hard to come up with a similar number of major figures in contemporary prose,[9] and few of these would be as well known as the poets mentioned. But while this is interesting in itself and worthy of analysis, the fact that poets of this stature continue to exist and write in Irish is, I would contend, a matter for celebration. To argue otherwise would be perverse and accepting of an outmoded binary, hierarchial view which has long ceased to have any validity or currency. Few people would question Seamus Heaney's measure of achievement in winning the Nobel Prize for Literature or think it any the less because he won it for poetry and not prose. People who would criticise contemporary Irish language literature and think it 'less than' because of the dearth of major contemporary novels, for example, are buying in to unquestioned assumptions relating to the hierarchy of genre which surface from time to time from both inside and outside the Irish-language tradition.[10]

It is interesting to find this distrust of poetry, and a refusal to accept it as a literary form on a par with prose, in a writer such as Ó Cadhain, or indeed his modern-day disciples, since this rests on an acceptance, at least on the conceptual level, of binary oppositions which flourish in theoretical paradigms of logocentric thought. These would privilege one axis over the other – for example, coloniser/colonised, masculine/feminine, prose/poetry – a paradigm which has been categorised in feminist and postcolonial practice as being the bedrock of colonial and patriarchal discourses. If the colonial stereotype of the Irish is that of a fey race given to poetry and drink whose wars are merry and songs are sad, then a postcolonial anxiety can seek to invert these categories as opposed to challenging the premise on which they are made. Prose therefore is, to continue Ó Cadhain's analogy, real man's work, getting one's hands dirty as opposed to the implied effeminate and dilettante nature of poetry, particularly that of the dreaded 'short lyric'. It is also interesting that Ó Cadhain – who as he avows, came from a community whose culture was oral, not literary but no less imaginatively wrought for that – sought to distance himself from his inherited folk tradition: 'saol an tseanscéil, an tseanamhráin, an tseanghnáis, na pisreoige'[11](the world of the old story, the old song, the old custom, of the *pisreog*), a stance in contradistinction, for example to Ní Dhomhnaill's later systematic mining of this tradition in her work.

But while Ó Cadhain's views on these matters are highly dubious, if understandable given the milieu of his time and specifically the folksification of the Gaelic world in state ideology to which he was strongly opposed, his pronouncements were simply wrong. Even a cursory glance at Louis de Paor's preceding essay in this volume on developments in poetry since 1940 shows that while the short lyric certainly has its place, it is not, by any means, the full story. Even as he spoke Ó Cadhain ignored the achievement of Eoghan Ó Tuairisc's 'Aifreann na Marbh', a long poem on the consequences of Hiroshima, published in the 1964 collection *Lux Aeternae* and categorised by de Paor in his essay as 'the single most ambitious poem in modern Irish'.

Since then poets such as Liam Ó Muirthile have experimented with the longer form, most notably in 'Tine Chnámh', a verse play from his first collection and more recently in 'Dialann Bóthair', the title poem of his 1992 collection from Gallery Press. This is an extended sequence, loosely based on the diaries of Wolfe Tone and on the poet's own journey, both actual and metaphysical, from Belfast to West Cork. In so far as it is a meditation on the contradictions and interstices of history and politics, language and religion, Ó Muirthile's poem could be likened to Richard Murphy's earlier achievement in English in 'The Battle of Aughrim'. Ó Muirthile is, of course, not the only contemporary poet in Irish to go beyond the short lyric.[12] Poets such as Cathal Ó Searcaigh and Belfast poet Gearóid Mac Lochlainn have practised the longer form: Ó Searcaigh most memorably in *Gort na gCnámh/The Field of Bones*, which looks quite literally at the skeletons beneath the surface of Irish rural life; Mac Lochlainn in his recent experimental macaronic performance piece *An Damhsa/They Danced*.

Given her presence on the occasion of Ó Cadhain's prediction, it is perhaps a sweet irony that it is Nuala Ní Dhomhnaill who, above anyone else, has pushed out the boundaries of the poetic form in Irish. Ní Dhomhnaill's work, I believe, can be read and best understood as a version of *écriture feminine* as that term is understood through the work of francophone theorists such as Kristeva, Cixous and Irigaray. Apart from her earlier poems, particularly her first collection *An Dealg Droighin*, where her impulse is still in the main lyrical, her later work develops her preferred form of the dramatic monologue, where she employs the technique of subversive ventriloquism much used by contemporary women poets internationally. It is a technique established by Ní Dhomhnaill's precursor Máire Mhac an tSaoi and also employed by her contemporary Biddy Jenkinson to great effect. But it is Ní Dhomhnaill who has developed this in a systematised way. This is particularly true of her last two collections in Irish, *Feis* (1991) and *Cead Aighnis* (1998). The thematic unity and highly ambitious nature of both collections, in particular that of her third collection *Feis*, with its highly developed and deliberate structure, has been insufficiently stressed in the past. The scope of her ambition and indeed of her achievement in these collections, however, is almost totally elided when her poetry is presented in bilingual editions.[13] I have argued elsewhere[14] that *Feis* can be read as the poetic equivalent of the Jungian journey of individuation reimagined from the specificity of a contemporary woman's perspective. Ní Dhomhnaill draws upon the imaginative resources available to her from the folk traditions of the West Kerry Gaeltacht as well as both Irish and Celtic literary and mythological traditions locating the universalised in the particular.

She thus reimagines and rewrites both Jungian narratives of the individuation journey and the traditional hero narrative. Moreover, I believe that it can be argued that Ní Dhomhnaill, in particular in *Feis*, and in the extended sequence from *Cead Aighnis*, 'Na Murúcha a Thriomaigh', is extending the lyric form to what can be best described as a form of contemporary epic.

However, whether short or long, epic or lyric, public or confessional, poetry in general remains the predominant literary form in Modern Irish and this will, likely as not, continue to be the case for the foreseeable future. Why this is so is an interesting question. But a prior question exists, a question which has a profound impact on the current and future state of literary production in Irish and one to which genre and form are inextricably linked. It is the very basic and highly pertinent question: why write in a beleaguered minority language when one has on the tip of one's tongue a language which instantly gives access to the widest domestic and world audience possible? Or, as the title of a recent essay by the writer Éilís Ní Dhuibhne has it: 'Why would anyone write in Irish?'[15] If, as a writer, being born in an English-speaking country is to be born 'with a silver spoon in one's mouth', as Ní Dhuibhne avers, why on earth would one choose to spit it out?

And choice is very much the operative word here. All contemporary writers in Irish are bilingual speakers of English. That they write in Irish is a choice based on a constellation of factors not only linguistic but also concerned with the interplay of creativity and personal circumstance not to mention cultural politics, ideology and aesthetics. For most creative writers throughout the world, although stylistic questions such as dialect and register do obviously arise, language choice is pretty automatic: they write in their mother tongue. For a number of writers in Irish this is also the case. The poet Cathal Ó Searcaigh, prose writers Micheál Ó Conghaile, Joe Steve Ó Neachtain, Pádraig Ó Cíobháin, Dara Ó Conaola and dramatist Antaine Ó Flatharta are, for example, native speakers from Gaeltacht areas, although some, such as Ó Cíobháin and Ó Flatharta, no longer reside there and Ó Flatharta also writes extensively in English.[16] Other writers such as Nuala Ní Dhomhnaill are, if you like, 'second-generation' native speakers and have strong familial links with the Gaeltacht. Many other established writers, Alan Titley for example, also poets such as Michael Davitt, Liam Ó Muirthile, Gabriel Rosenstock and, in what has been referred to as the 'post-*Innti*' generation, Louis de Paor, Colm Breathnach, Biddy Jenkinson and Gearóid Mac Lochlainn, are all urban-born with varying degrees of tangential linkages (or none) to the traditional Gaeltacht.

Other questions arise: is it valid to make this distinction? What does it mean to speak of Gaeltacht writers as opposed to Irish-language writers? And particularly in a situation where an increasing number of urban-based families are raising and educating their children through Irish, coupled with the fragmentation and atomisation of society from which traditional Gaeltacht areas are not immune and the increasing and pervasive nature of the creolisation of the language in the Gaeltacht heartlands, what does the term 'native speaker' mean? Should that term only apply to inhabitants of the geographical as opposed to the 'virtual' Gaeltacht increasingly connected through the internet, radio and television as well as the printed word? If the terms native speaker and Irish speaker, native language and national language are not coterminous do they operate as linguistic or cultural signifiers?

These questions point to the complex and unique position of the Irish language in Ireland today and by extension those who would write in it. Unlike other bilingual countries in Europe, such as Belgium or Finland, both of which, like Ireland, have two official languages, the choice of Irish as a medium of literary expression is not indicative of ethnic difference. Nor is it a question of a standard language and its dialects or regional varieties as it would be for example for a Scottish writer writing in Scots. It would be fair to say, however, that the motivatory factors at work here would be relatively similar, sharing both politico / cultural as well as aesthetic dimensions and above all the element of apparent choice and I use both terms advisedly: choice, because all writers in Irish are linguistically competent in English (in those cases where it is not actually their mother tongue); apparent, because for many writers this choice is experienced as a compulsion dictated by an amalgam of creative exigencies and personal sensibilities as is suggested by the title of a recent essay by Gabriel Rosenstock, 'How I Discovered Irish or How Irish Discovered Me.'[17]

If 'the act of poetry' is, according to Michael Hartnett, 'a rebel act',[18] then the act of writing poetry in Irish or indeed the act of writing anything in Irish can be seen to be doubly so. The writer and critic Alan Titley has stated, for example, that 'writing in Irish is an act of defiance'.[19] But defiance against what or whom? Certainly not 'Perfidious Albion', although there is no doubt that earlier generations were influenced and motivated primarily by cultural and political nationalism: 'he loved his native language / because it was his own' or variants on the theme.

The answer nowadays is more complicated and would increasingly appear to be positioned against a globalising monolingual homogenised view of culture, 'the stupefying mainstreams of our time', to quote Tim Robinson. Máire Ní Annracháin, for example, referred in a recent essay to what she terms the 'liberating and enhancing potential of the Irish language as an evocative, complex alternative to the mass culture of the western world'.[20] This is a view echoed forcibly by Gabriel Rosenstock, who also draws attention to the singularity of each writer and the effect of that on her or his choice of language: Irish suits, he says, 'the anarchist, the non-conformist in me . . . Had we an Ireland today that was 90% Irish speaking, I would probably join the other 10% – whatever that might be, Anglo-Irish, Hiberno-French . . . anything you wish to imagine. I like minorities. The world needs them more and more as we jostle towards consensus, towards homogeneousness.'[21] For Biddy Jenkinson, writing in the Irish language is 'a matter of love . . . a sustaining through my veins and verbs of something infinitely precious, a stretching back along the road we have come, a stand here in the present among the outnumbered and beleaguered but determined survivors of Gaelic Ireland'.[22] For Ní Dhomhnaill, writing in Irish is the postcolonial strategy 'par excellence': 'the use of the precolonial language as a creative medium is beginning to be appreciated for the revolutionary and subversive act which it undoubtedly is'.[23] The appreciation heralded above is perhaps overstated but it does indicate a sea-change in attitudes to the Irish language and the place it occupies in contemporary Ireland with resultant implications for Irish-language writing and the ways in which it is, and will be, received and perceived.

For centuries the Irish language has carried baggage. It has long been seen as more than a language, more than simply a means of communication. The realities and complexities of the relationship between language and politics in pre-Famine Ireland, however, have tended to be obscured and obfuscated if not totally ignored in the competing dominant discourses of nationalism and revisionism, although Declan Kiberd has recently drawn attention to what he terms the 'pluralist traditions'[24] within the Irish language. The revision of hitherto accepted orthodoxies, 'the delinking of the Irish language from political nationalism' to use Kiberd's phrase, is a salient feature of contemporary writing in Irish. This can be seen in Liam Ó Muirthile's long sequence on Wolfe Tone in *Dialann Bóthair*, already mentioned above, where he interrogates assumptions about language, identity and nationalism and refuses to partake in any facile binary opposition between language and cultural traditions in Ireland. His views are at odds with the older nationalist unproblematised equation of the Irish language as a signifier of national identity. Although the language is not seen here as any longer providing an overarching symbol as was the case in the founding mythos of cultural nationalism and the Irish state (however half-hearted or hypocritical this might have translated in practice), Ó Muirthile is adamant that Irish is a necessary and compelling piece of the mosaic that goes to make up a contemporary Irish identity – 'blúire eile den mhósáic a dhéanfadh / pictiúr nua iomlán' (another fragment of the mosaic that would complete the new picture). However, while he engages in a revision of the monoculturalism of certain sections of the Revivalist movement and underlines the necessarily fragmentary nature of any contemporary national identity, Ó Muirthile's poem equally refutes and challenges any attempt at a false pluralism or multiculturalism which would seek to elide the Irish language and its traditions, literary and cultural, from versions and visions of Irishness. Thus, while on the one hand challenging nationalist pieties, his poem is equally a riposte to those whom Biddy Jenkinson, drawing an analogy between the marginalisation of Irish speakers and the marginalization of travellers, describes as 'a comfortable settled monoglot community that would prefer we went away rather than hassle about rights'.[25] These views, I believe, reflect a new paradigm which will have a profound impact upon the future perception and reception of the language and by definition those who write and speak it, where Irish speakers are demanding language rights as a minority within Ireland as opposed to relying solely on the concept of Irish as the first official language or the national language.

The success of cultural nationalism in revitalising the language when it was on the verge of extinction was, however, a phenomenal and truly revolutionary act. The espousal of the language by a cadre of urban-based, politicised, intellectually progressive creative writers such as Pádraig Mac Piarais (Patrick Pearse), Pádraic Ó Conaire and Liam S. Gógan saw the creation of a new literature in Modern Irish as modern and as experimental in form as anything their European contemporaries were producing, as Philip O'Leary has clearly demonstrated in chapter 5 above.[26]

However, the 'official' status of Irish in the years since independence has been very much a mixed blessing. The fact that Irish has had 'the support of a nation-state', one of the factors proposed in recent linguistic studies as to the viability of a language,[27] and has a designated role in the state apparatus, no matter how tokenistic, has undoubtedly helped its survival. Yet the manner of the state's engagement with Irish, which in effect amounted to simultaneous patronage and marginalisation, led to great hostility among many whose experience of the language was confined to the educational system. For some of those who came of age in the late 1960s and 1970s and who would have seen themselves as modernising progressive forces within Ireland, the language itself – or more specifically the cultural baggage it carried, although these were too often conflated – was identified with the conservative ideology of a Catholic state that they were alienated from and rejected. Irish was also primarily identified with, at best, unimaginative and at worst, brutal teaching methods: Irish was a compulsory part of the primary and secondary school curricula and was famously needed for entry into and progression in the Civil Service, an important means of social mobility as well as secure employment, particularly for lower-middle-class and rural Ireland in pre-Celtic Tiger times.

In effect if not in essence, state educational policy until the 1980s could arguably be seen as a postcolonial inversion of the situation a century earlier when English was forced on Irish-speaking children in the National School system. The National School system was notorious in its attempts at anglicisation. As well as being subjected to use of the infamous 'tally stick', children were taught to recite a rhyme much quoted in nationalist narratives: 'I thank the goodness and the grace / That on my birth have smiled / And made me in these Christian times / A happy English child.' This colonial enterprise of linguistic and cultural coercion was not unique to Ireland, of course. It was duplicated in other countries. James McCloskey has recently pointed out the similarities between the experience of Irish children in nineteenth-century Ireland and that of Native American children in the infamous Bureau of Indian Affairs boarding schools as late as the 1970s. He also draws attention to the bitter personal cost and regret inherent in such language loss.

Interestingly, the four lines quoted above resurfaced in a poem written in the late 1970s by the English-language poet Michael O'Loughlin entitled 'The Irish Lesson'.[28] By prefacing his own poem with these lines, he makes a direct and overt analogy between the forced teaching of English to native Irish-speaking schoolchildren in the nineteenth century and the teaching of Irish during his own school days in the 1960s. The poem goes on to relate how Irish was forced down the poet's 'five-year-old throat'. He refused to 'learn their language / it wasn't mine'. The poem later switches to direct speech with the voice of authority, in parenthesis, telling him that he'll need it for the Civil Service. But as he tells us, 'I didn't want to join the Civil Service. / I still don't.'

Although the hurt and pain palpable behind the hostility in this poem is undoubtedly sincere and heartfelt and experienced by a not inconsiderable number of that generation educated in Ireland up to the late 1970s, there is a note of disingenuousness here. While admittedly Irish was necessary for the Civil Service in those days (it no longer is), its 'compulsory' nature stopped, often as not, at the school gate. English was, and continues to be, necessary for almost every aspect of public life. It was, in those pre-TG4 and Raidió na Gaeltachta days, very much the predominant language of television and radio, of newspapers and comics, popular books and magazines. Every time an Irish-speaking child looked or listened, English was being 'forced down their five-year-old throat' and of course English was, and still is, necessary for the

Civil Service, as indeed was Mathematics, teaching methods for which were hardly more enlightened. But Irish-speaking children were and continue to be totally written out of narratives of 'compulsory' Irish.

O'Loughlin's poem is interesting, however, not only in and of itself but because of the response it drew from the Irish-language poet Michael Davitt. Much of the engagement of contemporary Irish-language and English-language poets in Ireland has tended to be seen as a one-way street – often typified as having an element of patronage (whether latent or overt) – with the English-language poets translating from and giving their imprimatur to the country cousins and poor relations in Irish. Davitt's engagement with O'Loughlin's poem, in contrast, exemplifies much of the tone, tenor and sensibility of his generation of Irish-language writers as well as illuminating the socio-cultural semantics of language difference. For his riposte to O'Loughlin Davitt does not, for example, engage in some ringing defence of Irish. What he does is very simple but ingenious. He translates the poem into Irish. He does, however, change the title – a practice common among English-language translators of contemporary Irish language poetry, as it happens. Davitt's version is entitled 'That on my birth . . .' followed by the explanatory line 'saobhaistriúchán ar *The Irish Lesson* le Michael O'Loughlin', the word *saobhaistriúchán* meaning a slanted, skewed or crooked translation. One of the most interesting and ironic aspects of this particular 'skewed' translation is that it is far more literal than many of the versions of Irish-language poems that were being published as translations by their English-language peers.

Davitt begins his poem with the same four lines from the nineteenth-century rhyme exactly as O'Loughlin does, leaving them in the original English. He then gives a very faithful translation of the text, almost word for word, until the end of the poem when the teacher, the voice of authority, comes in. Davitt leaves this in direct speech but also leaves it in English, interpolating his own name into the text: 'But Mr Davitt, you're not being fair / to yourself, you know you can do better / than this. And don't forget / you'll need it for the Civil Service.' Davitt then switches back to Irish for the concluding lines: 'ach níor theastaigh uaim dul isteach sa Stát Seirbhís / Fós ní theastaíonn',[29] which is of course a direct translation of O'Loughlin's closing lines 'I didn't want to join the Civil Service / I still don't'. Davitt's use of Irish and of language difference in his 'translation' brilliantly deconstructs and subverts the meaning and intent of the original poem where Irish is 'their' language: 'they' being the voice of authority, of officialdom, those who regulate 'the nation's heritage', as well as, of course, social mobility. However, Davitt as an Irish speaker shows equal hostility to these forces in his poem. And by leaving the teacher's comments in English and switching back to Irish for his final refusal he dismantles the underlying essentialist assumptions inherent in O'Loughlin's poem as well as the hypocrisies inherent in the whole 'compulsory Irish' narrative which still continues to surface on occasion. What's sauce for the goose is even more so for the gander! This engagement between Davitt and O'Loughlin might well be designated as one all!

But there is, of course, no equivalence between the systematic extermination of a language and culture as was attempted during the nineteenth century in Ireland and the postcolonial state's policy of revival, however hamfisted that might have been. The fact that most Irish people colluded with the colonial intent in so far as they abandoned Irish as their mother tongue is read by Declan Kiberd as a sign of modernity, 'an anti-colonial gesture'; there was, he says, 'something heroic, as well as awfully desperate, about the ensuing achievement'.[30] While acknowledging the trauma – 'the psychic scar' in Ní Dhomhnaill's phrase – inherent in the loss of one language and the acquisition of another (the 'severed head' and the 'grafted tongue' in John Montague's haunting metaphor, 'as / harsh a humiliation / as twice to be born'),[31] Kiberd asserts that the most traumatic aspect of the loss of Irish as an everyday medium of communication for the majority of Irish people is 'the recognition that it was the Irish themselves who decided not to speak their own language'.[32]

But as James McCloskey points out, Irish people were not unique in abandoning their own language. It is a situation replicated in many parts of the world where local languages have come into contact with languages of imperial power, the knowledge of which in McCloskey's words 'supposedly provides access to a world of affluence, prestige and power'.[33] Although not automatic nor either necessary or inevitable according to McCloskey, the acquisition of the language of power, be that English, Spanish or French, has often meant taking the further step of abandoning the mother tongue, particularly when English was the imperial language. In Australia, for example, over 90 per cent of Australian languages extant when Europeans arrived are now moribund with many of them close to total extinction. Such language loss always entails and has to entail a measure of agreement or collusion or at the very least a decision on the part of the speakers of those languages: 'For every language that disappears, there has to be a group of people who decide either that they will themselves refuse to learn the language of their parents, grandparents, aunts and uncles, or who decide that they will not use that language with their own children.'[34] But far from being 'a free and rational choice', the step of 'abandoning the local language, the older community language' is always, according to McCloskey, taken 'in the presence of powerful and destructive external pressures'.[35] As Michael Hartnett's translation of Dáibhí Ó Bruadair's acerbic tongue-in-cheek epigram recognising the linguistic implications of power relations in seventeenth-century Ireland has it: 'Pity the man who English lacks / now turncoat Ormonde's made a comeback / As I have to live here, I now wish / to swop my poems for squeaky English.'[36]

The unspoken and often unacknowledged trauma involved in the loss of an indigenous mother tongue (particularly one which contrarily continues to exist as a mother tongue and a literary medium) has often been expressed in Ireland among those writers who write in English as, at best, a sense of unease and loss – Thomas Kinsella's dual tradition,[37] for example – and at worst rejection or downright hostility.[38] Dermot Bolger, writing in 1986, made the following rather telling comment about the attitude of what he calls, 'much of [his] generation':

> Irish was seen as a language of officialdom and oppression by much of my generation in the same way as English appeared to children a century before. It was also a language of tokenism . . . What we rebelled against mainly wasn't so much the actual language, as the way it was used to try and hem us within the idea of nationhood which simply could not contain the Ireland of concrete and dual-carriageways (which is as Irish as turf and boreens) that was the reality before our eyes.[39]

Bolger wrote the above, as it happens, as a foreword to *The Bright Wave: An Tonn Gheal*, one of the first dual-language anthologies of contemporary Irish-language poetry and one which did much to dispel the climate of ignorance to which Bolger himself alluded in the same piece. As a schoolboy in Dublin, he tells us, he was able to obtain poetry from Germany and Russia, but 'there seemed nothing available to even hint that an innovative and vibrant literature was developing here in my own country of which I knew nothing'.[40] He goes on to praise the 'emergence of a group of young writers who did not attempt to ignore or reject the contemporary world . . . [who] were willing to embrace all aspects of modern life and modern Ireland within their work, which has served not to destroy the Irish tradition but to take it out into the real world again where it has become a living and exciting discourse'.[41]

But the modernisation of Irish-language literature did not begin in the 1970s and 1980s with the *Innti* poets to whom Bolger is alluding in the above piece. The willingness to embrace 'all aspects of modern life and modern Ireland' and the struggle to find a commensurate form has been a marked feature of writing in Irish since the days of the Gaelic League. But this has long been ignored by the particular narrative to which Dermot Bolger's piece belongs, which equates Irish with anti-modernity and is basically essentialist despite his protestations to the contrary. This narrative totally ignores and occludes the work of writers such as Ó Conaire, Mac Grianna, Brian Ó Nualláin, Behan, Ó Cadhain, Liam S. Gógan, Máirtín Ó Direáin, Seán Ó Ríordáin, Máire Mhac an tSaoi, Eoghan Ó Tuairisc, Pearse Hutchinson. The list goes on.

In the introduction to his book *Transformations in Irish Culture*, Luke Gibbons, following Sean O'Faolain, states that 'modernization is not solely an external force, but also requires the active transformation of a culture from within, a capacity to engage critically with its own past'.[42] Writing in Irish, I believe, has always done this. Not, obviously, all writing in Irish – for every Seosamh Mac Grianna, there has also been a 'Máire'.[43] But the main current in Irish language writing has been highly subversive of the official ideology of the postcolonial state and has provided an alternative, if subalternised, discourse. This writing has contested the appropriation of the Irish language as a central symbol in state formation and legitimisation by those who simultaneously marginalised both the language and speakers of it. It also undermines the equation of the language with the other cornerstones of an Irish identity contained within the rubric of a Catholic, socially conservative, rural, Gaelic nation while, critically, speaking often from a position within that rural Gaelic nation. I am thinking here, for example, of Ó Cadhain's scathing deconstruction of, in the words of Gearóid Denvir, 'íomhá rómánsúil sin na Gaeltachta idéalaí nach raibh riamh ann ach in intinn an dreama a chruthaigh constráid na hÉireann oifigiúla'[44] ([that] romantic image of an idealised Gaeltacht that never existed except in the minds of those who created the construct of an official Ireland). Ó Cadhain's achievement was, however, ignored by anglophone Ireland as was that of his contemporaries Ó Direáin and Ó Ríordáin, a fact that allowed a writer like Patrick Kavanagh to claim that he was 'the only man who has written in our time about rural Ireland from the inside'.[45]

It is true to say, however, that the idealised Gaeltacht and Gaeltacht inhabitant were fetishised not only by official ideology but also by sections of the language movement itself, in particular, the figure of that exotic beast 'the native speaker'. But equally the strongest and most scathing critique of this has come from within the Irish-language tradition, in Brendan Behan's poem 'Guí an Rannaire',[46] for example, and most famously of course in Brian Ó Nualláin's comic masterpiece *An Béal Bocht* (The Poor Mouth).[47] Recent readings of *An Béal Bocht* by Louis de Paor[48] and Sarah McKibben have drawn attention to the ways in which it serves, in the words of McKibben, as 'a postcolonial riposte . . . which powerfully critiques a repressive and hypocritical nationalist discourse that replicated colonial attitudes and relations well after independence'.[49] 'Ultimately', she tells us, '*An Béal Bocht* restores the potential of Irish while simultaneously knocking it off the pedestal of ideological priority.'[50] That 'potential of Irish' is something that has always existed and continues to exist. The subversive power of parodic deconstructions and satirical critiques has a long history in Irish. Equally even the genre mercilessly and hilariously parodied in *An Béal Bocht,* that of the Gaeltacht autobiography, contained within it representations of women, for example, singularly out of step with the modest comely maidens and self-sacrificing mothers of de Valera's myopic vision of Gaelic Ireland which he enshrined in his 1937 Constitution. Interestingly enough, the position of the Irish language and of women in Ireland up to the Lemass era can be read as analogous. In her book *Outsiders Inside – Whiteness, Place and Irish Women*, Bronwen Walter observes the contrast between the 'high visibility [of Irish women] in symbolic representations of Ireland and a marginalized social position in Irish society'.[51] This is apposite in the case of the Irish language: both were accorded special status and importance in identity building; both were socially peripheral but symbolically central: both were made to bear others' meanings.

The fate of Irish-language writers up to the present generation, then, was either to be ignored and rendered invisible and/or misrepresented and conflated with a view of the language that was essentialist and value laden. And even as astute a critic and one as supportive of the Irish language as Declan Kiberd can contribute to this essentialism. In his essay 'Republicanism and Culture in the New Millennium', Kiberd talks about what he terms the split between 'what remained of the Gaelic mindset and the emerging political nationalism'.[52] He goes on: 'the signs of such strain are apparent in many Gaelic texts'.[53] He mentions in this context two examples from Blasket Island writing. The first is a piece in *Allagar na hInise* where Tomás Ó Criomhthain and his fellow islanders are having a conversation about political events on the mainland. Someone mentions the word republic – or 'republic' as it appears in the text. Tomás tells him he doesn't understand and asks him to say the word in Irish. He cannot, and Tomás ends the exchange with the sarcastic comment: 'agus is beag a chuir a soláthar imní ach oiread ort' (it's little its attainment bothered you either).[54] Having quoted the above exchange, Kiberd then goes on to give an account of an incident from *Fiche Blian Ag Fás* (Twenty Years a-Growing) where the young Muiris Ó Súilleabháin, arriving at the quay in Dingle, upon being asked if he is an Irishman, replies: 'Is Blascaodach mé' (I am a Blasketman).[55] Kiberd reads the above incidents as indicating a 'mind-set' incomprehensive of and distinct from political nationalism. He comments:

'Such persons were too Gaelic to feel Irish in terms of the new twin identities of nation and religion.'[56]

According to Declan Kiberd, therefore, these 'Gaelic texts' are representations of the 'Gaelic mindset' of Tomás Ó Criomhthain and Muiris Ó Súilleabháin, who are too 'Gaelic' to feel 'Irish', the term 'Gaelic' being used interchangeably to denote both language and presumably culture and also presumably shorthand for pre-modern, the rejection and jettisoning of Irish and the adoption of English being in Kiberd's thesis the necessary price to be paid for modernisation.

However, in another of the Blasket books, *Machtnamh Seanmhná*[57] (An Old Woman's Reflections), Peig Sayers relates an incident concerning a raid on the island during the War of Independence by the Black and Tans, who presumably, as they were raiding the island, did not share Declan Kiberd's view of the islanders as being too 'Gaelic' to sympathise with the nationalist cause. Before the raid, Peig and her neighbour Sean-Neil (Old Nell) discuss recent events in Dingle, where there had been a skirmish and a number of British officers killed. A street in the town had been burned down in retaliation. Peig first hears the news from a young boy, who tells her of the arrival of 'two boys from Dingle . . . who have escaped here with their lives'.[58] Because they were speaking English, he is unable to tell her much more than the phrase he overheard 'All John Street is burned'. When Peig asks him who burned it he replies: 'Ná fiafraigh díom . . . ní thuigim aon Bhéarla' (Don't ask me . . . I don't understand English).[59] Musing to herself, Peig concludes 'gurb amhlaidh a thug na Gaeil fogha fúthu sa Daingean' (that the Gaels made an attack on them in Dingle),[60] these particular 'Gaels' being English-speaking Gaels to whom she also refers as 'Óglaigh' (Volunteers) and with whom it is clear Peig makes common cause. Peig's neighbour Sean-Neil then arrives at Peig's door with the latest news. They discuss events on the mainland and the likelihood of further retaliation. Sean-Neil is convinced that the arrival of British soldiers, whom she describes as 'an namhaid' (the enemy), is imminent. Peig thinks the island's isolation will save them, but Sean-Neil is vindicated when a few days later the soldiers arrive. Peig is at home having a cup of tea when her daughter rushes in to tell her that soldiers are all over the island. Peig's husband arrives hot on her heels admonishing her for sitting there eating and drinking and orders her to take down the pictures of dead republican heroes which they have on their walls, among them a picture of Thomas Ashe, the Kerry-born leader of the Irish Volunteers who had been force-fed while on hunger strike in Mountjoy and had died as a result. Peig refuses, saying to do so would be an insult to their memory:

> 'Muise, leagadh is leonadh ar an namhaid a leag iad' arsa mise. 'Leagadar iad go míthrócaireach agus iad beo agus is cosúil go gcaithfead a bpictiúirí a chur i bhfolach anois uathu, agus iad marbh! Ach go rabhadsa marbh agus chomh marbh le hart má thógaim anuas iad le heagla roimh aon raispín Gallda . . . Throideadar sin is thiteadar ar ár son.'[61]

> 'Musha, mishap and injury be on the enemy that felled them', I said. 'They felled them mercilessly when alive and now it appears that their pictures have to be hidden from them and they dead. But may I be dead and stone dead if I take them down for fear of any English wretch . . . They fought for us and they died for us.'[62]

There is very little sign of 'the Gaelic mindset' that is 'too Gaelic to be Irish' here. But are we seriously suggesting that Peig was any less 'Gaelic' than Tomás Ó Criomhthain or Muiris Ó Súilleabháin because of her all-too-obvious and unhidden nationalist sympathies? Equally in *Rotha Mór an tSaoil* (The Hard Road to Klondike) Micí Mac Gabhann, a native Irish speaker from Donegal, has no difficulty in using religion as a marker of identity. He also shows a remarkably modern anti-colonial solidarity and sensibility when he equates the treatment of the Sioux that he meets in Dakota and the dispossession of their land with the treatment and dispossession of his own people in Cloch Cheannfhaola.

My point here is that it is impossible and highly dangerous to equate and conflate a 'mindset' with a language. Irish-language texts can equally support reactionary ideas and progressive ideas, can be pre-modern, modern or post-modern, can be folk-tales or treatises on quantum physics, can be handbooks on IT, volumes of poetry or post-modern novels. One particularly odious, if singular, book, a memoir entitled *Cé hÍ sin Amuigh*,[63] was published in 1992 and outlined the author's experience in, and support of, Nazi Germany. Although this text was published and written in Irish, I doubt if anyone would refer to it as a 'Gaelic' text.

There is in fact a wealth of confusion surrounding the use of the term 'Gaelic' when used to describe twentieth-century and contemporary writing. Does 'Gaelic' simply mean the Irish language? Invariably it does not. Gaelic was and is often used synonymously, often with conflationary implications, to denote not only the Irish language but also the rural and traditional. It also carried nationalist connotations (although these have recently been 'delinked' in Declan Kiberd's thesis). 'Gaelic' was a burden that Irish language writers were often made to carry on their backs by both friend and foe. This invariably has an impact on writers who wish to distance themselves from imposed stereotypes, particularly those writers such as the *Innti* poets and those following them, who were as at home in the world of 'concrete and dual-carriageways' as their contemporaries who write in English, and yet by virtue of writing in Irish are heirs to a long literary and oral tradition which was rooted, in the main, in the rural. Louis de Paor has articulated this particular dilemma and his own personal response:

> the determination of writers in Irish to refute colonial representations by proving the adaptability of Irish to the contemporary urban situation may have caused some of us at least to neglect or even deny crucial aspects of our own identity, an altogether unexpected consequence of our anti-colonial stance. Aspects of early Irish mythology, of folk tradition and belief as well as elements of my own family history which I had felt were irreconcilable with my own sense of myself as a thoroughly modern urban dweller, a chauvinistic townie, in fact, have gradually extended my sense of belonging in the entire history and geography of Ireland rather than being confined to the immediate here and now which I had felt was my proper place.[64]

The writer most associated with utilising traditional material in her work, Nuala Ní Dhomhnaill, has said in a recent essay that the job of the present generation of Irish speakers and writers is 'the de-Gaelicization of Ireland'.[65] In Ní Dhomhnaill's case, she has found in the oral traditions of Irish an alternative discourse, the dynamics of which she brings into her own work through transposition and intertextuality, which allows her to challenge logocentric binary modes central to the dominant strands in western discourse. But with Ní Dhomhnaill, as with Biddy Jenkinson, who also invokes traditional matter in her work, their engagement with the Irish-language tradition is a double-edged one. Their work not only offers an alternative discourse to an English-language tradition, it also revitalises, modernises and subverts the Irish-language tradition in which they write, in their case specifically from a woman's perspective.

Writing in *Éire-Ireland*, the writer and translator Hans-Christian Oeser made the comment: 'What singles out Ireland among other nations is the fact that Irish writers . . . face a challenging choice between two different languages in which to set down their experience – and are thus free, or compelled, to engage in either one or both of two different cultures.'[66] The question is, however, not as cut and dried as would appear from this. While Irish is obviously a distinct language, even in the highly creolised demotic version utilised in everyday speech by many in the Gaeltacht, how valid is it to say that there are two distinct and different cultures based on language difference? Increasingly, exclusive lines between two distinct traditions are blurring as both English- and Irish-language writers in Ireland, particularly poets, interact not only with each other and their traditions but are increasingly engaged in a cross-fertilisation process with other cultures, witness Gearóid Mac Lochlainn, undoubtedly the most important and exciting new poetic voice in Irish, and his engagement with the work of Jamaican poet Linton Kwesi Johnson and with the rhythms of hip-hop. Mac Lochlainn is also blurring even the distinction of separate languages with his macaronic performance pieces: *An Damhsa / They Danced*[67] mixes Irish, English, Spanish and the Lakota language. The influence of what Declan Kiberd has called the 'counter culture of the 1960s' on the *Innti* generation has long been attested, particularly the influence of the Beat writers on Michael Davitt and Cathal Ó Searcaigh. Gabriel Rosenstock has long invoked the spirit of Zen and eastern religions and has spoken recently of his preference for Rumi over Raftery, Basho over Ó Bruadair.[68] Indeed as Liam Ó Muirthile commented in an editorial while editor of *Poetry Ireland*:

> The act of writing poetry in Irish does not necessarily endow the poems with a gaelic voice. Many of the poems in English in this issue are more 'gaelic' than the poems in Irish . . . Is this a result of . . . the bleed-off factor, the blending of literary traditions in two languages? The fact is that some of the poems in English deal head-on with the Irish language, or engage aspects of what might be considered the Irish language tradition . . . Paradoxically, many Irish language poets are less 'within' the Irish language literary tradition than their counterparts writing in English.[69]

That this is so is I would contend a healthy sign, on both fronts. A tradition that does not change and absorb outside influence atrophies. And Irish has shown itself to be particularly adept at absorbing and indigenising such influences. It is also a sign of a new understanding that to live on the island of Ireland makes us all heirs to at least two languages and two traditions. This has particular importance in a country which is increasingly multicultural in ethnic terms, with 6 per cent of the current population of the state 'non-Irish national' according to the 2002 census.

The increasingly hybrid nature of Irish culture generally is one much commented upon. In a recent essay, Máirín Nic Eoin addresses the challenges of hybridity to what is termed 'Irish-language culture'.[70] But the very notion of there being a monolithic all-embracing 'Irish-language culture' even in the Gaeltacht heartlands is one that can be questioned and indeed is in a piece by Micheál Ó Conghaile quoted in the same essay. Here Ó Conghaile describes present-day Connemara, the Connemara in which he lives and writes. This is: '*Conamara an* discó, *an* rock an' roll. *An* chountry and western. *An* walkman *agus an* chairiócaí. *Conamara na* night clubs, *na* bpotholes *agus na* mobile homes. *Conamara na* videos, *Conamara* Chablelink, *Conamara* Sky *agus na* satailítí. *Conamara 'Home and Away' agus 'Coronation Street' . . . Conamara an microwave, na* mud wrestlers *agus an* Sunday World.'[71] It is, Ó Conghaile points out, a Connemara forced upon them by outside influences but one willingly embraced by many of them. It is, he says, 'the new Connemara that we are creating for ourselves. This is our culture now, not just one culture but cultures. At times we hardly recognise ourselves in the confusion of it all.'[72]

The picture painted here of cultural change and confusion, 'ar strae / áit inteacht / idir Cath Chionn tSáile / agus an *Chinese takeaway*' (astray / somewhere between / the Battle of Kinsale / and the Chinese takeaway) in the words of Cathal Ó Searcaigh,[73] is one, however, that would be immediately recognisable to many indigenous cultures throughout the world under pressure from the homogenising effect of late-capitalist consumerist culture. Máirtín Ó Cadhain spoke of his Connemara in very different terms – that of 'a local organic community', one where his family had lived 'cho fada siar agus bhí siar ann, le míle bliain, b'fhéidir, ar an gceird chéanna a bhfuil siad fós, ina dtalamhaithe beaga, anois sa darna leath den fichiú céad' [74] (as far back as one can go, maybe a thousand years, at the same trade as they are now, on their small holdings, in the second half of the twentieth century').

It is in contemporary Gaeltacht writing that the questions of hybridity and cultural and linguistic tensions are primarily expressed and problematised, although it is true to say that these issues surface in the work of most contemporary writers in Irish, to a greater or lesser degree. These issues, however, are foregrounded in the work of Gaeltacht writers such as Antoine Ó Flatharta in his plays *Gaeilgeoirí*, *An Solas Dearg* and *Grásta i Meiriceá*, as Máirín Nic Eoin points out in chapter 6 above. More recently Micheál Ó Conghaile's *Cúigear Chonamara*, ostensibly a kitchen sink drama set in present-day Connemara, uses the main character Danny, who is a transvestite, as a focus for exploring the breakdown and confusion of cultural and sexual identity in a play which is ultimately a study in liminality.

Declan Kiberd has recently spoken of the Gaeltacht as the 'crucible of Irish post-modernity',[75] a view echoed in the rather ironic lines from Cathal Ó Searcaigh's poem 'Trasnú' (Crossing) published on the cusp of the millennium: 'Tá muid leath-réamhstairiúil / agus leath-*postmodern intertext*úil' (we are half pre-historical / and half post-modern intertextual).[76] This poem is a wonderfully humorous, half-exasperated acknowledgement of the hybrid realities of Gaeltacht culture which draws attention to what has been lost while itself inhabiting the creative space made possible by hybridity.

Contemporary Gaeltacht writing ranging from popular cultural productions such as TG4's soap opera *Ros na Rún* to the work of Ó Conghaile and Ó Searcaigh has done much to deconstruct not only the stereotypes of 'the native speaker' but also to question constructs of the rural generally and of the Gaeltacht specifically. It has done this by acknowledging the contradictions and the incongruous juxtapositions inherent in the contested spaces of contemporary life. *Ros na Rún* has long mainstreamed its gay characters, has run storylines dealing with abortion, rape and youth pregnancy and introduced Irish television's first black Irish-speaking character without jettisoning the more traditional and stereotypical shenanigans of characters such as bachelor brothers Cóilín and Séamus. In 'Athair' (Father),[77] Ó Conghaile's wonderful short story of coming out, the father's acceptance of his son's gayness is indicated not by any meaningful heart-to-heart but by his asking the son to stand with him when he goes to milk one of the cows who has a sore teat – hardly a hip, *faux*-urban image but one true to the specificities of this story. Cathal Ó Searcaigh's poem 'Cainteoir Dúchais' goes further in linking issues of sexual and cultural identity. His 'native speaker' is described as having spent the morning 'flat out' 'hoovering' the flat, 'flashing' the floor, 'windowlene-ing' the windows and 'eau-de-cologne-ing' the beds. And after all that: 'Bhí sé *shag*áilte, a dúirt sé, / ach ina dhiaidh sin agus uile / rachadh sé amach a *chruise*áil; / b'fhéidir, a dúirt sé, go mbuailfeadh sé / le boc inteacht / a mbeadh Gaeilge aige' (He was shagged, he said, but even so / he would go out cruising. Maybe he might meet / a buck / who spoke Irish.)[78]

There has long been a self-conscious concern with the materiality of language that continues to attend writers in Irish. This concern is long attested as a preoccupation. It manifested and continues to manifest somewhat differently for Gaeltacht writers than for those writers who are not native speakers. Ó Cadhain, for example, spoke of the ontological fear of writers in the face of the very real worry that their language would pre-decease them. This had an obvious impact on his writing, stylistically and linguistically. Many Gaeltacht writers of that era either saw themselves or were regarded as custodians of the language, echoing rather literally Eliot's view of the writer's responsibility as being that of 'purifying the language of the tribe'. Contemporary Gaeltacht writers, in the main, no longer see themselves as being concerned with linguistic purity. Their work reflects a rupture in cultural and linguistic certainties, refusing what Maria Tymoczko and Colin Ireland (following Pierre Bourdieu) have termed 'the dual processes of naturalization, thereby facilitating new perceptions of personal and cultural identities by bringing unconsciously accepted aspects of culture and language to conscious awareness'.[79]

For non-Gaeltacht writers such as Ó Ríordáin, his sense of linguistic displacement mirrored his ontological unease.[80] Contemporary writers such as Gearóid Mac Lochlainn, who used a verse from Ó Ríordáin's 'A Theanga seo Leath-Liom' (O language that is half-mine) as a foreword to his most recent collection,[81] continue to inhabit 'the nether world of languages, / Lost in space between words / no longer mine' (Tá mé in idirdhomhan teangacha, / caillte sna spásanna idir focail / nach liom níos mó).[82] Mac Lochlainn more than any other writer, perhaps, articulates this state of liminality: 'Mise an teanga / a fhilleann san oíche, ceolta sí, Micí Mí-ádh . . . / eitlím trí na pasáistí dúdhorcha rúnda / faoi chathair bhriste ('I am Johnny Dark, Creole / I wing through secret pitch-black passageways / beneath the broken city').[83] Unlike Ó Ríordáin's generation, who still looked to the Gaeltacht not only as a linguistic source but as a place where they could decontaminate themselves of 'srathar shibhialtacht an Bhéarla',[84] a paradisal space where the contradictions and alienation inherent in the cultural confusion of the modern world did not exist, the present generation realises, not perhaps without some deep sense of loss, that in the words of Ní Dhomhnaill: 'there is no Ithaca to return to'. Writers such as Ní Dhomhnaill and Mac Lochlainn, among others, however, continue to inhabit the Gaeltacht and the Irish-language literary and oral traditions as imaginative space trying to achieve 'a delicate balance in the dual-language reality which is the lot of many of us on this island'.[85]

Contemporary Irish language writers have been to the fore in what is becoming a more general recognition of the plurality of our traditions and the increasingly hybrid nature of our culture. This increasingly takes the place of the polarised positions of yesteryear: on the one hand, those who contended that Irish was not only dead but a putrefying corpse infecting with its stench the bright, brand-new world they were creating and in need of a quick burial; on the other hand, those strict Revivalists who would brook no contamination from the foreign weed of English. Things have changed dramatically. From an Irish-language perspective this has led to a breakdown of exclusionist and protectionist practices and a de-ghettoisation of Irish-language production. It has also given a freedom to writers to be accepted as writers. As Michael Davitt put it: 'Is mar fhile a ghlactar leis an bhfile Gaeilge i measc an mhórphobail sa lá inniu seachas mar chaomhnóir oidhreachta, treallchogaí cultúrtha ná saoithín teanga. Is ina s(h)aothar mar dhéantús cruthaitheach atá suim an léitheora'.[86] (The Irish language poet today is accepted as a poet and not as cultural preservation officer, a cultural guerilla or a language expert. The reader is interested in his/her work as a piece of creative work.)

This reception has occurred for literary texts mainly through translation and in the case of television output through open subtitles. Translation is not of course without its inherent dangers and a caveat must also be entered because of the obvious disparity in power relations between the Irish and English languages. The whole question of translation has provoked differing responses among creative writers themselves and an ongoing and sometimes acrimonious debate aired in literary and academic journals.[87] Despite the much-debated and very real dangers inherent in such a strategy, the benefits of translation, I would contend, outweigh the drawbacks. Irish-language production now has a reach broader than ever before. The isolation suffered by Irish-language writers of Ó Ríordáin and Ó Direáin's generation no longer pertains. Indeed, the work of Ó Ríordáin, Ó Direáin and Máire Mhac an tSaoi is finally reaching new audiences by being included in dual-language form in contemporary anthologies side by side with their English-language contemporaries.[88] The work of Irish-language poets no longer appears solely in translations, even in English-language anthologies published outside Ireland.[89] At home, writers of *Ros na Rún* regularly see audiences of 280,000 for their work.[90] Irish-language writers appear at literary festivals alongside their English-language contemporaries and it would be a foolhardy editor indeed who would attempt an anthology of 'Irish writing' without some recognition of the presence of Irish-language writers.

There are other hopeful signs for the future. Publishing in Irish is thriving with well-established publishers such as Cló Iar-Chonnachta and Coiscéim joined by Cois Life, while the government-sponsored An Gúm continues to cater for the younger market. There continues to be a significant growth in genre literature: children's, young adults', detective and popular fiction as well as adult learners' short fiction. Writing for film and television is now very much a possibility for Irish-language writers, although the financial constraints and realities of television and film production have confined this in the main to low-budget genre TV drama such as children's drama, sitcom, soap opera and film shorts. It is interesting to note in passing that perhaps the only form of writing in Irish that has a financial imperative today is that of the film short, where the Oscailt scheme run jointly by TG4 and the Irish Film Board makes it more likely for a new writer/director to have a short film produced in Irish than in English (although this has led, more often than not, to a script originally written in English being translated rather than an original script conceived and written in Irish). The most significant and successful shorts made in Irish under Oscailt, however, have been those originated in Irish;

rather than ignoring questions of language and treating it as transparent, these works have taken the language itself as their theme as in *Lip Service* (dir. Paul Mercier, 1999) and the recent award winning *Yu Ming is Ainm Dom* (dir. Daniel O'Hara, 2003).

The Irish language, in the words of a Michael Hartnett poem, is, and has been in so far as historical exigencies have permitted, 'an líon / a bhailíonn gach iasc' (the net that catches all fish).[91] While long made to carry ideological baggage by both friend and foe, the Irish language is not in itself an ideology. However, choosing to speak or write in a minority language in an increasingly globalised anglophone world has undoubtedly ideological implications. That this is so is due to what might be best termed positionality and is central, I believe, to the choice of many writers to write in Irish. Eavan Boland, speaking of women writers, once made the point that 'marginality . . . however painful, confers certain advantages'.[92] To choose to write in Irish today is to invoke marginality while simultaneously either asserting the centrality of the margins or contesting the very notion of marginality as a fixed state. When Nuala Ní Dhomhnaill began to publish, she spoke about suffering what she called a 'double bout of invisibility', writing as a woman and writing in Irish. Although this patently is not the case for her today, due in no small part to translation, it is interesting to note that many of the best contemporary Irish-language writers write from similar positions of double marginality.

In the 1980s, for example, the strongest and most distinctive voices to be heard in Irish-language literature were arguably women poets such as Ní Dhomhnaill herself, Máire Mhac an tSaoi, Biddy Jenkinson, Áine Ní Ghlinn, Deirdre Brennan and Eithne Strong among others, who were speaking in what was then a zeitgeist alive with feminist struggles. In the 1990s, overtly gay male voices such as Cathal Ó Searcaigh and Micheál Ó Conghaile began to be heard in collections such as Ó Searcaigh's *Na Buachaillí Bána* and *Out in the Open* and in Ó Conghaile's fiction, in particular his novel *Sna Fir*, an overtly erotic work reminiscent of the work of Edmund White, detailing the sexual awakening of a young gay man from the Gaeltacht during his visits to gay bars and clubs in Dublin. And arguably one of the most marginalised and maligned communities within Ireland over the past thirty years, that of nationalist West Belfast, has found a voice in Irish in the person of Gearóid Mac Lochlainn, who speaks from a position within that community. Interesting also in this context is the winner of the Foras na Gaeilge Perpetual Trophy for best poem in Irish in the under-seventeen category in the 2003 Dún Laoghaire Poetry Festival. Her name is Hanan Youssef from Dublin, whose award-winning poem 'Cloch' (Stone) is about the Palestinian intifada.

In 2001 Field Day, in association with Cork University Press, published a volume in their Critical Conditions Series, a book by Elizabeth Butler Cullingford entitled *Ireland's Others*. The author expands on this title in her introduction: 'The price of insight into one injustice . . . may be blindness to a variety of others. The "Others" of my title are numerous, and they are both real and fictive. Ireland is accustomed to being stigmatized as the feminized object of English discourse, but in women, gays, abused children, travellers and the working class it has produced its own internal Others.'[93] Conspicuous by their absence from the above list are Irish-language and Gaeltacht voices who, I would contend, equally act in contemporary Ireland as 'internal Others'. Interestingly most of Butler Cullingford's categories have also found a voice in Irish and will likely continue to do so. Irish-language writers continue to be engaged, in the words of Nuala Ní Dhomhnaill, in 'the re-invention of the whole idea of homeland in terms that are much more inclusive and interesting'.[94]

Luke Gibbons has said of tradition, like the Irish language much maligned in certain narratives of modernisation, that 'it may often have a transformative impact, particularly if it activates muted voices from the historical past, or from marginalised sections of the community'.[95] This is apposite in the case of the Irish language. Irish-language writers in the new millennium will continue, I believe, to have a transformative impact in an increasingly pluralist multicultural country in an increasingly globalised, homogenising world. They are engaged in an act of hope, in the words of Gearóid Mac Lochlainn: 'san athshealbhú cainte / a thógann tú in airde, / le bheith ag snámh i measc / púdair réalta de bhriathra rúnda / ag damhsa gan chosc / i mbéal fairsing fuaime, / ar leathadh' (repossessing speech / that lifts you up / to swim / through the stardust of lost language / dancing in the deep open vowels / of articulation).[96]

Notes

1. Reg Hindley, *The Death of the Irish Language: A Qualified Obituary* (London: Routledge, 1990).
2. See Louis de Paor's discussion of this group of poets in chapter 7 above.
3. See James McCloskey, 'A Global Silencing', *Poetry Ireland Review* 52 (Spring 1997), pp. 41–6, p. 45.
4. See Máirín Nic Eoin's discussion of Ó Cadhain's work in chapter 6 above.
5. See Máirtín Ó Cadhain, *Páipéir Bhána agus Páipéir Bhreaca* (Dublin: An Clóchomhar, 1969).
6. Ibid., p. 37.
7. See chapter 7 above.
8. Nuala Ní Dhomhnaill, 'What Foremothers?', *Poetry Ireland Review* 36 (1992), pp. 18–31, p. 25.

9. See Máirín Nic Eoin's essay (chapter 6 above) for a discussion of these writers.
10. For a discussion of genre in Irish see Máire Ní Annracháin, 'Litríocht na Gaeilge i dtreo na Mílaoise', in Micheál Ó Cearúil, ed. *An Aimsir Óg* (Dublin: Coiscéim, 1999), pp. 14–25.
11. See Ó Cadhain, *Páipéir Bhána agus Páipéir Bhreaca*, p. 7.
12. See Louis de Paor's essay (chapter 7 above).
13. A similar point is made by Kaarina Hollo in 'From the Irish: On The Astrakhan Cloak', *New Hibernia Review* 3, 2 (Summer 1999), pp. 129–41.
14. Bríona Nic Dhiarmada, 'Immram sa tSícé; Filíocht Nuala Ní Dhomhnaill agus Próiseas an Indibhidithe', *Oghma* 5 (1993), pp. 78–94.
15. Eilís Ní Dhuibhne, 'Why Would Anyone Write in Irish?', in Ciarán Mac Murchaidh, ed. *'Who Needs Irish?': Reflections on the Importance of the Irish Language Today* (Dublin: Veritas, 2004), pp. 70–82.
16. See Máirín Nic Eoin's essay (chapter 6 above).
17. See Gabriel Rosenstock, 'How I Discovered Irish or How Irish Discovered Me', in Mac Murchaidh, ed. *'Who Needs Irish?'*, pp. 83–93.
18. Michael Hartnett, 'A Farewell to English', in *A Farewell to English* (Dublin: Gallery Press, 1975), p. 33.
19. See Alan Titley's introductory essay to Dermot Bolger, *The Bright Wave / An Tonn Gheal* (Dublin: Raven Arts Press, 1986), one of the first dual-language anthologies of contemporary poetry; this anthology featured the work of the *Innti* generation and did much to shatter the veil of invisibilty which still surrounded Irish-language writing at the time.
20. Neil Buttimer and Máire Ní Annracháin, 'Irish Language and Literature, 1921–84', in J. R. Hill, ed. *A New History of Ireland, Vol. VII: Ireland, 1921–1984* (Oxford: Oxford University Press, 2003), pp. 538–86, p. 586.
21. Rosenstock, 'How I Discovered Irish', p. 89.
22. See Biddy Jenkinson, 'Letter to an Editor', in *Irish University Review* 21 (Spring / Summer 1991), pp. 33–4.
23. Ní Dhomhnaill, 'What Foremothers?', pp. 18–23.
24. See Declan Kiberd, 'Republicanism and Culture in the New Millennium', in Robert Savage Jr, ed. *Ireland in the New Century* (Dublin: Four Courts Press, 2003), pp. 67–86.
25. Biddy Jenkinson 'Máire Mhac an tSaoi: The Clerisy and the Folk (*PIR* 24) – A Reply', in *Poetry Ireland Review* 25 (1989), p. 80.
26. See Philip O'Leary's essay (chapter 5 above).
27. James McCloskey, *Guthanna in Éag / Voices Silenced* (Dublin: Cois Life, 2001), p. 16.
28. Michael O'Loughlin, *Stalingrad: The Street Dictionary* (Dublin: Raven Arts Press, 1980), p. 14.
29. Michael Davitt, *Bligeaird Sráide* (Dublin: Coiscéim, 1983), p. 17.
30. See Kiberd, 'Republicanism and Culture', p. 77.
31. John Montague, *The Rough Field* (Dublin: Dolmen, 1972), p. 39.
32. Kiberd, 'Republicanism and Culture', p. 77.
33. James McCloskey, *Guthanna*, p. 24.
34. Ibid., pp. 24–6.
35. Ibid.
36. Michael Hartnett, *Selected and New Poems* (Dublin: The Gallery Press, 1994), p. 68.

37. See Thomas Kinsella, 'The Irish Writer', in *Davis, Mangan, Ferguson? Tradition and the Irish Writer* (Dublin; Dolmen, 1970), pp. 57–70; Kinsella, 'The Divided Mind', in Seán Lucy, ed. *Irish Poets in English* (Cork: Mercier Press, 1973), pp. 208–18.
38. For a discussion of these issues see Louis de Paor, '"Stepping Stones across a River in Spate": Images of Language Loss in Irish Writing in English and in the Guerrilla Poems of Lionel G. Fogarty', in Tadhg Foley and Fiona Bateman, eds. *Irish-Australian Studies: Papers Delivered at the Ninth Irish-Australian Conference, Galway, April 1 997* (Sydney: Crossing Press, 2000), pp. 34–44.
39. Bolger, *The Bright Wave/An Tonn Gheal*, pp. 9–10.
40. Ibid.
41. Ibid.
42. Luke Gibbons, *Transformations in Irish Culture* (Cork: Cork University Press in association with Field Day, 1996), p. 3.
43. 'Máire' was the pen name of Séamus Ó Grianna, brother of Seosamh (Mac Grianna). See Philip O'Leary's discussion of both writers in chapter 5 above.
44. Gearóid Denvir, *Litríocht agus Pobal* (Inverin: Cló Iar-Chonnachta, 1997), p. 96.
45. See Jonathan Allison, *Patrick Kavanagh – A Reference Guide* (New York: GK Hall, 1996), p. 13.
46. Brendan Behan, *Poems and a Play in Irish* (Dublin: The Gallery Press, 1981), p. 24.
47. See Máirín Nic Eoin's essay (chapter 6 above).
48. Louis de Paor, 'Myles na gCopaleen agus Drochshampla na nDealeabhar', *Irish Review* 23 (1998), pp. 24–32.
49. Sarah McKibben, '*The Poor Mouth*: A Parody of (Post) Colonial Irish Manhood', *Research in African Literatures* 34, 4 (Winter 2003), pp. 96–114, p. 96.
50. Sarah McKibben, 'An Béal Bocht: Mouthing off at National Identity', in P. J. Mathews, *New Voices in Irish Criticism* (Dublin, Four Courts Press, 2000), pp. 37–53, p. 40.
51. Bronwen Walter, *Outsiders Inside – Whiteness, Place and Irish Women* (London: Routledge, 2001), p. 18.
52. Kiberd, 'Republicanism and Culture', p. 78.
53. Ibid.
54. Tomás Ó Criomhthain, *Allagar na hInise* (1928) quoted in ibid., p. 78.
55. Muiris Ó Súilleabháin, *Fiche Blian ag Fás* (1933), quoted in ibid., p. 78.
56. Ibid., p. 78.
57. Peig Sayers, *Machtnamh Seanmhná* (Dublin: Oifig an tSoláthair 1939; new edition, 1980).
58. See extract from *Machtnamh Seanmhná* in Bríona Nic Dhiarmada, ed. 'Twentieth Century Irish Language Memoirs', with new translation by Bríona Nic Dhiarmada, in Angela Bourke et al., *The Field Day Anthology of Irish Writing*, vols. IV and V (Cork: Cork University Press in association with Field Day, 2002), iv, pp. 1,054–8.
59. Ibid., p. 1,055, 1,057.
60. Ibid.
61. Ibid., p. 1,056.
62. Ibid., p. 1,058.
63. Róisín Ní Mheara-Vinard, *Cé hÍ sin Amuigh* (Dublin: Coiscéim, 1992).
64. Louis de Paor, 'Disappearing Language: Translations from the Irish', *Poetry Ireland Review* 51 (1996), p. 67.

65. Nuala Ní Dhomhnaill, 'The Role of Irish in Contemporary Ireland', in Savage, ed. *Ireland in the New Century*, pp. 198–205.
66. Hans-Christian Oeser, 'Expansion and Seclusion: Internal, Outward, and Inward Translation of Literature in Ireland Today', *Éire-Ireland* 35, 1 and 2 (2000), pp. 29–38, p. 29.
67. Gearóid Mac Lochlainn, *An Damhsa/They Danced* (Belfast: Open House, 2003).
68. See Rosenstock, 'How I Discovered Irish', p. 88.
69. Liam Ó Muirthile, 'Editorial/Eagarfhocal', *Poetry Ireland Review* 51 (1996), p. 1.
70. Máirín Nic Eoin, 'Idir Dhá Theanga – Irish-language Culture and the Challenges of Hybridity', in Mac Murchaidh, ed. *Who Needs Irish?*, pp. 123–39.
71. Ibid., p. 126.
72. Ibid.
73. Cathal Ó Searcaigh, 'Trasnú', in *Ag Tnúth leis an tSolas* (Inverin: Cló Iar-Chonnachta, 2000), pp. 277–9, p. 277 (translation by this author).
74. Ó Cadhain, *Páipéir Bhána agus Páipéir Bhreaca*, p. 9 (translation by this author).
75. Kiberd, 'Republicanism and Culture', p. 78.
76. Ó Searcaigh, 'Trasnú', p. 277 (translation by this author).
77. Micheál Ó Conghaile, 'Athair', in *An Fear a Phléasc* (Inverin: Cló Iar-Chonnachta, 1997), pp. 147–56.
78. Cathal Ó Searcaigh, 'Cainteoir Dúchais', in *Ag Tnúth*, p. 255 (translation by this author).
79. Maria Tymoczko and Colin Ireland, editors' introduction, *Éire-Ireland: Special Issue – Language and Identity in Twentieth Century Ireland* 38, 1 and 2 (Spring/Summer 2003), pp. 4–22.
80. For a discussion see Máirín Nic Eoin, '"Severed Heads and Grafted Tongues" – The Language Question in Modern and Contemporary Writing in Irish', forthcoming.
81. Gearóid Mac Lochlainn, *Sruth Teangacha/Stream of Tongues* (Inverin: Cló Iar-Chonnachta, 2002).
82. Mac Lochlainn, 'Cainteoir Dúchais Eile', in *Sruth Teangacha*, pp. 50, 51 (the English translation is Mac Lochlainn's own).
83. Mac Lochlainn, 'Teanga eile', in *Sruth Teangacha*, pp. 56, 57 (translated by Séamus Mac Annaidh and Gearóid Mac Lochlainn).
84. Seán Ó Ríordáin, 'Fill Arís', in *Scathán Véarsaí* (Dublin: Sáirséal agus Dill, 1980), p. 96.
85. Nuala Ní Dhomhnaill, 'The Real McCoy', foreword to Mac Lochlainn, *Sruth Teangacha*.
86. Michael Davitt, 'Eagarfhocal', *Innti* 15 (December 1996), p. 3.
87. See for example Jenkinson, 'Letter to an Editor', and the special edition of *Éire/Ireland* (35, 1 and 2, Spring/Summer 2000) dedicated to the translation debate.
88. See Patrick Crotty, *Modern Irish Poetry* (Belfast: Blackstaff, 1995); Michael Longley, *Twentieth-Century Irish Poems* (London: Faber and Faber, 2002).
89. See Peggy O'Brien, ed. *The Wake Forest Book of Irish Women's Poetry* (Winston-Salem: Wake Forest University Press, 2002); Linda France, ed. *Sixty Women Poets* (Newcastle upon Tyne: Bloodaxe, 1993), for example.
90. This information is drawn from TG4's audited research figures for 2002/3.
91. Michael Hartnett, 'Teanga Mise', *Adharca Broic* (Dublin: The Gallery Press, 1978), p. 14.

92. Eavan Boland, *A Kind of Scar: The Woman Poet in the National Tradition*, LIP pamphlet (Dublin: Attic, 1989).
93. Elizabeth Butler Cullingford, *Ireland's Others* (Cork: Cork University Press in association with Field Day, 2001), pp. 6–7.
94. Ní Dhomhnaill, 'The Role of Irish in Contemporary Ireland', p. 203.
95. Gibbons, *Transformations in Irish Culture*, p. 4.
96. Mac Lochlainn 'Teanga/Tongue', in *Sruth Teangacha*, pp. 52–5 (the English translation is Mac Lochlainn's own).

Afterword: Irish literature in English in the new millennium

FINTAN O'TOOLE

Over a hundred years ago, in May 1897, an Irish fair was held at the Grand Central Palace on Lexington Avenue, New York, to raise funds for an Irish Palace Building, intended to contain a library, a shooting range and a riding school. The most popular exhibit was a giant topographical map of Ireland. In a long, rectangular room, surmounted by a huge green shamrock and surrounded by five columned archways, the map was spread across the floor. It was divided into thirty-two parts, each representing the exact contours of a county. But the special attraction of the map was that each of these 'counties' had been filled with 'the veritable Irish soil of the county . . . duly attested as truly genuine'. For ten cents, the visitor to the fair could walk the length and breadth of the island. The Irish immigrant could feel underfoot the land itself, the literal ould sod.[1]

As the New York *Irish World* reported, 'many a pathetic scene is witnessed daily'. One day, an eighty-year-old Fermanagh woman called Kate Murphy paid her ten cents and stepped across the coastline and made for her native county. She knelt down and kissed the soil,

> then, crossing herself, proceeded to say her prayers, unmindful of the crowd around her. While thus kneeling, a photographer took a flashlight picture of her. The flash was a revelation to the simple hearted creature, who seemed to think it a light from heaven, and was awed into a reverential silence. When she finally stepped off the Irish soil, she sighed sadly and clung to the fence, still gazing at 'old Ireland'. She kept looking backward as she walked away, as if bidding a long farewell.[2]

In 1997, I published an essay called 'No Place Like Home'.[3] It began with this vignette which I had come across in Ronald H. Bayor and Timothy J. Meagher's *The New York Irish*. To me, this image, with its strange collision of virtual reality and deep emotion, of ersatz gimmickry and genuine awe, of intimate memory and the flash of modern media, of a sense of place and a sense of displacement, seemed to say something about the nature of Irish culture. In May 2004, the Lola Gallery in San Francisco showed a piece by two Irish émigré artists that had been inspired by this essay and particularly by this image from the 1897 fair in New York. Claire McGovern and Susan Kennedy created a piece called 'Irish Air'. Their installation consisted of thirty-two jars mounted on thirty-two individual shelves, each bearing the richly coloured crest of a different Irish county in both the English and Irish languages. Underneath, in a deliberately archaic frame, was the caption 'Irish Air From The Thirty-two Duly Attested as truly Genuine'. As Clare McGovern wrote to me: 'Our intention was to create a parody of this "tangible map of Ireland" that you described (notwithstanding the fact that this map of so-called Irish soil in itself could also be construed as a parody). "Irish Air" is a commentary on the commodification of our nationality in a foreign land. The air references an identity that is perhaps undefined and elusive yet can still supposedly be packaged and given monetary value.'

McGovern and Kennedy's joke is witty and well aimed. The shift from solid earth to intangible air captures a widespread feeling that the word 'Irish' has become an airy nothing. The idea that a parody of a parody is the best way to get at the nature of Irish identity at the start of the twenty-first century makes an odd kind of sense. The concern with the commodification of culture is appropriate to a country that had become, around the start of the new millennium, the world's most globalised. The trick of successfully packaging a notoriously elusive product is indeed one of the keys to the privileged position of Irish literature in the international market-place of cultural goods and ideas. The idea of authenticity ('duly attested as truly genuine') is itself a part of the bargain. And yet, even as it poses so nicely the problem of Irish art in the twenty-first century, McGovern and Kennedy's installation also suggests part of the answer. The disruptions and discontinuities of a radically transformed Ireland have a history. Stories and images echo each other across time, even if it is only the call of one parody to another.

Framing that history is, however, a tricky business. Even to construct a narrative of Irish literature in the twentieth century is to imply a continuity that may be deceptive. In the early part of the century, the idea of a distinctively Irish literature was forged in the arena for a path-breaking revolt against one form of globalisation, the British Empire. In the last decade of the century, the Republic embraced another form of globalisation so thoroughly that it came to represent an extreme manifestation of the phenomenon. In 2004, the A.T. Kearney/Foreign Policy magazine *Globalization Index*, which ranks sixty-two countries for fourteen variables relating to economic integration, personal international contact, technological connectivity and global political engagement put the Republic of Ireland, for the third successive year, at number one. Ireland's position at the extreme edge of the process of globalisation has obvious cultural consequences, not least because market globalisation, in its dominant twenty-first-century form, is in part a deliberate attempt to create a homogeneous international culture. The Irish economy, especially as it emerged from the sustained boom of the 1990s, is dominated by transnational corporations. For them, cultural homogenisation is not a force to be feared, as it was for the writers and ideologists of the Irish Revival, but a welcome and even necessary aspect of economic globalisation. The leading Irish capitalist Tony O'Reilly, then CEO of the giant food conglomerate Heinz, put it succinctly in a speech in Belfast when he remarked that 'the communications revolution and the convergence of cultures have set the stage for truly global marketing'. The mass media's obliteration of the difference between one culture and another also obliterates the differences in taste and aspiration that form a barrier to the global marketing of products: 'Television will further homogenise the cultures of the developed world. It will in turn generate the cosmopolitan aspirations best satisfied by global brands. The capacity for transnational production is available . . . The final step in the process will be mass communication. And the technology of satellite and cable TV will make that possible.'[4]

As both an object of, and a participant in, this process, Ireland could hardly be immune from its effects and those effects are, from the point of view of literary history, rather paradoxical. On the one hand, the process of globalisation interacted, both as cause and effect, with the collapse of the classic markers of the Irish identity that was forged in the struggles that created an independent state in the early twentieth century. Daniel Corkery's well-known definition of authentically Irish literature in *Synge and Anglo-Irish Literature*, published in 1931, took it as axiomatic that it resulted from an interplay of 'three great forces which, working for long in the Irish national being, have made it so different from the English national being . . . (1) The Religious Consciousness of the People; (2) Irish Nationalism; and (3) The Land'.[5]

By the end of the twentieth century, those apparently secure landmarks no longer defined the Irish cultural landscape. Catholicism, which is what Corkery meant by religious consciousness, no longer served as a common culture, either in the Republic, where it was mired in scandal and uncertainty, or in the island as a whole, where, of course, it had long been one side of a divide. Irish nationalism, though it still had some emotional purchase, had been so radically redefined by the Belfast Agreement of 1998, with its complex mechanisms of consent, that even its perennial bedrock, the IRA, was crumbling into irrelevance. Corkery's capital-L Land, implying some mystical connection between

Irish writers and the soil, had become a platform for EU-regulated production inhabited by a minority of the population. When Corkery wrote, less than one-third of the population lived in urban areas. By 2002, approximately 60 per cent of the Irish population lived in towns and cities. Irish rural romanticism was dead and gone, and Corkery was turning in his grave.

On the other hand, one of the oddities of this process was that the writers whom Corkery's definition had been designed to exclude – Protestants and exiles – had been repackaged by the new Irish commercial culture as the essence of Irishness. Literary piety had replaced religious piety and patriotic piety, and was in general even less sincere than either of them. In the way Ireland sold itself, literary history had become a highly marketable commodity. Consumers could purchase 'quality heat resistant placemats & coasters' with the faces of Yeats, Joyce, Synge and even, just to remind us why satire is dead, Swift. They could eat Lamb Satay in the James Joyce Room at the Euro Bistro in Cork. At Cloghan Castle in Loughrea they could sleep in 'an ornate brass bed from And So To Bed . . . in the Lady Gregory Suite, while the Yeats Suite holds a solid wood masculine-style bed'. They could invest in an apartment in the Yeats Village in Sligo. At the Druid's Glen Hotel and Country Club in Wicklow they could dance in the James Joyce Ballroom, do unspeakable things in the Oscar Wilde Suite, get buried up to their necks in sand in the Samuel Beckett Room, muse in the William Butler Yeats Room, and hold a meeting of their company (which sells, presumably, succulent roasted babies) in the Jonathan Swift Boardroom. The Park West industrial estate in Dublin has streets called Joyce Way, Yeats Way, Kavanagh Avenue and Heaney Avenue.

Even as it was being embraced as a part of the commercial culture of the new Ireland, the literary past was also being adopted by the state itself as a convenient replacement for Corkery's awkward and outmoded branding. Looking for a cool, European, cosmopolitan and oddly uncontroversial emblem of Irishness for the twenty-first century, the state adopted James Joyce. The exile whose work had been so reviled in Ireland in his lifetime was now worth spending public money on. In 2000, when a previously unknown manuscript draft of the Circe episode of *Ulysses* turned up in New York, the state funded its purchase by the Irish National Library for $1.4 million. Two years later, the state purchased, for 12.6 million Euros (£8 million sterling), a collection of Joyce papers in the possession of the Leon family of Paris. The arrival of the manuscripts in Dublin, carried by Eamon de Valera's grand-daughter Síle, then Minister for Arts, was like the acquisition of a portion of the True Cross by a medieval city: 'After Ms Síle de Valera descended from the aircraft clutching the precious booty, it was put on display to the waiting media in the presence of the Taoiseach. Mr Ahern professed himself very glad to be in attendance at the acquisition of these memorials of the work of a fellow famous Drumcondra resident.'[6]

The official reinvention of the peripatetic Joyce as a 'Drumcondra resident' illustrated the irony of cultural branding in a globalised market-place. The very writers who might best serve as exemplars of the international nature of Irish writing – Joyce, Samuel Beckett, Oscar Wilde, Jonathan Swift – have instead been nationalised and even localised. Literary history, which in fact tells the story of an evasive, elusive, fragmentary and contested culture, has been seized on as a guarantor of authenticity and a symbol of distinctiveness. This authenticity is then sold both internally and externally as a proof that Ireland has not lost its true self in the process of becoming an extreme example of market globalisation.

Authenticity, of course, does not have to be real. In 1953, the Hollywood producer who was planning to make *Brigadoon* went to see the film correspondent of the *Scotsman* newspaper, Forsyth Hardy. He was looking for a suitable location in which to film, a Highland village that would look like it had not changed for centuries. Hardy took him to various places he thought might do the trick. The producer, however, was unimpressed. He returned a disappointed man to Hollywood and commented, 'I went to Scotland but I could find nowhere that looked like Scotland.'[7]

Fifty years on, it is fair to say that there is nowhere in Ireland that looks like Ireland and little in Irish literature that looks like Irish literature. John P. Harrington has, for example, highlighted the irony that notions of what is authentically Irish can be turned against representations of Irish culture in America. He has charted the history of the reception of Abbey Theatre productions by US critics and noted that there is, after a century of touring, 'a quite specific American notion of the Abbey'. Touring Abbey productions can thus be attacked for inauthenticity if they fail to match the familiar brand. Citing the hostile response to the 1988 Abbey production of Tom MacIntyre's *The Great Hunger*, Harrington suggests that 'the very negative critical and popular reception of *The Great Hunger* was based on disappointment that this was not the "real" Abbey at all'. As a commodity in the international cultural market-place, real Irish creations can be measured against their brand-image and found wanting in authenticity.[8]

More broadly, in an American-dominated global culture, Irish literature may be defined, not as a set of contradictory responses to actual Irish conditions, but as a set of telltale fingerprints that can be matched with a pre-existing data base. In the *New York Times* in 1998, the novelist Jack O'Connell remarked on the signifiers of national literature: 'If it's got adultery with a chamber maid in a haze of Gitanes, it's French lit, and if it's got mother love, xenophobic ballads and cirrhosis, it's Irish lit.'[9] In that, admittedly rather limited sense, 'Irish lit' died sometime in the late twentieth century. The gross national product of mother love, xenophobic ballads and cirrhosis declined rather catastrophically. Those supposed signifiers were probably always more imaginary than real, but in any case the Irish writers of the late twentieth and early twenty-first centuries had far more on their minds than the evils of Mammies, drink and the Brits. If those tropes appeared at all, it was in comic walk-on parts whose role was simply to show how distant from its clichéd past Irish literature then was. The markers that may seem from the outside to signify a continuity in Irish literary history actually have no meaning for Irish writers now.

How, then, will Irish writers react to their situation in a world where 'Irish' is as much a brand-name as a place of origin? Not, surely, by reacting against current complexities with a search for past simplicities. Part of the reason for taking a relatively sanguine view of the effects of globalisation on Irish culture is that reactions against globalisation, as we know, can often invoke an exaggerated sense of authenticity that is just as ludicrous and often much more dangerous. Joseph Roth, writing of Eastern European Jews before the Holocaust, noted ruefully and with terrible accuracy that 'the world isn't made up of "nations" and fatherlands that want only to preserve their cultural distinctions, and only if it means not sacrificing a single human life. Fatherlands and nations want much more or much less: they have vested interests that insist on sacrifices.'[10] The Irish experience of the sacrifices demanded by fatherlands and nations is too recent and bitter a memory to make any attempt at a new Irish Renaissance attractive.

A related reason for taking a calmer view is that 'traditional' Irish culture is itself inextricable from globalising currents. From Christianity to the British Empire to the immensely complicating factor of Ireland's disproportionately large diaspora, the Irish past has been so profoundly shaped by global forces that it is not all that easily distinguishable from the dislocated present. As the chapters in this history show, any attempt to contrast an authentic past with an impure present has to confront the awkward question of when, exactly, this authentic past existed.

A more productive answer to this question emerges when Irish literature is understood in an international context and through an interdisciplinary approach. This broader perspective can allow for the emergence of a critical practice that responds creatively to globalisation by exploring the possibilities of comparative literary history.

Just as Irish writers in the early twentieth century used both Irish and Greek mythology to create a hybrid of local and European influences, so too, at its end, there was a marked tendency to shift between Irish and European mythological frameworks. In 2000, Marianne McDonald counted more than thirty adaptations of Greek tragedy by fifteen Irish playwrights over the previous decade and a half.[11] What is perhaps more remarkable, though, is the relative ease with which Irish playwrights in particular could move between classical and European myth on the one hand and Irish folklore on the other. Brian Friel's hugely influential play *Faith Healer* is underpinned by the Irish myth of Deirdre, but his *Wonderful Tennessee* is a version of *The Bacchae*. Thomas Murphy's *The Sanctuary Lamp* draws on *The Oreisteia* and *The Gigli Concert* is his take on the story of Faust, but *Bailegangaire* is rooted in an Irish folk-tale. *Medea* haunts Marina Carr's *By the Bog of Cats*, and her *Ariel* is a version of the story of *Iphigenia*, but the action of *The Mai* is controlled by the local legend of Owl Lake and its figures of Bláth and Coillte. The renewed interest in myth and folklore probably represents a response to the conditions of globalised Ireland in the sense that these systems of imaginative meaning offer a substitute for the heightened language and ritual significance that a shared religious culture previously made available. But this ability to shift quite comfortably from one frame of reference to another is itself evidence of a kind of continuity with the Irish literature of a century ago. When you have a tradition of operating in the interstices between different national and international constructs, the cultural demands of globalisation don't necessarily involve a clean break with the past.

Another example of this same phenomenon is what might be called the Irish Gothic Revival. One of the reasons why the globalisation of Irish writing has been less traumatic a process than it might appear is that there was no fixed, national tradition of realism to disrupt. Ireland did not develop a national literature in the simple sense of a continuous set of realistic reflections on Irish society and Irish history. Even Joyce, the nearest thing to a classic realist in modern Irish writing, saw history as a bad dream from which one might awake into fiction. For all his unsentimental realism, Joyce was a historical escapologist in the Houdini class. Hanging over both *Dubliners* and *A Portrait of the Artist as a Young Man* is the feeling that history stopped with the fall of Joyce's political hero Charles Stewart Parnell and that what remains is an entropic purgatory of paralysis. In *Ulysses*, he comes up with a different strategy, expanding a single day so that it seems to fill the human universe and then preserving it up in his own magnificent prose so that it remains alive but unchanging forever. In *Finnegans Wake*, he replaces linear time with a circular notion of history in which, since everything has happened before and will happen again, no particular event can ever be said to have really happened in the here and now.

This very feeling that history is unreal is, ironically, one of the continuities of Irish literary history. John Banville has written of one of his own most important contemporary exemplars, Aidan Higgins, that 'for him the past is not the past but a kind of continuous, fixed present',[12] and this continues to be true of a great deal of Irish writing. The notion that the past has never ended is related to the idea that history has never really begun. Anthony Cronin expresses this idea directly in his poem 'Letter to an Englishman':

> We are exhorted much, but oftenest we
> Are told, don't think about your history.
> The truth is that we haven't had one yet
> And what you haven't had you can't forget.[13]

One of the open questions for twenty-first-century Irish literature is whether and when Irish writers will begin to feel that history has started. Will the achievement of a final settlement in Northern Ireland create a sense that the past is no longer contained in a continuous present? Will that in turn create the possibility both of a new realism and of a serious approach to the historical novel? Or will it, in a sense, be too late? Perhaps realism will never be appropriate to the dislocated, globalised culture of twenty-first-century Ireland. Perhaps the discontinuities will become so extreme that efforts at a fictive reimagining of the past will seem pointless because that past will seem to belong to someone else.

The immediate evidence in this regard is, again, that of a strange continuity of strategies for avoiding history. One of the great avoidance strategies adopted by nineteenth-century Irish writers was the sublimation of real horrors into imaginary ones. It is hardly accidental that a significant body of Irish fiction in the nineteenth century, when the English were using the novel to give an imaginative structure to industrial society and the Americans to elaborate potent national myths, is Gothic horror. What is *Dracula*, after all, if not Joyce's nightmare of history become literal, the past refusing to lie down but returning to haunt the uneasy dreams of nice Protestant gentlewomen? This strategy has its resonances in the work of later writers, from W. B. Yeats to Elizabeth Bowen.

What's striking, though, is that Irish Gothic again became almost the mainstream of the late twentieth and early twenty-first centuries. To contemporary Irish writers like Patrick McCabe, Dermot Bolger, Marina Carr and Conor

McPherson, ghosts, vampires, haunting and madness are the secular magic that serves the same purpose that Protestant magic served in the nineteenth century: to give non-believers access to the heightened sensibility that Catholicism offers its believers. The deranged mind of the murderer became the setting for novels like John Banville's *The Book of Evidence*, Patrick McCabe's *The Butcher Boy* and Eoin McNamee's *Resurrection Man*. The ghost story (as in McPherson's *The Weir* and *Shining City* or Carr's *Portia Coughlan*) and even the vampire story (as in *Saint Nicholas*) returned to the Irish stage. Dante's *Inferno* continued to exercise a powerful grip on Irish poetry, as evidenced most directly by Ciaran Carson's new version of the original poem in 2002. Introducing it, Carson wrote of how, not just Virgil's ghost, but Dante's too seemed to haunt his own corner of Ireland:

> . . . a British Army helicopter eye-in-the-sky is stationed overhead. As I write, I can hear its ratchety interference in the distance; and, not for the first time, I imagine being airborne in the helicopter, like Dante riding on the flying monster Geryon, looking down into the darkness of that place in Hell called Malebolge. 'Rings of ditches, moats, trenches, fosses / military barriers on every side': I see a map of North Belfast, its no go zones and tattered flags . . . And we see again the vendetta-stricken courtyards and surveillance towers of Dante's birthplace, where everyone is watching everyone, and there is little room for manoeuvre.[14]

This ghostliness is linked to both the inheritance of Irish writers from the literature of the past and to the oddly fractured condition of their culture. Realism has been discouraged both by the mystical inclinations of Catholicism and nationalism and by the hard facts of a society that saw itself essentially as a nursery for emigrants. In 1891, George Russell wrote that 'Every Irishman forms some vague ideal of his country, born from his reading of history, or from contemporary politics, or from imaginative intuition; and this Ireland in the mind it is, not the actual Ireland, which kindles his enthusiasm.'[15] Emigration itself has been part of this tyranny of fantasy over reality. Writing of rural Ireland in 1941, long before the influx of global capital, and describing life decades earlier, Jim Phelan noted that 'The Yank or returned American automatically owned the village. Young men who had not been in the States were looked upon as sissified fledgelings. It even reached the stage at which people *pretended* to have been in the States, for a quiet life. Sincere imitation could go no further.'[16] How could a writer be a realist in a society where a quiet life involves pretending to have been an emigrant and sincere imitation is an authentic response to reality?

Stendhal, in *Scarlet and Black*, published in 1830, could describe the novel as 'a mirror walking along a high road'. Four years later, his nearest Irish equivalent, Maria Edgeworth, wrote to her brother that 'It is impossible to draw Ireland as she now is in a book of fiction – realities are too strong, party passions too violent, to bear to see, or care to look at their faces in the looking-glass. The people would only break the glass, and curse the fool who held the mirror up to nature – distorted nature, in a fever.'[17] Half a century later, Oscar Wilde, in his dialogue *The Decay of Lying*, has one of the speakers complain that the notion of art as a mirror 'would reduce genius to the position of a cracked looking-glass'.[18] In *Ulysses* Joyce takes up the image again: as Stephen Dedalus points bitterly to Buck Mulligan's broken shaving-mirror: 'It is a symbol of Irish art. The cracked looking-glass of a servant.'[19]

The feverish, fragmented, distorted image that is reflected in a cracked mirror remains the best metaphor for Irish literature. One of the reasons, indeed, why attempts to explain in direct sociological terms the hugely disproportionate place of Ireland in global literary culture are so unconvincing is that the relationship of the books to the society that produces them is anything but direct. If there is some kind of collective imaginative energy that can account for the emergence of so many important writers from such a small and geographically marginal European culture, it is not to be found either in some ludicrous abstraction like the Celtic spirit, or in a vulgar Marxist calibration of economic base to intellectual superstructure. It is the energy generated by vacuums. What we encounter is the imagination occupying intolerable voids, distracting from unfathomable realities, filling in unbearable silences.

One of the constant refrains of recent Irish literature, indeed, is the acknowledgement of familial and social silences, and one of the likely themes for the future is the continuing search for alternative pasts. This search for memory itself, in a globalised context, becomes international. In Hugo Hamilton's memoir of his Dublin childhood his family's sense of its past is full of complications and occlusions, not simply because he has an Irish father and a German mother, but because those terms themselves are unstable:

> Some things are good not to know in Ireland. I had no idea that I had an Irish grandfather who couldn't even speak Irish. His name was John Hamilton and he belonged to the navy, the British navy, the Royal Navy . . . There's a picture in the front room of Franz Kaiser and Berta Kaiser with her head leaning on his shoulder, both of them laughing with a big glass of wine on the table in front of them. There's no picture of John Hamilton or his wife Mary Frances, alone or together, hanging anywhere in our house. Our German grandparents are dead, but our Irish grandparents are dead and forgotten . . . I didn't know that

> my Irish grandfather, John Hamilton, and my German grandfather, Franz Kaiser, must have stood facing each other in the Great War. Or that I was wearing the medals of two different empires side by side.[20]

Sometimes, in Irish memoirs of the late twentieth and early twenty-first centuries, even the basics of personal history are unknowable. The actor Peter O'Toole, in his vivid account of his early life, *Loitering with Intent*, is unable to say where he was born:

> For reasons which have never satisfactorily been explained, minor adjustments were made to the official record of [his parents'] lives and those of their kin. The family version of my date and place of birth is June, 1932 in Ireland; the same event is recorded as August of the same year at an accident hospital in England; my baptism was in November 1932, also in England. There are slight but charming variations of nomenclature on all three occasions.[21]

Even his father's name turns out to be partly fictional: 'In the twenties and thirties he had for a while flourished as Captain Pat O'Toole. His only known captaincy was of a minor professional soccer side.'

Near the start of her memoir *Nell*, the journalist Nell McCafferty, writes that

> One night a few years ago, my mother went mad, and her own secret came out of her . . . Suddenly she asked where Brian was. Luckily, I knew who Brian was, though my mother had never uttered his name in the presence of her children . . . 'Where's Brian?' she now asked. Brian was one of her older brothers. She had written him out of history, and her brothers and sisters and her relatives and our neighbours had observed the edict. Brian did not exist. He had murdered a woman in America who had worked as a prostitute, been sent to jail there, and wiped out of memory . . . I told her that he had died in London, that I had visited his grave, that there was a headstone with his name on it and that I had placed flowers there. She fell back, relieved. He had received a decent burial, at least. I was lying. I was delighted to bring her peace.[22]

These missing or mysterious origins have been woven into fictional work, too. In Roddy Doyle's *A Star Called Henry*, the narrator remarks that 'The family trees of the poor don't grow to any height. I know nothing real about my father; I don't even know if his name was real . . . He made his life up as he went along.'[23] Marina Carr's play *The Mai* puts an extended family of women on stage, ranging from Millie, aged sixteen, to Grandma Fraochlan, aged 100. Here, too, the notion of family origin is both mysterious and transactional.

Grandma Fraochlan, explains Millie, 'was known as the Spanish beauty though she was born and bred on Inis Fraochlan, north of Bofin. She was the result of a brief tryst between an ageing island spinster and a Spanish or Moroccan sailor – no one is quite sure – who was never heard of or seen since the night of her conception. There were many stories about him as there are about those who appear briefly in our lives and change them forever.'[24]

These broken family connections return in contemporary Irish writing as ghosts. Sebastian Barry has written of the lost ancestors that haunt his own extraordinary sequence of plays, set appropriately in Ireland, England and America, that 'they exist here in an afterlife, in another life, in a gallery of pictures painted freely, darkly. They are ghost plays, if ghosts are the images lingering of the vanished and the dead . . .'[25] This, perhaps, is why Irish Gothic has such a strong contemporary purchase. Yet since it is rooted in lived experience, this ghostliness can also be expressed as a metaphor for the condition of the individual in a globalised world, drawn between different frameworks and perpetually hovering between them.

The ghostly insubstantiality of Irishness can thus give Irish writers access to a set of experiences that are untypical of the rich, white world of which Ireland is now a part. Pato Dooley in Martin McDonagh's *The Beauty Queen of Leenane* (itself a product of a hybrid London-Irish culture) sums it up when he confesses to Maureen that although he is unhappy in London, he does not dream of returning forever to Leenane: 'when it's there I am, it's here I wish I was, of course. Who wouldn't? But when it's here I am . . . it isn't *there* I want to be, of course not. But I know it isn't here I want to be either.'[26] These people are neither here nor there. They don't know whether they're coming or going. The old exile's nostalgia has been replaced by a less tangible but more unsettling sense of hovering.

Imaginatively at least, this feeling can give Irish writers some access to the plight of others, creating a different kind of global connection. In Paul Muldoon's beautiful opera libretto *Bandanna*, for example, the chorus of Mexican illegal immigrants has a verse that locates Pato Dooley's feeling of being neither one thing nor the other in a very precise context:

> We strike across the river,
> Plastic bags between our teeth.
> We know what it's like to hover
> Between life and death.
> We move like shades between the two
> in the desperate hope of breaking through.[27]

As expressions of the feelings of Mexican migrants trying to sneak into the United States these lines have a realistic power. Yet they are also recognisably an expression of what has been felt both by Irish emigrants through the centuries and by Irish artists coming to terms with their culture now. These hoverings have a shape; these shades have substance.

It is, for example, already possible for Irish writers to invent their own literary genealogies with a relative freedom. Carson's ability to make Dante a Belfast man and himself a kind of Italian is one example. Colm Tóibín's novel *The Master* is a fictional biography of Henry James which both claims the American writer as an artistic ancestor by inventing for him a Jamesian encounter with Ireland and, at the same time, allows Tóibín to locate himself as a gay man and a writer in a new historical context. There is a sly moment when James's impressions of the Irish countryside remind the reader why he could not have existed as a novelist of manners in Ireland: 'Everything seemed ruined or partly ruined. Smoke appeared from half-rotten chimneys, and no one, emerging from these cabins, could refrain from shouting after a carriage as it passed or moving malevolently towards one if it slowed down. There was no moment when he felt free of their hostile stares and dark accusing eyes.' Yet, in a delicious turn, James himself is politely taunted at a dinner with the gentry in the Royal Hospital in Kilmainham with the implication that he himself might have emerged from those same malevolent cabins:

> 'Mr James, are you going to visit any of your Irish kinsmen while you are here?'
>
> 'No, Mr Webster I have no plans of any sort.' He spoke coldly and firmly. . . . 'What was the name of that place, Lady Wolseley? Bailieborough, that's right. Bailieborough in County Cavan. It is where you will find the seat of the James family.'[28]

This playfulness, where James – and by analogy Tóibín – shifts between contexts, horrified by an alien Ireland yet unable to escape being identified is a good metaphor for the odd mixture of entanglement and freedom that Irishness confers on contemporary writers.

There are, though, other ways of filling the silences and other kinds of imaginative genealogies to make for the uncertainty of one's origins. The ghosts that haunt twenty-first-century Ireland are not just missing family members, but also missing histories. One of the most powerful performances on the Irish stage in the early years of the new millennium was Gerard Mannix Flynn's *James X*, based around an examination of the state's official files on his own years as its guest and victim in schools, courts, industrial schools, psychiatric hospitals and prisons. Flynn used these documents as a kind of 'found' art, interrogating their tone and language to create, in a culture awash with works about the nation, a play about the state. This kind of direct but artful work, shifting the familiar language, so that it can articulate some of the things that it could not bear to say before, is one of the strategies that might prevent Irish writing from drifting into nebulousness. More broadly, it is possible to imagine both comparative cultural histories that might combine Tóibín's playful invention of new genealogies with Flynn's forensic scrutiny of the construction of an official version of the recent past. Already, feminist, gay, working-class and diaspora readings and reconstructions have done much to suggest the possibilities of a set of alternative pasts that can do in criticism what creative writers have been doing in prose, poetry and drama. Even if only as a vacuum, the past will remain a force in Irish writing.

Notes

1. *Irish World* (22 May 1897), quoted in Ronald H. Bayor and Timothy J. Meagher eds. *The New York Irish* (Baltimore: Johns Hopkins University Press, 1996), p. 285.
2. Ibid.
3. Fintan O'Toole, *The Ex-Isle of Erin: Images of a Global Ireland* (Dublin: New Island Books, 1997), pp. 129–30.
4. See ibid., p. 55.
5. Daniel Corkery, *Synge and Anglo-Irish Literature* (Cork: Cork University Press, 1931), p. 19.
6. *Irish Times*, 30 May 2002.
7. Quoted in David McCrone, *Scotland – the Brand* (Edinburgh: Edinburgh University Press, 1995), p. 49.
8. John P. Harrington's essay, 'The Abbey in America: The Real Thing', is, at the time of writing, unpublished.
9. Peter Applebome, 'Beating a Dead Mule, Partly in Fun', *New York Times* (13 June 1998).
10. Joseph Roth, *The Wandering Jews* (London: Granta, 2001), p. 19.
11. 'Classics as Celtic Firebrand', in Eamon Jordan, ed. *Theatre Stuff: Critical Essays on Contemporary Irish Theatre* (Dublin: Carysfort Press, 2000), p. 16.
12. John Banville, 'The Missing Link', *New York Review of Books* (2 December 2004).
13. Anthony Cronin, *Letter to an Englishman* (Dublin: Raven Arts Press, 1985), p. 28.
14. Ciaran Carson, *The Inferno* (London: Granta Books, 2002), pp. xi–xii.
15. See David Pierce, ed. *Irish Writing in the Twentieth Century: A Reader* (Cork: Cork University Press, 2000), p. 45.
16. Ibid., p. 496.
17. Maria Edgeworth to Michael Pakenham Edgeworth, 19 February 1834; reproduced in Frances Edgeworth, *A Memoir of Maria Edgeworth*, 3 vols. (privately printed, 1867), III, pp. 87–8.

18. Oscar Wilde, 'The Decay of Lying' (1891), reproduced in Seamus Deane, gen. ed. *The Field Day Anthology of Irish Writing*, 3 vols. (Derry: Field Day, 1991), II, p. 384.
19. James Joyce, *Ulysses* (1922; London: Penguin, 1992), p. 6.
20. Hugo Hamilton, *The Speckled People* (London: Fourth Estate, 2003), p. 12.
21. Peter O'Toole, *Loitering with Intent* (London: Macmillan, 1992), p. 10.
22. Nell McCafferty, *Nell* (Dublin: Penguin Ireland, 2004), pp. 3–5.
23. Roddy Doyle, *A Star Called Henry* (New York and London: Viking, 1999), p. 9.
24. Marina Carr, *The Mai*, in *Plays One* (London: Faber and Faber, 1999), pp. 115–16.
25. Sebastian Barry, *Plays: 1* (London: Methuen, 1997), p. xv.
26. Martin McDonagh, *The Beauty Queen of Leenane and Other Plays* (New York: Vintage Books, 1998), p. 31.
27. Paul Muldoon, *Bandanna* (London: Faber and Faber, 1999), p. 2.
28. Colm Tóibín, *The Master* (London: Picador, 2004), pp. 33, 47.

Guide to major subject areas

Chapter 1 Literature and politics

The artist and the social world 9
Catastrophism and art: the sense of an ending 10
The nomad as sign of the modern 12
Meltdown: literary form and social change 12
Virtual worlds 13
Underground codes: the Gaelic samizdat 15
Overground codes: Anglo-Irish anxieties 19
Some write to the future 21
Writing as exile: exile as writing 23
Bringing it all back home 25
A masked modernity? 26
The politics of dialect 29
Irish Modernism 31
Village Modernism and the compulsory Bohemia 33
The belated bohemians? 40
In a Free State? 43

Chapter 2 The Irish Renaissance, 1890–1940: poetry in English

Introduction 50
Yeats 53
Ascendancy poets 64
Women poets of the Revival 68
AE, Synge, O'Sullivan, Stephens 72
Translators 79
Colum, Campbell, Joyce, Gogarty 83
1916 and the Great War 91
In a Free State: Higgins, Lyle Donaghy, Donnelly, Devenport O'Neill, Salkeld, Coffey, Beckett, Devlin 98

Clarke and MacNeice 101
Select bibliography 111

Chapter 3 The Irish Renaissance, 1890–1940: prose in English
Non-Revival fiction 1890–1920 114
Popular fiction 114
Religion and the novel 116
The realism of poverty 120
New Woman fiction 122
Fin de siècle: Oscar Wilde 124
Category fiction 127
Fiction of the Great War 130
Revival fiction 1890–1924 134
Counter-Revival fiction 1903–1922 141
George Moore 141
James Joyce 145
Attempted realisms 153
The fiction of three Irelands 1922–1940 156
Writing of the Free State 156
The 'Ladies' Road' 160
Fiction from Northern Ireland 165
New directions 168
Select bibliography 180

Chapter 4 The Irish Renaissance, 1890–1940: drama in English
Myths of origin 181
Irish national theatre before the Irish National Theatre Society 182
Paris, Bayreuth and Dublin 185
The difficult case of Oscar Wilde 187
Irish theatre as Lady Gregory's theatre 189
J. M. Synge 192
Yeats's disappointment in Yeats's theatre 196
Holding the door against George Bernard Shaw 198
Realists and Catholics enter by the back 200
Out of Belfast 203
Sean O'Casey's masterpieces 205
Dublin Expressionism at the Gate 209

The late, great Yeats and Anglo-Irish drama 212
A last spell of excellence 216
Conclusion 218
Select bibliography 224

Chapter 5 The Irish Renaissance, 1880–1940: literature in Irish
Introduction 226
Building on the past: poetry 227
Breaking new ground: prose 233
The 'speech of the people' 234
The role of the native speaker 236
Revival institutions and publications 239
Short fiction 240
The novel 248
Gaeltacht autobiography 258
Drama 259
Literary criticism 263
Conclusion 266
Select bibliography 268

Chapter 6 Contemporary prose and drama in Irish 1940–2000
Introduction 270
Prose fiction and autobiography 271
New voices, new directions: 1940s and 1950s 271
Reacting to social and cultural change: 1960s and 1970s 282
A search for form: 1980s and 1990s 292
Drama and theatre: in search of an audience 299
Literary criticism and literary biography 306
Conclusion 310
Select bibliography 316

Chapter 7 Contemporary poetry in Irish: 1940–2000
Máirtín Ó Direáin and Liam S. Gógan 319
Brendan Behan 324
Máire Mhac an tSaoi 325
Seán Ó Ríordáin 328
Poetry in the 1960s 332
The *Innti* poets 336

Michael Hartnett / Mícheál Ó hAirtnéide 338
Nuala Ní Dhomhnaill 339
Biddy Jenkinson 342
Michael Davitt 344
Cathal Ó Searcaigh 345
Poetry from the Gaeltacht 346
Liam Ó Muirthile 347
Poetry since 1980 348
The question of translation 350
Select bibliography 354

Chapter 8 Contemporary poetry in English: 1940–2000

Introduction 357
Just after Yeats 358
Just after Yeats and Joyce: the 1940s and 1950s in the North 359
Just after Yeats and Joyce: emigrant poetry 363
Just after Yeats and Joyce in Éire 365
The 1960s and after: Murphy, Kinsella, Montague and the Dolmen Press 372
Seamus Heaney's career 382
The North: *The Honest Ulsterman*, Simmons, Mahon, and Longley 387
Growing up in the Troubles: Muldoon, Carson, McGuckian, Paulin 391
New models for the Irish woman writer 400
Bilingualism: Irish and cosmopolitan 407
Select bibliography 419

Chapter 9 Contemporary prose in English: 1940–2000

Introduction 421
The novel 423
Samuel Beckett and Francis Stuart 423
A new generation: McGahern, O'Brien and Higgins 425
The Big House novel 430
'The nightmare of history': O'Brien and Banville 433
The novel in Northern Ireland 436
Writing the Irish Republic 441
Women novelists 447

Short fiction 452
Continuities 452
Extending the tradition 455
The modern turn 457
Short fiction in Northern Ireland 459
Women's short fiction 463
Memoir, travel and miscellaneous 465
Travel writing 465
Memoir and autobiography 467
Cultural commentary 471
Select bibliography 475

Chapter 10 Contemporary drama in English: 1940–2000
The 1940s: conservation and continuity 479
The 1950s: innovation and breakthrough 485
The 1960s: change and development 493
The 1970s: tragic and comic disillusion 500
The 1980s: transcendence and achievement 508
The 1990s: the Celtic Tiger and the marketing of the 'Irish' play 519
Select bibliography 529

Chapter 11 Cinema and Irish literature
Early cinema and Irish literature 532
History on film, in the post-independence period 536
The Abbey Theatre and film 542
Breakthroughs in Irish cinema 546
The emergence of a new Irish cinema 553
Conclusion 558
Select bibliography 561

Chapter 12 Literary historiography, 1890–2000
Making readers 562
Revival projects: 'men have begun to co-ordinate their scattered impressions' 567
Revival criticism: 'no alien element' 575
Postwar histories: 'things of order' 581
After the 1960s: 'every mark of cultural identity' 584
Conclusions 589
Select bibliography 597

Index

Authorship, where known, has been identified in the index below. In many cases in Irish literature, particularly in the earlier periods, authorship was anonymous.

Abbey Theatre, Dublin, 182, 186, 196–203, 205–9, 211, 212, 214, 216–19, 262–3, 300–2, 480–5, 497–500, 501, 505, 506, 516, 517, 519, 521, 525, 632
  actors, 205, 206, 208, 482, 542–3
  and cinema, 534, 542–6
  and An Comhar Drámaíochta, 300–1
  fire at, 485–6
  and Irish language, 262–3, 300–2, 482–3
  pantomime, 483
  reopening, 497–8
  at the Queen's Theatre, 485, 494
  see Peacock Theatre
According to the Small Hours (Aidan Carl Mathews), 381
Across the Barricades (Joan Lingard), 567
Acts and Monuments (Eiléan Ní Chuilleanáin), 400
'Adam's Curse' (William Butler Yeats), 58
Adharca Broic (Michael Hartnett), 339
'Adhlacadh Iníon an Fhile' (Máire Mhac an tSaoi), 327
Adios (Tarlach Ó hUid), 273
'Ad Limina' (Joseph Campbell), 87
Adrigoole (Peadar O'Donnell), 157
'AE' *see* Russell, George William
'After Aughrim' (Emily Lawless), 67
After Babel: Aspects of Language and Translation (George Steiner), 510
'Afterlives' (Derek Mahon), 389
After Yeats and Joyce (Neil Corcoran), 566
Ag Stracadh leis an Saol (León Ó Broin), 247
Aids to the Immortality of Certain Persons in Dublin: Charitably Administered (Susan Mitchell), 71
'Aifreann na Marbh' (Eoghan Ó Tuairisc), 45, 333, 602
Aimsir Óg, An (journal), 271, 309
Aird ó Thuaidh, Na h-(Pádraig Ua Maoileoin), 282
'Aisling' (Paul Muldoon), 394
Aisling Mhic Artáin (Eoghan Ó Tuairisc), 303
Aistear (Diarmaid Ó Súilleabháin), 288
Aisteoirí an Damer, 302
Aisteoirí, Na h-(later An Comhar Drámaíochta), 262
Aistí Dána (Art Ó Maolfabhail), 333
'Aithrighe' (Brendan Behan), 325
'Alabama. Samhradh '98' (Biddy Jenkinson), 343
Alcock, Deborah, 117
  Crushed Yet Conquering, 117
Alexander, Eleanor, *The Rambling Rector*, 116
Algoland (Seán Mac Maoláin), 257
All Souls' Night (Joseph Tomelty), 482
All That Fall (Samuel Beckett), 44–5
Allagar na h-Inise (Tomás Ó Criomhthain), 258, 613
Amateur Army, The (Patrick MacGill), 131
Amharclann de hÍde, 304
'Among School Children' (William Butler Yeats), 61
Amongst Women (John McGahern), 430
Ancient Lights (Austin Clarke), 370–1
Anglo-Catholicism, 116
Anglo-Irish Literature (Hugh Law), 578
Anglo-Irish treaty 1921, 238
Anna Livia Plurabelle (James Joyce), 88
Annals of Chile, The (Paul Muldoon), 395
Another September (Thomas Kinsella), 374
Antarctica (Claire Keegan), 465

Anteroom, The (Kate O'Brien), 163
anthologies, 228, 229, 358, 565, 573–5, 587–90
dual-language, 611, 621
Field Day Anthology, 587–90
and the Revival, 573–5
of short stories, 452, 462, 463
Antoine, André, 185
Apollo's Blended Dream: A Study of the Poetry of Louis MacNeice (William T McKinnon), 585
'Ar an gCaorán Mór' (Michael Davitt), 344
Ar Bhruach na Laoi (Liam Ó Muirthile), 295
Árd-Chúirt Shochaide na Suadh (later Árd-Chúirt na hÉigse), 228
Ardmore Studios, 544–6
Aristocrats (Brian Friel), 506
Árus na nGábhadh agus Sgéalta Eile (León Ó Broin), 247
Ascendancy and Tradition (later revised as *From Burke to Beckett* by W. J. McCormack), 586
As the Beast Sleeps (Gary Mitchell), 526
Astronár (Piaras Béaslaí), 256
'Athair' ('Father' by Micheál Ó Conghaile), 619
Athnuachan (Máirtín Ó Cadhain), 277–8
Atlantic Rhymes and Rhythms (Emily Lawless) *see With the Wild Geese*
At Night all Cats are Grey and Other Stories (Patrick Boyle), 461
At Swim Two-Birds (Flann O'Brien), 40, 171–3
At the Hawk's Well (William Butler Yeats), 212–13
autobiography, 258–9, 271–5, 279, 280–1, 284, 467–71
collaborations, 259, 280–1
Gaeltacht, 258–9, 271–3, 274, 280–1, 284, 613
and incarceration, 468
Northern, 470
novelistic, 467
pseudo-autobiography, 272
see also memoirs, Blasket Islands literature
Autobiography of a Child (Hannah Lynch), 148–9
Autumn Journal (Louis MacNeice), 104–5, 360–1
Autumn Sequel (Louis MacNeice), 361
Avenue Theatre, London, 186
Awake! and Other Poems (W. R. Rodgers), 361

Backward Look: A Survey of Irish Literature, The (Frank O'Connor), 584
Baile an Droichid (radio soap by Joe Steve Ó Neachtain), 306
Bailegangaire (Tom Murphy), 515–16, 634
Baile seo Againne, An (Pádraig Ó Siochfhradha), 300
Bairéad, Tomás, 245
Cruithneacht agus Ceannabhán, 245
Cumhacht na Cinneamhna, 245
Geall a Briseadh, An, 245
Balcony of Europe (Aidan Higgins), 444
'Ballad of Reading Gaol, The' (Oscar Wilde), 64–5
Ballads and Lyrics (Katharine Tynan), 68
Banshee and Other Poems, The (John Todhunter), 65
Banville, John, 435–6, 457, 636
Birchwood, 435
Book of Evidence, The, 636
Nightspawn, 435
Untouchable, The, 436
Barbed Wire (Máirtín Ó Cadhain), 278
Bárd 'gus an Fó, An (Paul McSwiney), 260
Bards of the Gael and Gall (George Sigerson), 82
Bardwell, Leland, 401, 450, 465
Barnes, Ben, 492
Barrabas (theatre company), 525
Barracks, The (John McGahern), 427
Barrington, Margaret, *My Cousin Justin*, 164–5
Barry, Sebastian, 434, 441–2, 521–2, 639
Prayers of Sherkin, 521
Steward of Christendom, The, 521–2
Bás i dTír na nÓg, An (Seán Ó Tuama), 334–5
'Bás na Bó' (Liam O'Flaherty), 245
Bás san Oirthear (Lorcán Ó Treasaigh), 293
Bateman, Colin, *Divorcing Jack*, 542
Battle of Aughrim, The (Richard Murphy), 66, 373
'Beairtle' (Seán Ó Curraoin), 347
Bealach Buidhe, An (Fr Peter O'Leary), 260
Bealach chun a' Bhearnais, An (Tarlach Ó hUid), 273
Béal Bocht, An (*The Poor Mouth* by Myles na gCopaleen/Flann O'Brien), 271–3, 434, 612–13
Béal na h Uaighe agus Sgéalta Eile (León Ó Broin), 274
Bean Aonair agus Scéalta Eile (Pádraic Breathnach), 292
Bean Ruadh de Dhálach (Séamus Ó Grianna), 282–3

Béaslaí, Piaras, 229, 230, 231, 248, 256, 262
Astronár, 256
Danar, An, 262
Éigse na Nua-Ghaedhilge, 231
Beauty Queen of Leenane, The (Martin McDonagh), 522–3, 639
Becker Wives and Other Stories, The (Mary Lavin), 455
Beckett, Mary, 450
Beckett, Samuel, 99, 100, 169–71, 365, 423–25, 478, 489–91, 493
All That Fall, 44–5
Echoes Bones and Other Precipitates, 100
Molloy, 423
Murphy, 101, 169–71
Unnamable, The, 423
Waiting for Godot, 12, 210, 478, 486, 489–91
Bedmates (George Shiels), 481
Behan, Brendan, 318, 324–5, 466, 468, 472, 486–9, 491–2, 498
'Aithrighe', 325
'Do Bhev', 324
'Do Sheán Ó Súilleabháin', 325
Giall, An (later *The Hostage*), 301, 491–2
'Jackeen ag Caoineadh na mBlascaod', 325
Landlady, The, 486
Quare Fellow, The, 486–9
Behan, Dominic, 468
'Beirt Fhear' *see* Séamus Ó Dubhghaill
Belfast Confetti (Ciaran Carson), 397
'Belfast Group', 382, 388
Bell, Sam Hanna, 437, 466
December Bride, 437, 551–2
Bell, The (journal), 359, 422, 581
Bending of the Bough, The (George Moore and Edward Martyn), 185
Bennett, Ronan, 440
Bergin, Osborn, *Maidin i mBéarra agus Dánta Eile*, 231
Berkeley, Bishop George, 20
Berkeley, Sara, 464–5
Berlin Wall Café, The (Paul Durcan), 381
Best of Myles, The (edited by Kevin O'Nolan), 472
Beyond the Pale and Other Stories (William Trevor), 457
'Bhean Mhídhílis, An' ('The Unfaithful Wife' by Lorca, translation by Máire Mhac an tSaoi), 326
Bheirt Dearbhráthar agus Scéalta Eile, An (Máiréad Ní Ghráda), 246
Bhóinn agus an Bhóchna, An (Liam P. Ó Riain), 253
Bickley, Francis, *John Millington Synge and the Irish Dramatic Movement*, 580
Big Birthday, The (John Keyes Byrne, penname 'Hugh Leonard'), 493, 545
Big House novels, 430–3
Big Maggie (John B. Keane), 497
bilingualism, 226, 264, 290, 305, 328, 339, 349, 407–12, 489, 604, 611
in anthologies, 611, 621
in drama, 261, 300, 305
in journals, 226
in the national theatre, 300
in poetry, 79, 339, 346, 349, 350, 407–9, 603
in scripts, 305
Binchy, Maeve, 450, 555
Circle of Friends, 556
Birchwood (John Banville), 435
Bird Alone (Sean O'Faolain), 158–9
Birds of Innocent Wood, The (Deirdre Madden), 440
Bishop's Bonfire, The (Sean O'Casey), 480
Black, Cathal, 547, 554, 556
'Black Lace Fan My Mother Gave Me, The' (Eavan Boland), 403
Black List, Section H (Francis Stuart), 441–2
Black Soul, The (Liam O'Flaherty), 156
Blackwater Lightship, The (Colm Tóibín), 444
Blackwood, Caroline, 450
Blasket Islands, 258–9, 282
literature, 258–9, 274, 281, 283–4, 613–15
Blather (magazine), 257
Bliainiris (journal), 271, 309
Blind Fireworks (Louis MacNeice), 104
Blood and Water (Éilís Ní Dhuibhne), 463
Bloodaxe Book of 20th Century Poetry (Edna Longley), 585
'Bloody Sunday', 501
Blue Raincoat (theatre company), 525
Blundell, Mary *see* Francis, M. E.
Blunt, Wilfrid Scawen, 80
Blythe, Ernest (Earnán de Blaghd), 218, 262, 279, 480, 482–3, 485, 486, 499, 506, 542
Blyth, Oliver *see* Brinsley MacNamara
Bodkin, M. McDonnell, 130
Dora Myrl, The Lady Detective, 130
Paul Beck, The Rule-of-Thumb Detective, 130
Bohemia, 33–40
Boland, Eavan, 402–5, 622
'Black Lace Fan My Mother Gave Me, The', 403
'I am Ireland', 403–4
'Journey, The', 403

Kind of Scar, A: The Woman Poet in a National Tradition, 152–3
New Territory, 400
Nightfeed, 327
Object Lessons: The Life of the Woman and the Poet in Our Time, 153–4
War Horse, The, 402
'Woman in Kitchen', 154
Boland, Rosita, 466
Bolger, Dermot, 411, 443–4, 473, 611–12, 635
Bright Wave, The: An Tonn Gheal (editor), 611
Book of Evidence, The (John Banville), 636
Bord na Gaeilge, 302, 304
Bord na Leabhar Gaeilge, 299
Borges, Jorge Luis, 28
Boucicault, Dion, film versions of plays, 533–4
Bourke, Angela, 234, 308, 465
Bowen, Elizabeth, 161–2, 164, 430, 448, 454–5, 458, 466, 468, 469
Demon Lover and Other Stories, The, 454
Heat of the Day, The, 430, 448
Last September, The, 161, 540
Boyd, Ernest, 578–9
Ireland's Literary Renaissance, 579
Boyd, John, 471, 500–2
Flats, The, 500–1
Boyd's Shop (St John Irvine), 545
Boylan, Clare, 449, 464
Boyle, Patrick, 460–1
At Night all Cats are Grey and Other Stories, 461
Boyle, William, 203
Branar gan Cur, An (Breandán Ó Doibhlin), 286
Braon Broghach, An (Máirtín Ó Cadhain), 275
Breathnach, Colm, 349–50, 604
Croí agus Carraig, 349
Fear Marbh, An, 349
Scáthach, 349
Breathnach, Pádraic, *Bean Aonair agus Scéalta Eile*, 292
'Breith Anabaí Thar Lear' (Nuala Ní Dhomhnaill), 341
Breithiúnas (Máiréad Ní Ghráda), 301
Brennan, Deirdre, 342, 349
Brennan, Maeve, 455, 464
Bríde Bhán (Pádraig Ua Maoileoin), 283
Bright Wave: An Tonn Gheal, The (Dermot Bolger, editor), 611
Bring Everything (Peter Sirr), 410
British Board of Film Censors (BBFC), 537–9
British film industry and Ireland, 534, 542–3
Broderick, John, 428
Broken Soil (revised as *The Fiddler's House* by Padraic Colum), 202
'Broken World, A' (Sean O'Faolain), 158
Brooke, Stopford A, and Rolleston, Thomas William (editors), *A Treasury of Irish Poetry*, 69, 81, 575
Brosna (Seán Ó Ríordáin), 331
Broth of a Boy (screen title of *The Big Birthday* by Hugh Leonard), 545
Brown, Christy, *My Left Foot*, 549–50
Browne, Noël, 468
Brown, Terence, 566, 585
Louis MacNeice: Sceptical Vision, 585
Northern Voices: Poets from Ulster, 585
Bryans, Robin *see* Harbison, Robert
Buachaillí Bána, Na (Cathal Ó Searcaigh), 346
Bullaí Mhártain (Donncha Ó Céileachair and Síle Ní Chéileachair), 274
Burning Perch, The (Louis MacNeice), 361
Bush Theatre, 520
Butcher Boy, The (Patrick McCabe), 446, 524, 548, 636
Bute, Mary Ellen, 557
Butler, Hubert, 472
Byrce, Colette, 392
Byrne, John Keyes *see* Leonard, Hugh
By the Bog of Cats (Marina Carr), 524, 634

Cabinet of Irish Literature, The (edited by Charles A. Read and T. P. O'Connor), 573–4
Cad Ba Dhóbair Dó agus Sgeulta Eile (Liam Ó Rinn), 246
Cailín na Gruaige Duinne (Úna Bean Uí Dhíocsa), 255–6
'Caillte' (Eithne Ní Chonaill), 323
'Cainteoir Dúchais' (Cathal Ó Searcaigh), 619
caint na ndaoine ('speech of the people'), 234–6
Cairns, David *see* Richards, Shaun
Caisleáin Óir (Séamus Ó Grianna), 252, 281
Caitheamh Aimsire (Tadhg Ó Donnchadha), 230
Cal (Bernard MacLaverty), 439
Campbell, Joseph, 86–8
'Ad Limina', 87
Earth of Cualann, The, 87
Gilly of Christ, The, 86
Irishry, 86
'My Lagan Love', 86
Mountainy Singer, The, 87
'Raven's Rock', 87
'Vision of Glendalough, A', 87

Cannon, Moya, 407
Caoineadh Airt Uí Laoire (film; dir. Bob Quinn), 546
Caoineadh na Mná agus Duanta Eile (Séamus Ó hAodha), 233
Caoin Tú Féin (Diarmaid Ó Súilleabháin), 286
Captain Lavender (Medbh McGuckian), 399
Carbery, Ethna (penname of Anna Johnston), 69–70
  Northern Patriot (co-editor), 69–70
  'Passing of the Gael, The', 70
  'Rody McCorley', 70
  Shan Van Vocht (co-editor), 69–70
Carleton, William, *Willy Reilly and His Colleen Bawn*, 535–6
Carolan (Eoghan Ó Tuairisc), 304
Carr, Marina, 523–4, 634, 635
  By the Bog of Cats, 524, 634
  Portia Coughlan, 523–4
  Mai, The, 523–4, 634, 638
  On Raftery's Hill, 524
Carroll, Paul Vincent, *Shadow and Substance*, 216
Carson, Ciaran, 391, 392, 396–7, 636
  Belfast Confetti, 397
  'Hamlet', 396
  Irish for No, The, 396
  Last Night's Fun, 396
  New Estate, The, 396
  Twelfth of Never, 397
Casadh an tSúgáin (Douglas Hyde), 190
Cask, The (Freeman Wills Crofts), 169
Casquet of Literary Gems, 573
Castar na Daoine ar a Chéile 's ní Chastar na Cnuic nó na Sléibhthe (Séamus Ó Grianna), 250
Castle Rackrent (Maria Edgeworth), 14
Catalpa (Donal O'Kelly), 525
Catchpenny Twist (Stewart Parker), 503
Cathleen ni Houlihan (William Butler Yeats and Lady Augusta Gregory), 15, 183, 189, 190–1
'Catholic apologetics', 118
Cattledrive in Connaught, The (Austin Clarke), 101
'Cattle, The' (Katharine Tynan), 68–9
Cead Aighnis (Nuala Ní Dhomhnaill), 341–2, 603–4
Ceannracháin Cathrach (Seán Mac Maoláin), 247
'Ceasefire' (Michael Longley), 390
'Ceathrúintí Mháire Ní Ógáin' (Máire Mhac an tSaoi), 326
Céitinn, Seathrún (Geoffrey Keating), 13
'Celibacy' (Austin Clarke), 102
Celtic Theatre, 181
Celtic Twilight, 366, 367
Celtic Twilight, The (William Butler Yeats), 138
censorship, 44, 199, 323, 421, 423, 481, 490
  and cinema, 536, 537–9, 556
Censorship Board, 496
Censorship of Publications Act, 421, 423
Ceol Abhann agus Gleann (Donnchadh Ó Liatháin), 232
Chaise Gharbh, An (Peadar Ó hAnnracháin), 231
Chaise Riabhach, An (Peadar Ó hAnnracháin), 231
Chamber Music (James Joyce), 89–90
Changing Winds (St John Ervine), 132–3
Charabanc Theatre Company, 514, 525
Charwoman's Daughter, The (James Stephens), 138–9
Chéim Bhriste, An (Áine Ní Ghlinn), 342
Childers, Erskine, 130–1
  In the Ranks of the C.I.V., 131
  Riddle of the Sands, The, 130–1
Children of the Dead End (Patrick MacGill), 120
Churchill, Caryl, 513
'Cill Cais' (song), 18–19
cinema, 266, 368, 531–58, 621
  and Abbey Theatre, Dublin, 534, 542–6
  actors, 537–9, 542–3
  emergence of, 532–6
  and history, 536–42
  independent film sector, 549
  and the Irish Rebellion of 1916, 538
  and landscape, 534, 552
  and literature, 531–58
  and modernism, 547–8
  postmodern, 553
  see also screen adaptations
Ciontach (Diarmaid Ó Súilleabháin), 288
Cioth is Dealán (Séamus Ó Grianna), 244, 273
'Circus Animals' Desertion, The' (William Butler Yeats), 62
Circle of Friends (Maeve Binchy), 556
Cití (Siobhán Ní Shúilleabháin), 304
Civil Rights Movement, 499, 585
Claddagh Records, 378
Claidheamh Soluis, An (newspaper), 239
Claíomh Solais, An (Liam Mac Cóil), 295
Clancy Name, The (Lennox Robinson), 200
Clanking of Chains, The (Brinsley MacNamara), 155–6

Clarke, Austin, 101–3, 358, 369–72
Ancient Lights, 370–1
Cattledrive in Connaught, The, 101
'Celibacy', 102
'Lost Heifer, The', 101
'Martha Blake at Fifty-One', 371
Mnemosyne Lay in Dust, 370
Night and Morning, 102
'Penal Law', 103
Pilgrimage and Other Poems, 101, 102
Poems of Joseph Campbell, 87
'The Straying Student', 103
Tiresias, 371
Vengeance of Fionn, The, 101
'Young Woman of Beare, The', 102
as co-founder of the Lyric Theatre, 370
Clifton, Harry, 409
Clóchomhar, An, 307, 308
Cluysenaar, Anne, 401
Cochrane, Ian, 439
'Codail a Laoich' (Biddy Jenkinson), 343
Coffey, Brian, 99, 100
Third Person, 100
Coghill, Rhoda, 401
Coimhthigheach, An (Séamus Mac Conmara), 256
'Coinnle ar Lasadh' (Máirtín Ó Direáin), 322
Coinnle Geala (Máirtín Ó Direáin), 319
Cois Caoláire (Máirtín Ó Cadhain), 275–6
Coisithe, Na (Liam S. Gógan), 322
Cois Life (Seosamh Ó Torna), 248
Colum, Padraic, 52, 83–6, 139–40, 191, 202–3
Broken Soil (revised as *The Fiddler's House*), 202
Creatures, 85
Dramatic Legends and Other Poems, 85
King of Ireland's Son, The, 139–40
Land, The, 202
'Poor Scholar of the Forties, A', 84–5
Poet's Circuits: Collected Poems of Ireland, The, 85
Wild Earth, 83
C(h)omhairle Náisiúnta Amharclainne, An, 301
Comhar (magazine), 307
Comhar Drámaidheachta (Drámaíochta), An, 262, 300, 301
see Na hAisteoirí
Coming Back, The (Lady Constance Malleson), 166–7
Commitments, The (Roddy Doyle), 518, 557–8
Common Chord, The (Frank O'Connor), 453
Commotion Theatre Company, 524
Compántas Amharclainne, An, 300
Compántas Chorcaí, 302
'Conán Maol' (penname of Pádraig Ó Séaghdha), 240, 251, 258, 260
Confessions of a Young Man (George Moore), 142
Congreve, William, *Way of the World, The*, 188
Conlon, Evelyn, 451, 464
Conner, Reardon, *Shake Hands with the Devil*, 540
Connolly, James, 31
Connor, Elizabeth (penname of Una Troy), 481–2
Conradh na Gaeilge *see* Gaelic League
'Consolation' (William Larminie), 66
Conversations on a Homecoming (Tom Murphy), 505
Corcoran, Neil, *After Yeats and Joyce*, 566
Cork Dramatic Society, 202, 203
Corkery, Daniel, 153–4, 202, 228, 577–8
Hidden Ireland: A Study of Gaelic Munster in the Eighteenth Century, The, 228, 265, 564, 577
Synge and Anglo-Irish Literature, 154, 202, 630–1
Threshold of Quiet, The, 153–4
'Cork Realists', 200
Cormac Ua Conaill (Fr Patrick Dinneen), 249–50
Corp Eoghain Uí Shúilleabháin (Seán Ó Tuama), 303
Council for the Status of Women, 400
Countess Kathleen and Various Legends and Lyrics, The (William Butler Yeats), 57
Country Girls Trilogy, The (Edna O'Brien), 427
Coyle, Kathleen, 164–6
Flock of Birds, A, 165–6
Liv, 164–5
Cowboys and Indians (Joseph O'Connor), 445
Crab Apple Jelly (Frank O'Connor), 452
Crane Bag, The (journal), 586
'Crann na Tubaiste' (Biddy Jenkinson), 343
'Craoibhín Aoibhinn, An' *see* Douglas Hyde
Crawford, Robert, *Devolving English Literature*, 562
Cré agus Cláirseach (Tomás Mac Síomóin), 338
Creatures (Padraic Colum), 85
Cré na Cille (Máirtín Ó Cadhain), 275
'Crimson in the Tri-colour, The' (Sean O'Casey), 206
Crock of Gold, The (James Stephens), 78, 139
Crofts, Freeman Wills, *Cask, The*, 169
Croí agus Carraig (Colm Breathnach), 349

Croker, B. M., 122
Cromie, Robert, 127, 131
  Plunge into Space, A, 127
Cromwell (Brendan Kennelly), 381
Cronin, Anthony, 365, 472, 469, 635
Crossroads, The (Lennox Robinson), 200
Crucial Week in the Life of a Grocer's Assistant, A (formerly titled *The Fooleen* by Tom Murphy), 496, 499
Cruithneacht agus Ceannabhán (Tomás Bairéad), 245
Crushed Yet Conquering (Deborah Alcock), 117
Crystal and Fox (Brian Friel), 499
Cuaifeach mo Londubh Buí (Séamas Mac Annaidh), 293
'Cuchulain Comforted' (William Butler Yeats), 63
Cuchulain of Muirthemne (Augusta Gregory), 569
Cúigiú Díochlaonadh, An (Dáibhí Ó Cróinín), 294
Cúirt an Mheán Oíche (Brian Merriman), 22
Cuirtéis, Éamonn (Edmund Curtis), 317
Cullingford, Elizabeth Butler, *Ireland's Others*, 623
Cumhacht na Cinneamhna (Tomás Bairéad), 245
Cummins, Maria Susanna, *The Lamplighter*, 151
Curious Street, A (Desmond Hogan), 442
Cúrsaí Thomáis (Éamonn Mac Giolla Iasachta), 254–5
'Curse of Cromwell, The' (William Butler Yeats), 19
'Cú Uladh' *see* Peadar Mac Fhionnlaoich
Cyphers (journal), 402

Da (Hugh Leonard), 504
Daddy, Daddy (Paul Durcan), 381
Dalkey Archive, The (Flann O'Brien), 433
Dalton, Emmet, 543
D'Alton, Louis, 481
  Lovers' Meeting, 481
  This Other Eden, 545–6
Daly, Ita, 450, 451
Damer, An, 301–2
Dámh-Sgoil Mhúsgraighe Uí Fhloinn, 229, 231, 233, 317
Danar, An (Piaras Béaslaí), 262
Dancers Dancing, The (Éilís Ní Dhuibhne), 450
Dancing at Lughnasa (Brian Friel), 519–20, 550, 555
Dánta agus Amhráin (Séamus Ó Maoildhia), 231
Dánta agus Duanta (Liam S. Gógan), 232, 321
Dánta Aniar (Máirtín Ó Direáin), 319, 321
Dánta Eile (Tomás Ó Floinn), 322
Dark Rosaleen (M. E. Francis), 119
Daughters of Erin (Inghinidhe na hÉireann), 190
Daughters of Men (Hannah Lynch), 125
Davie, Donald, 583
Davitt, Michael, 336, 344–5, 609–10, 620
  'Ar an gCaorán Mór', 344
  'Poker', 345
Dawe, Gerald, 392
Day-Lewis, Cecil, 103, 360
'Dead at Clonmacnois, The' (Thomas William Rolleston), 81–2
Dead Kingdom, The (John Montague), 380
Dead, The (John Huston), 557
Dealbhóir sa nGairdín, An (Lorcán Ó Treasaigh), 293
Dealg Droighin, An (Nuala Ní Dhomhnaill), 339, 603–4
Deane, John F, 381, 411
Deane, Seamus, 43, 363, 392, 440, 467, 566, 587–9
  general editor of the *Field Day Authology*, I–III, 587–90
  'Heroic Styles', 566
  Reading in the Dark, 440, 470
Death and Resurrection of Mr Roche, The (Thomas Kilroy), 507
Death of a Chieftain and Other Stories (John Montague), 461
Death of a Naturalist (Seamus Heaney), 382
Death of Humpty Dumpty, The (Graham Reid), 503
De Bhailís, Colm, 228
De Bhilmot (Wilmot), Séamus, 262–3
  Mise Méara, 272
De Blaghd, Earnán *see* Blythe, Ernest
De Brún, Fr Pádraig (founder of *Humanitas*), 264
December Bride (Sam Hanna Bell), 437, 551–2
'De Civitate Hominum' (Thomas MacGreevy), 97
Deevy, Teresa, 216–18, 482
  Katie Roche, 217–18
  King of Spain's Daughter, The, 217
De hIndeberg, Risteárd *see* Henebry, Fr Richard
Deirdre (James Stephens), 135
Deirdre of the Sorrows (J. M. Synge), 75
Deirdre Wed (Herbert Trench), 66
Deirdre (William Butler Yeats), 197
Delanty, Greg, 409

Dé Luain (Eoghan Ó Tuairisc), 289
Demi-Gods, The (James Stephens), 135
Demon Lover and Other Stories, The (Elizabeth Bowen), 454
Deoraidheacht (Pádraic Ó Conaire), 246, 253
De Paor, Alín, 250
De Paor, Louis, 349, 616
De Paor, Pádraig, 308
Dermody, Frank, 301, 486
'Deserted Village, The' (Oliver Goldsmith), 21
Désirée (Liam Prút), 295
Devlin, Anne, 513
Devlin, Denis, 99, 364–5
  Heavenly Foreigner, The, 365
  Intercessions, 100, 364
  Lough Derg, 364
Dharmakaya (Paula Meehan), 407
Dialann Bóthair (Liam Ó Muirthile), 603, 606
Dialann Deoraí (Dónall Mac Amhlaigh), 279
Dialann sa Díseart (Eoghan Ó Tuairisc and Rita Kelly), 334
dialect, 29–31, 237, 238–9
Dianmhuilte Dé (Diarmaid Ó Súilleabháin), 286
Diarmuid agus Gráinne (Micheál Mac Liammóir), 263
Diarmuid and Grania (George Moore and W. B. Yeats), 187
'Digging' (Seamus Heaney), 385
Dillon, Eilís, 447
Dinneen, Fr Patrick (Pádraig Ua Duinnín), 228, 230, 231, 232, 234, 236, 249, 261
  Cormac Ua Conaill, 249–50
Divorcing Jack (Colin Bateman), 542
Dix, Elizabeth Rachel *see* Úna Bean Uí Dhíocsa
'Do Bhev' (Brendan Behan), 324
Dochartach Dhuibhlionna (Seosamh Mac Grianna), 253
Doctor's Wife, The (Brian Moore), 438
Dolmen Miscellany (John Montague, editor), 378
Dolmen Press, The, 372–3, 374, 378–9
Domestic Relations (Frank O'Connor), 452
Donaghy, John Lyle, 99
  Wilderness Sings, 99
Donnelly, Charles, 99
Donoghue, Denis, 583
  Warrenpoint, 470
Donoghue, Emma, 451–2
'Do Nuala Ní Dhomhnaill' (Máire Mhac an tSaoi), 327
Dora Myrl, The Lady Detective (M. McDonnell Bodkin), 130
Doras do Plabadh, An (Seoirse Mac Liam), 257
Dorcey, Mary, 451, 464
  Noise from the Woodshed, A, 464
Dorgan, Theo, 411
'Do Sheán Ó Súilleabháin' (Brendan Behan), 325
Double Cross (Thomas Kilroy), 511
Dowling, Joe, 492, 506
Doyle, Paddy, 468
Doyle, Roddy, 443, 557
  Commitments, The, 518, 557–8
  Paddy Clarke Ha Ha Ha, 443
  Snapper, The, 443
  Star Called Henry, A, 638
  Woman Who Walked into Doors, The, 443
Dozen Lips, A (pamphlet), 473
Dracula (Bram Stoker), 128–30
Drama in Muslin: A Realistic Novel (George Moore), 120, 121
drama *see* theatre, also plays
Dramatic Legends and Other Poems (Padraic Colum), 85
Dr Áthas, An (Liam Mac Cóil), 294–5
Drawing Ballerinas (Medbh McGuckian), 400
Druid Theatre Company, 507, 515, 523
Druma Mór, An (Seosamh Mac Grianna), 252, 272
Drums of Father Ned, The (Sean O'Casey), 480
'Dubh – ar thitim Shrebrenice, 11ú Iúil 1995' (Nuala Ní Dhomhnaill), 341
Dublin, 72, 300
  representations of, 442–4, 556–8
  theatres, 182
  theatre societies in, 203
  See also Abbey, Gate, Peacock, Pike theatres
Dubliners (James Joyce), 9, 33–43, 145–7
Dublin Magazine, 77, 401
Dublin Opinion (periodical), 258
'Dublin trilogy' (Sean O'Casey), 480
Duibhlinn (Ciarán Ó Coigligh), 296
Dúil (Liam Ó Flaithearta / Liam O'Flaherty), 274
Dún na mBan Trí Thine (Éilís Ní Dhuibhne), 306
Dunne, Mary Chavelita *see* Egerton, George
Dunne, Seán, 469
Dunsany, Lord Edward John, 93, 95, 173
  King of Elfland's Daughter, The, 173
  My Ireland, 173
  Tales of War, 132
Durcan, Paul, 380–1
  Berlin Wall Café, The, 381
  Daddy, Daddy, 381
Dutch Interior (Frank O'Connor), 158, 159

Éagnairc (Pádraig Ó Siadhail), 296
Éan Corr (Seán Mac Maoláin), 250
Earth Compels, The (Louis MacNeice), 104
Earth of Cualann, The (Joseph Campbell), 87
'Easter 1916' (William Butler Yeats), 16, 59
Easter Rising of 1916, 16, 27, 91–5, 205, 250, 255
Echoes Bones and Other Precipitates (Samuel Beckett), 100
Edelstein, Joseph, *Moneylender, The*, 121
Eden (Eugene O'Brien), 521
Edgeworth, Maria, 23
  Castle Rackrent, 14
Edwards, Hilton (co-founder of the Gate Theatre, Dublin), 211–2, 494, 495–7
Egan, Desmond, 409, 411
Egerton, George (born Mary Chavelita Dunne), 124–5
  Keynotes, 124
  Keynotes with Discords, 124
Eglinton, John, 578–9
'Éiceolaí' (Biddy Jenkinson), 343
Éigse na Nua-Ghaedhilge (Piaras Béaslaí), 231
Eireaball Spideoige (Seán Ó Ríordáin), 328, 329, 331
Éire-Ireland (journal), 616
Eiriceachtaí agus Scéalta Eile (Alan Titley), 291
Ellis, Conleth, 332–3, 339, 349
Ellis-Fermor, Una, *The Irish Dramatic Movement*, 580–1
Ellmann, Richard, 32, 566–7, 584
emigration, 25–6, 279–80, 458, 505, 636
  and cinema, 535, 538, 545
  and Irish-language literature, 279–80, 283
  and memoirs, 468
  novels of, 118, 142, 438, 445
  plays of, 484, 492–3, 494, 496, 497, 505
  poetry of, 72, 363–5
  see also exile; immigration; migration
Empire Theatre, 493
En Attendant Godot, see Waiting for Godot
End House, The (Joseph Tomelty), 482
Enemy of the People, The (Henrik Ibsen), 185
Enemy Within, The (Brian Friel), 494
Enright, Anne, 451, 465
  The Portable Virgin, 465
Eoghan Rua Ó Néill (Seosamh Mac Grianna), 243, 251
Ervine, St John, 132–3, 204–5, 482, 545
  Boyd's Shop, 545
  Changing Winds, 132–3
  Magnanimous Lover, The, 205
  Mixed Marriage, 204–5
Esler, E. Rentoul, 119
Esther Waters (George Moore), 141
Eureka Street (Robert McLiam Wilson), 441
Europa and the Bull and Other Poems (W. R. Rodgers), 361
Evelyn Innes (George Moore), 187
exile, 29, 44–5, 102, 156, 160, 216, 363–5, 389, 402, 421, 444, 631, 639–41
  writers in, 23–5, 44, 216, 363–5, 395
expatriates, 444, 448
Expressionism, 208–12, 480

Fáinne an Lae (newspaper, later titled *An Claidheamh Soluis*), 239
Fairy and Folk Tales of the Irish Peasantry (William Butler Yeats), 138
Faith Healer (Brian Friel), 517–18, 520, 634
Fallon, Pádraic, 366–7
  Vision of Mac Conglinne, The, 366–7
Fallon, Peter, 410–11
Familiar, The (Thomas Kinsella), 376–7
famine in literature, 26, 261, 262, 276, 283, 435, 499
Famine (Tom Murphy), 499
Fánaí (Seán Ó Caomhánaigh), 254
Fand and Other Poems (William Larminie), 65
Faoileán na Beatha (Seán Ó Tuama), 334
Faoistin Bhacach (Pearse Hutchinson), 333
Farewell to English, A (Michael Hartnett), 408
Farrell, Bernard, 504–5
  I Do Not Like Thee, Dr Fell, 504
  Last Apache Reunion, 504–5
Farrell, J. G., *Troubles*, 431
Farrell, M. J. (born Molly Keane), 161, 162, 430–1
  Good Behaviour, 431
  Loving without Tears, 430
  Mad Puppetstown, 162
Farrell, Michael, 426, 429
Farren, Robert (*see* Roibeárd Ó Faracháin), co-founder of the Lyric Theatre, 370
'Father O'Flynn' (Alfred Perceval Graves), 96
Father Ralph (Gerald O'Donovan)
Father Tim (Rosa Mulholland), 118
Fear an Tae (Liam Ó Muirthile), 305
Fear Dána, An (Alan Titley), 291
Fear in the Heart (Constance Malleson), 167
Fear Marbh, An (Colm Breathnach), 349
Féar Suaithinseach (Nuala Ní Dhomhnaill), 341
Feasta (magazine), 307
Feis (Nuala Ní Dhomhnaill), 603
Felicia's Journey (William Trevor), 432
feminism, 124, 184, 194, 400–1, 589, 602

'Fergus and the Druid' (William Butler Yeats), 57
'Fiachra Éilgeach' *see* Ristéard Ó Foghludha
Fiannaidhe Fáin, An (Pádraig Ó Miléadha), 232
Fiche Blian ag Fás (Muiris Ó Súileabháin), 258–9, 613–4
fiction, 113–73, 240–59, 271–99, 421–65
  counter-Revival, 141–56
  detective, 130, 257
  fin de siècle, 124–7
  of the Great War, 130–4
  Irish-language, 240–59, 271–99, 619, 622
  of Northern Ireland, 165–8, 436–41, 459–63
  New Woman, 122–4
  popular, 114–19, 279, 297–9
  post-World War II, 424
  of the Revival, 134–41
  science fiction, 127–8, 257
  spy, 130
  supernatural, 127–30
  thrillers, 257–8, 296, 435
  urban, 246–8
  World War II, 439
  see also novels; short stories
Fiddler's House, The (formerly *Broken Soil* by Padraic Colum), 202
Field Day Anthology of Irish Writing, 1, 357, 358, 509, 565–6, 587–90
Field Day Theatre Company, 495, 509–13, 514, 519, 525
Fielden, Olga, 168
  Island Story, 168
  Stress, 168
Field, The (John B. Keane), 550–1
Field Work (Seamus Heaney), 384
Figgis, Darrell ('Michael Ireland'), *The Return of the Hero*, 136
File Callánach (Seán Mac Maoláin), 253
Film Company of Ireland (FCOI), 534–5
Finnegans Wake (James Joyce), 31, 88, 557, 634–5
Fíon gan Mhoirt (Roibeárd Ó Faracháin), 248
Fire of Green Boughs, The (Mrs Victor Rickard), 133–4
Fishing the Sloe-Black River (Colum McCann), 458–9
Fitzmaurice, George, 203, 483
Flaherty, Robert, 266
Flanagan, Fionnuala, 34
Flats, The (John Boyd), 500–1
Flight (Vona Groarke), 407
Flock of Birds, A (Kathleen Coyle), 165–6
Flower Master, The (Medbh McGuckian), 397
Fly on the Wheel, The (Katherine Cecil Thurston), 123
Flynn, Gerard Mannix, 640
  James X, 640–1
Focus Theatre, 517
folklore, 137, 341, 634
folktales, 137–40, 233–4, 240–1
Fonn a Níos Fiach (Pádraig Ua Maoileoin), 283–4
Fooleen, The (retitled *A Crucial Week in the Life of a Grocer's Assistant* by Tom Murphy), 496
Fools of Fortune (William Trevor), 432, 540
Ford, John, 552
Foreign Affairs and Other Stories (Sean O'Faolain), 454
Fornocht do Chonac (Eoghan Ó Tuairisc), 304
'Fornocht do chonac thú' (Patrick Pearse, translation by Thomas MacDonagh), 92
Fortune Must Follow (D. G. Waring), 167
Fortune, The (Douglas Goldring), 132
Fox's Covert, The (Blanaid Salkeld), 100
Francis, M. E. (Mary Sweetman, later Blundell), 119
  Dark Rosaleen, 119
  In a North Country Village, 119
Francophile, The (Brian Friel), 494
Frankie Pig Says Hello (Patrick McCabe), 524
Freedom of the City (Brian Friel), 501–2
'Freehold' (John Hewitt), 362
Freeman's Journal, 571
Free State, Irish, 43–6, 156–9, 160, 238
French Life in Town and Country (Hannah Lynch), 149
Friel, Brian, 460, 478, 494–5, 496, 499–500, 501–2, 509–11, 517–18, 519–20, 526
  Aristocrats, 506
  Crystal and Fox, 499
  Dancing at Lughnasa, 519–20, 550, 555
  Enemy Within, The, 494
  Faith Healer, 517–18, 520, 634
  Francophile, The, 494
  Freedom of the City, The, 501–2
  Living Quarters, 506
  Making History, 510
  Molly Sweeney, 518
  Mundy Scheme, The, 500
  Philadelphia, Here I Come!, 494–5, 554
  Translations, 509, 510
  Volunteers, 506
From Ballybeg to Broadway (documentary), 520

From Burke to Beckett (formerly *Ascendancy and Tradition* by W. J. McCormack), 586
'Fuath, An' (Máire Mhac an tSaoi), 326
Full Moon in March, A (William Butler Yeats), 63
Furlong, Alice, 137

Gaeilgeoirí (Antaine Ó Flatharta), 305
Gael, The (Edward E. Lysaght), 154–5, 254
'Gaelic' (definition of term), 615–16
Gaelic Journal, The (*Irisleabhar na Gaedhilge*), 226, 229
Gaelic League (Conradh na Gaeilge), 35, 79, 226, 229, 230, 237–8, 261, 299
  publishing programme, 239–40
Gaelic theatre tradition, 260
Gaelic Union, 226
Gaeltacht, 604, 612, 617
  amateur drama, 304
  autobiography, 258–9, 271–3, 274, 280–1, 284, 613
  map of, 599
  non-Gaeltacht Irish language writers, 246, 273, 285, 290, 297, 604–5, 620
  official boundaries of, 282
  writing, 229, 234, 237, 242, 243, 248, 249, 252–3, 258–9, 261, 263, 270, 271–3, 274–5, 277, 278, 280–4, 293, 295–7, 298–9, 302, 304–5, 306, 317, 328–32, 346–7, 604–5, 618–19, 622
Gaiety Theatre, 183, 480, 494
Galvin, Patrick, 468, 553
  Song for a Raggy Boy, 553
Game Cock and Other Stories, The (Michael McLaverty), 460
Gaodhal, An (The Gael), 229, 239
Gap of Brightness, The (Frederick Robert Higgins), 98
'Gas from a Burner' (James Joyce), 88
Gate Theatre Company, 209–12, 494, 495–6, 497, 526
  actors, 211
  patrons, 212
  playwrights, 211, 496
Gealas i Lár na Léithe, An (Pádraig Ó Cíobháin), 295
Geall a Briseadh, An (Tomás Bairéad), 245
Gébler, Carlo, 434, 437, 445
genealogies, 640
Geographical Distribution of Irish Ability, The (D. J. O'Donoghue), 562–3
Ghosts (Henrik Ibsen), 185
ghost stories, 127
  see also gothic literature
Giall, An (Brendan Behan), 301, 491
Gibbons, Luke, *Transformations in Irish Culture*, 612
Gibbon, (William) Monk, 94, 96
Gigli Concert, The (Tom Murphy), 516, 634
Gilly of Christ, The (Joseph Campbell), 86
Girl Who Married the Reindeer, The (Eiléan Ní Chuilleanáin), 406
Glasshouse Productions (theatre company), 518
'Glass of Beer, The' (James Stephens), 79
'Gleann Maoiliúra' (Biddy Jenkinson), 344
globalisation, 629–35, 637, 639
Goblin, The (newspaper), 36
Gógan, Liam S., 230, 232, 262, 321–4
  'Coisithe, Na', 322
  Dánta agus Duanóga, 232
  Dánta agus Duanta, 232, 321
  Nua-Dhánta, 232
Gogarty, Oliver St John, 52, 90–1
  'Leda and the Swan', 91
  Selected Poems, 91
Golden Apple, The (Lady Augusta Gregory), 483
Goldring, Douglas, *The Fortune*, 132
Goldsmith, Oliver, 'The Deserted Village', 21–2
Good Behaviour (Molly Keane), 431
Goodbye to All That (Robert Graves), 262–3
Gore-Booth, Eva, 70
  'Little Waves of Breffny, The', 70
  'Visions of Niamh, The', 70
Gothic literature, 128, 431, 458, 547, 548, 635–6, 639
Grá agus an Ghruaim, An (Seosamh Mac Grianna), 42, 243
Grand, Sarah, 124
  Heavenly Twins, The, 124
Grásta i Meiriceá (Antaine Ó Flatharta), 305
Graves, Alfred Perceval (father of Robert Graves), 95, 96
  'Father O'Flynn', 96
Graves, Robert, 96–7
  Goodbye to All That, 262–3
  White Goddess, The, 96
'Great Breath, The' (George William Russell, 'AE'), 73
Great Cloak, The (John Montague), 379
Great Famine, the, 26, 368
  see also famine in literature
Great Hunger, The (Patrick Kavanagh), 517
Great War, The (World War I), 93–8, 130–4

Green Helmet and Other Poems, The (William Butler Yeats), 58
Gregory, Lady Augusta, 15, 80, 181–2, 189–92, 210, 219
Cathleen ni Houlihan (co-authored with Yeats), 190–1
Cuchulain of Muirthemne, 569
Golden Apple, The, 483
Kiltartan Poetry Book, 80
'Kiltartanese', 80, 191
Rising of the Moon, 192
Twenty-Five, 191
see also Yeats, William Butler
'Greidhlic' (Nuala Ní Dhomhnaill), 340
Grennan, Eamon, 358, 366, 409
Still Life with Waterfall, 409
Groarke, Vona, 407
Flight, 407, 411
Other People's Houses, 407
Shale, 407
Group Theatre, 493
'Gruagach an Tobair' *see* Pádraig Ó Séaghdha
'Guests of the Nation' (Frank O'Connor), 539–40
Guinan, Canon Joseph, 118
Gulliver's Travels (Jonathan Swift), 20
Gúm, An, 251, 266, 271, 621
Gunna Cam agus Slabhra Óir (Seán Ó Tuama), 302
Guthrie, Tyrone, 480, 494
Gwynn, Stephen, *Irish Literature and Drama in the English Language: A Short History*, 578
'Gyres, The' (William Butler Yeats), 63

Hail and Farewell (George Moore), 143
Halpin, Mary, *Semi-Private*, 513
Hamilton, Hugo, 445, 459, 637–8
Hamilton, M. *see* Mary Churchill Luck
'Hamlet' (Ciaran Carson), 396
Harbison, Robert, 467, 470, 471
Hard Road to Klondike, The (translation of *Rotha Mór an tSaoil* by Micí Mac Gabhann), 615
Hardie, Kerry, 407
Hartnett, Michael (Mícheál Ó hAirtnéide), 338–9, 408, 605, 611, 622
Adharca Broic, 339
Farewell to English, A, 408
Hayes, Maurice, 470
Hay (Paul Muldoon), 395
Healy, Dermot, 446, 469
Healy, Randolph, 411
Heaney, Seamus, 9, 31, 93, 95, 382–6
Death of a Naturalist, 382
'Digging', 385
Field Work, 384
North, 383–4
Preoccupations, 384
Redress of Poetry, The, 384, 385
Seeing Things, 384–5
Station Island, 384
Wintering Out, 383
Heather Blazing, The (Colm Tóibín), 444
Heather Field, The (Edward Martyn), 187, 190
Heat of the Day, The (Elizabeth Bowen), 430, 448
Heavenly Foreigner, The (Denis Devlin), 365
Heavenly Twins, The (Sarah Grand), 124
Hello Eternity! (Blanaid Salkeld), 100
Henebry, Fr Richard (Risteárd de hIndeberg), 234–6, 241
'Revival Irish' (essays), 234
Heritage and Other Stories (Eugene McCabe), 462
heroic romances, 135
'Heroic Styles' (Seamus Deane), 566
Hewitt, John, 362–3, 471
'Freehold', 362
as poetry editor of *Threshold*, 363
Hickey, Tom, 517
Hidden Curriculum, The (Graham Reid), 503
Hidden Ireland: A Study of Gaelic Munster in the Eighteenth Century, The (Daniel Corkery), 265, 564, 577
Higgins, Aidan, 427–8, 444, 457, 466, 467, 469, 635
Balcony of Europe, 444
Langrishe, Go Down, 427
Higgins, Frederick Robert, 98–9, 480
Gap of Brightness, The, 98
Higgins, Rita Ann, 407
High Island (Richard Murphy), 373
High Road, The (Edna O'Brien), 448
'High Talk' (William Butler Yeats), 63
Hill of Vision, The (James Stephens), 78
Hinkson, Pamela, *Ladies' Road, The*, 162–3
History of Ireland (Standish James O'Grady), 568
Hitchcock, Alfred, 536
Hogan, Desmond, 442, 458, 467
Curious Street, A, 442
Ikon Maker, The, 442
Leaves on Grey, The, 442
New Shirt, A, 442
Home is the Hero (Walter Macken), 544
Homer, *The Odyssey*, 28, 31

Homeward Thoughts by the Way (George William Russell, 'AE'), 73
Honest Ulsterman, The (journal), 387
Hopper Chesson, Nora, 71
Horniman, Annie, 186
Hostage, The (Brendan Behan), 491–2
'How Ferencz Renyi Kept Silent' (William Butler Yeats), 572
Howie the Rookie (Mark O'Rowe), 521
How Many Miles to Babylon? (Jennifer Johnston), 431
Hudson Letter, The (Derek Mahon), 389
Hughes, Declan, 518
Humanitas (journal), 264
Hunt by Night, The (Derek Mahon), 389
Hunter, Barbara (co-editor of *Rann* journal), 363
Hunt, Hugh, 216, 218, 498, 499
Huston, John, *The Dead*, 557
Hutchinson, Pearse, 401, 409
  Faoistin Bhacach, 333
Hutton, Seán, 349
hybridity, 617–18, 620
Hyde, Douglas, 79–80, 138, 229, 230, 236, 261, 563
  Casadh an tSúgáin, 190
  Love Songs of Connacht, 79
  'Necessity for De-Anglicizing Ireland, The', 79, 563–4, 572
  Úlla de'n Chraobh, 230
Hyde-Lees, Georgie, 59
Hynes, Garry (Gearóidín), 507–8, 523

'I am Ireland' (Eavan Boland), 403–4
Ibsen, Henrik, 185
  Enemy of the People, The, 185
  Ghosts, 185
Í Chearnaigh, Seán Sheáin, 284
Ideal Husband, An (Oscar Wilde), 189
identity, 429, 442, 584–9, 606
  politics of, 583
Idir na Fleadhanna (Áine Ní Fhoghludha), 233, 274
Idir Shúgradh agus Dáiríre (Máirtín Ó Cadhain), 248, 275
I Do Not Like Thee, Dr Fell (Bernard Farrell), 504
Ikon Maker, The (Desmond Hogan), 442
Imaginary Homelands (Salman Rushdie), 29
'I mBaile an tSléibhe' (Nuala Ní Dhomhnaill), 340
Imeachtaí na Saoirse (Antaine Ó Flatharta), 305
immigration, 45, 261, 404, 448, 527, 554, 628, 639
  see also emigration; migration
Importance of Being Earnest, The (Oscar Wilde), 188
Inalienable Heritage and Other Poems, The (Emily Lawless), 67
In a Little World of Our Own (Gary Mitchell), 526
In a North Country Village (M. E. Francis), 119
Independent Voice (Gary Mitchell), 525
'Informant, The' (Eiléan Ní Chuilleanáin), 405
Informer, The (Liam O'Flaherty), 539
Inglis, Brian, 468
Inishowen (Joseph O'Connor), 445
Inland Ice and Other Stories, The (Éilís Ní Dhuibhne), 463
Inniu (newspaper), 273
Innti (journal), 336–8, 348
Innti poets, 336–8, 345, 348, 611
  disappearance of, 338
  and women writers, 337
'Inquisitio 1584' (Máire Mhac an tSaoi), 326
inscape theory, 329
institutional abuse, 553–4
Insurrection in Dublin, The (James Stephens), 78, 139
Intercessions (Denis Devlin), 100, 364
internationalism, 199, 577, 582–3
Interpreters, The (George William Russell), 140–1
In the Land of Youth (James Stephens), 136
In the Middle of the Fields (Mary Lavin), 455
In the Seven Woods (William Butler Yeats), 58
In the Shadow of the Glen (J. M. Synge), 183, 193–4
Iolar agus Sionnach (Seán Mac Maoláin), 251
Íosagán agus Sgéalta Eile (Patrick Pearse), 241
'Ireland, Michael' *see* Figgis, Darrell
Ireland's Others (Elizabeth Butler Cullingford), 623
I Remember! I Remember! (Sean O'Faolain), 453
Iremonger, Valentin, 365, 480
Irish Classics (Declan Kiberd), 566
Irish Comic Tradition, The (Vivian Mercier), 583
Irish Constitution of 1937, 218
Irish Dramatic Movement, The (Una Ellis-Fermor), 580–1
Irish Fairy Tales (James Stephens), 136
Irish Fairy Tales (William Butler Yeats), 138
Irish Film Censor, 556
Irish for No, The (Ciaran Carson), 396
Irish Homestead, The (periodical), 20, 36, 73

Irish Independent Theatre Society, 181, 186
Irish language, commentary on, 3, 22, 234, 235, 600, 613, 622, 623
decline of, 282, 610–11
and identity, 606
and nationalism, 606–7
'official' status of, 607–10
revival of, 79, 285
television, 306, 621
Irish-language writing, 11–19, 40–3, 45, 600–23
drama, 259–63, 299–306, 482–3, 491, 498, 507, 516
fiction, 248–58, 271–99
film and television, 306, 621
literary criticism, 263–6, 306–10, 581–2
poetry, 227–33, 317–51
prose, 233-59, 271–99
short stories, 240–8, 274, 275–6, 288, 291–2, 293, 296
see also periodicals, Irish-language
Irish Lesson, The (Michael O'Loughlin), 608–10
Irish Literary Theatre, 181, 182, 186, 189–91
Irish Literature and Drama in the English Language: A Short History (Stephen Gwynn), 578
Irish Literature (Justin McCarthy, editor-in-chief), 573, 574
Irishman, The (Brinsley MacNamara), 155
'Irish Mode', 92, 578
Irish National Dramatic Society *see* Abbey Theatre
Irish National Theatre *see* Abbey Theatre
Irish National Theatre Society *see* Abbey Theatre
Irish Plays and Playwrights (Cornelius Weygandt), 580
Irish Press, the (newspaper), 422
Irish Rebellion of 1798, 397
Irishry (Joseph Campbell), 86
Irish Statesman (periodical), 73
Irish Studies, 2
Irish Theatre Company, 535
Irish Writers Co-operative, 442–3
Irisleabhar Mhá Nuad (journal), 285, 307
Irisleabhar na Gaedhilge (*The Gaelic Journal*), 226, 229, 233, 239
Iron Men, The (later retitled *A Whistle in the Dark* by Tom Murphy), 493
Is É a Dúirt Polonius (Críostóir Ó Floinn), 303
'I see His Blood upon the Rose' (Joseph Mary Plunkett), 93
Island narratives, 284
see also Blasket Islands
Island Story (Olga Fielden), 168
Is the Priest at Home? (Joseph Tomelty), 482

'Jackeen ag Caoineadh na mBlascaod' (Brendan Behan), 325
Jail Journal (John Mitchel), 24
James X (Gerard Mannix Flynn), 640–1
Jenkinson, Biddy, 342–4, 349, 606
'Alabama. Samhradh '98', 343
'Codail a Laoich', 343
'Crann na Tubaiste', 343
'Éiceolaí', 343
'Gleann Maoiliúra', 344
'Mo Ghrása mo Dhia', 343
'Suantraí na Máthar Síní', 343
Jewish life, 121
John Bull's Other Island (George Bernard Shaw), 30, 198–9
John Chilcote, MP (Katherine Cecil Thurston), 115, 123
John Inglesant (J. H. Shorthouse), 117
John Millington Synge and the Irish Dramatic Movement (Francis Bickley), 580
Johnston, Anna *see* Carbery, Ethna
Johnston, Denis, 209, 211, 466, 496, 539–40
Old Lady Says 'No!', The, 210, 480, 496
'Rhapsody in Green', 210
Johnston, Jennifer, 431, 451
How Many Miles to Babylon?, 431
Shadows on our Skin, 431
Johnstone, Robert, 392
Jones, Marie, 514, 524
Stones in his Pockets, 525
Jordan, Neil, 442, 458, 547–9
Past, The, 442
'Journal Intime' (Medbh McGuckian), 398
journalism, 472, 473
journals *see* periodicals
'Journey, The' (Eavan Boland), 403
Joyce, James, 10, 23, 24, 28, 31, 32–43, 44, 88–90, 145–53, 556–7, 579
Anna Livia Plurabelle, 88
Chamber Music, 89–90
Collected Poems, 88
Dubliners, 9, 33–4, 145–7, 634
Finnegans Wake, 31, 88, 557, 634–5
'Gas from a Burner', 88
Pomes Penyeach, 90
Portrait of the Artist as a Young Man, A, 9, 39–42, 88, 147–8, 557
'Tilly', 90

Joyce, James (*cont.*)
Ulysses, 18–19, 28, 33–40, 150–3, 556, 579, 631, 634
Joyce criticism, 579, 582
Joyce, Trevor, 381–2, 411
Judith Hearne (Brian Moore) *see Lonely Passion of Judith Hearne, The*
Juno and the Paycock (Sean O'Casey), 92, 537

Kalem (film company), 532–4
Katie Roche (Teresa Deevy), 217–18
Kavanagh, Patrick, 105–6, 367–70, 426
as diarist in the *Envoy* journal, 369
Great Hunger, The, 367–9, 517
Ploughman and Other Poems, 105–6
Tarry Flynn, 369
Kavanagh's Weekly (journal), 369, 581
Keane, John B., 492, 497
Big Maggie, 497
Field, The, 550–1
Many Young Men of Twenty, 497
Sive, 492
Keane, Molly *see* Farrell, M. J.
Keegan, Claire, *Antarctica*, 465
Keenan, Brian, 468
Kelly, Maeve, 464
Kelly, Rita, 334, 349 *see* Ó Tuairisc, Eoghan
Kennelly, Brendan, 380–1, 511
Cromwell, 381
Keogh, J. Augustus, 205
Kettle, Thomas, 96
Poems and Parodies, 96
Keynotes with Discords (George Egerton), 124
Kiberd, Declan, 566, 610, 613
Irish Classics, 566
'Republicanism and culture in the new millennium', 613–14
Kickham, Charles, *Knocknagow* (film version), 535
Kick, The (Richard Murphy), 373
Kiely, Benedict, 436–7, 460, 466, 471, 472
Land without Stars, 436
Kilroy, Thomas, 429, 434, 506–7, 508, 511–12
Death and Resurrection of Mr Roche, The, 507
Double Cross, 511
Talbot's Box, 506–7
'Kiltartanese' (Lady Augusta Gregory), 80, 191
Kiltartan Poetry Book (Lady Augusta Gregory), 80
Kinderszenen ('Robert Schumann', nom-de-plume), 294
Kind of Scar, A: The Woman Poet in a National Tradition (Eavan Boland), 152–3
King Goshawk and the Birds (Eimar O'Duffy), 137
King of Elfland's Daughter, The (Lord Edward John Dunsany), 173
King of Friday's Men, The (M. J. Molloy), 483
King of Ireland's Son, The (Padraic Colum), 139–40
King of Spain's Daughter, The (Teresa Deevy), 217
King of the Castle (Eugene McCabe), 497
Kinney, Blanaid, 458
Kinsella, Thomas, 372, 374–8, 386
Another September, 374
Familiar, The, 376–7
Lebor Gabála Érenn (*The Book of Invasions*) Kinsella's use of, 374
Madonna and Other Poems, 376
Messenger, The, 376
New Poems 1973, 375
One, 375
Starlit Eye, The, 372
Tain, The (translation of *Táin Bó Cúailnge*), 374
Knife, The (Peadar O'Donnell), 157
Knocknagow (Charles Kickham), 535
'Korea' (John McGahern), 541

Lá agus Oidhche (Micheál Mac Liammóir), 247
Lá Breá Gréine Buí (Diarmaid Ó Súilleabháin), 288
Lá Dár Saol (Seán Ó Criomhthain), 282
Ladies' Road, The (Pamela Hinkson), 162–3
Lá Fhéile Míchíl (Eoghan Ó Tuairisc), 303
Lagan (journal), 363
Lake, The (George Moore), 143
Lamb (Bernard MacLaverty), 553
laments, 11, 546
Lamplighter, The (Maria Susanna Cummins), 151
Landlady, The (Brendan Behan), 486
Land of Spices, The (Kate O'Brien), 163
Land of Youth, The (Richard Power), 428
Land, The (Padraic Colum), 202
Land without Stars (Benedict Kiely), 436
Lane, Temple, 401
Langrishe, Go Down (Aidan Higgins), 427
'Lapis Lazuli' (William Butler Yeats), 63
Larminie, William, 66
'Consolation', 66
Fand and Other Poems, 65
'Nameless Doon, The', 66
Last Apache Reunion, The (Bernard Farrell), 504–5

Last Night's Fun (Ciaran Carson), 396
Last Poems and Two Plays (William Butler Yeats), 53, 62
Last September, The (Elizabeth Bowen), 161, 540
L'Attaque (Eoghan Ó Tuairisc), 289
Laverty, Maura, 447–8, 496
Lavin, Mary, 447, 455
Becker Wives and Other Stories, The, 455
In the Middle of the Fields, 455
Patriot Son and Other Stories, The, 455
Single Lady and Other Stories, A, 455
Law, Hugh, *Anglo-Irish Literature*, 578
Lawless, Emily, 65, 66–8
'After Aughrim', 67
Inalienable Heritage and Other Poems, The, 67
Maria Edgeworth, 571
Point of View (Some Talks and Disputations), The, 67
With the Wild Geese, 66, 67
Lay Up Your Ends (Martin Lynch), 514
Leanbh sa Lamborghini, An (Liam Prút), 295
Leaves on Grey, The (Desmond Hogan), 442
'Lecture Delivered to the Royal Academy of Sweden, A' (William Butler Yeats), 564
'Leda and the Swan' (Oliver St John Gogarty), 91
'Leda and the Swan' (W. B. Yeats), 61–2
Ledwidge, Francis, 93–5
Songs of the Fields, 94
'Thomas McDonagh', 94, 96
'Wife of Llew, The', 94
Leitch, Maurice, 438–9, 551
Stamping Ground, 438
Leland, Mary, 450
Leoithne Andeas (Tadhg Ó Donnchadha), 230
Leonard, Hugh (born John Keyes Byrne), 469, 503–4, 545
Big Birthday, The, 493, 545
Da, 504
Life, A, 504
Patrick Pearse Motel, The, 503–4
Lendennie, Jessie, 411
Letts, W. M. (Winifred Mabel), 72, 116–17, 121, 401
Rough Way, The, 116
Lewis, C. S. (Clive Staples), 95, 96, 168
Out of the Silent Planet, 168
Spirit in Bondage, The, 96
Life, A (Hugh Leonard), 504
'Lighthouse with Dead Leaves' (Medbh McGuckian), 399
Lig Sinn i gCathú (Breandán Ó hEithir), 297
Lingard, Joan, *Across the Barricades*, 567
Línte Liombó (Seán Ó Ríordáin), 332
Lismoyle: An Experiment in Ireland (B. M. Croker), 122
Listowel Drama Group, 492
literary biography, 271, 308
literary canon, the, 1, 7, 358, 565–6, 585, 586, 587–9
literary competitions, 229, 251, 270, 299, 411
literary criticism, 263–5, 271, 306–10, 321, 562–4
in Irish, 263–6, 306–10, 581–2
journals of, 309
and Joyce, 579
poet-critics, 579
and the Troubles, 584–6
and Yeats, 580–1
literary history, 1–2, 562–7, 631–2, 633–4
and anthologies, 587–9
and globalisation, 629–35
and the idea of Ireland, 564–5
and Joyce, 582
and mythology, 568–71
Northern, 586
post-World War II, 581
and the Revival, 567–75
and the Troubles, 584
and Yeats, 582
literary societies, 572
literary theory, 586–9
see also individual theories: feminism, New Criticism, postcolonial theory
literary tradition, 2, 616
Literature in Ireland (Thomas MacDonagh), 92, 576–7
Litríocht, An: Infhiúcha ar Phrionnsabail, Fuirmeacha agus Léirmheastóireacht na Litríochta (Fr Seoirse Mac Clúin), 264
'Little Black Rose Shall be Red at Last, The' (Joseph Mary Plunkett), 93
'Little Waves of Breffny, The' (Eva Gore-Booth), 70
Littlewood, Joan, 491
Living Chalice, The (Susan Mitchell), 71
Living Quarters (Brian Friel), 506
Liv (Kathleen Coyle), 164–5
Loane, Tim (co-founder of the Tinderbox Theatre, Belfast), 525
Logan, Michael, 239
Lomnochtán, An (Eoghan Ó Tuairisc), 290
Lonely Passion of Judith Hearne, The (Brian Moore), 427, 550
Lonely Voice, The (Frank O'Connor), 33

Lonesome West, The (Martin McDonagh), 522
Longford, Christine, 496
Longford Productions, 212
'Long-legged Fly' (William Butler Yeats), 63
Longley, Edna, 363, 585
Bloodaxe Book of 20th Century Poetry, 585
Louis MacNeice: A Study, 585
Poetry in the Wars, 585
Longley, Michael, 390–1, 471
'Ceasefire', 390
No Continuing City, 390
'Mustard Tin, The', 391
Lord Edward, Or '98 (J. W. Whitbread), 183
Lost Belongings (television series), 502
Lost Fields (Michael McLaverty), 436
'Lost Heifer, The' (Austin Clarke), 101
Lough Derg (Denis Devlin), 364
Louise de la Vallière (Katharine Tynan), 68
Louis MacNeice: A Study (Edna Longley), 585
Louis MacNeice: Sceptical Vision (Terence Brown), 585
Lovers' Meeting (Louis D'Alton), 481
Love Songs of Connacht (Douglas Hyde), 79
Loving without Tears (Molly Keane), 430
Lucht Ceoil (Art Ó Riain), 251
Luck, Mary Churchill (M. Hamilton), 119
Lux Aeterna (Eoghan Ó Tuairisc), 333
Lynch, Hannah, 148–9
Autobiography of a Child, 148–9
Daughters of Men, 125
French Life in Town and Country, 149
United Ireland, 149
Lynch, Martin, 514
Lay Up Your Ends, 514
Lynch, Patricia, 447
Lyrical Poems (Thomas MacDonagh), 92
Lyric Theatre, 370, 501, 526
Lysaght, Edward E. (*see* Éamonn Mac Giolla lasachta), 154–5, 254
The Gael, 154–5, 254

Mac Amhlaigh, Dónall, 279–80
Dialann Deoraí, 279
Saol Saighdiúra, 280
Mac Annaidh, Séamas, 293–4
Cuaifeach mo Londubh Buí, 293
Mo Dhá Mhicí, 294
Rubble na Mickies, 294
Mac Anna, Tomás, 300–1, 483, 486, 492, 499, 501, 506
Mac Aonghusa, Criostóir, 317
Mac an tSaoir, Flann *see* Ó Floinn, Tomás
McAughtry, Sam, 466
McCabe, Eugene, 462
Heritage and Other Stories, 462
King of the Castle, 497
McCabe, Patrick, 446, 524, 635–6
Butcher Boy, The, 446, 524, 548, 636
Frankie Pig Says Hello, 524
McCafferty, Nell, 638
McCann, Colum, 445, 458–9
Fishing the Sloe-Black River, 458–9
Songdogs, 445
This Side of Brightness, 445
McCann, John, *Twenty Years A-Wooing*, 485
McCarthy, Justin (editor-in-chief of *Irish Literature*), 573, 574
McCarthy, Sean, 506
McCarthy, Thomas, 410
Mr Dineen's Careful Parade, 410
McCart, Martin *see* Martin, David
McCloskey, James, 600, 610–11
Mac Clúin, Fr Seoirse, 257
An Litríocht: Infhiúcha ar Phrionnsabail, Fuirmeacha agus Léirmheastóireacht na Litríochta, 264
Mac Cóil, Liam, 294–5
Claíomh Solais, An, 295
Dr Áthas, An, 294–5
Mac Conmara, Séamus, *An Coimhthigheach*, 256
McCormack, Mike, 458
McCormack, W. J., 469, 586
Ascendancy and Tradition (revised as *From Burke to Beckett*)
McCourt, Frank, 468, 553
McCrory, Moy, 464
Mac Cumhaill, Maoghnas ('Fionn'), 250, 251, 258, 281
MacDonagh, Donagh, 365
McDonagh, Martin, 522–3
Beauty Queen of Leenane, The, 522–3, 639
Lonesome West, The, 522
Skull in Connemara, A, 522
MacDonagh, Thomas, 91–2, 370, 576–7
Literature in Ireland, 92
Lyrical Poems, 92
MacDonald, Peter, 392
MacDonogh, Patrick, 365
McFadden, Roy (co-editor of *Rann* journal), 363
Mac Fhearghusa, Pádraig, 349
Mac Fhionnlaoich, Peadar ('Cú Uladh'), 246, 261
Mac Gabhann, Micí, *Rotha Mór an tSaoil* (*The Hard Road to Klondike*), 281, 615

McGahern, John, 14, 425–30, 429, 456–7
Amongst Women, 430, 554
Barracks, The, 427
'Korea', 541
'Wheels', 547, 554
MacGill, Patrick, 95, 120–1, 131–2
Amateur Army, The, 131
Children of the Dead End, 120
Rat-Pit, The, 120
McGinley, Patrick, 435
Mac Giolla Bhrighde, Eoghan, 263
Mac Giolla Bhrighde, Niall, 259
Mac Giolla Iasachta, Éamonn (*see* Edward Lysaght/MacLysaght), 254–5
Cúrsaí Thomáis, 254–5
Gael, The, 154–5, 254
Toil Dé, 254
Mac Giolla Léith, Caoimhín, 292
MacGreevy, Thomas, 95, 97–8
'De Civitate Hominum', 97
Poems, 97
Mac Grianna, Seosamh, 40–3, 243–4, 265, 271
Dochartach Dhuibhlionna, 253
Druma Mór, An, 272
Eoghan Rua Ó Néill, 243, 251
Grá agus an Ghruaim, An, 42, 243
Mo Bhealach Féin, 40–3, 243, 271–2
Pádraic Ó Conaire agus Aistí Eile, 243
McGuckian, Medbh, 391, 392, 397–400, 408
On Ballycastle Beach, 398
Captain Lavender, 399
Drawing Ballerinas, 400
Flower Master, The, 397
'Journal Intime', 398
'Lighthouse with Dead Leaves', 399
Marconi's Cottage, 398
'Realism', 398
Shelmalier, 397, 399
Soldiers of Year II, The, 400
'Time Before You, The', 398
McGuinness, Frank, 508, 514–15, 520–1
Observe the Sons of Ulster Marching Towards the Somme, 508, 514–15, 525
Machtnamh Seanmhná (An Old Woman's Reflections by Peig Sayers), 258, 614–15
McHugh, Roger, 480
MacIntyre, Tom, 304, 306, 459, 508, 517, 632
Macken, Walter, 434
Home is the Hero, 544
McKenna, Stephen, 265
McKinnon, William T., *Apollo's Blended Dream: A Study of the Poetry of Louis MacNeice*, 585
MacLaverty, Bernard, 439–40, 461, 462
Cal, 439, 541
Lamb, 553
Secrets and Other Stories, 462
McLaverty, Michael, 436, 460
Game Cock and Other Stories, The, 460
Lost Fields, 436
Mac Liammóir, Micheál, 188, 210, 211, 212, 247, 263, 279, 318, 347, 469, 496
Diarmuid agus Gráinne, 263
Lá agus Oidhche, 247
as co-founder of the Gate Theatre, Dublin, 211–12, 495
Mac Liam, Seoirse, *Doras do Plabadh, An*, 257
Mac Lochlainn, Alf, 435
Mac Lochlainn, Gearóid, 336, 603, 617, 620, 622
MacLysaght, Edward E. *see* Lysaght, Edward E.
MacMahon, Bryan, 426, 456, 466, 469
MacMahon, Ella, 117, 121, 122, 125
New Note, A, 125
Pitiless Passion, A, 117, 122–3, 125
MacManus, Francis, 426, 429
Mac Maoláin, Seán, 253, 273
Algoland, 257
Ceannracháin Cathrach, 247
Éan Corr, 250
File Callánach, 253
Iolar agus Sionnach, 251
Mac Mathúna, Seán, 292
Mac Meanman, Seán Bán, 244
MacNamara, Brinsley (born John Weldon, and who also wrote as Oliver Blyth), 155–6
Clanking of Chains, The, 155–6
Irishman, The, 155
Valley of the Squinting Windows, The, 155
MacNamara, Gerald, *Thompson in Tir na nÓg*, 204
McNamee, Eoin, 440, 462
Resurrection Man, 440, 541, 636
MacNeice, Louis, 103–5, 359–61, 471, 585
Autumn Journal, 104–5, 360–1
Autumn Sequel, 361
Blind Fireworks, 104
Burning Perch, The, 361
Earth Compels, The, 104
Modern Poetry: A Personal Essay, 103
Plant and Phantom, 104
Poems, 104
Poetry of W. B. Yeats, The, 581
Mac Néill, Eoin, 16

McNeill, Janet, 437–8
McPherson, Conor, 519, 521, 545, 635–6
Shining City, 636
Weir, The, 521, 636
Mac Piarais, Pádraig *see* Pearse, Patrick
McShane and Johnson, 261
Mac Síomóin, Tomás, 337, 338
Cré agus Cláirseach, 338
McSwiney, Paul, *An Bárd 'gus an Fó*, 260
MacSwiney, Terence, 73
Mac Thomáis, Éamonn, 468
Madden, Deirdre, 440
Birds of Innocent Wood, The, 440
'Madness of King Goll, The' (William Butler Yeats), 56–7
Madoc: A Mystery (Paul Muldoon), 394
Madonna and Other Poems (Thomas Kinsella), 376
Mad Puppetstown (M. J. Farrell), 162
Maeldún (Diarmaid Ó Súilleabháin), 287–8
Magdalene Sermon, The (Eiléan Ní Chuilleanáin), 405
Magnanimous Lover, The (St John Ervine), 205
Mag Shamhráin, Antain, 309
Maguire, Mary, 92
Mahon, Derek, 387–90
'Afterlives', 389
Hudson Letter, The, 389
Hunt by Night, The, 389
Night-Crossings, 388
Snow Party, The, 388
Yellow Book, The, 389
Mai, The (Marina Carr), 523–4, 634, 638
Maidin i mBéarra agus Dánta Eile (Osborn Bergin), 231
Máire *see* Ó Grianna, Séamus
Making History (Brian Friel), 510
Malleson, Constance (Colette O'Niel), 166–7
After Ten Years, 166
Coming Back, The, 166–7
Fear in the Heart, 167
Manannán (Máiréad Ní Ghráda), 257
Manning, Mary, 211, 496, 533, 539, 557
as editor of *Motley*, 211
Youth's the Season . . ., 211
Manning, Olivia, 448
'Man who Dreamed of Faeryland, The' (William Butler Yeats), 57
Man Who Was Marked by Winter, The (Paula Meehan), 407
Many Young Men of Twenty (John B. Keane), 497
'Maol Muire' *See* Sr Mary Vincent
'Marbhghin: Glaoch ó Liombó' (Derry O'Sullivan), 349
Marconi's Cottage (Medbh McGuckian), 398
Marcus, David (editor of *The Irish Press*), 422
Margadh na Saoire (Máire Mhac an tSaoi), 325
Maria Edgeworth (Emily Lawless), 571
'Martha Blake at Fifty-One' (Austin Clarke), 371
Martin, David (later Martin McCart), 437
Martin, Violet Florence *see* Ross, Martin
Martyn, Edward, 186, 190
The Heather Field, 187, 190
see also Moore, George
Mary Vincent, Sr ('Maol Muire'), 265
Masks and Faces (Tom Taylor and Charles Reade), 534
Mason, Patrick, 506, 508
Master, The (Colm Tóibín), 640
Mathews, Aidan Carl, 381, 459, 511
According to the Small Hours, 381
Maude, Caitlín, 45, 333, 366
Maurice Harte (T. C. Murray), 201–2
Max (Katherine Cecil Thurston), 123
Mayne, Rutherford, 204
Meade, L. T. (Elizabeth Thomasina), 115
Meehan, Paula, 407, 410
Dharmakaya, 407
Man Who Was Marked by Winter, The, 407
Meeting the British (Paul Muldoon), 394
Méirscrí na Treibhe (Alan Titley), 290
memoirs, 272, 279, 467–71, 638
by emigrants, 468
by Irish women, 470
Northern, 470
poetry as, 360
see also autobiography; Blasket Islands literature
Mercier, Paul, 518
Mercier, Vivian, 583–4
Irish Comic Tradition, The, 583
Merriman, Brian, *Cúirt an Mheán Oíche*, 22
Messenger, The (Thomas Kinsella), 376
Metre (journal), 411
Mhac an tSaoi, Máire, 325–8, 331, 342
'Adhlacadh Iníon an Fhile', 327
'Ceathrúintí Mháire Ní Ógáin', 326
'Fuath, An', 326
'Do Nuala Ní Dhomhnaill', 327
'Inquisitio 1584', 326
Margadh na Saoire, 325
translation of 'An Bhean Mhídhílis' ('The Unfaithful Wife' by Lorca), 326

Mhallacht An (León Ó Broin), 263
Mháthair agus Sgéalta Eile, An (Patrick Pearse), 242
Mhéar Fhada, An (Johnny Chóil Mhaidhc Ó Coisdealbha), 304
Michael Robartes and the Dancer (William Butler Yeats), 60, 62
migration, 552, 553, 554, 555
  see also emigration; exile; immigration
Miller, Liam, 372, 377
  as publisher, 372–3
Milligan, Alice (co-editor of the *Northern Patriot* and *Shan Van Vocht*), 69, 70, 190
  'When I was a Little Girl', 70
Milligan, Spike, *Puckoon*, 540–1
mime, 525
Miontragóid Chathrach (Cathal Ó Searcaigh), 345
Mise (Colm Ó Gaora), 281
Mise Méara (Séamas Wilmot), 272
Mise Raiftearaí an File (Críostóir Ó Floinn), 303
Mitchel, John, *Jail Journal*, 24
Mitchell, Gary, 525–6
  As the Beast Sleeps, 526
  Independent Voice, 525
  In a Little World of Our Own, 526
Mitchell, Susan, 71
  Aids to the Immortality of Certain Persons in Dublin: Charitably Administered, 71
  Living Chalice, The, 71
Mixed Marriage (St John Ervine), 204–5
Mnemosyne Lay in Dust (Austin Clarke), 370
Mo Bhealach Féin (My Own Way by Seosamh Mac Grianna), 40, 41, 42, 43, 243, 271–2
Modern Irish Poetry: A New Alhambra (Frank Sewell), 566
modernisation, 23, 43, 611–12
modernism, 11, 51, 52, 115, 319, 359, 365, 572, 582
  Catholic, 142, 147
  and cinema, 547–8
  European, 32, 51–2, 186, 359, 365
  Irish, 23, 31–46, 99–100, 210, 337, 359, 381–2, 582–3
modernity, 26–9, 129, 457
Modern Lover, A (George Moore), 141
Modern Poetry: A Personal Essay (Louis MacNeice), 103
Modest Proposal, A (Jonathan Swift), 20
Mo Chara Stiofán (Liam P. Ó Riain), 265
Mo Dhá Mhicí (Séamas Mac Annaidh), 294
Mo Dhá Róisín (Séamus Ó Grianna), 250
'Mo Ghrása mo Dhia' (Biddy Jenkinson), 343
Molloy, M. J., 483–5
  King of Friday's Men, The, 483
  Wood of the Whispering, The, 484–5, 508
Molloy (Samuel Beckett), 423
Molloy, Frances, 451
Molly Sweeney (Brian Friel), 518
Moneylender, The (Joseph Edelstein), 121
monologues, 34, 40, 286, 289, 384, 497, 517–18, 520, 521, 524–5
Montague, John, 27, 378–80, 393, 461
  Collected Poems, 380
  Dead Kingdom, The, 380
  Death of a Chieftain and Other Stories, 461
  Great Cloak, The, 379
  Smashing the Piano, 380
  Time in Armagh, 380
  as editor of the *Dolmen Miscellany*, 378
Mooney, Martin, 392
Mooney, Ria, 480
Moore, Brian, 427, 429, 436, 438
  Doctor's Wife, The, 438
  Lonely Passion of Judith Hearne, The, 427, 550
Moore, George, 120, 141–5, 185–6, 190
  Confessions of a Young Man, 142
  Drama in Muslin, A: A Realistic Novel, 120, 121
  Esther Waters, 141
  Evelyn Innes, 187
  Hail and Farewell, 143
  Lake, The, 143
  Modern Lover, A, 141
  Sportsman's Sketches, A, 120
  Story-Teller's Holiday, A, 143
  Untilled Field, The, 120, 141, 142
  'Wild Goose, The', 142
  and Martyn, Edward
  Bending of the Bough, The, 185
  and Yeats, W. B. *Diarmuid and Grania*, 187
Morning After Optimism, The (Tom Murphy), 505
Morrissey, Sinéad, 411
Morrissy, Mary, 450, 465
Morrow, John, 439, 461
Motherland (Timothy O'Grady), 434
Mountainy Singer, The (Joseph Campbell), 87
Mount Prospect (Elizabeth Connor/Una Troy), 481–2
Moy Sand and Gravel (Paul Muldoon), 395
Mr Dineen's Careful Parade (Thomas McCarthy), 410
Muintir (Diarmaid Ó Súilleabháin), 288
Muireann agus an Prionnsa, see Golden Apple, The, 483

Muldoon, Paul, 386, 391, 392, 393–6, 408–9
'Aisling', 394
Annals of Chile, The, 395
Bandanna, 639
Hay, 395
To Ireland, I, 393, 394
Madoc: A Mystery, 394
Meeting the British, 394
Moy Sand and Gravel, 395
Quoof, 394
'Sleeve Notes', 395
Why Brownlee Left, 395
'Yarrow', 395, 409
Mulholland, Rosa (Lady Gilbert), 118, 121
Father Tim, 118
Mulkerns, Val, 450, 464
Mullen, Marie, 507–8
multilingualism, 409
Mundy Scheme, The (Brian Friel), 500
Munster poetry, 14, 85, 228
Murdoch, Iris, 448–9
Murphy, Dervla, 467
Murphy, Richard, 372–4, 378
Battle of Aughrim, The, 66, 373
High Island, 373
Kick, The, 373
Sailing to an Island, 372
Murphy (Samuel Beckett), 101, 169–71
Murphy, Tom, 492–3, 496, 499, 505–6, 515–17
Bailegangaire, 515–16, 634
Conversations on a Homecoming, 505
Crucial Week in the Life of a Grocer's Assistant, A, 499
Famine, 499
Fooleen, The (retitled *A Crucial Week in the Life of a Grocer's Assistant*), 496
Gigli Concert, The, 516, 634
Iron Men, The (retitled *A Whistle in the Dark*), 493
Morning After Optimism, The, 505
Sanctuary Lamp, The, 505–6, 634
Whistle in the Dark, A (formerly *The Iron Men*), 493
White House, The, 505
and O'Donoghue, Noel, *On the Outside*, 492
Murray, T. C., 201–2, 203
Maurice Harte, 201–2
'Murúcha a Thriomaigh, Na' (Nuala Ní Dhomhnaill), 342, 604
'Mustard Tin, The' (Michael Longley), 391
My Cousin Justin (Margaret Barrington), 164–5
My Ireland (Lord Edward John Dunsany), 173
'My Lagan Love' (Joseph Campbell), 86
My Left Foot (Christy Brown), 549–50
Myles Na gCopaleen (pseudonym of Brian O'Nolan), 471; *see also* Flann O'Brien
mythology, 339, 341, 568–71, 634
Myths and Legends of the Celtic Race (Thomas William Rolleston), 569–70

'Nameless Doon, The' (William Larminie), 66
National School system, 608
National Theatre, 480, 481, 498–9, 506
National Theatre Society, 182
Native Speaker Examined Home, The: Two Stalking Fallacies Anatomized (Fr John M O'Reilly), 234
nativists, 234, 260
Néal Maidine agus Tine Oíche (Breandán Ó Doibhlin), 285–6
'Necessity for De-Anglicizing Ireland, The' (Douglas Hyde), 79, 563–4, 572
Nelson, Dorothy, 451
'Nelson Street' (Seamus O'Sullivan), 77
Nephew, The (film), 555
New Criticism, 564, 583
New Estate, The (Ciaran Carson), 396
New Gossoon, The (George Shiels), 544
New Irish Writing (series within *The Irish Press* newspaper), 422
'new journalism', 473
New Note, A (Ella MacMahon), 125
New Poems 1973 (Thomas Kinsella), 375
New Poems (William Butler Yeats), 63
New Shirt, A (Desmond Hogan), 442
New Songs (George William Russell, 'AE'), 76
New Territory (Eavan Boland), 400
New Woman, 122–5, 184
New Writers Press, 381
Niamh (Fr Peter O'Leary), 250
Ní Annracháin, Máire, 292, 605
and Nic Dhiarmada, Bríona (editors), *Téacs agus Comhthéacs: Gnéithe de Chritic na Gaeilge*, 309
Ní Bhrolcháin, Muireann, 299
Nic Éinrí, Tina, 299
Nic Eoin, Máirín, 617
Nic Gearailt, Máire Áine, 336, 342
Ní Chéileachair, Síle and Ó Céileachair, Donncha, 274
Bullaí Mhártain, 274
Ní Chonaill, Eithne, 'Caillte', 323

Ní Chuilleanáin, Eiléan, 386, 400, 401–2, 405–6, 408
  Acts and Monuments, 400
  Girl Who Married the Reindeer, The, 406
  'Informant, The', 405
  Magdalene Sermon, The, 405
  'Nuns: A Subject for a Woman Writer', 406
  Site of Ambush, 402
  as co-founder of *Cyphers* (journal), 402
Nic Mhaicín, Máighréad, 248, 249
Ní Dhomhnaill, Nuala, 308, 327, 339–42, 408, 601, 603–4, 616, 622
  'Breith Anabaí Thar Lear', 341
  Cead Aighnis, 341–2, 603–4
  Dealg Droighin, An, 339, 603–4
  'Dubh – ar thitim Shrebrenice, 11ú Iúil 1995', 341
  Féar Suaithinseach, 341
  Feis, 341, 603
  'Greidhlic', 340
  'I mBaile an tSléibhe', 340
  'Murúcha a Thriomaigh, Na', 342, 604
  'Súile Uaine, Na', 339–40
  'Venio ex Oriente', 340
Ní Dhuibhne, Éilís, 299, 306, 450, 463, 604
  Blood and Water, 463
  Dancers Dancing, The, 450
  Dún na mBan Trí Thine, 306
  Inland Ice and Other Stories, The, 463
  Pale Gold of Alaska and Other Stories, The, 463
Ní Fhoghludha, Áine, 233
  Idir na Fleadhanna, 233, 274
Ní Ghlinn, Áine, 342, 349
  An Chéim Bhriste, 342
Ní Ghráda, Máiréad, 246, 263, 301–2
  Bheirt Dearbhráthar agus Scéalta Eile, An, 246
  Breithiúnas, 301
  Manannán, 257
  Triail, An, 301
Night (Edna O'Brien), 448
Night and Morning (Austin Clarke), 102
Night-Crossings (Derek Mahon), 388
Nightfeed (Eavan Boland), 327
Nightspawn (John Banville), 435
Ní Ghuithín, Máire, 284
Níor Mhaith linn do Thrioblóid (Joe Steve Ó Neachtain), 306
Ní Shéaghdha, Nóra, 274, 281
  Peats na Baintreabhaighe, 274
  Thar Bealach Isteach, 274
Ní Shúilleabháin, Siobhán, *Cití*, 299, 304
No Continuing City (Michael Longley), 390
Noise from the Woodshed, A (Mary Dorcey), 464
Nóra Mharcuis Bhig agus Scéalta Eile (Pádraic Ó Conaire), 242
Northern Ireland, 46, 327, 336, 387–91, 392
  fiction of, 165–8, 436–41
  literary criticism, 584–8
  plays, 500–3
  short stories in, 459–63
  women playwrights, 512–13
Northern Patriot (magazine), 69
Northern Voices: Poets from Ulster (Terence Brown), 585
North (Seamus Heaney), 383–4
novel, the, 113–35, 141–2, 144, 147–53, 154–73, 248–58, 271–99, 421–52
  autobiographical, 467
  Big House, 430–6
  Catholic, 428, 437–8
  country house, 121–2, 161–5, 166
  of emigration, 118, 142, 438, 445, 458–9, 463
  historical, 134, 250–1, 279, 289
  Irish-language, 248–58, 271–99
  popular, 114–16, 118, 279, 297–9
  religion and the novel, 116–20
  see also fiction
novels
  in the Free State, 156–65
  in Northern Ireland, 165–8, 436–41
  in the Republic, 441–6
Nuabhéarsaíocht (Seán Ó Tuama), 317–18
Nuair a Bhí Mé Óg (Séamus Ó Grianna), 272–3
'Nuns: A Subject for a Woman Writer' (Eiléan Ní Chuilleanáin), 406

Ó Baoighill, Aindrias, 251
Ó Beirne, Pádraic, 260
Ó Beirne, Séamus, 261
Object Lessons: The Life of the Woman and the Poet in Our Time (Eavan Boland), 153–4
Ó Briain, Liam, 242, 279
O'Brien, Conor Cruise, 466, 472
O'Brien, Edna, 427, 429, 448, 456–7, 471–2, 556
  Country Girls Trilogy, 427
  High Road, The, 448
  Night, 448
O'Brien, Eugene, *Eden*, 521
O'Brien, Flann, (Brian O'Nolan, 'Myles Na gCopaleen'), 169, 171–3, 433, 434–5
  At Swim Two-Birds, 40, 171–3
  Best of Myles, The, 472
  Dalkey Archive, The, 433
  Poor Mouth, The (*An Béal Bocht*), 271–3, 612–13
  Third Policeman, The, 173, 433

O'Brien, Frank, 308
O'Brien, George, 468
O'Brien, Kate, 163–4, 447, 466
Anteroom, The, 163
Land of Spices, The, 163
Ó Broin, León, 247, 263
Ag Stracadh leis an Saol, 247
Árus na nGábhadh agus Sgéalta Eile, 247
Béal na hUaighe agus Sgéalta Eile, 247
Mhallacht, An, 263
Oíche Úd i mBeithil, An, 263
Rún agus Scéalta Eile, An, 247
Ó Bruadair, Dáibhí, 611
Observe the Sons of Ulster Marching Towards the Somme (Frank McGuinness), 508, 514–15, 525
O'Byrne, Cathal, 466
Ó Cadhain, Máirtín, 234, 248, 274–8, 298, 307, 600–2, 612, 618
Athnuachan, 277–8
Barbed Wire, 278
Braon Broghach, An, 275
Cois Caoláire, 275–6
Cré na Cille, 275
Idir Shúgradh agus Dáiríre, 248, 275
Páipéir Bhána agus Páipéir Bhreaca, 277, 601
Sraith ar Lár, An t-, 276
Sraith dhá Tógáil, An t-, 276–7
Sraith Tógtha, An t-, 276
O'Callaghan, Conor, 411
'Ó Caochlaigh, Barra' *see* Art Ó Riain
Ó Caomhánaigh, Seán, *Fánaí*, 248, 254
O'Carroll, Fr John, 260
O'Casey, Sean, 22, 205–9, 480, 493, 536–8
Bishop's Bonfire, The, 480
'Crimson in the Tri-colour, The', 206
Drums of Father Ned, The, 480
Juno and the Paycock, 92, 206, 207, 537
Plough and the Stars, The, 207–8, 498, 537–8
Shadow of a Gunman, The, 206
Silver Tassie, The, 208–9, 480–1, 498
Ó Catháin, Liam, 278
Ó Ceallaigh, Seán ('Sceilg'), 261
Ó Ceallaigh, An tAthair Tomás, 261
Ó Céileachair, Donncha and Chéileachair, Síle Ní, *Bullaí Mhártain*, 274
Ó Céilleachair, Séamus, 318
Ó Ciarghusa, Seán, 251, 258
Ó Cíobháin, Pádraig, 295, 604
Gealas i Lár na Léithe, An, 295
Ó Ciosáin, Seán, *Sgéalta Cois Laoi*, 247
Ó Coigligh, Ciarán, 296–7
Duibhlinn, 296
Slán le Luimneach, 296
Ó Coisdealbha, Johnny Chóil Mhaidhc, 304, 305, 347, 351
Mhéar Fhada, An, 304
'Raifteaíraí agus an File', 347
Ó Conaire, Breandán, 308
Ó Conaire, Pádraic, 236, 240, 242–3, 246, 248, 261
Deoraidheacht, 246, 253
Nóra Mharcuis Bhig agus Sgéalta Eile, 242
Seacht mBuaidh an Éirghe Amach, 243
Sgoláire Bocht agus Sgéalta Eile, An, 242
Síol Éabha, 242
Ó Conaire, Pádhraic Óg, 252, 273, 282
Ó Conaola, Dara, 293, 604
Ó Conchubhair, Domhnall, 228
Ó Conghaile, Caoimhín, 333
Ó Conghaile, Micheál, 296, 604, 617–18, 619, 622
'Athair' ('Father'), 619
Sna Fir, 296
O'Connor, Frank (born Michael O'Donovan), 44–5, 158–60, 247, 421, 452–3, 466, 467, 469
Backward Look, The: A Survey of Irish Literature, 584
Common Chord, The, 453
Crab Apple Jelly, 452
Domestic Relations, 452
Dutch Interior, 158, 159
'Guests of the Nation', 539–40
Lonely Voice, The, 33
Traveller's Samples, 452
O'Connor, Joseph, 445, 459, 467, 472
Cowboys and Indians, 445
Inishowen, 445
Secret World of the Irish Male, 472
O'Connor, Pat, 540, 555
O'Connor, Rory, 467
O'Connor, T. P. *see* Read, Charles A.
Ó Criomhthain, Seán, *Lá Dár Saol*, 282
Ó Criomhthain, Tomás (Tomás O'Crohan), 157, 228, 229, 230, 258, 259
Allagar na h-Inise, 258, 613
Oileánach, An t-, 157, 228, 258–9, 272
Ó Croiligh, Oilibhéar, 299
Ó Cróinín, Dáibhí, 294
Ó Cruadhlaoich, Pádraig ('Gaedheal na nGaedheal'), 229
Ó Cuaig, Mícheál, 347, 349
Ó Cuív, Shán, 265, 582
Ó Curraoin, Seán, 347, 349
'Beairtle', 347

Ó Dálaigh, Muireadhach Albanach, 291
Odd Man Out (Carol Reed), 543
Ó Direáin, Máirtín, 319–24, 335
'Coinnle ar Lasadh', 322
Coinnle Geala, 319
Dánta Aniar, 319, 321
Rogha Dánta, 319
Ó Doibhlin, Breandán, 285–6, 307
Branar gan Cur, An, 286
Néal Maidine agus Tine Oíche, 285–6
Ó Domhnaill, Hiúdaí Sheáinín, 280
Ó Domhnalláin, Pádhraic, 245, 246
Ó Donnchadha, Tadhg ('Torna'), 226, 228, 229, 230
Caitheamh Aimsire, 230
Leoithne Andeas, 230
O'Donnell, Peadar, 157
Adrigoole, 157
Knife, The, 157
as editor of *The Bell*, 157
O'Donoghue, Bernard, 408, 409
O'Donoghue, D. J., 562, 573
as editor of *The Poets of Ireland: A Biographical Dictionary*, 562, 573
Geographical Distribution of Irish Ability, The, 562–3
O'Donoghue, Gregory, 380
O'Donoghue, John, 467
O'Donoghue, Noel *see* Murphy, Tom
O'Donovan, Gerald (formerly Fr Jeremiah O'Donovan), 144–5
Father Ralph, 144
Waiting, 144
O'Donovan, Michael *see* O'Connor, Frank
Ó Drisceoil, Colmán, 299
O'Driscoll, Dennis, 409–10
Ó Droighneáin, Muiris, 265, 582
Ó Dubhghaill, Séamus ('Beirt Fhear'), 236, 240
Ó Dubhda, Peadar, 248, 250, 258
O'Duffy, Eimar, 137
King Goshawk and the Birds, 137
Wasted Island, The, 137
Ó Dúill, Gréagóir, 349
Ó Duinnshléibhe, Seán, 228
Ó Duirinne, Séamus, 261
Ó Dúshláine, Tadhg, 299
Odyssey, The (Homer), 28, 31
Oedipal theme, 32
Oeser, Hans-Christian, 616
O'Faolain, Eileen, 447
O'Faolain, Julia, 449, 463–4
O'Faolain, Nuala, 470
O'Faolain, Sean (born John Whelan), 157–60, 247, 359, 452–3, 454, 465–6, 469, 472
Bird Alone, 158–9
'Broken World, A', 158
Foreign Affairs and Other Stories, 454
I Remember! I Remember!, 453
Teresa, and Other Stories, 453
as founder and editor of *The Bell*, 359, 367, 422
Ó Faracháin, Roibeárd, 248, 370, *see also* Farren, Robert
Fíon gan Mhoirt, 248
Ó Farrelly, Agnes (Úna Ní Fhaircheallaigh), 244, 250
O'Flaherty, Liam (Liam Ó Flaithearta), 156–7, 245, 263, 274, 538–9
'Bás na Bó', 245
Black Soul, The, 156
Dorchadas, An, 263
Dúil, 274
Informer, The (film versions of), 539
Skerrett, 156
Ó Flaithbheartaigh, Máirtín, 249
Ó Flatharta, Antaine, 305, 604, 618
Gaeilgeoirí, 305
Grásta i Meiriceá, 305
Imeachtaí na Saoirse, 305
Solas Dearg, An, 305
Ó Floinn, Críostóir, 303
Is É a Dúirt Polonius, 303
Mise Raiftearaí an File, 303
Ó Floinn, Tomás (also Flann Mac an tSaoir), 307, 321
Dánta Eile, 322
Ó Foghludha, Risteárd ('Fiachra Éilgeach'), 228, 229, 262
Ó Gaoithín, Micheál, 274, 281
Ó Gaora, Colm, *Mise*, 281
Oghma (journal), 271, 309
O'Grady, Desmond, 409
O'Grady, Standish James, 134, 135
History of Ireland, 568
O'Grady, Timothy, *Motherland*, 434
Ó Grianna, Séamus ('Máire'), 224, 237–9, 250, 272–3, 282–3
Bean Ruadh de Dhálach, 282–3
Caisleáin Óir, 252, 281
Castar na Daoine ar a Chéile 's ní Chastar na Cnuic nó na Sléibhthe, 250
Cioth is Dealán, 273
Mo Dhá Róisín, 250
Nuair a Bhí Mé Óg, 272–3
Saoghal Corrach, 273

Ó Gríobhtha, Micheál, 245–6, 257, 258
O'Growney, Father Eugene, 260
Ó hAirtnéide, Mícheál *see* Hartnett, Michael
Ó hAodha, Séamus, 233, 264
Caoineadh na Mná agus Duanta Eile, 233
Uaigneas, 233
Ó hAodha, Tomás, 250–1
Ó hAnnracháin, Peadar, 231
Chaise Gharbh, An, 231
Chaise Riabhach, An, 231
Ó hÉigeartaigh, Diarmuid, 251, 259
Ó hEithir, Breandán, 297–8, 472
Lig Sinn i gCathú, 297
Sionnach ar mo Dhuán, 155
Ó hEodhasa, Eochaidh, 13
Ó hUid, Tarlach, 273, 279
Adios, 273
Bealach chun a' Bhearnais, An, 273
as editor of *Inniu* (newspaper), 273
Oíche Úd i mBeithil, An (León Ó Broin), 263
Oidhche i nGleann na nGealt (Ciarán Ua Nualláin), 257
Oidhche Sheanchais (film), 266
Oileánach, An t- (Tomás Ó Criomhthain), 157, 228, 258–9, 272
Oireachtas, An t-, 229, 231, 239, 270, 299, 302, 308
O'Kelly, Donal, *Catalpa*, 525
Ó Laighléis, Ré, 299
Old Lady Says 'No!', The (Denis Johnston), 210, 480, 496
O'Leary, Fr Peter (An tAthair Peadar Ua Laoghaire), 236, 240, 261, 300
Bealach Buidhe, An, 260
Niamh, 250
Séadna, 249, 300
Ó Leocháin, Seán, 349
Ó Liatháin, Annraoi, 279
Ó Liatháin, Donnchadha ('An Rí Liath')
Ceol Abhann agus Gleann, 232
Tiomna Naofa agus Dánta Eile, An, 232
Ó Lochlainn, Gearóid, 262, 263
O'Loughlin, Michael, 409, 410, 459
The Irish Lesson, 608–10
Olympia Theatre, 183, 480, 500
O'Malley, Mary, 363, 407, 409
Ó Maoildhia, Séamus, 231
Dánta agus Amhráin, 231
Ó Maolchathaigh, Séamas, 281
Ó Maolfabhail, Art, *Aistí Dána*, 333
Ó Miléadha, Pádraig, 318
An Fiannaidhe Fáin, 232
Ó Muilleoir, Máirtín, 299
Ó Muireadhaigh, Réamonn, 333
Ó Muirí, Daithí, 294
Ó Muirí, Pól, 299, 336, 349
Ó Muirthile, Liam, 305, 336, 347–8, 351, 603, 617
Ar Bhruach na Laoi, 295
Dialann Bóthair, 348, 603, 606
Fear an Tae, 305
Tine Chnámh, 347, 603
Walking Time agus Dánta Eile, 348
Ó Murchadha, Tadhg, 258
Ó Murchú, Micheál, 231
Tuaim Inbheir agus Dánta Eile, 231
On Ballycastle Beach (Medbh McGuckian), 398
'On Behalf of Some Irishmen Not Followers of Tradition' (George William Russell, 'AE'), 74
Ó Neachtain, Joe Steve, 306, 604
Baile an Droichid (radio soap), 306
Níor Mhaith linn do Thrioblóid, 306
O'Neill, J. M., 445
O'Neill, Mary Devenport (Agnes Nestor Skrine), 99
Prometheus and Other Poems, 99
O'Neill, Moira, 71–2
Songs of the Glens of Antrim, 71
Ó Néill, Séamus, 248, 263, 274, 299, 323
Máire Nic Artáin, 274
Tonn Tuile, 255, 274
One (Thomas Kinsella), 375
O'Niel, Colette *see* Malleson, Constance
Only Jealousy of Emer, The (William Butler Yeats), 213–14
O'Nolan, Brian (Ó Nualláin, Brian), *see* O'Brien, Flann, 'Myles Na gCopaleen'
O'Nolan, Kevin (editor), *Best of Myles, The*, 472
On Raftery's Hill (Marina Carr), 524
On the Outside (Tom Murphy and Noel O'Donoghue), 492
Ó Nualláin, Gearóid, 257
Ó Rabhartaigh, Tadhg, 278
Ó Raghallaigh, Criostóir, 264
Ó Raithbheartaigh, Toirdhealbhach, 265
oral narratives, 137, 234
O'Reilly, Caitríona, 411
O'Reilly, Fr John M., 344–5
Native Speaker Examined Home, The: Two Stalking Fallacies Anatomized, 234
Ó Riada, Seán, 337
Ó Riain, Art, *Lucht Ceoil*, 251, 257
Tost, An, 257
Ó Riain, Éamonn, 16–18

Ó Riain, Liam P. (William P. Ryan), 236, 253, 265
Bhóinn agus an Bhóchna, An, 253
Mo Chara Stiofán, 265
Plough and the Cross, The, 253
Ó Rinn, Liam, 236, 246, 323
Cad Ba Dhóbair Dó agus Sgeulta Eile, 246
Ó Ríordáin, Seán, 309, 328–32, 337, 344, 601
Brosna, 331
Eireaball Spideoige, 328, 329, 331
Línte Liombó, 332
Tar Éis mo Bháis, 332
Ormsby, Frank, 387, 411–12
O'Rowe, Mark, *Howie the Rookie*, 521
Ó Ruadháin, Seán, *Pádhraic Mháire Bhán*, 250, 251
Ó Ruaidhrí, Seán, 251
Ó Sándair, Cathal, 278
Ó Séaghdha, Pádraig ('Conán Maol'), 240–1, 251, 258, 260
Ó Séaghdha, Pádraig ('Gruagach an Tobair'), 240–1
Ó Séaghdha, Pádraig ('Pádraig na Léime'), 261
Ó Searcaigh, Cathal, 338, 345–6, 603, 618, 619, 622
Buachaillí Bána, Na, 346
'Cainteoir Dúchais', 619
Miontragóid Chathrach, 345
Suibhne, 346
Súile Shuibhne, 345
and Rosenstock, Gabriel, *Tuirlingt*, 345
Ó Siadhail, Mícheál (Micheal O'Siadhail), 338
Ó Siadhail, Pádraig, 296
Éagnairc, 296
Parthas na gCleas, 296
Peaca an tSinsir, 296
Ó Siochfhradha, Micheál, 244–5, 263
Ó Siochfhradha, Pádraig ('An Seabhac'), 234, 236, 244–5, 259, 262
Baile Seo Againne, An, 244, 300
Ossianic tales and ballads, 85
Ó Súileabháin, Muiris, 258, 259
Fiche Blian ag Fás, 258–9, 613–14
Ó Súilleabháin, Diarmaid, 286–9
Aistear, 288
Caoin Tú Féin, 286
Ciontach, 288
Dianmhuilte Dé, 286
Lá Breá Gréine Buí, 288
Maeldún, 287–8
Muintir, 288
Uain Bheo, An, 287
O'Sullivan, Derry, 349
'Marbhghin: Glaoch ó Liombó', 349
O'Sullivan, Seamus (James Sullivan Starkey), 76–8
'Nelson Street', 77
'Twilight People, The', 77
as editor of the *Dublin Magazine*, 77
Other People's Houses (Vona Groarke), 407
Ó Thuaidh! (Pádraig Ua Maoileoin), 283
O'Toole, Fintan, 473
Ó Torna, Seosamh, *Cois Life*, 248
Ó Treasaigh, Lorcán
Bás san Oirthear, 293
Dealbhóir sa nGairdín, An, 293
Sracfhéachaint, 293
Ó Tuairisc, Eoghan (Eugene Watters), 289–90, 303–4, 309, 318, 333–4
'Aifreann na Marbh', 45, 333, 602
Aisling Mhic Artáin, 303
Carolan, 304
Dé Luain, 289
Fornocht do Chonac, 304
Lá Fhéile Míchíl, 303
L'Attaque, 289
Lomnochtán, An, 290
Lux Aeterna, 333
and Kelly, Rita, *Dialann sa Díseart*, 334
Ó Tuama, Seán, 280, 291, 302–3, 308, 334–6, 337, 344
Bás i dTír na nÓg, An, 334–5
Corp Eoghain Uí Shúilleabháin, 303
Faoileán na Beatha, 334
Gunna Cam agus Slabhra Óir, 302
Nuabhéarsaíocht, 317–18
Saol fó Thoinn, 334, 335
Out of Joint (theatre company), 522
Out of the Silent Planet (C. S. Lewis), 168
Outsiders Inside – Whiteness, Place and Irish Women (Bronwen Walter), 613
Over the Bridge (Sam Thompson), 493
Owenson, Sydney (later Lady Morgan), 23

Paddy Clarke Ha Ha Ha (Roddy Doyle), 443
Pádhraic Mháire Bhán (Seán Ó Ruadháin), 251
Pádraic Ó Conaire agus Aistí Eile (Seosamh Mac Grianna), 243
Páipéir Bhána agus Páipéir Bhreaca (Máirtín Ó Cadhain), 277, 601
Pale Gold of Alaska and Other Stories, The (Éilís Ní Dhuibhne), 463
Park, David, 461
Parker, Lynne, 518

Parker, Stewart, 502–3
Catchpenny Twist, 503
Pentecost, 511–2
Spokesong, 502
Parnell, Charles Stewart, 184
Parnell's Funeral (William Butler Yeats), 63
Parthas na gCleas (Pádraig Ó Siadhail), 296
Partridge, Felix, 261
Passing Day (George Shiels), 481
Passion Machine (theatre company), 518
'Passing of the Gael, The' (Ethna Carbery), 70
'Passing of the Shee, The' (J. M. Synge), 74
pastoralism, 52, 83, 461
Past, The (Neil Jordan), 442
'Patch-Shaneen' (J. M. Synge), 75–6
Patrick Pearse Motel, The (Hugh Leonard), 503–4
Patriots (Lennox Robinson), 201
Patriot Son and Other Stories, The (Mary Lavin), 455
Patterson, Glenn, 440–1
Paul Beck, The Rule-of-Thumb Detective (M. McDonnell Bodkin), 130
Paulin, Tom, 391, 392
Peaca an tSinsir (Pádraig Ó Siadhail), 296
Peacock Theatre, 210, 300, 498–9, 506, 517–18, 521
Pearse, Patrick (Pádraig Mac Piarais), 28, 92–3, 232, 241–2, 255
'Fornocht do chonac thú', 92
Íosagán agus Sgéalta Eile, 241
Mháthair agus Sgéalta Eile, An, 242
'Renunciation', 92
Suantraidhe agus Goltraidhe, 232
Peats na Baintreabhaighe (Nóra Ní Shéaghda), 73, 77, 274
Peg Woffington (film), 534
Peig (Peig Sayers), 258–9
'Penal Law' (Austin Clarke), 103
Pentecost (Stewart Parker), 511
Peppercanister (imprint), 376
periodicals, 73, 77, 226, 237, 239, 271, 323, 365, 369, 372, 382, 387, 401, 402, 411, 452, 565, 571, 581, 583
Irish-language, 226, 237, 239, 248, 257, 271, 285, 307, 309, 348
Peter Abelard (Helen Waddell), 167
Phibbs, Geoffrey *see* Taylor, Geoffrey
Philadelphia, Here I Come! (Brian Friel), 494–5, 554
Piatt, Donn, 263–4
Picture of Dorian Gray, The (Oscar Wilde), 125–6, 531
Pike Theatre, Dublin, 486–92, 493
Pilgrimage and Other Poems (Austin Clarke), 101, 102
Pitiless Passion, A (Ella MacMahon), 117, 122–3, 125
Plant and Phantom (Louis MacNeice), 104
Playboy of the Western World, The (J. M. Synge), 194–6, 508
plays, 181–219, 259–63, 299–306, 479–527
adaptations of novels, 498
emigrant, 484, 494, 496
English-language, 181–219, 478–527
Irish-language, 259–63, 299–306, 482–3, 491, 498, 507, 516
Japanese Noh, 212
'New Woman', 184
verse, 196
Plough and the Cross, The (William P. Ryan/Liam P. Ó Riain), 253
Plough and the Stars, The (Sean O'Casey), 207–8, 498, 537–8
Plunge into Space, A (Robert Cromie), 127
Plunkett, James, 429, 443, 456, 466
Strumpet City, 429
Plunkett, Joseph Mary, 91, 93
'I see His Blood upon the Rose', 93
'Little Black Rose Shall be Red at Last, The', 93
Poems (Thomas MacGreevy), 97
Poems (Louis MacNeice), 104
Poems (J. M. Synge), 75
Poems and Parodies (Thomas Kettle), 96
Poems of Joseph Campbell (Austin Clarke), 87
poetic codes, 15–19
poetry, 10–12, 13, 50–106, 227–33, 317–51, 357–412, 602–3
aisling, 15
bilingual, 79, 350
dual-language, 79
of the Easter Rising, 1916, 91–5
emigrant, 363–5
of the Great War, 93–8
Irish-language, 227–33, 317–51, 600–4, 605–6, 608–10, 611–12, 616, 618–20, 622–3
macaronic, 408
translations of, 350–1, 407–9
and the war years, 322–3
women's themes, 401–4
Poetry in the Wars (Edna Longley), 585
Poetry of W. B. Yeats, The (Louis MacNeice), 581
Poets and Poetry of Munster, The (George Sigerson), 83

Poet's Circuits: Collected Poems of Ireland, The (Padraic Colum), 85
Poets of Ireland, A Biographical Dictionary, The (edited by D. J. O'Donoghue), 562, 573
Point of View (Some Talks and Disputations), The (Emily Lawless), 67
'Poker' (Michael Davitt), 345
Pomes Penyeach (James Joyce), 90
'Poor Scholar of the Forties, A' (Padraic Colum), 84–5
Portable Virgin, The (Anne Enright), 465
Portia Coughlan (Marina Carr), 523–4
Portrait of the Artist as a Young Man, A (James Joyce), 9, 39–42, 88, 147–8, 557, 634
postcolonial theory, 309, 401, 564, 577, 586–9, 602, 606
postmodernism, 553
Power, Richard, 428, 429
  Land of Youth, The, 428
'Prayer for My Daughter, A' (William Butler Yeats), 60
Prayers of Sherkin (Sebastian Barry), 521
Preoccupations (Seamus Heaney), 384
Professor Tim (George Shiels), 481, 543
Prometheus and Other Poems (Mary Devenport O'Neill), 99
prose, 12–13, 113–73, 233–59, 271–99, 421–73, 602
  see also autobiography; fiction; memoirs; novels; short stories
Prút, Liam, 295
  Désirée, 295
  Leanbh sa Lamborghini, An, 295
Puckoon (Spike Milligan), 540–1
Purcell, Lewis, 204
Purgatory (William Butler Yeats), 214–15

Quare Fellow, The (Brendan Behan), 486–9
'Queens' (J. M. Synge), 75
Queen's Theatre, 183
Quiet Man, The (dir. John Ford), 485, 494, 552–3
Quinn, Bob, 546–7
Quinn, Justin, 411
Quintessence of Ibsenism, The (George Bernard Shaw), 184
Quoof (Paul Muldoon), 394

Raftery, Anthony, 190
'Raiftearaí agus an File' (Johnny Chóil Mhaidhc Ó Coisdealbha), 347
Rambling Rector, The (Eleanor Alexander), 116
Rann (journal), 363
Rat-Pit, The (Patrick MacGill), 120
'Raven's Rock' (Joseph Campbell), 87
Read, Charles A. and O'Connor, T. P. (editors), *Cabinet of Irish Literature, The*, 573–4
Reading in the Dark (Seamus Deane), 440, 470
Real Charlotte, The (Edith Somerville and Martin Ross), 116
realism, 153, 154, 200–2, 367, 398, 481
  and drama, 198–203
  magic, 292, 293
  and myth, 28
  and poverty, 120–2
  social, 274, 279
'Realism' (Medbh McGuckian), 398
Redemption (Francis Stuart), 424–5
'Red-haired Man's Wife, The' (James Stephens), 78
Redress of Poetry, The (Seamus Heaney), 384, 385
Reed, Carol, *Odd Man Out*, 543
regionalism, 272, 281, 284, 307, 362–3
Reid, Christina, 513
  Tea in a China Cup, 513
Reid, Graham, 503
  Death of Humpty Dumpty, The, 503
  Hidden Curriculum, The, 503
Reincarnations (James Stephens), 78
'Renunciation' (Patrick Pearse), 92
'Republicanism and culture in the new millennium' (Declan Kiberd), 613–14
Responsibilities (William Butler Yeats), 58, 59, 62
Resurrection Man (Eoin McNamee), 440, 541, 636
Return of the Hero, The (Darrell Figgis), 136
'Revival Irish' (Fr Richard Henebry), 234
Revival, the, 74, 82, 101, 113–14, 134, 562–81
  and anthologies, 573–5
  and book collectors, 571
  canon, 134
  commentators and literary historians, 578–81
  and the 'English novel', 113–14
  fiction, 134–41, 240–58
  Irish-language Revival, 226–66
  and literary criticism, 562–3, 575–81
  and literary history, 567–75
  and modernism, 31–46, 572, 582–3
  and mythology, 568–71
  non-Revival fiction, 114–34
  plays, 183, 189–96, 259–63
  and poetry, 53–106, 227–33

and publication, 239–40
term 'Revival', 74, 113–14
and translation, 229
'Rhapsody in Green' (Denis Johnston), 210
Richards, Shaun, 586
and Cairns, David, *Writing Ireland*, 586
Richards, Shelagh, 480
Rickard, Mrs Victor (Jesse Louise), *Fire of Green Boughs, The*, 133–4
Riddell, Mrs J. H. (Charlotte, née Cowan), 115, 119, 127
Riddle of the Sands, The (Erskine Childers), 130–1
Ridireacht Liteartha, An, 246
Riders to the Sea (J. M. Synge), 194
Ridgeway, Keith, 444–5
'Righteous Anger' *see* 'The Glass of Beer' (James Stephens)
Ripley Bogle (Robert McLiam Wilson), 441
Robinson, Lennox, 200–1, 219
Clancy Name, The, 200
Crossroads, The, 200
Patriots, 201
Robinson, Tim, 466
Roche, Billy, 520
Roddy, Lalor (co-founder of the Tinderbox Theatre, Belfast), 525
Rodgers, W. R., 361–2
Awake! and Other Poems, 361
Europa and the Bull and Other Poems, 361
'Rody McCorley' (Ethna Carbery), 70
Rogha Dánta (Máirtín Ó Direáin), 319
Rolleston, Thomas William, 81–2
'Dead at Clonmacnois, The', 81–2
Myths and Legends of the Celtic Race, 569–70
see also Brooke, Stopford
Rosenstock, Gabriel, 337–8, 605, 606
Susanne sa Seomra Folctha, 337
see also Ó Searcaigh, Cathal
Ross, Martin (Violet Florence Martin) *see* Somerville, E. A.
Rossetti, Christina, 68
Rotha Mór an tSaoil (The Hard Road to Klondike by Micí Mac Gabhann), 281, 615
Rough Magic (theatre company), 518
Rough Way, The (W. M. Letts), 116
Rubble na Mickies (Séamas Mac Annaidh), 294
Rudkin, David, 551
Rugged Path, The (George Shiels), 481
Rún agus Scéalta Eile, An (León Ó Broin), 247
Rushdie, Salman, *Imaginary Homelands*, 29
Russell, George William ('AE', editor of the *Irish Homestead* and the *Irish Statesman*), 72–4, 140, 636
'Great Breath, The', 73
Homeward Thoughts by the Way, 73
Interpreters, The, 140–1
New Songs, 76
'On Behalf of Some Irishmen Not Followers of Tradition', 74
Russell, Thomas O'Neill, 234
Ryan, William P. *see* Ó Riain, Liam P.

'Sabháiste, Seán' *see* Seosamh Ó Torna
sagas, 135–7
Sailing to an Island (Richard Murphy), 372
'Sailing to Byzantium' (William Butler Yeats), 57
Salkeld, Blanaid, 99, 100
Fox's Covert, The, 100
Hello Eternity!, 100
Sally's Irish Rogue (screen title of *The New Gossoon* by George Shiels), 544
Salomé (Oscar Wilde), 188, 189, 531
Samhain (magazine), 218
Sanctuary Lamp, The (Tom Murphy), 505–6, 634
Sands of Pleasure, The (Filson Young), 127
Saoghal Corrach (Séamus Ó Grianna), 273
Saol fó Thoinn (Seán Ó Tuama), 334
Saol Saighdiúra (Dónall Mac Amhlaigh), 280
Sayers, Peig, 258, 614
Machtnamh Seanmhná (An Old Woman's Reflections), 258, 614–15
Peig, 258–9
Scáthach (Colm Breathnach), 349
'Sceilg' *see* Seán Ó Ceallaigh
school texts, 250
'Schumann, Robert' (nom-de-plume), *Kinderszenen*, 294
science fiction, 127, 257
scientific romances, 127
screen adaptations, 531–2
of Abbey Theatre plays, 543–6
of Brian Friel, 550, 555
of Brian Moore, 550
of Christy Brown, 549–50
criticism of, 547–9
of Dion Boucicault, 532–4
of Edna O'Brien, 555
of Frank O'Connor, 539
of historical novels, 534–6
of Hugh Leonard, 545
of James Joyce, 556–7

of John B. Keane, 550–1
of J. M. Synge, 531
of the lament for Art O'Leary, 546
of Liam O'Flaherty, 536, 538–9
of Louis D'Alton, 545
of Maeve Binchy, 556
of Maurice Walsh, 552
of Reardon Conner, 540
of Roddy Doyle, 557–8
of Sam Hanna Bell, 551
of Sean O'Casey, 536–8
of the War of Independence, 540–2
Scríobh (journal), 271
'Seabhac, An' *see* Pádraig Ó Siochfhradha
Seacht mBuaidh an Eirighe Amach (Pádraic Ó Conaire), 243
Séadna (Peadar Ua Laoghaire), 249, 300
'Second Coming, The' (William Butler Yeats), 60
Secret Rose, The (William Butler Yeats), 140
Secret World of the Irish Male (Joseph O'Connor), 472
Secrets and Other Stories (Bernard MacLaverty), 462
Seeing Things (Seamus Heaney), 384–5
Selected Poems (Oliver St John Gogarty), 91
Semi-Private (Mary Halpin), 513
Seod Do-Fhághala, An (Úna Bean Uí Dhíocsa), 251
'September 1913' (William Butler Yeats), 59
Sewell, Frank, *Modern Irish Poetry: New Alhambra, A*, 566
sexuality, 124, 254, 340, 343, 346, 428, 438, 619, 622
female, 448, 451–2, 464
homosexuality, 346, 619, 622
lesbianism, 451, 464
male, 451, 619, 622
Sgéalta Cois Laoi (Seán Ó Ciosáin), 247
Sgoláire Bocht agus Sgéalta Eile, An (Pádraic Ó Conaire), 242
Shadow and Substance (Paul Vincent Carroll), 216
Shadow of a Gunman, The (Sean O'Casey), 206
Shadows on our Skin (Jennifer Johnston), 431
Shake Hands with the Devil (Reardon Conner), 540
Shale (Vona Groarke), 407
Shame of Mary Boyle, The (American title of film version of *Juno and the Paycock* by Sean O'Casey), 536
Shamrocks (Katharine Tynan), 68
Shan Van Vocht (magazine), 69–70
Shaughraun, The (film), 533–4
Shaw, George Bernard, 184, 186, 187, 198–200, 205
John Bull's Other Island, 30, 198–9
Quintessence of Ibsenism, The, 184
Shewing-Up of Blanco Posnet, The, 199
Sheehan, Canon, 118–19
Triumph of Failure, The, 118–19
Sheehan, Ronan, 442–3, 458
Sheehy-Skeffington, Hanna, 27
'Sheep and Lambs' (Katharine Tynan), 68
Shelmalier (Medbh McGuckian), 397, 399
Sheridan, Jim, 549, 550
Sheridan, Richard Brinsley, 22
Shewing-Up of Blanco Posnet, The (George Bernard Shaw), 199
Shiels, George, 216, 481–2
Bedmates, 481
New Gosoon, The, 544
Passing Day, 216, 481
Professor Tim, 481, 543
Rugged Path, The, 481
Summit, The, 481
Shining City (Conor McPherson), 636
Shorthouse, J. H. (Joseph Henry), *John Inglesant*, 117
short stories, 120, 142–3, 145–7, 156, 240–8, 274, 275–6, 288, 291–2, 293, 296, 422, 452–65
in Northern Ireland, 459–63
by women, 462–5
Sigerson, George, 82–3
Bards of the Gael and Gall, 82
Poets and Poetry of Munster, The, 83
Sigerson Shorter, Dora, 70–1
Silence in the Garden, The (William Trevor), 432
Silver Tassie, The (Sean O'Casey), 208–9, 480–1, 498
Simmons, James, 387, 389
Simpson, Alan, 486, 489–90
Single Lady and Other Stories, A (Mary Lavin), 455
Síol Éabha (Pádraic Ó Conaire), 242
Sionnach ar mo Dhuán (Breandán Ó hEithir), 155, 409, 410, 411
Sirr, Peter
Bring Everything, 410
Site of Ambush (Eiléan Ní Chuilleanáin), 402
Sive (John B. Keane), 492
Skerrett (Liam O'Flaherty), 156
Skull in Connemara, A (Martin McDonagh), 522
Slán le Luimneach (Ciarán Ó Coigligh), 296
'Sleeve Notes' (Paul Muldoon), 395

Smashing the Piano (John Montague), 380
Smith, Michael, 381
Sna Fir (Micheál Ó Conghaile), 296
Snapper, The (Roddy Doyle), 443
Snow Party, The (Derek Mahon), 388
Society for the Preservation of the Irish Language, 226
Solas Dearg, An (Antaine Ó Flatharta), 305
Soldiers of Year II, The (Medbh McGuckian), 400
Somerville, E. A. (Edith) and Ross, Martin (Violet Florence Martin), 116
  Real Charlotte, The, 116
Song for a Raggy Boy (Patrick Galvin), 553
Songdogs (Colum McCann), 445
Songs from the Clay (James Stephens), 78
Songs of Myself (Thomas MacDonagh), 92
Songs of the Fields (Francis Ledwidge), 94
Songs of the Glens of Antrim (Moira O'Neill), 71
Southern Theatre Group, 497
Southwark Irish Literary Club, 572
sovereignty myths, 15
'speech of the people' (*caint na ndaoine*, 234–6)
Spender, Stephen, 16
Spirit in Bondage, The (Clive Staples Lewis), 96
Spokesong (Stewart Parker), 502
Sportsman's Sketches, A (George Moore), 120
Sracfhéachaint (Lorcán Ó Treasaigh), 293
Sraith ar Lár, An t- (Máirtín Ó Cadhain), 276
Sraith dhá Tógáil, An t- (Máirtín Ó Cadhain), 276
Sraith Tógtha, An t- (Máirtín Ó Cadhain), 276
Stamping Ground (Maurice Leitch), 438
Standish O'Grady, AE and Yeats (Michael McAteer), 568
Standún, Pádraig, 155–6, 297–8, 299
  Súil le Breith, 155–6
Starkey, James Sullivan *see* O'Sullivan, Seamus
Starlit Eye, The (Thomas Kinsella), 372
Station Island (Seamus Heaney), 384
Steiner, George, *After Babel: Aspects of Language and Translation*, 510
Stephens, James, 78–9, 135–6, 138–9
  Charwoman's Daughter, The, 138–9
  Collected Poems, 79
  Crock of Gold, The, 78, 139
  Deirdre, 135
  Demi-Gods, The, 135
  'Glass of Beer, The', 79
  Hill of Vision, The, 78
  Insurrection in Dublin, The, 78, 139
  In the Land of Youth, 136
  Irish Fairy Tales, 136
  'Red-haired Man's Wife, The', 78
  Reincarnations, 78
  Songs from the Clay, 78
  'Street Behind Yours, The', 78
stereotypes, 30–1
  stage Irish, 197, 523, 533
Steward of Christendom, The (Sebastian Barry), 521–2
Stiall Fhial Feola (Alan Titley), 291
Still Life with Waterfall (Eamon Grennan), 409
Stoker, Bram, 128–30
  Dracula, 128–30
'Stolen Child, The' (William Butler Yeats), 56, 57
Stones in his Pockets (Marie Jones), 525
Stories of Red Hanrahan (William Butler Yeats), 138, 140
Story of the Night, The (Colm Tóibín), 444
Story-Teller's Holiday, A (George Moore), 143
'Straying Student, The' (Austin Clarke), 103
'Street Behind Yours, The' (James Stephens), 78
Stress (Olga Fielden), 168
Strong, Eithne, 342, 349, 401
Strong, Leonard Alfred George, 105
Strumpet City (James Plunkett), 429
Stuart, Francis, 160, 423–5, 441–2
  Black List, Section H, 441–2
  Redemption, 424–5
  Women and God, 160
Studies (journal), 583
'Suantraí na Máthar Síní' (Biddy Jenkinson), 343
Suantraidhe agus Goltraidhe (Patrick Pearse), 232
Suibhne (Cathal Ó Searcaigh), 346
Súil le Breith (Pádraig Standún), 155–6
Súile Shuibhne (Cathal Ó Searcaigh), 345
'Súile Uaine, Na' (Nuala Ní Dhomhnaill), 339–40
Summit, The (George Shiels), 481
supernaturalism, 127, 128, 138, 342, 410
Susanne sa Seomra Folctha (Gabriel Rosenstock), 337
Sweeney, Matthew, 409
Swift, Caroline, 489
Swift, Jonathan, 20
  Gulliver's Travels, 20
  Modest Proposal, A, 20
Symons, Arthur, 185
Synge and Anglo-Irish Literature (Daniel Corkery), 154, 202, 630–1

Synge, J. M. (John Millington), 29, 74–6, 192–6, 483, 531
Deirdre of the Sorrows, 75
In the Shadow of the Glen, 183, 193–4
'Patch-Shaneen', 75–6
Playboy of the Western World, The, 194–6, 508
Poems, 75
'Queens', 75
Riders to the Sea, 194
'Passing of the Shee, The', 74
Well of the Saints, The, 194

Taibhdhearc, An, 262, 302, 303, 306, 507, 516
Táin Bó Cúailnge, 135
translated by Thomas Kinsella as *The Tain*, 374
Talbot's Box (Thomas Kilroy), 506–7
Tales of War (Lord Edward John Dunsany), 132
Tar Éis mo Bháis (Seán Ó Ríordáin), 332
Tarry Flynn (Patrick Kavanagh), 369
Taylor, Geoffrey (formerly Geoffrey Phibbs), 105
Taylor, Tom and Reade, Charles, *Masks and Faces*, 534
Téacs agus Comhthéacs: Gnéithe de Chritic na Gaeilge (edited by Máire Ní Annracháin and Bríona Nic Dhiarmada), 309
Tea in a China Cup (Christina Reid), 513
television, 553, 621
Irish-language, 306
Teresa, and Other Stories (Sean O'Faolain), 453
Thar Bealach Isteach (Nóra Ní Shéaghdha), 274
theatre, 181–219, 259–63, 299–306, 479–527
amateur, 271, 304, 485, 492–3
in English, 181–219, 478–527, 532, 639
experimental, 498–500, 517–18
Gaeltacht-based, 299, 302, 304–6
Irish-language, 259–63, 299–306, 482–3, 491, 498, 507, 516
Japanese Noh, 213
in Northern Ireland, 493–4, 499, 500–3, 509–15
origins of, 181–2, 185–7
see also plays
theatre companies, 301, 518
see also individual companies
theatre festivals, 526
Theatre of Ireland Society, 203
Théâtre-Libre de Paris, 185–7
theatre societies, 203
Third Person (Brian Coffey), 100
Third Policeman, The (Flann O'Brien), 173, 433
This Other Eden (Louis D'Alton), 545–6
This Side of Brightness (Colum McCann), 445
'Thirties Writers', 363
Thomas Campion and the Art of English Poetry (Thomas MacDonagh), 91
'Thomas McDonagh' (Francis Ledwidge), 94, 96
Thompson in Tír na nÓg (Gerald MacNamara), 204
Thompson, Sam, *Over the Bridge*, 493
Thomson, George, 259
Threshold of Quiet, The (Daniel Corkery), 153–4
Thurston, Katherine Cecil, 115, 123–4
Fly on the Wheel, The, 123
John Chilcote, MP, 115, 123
Max, 123
'Tilly' (James Joyce), 90
'Time Before You, The' (Medbh McGuckian), 398
Time in Armagh (John Montague), 380
Tinderbox Theatre Company, 525
Tine Chnámh (Liam Ó Muirthile), 347, 603
Tiomna Naofa agus Dánta Eile, An (Donnchadh Ó Liatháin), 232
Tiresias (Austin Clarke), 371
Titley, Alan, 290–1, 294, 306, 605
Eiriceachtaí agus Scéalta Eile, 291
Fear Dána, An, 291
Méirscrí na Treibhe, 290
Stiall Fhial Feola, 291
'To a Shade' (William Butler Yeats), 59
Todhunter, John, 65–6
The Banshee and Other Poems, 65
Tóibín, Colm, 444, 466, 467, 473
Blackwater Lightship, The, 444
Heather Blazing, The, 444
Master, The, 640
Story of the Night, The, 444
Tóibín, Nioclás, 251
Tóibín, Tomás, 317
Toil Dé (Éamonn Mac Giolla Iasachta), 254
To Ireland, I (Paul Muldoon), 393, 394
'To Ireland in the Coming Times' (William Butler Yeats), 57
Tomelty, Joseph, 482
All Souls' Night, 482
End House, The, 482
Is the Priest at Home?, 482
Tonn Tuile (Séamus Ó Néill), 255, 274
Tost, An (Art Ó Riain), 257
'To the Rose upon the Rood of Time' (William Butler Yeats), 57
Tower, The (William Butler Yeats), 57, 61–2

Tracy, Honor, 466
Transformations in Irish Culture (Luke Gibbons), 612
translations, 28, 29, 45, 79–83, 135, 229–31, 258, 262–3, 265, 277, 302, 304, 318, 321, 325, 339, 346, 349, 350–1, 374, 386, 397, 407–9, 434, 483, 488–9, 511, 574, 609, 521, 622
Translations (Brian Friel), 509, 510
Traveller's Samples (Frank O'Connor), 452
travel writing, 279, 465–7
Treasury of Irish Poetry, A (edited by Stopford A. Brooke and Thomas William Rolleston), 69, 81, 575
Treasury of Irish Poetry in the English Tongue, A (Katharine Tynan), 69
Trench, Herbert, 66
  Deirdre Wed, 66
Trevor, William, 431–3, 456–7, 469
  Beyond the Pale and Other Stories, 457
  Felicia's Journey, 432
  Fools of Fortune, 432, 540
  Silence in the Garden, The, 432
Triail, An (Máiréad Ní Ghráda), 301
Triumph of Failure, The (Canon Sheehan), 118–19
Troubles (J. G. Farrell), 431
Troubles, the (post-1969 Northern Ireland), 382, 383–4, 390, 436, 439–40, 461–3, 478
  and literary criticism, 584–6
  and literary history, 584
  plays on, 500–3
see also Northern Ireland
Troy, Una (penname 'Elizabeth Connor'), 481, 543
  Mount Prospect, 481–2
  We Are Seven, 543
Tuaim Inbheir agus Dánta Eile (Micheál Ó Murchú), 231
Tuirlingt (Cathal Ó Searcaigh and Gabriel Rosenstock), 345
Twelfth of Never (Ciaran Carson), 397
Twenty Years A-Wooing (John McCann), 485
'Twilight People, The' (Seamus O'Sullivan), 77
Tynan, Katharine, 68–9
  Ballads and Lyrics, 68
  'Cattle, The', 68–9
  Louise de la Vallière, 68
  Shamrocks, 68
  'Sheep and Lambs', 68
  Treasury of Irish Poetry in the English Tongue, A, 69

Ua Duinnín, An tAthair Pádraig *see* (Fr) Patrick Dinneen
Uaigneas (Séamus Ó hAodha), 233
Uain Bheo, An (Diarmaid Ó Súilleabháin), 287
Ua Laoghaire, Diarmuid, 251
Ua Laoghaire, An tAthair Peadar, *see* (Fr) Peter O'Leary
Ua Maoileoin, Pádraig, 234, 283–4
  Bríde Bhán, 283–4
  Fonn a Níos Fiach, 283–4
  hAird ó Thuaidh, Na, 282
  Ó Thuaidh!, 283
Ua Nualláin, Ciarán (Kevin O' Nolan), 256–7
  Oidhche i nGleann na nGealt, 257
Ua Tuathail, Lorcán, 261
Uí Dhíocsa, Úna Bean (Elizabeth Rachel Dix), 251, 255–6
  Cailín na Gruaige Duinne, 255–6
  Seod Do-Fhághala, An, 251
Uí Mhaolaoi, Nóirín, 299
Uladh (journal), 565
Úlla de'n Chraobh (Douglas Hyde), 230
Ulster Bridge Productions, 493
Ulster Group Theatre, 482, 493
Ulster Literary Theatre, 203–4
Ulster novelists, 119, 165
Ulster-Scots language, 86, 362
Ultach, An t-, 237, 307
Ulysses (James Joyce), 18–19, 28, 33, 36, 38, 150, 152–3, 556, 579
'Unappeasable Host, The' (William Butler Yeats), 57
'Under Ben Bulben' (William Butler Yeats), 63
'Unfaithful Wife, The' ('An Bhean Mhídhílis' by Lorca, translation by Máire Mhac an tSaoi), 326
United Ireland (Hannah Lynch), 149
Unnamable, The (Samuel Beckett), 423
Untilled Field, The (George Moore), 120, 141, 142
Untouchable, The (John Banville), 436
urbanisation, 39, 120–1, 184, 204, 245, 246, 247, 248, 270, 274, 299, 304, 320, 322, 348, 349, 471, 521, 554, 556–7, 600, 605, 616, 631

Valley of the Squinting Windows, The (Brinsley MacNamara), 155
Vengeance of Fionn, The (Austin Clarke), 101
'Venio ex Oriente' (Nuala Ní Dhomhnaill), 340
Vision, A (William Butler Yeats), 9, 60

'Vision of Glendalough, A' (Joseph Campbell), 87
Vision of Mac Conglinne, The (Padraic Fallon), 366–7
'Visions of Niamh, The' (Eva Gore-Booth), 70
Volunteers (Brian Friel), 506

Waddell, Helen, 167
Peter Abelard, 167
Wandering Scholars, The, 167
Waiting for Godot (Samuel Beckett), 12, 210, 478, 486, 489–90
Waiting (Gerald O'Donovan), 144
Walking Time agus Dánta Eile (Liam Ó Muirthile), 348
Wall, Eamonn, 409
Wall, Mervyn, 426
Walsh, Maurice, *The Quiet Man*, 552
Walter, Bronwen, *Outsiders Inside – Whiteness, Place and Irish Women*, 613
Wandering Scholars, The (Helen Waddell), 167
'Wanderings of Oisin, The' (William Butler Yeats), 56
War Horse, The (Eavan Boland), 402
Waring, D. G., 167–8
Fortune Must Follow, 167
Warrenpoint (Denis Donoghue), 470
Wasted Island, The (Eimar O'Duffy), 137
Watters, Eugene *see* Eoghan Ó Tuairisc
Way of the World, The (William Congreve), 188
We Are Seven (Una Troy), 543
Weir, The (Conor McPherson), 521, 636
Weldon, John *see* MacNamara, Brinsley
Weldon, Robert (Roibeárd Bheldon), 228
Well of the Saints, The (J M Synge), 194
West, Anthony C., 439, 461
Weygandt, Cornelius, *Irish Plays and Playwrights*, 580
Wheatley, David, 411
'Wheels' (John McGahern), 554
Whelan, John *see* O'Faolain, Sean
'When I was a Little Girl' (Alice Milligan), 70
Whistle in the Dark, A (earlier title *The Iron Men* by Tom Murphy), 493
Whitbread, J. W., *Lord Edward, Or '98*, 183
White Goddess, The (Robert Graves), 96
White House, The (Tom Murphy), 505
Why Brownlee Left (Paul Muldoon), 395
'Wife of Llew, The' (Francis Ledwidge), 94
Wild Earth (Padraic Colum), 83
Wilde, Oscar, 24, 30, 64–5, 187–9
'Ballad of Reading Gaol, The', 64–5
Decay of Lying, The, 637
Ideal Husband, An, 189
Importance of Being Earnest, The, 188
Picture of Dorian Gray, The, 125–6, 531
Salomé, 188, 189, 531
Wilderness Sings (John Lyle Donaghy), 99
'Wild Goose, The' (George Moore), 142
Wild Swans at Coole, The (William Butler Yeats), 60
Willy Reilly and His Colleen Bawn (William Carleton), 535–6
Wilmot, Séamus *see also* De Bhilmot, Séamus
Wilson, Robert McLiam, 440–1, 467
Eureka Street, 441
Ripley Bogle, 441
Wind Among the Reeds, The (William Butler Yeats), 57, 58, 60
Winding Stair and Other Poems, The (William Butler Yeats), 57, 62
Wingfield, Sheila, 401
Wintering Out (Seamus Heaney), 383
With the Wild Geese (Emily Lawless), 66, 67
'Woman in Kitchen' (Eavan Boland), 154
Woman Who Walked into Doors, The (Roddy Doyle), 443
'Woman Young and Old, A' (William Butler Yeats), 62
Women and God (Francis Stuart), 160
women's issues, 122–4, 400–1, 464
women writers, 1, 160–5, 299, 358, 400–7, 555
and Field Day Theatre Company, 512, 588
in the *Innti* poets, 337
Irish-language, 255–6, 274, 281, 299, 301, 325–8, 339–44
of memoirs, 274, 281, 470
novelists, 160–5, 165–8, 255–6, 422, 447–51, 452
playwrights, 496, 508, 512–13
poets, 66–72, 99, 325–8, 339–44, 398–407
of short stories, 462, 463–5
Wood of the Whispering, The (M. J. Molloy), 484–5
Woods, Macdara, 401
'Words for Music Perhaps' (William Butler Yeats), 62
Words upon the Window Pane (William Butler Yeats), 214
World War I, *see* Great War, The
World War II, 359, 423, 439
Writing Ireland (Shaun Richards and David Cairns), 586

'Yarrow' (Paul Muldoon), 395, 409
Yeats, John Butler, 65

Yeats, William Butler, 9, 15, 25, 30, 38, 53–64, 138, 140, 181–2, 187, 189, 191, 196–7, 212–16, 218–19, 569, 582–3
'Adam's Curse', 58
'Among School Children', 61
At the Hawk's Well, 212–13
Celtic Twilight, The, 138
'Circus Animals' Desertion, The', 62
Countess Kathleen and Various Legends and Lyrics, The, 57
'Cuchulain Comforted', 63
'Curse of Cromwell, The', 19
Deirdre, 197
'Easter 1916', 16, 59
Fairy and Folk Tales of the Irish Peasantry, 138
'Fergus and the Druid', 57
Full Moon in March, A, 63
Green Helmet and Other Poems, The, 58
'Gyres, The', 63
'High Talk', 63
'How Ferencz Renyi Kept Silent', 572
In the Seven Woods, 58
'To Ireland in the Coming Times', 57
Irish Fairy Tales, 138
'Lapis Lazuli', 63
Last Poems and Two Plays, 53, 62
'Lecture Delivered to the Royal Academy of Sweden, A', 564, 567
'Long-legged Fly', 63
'Madness of King Goll, The', 56–7
'Man who Dreamed of Faeryland, The', 57
Michael Robartes and the Dancer, 60, 62
New Poems, 63
Only Jealousy of Emer, The, 213–14
Parnell's Funeral, 63
'Prayer for My Daughter, A', 60
Purgatory, 214–15
Responsibilities, 58, 59, 62
'To the Rose upon the Rood of Time', 57
'Sailing to Byzantium', 57
'Second Coming, The', 60
Secret Rose, The, 140
'September 1913', 59
'To a Shade', 59
'Stolen Child, The', 56, 57
Stories of Red Hanrahan, 138, 140
'Unappeasable Host, The', 57
'Under Ben Bulben', 63
'Wanderings of Oisin, The', 56
Tower, The, 57, 61–2
Vision, A, 9, 60
Wild Swans at Coole, The, 60
Wind Among the Reeds, The, 57, 58, 60
Winding Stair and Other Poems, The, 57, 62
'Woman Young and Old, A', 62
'Words for Music Perhaps', 62
Words upon the Window Pane, 214, 531
and Gregory, Lady Augusta, *Cathleen ni Houlihan*, 183, 189, 190
and Moore, George, *Diarmuid and Grania*, 187
Yeats criticism, 580–1, 582–3
Yellow Book, The (Derek Mahon), 389
Young, Ella, 137
Young, Filson, *The Sands of Pleasure*, 127
Young Ireland, 84
'Young Woman of Beare, The' (Austin Clarke), 102
Youth's the Season . . . (Mary Manning), 211

B.S.U.C. - LIBRARY
00297145

THE CAMBRIDGE HISTORY OF

IRISH LITERATURE

*

VOLUME 2

1890–2000

This is the first comprehensive history of Irish literature in both its major languages, Irish and English. The twenty-nine chapters in this two-volume history provide an authoritative chronological survey of the Irish literary tradition. Spanning fifteen centuries of literary achievement, the two volumes range from the earliest Hiberno-Latin texts to the literature of the late twentieth century. The contributors, drawn from a range of Irish, British and North American universities, are internationally renowned experts in their fields. *The Cambridge History of Irish Literature* comprises an unprecedented synthesis of research and information, a detailed narrative of one of the world's richest literary traditions, and innovative and challenging new readings. No critical work of this scale and authority has been attempted for Irish literature before. Featuring a detailed chronology and guides to further reading for each chapter, this magisterial project will remain the key reference book for literature in Ireland for generations to come.

This second volume covers the long twentieth century, a period marked by the achievements of Irish writers in all genres, and looks forward to developments in the new millennium.

MARGARET KELLEHER is Senior Lecturer in the Department of English at the National University of Ireland, Maynooth. She has previously held the John J. Burns Visiting Chair in Irish Studies at Boston College. She is the author of *The Feminization of Famine* (1997), editor of *Making It New* (2000) and co-editor of *Nineteenth-Century Ireland: A Guide to Recent Research* (2005).

PHILIP O'LEARY is Associate Professor of Irish Studies at Boston College. He is the author of *Prose Literature of the Gaelic Revival 1881–1921: Ideology and Innovation* (1994), which won the ACIS First Book Prize, *Déirc an Dóchais: Léamh ar Shaothar Phádhraic Óig Uí Chonaire* (1995) and *Gaelic Prose in the Irish Free State, 1922–1939* (2004), which won the Michael J. Durkan Prize.